Personality Theories

To the late Dr. Albert Ellis, who was often a controversial iconoclast but always
a genuine genius. He was a visionary in psychology, psychotherapy, and human sexuality.
His influence has insinuated itself into every aspect of modern clinical psychology—*as it should.*

—M.A. & L.D.A.

To my late parents, Mr. Ben Abrams and Ms. Lilly Abrams, whose poverty
precluded secondary educations but who were able to inspire a passion for it nonetheless.

—M.A.

To my late parents, Dr. Edith Palfi Dengelegi and
Dr. Tiberius Dengelegi, who emerged from Auschwitz and a Russian work camp to
become physicians and loving parents, and set an example to all who face adversity.

—L.D.A.

To our daughters, Ms. Dax Abrams and Ms. Kira Abrams,
whose good behavior allowed their parents to contribute to this work.

—M.A. & L.D.A.

Personality Theories
Critical Perspectives

Albert Ellis
Albert Ellis Institute

Mike Abrams
William Paterson University and Albert Ellis Institute

with Lidia D. Abrams
Resolve Community Counseling Center

with contributions by Alexander Nussbaum, Saint John's University

and

Rebecca J. Frey, Yale University

SAGE

Los Angeles • London • New Delhi • Singapore

For information:

SAGE Publications, Inc.
2455 Teller Road
Thousand Oaks, California 91320
E-mail: order@sagepub.com

SAGE Publications Ltd.
1 Oliver's Yard
55 City Road
London EC1Y 1SP
United Kingdom

SAGE Publications India Pvt. Ltd.
B 1/I 1 Mohan Cooperative Industrial Area
Mathura Road, New Delhi 110 044
India

SAGE Publications Asia-Pacific Pte Ltd
33 Pekin Street #02-01
Far East Square
Singapore 048763

Printed in the United States of America

Library of Congress Cataloging-in-Publication Data

This book is printed on acid-free paper.

08   09   10   11   12   10   9   8   7   6   5   4   3   2   1

Acquisitions Editor:	Kassie Graves
Editorial Assistant:	Veronica K. Novak
Production Editor:	Catherine M. Chilton
Copy Editor:	Jacqueline A. Tasch
Typesetter:	C&M Digitals (P) Ltd.
Proofreader:	Doris Hus
Indexer:	Hyde Park Publishing Services LLC
Cover Designer:	Candice Harman
Marketing Manager:	Carmel Schrire

Contents

Introduction

This book is unique among more than 80 books and monographs I have produced in my half-century of authorship. It differs from all the others in three ways: It is the first college textbook I have ever produced, it devotes most of its pages to perspectives other than mine, and it is the first book to formally present my complete theory of personality. Why have I waited so long to write a textbook? For most of my career, I have sought to reach as many people as possible. Consequently, most of my books were for lay audiences or practicing clinicians. I have detailed the essence of my theory in several articles and chapters, but I have never presented a comprehensive theory set alongside that of other major theorists. To rectify this omission, I invited my longtime collaborators and good friends, Mike and Lidia Abrams, to work with me in preparing this textbook. I hope it will serve to expose a large audience to the principles that I and my students have been describing and applying since the mid-1950s. These principles, summarized under the rubric of Rational Emotive Behavior Therapy (REBT), have been used by thousands of clinicians to help millions of people to stop making themselves miserable.

Has REBT helped? In short, yes. It has done so by showing people that most human misery arises from an irrationality that is inherent but that also can be changed. People persist in demanding perfection of themselves, unconditional love from others, and fairness from the world. They whine when things are "too hard," and decide that they cannot stand doing things that are difficult, even if persevering is in their own best interest. Of course, a fair, easy, and loving world is a wonderful one to hope for or work toward, but it is profoundly irrational psychologically to expect and demand that life be that way. As is detailed in this text, some personality authors appear to have succumbed to the moralistic fallacy: They believe things that are morally wrong or undesirable simply cannot exist in the world. These authors insist that fairness, rationality, inherent goodness, or striving for goodness must be part of the world simply because they are desirable. Unfortunately for them and their clients, the world does not give a damn and goes merrily on its harsh, unfair, and irrational way. This is where I have differed from many of them. The world does not have to do what any of us want. Therefore, we had better learn to accept it without irrational demands or shoulds. Despite my admonitions and the several millennia of human history that have demonstrated that the things people irrationally demand are usually not forthcoming, their absolutistic demands are still going strong.

In 1955, when I began directing my practice away from psychoanalysis to a therapeutic approach based on rationality, I discovered a more effective and more rapid means to address people's problems. It was this rational approach to psychotherapy that evolved into REBT, which is practiced by numerous clinicians and is the intellectual foundation of virtually all of today's cognitive or cognitive behavioral therapies. When I developed REBT it represented a new theory of personality, radically different from those that dominated in that era.

Psychoanalysts, who were educated much the same way that I was, operated under the assumption that personality was an amalgam of powerful drives being kept at bay by largely unconscious mental structures. According to this model, people have very little direct control over their lives and, unless successfully analyzed, will live lives of continual turmoil as their internal forces perpetually battle. The other dominant view at that time was the behavioral view, which considered personality to be a complex construction of conditioned responses. This approach minimized human agency and made personality a function of conditioning. Current research shows that almost all theories have a kernel of truth. There is indeed a role for conditioning and behavioral change (hence my addition in the late 1990s of the B for *behavioral* in REBT), and there is a role for the nonconscious processes in personality.

Underlying all clinical approaches is a theory of human personality. This theory can be tacit or explicit, but it is requisite. One cannot diagnose an infirmity without a model of health. Nor can one treat it without a conceptualization of its etiology. A personality theory provides the foundation for understanding how both healthy and dysfunctional personalities develop, and it makes the distinction between the two. In addition, such a theory provides a framework for the research and experimental testing of both itself and the clinical approaches based on it. Karl Popper was indeed correct to require that all theories must be falsifiable in order to be considered scientific. Personality and other psychological theories are certainly no exception. I am perfectly open to being amended, or even proven wrong, as that is the role of science, to test and revise ideas, incorporate new knowledge, and devise theories that best fit our observable reality.

And there is much work to do in understanding human personality! Is it a composite of traits? Can it be explained by five factorial dimensions? Is personality really just a collection of learned behaviors? Is the person defined by striving for self-actualization? Alternatively, are we just social entities that come into being by adapting to the demands of interpersonal situations? These are just a few of the questions that are still to be resolved. Personality researchers have made great headway, yet the reader of this text will inevitably note that personality psychologists continue to set forth a medley of theories, many of which are incompatible with the others.

Prior to this text, my theory of personality was discussed in several articles and chapters. In these, I asserted that personality was a function of innate human irrationality, in which people make persistent demands that the world, and those in it, exist in a way that suits them. Further, this irrationality was expressed in the form of my original A-B-C theory of human behavior. It states that people in response to some activating event (A) will experience an emotional or behavioral (C) consequence. In most cases the person attributes the C as being a direct result of A. This in fact is quite wrong. A does not cause C, although it may significantly contribute to it. Instead, the person's beliefs (B) about the event are the essential predicates of the C. Rational beliefs lead to appropriate emotions and behaviors, whereas irrational beliefs lead to excessive emotional distress and poor choices. In short, my insight— which evolved into the cognitive behavioral approach—was that it is people's beliefs, attitudes, and biases that lead to their behavior and emotions—not the unconscious structures of Sigmund Freud, or the S-R connection of John B. Watson.

I have not rejected the notion that much of cognition is nonconscious. Indeed, most of the beliefs that influence our behavior are unconscious until evoked and often can be discovered only by inferring them from emotions and behavior. And I certainly do not reject behaviorism, as it is clearly instrumental in my therapeutic approach. However, I reject the notion that knowledge of stimulus response connections is sufficient to understand human behavior. An adequate theory of personality needs to include all of the elements of mind that interact to yield the human personality.

I have often written that hereditary factors play a major role in the development of personality. My A-B-C theory of human emotional distress does not in any way preclude a very strong role for genetic influences in personality and in how people view and experience the world. I have maintained throughout my career that people are constitutionally irrational and must learn through focused volition to behave rationally and avoid creating their own misery. More recently, this perspective has been implicitly supported by the evolutionary psychologists. In the evolutionary view, people have evolved psychological inclinations that were adaptations to environments humans faced eons ago. Since the world is radically different from the savannahs that early man evolved in, our psychology will often be at odds with our current world, which is vastly different from and more complex than that of our distant ancestors. Hence, we are inevitably inclined to be irrational. Based on this and related research, I have included the sociobiological influence into my most recent theory of personality.

In addition to providing a complete presentation of my theory of personality, I wanted my text to provide a more critical analysis than is typically offered in most textbooks. Many of the new clinicians whom I have supervised have been taught an assortment of incompatible personality theories, often without being provided any basis for judging which are correct, partially correct, or simply wrong. The failure to challenge the legitimacy of the theories that underlie many schools of psychology has harmed both the practice and science of psychology. One cannot find any other science in which historical theories are presented with equal standing to current research. Is there an astronomy textbook that presents the views of Ptolemy, Copernicus, and Carl Sagan as competing perspectives? Indeed not! The early astronomers are included to clarify their historical role in developing modern theories, but it is understood that modern theories are built on knowledge unavailable to earlier theorists and therefore are more valid representations of reality.

In the field of psychology, on the other hand, personality and history and systems textbooks often present the theories of Freud, Carl Jung, Alfred Adler, and others as complete and viable alternatives to modern, research-based theories. Unproven theories of personality, some a century old, are juxtaposed with recent research-based theories. Consequently, students are given inadequate direction for clinical practice and future research.

To help the student achieve an unbiased proper perspective, this book will provide supporting and contradictory evidence for each personality theory discussed. It is my goal to present the reader with a critical view of each theory, including my own. In addition, far less biographical information about the originators of theories will be offered. Although this is standard fare in most psychology texts, it is rarely found in texts in any other science. Discussions of Fermat's last theorem are rarely accompanied with a discourse on the conflicts Fermat faced in his childhood. Nor do biology texts precede each biological discovery with a brief developmental history of the discoverer. Throughout this book, my co-authors and I will seek to highlight the innovations as well as the weaknesses of early personality theories, which may have represented landmarks several generations ago but now fail to meet the standards of scientific empiricism. Too many of the theories remain in vogue based on the charisma and writing creativity of their formulators rather than on any extant scientific merit.

We cannot condemn many of the founding theorists in psychology, as they were developing a new field, without the benefit of prior research or even standards to perform such research. However, now with the benefit of more than a century of psychological research, their theories had better be reexamined. The burgeoning field of cognitive neuroscience has illuminated many mental processes that underlie personality and behavior, and much of this research is not compatible with the early theorists. For example, psychoanalysis emphasizes understanding universal unconscious mental structures, while phenomenology emphasizes the need for the unique qualities of each individual to be understood and accepted. However, recent psychological research seems to indicate that humans may never be fully able to apprehend the nonconscious systems that motivate or guide their behavior.

Freud was right that nonconscious processes do indeed represent the preponderance of mind. However, Freud may have given the unconscious too much cleverness. Instead, current evidence strongly suggests that the nonconscious mind is comprised of a multiplicity of specialized brain components that process information outside of awareness. Along these lines, researchers such as Michael Gazzaniga, Jerry Fodor, Daniel Dennett, and others propose that the psyche is comprised of many tiny robots or specialized brain modules that nonconsciously regulate cognition. Are these theoreticians correct, or is Freud? We can only know through the rigors of empiricism and science.

Another pressing problem with the field of psychology it that it is the only science that regularly teaches as dogma what other fields would call hypotheses. We seem to forget that a theory is only conjecture, and conjecture without supporting evidence is of little use. Many of our current theories of development and of the mind were the speculations of great thinkers, and they have remained essentially unchanged for nearly a century. And no matter how great the thinker, his or her speculations need to be formulated as a verifiable hypothesis and tested. Unfortunately, this was often not done. The many students of developmental psychology who have been taught Freud's psychosexual stages, Jean Piaget's genetic epistemology, or Erik Erikson's eight developmental stages, for example, and completed the course without knowing which of these theories is correct or least empirically supported, speaks to this problem. Is there any legitimate epistemology other than the scientific method for psychology, counseling, or personality theory? No, there is not. Intuition, faith, creativity, and insight are merely starting points for the development of theories and hypotheses, which then need to be tested by scientific methods.

Since REBT is a constructivist approach, I accept that people do create their own realities, and to an extent their own personalities. However, the type of reality or personality we construct is limited by our humanness. Being human comes with a range of intellectual, behavioral, and perceptual constraints that are boundaries within which we can conceive and be within the world. Thus, humans can both be unique and have common qualities that can be studied and defined.

I ask that the reader take the same skeptical view that I take when presented with any standard or novel theory in psychology. This field has become one in which television psychologists presenting personal opinion as psychological fact are given more weight than researchers who have spent careers diligently advancing the field with legitimate new knowledge. Beware of this, as many professionals in the field who are required to know better do not. They often advise clients based on popular nonsense rather than on the body of research that underlies this wonderful science, psychology. Those studying psychology, counseling, social work, and the allied fields must base their interventions and treatments on science. They must never stop learning and never stop questioning. Yes, there is an art to psychology, but the art must be continuously shaped by the best available evidence.

▣ ACKNOWLEDGMENTS

We wish to thank Professor Gordon Bear of Ramapo College of New Jersey, whose insightful comments were helpful in the development of several sections of this book, and Professor Arthur Reber and Professor Anthony Sclafani of the Graduate Center and Brooklyn College of the City University of New York, whose pioneering work into the cognitive unconscious, evolutionary psychology, and biological psychology laid the foundation of many of the concepts set forth in this book. We also offer our gratitude to the very professional staff at Sage Publications, including Kassie Graves and Veronica Novak, who patiently persisted through the many stages of the book's development, and Jacqueline Tasch, for her steadfast patience in copy editing this work. We would also like to thank the reviewers, who made both interesting and useful comments, and Gino J. Patti for many original drawings.

Chapter 1

The Study of Personality

Introduction

Chapter Goals

- Provide an overview of the controversies in the field of personality
- Explain the purpose and utility of studying personality to mental health professionals
- Review the various definitions of human personality
- Offer insights into the history of personality theories
- Introduce some of the methods used to measure or evaluate personality
- Present some of the major personality theorists who have developed the concepts we will be studying

---

Subdisciplines of psychology such as social psychology, cognitive psychology, and industrial psychology endeavor to find common principles that will explain everyone's behavior. These subfields have achieved considerable success in doing so, since we are all similar in many ways. Despite our similarities, however, there is little doubt that each human being is unique—different from every other individual on the planet. Seeking to understand human commonalities and seeking to account for individual differences are complementary, insofar as we cannot fully apprehend differences if we cannot identify our common characteristics.

Personality psychology looks for answers to numerous questions. In what ways do human beings differ? In what situations and along what dimensions do they differ? Why do they differ? How much do they differ? How consistent are human differences? Can they be measured? These are the issues that this text will explore. An important aspect of this exploration will be a critical examination of the numerous theories that have been proposed to explain personality. Some of these are competing and contradictory while others are supportive and complementary.

Personality psychology was a latecomer among the various disciplines within psychology. Before it was adopted as a subject for study, however, it was already well established as a topic of discussion in the public domain. People have always been practicing personality psychology whether they have recognized it or not. When we seek the right person for a mate, our judgment of his or her personality is indispensable in evaluating our hoped-for compatibility. And are personnel directors really doing anything other than analyzing the applicant's personality during a job interview? Similarly, when we describe a physician as a "good doctor," have we really assessed the caliber of his or her medical knowledge? Or are we saying that we are satisfied with the doctor's professional persona? When we listen to political speeches, how do we rate the orators? Are we looking at their command of the issues or their political acumen? Or is it essentially their personality that we appraise? In most cases, it would seem the latter. These examples illustrate the omnipresence of informal personality assessment. It is a subject of universal interest and continual relevance in all human interactions. On the other hand, although the study of personality is compelling and important, personality as such is also very hard to pin down.

Personality falls under the heading of things that most people believe they understand. In fact, there is probably no domain within any field of knowledge in which more people think they have achieved some expertise. Simply put, most people believe they can know or understand other people. We all try to predict behavior, interpret conversations, and make inferences about others' actions. If someone offends us, acts strangely, or seems excessively kind, we will quickly try to understand their motives. In addition, we often draw inferences about what kind of people they are; that is, what personality traits they may possess. Most of us regard ourselves as competent judges of personality. We make use of our skills in personality assessment on a daily basis; however, most of us would have a difficult time explaining exactly how we draw our conclusions about others.

Besides evaluating and rating each other's personalities, we also tend to be confident that we are very good in so doing. It is rare to find someone who admits that he or she is not a good judge of people and does not understand the behavior of others. As this text will show, most of us are not only often incorrect in our assessments of others but also overconfident of our abilities. Most people have an innate trust in their ability to impute underlying motives to the actions of others. We are personality experts, or at least think we are. Moreover, once we evaluate someone else's personal qualities, we tend to interpret their subsequent actions through the lens of our initial assessment, making it difficult to see that we might have been inaccurate in the first place.

We tend to go through our lives categorizing the people we encounter under various labels. Our language is replete with words that describe types or groups of people, many of them quite pejorative. Words like *macho*, *wimp*, *nerd*, *milquetoast*, *playboy*, *redneck*, *square*, and *hippie* are used to categorize a type of person, most often one we find undesirable. This tendency to categorize people makes a great deal of sense in some contexts because it is a universal human characteristic to impose order on complex situations. As complex as human behavior can be, repeating patterns can be discerned.

Almost all human encounters involve classifying and categorizing personalities. For example, business people typically judge their associates on their general demeanor, physical bearing, verbal style, and presumed ability to fit into the milieu of a specific organization. University professors presenting technical papers to their colleagues will be judged to some extent on their personality. Indeed, it is hard to conceive of any interpersonal interaction in which the appraisal of personality does not play an important role.

Can anybody really understand human personality? Furthermore, does it even exist? Or is it a convenient construct that is so intangible as to have no meaning? In fact, some experts do not accept the notion that people have consistent personalities. These experts espouse **situationalism**; the most extreme members of this group reject the concept of personality completely. Situationalists propose that differences in human behavior are artifacts of the various situations in which human beings find themselves, as well as their cultural environments or social surrounds. The authors of this text, however, are confident that the construct of personality is real and legitimate and will demonstrate its legitimacy in the chapter on individual differences.

▣ THEORIES OF PERSONALITY

The study of personality has a long history. For example, Plato, Aristotle, Descartes, and Machiavelli, among numerous other philosophers and writers, explored human personality in their works. Many of their books reveal compelling insights into the human psyche. Modern theorists to a large extent echo the theories set forth by these earlier thinkers.

Plato

Plato (427–347 BCE) saw the human soul as the seat of personality. In his well-known dialogue, *The Republic* (c. 390 BCE), he said that the soul consists of three basic forces guiding human behavior: reason, emotion, and appetite. Reason is given the highest value whereas emotion and especially appetite are regarded as the "lower passions." Plato believed the most powerful of these forces is reason, which keeps the more primitive forces of appetite and emotion at bay.

Aristotle

Aristotle (384–322 BCE), one of Plato's students and the teacher of Alexander the Great, referred to the seat of personality as the **psyche**. His description of the psyche suggests that he was the first biological psychologist. Aristotle proposed that the psyche is the product of biological processes. He also saw the psyche as including a set of faculties that he placed in a hierarchy of importance. The first faculty that Aristotle distinguished is the nutritive—the human organism's basic

Photo 1.1   Niccolò Machiavelli (1469–1527)

drives to meet its bodily needs. This faculty can be found in plants as well as in animals and people. The next and higher faculty is the perceptual, which Aristotle defined as the aspect of mind that interprets sensory data. Animals as well as people have a perceptual faculty. The last and highest faculty is the intellectual, which Aristotle saw as unique to human beings.

Descartes

René Descartes (1596–1650), a French philosopher, viewed human personality as the product of the interaction of divine and primal forces. He saw the essential force behind human personality as the immortal soul—pure, perfect, and intangible. Descartes set out to explain how this spiritual entity interacted with the physical body. His observation of an anatomical dissection led him to think he had resolved this mind-body problem. He noticed a small body in the apparent center of the brain known as the **pineal gland** or **pineal body**, so named by the Greco-Roman physician Claudius Galen (c. 130–c. 200 CE) because its shape reminded him of a pine cone.

Descartes (1649) came to the conclusion that that this cone-shaped endocrine gland must be the point of contact between the soul and the body. Cartesian dualism, which is the philosophical position that two substances—matter and spirit, or brain and mind—exist independently of each other although they interact—became the most common view in the Christian West after the seventeenth century because it "explained" the existence of human free will and consciousness in an otherwise mechanistic universe. Indeed, before the advent of the computer, it seemed impossible to allow for consciousness without appealing to nonphysical concepts. Cartesian dualism is still the dominant view on the mind-body issue among the general public, although it is not held by cognitive psychologists or neurologists.

Machiavelli

In contrast to Descartes, Niccolò Machiavelli (1469–1527), a Florentine diplomat and political thinker, believed that personality is best understood in a social context. According to Machiavelli's worldview, people are essentially selfish, greedy, ungrateful, and vengeful.

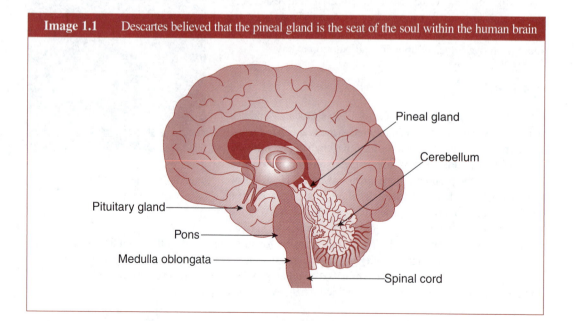

Image 1.1   Descartes believed that the pineal gland is the seat of the soul within the human brain

Furthermore, he saw two primary forces as defining human character. The first one is an almost untranslatable Italian term—**virtù**—which is best described as a combination of assertiveness, fearlessness, and self-confidence. Machiavelli called the second force *fortuna,* which is the Latin word for luck. A person could become a powerful leader with the help of a good dose of virtù and fortuna. Machiavelli (1546/1935) warned that leaders who act out of kindness and a belief in the essential goodness of humanity will always fail. This belief is sometimes expressed by contemporary people as "nice guys finish last."

Almost every major philosopher from ancient Greece and Rome through the Enlightenment proposed some form of personality theory, and many of their ideas served as the groundwork of theories set forth by modern psychologists. This text will concentrate on the theories that arose after the development of psychology as a distinct discipline. Because psychology is one of the social sciences, its practitioners seek not only to construct theories of personality or human behavior but also to find ways to test and validate them. As we will see, most of the more recent theorists in personality psychology claim to have discovered empirically verified principles as opposed to untested philosophical conjectures. Some have succeeded; some have not. The authors of this text, however, have little doubt that theories of personality should be held to the same standards used to judge theories in any other science.

▣ THE MAKING OF A THEORY

In attempting to explain natural phenomena, researchers systematically observe events or conduct experiments on the subject of interest. They then review their findings, looking for any patterns or consistent outcomes that they may have uncovered. Their final step is to assess their findings in light of prior studies in the field and then propose a comprehensive explanation that links these findings with earlier and current ones. This comprehensive explanation is called a **theory**.

We can consider an example from the history of medicine that illustrates the steps in the **scientific method.** In 1847, Ignaz Semmelweis (1818–1865), a young Austrian medical graduate who had just been appointed an assistant physician in midwifery at a large hospital in Vienna, noticed a puzzling phenomenon. There were two maternity wards in the hospital; patients in the first ward, attended by fully licensed physicians and medical students, had a rate of post-childbirth infection (called "puerperal fever" or "childbed fever") three times as high as that of patients in the second ward, who were attended only by nurses and midwives. Puerperal fever was a common cause of death following childbirth at the time that Semmelweis began his investigation.

Quantifications, observations, and measurements (sometimes called characterizations). Semmelweis began by keeping careful records of deaths from puerperal fever in the two wards under his care. In the 1840s, puerperal fever was commonly attributed to weather conditions, overcrowding in the hospital, or even the position in which the woman lay while giving birth. Semmelweis could find no correlation between climatic conditions or the number of patients in each ward and the number of cases of infection.

Hypotheses (theoretical or hypothetical explanations of the observations and measurements). Semmelweis tested the hypothesis, then widely taught in medical schools, that the position of the woman in childbirth was the cause of infection. He asked patients in both wards to lie in different positions during delivery. Again, he found no correlation.

Then a chance event led to the formulation of a new hypothesis. Semmelweis had a friend named Jacob Kolletschka, a professor of medicine, who died suddenly in March 1847 after performing an autopsy. During the autopsy, the professor had punctured his finger with a scalpel that had been used by one of his students to dissect an infected corpse. The description of the massive infection that killed Kolletschka haunted Semmelweis. In the younger doctor's own words,

> It rushed into my mind with irresistible clearness that the disease from which Kolletschka had died was identical with that from which I had seen so many hundreds of lying-in women die. The [patients] also died from phlebitis, lymphangitis, peritonitis, pleuritis, meningitis and in them also metastases sometime occurred. (Haggard, 2004, p. 86)

Semmelweis knew that the physicians and medical students who attended the women in the first of his two wards had usually spent the morning performing autopsies in another part of the hospital. Although the doctors washed their hands afterward with ordinary soap and water, Semmelweis suspected that this cleansing was not thorough enough and that the doctors were carrying infected material from the autopsy laboratory on their hands into the first delivery ward. The reason for the lower rate of infection in the second ward was that the nurses and midwives who attended the patients in that ward were not involved with autopsies. Semmelweis then formulated his new hypothesis:

> If this theory that the cadaveric material adhering to the hand can produce the same disease as the cadaveric particles adhering to the scalpel be correct, then if the cadaveric material on the hands can be completely destroyed by chemical agencies, and the genitals of the woman in labour or in the lying-in state, be brought into contact with the clean fingers only, and not simultaneously with cadaveric particles, then the disease can be prevented to the extent to which it originated by the presence of cadaveric material on the examining fingers. (Sinclair, 1909)

Predictions based on reasoning, including logical deductions from the hypotheses and theories. Next, Semmelweis predicted that the doctors' use of a strong disinfectant to cleanse their hands would lower the rate of infection among women in the first ward. He began with the nineteenth-century equivalent of chlorine bleach:

> I began about the middle of May, 1847, to employ *chlorina liquida* with which every student was required to wash his hands before making an examination. After a short time a solution of *chlorinated lime* was substituted because it was not so expensive. In the month of May, 1847, the mortality in the first Clinic still amounted to over 12 per cent, with the remaining seven months it was reduced in very remarkable degree. (Sinclair, 1909)

Experiments or Tests of All of the Above. Semmelweis continued to keep records of the infection rate in the two wards following the introduction of antisepsis:

> In the first seven months [from May through December of 1847] mortality was 3 per cent compared to 11.4 per cent prior to introduction of antisepsis. This compared to 2.7 per cent

in the Second Division [ward]. In 1848 the mortality fell to 1.27 per cent versus 1.3 percent in the Second Division. In 1848 there were two months, March and August, in which not one single death occurred among the patients of the First Division. (Sinclair, 1909)

Figure 1.2 is a visual review of the steps that psychologists and other scientists use to formulate a theory.

In any science, researchers construct a theory in such a way as to lead to **hypotheses**, or predictions based on that theory, that are subject to **verification** and **falsifiability**. That is, it must be stated in such a way that scientific experiments can be designed to test the applicability of the theory to real-world situations. Thus, a genuinely scientific theory must be precise, specific, and at least in some ways quantifiable.

To see the importance of these qualifications, let us suppose a theory that states that all manifestations of personality are a result of the soul's actions. How would we test this theory? First, we would have to define *soul* precisely. Then, we would have to devise a way to measure the soul and its effect on behavior. These measurements would be difficult at best. Although attempts were made by a Massachusetts physician named Duncan MacDougall to prove that the human soul has mass and weight (he weighed dying patients lying on a specially constructed bed in his office shortly before and shortly after death), his experiment—reported in the *New York Times* on March 11, 1907—would not have defined the soul to the satisfaction of all scientists, nor would he have proved that the soul affects human behavior even if he had succeeded in showing that it has a measurable weight.

Alternatively, suppose we have a theory that states that a person's response to fear and anger is mediated by the **amygdala** (an almond-shaped region of the brain associated with the emotions of aggression and fear). Here we have a proposition that is quite testable; it can be verified or falsified. This is exactly what Paul Whalen and his colleagues (2001) set out to do.

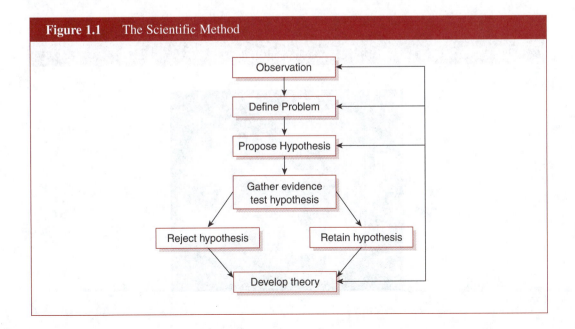

Figure 1.1   The Scientific Method

They showed participants photographs of faces expressing either fear or anger. The researchers then employed functional magnetic resonance imaging (fMRI), which is a technique that graphically depicts ongoing activity within the brain. In effect, fMRI can show the locations where thought is taking place within the brain while the subject is thinking. Whalen's team found that brain activity is significantly elevated in the amygdala when people viewed faces showing fear and is elevated to a lesser extent when they viewed angry faces.

It is important to understand that the word *theory* is used in formal science in quite a different way from its uses in ordinary speech. People often use *theory* informally to mean a guess or a hunch. In scientific usage, however, a theory is an organized set of principles that explains and makes verifiable predictions about some aspect or segment of reality. Theories are not opposed to facts; rather, facts are the building blocks of theories.

The ability to formulate specific and testable theories in personality psychology is vital if this field of study is to be a science in the full sense of the word. Yet personality psychology still lacks a full consensus as to what exactly is being studied. We can agree that the term *personality* describes enduring and reasonably consistent patterns of behavior, **perception**, attitudes, and cognition. But psychologists cannot as yet agree as to how these enduring patterns develop and come to be established in human beings.

As we move from descriptive accounts of personality to specific theories and models, we see progressive divergence among researchers in the field. When a descriptive account is founded on a theory of origin or structure, it gives way to an array of theoretical models or schools. In this context, *school* refers to a loose grouping of psychologists whose work and interpretation of data reflect a common conceptual foundation or the personal influence of a teacher. Each school attempts to provide a comprehensive and reasonably consistent understanding of patterns of human behavior. Personality psychology, more than any other area within psychology, is now defined and divided by these schools.

Image 1.2   Functional MRI Image of a Human Brain

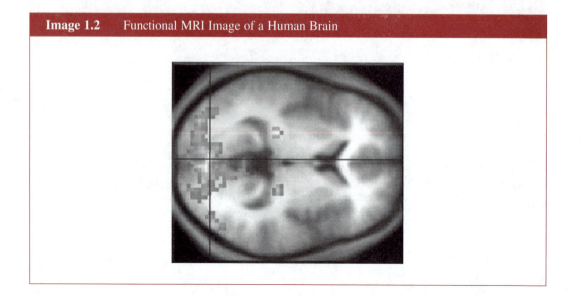

Jean-Martin Charcot, Pierre Janet, Sigmund Freud, Alfred Adler, Carl Jung, John Watson, B. F. Skinner, and Carl Rogers all set forth their own schools of personality psychology. As we will see, their models vary widely, and they were all highly individual thinkers. Such people frequently provide the impetus for new advances and ideas. However, no theorist, however gifted or original, should have his or her ideas accepted without testing and experimentation. The study of and research into human personality must proceed in an open and empirically based fashion in order to reach a point at which psychology will be able to explain and predict human behavior more accurately. A great deal of research is needed before we can even discriminate clearly between the so-called "normal" and the "pathological."

As of the early 2000s, there is little agreement about what portion of human personality can be attributed to **genes**, biology, or biochemistry. Indeed, the ancient mind-body problem has not yet been resolved. A significant number of psychologists believe that unconscious processes actively and independently guide all human behavior. While some theorists are firm in the belief that the **unconscious** is merely a by-product of neurological processes, still others believe that personality is derived from supernatural—or at least unobservable and unfalsifiable—entities.

The significance of personality psychology as well as the importance of its continued advance and improvement is evident whenever society is threatened by a human predator or a menacing despot. Fearsome people like a serial killer or a tyrannical leader are often analyzed for media consumption by personality experts who freely make predictions of and explanations for the behavior of these sociopaths. The earliest and best-known example of this type of analysis is the psychiatrist Walter Langer's (1899–1981) assessment of the mind of Adolf Hitler, undertaken in secrecy in 1943 for the U.S. Office of Strategic Services. Langer's (1972) study, finally published in the 1970s, was famous for predicting that Hitler would commit suicide rather than surrender when he was forced to recognize that the war was lost.

As Langer was recruited by a wartime intelligence agency, contemporary personality specialists are called on by law enforcement agencies to develop profiles to aid in the capture of serial murderers and other criminals. An example of psychological profiling that has been used in forensic casebooks is the case of John Duffy, an English serial rapist and killer who terrorized northwest London for four years between 1982 and 1986. A professor of behavioral science at Surrey University was asked in July 1986 to draw up a psychological profile of the offender. When Duffy was arrested shortly afterward, his personality characteristics matched 13 of the 17 points in the professor's profile (Evans, 1996, pp. 163–165).

This text will examine all the prominent schools of thought in personality psychology and will analyze and critique the numerous models offered by these schools. The authors will also present an integrative model of human personality built on the vast body of personality research and on the half-century of clinical experience of Albert Ellis and his associates.

PERSONALITY: A FUZZY SET

In mathematics, a **fuzzy set** is a set of objects in which each member is assigned a number that indicates the degree to which the member belongs to the set. For example, although people are often assigned to the set of conservative or liberal, any individual's actual assignment would, most appropriately, be a function of their accepting certain beliefs or principles over competing beliefs. Hence, as someone adopts more beliefs regarding minimal government intervention, the probability of their being assigned to the conservative set increases. In contrast, as someone adheres to an increasing number of beliefs in favor of social welfare programs, the probability of being assigned to the liberal set increases. Thus, unlike a more clearly defined set like gender, a membership in a fuzzy set is probabilistic.

Fuzzy set theory is often used in decision making with imprecise data. Some observers would define theories of personality as an example of a fuzzy set because the concept of personality seems so imprecise. Potter Stewart, a former associate justice of the Supreme Court, once made a telling statement about pornography. Stewart said, "I cannot define it, but I know it when I see it." He could just as easily have been describing personality. Most of us think we have a personality; we recognize personalities in others; but most of us would have a difficult time pinning down exactly what the word means. Here are some recent attempts at defining personality:

> The collective perceptions, emotions, cognitions, motivations, and actions of the individual that interact with various environmental situations. (Patrick & Léon-Carrión, 2001)

> The psychological forces that make people uniquely themselves. (Friedman & Schustack, 2006)

> The various styles of behavior that different organisms habitually reflect. (Rychlak, 1981)

> The visible aspect of one's character as it impresses others. (Random House *Webster's College Dictionary,* 1991)

> The characteristic manner in which one thinks, feels, behaves, and relates to others. (Widiger, Verheul, & van den Brink, 1999)

If we desired, we could fill an entire book with elegant but divergent definitions of personality. Most would bear a family resemblance to one another, but no two would be completely concordant. How can this be? How can a term that is used by both professionals and lay people on a daily basis not have a standard definition? Perhaps the variations exist for that very reason—that is, when a clinical or technical term enters everyday speech, it loses its original precision. For this and related reasons, the editors of the *Diagnostic and Statistical Manual of Mental Disorders* (DSM) of the American Psychiatric Association (APA) typically change the names of several psychological disorders in each new edition. An example of this transition is the term **psychosomatic**. This term originally referred to a physical symptom or disorder caused or notably influenced by psychological dysfunction. Over time, however, *psychosomatic* came to be used in popular magazines or newspapers to refer to imaginary or **psychogenic** symptoms. It was ultimately replaced in the fourth edition of the *Diagnostic and Statistical Manual* (DSM-IV; APA, 2000) by a diagnostic category titled Psychological Factors Affecting Medical Condition. The example given in the manual of a medical condition affected by a psychological factor is that of a person with weight-related diabetes who continues to overeat from anxiety.

The definition of personality that will be used in this text is: behaviors, styles of thought, speech, perception, and interpersonal interactions that are consistently characteristic of an individual. This definition includes both the overt and covert actions of an individual. Covert actions refer to all cognitive processes, both conscious and **nonconscious**.

It is important to note that our use of the term *nonconscious* is not the same as the psychoanalytic use of unconscious. As will be further discussed in the chapter on cognitive models of personality, the human brain processes a great deal of information outside its field of conscious awareness. These are called nonconscious cognitions.

▣ NORMAL AND PATHOLOGICAL PERSONALITIES

Although distinguishing between a normal personality and one that is dysfunctional, ill, or otherwise problematic may seem simple, it is not. The distinction between *normal* and *abnormal* remains one of the most vexing issues in personality psychology. When describing a normal personality, we can be certain of one thing—that our definition will be found lacking at least by some people. The Quaker saying, "All the world is queer save me and thee, and sometimes I think thee is a little queer," definitely captures the subjective nature of defining normality.

The distinction between *normal* and *pathological* is almost always arbitrary and, to some extent, an expression of the preferences of the individual making the distinction. Of course, in the case of such severe extremes as obsessive or compulsive personalities, or of individuals falling within the spectrum of **schizophrenia**, even a layperson can often determine that there is some pathology to be found in the afflicted person's personality. It is not, for example, normal for people to hear voices commanding them to kill someone, as the assassin of President James Garfield claimed after shooting him in 1881 (Rosenberg, 1968). By definition, however, such extreme conditions are unusual.

Another obvious means of determining pathology is by self-report. People who have personalities that cause them subjective misery can clearly be categorized as having pathological characteristics. Most personalities, however, cluster around the central tendencies of the more common personality configurations. Choosing the point at which a divergence from that mean becomes pathological is difficult. It involves making sharp divisions in what is basically a continuum—a problem that recurs in other contexts.

Each of the various schools of psychology has its own means of distinguishing the normal from the pathological. For example, a Freudian psychoanalyst would posit defects in the person's **intrapsychic** defense mechanisms, perhaps a breakdown of **ego** defenses against **id** impulses. Or the psychoanalyst might say that the overinvestment of mental energy in an intrapsychic **object** can result in a pathological personality. These terms will be explained in Chapter 4. A simpler model of pathology was proposed by the classical school of behaviorism. Behaviorists regard all personality pathology as resulting from aberrant conditioning and subsequent reinforcement. For example, a behaviorist would say that a perennially shy person was trained to be this way through parental **reinforcement**, and his/her personality remains shy due to reinforcers found in the person's present environment.

Exercise 1

Prepare a brief outline of what you see as the elements of a normal personality and the elements of an abnormal personality. Then describe your difficulty in making the determination.

VIGNETTE

According to the Old Testament (1 Samuel 16), David, the second king of Israel, had quite humble origins. He was an illiterate shepherd with two notable talents—fearlessness and deadly accuracy with a slingshot. These talents allowed David to rise rapidly in prestige and power when he employed them to slay the giant Philistine warrior, Goliath. After the death of King Saul in battle, David became the king of the Israelites (2 Samuel 2), but David did not fare well with the absolute power of a monarch. He became something of a tyrannical warrior king. After developing a passion for the wife of one of his officers, he conspired to send the man to his death in the front line of a battle (2 Samuel 11), essentially murdering a rival for a woman's love. In addition to David's other moral failings, he was prone to fits of exhibitionism, at one point dancing naked among his subjects (2 Samuel 6). King David is an instance of a Biblical figure whose personality became one dimension of his religious significance. Solomon was known for his wisdom and reflection (1 Kings 3), while Herod (Matthew 2) was known for his vanity and cruelty.

World history, like biblical history, is often guided by the vagaries of human personality. Alexander the Great's narcissistic conviction that he was a god, particularly after it appeared to be confirmed by an oracle at the oasis of Siwa during the Macedonian invasion of Egypt (331 BCE), played an essential role in his conquest of a great portion of the known world. Elizabeth I's reluctance to marry, possibly rooted in incestuous overtures from her stepfather during her adolescence as well as in her father Henry VIII's execution of her mother in 1536, kept England's domestic affairs free from interference by other European powers during the queen's lifetime. Mohandas Gandhi possessed a high degree of self-discipline and focus that rallied his people and led to the independence of India and Pakistan from Great Britain. In contrast, Josef Stalin's cruelty and paranoia led to a reign of terror in the Soviet Union that was responsible for the death of millions in the 1930s. The personality of key historical figures, past and present, is a major factor in the outcomes of significant events.

Each chapter of this text will include a vignette of a famous, infamous, or ordinary individual to illustrate the significance of personality in determining the fate of the individual or even the world.

Vignette Question

1. Why do you think David, despite clearly violating many social mores, is still presented as a biblical paradigm?

SCHOOLS AND MODELS OF PERSONALITY

Virtually all approaches to the study of personality can be divided into two categories, idiographic and nomothetic. The oldest approach and the one employed in literature for millennia is the **idiographic.** Idiographic personality theorists stress the uniqueness of individual personalities, suggesting that no two are exactly alike. A follower of this approach would study each person as a complete and unique entity and would not compare his or her personality to others. The Greek philosopher Theophrastus (372–287 BCE) took this approach more than 23 centuries ago, in his book *Characters*. In it, he described several prototypical personalities, most of which could easily describe a present-day person. His description of the flatterer is as follows:

> The Flatterer is a person who will say as he walks with another, "Do you observe how people are looking at you? This happens to no man in Athens but you. A compliment was paid to you yesterday in the Porch. More than thirty persons were sitting there; the question was started, who is our foremost man? Everyone mentioned you first, and ended by coming back to your name." With these and the like words, he will remove a morsel of wool from his patron's coat; or if a speck of chaff has been laid on the other's hair by the wind, he will pick it off; adding with a laugh, "Do you see? Because I have not met you for two days, you have had your beard full of white hairs; although no one has darker hair for his years than you." Then he will request the company to be silent while the great man is speaking, and will praise him, too, in his hearing, and mark his approbation at a pause with "True"; or he will laugh at a frigid joke, and stuff his cloak into his mouth as if he could not repress his amusement. He will request those whom he meets to stand still until "his Honour" has passed. He will buy apples and pears and bring them in and give them to the children in the father's presence; adding with kisses, "Chicks of a good father." Also when he assists at the purchase of slippers, he will declare that the foot is more shapely than the shoe. If his patron is approaching a friend, he will run forward and say, "He is coming to you," and then turning back, "I have announced you." He is just the person, too, who can run errands to the Women's Market without drawing breath. He is the first of the guests to praise the wine; and to say, as he reclines next the host, "How delicate is your fare!" and (taking up something from the table) "Now this—how excellent it is!" He will ask his friend if he is cold, and if he would like to put on something more; and before the words are spoken, will wrap him up. Moreover he will lean towards his ear and whisper with him; or will glance at him as he talks to the rest of the company. He will take the cushions from the slave in the theatre, and spread them on the seat with his own hands. (cited in Roback, 1928, p. 9)

Theophrastus depicts an ingratiating person whose primary goal is to gain standing with another person through psychological manipulation. Most of us have encountered or at least witnessed sycophants playing on another person's vanity to obtain some advantage. The question raised by such people is whether they differ in kind from the majority or merely in degree of some particular trait. Those who take a **nomothetic** approach to personality psychology would strongly affirm the latter proposition. The nomothetic approach stresses that uniqueness exists only as a combination of quantifiable traits. According to this model, we all have a number of traits in common, and we differ only in the amount of each trait we possess.

The first nomothetic personality psychologist may very well have been Claudius Galen, a Greco-Roman physician of the second century CE. We have encountered Galen earlier as the writer who gave the pineal body the name by which it is still known. He proposed that various combinations of the four **humors** or bodily fluids regulated human personality. The four humors he identified were blood, phlegm, black bile, and yellow bile. According to the

Photo 1.2   Sigmund Freud (1856–1939)

relative predominance of each humor in the individual, these fluids were supposed to produce temperaments designated respectively as *sanguine* (warm, pleasant), *phlegmatic* (slow-moving, apathetic), *melancholic* (depressed, sad), and *choleric* (quick to react, hot-tempered). From a historical perspective, Galen's four humors could be considered the equivalent of a modern four-factor (Lester, 1990) model of personality.[1]

Sigmund Freud (1856–1939), arguably the most influential personality theorist even in the twenty-first century, could be classified as nomothetic in his approach. He created a fascinating complex model of developmental stages, drives, and psychic structures. Indeed, he was an exceptional observer of human behavior. Freud is justly entitled to praise for developing his complicated explanations of personality: In so doing, he made the study of personality interesting and helped to start the process of research into personality in earnest.

Freud's first attempt at understanding personality is found in his *Project for a Scientific Psychology*, written in 1895 as part of his correspondence with Wilhelm Fliess. In this early model, Freud attempted to explain consciousness and human drives as outgrowths of the structure and interrelationships of neurons or nerve cells. Failing in this project, Freud moved on to his later topological and structural models of the psyche. His system resembled the celestial model of Ptolemy (c. 90–c. 168 CE), an Egyptian astronomer who became a Roman citizen. Ptolemy explained the observed motions of the planets while holding that the Earth was at the center of the universe. Specifically, Ptolemy's geocentric system appeared somewhat accurate in predicting planetary movements, but its faulty underlying assumptions necessitated increasingly complex modifications to explain apparent exceptions. We see the same process occurring with Freud's model of the psyche. His theory of human personality was superficially accurate in its descriptions of many human attributes. As his successors examined it more closely over time, however, they found a growing number of gaps and flaws. We can only hope that had Freud lived longer, he would have adjusted his model to accommodate the evidence of current research in personality.

Freud was followed by figures like Alfred Adler (1870–1937), who added the concepts of inferiority feelings and personal striving to the Freudian system. Then there was Carl Jung (1875–1961), who added numerous mystical elements, such as the collective unconscious shared by people across generations, archetypes of unconscious symbols, and a personality typology based on four functions of the mind—thinking, feeling, sensation, and intuition. Karen Horney (1885–1952), variously classified as a neo-Freudian or social psychologist, produced her own brand of psychoanalysis focused on the striving child.

The vast majority of contemporary textbooks in the field of personality psychology follow a common outline, classifying personality theories into three large groups: psychoanalytic, behavioral, and humanistic. And most of these texts continue to emphasize psychoanalytic theory as a viable explanation of human personality and behavior. This text will explore this fascinating starting point, but it will also show it as just that: a starting point. This text will examine it under the bright light of contemporary research in experimental psychology.

Table 1.1	Major Schools of Personality Psychology	
School	*Founders*	*Essential Premises*
Psychoanalytic	Sigmund Freud	Self-regulating and independent unconscious processes make up the essence of personality. They operate though mental structures that are in continual conflict.
Neo-psychoanalytic	Alfred Adler, Carl Jung, Karen Horney	Conscious individual, social, and interpersonal factors are powerful forces in shaping personality.
Humanistic	Albert Ellis, Carl Rogers, Abraham Maslow	People are basically good and strive toward maximum personal development or self-actualization.
Behavioral	John Watson, B. F. Skinner	Personality is the observable result of reinforcement.
Genetic/Biological	William Sheldon, Edmund O. Wilson, Hans Eysenck	Genes, hormones, and neurochemicals in the brain regulate the greater portion of human personality.
Trait	Raymond Cattell, Hans Eysenck	Differences among people can be reduced to a limited number of distinct behavioral styles or traits.
Cognitive/REBT	Albert Bandura, Ulric Neisser, Albert Ellis	Personality results from the interplay of learned and innate styles of thinking.

▣ PERSONALITY ASSESSMENT

Virtually all interpersonal interactions involve a personality assessment. All prospective lovers will have their personalities rated by those who arouse their passions. And what is a job interview if not a personality test (Yadav, 1990)? As we will discuss in detail in later chapters, assessments like those carried out in job interviews may lack standardization, reliability, and validity, but they are indeed personality tests.

Every human encounter is at least in part a personality assessment. Indeed, while some observers strongly object to formal, objective, and empirically evaluated personality tests, all of us are both subjects and administrators of a subjective personality test with each such encounter. People tend to identify with generic and positive descriptions of personality; that is, we all tend to be easily convinced that someone or some system (like astrology) has captured our essence, even though it actually presents only benign generic descriptions with which most people would identify. An American psychologist named Bertram R. Forer (1914–2000) conducted an interesting experiment in 1948, which he described in an article published in 1949. He gave his students a personality test and then gave each of them a personality analysis supposedly based on the results of the test. He then asked the students to rate their analysis as to how well it applied to them on a scale ranging from 0 = *very poorly* to 5 = *excellent*. The students gave their analyses an average rating of 4.27. Forer then revealed that he had given all the students the identical personality analysis and that he had compiled it from a series of newspaper horoscopes. Here is the analysis that Forer (1949) gave his students:

> You have a need for other people to like and admire you, and yet you tend to be critical of yourself. While you have some personality weaknesses you are generally able to compensate for them. You have considerable unused capacity that you have not turned to your advantage. Disciplined and self-controlled on the outside, you tend to be worrisome and insecure on the inside. At times you have serious doubts as to whether you have made the right decision or done the right thing. You prefer a certain amount of change and variety and become dissatisfied when hemmed in by restrictions and limitations. You also pride yourself as an independent thinker; and do not accept others' statements without satisfactory proof. But you have found it unwise to be too frank in revealing yourself to others. At times you are extroverted, affable, and sociable, while at other times you are introverted, wary, and reserved. Some of your aspirations tend to be rather unrealistic. (p. 120)

The principle that Forer studied was later designated the Barnum effect, after the famous showman Phineas T. Barnum, by the psychologist Paul Meehl (Dickson & Kelly, 1985).

Formal personality assessments, performed either with projective instruments like the Rorschach inkblot series, objective tests like the Minnesota Multiphasic Personality Inventory (MMPI), or an interview by a credentialed professional, must exceed a standard set by the Barnum effect (Andersen & Nordvik, 2002; Dickson & Kelly, 1985; Furnham & Schofield, 1987; Snyder, Shenkel, & Lowery, 1977). In other words, scientific assessment methods must be falsifiable and partly validated in ways other than by subjective agreement among examiners. Assessment tools must predict behavior better than chance, and they must be based on psychologically valid methods.

More than a modicum of research into personality has been confounded by the Barnum effect. The history of psychological research includes techniques like **phrenology**, which captivated both scientists and the lay population. For a nearly a generation the most widely known method for personality analysis, phrenology was based on the shape of persons' heads. Phrenological guidebooks sounded very much like horoscopes. Both participants and researchers endorsed personality profiles that sounded appropriate, even though the profiles did not have a meaningful association with the behavior of the individuals they sought to measure. The legacy we can derive from such techniques is caution. As we will show, all techniques used to assess personality must be at a minimum superior to methods that appear meaningful largely as a result of the Barnum effect.

The Rorschach, the Thematic Apperception Test, and the Draw-A-Person Test are all examples of personality tests predicated on the notion that dynamic unconscious forces lie at the foundation of human personality. These and similar assessment tools have a long and controversial history in the study of personality and will be examined in detail. Such objective tests as the Minnesota Multiphasic Personality Inventory, the Millon Clinical Multiaxial Inventory, the California Personality Inventory, and the Edwards Personal Preference Schedule have a slightly shorter history of use. These tests are generally based on empirical research

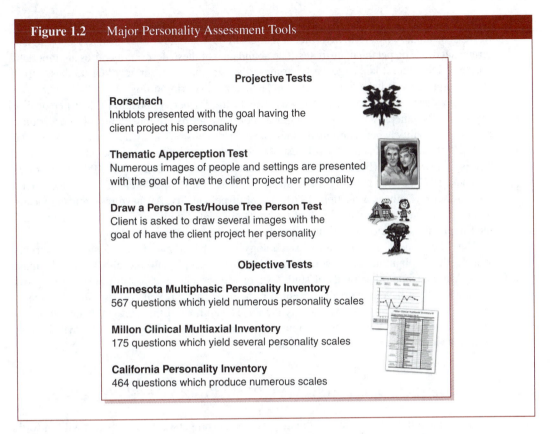

Figure 1.2   Major Personality Assessment Tools

Projective Tests

Rorschach
Inkblots presented with the goal having the client project his personality

Thematic Apperception Test
Numerous images of people and settings are presented with the goal of have the client project her personality

Draw a Person Test/House Tree Person Test
Client is asked to draw several images with the goal of have the client project her personality

Objective Tests

Minnesota Multiphasic Personality Inventory
567 questions which yield numerous personality scales

Millon Clinical Multiaxial Inventory
175 questions which yield several personality scales

California Personality Inventory
464 questions which produce numerous scales

and are continually evaluated and updated on the basis of more recent evidence. They have the marked advantage of avoiding the taint of administrative bias.

The specific meaning of the items or questions in these assessment instruments is not as important as the casual observer might think. The way a person responds to clusters of these items actually constitutes characteristic behavioral responses associated with personality types or traits. This approach to personality assessment has proven to have a high level of **validity**. On the horizon are new techniques utilizing fMRI, positron emission tomography (PET) scans, and others that directly associate personality with activity in specific areas of the brain. These techniques are in their infancy; but it is likely that the next generation of personality psychologists will have powerful tools to assist them in understanding human nature.

TRAITS, TYPOLOGIES, AND CHARACTER

Most of us are inclined to categorize people; psychologists are no exception. Freud proposed several character types based on his theory of childhood development. The so-called oral, anal, urethral, phallic, and genital personalities refer to persons whose sexual energies became diverted or stalled during certain phases of development. The English language is replete with far more terms that describe types of character or personality. Words like *shy*, *aggressive*, *kind*, *introverted*, *neurotic*, or *fixated* are just samples of the nearly 17,000 English terms that describe personal attributes. The abundance of these descriptors raises an important question: Did natural language evolve to describe personality accurately? Or do these terms really describe overt behaviors rather than lasting and enduring traits?

The evidence seems to suggest a weak *yes* to the former supposition. Most personality psychologists generally agree that composites of these terms are indeed useful in describing human personality when combined along specific dimensions known as factors. As of the early 2000s, the Five-Factor Model best describes the dimensions of personality. There are, however, a two-factor (Block, 2001), a three-factor (Eysenck, 1991, 1992, 1994; Eysenck & Eysenck, 1971), a four-factor (Brown, Strong, & Rencher, 1974; Merenda, 1987), and even a sixteen-factor (Delhees & Cattell, 1970) model of personality. All have research supporting them, and all have adherents. Some of the traits associated with the Eysenck two-factor and the Cattell sixteen-factor personality models are presented in Figure 1.4.

Thus the student of personality psychology must be prepared to examine the various systems that explain human personality and look more deeply into those that make the most sense. Unlike some other fields of study, personality psychology is still a work in progress that does not yet have universally accepted principles. Many psychologists still subscribe to one of the various schools of personality theory. The authors of this text will help you in this process of exploring the various options but we recommend that you engage the different points of view with an open and critical mind.

THE RATIONAL EMOTIVE BEHAVIORAL PERSPECTIVE

In addition to a thorough review of the major theories and perspectives, this text will set forth its own model and perspective, based on the work of its first author, Dr. Albert Ellis (1913–2007). His theory of personality, referred to as the Rational Emotive Behavioral Therapy (REBT) model, is described here. Dr. Ellis practiced psychoanalysis in New York City prior to 1955 but left the field of traditional psychoanalysis in that year to practice a more directive form of psychotherapy, which he first called Rational-Emotive Therapy or RET. He later changed its name to Rational Emotive Behavioral Therapy (REBT). For close to half a century the practice of REBT has been predicated on a theory of human personality, but prior to the early 2000s, Ellis's theory has largely been implied in his books rather than stated explicitly.

Ellis's formal break with his psychoanalytic training came with the publication of his paper, "Rational Psychotherapy," which was first delivered as a lecture at the American Psychological Association's annual convention in Chicago on August 31, 1956. The paper was then published in the *Journal of General Psychology*; it was one of the earliest contributions to cognitive theories of personality.

Unlike such theorists as George Kelly (1905–1966) and Albert Bandura (1925–), Ellis was a clinician who described his findings in clinical terms. And unlike most theoretical psychologists, his point of view was based on the accumulated experience of working closely with more than 10,000 persons in therapy over the course of half a century. Ellis (1958a, 1976) observed early in his career that a key component of human personality is irrationality, which often leads to cognitive, emotional, and behavioral dysfunction. An example of what Ellis meant by irrationality is the tendency of people to prefer short-term satisfaction of desires

Figure 1.3   Personality Traits: Two and 16 Dimensions

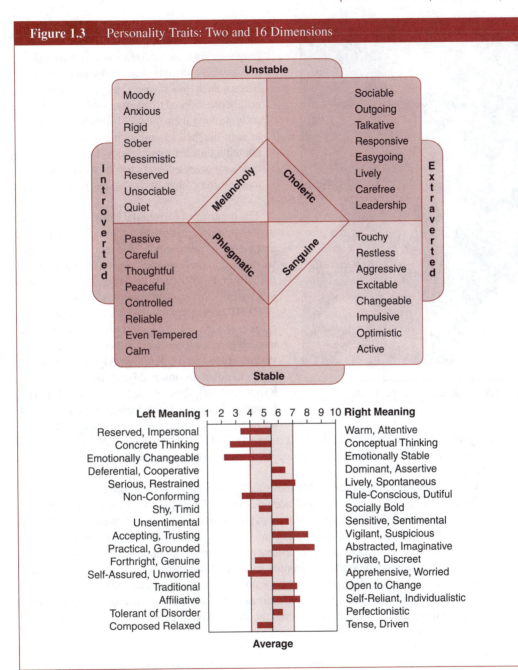

("I *must* have what I want *now*") to longer-term benefits ("It's better to build a good credit rating by paying my bills on time than a poor one caused by overspending"). Ellis said in 1987,

Photo 1.3   Dr. Albert Ellis (1913–2007)

I am still haunted by the reality, however, that humans—and I mean practically all humans—have a strong biological tendency to needlessly and severely disturb themselves and that, to make matters much worse, they also are powerfully predisposed to unconsciously and habitually prolong their mental dysfunctioning and to fight like hell against giving it up. No, I do not think they are masochistic—I think . . . that they are obsessed with the pleasures of the moment rather than of the future. (p. 365)

The treatment of irrational thinking became one of the primary predicates of his clinical method and theory of personality. This text will be the first work to comprehensively examine and integrate the vast body of thought and research on this subject by Ellis, his students, and his associates.

REBT uses a multifactorial and biological view of personality. Ellis's assertion that people are innately irrational has been validated by numerous studies (Ellis, 1976; Kendler, Myers, & Prescott, 2002; Kendler, Jacobson, Myers, & Prescott, 2002; Kendler, Myers, Prescott, & Neale, 2001; Knowles, Mannuzza, & Fyer, 1995; Ruth, 1992). This idea is not new, and in fact, it was a premise of the early psychoanalysts. For example, Morton Prince (1854–1929), the founder of the *Journal of Abnormal Psychology*, stated the following in an early text on personality theory:

> There is every reason to believe that intrinsically there is no essential difference between those physiological dispositions and activities of the lower nervous centers (subcortical ganglia and spinal cord), which condition and determine unconscious behavior, and those dispositions and activities of the higher centers—the cortex—which condition and determine both conscious and unconscious behavior. The former are undoubtedly innate in that they are primarily conditioned by inherited anatomical and physiological prearrangements of neurons and the latter are preeminently acquired through experience although probably not wholly so. (Our knowledge of the localization of function in the nervous system is not sufficiently definite to enable us to delimit the localization of either innate or acquired dispositions.) (Prince, 1921, p. 230)

Prince's proposition that personality can best be understood through the understanding of the brain is not new, but models of personality must integrate current neurological research to the greatest extent possible.

REBT views the brain as the seat of personality and genetics as the blueprint of the brain's development. It also regards these same factors as the basis of the irrationality that distorts much of our personality. Many behavioral dispositions are genetic in origin and, like most other genetic traits, developed as adaptations to the environment. This pattern of adaptation will be explored further in the section on natural selection. The connections between genetic endowments and personality can be better understood when we examine some other paradoxes of human evolution. For example, people born with the trait for sickle cell anemia have an adaptive advantage over those who lack the trait in countries where malaria is endemic. Evolutionary advantage may also explain genetic tendencies toward obesity in some populations. In times of famine, people who gain weight easily, have a lower metabolic rate, and are more motivated to seek food will be far more likely to survive and reproduce.

In the same manner as obesity and the sickle cell trait, many human behavioral tendencies evolved in very different ecological settings from those of our current world. The environment in which modern humans lived as hunters and gatherers for 99% of their existence has been termed the **environment of evolutionary adaptedness** (EEA) by John Bowlby (1907–1990) as part of his **attachment theory**. The human EEA is broadly identified with the Pleistocene era, a period of prehistoric time that began about 1.8 million years ago and ended about 12,000 years ago. Modern humans are left with behavioral and emotional residues that were probably quite adaptive in the Pleistocene era. For example, the well-known "fight or flight" reaction to stress increased a primitive human's chances of survival when confronted by a predatory animal. In the contemporary world, however, this same reaction may predispose us to respond with inappropriate and maladaptive emotions—as when a driver cut off in traffic gives in to "road rage" and behaves in ways that may actually cost lives (Gaylin, 1984, p. 124). It follows then that much of what is considered unacceptable behavior not only might be beneficial in a different environment but might actually endow some people with a distinct survival advantage. The concept of the EEA is integral to the REBT model of personality and psychotherapy. People are innately irrational partly because they have acquired a set of behavioral inclinations adapted to different times and places.

As Daniel Kahneman (1934–) and his colleague Amos Tversky (1937–1996) (Kahneman & Tversky, 2000; Tversky & Kahneman, 1973, 1983) have observed, people make decisions based on universal **heuristics**, or rules of thumb encoded in the human psyche by evolutionary processes. These rules of thumb are used by psychologists to explain how people make decisions or value judgments, or solve problems when they are dealing with incomplete information. Many of these heuristics may superficially seem logical and adaptive, but on closer examination, they lead to poor or biased decisions. A commonplace example, well-known to the advertising industry, is that people typically perceive an expensive name brand of food as tasting "better" than a generic store brand. Kahneman and Tversky concluded that people have a very poor ability to judge probabilities.

Such a universal tendency is unlikely to be accidental. These heuristics, like Bowlby's (1982) attachment theory, may be an evolutionary residue that allowed humans to make snap judgments in less complex times. The "quick and dirty" decision strategies essential in avoiding information overload but likely to lead to fallacies are called cognitive heuristics.

The REBT view of personality makes no use of a dynamic unconscious in the Freudian sense but fully acknowledges the significance of nonconscious processes in personality (Beck & Hollon, 1993; Ellis, 1995b; Kihlstrom et al., 1988; Lewicki, Czyzewska, & Hill, 1997). Given the vast accumulation of research by cognitive psychologists, neuroscientists, and other researchers, this finding must be accepted as beyond serious dispute. Furthermore, REBT differs dramatically from the psychodynamic schools of therapy in that the nonconscious foundations of personality are often viewed as secondary to the conscious.

As this book will show in detail, psychodynamic theorists believe that the most productive work takes place in therapy when the unconscious is made conscious. In contrast, altering nonconscious emotions and information is not the primary goal of REBT because the evidence shows that the nonconscious aspects of mental processing are frequently not directly accessible through talk therapy. REBT accepts people as conscious and free agents capable of overt volition. It acknowledges that all people have powerful innate inclinations, such as the tendency to experience fear or anger. When we examine the biological stratum of personality, we will see that our genes and physical constitution endow us with the primitive fundamentals of our being; the quintessence of personality, however, is the collection of beliefs and attitudes that overlie these basic endowments.

Another essential aspect of the REBT model is the notion that personality can be understood only as a synthesis of biological and behavioral psychology. Students of personality failing to consider both factors have frequently drawn defective inferences about human behavior. Failure to acknowledge these two dimensions of personality has led to what is called the cardinal causation error of personality psychology. This error occurs when mental health clinicians and researchers infer causal relationships between an adult's personality and the behavior of his or her parents. For example, an individual presents to a therapist as an introverted, insecure, and anxious individual. This individual then reports that he was emotionally and physically abused by his father. *Post hoc ergo propter hoc* (a Latin phrase that can be translated as "after this; therefore, because of this"): The therapist concludes that the cause of this individual's personality pathology is his father's treatment of him. This conclusion has been a mainstay of clinicians. REBT posits an alternative interpretation.

Parents with aberrant tendencies will tend to pass these unfortunate characteristics to all or some of their offspring. These aberrant parents will also tend to act out their behavioral disturbances with at least some of their children. When the situation is viewed superficially, it seems compellingly obvious that the abusive treatment is the direct cause of the child's ultimate behavioral disturbances, but the important genetic connection tends to be overlooked. In Chapter 16, evidence will show that it is not the disturbed upbringing that leads to the greatest portion of adult personality disturbances, but the child's genetic legacy combined with the overall social and environmental milieu.

Research will be provided to support this contention, and it will be contrasted with other prominent views. It is important to remember that the personality psychologist must keep an open mind to new ideas as well as continually challenge and test accepted ones. Consequently, the REBT model of personality takes a strongly scientific position that differs from those of many early schools of personality psychology. It advocates an open-ended process of continual testing of hypotheses and, when appropriate, modification of them. The authors believe this process to be the standard for any principle or theory in either applied or research psychology. The study of personality must be dynamic and not bogged down by undue regard for the past.

▣   CHAPTER SUMMARY

The study and understanding of personality is important within the field of psychology and many other disciplines in which people are evaluated. Personality theory is the study of the ways in which people differ from one another. It focuses on those differences in the way people think, behave, and process information. And it is these differences that define personality itself. Despite this working definition, personality is difficult to define precisely, as the many experts in the field of personality psychology differ in their standards and instruments of measurement.

Throughout history philosophers, politicians, physicians, jurists, and psychologists have developed theories to explain how and why the differences among people occur. Most had the goal of explaining or predicting human behavior. More recently, techniques have been developed to assess personality. These can include formal tests like the MMPI-II or such informal measures as simple observation. Assessment of personality is essential to understanding the individual and the ability to make generalizations about people. These generalizations commonly include classifying people by personality traits, which are the distinguishing characteristics of a person, and types that describe a person's overall pattern of interacting, behaving, and thinking. This chapter also introduced a new model of personality based on the work of Albert Ellis, who developed REBT.

▣ NOTE

1. A **factor** is an interpreted summary of multiple correlations combined in a statistical method called factor analysis. It is an approach that has been extensively employed in personality research. Galen, of course, did not use this mathematical method.

Chapter 2

Historical Perspectives on Personality

Chapter Goals

- Provide a comprehensive historical timeline of the development of personality psychology
- Give a brief synopsis of the various schools of thought on personality
- Provide an overview of the controversies in the field of personality
- Offer a closer look at the first comprehensive model of personality, psychoanalysis, Sigmund Freud's contribution, and its criticisms
- Present an overview of psychology's accomplishments and mistakes in its development of personality theories

The study of human personality long preceded the formal study of psychology. It was essential for people to form models of others' behavior. This type of analysis was vital, as the world has always been a dangerous place. Distinguishing accurately between friend and foe, and predicting the behavior of the latter, increased one's chances of survival. Even in the hunter-gatherer period of human evolution, people perennially sized up one another, looking for weaknesses, masked aggression, or reliability and other desirable qualities in a mate—just as we do today when encountering someone new. One might say that everyone has a personality theory, if only a naive or implicit one; and every philosophy encompasses a personality theory. Because an interest in personality is a universal part of human interaction, it stands to reason that it would become integrated into the lore and customs of most cultures. These informal bits and pieces of folk wisdom eventually became the logical foundations of today's more formal or scientific systems of personality. Early Greek, Roman, Asian, Hebrew, and Christian cultures have all presented models and typologies of human character. Most have set forth both ideal and more typical descriptions of human personality. Perhaps the earliest

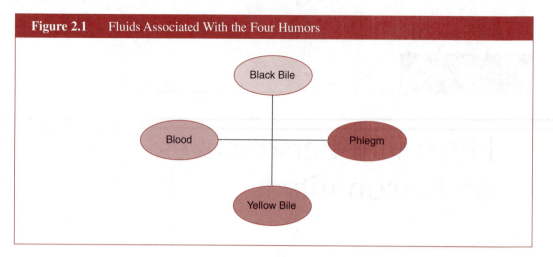

Figure 2.1   Fluids Associated With the Four Humors

theorist to seek naturalistic answers to the question of personality was Hippocrates, with his theory of the four humors.

Hippocrates of Cos (c. 460–c. 380 BCE), the "Father of Western Medicine." Hippocrates expanded on the contemporary Greek notion that the world consists of four elements: earth, wind, fire, and water. He proposed that human beings also are composed of four distinct life forces or elemental fluids, which he defined as blood, phlegm, yellow bile, and black bile. If these humors or life forces were maintained in their proper balance, the individual remained healthy. Hippocrates also believed that if the humors became imbalanced, the individual would develop an illness. Just as the balance of these body fluids was believed to be the basis of physical health, a proper configuration was also needed for mental health.

Claudius Galen, a Greco-Roman doctor who served as the personal physician of four successive Roman emperors, extended the Hippocratic theory of humors to explain differences in human temperament. Should any of the four humors dominate the others, specific changes in the individual's personality or mental outlook would take place. Thus, if blood became the predominant humor in a person's constitution, he or she would be sanguine—that is, content or cheerful. Should this individual have too much phlegm, he would become phlegmatic—slow-moving and impassive. Similarly, an oversupply of yellow bile would lead to a choleric or angry temperament, and too much black bile would produce a melancholy or depressed personality. Although Hippocrates' theory of the four humors and Galen's extension of it to personality have no empirical validity, their importance lies in the fact that for the first time in Western history, naturalistic or materialistic hypotheses were offered to account for personality differences and maladjustments rather than supernatural explanations involving gods or demons.

In the Far East, a somewhat similar system of explaining personality differences developed within traditional Chinese medicine, which will be discussed in more detail in Chapter 17. One of the basic theories of this medical system is that everything in the universe, including human well-being, is governed by five natural elements: fire, wood, earth, air, and water. Each element is correlated with one of the seasons of the year (the Chinese divided summer into two seasons) and with certain organs in the human body. An individual's personality is described in terms of an orientation toward a certain element; for example, aggressive people are said to have a wood personality, while fearful people are said to have a water personality. Although neither the classical Greco-Roman nor the traditional Chinese approach to classifying personality could be described as scientific in the modern sense of the word, both systems did attempt to organize informal observations and folk wisdom about personality differences into some kind of intelligible structure.

▣ PSYCHOLOGY: A DISCIPLINE WITH SUBDIVISIONS

Chapter 1 detailed several aspects of the study of personality as a subfield within psychology, a subfield that happens to be the foundation for all clinical psychology. It also briefly discussed the development of schools of thought within psychology and listed the major schools and their founders. All personality theories have developed out of one of these so-called schools, which are discussed in greater depth in this chapter. Understanding the major concepts and methodologies of the various schools in psychology is essential for an adequate understanding of the field as a whole.

A common difficulty encountered by beginning students in psychology is trying to gain a clearer understanding of exactly what psychology is. If you are reading this text, you probably have been exposed to articles about psychology or have even read other psychology textbooks in their entirety. If this is the case, you may have been a bit confused by the fuzzy definitions of psychology that you have been given. The reason for this uncertainty is that there is no universal consensus about the nature or scope of the discipline. Rather than being a distinct topic of study, the field of psychology is comprised of a cluster of closely related subjects. Most of these have their own research agendas, their own styles of practice, and their own views of the most desirable direction for the field as a whole.

The diversity of subfields within psychology has been a problem since the discipline's inception and remains so in the early 21st century. You can easily verify this observation by examining the constituencies of the American Psychological Association (APA). The APA is the largest organization dedicated to the advancement of the field of psychology. Table 2.1 lists the major subdivisions of the American Psychological Association. Although there is a large amount of overlap, the table makes clear that psychology as a field contains many distinct areas of study and practice.

An examination of these divisions reveals overlap in some areas and apparent disagreement in others. Nevertheless, this pattern of division and separation is the way psychology evolved in the 19th and 20th centuries. This chapter explains how and why it did so and the significance these divisions have had for the various theories of personality.

▣ THE BIRTH OF PSYCHOLOGY

Prior to the late 19th century, psychology was generally considered a subfield of philosophy. Philosophers debated such topics as the relationship between body and mind, the basis

Table 2.1   Divisions of the American Psychological Association (APA)

Society for General Psychology	Society of Psychological Hypnosis
Society for the Teaching of Psychology	State, Provincial, and Territorial Psychological Association Affairs
Experimental Psychology	Society for Humanistic Psychology
Evaluation, Measurement, and Statistics	Intellectual and Developmental Disabilities
Behavioral Neuroscience and Comparative Psychology	Population and Environmental Psychology
Developmental Psychology	Society for the Psychology of Women
Society for Personality and Social Psychology	Psychology of Religion
Society for the Psychological Study of Social Issues	Society for Child and Family Policy and Practice
Society for the Psychology of Aesthetics, Creativity and the Arts	Health Psychology
Society of Clinical Psychology	Psychoanalysis
Society of Consulting Psychology	Clinical Neuropsychology
Society for Industrial and Organizational Psychology	American Psychology-Law Society
Educational Psychology	Psychologists in Independent Practice
School Psychology	Family Psychology
Society of Counseling Psychology	Society for the Psychological Study of Lesbian, Gay, and Bisexual Issues
Psychologists in Public Service	Society for the Psychological Study of Ethnic Minority Issues
Society for Military Psychology	Media Psychology
Adult Development and Aging	Exercise and Sport Psychology
Applied Experimental and Engineering Psychology	Society for the Study of Peace, Conflict, and Violence: Peace Psychology Division
Rehabilitation Psychology	Group Psychology and Group Psychotherapy
Society for Consumer Psychology	Addictions
Society for Theoretical and Philosophical Psychology	Society for the Psychological Study of Men and Masculinity
Behavior Analysis	International Psychology
Society for the History of Psychology	Society of Clinical Child and Adolescent Psychology
Society for Community Research and Action: Division of Community Psychology	Society of Pediatric Psychology
Psychopharmacology and Substance Abuse	American Society for the Advancement of Pharmacotherapy
Psychotherapy	Trauma Psychology

of consciousness, the freedom of the human will, and the nature of goodness, truth, and beauty. Some, like Immanuel Kant (1724–1804), even theorized about nonconscious thought. Despite all the debates and publications, however, psychology remained an academic abstraction rather than an empirical science. This situation changed dramatically when William James (1842–1910) in the United States and Wilhelm Wundt (1832–1920) in Germany established laboratories dedicated to the study of psychology.[1] Psychology became a science in its own right; it was no longer a subtopic within philosophy.

Despite the separation of psychology from philosophy, however, there was still no consensus on the scope of the field. Over the course of the next few decades, psychology meandered, trying to find its focus as both a pure and an applied science. Psychology's development into a laboratory science as well as a field of clinical practice has also led to a lack of cohesion. That is, research psychologists in university laboratories were studying topics and deriving theories from their work—often with animals rather than people—that differed from those of the clinicians, who based their theories on their experiences with human clients. In turn, the different theories of personality derived by clinicians and researchers led to the development of different types of psychotherapies. More detail on these developments is provided in later chapters.

As background for some of the questions and arguments that have preoccupied psychologists during the process of the discipline's separation from philosophy, the accompanying box offers a summary of the mind/body problem, a recurrent source of disagreement among clinicians as well as researchers.

The Mind-Body Problem

How do mental events, such as thoughts, free will, consciousness, goals, or purposes relate to the physical aspect of man, that is, the body or the brain? This problem has been around for at least 2,500 years. It was a key religious issue for millennia. But as psychology separated from philosophy and attempted to become a science, this question became an issue for personality theories to tackle as well.
There have been a number of different approaches:

Dualism: In this view, there are two substances, mind and matter, which are fundamentally different. The two major versions of dualism are interactionism and parallelism.

Parallelism: Proposed by Baruch Spinoza (1632–1677), a Dutch philosopher, this view maintains that the activities of mind and brain are predetermined to agree but do not influence each other. For example, Spinoza (1677/1883) would maintain that when a person suffers brain damage because of a blow to the head, the mind was preordained to break down at exactly the moment of impact.

Interactionism: Proposed by René Descartes, a French philosopher, this view maintains that matter and spirit (the brain and mind) are different and interact in

(Continued)

(Continued)

some manner that we do not understand and are probably not permitted to understand. This dualism allowed Descartes to view some aspects of the universe as operating according to the laws of physics, while avoiding at least some problems with religious authorities. (He was however, condemned by the church, his books were banned, and he was brought before religious magistrates.)

Cartesian dualism became the most influential view in the Western world on the issue because it appeared to explain free will and consciousness in an otherwise mechanistic universe, while allowing that the immortal and immaterial "soul" existed and was the true source of identity. Dualism turned out to fit in perfectly with mainstream Western religions. Indeed, before the computer age, it was impossible to understand how the physical brain could produce consciousness.

It was only during the Enlightenment that physical objects were seen to move in lawful and predictable ways. Descartes applied this mechanical view of the world to the behavior of nonhuman animals and certain human behaviors—the ones controlled purely by reflexes (such as pulling one's finger away from a hot surface). The behavior of animals and the reflexive behaviors of humans were determined and subject to science. The unique and voluntary behaviors found in man alone were produced by the soul and a matter only for theology.

Monism: In this view, there is only one kind of existence. There are two basic forms of monism, depending on what the monist accepts as the fundamental reality—matter or ideas. These two types of monism are referred to respectively as materialism and idealism (also known as mentalism).

Materialism: According to this doctrine, everything that exists can be reduced to matter operating according to physical laws. Materialism is the version of monism that maintains that only the material world exists. Materialists thus subscribe to a mechanical view of the universe. Thus, all natural phenomena (including life and the mind) can be explained by the laws of chemistry and physics. All mental events, including consciousness, are thought of as physical or chemical processes in the brain

Idealism (or mentalism): According to this theory, mind is the ultimate reality. What humans perceive as the physical world is created by thought or the mind, either the mind of the individual or of God. According to idealists, the entire physical world is a by-product of mind.

The Contemporary Debate: The debate among psychologists in the early 2000s is heavily involved with the question of **artificial intelligence** (AI), and the question of whether consciousness can be built into computers. Some philosophers favor the position that consciousness cannot be ascribed to purely physical processes. Almost all neuroscientists disagree with that view, however, maintaining that consciousness arises completely from physical processes in the brain.

🔲 PERSONALITY THEORY TIMELINE

This timeline summarizes the development of psychology, especially those aspects most closely related to personality theories. It should help you get a better understanding of how the schools of thought evolved and how they came to differ with one another. In general, the events within each 20-year period are discussed in chronological order.

Late 1880s–1900

Wilhelm Wundt, a German researcher, established the first psychology laboratory in 1878 in the University of Leipzig after publishing the first volume *Principles of Physiological Psychology* in 1873. Wundt's (1899/1904) work led to the school of psychology called **structuralism**, disseminated in the United States by Edward Titchener (1867–1927), Wundt's student and translator.

Psychology became even more clearly demarcated as a field with the first doctoral degree awarded in experimental psychology in 1878. The United States established its first laboratory dedicated to psychological research at Johns Hopkins University in 1883, under the leadership of G. Stanley Hall (1844–1924), the first president of the American Psychological Association.

In Europe, Hermann Ebbinghaus (1850–1909) published *Memory: A Contribution to Experimental Psychology,* adding memory to the scope of psychological study (Ebbinghaus, 1885/1913). Francis Galton (1822–1911), a half-cousin of Charles Darwin, introduced batteries of psychological tests, thereby formalizing psychological testing as a legitimate area of research and establishing the field of **psychometrics**. Galton was an early proponent of attributing intellect, behavior, and personality traits to genetic endowment. He was also a pioneer in the introduction and development of statistical techniques that allow for a scientific study of personality.

This period saw the publication of the first comprehensive textbook in the field when William James published *The Principles of Psychology* in 1890 and a second edition 15 years later in 1905. James M. Cattell (1860–1944), who studied under Galton as well as Wundt, published an article, "Mental Tests and Measurements," in the journal *Mind* in the same year. Cattell's (1890) article further advanced the field of psychological testing as well as the position of psychology within the university in studying human consciousness and cognition. Cattell was influential in urging the widespread adoption of quantitative measurements and statistical analyses to bring psychology up to the level of the so-called exact sciences.

Independent of the English-speaking academic psychologists, two Austrian physicians, Josef Breuer (1842–1925) and Sigmund Freud, published *Studies on Hysteria* [*Studien über Hysterie*] in 1895 (Breuer & Freud, 1957). This book marked the emergence of the psychoanalytic school in German-speaking Europe. **Psychoanalysis** did not, however, make its way across the Atlantic until Freud was invited to give a series of lectures at Clark University in 1909.

While Freud and Breuer were developing the early principles of psychoanalysis in Vienna, the application of psychological theories to clinical problems formally began in the United States when Lightner Witmer (1867–1956) opened the first psychological clinic at the University of Pennsylvania in Philadelphia in 1896. Witmer was responsible for coining the term *clinical psychology*.

1901–1920

The biological or genetic study of behavior was formalized when Karl Pearson (1857–1936), a student of Galton and also a pioneer in statistics, published a study on the inheritance of human mental characteristics in 1909. Pearson also adopted and propagated Galton's views on eugenics.

While the psychologists were establishing departments of research psychology in major universities, the first major split in the psychoanalytic school took place in 1907, when Alfred Adler published his main work, *A Study of Organ Inferiority and Its Psychical Compensation*. In this book, Adler challenged many of Freud's premises, such as the notion that the prime motivator in life is the sexually charged libido. More of these challenges to Freud's intellectual system arose over the next few years. Adler was soon followed by Carl Jung, Karen Horney, and others who promoted their own variants of psychoanalysis. Freud, however, acquired an international reputation when his 1909 lectures at Clark University were translated into English the following year by a graduate student completing a dissertation on Freud's work (Freud, 1910).

Other psychologists in this period focused on the processes of human perception; the founders of **Gestalt psychology**, named for the German word for "shape" or "form," were early examples of this new area of interest. The Gestalt school may be seen as beginning around 1912, when Max Wertheimer (1880–1943) published the paper, "Experimental Studies of the Perception of Movement" (*Experimentelle studien über das Sehen von Bewegung*). The more formal establishment of the school was closer to 1925, when Wertheimer published a set of lectures titled *Gestalt Theory* (*Gestalttheorie*). In this book, he wrote:

> There are wholes, the behaviour of which is not determined by that of their individual elements, but where the part-processes are themselves determined by the intrinsic nature of the whole. It is the hope of Gestalt theory to determine the nature of such wholes (p. 2).

In other words, we are different from the sum of our parts.

The school of thought that set the tone for most of the 20th century, however, emerged in 1913, when John B. Watson (1878–1958), then a professor at Johns Hopkins University, published "Psychology as the Behaviorist Views It." Watson's article, which is sometimes called "the behaviorist manifesto," began as follows:

> Psychology as the behaviorist views it is a purely objective experimental branch of natural science. Its theoretical goal is the prediction and control of behavior. Introspection forms no essential part of its methods, nor is the scientific value of its data dependent upon the readiness with which they lend themselves to interpretation in terms of consciousness. The behaviorist, in his efforts to get a unitary scheme of animal response, recognizes no dividing line between man and brute. The behavior of man, with all of its refinement and complexity, forms only a part of the behaviorist's total scheme of investigation. (p. 158)

With this introduction, Watson rejected structuralism, the prevailing school of the day, and brought forth an entirely new movement in psychology.

1921–1940

If John Watson was the father of behaviorism, B. F. Skinner (1904–1990) brought it to maturity by developing the concept of **operant conditioning** (Skinner, 1938). Operant conditioning became the linchpin of the behavioral theory of personality.

Psychoanalysis obtained two new perspectives in personality theory in 1937. In that year Anna Freud (1895–1982), Sigmund Freud's youngest child and his academic collaborator, completed *The Ego and the Mechanisms of Defence*, establishing the field of **ego psychology**. Shortly afterward, Karen Horney (1937) published *The Neurotic Personality of Our Time*, commencing her contributions to social psychoanalytic theory. Amid the psychoanalysts and behaviorists, Edward C. Tolman (1886–1959) reported that learning can take place without external reinforcement. Tolman's (1932) research findings provided early support for the notion of intervening cognitive processes.

1941–1960

The first objective personality test was developed in 1942 by Starke R. Hathaway (1903–1984), a psychologist, and John Charnley McKinley (1891–1950), a neuropsychiatrist. The Minnesota Multiphasic Personality Inventory (MMPI), which was released for use in 1943, became the most widely accepted and researched personality instrument.

In the same year, Carl Rogers (1902–1987) published *Counseling and Psychotherapy; Newer Concepts in Practice*, which summarized a form of **nondirective** psychotherapy based on a **humanistic psychology** and its view of personality. Rogers's (1942) approach, originally called **client-centered therapy**, is now known as **person-centered psychotherapy**. Abraham Maslow (1908–1970) advanced the humanistic view of personality with his concept of a **hierarchy of needs**, first outlined in an article titled "A Theory of Human Motivation," published in *Psychological Review* in 1943.

The gradual advance toward a more accurate understanding of **cognition** proceeded further when Edward Chase Tolman published an article, "Cognitive Maps in Rats and Men," in *Psychological Review* in 1948. Tolman's work demonstrated that both humans and rats create and utilize mental representations of the world around them. This demonstration was in direct contradiction to the then-dominant behaviorist view of behavior. Behaviorism had all but ruled out internal mental states as an appropriate subject for psychological research. Leon Festinger (1919–1989) postulated the theory of social comparison process and **cognitive dissonance** theory, which indicate that people process information in complex ways—ways that are quite incompatible with behaviorism (Festinger, 1950).

Albert Ellis (1952) began the development of cognitive behavioral therapy in the form of what he initially called rational emotive therapy or RET. George Kelly, who began his career as an educational psychologist, published his two-volume *The Psychology of Personal Constructs* in 1955. George A. Miller (1920–) published his landmark article in *Psychological Review* in 1956 on the "magical number seven." The article demonstrated the existence of fixed limits to human cognitive processing—a contradiction of the behaviorists' premises.

B. F. Skinner published *Verbal Behavior* in 1957. The work ultimately proved to be the Achilles heel of strict behaviorism. In 1952, H. J. Eysenck (1916–1997), a European psychologist, published *The Effects of Psychotherapy: An Evaluation*, which concluded that psychoanalysis is no more effective in treating emotional disturbance than a placebo. It is important to note that Eysenck studied only psychoanalytic therapy, and not some of the other forms of psychotherapy practiced in the mid-20th century. In any event, his paper was the first outcome study of psychotherapy.

Allen Newell, Marvin E. Shaw, and Herbert A. Simon's article titled "Elements of a Theory of Human Problem Solving," published in *Psychological Review* in 1958, was the first elucidation of the information-processing approach to psychology. In 1959, Noam Chomsky (1928–) published a review of B. F. Skinner's book *Verbal Behavior*, in which he exposed profound flaws in Skinner's behavioral explanation of language acquisition. In 1960, George Sperling (1933–), a cognitive psychologist, published a monograph titled *The Information Available in Brief Visual Presentations*. In this monograph, Sperling demonstrated that elegantly designed experiments can provide inferences about the nature of hitherto hidden cognitive processes. He posited the existence of a so-called **iconic memory** in addition to short-term and long-term memory and also showed that humans have more information available to them for brief periods of time than they are able to report verbally.

1961–1980

Aaron T. Beck (1921–), a psychiatrist trained in classical psychoanalysis, published an article in the *Archives of General Psychiatry* in 1961 titled "An Inventory for Measuring Depression." The work contained the first version of the Beck Depression Inventory (BDI), one of the most widely used instruments for evaluating patients with mood disorders. Beck, Ward, Mendelson, Mock, and Erbaugh (1961) presented the notion that cognitive distortions are partially responsible for depression. Stanley Milgram (1933–1984), a psychologist then working at Yale University, published an article in 1963 called "Behavioral Study of Obedience" (expanded into a book titled *Obedience to Authority: An Experimental View* in 1974) in the *Journal of Abnormal and Social Psychology*. In the article, Milgram described an experiment that he conducted in 1961 to explore the social demand for obedience to authority that he believed underlay the Holocaust. Milgram's findings demonstrated that we all may share some less desirable personality qualities and that the demands of certain situations may erode or demolish our code of ethics. The notion that human personality is influenced by social situations and setting is supported by the work of Robert Zajonc (1923–), who developed the concept of **social facilitation** (Zajonc, 1965).

The information-processing metaphor for memory continued to develop during the 1960s with the publication of Saul Sternberg's (1932–) 1966 paper on "High-Speed Scanning in Human Memory." Sternberg's work revealed that humans search through memory in a serial manner. These and related works were finally organized in a comprehensive book when Ulric Neisser (1928–) published the first text on cognitive psychology in 1967.

Albert Bandura, a Canadian researcher in educational psychology, published *Principles of Behavior Modification* in 1969, in which he emphasized the process of observational learning. Joseph Wolpe (1915–1997), a psychiatrist who received his medical training in South Africa, wrote *The Practice of Behavior Therapy* in 1969. Wolpe was a pioneer of **behavior modification** therapy and assertiveness training, approaches that use the concepts of behaviorism to change responses to stimuli through a process of **desensitization**.

1981–2000+

Daniel Kahneman, Paul Slovic (1938–), and Amos Tversky served as joint editors of *Judgment under Uncertainty: Heuristics and Biases*, a collection of papers on risk taking, risk perception, and decision making that was ultimately rewarded with the Nobel Prize in economics (Kahneman, Slovic, & Tversky, 1982). John R. Anderson (1947–), a cognitive psychologist, published *The Architecture of Cognition*, which set forth a unified theory of human cognition in 1983. Roger W. Sperry (1913–1994), a pioneer in split-brain research, published "The Impact and Promise of the Cognitive Revolution" in *American Psychologist* in 1993. Sperry had already been awarded the Nobel Prize in Medicine in 1981 for his work in the lateralization of brain function. Cognitive behavioral therapy as practiced by Aaron Beck and Albert Ellis became the dominant approach in clinical practice to the treatment of depression, anxiety, and other mental disorders.

The preceding timeline has presented some of the key advances in the field of psychology as they relate to the growth and development of the various schools within the discipline. A careful review will have provided a better understanding of the partitioning of psychology into schools and subdisciplines.

As the number of psychology departments grew in universities throughout the world in the late 19th and early 20th centuries, so too did the number of topics under investigation. This is especially true in the subfield of personality psychology, which largely arose from the work of clinicians like Ellis, Freud, and Rogers, who developed models of personality to facilitate their treatment of people suffering from psychological disorders. The need to create a theoretical model becomes clear when one thinks of the complexity of the problems encountered in clinical practice. These practitioners of psychology must organize the continual stream of information conveyed by their patients in therapy. Imagine how difficult it would be for clinical psychologists who do not have a model of personality on which to base their work.

Without a theoretical model, the clinician would listen to patients' descriptions of everyday or past events, streams of consciousness, recitals of adversities, expressions of opinions, and evaluations of peers and adversaries. People in therapy have no obligation to organize or annotate their therapeutic sessions, so the therapist must take all of those random communications and weave them into a tapestry that includes the person, his or her nature, and the sources of his or her difficulties. Data must be organized to formulate a means for solving the client's problems.

For example, the REBT view of personality holds that most emotional distress results from irrational thinking. Therefore, the therapist listens for direct or indirect evidence of irrational premises in the client's view of the world and his or her life during a session of REBT. An example might be a patient's repeated statements of extreme upset when other people do not do what he or she wants, which are rooted in the irrational belief that it is a terrible disaster not to get his or her own way most or all of the time.

In contrast to the REBT approach, psychoanalysts hold that neuroses result from undesirable or unacceptable sexual or violent impulses forcing their way out of their restraints in the unconscious mind. Thus, the psychoanalytic therapist listens for themes in the patient's discourse that indicate the specific nature of the unconscious conflict. An example might be a patient whose verbally expressed worry about a parent's illness is a clue to underlying anger at the parent for being sick and draining the patient's resources of time or energy.

▣ SCHOOLS OF THOUGHT IN PSYCHOLOGY

In psychology, the term *school* refers to a group of loosely or informally associated individuals who practice, research, or espouse similar principles. As noted earlier, the formation of schools is especially important in personality psychology, which has its roots in clinical psychology and psychiatry. The clinicians needed to work out theories to explain the behavior of their patients.

In other words, a school is essentially a group of psychologists who profess a related set of ideas, theories, and research procedures designed for other psychologists to follow. Psychologists in each school tend to believe that if psychology is going to be a legitimate and meaningful science, it must follow the tenets of their particular school. Let us examine the historical development of several of these schools, as doing so will enhance our understanding of the various theories of personality.

Structural Psychology

Originating in Germany around 1879, structuralism may be seen as the first school of psychology. The first structuralists were interested in analyzing the human psyche in terms of what they considered its fundamental elements or structures. Wilhelm Wundt was a charismatic figure who had a great deal of influence on psychology through the work of his students as well as his own research. He set out to discover the basic "elements of consciousness." Wundt was no doubt influenced by the then-recent discoveries in physics and chemistry. He concluded that psychology could be like these exact sciences, which had rapidly advanced by discovering the fundamental particles of matter and the principles by which they interact. Wundt drew the logical parallel—that if one could determine the fundamental elements of mind, then one could also describe all aspects of human cognition and perception in terms of various combinations of these elements.

To best understand Wundt's approach, the reader should bear in mind that the early years of structuralism were contemporaneous with major advances in chemistry and physics. So as the more concrete sciences were describing the world in terms of chemical elements and subatomic particles, structuralist psychologists apparently concluded that the human mind can be similarly understood. Instead of elements, atoms, and subatomic particles, they identified sensations, images, and **affects** as the basic components of mind. The structuralists were concerned to study not only the fundamental elements of consciousness but also synthesis, or the process by which these elements of the mind combined to form more complex aspects of consciousness. The problem with the structuralist approach was that these elements of consciousness could be glimpsed only by **introspection**; thus the external objective evidence required by science was not possible on structuralist premises.

Photo 2.1 Wilhelm Wundt (1832–1920)

Functional Psychology

Unlike psychoanalysis and structuralism, which were European imports, the functionalist school of psychology began in the United States in the late 1890s. Its early leaders were William James at Harvard University, John Dewey (1859–1952) and James Rowland Angell (1869–1949) at the University of Chicago and Edward L. Thorndike (1859–1952) and Robert S. Woodworth (1869–1962) at Columbia University. Proponents of **functionalism** argued that psychologists should not try to understand consciousness by looking for its separate components and underlying structures. Instead, they proposed that psychologists should study the functions that consciousness serves. In other words, the functionalists were interested in the adaptive value of behavior.

The functionalists were clearly influenced by Charles Darwin (1809–1882), the English naturalist who was the dominant figure in the life sciences in the latter part of the 19th century. Scientists who accepted Darwin's theory of evolution usually attempted to infer the evolutionary advantages that certain traits conferred on their possessors when they explored any human or animal attribute. In psychology, the functionalists maintained the structuralists' emphasis on consciousness as the proper subject of study. While they did not reject introspection as a method of study, they did little to stop its transition into insignificance.

William McDougall (1871–1938) proposed a psychology based on purpose or striving, which never fully rose to the level of a school and can be considered a subtype of functionalism. He later named his approach **hormic psychology**; its basic premise is that all behavior is derived from goal-oriented instinctual impulses. According to McDougall (1923), all animals have instincts that push them toward basic survival behaviors. Their cognitive capacities aid them in their striving to survive. McDougall's hormic psychology did in fact anticipate many aspects of modern physiological psychology. His clinical work, especially with veterans of World War I (1914–1918) suffering from what would now be called post-traumatic stress disorder (PTSD), led to major contributions to the field of abnormal psychology. McDougall's explanation of human behavior relied more on innate instincts, conscious **repression**, and the resulting conflicts between the will and the instincts. In this work, he was among the first to challenge many of the arcane and inscrutable aspects of Freud's theories. In fact, McDougall continued his attacks on psychoanalysis for much of his career. You may wish to return to this section later when we discuss some functionalist influences on contemporary biological models of personality.

Empiricism/Associationism

Empiricism is a school of thought that has its origins in the philosophy of John Locke (1632–1704), an English physician and political thinker. Its basic premise is that people cannot construct complex ideas without first combining or associating more elemental ideas that are obtained through sense experience. For example, one cannot form the concept of a *plant* without combining the memories of sense impressions of specific plants (their color, taste, size, etc.).

Locke's empiricism stands in contrast to the positions of other theorists, who believed that humans have innate or inborn knowledge about the world. For example, Plato proposed, most notably in the *Republic* and another dialogue called the *Parmenides*, that there exist perfect abstract exemplars of every earthly category called ideas, forms, or **archetypes**. Our ability to know that a plant is a plant comes from recollecting or remembering our inborn knowledge of these archetypes, in this case, "plantness." The archetypes are beyond space and time and represent a higher degree of reality than the individual physical objects that they inform. The psychological **nativism** of Plato dominated the first 1,500 years of the Christian era and led to such notions as the idea that children not exposed to any language would spontaneously speak Hebrew.

During the Age of Reason, the French philosopher René Descartes, who also had a doctrine of innate ideas, asserted that certain essential concepts like God, infinity, and substance must be innate because experience could provide no model or example for them to be learned. Locke and other empiricists diverged widely from this notion. They took the position that experience is the sole source of all knowledge. Locke wrote, "Let us suppose the Mind to be, as we say, white paper, void of character, without any ideas. How comes it to be furnished? Whence has it all the materials of reason and knowledge? To this I answer, in one word, from Experience" (Fullerton, 1906, pp. 209–210). The notion that all ideas or abstract concepts come from sensory experience presents certain problems. After all, our eyes and ears can supply us only with sensations rather than organized ideas. On the other hand, our mind is not a disorganized jumble of sensations; ideas are organized into meaningful units. How is this organization achieved? The British empiricists proposed that some imaginary "mental string" held together the sensations or the "images" of the sensations, which aggregated to form an idea. These mental strings were formed by **associations.** Any two sensations that share certain features— let us say any two sensations that occur together, such as the taste and smell of a freshly cut orange—will become associated. Once two sensations are associated, the occurrence of one will evoke the memory of the other. According to these empiricist philosophers, associations are also formed between successive sensations. Thus, the ordering of ideas is also explained by associations.

Associationism became the logical foundation of the behavioral schools of psychology, which we will summarize shortly. But before behaviorism became established as a major psychological school, another was incubating—psychoanalysis.

Psychoanalysis: The First Comprehensive Model of Personality

Psychoanalysis is the most widely disseminated and best-known school of thought in psychology; thus, this discussion is somewhat longer than most of the other schools.

Psychoanalysis can trace its origins to the work of many people who proposed that both thought and motivation can take place outside of conscious awareness. One of these was Jean-Martin Charcot (1825–1893), a French physician who was the director of the Salpêtrière hospital in Paris. His students included such luminaries as Pierre Janet (1859–1947), a pioneer in the study of the post-traumatic and dissociative disorders; and Sigmund Freud, whose name was to become virtually synonymous with psychoanalysis. Charcot was known for his studies of hysterics—people (mostly women) who fainted or exhibited other dramatic physical symptoms that were believed to have a psychological basis. The term **hysteria** is no longer used as a clinical diagnosis. Notably, Charcot believed hysterical symptoms originated from unconscious conflicts that were usually sexual in nature.

Pierre Janet also studied people with hysterical symptoms and used the term **subconscious** to localize the source of their conflicts. Janet believed that subconscious thought is pathological and therefore a sign of mental dysfunction. He proposed the concept of integration as a goal for the healthy personality. According to Janet, hysterics, in contrast to healthy people, have failed to integrate all the different aspects of their personality. People with healthy personalities have all of their mental processes integrated and available to consciousness. Janet's perspective was in stark contrast to that of Freud, who asserted that the majority of mental processing takes place in the unconscious.

We can mark the birth of psychoanalysis with the publication of Freud and Breuer's *Studies on Hysteria* in 1895 (Breuer & Freud, 1895/1957). This work was a collection of case studies of people whom Freud and Breuer had treated. As the title indicated, the two physicians set out to examine the inner workings of hysteria. In short, their cases were set forth to provide evidence that unconscious processes were the basis of psychological disorders.

Despite the apparent originality of *Studies on Hysteria* (Breuer & Freud, 1895/1957), Freud and Breuer were actually synthesizing the work of many of their peers and predecessors, who had previously theorized that processes outside of awareness seem to guide human behavior. Freud's invention of the concept of the dynamic unconscious was his most original contribution to psychology. Freud brought the notion of an unconscious to life by suggesting that neurotic and even normal behavior results from motivational forces kept from conscious awareness. This position is in sharp contrast with those of contemporaries like Janet, who believed that the subconscious consisted of mental processes that would normally be conscious but were quarantined, or subject to **dissociation**, as a result of neurosis. Freud's theories were complex and comprehensive, including outlines of the stages of human and cultural evolution as well as individual development. These stages are briefly described here.

Freud's Stages of Psychosexual Development. An essential component of Freud's psychoanalytic approach is his theory of childhood development. To Freud, a child's psychological development is based on the quest for pleasure and the reduction of unsatisfied drives. He proposed in 1905, in a book translated into English in 1949 as *Three Essays on the Theory of Sexuality* (Freud, 1949c), that all children pass through five identical stages on their way to adulthood with varying degrees of success. The first stage is the **oral stage** (0–2 years), in which the focus of pleasure is located in the mouth. The next is the **anal stage** (2–4 years), in which sexual or libidinous pleasure is associated with defecation and control of the anal sphincter. The next stage the child enters is the **phallic stage** (4–7 years), in which the sexual drive is focused on the genitals. A **latency stage** (7–12 years) follows, in which the child's sexual drives are suppressed. The next and final stage is the **genital stage** (13 years +), in which the human being begins to desire members of the opposite sex and eventually participates in sexual intercourse (Freud, 1905/1949c). These and related theories, which are fundamental to contemporary personality theory, are examined in greater detail in Chapters 4 and 5.

The Oedipus Complex. Freud's theory of childhood development is based on a construct derived from a Greek myth, the story of Oedipus, the mythical king of Thebes. According to the legend, Oedipus unknowingly kills his father, Laius, and marries his mother, Jocasta. Freud appropriates the ancient story to describe a developmental phase, usually resolved by the end of the phallic stage, in which male infants experience sexual feelings for their mother and hostility toward the father. This phase continues until the boy's fear of castration by his father leads to him to give up competing with him. Instead, the boy chooses to identify with his father. According to Freud, a boy's close relation to his mother as the primary love-object leads to a desire for complete union with her. A girl, on the other hand, who is similarly attached to the mother and thus caught up in a "homosexual" desire, directs her **libido** (love, or sexual energy broadly construed) toward her father in what some have called the **Electra complex**. Freud himself usually used the term Oedipus complex for children of both sexes and disliked the introduction of the new term to describe the Oedipal stage in girls. This pattern of psycho-sexual development produces a triadic relationship regardless of one's sex, with the parent of the same sex cast in the role of a rival for the affections of the parent of the opposite sex.

The Unconscious. The linchpin of Freud's model of personality is the premise of a dynamic unconscious mind. To Freud, the unconscious does not refer to aspects of mental functioning taking place in the background. Quite the contrary—Freud proposed that most human think-ing, motivation, and goal setting take place in the unconscious. Significantly, Freud saw the unconscious as an active force that makes decisions on what or what not to allow into con-sciousness through the use of several censoring mechanisms. These internal censors will be explained in more detail in Chapter 4.

Topology and Structures of Mind. To explain the interactions between conscious and uncon-scious thought, Freud began with a simple model of mind based on three levels of thought: the conscious, the **preconscious**, and the unconscious. He expanded the complexity of this topo-logical model of mind by adding three sentient structures: the id, the ego, and the **superego**. The ego develops out of the id's interaction with the external world. It is produced from the non-biological (social and familial) forces brought to bear on a person's biological develop-ment and functions as an intermediary between the demands of the id and the external world.

Thus, the ego can be thought of as a flexible portion of the psyche consisting of a system of beliefs that mediate between a person's dealings with his or her internal drives and the external demands of life. This process of accommodating internal impulses follows what Freud referred to as **secondary process** thinking. Secondary process thinking reconciles the biological and instinctual demands and **drives** (both unifying and destructive in nature) of the id (which is governed by **primary processes**) with the socially determined constraints of the superego (internalized rules placing limits on the subject's satisfactions and pleasures) and the demands of reality. In fact, the ego is the only structure of personality that is in contact with and concerned about the real world.

Criticisms of Psychoanalysis. A common explanation for the prominence accorded to Freud in most basic texts is his position in the history of psychology close to the beginning of the discipline, coupled with his undoubted impact on the wider culture of the West. However, it is important to understand that Freud and the psychoanalytic tradition are widely rejected by many scientific psychologists as well as by a growing number of clinicians in the early 21st century.

Perhaps the most compelling challenge to Freudian theory is that Freud's hypotheses are stated in such a way as to make it difficult or impossible to test their truth. For example, Freud proposed that children pass through an anal stage of development. He further proposed that inadequate nurture during that phase can lead to an anal-retentive personality in which the individual is parsimonious and obsessive. Freud also stated, however, that excessive nurturing during this phase can lead to the exact opposite in personality, an anal-expulsive type of person who is messy and undisciplined. How, then, can someone verify the existence of such a phase?

Hans Popper is best known for this particular challenge to psychoanalysis, in that he maintains that its inability to be falsified precludes it being considered a science. Popper points out that the "so-called predictions [of psychoanalysis] are not predictions of overt behavior but of hidden psychological states. This is why they are so untestable" (Popper, 1986a). In addition, Freudian theory is based on the male psyche and gives women short shrift. The Oedipal crisis is a prime example of this focus on male development. Although a parallel Electra complex was added by some followers of Freud, he himself applied his understanding of the maturation of males to both sexes.

In addition, many critics maintain that Freud overemphasized the role of sexuality in human psychological development and experience. Freud's concept of libido defines the sexual drive as the primary life force and motivator. For Freud, sexual energy is the only source of energy and must be **sublimated** or redirected to serve all other actions. Many psychoanalysts after Freud allowed for other motivating forces in life.

Finally, many people think that a major flaw of psychoanalysis is its introduction of unnecessary complications into its understanding of human nature and personality. According to Farrell (1981), "[Psychoanalysis] appears to encourage analytic and psychodynamic practitioners to overlook the place and great importance of ordinary common sense" (p. 216). Because psychoanalysis deals chiefly with unconscious motives and repressed emotions, common sense no longer seems to be applicable. Farrell and other critics believe that it is increasingly important for analysts to be aware of the importance of common sense and the role that it can, should, and does play in psychoanalysis.

A unique feature of Freudian psychoanalysis is its premise of a motivational unconscious. To a Freudian, no actions result from chance, nor are they ever meaningless. Instead, they are always the result of quasi-conscious entities within the human mind that guide a person's behavior. These entities resist examination by the conscious portion of the mind. In fact, psychoanalysis posits that as one closes in on the true motivation of his or her behavior, censors within the mind will push these motivations deeper into the unconscious. Freud's approach to dream interpretation typifies his belief that the "true" meanings of events even in dreams are always disguised. He recounted his analysis of one patient's dream as follows:

> A patient's seemingly inoffensive, well-made dream. She was going to market with her cook, who carried the basket. The butcher said to her when she asked him for something: "That is all gone," and wished to give her something else, remarking; "That's very good." She declines, and goes to the greengrocer, who wants to sell her a peculiar vegetable which is bound up in bundles and of a black color. She says: "I don't know that; I won't take it."
>
> The remark "That is all gone" arose from the treatment. A few days before I said myself to the patient that the earliest reminiscences of childhood are all gone as such but are replaced by transferences and dreams. Thus I am the butcher [in the dream]. (Freud, 1920a, p. 51)

Other critics claim that psychoanalysis cannot be considered a science due to its inability to predict future behavior. Psychoanalysts, critics maintain, believe that certain childhood experiences, such as abuse or molestation, produce certain outcomes or neurotic conditions. To take this idea one step further, one should be able to predict that if children experience abuse, for instance, they will acquire certain personality traits. In addition, this concept would theoretically work in reverse. For instance, if individuals are diagnosed with a particular neurotic disorder, one should be able to predict that they had a corresponding causal childhood experience. Neither of these predictions, however, can be made with any accuracy (Colby, 1960, p. 55).

Hans Eysenck, a German psychologist who did much of his work in England, was the first researcher to challenge psychoanalysis on the basis of an outcome study of psychotherapy. He stated, "I have always taken it for granted that the obvious failure of Freudian therapy to significantly improve on spontaneous remission or placebo treatment is the clearest proof we have of the inadequacy of Freudian theory, closely followed by the success of alternative methods of treatment, such as behavior therapy" (Eysenck, 1986, p. 236).

Behaviorism

This school originated in the United States in 1912 and had a parallel beginning in Russia under the guidance of Ivan Pavlov (1849–1936), a researcher who was awarded the Nobel Prize in Medicine in 1904 for his experiments with the effects of **classical conditioning** on the salivation and digestive functions of dogs. In its strictest version, behaviorism rejected outright all unobservable mental processes. Consciousness, emotions, reflection, and attitudes were all made irrelevant and unscientific by the early behaviorists. John B. Watson, a professor at Johns Hopkins who eventually became a consultant to the advertising industry, discarded as irrelevant the entire foundation of both the structuralist and functionalist schools of psychology. Both of these schools regarded the internal operations of the mind as the primary subject matter of psychology and depended on introspection, or looking inward to scrutinize one's own mental processes, as the means of access to these operations.

Watson, however, asserted that an objective science cannot study something as **subjective** as someone's personal experience of consciousness. He went on to argue that even if consciousness exists, its subjective nature makes it inscrutable. He concluded that cognition is so subjective as to be unquantifiable. Behaviorism held that for psychology to be a science, it must limit itself to observable and quantifiable events. Stimuli and the consequent responses to those stimuli were just those events.

In 1920, Watson conducted an experiment at Johns Hopkins that would not be permitted by any medical ethics committee in the early 2000s. He deliberately conditioned an 11-month-old child known as Little Albert to experience fear in the presence of such originally neutral stimuli as tame white laboratory mice and rabbits by making a loud noise while the child was enjoying quiet play with the animals. Moreover, Watson never deconditioned Little Albert to remove the fears he had induced in the little boy. For nearly half a century, behaviorism was the overwhelmingly dominant school in psychology.

Under the influence of B. F. Skinner, one of the few psychologists to have published a novel (*Walden Two*) as well as scientific articles, behaviorism attempted to explain every facet of human behavior and development. Love, war, mating, language, and the development of societies were all explained in terms of contingencies of reinforcement. Language was a collection of those sounds that were reinforced after being distilled from the noises that the child randomly expressed during development. Affection, too, was a collection of behaviors reinforced by members of the opposite sex. At its high point, behaviorism was able to account for all actions of humans and the higher animals through the pattern of stimulus and response. But like Ptolemy's model of the celestial movements, behaviorism was based on some fundamental misconceptions. Its explanatory power then began to show severe weaknesses.

Gestalt Psychology

You have probably heard a variation of the maxim that "we are greater than the sum of our parts." This is a variant of the defining principle of the Gestalt school of psychology, which had its origins in Germany around 1912. *Gestalt* is the German word for form or shape. This school of psychology shares its name with a therapeutic method that is quite unrelated. The Gestalt school was founded and led by Wolfgang Köhler (1887–1967), Kurt Koffka (1886–1941), and Max Wertheimer, researchers who set forth the notion that the totality of the human mind is more than or different from the sum of its parts. They were primarily interested in perception and how the brain organizes the complex data coming from our senses into conscious perception. Interestingly, they concluded that our senses work quite differently from electronic recording devices. Rather than merely being imprinted by perceptual data, the human mind draws conclusions from the senses—so that what we see, hear, or otherwise perceive is a highly subjective experience.

Photo 2.2 Wolfgang Köhler (1887–1967)

The Gestalt psychologists presented several perceptual phenomena to support their thesis that analysis often fails to explain experiences. For example, our minds provide us with **object constancy**. For example, when we are looking at a table, if we walk around it or back and forth at a distance from it, we will continue to see the table as the same size and shape despite changes in viewing angle or distance. Similarly with sounds: If we transpose a tune into another key, we will still hear the same tune, even though the components (the individual notes) are all different.

Hence, the Gestalt psychologists could argue that experiences carry with them a quality of wholeness that cannot be found in the parts. For this reason, the German name *Gestalt* is appropriate to characterize their system because the word denotes form, figure, or configuration and carries with it the connotation that a reductionist analysis undermines the wholeness of the form or figure. The Gestalt psychologists quickly extended their observations and theoretical interpretations into such other areas as learning, thinking, and problem solving. They, like most advocates of other schools, tried to formulate a comprehensive model of psychology.

Cognitive Psychology

Behaviorism in its strongest form began to wane around the same time as the arrival of a new metaphor for the human mind: the computer. The early computer was a black box that processed information, which became a new metaphor for the human mind. It became hard to accept that the human brain was not at least as sophisticated an information processor as

Photo 2.3   Ulric Neisser (1928–)

the computer, which was obviously a completely physical object, made by human beings, and needed no appeal to nonmaterialistic concepts to explain its functioning. Human behavior began to be seen as a complex interplay of many mental processes whose existence and interactions could be inferred through subtle and elegant experimentation. With the opening of cognitive psychology as a new field of study, the concept of human beings as organisms that merely respond to environmental stimuli began to fall into disfavor.

The shift away from behaviorism's black-box model of the human psyche to the information-processing model of cognitive psychology was a gradual one. A logical birth year, however, would be 1967, when Ulric Neisser published the first text in the field. *Cognitive Psychology* consists of chapters on perception, attention, language, memory, and thought.

The information-processing approach to human cognition sees human thought as taking place in a series of stages, each of which requires a distinct mechanism that analyzes, parses, and routes information in a precise way. The early stages of thought involve the apprehension of sensory data relayed from our sense organs via the nervous system. Subsequent stages focus on the perception, interpretation, storage, and in some cases, awareness of the data. The final stages involve utilization of stored data and creation of such new information as reconstructed memories or the production of language.

Using the computer as a metaphor, we can easily see the absurdity of assuming that simply because we cannot observe the calculations taking place within such a device, we must limit ourselves to the study of its inputs and outputs. If we were to pinpoint a seminal event that resulted in psychology's shifting toward an information-processing view of the human mind, it would be Noam Chomsky's 1959 rebuttal of Skinner's model of language. Skinner (1957) had argued that language learning takes place when randomly emitted sounds are selectively reinforced. Chomsky countered that this theory of language learning is overly simplistic and, more importantly, impossible. He noted that there are too many ways to express the same idea and too many ways to organize a sentence for language skills to be learned by operant conditioning. He demonstrated quantitatively that there must be an inborn **language acquisition device** (LAD) in the brain that contains the elements of grammar.

Chomsky's rebuttal of Skinner's extreme behaviorist ideas resulted in a movement back to the examination of internal mental processing as a theme for psychology. Skinner's model fails to explain the human ability to innovate with language—that is, to construct sentences that are original, yet understood and judged to be grammatically correct by other speakers. According to behaviorists, each separate sentence would have to be emitted and then reinforced. Chomsky's famous example, "colorless green ideas sleep furiously," illustrates

Photo 2.4   Noam Chomsky (1928–)

that any one of us could construct a new and original sentence that follows the rules of English grammar. Chomsky proposes that we all possess a generative grammar that allows us to produce an infinite number of grammatically correct sentences, using a finite lexicon organized by a specific set of grammatical rules. Prior to this linguistic breakthrough, there had been a growing body of evidence that strict behaviorism could not account for all aspects of human personality or behavior; that there was more going on inside the "black box" than could be explained by the stimulus and response model.

As early as the 1920s, the Gestalt movement provided evidence for a cognitive model. The Gestalt psychologist Wolfgang Köhler performed some experiments with chimpanzees, which showed that primates cognitively process information. In a common experiment, a chimpanzee attempts to reach bananas hanging out of reach. After failing to reach the fruit by repeatedly jumping, he gives up in frustration. Then, after a pause involving what appears to be reflection, he scans his environment and notices various objects left in his enclosure, including a box. Without reinforcement or external direction, the animal places the box under the hanging bananas, grabs a pole that had previously been used as a toy, and engages it as a tool to strike at and obtain the bananas by knocking them down. This and similar events are in direct contradiction to the principles of behaviorism. There were no random operants that were shaped by reinforcement to create a complex behavior. The chimpanzees seemed to solve their problems through cognition, by developing mental representations of their situations and performing a virtual trial and error method (Köhler, 1925).

The concept of cognition was compellingly supported in the mid-1950s by the introduction of the computer, which could be programmed to emulate many aspects of human thought. Computers could calculate, perform rudimentary reasoning, and even perceive. And notably the processes that allowed the machines to carry out their tasks could be understood. This feature led to the adoption of the computer as a cogent symbol for human cognitive processes.

The computer has observable inputs and outputs and somewhat inscrutable processes occurring in between input and output. No reasonable person, however, would suggest that it is unscientific to explore these internal processes. Indeed, the introduction of computer science was synergistic with the growth of cognitive science in psychology. The computer as an information-processing device made the behaviorists' assertion that human behavior should be described in terms of stimulus and response increasingly untenable. The model of the human mind as an information-processing device was bolstered in 1956 by George Miller's discovery of the "magic number seven" (plus or minus two). Miller's (1956) meta-study indicated that there is a distinct short-term memory phase in human information processing and that it has specific limits.

In the later part of the 1950s, Leon Festinger, a social psychologist then teaching at Stanford University, described a new type of information processing within the human mind that was in harsh contrast to behavioral notions. Festinger found that the more widely our behavior differs from our self-image, the more we will modify our memory of our behavior. In effect, we reinvent our actions to accommodate our self-image. This finding disagreed with strict behaviorism, which held that reported memories are simply reinforced behaviors.

The evidence for information processing as a useful model of the mind continued to accumulate for every part of the life span. In 1962, Jean Piaget (1896–1980), a Swiss researcher, concluded that cognitive development in children took place in regular stages. These stages of cognitive development presented the same problems for behaviorism as language learning.

Figure 2.2   Topics in Cognitive Psychology

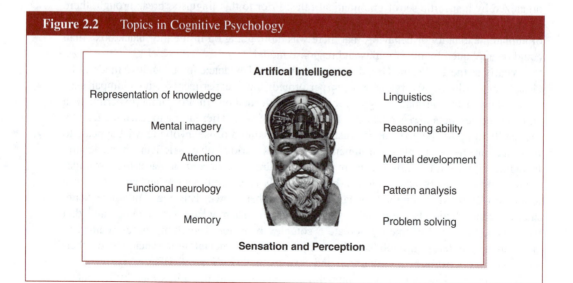

Cognition, Brain Modules, and Circuits. As the human mind was represented with increasing frequency as an information-processing device, some psychologists expanded the metaphor by describing the mind as a device with specialized modules. The reader should recall that the strict behaviorists saw the internal workings of the mind as either nonexistent or irrelevant. Now the pendulum had swung back to the point where new levels of complexity were once again being added to the researchers' picture of the mind. It is important to point out that the complexities introduced by the cognitive psychologists are different from those developed by the structuralists, who based their hypotheses on introspection and conjecture. The cognitive psychologists based their descriptions on strong clinical evidence and objective research as well as on computer models.

Jerry Fodor (1935–), an American philosopher and cognitive psychologist who studied under Chomsky, expanded his teacher's language hypotheses into a **modularity of mind** model. In his first two major books, *The Language of Thought* (1975) and *The Modularity of Mind* (1983), Fodor asserted that the mind is composed of functionally independent **modules**. The neuropsychologist Michael Gazzaniga (1939–) came to a similar conclusion from his work with split-brain patients—people who were treated for epilepsy with surgery that had effectively disconnected the two hemispheres of the brain. Gazzaniga's (1970) work with these people showed that the two hemispheres can act as two separate and sentient entities. By combining these findings with neuropsychological evidence, Gazzaniga was convinced that the brain has preprogrammed circuits or modules that act independently of one another to control specific mental functions.

One major implication of the work of these researchers is that it may be possible to study human perception, for example, without having to account for memory, or to model reasoning without taking account of emotion. More specifically, Fodor claims that such "higher" cognitive functions as reasoning do not interact with such low-level input and output functions as perception. This claim that the human mind is modular has philosophical antecedents in the notion of mental faculties. The problem of defining just what is included in the set of clearly isolated faculties has not gone away.

One more aspect in the concept of modules is contained in the work of some important neuroscientists, who have provided additional evidence that the structure of the human brain directs or shapes a significant portion of personality. Perhaps the first researcher to describe the operation of the human brain in terms of functionally distinct modules was Paul MacLean (1913–2008), a senior scientist at the National Institute of Mental Health (NIMH). This neurologist provided evidence that the human brain seems to have evolved with a set of distinct and somewhat independent sections that originated at different points in evolutionary history. MacLean's (1990) theory is known as the **triune brain** hypothesis. The oldest part of the brain, according to this hypothesis, is the so-called reptilian brain—the brain stem and cerebellum, which control breathing and other basic life functions. The second part, the **limbic system**, houses the amygdala and **hippocampus**, structures that are involved with the regulation of emotion and memory storage. The third part, the "new brain" or **neocortex**, involves the cerebral hemispheres. It constitutes about 83% of the human brain and governs such functions as speaking, writing, thinking, and planning for the future.

MacLean's triune model of the human brain offered a more satisfactory explanation for the inaccessibility of much of cognition to conscious awareness. During the course of human evolution, the limbic system and neocortex were added to the reptilian brain, which could not be replaced because it controls the basic life functions necessary to human survival. In addition, McLean and other neuroscientists tacitly undermined the idea that some aspects of cognition are difficult to access because of childhood trauma or toilet training problems. Rather, the human brain has evolved in such a way that communication within some regions of the brain is better than it is within others. This is essentially the conclusion that was reached by the neurologist António C. R. Damásio (1944–), who has observed that damage to key areas of the brain can result in profound and permanent changes to personality (Damásio, 1999). These issues will be discussed in more detail in Chapter 14.

Rational Emotive Behavioral Therapy and Cognitive Behaviorism

As shown in the outline of the history of personality psychology, behaviorism once dominated the field, but this dominance was eroded by several important insights that pointed to the importance of cognition. Experimental psychologists began to shift away from the study of behaviorism and toward cognition, in what is often referred to as the cognitive revolution. While this revolution was taking hold in the laboratories and universities, there was a parallel revolution taking place among the clinical psychologists.

Contemporaneous with the experimental psychologists' renewed focus on cognition, Albert Ellis asserted that clinical psychologists should take the same path. Unlike the experimental psychologists, who promoted a more complex model than the behaviorists, however, Ellis established a frugal cognitive approach to psychology. His approach lacked the Byzantine complexity of psychoanalysis, and it offered a new and compelling way for clinicians to understand both normal and abnormal behavior.

Ellis, like the other founders of modern psychology, first based his theory on anecdotal evidence and personal observation rather than laboratory research. At one time, this lack of experimental verification was a serious weakness of his rational emotive approach to psychotherapy. After half a century of research, however, it has ceased to be a problem. This book describes the research that supports Ellis's new cognitive behavioral approach, developed in earnest over the latter part of the 20th century and early years of the 21st. This research has validated most of his early intuitive conclusions.

Ellis noted that people are universally and inherently irrational. He based this generalization on his consistent observation that people tend to create arbitrary and absolute demands on the world around them—such as the person who "must have" a certain job, romantic partner, or new car. The universality of irrational thinking led Ellis to conclude that illogical thinking must be genetic and a result of adaptation to an earlier and simpler environment. Specifically, built into our psyche are styles of thought that would serve primitive humans quite well but often lead to emotional pain in modern humans living in complex environments. Interestingly, the psychologist and Nobel laureate Daniel Kahneman came to a similar conclusion about the universality of irrational thinking. He found that people consistently make inaccurate judgments about the probability of events, and that these judgments often lead to inefficient or self-defeating behavior. Ellis concluded that human irrationality results in people acting against their own best interests and leads to disturbances in personality. Why do these things happen? That question is examined in the following vignette and in greater depth in Chapter 16.

VIGNETTE

Dora's story is an example of a self-fulfilling prophecy. When she was still an infant, she emigrated with her parents and her older brother from Lithuania. After arriving in the United States, her parents both worked in blue-collar jobs and devoted their lives to their two children. Dora grew into a slight but pretty girl, with beautiful hair whose color was halfway between platinum and gold. Her attractive appearance, combined with a quiet and compliant nature, led to favorable treatment from her teachers. Her parents took great pride in her good grades and her helpfulness at home. Her success in school and her stable personality were in direct contrast to her brother, who became increasingly withdrawn and given to odd behavior. He was drafted into the Army at 18, only to be given a psychiatric discharge 2 years later when he was diagnosed with schizophrenia.

Dora thrived as her brother declined. She had a ready smile and a continuously happy demeanor. In all, she was as different as a person could be from the withdrawn, hostile, and bizarre person her brother had become. Dora went to college, completing her courses in 3 years with a degree in industrial engineering. Her parents were pleased with her excellent grades; however, they often pressured her about the importance of making friends. Dora replied to their suggestions with comments to the effect that other students were not serious about their work or that they would only distract her because they partied too much. Happily for Dora and her parents, her limited social life seemed to become irrelevant when she began dating a graduate student in engineering. Within a year, she married her beau.

The marriage prospered during the next 2 years; Dora worked as an engineer for a large computer manufacturer while her husband was employed by an international petroleum company. Dora did her job well, was quite socially appropriate at work, but stayed away from all optional social events. As she had in college, she did not feel comfortable around large numbers of people. There was only one coworker she could speak to about anything other than work—her boss. He was an elderly man who was trustworthy, in Dora's opinion. When he asked her why she rarely attended company holiday parties and the like, she complained about the malicious small talk she heard at these gatherings, and she added that she never wanted to provide any material for the gossip mill.

As Dora's life became more complicated, her suspicious nature became more manifest. Dora's belief that her coworkers harbored bad intentions toward her made her life increasingly uncomfortable. Despite all of her boss's attempts to dissuade her, Dora left the computer company to become an independent consultant. Her new career was put on hold, however, when she discovered that she was pregnant. The pregnancy had also created a respite in the marital problems that had been emerging with her husband. Although Dora had convinced herself that he was a sociopath, she

(Continued)

(Continued)

could find no one to agree with her diagnosis. She accused him of taking financial advantage of their joint income, of cheating on her, and of not helping out at home. When Dora's husband responded to her continual and unsupported accusations with anger and frustration, Dora saw it only as further evidence of his being a sociopath.

The marriage lasted 4 more years, largely because Dora's husband did not want to leave his family. But he could not bear her accusations any longer and filed for divorce. Now on her own, Dora returned to her career as a consultant. The personal computer had just been adopted as a tool by many large corporations, and Dora seized the opportunity to start a business that developed PC software for financial firms. As her financial success increased, so too did her social isolation. She had a few acquaintances whom she met occasionally for lunch or dinner, but her great suspicions of other people's motives always kept them at a distance.

Dora imparted her negative worldview to her son through her admonitions to be careful about trusting anyone else. She warned him regularly about the bad intentions of others and the importance of never letting down his guard. Unfortunately, her advice only annoyed and alienated him. Her son became closer to his father, and although he continued to live with his mother, he never became close to her emotionally. After Dora's son graduated from high school, he left for college and rarely returned to visit. He ultimately became a physician and in his early thirties cut off all contact with his mother.

Dora became quite wealthy and moved into a prestigious community of high-income professionals. Although her superficial charisma allowed her to make short-lived friendships, she remained largely alone. She never saw the connection between her personality, which regarded the world and those in it as hostile, and her loneliness. Instead, she considered her loneliness as confirmation of the world's malevolence.

Vignette Questions

1. Does Dora have a disturbance of her personality?

2. Or was she merely in the wrong time or wrong place?

3. That is, could her personality been more functional in a different time or different culture?

A brief synopsis of Ellis's rational emotive model of personality is set forth in Figure 2.4.

Following the REBT view of personality development, all humans are born with a unique set of dispositions, including level of arousal, sensitivity to noxious or pleasurable stimuli, and a preference for focusing on internal or external events. These innate characteristics will incline a person toward either neuroticism or placidity and will ultimately influence his or her tendency to think more or less rationally, depending on key development factors that will be discussed in Chapter 16.

Figure 2.3 Personality Development According to REBT

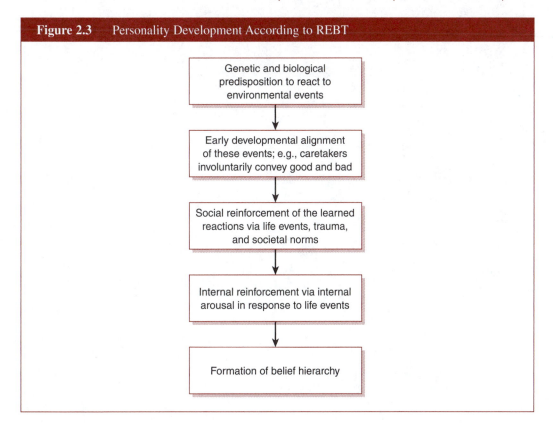

CHAPTER SUMMARY

This chapter traced the division of psychology into several schools of thought along the course of its history. This partitioning led to both the growth of psychology and some large mistakes related to the theorists' egos. One aspect of personality is the tendency to confuse one's worth with one's ideas. This confounding seems to have led many psychologists to uphold hypotheses or principles that had become unworkable and unsupported by the research evidence. If our understanding of personality is to grow and improve, it must be based unfailingly on the best available scientific evidence. It is important to note that there are no schools of thought per se in such fields as medicine, physics, or chemistry. These fields are guided almost exclusively by research and science. So, too, should psychology and the study of personality.

NOTE

1. Most historians credit Wundt with constructing the first free-standing laboratory dedicated to psychology, which was opened in 1879. Others note that William James's laboratory in Boylston Hall at Harvard was established in 1875.

Chapter 3

Personality Research

Chapter Goals

- Familiarize the reader with key terms used in the field of psychological research
- Provide a comprehensive understanding of the reasons for the research and testing of the various theories of personality
- Provide in-depth knowledge of the several testing approaches used in research as well as their advantages and disadvantages

---

Chapter 2 discussed the progress of personality theory from the general intuitions of great thinkers and innovators to a more formal science. A closer examination of the history of personality theory should make clear why a scientific approach is essential. Before the emergence of psychology as a discipline, the characteristics that define people as individuals were sometimes thought to result from the activity of spirits and demons. So, too, they were sometimes explained as the results of astronomical configurations. The apparent placement of the stars within constellations and the movements of the moon and the planets within the solar system were (and by some still are) believed to ordain the personality of those born under them.

Many of these explanations were quite understandable during eras in which there were few established means of testing their truth. Thus, if something seemed credible or could be convincingly argued, it might very well be accepted as a truth. After all, why do many people today study their astrological signs and explain their personality in terms of their sun sign in the zodiac? Perhaps this is so because such explanations are simple and easily understood and because the benign character descriptions for each zodiacal sign are universally appealing. The seductive attraction of other theories has led to large followings for phrenology, **spiritualism**, **animism**, and numerous similar movements that have failed to earn scientific support. It is only through unbiased and systematic examination of received ideas and rejection of those not supported by objective evidence that we can come ever closer to an understanding of what is true. The study of personality, as in all other subfields within psychology, is now conducted and evaluated by the same methods used in all other sciences.

Image 3.1

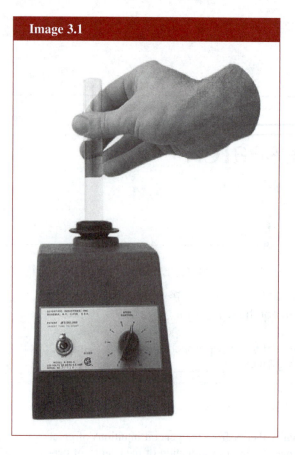

▣ THE SCIENTIFIC METHOD

What is science? Most people, if asked that question, would reply that science is an advanced body of knowledge in a so-called hard or technical area like chemistry or physics. But one of the most important things for college students to understand is that science is not so much a collection of information as a method that leads to knowledge about reality. A science can be defined as any discipline in which the scientific method is used.

During the last few centuries, a number of individuals sought methods of drawing conclusions objectively and in ways that can be communicated to other scholars. A major figure in this movement was Francis Bacon (1561–1626), an English nobleman who began his career as a lawyer and member of Parliament during the reign of Queen Elizabeth I. Bacon advocated an experimental approach to the acquisition of knowledge and encouraged using qualitative and inductive methods. In his *Novum Organum* (1620/1994), Bacon proposed that scientific knowledge is best advanced by an inductive rather than a deductive approach. According to Bacon, nothing should be accepted *a priori* but must be tested and examined. He suggested that the essential principles of any natural phenomenon can be understood if a sufficient number of observations are made to allow the induction of the underlying principles.

Contemporary science still uses the inductive method or **induction**. Let us clearly define what that method is and how it differs from **deduction.** Sherlock Holmes, the famous fictional detective created by Sir Arthur Conan Doyle, is typically described by his creator as using deduction. Actually, Holmes, or any wise detective for that matter, uses induction: building the case against a suspect by accumulating small facts to support it. In a short story called "The Five Orange Pips," which was published in 1891, Conan Doyle has Holmes compare himself to a famous French zoologist who reconstructed extinct animals from fossilized bones: "As [Georges] Cuvier could correctly describe a whole animal by the contemplation of a single bone, so the observer who has thoroughly understood one link in a series of incidents should be able to state all the other ones, before and after." (Doyle, 2002, p. 81)

A scientist is basically a detective. In contrast to deductive reasoning, which moves from general premises to specific conclusions, induction begins from small actual observations, using an accumulation of these to formulate some generalizations—generalizations that are useful only if they lead to testable predictions. Just as Holmes used such observations as the mud and scrape marks on his friend Watson's boots to infer that (a) Watson had been out in the rain that day and (b) had recently hired an incompetent servant who scratched the boot leather in attempting to remove the mud, a scientist might begin with some apparently unconnected phenomena and formulate a hypothesis to be tested by gathering further data.

Early scientists sought ways to study natural events without bias and to develop common sets of terms and systems of measurement for communicating their findings. One example was the development of the metric system, which began in 18th-century France when King Louis XVI charged a group of famous scientists to develop a universal system of measurement to replace the many different standards then in use in different parts of France. This process of standardization has led to a consensus among researchers in the many realms of science to examine events and understand their causes, effects, and even to predict their recurrence—as when astronomers learned to plot the courses of comets and predict the dates of their return.

Theories in personality psychology commonly offer an overarching explanation of the differences found among people, the degree to which they differ, and the sources of these differences. In seeking to answer these questions, researchers set forth propositions that can be tested against real-world events. Unless theories are testable and subjected to appropriate examination, the study of personality will not differ from the many pseudosciences that some people accept on faith. If you are taking the time to read a textbook, you most likely want something more than one individual's opinion, even if that person is reputed to have a first-rate intellect and deep insight. The following box contains an example of a hypothesis in personality theory, one that failed its tests.

Application of the Scientific Method to Personality Theory

In the mid-1790s, Franz Josef Gall (1758–1828) employed the consistently verified hypothesis that the brain is the seat of human personality. Gall combined this hypothesis with another proposal—that each personality characteristic is exclusively controlled by a specific and identifiable region of the brain. Consequently, he concluded that the skull overlying a particularly well-developed brain region would bulge in direct proportion to the strength of that characteristic. The graphic below illustrates this notion.

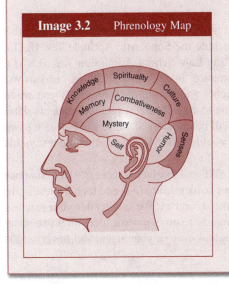

Image 3.2 Phrenology Map

The drawing illustrates the theory of phrenology, which became widely employed as a clinical method throughout Europe in the late 18th and early 19th centuries. In the early 1800s, however, experimental data presented by Jean Pierre Flourens (1794–1867) (Klein, 1970, p. 668) showed that Gall's notion of localization of function was a gross oversimplification of brain functioning. Consequently, a theory with very good *face validity* fell into oblivion.

Theoretical Research and Personality

Theories are essential for the growth of any field of study, provided that they are challenged, tested, and refined. Personality psychology is no exception to this rule. It is a field presently in flux, containing numerous theories—some new and others largely unchanged for a century. Irrespective of the pedigree of these theories, however, scientific personality psychology is based on philosophical **determinism,** which holds that all events are invariably caused by preceding events. This cause-and-effect relationship is governed by inviolable natural laws. The acceptance of this basic principle has profound consequences for the student of science. It means that anything one observes in the world can be traced to a preexisting cause that in turn can be understood on the basis of such invariant natural laws as those set forth in fields like mathematics and physics. Of course, human behavior is more complicated than the invariant world of chemicals and atoms. Predicting the behavior of people in a group, or even what one person will do in a given situation, is a far harder task than predicting what will happen when two chemicals are combined. It may, in any event, be a probabilistic matter, akin to tossing a die, but the essential concept is the same.

Determinism holds that events never occur as a result of spontaneous or magical causes. Moreover, determinists maintain that anything that does happen can ultimately be understood as a rule-governed event. For example, if a specific individual has an open and agreeable personality, we can look to preceding events or states to understand it. Such events may include the individual's genetic code, his or her parenting, or the behavior of peers. Only empirical study can be the basis of discovery of the causes of a person's behavior.

Once we accept the premise that human personality has identifiable causes and that these can be discovered through research, the next step is to use the procedures in Table 3.1 to develop an explanation of personality. Table 3.2 summarizes some of the more prominent theoretical approaches.

Reliability

If you are in college or graduate school, it is highly likely that you have taken some test of academic or intellectual ability. Such tests include the Scholastic Aptitude Test (SAT), the Graduate Record Examination (GRE), and the Law School Admission Test (LSAT). These tests are used to predict your performance in future educational endeavors. According to the publishers of these tests, the higher your score, the more likely you are to perform well in the school that you are competing to enter. If a test predicts students' later performance with a high degree of accuracy, it will be considered valid. But before we can even consider such a measure of legitimacy, we would need to know whether the test yields consistent results.

Let us suppose, for example, that you took the SAT and received a score of 1400. Suppose further that you felt that this result understated your academic aptitude and took the test again the next month, only to receive a score of 900 on the second try. We suspect that your reaction would be one of disappointment and disbelief. Wouldn't you wonder if there might be some quirk in the design of the test rather than a tremendous drop in your actual abilities?

Table 3.1	The Scientific Method

1. An event or object is observed that provokes interest and is thought to require further study or explanation.

2. A model is then formulated that either explains the observation or connects it to observations made by other scientists. This model is called a hypothesis, although made prior to a formal study; it is usually the product of a deep understanding in the applicable field of study.

3. The hypothesis is then employed to predict or create similar events in experimental settings or in observations in natural settings.

4. If the hypothesis turns out to be inaccurate in predicting experimental outcomes or worldly events, it is modified or replaced by a new hypothesis.

5. If the hypothesis proves consistently accurate, it is accepted and then becomes a theory, which is a set of connected propositions to explain a class of phenomena.

Table 3.2	Theoretical Approaches to Personality

Theoretical Approach	*Foundation*	*Typical Research Method*
Analytic	Personality is a function of dynamic and unconscious forces that control most human thought and behavior.	Idiographic case studies based on clinical encounters.
Trait	Personality comprises several discrete and enduring characteristics.	Statistical/correlational and psychometric research.
Social learning	Personality develops out of directly reinforced, observed, or socially encouraged behaviors.	Observation, quasi-experiments, and true experiments
Cognitive behavioral	Personality is a function of both thinking and behavior, reinforced through life events and interactions with others. Tendencies toward reinforcement can be biologically or genetically determined.	Observation, quasi-experiments, and true experiments.
Genetic/ biological	Personality is driven by genetic endowments and the resulting physiological processes	**Epidemiology** studies, quasi- and true experiments; statistical analyses.

If you were a bit research-oriented, you might check the published data on the SAT's reliability. You would likely find that it has a **reliability coefficient** of approximately .91. This number means that there is a .91 correlation between the scores people obtain on the first administration of the test and those obtained on a subsequent administration. We can conclude that although the test did not seem reliable to you, it is indeed a reliable instrument. On the other hand, if you had discovered that the test had a low reliability coefficient, that fact would indicate that the test is a poor measure of your ability.

Reliability in research or personality measurement refers to the dependability of the measure. A reliable test will yield very similar results in repeated administrations except in the face of basic changes that might have taken place between measurements. Logically, any test that yields unreliable results cannot be considered a valid measure of anything it claims to measure. For a test to serve as a valid measure of personality or any other attribute, however, assessing reliability is just the first step in evaluating the test.

Validity

If we were to provide a self-administered test that measures the quality of your soul, for example, we would run into some significant problems, not the least of which would be that we would not be clear as to exactly what we are measuring. The test may very well give

Image 3.3

consistent results. That is, you might take the test several times and always come out with the result that you possess a soul of the highest caliber. But we would still be left with the vexing problem of defining the soul.

Depending on your religious background and convictions, you may or may not accept the existence of a soul. And even if you do, your conception of *soul* may be radically different from that of someone accepting a different set of religious teachings. For a test of a human soul to be valid, a researcher must have a clear and precise definition of it. In addition, the test must yield some outcome that can meaningfully rate, categorize, or measure a soul. Thus, even if we could construct an operational definition of *soul*, we would still have the problem of measuring it in a meaningful way.

Validity in personality research refers to the same conceptual issue. To perform a valid measurement of personality, we are required to define precisely what we are measuring. Are we measuring a component trait? Or are we measuring the entire person? Does our measure of personality make some assumption about the nature of personality that other researchers may simply reject? These and related questions must be answered before moving on to the next step in developing a method to measure the construct we are studying. Once this step is completed, we must then find the appropriate individuals to serve as test subjects for the method.

For example, suppose researchers wish to ascertain if overcoming feelings of inferiority is a key factor in the development of a mature personality. They then construct an experiment in which a random sample of teenagers is divided into two groups based on their scores on a test that measures feelings of inferiority. Those who express a low level of inferiority feelings are placed in one group, and those with a high level of such feelings are placed in the second group. The participants are contacted 5 years later and retested to produce three groups.

The first group consists of young adults who scored high on both the first and second administration of the examination. The second group consists of those who were shown to

---

VIGNETTE

Buddy, as he liked to be called, lived up to his name. He worked hard at being everyone's friend; he loved to be liked. The youngest of three brothers, Buddy grew up in an ethnic neighborhood in the suburb of a large city. His mother was an elementary school teacher and his father a postal worker. The family was close-knit; moreover, all of the boys were good students and accepted into college. In fact, both of Buddy's brothers became doctoral-level professionals.

Buddy himself earned two master's degrees; however, these degrees were in fields that offered few prospects for faculty teaching positions. After earning an M.A. in Asian history, Buddy referred to himself as a historian, but he took a job as a corporate messenger that belied that appellation. Despite all exhortations by his brothers to get a teaching credential or some other training that would enable him to enter a more remunerative profession, Buddy went back to school for an M.A. in philosophy.

Buddy was somewhat diminutive, and his boyish demeanor made him seem even smaller. In fact, he would often come across as a prematurely aged child, always joking and allowing others to make him the object of ridicule. On several occasions, he was warned by friends in his workplace that he was sacrificing all chances to move up the company ladder by playing the clown. One friend even told him that he was liked by all but respected by no one and that he would always be a messenger if he did not stop his self-effacing silliness. Despite Buddy's high intellect, he could not absorb and learn from these well-intended admonitions.

In addition to Buddy's joking around, and in some contrast to it, he spent a significant portion of his spare time doing others' work. Although Buddy's job at the

(Continued)

(Continued)

company was considered low-level, he was bright enough to perform some higher level tasks for his superiors. Many of them exploited his ability and openly took credit for his work. Buddy never complained or objected; he was satisfied if they condescended to pat him on the head or offer some superficial compliment.

Outside the workplace, Buddy's self-defeating nature was most evident in his relationships with women. His typical relationship, which usually lasted only a few weeks, consisted of a series of expensive dates in which the woman would become increasingly critical of him. He would then respond to her criticisms with gifts or some other bit of submissive behavior. The woman would lose interest in him and leave him for another man.

Buddy seemed to be completely oblivious to the pattern of self-defeat that was evident to everyone else who knew him. He acted as though he sought out rejection and humiliation; this was not the case, however, as each additional rejection became increasingly painful to him. Unfortunately, with each blow to his self-image, he would become even more ingratiating and subservient to the people in his life. This behavior perpetuated Buddy's vicious circle of self-effacement: from contempt on the part of others to rejection to lowered self-image and back to self-effacement.

This pattern characterized most of Buddy's adult life. His self-defeating style exemplifies the way in which a personality can be both ineffective and opaque to the individual possessing it. Personality usually describes a pattern of behavior that is adaptive for an individual, but in some cases, the pattern can be quite destructive. In such cases, it is difficult for the afflicted individual to be aware of the interaction between his personality characteristics and his unhappy life, and the person will often fail to see the relationship when it is pointed out. This blindness was the situation with Buddy, who not only could not perceive his pattern of self-defeat but also seemingly did all he could to reinforce it.

Vignette Questions

1. Why do you think Buddy is the way he is: childhood, inborn events, or social learning?

2. Do you agree that Buddy is unaware of his self-defeating behavior?

3. Why or why not?

have low levels of inferiority feelings on both administrations. The third group, however, comprises those young people who overcame their former high level of inferiority feelings and now score low on the test.

Recall that the hypothesis being tested states that people who overcome feelings of inferiority will develop the highest levels of maturity. To test this hypothesis, the researchers must find out whether the participants in Group 3 are significantly more mature than those in Groups 1 and 2.

Let us assume that in order to make this determination, the researchers administered the Washington University Sentence Completion Test (WUSCT) to measure ego development (Loevinger, 1998). They found that the participants who had overcome feelings of inferiority had statistically higher levels of ego development, which the researchers posit as synonymous with emotional maturity. They have proven their hypothesis—or have they?

We can readily find several problems with the validity of the outcomes in this hypothetical experiment. First, the researchers seem to have a problem with the **internal validity** of the experiment. In experiments with high internal validity, almost all **confounding** factors are controlled, so that any change in the **dependent variable** can be attributed to the changes in the **independent variable**. The dependent variable in this experiment is feelings of inferiority. The researchers identified participants who showed reductions in this measure, but they did not control all the variables that could have produced the change. Moreover, they concluded that changes in feelings of inferiority *caused* differences in the subjects' level of maturity.

The researchers may very well have additional problems with their **construct validity.** Their outcome measure—the measure of maturity in this case—is determined by using the WUSCT, a test of ego development. Using this particular instrument implies that ego development is synonymous with maturity. This equivalence is true only if we have a precisely defined measure of ego development and if this measure has been demonstrated to be directly proportional with maturity.

Finally, there also seems to be a problem with **external validity** in this experiment. An experiment with satisfactory external validity can be applied in settings outside the original experimental area. If our experiment has a high level of external validity, we can reasonably conclude that all people everywhere can be expected to be more mature if they have overcome feelings of inferiority. But an obvious problem with this study lies in the selection of the participants, all of whom were university students. Are the individuals we select for our study truly representative of all people we are seeking to understand? These researchers, like many others, are inclined to study the groups most likely or available to participate in research—such as college psychology majors. Of course, there have been many important and elegant studies in all subdisciplines within psychology that recruited students as participants. We still face the troublesome concern, however, as to whether we can legitimately conclude that measures of personality among college students apply to people old enough to be their parents, or to people who never completed high school, or to people from other countries.

Replication and Verification

Irrespective of the specific theory of personality under consideration, relevant research must meet some basic criteria to be scientifically sound. One of the most essential of these criteria is **replicability**. This criterion requires presenting a study examining a principle of personality in a way that allows other researchers to repeat the study. Suppose, for example, a theorist concludes that stinginess and a need to control others results from restrictive parental toilet training. The theorist bases this conclusion on comments about childhood memories made by his clients during therapy sessions. He presents as further evidence that clients who gain insight into the origin of their controlling or stingy behavior during therapy showed marked reduction in compulsive or anal-retentive acts or attitudes.

We now have a theory or partial theory of personality based on idiographic or case study research. Can other personality psychologists accept this theory as fact? Or must they test it? Obviously, before scientists accept any new theory as an explanation of real-world observations, they must show that it is something other than a chance outcome, a biased interpretation of data, an error, or even a fraud or deception.

Next, given the requirement of testing this theory about the effects of toilet training on personality, how should we go about proving it? At best, it would be very difficult, at worst impossible. To replicate and confirm this therapist's findings, other researchers would have to answer several questions. Did this particular therapist record in detail every exchange in therapy sessions that led to his conclusions? Did he explain whether he combined observations from various clients or how much consistency he found across his client population? Was he able to confirm the accuracy of their reporting of their past? And was he able to correlate the magnitude of restrictive parental behavior among his clients? What was his **outcome measure**—that is, how did he quantify or set his standards for determining personality change or improvement? Did he discuss the adjustments he made for observed individuals who did not conform to what he considered typical conduct? Even if this therapist-researcher did document these and related questions, it would still be very difficult and time consuming for other psychologists seeking to confirm his findings.

▣ APPROACHES TO THE STUDY OF PERSONALITY

True Experiments

A **true experiment** is one in which the researcher controls all possible variables that can influence the outcome of the experiment. In a true experiment, the researcher wants to examine the results of changing one or more environmental factors to determine the effect these variables have on the measure being studied. All true experiments follow the same basic procedures. First, the subjects in a true experiment are randomly assigned to either the experimental or the control group. In this application, *random* assignment means that each participant has an equal chance of being assigned to either group. The randomness of the assignment minimizes the chances that the subjects in the experimental group are significantly different from those in the control group. It follows that the groups being compared do not differ in any meaningful or systematic way. Then any differences found after the experiment can be attributed to the treatment or **intervention** that the experiment sought to study.

Some questions, however, do not allow for random assignment of research subjects; thus the research they generate will of necessity be only quasi-experimental. As examples of **quasi-experiments**, let us assume that we are interested in the differences between blind and sighted people, young or old, males or females. Obviously, subjects cannot be randomly assigned to a blind or sighted group or to a group of men only or women only.

To give a specific example of a quasi-experiment, we can review an experiment (von Mayrhauser, 1989) in which the researchers wanted to study the phenomenon that people with introverted personalities tend to have central nervous systems (CNS) that are more easily aroused. Greater CNS arousal would then lead to a potentially uncomfortable level of mental stimulation when the person confronts ordinary life events, which would result in **introversion** as an effort to escape overstimulation. In contrast, **extroverts** with lower levels of baseline stimulation would be prone to seek stimulation and would need far greater levels of external activity to reach a comfortable level of stimulation. One result of this behavioral dichotomy is that extroverts tend to have shorter reaction times to events when compared to people classified as introverts. The researchers cite evidence that a **neurotransmitter** called **dopamine** (DA) seems to play a role in some of these differences between introverted and extroverted people.

The researchers further noted that the glutamate neurotransmitter system in the brain acts in concert with the dopaminergic system, but they found no evidence that glutamate plays a role in the extraversion/introversion dichotomy. They then set out to test the hypothesis that glutamate activity in the brain does indeed play a role in the dichotomy. Their experiment involved dividing 48 randomly selected and demographically similar participants into introversion and extraversion groups based on their scores on the Eysenck Personality Questionnaire, revised extraversion scale. Both groups were given a drug called **memantine**, developed in the 1990s to treat Alzheimer's disease. Memantine blocks the receptors in the brain to which glutamate binds.

This experiment was performed in a **double-blind** fashion. Double blinding means that neither the subjects nor the researchers who rated their performance knew who received the active drug and who received a **placebo,** an inactive substance given to the subject as if it were an active medication. The participants were given a series of reaction time tasks both with the drug and with a placebo. The results revealed that introverts taking the real drug had statistically significant longer reaction times than did the extraverts. These results provided meaningful evidence of the role of glutamate receptors in the personality dimension of introversion-extraversion.

The memantine test is an example of a true experiment. The researchers made reasonable efforts to control for every variable that might lead to a change in the dependent variable. When these precautions have been taken, virtually all changes in the dependent variable can be attributed to the independent variables that the researchers controlled.

Quasi-experiments

The prefix *quasi* means "approximately" or "as it were," so that a **quasi-experiment** is a research project that is virtually but not quite a true experiment. Quasi-experiments generally lack some of the precise control of confounding factors that true experiments provide. Quasi-experiments are employed when researchers cannot randomly allocate subjects to control or treatment groups because random assignment is either functionally or ethically impossible. As the control over any variable that might alter the outcome of an experiment decreases, however, the chance increases that some factor other than the independent variable will intrude or confound and produce an observed change in the dependent variable. The interfering factor is what is meant by the term *confound*. Quasi-experiments are the most common type of experiment used in psychological research (Mark & Reichardt, 2004). They are commonly used in non-laboratory settings in the study of personality and in clinical psychology.

The independent variable in quasi-experiments will often be a participant variable such as age, socioeconomic status, or a personality attribute. The independent variable also can be an environmental variable, such as a natural disaster, economic trend, or social change. Or the independent variable may involve a time variable, such as aging. Because each of these types of variables is inextricably linked with other factors, the experimenter always has other possible explanations for the conclusions he or she draws from the experimental results.

For example, let us suppose that one researcher studies achievement among people who score high on extraversion and discovers that they tend to earn higher incomes than individuals who score low on extraversion. Can we conclude that extraversion is the direct cause of higher incomes in those who possess this trait? Suppose extraverts are outgoing because they tend to be perceived as more physically attractive or because they come from more stable and affluent families. Suppose further that being physically attractive and coming from affluent homes often leads to high achievement. If these two suppositions are indeed the case, then these attributes lead to both extraversion and achievement, and the apparent connection between extraversion and income is illusory. Affluence and attractiveness are uncontrolled variables that are confounds in this study.

The greater the number of uncontrolled variables in a quasi-experiment, the higher the likelihood that the researchers will fail to draw a cause-and-effect relationship from their study. In fact, true experiments have the great advantage of being the only research method that does define cause-and-effect relationships. In quasi-experiments, the determination of cause and effect becomes more uncertain. Such nonexperimental methods as correlational studies cannot determine cause and effect.

Correlational Studies

Correlational studies are studies that aim to identify relationships between variables. They can yield three kinds of results: no relationship, positive correlation, and negative correlation. In a positive correlation, as one variable rises in value, the other rises as well. In a negative correlation, as one variable rises, the other falls. Correlation is measured by using a coefficient that ranges between 1 (perfect positive correlation) to 0 (variables not related at all) to −1 (perfect negative correlation).

The major limitation of correlational studies is that a correlation does not establish a causal relationship. For example, let us consider two variables, (A) high self-esteem and (B) academic achievement, which have a positive correlation. Does (A) lead to (B)? Or is it the other way around? Or are there some other hidden factors that produce both (A) and (B)?

As it turned out in real life, two carefully conducted independent studies found that there is no causal relationship between these two factors. They are correlated because both of them are linked to other factors, such as intelligence and the social status of the subjects' families. When these factors were controlled, the correlation between academic achievement and self-esteem disappeared. You must be very careful about not falling into the trap of assuming that a correlation implies a causal relationship; and you must recognize that in advertising, politics, or the media, people with an agenda may intentionally misuse correlations to "prove" their point. In men, for example, the degree of hair loss is positively correlated with length of marriage. Does marriage (or a certain number of wedding anniversaries) cause hair loss? No—age and an inherited tendency to male pattern baldness "causes" both variables.

To give another example, a statistically significant positive correlation has been found between stork populations and birth rates in Europe (Matthews, 2000). This finding might be taken as clear evidence for scientific storkism, a theory of human reproduction that should be taught in schools alongside the notion that sexual intercourse is necessary to make babies. Well, does it not? In a more serious example, does the completion of a college degree lead to a higher income for its possessor? Or does a student's socioeconomic background lead to both successful completion of a college education and a higher income? To study cause-and-effect relationships, we must hold socioeconomic factors and all other factors constant. That can be done in true experiments but not in correlational studies.

Correlational studies may suggest that variables influence one another, but they are never proof of causality. Without an explicit awareness of this difference between the two types of studies, none of us are immune from being misled by apparently scientific results. Even highly paid expert analysts of football games have a hard time understanding that running the ball a lot does not lead to wins even though the two are correlated. Rather, wins and attempts at rushing are correlated because teams in the lead typically run in order to run out the clock.

Case and Epidemiological Studies

When researchers are trying to document inductive reasoning and demonstrate by example behavioral phenomena, whether of people, animals, businesses, or systems of some kind, they often use a **case study** approach. In general, a case study is a relatively short and factual account of a sequence of events chosen to illustrate a broader principle.

Here we present a case study of a client treated by one of the authors:

Anita suffered from severe anxiety and depression that persisted despite high dosages of tranquilizers. She was the mother of a young son and was married to a man nearly twice her age who was afflicted with a life-threatening illness. Anita had left her husband on two occasions for what proved to be the illusory love of other men but returned in response to family pressure to attend to her dying husband, the father of her son.

In the initial stages of therapy Anita focused on stress at work and anxiety about her husband's illness. After more than 2 months of therapy, she revealed that she suffered from panic attacks that had begun when she was an adolescent. These episodes had been sufficiently severe for her school counselor to arrange for her to be placed in a school for emotionally handicapped students. This placement did not serve as a stabilizing influence in her life; rather, it led to sexual acting out. Despite becoming a social outcast, Anita continued this behavior.

This pattern of sexual acting out continued into her adult life. In Anita's complaints about the men in her life, it became clear that she selected men who were manifestly abusive, antisocial, or polygynous (having sex with many women). Despite her apparent high intellect and completion of advanced degrees, she initially denied seeing any danger in dating married men or men who had several other girlfriends. She also denied seeing the obvious self-harm inherent in her pattern of serial sexual relationships. This denial led to her becoming emotionally attached to men who would drop her after brief sexual relationships. Remarkably, she failed to see this pattern until it was pointed out in therapy. Anita said she enjoyed the sordid and demeaning aspects of her behavior and did not think beyond the initially positive reaction of her boyfriend of the moment.

At a later point in treatment, she indicated that she was aware of the double standard that most men have regarding sexual behavior but failed to see its significance in her own life. Specifically, most of the men in her life both encouraged and enjoyed her licentious behavior but then despised her for it. This dynamic created a vicious circle of rejection, increased self-contempt, a higher degree of arousal from participating in sexually degrading activities, and further rejection. In addition, most of Anita's nonsexual friendships were unstable, typically lasting a few months at most. This pattern was replicated in her career, in which she would leave her job impulsively after a brief period of employment.

When Anita's behavior was explored with the therapist, she admitted the existence of a painful conflict—she had grown to resent and distrust men, yet was strongly drawn to them sexually. She seemed to operate according to the tacit belief that because men and the act of sex would ultimately degrade her, she might as well accept degradation as part of sex. This persistent seeking of self-defeating relationships accelerated after her husband died. Anita reopened two relationships with married men, both of whom had promised to leave their wives for her. Neither of these men took any action to pursue his relationship with her beyond meeting her for furtive sexual encounters. She would become repeatedly enraged after each tired excuse they offered for not leaving their wives, yet she would accept their next call.

The underlying reason for Anita's behavior was clarified, however, when the topic of child abuse arose by chance during a therapy session. In a nonchalant fashion, she began to describe her mother's bizarre methods of disciplining her as a child. Anita was frequently spanked, beaten, and sexually violated throughout her childhood, although at unpredictable intervals. Discussions of this period of her life often precipitated periods of acute anxiety.

Anita was treated with Rational Emotive/Cognitive Behavioral Therapy, which addressed her failure to adhere to any regimen in her life—including work attendance, work performance, sexual self-restraint, and the maintenance of stable relationships. The central premise of her irrational behavior was her belief in the inevitability of failure and rejection by significant people in her life. Anita was also given help in her ability to cope with life stresses and taught that she had considerable control over her reactions to adverse events.

Anita's relationship problems were addressed in therapy by helping her examine her choices of men, and how these misguided choices were related to her poor self-concept. She was guided through behavioral changes in both her work and social life. In addition, she was helped to understand that satisfying her desire to debase herself would lead only to despair and anxiety when she was not sexually aroused. She came to understand how these behavioral vicious circles operated in her life and gradually improved.

Case studies like the example of Anita are widely used in the study of phenomena that by their nature cannot be reproduced in a controlled laboratory setting. The unit of analysis in a case study may be an individual, a group, or a complex social entity like a corporation or non-profit organization. Like the other research strategies discussed in this chapter, case studies have their advantages and disadvantages.

The advantages of case studies are considerable. They include giving researchers opportunities to study unusual or uncommon behaviors or conditions and providing a rich source of new hypotheses. A case study can uncover detailed individual experiences that may provide very powerful insights into real human experience and behavior. It can also generate rich and valid information that has not been altered by the subject's exposure to questionnaires, psychometric evaluations, or other tests. Using Anita's case as an example, the reader can see that such a study has high external ecological validity because the reported behavior comes from a real-life situation rather than the artificial environment of a psychology laboratory. And unlike the limited time frame of an experiment, in a case study, the therapist can follow the client for an extended period, during which he or she can build up a detailed picture of the client's behavior and monitor signs of progress. In addition, a case study often provides opportunities to meet with family members to garner further information related to the client. In the case of Anita, the therapist was able to meet with her son and with one of her current paramours. Last, the case study method provides opportunities to help subjects, as case studies are usually based on persons in psychological treatment.

The disadvantages of case studies include the possibility of bias on the observer's part. This bias includes the fact that the therapist will be using his or her preferred approach to therapy. Case studies being conducted by a therapist of one school will often neglect competing theoretical explanations of the observed behavior. For example, a psychiatrist might use a medical model to explain the patient's behavior whereas a therapist trained in family systems therapy might look for explanations in the patient's relationships with others. In addition, the data presented by the client are also subjective, which means that they are related from the client's own perspective rather than from the viewpoints of others involved in the client's life.

A second disadvantage of the case study approach is the difficulty of drawing generalizations from one instance—that is, observations of and conclusions about the psychological situation of one individual might not be meaningfully applied to others. A third disadvantage is that the client may be changed by the very act of undergoing treatment; that is, the familial, social, and psychological status of the subject of the case study may change as a result of the therapeutic process. Last, the data underlying most psychological research can be reviewed by peers and the experiment replicated if it seems necessary. Peer review, however, cannot be carried out for case studies because of the confidentiality required in mental health treatment.

There are, however, several important implications of the case study of Anita as an example of research. First, it explores the present status of a woman who was emotionally and physically abused in childhood; thus, it sheds some light on the impact the abuse may have had on her adult personality. Abuse often creates difficulties for children because it prevents them from resolving the conflicts at each stage of development in a normal fashion. In addition, Anita's lifestyle suggests a possible diagnosis of borderline personality disorder (BPD); thus, her case may encourage additional research into the origins of this pathology or of personality disorders in general. The case of Anita may provide evidence for the way personality disorders develop or are exacerbated. Finally, Anita's response to treatment with REBT/CBT suggests that even disorders arising from childhood trauma may be effectively addressed by changes in the client's present-day beliefs, attitudes, and behaviors.

🔲 PERSONALITY AND PSYCHOMETRIC TESTS

Objective Personality Measures

The term **objective test** does not necessarily mean that the test lacks bias in its construction, but rather that the scoring is objective and requires no judgment or subjective interpretation on the part of the examiner. Objective tests offer researchers the advantage of excluding the problem of having as many test evaluations as evaluators. In addition, objective tests can be scored by computer.

Minnesota Multiphasic Personality Inventory. Starke R. Hathaway, a psychologist, and J. Charnley McKinley, a psychiatrist, developed the Minnesota Multiphasic Personality Inventory (MMPI) over several years beginning in the late 1930s (Friedman, 2004), from a pool of more than 1,000 possible test items. Their goal was to develop a simple objective test that would measure many different types of psychopathology based on empirical rather than intuitively developed scales. Empirically derived tests rely on research data to determine the meaning of a pattern of responses. Hathaway and McKinley began with approximately 1,000 test questions culled from a wide array of sources, including other psychometric tests, case histories, and diagnostic reports.

The two researchers gave these questions to 724 adults who were mostly friends and relatives of patients in the University of Minnesota hospitals. The people in their sample had been assessed by clinicians to find if they met any major psychiatric diagnoses. They then tried to see which questions distinguished the various diagnostic groups from one another, and from those who did not warrant a diagnosis. Thus, if a majority of subjects answered a given question as "true," that question did little to distinguish one group from another and was rejected. On the other hand, if one diagnostic group endorsed an item much more frequently than another, the question would help to distinguish between it and other diagnostic groups and was retained. Hathaway and McKinley hoped that the inventory they designed would allow them simply to test someone and determine their diagnosis. Their finished product, although flawed by being normed on a very homogenous sample, set the standard for what became the most widely used and widely researched tests in psychology (Butcher, 1990).

Millon Clinical Multiaxial Inventory. The Millon Clinical Multiaxial Inventory or MCMI was developed by Theodore Millon, an American expert on personality theory, to put into practice his own model of personality or **personology**. Unlike the MMPI, the MCMI was developed from the responses of people in clinical treatment, and its results are keyed to the American Psychiatric Association's *Diagnostic and Statistical Manual of Mental Disorders*, fourth edition (DSM-IV). Millon served on the Personality Disorders Work Group for DSM-IV and its predecessor, DSM-III-R. Since the introduction of the MCMI in 1977, it has become one of the most widely used and researched clinical assessment instruments in use, investigated in more than 500 articles and at least six books. The MCMI is used to evaluate both the personality issues and clinical problems that a person seeking mental health treatment might confront. The test has 175 true/false questions. The MCMI-III version of the test includes 14 personality pattern scales coordinated with DSM-IV Axis II disorders and 10 clinical syndrome scales related to DSM-IV Axis I disorders. In addition, three modifying indices and a validity index help the administrator to detect careless, confused, or random responding.

With regard to validity, the MCMI has been shown to be a reasonably valid measure of personality disorders and other pathology defined by DSM-IV (Craig, 1999, 2005), including its measures of depression (Davis & Hays, 1997), antisocial personality disorder (Hart, 1991; Messina, Wish, Hoffman, & Nemes, 2001), and antisocial behavior (Kelln, 1998). Although MCMI scales may be related to depressive disorders (Choca, Bresolin, Okonek & Ostrow, 1988) most studies have found poor concurrent validity of the Major Depression scale for both the MCMI-I and MCMI-II tests.

Figure 3.1   Example of Millon Clinical Multiaxial Inventory–III

MCMI-III ™
ID 12566

Profile Report
Page 3

MILLON CLINICAL MULTIAXIAL INVENTORY - III

CONFIDENTIAL INFORMATION FOR PROFESSIONAL USE ONLY

ID NUMBER: 12566   Valid Profile

PERSONALITY CODE: 8A 3 2B 2A * * –* 8B 6A 1 + 6B 5 " 4 7 **// c **-*//

SYNDROME CODE: A ** T H D R * // CC**- *//

DEMOGRAPHIC: 12566/ON/F/44/W/D/--/--/--/-----/--/-----/

CATEGORY		SCORE		PROFILE OF BR SCORES				DIAGNOSTIC SCALES
		RAW	BR 0	60	75	85	115	
MODIFYING INDICES	X	163	93					DISCLOSURE
	Y	4	20					DESIRABILITY
	Z	28	91					DEBASEMENT
CLINICAL PERSONALITY PATTERNS	1	13	64					SCHIZOID
	2A	20	86					AVOIDANT
	2B	20	87					DEPRESSIVE
	3	22	88					DEPENDENT
	4	7	16					HISTRIONIC
	5	12	46					NARCISSISTIC
	6A	14	66					ANTISOCIAL
	6B	14	56					SADISTIC
	7	8	16					COMPULSIVE
	8A	24	98					NEGATIVISTIC
	8B	13	71					MASOCHISTIC
SEVERE PERSONALITY PATHOLOGY	S	16	64					SCHIZOTYPAL
	C	23	95					BORDERLINE
	P	15	70					PARANOID
CLINICAL SYNDROMES	A	17	95					ANXIETY DISORDER
	H	13	76					SOMATOFORM DISORDER
	N	11	63					BIPOLAR MANIC DISORDER
	D	17	76					DYSTHYMIC DISORDER
	B	8	61					ALCOHOL DEPENDENCE
	T	14	82					DRUG DEPENDENCE
	R	18	76					POST-TRAUMATIC STRESS
SEVERE CLINICAL SYNDROMES	SS	17	66					THOUGHT DISORDER
	CC	21	99					MAJOR DEPRESSION
	PP	7	66					DELUSIONAL DISORDER

California Personality Inventory. The California Personality Inventory (CPI), which is sometimes called the CPI-434 because the present version of the test contains 434 items, was designed by Harrison Gough, a professor at the University of California, Berkeley, in 1956. It is similar to the MMPI in the structure of its true/false questions; however, its goal is not to detect psychological maladjustment or severe mental disorders but rather to measure the more positive aspects of personality. The CPI is scored on 18 scales grouped into four categories: (1) measures of poise, self-assurance, and interpersonal adequacy; (2) measures of responsibility, intrapersonal values, and character; (3) measures of intellectual efficiency and the potential for achievement; and (4) measures of intellectual modes and interest modes. It is used most often by business corporations and other organizations to identify people with strong leadership potential and to form teams of employees who will work well together.

Projective Personality Measures

Projective personality measures invite the subject taking the **projective test** to respond to ambiguous stimuli and thus to reveal their inner thoughts, hidden feelings, and internal conflicts. More than half a century ago, the following explanation was given for the use of projective techniques in personality psychology:

> The concept of projection as used in projective procedures is one formed on the pattern of projector and screen. In this sense, a projection has occurred when the psychological structure of the subject becomes palpable in his actions, choices, products, and creations. Therefore, when a procedure is so designed as to enable the subject to demonstrate his psychological structure unstilted by conventional modes, it is projective. (Rapaport, Gill, & Schafer, 1946, p. 7)

Rorschach Inkblot Test. The Rorschach inkblot test, which is one of the best known and most frequently administered projective personality measures, was devised in the early 1920s by Hermann Rorschach (1884–1922), a young Swiss psychiatrist who published a book called *Psychodiagnostics* (*Psychodiagnostik* in the original German) in 1921. In this book, Rorschach detailed his method of using inkblots to reveal a person's unconscious thinking. He obtained his data by studying the responses of 305 psychiatric patients (Alexander & Selesnick, 1966). Since Rorschach had been strongly influenced during his medical school years by Eugen Bleuler (1857–1940) the professor of psychiatry who had also taught Carl Jung (Ellenberger, 1970) he believed that much of the patient's mental processes could not be accessed directly. That is, Rorschach thought that simply talking to patients about their emotions and how they understood their problems would not produce an accurate understanding of their minds.

Jung envisioned the unconscious mind as possessing a great degree of complexity represented by numerous symbolic entities, so it followed that Rorschach, who used Jung's word-association test in his own work with schizophrenics, would have sought a way to uncover these entities through a test that used vague and complex symbolic stimuli. It is thought that Rorschach's interest in inkblots as a stimulus was influenced by his father's work as an art teacher and his own early interest in becoming an art teacher as well. He entered medical school, however, on the advice of Ernst Haeckel, an eminent German biologist. Rorschach died from a ruptured appendix only a year after the publication of *Psychodiagnostics*, at the relatively young age of 37.

Rorschach himself usually used 15 inkblots in his examination of patients, but the test as it is administered nowadays consists of only 10 inkblots, each presented on a separate card. Five blots are in color (black and red or pastel colors), and the remaining five in black and gray. Rorschach's original method of presentation left most details of interpretation to the examiner. The subject is shown each card and asked what they see, and their response is recorded. The interviewer notes the speed of the subject's response as well as his or her social behavior—that is, whether the subject seems anxious, challenged, intimidated, indifferent, or cooperative.

Each inkblot card is shown to the participant twice. The first time is a free-association phase in which the participant freely discusses any impressions or images the card evokes. The second presentation of the card is used for the inquiry phase. In this phase, the examiner asks the participant to identify the part of each blot that reminded him or her of the image. The examiner notes whether the participant bases his or her response on the whole inkblot, on a common detail, on an unusual detail, or on a confabulatory detail—that is, whether the participant responded to something that is not actually on the card. The examiner will also score the determinant of the responses, the determinant being the portion of the blot that evoked the subject's response. The form quality of the response is also scored. Here the examiner determines whether the response is well fitted to the blot. If the participant sees movement in the blot, the examiner notes whether the participant sees a human, animal, or an inanimate object moving. Finally, the subject's reference to the use of color and shading in the card is also scored.

In Table 3.3 are some examples (Gilbert, 1980) of clinical judgments based on Rorschach responses. They are derived from either the Klopfer or Phillips and Smith scoring methods.

With regard to the validity of the Rorschach test, the advent of the Exner (1993) scoring system, which can be used with children over the age of 5 as well as with adults, improved the validity of this widely used measure of personality and pathology. A rigid insistence on the use of the Rorschach is questionable, however, as many clinicians see the inkblot test as

Table 3.3	Example of Clinical Judgments Based on Rorschach Responses
Clinical Interpretation	*Subject's Response to Card*
Obsessive-compulsive personality	Overelaboration of form content in responses; high number of animal responses; or a high number of responses focusing on an unusual detail of the blot
Hypochondriasis	Perceiving anatomical features in the whole of card
Antisocial personality disorder	Seeing internal organs in the blot; or a mediocre or poor use of form
Maturity	Simultaneous use of Form and Shading in responses
Extraverted personality	Low number of human movement responses; or more colors used in blot interpretation than human movement

an extension of the clinical interview rather than a separate evaluation. Most agree that the Rorschach should not be used as the only basis for diagnosing a mental disorder.

Is the Rorschach nonetheless a valid and scientific measure of personality or pathology? The overall evidence suggests a very weak yes. Atkinson (1986), in reviewing research articles examining the validity of the Rorschach from 1930 to 1980, concluded that there is evidence for its validity. He suggests that poor research was responsible for the impression among many psychologists that the test itself is not valid.

In recent meta-studies comparing the validity of both the MMPI and the Rorschach (Garb, 1998; Hiller, 1999), the latter is found to be a substantially less valid measure of personality and pathology than the MMPI. The Rorschach has been shown, however, to have some predictive validity in making a diagnosis of schizophrenia (Morgan-Gillard, 2003). This should not be surprising, as 188 of Hermann Rorschach's original sample of 305 subjects were schizophrenics.

Draw-A-Person Test. Some projective tests ask the subject to engage in a creative process, usually drawing a picture. In the Draw-A-Person (D-A-P) Test, developed by Karen Machover (1949, 1953), the subject, generally a child, is asked to draw a human being and then describe the person they just drew. Based on children's drawings of human figures, this test can be used with two different scoring systems for different purposes. One system measures nonverbal intelligence while the other system screens test subjects for emotional or behavioral disorders.

During the testing session, which can be completed in 15 minutes, the child is asked to draw three figures: an adult man; an adult woman; and him- or herself. To evaluate the child's intelligence, the test administrator uses the Draw-A-Person quantitative scoring system, or QSS. This system analyzes 14 different aspects of the drawings related to specific body parts and clothing, including the presence or absence of the body part or garment, the amount of detail, and the proportions of the figures in the drawing. In all, there are 64 scoring items for each drawing. A separate standard score is recorded for each drawing, and a total combined score is obtained for all three.

The administrator of the D-A-P has three pieces of plain white 8.5 × 11 paper ready for use. The first sheet is given to the child as the examiner says, "Here, I want you to draw a person as well you can." The examiner then asks such questions as: Who is this person? How old are they? What's their favorite thing to do? What's something they do not like? Has anyone tried to hurt them? Who looks out for them?

Then the child is given the second sheet of paper as the examiner says, "Now draw a [person of the other sex]." Again the examiner asks the child questions about the person's identity, age, likes and dislikes, and similar queries.

The child is then given the third sheet and told, "Now draw yourself." As with the previous two drawings, the examiner asks the child a series of questions about the person in the picture he or she just drew.

The use of a nonverbal and nonthreatening task to evaluate intelligence is intended to eliminate possible sources of bias by reducing such variables as primary language, verbal skills, communication disabilities, and sensitivity to working under pressure. The results of the D-A-P test, however, can be influenced by previous drawing experience—a factor that may account for the tendency of middle-class children to score higher on this test than lower-class children, who often have fewer opportunities to draw pictures.

To assess the test subject for emotional problems, the administrator uses the Draw-A-Person: SPED (Screening Procedure for Emotional Disturbance) to score the drawings. This system is composed of two sets of criteria. For the first type, eight dimensions of each drawing are evaluated against norms for the child's age group. For the second type, 47 different items are considered for each drawing.

Thematic Apperception Test. The Thematic Apperception Test (TAT) is a projective personality test that was designed at Harvard University in the 1930s by Christiana D. Morgan (1897–1967) and Henry A. Murray (1893–1988). Along with the MMPI and the Rorschach, the TAT is one of the most widely used psychological tests. It is regarded as more structured and less ambiguous than the Rorschach. The TAT consists of 31 pictures that depict a variety of social and interpersonal situations. The subject is asked to tell the examiner a story about each picture. The story must include a description of the card ("This is a picture of a young boy looking at a violin inside a shop window") and an explanation of what the characters are doing, what they have done in the past or what led to the situation, and what the characters might do in the future. The subject is also asked to describe the feelings and thoughts of the characters and the outcome of the story, if possible. The examiner records the subject's words verbatim and also notes the reaction time.

Of the 31 pictures, 10 are gender-specific while 21 others can be used with adults of either sex and with children. One card is blank. The pictures were intended to run the gamut of life situations; Murray thought that the first 10 cards would evoke descriptions of everyday situations, whereas the second set of 10 would encourage the subject to tell more unusual, dramatic, and bizarre stories about what he or she saw in the picture.

The original purpose of the TAT was to reveal the underlying dynamics of the subject's personality, such as internal conflicts, dominant drives and interests, or motives. The specific motives that the TAT assesses include the need for achievement, need for power, need for intimacy, and problem-solving abilities. After World War II, the TAT was used by psychoanalysts and clinicians from other schools of thought to evaluate emotionally disturbed patients. Another shift took place in the 1970s, when the influence of the **human potential movement** led many psychologists to emphasize the usefulness of the TAT in assessment services—that is, using the test to help clients understand themselves better and stimulate their personal growth.

The TAT is widely used to research certain topics in psychology, such as dreams and fantasies, mate selection, the factors that motivate people's choice of occupations, and similar subjects. It is sometimes used in psychiatric evaluations to assess disordered thinking and in criminal examinations to evaluate crime suspects, even though it is not a diagnostic test. As mentioned earlier, the TAT can be used to help people understand their own personality in greater depth and build on that knowledge in making important life decisions. Last, it is sometimes used as a screener in psychological evaluations of candidates for high-stress occupations (law enforcement, civil aviation, the military, religious ministry, etc.).

The TAT has been criticized for its lack of a standardized method of administration as well as the lack of standard norms for interpretation. Studies of the interactions between examiners and test subjects have found that the race, sex, and social class of both participants influence both the stories that are told and the way the stories are interpreted by the examiner. Attempts have been made to design sets of TAT cards for African American and for elderly test subjects, but the results have not been encouraging. In addition, the 31 standard pictures have been criticized for being too gloomy or depressing, therefore limiting the range of personality characteristics that the test can assess.

There is no standardized procedure or set of cards for administering the TAT, except that it is a one-on-one test. It cannot be administered to groups. In one common method of administration, the examiner shows the subject only 10 of the 31 cards at each of two sessions. The test sessions are not timed but average about an hour in length. There is no specific preparation necessary before taking the TAT, although most examiners prefer to schedule sessions (if there is more than one) over two days.

The chief risks involved in taking the TAT are a bad fit between the examiner and the test subject and misuse of the results. For example, the way the examiner asks the subject to tell the story may influence the results. Some researchers found that the examiner's use of loaded words produces distress in the subjects taking the TAT, thus skewing the results.

Because the TAT is used primarily for personality assessment rather than diagnosis of mental disorders, it does not yield a score in the usual numerical sense. The test has, however, more guides to evaluating the subject's responses than does the Rorschach. The examiner is expected to interpret the congruence between the subject's answers and the picture stimuli; the subject's compliance with the examiner's directions, the existence of conflict in the story, and finally the literal story content. Most psychologists who administer the TAT find Murray's scoring system to be overly elaborate, complex, and time-consuming.

With regard to psychometrics, many experts think that the TAT is unsound. For almost every positive empirical finding, there is a negative counterpart. On the other hand, exploration of such specific variables as the need for achievement produces respectably reliable results. The median test-retest correlation is only about .30; moreover, split-half reliabilities for the TAT have been consistently poor. Criterion-related evidence for the test's validity is difficult to document. A **meta-analysis** by Spangler (1992) indicated that average correlations between the TAT and other criteria run between .19 and .22.

Rotter Incomplete Sentences Blank. The Rotter Incomplete Sentences Blank (Rotter & Willerman, 1947), or RISB, is designed to screen for overall psychological adjustment. First published by Julian Rotter (1916–) in 1950, the RISB is a semi-objective projective measure that provides direct information about the subject's personality conflicts. The subject is given a set of 40 sentence "stems" and asked to complete the sentences. The stems, which are usually only two or three words long (for example, "I regret. . . ."), are worded to elicit responses that will reveal the subject's feelings. The RISB takes about 20 to 25 minutes to administer. The subject's answers are rated on a 7-point scale measuring omissions, incomplete responses, conflict responses, positive responses, or neutral responses. The minimum possible score is 0 and the highest possible score, 240. Most subjects score somewhere between 80 and 205. Higher scores indicate greater maladjustment. There are three forms of the RISB, for high school students, college students, and adults respectively.

The RISB has certain advantages compared to the Rorschach and the TAT. It elicits concise rather than diffuse responses; it purports to measure only one construct—adjustment—rather than three or four; answers are scored on a 7-point numeric scale; and the manual that accompanies the RISB provides detailed guidelines for scoring, similar to those for the Wexler Adult Intelligence Scale, the most widely used test to measure intelligence.

The psychometric properties of the RISB include good interscorer reliability (about .90) and an internal consistency reliability of about .80. The test-retest reliability for the RISB is close to .80 for one to two weeks after administration to the test subject; however, it drops to about .50 after several months or years. Validity studies tend to support the contention that the RISB measures adjustment; however, the evidence is weak since it is based almost entirely on a relatively small sample of college students (Lah, 1989).

▣ ETHICS IN PERSONALITY RESEARCH

The Milgram Study

The most famous—even parodied—study of human behavior was performed by Stanley Milgram (1963), a psychologist who was concerned with the problem of ordinary people's obedience to authority in relation to such atrocities as the Holocaust. Milgram's study, which in its original form would certainly not be permitted in the early 2000s, dramatically showed that ordinary individuals may comply with orders to inflict pain on others, leading to a collective outcry for firmer rules governing psychological research on human beings.

Milgram placed a classified advertisement in the local New Haven newspaper seeking participants for a psychological experiment at Yale University. The stated purpose of the experiment was to investigate the improvement of learning and memory through the use of punishment. People who responded encountered a formal-looking individual wearing a laboratory coat, who explained why the study might have important consequences. The subjects were paired with another participant who was actually a confederate of the researcher. All participants were told that they would be assigned either to the role of the teacher or the learner by chance. In actuality, one of Milgram's confederates, a middle-aged Caucasian male who had been trained for the part, was always assigned the learner's role.

Imagine that you are the subject. Drawing random slips of paper seemingly determines who will be the "learner" or "teacher." There is a 50-50 chance that you will become the teacher, or so you believe. You are, therefore, not surprised to be told that you will be the teacher. The three of you then proceed to an adjacent room, where the learner is strapped into a chair. The experimenter explains that this apparatus is to prevent excessive movement during the experiment, but it is obvious to you that the learner could not escape from the chair if he wished.

An electrode is then attached to the learner's arm, and conductive gel is applied to the electrode. The experimenter explains that this gel is to prevent burning and blisters. Both you and the learner are told that the electrode is attached to a generator in the other room and that electric shocks will serve as punishment for incorrect responses to the teacher's questions. The learner asks the experimenter if "the shocks will hurt," to which the experimenter replies, "Although the shocks will be painful, they cause no permanent tissue damage." You, the would-be "teacher," are given a sample 45-volt shock—a slightly painful experience—so that you will have some idea of what the higher voltages mean for the learner.

You leave the learner in his room and return to the other room, where the experimenter shows you the shock generator. The generator has 30 switches, each labeled with a voltage ranging from 15 volts up to 450 volts, in 15-volt increments. Each switch also has a rating, ranging from "slight shock" to "Danger: severe shock." The final two switches are simply labeled "XXX." You are told that your role is to teach the learner a simple word-pairing task, but that you must also punish him for incorrect responses. You are told that for every incorrect response, you must increase the voltage by 15 volts (that is, move up to the next switch).

Now, the experiment begins in earnest. The learner (pretends to) finds the task difficult and makes numerous errors. Each error results in a shock more intense than the previous one. The shocks are weak at first, but soon, they become more intense. At 75 volts, you can hear the "learner's" grunting noises through the wall. The same thing happens at 90 and 105 volts. At 120 volts, the learner says the shocks are getting painful. You know they are because you can hear him through the wall. At 150 volts, he cries, "Get me out of here! I refuse to go on!" Thus, despite the fact that there was no actual physical pain involved, the participants were exposed to what appeared to be great suffering.

The learner's protests continued as the voltage is set higher and higher. If at this point, or any other point, of the experiment, you question whether you should go on, the experimenter tells you that you must continue, using such reasons as "You can't stop now," "He is getting paid to participate in this experiment," or simply that "The experiment depends on your continuing compliance." The researcher may even say, "You have no choice." As the shocks increase, the learner screams, "I can't stand the pain!" At 300 volts, he begins pounding on the wall and demands to be released. After 330 volts, there is no longer any noise from the learner. At this point, the experimenter tells you that the learner's failure to respond should be interpreted as an incorrect response and that you must continue increasing the shock level. The learning task will be completed only when the highest shock level is reached.

Would you proceed to the end? That is, would you continue to give electrical shocks of dangerous intensity to a fellow subject, who may be dying or already dead, simply because you are told to do so? Of course not, you are probably thinking—only a deranged sadist would answer yes. When Milgram asked a group of 40 psychiatrists to estimate the percentage of subjects who would complete the task, the estimates he got ranged from 0 to 3 percent. The psychiatrists also predicted that most people would drop out at the tenth level (that is, administering a shock of 150 volts). They were dumbfounded to discover that 26 of Milgram's 40 subjects completed the task—65 percent!

The results of Milgram's experiment were shocking indeed. Here was dramatic evidence that it is relatively easy to get ordinary individuals to torture others simply because an authority tells them to do so. Two thirds of Milgram's subjects showed total obedience to the researcher's dictates, to the extent that they might well have been administering shocks to a corpse—the body of a fellow human being they had killed—all because an authority figure in a laboratory coat told them that they could not withdraw. And Milgram's confederate was indeed a "fellow man." The early 1960s were still a time of lingering racial and ethnic discrimination, so the learner was a white male of middle-class appearance who could well have been the subject's friend or neighbor.

What, however, was the effect of Milgram's experiment on the subjects? Did they gamely continue to "fry" the learner without any apparent qualms? No, as Milgram reported, the teacher-subjects showed intense emotional pain. Some trembled, sweated, stuttered, bit their lips, or dug their nails into their own flesh. Over a third exhibited a bizarre form of nervous laughter. Three went into seizures.

For this reason—the effect on the teacher-subjects—Milgram's experiment became as famous for generating ethical questions about the treatment of human subjects in psychological research as for the dark secret it revealed about humanity. It led to the enunciation of a set of principles on the ethical treatment of participants in research—the very term *subject* was now often seen as dehumanizing.

The Schachter-Singer Experiment

A basic ethical issue in psychological research using human subjects is transparency regarding the purpose of the experiment. Stanley Milgram's subjects, for example, were told that the experiment concerned the effects of punishment on learning and memory, which was not its true purpose. Rather, Milgram was interested in the psychology of human obedience to authority. Another famous experiment conducted around the same time as Milgram's raised the same question about the importance of full disclosure to human subjects. That was an experiment designed by Stanley Schachter and Jerome Singer (1962) to test their theory about the cognitive processes underlying emotional experiences.

Schachter and Singer hypothesized that identical states of physical arousal would produce different emotions if they were consciously attributed to different causes. The research subjects were told that they were participating in an experiment investigating the effects of a vitamin called Superoxin, which allegedly improved vision. They were divided into four groups, none of which received a vitamin injection. Subjects in the first three groups got a shot of **epinephrine** (adrenaline), a hormone naturally produced in the body by the adrenal glands, which is released when a person is under stress. Epinephrine speeds up the heartbeat, raises blood pressure, and raises blood-sugar levels. Subjects in the fourth (control) group received an injection of saline solution, a placebo.

The subjects in the first three groups were given three different types of information about the effects of the "vitamin" injection. One group was given accurate information about the physiological effects they would experience from the injection (feeling their heart racing, mild shakiness, etc.) A second group was told nothing. The third group was misinformed; the subjects were told that their extremities would feel numb as a result of the injection and that they would develop a slight headache.

Then, the subjects mingled with one of Schachter's assistants, who had supposedly been given the same injection. The assistant behaved in one of two ways: either euphoric or even silly, joking, making paper airplanes, and generally playing around; or angry and aggressive, freely insulting the subjects. Subjects in the second or third groups (uninformed or misinformed about the effects of the injection) proved to be quite susceptible to the assistants' behavior, feeling giddy and silly if the assistant had acted that way or angry and hostile if the assistant had displayed angry behavior. The subjects who had been given accurate information about the effects of epinephrine (even though they still thought they had been given a vitamin), however, were influenced very little by the assistants' behavior.

These findings confirmed Schachter and Singer's hypothesis that people who do not have an explanation for a state of physiological arousal become dependent on situational cues (in this case, the assistants' behavior) to understand what they are feeling, whereas people who have a satisfactory explanation for the physiological changes they are experiencing do not need their present social situation to help them make sense of what they are feeling.

Other psychologists have pointed out that the results of Schachter and Singer's 1962 experiment were inconclusive—there are many other factors that influence people's interpretation of feeling states. What is important in the present context, however, is the ethical legitimacy of deceiving subjects about the nature of a substance or device used in an experiment. In this case, three groups of subjects were given an injection that they were told was a vitamin when it was really a stress-related hormone.

Walster's Experiment With Self-Esteem

How does self-esteem affect receptivity to romantic overtures? Must we like ourselves before we can like others, or are we more receptive to affection from others precisely when our own self-esteem is low? The reader should remember that a true experiment requires subjects to be divided randomly into at least two groups. Elaine Walster (1965), however, decided to explore the question of romantic receptivity by actively manipulating the subjects' self-esteem rather than by dividing them into high self-esteem and low self-esteem groups based on responses to a self-esteem inventory.

All the subjects in this experiment were female. They were told that the study was intended to investigate "personality and the therapy process." The subjects were then given the MMPI or the CPI and were asked to return a few weeks later for a subsequent session. At that session, a handsome male confederate of the research team pretended to have a romantic interest in the subject and asked her for a date.

Each subject then received either a flattering or disparaging "report" from the personality test she had taken weeks earlier. She received a description of herself as either "immature" and "incapable of success," or having "great maturity" and "one of the most favorable personality structures." Subjects were then asked under the guise of further research to evaluate their feelings for the male confederate. Walster found that the subjects who had received the negative evaluations were more likely to report being attracted to the researcher's male confederate than were the subjects who had received positive evaluations. The researcher concluded that attacks on someone's self-esteem from an outside source can lead the person to like a potential date more rather than less.

The reader should note all the levels of deception involved in this experiment. First, the subjects were given false feedback from a bona fide personality test. Thus, they saw themselves, at least temporarily (until after the debriefing), as either wonderful people or failures. Second, the subjects were misled into thinking that a specific person—the handsome research assistant—found them attractive. On the strength of that misperception, many accepted the offer of a date with the assistant. Is the risk of potential psychological damage to the subjects acceptable for whatever—perhaps only slight—increase in knowledge about human psychology the experiment may provide? At least two publications (Diener & Crandall, 1978; Warwick, 1982) criticized Walster's work on the grounds that the subjects may have been hurt or angry about being deceived or about having a commonplace anxiety in the college population (about dating) exploited for purposes of research.

Using deception in research is considered ethically unacceptable by many researchers. Some psychologists will allow no exceptions to this principle, arguing that the use of deception delegitimizes science, as well as hurting participants and the reputations of researchers. A related danger is that if psychologists come to be commonly regarded as deceivers, they will not be able to function effectively as health providers in therapeutic settings. Among those who argue that deception violates basic human rights are Geller (1982), Kelman (1967), and Baumrind (1985).

Most psychologists, however, regard the use of deception as unavoidable at times if their research is to have external validity. So some point out that researchers will often be in the position of weighing the importance of discovery against the need for honesty. (Aronson, Ellsworth, Carlsmith, & Gonzales, 1990).

The American Psychological Association (APA, 2002) guidelines set three criteria that must be met for deception to be acceptable in research.

1. The benefits of the research must outweigh risks. Moreover, all alternatives to deception must be examined, and their rejection must be justified.

2. The deception must not be such that knowing about it would affect the participants' willingness to take part in the research. An example of unacceptable deception would be the concealment of physical risks.

3. Where deception is used, **debriefing** is required as soon as possible.

Debriefing involves the disclosure of any false information that may have been given to the subjects as part of the experiment. Full information about the experiment is also thought to prevent any lasting negative feelings. Researchers have a responsibility to prevent not only physical damage but also psychological damage to their participants. The empirical evidence shows that debriefing is generally effective, although some observers report mixed results. Walster, Berscheid, Abrahams, & Aronson, (1967) reported that debriefing is generally ineffective, but Holmes (1976a, 1976b) maintains that there is a preponderance of evidence supporting it.

Some researchers maintain that role playing can be as effective as deception. Evidence for the usefulness of role playing includes Greenberg (1967), Willis and Willis (1970), and Horowitz and Rothschild (1970), while other researchers (Simons & Piliavin, 1972; Yinon, Shoham, & Lewis, 1974) maintain that it is not effective. The reader should remember that when Milgram asked people how many subjects would deliver the highest level of electric shocks, estimates ranged from 0 to 3%.

And there is evidence that deception in psychological research does not hurt participants. Responding to Baumrind's (1964) criticism of the famous experiment regarding obedience to authority, Milgram (1964) wrote that fewer than 2% of his participants regretted having participated, while 84% said that they found their participation worthwhile. Gerdes (1979) found that participants did not object to deception across the 15 experiments that he surveyed. And Smith (1981) found that two years after participating in research that had involved deception and in a two-year follow-up study, none of the participants felt they had been harmed.

The debate regarding psychological research still goes on. Unlike other fields, psychology is particularly prone to a variation of the Heisenberg uncertainty principle of physics. In short, the act of measuring often alters that which is being measured. In physics, this is exemplified by the problem that detecting the location of a subatomic particle will change the state of that particle, thereby preventing complete knowledge of its condition. In psychology, letting people know that they are the subjects of an experiment will have a deep impact on the way they react to subsequent events. How is this resolved? An early answer was to either deceive the participants about the nature of the experiment or to hide the fact they were part of a research study. Deception is now rarely approved by the boards in universities that approve studies involving people. It is only done when there is no other way that the research can be performed, or the importance of the research far outweighs the risks to the subjects. Despite these requirements, human research still goes on. It does so by requiring a bit more cleverness in the design of experiments and by losing some insights that could be acquired only by deceit. Perhaps, this is a small price to pay when the alternative is the potential of doing harm.

▣ CHAPTER SUMMARY

Personality research is particularly important as it is one of the few fields where the preponderance of theorizing has been largely predicated on the intuition of key figures. In addition, a great portion of what is taught about personality has only minimal validation by the scientific method. Psychoanalytic, person-centered, and Gestalt theories are examples of principles set forth by iconic psychologists; all have strong face validity but weak experimental support. Virtually, every other science—especially those with clinical applications—employs the scientific method to test its hypotheses. This method, which can trace its origins back nearly half a millennium, holds that a hypothesis, no matter how intuitively appealing, must be tested using experimental techniques that vitiate the common tendency for people to see what they want to see.

This is especially important in psychology, in which people are studying the attributes of other people; it is a field in which bias, culture, or emotions can profoundly affect observations and conclusions. Personality research, therefore, typically strives to be both valid and reliable using true experiments when possible or quasi experiments when not.

Personality tests, which are usually the product of years of research and statistical analysis, are also an important means to study personality. Such tests include objective measures such as the Minnesota Multiphasic Personality Inventory and the Millon Clinical Multiaxial Inventory or projective measures such as the Rorschach and Thematic Apperception Test. The objective tests, being more statistically based, are generally regarded as more efficient means of studying personality. Finally, no matter what aspect of personality is being studied, ethical treatment of study participants is always paramount.

Chapter 4

Freud and the Dynamic Unconscious

Chapter Goals

- Place psychoanalysis in its historical context
- Discuss Freud the man and the time in which he wrote
- Explain the development of psychoanalytic theory
- Detail the components and complexities of Freud's theories
- Understand the pervasive influence of Freud and his theories
- List and explain some alternative points of view and the controversies surrounding Freudian theory

---

PSYCHOANALYSIS: THE FIRST COMPREHENSIVE THEORY OF THE PSYCHE

Chapter 2 put forward various historical views of personality and showed how these views have evolved over the last two millennia. There were a few critical points over the course of this history; one of them was Sigmund Freud's development of psychoanalytic theory. Freud is a pivotal figure not because he discovered previously unknown essential truths about human nature but rather because he set a standard for personality psychology. Freud proposed a comprehensive explanation of virtually all aspects of human behavior, both individual and collective. In addition, he attempted to explain how behavior developed in the individual and how the individual develops as a member of the human species (Ellenberger, 1970).

There are grave problems with many facets of Freud's theory. Even in Freud's inaccuracies, however, there is an intellectual elegance and intrigue that is at least in part responsible for the

Photo 4.1   Sigmund Freud
(1856–1939)

popularity of his ideas. Like them or not, Freud's theories have profoundly influenced many aspects of 20th- and 21st-century Western culture, from the graphic arts and literature to film and drama, as well as the practice of psychiatry. It is quite likely that you had heard of Freud before you opened this book or even before you took your first course in psychology. Terms like *neurotic*, *anal*, *penis envy*, *Oedipus complex*, or *repression*, were part of your vocabulary before you embarked on any study of psychoanalysis. And for better or worse, mental health professionals are inextricably linked with Freudian concepts in the minds of a large percentage of the lay public. The notion that psychoanalysis is synonymous with **psychotherapy** is almost universal. So, too, is the belief that psychotherapy is predicated on the uncovering of repressed memories or the release of long pent-up emotions.

Part of Freud's lasting appeal is the fact that a number of his postulates are widely accepted, even by critics of psychoanalytic personality theories. Few would deny that early childhood development plays a role in the formation of adult personality. Cognitive psychologists have demonstrated that a significant portion of information processing occurs outside our awareness, although in a manner very different from the way that Freud proposed. Similarly, many accept as self-evident that we use numerous **defenses** to protect our self-image from failures or insults. The question remains, however, as to whether the mobilization of these defenses is nonvolitional or whether it is a process of choice.

These and similar well-researched principles of psychology are recognized and understood by laypeople and professionals alike. However, the question that remains is the reason for the ubiquity of Freud's theories. Is Freud's renown due to his genius or to his ability to capture the imagination and engender medical controversy? This question will be addressed in the following sections as Freud's major theories are discussed, along with the positions of both adherents and opponents.

▣   THE BEGINNING

Freud's Early Career

Sigismund Schlomo Freud was born on May 6, 1856, in Austria-Hungary, in a region that is now part of Czechoslovakia. He later shortened his first name to the one by which he is generally known today. When Sigi, as his family called him, was 4 years old, his family moved to Vienna, the capital of the Hapsburg empire, where he lived until he fled the Nazi regime to safety in England in1938.

At age 17, he entered the University of Vienna to study medicine, graduating as a medical doctor in 1881, taking 3 years longer than usual to qualify for the degree. His mission in medicine was not so much to be a healer of the body but rather to "unravel the riddles of the world" (Jones, 1953, p. 28). Freud's protracted stay in medical school was the result of his spending a year in military service and a great deal of time translating into German the works of John Stuart Mill (1806–1873), the eminent British philosopher and political economist. For the next 3 years, Freud worked in several departments of the Vienna General Hospital, spending 3 months in the psychiatric department.

In 1885, he was appointed to the position of *Privatdozent*, or unsalaried lecturer, at the University of Vienna. This position, which has no direct equivalent in American or Canadian universities, is one in which the lecturer is approved by the university but is paid directly by fees from students. Shortly after his appointment as *Privatdozent*, Freud received funding to study under the French neurologist Jean-Martin Charcot at the Salpêtrière Hospital in Paris for several months in 1885 and 1886. Although Charcot is credited with coining the term *neurology* and with making several significant discoveries in this field, he is best remembered for his work on what was then called hysteria. Freud's experience with Charcot made such a deep impression on him that he named a son after him and redirected his career to pursue Charcot's interest in hysteria. This condition is generally referred to in the early 2000s as **conversion disorder** or **somatization disorder**. The specific symptoms associated with people suffering from hysteria have changed somewhat over the course of time (Blacker & Tupin, 1991; Micale, 1995).

In the early 2000s, somatization disorder is usually understood as a mental illness in which the patient has a long and complicated medical history and physical symptoms involving several different organ systems and pain in several different parts of the body, but with no known organic basis (Kroenke, 2007). For example, a person might complain of headache, nausea and vomiting, dizzy spells, lack of interest in sex, and pain in the lower back but have perfectly normal results on blood tests, X-rays, or other imaging studies. Conversion disorder, which is much less common in the developed world in the early 21st century than it was in Freud's day, takes its name from Freud's notion that the patient converts internal emotional conflicts into such external neurological symptoms as paralysis of a limb or a seizure resembling epilepsy.

An instructive example is that of an accountant who was ordered by his employer to falsify the company's books. His writing hand became paralyzed, which effectively prevented him from doing his employer's bidding. A specific form of conversion disorder known as camptocormia, in which the patient's trunk is bent completely forward at the waist, usually with the arms drooping, was frequently reported by military doctors in World Wars I and II (Miller & Forbes, 1990); it is still found in some adolescents as well as soldiers facing combat (Rajmohan, Thomas, & Sreekumar, 2004).

In Charcot's time, patients diagnosed with hysteria were generally much more dramatic in presentation than contemporary patients diagnosed with somatization disorder. Paralysis, blindness, hysterical anesthesias, grand mal seizures, bloated abdomens, and sexually aggressive behavior were common symptoms in the women hospitalized for hysteria in the mid-19th century. The great interest in this disorder led to Charcot's abandoning traditional hospital rounds in favor of dramatic clinical demonstrations and patient interviews in the hospital amphitheater. Freud reported hearing Charcot discussing the case of a couple in which the husband had erectile dysfunction and the wife subsequently suffered hysteria (Clark, 1980). Charcot reportedly said, "But in such cases, it is always a matter of sex—always—always—always—always."

Freud's experience with Charcot undoubtedly pointed him even more strongly in the direction of a psychobiological view of psychological illness. Freud was clearly convinced that hysteria is a physical manifestation of unseen psychological distress. His belief is evidenced by his proposal that hysteria is not an illness peculiar to women but can occur in men, too (Freud, 1957). It had been taken for granted that hysteria was strictly a female disorder to the extent that the very name of the disorder came from the Greek word for uterus.

Collaboration With Breuer and the Beginnings of Psychoanalysis

Freud brought his Parisian enlightenment with him when he returned to Vienna and began to collaborate with Josef Breuer, an older established physician who was sympathetic to Freud's advocacy of Charcot's ideas. Breuer had a young female patient who came to him in 1880, plagued by numerous hysterical symptoms that included periods of paralysis, numbness, visual disturbances, and repeated transient **aphasia** (inability to speak). Assigned the pseudonym Anna O., the patient developed symptoms after caring for her dying father.

Anna O. was identified by later writers (Jones, 1953) as Bertha Pappenheim (1859–1936), a woman who developed a negative attitude toward psychoanalysis later in life but went on to become a prominent feminist, director of an orphanage, and founder of a home for unwed mothers (Ellenberger, 1972). A postage stamp was issued in her honor by the Federal Republic of Germany in 1954. Breuer treated Pappenheim from 1880 to 1882, using hypnosis and discussion of her memories. Anna O. referred to this approach as "chimney sweeping" and the "talking cure." One of Anna's symptoms left her unable to drink water. Under hypnosis, however, she related to Breuer a story of a hated governess letting her equally hated dog drink from a dinner glass. After coming out of the hypnotic trance, she seemed relieved of this symptom.

Pappenheim suffered relapses and occasionally entered the Inzerdorf sanitarium during several years following her treatment by Breuer, until she relocated to Frankfurt in 1889. Based on their work with Anna O. and several other people suffering from hysteria, Freud and Breuer published *Studies in Hysteria* in 1895. This book documented their method of talk therapy, which Breuer called **catharsis,** a term derived from the Greek word for purification.

One day in 1882, however, a hysterical Anna accused Breuer of impregnating her. A shocked Breuer left Vienna with his wife and gave up this line of work. Freud, however, went on to elaborate on his psychological theories of pathology and human development. Freud eschewed hypnosis in favor of a new method called **free association**, in which the client talks about whatever comes to mind without controlling or organizing the flow of ideas or thoughts. Freud's later works, *The Interpretation of Dreams, Psychopathology of Everyday Life*, and *Three Essays on the Theory of Sexuality*, established his fame but increased sharp hostility on the part of other medical professionals toward him and his theories—especially those dealing with infantile sexuality.

▣   BRIEF OVERVIEW OF FREUDIAN THEORY

Freud envisioned personality as residing primarily in the unconscious. Decisions, judgments, attitudes, even our personal philosophy, are largely inscrutable to us, in his view. In describing how such a divided consciousness can function, Freud first developed what is known as the **topological theory of mind**. This theory contains the well-known three layers: the conscious, the preconscious, and the unconscious. The conscious refers to all the perceptions, memories, beliefs, and other mental contents that we are currently processing. If you would rather be watching television than reading this chapter at the moment, that fact may be present to your conscious.

Conscious and Unconscious

The preconscious refers to the components of mind that are not in immediate awareness but can be brought into conscious awareness voluntarily. If we are asked, for example, whether we like whole wheat bread, or to name our favorite color, we can immediately bring the answers into consciousness and expound upon them. Freud, however, did not regard either the conscious or the preconscious as containing the greatest portion of our identity. Rather, he identified this portion as lying within the unconscious, which is actively hidden from our conscious mind.

Freud used a hydraulic metaphor derived from 19th-century physics to describe the energy that powers both conscious and unconscious mental processes. He called this finite source of energy that he considered the essential motivating force of life the libido, from the Latin word for lust or desire. Although human libido can be expressed in many symbolic or indirect ways, it is basically the desire for sexual satisfaction. Thus, if a man builds a bridge or paints a picture, according to Freud, his bridge or artwork are only redirected expressions of sexual energy. In fact the bridge—or art or any other human achievement—can be viewed as a form of sexuality frozen in time.

Libido originally resides in a part of the psyche called the id, which is the reservoir of libido, and the source of all psychic energy. The id can engage only in primary process thinking, a form of ideation that consists of fantasy, disorganized fragments of thought, and demands for immediate gratification. Primary process thinking exists outside of linear time. As we develop through the various psychosexual stages—oral, anal, and phallic—our libido is increasingly repressed by parental figures who train us to delay gratification and to channel psychic energy in ways that are socially appropriate. With the formation of the unconscious, what is left over in the conscious portion of our mind is called secondary process thinking by Freud. Secondary process thinking concerns rational, logical, problem-solving thought. Solving an algebraic equation would be an example of secondary process thinking, as would translating Latin into English or fixing a clogged drainpipe.

Disruptions at any of the stages of psychosexual development, Freud observed, appeared to result in what he called **fixations**, which represent excessive preoccupation with that particular erogenous zone characterized either by over- or underindulgence. A fixation can be likened to an incomplete stage in a process. For example, signing up for an e-mail account with a provider often requires that you confirm your identity by responding to e-mail sent to a current account. Should you never receive the confirmation e-mail, you would be locked in this stage of the registration process indefinitely. This simple laminar or layered view of mind, however, was insufficient for Freud's efforts to explain the symptoms of people suffering from hysteria and other emotional problems. If the human psyche consists of three discrete layers, its structure then raises the question of how the layers interact and how conflicts between them arise. Moreover, if thoughts or feelings are repressed, or pushed down, into the unconscious, what mechanism moves them there? What keeps them there? Where does repression occur? An instance of forgetting that occurs in the conscious layer of the psyche is by definition not repression. But if repression occurs in the unconscious, as it must, then that fact implies that the unconscious itself has internal divisions.

Freud's Topological and Pathological Model

These and related questions necessitated mechanisms that moved across the boundaries between the different layers of the mind. These theoretical deficiencies led Freud to supplement his theory with a tripartite model of the mind. This model proposed that the topology of the mind has structures: the id, the ego, and the superego. The id, which takes its name from the Latin word for "it," represents the entire mind at birth. And as one would expect of an infant, the id is primitive, demanding, and completely lacking in a sense of time or priority. It has only one goal: the relentless seeking of pleasure through satisfying such life drives as hunger, thirst, and sexual desire.

Over time, as the infant develops, he or she must adjust to the reality that needs are not met instantly and cannot be met by wishing; that other people exist and have their own wishes or needs, which may be very different; and that the person must conform to the standards of parents, society, and other individuals. So out of necessity, some of the energy of the id is used to develop a structure called the ego, the Latin word for "I." This adjustment includes the adoption of defenses by the ego to protect against fearful impulses arising in the id. These defenses are necessary as the id, ego, and superego are in perennial conflict. When the id begins to dominate the ego, the individual will first experience anxiety (Freud, 1936); should the id's domination increase, the person's entire integrity of mind will break down.

Freud proposed three types of anxiety: realistic, neurotic, and moral. **Realistic anxiety** refers to all fears that arise from objective external dangers. Someone on an airplane who looks out the window and sees that one of the engines is on fire would experience realistic anxiety, as would someone confronted on the street by a large snarling dog. **Neurotic anxiety** ensues when unconscious impulses from the id begin to intrude into consciousness. Such behaviors as compulsive hand washing, checking, counting, or similar rituals may be related to neurotic anxiety about contamination or aggressive impulses; the person performs the compulsive acts as a way of warding off or preventing the feared consequences of getting dirty or behaving aggressively (Freud, 1930).

Moral anxiety develops when either id or ego impulses violate the proscriptions of the superego. An example of moral anxiety might be that experienced by a person who has grown up in a household in which alcoholic beverages are strictly forbidden and who then finds himself in a social setting in which people are drinking alcohol and seem to be enjoying themselves. The person might want to have a drink along with the others but feel quite anxious about wishing to do so. The three types of anxiety correspond to the ego's three harsh masters, the id, the superego, and reality.

The reader should note, however, that only realistic anxiety can be dealt with in a rational manner; that is, one can take such reasonable actions as telling a flight attendant about the engine fire or avoiding the hostile dog. According to Freud, the other types of anxiety can be transformed into quasi-realistic anxiety; in his opinion, this transformation of neurotic or moral anxiety explains the development of **phobias**. Phobias can be defined as objectively unfounded fears of objects or situations that produce a state of panic. Some phobias may have originated during earlier stages of human evolution (such as fears of snakes, spiders, or fire), while others represent individual responses to specific traumatic experiences. For example, a person who has a phobia about dogs in general may have been chased or bitten by a dog in childhood.

Shifting Boundaries

When you think of this dividing up of the personality into ego, superego, and id, you must not imagine sharp dividing lines such as are artificially drawn in the field of political geography. We cannot do justice to the characteristics of the mind by means of linear contours, such as occur in a drawing or in a primitive painting, but we need rather the areas of color shading off into one another that are to be found in modern pictures. After we have made our separations, we must allow what we have separated to merge again. Do not judge too harshly of a first attempt at picturing a thing so elusive as the human mind (Freud, 1933, p. 110)

While the id, the ego, and the superego helped Freud to clarify the workings of the unconscious and the minimally conscious mind, he did not see them as hard-and-fast divisions but constantly shifting boundaries within a dynamically divided psyche.

We shall now look upon the mind of an individual as an unknown and unconscious id, upon whose surface rests the ego, developed from its nucleus the Percept-system. If we make an effort to conceive of this pictorially, we may add that the ego does not envelop the whole of the id, but only does so to the extent to which the system Percept forms its surface, more or less as the germinal layer rests upon the ovum. The ego is not sharply separated from the id; its lower portion merges into it.

But the repressed merges into the id as well, and is simply a part of it. The repressed is only cut off sharply from the ego by the resistances of repression; it can communicate with the ego through the id. We at once realize that almost all the delimitations we have been led into outlining by our study of pathology relate only to the superficial levels of the mental apparatus—the only ones known to us. The state of things which we have been describing can be represented diagrammatically, although it must be remarked that the form chosen has no pretensions to any special applicability but is merely intended to serve for purposes of exposition. We might add, perhaps, that the ego wears an auditory lobe—on one side only, as we learn from cerebral anatomy. It wears it crooked, as one might say.

It is easy to see that the ego is that part of the id which has been modified by the direct influence of the external world acting through the Percept-Cs: in a sense it is an extension of the surface-differentiation. Moreover, the ego has the task of bringing the influence of the external world to bear upon the id and its tendencies, and endeavors to substitute the reality-principle for the pleasure principle which reigns supreme in the id. In the ego perception plays the part which in the id devolves upon instinct. The ego represents what we call reason and sanity, in contrast to the id which contains the passions. All this falls into line with popular distinctions which we are all familiar with; at the same time, however, it is only to be regarded as holding good in an average or "ideal" case.

The functional importance of the ego is manifested in the fact that normally control over the approaches to motility devolves upon it. Thus in its relation to the id it is like a man on horseback, who has to hold in check the superior strength of the horse; with this difference, that the rider seeks to do so with his own strength while the ego uses borrowed forces. The illustration may be carried further. Often a rider, if he is not to be parted from his horse, is obliged to guide it where it wants to go; so in the same way the ego constantly carries into action the wishes of the id as if they were its own.

It seems that another factor, besides the influence of the system Percept, has been at work in bringing about the formation of the ego and its differentiation from the id. The body itself, and above all its surface, is a place from which both external and internal perceptions may spring. It is seen in the same way as any other object, but to the touch it yields two kinds of sensations, one of which is equivalent to an internal perception. Psychophysiology has fully discussed the manner in which the body attains its special position among other objects in the world of perception. Pain seems also to play a part in the process, and the way in which we gain new knowledge of our organs during painful illnesses is perhaps a prototype of the way by which in general we arrive at the idea of our own body. (Freud, 1927, p. 28)

With the addition of these other structures to Freud's explanation of the workings of the human mind, he added a new level of complexity to his metaphor. He has added an ego and an id (the superego will come later). The ego is seen as a weak master metaphorically riding a far more powerful and primitive steed, the id. But unlike horsemen, we never dismount from our inner animal. For according to Freud, we are forever locked in a battle for control with our primitive inner side. While successfully riding a horse means maintaining control, there is a limit to the extent to which a horse can be forced to go where it does not want to—and if the horse really wants to go somewhere and takes the bit between its teeth, so to speak, there may be no stopping it.

FREUD'S STRUCTURAL MODEL

The Id

To Freud, the id is a metaphor for all primitive drives. He envisioned the id as chaotic, impulsive, and a vessel of pure stimulation. Its primitive nature does not allow it to conceive of or use time, so it cannot forgive or forget. Similarly, the id can engage opposite concepts simultaneously—like desire and revulsion. The id serves as the connecting factor between the physiological drives and basic behavioral control. By its very nature, the id has no ethical standards and cannot make judgments about good, evil, or moral choices. Its sole motivation is a relentless quest for pleasure—which Freud called the **pleasure principle.**

Freud envisioned the id as recapitulating or reenacting the most primitive stages of **phylogeny**, the evolutionary history of the human organism. In fact, he saw each phase of human development as reenacting a correlated stage of human evolution. He wrote, "Each individual somehow recapitulates in an abbreviated form the entire development of the human race" (Freud 1916a, p. 199); and "Ontogenesis may be regarded as a recapitulation of phylogenesis, in so far as the latter has not been modified by more recent experience. The phylogenetic position can be seen at work behind the ontogenetic process" (Freud, 1905/2000, p. xxvii). The id, which is primitive in its relentless groping for satisfaction, is faced with a real world with which it cannot deal. Eventually it comes into conflict with the standards of society as the person it controls grows into infancy. According to Freud, at this point in human development, another entity becomes necessary—the ego.

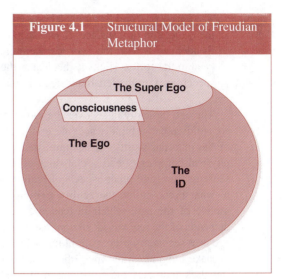

Figure 4.1   Structural Model of Freudian Metaphor

The Ego

The ego mediates and facilitates all sensation and perception from the outside world. Thus, it stands in contrast to the id, which is focused entirely within and can neither grasp nor understand external realities. The ego evolves out of necessity by channeling energy from the id because the growing person's needs and the demands of the external world cannot be met by the id's primary process thinking, which is capable of only fantasizing. Freud believed that if all human needs were met instantly, the human psyche would not develop beyond the id, as it would have no need to do so. Freud saw the ego as a metaphor for brain functions, specifically those located in the motor and sensory **cortex**:

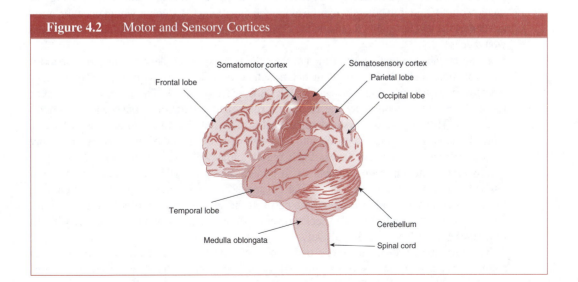

Figure 4.2   Motor and Sensory Cortices

The ego is first and foremost a body-ego; it is not merely a surface entity, but it is itself the projection of a surface. If we wish to find an anatomical analogy for it we can easily identify it with the "cortical homunculus" of the anatomists, which stands on its head in the cortex, sticks its heels into the air, faces backwards and, as we know, has its speech-area on the left-hand side. (Freud 1927, p. 21)

The ego basically takes over the job of engaging the external world from the id. In doing so, children cease blindly seeking gratification of their drives and begin to accept the reality of the external world. To accomplish this acceptance, the ego must be able to grasp the physical complexity and social rules of the outside world. It must make use of memory, a sense of time, and other aspects of reality testing to do so. The pleasure principle gives way to what Freud called the **reality principle**. That is, obtaining pleasure is not the primary motive of the ego, which instead focuses on accommodating the person's desires to the demands of the real world. In contrast to the primitive primary process thinking of the id, the ego uses secondary process thinking, which is rational, conscious, and logical. The ego is able to make judgments that meet the demands of external reality; it is therefore able to control impulses and delay the gratification of needs. The ego is the only part of the psyche that is self-preservative and the only part in contact with physical and social reality.

The Superego

To summarize briefly, Freud posited the existence within the human psyche of an irrational, craving id and a perceptually and socially aware ego. Left to themselves, these structures would produce a human being capable of self-regulation but only in response to the demands of the immediate situation. A person who had only an ego and an id would abstain from immoral or even criminal acts, but only if there were some authority figure continuously present. For example, a bank teller would steal as soon as the manager stopped observing, the dieter would binge immediately upon leaving the nutritionist, a student would cheat on a test as soon as the teacher stepped outside the classroom, and anonymous charitable contributions would cease.

Freud maintained that a part of the psyche called the superego develops in response to the need for moral behavior independent of immediate behavioral consequences. The superego emerges from the ego after the ego has developed from the id. The process of superego formation is put in motion by the restraints, rules, and regulations conveyed by a child's caretakers. This imposition of standards educates the child about the moral rules of society, which Freud saw as being integrated into the personality through the superego. The existence of the superego adds another layer of self-regulation as well as another source of intrapsychic conflict. The superego prompts us to punish ourselves when we transgress our own internalization of our society's rules. The existence of the superego adds another ongoing mental battle to the conflict between the ego and the id. The superego will be in continual conflict with the ego when the ego seeks to act expediently, and it will be in conflict with the id when the id pushes to act impulsively.

The development of the superego makes possible the existence of the emotion known as **shame**. Shame is an intensely painful feeling of humiliation, dishonor, or condemnation, usually associated with feeling generally defective as a human being. People feeling shame will typically wish they could disappear, "crawl into a hole and hide," or "never have to face those people again." According to Freud, without the superego, people would never feel shame because they would never be aware of having violated a moral or social standard. Like the ego, the superego is largely unconscious.

Parental proscriptions against the child's **polymorphous perverse** sexual behavior (Freud's term for a child's seeking of sexual gratification from any part of the body, before he or she internalizes the conventions of civilized society) are both consciously and unconsciously taken in as our own values during the first 3 years of life. Such parental interventions are to be expected as a result of Freud's belief that children are inclined to express their libidinous or sexual impulses in bizarre or inappropriate ways. The concepts of **infantile sexuality** and polymorphous perversity are some of the most controversial aspects of Freud's theory. He described the sexual drives of children as follows:

> It is an instructive fact that under the influence of seduction children can become poly-morphously perverse, and can be led into all possible kinds of sexual irregularities. This shows that an aptitude for them is innately present in their disposition. There is consequently little resistance towards carrying them out, since the mental dams against sexual excesses—shame, disgust and morality—have either not yet been constructed at all or are only in course of construction, according to the age of the child. In this respect children behave in the same kind of way as an average uncultivated woman in whom the same polymorphously perverse disposition persists. Under ordinary conditions she may remain normal sexually, but if she is led on by a clever seducer she will find every sort of perversion to her taste, and will retain them as part of her own sexual activities. Prostitutes exploit the same polymorphous, that is, infantile, disposition for the purposes of their profession; and, considering the immense number of women who are prostitutes or who must be supposed to have an aptitude for prostitution without becoming engaged in it, it becomes impossible not to recognize that this same disposition to perversions of every kind is a general and fundamental human characteristic. (Freud, 1905/2000, p. 57)

People who dismiss Freud's theory on the basis of their inability to recall such childhood desires are faced with an insurmountable obstacle, as Freud proposed that repression locks away these memories. The memories of childhood desires would arise symbolically, however, when the superego generates feelings of shame that are contrary to a decision made by the ego. An example of such shame would be the inhibition felt by a person who decided to

---

VIGNETTE

In his college years, Rich was the person others sought out if they were feeling blue or needed a dose of good humor. Not only was he constantly cheerful, he had what seemed to be an exhaustive mental repository of jokes. No matter how gloomy a situation might be, Rich could find something funny and clever to say about it. Not

(Continued)

(Continued)

surprisingly, his goal was to get into television as a comedy writer or performer. And no one doubted that Rich would succeed in reaching his goal. He was the very model of a person who could be funny without making himself the object of ridicule.

While Rich was a natural comedian, however, he was able to switch out of that persona into a mature and reflective adult whenever serious matters were at hand. And in situations when emotional support, friendly advice, or simple listening was called for, Rich always distinguished himself by offering what was needed.

He earned his degree in communications and media with honors. This field offered the precise training that he thought would get him into television. And as chance and an excellent interview would have it, he was offered a position at a small regional television station in the South. Although Rich was understandably elated about his start in television, his triumph was bittersweet as he had to leave his friends and family behind in Connecticut. His regret was assuaged, however, by the bon voyage party they gave him. Rich was in his glory on that occasion; he was both the guest of honor and the entertainer at the party. His stand-up comedy routines and improvisations left most of the attendees gasping for breath. By the end of the evening, no one doubted that they were saying goodbye to a future star.

The job itself turned out to be a bit of an anticlimax, as Rich did little more than run errands and assist the producers with the few shows that originated at the station. It seemed that they had little time or patience for his brand of charm and humor. For six months he did his best, but the job ended with an impersonal layoff notice when the station underwent a financial crisis. Rich took the setback in good humor and resolved to bounce right back into his dream profession. In spite of his disappointment, Rich resolved not to return to New England in defeat but to find a new job in television close to his new home. After two months of frustration and drained finances, however, Rich began to look for a provisional job until he could get back into television. After deciding to look for work elsewhere, he quickly took a job as an assistant manager in the electronics section of a department store.

For years Rich continued to apply for jobs in television, film, and even local theater productions while working in retail. His chronic feelings of disappointment were always kept at bay by his optimistic hope that his dream would become reality some time soon. For fifteen years, he was the happy and funny man that all of his friends had known. Then, seemingly abruptly, in his late thirties, Rich started to become a different man. It was then, it seemed, that his dreams had died. He was struck with the realization that he was just a department store manager and was likely to remain one. Rich was no longer funny; and when he tried to make jokes, his humor seemed forced and mordant.

Rich married and had two children, but he was never completely happy. With the loss of his dreams, the old Rich had died and been replaced by a bitter and somber man, not quite depressed but simmering with discontent. The funny avuncular man had become one who seemed lost in self-pity and resentment. His personality had changed with the loss of hope and his altered view of life. Rich's personality change demonstrates that in some people, personality is based at least in part on aspirations, hopes, and expectations for the future as well as experiences in the past or present. Should these visions undergo significant changes, so too will the personality.

Vignette Questions

1. What is the basis of Rich's unhappiness in the Freudian model?

2. Where in the structure of his mind would his problems reside?

3. Would Freud believe that Rich is aware of the real cause of his malaise?

engage in a sexual act that he has rationally considered to be both pleasurable and harmless; the person might, however, suddenly be stricken with **guilt** when he begins the act. According to Freud, his inhibition would result from the superego invoking its unconscious moral edicts. The superego develops two components, the **ego-ideal** and the **conscience**.

The Ego-Ideal. The ego-ideal is a subsystem of the ego that constructs an ideal image of the self. It could also be described as a norm or standard that the ego uses to measure its own performance. According to Freud, we all possess an internal image of the type of person we should be based on the standards presented to us as developing children. He described the ego-ideal as follows:

> This double aspect of the Ego-ideal derives from the fact that the Ego-ideal had the task of effecting the repression of the Oedipus complex, indeed, it is to that revolutionary event that it owes its existence. Clearly the repression of the Oedipus complex was no easy task. The parents, and especially the father, were perceived as the obstacle to realization of the Oedipus wishes; so the child's ego brought in reinforcement to help in carrying out the repression by erecting this same obstacle within itself. The strength to do this was, so to speak, borrowed from the father, and this loan was an extraordinarily momentous act. The superego retains the character of the father, while the more intense the Oedipus complex was and the more rapidly it succumbed to repression (under the influence of discipline, religious teaching, schooling and reading) the more exacting later on is the domination of the super-ego over the ego—in the form of conscience or perhaps of an unconscious sense of guilt. I shall later on bring forward a suggestion about the source of the power it employs to dominate in this way, the source, that is, of its compulsive character which manifests itself in the form of a categorical imperative. (Freud, 1927, p. 27)

The Ego-ideal, therefore, is the heir of the Oedipus complex and thus it is also the expression of the most powerful impulses and most important vicissitudes experienced by the libido in the id. By setting up this ego-ideal the ego masters its Oedipus complex and at the same time places itself in subjection to the id. Whereas the ego is essentially the representative of the external world, of reality, the super-ego stands in contrast to it as the representative of the internal world, of the id. Conflicts between the ego and the ideal will, as we are now prepared to find, ultimately reflect the contrast between what is real and what is mental, between the external world and the internal world. (Freud, 1927, p. 48)

In essence, the ego-ideal is created after the successful completion of the Oedipal phase of development (Freud, 1924). After the successful completion of this phase, the growing boy will develop an ego object or mental representation of the person he thinks he should be, based on the standards set by his father. Freud vacillated about the workings of this process in girls and so believed girls would develop a weaker superego and a weaker ego-ideal.

Conscience. Although the conscience is commonly seen as synonymous with the superego, Freud actually viewed conscience as one of the two components of the superego. As noted above, the ego-ideal contains the person's paradigm of behavior and public presentation. In contrast, the conscience, which is also unconscious, contains all of the proscriptions against immoral or inappropriate behaviors.

> What it is that the ego fears either from an external or from a libidinal danger cannot be specified; we know that it is in the nature of an overthrow or of extinction, but it is not determined by analysis. The ego is simply obeying the warning of the pleasure-principle. On the other hand, we can tell what lies hidden behind the ego's dread of the super-ego, its fear of conscience. The higher being which later became the ego-ideal once threatened the ego with castration, and this dread of castration is probably the kernel round which the subsequent fear of conscience has gathered; it is this dread that persists as the fear of conscience. (Freud, 1927, p. 85)

For Freud, then, the superego is formed out of a young boy's fear of castration and the resolution of the Oedipus complex. (Freud never came up with a fully satisfactory account of female moral development.) The way the Oedipus complex comes to pass, in Freud's account, is that the little boy realizes he has a hated rival for the affection of his mother, the source of all reward. The little boy then recognizes that this rival—his father—is not only more powerful than he is, but even more powerful than the mother—all-powerful, in fact. So the little boy gives up competing with his father but introjects his father's rules, thus identifying with and being like an omnipotent power, while at the same time being cared for by this omnipotent power. Later on, this omnipotent father becomes the Father in heaven—hence (according to Freud) the origins of religion.

Freud implies that the human conscience is punitive; in other words, it constitutes a person's capacity to punish himself. An example that Freud gave of such self-punishment is that of a professional man, a doctor or lawyer, who has gone further than his father in terms of educational credentials and income. Such a man might punish himself for outperforming his father by doing something scandalous that destroys his promising career (Freud, 1916b). In sum, an adult who has developed a complete personality structure (in Freudian terms) not only has an image that he or she strives to realize (the ego-ideal) but also passes judgment on him- or herself (conscience).

While the superego contains the conscience, Freud did not regard the conscience as the embodiment of goodness, for the superego operates by introjected imperatives—absolute rules, in fact. The superego can be savage and cruel—"as cruel as only the id can be" (Freud,

1901/1960, p. 44). The superego is not realistic or self-preservative. For example, it would be possible for a person's superego to lead him or her to commit suicide rather than suffer dishonor or loss of reputation; by this reasoning, the incidents of mass suicide by Japanese soldiers toward the end of World War II on such islands as Saipan and Okinawa were triggered by the soldiers' belief that surrender to the Americans was an intolerable blot on their honor as warriors. Another instance of a punitive superego according to Freud's definition would be the suicide of a teenager who feels that she should kill herself for failing to live up to her standards of competence. A 14-year-old girl who jumped off the Golden Gate Bridge in San Francisco in December 2001 left behind a suicide note in which she described herself as "fat, disgusting, and boring"; her mother described her as a self-motivated perfectionist, "the kid other kids called for help with homework" (Hamlin, 2005).

▣ FREUD'S VIEW OF ANXIETY

As we have discussed earlier, Freud saw the human psyche as a perennial battleground fought over by its internal structures. Since the greatest portions of all these structures are forever kept from our awareness, we can know about the battle inside us only indirectly. Anxiety is the way we are alerted to the conflict. Thus, understanding the nature of anxiety in Freudian thought is crucial to comprehending Freud's view of personality. Anxiety serves as the signal that a conflict exists among the three structures of the mind, and these conflicts are fundamental forces directing the nature of personality. It is quite clear that Freud viewed personality as arising from fundamentally unconscious constituents that exist in a constant state of tension. This dynamic tension directs our behavior, perceptions, and thinking.

What is more, the workings of this tension are actively kept secret from us by censors that block their emergence into consciousness or by mental devices that disguise them. Two forces power these conflicts, *thanatos* or aggression (sometimes called the death instinct) and libido or the sexual drive. We can see the origins of this concept in Freud's early writings, in which he described anxiety as resulting from lack of sexual activity. In one case, co-authored with Breuer, Freud refers to "the fact that the patient had been living for years in a state of sexual abstinence. Such circumstances are among the most frequent causes of a tendency to anxiety" (Breuer & Freud, 1895/1957, p. 88).

Thus, it followed for Freud that guiding a patient toward a more satisfactory sexual life could resolve most anxiety-related problems. When Freud revised his theory of anxiety in *The Ego and the Id,* however, he explained anxiety as a mental response to perceived danger, both external and internal. The ego, given its assigned task of self-preservation, has the job of alerting the individual to danger. If there is an external danger posed by something that can cause physical harm, the individual will seek to fight the danger or flee from it. If the danger arises within, however, from id impulses that threaten the ego, the ego must contrive defenses against this danger. Obviously, the need for defenses raises some complex problems, because the ego also works to keep the id's impulses secret from itself. It must, therefore, contrive ways to protect the individual and itself from the impulses that it strives to keep from conscious awareness. So for Freud, our conscious knowledge of ourselves is similar to the contents of an official newspaper in a dictatorship—we know only what the internal autocrat permits us to know. Here we present a case study of a patient whose anger at his wife emerged in the disguised form of headaches and other physical symptoms:

The Case of Carlo

Carlo was referred to one of the authors by a physician who reported that he had exhausted all possible medical explanations for the patient's symptoms, based on several months of diagnostic testing. The physician reported that Carlo sought treatment for severe headaches characterized by feelings of intense pressure within his head and dizziness. He was initially referred to a neurologist who performed a basic neurological examination and found Carlo to be completely normal in all measures. The neurologist suggested, however, that Carlo be evaluated for depression, a suggestion that Carlo adamantly rejected. He did experience several days of relative well-being after the specialist repeatedly assured him that he had no medical illness.

Unfortunately, the headaches returned, and Carlo returned to his primary physician, who once again referred him for additional testing—this time for a CAT scan of his head. The radiologist who administered the scan reported absolutely no abnormality. Again, Carlo experienced several days of relief after receiving the good news that he did not have a potentially lethal disorder like the brain tumor he feared.

Shortly thereafter, the symptoms returned again, although not exactly the same as before. With each relapse, Carlo's symptoms would always assume subtle changes; the pain might shift from the temple to the top of the head, or he might notice a vague change in the quality of the dizziness. These "new" symptoms would once again provoke Carlo to seek medical attention. After close to eight months of pain, anxiety, and medical testing, Carlo agreed to see a psychologist.

Carlo then met with one of the authors of this text. The initial sessions focused on his physical symptoms. He denied any problems worthy of discussion and stated that the only issue in his illness was the pain and tightness in his head. Over the following weeks, however, Carlo gradually disclosed that he was unhappy in his marriage. In fact, he came to acknowledge that he absolutely loathed his wife.

Carlo was a first-generation immigrant from southern Italy who had come to the United States with his parents and sister. After the family's first years of struggle, his parents purchased a home in the suburbs of a large city. Carlo had worked as a tradesman with his father during his entire youth and young adulthood. His mother had died when he was still in his teens; his father died just after Carlo turned 30. At 34, Carlo had little contact with his sister, who had married and moved out of state. His only connection to his familial legacy, then, was the house in which he had grown up.

Carlo's wife was a native-born American who held a degree in business. She was an independent and assertive marketing executive. Carlo had been raised, however, to believe that a woman should play a different role in life. He deeply resented her tacit refusal to accept his authority as the head of the household. This resentment grew to a silent rage. When he finally expressed his anger in therapy, he was asked why he would stay in such a marriage. "Because I would never let her get the house," was his response. Carlo was informed that the house was not part of community property, as he had inherited it prior to the marriage. With a look of sudden intensity, he asked the therapist, "If I divorce her, I can keep the house? I would rather kill her than let her get it." The psychologist told him that this was the law in Carlo's state of residence as the psychologist understood it, but that Carlo should confirm the information with an attorney. He did find it to be true and immediately asked his wife for a divorce.

Carlo's symptoms dissolved within weeks of the divorce. Carlo had revealed that he believed himself to be in an inescapable trap, one that was associated with frustrated rage. When his frustration and anxiety were resolved, so, too, were his physical symptoms.

Carlo's plight is paradigmatic of psychological problems that, according to psychoanalysts, arise as a result of unconscious conflicts. However, for cases like Carlo's to provide cogent evidence for Freud's theories, more frugal theories would have to be ruled out. For example, was Carlo's rage unconsciously repressed, or was he suppressing it because he felt powerless to act on it? Were his headaches a symbolic presentation of unconscious conflicts, or did his continual anger simply lead to headaches?

Realistic Anxiety. Realistic anxiety refers to fear of an external object or action that others would generally regard as dangerous or as posing a real threat to the concerned individual. It is what a soldier might feel while marching into battle or what a woman might feel walking home alone after dark and hearing footsteps behind her. The danger that provokes realistic anxiety can generally be observed by others, who would understand how the situation would produce dread. By definition, realistic anxiety is fully conscious.

Neurotic Anxiety. The danger that leads to neurotic anxiety cannot be observed or perceived by anyone other than the afflicted person. According to Freud, it is the dread that permeates consciousness when the ego is threatened by desires emanating from the id that are both unacceptable and uncontrollable. Neurotic anxiety is kept at bay through the use of one or more of the **defense mechanisms** discussed below. Should these defenses fail, the person will tend to become increasingly dysfunctional. Such dysfunction may lead to a **neurosis** or what would be called today a **personality disorder**. According to Freud, unrelieved neurotic anxiety may lead to **psychosis**—a complete breakdown of the integrity of the psyche. A psychosis is a severe mental disorder, typically characterized by delusions or hallucinations, which causes gross distortions in a person's ability to recognize reality and respond appropriately. A psychosis may be shared between two people, most often spouses or siblings; a Boston psychiatrist reported a case study involving a suicide pact between a husband and wife who believed they were about to be abducted by aliens from outer space and attempted suicide to prevent the imagined abduction (Neagoe, 2000).

Moral Anxiety. This type of anxiety enters consciousness when a person's ego has acted or desires to act in such a way as to violate the unconscious superego. The impulse that might propel the ego toward unacceptable behavior will typically arise from the id, but the superego is essentially concerned with regulating the ego. For example, if an impulse from the id drives the ego toward sexual infidelity, the person considering this act may feel moral anxiety when thinking about having an affair. The essential distinction between neurotic anxiety and moral anxiety is that the former is a fear of external consequences and the latter is related to fear of rebuke from the superego acting through the conscience.

▣ MECHANISMS OF EGO DEFENSE

The ego develops a number of strategies that assist it to ward off the irrational demands of the id and allow it to function in the world of reality. The impulses are kept unconscious by defense mechanisms, which are also unconscious. This lack of conscious awareness of defenses is a particularly important point because some observers see defense mechanisms in the behavior of others on a regular basis. For example, we all tend to deny painful aspects of our lives to varying extents. Many of us can be seen by others to project blame or regress to less mature levels of development under severe pressure. The key issue is not whether defenses are employed in daily life but whether they are operated by entities within us that are outside of our awareness. Freud did not consider the ego defenses as volitional or intentional. Rather, these mechanisms are by their very nature unconscious and beyond our control. The Freudian scholar Matthew Erdelyi (2001) points out that Freud originally envisioned ego defenses as conscious or unconscious and only later defined them as exclusively unconscious.

Exactly how deep in the unconscious the defense mechanisms lie is debatable; nevertheless, they are often far easier to see in others than in ourselves. In fact, they are often transparently obvious in others to an extent that makes their operations laughable. An example would be that of a drunk driver pulled over by a highway patrol officer who denies that he has been drinking, even though his speech is slurred, he smells of alcohol, and he can barely stand up. Freud would say that the defenses have this one-way quality because they are designed to fool not others, only ourselves. Notably, Sigmund Freud himself only hinted at the existence of the more elaborate defense mechanisms. The actual naming and elaborate explanations of these mechanisms come from the writings of his daughter, Anna Freud. We will discuss a few of these as they have become inextricably associated with Freudian theory.

Repression

Freud believed that we all use repression as a defense against anxiety while rarely if ever being aware we are doing so. Repression is a fundamental primal defense that serves the ego by defending it from impulses from the id that threaten its psychological stability. When a wish or desire that we cannot consciously recognize without experiencing anxiety or other distress approaches consciousness, it is pushed into the unconscious mind by a self-regulating censoring mechanism, in this view. Freud first elaborated on this idea in the book he co-authored with Josef Breuer, *Studies in Hysteria*:

> Now I already knew from the analysis of similar cases that before hysteria can be acquired for the first time one essential condition must be fulfilled: an idea must be *intentionally repressed from consciousness* and excluded from associative modification. In my view this intentional repression is also the basis for the conversion, whether total or partial, of the sum of excitation. The sum of excitation, being cut off from psychical association, finds its way all the more easily along the wrong path to a somatic innervation. The basis for repression itself can only be a feeling of unpleasure, the incompatibility between the single idea that is to be repressed and the dominant mass of ideas constituting the ego. The repressed idea takes its revenge, however, by becoming pathogenic. (Breuer & Freud, 1895/1957, p. 116)

According to Freudian dynamic theory, this act of repression—of pushing a drive that has a force and energy of its own into the unconscious—takes a certain amount of mental or libidinal energy. Because Freud viewed a person's mental or libidinal energy as finite, using this energy for repression leaves less for those mental functions essential for healthy living.

The reader should note that repression is not to be confused with the conscious suppression of thoughts, desires, or impulses. Repression is unconscious; it is a process that blocks material from consciousness without the individual's awareness, whereas suppression is a fully conscious act involving the will. An example of suppression would be a person's decision to continue studying or working on a project rather than yielding to the impulse to play computer games, watch television, or otherwise procrastinate.

It is true that a repressed thought or impulse may surface in the form of a symptom or series of symptoms called the **return of the repressed**. A common example of this kind of symptom is a slip of the tongue (or pen), sometimes called a Freudian slip or **parapraxis**. One such incident concerned a secretary in a legal firm whose boss had a reputation for trying to seduce his female employees. The secretary referred to him in an e-mail to a friend as "pubic enemy number one" and was unaware of the typo until her friend commented on it. Repression is the basic defense mechanism and underlies all the other defenses.

Regression

According to Freud's theory of psychosexual development, as we saw, people progress through a series of standard stages as they advance toward maturity. But people may move backward as well as forward along this path; that is, they may revert to an earlier phase instead of advancing or maintaining their position. When they move backward in their psychosexual development, **regression** is said to have taken place. For example, a child who has been toilet-trained may begin soiling again when the parents present her with a new baby brother or sister; or an adolescent who has begun dating members of the opposite sex may give up heterosexual courtship. It is, for example, not uncommon to see a teenage girl undergoing stress to retrieve her old stuffed toys from the attic or a teenage boy under similar pressure to rediscover his earlier hobby of building model airplanes.

A person characteristically resorts to regression when facing an anxiety-producing conflict; for example, the young child who regresses in regard to toilet training is typically torn between affection for the new baby and jealousy stirred up by the parents' preoccupation with the new arrival. Regression, therefore, constitutes a dysfunctional response to preserve the person's ego from an inner or external threat of some type. In the example of sibling rivalry, older children are most likely anxious about losing the parents' love if they allow resentment of the newborn to show.

Regression may be a psychoanalytic explanation for the sudden onset of enuresis (bedwetting), for example. Children with enuresis that has no identifiable medical cause (such as an abnormally structured bladder or a urinary tract infection) may feel threatened by increasing parental demands to act like a big boy or girl and a perceived loss of love. Regression to an earlier level of functioning seeks to restore the lost love. Regression in Freud's theory is associated with the flow of libidinal energy backward from mature to immature sexuality. So a regressed person is typically believed to become less outwardly sexual and more autoerotic.

Regression in Freud's system of thought is not the same as fixation, in which the person's libido is "stuck" at an earlier stage; regression rather involves detaching the libido from the person's current stage of development and redirecting it backward in time to previously satisfying states or activities.

Projection

This mechanism of defense has two unconscious components. People who are employing **projection** begin by denying to themselves that they have a feared or undesirable impulse or trait. They will then impute that impulse or motive to someone else. Projection is exemplified in the case of a man who harbors homicidal jealousy toward another. An unconscious censor within the potential killer will block the knowledge of his rage from his consciousness. It will then lead him to believe that the arousal he feels when encountering his enemy results from the enemy's homicidal rage toward him. People using projection have absolutely no awareness of their own rage; they are aware only of their perceived foe's apparent motive.

As in the case of most defense mechanisms, projection helps to spare libidinal energy by allowing some release of the feared impulse, even if in disguised form. Hence, a key characteristic of projection, and one often neglected in descriptions of it, is that in the process of projecting unacceptable impulses onto others, one allows oneself to act on these precise impulses. To return to our example, a person who attributes his aggressive impulses to everyone he meets has a constant excuse to get into fights. A person who sees everybody else as dishonest may feel entitled to take from others on the grounds that she isn't a thief—she is only taking back what is owed her. This type of projection is commonly seen in persons sent to prison for embezzlement or forging checks—they will often say that the "really big crooks," white-collar criminals such as dishonest financiers or securities traders, are never sent to jail.

Typically, projection is used by individuals who suffer feelings of impotence or weakness; thus, mothers who abuse their children may interpret the child's behavior as "asking for punishment" and view themselves as helpless victims of a "mean" or aggressive child even though they are older and, in most cases, much larger than the child (Hamilton-Giachritsis & Browne, 2005). The reader should remember the saying that a man never checks under the bed unless he has hidden there himself.

Introjection

People are said to be using the defense mechanism of **introjection** when they take into themselves the characteristics of another, usually more powerful, individual. Introjection is the principle behind the formation of the superego, in which youths introject the values of their parents. This defense is most common when one has values opposed to the values held by a majority, values that might be seen as threatening. To avoid the real or imaginary fear of rebuke or rejection, people instead adopt the new values as their own. As with the other defenses, someone experiencing introjection is not aware of the reason for the shift in values; rather it is managed by an unconscious force. In extreme situations, individuals even introject the values of persecutors; the phenomenon of concentration camp prisoners modeling their ragged clothes after Nazi uniforms and treating other prisoners under their authority the same way as the guards treated them is well documented. Another example of this type of introjection is the abused children who internalize the hostile attitudes of their caretakers and act aggressively and cruelly toward younger siblings or family pets.

Intellectualization

Intellectualization is a defense mechanism that strips away the emotional content of a situation or experience. People appear to be reacting to the event in a purely analytical way devoid of passion or emotion, thus separating the threat from the negative feelings that it would normally cause. An example of intellectualization concerns a patient who was told by his primary physician that he had cancer. He immediately began to do large amounts of research on his form of cancer, the treatments for it, the success rates of each form of treatment, and the names and locations of specialists who had published studies of his type of cancer. A related form of intellectualization is the use of jargon or specialized terminology as a way of distancing oneself from the emotional implications of one's situation. To return to the case of the cancer patient, he began to use technical words like *carcinoma* or *malignant neoplasm* when talking about his disease and using the chemical names of the drugs used in his chemotherapy.

Another form of intellectualization is the use of euphemisms for unpleasant realities, such as saying that someone has *passed away* rather than *died* or that a sick or injured animal was *put to sleep* rather than *euthanized*. In one survey of British doctors, a sizable number reported that they used euphemisms rather than direct communication when telling patients that they had a terminal illness (Todd & Still, 1993). One need not be "challenged" or "special" to see that the use of euphemisms for various disabilities or diseases is common, as in the use of the phrase "special education."

Rationalization

Rationalization is a widely practiced defense that would provide clear evidence of the cogency of psychoanalytic theory, were it not for the fact that many of us are quite aware when we are rationalizing. When people rationalize, they excuse their inappropriate or inadequate behavior by offering an explanation that is more acceptable than the real and unconscious (or partially conscious) motive. This defense leads them to deny feelings associated with a failure, rejection, or similar emotional setback. For example, if an executive fails at her dream of becoming the chief executive officer of a corporation, she may rationalize it by stating that she is happy not to have been burdened with such a taxing job. Another example of rationalization is the person who justifies the purchase of a large and expensive truck or sport utility vehicle on the grounds that he needs the extra space for hauling equipment or taking the family on trips, when the real motivation is to impress others with a display of wealth or to intimidate other drivers on the highway (Bradsher, 2002, pp. 120–123).

Reaction Formation

Freud considered **reaction formation** to be a more primitive version of sublimation. Sublimation is a defense mechanism in which a wish that cannot be directly expressed is diverted toward socially or morally acceptable behavior. The fine arts and the performing arts offer many people satisfying opportunities for sublimation.

In contrast to healthy sublimation, however, reaction formation is a harsh and primitive form of sublimation that turns an unacceptable or anxiety-provoking impulse into its opposite. Freud describes the difference as follows:

A lower form of sublimation is the suppression through reaction formation, which, as we have found, begins early in the latency period of infancy, and may continue throughout life in favorable cases. What we call the character of the person is built up to a large extent from the material of sexual excitations; it is composed of impulses fixed since infancy and won through sublimation, and of such structures as are destined to suppress effectually those perverse feelings which are recognized as useless. The general perverse sexual disposition of childhood can therefore be esteemed as a source of a number of our virtues, insofar as it incites their creation through the formation of reactions. (Freud 1938, pp. 625–626)

Unlike sublimation, in reaction formation, people's conscious experience of their impulse is reversed in such a way that the individual is aware of exactly the opposite feeling. Followers of Freud typically attribute this reversal to the influence of the superego's standards. But the point of a reaction formation is that in feeling the exact opposite of our true feelings, we get to express our true forbidden desires, but in disguised form. Thus, a mother feels resentment against her child for thwarting her career plans. It is unacceptable to her to express her hostility directly, so she becomes an overly "loving" mother to the extent that she smothers her child's life through overprotection. She may say such things as, "I'm not letting you play with the other children because you will get hurt."

Other examples of reaction formation would include anti-pornography crusaders who accumulate huge collections of pornography "only to show people how bad it is," or animal rights activists who harass medical researchers. In one instance, an activist of this type posted a letter to a scientist that said the activist would laugh out loud when he heard about what he hoped would be a long painful death of the scientist (Masserman, 1961).

Sublimation

According to Freud, sublimation is the most mature and functional defense mechanism:

Sublimation, too, gives justification for broadening the concept of sex; for investigation of cases of the type mentioned conclusively show that most of our so-called feelings of tenderness and affection, which color so many of our activities and relations in life, originally form part of pure sexuality, and are later inhibited and deflected to higher aims. Thus, I have in mind a number of benevolent people who contributed much of their time and money to the protection and conservation of animals, who were extremely aggressive in childhood and ruthless Nimrods as adults. Their accentuated aggression originally formed a part of their childhood sexuality; then, as a result of training, it was first inhibited and directed to animals, and later altogether repressed and changed into sympathy. Now and then, we encounter cases in which repression and sublimation do not follow each other in regular succession, owing to some weakness or *fixation* which obstructs the process of development. This may lead to paradoxical situations. For example, a man, who was notorious as a great lover of animals, suffered while riding his favorite pony from sudden attacks during which he beat the animal mercilessly until he was exhausted, and then felt extreme remorse and pity for the beast. He would then dismount, pat the horse, appeasing him with lumps of sugar, and walk him home—sometimes a distance of three or four miles. We cannot here go into any analysis of this interesting case; all we can say is that the horse represented a mother symbol, and that the attacks, in which cruelty alternated with compassion, represented the ambivalent feeling of love and hatred which the patient unconsciously felt for his mother. (Freud, 1938, p. 19)

Sublimation is the foundation of all creativity, aesthetics, and societal progress. Freud considered all productive endeavors to be the fruit of sublimated, or converted, sexual or aggressive impulses. In sublimation, the individual repressing these drives releases them by radically changing their expression into creation, invention, artistic appreciation, charity, worship, or other laudable endeavors. For example, someone who feels sad about the end of a relationship might decide to go to a play, movie, or opera about a romantic tragedy, or perhaps write a poem or paint a picture that represents sorrow or loss, as a way of sublimating anger related to the lost relationship. In a specific instance, the English poet Alfred Lord Tennyson was saddened in 1833 by the sudden death of his closest friend, who was also engaged to marry Tennyson's sister. Over the next 17 years Tennyson wrote a series of 133 poems in response to his friend's death; the poems were published in 1850 as a collection titled *In Memoriam*. In coping with his own grief, Tennyson wrote some often-quoted lines that still comfort many bereaved people:

> *I hold it true, whate'er befall;*
> *I feel it, when I sorrow most;*
> *'Tis better to have loved and lost*
> *Than never to have loved at all.*

Sublimation, in short, is the source of emotional energy underlying many great works of art or medical or scientific research; it is a defense mechanism that allows people to channel pain in socially productive as well as personally beneficial ways.

Freud proposed that a balanced individual has an ego that can discharge the greatest portion of its pent-up psychic energy in meritorious ways. The reader should recall that in Freud's system, inability to release pent-up psychic energy results in anxiety, psychopathological symptoms, or aberrant behavior.

▣ FREUD'S PSYCHOSEXUAL STAGES OF DEVELOPMENT

Any full theory of personality will usually include an account of human development, and Freud's theory was quite complete in this regard. He proposed five developmental stages that all humans pass through from childhood to adulthood (Freud, 1905/2000). Each stage is defined by a specific focus for the person's libidinal or sexual energy. As we move from stage to stage, most of our sexual energy is redirected from a less mature focus to a more mature one, from the mouth to the anus, for example. Conflicts, inadequate satisfaction, or excessive pleasure at any point during these stages can lead to something called a fixation, in which the target of the sexual energy remains attached to an object associated with a lower level of maturity. For example, a person might remain focused on the pleasures associated with the mouth; they are then said to be orally fixated. The reader should note that Freud thought fixations could result from frustration as well as too much stimulation; thus, an oral fixation could result from being weaned too soon as well as from being allowed to nurse too long.

Fixation is a very important aspect of Freud's personality theory, as the nature of one's personality is based on one's preferred sexual focus. So in the case of people with the oral fixation, they will tend to seek oral pleasures (food, smoking, alcoholic beverages, certain drugs); develop a dependent personality (like a suckling infant); and interact with others in a docile and submissive manner.

Oral Phase

The oral phase of development begins at birth; during this period the infant's erotogenic (sexually sensitive) region is the mouth. The sexual energy of the libido focuses on the mouth and is therefore gratified by oral stimulation. This focus is also referred to as **cathexis**, a Freudian term referring to the emotional charge associated with the instinctual investment of psychic or libidinal energy into a part of the body or other instinctual object. One of the problems in understanding Freud is that while he wrote in German, using powerful and vivid terms, standard translators have chose to translate those terms into Latin or Greek. The word Freud used for cathexis was *Besetzung*, which in German means "sitting there" or "occupying." Infants in this stage are said to be in a state of autoerotic primary narcissism, in which all sexual energy is directed at themselves. When libidinal energy is directed toward the mouth, the infant is concerned to obtain gratification from oral stimulation. This gratification would ordinarily be satisfied by eating, sucking, biting, or swallowing. Here, according to Freud, we see the early expression of **eros**—the sexual and self-preservative instinct. Some psychoanalysts propose that biting or other acts of oral aggression are manifestations of what Freud called the **death instinct** or **thanatos.** The death instinct is the conjectured drive that

Table 4.1	Freud's Stages of Psychosexual Development

Age	Stage	Pleasure Source	Conflict
Birth to 2 years	Oral	Mouth: sucking, biting, swallowing	Weaning
2–4 years	Anal	Anus: defecating or retaining feces	Toilet training
4–5 years	Phallic	Genitals	Oedipus complex (boys); **Electra complex** (girls)
6 years to puberty	Latency	Sexual urges sublimated into sports and recreation. Social activities with same-sex friends help to channel sexual impulses.	
Puberty to adult maturity	Genital	Physical sexual changes reawaken repressed needs. Direct sexual feelings toward others lead to sexual gratification.	Social rules; need to complete education or job training

urges us toward aggression and ultimately self-destruction. A child exhibiting a period of oral aggression is considered by some Freudians as going through the oral-sadistic phase.

In the oral stage, we see the beginnings of identification, a mechanism that does not reach maturity until the child enters the phallic stage of development. In identification, infants begin to take on the identity of (to identify with) significant others in their life; this identification can include the mannerisms, dress styles, beliefs, or attitudes of other family members. This less mature behavioral style was considered by Freud to be a more primitive variant of object cathexis for, in the latter, sexual energy is directed toward a person rather than oneself. Freud saw the oral stage as the most narcissistic stage of human development, leaving those who fail to resolve it permanently immature and focused on themselves.

Anal Phase

The child who outgrows the oral stage must next complete the **anal stage** of development. As children progress from one stage to the next, so too does the focus of the libidinal energy. In the anal stage, the libido cathects the anus and activities associated with it. The control and release of feces is the source of the child's sexual pleasure during this phase of maturation. Freud discusses the sexual nature of the anal phase as follows:

> Children utilizing the erogenous sensitiveness of the anal zone can be recognized by their holding back of fecal masses until through accumulation there result violent muscular contractions; the passage of these masses through the anus is apt to produce a marked irritation of the mucous membrane. Besides the pain, this must also produce a sensation of pleasure. One of the surest premonitions of later eccentricity or nervousness is when an infant obstinately refuses to empty his bowel when placed on the chamber pot by the nurse, and controls this function at his own pleasure. It naturally does not concern him that he will soil his bed; all he cares for is not to lose the subsidiary pleasure in defecating. Educators have again shown the right inkling when they designate children who withhold these functions as naughty.
>
> The content of the bowel, which acts as a stimulus to the sexually sensitive surface of mucous membrane, behaves like the precursor of another organ which does not become active until after the phase of childhood. In addition, it has other important meanings to the nursling. It is evidently treated as an additional part of the body; it represents the first "donation," the disposal of which expresses the pliability while the retention of it can express the spite of the little being towards his environment. From the idea of "donation," he later derives the meaning of the "babe," which according to one of the infantile sexual theories, is supposed to be acquired through eating and born through the bowel. The retention of fecal masses, which is at first intentional in order to utilize them, as it were, for masturbatic excitation of the anal zone, is at least one of the roots of constipation so frequent in neurotics. The whole significance of the anal zone is mirrored in the fact that there are but few neurotics who have not their special scatologic customs, ceremonies, etc., which they retain with cautious secrecy. Real masturbatic irritation of the anal zone by means of the fingers, evoked through either centrally or peripherally supported itching, is not at all rare in older children. (Freud, 1938, pp. 589–590)

Freud's view of developmental stages as expressions of sexual energy is made clear in the preceding excerpt. In the anal stage, as in all stages of development, the personality is formed through the appropriate focus of sexual energy. In the anal stage, the child's ability to control and respond to parental demands for bowel control is the key to the personality styles that can develop out of this stage. Prior to the anal stage, children's source of pleasure was located entirely within, but now, children must interact with outside entities who demand that they delay gratification. In the anal stage lie the beginnings of the reality principle and secondary process thinking. And with the demands of the outside world to conform to the needs of reality, the ego begins to form out of the child's id.

Phallic Phase

The phallic phase of psychosexual development commences between the ages of 4 and 6 years. It is characterized by the penis (in boys) becoming the focus of libidinal energy or cathexis. Thus, activities involving the penis, including self-stimulation and urination, are central to the boy's erotic life. Urination is experienced as pleasurable, in both the expulsion and retention of urine, Freud believed. In the phallic period, the child's libidinal energy is directed toward the genitals and subsequently toward the parent of the opposite sex. When children cathect the parent of the opposite sex, they become wary of their other parent, who is now a competitor.

Freud saw this conflict as comparable to that of Oedipus, a tragic hero in Greek legend. According to the legend, Laius, the king of Thebes, was warned by an oracle that he would be killed by his own son. When his wife, Jocasta, gave birth to a son, Laius ordered the baby to be bound by his ankles and exposed to the elements. A shepherd found the infant and saved him from death by exposure. The child was ultimately adopted by King Polybus of Corinth. Now a young prince, the adopted boy visited the same oracle as his father. The oracle told him that he was fated to kill his father and marry his mother; on hearing this, Oedipus fled from his home to avoid his fate. He traveled to Thebes, where he came upon King Laius, who challenged him. Oedipus, not knowing that Laius was his father, killed him in combat. After some additional adversity, he won the throne of Thebes and married Jocasta, the queen—thus fulfilling the prophecy that he would kill his father and marry his mother.

From Freud's own self-analysis, he concluded that the myth of Oedipus was an expression of a developmental impulse found in all children. He believed that children fantasize about eliminating the parent of the same sex so that they can have sexual union with the parent of the opposite sex. This desire, in turn, leads to an epiphany in a male child, namely that his father will take revenge on his little competitor by castrating him. This fear is what Freud called castration anxiety. The growing dread of impending castration forces the boy child to give up competing with his father and instead identify with him. By doing so, the little boy can achieve his goal vicariously. The boy's allying with his father leads to introjection of his father's moral and motivational values, the foundation of the boy's superego.

In sharp contrast, Freud did not think that this path of development was the case for little girls. He saw girls as unable to experience castration anxiety; as a result, girls are far less motivated to give up their quest for the parent of the opposite sex and introject the values of the same-sex parent, their mother, he thought. Girls supposedly experience **penis envy** during this stage of development. Freud theorized that children do not recognize the external anatomical differences between males and females prior to the phallic phase. In the phallic stage, however, the girl often takes her mother as the focus of libidinal energy. She will then compete with her father with the goal of impregnating her mother. With the formation of this goal, the girl becomes painfully aware of her lack of a penis to accomplish the task of impregnating her mother. Freud suggested that girls make temporary adjustments to this discomfort through fantasies about acquiring or reacquiring a penis. But eventually the girl will acknowledge defeat. She then blames her mother for her deficiency and turns to her father with the fantasy of obtaining a penis from him, which is later replaced by the wish to receive a child from him.

Because Freud believed that satisfactory completion of the phallic stage through the resolution of castration anxiety is required for the proper development of the superego, it follows then that he thought women were anatomically destined to have weaker moral values and ethical convictions than men. Moreover, because women never completely resolve their penis envy according to Freud, they are left feeling inadequate, less mature, and less capable of sublimating their impulses toward such productive activities as intellectual or artistic accomplishment.

Here Freud's account of female psychosexual development becomes far more shadowy and incomplete. In his system, females also develop an Oedipus complex and a superego; they also pass through a latency period. May one ascribe to girls also a phallic organization and a castration complex? Freud's answer is in the affirmative, but it cannot be the same for the girl as for the boy. The feminist demand for equal rights between the sexes does not carry very far here; Freud thought that the morphological differences between males and females must express themselves in differences in the development of the mind. Freud is frequently quoted as saying that "anatomy is destiny." The little girl's clitoris behaves at first just like a penis, but by comparing herself with a male sibling or playfellow, the female child perceives that she has "come off short" and takes this fact as proof of ill treatment and as a reason for feeling inferior. Freud says:

> For a time [the girl] still consoles herself with the expectation that later, when she grows up, she will acquire just as big an appendage as a boy. Here the woman's "masculine complex" branches off. The female child does not understand her actual loss as a sex characteristic, but explains it by assuming that at some earlier date she had possessed a member which was just as big and which had later been lost by castration. She does not seem to extend this conclusion about herself to other grown women, but in complete accordance with the phallic phase she ascribes to them large and complete, which is, male, genitalia. The result is an essential difference between her and the boy, namely, that she accepts castration as an established fact, an operation already performed, whereas the boy dreads the possibility of its being performed The castration-dread being thus excluded in her case, there falls away a powerful motive towards forming the super-ego and breaking up the infantile genital organization.
>
> These changes seem to be due in the girl far more than in the boy to the results of educative influences, of external intimidation threatening the loss of love. The Oedipus-complex in the girl is far simpler, less equivocal, than that of the little possessor of a penis; in my experience it seldom goes beyond the wish to take the mother's place, the feminine attitude towards the father. Acceptance of the loss of a penis is not endured without some attempt at compensation. The girl passes over—by way of a symbolic analogy, one may say—from the penis to a child; her Oedipus-complex culminates in

the desire, which is long cherished, to be given a child by her father as a present, to bear him a child. One has the impression that the Oedipus-complex is later gradually abandoned because this wish is never fulfilled. The two desires, to possess a penis and to bear a child, remain powerfully charged with libido in the unconscious and help to prepare the woman's nature for its subsequent sex role. The comparative weakness of the sadistic component of the sexual instinct, which may probably be related to the penis-deficiency, facilitates the transformation of directly sexual trends into those inhibited in aim, feelings of tenderness. It must be confessed, however, that on the whole our insight into these processes of development in the girl is unsatisfying, shadowy and incomplete. I have no doubt that the temporal and causal relations described between Oedipus-complex, sexual intimidation (the threat of castration), formation of the super-ego and advent of the latency period are of a typical kind; but I do not maintain that this type is the only possible one. Variations in the sequence and the linking up of these processes must be very significant in the development of the individual. (Freud, 1908/1959, vol. 2, pp. 275–276)

Latency

The psychosexual stage known as latency takes place in children between the ages of 6 and 12 years. During this period, the libidinal or sexual forces are held in abeyance or sublimated through such other activities as sports and schoolwork. The Oedipal conflicts are repressed in this stage as children are approaching adulthood. Children are, however, becoming concerned with independence from their parents. According to Freud, children in latency are beginning to learn to use sublimation to divert sexual impulses to socially acceptable and constructive directions.

When the more primitive sexual impulses are repressed, children learn to replace them with affection. Children at this age may take a great interest in pets or farm animals as well as socializing and playing with other youngsters. These activities become more complex during this period. Freud proposed that the defense mechanism of identification emerges during this period so that children will seek out others who are similar to them. Identification is the reason why young boys will tend to seek out male companions and girls will seek out females. Freud describes the latency period as follows:

The sexual instinct of man is very complex and is made up of contributions from numerous components and partial impulses. The peripheral stimulation of certain specialized parts (genitals, mouth, anus, urethra), which may be called erotogenic zones, furnishes important contributions to the production of sexual excitation, but the fate of the stimuli arising in these areas varies according to their source and according to the age of the person concerned. Generally speaking, only a part of them finds a place in the sexual life; another part is deflected from a sexual aim and is directed to other purposes, a process which may be called sublimation. During the period of life which may be distinguished as the "sexual latency period", i.e. from the end of the fourth year to the first manifestations of puberty at about eleven, reaction-formations, such as shame, disgust, and morality, are formed in the mental economy at the expense of the excitations proceeding from the erotogenic zones, and these reaction-formations erect themselves as barriers against the later activity of the sexual instinct. (Freud, 1908/1959, Vol. 4, pp. 46–47)

Genital Phase

The genital stage begins when children enter puberty, a point in development at which reproduction is now possible. Physical sexuality is becoming a strong force at this time of life, and the symbolic dimension of sexuality becomes less significant. Freud believed that the available libido increases during puberty with the surge of sex hormones in the young person. He predicted a range of psychic manifestations, given the conflicts and demands of young adulthood. For example, he explained the social sensitivity of young adults as libidinal sublimation and their rebelliousness as expressions of thanatos or the death instinct.

The latter portion of the genital phase is associated with adulthood. At this point, mature adults can express their sexuality through procreative heterosexual intercourse. Freud considered homosexuality to be a permanent pathology associated with inadequate completion of the phallic stage. He, therefore, considered it to be the result of a severe phallic fixation.

The healthy genital stage is associated with a high degree of maturity. Fixations from prior stages are minimal. People can have both a satisfying sexual life and combine sexual gratification with genuine affection for others. They exhibit little or no infantile narcissism and use the defense mechanism of sublimation to redirect libidinal energy toward productive work and socially acceptable endeavors.

▣ CHAPTER SUMMARY

Sigmund Freud developed the first comprehensive theory of personality, which included a theory of human development, a theory of mental functioning, and a set of propositions suggesting the ways in which disturbances in mental functioning lead to psychopathology. In addition to these formulations, Freud applied his psychoanalytic concepts to social and group psychology and to the patterns he saw in human history. This made him the first writer to develop a comprehensive theory of human behavior, one that would include, at a minimum, today's disciplines of social psychology, clinical psychology, personality theory, and historical psychology. It is probable that his all-embracing theory, combined with a fascinating and accessible writing style, made the icon that he has become.

His remarkably complex set of theories began with Freud's training in Paris and his collaboration with Josef Breuer. Using the concept of unconscious conflicts as both the basis of psychological problems and of personality development, Freud and Breuer's "talking cure" as a way to address these problems is generally considered the first modern form of psychotherapy.

Freud's structural model of the human mind provoked a great deal of research and experimentation on the nature and function of thought and consciousness, even though Freud's model was and still is controversial. Freud's concepts of the id, ego, and superego pervaded every aspect of the mental sciences and, for several generations, served as the framework for most models of personality.

Freud's positing of oral, anal, phallic, latent, and genital stages in human growth served as a founding model for developmental psychology. Freud first formally proposed that all people progress through fixed stages of development; he is, thus, the father of all subsequent stage theories. His notion that trauma or other disturbances during these stages have a fundamental impact on adult personality has been profoundly influential on generations of psychologists as well as on physicians, educators, clergy, social workers, jurists, and other professionals.

Chapter 5

Psychoanalysis in Theory and Practice

Chapter Goals

- Reveal some of the complexities of Freud's theories
- Present some of the controversies regarding Freud and psychoanalysis
- Contrast the Freudian view of the unconscious with those of recent neuroscientists
- Detail the theory behind psychoanalysis as a treatment
- Explain the process of psychoanalytic treatment

FREUD'S CONCEPT OF PERSONALITY TYPES

Psychoanalytic theory holds that as children progress through the five stages of psychosexual development, their libidinal energy continually reattaches itself—or cathects—to other objects. In Freud's terminology, an object is an unconscious mental representation of the target or focus of sexual or aggressive desires. In the early stages of development, the child's libidinal energy is focused on infantile objects. If all goes well in the child's development, however, cathexes are redirected toward more mature objects. On the other hand, the individual can become fixated or regressed if any of the earlier developmental stages is marked by either overindulgence or trauma. In other words, such a person's libidinal energy remains locked within a less mature stage. The personality typology that Freud proposed was founded on this notion. In his opinion, people who have a disproportionate amount of libidinal energy invested in one of the developmental stages will exhibit personality characteristics associated with that stage.

Freud's explanation of both normal and pathological personalities is based on the many ways a person can move through the stages of development. The healthiest passage is afforded to the person who completes the stages without having any of his or her libido fixated on earlier stages. He used the analogy of an advancing army. If an army tends to leave behind groups of soldiers at various bases along the line of march, it will have less strength for the real battle—in this case, the battle against cruel reality and the ordinary miseries of life. Sadly, Freud considered some amount of fixation inevitable; all of us, as he saw it, will develop fixations to some degree. In his system, people are constitutionally predestined to be always somewhat immature and attached to childish things.

Freud's account of this process begs the question as to exactly how fixation takes place. He answered this question by first proposing that the general tendency toward fixation is constitutional or hereditary. In other words, whatever the cause of a specific fixation, some people are by their essential nature more susceptible to develop it than others. The specific triggers of fixation are quite problematic, irrespective of a person's susceptibility. A fixation can take place in a given psychosexual stage if the child feels too comfortable in that stage, so that moving on to the next phase results in distress and frustration. Conversely, if a child is traumatized or even displeased during a specific stage, he or she can also become fixated in that stage.

Freud compared the process of fixation to the flow of fluid under pressure. Water or some other fluid will naturally flow from higher to lower pressure; however, if openings occur along the path of flow, the fluid will collect in or leak through those openings. The fluid in this metaphor is the libido, which Freud viewed as a finite form of psychological energy. Should some of a person's life energy be diverted into an opening (fixation) associated with a particular stage, it will collect there until it is released through the process of psychoanalysis. An obvious problem with this metaphorical explanation is that libido itself is a metaphor. There is no objective or measurable process in psychology or physiology that corresponds to this metaphorical concept. The exact concept of a fixation must therefore remain vague in Freud's system.

Oral Personalities

Freud viewed people as existing in a state of perpetual internal conflict. The human psyche is a set of irreconcilable forces drawing on a limited amount of mental energy. His view of personality types is similarly negative in that he regards them as the result of aberrations in the developmental process. The unsatisfactory completion of a psychosexual stage will lead to a personality type that confines the individual within that stage. For example, if one's libidinal energy becomes fixated on oral pleasure, the individual will manifest a personality style that distinctly reflects this focus. It follows that because infants in the oral stage are passive and dependent, adults who are fixated in this stage will tend to be dependent, ingratiating, and compliant. Just as the child tends toward optimism, equanimity, and delight, so, too, is the orally fixated adult. Such a person will tend to be a Pollyanna, gullible, and easily led.

The oral personality regards the mouth as the greatest source of pleasure, so that eating and drinking will often be taken to excess. Obesity, alcoholism, smoking, and even drug abuse are blamed by Freudian theorists on oral fixations. Because people with substance addictions or eating disorders are dependent and prone to excessive intakes of food or their drugs of choice, Freud's theory of fixation as the root of their personality type seems to have **face validity**— that is, it looks like it offers a satisfactory explanation of what it is intended to explain.

Some of Freud's followers divided the **oral personality** type into two subcategories, the more common of which is referred to as the oral dependent, oral passive, or oral receptive personality The other subtype is the oral aggressive personality, which is negativistic and given to sarcastic or biting comments. In direct contrast to their passive counterparts, oral aggressive individuals will be distrustful, demanding, and manipulative.

Anal Personalities

The anal personality has an excessive amount of libido fixated on the pleasures discovered during the period of toilet training. In learning to control bodily wastes, children become concerned with avoiding soiling themselves by defecating in appropriate locations at acceptable times. They will also derive great pleasure from the act of defecating and the associated parental accolades for doing so. A libido fixated at this stage leads to a personality style in which the person seeks order, control, and precision. Because the anal personality arises during the time when the superego is formed, a fixation at this stage can lead to a highly moralistic and overly controlled personality style.

Freud suggested that children in the anal stage of development regard the release of their feces as a gift to the parent—a gift that can be given or withheld. Children will release the feces if given sufficient love and withhold them if not. In Freudian thought, fecal matter becomes a type of currency in the parent-child relationship, which can be withheld or dispensed, thus giving the child a sense of control. The word *currency* is appropriate in this context; Freud assumed that the human unconscious makes a symbolic equation between feces and money. In a 1911 paper on dreams in folklore, he noted that according to ancient Eastern mythology, "gold is the excrement of hell" (Freud & Oppenheim, 1911/1958, p. 157).

As with the oral personality, there are two types of **anal personality,** anal-retentive and anal-expulsive. Anal-retentive children hoard their feces in miserly fashion, releasing wastes only when strongly encouraged or rewarded. These characteristics are supposedly present in anally fixated adults who demand that others offer them devotion and sacrifice. Anal-retentive adults hoard love and affection while commonly withholding their own affection from others. Another type of anal-retentive person is the individual who seeks to obsessively control his or her environment and the people in his or her life, often by being stingy or miserly. Anal-retentive personalities are symbolically seeking to control their feces and the soiling associated with elimination. The anal-retentive is the more stereotypical and common type of anal personality. The latter, the anal-expulsive type, is the direct opposite. Anal-expulsive people tend to be sloppy, profligate, careless, emotionally disorganized, and defiant, although some of them display some artistic talent as well.

Phallic Personalities

Freud thought that fixations in the phallic stage of development can lead to a few additional distinct personality types. As discussed previously, the so-called Oedipal crisis takes place during the phallic stage; thus fixations at this point are believed to have a profound impact on the growing child's personality. Since the Oedipal crisis is especially sexual in nature, fixations associated with it will tend to have a sexual focus. A phallic fixation can lead to an individual with a narcissistic, egotistic, or overly sexualized personality that may include serial marriage, polygamy, or polyandry. The phallic personality will tend to use sex as a means to discharge emotional tensions and will often have sexual relationships that are superficial and lacking in love or affection. Should the fixation take place in a male child during the period of most intense castration anxiety, he may well turn out to be attracted to countercultural movements, to be supportive of radical causes, or to be an advocate of social change.

Freud thought that assertiveness or strength in a woman was evidence of a phallic stage fixation and failure to resolve the Oedipal crisis in a satisfactory fashion. This failure led to what Freud called a **masculinity complex:**

> It points to a complication in the case of girls. When they turn away from their incestuous love for their father, with its genital significance, they easily abandon their feminine role. They spur their masculinity complex into activity, and from that time forward only want to be boys. (Freud, 1959, p. 186)

The girl's failure to accept her lack of a penis means that she will become a woman fixated on acting like a man. Consequently, all professional women would be regarded by traditional Freudian theorists as exhibiting a pathological fixation. The concept of the masculinity complex is clearly bound to the Central European culture of Freud's time. So, too, is his notion that competitive women are castrating females, as he believed that they competed with men with the unconscious goal of stealing the male penis. The unwillingness to accept the absence of a penis can also lead to a focus on the clitoris as the central sex organ rather than the vagina, Freud thought. Lesbianism is also viewed as a variant of these kinds of phallic fixations. According to Freud, a lesbian has taken this masculine fixation to its extreme and seeks to play the male role with another female.

Homosexuality in men is also considered a type of phallic fixation. Freud thought that the typical homosexual male was pampered by an overly protective mother during his phallic stage. An unusual degree of closeness and comfort with his mother leads to his identifying with her rather than making her an object of sexual interest. By identifying with his mother, the gay man develops a feminine type of sexuality. His fixation on this highly satisfying period of his life leads to his seeking a way to preserve the bond between mother and son. To accomplish this goal, he will take on the role of a mother with other boys, making them the focus of his libidinal drives. The boys, however, are only proxies for him in that they play the role of the loved son. Hence, homosexual love is considered by traditional Freudians to be an immature and narcissistic form of self-love. Given Freud's theory of psychosexual fixations, one can readily understand one potential source of criticism of Freudian theory. Specifically, Freud's system of thought tends to view all human behavior as symptomatic of some kind of pathology.

Genital Personalities

If Freud believed there were any people free of neurosis, they would be adults with a fully developed genital personality. Freud only implied the existence of a genital personality and never actually proposed a distinct personality type associated with this stage of development. However, an early follower of Freud named Wilhelm Reich (1897–1957) described the genital personality in this way:

> Since [the genital character] is capable of gratification, he is capable of monogamy without compulsion or repression; but he is also capable, if a reasonable motive is

given, of changing the object without suffering any injury. He does not adhere to his sexual object out of guilt feelings or out of moral considerations, but is faithful out of a healthy desire for pleasure: because it gratifies him. He can master polygamous desires if they are in conflict with his relations to the loved object without repression; but he is able also to yield to them if they overly disturb him. The resulting actual conflict he will solve in a realistic manner. There are hardly any neurotic feelings of guilt. (Reich, 1929/ 1948, p. 161)

The genital personality can be said to be exemplified by those people who pass through all prior stages of psychosexual development with a sufficient supply of libido to perform productive work, love others in a mature fashion, and reproduce. In contrast to these healthy specimens of humankind, people with fixations in earlier stages will tend towards **narcissism**, **fetishism**, and other barriers to mature heterosexual gratification. Thus, men with **paraphilia** and women with frigidity or other arousal disorders would be examples of people who fail to achieve the level of maturity required for genital personalities.

▣   PSYCHOANALYTIC NOSOLOGY

Psychoanalytic treatment sought to resolve conflicts that were typically centered on maladaptive sexual functioning. The reader should recall that libido, which refers to both the sexual energy within a person and the person's general life force, can lose its direction. It can become detached from appropriate targets, attached to inappropriate objects, and thereby cause emotional and personality malfunctions. *Neurosis* is the term Freud used to describe the state of libidinal dysfunction.

Actual neurosis. **Actual neurosis** was a term first used by Freud in 1898. He used it to describe an inversion of libido resulting in acute impairments of sexual functioning and physiological consequences of present disturbances in sexual functioning. He distinguished actual neuroses from psychoneuroses, which he regarded as due to psychological conflicts and past events. He further distinguished two types of actual neurosis—**neurasthenia**, which he attributed to sexual excess, and **anxiety neurosis**, which he saw as the result of unrelieved sexual stimulation. Freud later also included hypochondria, or excessive concern with one's health, among the actual neuroses.

Psychoneurosis. This term appears in Freud's early writings and is used to define a series of transference neuroses, including hysteria, phobias, and obsessional neurosis. The symptoms of the psychoneuroses are symbolic expressions of infantile conflicts in which the ego defends itself from disagreeable representations from the sexual sphere.

Transference neurosis. Transference neuroses, according to Freud, are childhood neurotic patterns played out by patients during psychoanalytic sessions. He defined **transference** itself as the process in which the **analysand** transfers to the analyst emotions experienced in childhood toward parents or other important figures. The transference neuroses include: (a) conversion hysteria, in which the symptoms are physical complaints; (b) anxiety hysteria, in which the patient experiences excessive anxiety in the presence of an external object (phobia); and

(c) obsessional neurosis, in which the predominant symptoms are obsessive thoughts and compulsive behavior. According to Freud's student and translator Abraham Brill (1938), all transference neuroses are rooted in disturbances of the patient's libido:

> The transference neuroses, hysteria and compulsion neuroses, are determined by some disturbance in the give-and-take of object libido, and hence are curable by psychoanalytic therapy, whereas the narcissistic neuroses, or the psychoses which are mainly controlled by narcissistic libido, can be studied and helped, but cannot as yet be cured by analysis. The psychotic is, as a rule, inaccessible to this treatment because he is unable to transfer sufficient libido to the analyst. The psychotic is either too suspicious or too interested in his own inner world to pay any attention to the physician. (Brill, 1938, p. 16)

Narcissistic neurosis. Freud used this term to distinguish conditions inaccessible to psychoanalytic treatment from the transference neuroses, which were more amenable to psychoanalysis. The narcissistic neurosis represents a conflict between the ego and the superego, as opposed to the transference neurosis, which involves a conflict between the ego and id. Freud believed narcissistic neuroses are refractory to psychoanalytic treatment:

> In the transference neuroses we also encountered such barriers of resistance, but we were able to break them down piece by piece. In narcissistic neuroses the resistance is insuperable; at best we are permitted to cast a curious glance over the wall to spy out what is taking place on the other side. Our technical methods must be replaced by others; we do not yet know whether or not we shall be able to find such a substitute. To be sure, even these patients furnish us with ample material. They do say many things, though not in answer to our questions, and for the time being we are forced to interpret these utterances through the understanding we have gained from the symptoms of transference neuroses. (Freud, 1920b, p. 365)

Traumatic neuroses. Some psychoanalysts after Freud conjectured that a neurosis can arise as a direct result of a trauma, thus the designation traumatic neurosis. Such a neurosis would not have unconscious causes and therefore could be addressed directly. Freud, however, rejected this notion:

> If anxiety is the reaction of the ego to danger, then it would be the obvious thing to regard the traumatic neuroses, which are so often the sequel to exposure to danger to life, as the direct result of life- or death-anxiety, with the exclusion of any dependence, in its etiology, upon the ego and castration. This is what was done by the majority of observers in the case of the traumatic neuroses of the last war, and it has been triumphantly claimed that proof is now at hand that jeopardy to the instinct of self-preservation is capable of giving rise to a neurosis without the participation of sexuality at all, and without regard to the complicated hypotheses of psychoanalysis. It is, as a matter of fact, extremely to be regretted that not a single reliable analysis of a case of traumatic neurosis exists. (Freud 1936, p. 66)

Psychosis. Freud saw psychosis as a condition characterized by hallucinations, paranoia, and hysterical psychosis (which he distinguished from hysterical neurosis). Freud explained the essential difference between neurosis and psychosis as follows: "Neurosis is the result of a conflict between the ego and its id, whereas psychosis is the analogous outcome of a similar disturbance in the relation between the ego and its environment (outer world)" (Freud, 1959, pp. 250–251).

Psychoanalytic theory would therefore view a psychotic individual as one whose ego is too weak to handle the vicissitudes of life. Or the psychotic might be a person with an adequate ego who faces such severe adversity as to cause a complete collapse of ego functioning.

◫ PSYCHOANALYTIC PSYCHOTHERAPY

Despite any criticisms of his theories, Freud deserves credit for a comprehensive model of what it means to be human. In addition to his attempts to explain the nature of human personality and the course of its development, he provided accounts of group behavior and the role and origin of spirituality, regarding that what we consider the highest and most noble aspects of human thought and behavior arise from our lower instincts. Although Freud was pessimistic about the possibility of curing neuroses or effecting lasting changes in personality, he developed the first form of psychotherapy: psychoanalysis. This method of psychotherapy involves a therapist who plays the role of a blank screen on which the patient can project his unconscious impulses or conflicts. The psychoanalyst encourages the client to free-associate, or speak freely, about whatever comes to mind. In doing so, the client is expected to reveal portions of his or her unconscious conflicts from time to time. This method was also applied to dream analysis, in which the client would relate recent dreams and the analyst would seek to uncover the impulses and wishes that the dream disguised. The analyst also would interpret all behaviors directed toward him, whether positive or negative, as representations of conflicted emotions toward parental figures.

If clients displayed affection or sexual attraction to the analyst, the analyst would regard them as transferring repressed feelings for their parent to the analyst. The reader should recall Anna O's phantom pregnancy in this context. Conversely, if clients were angered or displeased with the analyst, the analyst would consider their negativity as repressed hostile impulses toward a parental figure rather than directed at the analyst. These specific psychoanalytic techniques are largely explorative even though they seek to reduce patients' suffering and improve their ability to function. Although Freud believed that personality change is possible, he was pessimistic about the practical merits of psychoanalysis in effecting such a change. The long and grueling nature of analysis, the verbal and intellectual skills required of the analysand, the anxiety and distress provoked by the exploration of one's past, and the limited effectiveness of psychoanalysis in treating the more severe mental disorders were some of the reasons for Freud's pessimism. He expressed himself on this and related issues as follows:

> Allowing "repetition" during analytic treatment, which is the latest form of technique, constitutes a conjuring into existence of a piece of real life, and can therefore not always be harmless and indifferent in its effects on all cases. The whole question of "exacerbation of symptoms during treatment," so often unavoidable, is linked up with this. The very beginning of the treatment above all brings about a change in the patient's conscious attitude towards his illness. He has contented himself usually with complaining of it,

with regarding it as nonsense, and with underestimating its importance; for the rest, he has extended the ostrich-like conduct of repression which he adopted towards the sources of his illness on to its manifestations. Thus it happens that he does not rightly know what are the conditions under which his phobia breaks out, has not properly heard the actual words of his obsessive idea or not really grasped exactly what it is his obsessive impulse is impelling him to do. The treatment of course cannot allow this. He must find the courage to pay attention to the details of his illness. His illness itself must no longer seem to him contemptible, but must become an enemy worthy of his mettle, a part of his personality, kept up by good motives, out of which things of value for his future life have to be derived. The way to reconciliation with the repressed part of himself which is coming to expression in his symptoms is thus prepared from the beginning; yet a certain tolerance towards the illness itself is induced. Now if this new attitude towards the illness intensifies the conflicts and brings to the fore symptoms which till then had been indistinct, one can easily console the patient for this by pointing out that these are only necessary and temporary aggravations, and that one cannot overcome an enemy who is absent or not within range. The resistance, however, may try to exploit the situation to its own ends, and abuse the permission to be ill. It seems to say: "See what happens when I really let myself go in these things! Haven't I been right to relegate them all to repression?" Young and childish persons in particular are inclined to make the necessity for paying attention to their illness a welcome excuse for luxuriating in their symptoms. There is another danger, that in the course of the analysis, other, deeper-lying instinctual trends which had not yet become part of the personality may come to be "reproduced." Finally, it is possible that the patient's behavior outside the transference may involve him in temporary disasters in life, or even be so designed as permanently to rob the health he is seeking of all its value. (Freud, 1959, pp. 371–373)

Despite Freud's pessimism, however, psychoanalytic treatment has attempted to bring about both symptom relief and long-term personality change by liberating unconsciously invested psychic energy by bringing it to consciousness. This task is accomplished through several phases of treatment.

First Phase: Establishing the Therapeutic Alliance

The first phase involves developing a **therapeutic alliance** between the analyst and the analysand through a process in which the analyst elicits trust and faith from the analysand. The establishment of a therapeutic alliance is inherently more difficult in psychoanalysis than in other forms of psychotherapy, however, because the analyst must scrupulously avoid revealing any aspects of his or her own personality. Self-disclosure, whether biographical or attitudinal, would negate the therapist's usefulness as a blank screen. For example, the analyst could not be certain that behavior related to the transference was indeed issuing from the patient's unconscious instead of being a response to the therapist's behavior. Trust and confidence in psychoanalysis must, therefore, be earned by the therapist's steadfast consistency to the correct method.

Once this takes place, the client is encouraged to relate anything that comes to mind, no matter how trivial or irrelevant it may seem on the surface. Over time, the patient's free associations will result in a cathartic release of libidinal energy along with the strong emotions that Freud expected clients to experience during such a discharge. These strong emotions in the presence of the analyst will further strengthen the therapeutic alliance and bring about the next phase of the analysis: the expression of the patient's **countertransference** and resistance.

Second Phase: Analyzing the Resistance

Based on Freud's experience with his own patients, he concluded that they would typically devise barriers for the analyst as the treatment moved toward issues closely related to their pathology. Freud suggested that what he called **resistance** to the analysis signified progress in the therapy: the greater the resistance, the closer the analyst was getting to the source of the patient's neurosis. Resistance is an unconscious process; consequently, the analysand will tend to believe that his or her behavior is externally caused or is a legitimate voluntary action. For example, coming late to or missing a session with the therapist is usually considered an instance of resistance. Even if the analysand is called to work at the last moment or has a bona fide family crisis, the analyst will usually invoke the principle of psychic determinism to judge the missed appointment to be a volitional act of the unconscious mind to avoid the anxiety provoked by the therapy. Other acts of resistance include silence, irrelevant discussions, refusing to pay the analyst's bills, or complaining of physical symptoms.

Third Phase: Analyzing the Transference

Freud believed that the analysand's feelings of affection for or anger at the analyst were actually emotions transferred from a significant figure from early life to the present-day therapist. The reader should recall that psychoanalysis holds that we create internal representations of people who have played important roles in our development. These representations are referred to as objects. Because Freud saw all mental or emotional energy as finite, if a portion of it is attached to an object from the past, less will be available to the analysand in his or her present-day life. Freud called the attachment itself a cathexis and spoke of either cathecting (attaching emotional significance to) or decathecting (withdrawing emotional significance from) an object. A corollary to the principle of the limited quantity of emotional energy is that feelings will be expressed toward the analyst during therapy. Freud first used the term transference in *Studies in Hysteria* and explained it this way:

> [Occasionally] the patient is frightened at finding that she is transferring on to the figure of the physician the distressing ideas which arise from the content of the analysis. This is a frequent, and indeed in some analyses a regular, occurrence. Transference on to the physician takes place through a *false connection*. I must give an example of this. In one of my patients the origin of a particular hysterical symptom lay in a wish, which she had had many years earlier and had at once relegated to the unconscious, that the man she was talking to at the time might boldly take the initiative and give her a kiss. On one occasion, at the end of a session, a similar wish came up in her about me. She was horrified at it, spent a sleepless night, and at the next session, though she did not refuse to be treated, was quite useless for work. After I had discovered the obstacle and removed it, the work proceeded further; and lo and behold! The wish that had so much frightened the patient made its appearance as the next of her pathogenic recollections and the one which was demanded by the immediate logical context. What

had happened therefore was this. The content of the wish had appeared first of all in the patient's consciousness without any memories of the surrounding circumstances which would have assigned it to a past time. The wish which was present was then, owing to the compulsion to associate which was dominant in her consciousness, linked to my person, with which the patient was legitimately concerned; and as the result of this *mésalliance*—which I describe as a "false connection"—the same affect was provoked which had forced the patient long before to repudiate this forbidden wish. Since I have discovered this, I have been able, whenever I have been similarly involved personally, to presume that a transference and a false connection have once more taken place. Strangely enough, the patient is deceived afresh every time this is repeated. (Freud, 1957, p. 303)

Seventeen years later, Freud elaborated on the concept of transference and linked it to his notion of the object or love-object.

Let us bear clearly in mind that every human being has acquired, by the combined operation of inherent disposition and of external influences in childhood, a special individuality in the exercise of his capacity to love—that is, in the conditions which he sets up for loving, in the impulses he gratifies by it, and in the aims he sets out to achieve in it. This forms a cliché or stereotype in him, so to speak (or even several), which perpetually repeats and reproduces itself as life goes on, in so far as external circumstances and the nature of the accessible love-objects permit, and is indeed itself to some extent modifiable by later impressions. Now our experience has shown that of these feelings which determine the capacity to love only a part has undergone full psychical development; this part is directed towards reality, and can be made use of by the conscious personality, of which it forms part. The other part of these libidinal impulses has been held up in development, withheld from the conscious personality and from reality, and may either expend itself only in fantasy, or may remain completely buried in the unconscious so that the conscious personality is unaware of its existence. Expectant libidinal impulses will inevitably be roused, in anyone whose need for love is not being satisfactorily gratified in reality, by each new person coming upon the scene, and it is more than probable that both parts of the libido, the conscious and the unconscious, will participate in this attitude.

It is therefore entirely normal and comprehensible that the libido-cathexes, expectant and in readiness as they are in those who have not adequate gratification, should be turned also towards the person of the physician. As we should expect, this accumulation of libido will be attached to prototypes, bound up with one of the clichés already established in the mind of the person concerned, or, to put it in another way, the patient will weave the figure of the physician into one of the "series" already constructed in his mind. If the physician should be specially connected in this way with the father-imago (as Jung has happily named it) it is quite in accordance with his actual relationship to the patient; but the transference is not bound to this prototype; it can also proceed from the mother- or brother-imago and so on. The peculiarity of the transference to the physician lies in its excess, in both character and degree, over what is rational and justifiable—a peculiarity which becomes comprehensible when we consider that in this situation the transference is effected not merely by the conscious ideas and expectations of the patient, but also by those that are under suppression, or unconscious. (Freud, 1959, pp. 312–314)

Late Stages of Psychoanalysis

The later stages of psychoanalytic therapy are lengthier than either the early or middle stages, for the later phases are those in which interpretation assumes cardinal significance. Interpretation, or the analyst's explanations of the patient's emotions and behavior, can occur at any stage of psychoanalysis, but regular interpretation must wait until a solid therapeutic alliance has been formed and the therapist has become familiar with the patient's personality and major unconscious conflicts. The meanings of dreams, parapraxes, resistance, and transference reactions are among the topics that psychoanalytic therapists discuss with their patients. The goal of interpretation is to provide the client with insight, defined as an intellectual and emotional understanding of the unconscious determinants of one's behavior; and then to work through these unconscious issues to strengthen the ego, loosen the restrictions imposed by the superego, and gain better control over the id. In Freudian terms, the libidinal energy consumed by the neurosis itself and the defenses that keep it out of awareness can be freed to strengthen the ego. According to Freud, the goal of psychoanalysis was "Where id was, there ego shall be . . . where superego was, there ego shall be" (*Wo Es war, soll Ich werden*, a literal translation being "Where 'it' was, 'I' shall come to be" (Freud, 1933, p. 80).

While simply talking about unconscious conflicts can lead to catharsis and an intensification of the therapeutic alliance, Freud soon discovered that it is necessary to supply the patient with emotional insight into and an opportunity to work through his or her problems by addressing the transference reactions occurring in the therapy sessions. Freud viewed offering interpretations too early in the therapeutic process as equivalent to reading a cookbook to a starving person.

Risks of Psychoanalysis

Such critics of psychoanalysis as Hans Eysenck and Jeffrey Masson, who worked for a time in the Freud archives, have argued that in addition to the theoretical problems with Freud's theories, its clinical applications have violated the Hippocratic maxim: first, do no harm. One example of the potential of psychoanalysis to damage patients, however, is the term "schizophrenogenic mother," coined by Frieda Fromm-Reichmann (1889–1957) in 1948 in an attempt to explain the origins of schizophrenia (Fromm-Reichmann, 1948). For nearly a generation, psychoanalysts made use of this term, which implied that schizophrenia is caused by a mother who placed her child repeatedly in a **double bind** (Bateson, Jackson, Haley, & Weakland, 1956), which gives the child conflicting messages from a single source. A double bind in essence forces children into a psychological dilemma in which any response they make will be considered inappropriate. For example, a mother who scolds a child for not being affectionate enough but later punishes the child for being too dependent when the child tries to kiss her would be placing the child in a double bind. Despite the complete lack of evidence that double binding causes schizophrenia, many mothers were hurt by psychiatrists who falsely fixed the blame on them.

Similarly, psychoanalysts once said childhood autism was caused by parents. Parental indifference, a cold rejecting mother, or a failure to bond between parents and children were seen as the cause of this disorder, which is now almost universally considered to result from brain dysfunction. Moreover, autistic children were treated with psychoanalysis, which is now regarded to be an ineffective form of therapy for this disorder. Others criticize psychoanalysis as being an excessively long and costly, thus causing indirect financial harm, as more direct and less expensive therapeutic approaches are available.

▣ CRITIQUES OF FREUD'S THEORIES

As Freud's theories and clinical techniques grew, so did the criticisms of his work. Some criticisms came from other physicians and others from the lay public. For example, the well-known writer Franz Kafka described psychoanalysis as follows:

> You say you do not understand it. Try to understand it by calling it illness. It is one of the many manifestations of illness that psychoanalysis believes it has revealed. I do not call it illness, and I regard the therapeutic claims of psychoanalysis as an impotent error. All these so-called illnesses, however sad they may look, are facts of belief, the distressed human being's anchorages in some maternal ground or other; thus it is not surprising that psychoanalysis finds the primal ground of all religions to be precisely the same thing as what causes the individual's "illnesses." . . . And does anyone really think this is a subject for treatment? (quoted in Szasz, 1988, p. 105)

The most common criticism of Freud's theories is that they are neither scientific nor stated in such a way that they can be tested empirically (Lynn & Vaillant, 1998; Macmillan, 1992; Webster, 2004). Some of these critics have even likened psychoanalysis to a religion (Sulloway, 1991) or secret society in which only members or initiates—in this case, researchers who have themselves been analyzed—are qualified to judge it, and that believing in its truths is a common starting point for those who wish to study it.

Is It Science?

The psychologist Hans Eysenck and the philosopher Karl Popper (1963, 1986b) have both challenged the notion that psychoanalysis meets the criteria of a science. Popper argued that for Freudian theory to qualify as a science, it should be accessible to tests constructed by others. Science cannot be based on belief or personal philosophy but must be based on evidence that others can attempt to disqualify. Popper believes that the predictions made by psychoanalysis are not predictions of overt behavior but of unseen psychological states. This reference to hidden states makes them untestable, to Popper's way of thinking. For example, Popper suggests that only when some individuals are not neurotic is it possible to experimentally determine if prospective patients are currently neurotic. He goes on to point out that because psychoanalysis holds that every individual is neurotic to some degree, it is impossible to design an experiment that would demonstrate the contrast between neurotic and non-neurotic people.

Eysenck (1986), who conducted the first study of the efficacy of psychotherapy, challenged the legitimacy of psychoanalysis based on his conclusion that it is ineffective:

> I have always taken it for granted that the obvious failure of Freudian therapy to significantly improve on spontaneous remission or placebo treatment is the clearest proof we have of the inadequacy of Freudian theory, closely followed by the success of alternative methods of treatment, such as behavior therapy. (p. 236)

Adolf Grünbaum (1923–), an eminent philosopher of science, has been a long-time cogent critic of Freudian theory. He has systematically challenged the major planks of psychoanalysis

(Grünbaum 2002, 2006, 2007): (a) its "cornerstone" that unsuccessful repression is the cause of neurosis; (b) the wish-fulfillment theory of dream-production; (c) its explanation of seemingly unmotivated bungled actions ("slips") as induced by repressed motives; (d) Freud's claim that his innovative method of clinical investigation by free association can identify the causes of neuroses, dreams, and slips; and (e) the contention that the psychoanalytic dissection of the adult patient's infantile behavior toward the analyst during treatment is the key to fathoming the pathogenesis of his/her disorder. Moreover, Grünbaum maintains that none of the evidential defects of Freud's edifice have been remedied by the post-Freudian modifications of psychoanalysis.

Photo 5.1 Adolph Grünbaum (1923–)

In Freud's view, neurotic symptoms, the manifest contents of dreams, and our various "slips" are each constructed as "compromises between the demands of a repressed [instinctual] impulse and the resistances of a censoring force in the ego" (Grünbaum, 2001, p. 106). He assumes axiomatically that distressing mental states, such as forbidden wishes, trauma, disgust, anxiety, anger, shame, hate, and guilt—all of which are unpleasurable—almost always actuate, and then fuel, forgetting to the point of repression. Thus, repression wards off negative affect by banishing it from consciousness. Grünbaum does not deny the existence of this mechanism of repression, but he objects that Freud was disingenuously evasive in handling a genuine challenge to this scenario. Thus, Grünbaum writes:

> As Freud put it dogmatically: "The tendency to forget what is disagreeable seems to me to be a quite universal one" and "distressing memories succumb especially easily to motivated forgetting." Yet he was driven to concede that "one often finds it impossible, on the contrary, to get rid of distressing memories that pursue one, and to banish distressing affective impulses like remorse and the pangs of conscience." Furthermore, he acknowledged that "distressing things are particularly hard to forget." Thus, some painful mental states are vividly remembered while others are forgotten or even repressed. Yet Freud's account is vitiated by the fact that factors *other than* the degree of their painfulness determine whether they are remembered or forgotten. (Grünbaum, 2001, p. 107)

Furthermore, Grünbaum points out that Freud explicitly failed to come to grips with this very damaging fact, when he tried to parry it, declaring: "Mental life is the arena and battleground for mutually opposing purposes [of forgetting and remembering]. . . . there is room for both." Finally, Grünbaum contests in depth the popular notion that psychoanalytic insight is curative.

Challenging Freud's Model

It has been close to a century since Freud proposed the three-layered model of the human mind, and in that time, research has not supplied evidence to support that the psyche works in the way that Freud proposed. The same is true for Freud's structures, the id, ego, and superego. With the advent of **cognitive psychology,** however, has come a large body of work providing a more complex view of nonconscious processes. The term *nonconscious* is used here to describe mental activities that operate outside awareness, in contrast to the term *unconscious,* which implies a dynamic Freudian process.

Over the course of the last few decades, the trend in psychology has largely shifted from a behavioral paradigm to one of cognitive information-processing. Within this paradigm, researchers have moved toward both an acceptance and a new understanding of nonconscious thinking. Nonconscious processing has been shown to play a role in such aspects of our being as emotions, perception, attribution of meaning (Marcel, 1983a, 1983b), and *learning* (Reber, 1967). Exploring the development of this work will facilitate understanding of how recent research and thinking stand in contrast to Freud's models.

Ulric Neisser (1928–), a professor who published the first text on cognitive psychology in 1976, coined the term **preattentive processes** to describe those mental functions that occur without the subject's conscious attention.

The **Stroop effect**, a color-word task, is a classic example of this phenomenon. John R. Stroop (1897–1973), a psychologist in Tennessee, described the effect that bears his name in his doctoral dissertation, completed in 1935. Stroop noted that when individuals are asked to name the colors of the words in a chart similar to the one in Figure 5.1, they would often read the word itself rather than naming the color of its letters. Psychologists generally believe that the processing of lexical (word-related) information becomes automatic and preattentive in the sense that it has ceased to require conscious attention. In contrast, the naming of the colors of words is unusual, making it effortful and demanding conscious mental processing on the subject's part. More recently, the term *preattentive* has largely been dropped in favor of terms like *nonconscious* or *automatic* to describe mental activities that require little or no conscious awareness to complete.

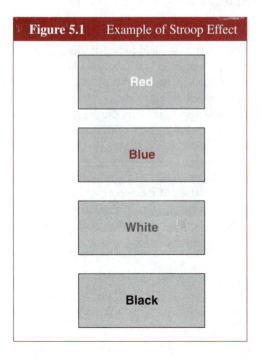

Figure 5.1   Example of Stroop Effect

Red

Blue

White

Black

For example, people are quite capable of accumulating information about the frequency of events without conscious effort or attention; that is, they learn it nonconsciously. If people are asked a question like "Have you seen more German shepherds or cocker spaniels in your neighborhood?" they will usually deny any conscious knowledge about what dogs they may have seen recently but tend to be accurate when asked to guess. Hasher and Zacks performed extensive research into this phenomenon (Hasher & Zacks, 1979; Zacks, Hasher, & Sanft, 1982), and have provided evidence that people acquire information about the frequency of events without conscious effort and without being conscious that they have even done so. In fact, this automatic ability to acquire information about the frequency of events is largely independent of age, education, emotional state, and effort. In one early study, Hasher and colleagues (Hasher, Goldstein, & Toppino, 1977) presented a list of 48 words to elementary students in Grades 2, 4, and 6. They then presented the same word list to college students. The participants were given word lists to study in which the words were presented from one to four times. In addition, the subjects were randomly assigned to one of two instructional groups. The first group was told that they should study the frequency of the words because they would be tested on that. The second group was not informed that they would be tested on the frequency of the words. After the participants had completed the study period, they were given a new word list and asked to measure how often the words in this second list had appeared in the study list. The new list contained all of the words in the study list plus 10 words that had not appeared. The results revealed that all subjects irrespective of age or instructional set (to study or not study frequency) did well in estimating the frequency of the words.

Implicit Learning

Arthur Reber, a professor of psychology at Brooklyn College, originated the expression **implicit learning** to describe "the process by which knowledge about the rule-governed complexities of the stimulus environment is acquired independently of conscious attempts to do so" (Reber, 1989, p. 219). In other words, Reber proposed that people have the ability to nonconsciously learn the relationships or rules of complex events that they encounter in daily life. To provide evidence of implicit learning, Reber and other psychologists developed artificial grammars based on rules similar to those set forth in the schematic shown in Figure 5.2. Letter strings generated from such rule systems were first presented to participants in the learning phase of experiments. The subjects were not informed that these letter strings exemplified a complex set of rules. They were, however, able to classify new letter strings as to whether or not the strings were formed according to these grammatical rules despite little conscious insight into the rule structure.

Subsequent researchers have demonstrated that implicit learning plays a crucial role in such basic human functions as language acquisition and the development of social and motor skills (Gomez & Gerken, 1999; Reber, 1992, 1993). Reber and his colleagues have proposed that conscious or explicit learning is an ability that humans acquired relatively late in their evolutionary history. In contrast, implicit learning, which occurs without consciousness, is thought to be a phylogenetically older form of learning that operates in organisms that have no conscious awareness (Reber, 1992; Reber & Squire, 1994). Evidence for the earlier development of implicit learning has been compiled through studies that showed that implicit learning is operative in people despite differences in age, neurological illness, psychological disorders, or basic intelligence level (Abrams & Reber, 1988; Reber, 1992; Reber, Walkenfeld, & Hernstadt, 1991).

A parallel line of research has been developed by the neurologist and neuroscientist António Damásio. Damásio's research into the role of emotions in cognition has led him to conclude that most models of human information-processing lack this important component. The emotional centers of the brain, according to Damásio, acquire frequency-related information that guides our decisions. He points out that people face a constant barrage of information through all five senses that far exceeds the capacity of consciousness. Damásio's research (Bechara, Dámasio, & Dámasio, 2003; Bechara, Dámasio, Dámasio, & Anderson, 1994; Holmes, 2004) suggests that decisions made in almost every situation require input from the emotional centers in the limbic system of the brain, feedback that is nonconscious and nonverbal but vital. These emotional memories are also acquired nonconsciously through automatic frequency associations. For example, a person who has gambled intermittently

Figure 5.2   Example of Artificial Grammar in Implicit Learning

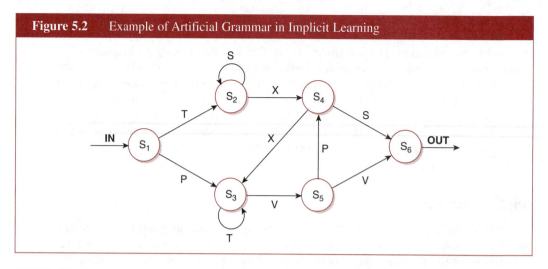

NOTE: In this schematic, grammar strings are produced by following any path of arrows leading from the initial State 1 to the terminal State 6. The following are the five basic strings in this grammar with the loops or recursions in brackets: 1. T[S]XS; 2. T[S]XX[[T]VPX]VV; 3. T[S]XX[[T]VPX]VPS; 4. P[[T]VPX]VV; 5. P[[T]VPX]VPS.

across many years with very poor outcomes may not have any conscious awareness of his actual gambling performance. According to Damásio, the man's emotional centers will store the negative affect associated with gambling so that thinking about doing it again will result in an uncomfortable or uneasy feeling. This hypothesis makes a great deal of sense from an evolutionary perspective, as our precognitive progenitors would benefit from a mechanism guiding them to avoid situations that had caused fear or pain.

Damásio (1995) demonstrated the way in which emotional guidance works nonconsciously in a study using a card game. In this study the participants were asked to sit in front of four decks of cards labeled A, B, C, and D. The players were each given a loan of $2,000 in play money that looked genuine and instructed to try to lose as little of their stake as possible while trying to win as much money as they could.

The game involved turning over cards one at a time from any of the four decks until the experimenter told the participants to stop. The subjects were not informed how many card turns they would be allowed. They were also told that most card turns would result in winning some money but that certain others would result in paying a fine to the experimenter. The subjects were given no other information about the amounts to be won or lost. The participants were encouraged to learn the best strategy to win the most money. An important feature of the experiment was that the four decks differed markedly in their payouts. Some of the decks contained cards with bigger payouts but also held cards with very large fines.

The participants in the study consisted of two groups of people; the first group were healthy subjects, while the second included people who had suffered prior damage to the ventromedial prefrontal lobes of the brain. Despite the complexity of the card payout system, the intact participants generally discovered the correct strategy to maximize their rewards. The participants with damage to the frontal lobes of their brains, however, would almost always persist in a strategy that would be profitable in the short run but cause losses in the

| Table 5.1 | Damásio's Gambling Experiment | | | |

Variables	Deck 1	Deck 2	Deck 3	Deck 4
Reward	$100	$100	$50	$50
Probability of the reward	1	1	1	1
Fines	$150–350	$1,250	$25–75	$250
Average fine	$250	$1,250	$50	$250
Probability of a fine	0.5	0.1	0.5	0.5
First punishment appears at	Card 3	Card 9	Card 3	Card 10
Expected value of a card	−$25	−$25	+$25	+$25

SOURCE: Damasio, A. R. (1995). *Descartes' error: Emotion, reason and the human brain.* New York: Quill.

long run. Interestingly, the brain-damaged individuals had IQs comparable to those of the intact participants but lacked the ability to express emotions.

Damásio proposes that it is emotional feedback that helps people intuit optimal choices nonconsciously in tasks like the card game. To help the investigators examine the subjects' underlying responses, the subjects had electrodes placed on their skin to measure their galvanic response (resistance of the skin to a mild electrical current). Remarkably, the participants with intact brains began to exhibit subtle levels of emotional arousal when confronted with the decks that contained a disproportionate number of bad choices before they were able to explain their choices in words. In contrast, the participants with damaged prefrontal lobes were never able to master the card game despite normal intelligence; moreover, they never showed any significant level of emotional arousal when facing bad choices.

Nonconscious Processes

The notion of nonconscious automatic processes has grown with the development of cognitive psychology (e.g., Anderson, 1985; Erdelyi, 1985; Lachman, Lachman, & Butterfield, 1979). We can see the beginnings of this distinction from researchers like Broadbent (1958), who represented the conscious mind as a system with limited capacity. He suggested that the role of consciousness is to filter out the less relevant stimuli from the sensory barrage that we encounter at all times. An example of such filtering would be a parent's ability to detect his or her child's face in a crowd of other children on a large playground. Broadbent's original model, however, did not allow for any processing of the ignored or filtered stimuli.

A classic experiment by Moray (1959) then established that the role of attention is not merely to filter out less relevant sensations or stimuli. He employed a task known as shadowing, in which subjects wearing headphones had to monitor a message that entered one ear and repeat the message back to the experimenter. While the subjects were monitoring, their names would be occasionally sounded through the headphone into the unattended ear. Rather than filtering out this stimulus, many of the subjects reported being aware that their names were sounded. Moray concluded that some subjects were able to shift attention rapidly from the attended ear to the unattended one. Other researchers (Deutsch & Deutsch, 1963; Norman, 1968) then presented evidence to show that all sensory input is monitored outside prior to reaching a person's attentional or conscious levels. The consensus was that this monitoring operates in a manner quite different from that envisioned by Freud; that is, the mind's filters do not include censors based on social standards, sexual impulses, or aggressive drives.

This research prompted others to further investigate consciousness as a system with limited capacity encompassing attended as well as unattended channels. Posner and Boies (1971) demonstrated that a task requiring little or no attention can be performed at the same time as a task that requires participants to focus or concentrate. Their research led them to conclude that attention has three components: alertness, selectivity, and processing capacity. They further concluded that while these three components of attention are related to conscious awareness, many tasks do not require all three components and therefore remain unconscious. They proposed that "conscious awareness is rather late in sequence of mental processing" (p. 407); such operations as relating sensory input to long-term memory can occur outside of consciousness.

In a related study, Posner and Snyder (1975) performed an experiment to demonstrate the functional dichotomy between automatic and attentional processes. The subjects were given priming letters that would either correctly or incorrectly cue the first letter of a letter pair. Their task was to determine as rapidly as possible whether both letters in the pair were the same or different. The primes are predictors of varying likelihoods depending on the letter. If the prime was presented rapidly before the pair of letters, the subjects' ability to determine sameness or difference was facilitated if the prime was an accurate predictor. If the predictor was incorrect, the subjects were not inhibited in their reaction time. If the subjects were presented with a long interval between the prime and the pair of letters, their reaction times tended to increase. These findings demonstrate that automatic processing occurs on two levels, one requiring some attention or consciousness, the other virtually nonconscious or preattentional. The work of Posner and Snyder also showed that conscious expectations can impair the automatic processes.

Shiffrin and Schneider (1977) demonstrated that conscious effort can indeed affect the automatic processes. In fact, their research indicated that **automaticity**—the ability to perform an action without conscious attention to minor details of the action—is acquired through conscious practice. Subjects who had practice in doing their experiments were able to monitor a large number of simultaneous sources of signals for a single target. Thus, a task that originally required conscious mediation required less and less attention as the subjects gained practice until it became entirely unconscious with virtually no central limitations. The subjects, however, still viewed the process as being consciously controlled. It is processed so rapidly in short-term memory that cognizance is not attained. An important secondary aspect of this theory is that controlled processes are required for storage in long-term memory.

Learning to operate a car or truck with a manual transmission is a typical illustration of the phenomenon of acquired automaticity. When we first begin to learn to shift gears, each step of the process is completely conscious and frequently precludes other complex tasks. When we have practice doing this, however, we can carry on a conversation, read street signs, or plan future activities while shifting gears. We may even complete a trip with little or no memory of ever shifting gears or even of driving at all. Yet, at any time, we can apply focused attention to gear shifting—for example, if we notice a hazardous condition on the roadway—and the process will become fully conscious. Automaticity exemplifies the notion that the unconscious is acquired through learning.

This point of view contrasts with Freud's idea that the unconscious contains fundamental processes unique to itself. Posner in a review (1982) of the research on automatic processes agreed that automaticity is a function of reduced demands on attentional resources. He suggested that people can monitor two channels of sensory information simultaneously because no interference occurs over the sensory channels employed, but that conscious awareness of any of the information coming across the channels imposes a drastic limit. An example might be a piano student who is playing a difficult piece from memory. The student can be aware of the feel of the keys beneath his fingers and the sound of the notes at the same time without interference, but if one of the notes sounds out of tune, it will intrude on the pianist's conscious awareness.

Cognitive psychology's support for the concept of a nondynamic unconscious has led some Freudians to use it as a basis for supporting Freud's conjectures. Other researchers (O'Brien & Jureidini, 2002) suggest that this effort is inherently ordained to fail, as they maintain that the human brain is inherently structured for nonconscious mentation in a way incompatible with Freud's models. Indeed, studies of cognition, cognitive neuroscience, and related fields have revealed that a large portion of our brains do function without conscious intermediation. Similarly, functions that are sometimes conscious, like the example of driving with a manual transmission, can operate at other times without the subject's conscious awareness. These observations differ from Freud's premises in that his dynamic unconscious had its own volition arising from developmental pressures, societal mores, and biological predispositions—premises that are essentially at odds with more recent findings. Cognitive models of nonconscious mentation depict the processes of attention, sensation, perception, memory, and related functions all interacting in a logical fashion. This picture stands in direct contrast to the Freudian notion of an irrational unconscious driven by an id.

Freud originally attempted to link hysteria and other manifestations of the unconscious to the workings of the brain in his reductionistic *Project for a Scientific Psychology* (1950; published in German in 1895 as *Entwurf einer Psychologie*). He gave up, conceding that his knowledge was insufficient to explain the brain in terms of the internal connections between two different types of neurons or nerve cells. More recent neuroscientists have provided evidence that the unconscious is an essential aspect of the structure of the human brain. This concept was cogently set forth through the work of Paul D. MacLean, who researched this issue for several decades (MacLean, 1954, 1972).

The Triune Brain

MacLean concluded that the human brain is a triune brain in that it can be anatomically and functionally divided into three distinct subbrains (see Figure 5.3), which he named the reptilian, paleomammalian, and neomammalian brains (MacLean 1977a, 1977b). MacLean observed that each of these regions has internal connections among its various structures that are more efficient than its connections to the other subbrains. The reptilian brain contains the brain stem, the midbrain, the **basal ganglia**, the **hypothalamus**, and the reticular activating system. These structures resemble the complete brains of the reptiles, our distant ancestors. In reptiles, these structures are sufficient for the tasks of learning, aggressive and defensive behaviors, and intake and reproduction (MacLean, 1985).

Figure 5.3 McLain concluded that the brain is a triune brain: divided into three subsections

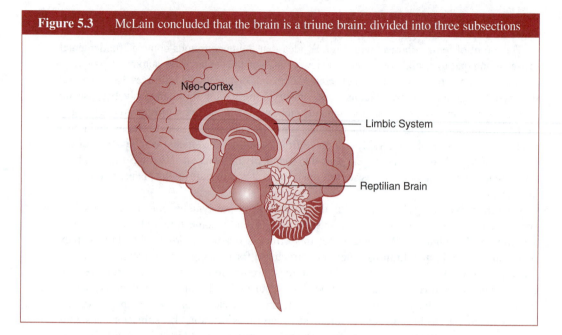

The paleomammalian brain, according to MacLean, comprises the brain's limbic system, whose name comes from the Latin word for "edge." The paleomammalian brain is a complex of brain centers that serve the role of mediating survival behaviors and the associated drives, rewards, and punishments. In other words, the paleomammalian brain is the set of structures in which we feel the delight of pleasure as well as the unpleasant sensations of hunger and the torment of pain. The paleomammalian brain regulates all of our behaviors through its ability to impose the rewards and punishments that guide our decisions. These two older subbrains, according to MacLean, contain the legacy of our distant ancestors passed down through evolution and genetic transmission. Territoriality, group aggression, courtship, mating, and socialization are all behaviors that these less conscious systems regulate. It follows that the essential qualities of human personality arise there.

This hypothesis is supported by studies of people with damage to the limbic structures of their brains, who almost invariably undergo marked personality changes. There is the famous case of Phineas Gage, a 28-year-old railroad worker in Vermont, who was injured in an accident in 1848 in which an explosion blew a 30-inch-long tamping iron through his skull; it entered through his lower left cheekbone and exited the top center of his head. Remarkably, Gage survived the accident, living for 12 years after the event. However, all who knew him reported a marked change in his personality. Originally polite and diligent, he became an impulsive ne'er-do-well who could not sustain work, was foul-mouthed and aggressive. Gage's case is usually cited as one of the earliest pieces of evidence in neurology that damage to various parts of the brain can affect personality as well as vision, hearing, and other forms of sense perception (Haas, 2001).

Animals with lesions in the limbic system tend to lose some or all of their species-specific behavior. Lesions in the amygdala are known to cause overeating and obesity in rats, dogs, mice, and monkeys (King, 2006), and damage to the hippocampus causes epileptic seizures in cats (Fatzer, Gandini, Jaggy, Doherr, & Vandevelde, 2000). Veterinarians have also discovered that certain types of anesthetics used during veterinary surgery selectively affect the limbic system in cats, dogs, and other small mammals, slowing the animals' response to signs of danger or pain. Traumatic damage to the limbic system in dogs and cats removes interest in as well as the ability to mate (Kohn, Wixson, White, & Benson, 1997).

In humans, it appears that emotional memories are mediated by limbic structures like the hippocampus and the amygdala. MacLean concluded that each subsystem of the human brain evolved as a superimposition on the older system. This evolutionary process has led to a complex brain that can be at odds with itself on occasion. The more primitive subbrains send impulses that are inscrutable or even uncomfortable to the neomammalian brain, the set of structures in which consciousness most likely has its locus.

MacLean (1954) coined the term *schizophysiology* to describe the inevitable conflicts that arise within a brain constructed of layers that are phylogenetically distinct. Such conflicts result from the fact that our verbal knowledge and moral values are stored in different areas of the brain from those that house our emotions and feelings. MacLean (1977a) referred to these internal discontinuities as "conflicts between what we feel and what we know" (p. 319). An example of this type of conflict would be the situation of a person who has gotten into an angry argument with an office coworker. He may feel like punching the colleague in the face but knows that a physical assault would cost him his job. If MacLean is right, then irrational behaviors, aggression, and sexual conflicts can be explained by the activity of a brain that contains some structures that are not always compatible with others.

Interestingly, the conflicts that Freud had described in terms of metaphors drawn from physics can be explained by the model of MacLean's triune brain, each component of which works somewhat independently. For example, a person whose limbic system is reacting to external events may experience anxiety without the person's having a conscious apprehension of the source of the anxiety. A high level of arousal would in many circumstances provide an adaptive advantage, for it would allow the person to flee more quickly when confronted with a predator or other danger. In other circumstances, stimulation of the limbic system yields only a vague anxiety that Freud interpreted as a sign of neurotic conflict.

Why did the human brain evolve in such an unsystematic manner? The reason is that at every stage in its development, the human brain had to remain functional. There was no point at which the human brain could be shut down and redesigned from scratch. New cities, or new parts of older cities whose construction was planned, are laid out in even parallel streets, while the streets of such older cities as London or Boston resemble a maze. That is because those old cities could not be torn down completely and rebuilt from scratch; rather, an already existing circuitous path had to be maintained while the newer buildings or roadways were constructed. Similarly, archaeologists often find the ruins of ancient buildings in cities like Rome or Jerusalem, whose origins go back over several millennia, when construction workers preparing the foundation of a new building or highway uncover objects that are centuries old. The human brain is something like an old city, with several layers of "streets" or "buildings" lying on top of one another.

A Network of Modules

MacLean's research has been corroborated by numerous other scientists who see the brain as a network of integrated modules that can function with varying degrees of autonomy. For example, the neuroscientist Michael Gazzaniga (1985) writes:

I argue that the human brain has a modular-type organization. By modularity I mean that the brain is organized into relatively independent functioning units that work in parallel. The mind is not an indivisible whole, operating in a single way to solve all problems. Rather, there are many specific and identifiably different units of the mind dealing with all the information they are exposed to. The vast and rich information impinging on our brains is broken up into parts, and many systems start at once to work on it. These modular activities frequently operate apart from our conscious verbal selves. That does not mean they are "unconscious" or "preconscious" processes and outside our capacity to isolate and understand them. Rather, they are processes going on in parallel to our conscious thought, and contributing to our conscious structure in identifiable ways. (p. 4)

Gazzaniga (Le Doux & Gazzaniga, 1981) proposes that many of our social judgments and behaviors take place outside consciousness as a result of background processing by specialized brain modules. Gazzaniga was instrumental in conducting much of the research into the so-called split-brain phenomenon. Based on his research with people whose **corpus callosum** has been severed, Gazzaniga went on to suggest that information may be processed simultaneously by a number of functionally isolated modular mental systems. He, like MacLean, Reber, and Damásio, believes that humans process conscious, verbally accessible information separately from information related to the emotions. Gazzaniga also theorizes that humans possess a master module that he calls "the interpreter," which corresponds to our personal consciousness. The interpreter is the "I" that we refer to in subvocal self-talk when we are reasoning about a problem. The numerous other modules in the brain are processing visual, auditory, and other sensory information largely independently of the interpreter module. Quite often, the interpreter might be so much out of the processing loop that it forms inaccurate conclusions about the information processed by other brain modules.

Such errors are dramatically exhibited in studies of individuals with split brains.[1] In one experiment, such people are seated before a computer, and a request to pick up an object is flashed rapidly on the display screen. The request is seen only on the left side of the retina as it is flashed too rapidly on the screen to allow subjects to move their eyes to scan the image across the full retina. Because the left half the retina of each eye connects to the right hemisphere (as the right half does to the left hemisphere), the message to pick up the object is relayed only to the right side of the brain, the nonverbal hemisphere. If patients are asked to "pick up the pen on the table," they will typically do so. When asked why they did so, however, they will usually explain that they decided on their own that they wanted to pick up the pen. This **confabulation**, which is an attempt to fill in a memory gap and not a deliberate lie, results from the fact that the spoken answer is generated by the verbal side of the brain—the left brain, which did not see the message and therefore cannot know why the right brain directed the person to pick up the pen.

In a similar experiment, the researcher asked a split-brain subject to point to the picture that went best with several other pictures presented on a display screen. A snow scene was presented in such a way that it could be seen only by the subject's nonverbal right hemisphere. The participant then pointed to the image of a snow shovel with his left hand—which is controlled by the right hemisphere. When the right hemisphere was presented with the snow scene, the verbal left hemisphere was shown a drawing of a chicken claw. The split-brain participant then pointed to the image of a chicken. When asked to explain why his left hand pointed to a snow shovel, the participant responded: "The chicken claw goes with the chicken and you need a shovel to clean out the chicken shed."

This experiment is typical of split-brain studies in two respects. First, research has shown that each hemisphere of the brain is able to think and act independently of the other. Second, when split-brain subjects are queried about volitional acts governed by the nonverbal hemisphere, their verbal hemisphere tends to confabulate an explanation of the act's intent or purpose. It seems as though our conscious mind dislikes any awareness of nonconscious processes.

Taken as a whole, the evidence is quite strong that nonconscious processing is an inherent feature of the human brain. The evidence is also strong that it underlies many other phenomena in psychology. For example, researchers have proposed that conflicts among the various brain modules can result in some psychopathologies (Grigsby & Schneiders, 1991). One researcher explains that nonconscious memories (Moscovitch, 1995) result from specialized brain modules that process consciously perceived events separately from those that are apprehended without awareness. As evidence for the existence of nonconscious processing in specialized brain modules, neuroscientists cite the process of facial recognition (Nachson, 1995). This hypothesis has a great deal of face validity because we all can recognize or distinguish among thousands of faces, but we cannot explain how we do it. Further, a condition known as **prosopagnosia** or face blindness can result from damage to these specialized modules. Prosopagnosia, which takes its name from the Greek words for "face" and "not knowing," is a condition in which a person loses the ability to distinguish one human face from another. Once this specialized ability is lost, no amount of conscious training can restore it.

VIGNETTE

Ian was determined to work his way out of the Brooklyn ghetto in which he had grown up. In the inner city, a student who took his schoolwork seriously was demeaned and ridiculed because studying hard was a sign of capitulation or allying with the enemy. But Ian had a singular ability to focus his attention on his studies—he resisted both the drugs and the other aspects of street life that had consumed the futures of most of his peers. Ian was strong-willed, laconic, and gifted with an ironic sense of humor that he used to slyly mock his detractors. He sometimes had to fight his opponents in the tough streets he had to traverse daily, but when he did fight, he was effective enough to be treated with caution by those who resented his resolve.

(Continued)

(Continued)

In short, Ian was an emotionally strong and single-minded young man who knew who he was and where he was going. His future became even brighter when he scored in the 96th percentile on the Scholastic Aptitude Test; he was virtually assured a scholarship to a first-tier university.

This promising future was suddenly clouded, however, by what seemed at first to be nothing more than a bad cold with a severe headache. Ian was in great pain from the pounding in his head. His grandmother, who had reared him, insisted that he go to the hospital emergency room. At first, he rejected her entreaties, but with the pain becoming unbearable, he finally agreed. After waiting nearly 4 hours, Ian was examined by a resident physician, who dismissed his symptoms as just a sinus infection. He was sent home with some pain medication and told to rest. Within 24 hours after leaving the hospital, however, Ian had an epileptic seizure and was brought back to the same hospital. He did indeed have a sinus infection—but one so severe as to have infiltrated the frontal lobes of his brain. Now his medical complaint was taken seriously, but far later than it should have been. Ian required emergency neurosurgery to relieve the pressure on his brain and remove a portion of his left frontal lobe that had been damaged by the infection.

Ian was able to leave the hospital after the surgery but continued to have seizures that could only be partially controlled by medication. But the epilepsy was not the worst of what he was facing; his personality had also been affected by the surgery. Ian, once strong and unflappable, now burst into tears when he had to deal with even slight difficulties; and even when all was going well, he was sullen and pessimistic. Reading and studying became far more difficult for him; although he was able to graduate from high school, his final grades were a big disappointment. Ian lost interest in attending college and had to be pushed to complete the forms required for him to receive disability payments. Sadly, Ian was no longer the Ian he had been before the infection. With the loss of part of his brain also went much of his will and previous personality. He was now a sullen and easily distracted young man who surprisingly failed to see the changes that had taken place in him. He reported to his doctor that he had just lost interest in the goals that used to motivate him.

The neurosurgeon who had operated on Ian had assured his grandmother that Ian would experience only slight changes in his functioning. The surgeon was wrong, however. Although the amount of tissue that had been removed was not great, it was sufficient to radically alter key aspects of Ian's personality.

Ian's case illustrates several noteworthy points about the relationship between the brain as an organ of the body and human personality. In some cases, there can be marked trauma to the brain with no personality change, while in others, small lesions can lead to radical differences in behavior and cognitive style. In both types of cases, however, the changes are rarely apparent to the affected individual.

Vignette Questions

1. What do the changes in Ian say to those who opine that personality is primarily a result of social learning?

2. Do you think that Ian will be able to recover his old personality with time?

3. Why or why not?

Reviewing the Concept of Repression

Perhaps the most important element of Freud's psychoanalytic theory is repression, the process in which unconscious censors hide or disguise memories, emotions, and impulses that threaten the conscious ego. Repression is part of Freud's earliest explanation of neurosis. He proposed that traumatic events are actively blocked from consciousness, resulting in a loss of mental energy and efficiency. The clinician's task is to help the patient uncover these repressed memories in the expectation that this recovery will unblock psychic energy and relieve the neurotic symptoms.

Recent research into the psychology of memory, however, seems to contradict Freud's premise. Despite the belief that is common even among psychologists, that memory is accurately and permanently recorded (Legault and Laurence, 2007; Loftus & Loftus, 1980) in the brain, various experiments show that memory can be readily manipulated. Roediger and McDermott (1995) presented lists of 12 words to college students and then asked them to recall the words. All the words in each list were semantically associated with a target word, known as a critical lure or a **lure word**, which was not presented. For example, one list contained words related to the word *chair*, such as *table*, *sit*, and *legs*, but the word *chair* itself was not presented. After listening to six such word lists, the students were asked to write down all the words they recalled. The critical lure, which had *not* appeared on the lists, was "remembered" 40% of the time. When the students were given a recognition test, they falsely believed that they recognized the lure words 84% of the time. In a second experiment using 15-word lists, Roediger and McDermott reported a false recall rate of 55% for the critical lures and a false recognition rate of 81%. This finding is known as the **Deese-Roediger-McDermott (DRM) paradigm**; it elegantly demonstrates how inaccurate human memory can be and how easily it can be manipulated.

Loftus and her coworkers found that people can be confident about memories that have been manipulated or changed by others. For example, people who are asked a leading question about an event will tend to have their recall of the event altered by the question. For example, if subjects are asked one of two questions after watching a film of an automobile collision, "How fast were the cars going when they smashed into each other?" or "How fast were the cars going when they hit each other?" they will tend to recall the speed of the vehicles as being higher when asked the first version of the question (Loftus, 1979a, 1979b). Loftus found that merely by changing the wording of a question, she could alter a person's recalled memories. This characteristic of human memory is important in evaluating what has been called false memory syndrome, in which a susceptible person is induced to "remember" an event that never occurred, either by hypnosis or by constant rehearsal (repeated description) of the "event" by another person.

Ceci and coworkers found that children are particularly susceptible to having false memories implanted (Ceci, Huffman, Smith, & Loftus, 1994; Ceci, Loftus, Leichtman, & Bruck, 1994). In one study, 96 preschoolers between the ages of 3 and 6 years were administered seven interviews by the experimenters. During these interviews, the children were presented with both actual events from their lives and false events fabricated by the experimenters. The children were then asked to state whether the events really happened. The results indicated that the true events were almost always accurately recalled. Slightly more than one third of the children, however, maintained that the fictitious events actually happened. According to Ceci et al., the results suggest that children can readily be misled into believing that imaginary events actually took place.

Loftus (Loftus & Pickrell, 1995) obtained similar results in a study in which participants were given short narrative descriptions of childhood events and then prompted to remember those events. The participants were told that the descriptions were all provided by family members and were true. One event, however, was actually a pseudo-event in which the subjects were told about their having been lost for an extended period of time in a shopping mall at the age of 5 or 6. They were told that they had been quite disturbed about being lost but were rescued by an elderly person who reunited them with their family. Approximately 25% of the participants stated that they recalled this event, and some even expanded the story with confabulated details. The plasticity of memory has highly significant implications for Freud's premise that the recovery of repressed memories is critical to recovery from neurosis. If people can be persuaded to recall "events" that never took place, then it is difficult to see how they can be healed by uncovering memories that had been repressed.

Challenge to Psychosexual Stages

Freud is supported in his observation of many individuals with the characteristics that he identified with an oral personality (Kline & Storey, 1977, 1978). It is doubtful, however, whether dependent, passive, or orally focused people acquire those characteristics as the result of an early fixation (Kline & Storey, 1980); likewise, for anal personalities and those associated with fixations during other stages of development. Researchers examining Freud's theory have found weak or contradictory evidence for the existence of these stages and the personality types they supposedly form.

For example, Stone and Gottheil (1975) administered a 186-item questionnaire to hospital inpatients regarding behavioral traits associated with oral and anal personalities. The data were analyzed using factor analysis, which yielded results that were weakly consistent with Freud's oral and anal personalities. Stone found that the patients with proctologic (anal) problems had factor scores closer to those of patients with digestive ulcers than to those of patients with obsessive-compulsive disorders, which Freud would have associated with anal fixations. The obsessive-compulsives were actually more similar to passive-dependent patients. Most notably, Stone found that patients suffering proctologic and obsessive-compulsive disorders were the most dissimilar of all the groups studied.

Freud assumed that people with orally fixated personalities were excessively inclined to seek pleasure through oral stimulation. This premise was not validated in a study (Keith & Vandenberg,

1974) that compared obese and normal-weight subjects, using the Dynamic Personality Inventory, a test designed to measure Freudian constructs. The author failed to find any differences between the two groups. This result is mirrored in a small study (Castelnuovo-Tedesco, 1975) that compared 12 superobese (approximately double the standard body weight) individuals with those of normal weight. The superobese were found to be mildly depressed and somewhat passive-aggressive, but they did not fit any model of the oral personality.

Torgersen (1980) studied a Norwegian sample of 99 pairs of female and male twins between the ages of 20 and 70 with no notable psychopathology. He found that hysterical traits in the female participants and oral traits in the male participants seemed to have a genetic component. This finding is not compatible with fixation as the sole basis of pathology in so-called oral personalities.

There have been fewer scientific studies of the anal personality than of the oral personality. One such study (Gottheil & Stone, 1974) looked at relationships between anal and oral personality styles in five groups of patients: those with gastric ulcers; those with proctologic ailments; those with passive-dependent personality disorders, those with obsessive-compulsive disorders and a control group. The study employed a personality questionnaire. The author found that the patients diagnosed with passive-dependent and obsessive-compulsive personality disorders received slightly higher scores on the oral and anal trait scales, respectively. Although the study weakly confirmed Freudian theory, the small sample size and the methodology made it somewhat questionable. Another researcher (Fischer & Juni, 1982) administered the Kline Anality Scale to see whether participants scoring high on Freud's anal characteristics possessed associated personality characteristics. The study found that those with high scores on anality tended to have lower levels of self-disclosure, but it found no links to self-esteem, socioeconomic status, or more significantly, to negativism (Juni, 1982).

To test Freud's premise that early fixations predispose individuals to oral or anal personalities, researchers administered the Rorschach test to 54 participants and gave them an attitude survey. The Rorschach content analyses were assumed to show fixation scores. The author concluded that the prediction of oral fixations was confirmed for females only and anal fixations for males only. Another researcher (Lewis, 1994) failed to find an association between scores of anality using the Ai3Q, which is an instrument designed to measure obsessional personality traits and anal characteristics.

Taken as a whole, the research examining Freud's predictions of distinct character types resulting from psychosexual fixations appears to yield weak or contradictory results. In fact, it seems that some personality styles can be made to fit into the Freudian constructs of oral and anal personalities. There are certainly people who are passive, dependent, and ingratiating or placating. There are people who are orderly, overly concerned with details, and stingy. And there are people who either suppress their emotions or display them flamboyantly. Recent personality research, however, provides only weak support for Freud's precise formulations of fixations and personality styles.

The Oedipal Complex Examined

Freud proposed that all infants compete with the parent of the same sex for the affections of the parent of the opposite sex. Is this hypothesis true? To date, there is no definitive evidence that it is so, but there is a body of research showing that the so-called **Oedipus complex** is not universal. Bronislaw Malinowski (1884–1942), an anthropologist who studied the Trobriand Islanders during World War I, concluded that they had a matriarchal society and experienced a very different Oedipal phase from the one that Freud described. Malinkowski observed that in the Trobriands, the father is not a figure of authority; a boy's maternal uncle is the male authority figure. Consequently, boys did not experience a paternal conflict nor the castration fears central to Freud's Oedipal crisis. The Trobriands exhibited no resulting pathologies (Malinkowski, 1929). Newman and Stoller (1971) concluded many years later that they found no evidence of Oedipal conflicts in transsexual men.

Lloyd Silverman and his colleagues (Silverman, 1978) designed experiments to provide evidence of repressed Oedipal conflicts. Silverman was testing the psychoanalytic principle of **symbiosis** (Silverman & Weinberger, 1985), which was suggested by Freud and elaborated by subsequent psychoanalysts. The concept of symbiosis holds that all people harbor strong unconscious desires to fuse with or create a state of oneness with another person, usually a parent or spouse. Psychoanalysts refer to these desires for fusion as symbiotic wishes to recreate the experience that people have with a good mother in early childhood. The technique that Silverman used in his many studies is called subliminal psychodynamic activation. It involved flashing phrases on a screen for approximately 4 milliseconds, too rapid to be consciously apprehended but long enough, according to Silverman, to stimulate unconscious thinking.

The phrases were either menacing or soothing. They included: "Beating Daddy is wrong," "Mommy and I are one," or "I am losing Mommy." In an early experiment using this paradigm (Silverman, Spiro, Weisberg, & Candell, 1969), Silverman evaluated the levels of pathology in 24 men suffering from schizophrenia. They were then presented with the subliminal phrase, "Mommy and I are one," combined with a visual image of a man and woman fused at the shoulders. They were then shown the subliminal phrase "People are thinking," along with a picture of two men who appeared to be thinking. Finally, they were presented with the subliminal phrase "Destroy mother," along with a picture of a man attacking a woman with a knife. Silverman found that those who were presented with the phrase "Mommy and I are one" showed some reduction of pathology, whereas those who were presented with "People are thinking" showed virtually no change. Presentation of the phrase "Destroy Mommy" tended to worsen their symptoms.

Silverman's general approach was used to test college students, obese women, stutterers, and a range of individuals with and without psychopathology. The results generally showed that that the subliminal presentation of phrases that stimulated symbiosis tended to be beneficial in such ways as improving academic performance (Bryant-Tuckett & Silverman, 1984), reducing weight (Silverman, Martin, Ungaro, & Mendelsohn, 1978), or diminishing the frequency of stuttering (Silverman, Bronstein, & Mendelsohn, 1976). Interestingly, Silverman found that these same phrases presented superliminally, that is, consciously, did not produce any beneficial effects. The subjects benefited only when the stimulus phrase was presented subliminally or unconsciously.

The major question is whether Silverman's studies have actually substantiated Freudian theory or called it into question. First, Silverman's work with schizophrenics is problematic because schizophrenia is regarded as an organic illness of the brain as of the early 2000s, not as a result of a conflict between the id and the ego resulting from poor bonding with parents or from Oedipal conflicts. In addition, the mitigation of schizophrenic symptoms is not uniquely supportive of psychoanalytic theory because the illness follows a roller-coaster pattern of remissions and acute episodes in some patients. Silverman did, however, present evidence that information presented too rapidly to be consciously perceived can have beneficial effects in test subjects. These results are consistent with studies of cognition that demonstrate the existence of nonconscious processing of rapidly presented information (Lewicki, Hill, & Czyzewska, 1992). Thus the salient issue in relation to Freud's theory is whether people have an unconscious desire for symbiotic union with their mothers. This question was addressed by Watson (1975), who challenged the entire premise that subliminal activation is at all related to psychoanalytic theory.

Watson questioned the validity of the projective procedures used by Silverman as outcome measures and pointed out the difficulty of determining a direct relationship between Silverman's results and psychoanalytic constructs. This conceptual challenge has been extended by researchers who state that benign statements like those that Silverman presented to his subjects do no more than temporarily elevate the participant's mood (Sohlberg, Billinghurst, & Nylén, 1998). Others have simply failed to replicate Silverman's paradigm (Balay & Shevrin, 1988; Heilbrun, 1980; Malik, Apel, Nelham, Rutkowski, & Ladd, 1997; Oliver & Burkham, 1982). These researchers have performed similar experiments with populations comparable to those tested by Silverman and found no improvements after subliminal activation. Their studies have raised doubts about the significance of Silverman's findings. What is clear is that Silverman was able to demonstrate that with sufficient creativity, even the more abstract principles of psychoanalysis can be subjected to scientific testing.

▣ CHAPTER SUMMARY

Freud's influence in personality theory was explored by detailing how he linked developmental psychosexual theory to derived personality types. He proposed that life (libidinal) energy fixations—at any stage—will yield a personality type derived from the conflicts that need to be resolved at that stage. According to Freud, the developmental juncture that is most critical to personality is the Oedipal period. Here, the individual who adequately matures through this personal epoch will be endowed with a more mature and productive personality.

The clinical applications of psychoanalysis were also explored. Psychoanalytic therapy typically requires nondirective therapists whose neutral posture allows them to serve as a representation of significant individuals in the client's past. Consequently, the client will unconsciously project unto the psychoanalyst the unresolved or fixated emotions that are the basis of neurosis. The process of analysis typically involves several stages and faces emergent barriers such as anxiety and resistance, which require interpretations by the psychoanalyst to allow for successful completion of analysis.

The controversies of Freud's personality and clinical theories were enumerated. Most of these are predicated on the absence of convincing research evidence for either the clinical approach or its underlying psychoanalytic explanation of personality.

Recent research into the cognitive unconscious was presented as a contrast to psychoanalytic views of unconscious mentation. The current view of the cognitive unconscious sees the mind as automatically processing information outside of awareness as a fundamental and normal aspect of the human brain. Nonconscious cognition appears to serve the adaptive role of supplementing the brain's limited capacity when consciously processing information.

◨ NOTE

1. Split-brain patients are people who have received surgery that severed their corpora callosa (the bundle of fibers connecting the right and left hemispheres of the brain) in order to treat seizure disorders. This procedure leaves the two hemispheres with minimal means of communication, virtually creating two separate brains.

Chapter 6

Freud's Followers

Chapter Goals

- Examine Alfred Adler's and Carl Jung's contributions to personality theory and contrast to those of their mentor, Sigmund Freud
- Explore the theoretical or personal issues that led to their break with Freud
- Look at controversies regarding each of their theories
- Evaluate their current relevance to psychology and mental health

Freud himself was afraid to the point of obsession that others might revise his ideas. Which of his ideas came most frequently under attack, even by those who would consider themselves his intellectual heirs? Libido, the life energy that powers the psyche, is entirely sexual; the ego is merely "the clown in the circus"; and the idea that people have spiritual needs is simply "the mud of occultism" and stems from our basest parts.

Alfred Adler and Carl Gustav Jung started out as the two crown princes in the Freudian kingdom, then rebelled to create their own realms. What was the source of their problems with Freud beyond simply not wishing to stand in his shadow? Their essential disagreement with Freud stems from the answer to the seemingly simple question, "Are human beings reasonable?" For Freud, rationality was not a birthright but a battle, a lifelong struggle, a combat waged with limited resources and no help from spiritual powers. Reason is a balancing act precariously maintained over an abyss of darkness, he thought. Freud was a rationalist but recognized the fragility of human reason. Even so, he maintained that "the voice of the intellect is a soft one, but it does not rest until it has gained a hearing" (Freud, 1928, p. 93).

Adler and Jung, in effect, each took one aspect of the rationality question. For Adler, the battle for reason is only a sham conflict because being reasonable is no problem. Rather, the central issue of life is the ability to express an interest in society. Jung can be pictured as raging against this very question: "Reason! Reason! That is the Western sickness! Let the power of

unreason envelop us!" Jung believed in the autonomy of the human psyche, meaning that he considered thoughts and fantasies to be independent events; he said they must be allowed freedom from the constraints of reason. Therapy for Jung was thus a conversation with and freeing of the unconscious, the true source of human creativity. The chapter begins with these two, then looks at the neo-Freudians.

⊞ CARL GUSTAV JUNG

Carl Gustav Jung was born in Switzerland in 1875, 19 years after Freud. He was the son of a poor country pastor who eventually suffered from clinical depression and of a mother with her own set of emotional problems. By Jung's own account, his childhood was lonely, psychologically stressful, and unhappy. He was 9 years old when his younger sister was born, meaning that she was too young to be a playmate or companion when he needed one to ease his loneliness. Jung's father was a pastor of the Swiss Reformed Church who was sometimes moody and irritable but nonetheless took care of the child when Jung's mother, Emilie, was hospitalized. Jung later said that for him, *father* implied two characteristics: reliability on the one hand and powerlessness on the other (Bair, 2003, p. 21; Jung 1961, p. 8).

Emilie suffered from severe mood swings, exhibited erratic behavior, and left the family periodically for long stays in a rest home near Basel. Jung remembered her as being able to change in an instant from a relatively normal housewife to an incoherent mystic who spoke to Carl as well as her village neighbors of mysterious spirits who visited her at night. As a boy, Jung could not understand how his mother could manifest two vastly different personalities. He later attributed his distrust of women and his association of them with unreliability with his mother's absences from the household. "I was deeply troubled by my mother's being away. From then on, I always felt mistrustful when the word 'love' was spoken" (Jung, 1961, p. 8).

From an early age, Jung was given to spending time by himself, dreaming and fantasizing. At one point, he seems to have thought he had two personalities, one a modern Swiss and the other an 18th-century man. He was prone to neurotic fainting spells that drew him into the world of his unconscious as well as causing physical injuries. On one occasion, he fell against the corner of a stove and cut his head open, an injury that left a lifelong scar (Bair, 2003, p. 21–22). He also began to play with fire, building small fires inside a hollow space that he had found inside an old wall in the garden of the family house (Jung, 1961, p. 20). Jung would continue throughout his life to make decisions based on what his unconscious told him in his dreams and on conversations he had with his unconscious. He would often talk out loud to his **anima**, the contrasexual part of his personality.

When Jung chose psychiatry as his adult profession, he was choosing a branch of medicine that was not highly respected at the time. He had originally wanted to study archaeology, but his parents could not afford to send him to any of the Swiss universities where that subject was taught. Jung settled for medicine because he could go to medical school close to home, at the University of Basel. Jung eventually developed a highly original and complex map of the human personality that might have owed something to his frustrated dreams of becoming an archaeologist. He studied Eastern religions, medieval mysticism, Egyptian mythology, alchemy, the occult, different cultures (including those of the American Southwest), his own dreams, and the dreams of his many patients to help develop his theories. Such an assortment of miscellaneous methods and sources would not be considered scientific today.

Certainly by mid-career, Jung's writings had more in common with New Age beliefs than psychology; it is not surprising that many New Age writers later thought of him as a father figure or mentor (Schwartz, 1996, p. 342, p. 350). Jung (1959c) even published a book, translated into English as *Flying Saucers: A Modern Myth of Things Seen in the Skies*, in which he speculated that reported sightings of UFOs were human psychological projections that could be picked up on radar. Most of Jung's concepts, fascinating and mythical as they may appear, have not found validation in modern psychological research. Some Jungian concepts, however, do have parallels in modern psychological theories, at least in a very broad sense.

Early Career

After completing medical school, Jung worked in a famous mental hospital near Zürich called the Burghölzli, under the supervision of a well-known psychiatrist named Eugen Bleuler. Bleuler had coined the term *schizophrenia,* or "split mind," for the psychotic disorder that still bears the name. Jung's was an intensive internship under a very demanding supervisor, and it gave Jung the opportunity to study a large number of patients with schizophrenia and other severe mental illnesses. He devised word association tests for studying the Burghölzli patients. After his internship, Jung opened a private practice that became extremely successful. He also became a lecturer at the University of Zürich. While there, he read Freud's book, *The Interpretation of Dreams*, and became interested in Freudian theory.

Jung met Freud in 1907 after starting a correspondence with the older man and sending him a copy of his book on word associations, and the two became close personally and professionally. Their first meeting lasted for 13 hours of nonstop discussion, and their relationship initially continued on that intense note. When Freud formed the International Psychoanalytic Society, he chose Jung to be its first president—a position that Jung held until 1910. Freud thought it important to elect a non-Jew to this position because many European psychoanalysts at that time were Jews, and Freud was afraid psychoanalysis would be seen as a purely Jewish movement. In addition, Jung's association with the Burghölzli hospital gave him considerable professional prestige, which in turn boosted Freud's reputation. Jung traveled with Freud to the United States in 1909, when Freud gave his famous set of lectures in September at Clark University in Worcester, Massachusetts.

Freud had hoped that Jung would be his heir apparent, carrying on and further developing his work in psychoanalysis. The actual outcome was far less pleasant. One reason may have been Jung's personality: He was the kind of person who needed to strike out on his own rather than being someone else's disciple. Another reason was theoretical: Jung disagreed with Freud on several points, most strongly regarding Freud's emphasis on sexuality as the root of all psychopathology. According to Jung,

> Freud never asked himself why he was compelled to talk continually of sex, why this idea had taken such possession of him. . . . He was blind toward the paradox and ambiguity of the contents of the unconscious, and did not know that everything which arises out of the unconscious has a top and a bottom, an inside and an outside. . . . There was nothing to be done about this one-sidedness of Freud's. Perhaps some inner experience of his own might have opened his eyes; but then his intellect would have reduced any such experience to "mere sexuality" or "psychosexuality." (Jung, 1961, pp. 152–153)

Freud was so upset and disappointed about Jung's disagreement with his theories that he actually fainted on several occasions (Jones, 1955). Ironically, there was another source of friction between the two men, and it was related to sex: Freud's disapproval of Jung's extramarital affairs with two female colleagues, Sabina Spielrein and Toni Wolff. Jung had married Emma Rauschenbusch, the daughter of one of the wealthiest families in Switzerland, in 1903; the couple eventually had five children. Emma was unhappy about her husband's affairs and threatened to divorce him on at least three separate occasions, but she accommodated herself to the situation by continuing her education and developing her own analytic practice (Bair, 2003, pp. 318–321).

"Promise me never to abandon the sexual theory. This is the most essential thing of all. . . . You see, we must make a dogma of it, an unshakable bulwark . . . against the black tide of mud . . . of occultism," Freud asked of Jung (Jung, 1961, p. 150). But when Freud thought Jung was the right man to carry on his work, he made a grave error, proving that even a great psychiatrist could completely misjudge someone else's character. Ultimately, Freud and Jung turned out to have very little in common except the German language and their medical training. Freud was a rationalist who described himself as an atheist Jew, whereas Jung— after Hitler came to power in the 1930s—sought to free the irrational Aryan barbarian that he saw lurking in the psyche of the German people from the bonds of Enlightenment rationality.

Jung's school of thought came to be known as **analytical psychology**. Jung described the structure of human personality as a complex network of interacting systems, some conscious and many unconscious, but all seeking balance and harmony. The goal of psychotherapy from Jung's perspective is to allow the person to achieve self-realization. Jung's writings about self-realization can be traced back to Aristotle, who proposed the concept of a *telos*, a purpose or goal that everything and every person has and is essential to their being. Just as, Aristotle thought, a seed has in it all the potential of becoming a mature plant of its kind, so a human has the potential to become what he or she is meant to be.

The reader should note that Jung's concept of self-realization sounds vaguely like humanistic psychology, a therapeutic movement that emerged in the late 1950s in the United States in opposition to both psychoanalysis and behaviorism. A key difference between Jung's analytical psychology and humanistic psychology, however, is that humanistic psychology emphasizes individual achievement, freedom from social rules, the importance of rights rather than duties, and each person's uniqueness; in short, it places the individual at the center. In contrast, Jung's analytical psychology entails integrating all parts of the psyche, the conscious and the unconscious, with their many independent archetypes. The archetypes are inherited unconscious thought patterns, images, or ideas that Jung thought are present in all individual psyches. Self-realization for Jung means integrating the permissible and socially

A person may not be aware of these complexes because they are unconscious, but they do affect the person's thoughts and feelings and interactions with the environment. In a Jungian analysis, the analyst helps patients become aware of their complexes, most notably through the use of word association, which will be discussed later in more detail. Jung agreed with Freud that some complexes may arise from past traumatic experiences; however, Jung placed more importance on the complexes that he saw as products of what he called the collective unconscious.

Collective Unconscious. The collective unconscious is an important component of Jung's analytical psychology that has no counterpart in Freud's system of thought. Whereas Jung saw the personal unconscious as consisting of material that was conscious at one time but has been either forgotten or repressed, he regarded the collective unconscious as an entity that has never been part of the conscious mind and, moreover, is not particular to any individual. According to Jung, the contents of the collective unconscious are common to all human beings and owe their existence exclusively to heredity. Jung wrote that humans who may belong to different races and cultures nonetheless have stored within a collective unconscious the cumulative memories of their ancestors. He thought that people of different races differ from each other because they have different racial memories (Jung, 1969). Jung also attributed coincidences to the working of the collective unconscious. On one occasion, he awoke from fitful sleep with a dull pain in the back of his head, "as though something had struck my forehead and then the back of the skull." The next day he found out that one of his patients had committed suicide by shooting himself, the bullet lodging in the back of the skull. Jung continues: "The collective unconscious is common to all; it is the foundation of what the ancients called the 'sympathy of all things.' In this case the unconscious had knowledge of my patient's condition" (Jung, 1961, pp. 138–139).

Archetypes. Jung proposed as early as 1919 that the collective unconscious is a storehouse of **archetypes,** which are prototypical images, objects, and types of people or experiences that our ancestors have encountered generation after generation. Jung (1959a) wrote,

> There are as many archetypes as there are typical situations in life. Endless repetition has engraved these experiences into our psychic constitution, not in the form of images filled with content, but at first only as forms without content, representing merely the possibility of a certain type of perception and action. (p. 48)

Jung's archetypes are akin to a blueprint or template on which our individual experiences are formed. So, for example, everyone has an innate mother archetype, a preformed or general image of a mother, which results from and summarizes our ancestors' cumulative experiences of mothers. When an infant interacts with its mother, the specific mother's characteristics fill in the details and help to fully develop the child's image of a mother.

Jung went into a great deal of detail describing certain archetypes that he considered central to the collective unconscious. Some of these are: Birth, Death, Rebirth, the Great Mother, the Wise Old Man, the Child, the Trickster, the Demon, God, Power, Magic, and the Hero. These archetypes can then combine to form complexes, such as the Hero archetype combining with the Demon archetype to yield a Ruthless Leader archetype. To give another example, if a person has many experiences surrounding religion and God, the God archetype is attached to these experiences and forms a God complex. This God complex is now no longer in the collective unconscious but has moved into the personal unconscious. Then, if the experiences that formed that God complex are powerful enough, the God complex will push its way into our personal conscious experience. A dominant God complex, or a complex around any other archetype, will have a great deal of influence on our choices, perceptions, and beliefs.

The complexes may express themselves in literary creations or other works of art. There is, for instance, a large and influential school of criticism that interprets the characters in novels, dramas, or even popular culture as examples of archetypes and complexes. For example, some critics interpret Obi-Wan Kenobi in *Star Wars* as an archetype of the Wise Old Man, while Bugs Bunny represents the Trickster, Linus in the *Peanuts* comic strip is the Child, and Batman exemplifies the Hero.

Critique of Archetypes. There are a number of objections that can be raised to Jung's notion of a collective unconscious populated by archetypes. Jung based his theory of archetypes on a now discredited theory of evolution developed by the late 18th-century French biologist Jean-Baptiste Lamarck (1744–1829). Lamarck propounded a theory about the inheritance of acquired traits known as Lamarckism. This theory holds that traits acquired (or diminished) during the lifetime of an organism can be passed on in their acquired (or weakened) form to the offspring. So, for example, if a blacksmith works hard and develops muscular arms, it is likely that his sons will also have muscular arms when they grow up. Lamarck made a logical error in that he confused correlation with causation. That is, the blacksmith's sons likely inherited their father's genes for muscular arms. Furthermore, if they joined their father in his trade, their arms were likely to become well-muscled from the physical effort involved in forging iron. But their father's actual experience with blacksmithing had no way of affecting his genetic composition, and thus it would not be passed on to his sons.

There is no mechanism consistent with what is known about heredity that would explain how our ancestors' experience with mothers, children, life and death, journeys, heroic achievement, and magic would be transmitted from one generation to another. It is certainly the case that most human beings encounter comparable or similar situations in life. People are born; reared by parents or parental figures; educated; encounter various physical, emotional, and spiritual challenges in life; and face the finality of death. People whose lives may depart from this pattern for one reason or another often encounter this common stock of experiences through art or literature. The general pattern offers sufficient explanation for why people come to develop powerful feelings about their mothers, fathers, children, religion, life tasks, and the like. Jung's addition of the concept of archetypes is not only impossible to prove, but also unnecessary in explaining human experiences and personalities.

Central Archetypes

Jung described four core archetypes that play important roles in shaping our personalities. These are the persona, the anima or animus, the shadow and the Self.

Persona. The **persona** is named after a Latin word meaning mask—the mask an actor might wear while impersonating a character in a classical drama. Shakespeare made the observation centuries ago that the world is a play and that people are all actors on the stage. Jung believed that the persona or mask that people wear to be able to fit in and carry out their social responsibilities is actually an archetype, a piece of the collective unconscious. He thought the persona is related to the collective unconscious because all people who are not psychotic must at least to some extent sacrifice the free expression of their individuality to society's requirements for appropriate behavior.

Different workplace requirements, family settings, or social positions, however, require people to put on different masks, and some situations allow them to peek through the mask more than others. For example, a corporate lawyer is expected to behave in much more standardized ways than, say, an artist. Furthermore, the same person is expected to put on different masks at work, while interacting with family, or other situations. The totality of all of our masks is called the persona.

Jung writes about the dangers of having an overdeveloped persona, wherein we might become so caught up in the role we feel must be played that the self becomes distorted. He writes about ego inflation, resulting from an overdeveloped persona. An overdeveloped persona can lead to an exaggerated sense of self-importance deriving from how well we are fulfilling our role in the community. On the other hand, feelings of inferiority, alienation, and loneliness can develop when we feel unable to live up to standards expected of us.

A critique of Jung's description of the persona can begin with the observation that the roles that all people play in society and the ways in which role-playing can affect them are valid and observable facts. Indeed, persons who refuse the roles prescribed by society will not do well in life, while those who accept socially prescribed roles without allowing themselves the freedom to be genuine in appropriate contexts will have different kinds of problems.

What is problematic about Jung's concept of the persona is his assertion that the need to wear a social mask derives from the collective unconscious. There is no empirical evidence to support or disprove the existence of a collective unconscious or of a persona within it. Furthermore, it is not necessary to appeal to the notion of a collective unconscious to explain the reality of living in a society in which people must accommodate to some of its demands in order to complete their education, enter the workforce, and start families of their own.

Anima and Animus. These terms refer to the contrasexual components of the adult personality. According to Jung, the anima represents the feminine side of an adult male. On the outside, a male may appear to have masculine characteristics, but feminine characteristics are hidden within his psyche. Conversely, a woman may look and act in a conventionally feminine way, but she also has an inner masculine component, her **animus.** The anima incorporates the man's unconscious notions of womanliness, based on his ancestors' many encounters with women in their lives. Conversely, a woman's animus is based on her ancestors' experience with men and masculinity.

Jung asserts that a man inherits his image of woman in the form of his anima, thereby unconsciously establishing standards for accepting or rejecting any specific women he may meet, depending on how well these women fit his anima. Jung writes:

> Every man carries within him the eternal image of the woman, not the image of this or that particular woman, but a definite feminine image. This image is fundamentally unconscious, an hereditary factor of primordial origin engraved in the living organic system of the man, an imprint or archetype of all the ancestral experiences of the female, a deposit, as it were, of all the impressions ever made by woman. . . . Since this image is unconscious, it is always unconsciously projected upon the person of the

beloved, and is one of the chief reasons for passionate attraction or aversion. (Jung, 1954, p. 198)

Jung proposes that healthy people should have a good balance between their masculine and feminine sides. A man who attempts to totally ignore his anima—his feminine side—may appear strong on the outside but is likely to be internally weak and submissive. A woman who attempts to be ultra-feminine and suppresses her animus will have to deal with periodic outbursts of anger and aggression as well as unconscious qualities of stubbornness and willfulness.

One obvious criticism that can be leveled against Jung's descriptions of feminine and masculine qualities is that Jung showed himself to have a poor view of femininity. He wrote that a man's anima leads him to feel attracted to all that is vain, helpless, uncertain, and unintentional in women. He attributed this low view of women to his difficult relationship with his mother. On the other hand, a woman's animus draws her to heroic, intellectual, artistic, or athletic men. Women's consciousness is characterized by the ability to enter into relationships, whereas men's consciousness is geared toward rational and analytical thinking. Despite Jung's allowing that each person has some characteristics of the opposite sex inside him or her, he was nevertheless quite rigid in his opinion regarding overstepping our boundaries in behaving too much like a member of the opposite sex.

The main problem, however, arises from Jung's assertion that the anima and animus are inherited. Here again he made the Lamarckian error—namely, that our ancestors' lived experiences became part of their genetic material, were transmitted through the human genome, and then formed a world of experiences to which we cannot gain full access, as they are part of our collective unconscious. Given what is known about genetics and the functioning of the brain in the early 21st century, this notion of hereditary transmission of experience cannot be proved.

Shadow. Whereas the anima and the animus are unconscious forces that affect our adult relationships with members of the opposite sex, the shadow is an unconscious archetype that affects our relationship with members of our own sex. It is also the stimulus of behaviors that we consider atypical of our better selves. For example, if a normally budget-conscious person goes on a wild spending spree, Jung would attribute that act to the person's shadow. Jung proposed that the shadow is our dark side, containing all our uncivilized and disowned raw urges and desires. He describes it as having deep roots in our evolutionary history and being the most powerful and dangerous of all the archetypes. It contains violent and uncontrolled animal spirits. We must work on taming our shadow in order to be able to live in a community. The ego—the conscious mind—must develop a strong persona in order to set limits to the shadow's urgings.

On the other hand, however, Jung also maintains that the shadow must not be fully suppressed, lest the person come to lead a shallow and spiritless life. It is a necessary tool in the process of individuation. The shadow supplies zest, vitality, and pleasure in life as well as some wisdom from its instinctual nature when it is properly managed. The struggle to find a balance between the shadow's desires and society's demands is constant, as the shadow never relents in asserting its will.

Jung's concept of the shadow does present difficulties, however. We have all been able to observe in ourselves and in others the very human tendency to drop our social mask or persona and do what feels good at the time. The ability to control these urges is critical to survival in a community. Another problem with Jung's concept of the shadow is that it became a vehicle for his racist ideas. At one point, Jung described his experience of North African culture as "an unexpectedly violent assault of the unconscious psyche . . . an ethnic shadow . . . the first hint of 'going black under the skin,' a spiritual peril which threatens the uprooted European in Africa to an extent not fully appreciated" (Jung, 1961, p. 245). In another instance, he explained his interest in the Pueblo Indians of the American Southwest as a desire to explore "the cultural consciousness of the white man . . . by descending to a still lower cultural level" (Jung, 1961, p. 247).

Self. The archetype of the self represents the totality of our personality. It is the central archetype of the collective unconscious, the organizing principle of an individual's personality, and a stimulus toward unity and wholeness. For Jung, the ego was the organizer of consciousness; thus, it is inevitably one-sided. The self, on the other hand, is the organizer of our total being (Jung, 1946). In Jung's own words, "The self is by definition always a *complexio oppositorum* [collection of opposites]" (Jung, 1954/2002, p. 133).

Jungian Psychotherapy

Unlike Freud, Jung (1959b) believed that "the doctor must emerge from his anonymity to give an account of himself, just as he expects his patients to do" (Vol. 16, p. 23). The therapist is not to be a blank slate onto which patients can project their neuroses. Furthermore, the therapist must be emotionally healthy and demonstrate high ethical standards to be successful.

> The art of psychotherapy requires that the therapist be in possession of avowable, credible, and defensible convictions which have proved their viability, either by having resolved any neurotic dissociations of his own or by preventing them from arising. A therapist with a neurosis is a contradiction in terms. (quoted in Masson, 1988, p. 154)

The ironic contradiction is that although Jung did possess a great many strongly held beliefs and convictions, he was biased against the majority of human beings. He had negative views—which he made known in his writings and his speeches—of women, Jews, blacks, and Asians. Jung has been quoted as supporting colonialism in South Africa and lamenting the hardships of the white settlers: "in South Africa, the Dutch, who were at the time of their colonizing a developed and civilized people, dropped to a much lower level because of their contact with the savage races" (quoted in Masson, 1988, p. 155–156). In another instance, Jung was commenting on the sexual repression that Freud described among his patients when he wrote:

> The causes for the [sexual] repression can be found in the specific American Complex, namely in the living together with lower races, especially the Negroes. Living together with barbaric races exerts a suggestive effect on the laboriously tamed instinct of the white race, and tends to pull it down. (quoted in Masson, 1988, p. 156)

How could Jung possibly help a non-Caucasian client while he held such views? Fortunately for his patients, Jung's clientele was almost exclusively white. On the other hand, he also had very specific and traditional ideas about women, and most of his clients were women. As late as 1955, when more enlightened ideas had been put forth by others, Jung wrote, "a home is like a nest—not enough room for both birds at once. One sits inside, the other perches on the edge and looks about and attends to all outside business" (Jung, 1977, p. 244). Noting a change in women's roles toward the end of his life, Jung wrote, "I asked myself whether the growing masculinization of the white woman is not connected with the loss of her naturalness . . . whether it is not a compensation for her impoverishment" (Jung, 1963/1983, p. 216).

One wonders how helpful Jung was to women patients who were unhappy sitting inside their "nests." Did he endeavor to persuade them that they were misguided and "compensating for their impoverishment"? Given Jung's premise that much of our motives are unconscious, as long as the patient accepted this premise, she had nowhere to stand to legitimize her feelings.

An example of Jung's imposing his own standard set of interpretations on a female patient's dream is as follows: A 25-year-old female client of Jung's, whom he characterized as argumentative—perhaps for not agreeing with him—had a "most singular fantasy of a quite unimaginable erotic adventure that surpassed anything I had ever come across in my experience. I felt my head reeling, I thought of nymphomaniac possession, of weird perversions, of completely erotic fantasies" (Jung, 1966, p. 331–332). Jung was convinced, and worked hard at convincing his patient, that this dream symbolized her wish to get married. Jung accounted for the dream's strong sexual content by the influence of this woman's childhood nanny, a native of the West Indies.

Jung also had very specific ideas about the problems of people in midlife:

> Among all my patients over thirty-five—there has not been one whose problem in the last resort was not of finding a religious outlook on life. It is safe to say that every one of them fell ill because he had lost that which the living religions of every age have given their followers, and none of them has been really healed who did not regain his religious outlook. (Jung, 1933, p. 244)

It takes quite a leap of imagination to maintain that everyone over 35 is in need of religious guidance—some are and some are not—but this generalization is what Jung offered his patients. He attributed the healing of the portion of his patients who did get better to overcoming a religious crisis. Yet, for the many clients who had other issues with which they needed help, the causes of improvement or lack thereof may have had nothing to do with religion. Ironically, Jung himself never attended church services as an adult, retaining his membership in the Reformed Church only as a technicality (Bair, 2003, p. 321).

Jung believed that he was not a theoretician but rather a scientist in search of facts. Jung, however, used data that do not belong to the realm of science, such as occult séances, to help understand his clients. Not only did he put a great deal of stock in his patients' dreams to help understand their personalities, but also he used his own dreams about the client in the course of this analysis. On one occasion, he used a dream he had about a female patient who was a completely secular Jew to try to convince her that she had "the makings of a saint." Jung dreamed that his patient had come to a reception at his house, noticed that it was raining, and asked him for an umbrella. He handed her an umbrella "on my knees, as if she were a goddess." He then commented,

> The dream had showed me that she was not just a superficial little girl. . . . She knew only the intellect and lived a meaningless life. In reality she was a child of God whose

destiny was to fulfill his secret will. I had to awaken spiritual and religious ideas in her, for she belonged to that class of human beings of whom spiritual activity is demanded. (Jung, 1961, pp. 139–140)

Synchronicity and the *Numinosum*

Jung did not believe that cause and effect, which are central to scientific analysis, could explain all of human behavior. They could, therefore, not explain psychic phenomena. Thus, Jung introduced the concept of **synchronicity,** which allowed him to ascribe underlying patterns to temporal coincidences. Meaning emerges in the pattern of events only when we go beyond the Western "blindness" that requires causes to occur before events, he thought. For Jung, events fall into patterns that cut across the concepts of antecedent and consequent or the Western notion of time as linear. At one point in the early 1950s, Jung hired four different astrologers to interview accident victims—particularly those who had been involved in motor vehicle accidents—to find recurrent patterns between the patients' horoscopes and the timing of their accidents. He seemed to think that this research would demonstrate the existence of synchronicity. Thus, Jung did not believe that human personality has a cause in the Western sense of that word; rather, it exhibits patterns that are not bound by time and logic. For Jung, the mind is not a physical entity, and the essence of humanity is not bound by the laws of physics or the physical world.

In contrast to Jung, Freud was a materialist who did not regard people as having any spiritual needs. He perceived the spiritual dimension of life to be "the black mud of occultism," as he put it (Jung, 1961, p. 150). While Freud—and Adler, too, for that matter—were materialists, Jung was a spiritualist, incorporating some of humanity's most primitive beliefs with his own unique brand of spiritualism. Although Jung had been Freud's hand-picked successor at one point, he split from Freud in part over the issue of the content of the unconscious. While Freud believed that the unconscious contains repressed sexual material, for Jung, as we have seen, it holds inherited communal memories. Jung theorized on the basis of his own experience that it also contains religious belief.

For Jung, the ego can identify with a potent complex, with the personality under direction by the unconscious. This power under which the individual falls is the "big image," the so-called **numinosum.** The numinosum, which could be defined as a center of authority and value within humans that allows for the emergence of a religious attitude toward life, manifests itself through archetypes that are sacred and eternal. Unfortunately, the numinosum that became Jung's center was nothing other than Nazism. "There is no question but that Hitler belongs in the category of the truly mystic medicine man. . . . So you see, Hitler is a medicine man, a form of spiritual vessel, a demi-deity" (Jung, 1939, quoted in Masson, 1988, p. 106).

Jung fell into a trance in which he had a vision that an Aryan god existed within him; that he was the Aryan Christ, with the truth to give the select (Noll, 1997). Jung became president of the International General Medical Society for Psychotherapy, formed by a group of German analysts in the 1920s. In the early 1930s, however, the society was subverted by those among its members who were in sympathy with Hitler, and it redefined its task as separating true Aryan psychology from Jewish subhuman psychology. After the war, Jung justified his acceptance of the presidency of the society by maintaining that he did it only to "save" psychology. Jung did not think the life of a "people" differed from the life of an individual.

As has already been noted, Jung was a racist. Jung was more than just simply extremely racist; for Jung, it was the race that existed, not the individual. The term *race* for Jung had a broad meaning, encompassing culture as well as the physical characteristics usually associated with racial differences. For Jung, the ancient pagan gods of Europe were just as much a part of the European race as skin color or the shape of skulls.

Ironically, while Jung's work is often used in the early 2000s as a springboard to the study of yoga or Zen Buddhism, Jung was in actuality opposed to both practices for a European, because both yoga with its great control over consciousness and Zen Buddhism with its attunement to unconscious promptings were neither meant for nor appropriate for the European unconscious, he thought.

Europeans must find their own way, he said, not one transplanted from another historical or cultural tradition. Jung became convinced during the 1930s, however, that an upheaval from the unconscious was about to end the one-sided materialism of Western society, and the glorious Aryan barbarian would rise again. And Jung would be the prophet, the messiah to unleash the "magnificent beast."

Jung saw Christianity as a "foreign growth" that cut the *Volk* away from the ancient Germanic gods and thus from their collective unconscious. For this reason, "the Germanic man is still suffering from this mutilation. We must dig down to the primitive in us, for only out of the conflict between civilized man and the Germanic barbarian will there come what we need: a new experience of God" (Jung, letter to Oskar Schmitz, quoted in Noll, 1997, p. 264).

Jung believed that the vast majority of mental illnesses are due to the disintegration of consciousness caused by the invasion of the contents of the unconscious. In other words, emotions are not willfully produced by people but just happen to them. "I don't know what came over me" is thus literally the case. People are most in danger of being taken over by the collective unconscious when an archetype no longer has a symbol through which it can express its meaning in a conscious form and give balance to the personality, Jung thought. Symbols have a very important function in mental health. They occur in all societies, for they are like bridges between the conscious and unconscious parts of the psyche, and thus there are similarities among the symbols from very different cultures.

Jung saw the self as the striving for wholeness manifesting an archetype that is expressed in all ways and through sensing, intuition, emotions and rationality. Rationality is only a small part of the human self, distorted by Western society to occupy a greater place than it should. Western man is consequently cut off from the magnificent barbaric animal within, Jung said, and, of course, Nazism freed the magnificent barbarian.

To achieve unity and wholeness, Jung thought, people must become increasingly aware of the collective unconscious. The main strategy of therapy in Jung's analytic psychology is to engage the unconscious in the therapeutic encounter in order to bring it to the fore. This approach permits the individual to face aspects of the self that have previously been suppressed, and therefore to integrate them within the self. If people can gain access to the dark, previously prohibited parts of the psyche, then they can accept them and assimilate them. To accomplish this assimilation, Jung believed that the unconscious complex must be viewed as a separate personality to be debated. Analytical treatment is, thus, a conversation with the unconscious (Jung, 1939).

Jung's Legacy

Jung's most enduring legacy is found in contemporary popular culture. Some of his work can be read as a preview of the current obsessions of pop culture, such as UFOs, superheroes, astrology, tarot cards, ESP, and "spooky" coincidences—and it lends them a gloss of academic responsibility. Jung, in fact, used patients' horoscopes and other parapsychological techniques, including the *I Ching,* a classical Chinese system of divination, as ways of amplifying the voice of the unconscious and breaking the hold of everyday rationality. The reader should recall that dream interpretation is one of the weaker aspects of classical Freudian theory. Jung, however, took dream interpretation to new heights. To him, dreams are more than the working out on an unconscious level through symbolism what the dreamer could not admit to conscious recognition. Rather, Jung saw dreams as the source of spiritual insight from what he called the inner "superior man"—who knows all the answers. Unfortunately, Western culture's emphasis on rationality cuts off the voice of the inner superior man in our daily functioning.

Jung is certainly held in higher regard outside the field of experimental psychology. His ideas have been taken up by writers of artistic and literary criticism—and in those fields, he is a true rival to Freud. Jung's concept of archetypes and his theories about dream analysis, gleaned from such various mythological sources as the Tibetan *Book of the Dead,* set the stage for Joseph Campbell, who was known for such popular books as *The Hero with a Thousand Faces* as well as television documentaries. Campbell's work was dependent on Jung, while Campbell in turn influenced the creation of such contemporary myth-dependent fantasies as the *Star Wars* series. Jung's concept of the collective unconscious has become a staple of such works of science fiction as the *Dune* novels and *Babylon 5.*

Experimental Testing

Experimental testing of Jung's theories has been limited by the nature of the theories themselves. Jung's ideas were far-ranging and subjected to constant revision, with no consideration of making concepts amenable to operational definition and a pronounced hostility to the possibility of illuminating the human situation through experimentation.

The one aspect of Jung's theory that is amenable to scientific analysis, namely his distinction between introversion and **extraversion,** has been extensively and successfully investigated, although not through reliance on Jung's methods or theories. A popular current personality test, the Myers-Briggs Type Indicator (MBTI), assigns test subjects to 1 of 16 categories based on three other dichotomies (sensation/intuition, thinking/feeling, and perception/judgment) in addition to Jung's introversion/extraversion distinction. The MBTI (Briggs & Briggs, 1995) is commonly used in career counseling, workplace team building, life coaching, and personal development. Many academic psychologists, however, regard the instrument as lacking convincing validity data (Hunsley, Lee, & Wood, 2004, p. 65).

With regard to research technique, Jung made use of word association as a way to tap into a client's personal unconscious and psychic complexes, although he modified standard word association techniques to fit his theory of complexes. His usual approach to the study of the collective unconscious, however, was his own dreams and visions as well as mythology, ranging from Native American, Indian, and African legends to the classical mythologies of ancient Egypt, Greece, and Rome. Jung claimed that the specific hallucinations of psychotic patients could be found in ancient mythologies, and as the patients had not learned such mythologies, their visions must have reflected the collective unconscious.

The best-known instance of Jung's fascination with such patients was Emile Schwyzer, the so-called "solar phallus man," who suffered from psychotic delusions in which he saw the sun as having a gigantic phallus that he himself could control, causing it to move from side to side and produce the wind and other weather phenomena. When Jung came across a book about ancient rituals published in 1910 that described a "tube hanging down from the sun" that produced the wind, he assumed that Schwyzer—who could not possibly have read this particular book—had somehow derived the image of the sun with a phallus from a collective unconscious (Bair, 2003, pp. 171–190).

🔲 ALFRED ADLER

Alfred Adler, like Jung, started out as one of Freud's followers, and like Freud, he was an Austrian. Born the second child of a middle-class Jewish family in 1870, he received his M.D. from the University of Vienna in 1895. Interestingly, Adler specialized in ophthalmology before he became a psychiatrist. One of the charter members of the Vienna Psychoanalytic Society, Adler broke with Freud in 1911 because of his disagreements with some of the principles of classical psychoanalysis. In 1912, Adler founded his own group, which he called the Society of Individual Psychology.

Image 6.3　Alfred Adler (1870–1937)

Adler emphasized in his work that individuals are shaped by social and familial factors rather than by innate instincts (Freud) or unconscious archetypes (Jung). Feeling weak and inept during his own childhood, Adler concluded that everyone feels inferior to others because all humans are born weak and helpless and initially totally dependent on their caregivers for survival. This feeling of inferiority prompts people to strive for superiority by way of compensation, which is the basic mode they adopt in interacting with the world. According to Adler, everyone pursues this same basic goal but takes different routes, which determine each person's style of life and are set by age 5.

The style of life is reflected in the three major areas of life—sex and marriage, school and employment, family and social relationships. People must also develop a wider social interest, however, demonstrated in their contributions to society. Adler thus did not posit a distinction between the conscious and unconscious parts of the mind; moreover, he did not emphasize the intrapsychic phenomena that play such a large part in Freudian theory. He was more concerned with interpersonal relationships and an individual's behavior in the social world. Holding as he did that people are primarily social beings, with sexuality playing a subordinate role, Adler's break with Freud was ostensibly over the importance of sexuality. The major reason for the break, however, was Adler's own striving for superiority and refusal to subordinate himself to Freud.

Adler was the second of six children, sickly from birth and inclined to have problems with his studies. He later described his childhood as unhappy. He tried to outdo his "perfect" older

VIGNETTE

Former President Clinton is arguably an example of the extent to which intelligence, talent, and motivation can be subverted by personality flaws, in his case a driving need for recognition and approval.

Clinton was raised until he was 7 years old in rural Arkansas by his widowed mother, his father having been killed in an auto accident before he was born. His mother then married an alcoholic car dealer who showed the boy little affection or attention and would often assault his mother when he was drinking. Instead of despairing over his dismal home life, however, Clinton merely set his goals higher. And he seemed to have offset the negative attention he received at home by making himself a popular figure in school. In addition to his interpersonal charm, he was a skilled musician and was awarded the position of first saxophonist in an Arkansas state band.

Despite his troubled family of origin, Clinton moved along a path of nearly uniform success. While still in high school, he became a senator in Boys Nation, a political organization for young people; in that position he was able to meet then-President John F. Kennedy. Clinton's political activism, musical skills, and academic performance then won him a scholarship to Georgetown University. His academic excellence continued in college, where he interned for a U.S. senator, was elected to Phi Beta Kappa, and was awarded a Rhodes scholarship to Oxford University. With all of his academic and extracurricular activities, Bill even ran for president of the student council; it seemed that he was driven not only to succeed but also to obtain public acclamation of his successes.

After the completion of his studies at Oxford and graduation from Georgetown, Clinton attended Yale Law School. There, too, he managed to become a prominent figure in campus. Within 3 years of graduation from Yale, he was elected attorney general of Arkansas at the age of 28. By the age of 32, he was the governor of the state, the youngest governor in the United Sates.

Clinton was the third-youngest president of the United States when he took office in 1993. During his presidency, Bill was the subject of extensive media attention that was critical of his private life and behavior. Bill was repeatedly accused of sexual liaisons with numerous women. During his presidency, three women affirmed that he had sexual relationships with them. One, Gennifer Flowers, eventually sued Bill for defamation of character as a result of his official denials of the affair. The most notorious of these affairs involved a young aide, Monica Lewinsky, with whom Clinton had sexual encounters in the Oval Office of the White House. Clinton's denials under oath and subsequent admission of his involvement with Lewinsky led to his impeachment. Though he was acquitted of committing offenses worthy of removal from office, he did have his law license suspended for his perjury.

Clinton remained in the public eye after leaving the presidency, including frequent appearances on television talk shows, attendance at high-profile international conferences, and making controversial statements about current political matters to

(Continued)

(Continued)

the media. In sum, he illustrates Adler's concepts of compensation and striving for superiority.

Vignette Questions

1. Do you think that President Clinton's personality was important in his achieving the positions he did?

2. Is it possible that some of the very same personality forces that led him to fame and power also led to his sexual embarrassments?

3. How might Adler and Jung have characterized or explained his behavior?

brother (named Sigmund, ironically) but failed to surpass him; he was also jealous of his younger siblings. Adler was very concerned with fitting in and being popular with classmates during childhood. He himself noted the relationship between his younger years and his later theories. All these social dynamics would leave their mark in Adler's concepts of inferiority feelings, the striving for superiority, social interest, and the importance of birth order. Trying to fit in better, Adler converted from Judaism to Protestant Christianity despite being an atheist. To Adler, being part of the majority with regard to one's religious label serves to overcome feelings of inferiority. His ideas about the so-called masculine protest in women were based on his own marriage, which turned into a battle for control between husband and wife.

Personality theorists at times enter the field to come to terms with their own unresolved problems, and Adler was no exception. He soon left the practice of ophthalmology and entered psychiatry. After writing a newspaper article defending Freudian theory in 1902, Adler was invited by Freud to join a new group holding weekly discussions of psychoanalysis. This group eventually organized itself as the Vienna Psychoanalytic Society, with Adler as its first president. From the start, Adler behaved like a typical middle child, constantly quarreling with other members over the priority of his ideas. He was in effect reenacting with Freud the sibling rivalry of his childhood, wondering why he always had to work in someone else's shadow. Adler and Jung together gave Freud a considerable amount of bad press. Although they did not agree with each other on anything, they joined forces to attack Freud. Adler said that Freud was a threat to humanity and described Freud's theory as "filth" and "fecal matter" (Kaufmann, 1980, p.199). Taking an almost messianic attitude, Adler expected his movement to transform the world through adult education and psychotherapy.

Adler's theory of personality has been described by Henri Ellenberger (1970) as follows: "This kind of pragmatic psychology . . . does not pretend to go into matters very deeply, but to provide principles and methods that enable one to acquire a practical knowledge of oneself and of others" (p. 608). Freud commented, "I would never have expected a psychoanalyst to be so taken in by the ego. In reality the ego is like the clown in the circus, who is always putting in his oar to make the audience think that whatever happens is his doing" (Freud & Jung, 1974, p. 400).

Theories

The reader should recall at this point that in spite of the weaknesses in Freud's system, he did set out to construct a scientific psychology. His view of human nature was that it is a complex energy system that evolved to serve the species' biological survival. Adler discarded Freud's concept of biological drives or instincts and substituted a notion of human personality as the product of society. Human motivation is, therefore, not a matter of drive reduction but rather of establishing a position in society. Humans are primarily social rather than biological beings. In later Adlerian theory, the goal of life is defined as a manifestation of social interest.

Adler's work is constructed on six basic concepts: (1) fictional finalism, (2) striving for superiority, (3) inferiority feelings and compensation, (4) social interest, (5) style of life, and (6) the self as creative.

Fictional Finalism. Freud saw people as the products of their pasts. In contrast, Adler believed that people are motivated by expectations of the future. Freud stressed inherent constitutional structures and childhood events as the primary factors in the development of personality whereas Adler postulated that self-created fictions or assumptions are the central explanation of human motivation. "Honesty is the best policy," "God loves us," "winning is the only thing," or "if at first you don't succeed, try, try again" are examples of what Adler meant by fictions. He borrowed this concept from a philosopher named Hans Vaihinger, who had published a book in 1911 called *The Philosophy of "As If."*

Referring to the ideals or assumptions that people live by, Vaihinger used the term *fiction* not because these ideals are always false or wrong but because they are not hypotheses that can be tested. Whether or not these fictions are "true," they motivate people to complete tasks and achieve various goals. Some fictions, such as "virtue is its own reward" or "one should work for the common good" lead to positive behaviors, whereas others, such as "win at any cost," lead to negative outcomes. The healthy personality, according to this view, can abandon fictions when they are no longer useful. As Adler expressed it, "The neurotic is nailed to the cross of his fiction. . . . The normal individual, too, can and will create his deity. . . . But he will never lose sight of reality, and always takes it into account as soon as action and work are demanded" (Adler, 1912/1956, pp. 246–247). The distinction between the healthy person and the neurotic, then, is that the healthy individual conforms to reality while the neurotic cannot.

Striving for Superiority. Adler believed that a striving for superiority exists in everyone, concluding that aggression is a more important source of motivation than sexual desire. Adler (1930) first borrowed the phrase "will to power," used by Nietzsche (1883/1969) in *Thus Spake Zarathustra,* and saw the striving for superiority or the will to power as the primary human drive. But given Adler's later emphasis on social interest, his later phrase, "striving for superiority," did not refer to the desire to win in direct competition with others (although it could) as much as it referred to the desire for competence and mastery over one's environment. Thus, completing a degree program, sculpting a statue, learning a new language, or fixing a broken window without having to call in a professional carpenter could all be seen as expressions of the striving for superiority, whether or not the person engaged in these projects is being compared to others. Adler once described what he called "the great upward drive":

I began to see clearly in every psychological phenomenon the striving for superiority. It runs parallel to physical growth and is an intrinsic necessity of life itself. It lies at the root of all solutions of life's problems and is manifested in the way in which we meet these problems. All our functions follow its direction. . . . The impetus from minus to plus never ends. The urge from below to above never ceases . . . self-preservation, pleasure principle, equalization—all these are but vague representations, attempts to express the great upward drive. (Adler 1930, p. 398)

Inferiority Feelings. The inferiority complex is the best known of Adler's concepts; the term is thoroughly familiar to us all. Inferiority feelings can result from real or imaginary shortcomings, for which people try to compensate. An example of compensation is seen in the history of John Randolph of Virginia, an early American politician who was impotent, never reached puberty, and suffered from undescended testicles. In spite of his deformity and high-pitched voice, he became a master orator and a powerful member of Congress in the early 19th century. Randolph took to brandishing whips and firearms on the floor of Congress while arguing for states' rights.

In compensating for feelings of inferiority, some people act selfishly and in self-defeating ways. Others, however, turn compensation into an engine, so to speak, of positive accomplishment. Augustus Caesar, for example, knew that he lacked the robust physique, charismatic personality, and military aggressiveness of his uncle, Julius Caesar. An intelligent and patient man in spite of asthma and other lifelong health problems, Augustus chose to focus his energies on less spectacular but nonetheless necessary long-term changes in Roman government, such as reforming the taxation system, cutting administrative expenses, rebuilding the roads and aqueducts, and providing the city of Rome with its first professional fire department and police force. Adler early on termed compensation the masculine protest, associating femininity with weakness, as did Freud and many others at the time.

Social Interest. Before World War I, Adler placed aggression, the masculine protest, or the desire to be on top at the center of his psychological system. After the war, Adler in effect had an intellectual conversion, compensating for his earlier views by placing desire for community feeling at the core of his theories. He had spent 2 years as an army physician with Austrian troops near the Russian front. The effect of seeing the horrors of warfare changed his theories from a position of moral relativism to a strong positive morality with an emphasis on social interest. Social interest, according to Adler, is an inborn trait that makes all humans value contributing to society and the common good. The productive way to compensate for individual feelings of inferiority is to work to make the world a better place. The concept of social interest shifted Adler's brand of psychology in the direction of a focus on the human community rather than the individual psyche.

Style of Life. Adler regarded people as having unique personalities. Our style of life is our unique combination of motives, interests, experiences, attitudes, and values. The style of life became a major focus of Adler's later writings (Adler, 1931). The style of life determines how a person will act in any situation. Adler described three general styles of life that he considered misguided: an overaggressive style, an avoidant style, and a dependent style; and one positive general style of life, a socially useful one (Adler, 1927). Obviously, an individual with a socially useful style of life expresses a great deal of social interest.

To return to Augustus as an example, his concern for the ordinary citizens of Rome as well as the aristocracy was evident in his attention to public works and safety measures. In 29 BCE, he paid each citizen (about 250,000 people) a sum of money worth about $800 in contemporary dollars from funds saved by administrative cost-cutting measures. Presumably, Adler would have considered the emperor an instance of a socially useful style of life.

The Creative Self. Later, Adler proposed the creative self as the core of human personality. The creative self is the dynamic force that allows us to use our experiences and heredity to construct and elaborate a style of life. For Adler, the notion of the creative self became the logical climax of his evolving theory (Adler, 1964). The concept of the creative self means that people are not the slaves or victims of their heredity; they are in effect totally conscious, aware of everything about them, and the architects of their own lives.

The Significance of Birth Order

The importance of birth order within the nuclear family is an Adlerian concept. Adler considered birth order and family structure as playing a large role in the formation of the personality. For example, Adler thought that the oldest child in a sibling relationship will often acquire feelings of responsibility since he or she is the one who cares for younger siblings, but the eldest also suffers the loss of centrality in the family with the birth of younger siblings. This loss of parental attention can result in feelings of insecurity, and Adler noted that oldest children have the highest likelihood of becoming criminals or neurotics. On the other hand, as a source of authority over the younger siblings, the oldest child can also become the conservative upholder of societal rules or intellectual traditions. Thus, oldest children are overrepresented in such fields as medicine, religion, engineering, law, and the military.

The middle child must compete with the stronger and more mature older sibling for accomplishment and with the youngest sibling for attention. But middle children also learn about cooperation, compromise, and social interest. (Adler himself was a middle child.) Youngest children are often pampered, which may lead to being spoiled and having a hard time coping with setbacks in later life.

Sulloway (1996) conducted extensive statistical analysis to demonstrate the centrality of birth order in the development of personal traits from an evolutionary Darwinian perspective. First-borns tend to be conservative and authoritarian and to favor the current social order, whereas later-born children tend to be liberal, rebellious, and committed to changing the world. Sulloway found, for example, that among the scientists who were involved in the controversy over Darwin in the years immediately following his publication, those who were later-born children were 4.6 times more likely to accept evolution than first-born children.

Concept of Neurosis

Adler considered neurosis to be the product of rationalizing our shortcomings, asserting that mental diseases are arrangements. He based this definition of neurosis on Vaihinger's (1924) theory that people engage the world on an "as if" basis, the idea being that because ultimate reality is beyond human comprehension, we construct partial truths or constructs for managing our day-to-day lives. It is not that reality is totally subjective, but rather that our constructs work or do not work in the real world and thus are either useful or not useful. For Adler, the neurotic could be defined as a person who clings to destructive constructs. Although neuroses are compensatory devices that ward off increasingly painful feelings, they are maladaptive rather then adaptive, unlike the strategies for living that normal people adopt. Here are Adler's ideas about some specific neuroses and psychoses:

Depression. Depressed people, in Adler's view, have extremely deep-seated feelings of inferiority. Thus, they restrict their activities because they cannot be judged a failure if they do not attempt to achieve something. In extreme cases, depression may lead to suicide, which is a final act of asserting control over one's environment by leaving it.

Paranoia. Paranoid people, according to Adler, move their battle for superiority into an imaginary world in which they are the champion or hero pursued by those inferior to themselves.

Schizophrenia. Schizophrenic individuals became totally discouraged early in life. With no chance of even getting into the game to achieve superiority, they withdraw completely from the world.

Homosexuality. Adler regarded homosexuality as a strategy for reducing the "playing field" by excluding half the world through complete denial of the other sex. Contemporary Adlerians have attempted to modify Adler's view of homosexuality with varying degrees of success.

Criminality. Adler understood criminal behavior as a deficiency of social interest. Criminals are unable to pursue the social interest, cannot achieve their goals within society, and thus act against society.

Adlerian Psychotherapy

Adler was not an experimental or research psychologist, but rather a clinical psychotherapist, which reflected his early training as a medical doctor. In Adlerian therapy, however, the patient and therapist sit facing each other on chairs of the same size, in contrast to Freudian therapy, in which the patient lies on a couch unable to see the analyst's face. Adlerian sessions are shorter and less frequent than in Freudian psychoanalysis; in fact, Adler's approach has been regarded as the forerunner of cognitive-behavioral therapy (CBT) and other brief or time-limited therapies (Ansbacher, 1972; Dowd & Kelly, 1980). The reader should note that each of Adler's innovations have been retained in humanistic approaches to therapy and have a more modern feel to them than Freudian psychoanalysis.

The Adlerian therapist must understand the client and the history of his or her problem, but the focus is more on the here and now than in Freudian therapy. The therapist takes a more active role in disclosing what is wrong with the patient's style of life. Adler had a strong messianic streak and made moral judgments, whereas Freud considered it a point of honor that he refrained from doing so.

Adler's approach also involved asking the patient about his or her earliest memory of childhood as a clue to the patient's present-day difficulties. An example is his work with a young man who suffered from severe anxiety attacks. The patient reported that his earliest memory was of watching workmen building a house across the street from his home, while his mother knitted stockings. Adler deduced from this recollection that the young man had an overly solicitous mother and that he considered himself a spectator of life rather than a participant in it. Furthermore, Adler noted that the patient's anxiety attacks were most acute whenever he tried to think through which occupation he should take up when he completed his education. Adler suggested that the patient consider a line of work that would use his interest in looking and observing. The young man took Adler's advice and became a successful dealer in art objects (Hall & Lindzey, 1970, p. 129).

Adler's favorite question for his patients was, "If you didn't have this affliction, what would you do with your life?" The answer clearly showed what patients were avoiding through their symptoms and thus pointed to the source of the symptoms. When patients become aware of the ways in which they use neurosis to avoid a certain task, relationship, or problem, they must decide whether and how to change their lifestyle and behaviors. Adler saw psychotherapy as a process of reeducation, which made the treatment a much easier process. He initiated face-to-face interviews, with patients attending only once or twice per year. His therapy focused on changing a person's thinking rather than on coming to terms with deep

Table 6.1   Summary Comparison of Freud, Jung, and Adler

	Adler	*Jung*	*Freud*
Human motivation	Originally inferiority complex but ultimately social interest	Expressing all parts of the psyche (including the inherited unconscious)	Sexual and aggressive drives; reducing their tension level
Cause of neurosis	Misguided style of life	One-sidedness; not allowing an inherent characteristic to come to fruition; the attempt to deny one's true inner nature disrupts harmony between opposites	Arrested libidinal development; realistic satisfaction of erotic needs denied; neurosis begins with an unresolved oedipal complex
Symptoms of neurosis	Cheap tricks	Neglected parts of the psyche expressing themselves	Compromises
Goals of analysis	Reeducation toward a style of life expressing social interest; the key question to determine what the person should be doing is "if you didn't have this ailment, what would you do?"	Conversation with the unconscious; believed in "autonomy of the psyche," meaning that thoughts and fantasies are autonomous events, and must be allowed freedom; the goal of therapy is individuation; all parts of the psyche are developed and allowed expression and transcendence; integration of all the parts of the psyche toward balance and perfect wholeness by the self	Strengthening the ego's secondary process

dark secrets or ancestral residue. All this made for a more popular and more easily accessible form of psychotherapy.

Elements of Adlerian psychology have been retained in humanistic, client-centered, and cognitive schools of therapy. Psychiatrist Joseph Wilder has written (Adler & Deutsch, 1959) that Adler's ideas have so completely permeated various psychotherapies that "the proper question is not whether one is Adlerian but how much of an Adlerian one is" (p. xv). Adler's approach differed from more modern cognitive approaches primarily in the importance it ascribed to motivation and goal-setting and its emphasis on social interest.

▣ CHAPTER SUMMARY

Both Alfred Adler and Carl Jung came to prominence as acolytes of Sigmund Freud. Jung broke with Freud primarily as a result of his personal ascendance in the psychoanalytic community and secondarily over theoretical differences. Jung disposed of Freud's unconscious structures and replaced them with a new complex of unconscious motivating entities. Jung's model of personality was predicated on numerous archetypes. He thought there were innate and inherited mental constructs that unconsciously direct human behavior. These include the feminine anima and masculine animus, both of which are present to varying degrees in both men and women; the shadow, which includes all repressed and inchoate personality inclinations; and the Self, which represents each individual's link to a divine spiritual consciousness and the collective human experience. Jung's theories, although still present in many clinical settings, play a very small role in current personality research and models.

Adler broke with Freud primarily over conflicts with the latter's emphasis of unconscious sexual motives as the primary motivation in life. In doing so, Adler became the first to stress social and interpersonal forces in personality development. Rejecting repressed sexual urges as the essential factor in personality, he proposed that the individual's striving for feelings of social adequacy is the guiding force in life. Adler was the pathfinder for other psychoanalytic theorists, such as Karen Horney, who would de-emphasize sexual drives and elevate social and interpersonal motives in personality. Although Adler's theories are no longer major factors in personality research, they have been subsumed into many more recent models. These include both the social-learning and humanist models of personality.

Chapter 7

Psychiatric and Medical Models

Chapter Goals

- Explore the history of the medical models of mind and personality
- Trace the changing medical view of personality from ancient times
- Explore the differences between the psychiatric and psychological concepts of personality
- Explain some of the controversies in medicine that have shaped modern views of the person

Psychiatry and medicine have focused primarily on the study of pathological personalities. Of course, to properly understand pathology, one must have a baseline determination of health. Psychological health, however, has yet to be clearly defined. That is, researchers who study personality have yet to come to a consensus as to the nature of personality itself. Consequently, a definition of what a healthy or normal personality is has yet to be universally accepted. This situation makes defining an abnormal or pathological personality all the more difficult.

Attempts to understand the nature of and explain the origins of mental pathology go back to antiquity. The Bible contains several notable descriptions of psychological disorders. For example, in 1 Samuel 16:14 we find a description of King Saul's emotional difficulties explained in terms of the loss of spiritual connections: "But the Spirit of the Lord departed from Saul, and an evil spirit from the Lord troubled him." Similarly in Daniel 2:1, King Nebuchadnezzar seems to be suffering from depression: "And in the second year of the reign of Nebuchadnezzar, Nebuchadnezzar dreamed dreams, wherewith his spirit was troubled, and his sleep departed from him."

Virtually every culture that has left a written legacy has some description of madness and unusual behavior. Sometimes such behavior has been attributed to prophetic ecstasy, as in the ancient Greek oracle of Delphi, and in other times to demonic possession. But one thing has been clear—most people are attuned to deviations from normal behavior. Just as people can distinguish the beautiful from the ordinary without being able to define the features used in making this judgment, they can distinguish abnormal behavior from the mundane. Most of us are quite adept at labeling those we believe are abnormal or deviant in character. We can't define it, but we know it when we see it. Or at least we think we do.

▣ MENTAL ILLNESS IN WESTERN MEDICINE

Classical Antiquity

The ancient Greeks developed and documented the organized practice of medicine around 400 BCE. Their physicians rejected the notion of supernatural forces as the basis of pathology. Instead, they began to describe disease in the same terms as other natural phenomena, as events that can be measured, understood, and explained. Hippocrates of Cos, the so-called father of Western medicine, proposed that psychopathology is caused by infirmity of the brain. This hypothesis stood in contrast to that of many of his contemporaries, who believed the brain served the purpose of temperature regulation. Hippocrates' treatment of the mentally ill included exercise, medication, and essentially the same treatment recommended for physical ailments. A major portion of ancient Greek clinical observation is known as the Hippocratic Corpus, a collection of about 60 treatises on medicine (Hippocrates, 1978).

Later commentaries on Hippocrates' writings also include a notion that later lay buried for centuries and even now requires constant reiteration and emphasis. This is the recognition that there is no sharp dividing line between normality and abnormality. Notably, Hippocrates developed a very early classification of mental illness. He proposed three disorders of personality: mania, melancholia, and dementia. Today, these disorders would correspond to the mania of **bipolar** disorder, depression, and psychosis or dementias such as Alzheimer's or Korsakoff's disease.

The Roman physician Claudius Galen developed his own model of the causes and treatment of mental disease on the basis of Hippocrates' classification (Adams, 1891). This model included the four humors, or bodily fluids, discussed in Chapter 1. Galen's approach was distinguished by his notion that both physical and mental diseases were caused by irregularities in physical processes represented by the humors.

The Greek philosophers before Socrates are often known as pre-Socratic, as if their work were inferior to or at least only led up to the ideas of Socrates and Plato. The approach of the pre-Socratic thinkers was naturalistic and proto-modern, however; it was far different from the spiritualistic tradition that followed. Plato's influence served to eradicate the naturalism of Hippocrates, as Plato believed that gods cause the symptoms of mental illness. In fact, the philosophy of Plato, with its separation of mind from body and its belief in ideal forms existing in a nonphysical space, continued to influence the Judeo-Christian concept of mental illness for millennia.

The principle of physical factors as the basis of mental pathology was carried forward by the Iranian physician Avicenna (980–1037 CE), who wrote a book called the *Canon of Medicine*. Avicenna added to Galen's understanding of the four humors by elaborating on the importance of dietary modification and reduction of emotional stress in the treatment of mental disturbances. In fact, he was among the earliest to describe the connection between stress and clinical disease. Avicenna attempted to explain the cause of depression and numerous other psychopathologies with reference to the four humors, but he also played a key role in drawing connections between brain pathology and behavioral disturbance. He explained that psychopathologies were the result of imbalances among the humors leading to brain dysfunction.

The Middle Ages and the Early Modern Period

Advances toward a biological or physical explanation of psychopathology came very slowly and haltingly during the European Middle Ages. During this era, the influence of the Catholic Church and the need of feudal rulers to maintain some kind of governmental control over their populations led to oversimplified interpretations of aberrant behavior. The philosophy of interactional dualism played a large part in the study of mind and behavior. This understanding of the human psyche held that the immortal and incorporeal soul governs the entire body and its behavior, except when the human organism is disrupted by Satan or his minions. Thus, when people act rationally and appropriately, their actions are understood to be governed by the inherently good soul. When they behave badly or irrationally, however, they might be under the influence of evil forces.

Medieval physicians did not, however, necessarily attribute all instances of mental derangement to the supernatural. Like their predecessors in ancient Egypt and the Roman Empire, they knew that some psychiatric disturbances were caused by head injuries, alcoholic intoxication, or such diseases as ergotism, which is caused by a fungus that contaminates rye and barley. Some medieval clergy also recognized that depression and other mood disorders might well respond to simple friendly concern from others and were not always signs of demonic activity. In other cases, however, evil and psychopathological behaviors were regarded as having the same cause: Satanic forces. From the late Middle Ages through the seventeenth century, individuals who behaved bizarrely might be accused of demonic possession. The penalty for such violations of proper morality could be torture or death.

A text that could be considered a guide to the different types of demonic possession was the *Malleus maleficarum* ("The Witches' Hammer"). Written by the Dominican monks Heinrich Kramer and James Sprenger in 1486, the book detailed the symptoms of witchery and demonic alliance. Kramer and Sprenger (2000) apparently believed that women are, as a group, inclined to yield to the temptations of evil. The excerpt below makes this point:

As to our second inquiry, what sort of women more than others are found to be superstitious and infected with witchcraft; it must be said, as was shown in the preceding inquiry,
that three general vices appear to have special dominion over wicked women, namely,
infidelity, ambition, and lust. Therefore they are more than others inclined towards witchcraft, who more than others are given to these vices. Again, since of these vices the last

chiefly predominates, women being insatiable, etc., it follows that those among ambitious women are more deeply infected who are more hot to satisfy their filthy lusts; and such are adulteresses, fornicatresses, and the concubines of the Great. (p. 47)

Most significant, many of the symptoms attributed to witchcraft bore a marked resemblance to those of people suffering from psychiatric disorders. The monks' description of the symptoms and "treatment" of these aberrations makes the *Malleus maleficarum* one of the earliest mental health **nosologies**. Abstractly, the treatise introduced the concept of differential diagnosis, and its directions help to differentiate between witchcraft and conditions arising from such natural afflictions as disease. It specifies that investigating clergy must confer with a physician if there is any evidence that the accused is suffering from mental or physical illness. If the disease could not be cured by drugs or current medical interventions, it was presumed to arise from supernatural causes. Such psychiatric symptoms as hallucinations or delusions were considered products of an evil mind and evidence of witchcraft. This explanation was generally applied to any abnormal behavior or personality style.

Supernatural explanations for aberrant behavior reached their peak in the late 16th and early 17th centuries, however. Examinations for the two types of demonic possession were common. In the beginning of this era, there were two categories of possession: willing and unwilling. The unwilling victims of possession were the mentally ill. The second and more pernicious group included those who voluntarily joined Satan. Unfortunately, the distinction between the willing and the unwilling hosts of Satan was lost after the beginning of the 16th century, and the mentally ill were sometimes punished as witches.

Witch hunting reached its peak in Western Europe between 1450 and 1650, and the "Witches' Hammer," which was reprinted until 1669, established the officially enforced view. Symptoms of mental illness became proof of demonic possession. The possessed were identified through subjection to torture and judicial ordeals; and the treatment was more torture, burning, or dismemberment—all to make the body an uncomfortable dwelling place for the demon.

Some echoes of a belief in possession persist to the present day. Exorcism is still considered a valid procedure (although only in extreme and carefully reviewed cases) by the Roman Catholic Church as well as by other Christian denominations; however, it captured the popular imagination through a well-known movie (1973) based on a best-selling book, *The Exorcist*. In some respects, the practices and rationale of Scientologists in "clearing" people of past traumas, "engrams," and "implants" resulting from brainwashing by extraterrestrial beings resemble exorcism.

Witch hunting was rampant in the century that produced Galileo Galilei and Thomas Hobbes, links to the modern world. The popes of the Renaissance all endorsed the *Malleus maleficarum*, and it was equally popular in such Protestant countries as Scotland and Switzerland. Untold thousands of people were killed across Europe for supposedly being in league with Satan, estimates running as high as 150,000 (Brems, Thevinin, & Routh, 1991). In Trier, Germany, alone, 7,000 people were burned in a period of just several years in the 16th century (Bromberg, 1959). Most of those executed in Europe were probably the victims of personal enemies or simple bad luck (and the added motivation of executed witches' property being confiscated by the state, with part of it assigned to the religious judges), but many were afflicted by mental disorders.

Ignorance may have been widespread European medicine during this time, but it was not universal. Pioneers like the Dutch physician Johann Weyer (sometimes spelled Weir; 1515–1588) took a more rational stance. In his prescient work, *De praestigiis daemonum*, written in 1563 (1967), he refuted the premises of the *Malleus maleficarum*. His alternate hypothesis about those accused of witchcraft was that they were mentally ill and in need of medical care, not punishment; in fact, he is thought to be the first person to use the phrase "mentally ill" in reference to those accused of witchcraft. Of course, Weyer was not unopposed; his works were banned by the Roman Catholic Church, and as reported by a church official, Satan himself appeared and praised Weyer for making his job easier (Castiglioni, 1946).

Also taking a more humane position was St. Vincent de Paul (1581–1660), a French priest who founded a number of orphanages, schools, and other charitable institutions. He explicitly stated: "Mental disease is no different from bodily disease. Christianity demands that the powerful must protect, and that the skillful must relieve one condition as well as the other" (Vincent de Paul, 1851).

The Enlightenment and the Early Nineteenth Century

The view that those with mental impairments are evil was reflected not only in churches but also in the wider society. The notorious asylum known as Bethlehem Royal Hospital in London, its name the source of the word *bedlam*, exemplified the prevailing view of the insane as morally bad. In the 16th and 17th centuries the inmates were allowed to lie in their own filth and might be put on public display. The treatment in this institution consisted of isolation at best and beatings and public humiliation at worst. Other citizens of London would visit the asylum for cheap entertainment, much as some people nowadays might watch Jerry Springer or similar television shows that encourage people to act foolishly in public.

Even before the 18th-century Enlightenment, however, there were also writers like Michel Eyquem de Montaigne (1533–1592) who, in his famous *Essaies*, argued that life stresses and the resulting emotions can be strong enough to produce both physical and mental illness. Similar concepts were expressed by François-Marie Arouet de Voltaire (1694–1778), a later French writer who suggested that the insane be treated as "poor unfortunate sufferers." Moreover, Voltaire's definition of the word *folie* (insanity) in his dictionary of philosophy was "a brain disease that keeps a man from thinking and acting as other men do. If he cannot take care of his property he is put under tutelage; if his behavior is unacceptable, he is isolated; if he is dangerous, he is confined; if he is furious, he is tied" (cited in Ellenberger, 1974, p. 18). Thus, mental illness was not identified with witchcraft or the work of demons, but with disease.

Unfortunately, the antecedents of psychiatry and the introduction of the medical model of mental illness in the 18th century did not immediately result in more humane standards of care. The mentally ill were viewed as sideshow freaks, ridiculed, maltreated, bled to "adjust body fluids," and starved "to prevent excess production of body fluids."

Philippe Pinel and Benjamin Rush. The notion that mental disturbance is a disease did not become operationalized until the time of the French Revolution. The pioneer in this regard was a French physician named Philippe Pinel (1745–1826), sometimes called the father of modern psychiatry. Pinel, who regarded Hippocrates as his role model, became an innovator by reforming a hospital in Paris for the mentally ill; the Bicêtre had been run more like a prison than a caregiving institution prior to Pinel's directorship. Pinel attempted to treat the patients of the Bicêtre to restore them to health rather than to punish, isolate, or humiliate them. His interest in mental illness was stimulated in part by the suicide of a close friend, a tragedy that Pinel thought resulted from the friend's mismanagement by his doctors. Pinel wrote a book on the classification and treatment of mental illness that was translated into English and used by generations of British medical students.

At about the same time in the United States, Benjamin Rush (1745–1813) was treating mentally ill patients at Pennsylvania Hospital. He advocated treating patients with psychiatric disorders with the same quality of care as those who were physically ill. Rush's 1812 text, *Medical Inquiries and Observations upon the Diseases of the Mind*, was the first textbook in psychiatric medicine; it recommended treating psychiatric disorders humanely and scientifically.

Franz Josef Gall. The growing acceptance of the notion that mental illness is related to structural abnormalities or malfunctions of the brain led to a movement away from supernatural or occult explanations. During the later part of the 18th century the anatomy of the brain was studied in greater detail and precision. Along with more intensive mapping of the brain came research and theories regarding the localization of brain function and behavior. Investigators also applied the same concepts to find relationships between aberrant behavior and structural variations or dysfunctions in the brain. An important figure in this movement—one who was wrong, but brilliantly so—was Franz Josef Gall, a German physiologist who was the founder of phrenology. After several years of observation, Gall (1810) concluded that all major personality traits are localized within 37 brain regions that he called organs. A corollary to this principle of localization was that the brain organs that are the most developed, and therefore have the most influence on an individual's behavior, are larger than the less influential organs. Consequently, the skull overlying these larger organs must exhibit bumps or bulges

Image 7.1   Wilhelm Griesinger (1817–1868)

to accommodate them. Gall's phrenology was based on his physical measurements of several hundred patients' heads; and it also involved personality analysis based on the configuration of bumps on the exterior of the skull. According to the principles of phrenology, not only normal personality but psychopathological states could be inferred from the surface terrain of the head.

Today's scientists know that personality, intelligence, and character are not nearly as neatly localized as Gall proposed. His ideas, however, contained the seeds of some important principles. First, phrenology was firmly rooted in the principle that the human psyche originates in the brain and that consciousness and personality have a material basis. Second, implicit in Gall's theories is the notion that personality traits do exist and have their basis in brain function. Third, these traits lie along a continuum from the normal to the pathological. For example, if a person has a small bump for cautiousness, he or she would likely be appropriately suspicious of new situations. If the underlying brain organ were unusually large, however, the person would likely suffer from social phobia.

Phrenology had its critics, even in Gall's lifetime. The most vocal of these were the Roman Catholic hierarchy of Austria, and, after Gall moved to Paris, the Emperor Napoleon and the French scientific establishment. All three thought that Gall's phrenology was too materialistic in localizing the source of the human psyche. Gall's ideas were well received only in England, where some members of the ruling class found them useful in demonstrating the "inferiority" of the Irish, the Indians, the Zulus, and other colonial peoples.

Wilhelm Griesinger. Wilhelm Griesinger (1817–1868), a German neurologist and psychiatrist, advanced many of these same principles in his text, *Mental Pathology and Therapeutics*, which first appeared in 1845 and was extensively expanded in a second edition in 1867 (1965). In this work, he described the symptoms of numerous mental disorders and suggested their causes. Most important, Griesinger presented case histories involving abnormalities of brain structure in which he attempted to show the links between brain disease and mental illness. He clearly stated his conviction that mental illnesses are manifestations of organic brain disorders. Griesinger maintained that these problems would be cured when the anatomical abnormalities of the brain were better understood.

Diagnostic Classification of Mental Disorders

Emil Kraepelin. Although both Philippe Pinel and Benjamin Rush had attempted to construct a workable classification of psychiatric disorders, the first widely accepted system was the work of Emil Kraepelin (1856–1926), the founder of modern psychopharmacology and psychiatric genetics. Influenced by the work of Griesinger and, to a lesser extent, Pinel, Kraepelin developed a nosology that would systematically categorize mental illnesses on the basis of their clinical presentation. While working in a hospital in what is now Estonia, Kraepelin set out to document and describe the numerous disorders that were being treated in his clinic. Without a complete listing and description of the numerous illnesses, causal explanations would tend to be wanting at best, he thought. Only after mental disorders were described and classified could their etiologies be understood and suitable treatments found. In addition to these principles of research, Kraepelin (1921) proposed replacing the numerous theories of mental illness then in circulation with research into documented pathologies.

Kraepelin claimed that he had discovered a better way to approach mental illness; he described his method as *clinical* as opposed to the traditional method, which he referred to as *symptomatic*. Having studied experimental psychology under one of the founders of that field, Wilhelm Wundt, Kraepelin applied Wundt's methods to his new clinical psychiatry. This approach led to the identification of bipolar disorder, schizophrenia (which Kraepelin called dementia

Image 7.2   Emil Kraepelin (1856–1926)

praecox, or youthful dementia), and Alzheimer's disease, a disorder he described but named for its codiscoverer, a colleague named Alois Alzheimer.

Kraepelin designed numerous experiments to find the connection between such factors as drugs, physical stress, or alcohol on mental performance. Using clinical observations, which he meticulously organized and his research, he published his *Lehrbuch der Psychiatrie* in 1883. The original *Lehrbuch* was the first of eight editions that Kraepelin expanded and refined until 1915. The *Lehrbuch* contained much of what would become the *Diagnostic and Statistical Manual of Mental Disorders* (DSM) of the American Psychiatric Association. By its sixth edition, the *Lehrbuch* included several clinical types of dementia praecox: disorganized, paranoid, and catatonic. Although Kraepelin employed the terms neurosis and psychosis in his nosology, he did not use them in the same way as Freud. To Kraepelin, neurosis describes a maladaptive personality whereas psychosis refers to a disorder of personality severe enough to lead to impaired reality testing and to require inpatient care.

According to Kraepelin, all personality disorders are either functional or organic. Organic mental disorders are those for which a physical disease process can be identified, such as the microbial infection responsible for the psychiatric symptoms of tertiary syphilis or the amyloid plaques and neurofibrillary tangles of Alzheimer's disease; all other pathological mental states were functional disorders. Kraepelin also noted the familial or genetic patterns in numerous psychiatric illnesses. He observed that dementia praecox runs in families, as do most of the mood and anxiety disorders (Kraepelin, 1919/1971).

Image 7.3   Adolf Meyer (1866–1950)

Kraepelin's classification and nomenclature were disputed by Eugen Bleuler, Carl Jung's supervisor at the mental hospital in Zürich, who first used the term schizophrenia. Although Bleuler (1950) agreed that this form of psychosis represented a diverse but related group of disorders, he believed that it involves a breakdown of neurological coordination, as opposed to an early onset dementia.

Interestingly, the growing psychoanalytic community was critical of Kraepelin's experimental method (Hollingworth, 1930, p. 66). His nomothetic approach was said to be clinically irrelevant by psychoanalysts who advocated the idiographic approach, which, they maintained, accounts for the whole of the human personality. They argued that Kraepelin placed too much stress on cognition as opposed to will, emotion, and inner conflict. Edward Shorter (1997), in his text on the history of psychiatry, refutes their position by saying:

It is Kraepelin, not Freud, who is the central figure in the history of psychiatry. Freud . . . did not see patients with psychotic illness. His doctrine of psychoanalysis, based on intuitive leaps of fantasy, did not stand the test of time. By contrast,

Kraepelin . . . provided the single most significant insight that the late nineteenth and early twentieth centuries had to offer into major psychiatric illness: that there are several principal types, that they have very different courses, and that their nature may be appreciated through the systematic study of large numbers of cases. (p. 100)

Adolf Meyer. Kraepelin's task of classifying personality and other mental disorders was initially advanced in the United States by the Swiss-born physician Adolf Meyer (1866–1950), although a change in perspective in Meyer's later life led to a major change of emphasis. Trained in Europe, Meyer relocated to the United States early in his career, where he first worked in both general practice and neuropathology at the University of Chicago. In 1893, he was offered a position as a pathologist in the Illinois Eastern Asylum in Kankakee, Illinois. In this large facility, he had the opportunity to work with people suffering from a wide range of mental disorders. Although the asylum was intended to be a progressive institution—its inmates were housed in numerous small buildings rather than large dormitories—Meyer was disappointed by the quality of care that he witnessed. He even wrote to the governor of Illinois with specific suggestions regarding more humane care. Meyer (1957) thought that mental hospitals should be more like hospitals for the physically ill and less like prisons.

After Meyer moved to New York and began working with the New York State system of hospitals, he also advocated for better training in the neurological sciences for the medical staff. In his own practice, he was known for collecting great masses of detail in his case histories of patients and for attempting to understand the patient's life story and relationships as they impacted his or her psychological condition. Meyer had brought Kraepelin's system of classification and diagnosis with him from Europe, and he was a strong advocate for it early in his career.

Meyer's advocacy of Kraepelin's system began to wane, however, as he refined his own sociobiological reactive concept of psychopathology. Meyer coined the term **psychobiology** to encourage clinicians to regard patients in their care as whole beings, not collections of symptoms and genetic legacies. He wanted a patient's full history, environment, and personality considered in assessment and treatment. The idea of separating mind and body was contrary to what he had learned and observed. Meyer saw each person as an individual responding to external and biological events in a unique and characteristic way. He referred to this response as the psychobiological whole.

Consequently, Meyer thought Kraepelin's precise nomothetic nosology failed to apprehend the complexity of a specific individual's unique reaction to his or her ever-changing environment. Moreover, Meyer's adoption of many of Freud's theories put him at further odds with Kraepelin. He did not, however, accept psychoanalysis as a whole, as he regarded it as too bound by complex theories. But Meyer's conceptual framework was closer to Freudian psychoanalysis than to Kraepelin's thought in rejecting the disease model of mental disorders. Meyer had in common with Freud the belief that personality and psychological problems are primarily due to life stressors rather than organic illness. Meyer's concordance with these psychoanalytic principles did much to bolster the psychoanalytic movement in the United States.

Meyer ultimately developed his own nosology of disorders based on his reaction model. His system never received wide acceptance, however, partly as a result of his awkward writing style and partly due to the ambiguity of his terminology. Meyers's system was sufficiently influential, however, to shape some of the classifications in the first *Diagnostic and Statistical Manual of Mental Disorders* (DSM-I) published by the American Psychiatric Association in 1952.

🔲 PHYSICAL TREATMENTS FOR MENTAL ILLNESS

With psychiatry's growth as an independent specialty within medicine, the medical model of personality and mental disorders also gained increased status. The inclination to view disturbed behavior of any kind as a disease that needed to be treated by medical means became pervasive. Of course, this model was developing in parallel with the psychoanalytic model. The medical perspective tended to hold sway in hospital settings, especially in the United States, while the psychoanalytic model tended to dominate outpatient therapy. On occasion, the quest to find medical treatments for psychiatric disorders led to poor outcomes, sometimes even violating the Hippocratic oath by inflicting harm. Nevertheless, these procedures were developed in a time when practitioners were armed with a depth of theories and descriptions but had very little in the way of effective treatments.

Shock Treatments

Psychiatrists in the early 20th century used chemicals and electricity in the various forms of shock therapy that were tried in the treatment of mental illness.

Insulin Shock Therapy. An early and dramatic method that fell under the rubric of shock treatments was developed by Manfred Sakel (1900–1957), a Polish psychiatrist and neurophysiologist working in Vienna, who emigrated to the United States when the Nazis annexed Austria in 1936. As early as 1927, Sakel (1937) had developed a technique for treating people suffering from schizophrenia by injecting insulin to induce a coma. He reported that the patients' psychotic symptoms were relieved and that their personalities were profoundly and favorably improved. He had made his discovery by accident when he inadvertently gave a psychiatric patient an overdose of insulin. Noting a marked improvement in the patient's state of mind, Sakel formalized his discovery into a systematic treatment regimen. It consisted of daily overdoses of insulin followed by glucose fed through a nasogastric feeding tube to bring the patient out of the coma.

Sakel traveled widely, demonstrating and promoting his technique, claiming that it was 88% effective. Critics of the insulin shock technique pointed out that insulin interferes with the uptake of glucose by the brain and that a lowered supply of glucose increases the risk of brain damage, especially in those areas of the brain related to memory. Moreover, very little explanation was offered about how insulin could produce changes in personality or pathology. One exception was an American psychoanalyst named Smith Ely Jelliffe (1866–1945), who suggested that the efficacy of insulin shock therapy was derived from its "withdraw[al of] the libido from the outside world and fusing it with the death impulse for the maintenance of the narcissistic ego" (Jelliffe, 1918, quoted in Shorter, 1997, p. 312).

Metrazol. Ladislas von Meduna (1896–1964), a Hungarian researcher working in Budapest, hypothesized that an even more dramatic type of shock would change the character of schizophrenic individuals. Meduna proposed the deliberate induction of epileptiform seizures. After analyzing the brains of both epileptic and schizophrenic patients, he noted an interesting contrast. Specifically, the density of the glial cells in the brains of epileptics had increased, whereas people suffering from schizophrenia had a deficiency of glial cells. Meduna thus reasoned that the induction of epileptiform seizures in schizophrenics would stimulate the production of glial cells in their brains and thus help them to recover from their disorder.

Both Meduna and Smith Ely Jelliffe advocated the use of a drug called Metrazol (or Cardiazol) to induce these therapeutic seizures. Metrazol, the commercial name of a stimulant compound called pentamethylenetetrazol, is even more effective than insulin in inducing seizures. It has, however, a disconcerting drawback. While coma or seizures induced by insulin can be rapidly reversed by the administration of glucose, a simple sugar, Metrazol has no corresponding fast-acting antidote. Thus, seizures resulting from the administration of the drug are not easily controlled. Broken bones, shattered teeth, and even fatal outcomes were not uncommon in patients who were given Metrazol. Another shortcoming was the unpredictability of the latency period between injection of the drug and the seizure. People who were given Metrazol reported great distress prior to the onset of the convulsions.

Thus psychiatrists who accepted the notion that epileptiform convulsions relieve personality disturbances sought another method to produce such convulsions in the mentally ill. In addition, the Food and Drug Administration (FDA) stepped in and revoked its approval of Metrazol in 1982.

Electroconvulsive Therapy (ECT). The replacement for Metrazol emerged from the work of Ugo Cerletti (1877–1963), an Italian researcher studying the neurological basis of epilepsy. Cerletti had begun research on dogs to determine the level of electric shock that can be administered with relative safety to induce epileptic-like seizures to model the disorder. A chance piece of additional information led to a different application of his data. Cerletti learned that pigs being led to slaughter seemed more controllable when given electrical shocks. His research with dogs and the anecdotal information from the slaughterhouse rapidly led to a new treatment for the mentally ill. Cerletti wrote about his new method:

> Nevertheless I, who had gone to such lengths in striving to preserve dogs from death when given electrically induced convulsions, had now come to the conviction that a discharge of electricity must prove equally harmless to a man if the duration of the current's passage were reduced to a minimum interval. Continually turning the problem over in my mind I felt that I would sooner or later be able to solve it; so much so that in 1937, not being able to go to the Munsingen Congress, I allowed Bini to hint at these vague hopes, and I myself at the 1937 Milan Assembly concerning the therapeutics of schizophrenia, announced these hopes that I had been nourishing. (Cerletti, 1950, cited in Szasz, 2007, p. 129)

In a relatively short time, electrical shock treatments, now called **electroconvulsive therapy** (ECT), became widely used for people suffering from most major psychiatric disorders.

ECT grew in popularity with only a few modifications—including the introduction of light anesthesia and the use of a muscle relaxant to reduce the number of bone fractures occurring during the convulsions. Today, about 150,000 patients receive electroconvulsive therapy each year. Despite advances making the treatment less traumatic and more safe, one of the most authoritative recent psychiatric texts cautioned practitioners about the fear this treatment could still evoke:

> The major reason for the underuse is hypothesized to be misconceptions and biases about ECT, at least partly fueled by the widespread misinformation and inflammatory articles in the lay press. Because ECT requires the use of electricity and the production of a seizure, ECT understandably frightens many laypersons, patients, and patient's families. (Kaplan & Sadock, 1996, p. 466)

Psychosurgery

Psychosurgery is a general term for the use of surgical treatments for mental disorders. There are two major types of procedures in this category, those that involve leaving a permanent opening in the skull, which is then covered with skin, and those that involve removal or destruction of brain tissue.

Trephination. The oldest surgical procedure to treat mental illness is trephination, which is also called trepanation. This operation involves drilling holes in the skull, with goals that range from allowing evil spirits to escape to treating epilepsy. It was practiced as far back as 6500 BCE, judging from prehistoric skulls found in a burial site in France. Archaeological evidence indicates that the Maya of Central America and the Inca of Peru also practiced trephination as early as 1400 BCE. According to the Hippocratic corpus, the ancient Greeks used trephination for the more sophisticated purpose of relieving pressure on the brain due to head trauma, and it is still occasionally used today for the emergency treatment of head injuries in which blood has collected under the membranes overlying the brain.

No practice of the past is truly ever dead, however, and amazingly, trephination has had a thankfully minor resurgence as a New Age technique for expanding consciousness. A few dozen people, primarily in Europe, have undergone this procedure. It is often self-administered in spite of the obvious risks of infection as well as permanent neurological damage (Michell, 1999, pp. 144–151). Needless to say, no reputable medical authority endorses self-trephination.

Many psychiatric procedures of the recent past were no more effective or humane than trephination. These were desperate measures that came into being and were used for a time because nothing better was available. The fact remains, however, that psychiatric practice based on a medical model but not very advanced in its knowledge has instituted procedures designed for roughshod treatment of mental disease that have not contributed to the understanding of personality. Nevertheless, when the need was regarded as pressing, it was natural for therapists to embrace any treatment that offered some hope of alleviating the suffering that many encountered in their patients on a daily basis.

Frontal Leucotomy (lobotomy). The first systematic effort to change a disordered personality through surgery on the brain itself can be credited to António Egas Moniz (1874–1955), a Portuguese neurosurgeon. By intentionally damaging the frontal lobes of the brain or severing their connections to the limbic region, Moniz believed he had cured a wide range of disorders. Despite the popularity of the term *lobotomy* for this surgery, Moniz's procedure is better termed leucotomy. It did not involve removal of the frontal lobes; rather, the surgery severed the corticothalamic tracts in the prefrontal cortex. Moniz (1936/1964) hypothesized that the pathways in the brain between the frontal lobes and the thalamus control the level of the patient's emotion. Moniz and his colleagues were aware that the frontal lobes are essential for the executive tasks of planning for the future and applying knowledge gained from past experience. They observed that natural damage to the prefrontal cortex resulted in severe impairments in the individual's judgment, ethical behavior, creativity, and sense of personal identity.

| Image 7.4 | António Egas Moniz (1874–1955) |

Moniz postulated that many sufferers of mental illness had abnormal circuits between their frontal lobes and the limbic structures. It was these abnormal connections that needed to be severed to interrupt the disordered thinking they induced. He dubbed the new cure the **prefrontal leucotomy** and developed an instrument called a leucotome, used to inject alcohol into the tissue connecting the frontal lobes in order to destroy it. Moniz announced that he had effected remarkable cures with his new procedure and traveled extensively to promote its use. The prefrontal leucotomy did seem to calm even the most disturbed psychotic individuals. Given the lack of compelling alternative treatments, it appeared that Moniz had indeed made an extraordinary advance—one that led to his receiving the Nobel Prize in Medicine in 1949.

The high level of optimism in the popular press about Moniz's new treatment for mental illness was reflected in this quotation from *Time* (November 30, 1942; see Psychosurgery):

> The surgeon's knife can reach into the brain to sever the tensions which underlie a psychopathic personality. This drastic method of rescuing psychotic patients from complete insanity is not exactly a new invention. It has been developed in Lisbon by Dr. Egas Moniz since 1935. But now two men who have pioneered this treatment in the U.S.—Neurologist Walter Freeman and Neurosurgeon James W. Watts of George Washington University—have published a book, *Psychosurgery* (Charles C Thomas; $6), based on their work. Some 300 people in the U.S. have had their psychoses surgically removed.

The two psychiatrists named in the *Time* article cited above, Walter Freeman II (1895–1972) and James Watts (1904–1994), changed the name of the surgery to lobotomy (Freeman,

1971). Watts was the only one of the pair who had been trained as a surgeon; he was also the unfortunate doctor who performed the unsuccessful leucotomy on Rosemary Kennedy, the younger sister of the late president. Freeman introduced a newer version of the lobotomy that did not require general anesthesia and a sterile field, as did Watts's technique. Impatient with the slowness of a procedure that had to be performed inside a hospital operating room, Freeman developed the so-called ice-pick lobotomy, which could be done in a doctor's office. It involved using a mallet to force an implement resembling an ice pick through the thin layer of bone at the top of the patient's eye socket. The instrument was then wiggled back and forth inside the skull to damage the frontal lobes of the brain.

There has always been a tendency on the part of some people to attribute near-magical qualities to people who have some knowledge in a domain in which they have none; it certainly seems to have been the case with leucotomy. Elliot Valenstein (1986), who studied the rapid growth in popularity of this procedure, observed that "there was nothing compelling about any of [Moniz's] arguments that should have persuaded a prudent man to attempt psychosurgery. It was not genius that enabled Moniz to see beyond the risks; rather, it was his willingness to take these risks" (p. 100).

Valenstein (1986) noted that the number of leucotomies performed increased tenfold between 1946 and 1949, and by the end of that period, 5,000 were being performed each year. By the time the annual number of leucotomies had exceeded 20,000, most experts in psychiatry had reached a consensus that the procedure did not actually help patients diagnosed with schizophrenia (Flor-Henry, 1975).

The number of lobotomies performed in the United States from the late 1930s through the late 1950s well exceeded 40,000. The improbability of clinical efficacy and probability of great harm is evidenced by the rarity of psychosurgery today. Lobotomies are no longer performed at all. As of 2007, there are no more than 20 surgeries a year performed in the United States to treat psychiatric disorders. In those cases, they are typically limited to laser-induced lesions of the **cingulate gyrus** (a ridge of tissue in the medial part of the brain that functions as part of the limbic system) for intractable obsessive-compulsive disorder (OCD).

The former popularity of lobotomies, however, serves as a reminder that barbarous treatment of the mentally ill did not end in the Middle Ages and that a little knowledge combined with overconfidence on the part of those with professional titles does not serve patients well. Walter Freeman kept records of the 3,439 lobotomies he performed in the course of a career that lasted from 1936 until 1967, when one of his patients died after the procedure. The hospital then revoked his privileges. Freeman was a psychiatrist with no surgical training except what he received "on the job" from Watts, but with the air of a natural showman, he turned lobotomies into media events. Promoted and popularized by Freeman, lobotomy became the "miracle cure" for schizophrenia, depression, criminal behavior, all sorts of manias, and even simple eccentricity. Freeman, in fact, considered seriously disturbed patients too ill to be helped and maintained that lobotomy would be most beneficial for patients in the "early" stages of a mental disorder. Lobotomies would be performed the world around. Criminals were common victims of the procedure, and in Japan, lobotomy was an option for children considered hard to manage.

Consider the following scene: A woman is strapped down on an operating table. A man with a sharp tool approaches her. "What's he going to do to me? Tell him to go away," she says. Then she screams (El-Hai, 2005). No, this is not a scene from a slasher movie—it was Walter Freeman performing his first ice-pick lobotomy.

Freeman traveled from one mental hospital to another. Wearing a surgical gown, its sleeves cut off to reveal his powerful biceps, and wielding a gold-plated ice pick, Freeman would lobotomize patient after patient with his **transorbital** technique. He tried to set speed records, having assistants time him. He sometimes cut into both eye sockets simultaneously, and delighted in shocking and sickening observers, including surgeons. Freeman had himself filmed and photographed performing transorbital lobotomies and played up to the media of his day as a combination ringmaster and lobbyist for lobotomies. One of Freeman's patients died on one occasion when he paused to allow a photograph to be taken in the middle of the procedure, and the leucotome sank too deeply into the patient's brain (El-Hai, 2005).

Freeman and Watts's most famous failure was Rosemary Kennedy, the younger sister of John F. Kennedy. She was mildly retarded rather than mentally ill, and when she started to show some interest in boys, her father, Joseph Kennedy, decided that she should undergo the procedure. Watts performed the actual lobotomy on Rosemary under Freeman's supervision. The operation was described later by an investigative reporter named Ronald Kessler:

> [Watts said,] "We went through the top of the head, I think she was awake. She had a mild tranquilizer. I made a surgical incision in the brain through the skull. It was near the front. It was on both sides. We just made a small incision, no more than an inch." The instrument Dr. Watts used looked like a butter knife. He swung it up and down to cut brain tissue. "We put an instrument inside," he said. As Dr. Watts cut, Dr. Freeman put questions to Rosemary. For example, he asked her to recite the Lord's Prayer or sing "God Bless America" or count backwards. . . . "We made an estimate on how far to cut based on how she responded." . . . When she began to become incoherent, they stopped. (Kessler, 1996, p. 226)

After the lobotomy, Rosemary Kennedy was reduced to a virtually infantile condition; she lost her ability to talk intelligibly and to control her bladder. She lived for the last 60 years of her life in an institution. Even many of Freeman's "successes" lost the ability to eat or go to the bathroom on their own, lost their normal emotional responsiveness, and sat motionless for hours. They were successes by Freeman's reckoning only because they were no longer violent, overly emotional, or self-absorbed. The loss of the sparkle of the individual personality was true of even those patients who managed to return to a semi-normal life.

▣ PERSONALITY AND BODY TYPE

Kretschmer's Biotypology

After the growing consensus in the 19th century that the brain is the seat of human personality, other researchers came to think that personal characteristics are transmitted genetically. Just as many genetic traits are linked, it followed that many personality characteristics could be linked to other genetic traits. Ernst Kretschmer (1888–1964), a German psychiatrist, was a prominent proponent of this concept. Kretschmer (1970) linked personality to body type in his system of **biotypology**. He concluded on the basis of his clinical experience that there are three basic body types and that body type influences behavior and susceptibility to psychopathology, especially manic-depressive illnesses and schizophrenia. Kretschmer defined three basic body types: asthenic, athletic, and pyknic, as well as a fourth pathological type—the dysplactic—which included the more atypical body types that are usually associated with glandular imbalances.

The essence of Kretschmer's theory is that each body type is fundamentally associated with a personality or character style. The pyknic type includes stocky, rotund, and shorter individuals, who, in Kretschmer's opinion, are predisposed to develop such cyclical mood patterns as manic depression. He also thought of pyknics as inclined to be gregarious, generous, and friendly. The second basic category is the asthenic, the tall and thin type of person. Kretschmer regarded these individuals as likely to develop schizoid styles or schizophrenia. When they are not ill, he believed them to be reserved, anxious, and socially withdrawn. The athletic type of individual in Kretschmer's biotypology tends to be muscular and well-proportioned. Kretschmer believed that athletic individuals are the least likely to suffer from mental illness, but when they are so afflicted, they are likely to be diagnosed with schizophrenia.

Sheldon's Somatotypes

The principle that personality is an expression of body type was expanded upon by William H. Sheldon (1898–1977), an American psychologist, in the 1940s. He also postulated three body types (Sheldon, Stevens, & Tucker, 1940), which he called **somatotypes** (see Table 7.1). Each body type was presumed to be dominated by one of three tissue layers of the body. Sheldon called the first type the endomorph because he believed this body type is related to the endoderm, the innermost cell layer of the human embryo. The lining of the mature digestive tract develops from this cell layer, which led Sheldon to conclude that endomorphs are dominated by their digestive system, which explains their tendency to obesity. Sheldon also believed that essential personality characteristics were associated with his body types. Endomorphs tend, like Kretschmer's pyknics, to be gregarious and affectionate. Sheldon also thought of endomorphs as pleasure-seekers but not as particularly aggressive or competitive.

Sheldon called the second body type the mesomorph. People who belong to this type are supposedly dominated by the mesoderm, which is the middle layer of embryonic tissue, which gives rise to connective tissue, muscles, and blood vessels. Sheldon thought of mesomorphs as typified by a muscular build and physical symmetry. As people, they are aggressive, brave, socially dynamic, and energetic.

Sheldon called his third body type the ectomorph, whose physiology is directed by the ectoderm, the outer layer of embryonic tissue from which the brain and central nervous system develop. Ectomorphs are characteristically tall and slender. They are also, according to Sheldon, artistically inclined, introverted, passive, and sensitive in their interpersonal interactions.

Sheldon theorized that although some individuals are nearly pure representatives of their respective types, most people have some components of each type. In his *Atlas of Men,* he set forth a system that rated people on a scale of 1 to 7 according to the degree to which they possessed the characteristics of each type. In Sheldon's system, a person scored as 5-3-1 was

Table 7.1	William Sheldon's Somatotypes		
Body Type	*Endomorph*	*Mesomorph*	*Ectomorph*
Physical characteristics	• Fleshy and rounded • Large abdomen and digestive system • Weak musculature	• Well-defined musculature • Very mature in appearance • Large shoulders and arms • Upright stance	• Thin and frail • Flat chest • Tall with stooped stance • More childlike • Large brain
Personality characteristics	• Forgiving • Stable emotionality • Gregarious • Focuses on food and physical comforts • Seeks affection	• Dominant and aggressive • Competitive • Unconcerned with the opinions of others • Seeks activity	• Introverted and anxious • Shy or self-conscious • Creative or artistic • Mentally focused

SOURCE: Hemera.

primarily an endomorph with some mesomorphic and a few ectomorphic traits. Sheldon scored himself as a 3-4-5.

The work of Kretschmer (1970) and Sheldon stimulated a great deal of research and, for a while, was a key topic in personality research. With continued scrutiny, however, researchers found that the notion of body type as a key to personality had little if any merit. There are a number of reasons for doubting the validity of this typology. First, fitting a person into a category based on physical characteristics is a highly subjective task. The areas of the body that are measured to fit a person into a type are continuous with one another. The point at which one category begins and another ends tends to be arbitrarily defined by each investigator. This subjectivity invariably calls into question the basic notion of body types. Sheldon and his adherents did find a few correlations between the proposed body types and personality characteristics. The correlations were sufficiently small, however, as to lack any validity for a scientist seeking to understand individuals.

In addition to the subjectivity involved in his measurements, Sheldon failed to use basic caution in using correlative data. That is, the correlation of two factors does not by itself demonstrate a cause-and-effect relationship. In the case of body type and personality, social factors may be more powerful forces in shaping personality than linked genes. For example, a person with a large symmetrical muscular body may be treated with greater deference, receive more attention from parents and teachers, and be held to higher expectations. Similarly, an undernourished person reared in a socially deprived setting will tend to be both slender and introverted. Thus, social and environmental factors may contribute as much as genetic factors to systematic differences between body type and character. Although body type may appear on superficial examination to be directly linked to personality or character, in actuality, other unmeasured variables are usually in play.

◫ CHALLENGES TO THE MEDICAL MODEL

Thomas Szasz (1920–), a Hungarian-born psychiatrist, has become psychiatry's best-known and most enduring adversary. Few would argue that the abandonment of demonology has been beneficial to those with mental disorders, but there are some who argue against the medicalization of mental disorders. Szasz has been the most prolific writer and polemicist of this school.

Image 7.5   Thomas Szasz (1920–)

SOURCE: Schaler.

The medical model of illness in general maintains that there are identifiable diseases and disorders, all of which have causes, courses, and outcomes. These diseases are presumed to be caused by some organic pathology such as an infection, a traumatic injury, a biochemical imbalance, or a genetic mutation. As applied to psychiatry, the medical model holds that most or all mental illnesses are diseases and should be treated accordingly. In part, the medical model is the legacy of people like Pinel and Griesinger, who endeavored to make the practice of psychiatry more scientific.

In Szasz's (1960) book, *The Myth of Mental Illness*, he charges that this effort far exceeds any legitimate foundation in science. He points out that virtually none of the common psychiatric diagnoses can be directly linked to lesions or pathology of the nervous system. He likens the collective use of the term *mental illness* to the repetition of a myth—passed along unchallenged and accepted as part of a culture.

In this case, the myth of mental illness is the mythical culture of psychiatry, which, according to Szasz, labels behaviors that are socially undesirable or unacceptable to the psychiatrist as symptoms. Szasz puts it this way: "Mental illness is a myth whose function it is to disguise and thus render more palatable the bitter pill of moral conflicts in human relations" (p. 118).

Szasz has never denied that there are people who suffer emotional anguish, but he states that these result from problems in living, not disease. The medicalization of life problems, he asserts, has led to one group of people losing their freedom to others who seek to protect them from their own unhappy lives. As evidence supporting his position, he points to the use of insulin shock therapy, ECT, psychosurgery, and other less propitious psychiatric "cures" for vaguely defined illnesses. In addition, he notes that many so-called diseases of the past that resulted in extreme treatments are no longer even considered illnesses. Examples of this reclassification are homelessness, masturbation, homosexuality, and illegitimacy.

Szasz has always made a compelling case for his position, and if he is considered a cautionary figure, reminding people of past abuses and warning against future mistreatment, then he may be considered a major figure in the fields of psychology and psychiatry. The history he summarizes is undeniable. Physicians who had the right to confine people in medical settings sometimes abused that privilege. They have also been shown to be guilty of applying personal social judgments in their determination of pathology.

On the other hand, Szasz's requirement that the profession must demonstrate a direct link between mental pathology and organic dysfunction seems too harsh. It is similar to the situationalist view of personality, which holds that a person has no constant personality. Rather the situation will demand or elicit behaviors that are associated with personality. A strong adherent of situationalism will argue that all people will act outgoing when placed in a position of power, for example. Szasz applies this concept to psychiatric diagnoses. Many of what are now called illnesses used to be called demonic possession. Thus, those who control the definition of diagnostic criteria create the illness, he argues, which does not exist independently of the diagnosis.

Although most observers would regard Szasz's views as extreme, the fact remains that the psychiatric diagnoses of the type used by the American Psychiatric Association's official manual are descriptive rather than etiological; that is, they are little more than labels applied to a specific set of problematic behaviors rather than causal explanations. The labeling problem is not unique to psychiatry. The problem with labels is that once one is applied to a person or situation, it feeds into the commonplace illusion that naming a phenomenon is equivalent to understanding it. Then anyone studying the phenomenon in question is likely to see any additional information about it through the filter of the original label. With regard to the effects of labeling on human beings, once a person is labeled by others, he or she may accept, identify with, and meet the expectations attached to that label; hence, it becomes a self-fulfilling prophecy.

▣ CONTEMPORARY AMERICAN PSYCHIATRIC NOSOLOGY: THE *DIAGNOSTIC AND STATISTICAL MANUAL*

The Road to DSM-I (1952)

Kraepelin's work established psychiatric nosology as the basis of sound diagnosis and treatment of mental disorders. In the United States, the Bureau of the Census first began to classify and quantify the frequency of psychiatric disorders among Americans in the 1840s. Isaac Ray, superintendent of the Butler Hospital in Rhode Island, presented a paper at the 1849 meeting of the Association of Medical Superintendents of American Institutions for the Insane (the forerunner of the present American Psychiatric Association) in which he called for a uniform system of naming, classifying, and recording cases of mental illness. The same plea was made in 1913 by Dr. James May of New York to the same organization, which by then had renamed itself the American Medico-Psychological Association. The growing interest in psychiatric disorders by researchers in the social sciences led to a collaboration between the Census Bureau and the American Medico-Psychological Association in developing a psychiatric nosology. At the request of the Bureau, and following Dr. May's request, the Association formed a committee on statistics in 1913 that led to the 1918 publication of the *Statistical Manual for the Use of Institutions of the Insane*. This early version of the current

Image 7.6 The DSM is currently in its fourth edition, which has also been revised.

DIAGNOSTIC AND STATISTICAL MANUAL OF MENTAL DISORDERS

FOURTH EDITION

TEXT REVISION

DSM-IV-TR®

AMERICAN PSYCHIATRIC ASSOCIATION

nosology took a clearly biological perspective; it described psychiatric disorders as essentially physical problems.

The reader should recall that at this time, just prior to World War I, there were no clinical schools of thought. There were competing theories of etiology in mental health, but there were no theories of treatment methodology. Given this lack of a standard of care, there was no perceived need for more accuracy in diagnosis. As a result, 34 years went by before the next official revision of the diagnostic criteria for mental illness.

The revision of the *Statistical Manual* that was published in 1952—by the renamed American Psychiatric Association (APA)—was the first edition of the *Diagnostic and Statistical Manual of Mental Disorders,* or DSM-I. The 60 diagnoses catalogued in DSM-I reflected Meyer's psychobiological view that mental disorders represented reactions of the personality to psychological, social, and biological factors. Meyer held that the human psyche functions as a whole; and when it functions well, all of its components are well integrated with one another. Meyer considered Freud's notion of the unconscious irrelevant to understanding human personality. Instead, he saw functioning in response to life events as a much more significant factor. From a psychobiological perspective, then, psychiatric illnesses and personality disorders result from faulty patterns of response to life events.

DSM-I outlined four categories of mental disorders: (1) disturbances of pattern; (2) disturbances of traits; (3) disturbances of drive, control, and relationships; and (4) sociopathic disturbances (see Table 7.2). While tacitly accepting Meyer's principles, the framers of DSM-I also made room for a psychoanalytic perspective. Freud's concept of a dynamic unconscious is reflected in the use of the term neurosis to describe several disorders. This homage to Freud is made clear in the following excerpt describing the psychoneurotic disorders:

The chief characteristic of these disorders is "anxiety," which may be directly felt and expressed or which may be unconsciously and automatically controlled by the utilization of various psychological defense mechanisms (depression, conversion, displacement, etc.). In contrast to those with psychoses, patients with psychoneurotic disorders do not exhibit gross distortion or falsification of external reality (delusions, hallucinations, illusions) and they do not present gross disorganization of the personality. Longitudinal (lifelong) studies of individuals with such disorders usually present evidence of periodic or constant maladjustment of varying degree from early life. Special stress may bring about acute symptomatic expression of such disorders.

Table 7.2   Disorders of Personality in DSM-I (1952)

Disorders of Psychogenic Origin or Without Clearly Defined Tangible Cause or Structural Change		
00D—x00	Psychoneurotic reactions	(318.5)
000—x0i	Anxiety reaction	(310)
000—x02	Dissociative reaction	(311)
000—x03	Conversion reaction	(311)
000—x04	Phobic reaction	(312)
000—x05	Obsessive compulsive reaction	(313)
000—x06	Depressive reaction	(314)
000—x0y	Psychoneurotic reaction, other	(318.5)
Disorders of Psychogenic Origin or Without Clearly Defined Tangible Cause or Structural Change		
Personality Disorders		
000—x40	Personality pattern disturbance	(320.7)
000—x41	Inadequate personality	(320.3)
000—x42	Schizoid personality	(320.0)
000—x43	Cyclothymic personality	(320.2)
000—x44	Paranoid personality	(320.1)
000—x50	Personality trait disturbance	(321.5)
000—x51	Emotionally unstable personality	(321.0)
000—x52	Passive-aggressive personality	(321.1)
000—x53	Compulsive personality	(321.5)
000—x5y	Personality trait disturbance, other	(321.5)
000—x60	Sociopathic personality disturbance	(320.7)
000—x61	Antisocial reaction	(320.4)
000—x62	Dyssocial reaction	(320.5)
600—x63	Sexual deviation. Specify Supplementary Term	(320.6)

Table 7.2 (Continued)

000—x64	Addiction	
000—x641	Alcoholism	(322.1)
000—x642	Drug addiction	(323)
000—x70	Special symptom reactions	(321.4)
000—x71	Learning disturbance	(326.2)
000—x73	Enuresis	(321.3)
000—x74	Somnambulism	(321.4)
000—x7y	Other	(321.4)
Transient Situational Personality Disorders		
000—x80	Transient situational personality disturbance	(326.4)
000—xSl	Gross stress reaction	(326.3)
000—x82	Adult situational reaction	(326.6)
000—x83	Adjustment reaction of infancy	(324.0)
000—x84	Adjustment reaction of childhood	(324.1)
000—x84I	Habit disturbance	(324.1)
000—x842	Conduct disturbance	(324.1)
000—x843	Neurotic traits	(324.1)
000—x85	Adjustment reaction of adolescence	(324.2)
000—x86	Adjustment reaction of late life	(326.5)

"Anxiety" in psychoneurotic disorders is a danger signal felt and perceived by the conscious portion of the personality. It is produced by a threat from within the personality (e.g., by supercharged repressed emotions, including such aggressive impulses as hostility and resentment), with or without stimulation from such external situations as loss of love, loss of prestige, or threat of injury. (DSM-I, APA, 1952, p. 31)

DSM-II (1968)

In 1968, the APA released the second edition of the *Diagnostic and Statistical Manual,* or DSM-II. This edition made the demarcation between pathology and normal mental functioning more precise. It also represented the first attempt to coordinate the American manual with the World Health Organization's (WHO) *International Classification of Diseases,* or ICD. DSM-II still reflected a preference for psychoanalytic nomenclature, however. Psychoneurotic illnesses were now called neurotic disorders, while psychoneurotic reactions gave way to neurotic disturbances, an indication that the influence of Meyer had faded while Freudian influence remained strong.

DSM-II's classification system placed all psychiatric disorders under eight major categories:

1. Transient situational disturbances

2. Personality disorders

3. Neuroses

4. Psychophysiologic disorders

5. Psychoses not attributable to physical conditions

6. Psychoses associated with organic brain disorder

7. Mental retardation

8. Behavior disorders of childhood and adolescence

The addition of these categories to DSM-II, however, did little to improve the manual's contribution to diagnostic reliability. Like DSM-I, DSM-II provided imprecise diagnostic criteria and yielded poor reliability among clinicians.

DSM-III (1980) and DSM-III-R (1987)

The publication of DSM-III in 1980 introduced a new five-axis diagnostic system that distinguished between clinical syndromes, defined as Axis I disorders, and personality disorders, which comprised most of Axis II. The intent of the multiaxial system was to clarify the relevant diagnostic criteria for mental health practitioners. By adding precision, the multiaxial system and the atheoretical approach of DSM-III added greater legitimacy as well as consistency to mental health diagnoses. DSM-III also contributed to advances in research into personality disorders, as more precise definitions made experimentation and study far more practical.

The descriptive classification of personality disorders within DSM-III, however, was found to be unsatisfactory in terms of diagnostic reliability. As a consequence, a revision of DSM-III, known as DSM-III-R, was published in1987. The newer criteria highlighted some of the major problems in achieving adequate descriptions of personality disorders, even though they promoted the study of these disorders. Clinicians found that the distinctions among the disorders have limited utility in actual clinical practice because the personality disorders tend to have a high rate of comorbidity. For example, people diagnosed with histrionic personality disorder will also meet many of the diagnostic criteria of borderline personality disorder, while some individuals will meet the criteria for both disorders. In the same way, the criteria for schizotypal personality disorder overlap somewhat with those of paranoid personality disorder.

DSM-IV (1994) and DSM-IV-TR (2000)

Background of DSM-IV. The fourth edition of the *Diagnostic and Statistical Manual,* or DSM-IV, was published in 1994 after a preparatory review period lasting 2 years. DSM-IV built upon the research generated by the empirical orientation of DSM-III and DSM-III-R. By the early 1990s, most psychiatric diagnoses had an accumulated body of published studies or data sets. Conflicting reports or lack of evidence were handled by data reanalyses and field trials. The National Institute of Mental Health sponsored 12 DSM-IV field trials together with the National Institute on Drug Abuse (NIDA) and the National Institute on Alcohol Abuse and Alcoholism (NIAAA). The field trials compared the diagnostic criteria sets of DSM-III, DSM-III-R, ICD-10 (which had been published in 1992), and the proposed criteria sets for DSM-IV. The field trials for DSM-IV recruited subjects from a variety of ethnic and cultural backgrounds, in keeping with a new concern for cross-cultural applicability of diagnostic standards. In addition to its inclusion of culture-specific syndromes and disorders, DSM-IV represented much closer cooperation and coordination with the experts from the WHO who had worked on ICD-10.

DSM-IV-TR (2000). DSM-IV-TR, which was published in 2000, does not represent either a fundamental change in the basic classification structure of DSM-IV or the addition of new diagnostic entities. The textual revisions that were made to the 1994 edition of DSM-IV fall under five categories: corrections of factual errors in the 1994 text; review of currency of information; changes reflecting research published after 1992, which was the last year included in the literature review prior to the publication of DSM-IV; improvements to enhance the educational value of DSM-IV; and updating of the ICD diagnostic codes, some of which were changed by WHO in 1996.

The Multiaxial System of DSM-IV. Axis I in the DSM-IV system is used to report various disorders or conditions that fall into 1 of 14 categories, including anxiety disorders, childhood disorders, cognitive disorders, dissociative disorders, eating disorders, factitious disorders, impulse control disorders, mood disorders, psychotic disorders, sexual and gender identity disorders, sleep disorders, somatoform disorders, and substance-related disorders. Other conditions known as adjustment disorders may also be a focus of clinical attention; these include medication-induced movement disorders, relational problems, problems related to abuse or neglect, noncompliance with treatment, malingering, adult antisocial behavior, child or adolescent antisocial behavior, age-related cognitive decline, bereavement, academic problem, occupational problem, identity problem, religious or spiritual problem, acculturation problem, and phase of life problem. In brief, any DSM diagnosis or diagnoses for an individual are noted on Axis I, with the exception of the personality disorders and mental retardation. These diagnoses can include anything from an adjustment disorder to schizophrenia of the paranoid type.

Diagnoses noted on Axis II include the personality disorders and mental retardation. Clinicians will give consideration to additional intervention and treatment choices. The reader should recall here that personality represents the qualities and traits of a unique individual. It is the enduring pattern of our thoughts, feelings, and behaviors—how we think, love, feel, make decisions, and take actions. Personality is determined partly by genetics and partly by the social environment. It is the determining factor in how we live our lives. Individuals with personality disorders have more difficulty in every aspect of their lives. Their individual personality traits reflect ingrained, inflexible, and maladaptive patterns of behaviors that cause discomfort and distress and impair the individual's ability to manage the daily activities of living.

Mental retardation is usually caused by problems in brain development and will affect virtually all aspects of the individual's cognitive functioning. Borderline intellectual functioning, as well as learning disabilities, may also be a consideration for clinical focus. The logic of the multiaxial system here is that the clinical syndromes on Axis I will manifest in different ways if there is an underlying personality disorder. For example, a person diagnosed with an anxiety disorder who is also diagnosed with avoidant personality disorder may be better understood if his or her lifestyle requires a great deal of social contact or pressure.

Axis III is used to list any medical disorders that may be relevant to the individual's current or past mental health diagnoses. Like a personality disorder, a medical problem can alter or mimic the presentation of a mental health disorder. For example, someone seeking help for major depression who is found to suffer from hypothyroidism might in fact have developed all symptoms as a result of low levels of thyroid hormone.

Psychosocial stressors are recorded on Axis IV. These include adverse life events that may affect the individual's psychological stability. Such events as the loss of a job, marriage or divorce, the birth of a child, a traumatic event, or a death in the family are examples of such stressors.

Axis V notes the individual's general level of functioning. To use this axis, the clinician or therapist assesses the level of function that the individual has attained at the time of assessment. In some cases, the scale, which is called the Global Assessment of Functioning or GAF Scale (see Table 7.3), is used to indicate the highest level of function that the person has attained in the past year. Level of function is coded on a 0–100 scale, with 100 being nearly perfect functioning.

VIGNETTE

Maury had an unremarkable upbringing. His parents both worked to provide him and his brother with a middle-class home. They were not harsh disciplinarians but tried to instill appropriate values in their sons. Most important, they did so through their lived example. Maury's parents were honest, generally kept their promises, and earned the respect of their peers. It would seem that Lewis, Maury's brother, had benefited from his parents' examples. Lewis did well in school and was awarded a partial scholarship to a large private university in a nearby state. He ultimately earned a master's degree in education and became the assistant principal of a high school.

Maury, however, took a different path. By the age of 14, he was cutting school and leading a group of like-minded boys to hangouts where they drank malt liquor and smoked marijuana. From that time on, he was always in some sort of trouble, either with school officials or with the police. Despite every intervention his parents could

(Continued)

(Continued)

think of or afford, Maury was focused on immediate pleasures and satisfactions. Accomplishments like graduating from school and becoming a professional or tradesman were too abstract to motivate him in any way. Sadly, the obvious distress of his parents produced no remorse or shame. It seemed that Maury's emotional repertoire was limited to two basic emotions: fear and anger. The only goals that Maury had were obtaining drugs and finding willing sexual partners.

After a youth spent in and out of family court and juvenile facilities, Maury ended up in an adult prison by the age of 19 for selling cocaine. Rather than being traumatized by the experience, however, Maury was invigorated by it. He had done "hard time" and it did not faze him—he actually took pride in surviving "the system." And the only lesson he learned from prison was to avoid getting caught again. His social life followed a similar pattern. Sex was most enjoyable when he felt he could fool a woman into loving him. The woman's anguish when she discovered that he either had other girlfriends or that he simply did not care for her beyond sexual satisfaction was laughable to Maury. He believed that "stupid" people deserved what they got. And he held most women with whom he had sex to be quite stupid. After all, how could any ordinary woman be anything but stupid to think someone as wonderful as Maury could be in love with her?

Maury spent his early adult life committing petty crimes, dealing drugs, and betraying friends and family members. He never showed any evidence of remorse, feelings of social obligation, or values. Maury fathered a child in his late thirties and paid child support only when his assets were attached. By this time in his life, however, he had found a vocation in auto sales, where his talent for sincere deception led to a better income than drug dealing. Although he probably could have done well without deceiving others, he took special pride in exploiting naïve first-time car buyers. Although many clinicians would classify Maury as having an antisocial personality disorder, he would not have accepted that diagnosis. He managed to function quite satisfactorily by his standards and actively enjoyed his life. Maury surely exemplifies some of the complexities in classifying personality.

Vignette Questions

1. Does Maury have a personality disorder?

2. Or did he learn a style of behavior that is socially undesirable?

3. What type of treatment might Maury have received from a psychiatrist versus a nonmedical therapist?

In DSM-III-R personality disorders were organized into three conceptually related clusters with several modifications. This classification scheme was retained in DSM-IV (see Table 7.4).

The DSM is now in its fourth edition, but due to textual revisions made in 2000, it is now referred to as DSM-IV-TR. The operational approach to diagnoses, first introduced in DSM III, provided a clear step-by-step "shopping list" of criteria and has at least eliminated some of the

Table 7.3   The GAF Scale

	Global Assessment of Functioning Scale
100–91	Superior functioning in a wide range of activities, life's problems never seem to get out of hand, is sought out by others because of his or her many positive qualities. No symptoms.
90–81	Absent or minimal symptoms (e.g., mild anxiety before an exam), good functioning in all areas, interested and involved in a wide range of activities, socially effective, generally satisfied with life, no more than everyday problems or concerns (e.g., an occasional argument with family members).
80–71	If symptoms are present, they are transient and expectable reactions to psychosocial stressors (e.g., difficulty concentrating after family argument); no more than slight impairment in social, occupational, or school functioning (e.g., temporarily falling behind at work or in school work).
70–61	Some mild symptoms (e.g., depressed mood and mild insomnia) or some difficulty in social, occupational, or school functioning (e.g., occasional truancy, or theft within the household), but generally functioning pretty well, has some meaningful interpersonal relationships.
60–51	Moderate symptoms (e.g., flat affect and circumstantial speech, occasional panic attacks) or moderate difficulty in social, occupational, or school functioning (e.g., few friends, conflicts with peers or coworkers).
50–41	Serious symptoms (e.g., suicidal ideation, severe obsessional rituals, frequent shoplifting) or any serious impairment in social, occupational, or school functioning (e.g., no friends, unable to keep a job).
40–31	Some impairment in reality testing or communication (e.g., speech is at times illogical, obscure, or irrelevant) or major impairment in several areas, such as work or school, family relationships, judgment, thinking, or mood (e.g., depressed, avoids friends, neglects family, unable to work, child frequently beats up younger children, defiant, falling behind in school).
30–21	Behavior is considerably influenced by delusions or hallucinations or serious impairment in communication or judgment (e.g., sometimes incoherent, acts grossly inappropriately, suicidal preoccupation) or inability to function in almost all areas (e.g., stays in bed all day, no job, home, or friends).
20–11	Some danger of hurting self or others (e.g., suicide attempts without clear expectation of death, frequently violent, manic excitement) or occasionally fails to maintain minimal personal hygiene (e.g., smears feces) or gross impairment in communication (e.g., largely incoherent or mute).
10–1	Persistent danger of severely hurting self or others (e.g., recurrent violence) or persistent inability to maintain minimal personal hygiene or serious suicidal act with clear expectation of death.
0	Inadequate information.

Table 7.4   Personality Disorders in DSM-III and DSM-IV

Cluster A: disorders marked by odd or eccentric behaviors

- Paranoid personality disorder
- Schizoid personality disorder
- Schizotypal personality disorder

Cluster B: disorders characterized by dramatic, emotional, or erratic behaviors

- Antisocial personality disorder
- Borderline personality disorder
- Histrionic personality disorder
- Narcissistic personality disorder

Cluster C: disorders characterized by anxious or fearful behaviors

- Avoidant personality disorder
- Dependent personality disorder
- Obsessive compulsive personality disorder
- Passive-aggressive personality disorder

Table 7.5   Comparison of Successive Editions of DSM

Release	Date of Publication	Theoretical Orientation	Diagnostic Entities
DSM-I	1952	Sociobiological model derived from Adolf Meyer combined with psychoanalytic orientation derived from Sigmund Freud	106
DSM-II	1968	Reaction terminology dropped but psychoanalytic terms retained	182
DSM-III	1980	Psychoanalytic terms dropped in favor of an atheoretical approach	265
DSM-III-R	1987	Atheoretical	296
DSM-IV	1994	Atheoretical/descriptive	290
DSM-IV-TR	2004	Atheoretical/descriptive	290

subjectivity in diagnoses and improved reliability. Reliability may not guarantee validity, but lack of reliability guarantees lack of validity. Table 7.5 provides a summary of the differences.

Critiques of DSM-IV. DSM-IV is not without its critics. First, critics maintain that the retention of the medical model of mental illness in DSM-IV perpetuates the social stigma attached to mental disorders (Wahl, 1999). Second, the symptom-based criteria sets of DSM-IV have led to an endless multiplication of mental conditions and disorders. The unwieldy size of DSM-IV is a common complaint of doctors in clinical practice—a volume that was only 119 pages long in its second (1968) edition has swelled to 886 pages in less than 30 years.

Third, some critics contend that the DSM-IV criteria do not distinguish adequately between poor adaptation to ordinary problems of living and true psychopathology. One by-product of this inadequacy is the suspiciously high rates of prevalence reported for some mental disorders. Some critics point out that with one-year prevalence of psychiatric disorders close to 30% and lifetime close to 50% (Jacobi et al., 2004; Kessler, McGonagle, Zhao, & Nelson, 1994), one might judge psychopatholgy to be a normal condition based on the DSM.

Another criticism of DSM-IV is that the current classification is deficient in acknow-ledging disorders of uncontrolled anger, hostility, and aggression. Even though inappropriate expressions of anger and aggression lie at the roots of major social problems, only one DSM-IV disorder (intermittent explosive disorder) is explicitly concerned with them. In contrast, entire classes of disorders are associated with depression and anxiety.

Last, some observers think that DSM-IV's emphasis on biological psychiatry has con-tributed to the widespread popular notion that most problems of human life can be solved by taking pills. In addition, DSM-IV's emphasis on the use of medications in treating mental disorders has come under fire by critics who note that about 50% of the members of the panel that brought out DSM-IV have or have had ties to major pharmaceutical companies.

The tremendous differences between DSM-I and DSM-IV—in the length of the manual and in the number and categorization of disorders—reflects, of course, not changes in actual patient symptoms, but rather changes in psychiatric thinking. No stronger example can be brought to illustrate this than the changing views of homosexuality. It took a heated battle to remove homosexuality from being listed as a mental illness in DSM-II, and the APA vote at the time to remove it was a close 5,854 to 3,810. Recall Szasz's view above that the term "mental disorder" may reflect no more than behavior that runs counter to the values of authority figures. The reader should remember that regardless of our own affinities, even if mental disorders reflect more than just the subjective views of therapists, they undeniably at least partially reflect those views.

Kurt Schneider (1887–1967) was a pioneering German psychiatrist famous for his contri-butions to the diagnosis of schizophrenia through listing symptoms. Some of the symptoms of the disorder are still called Schneiderian or first-rank symptoms. This is what he wrote:

> Psychopathic types look like diagnoses but the analogy is a false one. A **depressive** psy-chopath is simply a "certain sort of person." People or personalities cannot be labeled diagnostically like illness or like the psychic effects of illness. At most, we are simply emphasizing and indicating a set of individual peculiarities which distinguish these people and in which there is nothing comparable to symptoms of illness. (quoted in Schwartz, Wiggins, & Norko, 1995, p. 429)

▣ CHAPTER SUMMARY

An understanding of personality requires an understanding of what constitutes an abnormal personality. In ancient Greece, Hippocrates proposed that psychopathology is caused by infirmity of the brain, but this naturalism was later undermined by religious views. For over a millennium, the mentally disordered were seen as possessed by demons or as being in league with Satan. With the Enlightenment, mental disorders were once again regarded as diseases, but the clinical treatment of the mentally ill did not immediately improve. The introduction of the medical model, however, led to mental illness being seen as a condition requiring treatment rather than punishment; it also resulted in advances in classification. On the negative side, the medical model produced such treatments as insulin shock and lobotomy, which did at least as much harm as good.

Kretschmer and Sheldon classified body types and held them responsible for personality characteristics. These ideas led to new research but proved to be false leads. Thomas Szasz challenged the medical model and considered mental disorders to be a myth. His views are at least a warning of the dangers of labeling people.

The Diagnostic and Statistical Manual (DSM), put out by the American Psychiatric Association, has become the North American standard for diagnoses, and it undergoes periodic revision. It eventually took on an atheoretical and operational view of diagnoses. Later editions using this approach have resulted in increased reliability of diagnoses.

Chapter 8

The Neo-Freudians

Chapter Goals

- Trace the influence of psychoanalytic thought from the early 20th century to the present
- Provide an understanding of recent psychodynamic approaches including those of the self, ego, and object relations schools
- Explain the essential ideas of major psychodynamic theorists such as Karen Horney, Melanie Klein, Harry Stack Sullivan, Heinz Kohut, Otto Kernberg, Erich Fromm, and Erik Erikson
- Clarify how these theoreticians have diverged from Freud's original psychoanalysis
- Provide an understanding of these theories to modern personality theory

Freud's theories were so influential that they became benchmarks for rebellion as well as starting points for modifications. To some observers, Freudian theory stood for everything a personality theory should *not* be, and they rejected the entire psychodynamic approach; these writers will be considered in other chapters. This chapter introduces those theorists who—to a greater or lesser extent—remained within the psychoanalytic camp while modifying and adding to Freudian theory. Most of these heirs of Freud sought to give the human ego a greater role in personality development and attributed more power to it than Freud had. Freud, of course, regarded the ego as having no energy of its own; he thought it derived its existence only by draining part of the libido's energy; he considered it a rational force rather than an authority figure. For the ego psychologists who followed Freud, however, the ego is not Freud's "clown in the circus," but a part of the personality with its own independent energy. For ego psychologists, adult activities and pleasures are truly carried out for their own sake; they are not merely poor substitutions for unacceptable primitive and nonconscious yearnings.

In the following discussion, the term *theory* as used in some personality theories is somewhat different from how the term is used in the physical sciences. These theories are coherent sets of interdependent principles, but they do not function with the goal of generating hypotheses that will be tested using controlled experiments.

Breaking Away From Freud

Ego psychology describes a range of neo-psychoanalytic thinking that allows for the existence of an entity that Freud did not recognize—namely, an autonomous ego. The appeal of ego psychology is that it restores some of the dignity that Freud supposedly stripped from the human condition. Indeed, Freud himself looked at his own theory as the third great blow to human self-importance, the first two being Copernicus's disproof of the notion that the Earth is the center of the universe and Darwin's account of human beings as creatures that had evolved from other animals rather than being directly created by God.

Ego psychologists, however, point out that Freud's view of the human psyche ignores the true potential of humans. According to their account, people are not mere slaves of the unconscious. "I," the thinking human subject, truly am; and the first-person singular pronoun is not merely an illusion, a side effect of the battles taking place among the nonrational entities in the unconscious. Ego psychology, like most modifications of Freudian theory, offers a view of the human species that is far more optimistic than that of the pessimistic founder of psychoanalysis.

Basic Concepts of Ego Psychology

Conflict-Free Ego. In contrast to Freudian theory, ego psychology posits that the ego, which after all is the rational part of the psyche, has its own autonomous energy from birth—energy that is neither derived from nor beholden to the id. The processes of rational thought rely on this energy. They are, thus, truly reasonable; they are not mere sublimations and rationalizations derived from the id. It is not an overstatement to say that ego psychology implies that human beings are free and independent creatures, not the servants or playthings of internal forces that Freud postulated. Ego psychology also implies a self-subsistent quality to human activities; that is, a chess player plays chess because he enjoys the game, not because he really wishes to sleep with his mother and kill his father. Similarly, a college student majors in bio-chemistry because she genuinely wants to be a doctor, not because she feels defective about the lack of a penis and wishes to compensate for it through discoveries in the laboratory and other academic successes.

Source of Conflicts. According to most psychologists, neurotic development results from unresolved or unsuccessfully resolved internal conflicts. In Freudian theory, the individual psyche provides all the contending forces in this conflict. Freud regarded neuroses as com-promise settlements of the conflict between the desires of the id and the moral imperatives of the superego. Ego psychology, however, regards the source of conflict as external rather than internal. Instead of life being an uneasy truce among the various components of the psyche, it is better understood as an ongoing need to make adjustments between the desires of the individual and the requirements of the wider society. Thus, humans are seen primarily as social animals in ego psychology—a shift in perspective that allowed some neo-Freudians to incorporate Marxist thought into their systems.

A short answer to the question of whether the ego is genuinely conflict-free is that there is scant empirical evidence for most theoretical constructs in personality psychology, Freudian or otherwise. Studies of creative or brilliant individuals offer evidence that such individuals are doing more than merely sublimating unresolved internal conflicts. Rather, they are oblivious to their surrounding society; convinced of their own greatness, they simply enter a field that attracts them and create works of art, invent new machines or techniques that improve the lives of others, expand the scope of human knowledge, or contribute to the world in some other way. MacKinnon's (1965) pioneering study of architects showed that the more creative architects differed from their less creative colleagues in that they had little regard for social rules, demonstrated an intense sense of purpose, and had self-confidence.

🔲 KAREN HORNEY

In spite of Freud's underestimation of women's talents and abilities, one of his most notable successors was a woman, Karen Horney (pronounced "horn-eye"). Born Karen Danielsen in Hamburg in 1885, Horney was trained as a medical doctor and psychoanalyst at the University of Berlin. She entered medical school in 1906, only 6 years after the German universities began to admit women to their degree programs. In 1909, during her years in medical school, she married Oskar Horney, a lawyer, with whom she had three daughters. She left her husband in 1926 and emigrated to the United States in 1930 with her children. In 1932, she moved to Chicago at the invitation of the director of the Chicago Psychoanalytic Institute. She then moved to New York in 1934, where she eventually became the founder and dean of the American Institute of Psychoanalysis after she became dissatisfied with the "old school" psychoanalytic institutes. Horney remained at her new institute until her death in 1952.

Career

Horney departed from traditional psychoanalytic thought in a number of respects. While acknowledging the contributions of Freud, Horney was especially critical of Freud's understanding and treatment of women, particular his concept of penis envy as the determining factor in the psychology of women. She considered her work as falling within the framework of Freudian thought, but her deviation from the classical psychoanalytic line led to her resignation from the New York Psychoanalytic Institute.

This particular pattern of professional development—obtaining a position in a traditional Freudian institute, increasingly deviating from the Freudian "party line," being forced out of the traditional Freudian institute, and opening one's own institution—is a recurrent theme among the neo-Freudians. Young psychoanalysts were often eager to add their own improvements to the ideas of the "great man," only to find that the traditionalists disapproved their alterations. When Horney quit the New York Psychoanalytic Institute in 1941, she actually walked out singing the spiritual, "Go Down, Moses."

Horney (1939) was among the earliest theorists to take exception to Freud from a feminist point of view. Indeed, some of her ideas about the role of women, which were of course not unique to her, have become standard in modern Western societies. When Horney proposed that women should form identities independent of their husbands by developing their own potential and seeking achievement through careers that interested them, however, such ideas were still revolutionary. Horney's own father, a fundamentalist sea captain nicknamed "the Bible-thrower" by his children, believed not only that women are inferior to men but that they brought sin into the world. Horney became skeptical of both religion and the expectations of a male-dominated society. She also battled depression and had made at least one suicide attempt by 1923, when her husband's firm declared bankruptcy and a beloved brother died suddenly of a lung infection.

Horney regarded the differences between male and female gender roles as essentially cultural artifacts rather than biological mandates. "My conviction, expressed in a nutshell," she said, "is that psychoanalysis should outgrow the limitations set by its being an instinctivistic and a genetic [biological] psychology" (Horney, 1939, p. 8). This position led her to maintain that the great flaw in Freud's theory was his underestimation of the power of cultural influences. She wrote, "When we realize the great import of cultural conditions on neuroses, the biological and physiological conditions, which are considered by Freud to be their root, recede into the background" (Horney, 1937, p. viii). The culture's "influence on our ideas of what constitutes masculinity or femininity was obvious, and it became just as obvious to me that Freud had arrived at certain conclusions because he failed to take them into account," she added (Horney, 1945, p. 11). Horney maintained that the psychological traits considered feminine arise from women's lack of self-confidence and society's overemphasis on love relationships with men as the mark of female "success" rather than resulting from the anatomy of the female sex organs. She may have come to this insight about society's tendency to define women by their relationships with men through her disastrous intimate relationship in the 1930s with Erich Fromm, a social psychologist discussed later in this chapter, as well as her failed marriage.

The primacy of culture and society in shaping interpersonal relationships and the role of interpersonal relationships in defining personality, both healthy and impaired, was also evident for Horney in the differences she saw between the patients she had treated in Europe and those she encountered in the United States. She decided that social experiences determine personality and led to the development of personality disorders; therefore, society and the environment to which it gave rise molded the personalities of individuals. Thus, Horney also anticipated the trend of giving greater importance to the social environment in the classic nature-versus-nurture debate. In addition, she regarded Freud's tripartite division of the mind as misleading, and his emphasis on sex as culture-bound. In her opinion, his notion of sexuality was the product of a specific time and place—the troubled capital city of a disintegrating empire at the end of the 19th century—and therefore inapplicable to the setting in which she was then practicing, half a century later on a different continent.

Theory of Personality

Familial and Social Origins of Personality Disturbances. For Horney (1937), personality disturbances (or neuroses) are rooted in troubled social relationships. This was a major departure from the Freudian model, which held that neuroses arose in individuals whose ability to repress unconscious urges were impaired due to developmental perturbations. In fact, Horney challenged a preponderance of Freud's crucial premises. For example, she asserted that he was mistaken about the universality and importance of the Oedipus complex:

Freud's observations concerning the Oedipus complex were made on neurotic persons. In them he found that high-pitched jealousy reactions concerning one of the parents was sufficiently destructive in kind to arouse fear and likely exert lasting disturbing influences on character formation and personal relationships. Observing this phenomenon frequently in neurotic persons of our time he assumed it to be universal. Not only did he assume the Oedipus complex to be the very kernel of neuroses, but he tried to understand complex phenomena in other cultures on this basis. It is this generalization that is doubtful. . . . But there is no evidence that destructive and lasting jealousy reactions—and it is these we think of when talking of the Oedipus complex—are in our culture, not to speak of other cultures, so common as Freud assumes. (Horney, 1937, pp. 82–83)

Horney posited that social relations and their development determined whether a person developed a healthy or neurotic personality. A child's first social relationship is, of course, with its parents, and the nature of this relationship sets the pattern for future personality development as well as problems therein. All children start out in life feeling powerless. They have two primary needs, namely, *safety* and *satisfaction*. The parents will either satisfy the child's need for safety by providing nurturance or fail to do so by subjecting the child to indifference or hostility. A child subjected to mistreatment by its parents develops basic hostility to the parents. Even a maltreated child, however, is dependent on the parents for simple survival, which requires the angry child to repress this basic hostility. The emotional conflict that results leads in turn to a generalized fear of others, hostility toward all the world, and **basic anxiety.**
Horney described basic anxiety as

the feeling a child has of being isolated and helpless in a potentially hostile world. A wide range of adverse factors in the environment can produce this insecurity in a child: direct or indirect domination, indifference, erratic behavior, lack of respect for the child's individual needs, lack of real guidance, disparaging attitudes, too much admiration or the absence of it, lack of reliable warmth, having to take sides in parental disagreements, too much or too little responsibility, overprotection, isolation from other children, injustice, discrimination, unkept promises, hostile atmosphere, and so on and so on. (Horney, 1945, p. 41)

Thus the foundations of a neurotic personality are laid. So damaging is parental behavior that does not meet the child's fundamental need for safety that Horney called parental mistreatment the **basic evil.**

Neurotic Needs. According to Horney, dealing with basic anxiety manifests itself in an unhealthy preoccupation with one of ten neurotic needs. These develop in childhood as defense mechanisms against basic anxiety, but then continue through adolescence into adult life. Horney defined the ten neurotic needs as follows (Horney, 1942):

1. need for affection and approval

2. need for a partner to direct one's life

3. need to confine one's life within narrow limits

4. need for power over others

5. need to exploit others

6. need for recognition and prestige

7. need for personal admiration

8. need for superior achievement

9. need for self-sufficiency and independence

10. need for perfection in order to be unassailable

As the reader surveys this list, some of the needs that Horney identifies do not appear to be particularly neurotic, but rather commonplace human drives. Her point, however, is that these needs become neurotic when their intensity is unrealistic, when the goals they reflect are regarded as more desirable than they really are, and, most of all, when one need overshadows all others to become an obsession that rules the neurotic's life. Horney noted that a person may try to fulfill neurotic needs in an unconscious manner, which results in self-defeating behavior.

Three Basic Life Strategies. Horney (1945) later summarized her list of 10 neurotic needs under the headings of three fundamental life strategies, which she also called coping strategies:

1. *Moving toward people.* This strategy of compliance and self-effacement includes the neurotic needs for approval and a partner who will solve one's problems (seen in neurotic needs 1 and 2)

2. *Moving against people.* This is a strategy of aggression, which incorporates neurotic needs for power and superiority; others are seen as pawns to one's one ends (seen in neurotic needs 4 through 8).

3. *Moving away from people.* A life strategy of withdrawal meets the neurotic need for complete independence from others, who are seen as problems to be avoided (seen in neurotic needs 9 and10).

Gender Roles. With regard to Horney's rejection of Freud's concept of penis envy, the term **"vagina envy"** was subsequently and ironically proposed by feminist writers (Peterson, 1980) to illustrate the way in which Freud's phrase can be turned back on traditional psychoanalysis. According to Peterson (1980), the three-piece masculine "power suit," with its overabundance of pockets—in the pants, jacket, vest, and jacket lining—offers men a symbolic compensation for their lack of a vagina.

All people are products of their respective times, and perhaps, it was in response to such ideas as Horney's that Freud wrote shortly before his death, "A woman analyst who has not been sufficiently convinced of the intensity of her own wish for a penis also fails to attach proper importance of that factor in her patients" (Freud, 1949b, p. 54). For her part, Horney believed that as men cannot create life, they attempt to hide their basic inferiority through achievement and through denigration of women.

In summary, Karen Horney was a pioneer in the development of the view that differences between the behavior of males and females are due primarily to the influence of society, which minimizes the contributions of biological nature to personality. As she said in 1937, "The person who is most likely to become neurotic is one who has experienced the culturally determined difficulties in an accentuated form, mostly through the medium of childhood experience" (Horney, 1937, p. 290). Horney's position became almost universally accepted by Western psychotherapists, but it has been challenged in recent decades by evolutionary psychologists, who maintain that psychological traits in both men and women are biologically based and are products of the evolutionary process of natural selection.

VIGNETTE

Mark, a 23-year-old banker, was engaged as an entry-level financial analyst by one of the premier financial institutions in the world. Unlike many of his cohorts, however, he did not come equipped with top grades from a high-status university. The only quality that made Mark stand out from the new cadre of grey suits and white shirts was his Doberman pinscher-like intensity and his bull-like physique. The elite members of the firm, although cautious in his presence, generally disregarded him.

In addition to these physical stature and educational shortcomings, however, Mark had one further attribute that eventually enabled him to surpass his detractors: He was not intimidated by protocol. This self-assurance came into play on the day he was told that the president of the organization would be taking a limousine to the airport. The president's forthcoming talk to key economists was well publicized. What Mark did next defined his career. He left work half an hour before the president's scheduled departure. He rushed to the parking area a quarter-mile away and brought his own car to the front of the building. After a short wait, Mark saw the president and his assistant leaving the building. Mark leaped from his car and obsequiously accosted his chief operating officer: "Mr. Callahan! Hello! I'm Mark M. from finance. *I* can take you to the airport."

The president blandly thanked him and informed Mark that he had already ordered a limousine. But Mark insisted that he was going to the airport anyway—without offering an explanation or reason for his going there—and said that they could save the organization money. Mark opened the rear door for Mr. Callahan, and the boss of his boss's boss duly got into his car. The 40-minute ride to the airport was essentially silent, but Mark would occasionally break the silence with ideas for making the organization more competitive with some of its smaller but more technologically advanced competitors. The president attended to Mark somewhat casually while studying some documents. When they arrived at the airport, Mark knew the trip had all been worth it. The president said as he left the car, "Good job, Mark."

Over the next year, Mark prepared unsolicited reports and presentations for corporate senior staff. He continually insinuated himself into meetings, luncheons, and seminars for corporate leaders far above his rank. He was a driven young man. "Sh-t for brains" was his appellation for even the best of his staff who could not immediately provide him with the data he requested. He was, however, far more forgiving of errors than he was of any challenge to his authority. For those bold enough to provoke him in this way, he would always respond by inducing fear in the challenger. His typical technique was a closed one-on-one meeting. Once the door

(Continued)

(Continued)

closed behind his competitor, Mark would physically close in on him. While standing only inches away from the other's face, Mark would affect a demeanor of volatile but controlled rage. In short, Mark was the stereotypical alpha male.

By the age of 26 he had achieved the level of division director, an extremely young age for this position. Like most who become powerful leaders, Mark had acquired a sense of entitlement, and his most recent accomplishment did little to temper his drive for corporate ascendancy. He pursued his rise to power, which involved not only bypassing but also firing some of the very people who had hired and mentored him. They included Stan Straussman, a pedantic honors graduate of Princeton with a Harvard MBA. Stan had actually hired Mark but had nevertheless provoked Mark's resentment. Stan was an aristocratic elitist, unabashed about displaying his intellect. Mark, who came from a working-class background, perceived Stan's elitism as a personal affront. Consequently, Mark outwardly expressed loyalty and gratitude to Stan but worked behind the scenes to undermine and embarrass him.

Mark's strategy reached fruition when a marketing plan developed by Stan began to fail. Mark closed in and not only made certain that senior management was aware of Stan's misstep but also made it seem that Stan had been insubordinate. Within weeks of this behind-the-scenes drama Stan announced his early retirement. Shortly thereafter, Mark was awarded Stan's position, making him the youngest vice president in the firm's history.

Over the next decade Mark became the youngest person to hold each corporate title in succession. Each promotion was invariably coupled with the destruction of the career of anyone Mark saw as an adversary. Mark's predatory personality, despite its harsh and unpleasant qualities, led to his success within this particular organization. There were aspects of Mark's personality that would be considered undesirable by many people and sociopathic by others. But despite the disapproval of some who knew his history, Mark seemed quite pleased with himself.

Vignette Questions

1. Was Mark a sociopath?

2. Was his behavior a product of his times—the 1980s, the decade of greed?

3. Do you admire anything Mark did?

4. How do you think you would behave in similar circumstances?

HARRY STACK SULLIVAN

Born Herbert Stack Sullivan (1892–1947) in upstate New York in 1892, Sullivan, like Horney, Kohut, and other neo-Freudians, was trained as a physician. Unlike the medical schools attended by many of his colleagues, however, the Chicago school that awarded Sullivan his

MD was what he himself called a "diploma mill"—in fact, it closed in 1917, the same year he completed his degree. The poor quality of Sullivan's education affected later work, in that he did not receive a solid grounding in scientific method and research techniques; also, he did not learn to write well, and he published little during his lifetime.

Sullivan's relative lack of recognition during his lifetime has been attributed to his homosexuality; he lived with a younger man, who was supposedly his foster son although there was no legal relationship between them. It may well be, however, that Sullivan's sexual orientation helped him to understand the psychiatric problems of racial minorities; he pioneered research into the mental disorders of African Americans in the North as well as the South in the 1930s.

Sullivan did not receive any formal training through a residency program in psychiatry; he learned to be a psychiatrist "on the job," when he joined the staff of Saint Elizabeth's Hospital in Washington, D.C., in 1922. He then moved to the Sheppard and Enoch Pratt Hospital in Baltimore, where he made his reputation as a clinician from 1925 to 1929 by setting up an innovative closed ward for the treatment of patients with schizophrenia. In 1930, he moved to New York and underwent a personal psychoanalysis; he joined with Erich Fromm and Frieda Fromm-Reichmann to establish the William Alanson White Foundation, considered by many to be the world's leading independent psychoanalytic institute; and he started the journal *Psychiatry* in 1937.

Interpersonal Theory of Psychiatry

Sullivan's major innovation was his **interpersonal theory of psychiatry**, which underlies his view of personality. Sullivan thought of personality as an "illusion" (his word) that cannot be understood apart from interpersonal relations. Thus, the proper object of study in personality research for Sullivan is the interpersonal situation, not the individual person. Sullivan also maintained that interpersonal situations could include an individual's relationship with a historical figure, legendary hero, fictional character, or ancestor—that is, with significant others who are not present here and now. In a lecture series published after his death, Sullivan said, "Psychiatry is the study of phenomena that occur in interpersonal situations, in configurations made up of two or more people all but one of whom may be more or less completely illusory" (Sullivan, 1964, p. 33). Sullivan's broad definition of interpersonal situations helps to explain the fact that some determined individuals are able to overcome painful experiences in their families of origin by taking a hero or great moral teacher as their role model rather than their troubled parents. In addition, Sullivan's definition of personality as the characteristic ways in which a person interacts with others emphasizes externally observable actions, words, and other behaviors rather than intrapsychic processes that cannot be directly observed.

In fact, Sullivan is the source of the phrase "significant other," which appeared for the first time in his posthumous book, *The Interpersonal Theory of Psychiatry* (1953). Sullivan's emphasis on the interpersonal dimension of human life also guided his clinical practice; he laid great stress on the psychiatric interview, the term he preferred for the process taking place between therapist and patient—whether the interview consisted of a single meeting or a series of appointments over a long period of time. Two series of lectures that Sullivan gave in 1944 and 1945 were collected after his death into a book titled *The Psychiatric Interview* (1954). Sullivan divided the interview into four stages or phases: (1) inception (during which the therapist observes how the patient speaks and behaves, as well as the content of what he or she says); (2) reconnaissance (Sullivan's term for requesting biographical information or such personal data as occupation and marital status); (3) detailed inquiry into the patient's problems; and (4) termination (in which the therapist summarizes what he or she has learned about the patient and prescribes a course of action to follow).

Dynamisms. Anxiety is a central concept in Sullivan's theory. He defined it as any painful feeling that might arise from either bodily needs or social stress. To ward off anxiety in dealing with others, people engage in what Sullivan termed **security operations**, which include selective inattention and sublimation. Sullivan regarded people's interactions with one another as energy transformations and referred to patterns in these interactions as **dynamisms.** An energy transformation in Sullivan's theory is any form of behavior—it may be open and public (such as talking or playing a musical instrument) or internal and private (such as thinking or daydreaming), but it is always derived from experiences that the person has had with other people. Any habitual reaction to others constitutes a dynamism. Thus, a child who is afraid of the pediatrician is showing a dynamism of fear, while an adult who is habitually nasty to members of other races has a dynamism of malevolence.

The Self-System. The most important dynamism for Sullivan is the **self-system**, which he saw as the composite of all of a person's security operations to defend against anxiety and protect self-esteem. The self-system originates in childhood experiences of parental disapproval and rejection and the anxiety these experiences generate. The self-system is, thus, somewhat isolated from the rest of the personality and usually prevents us from making objective evaluations of our behavior or learning from experience. Sullivan apparently believed that children are often made anxious for reasons that would not exist if society as a whole were more rational; on one occasion, he stated that the self-system in the typical modern person "is the principal stumbling block to favorable changes in personality" (Sullivan, 1953, p. 169).

Theory of Cognition

Sullivan's theory of cognition represents his other major contribution to personality theory. He defined three cognitive processes through which people experience the world and relate to others in the course of their development. The first is what Sullivan called **prototaxic experience**. This is the lowest level, characteristic of the infant. The baby perceives the world as a series of disconnected sensory experiences (of warmth, hunger, fullness, pain, and so on) that have no connection with one another and no particular meaning.

The second level is **parataxic experience**, in which the older child begins to perceive causal relationships between events that occur close together in time but are not necessarily logically related. For example, two children whose playground argument is interrupted by a thunderstorm may assume that their fight "caused" the storm. Superstitions, such as the notion that Friday the 13th is an unlucky day or that a cat licking itself means rainy weather to come are commonplace examples of parataxic thinking. Sullivan thought that many adults never move beyond the level of parataxic experience. The third level of cognition is **syntaxic experience**, which depends on symbols (such as language or numbers) that have a standard meaning shared with others in one's culture. Syntaxic thought allows individuals to communicate with one another and understand their shared experiences.

▣ ERIK HOMBURGER ERIKSON

Erik H. Erikson (1902–1994) was a German developmental psychologist whose main thrust was not just the revision of Freudian theory, but rather the extension of the Freudian developmental stages throughout the entire life span. In the process of his work, Erikson took a theory of psychosexual development and turned it into a theory of psychosocial development. Freud's psychosexual stages of development emphasized the first 6 years of life as the foundation of the adult personality; latency and the genital stage of development were almost afterthoughts. Freud reasoned that the first few years of life are of critical importance and set the stage for everything that follows.

For Freud, the human personality is largely set in stone during the first 5 years of life. Erikson, however, believed that no single phase of life is more important than any other and that personality evolves throughout the entire life span. In fact, just as the first few years of life present opportunities and conflicts, so does every stage of life present opportunities and conflicts. Like many neo-Freudians, Erikson saw the primary motivation in life as social acceptance and integration rather than sexual development, as it was for Freud. Erikson was a pioneer of life span development, and as such, his theory became one of the most influential contributions to psychology in the 20th century. It still figures prominently in child psychology, adolescent psychology, and theories of adult development.

Early Years

Erik H. Erikson was born on June 15, 1902, near Frankfurt, Germany, as the product of an extramarital relationship. He never knew his biological father, and the circumstances of his birth were hidden from him until he was an adult. His biological father, whose name is lost to history, was apparently Danish and abandoned Erik's mother once she became pregnant. His mother, Karla Abrahamsen, who was Jewish, married a Jewish pediatrician, Dr. Theodor Homburger, when Erik was 3 years old. Dr. Homburger officially adopted Erik as his son in 1911, and Erik was known as Erik Homburger until he was a young adult.

When he found out the truth about his parentage, he experienced an **identity crisis**—a concept he later helped to name. It is no wonder that the development of identity became the great concern of Erikson's later theorizing. As a youth, Erik Homburger did not seem to fit in anywhere. He was a tall, blond, blue-eyed boy who was teased for his Nordic appearance in temple school but rejected as a Jew by his classmates in the local grammar school. For Erik Homburger, acceptance did not come either from his Jewish peers or the surrounding Gentile society.

After graduating from high school, Erikson hoped to become an artist and adopted a carefree bohemian lifestyle. Rules and formality did not sit well with him, and a university degree was not an option. Late in life, he admitted that he used the label *artist* as a euphemism for shirking life's responsibilities (Erikson, 1964). He briefly took art classes at two different schools, but there, too, regulations annoyed him. He then wandered around Europe, filled journals with his thoughts, and took shelter where he could find it. He became an art instructor himself, and his teaching led him at age 25 to a school run by a friend of Anna Freud. The students in the school were mostly children of parents involved with psychoanalysis and were psychoanalyzed by Anna Freud herself.

Once settled in Vienna, Erikson established a progressive ungraded school. He also became a member of the Vienna Psychoanalytic Institute and an intimate of the Freud family; he finished his training in psychoanalysis, graduating from the institute in 1933. This certification was actually his only formal training and academic credential. Later, after he moved to the United States and was urged to acquire some academic respectability, he entered a doctoral program at Harvard University but almost immediately dropped out.

Later Career

When the Nazis annexed Austria in 1936, Erikson left Vienna, now with a Canadian wife and two children, first for Copenhagen, but soon settling in Boston, where he became a child psychoanalyst. He arrived in the United States knowing only a few English words and phrases learned on shipboard, but apparently had no trouble establishing a practice in Boston. His move to the United States allowed Erik Homburger to create a new and final identity for himself, one that harkened back to his Scandinavian heritage—he took the name Erik H. Erikson when he became an American citizen and made it famous around the world.

Erikson moved to the West Coast in the late 1940s and became a professor at the University of California at Berkeley, a job he lost in 1950 because he refused to sign a loyalty oath—apparently not because of sympathy toward communism, but because of his characteristic refusal to accept institutional rules. He returned to Stockbridge, Massachusetts, where he held a senior position at Austin Riggs Center, an institution for emotionally disturbed adolescents. In 1960, he became a professor at Harvard, an unusual distinction in light of the fact that he had never received any college degree. At various times in his career, he studied child rearing among the Oglala Sioux and the Yurok Indians, and he analyzed such historical figures as Martin Luther and Mahatma Gandhi. His book *Gandhi's Truth* (1969) won a Pulitzer Prize for general nonfiction as well as the National Book Award. Erikson retired from Harvard in 1970 but remained active, writing and lecturing in the center that he founded until his death in 1994. His last book, *Vital Involvement in Old Age* (Erikson, Erikson, & Kivnick, 1986), contained his views on the last stage of human life.

Theory of Human Identity Formation

Identity formation, according to Erikson, is the specific task of adolescence. Erikson thought of each stage of the life span as posing a particular challenge for resolution; however, special attention has been given to the fifth of his eight developmental stages, which he labeled "identity vs. role confusion." During adolescence, teenagers become concerned with who they are and their role in society. This is a difficult crisis to resolve, he thought, because the emerging adult must balance the fulfillment of societal expectations and roles with the establishment of a unique sense of self. To accomplish this goal, the person requires a psychosocial moratorium—Erikson's term for the period of time when we are no longer children but have not yet undertaken adult responsibility. The moratorium is a sort of "time out" in which we are free to explore different roles, identities, and values to test their fit. For the first time in their lives, adolescents face significant choices and decisions, perhaps too many—vocational preparation, further education, sexual orientation, group participation— but are simultaneously confronted by obligations and responsibilities. These decisions and

Table 8.1	Marcia's Identity Statuses in Adolescence	
	Commitment Made	*Commitment Not Made*
Crisis Has Occurred	Identity achievement	Moratorium
Crisis Has Not Occurred	Identity foreclosure	Identity diffusion

choices need to be made by early adulthood and are often irrevocable. But before that point, Erikson (1968) thought, there should be experimentation and the freedom for it.

Erikson believed that identity gained during adolescence can be lost and a new identity gained, only to be lost once again, until at some point, a persona is established. Research on identity development has tended to support Erikson's theory, but with several modifications. Erikson saw the task of identity formation as beginning in adolescence whereas research shows it to be a process that begins in late adolescence and extends well into young adulthood (Adams & Jones, 1983; Archer, 1982). Moreover, Erikson's use of the term *crisis* (as all of his stages had crises) leading to a resolution does not adequately describe or capture the length and slowness of the process of identity development (Baumeister, 1991), as it suggests a sudden or time-limited event.

Erikson's theoretical work on identity formation, however, has been fruitful for later research. James Marcia, a Canadian developmental psychologist who considers himself an Eriksonian, has refined his mentor's identity theory by suggesting that there are four different stages in identity formation that adolescents undergo. He termed these stages **identity statuses**: identity diffusion, identity foreclosure, identity moratorium, and identity achievement. Marcia (1994) designed a semistructured interview known as the Identity Status Interview to test his hypothesis, and he believes his experimental findings support it. The four identity statuses can be plotted in a table with four cells, the two axes referring to whether the young person has undergone an identity crisis and whether a commitment to a certain value or role has been made.

Marcia's conceptualization is still influential as of the early 2000s but is not without its critics—not only psychologists who reject Erikson but also some who are firmly in the Eriksonian camp. The critics regard Marcia's tabular approach as a dilution of Erikson's concept of crisis. They point out that Erikson meant by that term an almost gut-wrenching need to question the expectations of society (Cote & Levine, 1988; Van Hoof, 1999).

Psychosocial Stages

Extending Freud's stages of development to encompass the entire human life span, Erikson assigned to each stage its characteristic conflict—a life crisis—that must be successfully resolved so that the individual is prepared to face the conflict of the next stage. When the resolution is successful, we grow stronger and acquire a new positive quality as a dimension of our personality that will help us face life's struggles. Erikson calls these positive qualities ego strengths or **virtues**. If the resolution is unsuccessful, we acquire a negative quality that will handicap us in later stages of life. In Erikson's (1969) own words, "In each stage of life a given strength is added to a widening ensemble and reintegrated at each later stage in order to play its part in a full cycle" (p. 39). While the stages are sequential, the ages at which they occur may vary somewhat, as people differ in their rate of maturation.

▣   HEINZ KOHUT

Heinz Kohut (1913–1981), like most of the neo-Freudians, was a medically trained psychoanalyst. Born in Vienna, Austria, Kohut was the only child of Jewish parents. His father was an accomplished pianist who contributed to Kohut's lifelong interest in music. His mother, however, suffered from mental illness during his childhood and was alternately smothering and rejecting. He received a medical degree from the University of Vienna at age 24, but like many European intellectuals, he was forced to flee abroad after Adolf Hitler came to power. Kohut left Vienna in 1939, stayed in England for a year with an uncle who lived in London, and left for the United States in 1940. He settled in Chicago, where he had a childhood friend who had gotten a position at the University of Chicago. Kohut completed a residency in neurology at Chicago and went on to complete his qualifications to become a psychoanalyst. Kohut had begun his own analysis in Austria with a friend of Freud's named August Aichhorn. He continued being in analysis with Ruth Eissler at the Chicago Institute for Psychoanalysis, and he joined its faculty upon his graduation in 1950.

At that time, Kohut considered himself a traditional Freudian, even jokingly referring to himself as "Mr. Psychoanalysis" at one point. He was not to remain a traditionalist for long. Kohut's innovations and departures from Freudian psychoanalytic theory were rooted in the perceived nature of the patients he treated. He was not able to fit his postwar patients into the categories that Freud had derived from his Viennese clientele half a century earlier. Kohut's patients seemed to be suffering less from sexual repression than from a pervasive sense of alienation, absence of meaning in life, powerlessness, and emptiness. They also tended to camouflage these feelings under a protective shell of narcissism—which Kohut defined as a narcissistic personality disorder.

Kohut was influenced by the approach pioneered by Carl Rogers, the founder of humanistic psychology and nondirective therapy. Rogers, whose work will be described more fully in Chapter 12, conceived the therapist's task as providing an unconditionally accepting environment that enables a patient to develop **positive self-regard**. Rogers interpreted positive self-regard as consisting of healthy narcissism and becoming a connected (rather than alienated) member of society. The therapist, thus, supplies what the patients' parents should have given them but probably did not. Kohut maintained that most of his patients suffering from what he called disorders of self had had parents who were lacking in **empathy**. In Carl Rogers's usage, empathy refers to the therapist's ability to suspend his or her own judgments and beliefs and enter as fully as possible into the client's perspective. Kohut believed that empathy—which he defined somewhat differently from Rogers as vicarious introspection—could contribute to the effectiveness of psychoanalysis as well as it had to Rogers's humanistic form of therapy. Kohut saw the parent-child relationship as reenacted in the course of treatment through **transference**, but with the patient achieving a better result.

Kohut eventually broke with classical Freudian theory. His departure led, as it did for so many other former Freudians, to the rupture of his organizational ties and an end to many

Table 8.2   Life Stages According to Erikson

Life Stage	Age	Crisis (Conflict)	Virtue
1. Oral-sensory	0–1 years	Basic trust versus mistrust: If caretakers are consistent, adequate, and loving, babies learn to trust others and see the world as a safe place. If caretakers are inadequate or unloving, infants develop basic mistrust.	Hope
2. Muscular-anal	2–3 years	Autonomy versus shame and doubt: If parents provide rules while praising and allowing children some independence, they develop will and self-esteem. If parents are either too permissive or too autocratic, children will either experience excessive shame and doubt or lack self-control.	Will
3. Locomotor	3–5 years	Initiative versus guilt: If parents are supportive of children's efforts to show initiative, children develop a sense of purpose, the ability to set goals, and the ability to meet them. If parents are not supportive of initiative, children develop an inappropriate sense of guilt. On the other hand, if children's initiatives are never restrained, they may become ruthless.	Purpose
4. Latency	6–12 years	Industry versus inferiority: Children must begin to master the social rules of their culture and develop the skills to do well in school.	Competence
5. Adolescence	13–19 years	Identity versus role confusion: Teenagers must form peer relationships as well as a sense of stability and continuity to the self. Role confusion has been summarized as an inability to see oneself as a productive member of one's society.	Fidelity
6. Young adulthood	20–40 years	Intimacy versus isolation: Young adults must develop the ability to form lasting close relationships and readiness for marriage rather than sexual promiscuity or isolation from others.	Love
7. Middle adulthood	40–65 years	Generativity versus stagnation: Adults must learn to undertake the challenges of parenting the next generation or to otherwise make their contribution to the world.	Caring
8. Maturity	65 years+	Integrity versus despair: Elders must develop the ability to accept their lives and their contributions as a whole.	Wisdom

personal friendships. Kohut eventually called his modification of psychoanalysis self theory (Kohut, 1971). He replaced Freud's structural model of id, ego, and superego with a model of the self as an entity that develops through relationships with others. Kohut's problems with his colleagues began at a 1957 meeting of the Chicago Institute for Psychoanalysis. In that meeting, he presented a paper in which he stated that empathy on the part of the therapist has a primary role in psychoanalysis. He was literally shouted down and booed, as some of the postwar splintering of Freud's tradition took the form of power battles as well as the punishment of "heretics."

At the time that Kohut presented his controversial paper, he was still in the orthodox Freudian camp; he was president of the American Psychoanalytic Institute and vice president of the Freud archives. Together with Anna Freud, he stood in the upper ranks of practicing psychoanalysts. Total allegiance to classical Freudianism, however, left no room for creativity. Like radical behaviorism, Freudianism handcuffed its adherents who sought to put their own brand on personality theory. Not until 1971 did Kohut publish his first book-length deviation from classical Freudianism, *The Analysis of the Self*. As a result of this publication, however, he became a nonperson to those who had once looked up to him. In 1977, he went a step further and finally abandoned Freudian drive theory. This defection created a major stir in the psychoanalytic world. Kohut was now completely on his own. For the rest of his career, he devoted himself to writing and scholarship rather than holding administrative positions in professional organizations.

Donald Winnicott (1896–1971), who will be discussed in more detail below, pioneered a different brand of post-Freudianism from Kohut, but what they had in common was being among the first to note the disappearance of so-called classical neurotics, the types of patients who had found their way to Freud's consulting room. Freud had analyzed people suffering from severe repressions and moral rigidity resulting from a harsh internal censor. The symptoms in the patients that Freud had treated often took the form of somatization disorder, conversion disorder, phobia, and obsessional neurosis. Classical Freudianism was no longer adequate in the postwar period, however, because its theory and treatment of neurosis presupposed the parenting style characteristic of the late 19th century. In contrast, the patients of the 1950s were sometimes called "Watson babies" (Blanck & Blanck, 1974), as they had been reared according to the behaviorist theories advocated by John B. Watson. Rather than having an overly strict superego produced by resolution of the Oedipus complex and **identification** with an all-powerful father, these patients suffered from character disorders—in particular, narcissistic distortions of personality produced by a cold and uncaring upbringing that left the child no one with whom to identify.

Even though Kohut had earned a medical degree and had completed a specialized residency in neurology, he saw the medical model of mental illness as inappropriate (Kohut, 1981, quoted in Lichtenberg, Bornstein, & Silver, 1984). Interestingly, Kohut saw the theories of physicists like Einstein and Heisenberg as showing that there can be no purely objective judgments unless one takes into account the subjective perspective of the observer. Kohut (1981) said:

I have . . . been familiar with the relativity of our perceptions of reality and with the relativity of the framework of ordering concepts that shape our observations and explanations. And the same was true when . . . I acquired an . . . at least superficial acquaintance with the scientific outlook of modern physics—Einstein's and . . . that of Planck and Heisenberg . . . namely that an objective reality is in principle unreachable . . . that reality per se . . . is unknowable and that we can only describe what we see within the framework of what we have done to see it. (quoted in Lichtenberg et al., 1984, pp. 90–91)

Culture and the Unconscious

One of the reasons for Kohut's departure from old-line Freudianism, then, was his observation that Western culture had undergone major transformations since Freud's time and had thereby changed the course of human development and the origins of neurosis. Kohut's self theory focused on narcissistic character disorders. According to the ancient Greek myth, Narcissus is a handsome youth who falls in love with his own reflection in a pool of water. Waiting for the reflection to respond to him, he pines away and eventually dies. In line with this myth, a narcissistic personality is characterized by total self-involvement, lack of empathy, no concern for others, and feelings of grandiosity.

In Freudian terms, narcissists have invested all their libidinal energy in themselves, never reaching the genital stage of development in which libidinal energy is invested in attachments to others. Kohut saw the increasing numbers of patients in his practice who were diagnosed with narcissistic disorders as evidence of the changes in society, which had produced changes in the nature of the problems for which people sought help. Where Freud's patients were oppressed by an overly strong superego, the patients Kohut saw suffered from the consequences of a weak or absent superego. If a child's parents are too weak to fear or too neglectful and distant to idealize, or even missing altogether, the child has no psychic material for the formation of a superego. Adults lacking an adequate superego have no understanding of rules, of social justice, or of the finer points of interpersonal interaction. Rather than being burdened with excessive guilt or feeling overly inhibited, narcissistic individuals feel empty; they experience an emotional void, an inability to connect to anything, and they may seek high levels of artificial stimulation in a fruitless quest to fill the inner vacuum.

The superego is the one personality structure, according to Freudian psychology, that is accessible to societal influence. Kohut concluded that changes in society were generating character disorders related to a defective superego rather than a punitive one. This conclusion led him to leave the Freudian fold, but in the eyes of his supporters, it resulted in rescuing and revitalizing psychoanalysis (Strozier, 2001). Although Kohut himself wrote in a difficult style, he has become highly influential over the past two decades through his students and his influence on other therapists concerned with **holistic** notions of the self. Kohut's work has been particularly valuable to feminist psychologists because his concepts avoided much of the sexism in classical psychoanalysis.

▣ ERICH FROMM

Erich Fromm (1900–1980), a social psychologist and psychoanalyst, was born in Frankfurt, Germany, in 1900. He began his university studies intending to become a lawyer but switched from jurisprudence to sociology, receiving his Ph.D. in that field from the University of Heidelberg in 1922. He underwent psychoanalysis with Frieda (Fromm-) Reichmann in 1925;

in spite of the differences in their ages, she seduced him while he was her patient. In 1926, they commenced what would be a contentious and, ultimately, failing marriage.

Fromm began his own clinical practice as a **lay analyst** (an analyst who does not have a medical degree) in 1927 and moved to Geneva in 1933 after separating from Frieda. He then came to the United States. Like a number of other theorists covered in this chapter, Fromm lectured at the Chicago Psychoanalytic Institute. He later accepted a position at Columbia University in New York, where he had an affair with Karen Horney. (Horney wrote a book on self-analysis in 1942; sometimes described as the first self-help book, it was based on her infatuation with Fromm.) Fromm's training in sociology and political science led him to adopt a Marxist view of the effects of economic factors on individuals, while his experiences in prewar Germany showed him that individuals can be profoundly harmed by society.

In 1950, Fromm moved to Mexico City, where he taught at the medical school of the National University of Mexico until his retirement in 1965. In 1974, he returned to Switzerland, where he lived until his death in 1980. He maintained a private clinical practice throughout his teaching career.

Freedom and Psychological Conflicts

Fromm's writings are notable as much for their social and political commentary as for their philosophical and psychological underpinnings. He identified freedom as the basic human condition that poses, in his words, a "psychological problem." Humans have gained freedom through their relative mastery of nature; however, the price of this freedom is a pervasive sense of separation and loneliness. To be human, according to Fromm, is to be lonely because we are separated from other people and from nature. The temptation for us is to try to escape these feelings of loneliness, not by creating a society that might better fulfill our needs, but by creating new forms of dependency and domination.

In Fromm's best-known book, *Escape from Freedom* (1941), he outlined three mechanisms that he saw as ways in which people try to evade the demands of freedom: **automaton conformity,** authoritarianism, and destructiveness. Automaton conformity is a term that Fromm coined to describe changing our ideal self into what we perceive to be the preferred personality type in our society or social reference group, thus losing our true self. Fromm sometimes described the person who chooses this escape mechanism as a social chameleon who adopts the prevailing personality pattern as a kind of protective coloration to avoid standing out from the crowd. Authoritarianism refers to allowing ourselves to be controlled by another. The third mechanism, destructiveness, includes any process that attempts to eliminate other people or the world as a whole in order to escape freedom. All psychological conflicts, in Fromm's opinion, are rooted in the use of these escape mechanisms.

Fromm described his ideal society in 1955:

[a society] in which man relates to man lovingly, in which he is rooted in bonds of brotherliness and solidarity. . . . A society which gives him the possibility of transcending nature by creating rather than destroying, in which everyone gains a sense of self by experiencing himself as the subject of his powers rather than by conformity, in which a system of orientation and devotion exists without man's needing to distort reality and to worship idols. (p. 362)

Basic Human Needs

Fromm originally postulated that humans have five basic needs: relatedness, transcendence, rootedness, a sense of identity, and a frame of reference or orientation. Relatedness refers to the need to form productive love relationships with other people. It is noteworthy that Fromm did not define love as an emotion or sexual passion, but rather as an attitude or capacity requiring mutual understanding, care, responsibility, and respect. Rootedness refers to the need to belong to a family or group. Transcendence concerns the need to rise above the animal level and become an active creator. A sense of identity refers to awareness of ourselves as distinctive and unique individuals. The frame of reference is a stable and consistent perspective on the world that provides us with a way to organize our perceptions and make sense of our environment; it may be rational, irrational, or a mixture of both.

In the 1970s, Fromm (1973) added a sixth basic need, a need for excitement and stimulation, to his earlier list of five. He defined the need for excitement as a need to actively strive for or work toward a goal, as distinct from a passive response to our environment.

Character Orientations

Fromm identified five types of character orientation that he derived from what he understood to be five different strategies for achieving significance in our lives. The first four cause more problems than they solve, in contrast to the fifth strategy, the only character orientation that Fromm considered productive. The four nonproductive strategies are:

1. *Receptive.* The receptive person expects others, whether parents, lovers, or political leaders, to provide meaning or affection in life. This character orientation holds that the only way to obtain anything is to receive it from an outside source.

2. *Exploitative.* This type of person achieves significance by exploiting others through force or cunning for their own ends. Others are seen as merely resources to be manipulated and used in the quest for importance.

3. *Hoarding.* A person characterized by the hoarding orientation is miserly, keeping what he or she has, refusing to share with others, and often regarding people as possessions as well. This orientation has much in common with Freud's anal-retentive personality.

4. *Marketing.* Fromm's identification of the marketing orientation is considered one of his most original contributions to personality psychology. The marketing personality thinks of him- or herself as a commodity. Aspects of the self are simply units of exchange that can be modified or altered as soon as the forces of the market change.

And finally, there is the beneficial strategy:

5. *Productive.* This character orientation represents genuine achievement and is similar to what Abraham Maslow later called **self-actualization**. The productive person perceives the world accurately and enriches it by fully using his or her talents in a positive and generous manner.

Approach to Therapy

Unlike some other therapists, Fromm opposed the traditional reserve and detachment considered appropriate and "professional" for therapists to maintain. On the contrary, because his patients' problems often stemmed from living in a society in which few people are honest about feelings, it is up to the therapist to interact with the patient in an honest fashion. Fromm maintained that patients enter therapy to obtain a frank evaluation of themselves that they cannot get outside the therapy relationship. Although Fromm wrote relatively little about his therapeutic techniques, he sometimes described his approach as "activating," meaning that he believed the therapist must make active interventions during therapy to help the patient progress.

▣ MELANIE KLEIN

Melanie Klein (1882–1960), considered one of the founders of **object relations theory**, was born in Vienna on March 30, 1882. Her father, Dr. Moriz Reisez, had broken away from his orthodox Jewish family to study in a university and became a doctor. Reisez married Klein's mother after his early arranged marriage failed. Although Klein was not close to her father, who favored her older sister, she was impressed by his rebellion against his strict orthodox Jewish family and his arranged marriage to enter a world of knowledge and literature. Klein considered herself an atheist although she clung to her Jewish roots.

She became engaged at the age of 19 to Arthur Stephen Klein, a friend of her brother (Segal, 1979). The death of this brother, as well as her sister's death, contributed to a lifelong battle with depression. During her engagement, Klein entered the University of Vienna, but her marriage ended her studies, as she quit school to be with her husband, who had to move for the sake of his job. The marriage was not happy except for the birth of her three children between 1904 and 1914 (Segal, 1979).

In 1910, Klein read Freud's book on dream interpretation, which changed the course of her life. She entered psychoanalysis with Sandor Ferenczi and met Freud himself. She separated from her husband in 1919, divorcing him a few years later, and in 1921 established a psychoanalytical practice in Berlin, where she worked with children. Klein's ideas about child development conflicted with those of Anna Freud as well as those of Anna's father. For example, Klein believed that the superego emerges at a much earlier point in life than Freud thought; she traced its origins to the first and second years of life rather than the Oedipal phase. In addition, Klein disagreed with Anna Freud as to whether children can be psychoanalyzed; Freud thought they could not.

In 1925, Klein met Ernest Jones, who saw the potential in child psychoanalysis. In 1926, he invited her to come to England to lecture; these lectures became the core of her first book, *The Psychoanalysis of Children* (1932) (Segal, 1979). In 1927, she moved her practice to England.

Klein was a pioneer in the application of psychoanalytic methods to children. Because children are not capable of free association, she observed them at play; she decided that children's unconscious could be glimpsed through their playtime activities. She was an innovator in understanding play as a mode of communication. She gave her young patients dolls, drawing paper, modeling clay, and other materials to help them express their feelings about parents and other significant figures in their lives. In her opinion, this form of communication was an adequate substitute for free association. Klein tried out her theory of play on her youngest son, Eric. In doing so, Klein developed the now widely used technique of play therapy. In treating children, she tried to redirect to the therapist the unconscious feelings that the child held toward the parents or other caretakers (Groskurth, 1986).

Klein helped post-Freudian psychoanalysis move away from Freud's drive theory and put interpersonal relationships in the foreground, especially the relationship between the child and its mother. Her emphasis on the importance of relationships in individual development is the reason that she is regarded as an important figure in the establishment of object relations theory (Hergenhahn, 2001). In object relations theory, as in Freudian theory in general, the word *object* refers to other people, and Klein too used the word in that sense. The infant's first object is its primary caregiver, usually the mother.

Klein coined the term **part-object** to refer to one organ (or other part) of a human being, as the mother's breast plays an important part in the development and developmental disturbances of infants. Similarly, Klein used the term **whole-object** to refer to the person as a whole in the child's mental representations. Older children may develop preoccupations with parts of a person, whether body parts or internal aspects, rather than seeing the whole person. One of Klein's theoretical innovations was her understanding of the dynamic of envy, which results in the person attacking the very thing they value when it does not provide constant and unending satisfaction (Klein & Riviere, 1964). Envy results in the splitting of objects into a good part and a bad part, so that the frustrated child can attack the bad part without perceiving that the good part is also harmed. Thus, attacks issuing from envy can continue with an absence of guilt on the envious person's part. Only by understanding that the other person is an integrated whole can a growing child experience guilt, which is necessary to develop a sense of personal responsibility for the consequences of our behavior.

Klein, however, retained Freud's concept of a death instinct and with it the concept of aggression and destruction as built-in characteristics of the human infant. This notion led to a break between Klein and later object relations theorists, particularly the British school of thought, which included figures like John Bowlby. Bowlby and his colleagues tended to regard infants as prepared by nature for harmonious and loving interactions with their environment and caretakers, a harmony that is more likely to be marred by an uncaring and inadequate mother rather than by primitive destructive and aggressive impulses originating in the infant. In challenging the Kleinian premise that aggressive mother-child relationships are natural and universal fantasies, Bowlby said, "But there is such a thing as a bad mother" (cited in Mitchell, 2000, p. 84). This challenge was the hallmark of the later British approach to object relations theory (Scharff, 1996).

POSTWAR BRITISH OBJECT RELATIONS THEORISTS

After World War II, the British Psychoanalytic Society divided into three groups: those who considered themselves mainstream Freudians, including the followers of Anna Freud; the disciples of Melanie Klein; and the newer object relations tradition of Donald Winnicott, John Bowlby, and W. R. D. Fairbairn (1889–1964). Winnicott, an English pediatrician and psychoanalyst, broke away in the 1930s from Klein's emphasis on envy and aggression to focus instead on the mother's importance and capability in nurturing a child. Bowlby is best known for his work on attachment theory, a concept he developed in the course of his work with children traumatized by wartime separation from their parents, to explain children's tendency to seek closeness to a parental figure and to feel secure in the presence of that person. Bowlby (1969) regarded human attachment as an evolutionary survival strategy that developed to protect human infants from predators. Fairbairn, who spent his entire career in Scotland, reinterpreted Freud's concept of libido as object-seeking rather than pleasure-seeking and called in 1954 for a complete break with Freud. The title of a compilation of Fairbairn's papers, *From Instinct to Self* (Fairbairn & Scharff, 1994), captures the central theme of his work.

Object relations theory, like other most psychoanalytic schools, did not produce a unified theoretical framework, let alone specific hypotheses. The difficulty of pinning down object relations thought with precision is a function both of the nebulous writing style of its originators and of subtle differences among the individuals grouped together as object relations therapists.

In general, however, therapists in this tradition concentrate on the development of a self defined by its relations with objects—especially the first object, the primary caregiver. The components of the human self in object relations theory are self-image, object images (our images of other people), and affect-dispositions (emotional states). The stages of development consist of differentiating the self from objects; developing a sense of independence from objects; splitting others into good and bad objects; and finally achieving a state of integration in which the developing child is able to see others as combinations of both good and bad and to have a stable concept of his or her own self. According to object relations theorists, the characteristics of a mature self are as follows: an ability to form and maintain deep relationships with others; an ability to tolerate separation from and ambivalent feelings toward relational objects; and the development of an integrated self-concept and congruence between behavior and self concept (Kernberg, 1976).

It may seem odd to the contemporary reader that the object relations theorists maintained the use of the term object to refer to persons other than the self. This use of the term originated with Freud, and it seems appropriate in Freudian theory, with its mechanistic view of development driven by instincts (libidinal energy) and leading to conflicts in which others are perceived as possibilities for the release of pleasurable energy. Object relations theorists retained the term but redefined it by affirming the centrality of relationships with others in the process of human development and by regarding these relationships as having the potential to be genuinely satisfying rather than controlled by a destructive death instinct.

The onus for the foundation of satisfactory relationships leading to healthy mature functioning is shifted in object relations theory from the individual infant to the primary caregiver, usually the mother. Whereas Freud saw human infants as put by nature in an impossible situation of tension between instinctual drives and the demands of civilization, object relations theorists saw infants not as programmed for conflict but rather as endowed by nature for tranquil and successful relationships with the mother and the larger world (Bowlby, 1988). All neuroses, then, have their genesis in inadequate mothering. Object relations theory is concerned with psychopathology and attributes it to an unsatisfactory relationship with the baby's first object.

▣ OTTO KERNBERG

Otto Kernberg (1928–) is a psychoanalyst in the object relations tradition who has specialized in the treatment of borderline personality disorder and narcissism. He was born in Vienna on September 10, 1928. In 1939, his family left Europe to escape the Nazis and moved to Chile, where Kernberg attended medical school. He also studied psychiatry in Chile and became a member of the Chilean Psychoanalytic Society. Kernberg first visited the United States in 1959, when he received a Rockefeller Foundation fellowship to study under Jerome Frank at Johns Hopkins University. In 1961, he moved to the United States permanently to take a position at and eventually become the director of the C. F. Menninger Memorial Hospital in Topeka, Kansas. In 1973, Kernberg moved to New York City, where he now serves as a professor of psychiatry at Weill-Cornell Medical Center and as director of the Personality Disorders Institute at New York-Presbyterian Hospital.

As a psychoanalyst within the object relations framework, Kernberg adapted and elaborated on Kohut's theory of narcissism, and has written widely on borderline personality disorders and pathological narcissism. Kernberg (1975) attributes narcissistic disorders of personality to coldness and indifference on the part of caregivers. There are, however, differences between Kernberg's and Kohut's theories of narcissism. Kohut viewed narcissism as the result of empathic failure between caregiver and child, whereas Kernberg regards narcissism in terms of drive theory. He maintains that Kohut failed to recognize the importance of analyzing anger, hate, and envy in narcissistic patients; the therapist should maintain a position of functional authority as well as neutrality in working with borderline patients, he thought.

Kernberg has popularized the term *borderline* in reference to a psychological condition that has been difficult to categorize. **Borderline personalities** were a puzzle in the 1930s, when therapists began to encounter patients who seemed to see life as either all black or all white and who also swung between a general level of neurotic functioning and episodes of psychotic behavior. Kernberg regards such individuals as unable to understand that a specific person in their lives might have different moods yet still be the same person. He described borderline behavior to an interviewer in the early 1980s:

> In one session, the patient may see me as the most helpful, loving, understanding human being and feel totally relieved and happy, and all the problems solved. Three sessions later, she may berate me as the most ruthless, indifferent, and manipulative person she has ever met. Total unhappiness about the treatment, ready to drop it and never come back. (quoted in Sass, 1982, p. 66)

Kernberg treats such patients with what he calls **expressive psychoanalytically oriented psychotherapy**, which differs from classical psychotherapy in that the therapist prevents the development of a complete transference, openly discusses the patient's distortions of reality, and even confronts the patient with them. This approach to treatment is intensive, requiring three or more sessions a week. Kernberg (1992) views his life's work as changing Freud but not abandoning him.

▣ CHAPTER SUMMARY

Psychoanalysis evolved from the hydraulic and repression system of Freud to an entirely new system involving people often referred to neo-Freudians. Like Adler, Horney emphasized social forces and cognitive styles in her model of personality and psychopathology. Although still embracing unconscious motives in human behavior, her theory was much more focused on social learning. Very much *unlike* Freud, she set forth a psychology that viewed women as the social and psychological equals of men. In a similar manner, Harry Stack Sullivan's interpersonal psychiatry sought to find the conscious social factors that underlie personality. Sullivan described a personality that develops though life experience and pathology arising from unfavorable experiences.

Erik Erikson also largely disposed of a dynamic unconscious as the predicate of personality. Rather, he envisioned a lifetime of growth that is maximized by successfully navigating through universal life stages. Erich Fromm took a similar approach to explaining human nature. He synthesized social psychology and psychoanalysis to develop a perspective that sees the person developing out of a striving for personal freedom.

Heinz Kohut, Melanie Klein, Otto Kernberg, and others who fall in the self, ego, and object relations schools continued to emphasize unconscious forces in personality, however, each did so in a quite different way. Kohut's self psychology holds that unconscious forces are important in personality but so, too, are external factors like empathy and social relationships. Melanie Klein and the derivative object relation theorists posited that unconscious representations of significant people in our development provide the foundation of our personality. Other recent psychoanalytic theorists such as Otto Kernberg emphasized ego functioning, but they do so in a way quite different from both Freud and the other modern psychoanalysts.

In all, the followers of Freud evolved away not only from their intellectual founder, but also from each other. Today, the legacy of Freud appears to exist among numerous competing schools of thought with typically mutually exclusive explanatory theories of human behavior. They differ in their concept of the unconscious, the methods to be used to illuminate it, its internal structure, the etiologies of its pathology, and the means to treat it. Freud's original theories, when viewed from the whole of modern psychoanalysis, seem to have been so divided against themselves as to barely even exist as a definable school of psychology.

Chapter 9

Personality and Traits

Chapter Goals

- Explain the meaning and origin of the trait in personality theory
- Discuss how the trait approach to psychology both complements and competes with other perspectives
- Review the methods by which traits are discovered and tested
- Compare the leading trait models of personality
- Examine the biological and evolutionary basis of traits

A **trait** in personality psychology can be generally defined as a component or distinguishing characteristic of an individual's personality that is stable across time and external situations—although, as we shall see, different researchers have used the term in somewhat different ways. **Trait psychologists** or **trait theorists** are those who regard human personality as being composed primarily of traits.

The trait perspective has been criticized for its reductionist approach because it seems to be the very antithesis of humanistic psychology—of seeing humans as unified, free, conscious beings seeking self-fulfillment. Yet, a number of personality theorists, for example, Gordon Allport (1897–1967), have built bridges between humanistic psychology and trait theory, seeing traits as the means or medium through which individual uniqueness is expressed.

Furthermore, and perhaps more important, trait theory is the single approach to personality theory that is most directly based on and corroborated by research data. Most personality theories pay at least lip service to the importance of empirical research, but trait theories can lay claim to being defined by it. The very usefulness of the concept of a trait is that it can be operationally defined and investigated through use of the scientific method. In this chapter, this operational approach is shown at work in the various definitions of traits.

Preliminary Definitions

Allport (1961) defined a trait in partly biological terms as a "neuropsychic structure having the capacity to render many stimuli functionally equivalent, and to initiate and guide equivalent forms of adaptive and expressive behavior" (p. 347). Another definition of trait from Pervin, Cervone, and John (2005) is that a trait represents "the consistency of an individual's responses to a variety of situations" (p. 8). A trait, therefore, is an element of personality that causes individuals to act in a similar fashion across different social settings. For example, a person who has the trait of extroversion is likely to be outgoing and sociable in most situations rather than shy and inhibited.

If human beings differ in terms of personality—and most of us would agree that they do—traits are one way to measure those differences. The definitions of traits offered by different psychologists tend to have these elements in common:

1. Traits are stable within a given individual.

2. Traits vary among individuals.

3. Traits can be measured.

4. Traits are responsible for closely related behaviors.

Traits and Attitudes

There are clear relationships between traits and **attitudes**, although the distinction between them is often arbitrary. If these concepts are to have any value, however, they must first of all correlate with and predict behavior. Penrod (1986) made the point that although attitude refers to a behavioral disposition, the tacit assumption in attitude research is that there is a direct correlation between our attitudes and our behaviors. The literature on the relationship between attitudes and behaviors has uncovered problems with postulating any sort of simple relationship between them. In fact, psychologists have often had to construct complex models to find a connection. It has been said that attitudes, whether based on the noblest ideals or the basest prejudices, often melt before the perceived requirements of specific social situations.

Let us look at a specific example. Imagine traveling back in time to the early 1930s, when America was a very different place from what it is today. Hotels and restaurants regularly posted signs reading "No Negroes, Dogs, or Jews Allowed." A professor of sociology from Stanford University named Richard T. LaPiere (1899–1986) traveled across the United States by car with a young Chinese couple. One might have expected the travelers to be in for a rough time. In 184 restaurants and 66 hotels, however, they were refused service only once—at a rural campground. In fact, their treatment generally reflected, in LaPiere's (1934) words, "more than ordinary consideration" (p. 232). Six months after his jaunt, LaPiere mailed the following question to the establishments that he and the Chinese couple had patronized on their trip: "Will you accept members of the Chinese race as guests in your establishment?" Of those who replied, more than 90% said they would not accept Chinese guests. Something was amiss.

The article that LaPiere published on his findings, which proved to be influential in the study of discrepancies between attitudes and behavior, can easily be criticized for its methodological flaws, and indeed, it has been. For example, the clerks who answered LaPiere's inquiry about their willingness to serve or admit Chinese individuals were not the same people who actually admitted the couple. Moreover, the Chinese who accompanied the professor were well dressed in Western clothes and may not have fitted the image of Chinese commonly held at the time. Nevertheless, the unexpected results of LaPiere's simple experiment called into question the existence of a straightforward relationship between attitudes and behaviors.

Many studies have been done on the willingness of passersby to help (or fail to help) people who are having an emergency. Although the link between personality traits and the likelihood of helping others in an emergency is weak at best, the perceived number of others available to help, which is a situational factor, has an important effect on the outcome.

Another famous experiment showing the gap between attitudes and behaviors was conducted by Darley and Batson (1973). Students in a theological seminary were recruited for a study on religious education. They began by taking a survey in one building and were then told to go to another building. On the way, they encountered a man slumped in a doorway and moaning. The experimenters manipulated the time constraint that the students were under to get to the next building, as well as the talk each student was supposed to deliver there. One talk was about the seminary, the other was on the parable of the Good Samaritan in Luke 10:25. In Jesus' story, it is a Samaritan, a member of a sect considered heretical by most first-century Jews, who stopped to help a wounded man lying on the edge of the road after two religious leaders—a priest and a Levite—ignored him. In the Darley and Batson experiment, the situation (whether the seminary student was under time pressure or not) was the major determinant of the likelihood that the student would help the man moaning in the doorway. There was no correlation between the student's score on a "religious types" survey and whether help would be offered. In the low time-pressure situation, 63% of the students assisted the sick man. In the high time-pressure situation, however, only 10% helped. Ironically, having to speak about the parable of the Good Samaritan, with its pointed reference to the indifference of supposedly pious religious professionals, made no difference in the students' behavior. Those who felt pressed for time were still highly unlikely to offer assistance—some even stepped over the moaning person in their rush to be on time.

Such experiments as the foregoing indicate that the concept of attitude itself is useful but that a more complicated model is required for evaluating the correlation between attitudes and behaviors. A rough consensus developed among psychologists that general attitudes do correlate with general behaviors, but that specific behaviors do not show a high degree of correlation with specific attitudes.

Do Traits Exist?

Whether or not traits are essential for personality theory, they seem to be required for effective communication. If we are asked to describe someone else's personality, we will most likely come up with a list of traits—there really is no useful alternative. Traits are universally used to describe and explain the behavior of others; they are part of everyone's implicit or unstated personality theory. We are motivated to see other people as more consistent than they really are because we need to understand others for our own social and economic survival. The notion of traits, then, gives us at least the illusion of understanding others. If we see people behave in a particular way in a given situation and we attribute that behavior to their traits, we will think that we have learned something about them and can predict their behavior in the future. On the other hand, if we attribute people's behavior to the situation, we have not learned very much about them and will have no clue as to what we can expect from those people in the future. There appears to be a built-in tendency in humans to overestimate the importance of internal dispositions and underestimate the contribution of the specific situation in explaining the behavior of others. Social psychology has a name for this bias—the **fundamental attribution error** (Ross, 1977). The very name indicates how pervasive this error is.

The fundamental attribution error is reversed when it comes to analyzing our own behavior. While we attribute the behavior of others to dispositional factors, that is, to traits, when it comes to our own behavior, we attribute it to situational or external causes. This bias also has a name, the **actor-observer bias.** It can be summarized as "When you fall, it's because you are clumsy; when I fall, it's because the floor was slippery." To take another example, suppose we have a classmate who often misses lectures. If we are asked to explain the absences, we might say that the classmate is irresponsible, does not take things seriously, is undependable and lazy—all of which are trait descriptions. How would the students explain their absences? The authors of this text can attest from their experiences as professors that no student has ever approached them to say, "I'm sorry I missed the last class, but I'm just a lazy, irresponsible jerk." Rather, they usually explain their absences as the results of illness, car trouble, a traffic accident, or a family emergency of some kind.

Although we are motivated to overestimate the consistency of others, we still recognize that people can be inconsistent. In fact, we are also attuned to the ways in which situations affect behavior. Our friends behave one way at home with parents, another way with their friends; they behave differently with peers than with professors. Some people may be outgoing with same-sex friends but shy around members of the opposite sex. The vicious tattooed thug proudly sporting his gang colors on the street invariably wears a conservative suit, clean shirt, and fresh haircut when he has to appear in court. Moreover, some situations are regarded as demanding conformity to certain behavioral standards from everyone, such as worship services, weddings and funerals, graduation ceremonies, and courtroom proceedings. At the other extreme, members of a mob typically abandon their usual inhibitions and feel free to riot, loot, set fire to buildings, or even kill people. Violent attacks between rival groups of fans at soccer games, sometimes called football hooliganism, are a major topic of research among European psychologists (Hagmann, 2000).

In the 19th century, Le Bon (1896) pointed out that participants in a mob lost all their customary inner restraints against violence. Being part of a mob leads to **deindividuation** (Festinger, Pepitone, & Newcomb, 1952), a condition in which people lose their sense of personal identity. The sense of anonymity that is one dimension of deindividuation means that a person no longer feels accountable as an individual but is free to behave as badly as the least inhibited members of a group. Riots and other ugly scenes that make the news can be understood as instances of a situation determining behavior rather than individual differences among the rioters.

The Person/Situation Debate

Most people appear to display some consistency across situations and thus can be usefully described in terms of traits. Some psychologists have said that situations are of paramount importance in determining behavior and that individuals are so inconsistent as to render the existence of traits a mere illusion—so much so that the very concept of personality is rendered meaningless.

Perhaps the most curiously titled book of all time was published in 1968 by an Austrian-born psychologist named Walter Mischel (1930–). It bore the title *Personality and Assessment*. At the time, Mischel claimed that there is no such thing as a stable personality and thus assessment of it is impossible. According to Mischel, the evidence shows that individuals' behaviors are too inconsistent across situations to allow categorization by traits. Of course, other psychologists disagreed, and sides were taken on the great "person-situation" debate. Mischel himself later stated that others attributed more extreme views to him than he actually held and that he did not quite mean that personality as such does not exist. By 1995, he took a softer line (Mischel & Shoda, 1995), which led some researchers to say sarcastically that Mischel is no longer a Mischelian. Nevertheless, the debate between trait psychologists and situationists goes on.

Evidence for the Existence of Traits

The concept of a trait is useful only if it predicts future behavior. The basic measure of predictability—what in testing is called predictive validity—is the **correlation coefficient,** which defines the direction and the strength of the relationship between two random variables. You may recall that the correlation coefficient can range from 1 to –1. A positive correlation means that as one variable goes up in value, so does the other, whereas a negative correlation means that as one variable goes up in value, the other goes down. A correlation of 0 means that there is no relationship between the two variables under examination.

One way of interpreting what a given correlation means is to square it, thus obtaining the **coefficient of determination.** This coefficient gives the percentage of variation in one variable that is explained by the variation in the other variable. Although this method is useful because it reduces the likelihood of error when predicting one variable from the other, it also yields a number that is open to misunderstanding and may result in a subjective underestimation of the magnitude of the correlation.

Such situationists as Richard Nisbett (1980) have claimed that the correlations between traits and behavior, and between behaviors across situations, cannot be expected to exceed a correlation of .4. Furthermore, they maintain that correlations this "small," which some even derisively termed "personality coefficients" (Mischel, 1968), are incontrovertible proof that personality (and traits) do not exist.

Most personality psychologists, to say nothing of trait theorists, countered that the situationists are wrong on two points. First of all, there is no rule that correlations between behaviors on the one hand and traits or personality on the other cannot significantly exceed the .4 "barrier" through improved measurements on both ends. If the predictions made by a model are not satisfactorily accurate, this fact does not mean that an accurate model is impossible. Specifically, behavioral trends may provide greater predictability than single behaviors.

In addition, consistency across situations may in itself be a trait (Bem & Allen, 1974). That is, the behavior of some people may be more consistent that the behavior of other people because consistency of behavior is one of the traits on which they score high. Kenrick and Springfield (1980) found that individuals may be quite consistent on some behavioral dimensions but not on others and that other people are well attuned to the behavioral dimensions on which someone is consistent. We may know, for example, that one friend is almost always in a good mood while another's moods cannot be predicted or that one friend is almost always dependable while another is not. Both of these behave highly consistently with regard to their reliability while a third person may be totally unpredictable with regard to reliability.

Second, .4 is not necessarily an unimpressive correlation. Specific attitudes predict specific behaviors. For traits, which are by their nature global, a correlation of .4 with a given behavior is significant and meaningful. In fact, according to calculations by Rosenthal and Rubin (1982), a correlation of .4 means that the trait score will improve, predicting a behavior that has a base rate prediction of .5 to .7.

Let us look more closely at what these numbers mean. Suppose that applicants to a police department are accepted without a preliminary weeding-out process. About 50% will complete basic training, and 50% will wash out. Suppose further that the candidates have taken a test measuring conscientiousness (a major factor that will be further discussed below) and that the correlation between this test and successful completion of basic training is .4. By using this test, and no other measurement, to determine which applicants will succeed in being accepted into the police force, the trainee success rate would improve from .5 to .7. In other words, out of every 1,000 trainees, 700 would become officers instead of only 500. This is a great difference that would result in substantial savings to the police department during the screening process. That result may be counterintuitive, but the mathematics is unassailable. The reader should note here that there is only one predictor in this model; a larger number of predictors would lead to an even better model.

To return to the .4 correlation, squaring it to obtain the coefficient of determination yields .16 or 16%, which gives the percentage of variation in one variable—behavior in this case—explained by the variation in the other variable—in this case, the situation. So far so good. Situationist psychologists, however, automatically ascribe that "missing" 84% as caused by the situation. But this is a double error. Explaining the percentage of the variance in one variable as caused by the variance in another is not the same as saying that the one variable—that is, the score on that variable—is responsible for that percentage of the score on the other variable. And the other 84% of the variance is not due to the immediate situation only but to everything else, including all the personality traits not being measured in the study, or not measured optimally. Although no one would say that situations have no effect on behavior, theoretically, it is possible for this absence of situation effect to be the case and for measured correlations between traits and behavior to remain in the .4 range.

If correlational studies involving traits and behavior produce correlations in the range of .4, what about studies involving situation and behavior? Funder and Ozer (1983) looked at some of the classic studies on the relationship between situations and behavior, such as Festinger and Carlsmith's (1959) cognitive dissonance experiment and Milgram's obedience experiment—projects familiar to every student of psychology. They found that the relationships, when expressed as correlations, are about the same order of magnitude as those disparaged by the situationists' "personality coefficients."

Are Traits and Behavior the Same?

Even so, the value of ascribing behavior to traits has been doubted. Some observers have pointed out that even if traits are measurable, using them to explain behavior is simply circular thinking. For example, saying that a hypothetical person named Joe assaulted someone because he's aggressive really explains nothing; it mistakes labeling someone for understanding him. How do you know that Joe is aggressive? Well, because he assaulted somebody. While there is some truth in that, it is nevertheless useful to know that Joe is aggressive because he is likely to assault someone else in the future, and he may be a good person to avoid. That is why everyone intuitively makes trait attributions when describing other people.

It has also been pointed out that the most ardent situationists, when asked to write a letter of recommendation for a student, will still refer to the student's traits. Imagine a letter that states, "She received an A in my class, but that success was completely due to the situation and not to any stable internal dispositions on the part of the applicant." But if personality differences are real, and if trait theory is an extremely powerful and perhaps the most fruitful approach to the study of personality, the study of situations is not without value either, as seen in the progress made in empirical social psychology. The study of situations also includes the study of environments and **ergonomics** or engineering psychology.

Interactionism and Situation Choice

The debate between trait theorists and situationists may remind the reader of the older debate between those who attribute differences among people primarily to the environment and those who look to heredity. The quick answer to that argument is that both play a role, but also that the environment and a person's genetic endowment interact. The two factors are not simply additive, which makes it difficult if not impossible to separate their effects. Interactionist psychologists give the same answer to the personality traits/situation debate. They maintain that personality traits and situations interact to produce behavior (Ozer, 1986). Being frustrated or cheated, for example, may lead to aggressive behavior, but only in people who are prone to aggressive behavior. Certainly, situations play a part in human behavior; after all, your instructors hope that the situation of being a student and attending class will be an exceptionally powerful determinant of your behavior; that you will all sit quietly in your seats during class and pay attention to the lecture, regardless of differences in personality—differences that are nevertheless real.

Moreover, there is another factor that the situationists overlooked. It is well understood that situations differ as to how much influence they exert over individual behavior; we have already touched on this matter. Roll call in the military or being sworn in on the witness stand during a jury trial allows for no differences in personality among individuals, whereas a casual get-together among friends allows for individual personalities to shine through. Some researchers refer to these different types of situations as strong and weak situations respectively. Sitting in a classroom, while not quite as regimented or strong as the roll call, is not as free or weak as the party. The reader may recall the example given earlier of people behaving the same during a worship service—a strong situation. Individuals do have a choice, however, as to whether they enter that situation. (They may have less of a choice about providing testimony in a courtroom.)

Individuals choose most of the situations they encounter in life, insofar as they choose whether to attend church or synagogue, enlist in the armed forces, or enroll in a college. In other words, based on our personality, our traits, and other individual differences, we select most of our situations, even those that, once chosen, allow seemingly few of those individual differences to show. Even in cults, where the goal is often the total negation of personality,

Image 9.1   Gordon W. Allport
              (1897–1967)

people have an element of choice about their initial decision to join the group, at least in the Western world.

It seems that personality differences can indeed be fruitfully measured in terms of traits, measurements which then within reason predict and explain behavior. We will now explore some of the techniques of that measurement as well as examine the ideas and concepts of some of the pioneers of trait theory.

GORDON W. ALLPORT

Gordon Allport, the son of a country doctor in Ohio, became interested in trait theory after coming to reject Freud's emphasis on unconscious motivations and the dark side of personality. Allport bridged humanistic psychology and trait theory. He emphasized the uniqueness of the individual, just as humanists do, and regarded traits as the forms in which uniqueness is achieved and expressed. Allport saw traits as the true manifestation of a person's uniqueness and a genuine part of the self, not simply a convenient catchall term for a group of related behaviors.

The Mature Personality

True to his humanistic leanings, Allport was among the earliest psychologists to attempt to describe a healthy mature personality. A major humanist criticism of psychoanalysis is that it deals only with neurotic distortions of personality. Allport came up with a definition of a mature personality as one that exhibits the following characteristics:

- Realistic assessment of self, one's skills, and one's external reality
- Acceptance of self and others; ability to relate warmly to others in appropriate situations
- Ability to plan and delay gratification
- Self-insight and being able to laugh at oneself
- Participating in diverse activities and deriving gratification from diverse sources, sometimes called a capacity for self-extension
- A unifying philosophy of life or spiritual orientation; it includes having a conscience and ethical principles or guidelines

In summary, mature individuals can cope in a healthy fashion with the problems of life, find ways to obtain pleasure, and pursue realistic goals. Allport believed that the mature individual has genuine values and a clear philosophy of life. For Allport (1955), the essence of being human is the process of becoming, a concept often found in the writings of humanistic psychologists.

Allport taught courses in social ethics as well as psychology and had a number of interdisciplinary interests. He was not a practicing psychotherapist and was not interested in the study of emotionally disturbed people. True to his humanistic inclinations, he believed that studying neurotics cannot inform us about normal adult functioning, any more than the study of animals can define human nature. Abraham Maslow acknowledged Allport's contribution toward his own concept of self-actualization, which will be discussed in a later chapter.

Idiographic Research

Given Allport's emphasis on individual uniqueness, his preferred type of study was idiographic research, in which individuals are studied in depth. This method uses sources of information that are specific to each individual, such as diaries, letters, and interviews; it does not compare people with one another. The goal of idiographic research is clearly not to measure how an individual scores on certain personality traits compared to others, or to objectively measure an individual's trait profile. Rather, the goal is to discover the particular constellation or organization of traits within the individual.

The alternative approach, used by most other trait theorists and empirically inclined psychologists in general, is the nomothetic approach, which involves the study of large groups, that is, population samples, to discover regular or recurrent features in the population of interest. Allport believed, however, that each individual possesses traits unique to him or her that cannot be discovered or measured by science. One of his most famous research projects involved a collection of several hundred letters written during the 1940s by a woman in late middle age to a young married couple. In 1965, Allport published an analysis of the letters. He identified eight central dispositions in the woman's personality, subjected the letters to a formal content analysis, and then asked other researchers to explain, if they could, why the writer of the letters had behaved in a persistently self-defeating manner. Allport's point, at least in part, was that the letter writer's personality had a dimension of uniqueness that could not be derived from a statistical analysis of the contents of the letters.

The idiographic approach to research is congenial to humanism, with its conviction that science cannot fully capture the essence of what it means to be human. Allport disapproved of what he saw as a devaluation of aspects of the human personality that do not lend themselves to study using the empirical method. Allport's approach does not advance the scientific study of personality in the same way as the approach taken by Raymond Cattell, who will be discussed later. Allport worked together with H. S. Odbert (1936) in deriving from a dictionary a list of 17,953 words that can be used to describe a person, then eliminating synonyms and redundancies to arrive at a smaller but still large list of personality traits.

Allport initially used the word *dispositions* as equivalent to traits; he divided dispositions into three categories. As Allport's theory matured, he reserved the term *trait* to describe the characteristics of groups; in describing individuals, he used *disposition*. His three categories vary as to their generality: a cardinal trait or **disposition** in Allport's system is all-pervasive, influencing nearly every behavior and nearly all aspects of an individual's personality. Most people do not possess cardinal dispositions. Cartoon characters sometimes have a cardinal disposition; and if a fictional character has a cardinal disposition, we would describe that character as being not "filled out" and a caricature. Central dispositions are those that are quite characteristic of a person. Allport thought that most people have between 5 and 10 central dispositions; as was noted above, he found eight central dispositions in the author of the collection of letters that he analyzed in the early 1960s. If you were asked to describe a friend, you would probably list their central dispositions. Secondary dispositions are limited in their effects and may be restricted to specific situations in the person's life. While Allport distinguished between traits on the one hand and habits or attitudes on the other, the distinction vanishes at the level of secondary dispositions. Secondary dispositions include such preferences as favorite foods or colors.

Allport (1954) was also known for his work on religion and spirituality and for his important study of a negative trait, social prejudice. His book on the subject, which dealt with gender as well as racial prejudice in the 1950s, well before the civil rights and feminist movements of the 1960s, is still widely read.

The Proprium

Allport used two other concepts that also clearly underline his humanistic approach to psychology. The first is the **proprium,** a word taken from the Latin for "own" (in the sense of "one's own"). In Allport's usage, the proprium encompasses one's sense of self, which develops during childhood and includes a sense of one's body, self-identity, and self-awareness. The term *proprium* itself had a number of significant aspects for Allport; he adopted it to avoid the use of ego—in his opinion, an overused term with unwanted connotations. In addition, the prefix *pro-* in *proprium* suggested progress and moving forward. Allport (1961) attributed seven functions to the human proprium, which he called propriate functions: bodily self; self-identity; self-esteem; self-extension; self-image; rational coping; and striving. The full elaboration of these concepts came rather late in Allport's career and illustrates the evolving and developing nature of many personality theorists' ideas.

According to Allport, these seven propriate functions develop at different points in the life cycle:

1. *Bodily self.* The sense of one's body, its separateness from other bodies, and its basic parts, emerges at about 15 months of age.

2. *Self-identity.* The sense of inner sameness, of continuity to the self, and having a distinctive name emerges around the age of 2 years.

3. *Self-esteem.* The sense of competence, to feel some control over one's environment, to "look good," is achieved between 2 and 3 years of age.

4. *Self-extension.* The sense of possession or ownership of toys or certain people ("my ball," "my puppy," "my daddy") emerges between ages 4 and 6.

5. *Self-image.* The sense of being evaluated, that others have expectations of the self ("I'm the best at marbles," "I did what mommy asked me to do") also emerges between the ages of 4 and 6. Allport saw this propriate function as the foundation of the adult conscience.

6. *The self as rational coper.* The ability to think rationally to solve problems develops between ages 6 and 12.

7. *Propriate striving.* The identification of a life goal and the formation of plans to achieve it emerge during adolescence.

Functional Autonomy

A final Allportian concept is **functional autonomy**. Allport differed from Freud, who regarded the motives even of mature adults as sublimation. Allport thought that a mature adult might pursue activities for their own sake, even though they may have been performed originally for an external reward. For example, students may do their homework for history class in junior high school because they are rewarded for doing a good job and scolded if they do not do well. Grown to adulthood, one of those students may become a professional historian because he loves the study of history for its own sake and not because he is sublimating a forbidden desire (such as uncovering secrets or trying to surpass his father). Allport's notion of the functional autonomy of adult behaviors is related to the post-Freudian concept of the autonomous ego (Hartmann, 1958). However, Allport's concept of functional autonomy illustrates the influence of Freud, even on the majority of theorists who disagreed with him, because the concept would not have required elaboration without the Freudian notion of sublimation in the background.

回 RAYMOND BERNARD CATTELL

Early Career

Raymond Cattell (1905–1998) was born in England in 1905 and graduated from the University of London at age 19 with a double major in physics and chemistry. He became convinced, however, that the so-called hard sciences did not hold the answer to the social problems he saw around him during the period of social upheaval that followed World War I. He thus turned his attention to psychology and earned a Ph.D. in the field from the University of London in 1929. Cattell had decided that psychology could be a source of solutions to the problems of postwar society in a way that the more traditional physical sciences could not be. In graduate school, he worked with Charles Edward Spearman (1863–1945), the inventor of factor analysis. Spearman had applied this technique to the study of intelligence in 1904. Cattell made Spearman's technique the basis of his study of personality.

Spearman's own story is a fascinating one. For 15 years, he was a British army officer in India, but this particular military officer was also a mathematical genius. He did not complete his Ph.D. until the ripe age of 48. While he was still a graduate student, his papers on intelligence revolutionized the field. Spearman invented the term *general intelligence,* also known as the psychometric **g factor**. Spearman desired to prove his theory of intelligence through empirical testing. The question of whether intelligence is a single entity or whether there are many types of intelligence is still debated, although the latter approach probably has the upper hand as of the early 2000s (Goleman, 2006). But regardless of the status of Spearman's theory of intelligence, factor analysis may well rank as the single most important contribution to the study of personality. It also ranks as an example of one of the many statistical techniques created by psychologists that are now used by scientists in many other disciplines.

After Cattell completed his studies under Spearman, success did not come immediately or easily for him. There were few positions in postwar London for academic psychologists, and he had to work at a series of part-time jobs to support his family. His interest was in the application of factor analysis to the study of personality, but Cattell could not find a teaching position that would allow him to pursue that work; also the technology did not exist in the

1920s and 1930s to allow him to do further work. Innovations in science have sometimes had to wait until the technology was invented that would permit further exploration.

In 1937, Cattell moved to the United States. Finally, in 1945, he became a research professor at the University of Illinois. He was free from teaching courses, and at Illinois, he had access to one of the first electronic computers, the Illiac I, which made it possible for the first time to do the kind of analyses that Cattell's research required. He could now perform large-scale factor analyses to reach his goal of creating an empirically derived model of personality. And Cattell was tireless in pursuing that goal. He founded the Laboratory of Personality Assessment and Group Behavior and began a period of intense creativity with a hand-picked staff of research associates. In addition to hundreds of research publications, Cattell wrote some 50 books. Cattell's career exemplifies the adage about genius being 99% perspiration. Cattell wrote books and articles almost until his death; over the course of a 70-year career, he averaged a book or article every month and a half. Colleagues used to joke that Cattell wrote faster than others could read. Cattell died in 1998.

Factor Analysis

Factor analysis is easy to perform using a statistical software package but extraordinarily difficult when it comes to having a deep understanding of what the technique actually accomplishes. It is, however, easy to describe the underlying logic of factor analysis. Factor analysis is based on correlation. The correlation coefficient is the statistical measurement of the relationship between two sets of scores; the larger the correlation in absolute terms, the stronger the relationship. Let us say that a large number of individuals take six tests: a math test, a history test, a science test, a basketball dribbling test, a football throwing test, and a baseball hitting test. Every score is correlated with every other score. The scores indicate that the science, history, and math tests have a strong positive correlation, and the football, basketball, and baseball tests also have a strong positive correlation; but the correlations between any test score from the first group and any test score from the second group is close to zero.

Consider the imaginary correlation matrix in Table 9.1.

Table 9.1   Example of a Correlation Matrix

	Math	History	Science	Basketball	Football	Baseball
Math	—	.8	.9	.0	.0	.0
History	.8	—	.8	.0	.0	.0
Science	.9	.8	—	.0	.0	.0
Basketball	.0	.0	.0	—	.9	.8
Football	.0	.0	.0	.9	—	.8
Baseball	.0	.0	.0	.8	.8	—

Most people would look at these results and conclude that there are two factors underlying these scores; in other words, that two separate and real things are being measured—perhaps we could call them school knowledge and athletic ability. If the scores on two measures rise and fall together when examined across a large number of people—in other words, if the two measures covary—they are in a sense measuring the same thing, namely, a common underlying trait, in two different ways. But factor analysis does not look at the relationship between two measures; rather, it looks at a matrix of the correlations among many measures. This analysis can be performed only by using computer programs. Once the computers were available and became sufficiently powerful, however, more sophisticated factor analytic techniques also became possible.

The strength of factor analysis in psychology is that it can take a large number of different measurements from a wide variety of different sources, such as paper-and-pencil self-assessment tests; assessments made by others; observer ratings from friends, teachers, or workplace colleagues; and existing records of past behaviors, and then compute the correlations.

The strengths of factor analysis far outweigh its limitations, but it does have one major weakness. For the imaginary correlation matrix above, factor analysis will show that two factors emerge. That much is clear and objective. What is not clear and objective, however, is the best names for the factors. What if we decide to call the first factor in the example above "intelligence"? We will see this problem recur in five-factor theory, which will be discussed below.

Theory of Personality

Cattell (1950) defined personality as "that which permits a prediction of what a person will do in a given situation" (p. 2). Traits are the elements or building blocks of personality. Cattell thought that traits could be statistically measured from observing our own behavior as well as the behavior of others; these measurements then permit the prediction of behavior.

Cattell introduced a distinction between **surface traits** and **source traits**. A surface trait is inferred from and manifested in a series of behaviors that obviously go together and are related to one another. Someone who is easily provoked to anger, brusque in speech, and quick to put down others will be categorized by them as hostile. A surface trait is just that; it lies on the surface of personality, is apparent on casual observation, and is somehow related to other surface traits. A surface trait does not, however, explain the underlying structure of personality. How are casual observations of "unfriendliness," "suspiciousness," or "hostility" related beneath the surface? For that, we need the concept of source traits. The comparatively large number of surface traits in an individual's personality is the overt manifestation of a much smaller number of what Cattell called source traits. He identified 16 of them and described them as bipolar dimensions.

For Cattell, source traits are real, objectively derived through factor analysis, and form the structural core of personality. All people have the same 16 source traits; however, they differ on the extent or degree to which they manifest each one. For example, everybody has the source trait of *assertiveness*. Some individuals score very high on this trait and thus have dominant personalities, whereas others score closer to the *humble* end of this particular dimension of personality and thus are relatively submissive. Cattell subdivided his 16 source traits into two categories, hereditary or environmental traits.

Whether environment does more to shape personality than heredity, or vice versa, is one of the oldest arguments in all of philosophy as well as in psychology. The usual answer is both/and rather than either/or. That was the answer Cattell, too, adopted, but oddly, he seemed to believe that a particular source trait arises from heredity or the environment rather than a combination of both. He further categorized his 16 source traits as ability, **temperament,** and dynamic traits. Ability traits reflect the effectiveness of our functioning in our environment and our capacity to attain our goals. Intelligence is a prime example of an ability trait in Cattell's classification. Temperament traits govern the emotions, whereas dynamic traits move the individual to act.

Research Methods

Cattell also systematically distinguished between sources of data. L-data refer to life data, which are objective life occurrences and observer ratings. Q-data are questionnaire data, namely self-reports derived from questionnaires. OT-data are data from objective personality tests. Cattell believed that factor analysis should uncover the same factors or traits from all three data sources. He clearly saw factor analysis as the best way to do just this.

In addition, Cattell noted in 1959 that personality theory research used one of three approaches. The classical model of science pioneered by the physical sciences is the experiment, which uses two variables, an independent variable and a dependent variable. The independent variable is manipulated by the experimenter while everything else is held constant, and the effects on the dependent variable are measured. Cattell notes that while this method ensures objectivity, examining one independent variable at a time is woefully inadequate when seeking to understand the complexity of human personality. The clinical method, which works with data gathered by an observant clinician, allows the examination of many factors at once, thus more closely paralleling personality complexity. It has a fatal flaw, however, in that it is totally subjective. Cattell thought that the overwhelming advantage of factor analysis is its combination of scientific objectivity with simultaneous consideration of many clinically derived variables.

The 16 PF Questionnaire

Cattell derived 16 factors that represented the best solution to the question of personality, in his opinion, and developed a questionnaire known as the Sixteen Personality Factors (16 PF) Questionnaire. From 200 potential trait names, Cattell found 36 surface traits and 16 source traits. But what should he call them? Recall that in factor analysis, the naming of the factors is a subjective affair. To avoid unwanted connotations and charges of subjectivity, Cattell initially made up imaginary words for his personality factors, such as *parmia, premsia,* and *autia.* Here are his traits, as presented by Conn and Rieke (1994), and a brief explanation where needed in parentheses.

1. Warmth (warm vs. reserved)
2. Reasoning (less vs. more intelligent)
3. Emotional stability (low vs. high ego strength)
4. Dominance (dominant vs. submissive)

5. Liveliness (serious vs. spontaneous)

6. Rule-consciousness

7. Social boldness

8. Sensitivity

9. Vigilance (trusting vs. suspicious)

10. Abstractedness (practical vs. imaginative)

11. Privateness (open vs. shrewd)

12. Apprehension (fearful vs. self-assured)

13. Openness to change

14. Self-reliance

15. Perfectionism (neat and careful vs. disordered)

16. Tension (nervous vs. relaxed)

Contributions

We have barely touched on the sheer volume of Cattell's work, and it is also remarkable for its breadth. Although Cattell was primarily concerned with the stability of human personality, he also focused on situations, differentiating between states and traits. States are responses that depend on particular situations. While Cattell (1979) was the ultimate trait theorist, he also wrote, "Every intelligent observer of human nature . . . realizes that the state of a person at a given moment determines his or her behavior as much as do his or her traits" (p. 169). He made a distinction between innate tendencies, which he called **ergs,** and environmentally determined tendencies, which he called **sentiments**. An erg is similar to an instinct; hunger, sexual desire, security-seeking, and self-assertion are examples of ergs. Sentiments, such as valuing a career or a relationship, are learned.

Cattell recognized that group affiliations influence behavior, and he used the term **syntality** to describe the traits of a group. Syntality refers to the trait structure of groups in the same way that personality describes the trait structure of individuals. For all his cold scientific precision, Cattell (1972, 1987) was very aware of the human situation outside the laboratory, writing several books on what he termed **beyondism**. Beyondism is, according to Cattell (1987), "a system for discovering and clarifying ethical goals from a basis of scientific knowledge" (p. 1). Unfortunately, his 1987 publication of *Beyondism: Religion from Science* touched off a firestorm of controversy. Although Cattell intended in the book to do no more than discuss his theories of evolution and natural selection, his references to eugenics, or selective mating and reproduction among humans, led to his being called a fascist and racist.

There was no aspect of personality, even in its broadest sense, that Cattell did not discuss. He is best known for his use of multivariate techniques and for founding the Society for Multivariate Experimental Research. Cattell's fingerprints are all over trait theory. Yet, at the same time, his work may become obsolete as a simpler, better solution to the data he dealt with is being uncovered, namely five-factor theory.

▦ HANS EYSENCK

Hans Eysenck was born in 1916 in Germany but emigrated to England in the 1930s because of his opposition to the rise of Hitler. He was influenced by a variety of different theorists, including C. G. Jung and Charles Spearman, from whom he learned to value the use of statistics in psychological research. He was also influenced by Cyril Burt (1883–1971), an edu-

Image 9.2   Hans Eysenck (1916–1997)

cational psychologist and strong proponent of genetics as the primary determinant of intelligence. After Burt's death, Burt was accused of making up or misrepresenting data for his twin studies—even to the point of creating fictitious research assistants—a charge still disputed by supporters. Eysenck himself became involved in a rather heated debate on the heritability of intelligence with Leon Kamin, one of the psychologists who had accused Burt of fraud.

A supporter of many controversial positions, including downplaying the role of smoking in causing cancer and regarding psychoanalysis as worthless, Eysenck held beliefs about the heritability of intelligence that made him the target of a number of other psychologists. Ironically, the refugee from Nazism was himself labeled a Nazi in the 1970s. In 1973, while Eysenck was lecturing at the London School of Economics, he was punched in the nose by a group of opponents. His children even had to change their last name to avoid abuse.

Eysenck regarded psychoanalysis as totally without value; more interesting, he believed that traditional psychotherapy in general owed any success it had to behavior therapy unknowingly conducted by the therapist. By the time of his death in 1997, Eysenck had dozens of books and hundreds of articles to his credit.

Like Cattell, Eysenck used factor analysis in his work and regarded his research as adhering strictly to the scientific model. In his opinion, the biological basis of human personality traits had to be demonstrated to establish their reality. To Eysenck, biology is the key to solving the problem of circularity mentioned earlier, namely, how do we know Joe is aggressive? Because he assaulted someone. Why did Joe assault someone? Because he is aggressive. Although Eysenck used factor analysis, however, the overall conclusion that he derived from it was diametrically opposed to that of Cattell. Unlike Cattell's theoretical system, with its many different traits and categories of traits—surface traits, the 16 basic source traits, environmental versus constitutional traits, ability, temperament, and dynamic traits—Eysenck focused on just two major factors, introversion versus extroversion and emotional stability versus instability (neuroticism). He later added a third, psychoticism. Eysenck also defined types differently; a type for him was not a category that a person fits but rather a broad dimension or continuum.

Thus, Eysenck would not label a specific individual an introvert but rather would state that the person is located closer to the introversion end of the introversion/extroversion dimension. Some people may score very close to the extreme ends of this continuum, but most people will fall close to the middle. Obviously, individuals scoring high in extroversion will be outgoing, impulsive, lacking in self-consciousness, and able to easily initiate conversations with strangers. Those toward the introversion end of the dimension will be shy, quiet, and closed within a kind of shell. Note the similarity of Eysenck's continuum to Jung's two basic attitudes.

Eysenck's stability versus instability dimension describes an individual's adjustment to the environment. Instability refers to neuroticism, unreliability, and poor adjustment. Individuals high in stability, by contrast, are mature, even-tempered, and well adjusted to their social environment. This two-by-two dimensional classification produced four quadrants; it is highly reminiscent of the four temperaments postulated by the ancient Greek physician Hippocrates. In fact, Eysenck's four quadrants mirror Hippocrates' four temperaments (see Figure 9.1).

Later Eysenck added a third dimension, which he called *psychoticism*. Scoring high on this dimension means that a person is insensitive and uncaring. Eysenck developed questionnaires to measure his dimensions, such as the Eysenck Personality Questionnaire (EPQ) and the Eysenck Personality Inventory (EPI).

The Biological Basis of Eysenck's Factors

There is some evidence that Eysenck's three factors are heritable, thus that they have a biological basis. They also appear to occur across cultures (Eysenck & Long, 1986). Eysenck (1967) proposed that the differences between extroverts and introverts are due to differences in their ascending reticular activating system, or ARAS. This system of nerves, which connects the **reticular formation** in the brain stem with various areas in the

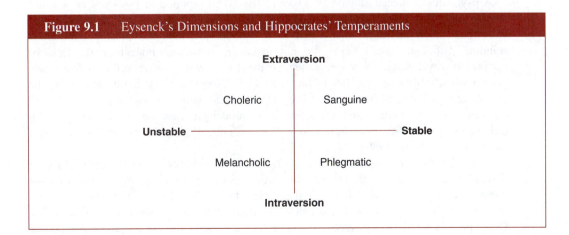

Figure 9.1   Eysenck's Dimensions and Hippocrates' Temperaments

thalamus, hypothalamus, and cerebral cortex, accounts for a person's general level of arousal. Eysenck maintained that introverts have a more active ARAS than extroverts, which means that they are more easily stimulated and thus less eager to seek arousal from the environment.

There have been many findings that introverts and extroverts differ in just that way in the level of stimulation they seek. They appear to be brought to the same level of nervous arousal by the differing levels of stimulation that they seek; in addition, introverts appear to be more aroused than extroverts by identical stimuli (Geen, 1984; Gilbert & Hagen, 1985; Ludvigh & Happ, 1974). Eysenck's own demonstration of the differences in level of arousal between introverts and extroverts used something as simple as lemon juice (Eysenck & Eysenck, 1967). Imagine that the differences between the so-called life of the party and the wallflower extend to their respective reactions to lemon juice. When drops of lemon juice were simply placed on subjects' tongues, Eysenck and his wife, Sybil, found a strong negative correlation between extroversion and the amount of saliva secreted in response to the acidic liquid. In other words, extroverts secreted less saliva than introverts.

▣ THE FIVE-FACTOR THEORY

In our discussion of individual trait theorists up to this point, you may have noticed that while they all have in common an acceptance of the reality and importance of traits, there are also large differences among them. That situation holds true for every major school of personality theory. The problems associated with the study of personality stem from the fact that theories are accrued rather than replaced. Old theories are not replaced by better ones; rather, newer theories are often simply studied alongside the older ones. Trait theory, however, is well placed to overcome some of these problems. A recent consensus about the so-called "Big Five" personality factors may be regarded as a step toward replacing some of the older theories altogether.

A psychologist named Donald W. Fiske (1916–2003) reported in 1949 that he was not able to replicate Cattell's 16 factors when he performed factor analysis on data he had collected; rather, he found that a five-factor model provided the most parsimonious solution. Although Fiske's paper did not make an immediate impact on the field of personality psychology, other researchers in the 1960s were also reporting a five-factor pattern when subjecting trait data to factor analysis (Norman, 1963; Smith, 1967). By the 1980s, enough data had been accumulated from a wide variety of sampling methods and cultures to lead to a consensus that a five-factor model provides the best fit across rating techniques, personality measures, and cultures (John, 1990; McCrae & Costa, 1987; Peabody & Goldberg, 1989).

Lewis Goldberg coined the term *Big Five* in 1981 after reviewing the consistency of findings that a mere five factors are the basic units of personality. *Big* emphasizes the importance of these factors, but it also makes clear that each of these factors contains many related traits. The Big Five are broad factors, each an umbrella that covers many other traits. Developments in trait theory eventually showed that the five factors have a genetic component and appear to be evolutionary adaptations in terms of their origin. The *Journal of Personality* once devoted an entire issue to the five-factor model.

There is still some disagreement, however, regarding the best names for the factors. The reader should recall that naming is the subjective part of factor analysis. A simple way to remember the names of the five factors is the acronym OCEAN, coined by John in 1990.

O = Openness (open vs. conventional)

C = Conscientiousness (reliable vs. unreliable)

E = Extroversion (vs. introversion)

A = Agreeableness (vs. uncooperative)

N = Neuroticism (vs. stable)

While other five-factor theorists have used somewhat different names for the factors, there is widespread agreement about the way they line up. Fiske's pioneering study in 1949 referred to the five factors as "inquiring intellect," "will to achieve," "social adaptability," "conformity," and "emotional control." Borgatta in 1964, at a point when personality psychologists first started taking notice of the five-factor model, called the factors "intelligence," "responsibility," "assertiveness," "likeability," and "emotionality." Notice again that these names correspond quite closely to those of the OCEAN mnemonic.

Some inquirers have asked why there are five dimensions of personality rather than some other number. McCrea and John (1992) have responded that "it is simply an empirical fact, like the fact that there are seven continents" (p. 194). Trait theorists have also tied the five-factor model to an evolutionary perspective, however, and evolutionary adaptation may provide part of the answer. Goldberg (1981) claimed that individuals from a wide variety of different cultures seek answers to five basic questions when they interact with another. These five questions correspond to the five factors, as seen below:

1. Is the other person smart? (O)

2. Can I depend on her or him? (C)

3. Is she or he dominant or submissive? (E)

4. Is he or she easy or hard to get along with? (A)

5. Is she or he sane and stable or emotionally volatile? (N)

These five factors, then, are important in mate selection and intra- as well as intergroup relations. It has also been pointed out that individual great apes, who share 98% of their genetic material with humans, also demonstrate different levels of sociability, dominance, adaptiveness, aggressiveness, and predictability.

VIGNETTE

Emma's case exemplifies the way in which a personality style may be quite functional in one setting and then allow the emergence of an emotional disorder with a change of milieu. Emma, a former schoolteacher, had frequent complaints of physical illness that increasingly worried her husband, Derek. She experienced sudden bouts of weakness and numerous aches and pains that moved at random through her body. Emma had even stopped socializing with other homemakers— which had been her only avocation. At Derek's urging, she went for a complete medical examination. The results of the examination and medical tests were a source of both relief and frustration for Emma and Derek. The doctor found that Emma was in excellent health for a woman in early middle age; absolutely nothing was wrong with her. For several days, Emma returned to her previous level of activity. It seemed that her physician's assurance that she was not fatally ill had invigorated her.

A careful scrutiny of recent events in Emma's life, however, revealed a major change that might have been a factor in her recent malaise. Derek had been promoted to a new position—national marketing director of his firm, a leading electronics company. This new role required him to spend several days each week traveling or working late. The job promotion was the fulfillment of a dream for Derek but not for Emma. Prior to marrying, Emma had been an elementary teacher, but she had quietly longed for marriage to a strong and supportive man. She was a physically small woman, shy and not very talkative. Emma gave up her teaching career shortly after her marriage to Derek. She cooked, cleaned, and indulged her husband so that the loss of her salary seemed a small price to pay to have such a woman at home. What Derek did not know, however, is that people often express what they want from another through what they offer them. Emma took good care of her husband because that is what she wanted—to be cared for.

Emma's greatest fear was to have to make her way in the world without a strong figure guiding her and supporting her emotionally. She cared for the house with the tacit understanding that she would now be safe and protected by her husband for the rest of her life. Thus, when Derek's promotion forced him to spend increasingly longer periods of time away from Emma, her dependent personality traits began to become quite evident. Of course, she did not intend to undermine her husband's performance in his new job, but her panicky calls and demands that he take her illness more seriously had that distinct effect.

After repeated medical examinations with an assortment of specialists, all with inconclusive findings, Derek confronted Emma with a pattern that was becoming increasingly evident to him: Emma would almost always get sick when he was away for a long time. Emma reacted with sincere hurt and grief to what she perceived as an insensitive accusation. Like virtually all people with conversion symptoms, Emma was not aware of the connection between her emotional distress and her illnesses.

It took a great deal of persuasion for Emma to see a therapist. At the outset of therapy, her main complaint was her husband's callous indifference to her needs. Over time, Emma gained a modicum of insight—namely, that her extraordinary dependency created a high level of anxiety that she perceived as physical illness. Her dependent personality remained a troubling aspect of her nature but her functioning did improve.

Vignette Questions

1. Are Emma's problems a result of her personality?

2. If not, what is?

3. If so, what in her personality leads to her symptoms and conflicts?

4. How would you describe her traits as a person?

The Big Five and Cross-Cultural Evidence

Cross-cultural studies of five-factor theory have proved to be a fruitful line of inquiry. Are the Big Five, however, found in non-Western cultures? The evidence indicates that indeed they are. The five factors reappeared when questionnaires were translated into Hebrew (Montag & Levin, 1994), Chinese (McCrae, Costa, &Yik, 1996), Korean (Piedmont & Chae, 1997), and Turkish (Somer & Goldberg, 1999). Interestingly, only four of the Big Five were present when the questionnaires were translated for use in Japan (Bond, Nakazato, & Shiraishi, 1975). The one factor that was missing was "openness." These preliminary findings perhaps offer clues to the extent of cultural influence as well as the universality of the five factors. The studies mentioned above relied on translating questionnaires originally written in English into the various languages. What if one were to begin with a non-Western language like Mandarin Chinese, make a list of its descriptive terms, and then analyze the factors? Yang and Bond (1990) did just this. They found five factors that overlapped to some extent with the standard list, although the overlap was far from perfect. What is noteworthy here is not that culture plays a role—one needs only to travel abroad or indeed pick up a newspaper to see cultural differences at work—but that the Big Five personality traits resurface across such a variety of cultures and studies. There is something robust about them and—dare we say—something real.

The Big Five factors have been found to be reliable and stable across a person's lifetime (McCrae & Costa, 1994). Five-factor theory owes its genesis to factor analysis and to the fact that a five-factor solution emerges over and over in such studies. But other avenues of research also lend support for five-factor theory. The fundamental lexical hypothesis, which originated with Sir Francis Galton, predicts that people's language will form words for precisely the traits that are important to them in interpersonal relationships. There is evidence that the terms for character traits contained in diverse languages do in fact reflect traits subsumed under the Big Five (Church, Katigbak, & Reyes, 1996).

Questionnaires have, of course, been established to measure the five factors. One such questionnaire is the Revised NEO Personality Inventory (NEO PI-R) by Paul T. Costa and Robert R. McCrae (1992). It is intended for use with adults (18 years and older) without obvious mental disorders. It has 240 items and takes about 40 minutes to complete. A shorter version is called the NEO FFI. The mysterious name of this questionnaire derives from the fact that it was originally designed to measure only three of the five factors: neuroticism, extroversion, and openness. Measurements for the other two factors were added in revisions. Since 1992, the NEO PI-R has been translated into more than 40 languages. These translations have helped to show the universality of the five factors. Additional proof for the adequacy of five factors is that the results of this questionnaire correlate well with findings from other personality measures.

As we saw earlier, trait theories of personality fell into some disfavor following Mischel's (1968) attack on the usefulness of the concept of traits. Trait theory rebounded, however, and in addition, five-factor theory for the first time made possible a study of personality that can claim to be fully scientific.

Biological Basis of Traits

There is certainly a biological basis for traits, as many personality psychologists and the evidence agree. Many people, however, find the notion that their personality is the by-product of their genetic material distasteful. They overlook two things. One is that if something is an empirical fact, it does not depend on whether humans like it; this childish illusion is responsible for untold suffering. Hans Eysenck made this point in his 1997 autobiography:

> I always felt that a scientist owes the world only one thing, and that is the truth as he sees it. If the truth contradicts deeply held beliefs, that is too bad. Tact and diplomacy are fine in international relations, in politics, perhaps even in business; in science only one thing matters, and that is the facts. (p. 229)

The second point is that understanding the genetic dimension of traits will help us also to understand the environment's contribution to them. This knowledge, in turn, will be useful in designing environmental conditions that will foster productive behavior and discourage destructive behavior.

The biological basis of traits can be seen in that traits have a large inherited component (Plomin, 1994). Some of the research in this area has been done with twin studies. Bouchard, Lykken, McGue, Segal, and Tellegen (1990) found remarkable personality similarities between twins raised apart. In the 1990s, the U.S. Department of Education conducted a large-scale study on the school progress of children called the Early Childhood Longitudinal Study. The results seem to strongly support the hypothesis that the most important contribution that parents provide for their children is their genes rather than their household environment (Levitt & Dubner, 2005).

Finding a specific gene that is related to a personality trait, however, is not possible because many genes are responsible for the brain functioning that affects many traits simultaneously. Moreover, human genes interact with other genes in a literally mind-boggling complex pattern that affects all a person's traits. "I" am the result of 100 billion **neurons**, each having many thousands of connections with other nerve cells and influenced by neurotransmitters whose level of secretion depends on genes. All these different levels of functioning within the central nervous system go together to produce the conscious human being with his or her individual personality. Nevertheless, more and more researchers are constantly doing better and better work in behavioral genetics. An understanding is emerging of the extent to which human personality traits, in both normal and pathological conditions, are a function of genes.

The growing consensus that there are five cross-cultural personality dimensions has spurred the hope that specific neurotransmitters can be associated with a particular dimension. For example, high levels of the neurotransmitter dopamine have been linked to novelty seeking (Bardo et al., 1993). In addition, a gene has been identified in association with production of the protein that creates a dopamine receptor called DRD4. A number of studies have found a connection between this gene and novelty-seeking behaviors (Benjamin et al., 1996; Ebstein et al., 1996; Ono et al., 1997).

On the other hand, other researchers have not found a relationship between D4DR polymorphism and novelty seeking (Gelernter et al., 1997; Herbst, Zonderman, McCrae, & Costa, 2000; Sullivan et al., 1998). No one has ever promised that the task of understanding the genetic nature of personality would be easy. But it is clear that an essential aspect of understanding personality is further research into its genetic basis.

回   CHAPTER SUMMARY

The quest to explore and understand personality can take the form of viewing as a unique whole or as a composite of universal components. The trait approach uses the latter. Primarily beginning with Gordon Allport and Raymond Cattell, trait researchers have worked with the premise that personalities differ only as to the degree to which they contain any of a number of stable inclinations or traits. In other words, each personality is a unique compound made up of elements common to all people.

Trait researchers, working under this assumption, have sought to discover what these elements are. The modal approach was to distill natural language terms used to describe human characteristics down to the most incisive and potent descriptors. Such elemental descriptive terms would represent the most basic dimensions of personality, according to this thinking, and we could be defined and understood in terms of how much we possess of each dimension. This approach has received significant support from genetic and biological researchers, who have discovered specific genetic markers for several traits.

Today, research into traits continues as a major force in personality psychology. The trait model that has received the greatest consensus among psychologists is the five-factor or Big Five model of personality. According to the five-factor model, the essence of anyone's personality can be reduced to the level of (1) openness to experience, (2) conscientiousness, (3) extroversion, (4) agreeableness, and (5) neuroticism. Whether or not our position in this five-dimensional personality truly captures who we are remains to be seen, but right now, it is quite a good estimator.

Chapter 10

Behaviorist Views of Personality

Chapter Goals

- Show how older systems of psychology set the stage for the advent of behaviorism
- Explain the logic behind the rejection of consciousness in personality by behaviorists
- Provide a link between the work of physiologist Ivan Pavlov and psychological behaviorism
- Make clear the distinction between the radical behaviorism of psychologists like B. F. Skinner and neo-behaviorism of theorists like John Dollard and Neal Miller

Psychology had its origins as a subdiscipline of philosophy that sought to discover the nature of human thought, mind, and soul. It attempted to answer such profound questions as whether people have souls. Are the qualities that make us human, that allow us to reason or to ponder the nature of our being, derived from a soul? Is the mind a unique entity separate from the body? Or is it merely a by-product of organic functions?

Psychology became independent from philosophy during the era in which Western thought began to move toward materialism and empiricism. Psychology's separation from philosophy was similar to the earlier separation of philosophy from religion or theology. Despite their divergent methods, all these fields had in common the goal of understanding human beings through exploring the nature of thought, consciousness, self-awareness, and moral vision. This quest represented the domain of psychology until the early part of the 20th century, at which time psychologists began to reject this view of human beings in its entirety. Soul, mind, and consciousness were all discarded as irrelevant to the study of psychology; they were seen as mere "ghosts in the machine," phantoms that could not be seen, heard, or measured.

A signal of this change was that psychologists began to draw their data from experimentalists like Gustav Theodor Fechner (1801–1887), who began his teaching career as a professor of physics. His research demonstrated that the properties of mind can be measured like the functions of the body. Fechner, who became interested in visual phenomena when he suffered a temporary eye disorder in the 1830s, showed that human sensations, or **percepts**, can be understood in terms of differential thresholds of stimuli. His work led to a new field called **psychophysics,** which employs the same scientific methods as physics itself. Psychophysicists usually make use of experimental stimuli that can be objectively measured, such as musical tones of different pitches or loudness or lights of varying intensity or color.

Similarly, Hermann von Helmholtz (1821–1894) applied the methods of physiology to measure the relationship between neural conduction and the functions of vision and hearing. His work showed that at least some functions of mind are bound to the same laws of physiology that govern all other bodily functions. Perhaps most significant was the influence of Charles Darwin, whose work led the way to the study of animals in order to better understand human behavior. The similarity between the higher animals and humans became an essential principle of behaviorism, a school of psychology that used experiments with animals to discover universal laws of behavior.

With these intellectual antecedents, behaviorism dominated the field of psychology for nearly 60 years. Like psychoanalysis, it has left a deep imprint on the popular psyche. This influential imprint extends well beyond psychology to such fields as marketing, education, and forensic psychology, all of which predicate many of their interventions on behavioral principles. As a discipline, behavioral psychology is both pragmatic and egalitarian because it is concerned solely with the principles of learning. Consequently, behaviorists view all psychological differences among people as products of differential learning experiences. Human beings are regarded as completely malleable, each person differing from others only in the type and degree of learning of which he or she is capable. Although behaviorism no longer represents an independent model of personality, it has been integrated to varying degrees within every extant model. Behaviorism remains a component of almost every modality of applied psychology, including clinical, educational, forensic, and even evolutionary psychology.

During the period in which behaviorism dominated American departments of psychology, almost all students studying psychology, professors teaching it, and researchers exploring it were behaviorists. Behaviorism was not merely a matter of style or emphasis but a creed so dominant that it pushed aside all other explanations of human behavior, personality, or development as irrelevant. Behaviorism so dominated experimental psychology for a time that some later writers asserted that it had virtually eliminated research into cognitive processes (Miller, 1988; Neisser, 1976; Solso, 1979). In many psychology departments, such words as *consciousness*, *awareness*, *thought*, or *feelings* could not be used in any research or scientific context. According to Gregory Kimble, a historian of psychology, "In mid-century American psychology, it would have cost a career to publish on mind, consciousness, volition, or even energy" (quoted in Koch & Leary, 1985, p. 316). Although Kimble was being a bit hyperbolic, he captured the essence of the times.

This exclusionary approach to the study of psychology was most closely associated with those referred to as **radical behaviorists**, psychologists who generally rejected any explanation or model that could not be directly observed. Rejected terms included such words as *motivation*, *drives*, *insight*, *ego traits*, *needs*, or *appetites*. As a result, many psychologists eschewed such terms for fear they would be banished as adherents of unscientific **mentalism**; that is, people who valued data gained from introspection or other internal mental processes to understand human behavior.

Inherent in radical behaviorism is extreme determinism. Determinism is the philosophical doctrine that holds that all observable phenomena, including social and psychological events and natural occurrences, are causally determined by preceding events or natural laws. Thus, a behaviorist psychologist maintains that people do not act out of free agency or will; rather, their behavior is determined by the environment or by events outside their control. All human actions result from prior reinforcement, not from the free will of the individual.

Experimental psychology, doctoral dissertations, and research funding tended to exclude all but behavioral topics (Hunt, 1999). Although consciousness and mind were banished from most laboratories, they did find safe havens in some quarters. These refuges included the growing fields of clinical psychology and psychoanalysis, as well as the work of Jean Piaget, an eminent Swiss psychologist well known for his studies of the cognitive development of children. In most laboratories and university departments, however, behaviorism reigned supreme. This dominance grew primarily out of work done in the Soviet Union and the United States, countries in which two outstanding figures established nearly exclusive intellectual domains. In Russia, the physiologist Ivan Pavlov, winner of the 1904 Nobel Prize in medicine, advocated the reduction of psychological principles to basic reflexes. In the United States, John B. Watson rejected consciousness and feelings in favor of observable stimuli and responses. The influence of the movement they began is exemplified by the following excerpt from *A Textbook of Psychology* by Donald Hebb (1958):

> It is difficult to give a precise and unequivocal definition of psychology, partly because the terms which must be used in a definition are themselves equivocal, meaning different things to different people. To define it as the study of behavior is not quite satisfactory, because this includes a large segment of physiology. Mouth-watering is behavior, and so is clenching the fist; to find out how the parotid gland secretes saliva, or how muscle cells produce finger movements, is a problem for the physiologist. (The psychologist is more concerned with the way in which many such small single items of behavior combine to form complex actions over longer periods of time.) On the other hand, the older definition—that psychology is the study of mind—does not cover the full range of phenomena with which we are concerned. Psychologists for example have traditionally been students of learning, not only in higher species but also in the earthworm and the ant. These organisms do not have the complexity of function which is referred to by the terms "mind" and "mental," so when a psychologist studies learning in the ant he is not dealing with mental processes, in any reasonable use of the term. (p. 2)

Like most texts of the time, Hebb's book described psychology as the study of behavior, not merely as the external expression of cognition, affect, or other less discernible processes; the human organism was basically reduced to its observable behavior. This trend reached its peak in the 1960s, when behaviorism was referred to in an influential text as "the psychological revolution in the twentieth century" (Kantor, 1963, p. 365). Although the beginnings of human observation of behavioral principles can be traced to the earliest domestication of animals around 15,000 BCE, the formal beginning of behaviorism as a school of psychology began in the physiology laboratory of Ivan Pavlov in the 19th century.

IVAN PETROVICH PAVLOV

Ivan Pavlov was one of the founders of behavioral psychology. He was not a psychologist, however, and tended to hold psychologists in low regard, as he accused them of wanting "their subject to remain forever unexplained. How they love the mysterious! Everything that can be explained physiologically they reject" (Kimble, Wertheimer, & White, 1991, p. 27). Pavlov was a physiologist who had received a medical degree from the University of St. Petersburg. Given his medical background, he was confident that most psychological events could be traced to physiological functions. For most of his career, he studied the digestive tract of dogs, seeking to define the interactions between the brain and the gut. It was for this research that he was awarded the Nobel Prize in Physiology or Medicine in 1904.

Image 10.1   Ivan Petrovich Pavlov (1849–1936)

Classical Conditioning

Pavlov's involvement with human psychology was somewhat fortuitous; it was a by-product of his work with dogs. Many of his experiments in the 1890s and the first decade of the 20th century required him to feed dogs through *fistulae* (tubes) placed directly into their stomachs. In these early studies, Pavlov noted that feeding the dogs, even through the fistulae, initiated immediate neural responses that caused the dogs to salivate. Pavlov referred to this response as an unconditioned reflex. He then discovered that digestion could be initiated without the animal's actually tasting the food. He found that merely presenting the food to a dog would cause the dog to salivate and secrete digestive juices in the gut. Pavlov's most momentous discovery, however, was that if a neutral stimulus like the sound of the feeding machine were repeatedly associated with the dog's food, the stimulus would eventually cause the dog to salivate, even in the absence of food.

Pavlov called this learned reaction a conditioned reflex. He regarded it as a brain circuit that became specific to the animal (or person) through external intervention; it is not a reflex common to every member of the species. Put slightly differently, the act of salivation in response to the sound of a bell when no food was present is a conditioned reflex because the instinct to salivate had been acquired through a type of learning. Pavlov concluded that all these reactions or reflexes were a result of the dog's learning that the appearance of food would shortly be followed by a meal. Thus, mental or "psychic" processes could directly influence physiological actions. In fact, Pavlov believed that all cerebral processes could be described in terms of unconditioned or conditioned reflexes (Babkin, 1974, p. 273).

The unconditioned reflexes are those that each organism possesses through evolution and inheritance. Such emotions as joy, anger, or fear are defined as subcortical reflexes—that is, they are located in the portions of the brain that lie below the cerebral hemispheres. The more complex cognitions are reflexes that originate in the cortex, the layer of tissue that covers the cerebral hemispheres in humans and other mammals. Pavlov regarded the brain as the operative center of a vast number of switching circuits, each circuit receiving an input from sensory neurons and responding with a predictable output:

> An external or internal stimulus falls on some one or another nervous receptor and gives rise to a nervous impulse; this nervous impulse is transmitted along nerve fibers to the central nervous system, and here, on account of existing nervous connections, it gives rise to a fresh impulse which passes along outgoing nerve fibers to the active organ, where it excites a special activity of the cellular structures. Thus a stimulus appears to be connected of necessity with a definite response, as cause with effect. (Pavlov, 1927, p. 7)

From this explanation, it is clear that Pavlov thought he had no need to hypothesize about constructs like free will, consciousness, or cognition. In his more frugal model, the human brain receives sensory inputs and responds in fixed and predetermined ways with a neurological or behavioral output. Consequently, Pavlov proposed that all mental processes must ultimately be understood as functions of the central nervous system. As such, he viewed psychological explanations as provisional speculations. He wrote elsewhere:

> But if we attempt and approach (to understand brain function) from this science of psychology to the problem confronting us we shall be building a superstructure on a science which has not a claim to exactness. . . . In fact, it is still open whether [psychology] can be regarded as a science at all. (Pavlov, 1927, p. 3)

Pavlov's fame as a physiologist and his discovery of what is now called classical conditioning set the dominant theme in psychology for more than half a century. Just as Pavlov rejected the subjective dimension of psychology, so too did the psychologists who embraced his efforts to employ scientific methods only on observable and measurable events. There were, however, such psychologists as Edward L. Thorndike, who were also studying learning and conditioning without completely rejecting the study of conscious states. We will look at Thorndike more closely later in this chapter.

While behaviorism was in its infancy, there were psychologists in the German universities working along parallel lines. These psychologists studied the mind in a distinctly different fashion from either Pavlov or the structuralists. The predominantly European school of Gestalt psychology explored the means by which the human psyche creates forms that are inherently processed as a whole. The Gestalt school, like the behaviorists, set forth ideas that were in direct contradiction to those of the structuralist psychologists, who attempted to analyze consciousness and reduce it to its molecular components. The Gestalt psychologists' research showed that the human mind constructs a reality that is greater than or different from the sum of the parts of conscious experience.

EDWARD L. THORNDIKE

Edward L. Thorndike, an educational psychologist who spent almost all of his career at Teachers College of Columbia University, was an early proponent of what would become behaviorism. Thorndike believed that the results of studying animal learning and thought can be applied to gaining a better understanding of human learning and behavior. This idea was not at all acceptable to the structuralists, the psychologists who dominated the study of psychology in the United States when Thorndike was in graduate school. The structuralists studied human consciousness exclusively.

Thorndike anticipated some key elements of behaviorism, with the exception that he allowed for species-specific behaviors and individual differences among humans. Such reservations would become anathema to the more strict behavioral theorists. Thorndike's role in establishing the basis for animal models of human behavior was nonetheless critically important. He proposed that humans do not differ qualitatively from other animals but do differ in the quantity and complexity of associations acquired by their brains. He was instrumental in helping define psychology as a separate science rather than a branch of philosophy. He emphasized that psychology must be based on standard scientific procedures, like those used by the physical sciences.

The Law of Effect

Thorndike proposed this law of learning, called the **law of effect**: If an animal makes several responses to the same situation, those responses that are associated with or are closely followed by satisfaction to the animal will become associated with the situation. Consequently, when the situation presents itself again, the animal will be likely to exhibit those responses that were associated with satisfaction. Conversely, actions expressed in a situation leading to discomfort will be less likely to be repeated. Anyone who has tried to take a pet to the veterinarian for vaccinations more than once knows that the dog or cat is considerably less cooperative the second time around. The greater the intensity of the animal's satisfaction or the discomfort, the stronger will be the connection between the response and the situation. In short, animals can learn which behaviors bring positive reinforcement and which bring aversive ones, and they will repeat the behaviors that bring positive outcomes.

Thorndike (1898) presented this concept in his doctoral dissertation, *Animal Intelligence*, in which he clearly inferred the existence of cognitive processes within animals. He believed that animals have the ability to make choices regarding the stimuli to which they respond and the type of response that they make. Thorndike did not think that Pavlov's model of

Image 10.2   Edward L. Thorndike (1874–1939)

classical conditioning is sufficient to explain the scope of behavior observed in nature. His paradigmatic experiment involved a puzzle box in which a cat was placed in a cage with a latched door. Outside the cage was an enticing piece of salmon, which the cat first tried to reach by clawing at the cage. During its aggressive attempts to get out of the cage, the cat struck the latch that opened the door. With each repetition of the experiment, the time it took the cat to hit the latch diminished until it would swat the latch immediately to open the door when the salmon was presented. Thorndike attributed this behavior at least in part to the cat's anticipation of the reward, not merely to the classical conditioning described by Pavlov.

Significantly, Thorndike believed that human beings differ in degree from animals as the result of natural selection, but they do not differ in kind. That is, because humans evolved in parallel with other animals, they share many characteristics with them, thus making animal behavior a legitimate model for the understanding of human behavior. This principle has guided generations of experimental psychologists.

The Law of Exercise

A fundamental commonality between humans and animals is that they learn via the laws of effect and exercise. The law of exercise states that a response will be more strongly connected with a stimulus the more often a connection is made between stimulus and response and that the response will weaken if it is not repeated. Thus, according to Thorndike, animals differ from humans in the number, precision, complexity, and duration of associations, but both humans and animals learn in a similar fashion. Thorndike believed that humans are unique in their ability to formulate concepts and ideas, but he also thought that the ideas themselves issued from the laws of exercise and effect.

▣ JOHN B. WATSON

John Broadus Watson was a creative iconoclast who offered psychology a uniquely hopeful albeit mechanical view of humankind. Psychology as a separate discipline was in its infancy when Watson began his work. Clinical psychology existed only in its most rudimentary forms, primarily in the form of psychometrics, which is the quantitative measurement of psychological characteristics. The major universities had only recently added psychology departments as independent centers of research, and the work of psychology was seen as largely esoteric and irrelevant to the lives of most people. The beginning of the 20th century saw most psychologists fruitlessly working to understand the abstract nature of consciousness. They had little to do with psychiatry, which was a separate field carried out either in hospitals following a medical regimen or as a form of outpatient treatment adopting some of the principles of psychoanalysis.

Early Career

Watson graduated from Furman University in South Carolina and went to the University of Chicago for graduate work. His dissertation, completed in 1903 under James Rowland Angell, a leading functionalist psychologist who later served as president of Yale University,

Image 10.3   John B. Watson
(1878–1958)

was a study of the learning ability in rats of different ages. Watson seized the day 10 years later by publishing a philippic titled "Psychology as the Behaviorist Views It," in which he accused his peers of losing touch with the real world. Psychology as represented by both structuralism and functionalism had not yielded any useful or meaningful discoveries, he thought. The field, he pointed out, was considered irrelevant by most other professions and desperately needed to become both scientific and useful.

The psychology Watson espoused saw humans as just one type of organism that could be completely molded by conditioning. His 1913 manifesto plainly stated that conviction:

> Psychology as the behaviorist views it is a purely objective experimental branch of natural science. Its theoretical goal is the prediction and control of behavior. Introspection forms no essential part of its methods, nor is the scientific value of its data dependent upon the readiness with which they lend themselves to interpretation in terms of consciousness. The behaviorist, in his efforts to get a unitary scheme of animal response, recognizes no dividing line between man and brute. The behavior of man, with all of its refinement and complexity, forms only a part of the behaviorist's total scheme of investigation. (p. 158)

Watson seized upon the discoveries of Ivan Pavlov and his coworkers to advocate an entirely new method of understanding behavior. And behavior, he avowed, was all that needed to be understood. Watson's *tabula rasa* (blank slate) view of the human mind became widely known and popularized by the mass media. A 1939 quotation from *Time* magazine makes clear that behaviorism was widely known as proposing that humans are all fundamentally the same. "Some researchers, such as Behaviorist John Broadus Watson, have tried to show that emotional endowments are all the same at birth and that differences appearing later are due to environment" ("Emotional Rats," 1939).

This same sentiment was expressed by Watson some years earlier in his behavioral creed:

> [W]e have no real evidence of the inheritance of traits. I would feel perfectly confident in the ultimately favorable outcome of careful upbringing of a healthy, well-formed baby born of a long line of crooks, murderers, thieves, and prostitutes. Who has any evidence to the contrary? Many, many thousands of children yearly, born from moral households and steadfast parents, become wayward, steal or become prostitutes, through one mishap or another of nurture. Many more thousands of sons and daughters of the wicked grow up to be wicked because they couldn't grow up any other way in such surroundings. But let one adopted child who has a bad ancestry go wrong and it is used as incontestable evidence for the inheritance of moral turpitude and criminal tendencies. As a matter of fact, there has not been a double handful of cases in the whole of our civilization where records have been carefully enough kept for us to draw any such conclusions—mental

testers, Lombroso [Cesare Lombroso, an Italian criminologist who thought that criminal tendencies are inherited], and all other students of criminality to the contrary notwithstanding. All of us know that adopted children are never brought up as one's own. One cannot use statistics gained from observations in charitable institutions and orphan asylums. All one needs to do to discount such statistics is to go there and work for a while, and I say this without trying to belittle the work of such organizations. I should like to go one step further tonight and say, "Give me a dozen healthy infants, well formed, and my own specified world to bring them up in and I'll guarantee to take any one at random and train him to become any type of specialist I might select—a doctor, lawyer, artist, merchant chief and, yes, even into beggar man and thief, regardless of his talents, penchants, tendencies, abilities, vocations, and race of his ancestors." I am going beyond my facts and I admit it, but so have the advocates of the contrary and they have been doing it for many thousands of years. Please note that when this experiment is made I am to be allowed to specify the way they are to be brought up and the type of world they have to live in. (Watson, 1926, pp. 9–10)

Structuralist Psychology. To some extent, Watson was rejecting the hereditarian psychology of Francis Galton and those who, like Lombroso, made use of Galton's views to justify **eugenics**. But Watson's radical new approach was primarily a reaction to the psychological school of thought called structuralism. Followers of this approach studied the human psyche through introspection of their own thoughts, sensations, or perceptions. This method asked researchers trained in specified methods to examine their own sensations, perceptions, and mental processes with the goal of identifying all of the molecular units of cognition down to their fundamental components.

Structuralism grew out of the work of Wilhelm Wundt in Germany and was advanced in the United States by Edward Bradford Titchener. In seeking to distinguish his approach from the functionalism of psychologists like John Dewey (Flugel, 1964), Titchener invented the term structuralism to describe his methods and research. Both Titchener and Wundt shared the goal of making psychology as scientific as physics, whose advancements had clearly supplied a model for structuralism.

Titchener sought to discover the basic components and subcomponents of mind in the same way that physicists had been discovering the quantum nature of matter. Titchener referred to these basic elements of mind as "simple elementary constituents" (Titchener, 1899), which could be combined in various ways to explain all perceptions, mental states, and behavior. Just as subatomic particles could be structured to make any atom or molecule, the simple elementary constituents could be constituted to produce any mental state. Titchener regarded the purposes of psychological science as the definition of the most elementary constituents of consciousness, the discovery of the laws by which these elements are related or combined, and the description of the relationships of these elements to bodily states.

Structuralism and Introspection. Titchener proposed that trained introspection of one's own consciousness is the only legitimate method of research in psychology. The fundamental weakness of the structuralist approach, however, is that there was never any objective evidence for the existence of these elementary aspects of mind. Titchener's lack of objective evidence did not stop him or his students from producing a wealth of papers, reports, and symposia that described an astounding number of simple elements. With the number of elements to be discovered limited only by the introspective talents of the observers, the number of sensations Titchener identified eventually exceeded 44,435 (Titchener, 1899, p. 74).

The structuralist method of research and its prolific output of publications (Boring, 1942), which increasingly lost contact with most mundane problems of life, was distasteful to Watson, who believed it to be both unscientific and unproductive. Watson, like a number of psychologists of his time, became increasingly uncomfortable with unquantifiable constructs like *thought, feeling, consciousness,* or *emotion.* Aided by Titchener's bewilderingly complex system of sensations derived by introspection, Watson had a negative paradigm to reject. With the rejection of introspection went everything that could not be observed, which included all mental states and processes. Watson responded with a proposal for a new psychology unfettered by hypothetical constructs, one that would be both scientific and practical. His 1913 article, which was followed by a book 6 years later (Watson, 1919), reshaped the field of psychology for the next half century.

Clinical Paradigm

Watson redirected the entire field of experimental psychology with his advocacy of a strict behavioral perspective. He proposed in a later book titled *Behaviorism* (Watson, 1930) that human beings, unlike other animals, can be conditioned across three domains of behavior: manual, verbal, and emotional (visceral). Manual behaviors in Watson's terminology referred to all observable physical actions, all of which can be manipulated by conditioning. Watson proposed that training young people to have more reliable work habits was the foundation of productivity, even genius. He advocated **distributed practice** (short frequent sessions of study or exercise rather than longer but less frequent sessions) as the means to perfecting any

Table 10.1   Titchener's Elements of Sensation

Organ	Sensations	Organ	Sensations
Eye	32,820	Alimentary canal	3?
Ear (hearing)	11,600	Blood vessels	?
Nose	?	Lungs	1?
Tongue	4	Sex organ	1
Skin	4	Ear (static sense)	1
Muscles/tendons/joints	2/1/1	Total	44,435

NOTE: A question mark denotes an undetermined or uncertain number of sensations.

motor skill or form of learning. This is in contrast to **massed practice**, in which one learns a skill through a few intensely repetitive sessions. Interestingly, by not emphasizing external conditioning or behavioral control, Watson allowed for a higher degree of self-motivation and regulation than some of the more radical behaviorists who followed him. Watson regarded thought as nothing more than internalized speech. This explanation of thought only superficially avoids postulating internal constructs because there is a minimal difference between an unheard internal dialogue and a nonobservable thought. Nevertheless, Watson thought of verbal habits or behaviors as a type of serial ordered behavior that arises from what he allowed could be innate instincts to produce rudimentary sounds (Watson, 1926). He applied these principles to psychopathology (Watson, 1916), being the first to reject Freudian and other approaches that used mental constructs to explain disturbed behavior.

The Little Albert Experiment

If one were to pick Watson's second most influential contribution, it would probably be his study of Little Albert. This experiment has been cited thousands of times in research articles and is presented in almost every textbook in introductory psychology. It represents the behaviorist explanation of the etiology of phobias and by extension all other psychopathologies (Eysenck, 1965). Unfortunately, a careful examination of the Little Albert experiment reveals a study so poorly designed that if it had been completed in more recent times, it would not have been accepted for publication. In this paradigmatic 1920 study, Watson and his assistant, Rosalie Rayner, had one participant, an 11-month-old infant named Albert B. Albert, now known to psychological posterity as Little Albert, was variously exposed to a white rat, a rabbit, a dog, a monkey, masks (with and without hair), cotton wool, and burning newspapers. None of these objects caused any apparent fear in Albert; in fact, the authors reported that the little boy was virtually always placid and "practically never cried."

Albert was then subjected to loud noises, beginning with the sound of a hammer striking a steel bar, which startled him. At the third repetition of the noise, the child began to cry. Watson and Rayner reported that this was the first time that Albert was seen to react with fear or crying. The authors, who apparently assumed that fear of loud noises is an unconditioned or innate response, sought to condition Albert to fear a white rat by pairing the animal with the loud noise. In this way, they supposedly created a conditioned emotional response. Over the course of several weeks, Watson and Rayner conducted a program of repeatedly startling Albert when presenting him with a white rat, a white rabbit, a cotton ball, and a fur coat. The way in which they did so has been criticized for being unsystematic and poorly designed (Rilling, 2000). In addition, their conclusion that Albert was conditioned to experience a specific emotional reaction was based entirely on the observation of the researchers seeking this goal. Despite Watson and Rayner's claims that Albert was conditioned to fear the white rat and other white furred objects, he was quite inconsistent in his responses. The following excerpts describe Albert's responses to his conditioning (Watson & Rayner, 1920):

1. Rat presented suddenly without sound. There was steady fixation but no tendency at first to reach for it. The rat was then placed nearer, whereupon tentative reaching movements began with the right hand. When the rat nosed the infant's left hand, the hand was immediately withdrawn. He started to reach for the head of the animal with the

forefinger of the left hand, but withdrew it suddenly before contact. It is thus seen that the two joint stimulations given the previous week were not without effect. He was tested with his blocks immediately afterwards to see if they shared in the process of conditioning. He began immediately to pick them up, dropping them, pounding them, etc. In the remainder of the tests the blocks were given frequently to quiet him and to test his general emotional state. They were always removed from sight when the process of conditioning was under way.

2. Joint stimulation with rat and sound. Started, then fell over immediately to right side. No crying.

3. Joint stimulation. Fell to right side and rested upon hands, with head turned away from rat. No crying.

4. Joint stimulation. Same reaction.

5. Rat suddenly presented alone. Puckered face whimpered and withdrew body sharply to the left.

6. Joint stimulation. Fell over immediately to right side and began to whimper.

7. Joint stimulation. Started violently and cried, but did not fall over.

8. Rat alone. The instant the rat was shown the baby began to cry. Almost instantly he turned sharply to the left, fell over on left side, raised himself on all fours and began to crawl away so rapidly that he was caught with difficulty before reaching the edge of the table. (pp. 4–5)

Watson and Rayner concluded from their efforts with Albert that emotions can be conditioned by standard stimulus-response (S-R) techniques. In this particular experiment, fear was the focus.

Although Watson was attempting to demonstrate that all emotions can be both explained and manipulated by prior reinforcement, it is questionable that his experiment with Albert provided compelling evidence. This ambiguity can be seen in Watson's notes taken when Albert was 1 year and 21 days old, approximately a month after the conditioning was completed.

1. Santa Claus mask. Withdrawal, gurgling, then slapped at it without touching. When his hand was forced to touch it, he whimpered and cried. His hand was forced to touch it two more times. He whimpered and cried on both tests. He finally cried at the mere visual stimulus of the mask.

2. Fur coat. Wrinkled his nose and withdrew both hands, drew back his whole body and began to whimper as the coat was put nearer. Again there was the strife between withdrawal and the tendency to manipulate. Reached tentatively with left hand but drew back before contact had been made. . . .

3. Fur coat. The coat was taken out of his sight and presented again at the end of a minute. He began immediately to fret, withdrawing his body and nodding his head as before.

4. Blocks. He began to play with them as usual.

5. The rat. He allowed the rat to crawl towards him without withdrawing. He sat very still and fixated it intently. Rat then touched his hand. Albert withdrew it immediately, then leaned back as far as possible but did not cry.

6. Blocks. Reaction normal.

7. The rabbit. The animal was placed directly in front of him. It was very quiet. Albert showed no avoiding reactions at first. After a few seconds he puckered up his face, began to nod his head and to look intently at the experimenter. He next began to push the rabbit away with his feet, withdrawing his body at the same time. Then as the rabbit came nearer he began pulling his feet away, nodding his head, and wailing "da da." (pp. 10–11)

What do the above results show? Albert was mildly afraid of a Santa Claus mask (with the white beard) but cried only when he was *forced* to touch it three times. His reaction of fear to the white fur coat consisted simply of wrinkling his nose; he whimpered only when the coat was placed very close to him—as any child might when a large unfamiliar object is forced upon him. In addition, Watson and Rayner conjectured that Albert experienced "strife between withdrawal and the tendency to manipulate." There was no evidence of such a conflict, perhaps because Albert was not particularly fearful of the coat. Finally, and most telling, was the fact that Albert actually crawled toward the rat—the very rat he had supposedly been conditioned to fear. Watson and Rayner attempted to explain this anomaly by stating that Albert was able to block "fear and noxious stimuli" whenever he was close to crying or becoming emotionally upset (p. 13). In addition to the questionable methodology and results, Watson also described the study differently across the course of several of his publications, adding some doubt to its overall veracity (Cornwell, Hobbs, & Prytula, 1980; Harris, 1979).

Despite these historical problems, the Little Albert study is presented as the behaviorist paradigm in most introductory and behavioral psychology textbooks. Remarkably, according to Harris (1979), the description of the Little Albert experiment differs widely in various psychology textbooks. He notes that Albert's age, the animal he was conditioned to fear, the objects to which he generalized the fear, and the process of Albert's reconditioning (there was none, an omission that would now be considered unethical) are among the discrepancies that are found in textbook accounts of this experiment.

Theory of Personality

Watson, as did his students and followers, viewed human personality as devoid of any preexisting traits or hypothetical structures (Watson, 1913). Watson believed that there are only three basic emotions: fear, rage, and love. We are born afraid of loud noises and loss of support; we feel rage at being hampered; and we feel love in response to being stroked, rocked, and patted. Our "personality" is formed in our family as unique stimuli are attached to these emotions via classical conditioning. Watson did allow for basic and universal temperaments or instincts, but these were of the most rudimentary nature. Therefore, his model of personality had the distinct advantage of parsimony: it required mastering very few concepts for the student to understand it.

Watson also made a distinction between character and personality. He saw human character as a subset of a more global characteristic that he referred to as personality. Accordingly, character refers to an individual's reactions to specific moral and social situations. Personality, according to Watson, included these basic reactions as well as global behavioral responses to long-standing problems viewed in the context of the person's life history. Watson clarified his distinction between character and personality with the example of a thief or liar who could be said to have no character while possibly having a very interesting personality (Watson, 1919, p. 392).

> Let us mean by the term personality an individual's total assets (actual and potential) and liabilities (actual and potential) on the reaction side. By assets we mean first the total mass of organized habits; the socialized and regulated instincts; the socialized and tempered emotions; and the combinations and interrelations among these; and secondly, high coefficients both of plasticity (capability of new habit formation or altering of old) and of retention (readiness of implanted habits to function after disuse). Looked at in another way, assets are that part of the individual's equipment which make for his adjustment and balance in his present environment and for readjustment if the environment changes. By liabilities we mean similarly that part of the individual's equipment which does not work in the present environment and the potential or possible factors which would prevent his rising to meet a changed environment. In more detail, we mean that we can enumerate the reasons for his present lack of adjustment in such terms as insufficiency of habits, lack of social instincts (instinct not modified by habit), violence of emotion or insufficiency or lack of emotion, and that we can infer that with his present equipment and plasticity the individual cannot make a satisfactory adjustment either to his present environment or possibly to any other environment. In case his potential assets are sufficient we can enumerate and begin the inculcation of those factors which will make for his adjustment. (Watson, 1919, p. 397)

Thus, people differ solely based on the type and degree of the **reinforcements** they received in childhood. If someone had exhibited outgoing behavior (or some external event elicited it) and it was sufficiently reinforced, then that person would be outgoing. The same is held to be true for every personality measure, from sociopathy to sensitivity. Watson allowed for innate differences in people's ability to respond to reinforcement; these differences are an additional factor in the development of personality. Differences among people also include social instincts, which Watson thought could exist without conditioning or learning.

Watson did believe, however, that innate inclinations can be modified by conditioning. Once conditioned, a personality could be qualitatively evaluated based on its range and flexibility because personality is only a repertoire of prepared responses to social and situational stimuli. That is, a person who has in her behavioral repertoire a greater number of potential responses to a larger range of situations would have an advantage in personality over someone with a less comprehensive repertoire.

Watson believed that personality is a useful construct from the behavioral perspective as it represents a history of response patterns to various life stimuli. It therefore makes prediction of a person's behavior more feasible. Watson pointed out that someone's perception of another's personality might be a conflation of prior conditioning to defer to someone of similar status. An example would be that a child raised to respect certain authority figures will in later life describe people of similar status as having powerful or compelling personalities as a result of this early conditioning. People differ solely based on the type and degree of reinforcements they received, Watson held.

In his behaviorist manifesto, Watson rejected both the dominant school of structuralism and the popular school of functionalism. Both, he said, predicated their theories and research on precepts that were neither necessary nor provable. Watson saw the concept of consciousness as a means of bringing the unscientific topic of the soul back into psychology through the back door. Introspection had produced as many psychologies as psychologists, he thought. For Watson, only stimuli and responses are available for study. In addition, this barebones outline of a science is what it means to be human. Watson did leave open the possibility that at some point in the future, psychologists might be able to study and apply mental states to the field of psychology, but given the state of technology in his time, he believed such analysis served only to make psychology useless to all other professions. He pointed out that most other professions saw no use or relevance for psychology. Physicians, lawyers, and business people did not look to the field to aid in their decisions. Watson noted that there was an incipient field of applied psychology, but he felt it need not be necessary to create an adjunct discipline to make the profession relevant or useful.

For Watson, the conditioned response is the basic unit of behavior. His theory of learning—and so, in effect, his theory of personality—rely solely on classical conditioning. But the reader should note that in classical conditioning the animal does not learn a *new* behavior—Pavlov's dogs already knew how to salivate. For a behaviorist account of the way in which people learn complex and novel behavior, we must look at B. F. Skinner's ideas later in this chapter.

From Academia to Madison Avenue

Watson's lasting influence is more extensive than most people think. Academic psychology has moved away from Watson's behaviorism, but his legacy touches all of us daily through the advertising that pervades the mass media. Watson, in effect, invented modern advertising, in which the product becomes the conditioned **reinforcer.**

Watson earned $70,000 a year during the Depression as an advertising executive—a huge sum at the time. His transition from professor to advertising guru was the result of his lively libido. His collaboration with Rosalie Rayner, a graduate student young enough to be his daughter, extended beyond the Little Albert study into the bedroom. Watson hid his affair with Rosalie very poorly (which Freud would have attributed to an unconscious wish to be found out, no doubt).

Watson's wife, Mary, grew quite suspicious and acquired more than 10 graphic love letters through the ruse of paying a social visit to Rayner's home, then stealing the letters from Rosalie's bedroom. The letters found their way to the president of Johns Hopkins University. Watson's academic career was finished. He found a job in advertising in New York, and with it more money than he had previously dreamed of and the opulent lifestyle to go with it.

(Continued)

(Continued)

Watson saw that people, just like the rats he had studied in the laboratory, reach for easily available objects. Thus, he advised retailers that candy and magazines could be profitably placed close to checkout lines. He developed advertising campaigns based on guilt; thus, mothers could be made to buy baby powder and men to purchase deodorant. He showed that smokers may claim loyalty to their favorite brand, yet cannot identify their brand by taste. They were buying only a conditioned image; thus, image is the most important aspect of salesmanship. In addition, in 1928, Watson invented a secular ritual as part of a campaign to sell more Maxwell House coffee, a ritual still reenacted in thousands of offices and factories—the coffee break.

As for Rosalie, she and Watson were married in 1921 after his divorce from Mary became final. She bore Watson two sons, one of whom later became a psychiatrist and still later committed suicide. Her life was darkened by Watson's other infidelities and her misgivings about his behaviorist theories of childrearing. In 1930, she wrote an article "I Am the Mother of a Behaviorist's Sons," for *Parents' Magazine*. She died of pneumonia in 1935.

She wrote, "In some respects I bow to the great wisdom in the science of behaviorism, and in others I am rebellious. I secretly wish that on the score of [the children's] affections, they will be a little weak when they grow up, that they will have a tear in their eyes for the poetry and drama of life and a throb for romance. . . . I like being merry and gay and having the giggles. The behaviorists think giggling is a sign of maladjustment."

VIGNETTE

John Watson was a pioneering behaviorist psychologist whose career illustrates the detrimental effects of a conflict between a drive for achievement and reluctance to compromise with social conventions in order to advance professionally.

Watson was born in South Carolina, a part of the country known in the late 19th century for its social conservatism. In his youth, he received conflicting messages from his parents. His mother espoused the tenets of a Southern fundamentalist form of Christianity, while his father was an alcoholic womanizer. It was not surprising that Watson was a poor student in his early years and known for his disruptive classroom behavior. But despite all of these obstacles, he was a precocious student. Watson graduated from high school at the age of 16 and entered Furman University in Greenville, South Carolina. During his undergraduate years, he kept to himself, developing a pattern of emotional reserve that continued into his later life. Close friendships and genuine intimacy always eluded him to varying degrees throughout his life.

Watson began his college career by studying philosophy and religion—largely to please his mother, who wanted him to become a minister. Because he was not fully committed to his schoolwork, however, his grades were only passable. In addition, Watson took a nonconformist approach to his studies; thus, in spite of the intellectual gifts that were apparent to some of his professors, he did not receive top marks. Consequently, it took him 5 years to earn his bachelor's degree. Despite his weak undergraduate record, however, Watson was able to earn his master's degree from Furman in just 1 year.

As Watson's college career indicated, his drive to succeed was always at odds with his resistance to convention. This conflict came into play when he began his doctoral studies at the University of Chicago. Watson was given the opportunity to study under the famed philosopher John Dewey, but he was not at all impressed with his teacher. In fact, he called Dewey incomprehensible and left Chicago's department of philosophy to study psychology instead. With the death of his mother in the previous year, he was no longer under pressure to study for the ministry. Psychology became a passion for Watson; he requested a functionalist psychologist, James Rowland Angell, as his new adviser, and he began to distinguish himself during his doctoral studies in a way that he had not done as an undergraduate.

At the outset of his budding career, however, Watson suffered an episode of major depression. In 1902, he suffered from what was then called a nervous breakdown, which had been a long time coming. This collapse was prefigured by bouts of anxiety that he had had in his youth. He interpreted literally the tales of Satan and his minions that his mother had told him. These stories of hellfire and damnation produced on-and-off periods of dread that culminated with his emotional breakdown in 1902. After a few months of slowing the pace of his doctoral studies and taking more time to rest, Watson recovered. For the remainder of his life, he vigorously rejected his mother's faith and openly proclaimed that he was an atheist.

Within a year of Watson's crisis, he completed his Ph.D. in experimental psychology with highest honors. In addition to his academic success, the very handsome new psychologist was developing a reputation for being a Lothario. He had numerous love affairs prior to his marriage to one of his students when he was 26, the year after he completed his doctorate. In 1913, still a junior faculty member at Chicago, Watson published a paper that had an impact on psychology for decades to come. Titled "Psychology as a Behaviorist Views It," this article-cum-manifesto rejected the then-dominant schools of psychology for a new approach—behaviorism. Watson's replacement for functionalist psychology became so influential that it completely dominated the field for the next 75 years.

Some aspects of Watson's personality led both to his becoming a legend in psychology and to his downfall as an academic. He was a driven but vulnerable man who seemingly had a great deal to prove after his troubled upbringing. His drive for achievement led to his ability to escape the constraints of conventional thinking within the field of psychology; however, it also made him impatient with social mores, which led to behavior that precipitated personal and professional disaster.

Vignette Questions

1. What aspects of Watson's personality that led to his downfall might also have been responsible for his ascendance in the field?

2. List some other personality characteristics that could be advantageous in some situations and disadvantageous in others.

回   CLARK L. HULL

Watson had been the leader of many behaviorally oriented psychologists, who ventured to create a scientific psychology based on S-R behavioral principles. After Watson's unceremonious departure from academic psychology, Clark L. Hull (1884–1952) assumed the mantle of the most influential behaviorist. Hull, who had started out in engineering before he became a psychologist, attempted to expand upon the work of early behaviorists like Thorndike by determining the quantitative foundations of learning. He wrote:

> [I believe that] psychology is a true natural science; that its primary laws are express-ible quantitatively by means of a moderate number of ordinary equations; that all the complex behavior of single individuals will ultimately be derivable as secondary laws form. (quoted in Hunt, 1993, p. 267)

Hull was motivated by his conclusion that such major philosophers as Immanuel Kant, Thomas Hobbes, and David Hume had failed to develop a cohesive and consistent explana-tion of human knowledge, learning, and reason. They had failed for the same reason as the structuralists—their theories were all founded on human consciousness. Hull proposed an approach based on learning. He said, "I shall start with action—habit—and proceed to deduce all the rest, including conscious experience, from action, i.e., habit" (quoted in Ammons, 1962, p. 837).

Hull differed from many of his contemporaries in two respects. First, reflecting his engineering background, he wanted to explain human behavior in terms of mathematical equations that would define the relationships between learning and reinforcement, and through this means, he hoped to discover the basis of conscious experience. Unlike the more radical behaviorists, Hull thus accepted the concept of consciousness but thought that it must be understood through its essential S-R components.

Hull's (1951) formal theory was presented in his text, *Essentials of Behavior.* His approach essentially expanded upon the intervening variable approach of Edward C. Tolman, which posited that organisms do not merely respond to a stimulus but make choices among a variety of possible internalized responses. Hull's work was founded on a collection of mathematical postulates and corollaries that provide the basis of his learning theory. For example, he expressed an organism's habit strength (Hull, 1952, p. 8) through the following equation: $_sH_R = 1\text{-}10^{-aN}$. In other words, habit strength or $_sH_R$ (stimulus-habit-response) equals 1 minus 10 raised to the negative power of the constant a multiplied by N (the number of times a stimulus has been reinforced).

In addition to Hull's mathematical models, he also detailed all of the antecedents, environmental variables, and resulting behavioral outcomes involved in the conditioning of behavior. He described the lower and higher level constructs within an organism that make it more or less receptive to learning or conditioning. Unfortunately for Hull's legacy, his complex series of postulates describing the reactions to physical stimuli in terms of power functions, momentary effective reaction potentials, behavioral oscillations, and similar expressions was difficult to understand and left many behaviorists confused at best.

Despite Hull's complex manner of presentation, however, he did advance the behaviorist perspective by proposing that apparently simple stimulus-response connections are typically far more complex than meets the eye. His system allowed for a network of internalized stimulus-response links that would permit behaviorism to explain complex behaviors precisely through predictable and quantifiable laws. Equally important was Hull's premise that the entire S-R process begins with a drive that exists within the organism. Accordingly, organisms engage in purposeful behaviors. That is, they seek to reduce the strength of the drives that ensure their survival, such as hunger and thirst. Like Dollard and Miller, who will be discussed later, Hull's drive reduction theory was most likely influenced by psychoanalysis.

🔲 BURRHUS FREDERIC (B. F.) SKINNER

Watson's departure from psychology briefly deprived behaviorism of a persuasive emissary for its point of view because the verbal and mathematical complexity of Hull's theories made them inaccessible to many psychologists. These developments set the stage for B. F. Skinner to dominate the field of behavioral psychology for more than a quarter of a century. Skinner was the virtual incarnation of behaviorism, having a greater influence on psychology than any other researcher of his era. The American Psychological Association honored him with the Presidential Citation for Lifetime Contribution to Psychology and stated, in awarding him the Distinguished Scientific Contribution Award, that his impact on the field of psychology was both profound and widely influential. In addition to his own discipline's honors, he was awarded the National Medal of Science by the United States and the Gold Medal Award by the American Psychological Foundation.

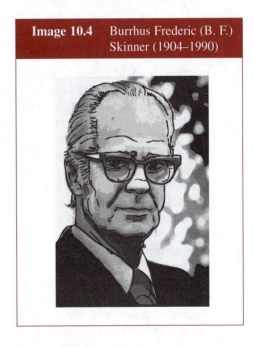

Image 10.4 Burrhus Frederic (B. F.) Skinner (1904–1990)

Skinner earned these honors by way of his radicalism. That is, he rejected all explanations of behavior, animal or human, that could not be observed. Skinner's radical behaviorism differs somewhat from Watson's strong behaviorist position. Watson rejected introspection as a technique for obtaining psychological data but was open to cognitive explanations when they could be fully explained and applied. In contrast, Skinner rejected any such concepts. He neither accepted nor foresaw that there would ever be a need for anything other than a stimulus-response explanation of behavior. He said in 1959:

> Freud's explanatory scheme followed a traditional pattern of looking for a cause of human behavior inside the organism. His medical training supplied him with powerful supporting analogies. The parallel between the excision of a tumor, for example, and the release of a repressed wish from the unconscious is quite compelling and must have affected Freud's thinking. Now, the pattern of an inner explanation of behavior is best

exemplified by doctrines of animism, which are primarily concerned with explaining the spontaneity and evident capriciousness of behavior. The living organism is an extremely complicated system behaving in an extremely complicated way. Much of its behavior appears at first blush to be absolutely unpredictable. The traditional procedure had been to invent an inner determiner, a "demon," "spirit," "homunculus," or "personality" capable of spontaneous change of course or of origination of action. Such an inner determiner offers only a momentary explanation of the behavior of the outer organism, because it must, of course, be accounted for also, but it is commonly used to put the matter beyond further inquiry and to bring the study of a causal series of events to a dead end. (Skinner, 1959, p. 187)

Skinner clearly rejected Freud's and all other models of human behavior based on invisible structures. Moreover, he accused all such psychologists of directly blocking the path to the truth by formulating constructs that can be neither verified nor studied.

Operants, Respondents, and Reinforcers

Skinner added a remarkable degree of complexity to the simple stimulus-response model of his predecessors. His work appeared both necessary and completely sufficient for more than a generation to explain all behaviors of all organisms. A key component of his new model was the operant, a concept that referred to any behavior produced by an organism that can be defined by its effect on the organism's environment. Skinner placed all behavior into one of two categories, respondent or *operant* (Skinner, 1938). According to Skinner, a respondent behavior is elicited by some external event or stimulus. The paradigmatic respondent is the salivation exhibited by Pavlov's dog. The salivation was initially provoked or elicited by the presentation of meat. This type of response is the focus of classical conditioning, which Skinner referred to as respondent conditioning. In fact, Skinner uses the term *response* to refer to a single occurrence of an operant. Operants are expressed without any associated stimulus; thus, they are the natural behaviors of an organism. A baby swinging its arm, a chicken making a random peck, or a bird alighting on a branch could all be considered operants (Skinner, 1948a; Skinner, 1963). In essence, any movement that an animal makes that cannot be attributed to some provocation or an eliciting stimulus is an operant. Skinner held that learning results from voluntary responses that operate on the environment. These responses can either be strengthened or weakened by the consequences that follow their expression. This is Skinner's **law of acquisition,** which states that the strength or frequency of an operant behavior increases when followed by a reinforcer. This principle diverges from those enunciated by some of his behaviorist peers, like Thorndike or Hull, who wrote of pleasure or satisfaction as factors in reinforcement. Skinner tacitly rejected these theories as requiring suppositions about inscrutable internal states.

Reinforcers and Punishments

Skinner elaborated on the work of Watson and earlier behaviorists by expanding the ways that organisms can learn or change their behavior through reinforcement. According to

Skinner (1971), "When a bit of behavior is followed by a certain kind of consequence, it is more likely to occur again, and a consequence having this effect is called a reinforcer" (p. 27). Skinner described two basic types of reinforcers, positive and negative. In general, the use of a positive reinforcer is a more efficient way to increase the probability that an operant will be repeated. Positive reinforcers are often described as pleasurable or satisfying to the organism. Skinner eschewed all definitions that imply unobservable internal states; he simply defined a positive reinforcer as any event that follows an operant and increases the frequency or likelihood of its occurrence. Examples of positive reinforcers are appetizing food or drink, cheerful colors, or signs of social approval. Similarly, a negative reinforcer is any event that increases the probability or frequency of an operant when it is removed. For example, the removal of such an aversive stimulus as an electrical shock when an animal emits a desired response is a negative reinforcer. In humans, the act of taking an aspirin for a headache is an example of a negative reinforcer because the dose of analgesic usually removes the aversive headache. Because aspirin (unlike alcohol or opioids) does not have any inherently positive reinforcing qualities of its own, it reinforces the operant (taking the tablets) by removing a negative event, the headache. Here again, Skinner would not appeal to the **hedonic** or phenomenological properties of any event in determining its reinforcing value. He was concerned only with its effect on the frequency or likelihood of the operant being studied.

In Skinner's system, some reinforcers can be positive in some circumstances and negative in others. For example, food can be a positive reinforcer because of the hedonic properties associated with pleasant tastes or smells or attractive presentation of the food (such as a beautifully decorated cake or a tastefully arranged platter of appetizers). But food can also be considered a negative reinforcer because it relieves hunger. Skinner avoided paradoxes like these by concentrating only on the changes in behavior instead of the organism's internal states.

Skinner also maintained that punishment—which he defined as any event following an operant behavior that reduces the frequency or probability of that response in the future—can alter behavior or affect learning in three ways. It can reduce the rate of expression of an undesired behavior; it can increase avoidance behaviors; and, in the case of strong punishments, it can paradoxically increase the undesired behaviors when it is terminated. Skinner generally avoided terms like *aversive*, *unpleasant*, or *painful,* as such words require the researcher to acknowledge the organism's mental states. Punishment was not Skinner's preferred means for altering or **shaping** behavior. He believed its effects were more transient than those obtained through the use of positive reinforcers. Punishment may reduce or even temporarily stop the undesired behavior, but because these behaviors had to have been positively reinforced or have positive reinforcers waiting for them, they are likely to resume.

For Skinner, a preferable alternative to punishment is **differential reinforcement** of desired behaviors. In other words, rather than punish the individual to suppress a proscribed behavior, the parent or teacher reinforces the person for performing preferred behaviors. In Skinner's ideal of differential reinforcement, a thief would not be punished for stealing but strongly reinforced for socially responsible behaviors. This view of punishment is clearly expressed in the following excerpts from Skinner's novelized credo, *Walden Two* (1948b).

For one thing, we don't punish. We never administer an unpleasantness in the hope of repressing or eliminating undesirable behavior. (p. 114)

The old school made the amazing mistake of supposing that the reverse was true, that by removing a situation a person likes or setting up one he doesn't like—in other words by punishing him—it was possible to reduce the probability that he would behave in a given way again. That simply doesn't hold. It has been established beyond question. What is emerging at this critical stage in the evolution of society is a behavioral and cultural technology based on positive reinforcement alone. (p. 260)

The immediate, temporary effect of punishment overshadows the eventual advantage of positive reinforcement. We've all seen countless instances of the temporary effect of force, but clear evidence of the effect of not using force is rare. (p. 261)

In contemporary research, Skinner's principle of differential reinforcement has been applied to understand the relationship between stress and depression (Pizzagalli, Bogdan, Ratner, & Jahn, 2007) and to prevent acts of self-mutilation in psychiatric inpatients (Kumar & Geist, 2007).

Schedules of Reinforcement

Skinner's work in refining methods of reinforcement has played a major role in many disciplines, including fields as diverse as education, psychopharmacology, and forensics. His research with animals provided evidence that behavior can be progressively shaped by manipulating the timing, frequency, or type of reinforcement according to specific regimens. According to Skinner and the behaviorists aligned with him, all human behaviors—even complex social interactions—are products of such reinforcement. Skinner showed that reinforcement is often more effective in regulating behavior when it is not continuous; that is, the organism need not be reinforced each time to produce the desired behavior. In fact, Skinner demonstrated that less predictable reinforcements can produce far more consistent and lasting behavioral change. The reinforcement's unpredictability can be used to develop programs of reinforcement based on either the duration or the frequency of the response. Skinner referred to this approach as *contingencies of reinforcement*.

For example, if a person in strict behavioral treatment for avoidant personality disorder is given a verbal reinforcer immediately after every 3 consecutive days of public activity, this reinforcement would be an example of a fixed-interval schedule of reinforcement. In this approach, the first response following a specified interval is reinforced. Thus, if the individual being reinforced on this schedule fails to speak at the end of the third day, he will not be reinforced. Over time, the person will begin with virtually no speaking and will gradually reach a peak at the moment of reinforcement. This pattern of responding is called scalloping (see Figure 10.1) and is characteristic of fixed-interval reinforcement. This problem is resolved with a less predictable schedule like a **variable-interval reinforcement.** Here the reinforcement is provided after variable time intervals but with a predetermined average time. So reinforcement is provided without regard to the number of responses, as long as there are some responses being emitted during a time period. An example of such a schedule of reinforcement is the Internal Revenue Service's pattern of tax audits. Among the ways in which the IRS selects taxpayers for review is random selection, which effectively means that the average individual will be audited every few years but exactly how often is known only to the IRS. The unpredictability of this negative reinforcer keeps most taxpayers quite honest.

If the reinforcer is contingent on a specific number of responses, it is called a **fixed-ratio reinforcement** schedule. An example of the application of a fixed-ratio schedule is the allocation of sales commissions, in which a salesperson is paid each time after meeting a specific sales quota. If the reinforcement is awarded after a fluctuating number of responses, it is called a **variable-ratio reinforcement** schedule. In such a schedule, the organism is reinforced in an unpredictable pattern. Only the average number of responses in a particular time period is predetermined, but the number of responses required for each subsequent reinforcer is random. An application of this type of reinforcement, familiar to anyone who has ever visited a casino, is the slot machine. These devices are programmed to pay out over time about 90% of what they take in. However, if each time players put a dollar into the machine they got 90 cents back, they would quickly lose interest. So the machine reinforces gamblers with periodic but unpredictable wins. The power of such reinforcement is evident to anyone watching the rows of seated gamblers placing coin after coin into the slots. Most of these people lose money over time but remain reinforced as a result of variable payoffs.

Figure 10.1 graphically depicts Skinner's basic schedules of reinforcement. As the chart implies, the variable-ratio schedule of reinforcement leads to the greatest number of responses in any time period and the fixed-interval schedule the lowest.

In addition to the changes in duration and frequency of reinforcement, Skinner added several other principles that added to the understanding and methodology of behaviorism. One of these is **discrimination.** Skinner showed that even pigeons can learn to discriminate between very similar stimuli if they are gradually reinforced to do so.

Skinner used the term *response induction* to refer to the reinforcement of behaviors similar to ones that were reinforced. This phenomenon has been used to explain superstitious or ritualistic behaviors. For example, Skinner pointed to the body movements that bowlers make after they throw the bowling ball down the alley (Skinner, 1948a). The original movements were reinforced when they led to the ball hitting the pins successfully. The bowler has been reinforced to make certain movements during the delivery of the bowling ball but will often generalize these reinforcers to motions that cannot have any effect on the ball's trajectory. Similarly, stimulus induction refers to the expression of a conditioned response to a reinforcer similar to one that originally conditioned the behavior.

For example, in the much touted case of Little Albert, the baby's startle response was initially paired with the sight of a rat. Over time, he reportedly began to show fear in response to objects that had some of the characteristics of the rat, such as other white furry objects like a rabbit or a fur coat. Thus, Little Albert—at least in theory—induced or generalized his fears to other stimuli.

The reader should think of inductive reasoning when considering Skinner's concept of stimulus induction. In inductive reasoning, we infer a general rule after observing a series of relationships among events. For example, if we notice that heavy rain is usually preceded by a certain cloud formation, we will learn to carry an umbrella the next time we see that type of

Figure 10.1   Skinner's Schedules of Reinforcement

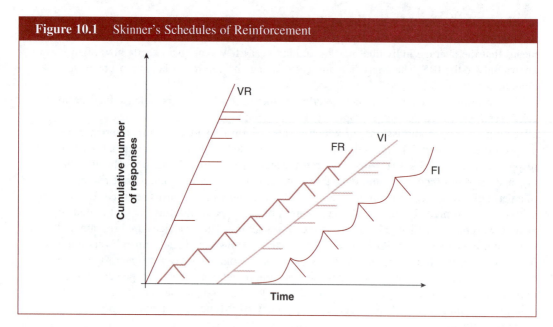

NOTE: VR = variable ratio; FR = fixed ratio; VI = variable interval; FI = fixed interval.

cloud. Similarly, in both response and stimulus induction, the organism makes generalizations about the connections between stimuli and responses. Like Watson, Skinner pointed out that no matter how strongly a stimulus and response connection was reinforced, repeated pairings without reinforcement would face **extinction**. Thus, if a student is strongly motivated to study though the positive reinforcement of high grades, this S-R connection will inevitably become extinct if his or her work fails to lead to high grades or if the work is not graded at all.

Skinner's additions to research in reinforcement techniques provided support for the belief that operants can be shaped and manipulated with great control and precision. In fact, he explained all human action, history, language, and culture in terms of reinforced operants. In his view, all creatures will emit numerous behaviors as they develop. Some of these will result in positive outcomes that will reinforce the behavior and thus increase the probability of that behavior or operant occurring again. If on its repetition, the behavior meets with additional positive outcomes, it will become part of that animal's behavioral repertoire. Over time, the animal's responses will be shaped by the demands of the environment. Shaping takes place when a behavior solves a survival or experiment problem closely but not completely. For example, a lion emits numerous behaviors, one of which includes a rapid charge. Eventually, this rapid charge will result in the downing of an antelope, and the lion would thereby be reinforced to charge at antelopes at a high rate of speed. If, in the process of charging at the antelope, however, the lion by chance makes a circular movement and thereby brings the prey down faster, his charging behavior will be shaped accordingly. Eventually, the lion will be shaped through successive approximations in which the behavior is gradually reinforced to an optimal level.

A similar concept is response shaping, in which a human or animal is reinforced to make a basic response to a stimulus and then, through progressively more specific reinforcement, to respond with a very precise behavior. In a notable experiment, Skinner was able to have two pigeons engage in a match of table tennis through this method (Skinner, 1953). Response shaping has been applied in psychotherapy; for example, a woman who was diagnosed with anorexia nervosa, an eating disorder, and had not been helped by eight previous hospitalizations was placed in a bare hospital room with no television or magazines and no visits permitted. The only reinforcer she was allowed was her knitting. The nurses were instructed to avoid coaxing the patient to eat and to keep their social interactions with her to a minimum. The patient's therapists then described their method of response shaping:

> The authors shaped [the patient's] eating behavior by talking with her when she picked up her fork, lifted food toward her mouth, chewed food, and so forth. They also shaped the amount of food eaten by allowing her the radio or television after meals at which she ate increasing amounts of the food on her plate. Later on, as she began to gain weight, other reinforcers were introduced; she was allowed to choose her own menu, invite another patient to dine with her, or dine with the other patients. Note that these reinforcers were directly related to, as well as contingent upon, eating behavior. Still later the reinforcers included walks, visits, and mail. (Bachrach, Erwin, & Mohr, 1965)

Misbehavior of Organisms: Breland and Breland

Keller and Marian Breland (later Marian Bailey) were graduate students of Skinner who assisted him during World War II to train pigeons to guide bombs for the U.S. Navy. Pinpoint bombing was difficult in the 1940s because of the technological limitations of the guidance systems then in use. Although the trained pigeons proved to be successful at their unusual task, the Navy abandoned the project in 1943 because the admirals knew that the atomic bomb was nearing completion and that there would not be any further need for pinpoint bombing in World War II.

Having become thoroughly familiar with the principles of operant conditioning through their work with Skinner, the Brelands went on to put these principles to practical use in the training of animals, starting a business that they called Animal Behavior Enterprises (ABE). The Brelands trained thousands of animals and dozens of species for fairs, circuses, and television commercials. Although they were commercially successful—General Mills was one of their corporate clients—what they discovered in the course of training the animals would threaten the very basis of behaviorist psychology.

Behaviorists believed they were discovering universal laws of behavior that are identical across species. Skinner (1956) iconoclastically stated, "Pigeon, rat, monkey,

(Continued)

(Continued)

which is which? It does not matter" (p. 230). Skinner maintained that there is an arbitrary relationship between the response and the reinforcer, thus assuring that the conditioning phenomena observed would not be specific to either the species or the situation being studied. The relationship between the stimuli, the operants, and the reinforcers could thus be shaped to suit the requirements of the individual doing the conditioning.

Breland and Breland found that this assumption is just plain wrong. There are instinctual, species-specific constraints on the effective pairing of reinforcers and responses, and whenever instincts can interfere, they do. Skinner had used pigeons, pecking, and food, which was effective because pecking is the pigeon's instinctual way of getting food. Thus, it was easy to condition a pigeon to peck for food. But if conditioning did not happen to match species-specific instinctual behavior, innate behavior patterns would gradually overcome and replace any conditioned new behaviors. The Brelands coined the term *instinctual drift* to describe this tendency. They titled the article describing their findings "The Misbehavior of Organisms" (Breland & Breland, 1961), a play on the title of Skinner's (1938) book *The Behavior of Organisms*.

They found that there are significant biological constraints on what organisms learn and which unconditioned stimuli (US) can be used with which conditioned stimuli (CS). Thus, the search for species-independent learning principles was doomed. In the Brelands' (1961) words, "The general principle seems to be that wherever an animal has strong instinctive behaviors in the area of the conditioned response, after continued running the organism will drift toward the instinctive behavior to the detriment of the conditioned behavior and even to the delay or preclusion of the reinforcement" (p. 684). Breland and Breland found that a raccoon conditioned to deposit coins in a box for reinforcement would increasingly pick up the coins and rub them together, even though this gesture delayed or prevented reinforcement. Rubbing the coins together to wash them was the raccoon's instinctive response with food.

Pigs conditioned to do the same would drop the coin, push it with their snout, pick it up, drop it, and push it with their snout over and over instead of depositing it for food. Instincts were far more powerful than any reinforcement, taking over for conditioned behaviors even if they eliminated reinforcement. Breland and Breland (1961) would encounter other problems: "hamsters that stopped working in a glass case after four or five reinforcements . . . cats that will not leave the area of the feeder, rabbits that will not go to the feeder, the great difficulty in many species of conditioning vocalization with food reinforcement, problems in conditioning a kick in a cow," and all of these "egregious failures came as a rather considerable shock to us, for there was nothing in our background in behaviorism to prepare us for such gross inabilities to predict and control the behavior of animals" (p. 683).

The Brelands commented in 1961, "It is our reluctant conclusion that the behavior of any species cannot be adequately understood, predicted or controlled without knowledge of its instinctive patterns, evolutionary history, and ecological niche. . . . as we have recently discovered, if one begins with evolution and instinct as the basic format for the science, a very illuminating viewpoint can be developed which leads naturally to a drastically revised . . . conceptual framework." And Skinner's pigeons pecking for reinforcement? Jenkins and Moore (1973) found that if food pellets were the reinforcement, pigeons pecked the key in an eating posture, and if water was the reinforcement, they used a drinking posture.

After her work with animal behavior, Marian went on to apply her understanding of behavioral modification to working with mentally retarded children. In 1965, she contributed a chapter to a book, *Teaching the Mentally Retarded* (Bensberg, 1965), that was intended to help train such children in self-care and other activities of daily living so that they could live in group homes rather than being placed in institutions.

Downfall of Radical Behaviorism: Language

Skinner was accustomed to explain the acquisition of language in humans by noting that a baby in its first year of life will make numerous vocalizations, most of which will have no resemblance to actual words. At some point, it will make a sound like "ma": this verbal operant, unlike the other verbal operants, will tend to be met by a parental positive reinforcement because it is similar to a desired word. Consequently, the baby will be reinforced by being picked up, cuddled, or smiled at. According to Skinner, this reinforcement of a chance vocalization begins the process of learning language. As the "ma" sound is emitted more frequently, it will by chance be emitted twice in succession, producing the sound "mama," which will be further reinforced. According to Skinner (1957), this process will continue until all words and grammar are learned through reinforcement. Skinner made no distinction between verbal utterances and any other physical behavior:

> We have no more reason to say that a man "uses the word *water*" in asking for a drink than to say that he "uses a reach" in taking the offered glass. In the arts, crafts, and sports, especially where instruction is verbal, acts are sometimes named. We say that a tennis player uses a drop stroke, or a swimmer a crawl. No one is likely to be misled when drop strokes or crawls are referred to as things, but words are a different matter. Misunderstanding has been common, and often disastrous. (Skinner, 1957, p. 7)

Some researchers who initially accepted Skinner's hypothesis of the way in which humans acquire language were troubled by the fact that all children in all cultures seem to learn language at approximately the same rate and age. If language acquisition were a random process of operants being shaped through successive approximation, it would not follow such a predictable pattern, they thought. In Noam Chomsky's (1959) review of Skinner's theory, he embraced these concerns by challenging Skinner's entire premise in his review of Skinner's (1957) book, *Verbal Behavior*. Chomsky produced a set of trenchant refutations of Skinner's premise that operant reinforcement explains language acquisition. Chomsky pointed out that much of the infant's babbling meets no reinforcement. Skinner explained this by asserting that automatic self-reinforcement takes place. Thus, babies automatically reinforce their own random utterances; by extension, novelists write what they have been reinforced by reading and so on. Chomsky rejected the circularity of Skinner's defense by pointing out that people do what they like to do, and calling this behavior a reinforcement does nothing to advance the understanding of behavior.

Chomsky also pointed out that all people have a finite exposure to any aspect of a language. They can hear only a finite number of words, phrases, and sentences—and not all of these are grammatical or even an adequate means for the expression of ideas. Yet, despite the virtually infinite number of possible grammatical combinations and permutations of words, most children develop a grammatical competency to both speak and interpret a language in the first 5 to 6 years of life. Chomsky points out that both children and adults can generate and understand phrases that they have never heard before. This linguistic creativity should not be possible if all behavior results from reinforcement. Instead, Chomsky proposed the existence of an innate neural structure that he called the language acquisition device (LAD), which is genetically ordained to recognize, interpret, and generate linguistic grammars. The LAD is capable of understanding the way in which events and objects are represented by noun and verb phrases and how these phrases represent what is doing the acting and what is being acted upon.

Chomsky did not deny that language is learned; instead, he argued that its learning is innately facilitated by a brain structure that rapidly decodes the structure of a natural language without any necessity of that structure's being taught or reinforced. Most grammatical errors that children make when learning their native language are due to the particular grammatical irregularities of their language, not the failure of caretakers to reinforce the proper rules of grammar. The grammatical structures of all human languages have a unique surface structure that overlies a deep or universal grammatical structure that is common to all languages. According to Chomsky, the LAD will immediately convey a feeling of propriety when a phrase conforms to the rules of grammar. For example, Chomsky (1957) pointed out that the phrase "colorless green ideas sleep furiously," is perceived as grammatically correct despite the fact that it makes no literal sense (p. 15). This is in direct contrast to a phrase like "furiously sleep ideas green colorless," which is immediately perceived by a native speaker of English as both ungrammatical and nonsensical.

Chomsky pointed out that if language were learned by the reinforcement of operants, it should be acquired gradually and at a fairly consistent rate. This is not the case. Language is learned rapidly, with the typical infant demonstrating a burst of language acquisition between the third and fifth year of life. Most 5-year-olds speak as well as adults in terms of grammar and syntax, although their vocabulary may not be as sophisticated as that of an adult. This process is referred to as the "vocabulary spurt" (Bates & Carnevale, 1993) and is at direct odds with processes that result from operant conditioning.

Perhaps most compelling was Chomsky's implication that the human brain with its billions of neurons, each with thousands of connections, is still finite, but the ability to generate language is infinite. That is, the innate system of grammar in all our brains is capable of generating an infinite number of grammatically consistent expressions. This capacity was demonstrated by Jackendoff (1994, p. 11), who pointed out that English has tens of thousands of nouns and that each one can be used to create sentences following a simple rule: noun X is not noun Y, which could produce sentences of the form:

A table is not a dog

A table is not a doggerel

A table is not a dogcatcher. . . .

A dog is not a table, and so on.

Although these sentences are not particularly eloquent, they conform to the rules of English grammar. And if the generation of sentences is continued, Jackendoff's (1994) simple rule—X is not Y—will yield billions of sentences. Compounding the vast number of simple sentences that can be produced by the rule is the profound number of sentences that can be generated by combining the simple sentences formed by Jackendoff's simple rule.

Since a table is not a dog, a dog is not a table.

Since a table is not a doggerel, a doggerel is not a table.

Since a table is not a dogcatcher, a dogcatcher is not a table.

According to Jackendoff (1994), this process of sentence generation will ultimately produce more than 100 sentences per neuron in the brain, far more than could be stored by any system of learning or memorization. Jackendoff used just one simple rule of generating sentences, when even the least gifted linguist is capable of generating more complex systems that could be used to produce a vast number of sentences. Jackendoff, like Chomsky, affirmed that the brain does not learn language through reinforcement of unique expressions but instead stores words, their meanings, and a grammatical system that guides their organization to create meaningful expressions.

Chomsky (quoted in Sternberg, 2003) proposed that to understand the acquisition of language, we must understand the connections among phrases within sentences and the syntactical relationships between sentences. This understanding requires the study of transformational-generative grammar, which first examines the deep structure of each sentence and then examines the means by which this deep structure is mapped via specific rules to create the surface structure of spoken language. For example, the sentence "Bill hates to study" essentially means the same thing as "studying is hated by Bill." Thus, both sentences are derived from similar deep syntactic systems. Given the innate human ability to transform concepts into many forms of verbal expression, people are able to generate far more utterances than those that could be learned by reinforcing operants, in which each phrase would have to have been reinforced.

Children can typically produce numerous synonymous sentences to express an idea, such as "My head hurts," "I have a headache," and "There is a pain in my head." Even allowing for stimulus generalization, such that similar phrases would evoke a like response, operant conditioning still fails to account for language acquisition, according to Chomsky (1957). Conversely, both children and adults can understand an infinite number of sentences despite not having been previously exposed to them. This type of understanding would not be possible if language were acquired by reinforcement.

Skinner was unable to respond to Chomsky's criticisms of the behaviorist model of language acquisition and to subsequent criticisms by Chomsky. His failure to challenge the opening of the "black box" by Chomsky occurred at the early stages of cognitive psychology, which sought, once again, to make the human mind the proper subject of psychology. Chomsky's rebuke of Skinner had implications more extensive than that of linguistics. He showed that the processes of the brain can be illuminated through modeling and inference. His work meshed with the nascent field of cognitive psychology, which came armed with the ability to use the computer to model theories of mental operations. Learning, motivation, thought, and even emotions could be represented using computer programs. With this new tool to study the mind—as opposed to behavior—Skinner and radical behaviorism entered on an inexorable decline.

Skinner's View of Personality

Personality, as Skinner saw it, is simply a repository of learned responses within a specific individual. Throughout life, we will emit random operants, according to his view: some will be weakly reinforced, some strongly, some only in certain circumstances, and some not at all. Thus, people in identical or similar situations (through stimulus generalization) would tend to behave similarly. This similarity, in short, is the human personality, according to Skinner. He advocated greater theoretical parsimony that most inferred constructs required. Personality required inferring the existence of traits, temperaments, cognitive styles, and so on. Such unobservable entities make the human more inscrutable than understandable, from Skinner's perspective.

Skinner rejected even a concept as fundamental as the self. In effect, he stated that there is no essential self within a person. He referred to the self as a "hypothetical cause of action" (Skinner, 1953, p. 283), explaining that all personality characterizations are the result of a failure to observe the explanatory external variables that elicit the behavior summarized as a personality. Without the knowledge of these variables, people tend to assume that the behavior originates within themselves. Skinner (1953, p. 283) said that explaining behavior in terms of such vague constructs as the self or the personality was as unscientific as the ancient Greeks positing that the wind is the blowing of Aeolus and that Zeus causes the rain to fall. In sum, he stated that all human behavior, despite any inferred consistency within an individual, is the result of a failure to determine the behavioral antecedents. This failure, according to Skinner, often leads to unnecessarily complex explanations of the person. Personalities, multiple personalities, and Freudian psychic structures are all unnecessarily elaborate models invented to account for behavior that is observed without first understanding the operants that were reinforced at an earlier point in time to create the behavior (Skinner, 1953, p. 284).

Skinner, like more recent situationalist psychologists, rejected the idea that personality is a constant representation of the persona. Instead, he suggests that it would change across scenarios that offer different types and degrees of reinforcers. In making this point, he stated:

> The libertine is very different from the ascetic who achieves his reinforcement from the ethical group, but the two may exist side by side in the same organism. . . . Under the proper circumstances the timid soul may give way to the aggressive man. The hero may struggle to conceal the coward who inhabits the same skin. (Skinner 1953, pp. 285–286)

Accordingly, Skinner's view of interpersonal differences comes quite close to Watson's paradigm that the thief and scholar differ only by the type and degree of reinforcement they received. Skinner, thus, rejected the utility of dividing the personality into components, at least until psychology fully understands what these components are. Traits, intellectual measures, temperament scales, and similar measures of individual differences add little to the understanding of human being, according to Skinner. A model of the human person should not require placement in a hierarchy but allow for understanding of the individual without comparisons to others. From the following excerpt, we can infer that Skinner's radical behaviorism was more a rejection of unsupported conjecture than an actual belief that the human psyche is no more than a physiological switching device.

> Abilities and traits have been made respectable through correlational analyses, which give them the status of "individual differences." Although most psychologists think

of an ability as something which has meaning in the behavior of a single individual, current techniques of measurement find it necessary to make use of the position of the individual in a population. . . . A proper theory at this stage would characterize the behavior of an individual in such a way that measurement would be feasible if he were the only individual on earth. This would be done by determining the values of certain constants in equations describing his behavior—clearly a third-stage enterprise. The individual proves to be no more undividable than the atom was uncuttable. Many sorts of metaphorical schemes have been devised to represent this fact. A single personality may be regarded as moving about from one level of consciousness to another, or personalities may be frankly multiple. A proper theory must be able to represent the multiplicity of response systems. It must do something more: it must abolish the conception of the individual as a doer, as an originator of action. This is a difficult task. The simple fact is that psychologists have never made a thoroughgoing renunciation of the inner man. He is surreptitiously appealed to from time to time in all our thinking, especially when we are faced with a bit of behavior which is difficult to explain otherwise. Eventually we may expect the main features of a behavioral theory to have physiological significance. As the science of physiology advances, it will presumably be possible to show what is happening in various structures within the organism during particular behavioral events, and the theoretical systems of the two sciences may also be seen to correspond. An example of this rapprochement is the way in which facts and principles of genetics arrived at from the study of the characteristics of parents and offspring are seen to correspond to facts and principles of cell structure. The science of genetics has already reached the stage at which it is profitable to investigate both subject matters at the same time. (Skinner, 1959, p. 236)

A comparison can be made between the positions of Skinner and the psychiatrist Thomas Szasz, who was discussed in Chapter 7. Szasz rejects the profession of psychiatry as a branch of medicine that does no more than treat metaphorical illnesses. He pointed out that the term *mind* is a metaphor for all functions of the brain and body that yield behavior. Consequently, the treatment of mental illness is the treatment of metaphorical illnesses. Szasz has never argued that brain diseases or injuries do not exist; rather, he holds that the classifications made by psychiatry are not predicated on any direct correspondence with brain dysfunctions.

Toward the end of his life, Skinner softened his position regarding the importance of understanding the processes of the brain. In effect, he acknowledged the importance in developing an understanding of the mechanics that take place within the "black box" of the human psyche. Perhaps his travails after suffering a stroke forced him to confront the fact that operant conditioning can work only within the constraints of a living brain, and those brains differ among species and among individual human beings. His behaviorism had focused on universal laws of learning that disregard both levels of differences.

In recent years, the field of psychology has been gradually moving away from behaviorism as its central tenet. Operant conditioning is now just one tool for manipulating and understanding behavior. Skinner played a major role in education, behavioral pharmacology, and behavior modification but, in retrospect, contributed little to the understanding of personality.

Skinner Shapes Society

Skinner was interested in putting his ideas into practical use, as were behaviorists in general, and he saw behaviorism's "technology of behavior" as having the potential to bring about social utopias. Therefore, like Watson, he wrote for a wide audience. But first, "useless" concepts like "freedom" and "dignity" must be abandoned, he thought. Skinner's long essay, *Beyond Freedom and Dignity,* summarized not only his thinking but also what behaviorism meant for the general population.

Summary of Beyond Freedom and Dignity

1. A technology of behavior comparable in precision to physics is needed to solve social problems. An integrating consciousness is an illusion, and postulating internal states is pointless, as what is deemed "personality" is simply the sum total of behavior.

2. Behavior is totally explained by the organism's reinforcement history. A better world means improving human behavior. It is the environment that must be changed, not the individuals in it.

3. Greek physics personified natural phenomena. Aristotle argued that a falling body accelerated because it grew more jubilant as it found itself closer to its proper place. Attributing human behavior to internal states is just as unscientific and unproductive.

4. Evolution, shaped by contingencies of survival, would create, for example, the tendency to act aggressively, not "feelings" of aggression, so there is no need to look for internal states.

5. Comparing a human being to a dog (a frequent criticism of Skinner and behaviorists in general) is a huge step forward, for a dog is within the range of scientific analysis while a "soul" is not.

6. While behaviorism sounds "controlling" and "anti-freedom", in truth we cannot "free mankind from control." Instead, we must analyze and change the environmental contingencies that control us. "Freedom" refers only to knowing how to act in an environment to receive positive reinforcement.

7. Humanistic theories preach the elimination of aversive control but ignore the effects and dangers of positive reinforcement. Freedom is just another word for abundant positive reinforcement.

8. The amount of credit we give an individual for performing the "right" behavior is inversely proportional to how apparent the cause of the behavior is. In other words, someone who does the "right" thing because the police are watching receives no credit, whereas someone who does the right thing because he was reinforced for it through praise given years before receives a great deal of credit.

9. Punishment may reduce the incidence of wrong behavior but is not effective for teaching proper behavior. The individual simply learns to avoid the punishment. (This principle runs contrary to the incorrect popular assumption that behaviorism is "all about punishment.")

10. Conflicts between feelings are really conflicts between conditions of reinforcement. What we mean by a "culture" is the rules of reinforcement in a particular environment.

11. As all control is exerted by the environment, we must design better environments (rather then "better people").

12. And the main point: Humans are controlled by their environment, but it is an environment of their own making. (Skinner became aware of this paradox at a later point in his career. While he had once been optimistic that his program for a better world would be carried out, he became pessimistic near the end of his life, recognizing that the problem of the circular relationship between humans and the environment would prevent the construction of a behaviorist utopia.)

🔲 JOHN DOLLARD AND NEAL E. MILLER

In the early 20th century, psychology was largely a research science with few clinical applications. Theories related to psychopathology and its treatment fell largely within the domain of medicine, with psychoanalysis as the paradigmatic form of therapy. As behaviorism's influence grew within experimental psychology, so, too, did psychoanalysis dominate the field of medicine. By the late 1940s, there were two independent paradigms dominating the science of mind, with practitioners in each field largely ignoring the other. This situation understandably presented a problem for the expanding field of psychology as it moved into the clinical realm.

The practitioners of clinical psychiatry subscribed to the labyrinthine complexities of the Freudian model of the psyche; thus, something as simple as a stimulus-response model could not be seriously considered. With the growth of psychology as a discipline, psychologists became increasingly interested in the clinical applications of their work. They began to look for ways to bridge the divide between S-R experimental psychology and psychoanalysis. Neil E. Miller (1909–2002) and John Dollard (1900–1980) did so with the development of a comprehensive theory of personality combined with clinical applications. Their goal was to "combine the vitality of psychoanalysis, the rigor of the natural-science laboratory, and facts of culture" (Dollard & Miller, 1950, p. 3).

Something like their attempt was inevitable. Whenever there are two competing philosophies that become important, someone will try to reconcile and combine the two. The reader may think of theistic evolution, an attempt to combine the Darwinian concept of evolution with the biblical doctrine of creation, and liberation theology, which attempted to combine Roman Catholic social teaching and Marxist political theory. Dollard and Miller were in good company when they sought to combine and reconcile the seemingly opposed approaches of Freudianism and behaviorism. Although Dollard and Miller completed their undergraduate and graduate work at different institutions, both were originally from Wisconsin, and both held teaching appointments at Yale University's Institute of Human Relations, founded in 1933 by James Rowland Angell, a functionalist psychologist who was president of Yale at that time. Miller had been a research fellow at the Institute of Psychoanalysis in Vienna from 1935 to 1936, and Dollard had studied psychoanalysis in Berlin.

Learning Theory

Dollard and Miller accomplished their goal by demonstrating that most psychoanalytic constructs can be expressed and explained in behavioral terms. In doing so, they adopted a softer behavioral perspective that allowed for internal states; they maintained that individuals can receive indirect reinforcement by observing others. In effect, Dollard and Miller developed a social learning theory that anticipated the more influential one proposed by Albert Bandura a decade later. Like learning theorists before them, Dollard and Miller posited that stimulus-response connections underlie the formation of habits, which provide the basic structure of human personality. Their model added some complexity to the more straight-forward model of Watson in that they added internalized drives and **cues** to the behaviorist model. They described drives and cues as follows:

> What, then, is learning theory? In its simplest form, it is the study of the circumstances under which a response and a cue stimulus become connected. After learning has been completed, response and cue are bound together in such a way that the appearance of the cue evokes the response. . . . Learning takes place according to definite psycholog-ical principles. Practice does not always make perfect. The connection between a cue and a response can be strengthened only under certain conditions. The learner must be driven to make the response and rewarded for having responded in the presence of the cue. This may be expressed in a homely way by saying that in order to learn one must want something, notice something, do something, and get something. Stated more exactly, these factors are drive, cue, response, and reward. These elements in the learn-ing process have been carefully explored, and further complexities have been discov-ered. Learning theory has become a firmly knit body of principles which are useful in describing human behavior. (Miller & Dollard, 1941, pp. 1–2)

Drive Reduction. Specifically, Dollard and Miller proposed that learning has several parts or steps: It requires an individual who has a desire, notices the object of that desire, and takes action to get it. In more general terms, learning takes place after an organism has encountered a drive, a stimulus, a cue, a response, and a reward. Like Watson before them, Dollard and Miller believed that humans share many behavioral inclinations and drives with animals and that the study of animal learning can illuminate the nature of human behaviors. Such drives as hunger and thirst are innate in humans as well as animals and provide the initial motivat-ing force behind all learning and behaviors. And like Freud, Dollard and Miller posited that the basic motivational force is drive reduction; that is, a person will tend to behave in ways that relieve tensions created by strong drives.

Primary and Secondary Drives. Dollard and Miller distinguished between **primary** and **secondary drives.** Primary drives are innate and are related to physiological processes associated with survival, such as hunger, thirst, and needing to sleep. In contrast to these innate primary drives, secondary drives result from learning indirect or more complex ways to satisfy the primary drives. "These learned (secondary) drives are acquired on the basis of the primary drives, represent elaborations of them, and serve as a façade behind which the underlying innate drives are hidden" (1950, pp. 31–32). An example of the distinction between the two types of drives would be a person's picking up groceries on the way home from work (secondary drive) to have something to cook for dinner (secondary drive) to satisfy hunger (primary drive). This primary/secondary drive concept is directly related to psychoanalytic theory, in which personality is driven by hidden forces.

Another example of Dollard and Miller's drive concept is that the secondary drive to be creative may arise from the primary drive of hunger because creativity (whether intellectual or physical) generates the income that allows its earner to purchase food. Other examples of secondary drives are those associated with social interactions. These include anger, shame, and desire for social approval. Over time, the primary drives tend to be replaced by secondary ones, so that the desire for praise from our workplace supervisor may replace the drive for higher income (which work-related commendations generally lead to), which in turn has replaced the drive for food.

Hierarchies of Response. Concordant with Dollard and Miller's concept of primary and secondary drives is the proposition that humans are born with an innate **hierarchy of response**. A hierarchy of response refers to a group of possible responses to a situation, arranged in the order in which they are likely to be used as a result of prior learning about their effectiveness. For example, a newborn confronting the aversive stimulus of an uncomfortable diaper will first try to push it away. When this attempt at drive reduction fails, he may respond by crying. Because this response is usually more likely to result in getting the diaper changed (by a nearby caregiver), it will be the response that is reinforced.

Dollard and Miller's model of personality, like Skinner's, was based on a stimulus-response theory of learning. They differed from Skinner in that they adapted a model of learning that was conceptual similar to the stimulus-organism-response or S-O-R model of Edward C. Tolman, a behavioral psychologist who taught at the University of California, Berkeley. Specifically, Dollard and Miller believed that an organism could react to the same stimulus with different responses, depending on the way in which that organism processes the response. In their model, the more direct S-R responses were referred to as instrumental responses. They referred to the S-O-R pattern as a cue-producing response, in that a stimulus leads to an internal response, which in turn leads to an internal cue and then an external response. A commonplace example of a cue-producing response is the way we might talk to ourselves when following written directions to a friend's house. As we watch for street signs, we may say, "Let's see . . . there's the sign for Willow Valley Road. . . . I'm supposed to turn left here" and then put on our turn signal and move the steering wheel to turn the car to the left.

Dollard and Miller also proposed that prior responses to stimuli are remembered and can mediate future responses. This mediation can be accomplished in two ways. The first way is self-talk, in which the individual internally recounts the consequences of prior responses to a stimulus and then decides on the most desirable outcome. Self-talk is a form of self-regulation and is often used to remind ourselves to do something, as when we think on our way to class, "I've got to drop the letter inside my backpack in a mailbox on the way home." The second way is visual imagery, in which images of various responses are used to make a similar determination of a response. Visual imagery is sometimes used to help change habits: If we are trying to cut down on food intake, we may visualize the way we looked in a swimsuit before gaining the weight we are trying to lose now. Clearly, Dollard and Miller's model is distinctly different from Skinner's more mechanical operant conditioning model, in that Dollard and Miller allow for some types of internal mediating states.

Cues. A cue (Miller & Dollard, 1941) is a stimulus that determines the specific manifestation of a response. We are subjected to more environmental stimuli than we can respond to, so for a response to be elicited, a stimulus must have distinct defining characteristics—which identify it as a cue. For example, Pavlov's paradigmatic dogs salivated as the result of a number of cues: the sight of food, the smell of the food, or hunger itself. When the dog had been conditioned to salivate at the sounding of a bell, then the sound acquired a cue function.

Cues can take any form and can vary in both intensity and duration. A cue can be a soft voice or a flashing red light, and each of these can generally be expected to lead to a very different type of response. According to Dollard and Miller, a cue cannot be linked to a response; the response must first actually occur. The ability to distinguish cues originates in childhood:

> In the first year of its life the human infant has the cues from its mother associated with the primary reward of feeding on more than 2,000 occasions. Meanwhile the mother and other people are ministering to many other needs. In general, there is a correlation between the absence of people and the prolongation of suffering from hunger, cold, pain, and other drives; the appearance of a person is associated with a reinforcing reduction in the drive. Therefore the proper conditions are present for the infant to learn to attach a strong reinforcement value to a variety of cues from the nearness of the mother and other adults. (Dollard & Miller, 1950, pp. 91–92)

Learning and the Rearrangement of Hierarchies. Clearly, for the connection between cue and response to be created, there must be reinforcement. Dollard and Miller viewed reinforcers in a manner concordant with Freudian theory: Reinforcers are those entities that reduce drives. In Freud's model of personality, drive reduction is an essential motivating force of life. Consequently, any response that reduces a drive serves to reinforce that response and thereby increases the probability that the response will be repeated. For example, if we find that a cup of strong coffee reduces the drive to sleep when we are tired, we will be more likely to drink coffee the next time we need to stay awake and alert. Dollard and Miller postulated that within each organism, each cue tends to elicit numerous simultaneous responses. The one that is most likely to occur is called the dominant response, which is usually the one that has previously been most successful in reducing a drive. The organism can, however, rearrange these hierarchies through learning, resulting in new dominant responses. Learning, therefore, is most likely to take place when a response fails to produce a satisfactory reduction in drive.

In Dollard and Miller's formulation, fear is an important drive that all organisms seek to reduce, and they are strongly reinforced for doing so. This type of learning is particularly resistant to extinction because fear tends to force the organism to avoid stimuli that arouse fear. Because exposure is required to extinguish the response, extinction usually cannot take place. As the individual matures, the hierarchy of responses will change to become concordant to the demands of each particular stage of life. For example, as we mature, we are less likely to respond with laughter at another's embarrassment in the way that a child might. Dollard and Miller believed, however, that we can begin to exhibit childish responses in times of distress. This was their equivalent of the psychoanalytic process of regression.

Frustration-Aggression Hypothesis

Dollard and Miller proposed that all human aggression is a result of frustrated efforts at drive reduction. For example, if someone has learned to avoid rebuke by walking away, but this response is blocked because the individual is in a controlled environment—such as a student in a classroom or a person on the witness stand in a courtroom—the learned response will be frustrated. The concept of catharsis (release of tension)—rooted in Freudian psychoanalytic theory and extended by Dollard, Miller, and their coworkers (Miller, Mowrer, Doob, Dollard, & Sears, 1958)—is important in frustration-aggression theory. They proposed that aggression results primarily from frustrated drive satisfaction. Dollard and Miller concluded on the basis of a series of experiments that many of the psychodynamic defense mechanisms can be explained in terms of frustrated drives.

Dollard and Miller performed a series of experiments designed to test the hypothesis that frustrated drives can explain psychoanalytic defense mechanisms like projection. In the following study, Dollard and his coworkers concluded that the use of defense mechanisms does in fact take place.

By chance it was known that, as a part of a general testing program, boys at a camp were going to be forced to sacrifice a portion of their leisure activity in order to take long, dull examinations composed of questions which, on the whole, were too difficult for them to answer. At the outset the boys were relatively unaware of what was in store for them. Later, it became obvious that the tests were running overtime and were preventing them from making the strongly instigated response of attending Bank Night at the local theater; thus they were compelled to miss what they considered to be the most interesting event of the week. In order to exploit this situation, so loaded with frustrations, all of the boys were given brief attitude tests before and after the main examination. Half of them rated Mexicans before and Japanese after the main examination. As would be expected, the attitude toward either set of foreigners was more unfavorable after the frustration of taking the examinations and missing Bank Night than before. (Dollard et al., 1939, pp. 43–44)

Conflicts and Gradients

Dollard and Miller proposed that people are reinforced to seek out or approach previously reinforced stimuli. Conversely, they are reinforced to avoid feared or aversive stimuli. The internal conflicts that organisms experience when having to simultaneously encounter reinforced and feared stimuli was explained in terms of four gradients:

1. *Gradient of approach*: the tendency to approach a goal is stronger the nearer the subject is to attaining the goal.

2. *Gradient of avoidance*: the tendency to avoid a feared stimulus is stronger the closer the subject is to the feared stimulus.

3. The gradient of avoidance is steeper than the gradient of approach.

4. Increasing a drive raises the height of the entire gradient.

In essence, Dollard and Miller stated that as we get closer to obtaining a desired goal, the desire to obtain it is progressively strengthened. An example would be a marathon runner's increased desire to complete the race the closer he or she gets to the finish line. In contrast, as we are pushed toward an object or situation we fear or find otherwise aversive, the feelings of dread progressively increase. Most of us, having sat in a dentist's waiting room, are familiar with this sense of increased dread. Dollard and Miller proposed that fear and aversion are more powerful forces than rewards in directing behavior; thus, the gradient of avoidance is stronger (or steeper) than that of approach. They allowed, however, for changes in the strength of a gradient if there is a corresponding change in the strength of a drive. Thus, if we are getting progressively hungrier, our gradient of approach to food will increase.

Because Dollard and Miller were in effect synthesizing psychoanalytic theory with behaviorism, they used their concept of gradients as a basis for explaining neurotic behavior. Psychoanalytic theory saw the reduction of drives as a prime mover in human behavior. Freudian theory also posited the existence of internal conflicts that serve as barriers to drive reduction. These internal conflicts took place among the structures of mind that Freud termed the id, the ego, and the superego. Dollard and Miller's parallel system predicated the existence of conflicts among differentially reinforced behaviors. Dollard and Miller allowed that we can effectively choose our responses to stimuli, and this power of choice can lead to internal conflicts regarding the best response to effect drive reduction. On the other hand, Dollard and Miller also thought that our gradients of approach or avoidance are unconscious; thus, the conflicts that can arise when we are faced with incompatible choices can lead to an experience of distress that baffles the individual.

Types of Conflicts. Because the conflicts that arise from these different gradients tend to be unconscious, a person facing incompatible gradients will tend to feel fear without fully understanding why. According to Dollard and Miller, the reinforcement of cues is not a conscious process. Consequently, we will be either drawn to or repelled by objects or situations without necessarily understanding the reason for our attraction or aversion. The three basic conflicts that people face are the **approach-avoidance conflict**, the **avoidance-avoidance conflict**, and the **approach-approach conflict**. An example of an approach-avoidance conflict is as follows: Suppose a person has been reinforced to enjoy fine dining but fear social encounters;

he or she would tend to experience a great deal of frustration if invited to a free meal of haute cuisine in a crowded restaurant. According to Dollard and Miller, the desire to reduce the drive for food would be frustrated by the barrier presented by the feared crowd. In this approach-avoidance conflict, the individual will initially be increasingly drawn to the food by the gradient of approach. Frustration would begin to intensify even more rapidly, however, by the steeper gradient of avoidance. So the person's fear of entering the restaurant would likely overpower the desire for a fine meal.

To understand the avoidance-avoidance conflict, suppose the same socially phobic individual were forced through a work obligation to join a client for a grease-laden meal in a fast food restaurant—an avoidance-avoidance conflict. The predicted response would be prolonged vacillation and anxious distress, even to the point of risking losing a sale and possibly losing his job as well.

The third type of conflict in Dollard and Miller's system is the approach-approach conflict. Suppose this same fearful person is offered a fine meal to enjoy by himself in his hotel room. He can choose a meal prepared by one of two renowned chefs. In this situation, he would likely face an approach-approach conflict. He can choose only one chef's style of cooking but wants very much to try both, so he would also suffer distress. In general, the level of anxiety in the approach-approach conflict is the least distressing and most easily resolved of the three types, as the worst possible outcome is simply failing to pick the better of the two choices.

Unconscious Conflicts. Dollard and Miller hypothesized that if these anxiety-producing conflicts take place frequently during childhood, they can result in long-term unconscious conflicts. They believed that the ability to reflect verbally on an internalized conflict is necessary for its resolution. As childhood conflicts may occur before the child acquires the ability to assign verbal labels to events, they consequently become inaccessible. As Dollard and Miller (1950) described the process, "Early conflicts [are] unlabeled, [and] therefore unconscious. . . . What was not verbalized at the time cannot well be reported later" (p. 136). Consequently, they recommended that parents set minimal restrictions on their children to avoid provoking conflicts prior to the development of verbal abilities.

Similarly, they believed that parental maltreatment in the form of excessive punishment is a common source of emotional disturbance later in life. Children who are punished for emotional expression or assertiveness will learn to fear their own anger, which may lead to blocking the ability to express anger: "Robbing a person of his anger completely may be a dangerous thing, since some capacity for anger seems to be needed in the personality" (Dollard & Miller, 1950, p. 149). The loss of the ability to express anger will lead to an anger-anxiety conflict (Dollard et al., 1939, p. 148) that will inhibit this person from being assertive and self-confident later in life. Instead, she will experience conditioned anxiety each time she feels outrage at some act of oppression. This conflict may lead to neurotic behavior in the form of a clinical depression, **passive aggression,** or other disturbed expressions of anger.

This type of internalized conflict in their model is difficult to resolve, but not nearly as difficult as the conflicts that arise from sex. Dollard and Miller did not believe that sex is the most fundamental drive because it is not necessary for the survival of the individual, as are food, drink, and sleep. They did assert, however, that internalized conflicts related to sex tend to be very deep-seated. In addition, they believed like Freud that conflicts related to sex can result in great emotional distress for those so conflicted. It is precisely because sex is not absolutely necessary for life that it is more easily inhibited by fear than the more primary drives. One source of sexual fears is an unresolved Oedipal conflict, which Dollard and Miller adopted from Freudian theory.

Unlike Freud, however, Dollard and Miller interpreted the Oedipal conflict as a learned response to a situation in which a boy's father is openly competitive with him, or his mother seeks an excessively close relationship with him as a result of an inadequate sexual relationship with his father. According to Dollard and Miller, the son will learn to view his genitals and sexual feelings as a source of fear because he will tend to dread his father's retribution. This learning theory equivalent of castration anxiety would be generalized to all heterosexual relationships and lead to sexual anxiety or impotence later in life.

Dollard and Miller also theorized that sexual anxiety will occur when a child is not treated in a gender-appropriate fashion or is rebuked for masturbation. People who have been reinforced to fear aspects of their sexuality will be drawn to sexual encounters from a distance. As they move closer to consummating their sex drive, however, the gradient of avoidance will begin to prevail, which will inhibit them from completing the act. They may attempt to escape the sexual situation or have difficulty in performing. Such people will be tormented and conflicted, as their sex drive and fears are unconsciously at war with each other.

Repression. According to Dollard and Miller (1950), unconscious conflicts can lead to the equivalent of repression, which they defined as the "automatic tendency to stop thinking and avoid remembering" (p. 220). This tendency arises through an unconscious process of learning to avoid the cue-producing responses that generate anxious conflicts. This avoidance may take the form of overt inhibition of an instrumental response such that no verbal labels are required. An example would be the inhibition of a sexual drive without any awareness of ever having it. If a thought is required to resolve a conflict but the person lacks the cue-producing responses (words or labels), this lack will tend to result in repression of the event.

Dollard and Miller proposed three types of repression. The first takes place when we unconsciously inhibit the behavioral response that generates a verbal label for a drive. In this case, we may respond to an affront with rage but will inhibit our own response to label the rage, so we would report feeling "strange" without knowing the reason for the feeling. The second type of repression occurs when we inhibit the cue-producing responses that would generate a drive. In this second case, although expected to respond with anger, we would inhibit thoughts about the offensive action and thereby block the drive from arising in the first place. Like Freud, Dollard and Miller believed that repression exacts a high cost in mental energy. The third type of repression takes place when we respond to a stressor by producing cue-mediating responses to yield a different emotion from what would be expected. For example, if we are provoked by our boss to the point of rage, we could produce a cue-mediated response labeling the boss's actions as paternal. We might then feel dependent or even grateful rather than angry. It is evident that virtually all of the psychoanalytic defense mechanisms can be presented in the terms of Dollard and Miller's system.

The Stupidity-Misery Syndrome and Neurosis

Dollard and Miller framed neurosis in their adaptation of psychoanalysis as the loss of the origin of a learned fear. If we are inhibited by a gradient of avoidance to reduce a drive but have no understanding as to why we feel anxious, we will fall into a cycle of irrational behavior leading to distress. Our distress, in turn, leads to more irrational behavior and even further distress. Dollard and Miller (1950) referred to this cycle as the **stupidity-misery syndrome** (p. 223). Neurotic people will appear stupid to others because they will act in a self-defeating way, engaging in behaviors that only make their situation worse. People with a learned neurosis are fighting powerful emotions arising from unlabeled and unconscious conflicts. In essence, they are driven to act constructively but effectively block themselves from doing so.

People caught up in the stupidity-misery syndrome will also be prone to self-defeating stimulus generalizations. For example, a woman who was abused by her father may respond to all men by keeping an anxious distance from them, acting as though each was her father. Because she has long ago blocked the connection between her fear of men and her childhood experiences with her father, she faces a painful barrier to a healthy relationship. Dollard and Miller (1950) posited that neurotics learn to be so in childhood: "Our answer is that the neurotic conflicts are taught by parents and learned by children. . . . Out of confused instructions to parents, combined with the character faults of parents themselves, arise the situations in which children are put in severe conflict" (p. 127).

From the perspective of an outside observer, neurotic people repeatedly stop short of achieving the goal that would resolve their distress. For example, the person who was conditioned to fear his own anger and becomes excessively passive may desperately desire a new job. His fear of asking for a promotion or seeking a new position, however, will lead him to abort his efforts and return to the job he has been miserably complaining about. His efforts to confront the situation lead to anxiety and the physical symptoms (nausea, insomnia, shortness of breath, and others) typical of anxious states. His misery will worsen and return him to his passive, change-resistant behavior, which, in turn, leads to additional misery for not having made the change.

The stupidity-misery cycle may be exacerbated by repression of thoughts related to the situation. In the case of the person who might like to ask his boss for a raise, he will tend to feel anxious at the prospect of making such a request, so he will be inclined to block all thoughts about doing so. He thereby undercuts his own ability to find a solution to the problem. In addition, his behavior will seem stupid to an outside observer, who sees an otherwise capable person unable to imagine an apparently simple solution to his conflict.

Personality Theory

According to Dollard and Miller, personality is in essence an individual's unique collection of habits. An individual's repertoire of habits, however, is constantly changing as a result of recent reinforcements or the lack thereof. Recent experiences and reinforcers produce continual adjustments in a personality, making it both flexible and adaptive. Consequently, personality in their framework is far less fixed than in the nonbehavioral perspectives. Moreover, Dollard and Miller attribute individual differences in personality entirely to differences in life experience. Different people will face different stimuli and yield different cues and responses based on the reinforcers they receive. This concept of personality has led some to criticize Dollard and Miller on the grounds that they, like other behaviorists, ignore or reject the role of cognition in personality formation.

Dollard and Miller understood early on that there are many similarities between human and animal behavior, but they saw that for the most part, animal behavior tends to be less complex than human. Thus, it is often easier to identify basic principles of behavior by studying animals. Another factor that contributes to the ongoing use of animal subjects in behavioral studies is the fact that psychologists can observe most animals across their entire lifespan (with a few exceptions like cockatoos, tortoises, and certain whale species), whereas tracking such changes in humans would take many decades of research and would be quite expensive. Moreover, psychologists can exercise a much higher degree of control over animal subjects than human participants. Researchers can control almost every aspect of an animal's environment and even their genetic background, whereas this degree of control would be impossible with human subjects because of ethical considerations.

🔲 CHAPTER SUMMARY

The dominance of radical behaviorists in psychology departments has clearly declined over the past two decades to the point of virtual extinction in the early 2000s. This shift in perspective is in a large part a result of the advance of cognitive psychology and cognitive neuroscience. Both fields have demonstrated that humans can peer into the "black box" of the mind both directly and inferentially. Cognitive psychologists have been able to make inferences about the speed of thought, the nature of different types of thinking, and the ways in which emotions can both impede and guide mental processes. The improved understanding of the brain that has been obtained through various imaging techniques like functional magnetic resonance imaging (fMRI) and positron emission tomography (PET) have demonstrated that the human brain processes information in far more complex ways than even Clark Hull imagined. For example, simple S-R learning has been localized to take place at least partially in the basal ganglia, while emotional learning, especially that of fear, is strongly associated with the amygdala and its connections to both the **thalamus** and the frontal lobes. In short, learning takes place in the brain in many different ways; S-R psychology presents a summary of some of these but is grossly incomplete.

The invention of the computer played a twofold role in the fading of behaviorism. While many people regard computers as anti-humanistic, cold mechanical devices, they have actually served as humanizing influences within psychology because they legitimized the discussion of information processing and complex recognition programming. If these processes could be installed within computers, then there is nothing about them that requires a metaphysical explanation. How can a process be mentalistic if a machine manufactured from metal and silicon can do it? And if a computer is able to make decisions, how can researchers argue, as the behaviorists did, that a human being cannot? If a computer is a far more sophisticated information processor than a mere conditioning machine, how can someone maintain that a human being is simply a conditioning machine?

In the early 1960s, the word *mind* was taboo in academic psychology; four decades later, psychology is largely cognitive in orientation. Second, and equally important, the computer greatly expanded the feasibility of certain types of psychological experiments. Technology plays a role equal to that of theoretical and social realities in determining what research can be done.

Behaviorism does not offer a complete explanation of personality, nor even one for learning. As we shall see in Chapter 13, the social cognitive psychologists have shown that many types of learning do not require direct reinforcement. In fact, learning does not require reinforcement at all; mere observation is all that is required for human learning. Reinforcement enters the picture only in raising the probability that a learned behavior will be repeated; and even then it is not reinforcement that plays a part but the expectation of reinforcement. Cognition again. Both humans and animals can learn by watching the outcome of others' behaviors. This fact directly contradicts the theories of the radical behaviorists, who maintained that all learning takes place when the organism itself is reinforced. We learn simply by observing. We perform an action that we learned if we expect it to yield a positive outcome. But we can be very wrong. Thus, much of what we label "psychological problems" is simply faulty expectation.

From Behaviorism to Cognitive Psychology

"I thought it was crazy. It was so constrained, uptight, full of prohibitions. There was nothing you could do."

These sound like the words of a defector from a cult, and in a way they are. This is how Ulric Neisser (quoted in Baars, 1986, p. 276) described behaviorism. Neisser (1967) would popularize the term *cognitive psychology* in his book of that title. Ironically, behaviorism, which rejected competing approaches as unscientific, became so itself in its intolerance of competing theories.

Such animal researchers as Temple Grandin (2005) point out that if animals acquired all of their knowledge via operant conditioning—which in the wild would amount to learning by trial and error, they would be at a distinct disadvantage compared to animals that can learn by observation. Evidence for the ability to learn in this way can be seen in an African Grey parrot that learned concepts by observing laboratory assistants being rewarded with parrot treats when they identified colors. Before long, the parrot not only was able to learn the concept of colors and shapes but even asked about his own color. Humans, parrots, and moving down the phylogenetic spectrum, even bacteria have characteristic behaviors that require little or no conditioning. The preponderance of evidence indicates that it is not to the advantage of organisms to begin life as a blank slate. All species are born with some behavioral predilections, and most species are more readily conditioned to some stimuli and less to others, according to the evolutionary demands that their ancestors faced. Because different evolutionary milieus yielded different behavioral inclinations, it follows that the behaviorist premise that learning can be generalized from any animal to humans is highly questionable. In fact, even within a single species, the penchant for learning certain behaviors differs. For example, it is far easier to condition a golden retriever to retrieve than it is a pomeranian.

But behavioral theories need not be discarded together with their inflexible radical dogma. The behaviorists contributed a great deal to the advancement of psychology, the understanding of personality, and the treatment of neurotic disorders. The modal psychotherapeutic approach, and the one advocated by the authors of this text, is cognitive-behavioral. Both terms are emphasized, as the treatment of personality and emotional disorders requires the patient to change both thought patterns and behavioral habits. Behaviorist psychology contributed a great deal to the understanding of that portion of personality that results from learning. It also became the foundation of the most effective clinical approach to treating personality and other psychological disorders.

Chapter 11

Humanistic Views of Personality

Chapter Goals

- Outline the development of the humanistic school in psychology
- Show how humanism came into being, in part as a response to the pessimistic concepts of psychoanalysis and the mechanistic methods of behaviorism
- Explain the importance and role of Abraham Maslow in the humanistic movement in psychology
- Trace the growth of the existential movement in psychology and detail its connection to humanism
- Explore both the strengths and weaknesses of humanistic psychology in explaining human personality

The fact that we speak at all of a humanistic approach to psychology leads to an obvious question: Why did some psychologists feel this approach was necessary? After all, to propose a humanistic approach to psychology implies that psychology in its essence is not concerned with human beings. In fact, this was precisely the point the early humanist psychologists were making.

By the middle of the 20th century, psychiatry was dominated by psychoanalytic views of personality as well as of mental pathology. The leading school of thought in the field of psychology itself was behaviorism, which was taught and practiced in most universities and clinical centers, especially in the United States. A majority of psychologists approached all organisms, including humans, in terms of their responses to stimuli. Such internal events as thoughts and emotions were considered to be irrelevant to psychology. They could neither be observed nor directly tested; thus, including them in analyses of human nature was considered unscientific. This restriction led some psychologists to find the dominant view far too limiting. They maintained that behaviorism had eliminated some of the most important dimensions of the human psyche. This point of view had been indirectly supported in an earlier generation by such psychologists as Max Wertheimer, Kurt Koffka, and Wolfgang Köhler. These theorists are generally credited with developing the Gestalt (from the German word for *form* or *shape*) approach to experimental psychology.

HUMANISTIC PSYCHOLOGY—A "THIRD FORCE"

What gives life meaning? What makes us human? Love and hate, hope and fear, happiness and sorrow, satisfaction and creativity. These essences of what it means to be human are not amenable to operational definitions. How can one explain the human need for independence and creativity through laboratory experiments? Even if they cannot be proved, can a psychology that ignores them really be a "human" psychology?

The first president of the American Association for Humanistic Psychology, James Bugental (1967), described the goal of humanistic psychology as providing "a complete description of what it means to be alive as a human being" (p. 7). Humanistic psychology was—in the mind of one of its pioneers, Abraham Maslow—a "**third force**," created to battle with the established forces of behaviorism and psychoanalysis. It sees behaviorism as seeking to reduce the human to a large rat and as having nothing to do with the human experience. It sees psychoanalysis as the study of only disturbed individuals; studying only the disturbed will, in the words of Maslow (1970, p. 180), "only lead[s] to a crippled psychology."

So what does it mean to be human? Humanists would say three answers have been given: being enslaved by the garbage of the past, being enslaved by the environment, or being free to pursue the possibilities of the future.

The Gestalt psychologists who were trained in German universities prior to World War I and emigrated to the United States in the 1920s and early 1930s argued that behaviorism and other systems that attempted to reduce the human psyche to its essential elements were on the wrong track. The Gestalt approach is predicated on the notion that the human mind is more than the sum of its parts and can be understood only by studying its functioning in its natural ecology. Trying to understand it by breaking it down into its components misses the unique function of the mind as a whole. The Gestalt approach began largely as a result of Wertheimer's research into the **phi phenomenon,** which refers to the illusion of movement created by a rapid succession of still images. A familiar example of the phi phenomenon is the theater marquee with lights that blink in succession, giving the observer the impression that a wave of light is moving around the marquee. The movement of the light, of course, exists only in human perception, which, the Gestalt psychologists believed, has the innate capacity to organize sensory experience.

The Gestalt hypothesis—that the human mind creates a whole that is different from its sensory components—is supported by other phenomena. For example, if we view a building from a distance, we still perceive the object as a building, even though the image on the retina of the eye is that of a small rectangle. This capacity to perceive objects accurately even though they change their apparent shape or size as they move in space (or as the observer moves around them) is referred to as object constancy. Object constancy implies that our minds interpret and manipulate sensory data to create a new whole that is not uniformly connected to the data that our senses convey. The word *Gestalt* itself is a German term that is most closely translated as *form* or *shape*. This derivation connotes something that is irreducible, that exists only as a whole that cannot be fully understood or appreciated when considered simply as the sum of its parts. The Gestalt approach stood in contradiction to the perspective of the behaviorists, who viewed the mind as a simple compound of reinforced behaviors, or that of the structuralists, who viewed the psyche as being made up of elementary components, much like the atom.

The structuralists were psychologists who sought to understand the psyche by seeking to define the fundamental units that comprise it and then studying those units. The structuralists, in modeling their approach on physics, thought that psychologists, just like their colleagues in the physics laboratories, need to understand the basic building blocks of the mind. Behaviorists, on the other hand, viewed the stimulus-response connection as their equivalent of the atom; all behavior would be explained through this unit, just as all matter is made up of atoms.

回　ABRAHAM MASLOW

The Gestalt school posed a direct challenge to behaviorism's molecular view of the human mind. The Gestalt psychologists' challenge was predicated on the principle that the human brain is more than a switching circuit; instead, it interprets and transforms information. This principle was expanded on in the middle of the 20th century by an experimental psychologist named Abraham Maslow. While teaching at Brooklyn College of the City University of New York and later at Brandeis University, Maslow advanced the idea that psychology should consider the unique aspects of humankind. He was somewhat stifled by the predominance of behaviorism, even though he had completed a Ph.D. dissertation at the University of Wisconsin on the dominance characteristics of monkeys. He later said that a happy marriage and the birth of his first daughter convinced him that behaviorism is inadequate to explain the richness of human experience.

Frustrated by his difficulty in publishing articles in psychology journals with behaviorist reviewers, he began to contact like-minded psychologists. His networking ultimately led to the formation of the Association of Humanistic Psychology (AHP) and the *Journal of Humanistic Psychology* and to the beginning of what Maslow called the **fourth force** in psychology. The first three forces were (1) psychoanalysis, (2) behaviorism, and (3) humanistic psychology. The fourth force or **transpersonal psychology** added a spiritual element to humanism. Maslow's novel approach to psychology was first seen in his 1943 article titled "A Theory of Human Motivation." In it he proposed that people seek to fulfill a range of motivational needs and outlined 13 principles of motivation:

1. The integrated wholeness of the organism must be one of the foundation stones of motivation theory.

2. The hunger drive (or any other physiological drive) was rejected as a centering point or model for a definitive theory of motivation. Any drive that is somatically based and localizable was shown to be atypical rather than typical in human motivation.

3. Such a theory should stress and center itself on ultimate or basic goals rather than partial or superficial ones, on ends rather than means to these ends. Such a stress would imply a more central place for unconscious than for conscious motivations.

4. There are usually available various cultural paths to the same goal. Therefore, conscious, specific, local-cultural desires are not as fundamental in motivation theory as the more basic unconscious goals.

5. Any motivated behavior, either preparatory or consummatory, must be understood to be a channel through which many basic needs may be simultaneously expressed or satisfied. Typically an act has more than one motivation.

6. Practically all organismic states are to be understood as motivated and as motivating.

7. Human needs arrange themselves in hierarchies of **prepotency**. That is to say, the appearance of one need usually rests on the prior satisfaction of another more prepotent need. People are perpetually wanting animals. In addition, no need or drive can be treated as if it were isolated or discrete; every drive is related to the state of satisfaction or dissatisfaction of other drives.

8. Lists of drives will get us nowhere for various theoretical and practical reasons. Furthermore, any classification of motivations must deal with the problem of levels of specificity or generalization of the motives to be classified.

9. Classifications of motivations must be based on goals rather than on instigating drives or motivated behavior.

10. Motivation theory should be human centered rather than animal centered.

11. The situation or the field in which the organism reacts must be taken into account, but the field alone can rarely serve as an exclusive explanation for behavior. Furthermore, the field itself must be interpreted in terms of the organism. Field theory cannot be a substitute for motivation theory.

12. Not only the integration of the organism must be taken into account, but also the possibility of isolated, specific, partial, or segmental reactions. It has since become necessary to add to these another affirmation.

13. Motivation theory is not synonymous with behavior theory. The motivations are only one class of determinants of behavior. While behavior is almost always motivated, it is also almost always biologically, culturally, and situationally determined as well.

From this list, we can see that Maslow was likely influenced by the Gestalt theorists, who wanted people to be regarded as wholes rather than composites of stimulus-response (S-R) connections or unconscious structures in continual conflict. In contrast to Freud, Maslow saw such basic drives as hunger as secondary to higher level drives to affiliate with others, accomplish positive goals, and find an overarching meaning in our existence. We would, of course, need to satisfy the drives related to physical survival before we could proceed to meeting the higher needs. But satisfying these basic drives is simply a prerequisite for moving higher; it is not the driving force of the psyche, he thought. Like Freud, Maslow postulated that our drives are complex and unconscious. He tacitly criticized the behavioral psychologists of his time for using animals in their behavioral paradigms to model human learning and behavior.

The Work of Kurt Lewin. Maslow's 13 principles demonstrate that he similarly contrasted his view with that of Kurt Lewin (1890–1947), who set forth the social-psychological system called **field theory**. Lewin thought that an individual's field is built up from a number of factors, including the person's motives, values, needs, moods, goals, and ideals. Like Maslow, Lewin was influenced by the Gestalt psychologists. Educated in Germany in the early part of the 20th century, Lewin came to the United States when Hitler took power in the 1930s. Like the Gestalt psychologists, Lewin also wanted human actions to be viewed as wholes, which to him included people's internal states, their social environment, and their unique life situations. This combination of factors in a person's life is what Lewin called the **field**. Lewin saw the behavior of an individual as a function of the precise conditions and forces in operation at the time the behavior occurs. Lewin also described what he called the **life space**, which he defined as an entity consisting of the person and his or her psychological environment.

Lewin was a pioneer in the subdiscipline of social psychology, studying the effects of group membership on attitude change. Lewin invented the concept of **group dynamics**, in that he saw a group as constituting a dynamic field influencing the behavior of its members. In particular, he noted that people seek to avoid discrepancies between their attitudes and those of the groups to which they belong. Although Lewin's approach took social factors into account, his theories were still too much like physics or applied mathematics for humanist tastes.

Hierarchy of Needs

Maslow is best known for the hierarchy of needs that he defined in the 1943 paper mentioned earlier. According to Maslow, these needs must be satisfied in a certain order: first, biological needs, followed by safety needs, love needs, esteem needs, and finally, the need for self-actualization, an innate tendency of human beings to fulfill and enhance their potential, provided that basic physical and social needs are met. Maslow referred to this hierarchical arrangement

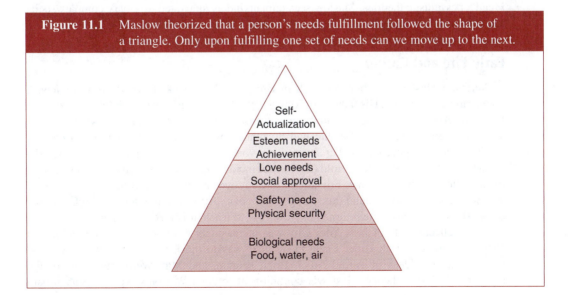

Figure 11.1   Maslow theorized that a person's needs fulfillment followed the shape of a triangle. Only upon fulfilling one set of needs can we move up to the next.

as the prepotency of needs. He considered these needs as inherent in people and the foundation of all motivated action. Accordingly, all people are primarily motivated by biological needs common to all animals, he thought, but once satisfied, people move on to satisfy the higher needs that are uniquely human. Maslow thought that the higher needs came later in human evolutionary development and are by their nature less necessary for physical survival.

The most basic human needs are biological, namely the fundamental requirements to sustain life: water, oxygen, and nutrients. Maslow believed that a deficiency in any one of these, even a specific vitamin, will lead to a craving that will bring the person back to **homeostasis**, or a condition of stable equilibrium. Only after the first set of prepotent needs is met will the individual become increasingly desirous of safety, family structure, and stability. In a simple society, stability might consist solely of shelter, membership in a tribal group, or weapons.

In a more complex society, stability might include such security measures as life insurance, retirement plans, or bodyguards. When the physical needs are satisfied, however, a person begins to focus on satisfying needs involving love, social approval, and affiliation. When our appetites are satisfied and we feel secure and loved, we will then focus on satisfying needs related to esteem. These needs include wealth, status in our profession, or academic achievement. They also include the need to feel competent or confident in our own eyes, whether or not others are favorably impressed. Maslow referred to the four lower need categories as deficit needs or **D-needs** and contrasted them with the higher, exclusively human needs, which he called meta-needs, the need for growth, being-needs, or **B-needs** (Maslow, 1970). B-needs include noble love, artistic creation, the quest for knowledge, and altruism. When B-needs are fulfilled, they do not go away but motivate the individual to strive for satisfaction of needs even higher in the hierarchy.

By proposing that humans are motivated in life by factors other than drive reduction, Maslow rejected a key element of Freudian theory. Freud thought that people are primarily motivated to reduce cravings related to primitive drives, with libido or the sexual drive being predominant. This difference is a fundamental feature of Maslow's humanism. Humans to him are more oriented toward positive goals than the impulse-driven beings described in Freud's pessimistic theories. Maslow sees humankind as motivated to satisfy complex social and even spiritual needs.

Early Life and Career

Abraham Maslow was born in 1908 in Brooklyn, New York. His parents were Jewish immigrants from Russia. His father's making a better living actually led to childhood problems for young Abraham because the family moved from a slum where other Jews were living to a better neighborhood, but one that had no other Jewish families. Maslow described his childhood as unhappy; his mother favored his younger siblings and punished him for the smallest offense. In later life, he told of a painful incident in which his mother killed two stray cats that he had brought home. Friendless, without even a pet for comfort, and the target of anti-Semitism, Maslow found his refuge in books. After completing his Ph.D. at the University of Wisconsin, he returned to New York to teach at Brooklyn College.

The intellectual life of New York City was increasingly cosmopolitan in the 1930s and 1940s, as refugees from Hitler's rule made their way to the United States. Maslow made contact with the ideas of Alfred Adler, Erich Fromm, and Max Wertheimer, one of the founders of Gestalt theory. Maslow's commitment to John Watson's type of behaviorism

Table 11.1	Need Fulfillment in Maslow's Hierarchy	

Need	*Examples*	*Satisfaction*
Physiological	• Hunger, thirst • Sexual frustration • Fatigue • Illness	• Relaxation • Release from tension • Experiences of pleasure derived from the senses • Physical comfort
Safety	• Insecurity • Fear • Anxiety	• Security • Poise • Calm
Love	• Social anxiety • Feeling rejected • Feeling worthless • Loneliness	• Free expression of emotions • Sense of wholeness • Sense of warmth • Renewed sense of life and strength
Esteem	• Feeling of incompetence • Negativism • Feeling of inferiority	• Confidence • Sense of mastery • Positive self-regard
Self-Actualization	• Alienation • Absence of meaning in life • Boredom • Routine living	• Healthy curiosity • Realization of one's potentials • Pleasurable and meaningful work • Creative living

began to weaken even before the birth of his first child spurred him to think that humans are more than just overgrown laboratory rats. In addition, the horrors of World War II further convinced Maslow that the study of personality should show that humanity is capable of something better than genocide. Maslow died in 1970 after several years of poor health.

Self-Actualization

Maslow's concept of self-actualization became the focal point of the humanistic movement in psychology. This term, which had originated with Kurt Goldstein (1878–1965), a neurologist and adherent of **organismic psychology**, referred to a motive that is universal among humans—namely, to achieve our potential. Goldstein's approach to psychology was termed organismic because he emphasized the unity of the human organism and held that anything that occurs in any part of it affects the whole. Goldstein's concept of self-actualization was adopted by Maslow and became the core of his personality theory. In addition, Maslow attempted to operationalize the term by investigating the specific characteristics of individuals who had achieved this level in his hierarchy. Although he acknowledged that he had no standardized tests to evaluate his findings, he studied people, both historical figures and contemporaries, whom he considered self-actualized, and sought to define their common features.

Table 11.2   Maslow's Examples of Self-Actualized People

Type of Person	Name of Person	Level of Self-Actualization
Leader	Thomas Jefferson	probable
	Abraham Lincoln	probable
	Franklin Delano Roosevelt	partial
	Eugene V. Debs	potential
Social innovator	Eleanor Roosevelt	probable
	Jane Addams	probable
	Albert Schweitzer	potential
Scientists and developers	Albert Einstein	probable
	Sigmund Freud	partial
	George Washington Carver	potential
	Albert Schweitzer	potential
Philosophers	Baruch Spinoza	probable
	William James	probable
Poets and writers	Johann Wolfgang von Goethe	potential
	Walt Whitman	partial
	Henry Thoreau	partial
Painter	Thomas Eakins	potential
Composer	Ludwig von Beethoven	partial

Maslow's study involved the highest functioning 1% of college students based on the absence of neurosis, psychopathic personality, psychosis, or related disorders; some of his friends and acquaintances were also included, as well as those who possessed "positive evidence of self actualization" (Maslow, 1954). This positive evidence consisted of the subject's making full use of his or her talents, capacities, and personal potential. In selecting self-actualized individuals, Maslow studied the younger subjects directly and the historical figures indirectly. According to Maslow, his study was iterative, in that it began with a rough a priori definition of self-actualization and then sought individuals who fit this definition. Maslow's research was not scientific, which he himself acknowledged. His descriptions were not based on standardized personality tests, and his choice of individuals who were self-actualized was totally subjective. Indeed, the list of potential self-actualized individuals in Table 11.2 contains individuals who, while unquestionably accomplished, also had profound character problems, including severe depression.

After Maslow selected people he considered appropriate, he modified his definition of self-actualization to fit the characteristics of the selected people. When the characteristics were finally analyzed, Maslow and his coworkers concluded that self-actualized people have the following qualities:

- *Acceptance* (of self, others, and the natural world). This quality refers to a lack of self-consciousness, shame, and guilt, as well as the ability to interact with others without judgment or discomfort related to their differences and foibles. So just as we accept water as being wet and rocks as hard, the self-actualized person will accept the attributes of others, even if problematic, as aspects of their reality.

- *Spontaneity*. Actualized people spend less time considering the judgment of society or of other people about their actions. Thus, their decisions to act are simpler and more spontaneous. They are capable of being unconventional when necessary, but they do not act unconventionally just for effect. Spontaneity allows self-actualized people to take novel approaches to problems.

- *Problem-centered*. Self-actualized people have the ability to put themselves and their egos aside and focus entirely on the problem at hand. Such people generally have a vital interest or mission that they are pursuing, and they do so with minimal concern about their own benefit in the undertaking.

- *Detachment: A need for privacy.* In contrast to the typical person, who has a minimal desire for solitude, the actualized person has a distinct need for it. This desire for solitude is associated with detachment from the conflicts of more mundane people. Consequently, self-actualized people can view events more objectively with little emotional investment, allowing them to maintain their identity and dignity in difficult situations and to maintain their point of view despite social pressure.

- *Autonomy: Independence of culture and environment.* Actualized people are motivated by the need for growth rather than the need to satisfy a D-need; they are less dependent on external reinforcement. They do not need social encouragement to motivate them; rather they are motivated from within, by their own desires to explore and create. The quality of autonomy makes them relatively immune to social changes, physical illness, and other hardships.

- *Continued freshness of appreciation.* The pleasurable experiences of life continue to offer their original satisfactions to actualized people. They tend not to become jaded by the delights of life. Maslow thought that this quality of appreciativeness is especially true of both sexual and romantic love.

- *Mystic or peak experiences: The oceanic feeling.* Maslow likened what he called **peak experiences** to the religious rapture experienced by devout people but experienced in secular situations. Actualized people will experience sexual and other intense pleasures, as well as such "ordinary" events as a sunrise, with sensations of "limitless horizons opening up to the vision, the conviction that something extremely important has happened, so the (actualized person) is to some extent transformed and strengthened even in his daily life by such experiences"

(Maslow, 1970, p. 216). This experience of transcendence is what Maslow meant by a peak experience. A peak experience can be compared to a sexual climax in nonsexual situations. It involves a feeling that all is well, a loss of the boundaries of the self, and a feeling of oneness with the universe. The actualized person is not going somewhere but *is there*. Neither the past nor the future is meaningful in a peak experience, only the total *now*.

- *Gemeinschaftsgefühl.* Maslow adopted this term, which literally means "a sense of community," from Alfred Adler to describe a consistent ability to feel identification, sympathy, and affection for other people, despite occasional negative feelings about them. **Gemeinschaftsgefühl** elicits a genuine desire to be of service to others, whether through volunteer work of some kind or other forms of generosity.

- *Deep interpersonal relations.* While self-actualized individuals have deep interpersonal relationships, they are also selective; they have a few close friends rather than a large number of casual acquaintances. This is how Maslow saw himself. The depth and intensity of interpersonal feelings of actualized people are closer to those of children than of other adults, in his view. "They are capable of more fusion, greater love, more perfect identification, more obliteration of the ego boundaries than other people would consider possible" (Maslow, 1970, p. 212). In addition, when the actualized person is hostile to another person, the hostility is usually deserved and often benefits the targeted person. Self-actualized people condemn behaviors rather than other persons—an attitude often expressed in religion as hating the sin and not the sinner.

- *Democratic character structure.* Actualized people are nonauthoritarian; they are "friendly with anyone of suitable character regardless of class, education, political belief, race, or color" (Maslow, 1954, p. 220). They are open to learning from anyone with something to teach them without regard to the other person's status, and they do not condescend to anyone. The reader should recall that Maslow himself had been a target of anti-Semitic prejudice.

- *Ability to discriminate between means and ends.* Maslow concluded that actualized people have crystallized standards of right and wrong. They are moral people without the need of a religious or other external authority for their morality. He concluded that "self-actualizing people most of the time behave as though, for them, means and ends are clearly distinguishable. In general, they are fixed on ends rather than on means, and means are quite definitely subordinated to these ends" (Maslow, 1954, p. 221).

- *Gentle and philosophical sense of humor.* Actualized people do not laugh at someone else's pain, suffering, or humiliation. Taking Abraham Lincoln as an example, Maslow believed that "Lincoln never made a joke that hurt anybody else; it is also likely that many or most of his jokes had something to say, had a function beyond just producing a laugh" (Maslow, 1954, p. 222).

- *Creativity.* Maslow emphasized that without exception, all actualized people have a quality of creativity. Self-actualized people are original, inventive, and unrestrained by convention in everything they do.

- *Resistance to enculturation.* Actualized people do not adjust to their culture, in a process called **enculturation**; instead, they peacefully coexist with it. They have an inner detachment that prevents them from being shaped or biased by external mores or cultural norms. They do not let conventionality hamper them. Maslow (1970) defined conventionality as the "pervasive psychopathology of the average" (p. 177). Self- actualized individuals view themselves as members of humanity as a whole rather than of any sectarian group.

- *Freedom.* Self-actualized individuals are free to be themselves and to allow others the same freedom. They reject the slogan, "Lead, follow, or get out of the way." Self-actualized individuals, if they had a slogan, would adopt one like, "Calmly pursue one's bliss while neurotics run around aimlessly."

Those who achieve this rare state tend to have the preceding characteristics in common, although a given self-actualized individual will not possess all of them. Self-actualized individuals are also not perfect human beings; they are simply the best that they can be. Despite the difficulty of reaching self-actualization, Maslow argued that all people are drawn toward achieving it. He further believed that human personality is a function of higher forces motivating people toward personal excellence. But as we shall see, there are some lingering problems with some of Maslow's ideas.

Critiques of Maslow

A number of Maslow's concepts are self-evident. First, it is obvious that people cannot be concerned with fulfilling a higher desire if they have an unmet fundamental need. Such other writers as the historian Will Durant made similar observations long before Maslow. Someone deprived of water will be concerned only with slaking their thirst, not about philosophy. Second, even if one accepts that there is a hierarchy of human needs, is the highest one necessarily self-actualization? In addition, the concept of prepotent needs is challenged by actualized people throughout history who lived with hunger, physical discomfort, and other privations. Mohandas Gandhi and Henri de Toulouse-Lautrec are examples of people who achieved self-actualization while having some of their basic needs unmet for much of their lives. The authors of this text have counseled people who were still motivated by such socially affirming rewards as fame or professional recognition while living in poverty and with needs for safety and stability unmet. The concept of the starving artist is so well known as to be a cliché. Of course, if the artist is literally starving, on the brink of losing consciousness from hunger, he will think of nothing but food. On the other hand, it is common for artists to continue to work while living in wretched conditions. So, perhaps, Maslow's hierarchy of needs is obvious on one level and only questionably true on another. And even if one subscribes to the idea that our ultimate need is to fulfill our potential, the fact is that many creative people are actually fueled in their creativity as compensation for other needs that are not met.

Although Maslow's concept of self-actualization is widely taught and appears in textbooks as a fundamental tenet of personality psychology, it has weak empirical support at best (Williams & Page, 1989). Maslow's own attempt to find empirical support for it incorporated a tautology. That is, Maslow arbitrarily designated some people as self-actualized and then looked for characteristics to confirm his a priori designation. Even more problematic is the fact that he categorized historical figures such as Abraham Lincoln as actualized individuals and then made behavioral attributions based on his own classification that would be expected of an actualized person. For example, Maslow concluded that Lincoln did not make use of disparaging humor. In effect, he says that Lincoln was self-actualizing, and such a person would not employ hostile humor, and because he believes Lincoln didn't do so, that is evidence that he was self-actualized.

There are also some troubling aspects of Maslow's conceptualization of self-actualization itself. In contrast to both Carl Rogers (discussed in Chapter 12) and Goldstein, who coined the term, Maslow viewed self-actualization as a rare state of being. In fact, he freely acknowledged that he himself had not achieved it. Rogers and Goldstein, however, both regarded self-actualization as a goal that all people can eventually attain. We may need a bit of guidance to get there, they believed, but it is nevertheless within our power. Rogers chose to name his comparable concept "**the fully functioning person**." An essential difference between Rogers's and Maslow's concepts is that Rogers viewed full functioning as a goal that we all approach, even though we move toward it at various rates of speed. Maslow's concept was a goal line that a person either succeeded in crossing or failed, with the overwhelming majority of people fated to fall short of the line.

Maslow wrote during a time of rapid cultural change in America, of student protests, of open advocacy of hallucinogens and other drugs, of active sexual exploration. His ideas, although meaningful, seem to bear the stamp of that era. This time-bound quality of his work and related problems have led some researchers to believe that like those of other early personality theorists, Maslow's theories require revision (Neher, 1991; Rowan, 1998) or should be subsumed under more recent theories.

Interestingly, although Maslow is often seen as one of the architects of the human potential movement of the 1960s, he came to criticize the movement toward the end of his life for its focus on sensory experience, touchy-feely language, and emotion-laden group encounters to the exclusion of the intellect. He did not abandon his concept of self-actualization but warned his followers that work on their underlying conflicts and neuroses is necessary before reaching for the higher levels of the hierarchy of needs. Recognizing that he had built his life around avoiding anger and other negative emotions, Maslow entered psychoanalysis for the first time at the age of 61 in order to deal with his long-repressed anger, which had been a factor in his first two heart attacks. He never lived to complete his analysis, dying of his third heart attack in June 1970 (Schwartz, 1996, pp. 107–109).

A Sign of the Times

As we have seen, prior to the 1960s, the two established schools of psychology were psychoanalysis and behaviorism. Both were products of the specific times and places that produced them. Psychoanalysis was popular and originated in Europe, spawned by the sexual repression that was commonplace among middle-class Europeans of all nationalities and given increased popularity by the irrational disaster that was World War I. In the late 19th century, sex was a problem for both men and women. Respectable women did not engage in premarital sex. Men could avail themselves of prostitutes, but there was no safe cure for syphilis prior to Paul Ehrlich's discovery of arsphenamine in 1909. "Self-abuse," the polite term for masturbation, was considered a sin and a cause of insanity. Most men married only when they could support a wife financially.

The late 19th century saw progress in the sciences, slow improvement in social problems, and the spread of the optimistic belief that human rationality could create a secular utopia. Then came World War I, 4 years of total war leaving 40 million dead, an entire generation of Europe's youth wiped out. The disillusionment that followed the war was a tremendous boost to such mind-sets as Freud's, which emphasized the primitive and irrational forces lurking beneath the surface of civilization.

Behaviorism was born in turn-of-the-century America, with its emphasis on the practical, its distrust of European intellectuals and philosophy, where "common sense" was better than "book larnin'." Behavior was seen as simple and controllable; what could be better for the optimistic American spirit? In addition, the European belief that people are influenced by their genetic predispositions was elitist and out of step with American egalitarianism.

Humanist psychology emerged in the 1960s, bringing with it the human potential movement. Both mirrored the rebellion against tradition that characterized the time, the rejection of materialism and "cold science," the opposition to all social forces that "reduced" humans to numbers. Humanism tried to restore the belief in free will that the other two psychological traditions seemed to deny to humanity. As the imprisoned agent on the seminal 1960s British TV cult series, *The Prisoner,* shouts, perhaps in vain, "I am not a number, I am a free man." As life becomes ever more complex, as people are ever more seen as strings of numbers, these concerns remain pertinent in the early 21st century, and there is a good chance that you can identify with them.

VIGNETTE

Timothy Leary (1920–1996) was a bright and innovative young man. Not only did he tend to see things differently from others, he generally insisted that his view was the correct one. His impulsive and iconoclastic nature, however, put off as many people as it favorably impressed. Despite Leary's obviously high intellect, his college years were marred by volatile behavior that included continual aggressive pursuit of young women, drunkenness, and failure to attend classes. His superior IQ was hampered by his temperament and drives, leading to disciplinary problems at three different colleges.

After an erratic period at the College of the Holy Cross in Massachusetts, he was admitted to the prestigious West Point Military Academy, only to be forced to leave for violating the ban on bringing liquor onto the campus. He left West Point without his degree or officer's commission. Instead, he remained in the Army as an ordinary soldier and managed to earn his bachelor's degree from the University of Alabama in 1943. Not surprisingly, he was often cited by the school for violating its rules. Despite never quite finding academic settings a comfortable fit, Leary managed to earn a master's degree from Washington State University in 1946 and a Ph.D. in psychology from the University of California, Berkeley, in 1950. His dissertation was titled *The Social Dimensions of Personality: Group Structure and Process*. He was only 30 years old at the time.

(Continued)

(Continued)

Despite Leary's checkered personal history, he made many creative contributions to personality psychology. He was an assistant professor at Berkeley from 1950 to 1955 and director of psychiatric research at the Kaiser Foundation from 1955 to 1958. He then became a lecturer in psychology at Harvard University at the age of 39. Harvard's reputation enabled Leary to become instrumental in shaping both personality psychology as a subdiscipline and the burgeoning humanistic movement in psychology. He associated largely with other iconoclastic figures, however, and as his past might have led an observer to predict, he switched friends and lovers as often as his life priorities. Leary was married five times and divorced three of his wives; moreover, he seemed to have few long-lasting friendships.

The tempering that usually comes with age only minimally dampened his radical style. Not long after his Harvard appointment, Leary traveled to Mexico to explore the hallucinogenic high provided by psilocybin mushrooms. His investigation turned out to be an experience he liked a bit too much. This new passion led to experimentation with other more potent hallucinogens, ultimately leading Leary to LSD—a drug that he believed gave him a deeper understanding of his own mind and of the meaning of the world in general.

Before long, Leary was enthusiastically advocating the use of hallucinogens to his students, peers, and all who would listen. It appears that the risks of indiscriminately encouraging people to take drugs with unpredictable effects were lost on Leary. Despite all his skill and success in psychological research, these gifts of mind did not rein in his tendency to make judgments based on his feelings. As his bumpy academic history might have shown, his judgments probably required far more reflection than he possessed. He had earned the privilege of teaching at Harvard by conducting forward-thinking research, publishing important articles, and writing an innovative textbook. Unfortunately, many of the very same characteristics that guided him to originality in research led him to self-destruct.

Timothy Leary was a brilliant psychologist with a deeply flawed personality. Extreme personality attributes can be gifts or curses and sometimes both at the same time. Leary was an illustrative example of that third possibility. He was unrestrained by social mores and standards, a freedom that helped him consider human personality from a fresh perspective. This novel perspective produced a noteworthy body of psychological research and publication. Unfortunately, these very same personality characteristics also blinded him to the professional and social consequences of his position on hallucinogenic drugs and the lifestyle associated with them.

Leary spent the remainder of his life as a social outcast, often encountering rebuke and legal consequences. He served time in prison more than once, at one point being placed in a cell next to Charles Manson at Folsom Prison. Although he tried to remake himself as a Hollywood figure in the 1980s, the studios were reluctant to hire him for any major project. He eventually died of prostate cancer, experimenting with heroin, morphine, and other drugs in his last days. Timothy Leary was a classic example of personality as a force that can negate the gifts of both reason and intellect.

Vignette Questions

1. Do you think if Humanism had been more dominant in Leary's time, his actions might have been more tolerated? Explain.

2. Was Leary a humanistic psychologist?

3. If yes, why? If not, how would you have characterized him?

4. What in Leary's personality do you think led to his downfall as a psychologist?

回 GORDON W. ALLPORT

Gordon W. Allport's work as a trait theorist was discussed in Chapter 9. Trait theory, with its emphasis on studying personality by analyzing its component traits, which can then be identified and measured with scientific precision, appears to be the very antithesis of humanistic psychology. Yet, Allport effortlessly combined the two approaches within his far-reaching theories, and for this reason, he also merits inclusion in a chapter on humanistic psychology. In fact, Allport is difficult to fit neatly into any of the categories used to classify personality theorists. He was at once a **phenomenologist** (Allport, 1961), an approach that emphasizes a person's interpretation of events over an "objective" account of the events; a trait theorist; and a humanistic psychologist.

Allport was attracted to trait theory, not because of the reductionism and scientific precision associated with that approach, but because of his enduring conviction that every individual is unique and valuable and that traits are the way in which that uniqueness finds expression. In addition to the traits that are commonly identified as such by trait theorists, Allport suggested that each person may have unique traits that cannot be adequately captured by scientific methodology. He incorporated many sources into his theories, even to the point of spending a year in Europe working with Carl Jung; this eclecticism meant that he founded no school and did not seek to form his students into followers, as was true of some of the other theorists considered in this book. On the other hand, Allport's wide range of interests, his open use of many sources, and his clear and accessible writing style had a subtle influence on several generations of psychologists, including former students as otherwise different as Stanley Milgram and Jerome Bruner. In fact, Allport's pioneering 1937 textbook practically invented the field of personality as a separate domain within psychology.

Allport's contributions to the humanistic tradition within psychology include his concept of the proprium, which, as explained in Chapter 9, is a person's subjective experience of the self and self-awareness, and which provides coherence and meaning to experiences. Allport deliberately avoided using the term *ego*. In addition, he believed that people need and are guided by unifying values that provide meaning to life. He postulated six such values:

1. *Theoretical:* This value is seen in the work of a scientist searching for truth.

2. *Economic:* A businessperson who values usefulness would score high on this value.

3. *Aesthetic:* An artist, musician, poet, or dancer who loves beauty is motivated by this value.

4. *Social:* Someone attracted to medicine or social work to help others exhibits this value.

5. *Political:* This value represents the search for power and influence.

6. *Religious:* The religious person values a sense of unity with God and the universe.

In 1931, Allport formulated a personality test called the Study of Values (SOV), working with an educational psychologist named Philip E. Vernon (1905–1987), to identify these values within a given individual's motivations. The SOV was a major influence on the many vocational aptitude tests given to contemporary high school and college students to help them find the careers best suited to their personalities.

Allport's concept of functional autonomy was meant to emphasize the rejection of the past as the cause of behavior, allow for freedom of the will, and recognize that mature adult activities are enjoyed for their own sake—all in opposition to Freud's position. An amusing personal anecdote that Allport related in later life helps to explain his rejection of Freudian theory.

After completing his undergraduate education, Allport took a year off to teach English in a school in Turkey. On his way home in 1920 to begin his graduate studies at Harvard University, he boldly sought a meeting with the great man himself, Sigmund Freud. Allport succeeded with his brash plan and found himself in Freud's inner office, in the presence of the living legend. Freud said nothing. Nervously, Allport tried to break the ice by describing a young boy he had seen on the streetcar on his way to Freud's office. The lad was clearly anxious about not getting dirty. Freud responded with a question: "And was that little boy you?" (Allport, 1967, p. 8). This incident confirmed Allport's recognition that seeking deep, dark, unconscious reasons for human behavior may miss the mark.

The Significance of Religion

Both behaviorism and psychoanalysis were quite hostile toward religion. Freud viewed religion as the "black mud of the occult" and an excuse to give expression to the id's barbaric impulses while satisfying the superego's desire to inflict harsh punishment. Humanism, while in general hostile to fundamentalist religion, presents a more complex and nuanced view of religion as a whole. Allport, in fact, wrote extensively on the place of religious faith in the mature personality. He differentiated between what he termed extrinsic religion, which he considered problematic, and intrinsic religion, which he considered healthy (Allport, 1950a). He defined extrinsic religion as a religion that a person adopts because it is the religion of his or her group; it concerns receiving rewards and excluding "unbelievers." Intrinsic religion to Allport lies closer to what some people think of as spirituality. It is related to Allport's concept of the unifying values that provide meaning in a person's life.

◫   EXISTENTIAL PSYCHOLOGY

Existentialism is generally considered a form of philosophy rather than psychology in the strict sense. It arose in Europe after World War II, in large part as a response to that horror. Its two best-known philosophers were Jean-Paul Sartre (1905–1980) and Albert Camus

(1913–1960)—although Camus always protested that he was not an existentialist. Existentialism is essentially a philosophy of being. What does it mean to be a human for one fleeting and random moment in an eternity of time in an infinite universe?

Psychologists influenced by existentialism attacked both behaviorism and psychoanalytical theory for the very same reason humanism did—for being deterministic, for seeing a human's behavior determined by the past rather than freely chosen in the present. To an existentialist, what we do at the present moment is by definition freely chosen and independent of any previous moment. Choice is our ongoing responsibility; we cannot blame present circumstances on childhood or conditioning.

How does existentialist psychology compare to humanistic approaches? Some critics regard humanism as a sanitized and optimistic version of the bleak view of the human condition presented by European existentialism. Humanistic psychologists, in their opposition to determinism, are generally hopeful about the possibilities of freedom. As we saw, Carl Rogers thought of human nature as essentially benign and predisposed to make positive use of its innate tendency toward growth. Existentialists, on the other hand, while agreeing with humanists that human beings have free will, are pessimistic; to them, freedom is more of a curse than a blessing. One could say that human beings are condemned to be free. This darker side of European existentialism was played down in American humanistic psychology.

An example of the existentialist ambivalence toward freedom may be found in Jean-Paul Sartre's reminiscences of life in Nazi-occupied France in the early 1940s. "We were never more free than during the German occupation," wrote Sartre (1947, p. 498) at the beginning of his essay, "The Republic of Silence." What Sartre meant was that at that time, every French citizen was faced with the choice of how to react to the Nazi occupiers; moreover, the choice was completely free. But this freedom of action was terrifying. The French might try to throw it away. But how? They could ask someone else what to do. But whom should they ask? A member of the resistance or a collaborator? If they are practicing Catholics, they might decide to ask a priest. But should they ask a priest who is resisting or a priest who is collaborating? The choice returns to the individual! In sum, in Sartre's view, each of us is free but also totally responsible to find our own meaning in a meaningless world. Responsibility and blame for our choices and their consequences cannot be shifted to parents or priests or society at large.

Binswanger and Boss

Ludwig Binswanger (1881–1966) and Medard Boss (1903–1990) were two Swiss psychiatrists who combined an existentialist approach to psychology with extensive clinical practice. Both influenced American humanistic psychologists and existentialists. Binswanger, a contemporary of Jung and Adler, was an early follower of Freud and maintained a friendship with him for the rest of Freud's life. After completing his M.D. in 1907, Binswanger studied under Eugen Bleuler, Jung's former supervisor at the famous Burghölzli hospital in Zürich. By the 1920s, however, Binswanger began to incorporate the concepts of existentialism in his practice.

A lengthy case study that Binswanger first published in 1944 called "The Case of Ellen West" has become a classic of existentialist psychology. Ellen West is the pseudonym that Binswanger gave to a young woman who developed what is now termed anorexia nervosa and committed suicide in her early thirties after being unsuccessfully treated by several of the most eminent psychiatrists of the early 20th century, including the great Emil Kraepelin himself. West is now regarded as a tragic example of the intellectually gifted woman who could find no outlet for her creativity in the years preceding World War I. At the end of her life, she came under Binswanger's care after she had already made several suicide attempts and signed herself into the Kreuzlingen Sanatorium, Binswanger's hospital. She was using 60 to 70 laxative tablets a day to lose weight and vomiting every night.

After counseling Ellen in a series of interviews, and coming to know her through her poetry and her own handwritten account of her eating obsession, Binswanger gave her and her husband a choice: He could commit Ellen to a closed ward, in which her mental and physical health would continue to deteriorate, or he could release her. She and her husband chose release. After returning home, Ellen felt better, largely because she knew what she needed to do. Binswanger's case study closes with the following:

> On the third day of being home she is as if transformed. At breakfast she eats butter and sugar; at noon she eats so much that—for the first time in thirteen years—she is satisfied by her food and gets really full. . . . She takes a walk with her husband . . . is in a positively festive mood, and all heaviness seems to have fallen away from her. . . . She writes letters, the last one a letter to the fellow patient [in Binswanger's hospital] to whom she had become so attached. In the evening she takes a lethal dose of poison, and on the following morning she is dead. (Binswanger, 1958, pp. 237–364)

Binswanger interpreted Ellen's conflict as an existential dilemma: In her poetry she described herself as living in a "tomb world"—her physical and social existence, which she tried to escape by starving her body. Desiring to flee the "tomb world" into what she called the "ethereal world," in which the mind is free of the cumbersome body and its "low" needs, she could succeed only by discarding the body and ending her entire existence.

Medard Boss associated with many prominent personality theorists, including Freud, and was a friend of Martin Heidegger (1889–1976), an existentialist philosopher whose reputation has been compromised by his cooperation with the Nazis in the 1930s. Boss called his approach to psychotherapy **Daseinsanalysis,** which can be loosely translated into English as "analysis of being."

The flavor of existential psychology can be seen in Boss's writing. The following excerpt is taken from his book, *Existential Foundations of Medicine and Psychology* (Boss, 1977):

> We declare that only man exists. This is not to say that material, inorganic nature and nonhuman beings—animals and plants—are in any sense unreal, insubstantial, or illusory. . . . We merely state that the reality of these nonhuman realms differs from that of human existence, whose primary characteristic is Dasein [being there]. (p. xxix)

Boss was also well known for his emphasis on dream interpretation as a technique in therapy and his use of the term **attunement** for describing moods. If a person is in an angry mood, for example, Boss would describe him or her as attuned to angry things or angry thoughts, while a person in an anxious mood is attuned to threats or to what they perceive as threats.

Major Concepts in European Existential Psychology

Dasein. **Dasein** is a German word taken from Heidegger's work that is often left untranslated in the works of existentialist psychologists. A literal English translation would be "being there" or "being-in-the-world." For an existentialist psychologist, there is no such thing as causality in human actions; the present neither follows from the past nor determines the future. The immediate present is all that we have. Dasein, therefore, conveys the special nature of human existence as opposed to the existence of plants, animals, and inanimate objects. There is no "there," no true existence, without human beings.

Being-Beyond-the-World. This phrase originated with Binswanger, who used it not to refer to an afterlife or an otherworldly dimension but to express the manifold possibilities open to human beings. For Binswanger, humans are beings-in-the-world and have a world but long to transcend their present situations. Thus **being-beyond-the-world** represents openness to our future and the realization of our full potential. This concept is not far removed from Abraham Maslow's notion of self-actualization and Carl Rogers's definition of the fully functioning person.

Thrownness. **Thrownness** in existentialist parlance refers to the condition of finding oneself in and having to respond to the external world. It is the English word most commonly used to translate Martin Heidegger's term *Verworfenheit.* Existentialism regards each of us as endowed with free choice, responsible for our actions and the creation of our own destiny. Yet, there are external situations that affect our freedom. We are all born in a particular place, in a particular time, in particular circumstances. For existentialists, we are thrown into a ground of existence (time, place, circumstance) over which we had no choice. To return briefly to Binswanger's case study, Ellen West had no choice about being born female at a time and in a place in which her sex was a barrier to her full development.

Many terms in existentialism have a dual connotation. Thrownness means first that each of us has our own unique experience of the contingencies of human existence; no two people are born into the exact same set of circumstances. Second, all people are thrown into a universe with no rules and no absolutes, a world devoid of ultimate purpose. Camus used to speak of Sisyphus, the mythological figure condemned forever in the afterworld to push a boulder up a hill, only to have it fall back down again. Camus compared the endless task of Sisyphus to humankind's inescapable dilemma; the boulder represents reality, which always falls back on people. Yet, human beings can and must still create all meanings in their lives.

Authenticity. **Authenticity** is an important concept in existentialist psychology, generally understood to include retaining our own individuality and character in spite of external pressures to conform to alien or imposed standards. We become inauthentic if we allow others (culture, religion, family, or political "isms") to define who we are. Lack of authenticity results in alienation and failure to actualize our potential. We are living inauthentically if we fall prey to authoritarianism or excessive respect for tradition. The reader should notice the similarity here to Erich Fromm's account of the ways in which humans seek to escape from freedom, discussed in Chapter 8. Anxiety, dread and despair are "the three horsemen of inauthentic experience," the emotions that result from inauthenticity.

Anxiety. Anxiety results from living inauthentically and also from the limitations of human existence. Every action taken and choice made involves the rejection of all other possibilities. If we decide to go to medical school, for example, we cannot at the same time plan to attend a music conservatory or enter law school. The ultimate anxiety, of course, results from the painful awareness, unique to humans, of the inevitability of death. The basic source of existential anxiety is the awareness that we are going to die and may do so at any time. To defend against these feelings of anxiety, we can cling to social conformity; that is, merge with a larger group—cultural, professional, ethnic, religious, or national—all in an effort to deny our own mortality. This defense, however, causes people to be inauthentic and lose their single moment of existence, according to the existentialist view.

The answer to existential anxiety is confronting the inevitability of death head-on. As put by Rollo May, an American psychologist who will be described more fully in the next section,

> To grasp what it means to exist one needs to grasp the fact that he might not exist, that he treads at every moment on the sharp edge of possible annihilation and can never escape the fact that death will arrive at some unknown moment in the future . . . but with the confrontation of nonbeing, existence takes on vitality and immediacy. (May, 1958, p. 47)

Absurdity. Absurdity is a term with two meanings in existential psychology. On the one hand, it means that a person is not authentic; to live inauthentically is to live in absurdity. On the other hand, the ultimate absurdity is being born only to die.

Fallenness. Fallenness, or falling into nothingness, is another existential term with two meanings. Like absurdity, it may refer to living inauthentically or living conventionally. Conventionality, living a life defined by others, is a common way to fall into nothingness, as we lose our essential being through enslavement to the standards or values of our society. The ultimate fall into nothingness is, of course, death.

In sum, existentialist psychology regards human life and its inescapable dimension of freedom as a tragic personal experience. Human beings must strive to create themselves in the face of futility in a meaningless universe into which they have been thrown, all the while knowing that death and nothingness await them at the end of life. People are responsible to themselves but are also totally responsible for themselves. There is nothing they can hide behind, though they may try. Human beings are truly condemned to be free.

▣ ROLLO MAY

Rollo May (1909–1994) is often credited as being the first American theorist to incorporate existential and philosophical concerns with psychology. He has sometimes been called the father of existential psychotherapy. Intensely interested in the work of Ludwig Binswanger and other European existential therapists, May helped to introduce American psychologists to their work through one of his early publications, *Existence,* a collection of essays by Binswanger and other Europeans that he edited together with Ernest Angel and Henri Ellenberger in 1958. *Existence* had a great influence on both Abraham Maslow and Carl Rogers. In 1961, May edited a second collection of essays called *Existential Psychology,* which included contributions by Gordon Allport as well as essays written by Maslow, Rogers, and May himself.

Early Career

May was born in Ohio but grew up in Michigan. His father was somewhat anti-intellectual, blaming his older sister's psychotic illness on "too much education." In 1930,

May completed his undergraduate degree at Oberlin College and then traveled to Greece to teach English in an American school in Salonika for 3 years. During his stay in Greece, May occasionally traveled to Vienna to attend seminars offered by Alfred Adler. His exposure to the tragic view of human nature and history that characterized European thought led him to think that the behaviorist psychology then dominant in American universities was too mechanistic and simplistic.

Returning to New York, May entered Union Theological Seminary, but his studies were interrupted by his parents' divorce and a family crisis that followed it. He finally completed his theological degree in 1938. After serving as the pastor of a Congregational church in New Jersey for 2 years, May went back to New York, where he studied psychoanalysis at the William Alanson White Institute and met such neo-Freudians as Harry Stack Sullivan and Erich Fromm. May then enrolled at Columbia University, receiving in 1949 the first Ph.D. in clinical psychology that the school ever granted. His studies had again been interrupted, this time by contracting tuberculosis—for which there was no cure at the time. May spent 3 years at a sanatorium in upstate New York, uncertain whether he would even survive the illness. He read both Freud and the philosopher Søren Kierkegaard during that time. His first book, *The Meaning of Anxiety* (1950), was based on his doctoral dissertation, a study of Kierkegaard. He quoted the Danish thinker's definition of anxiety: "Anxiety is the dizziness of freedom," and then added his own: "[Anxiety is] the apprehension cued off by a threat to some value which the individual holds essential to his existence as a self" (May, 1950, p. 72).

Four Stages

May is unique among existential psychologists for positing four stages of consciousness of self, a quality in general that he considered unique to human beings. These are not stages in the traditional sense of being age-defined phases that succeed one another in time; they can and do overlap in everyday life. A child may certainly be innocent, ordinary, or creative at times, and an adult may be rebellious—as the expression "midlife crisis" suggests. May's (1953) four stages are as follows:

- *Innocence.* This stage is characteristic of infants, who do not yet have consciousness of self. Innocent people are premoral, that is, they are neither bad nor good but only doing what they must do. The innocents do, however, have a degree of will in the sense of a drive to fulfill their needs.
- *Rebellion.* According to May, rebellion is the stage of consciousness of self in which people define themselves in opposition to or defiance of another. Rebellious people desire freedom but have as yet no full understanding of the responsibility that goes with it.
- *Ordinary.* Ordinary consciousness of self to May is the normal adult ego, or what people mean when they say that someone they know has a healthy mature personality. People with ordinary consciousness of self can learn from mistakes and take responsibility for their life.
- *Creative.* May believed that not everyone reaches creative consciousness of self, as that stage involves transcending our usual limited viewpoint and catching a glimpse of ultimate reality. The creative stage is roughly similar to Maslow's peak experience.

Major Concepts in May's Thought

Destiny and Courage. May's understanding of destiny may be thought of as an American translation of Binswanger's notions of thrownness and fallenness. In his 1981 book titled *Freedom and Destiny,* May defined destiny as the design of the universe working itself out in each person's unique life. Destiny sets limits to us because of the specificities of our family, our culture, and the period of history into which we are born, but it also gives us the tools we need to accomplish our life's purpose. May uses the word *courage* where a European existentialist would speak of *authenticity.* Courage for May means facing our anxiety and surmounting it.

The Daimonic. May introduced the concept of the **daimonic** in what is probably his best-known book, *Love and Will* (1969). The English word comes from the Greek word *daimon,* which originally meant "little god" rather than "demon" in the modern sense. For May (1969), the daimonic is "any natural function which has the power to take over the whole person" (p. 123). It includes such motivations as sex, anger, craving for food, the drive for power, and the like. The daimonic can be either creative or destructive; what counts is our ability to acknowledge its presence and integrate it within our personality. Trying to repress the daimonic by pretending it does not exist or by overvaluing the rational intellect puts a person at risk of being overcome by the daimonic.

The Importance of Myth. Toward the close of his life, May wrote a book called *The Cry for Myth* (1991), in which he argued that contemporary people find their lives increasingly senseless because they have lost the myths that once gave an overarching structure to people's lives. In that book, May defined myths not as made-up stories but as "narrative patterns that give significance to [human] existence" (p. 19). A myth or "guiding narrative" may be conscious or unconscious, personal or collective. For example, some people still find that the story of a Bible character speaks to them and their life histories in a very deep way. Examples of American myths that have shaped the national character are those of frontier explorers like Lewis and Clark or the 20th-century astronauts; self-made successes like the fictional Horatio Alger or the real-life Bill Gates; and radical individualists like Henry David Thoreau or Walt Whitman. Some psychologists have noted the similarity between May's myths and Carl Jung's archetypes, although May's theory has nothing comparable to Jung's concept of the collective unconscious.

▣ EXISTENTIALISM AND THE QUESTION OF FREE WILL

Existentialist psychology makes the question of free will an urgent matter for the clinician as well as the researcher. Belief in free will is a central doctrine of the monotheistic Western religions. Most people certainly think they have free will. There is a concept in the field of social psychology termed **reactance**, which is the negative affect that people experience when they perceive that a choice they think is theirs to make is being taken away. Individuals experiencing reactance are motivated to reassert their right to the endangered freedom (Brehm, 1966). A commonplace example is a child's insistence on using bathroom talk on every possible occasion after being chided by a parent for referring to bodily functions in inappropriate settings. Another example of reactance is the person who defiantly lights up a cigarette right beneath a "No Smoking" sign.

But perhaps free will, as classical philosophy has understood it, may be an illusion. In the early phase of the European Enlightenment, there were thinkers who dared to see humans as machines, which certainly do not possess free will. In science, if Event A occurs before Event B and B occurs before Event C, then it is possible (although not necessarily the case) that A caused B. One cannot, however, explain B as caused by C because causes must precede outcomes. Furthermore, if we establish A as the cause of B, then B has no "choice" in occurring if A occurs. Pick up a stone, then drop it, and it will fall to the ground. If the stone is dropped from a height, it will accelerate according to the distance it falls. Why? We know that the explanation involves the laws of motion and gravity; the stone has no purpose or goal.

The English words *teleology* and *teleological* come from the Greek word *telos,* meaning end or purpose. A dictionary definition of teleology is "explaining [something] in terms of purpose, as opposed to a mechanical explanation." A teleological explanation is one that refers to the realization of some end or purpose on the part of some intelligence; it deals with the relation of a thing to a goal being realized. Why does the sun shine? Some ancient people (and many today) would give a teleological explanation: The sun shines to warm the human race. A mechanistic explanation of the sun's shining, however, would use the language and formulae of astronomy or nuclear physics. There is a constant conflict between these two views in the history of thought.

The first rule of science is that teleological explanations are forbidden in accounting for natural phenomena. But what of explanations for human behavior? Can science admit to the existence of free will? The reader may recall an old joke—why did the chicken cross the road? Answer: to get to the other side. That is how most of us explain our own behavior—in terms of purposes and goals. But achieving the goal follows the behavior. Does not science have to explain behavior in terms of what preceded it? Science insists on lawful cause-and-effect relationships.

In a materialistic universe, if we know everything that there is to know about chemistry, could we predict what would happen when two or more chemicals are combined? Obviously, we could predict the result. If we knew everything about a person, however, could we be certain of what that individual would do in any specific situation?

Between the time of the ancient Greek and Roman atomists and the 18th century, there were very few defenders of a materialistic view of nature, much less of human behavior. Such views would not only conflict with the spirit of the times, they would result in death for their proponents.

Julien Offray de La Mettrie (1709–1751), a French physician of the Enlightenment, wrote an infamous book titled *L'homme machine (Man Is a Machine),* which was banned in most European countries. La Mettrie was among the first to state that, just as the title of the book suggests, humans are simply complicated machines and entirely material. He appears to have adopted this view as a result of studying the effects of a fever he suffered in 1742 on speeding up his circulation and thereby affecting his ability to think. He concluded that physical phenomena can be regarded as the effects of organic changes in the brain and nervous system. La Mettrie's views led him to be constantly on the run, but he is sometimes regarded as a pioneer of the approach taken by modern cognitive science.

People use free will to explain human behavior when they no longer understand the cause. That was the bold assertion of another great Enlightenment figure, Paul-Henri Thiry, baron d'Holbach (1723–1789). D'Holbach was German by birth but inherited his French uncle's fortune and title, moved to Paris, established a salon, and hosted the leading thinkers of the time. A materialist and determinist, Holbach maintained that free will does not exist and that nothing could occur other than for lawful, natural causes.

D'Holbach published a book titled *Le système de la nature* (The System of Nature) in 1770 but anonymously for "health" reasons. The book was banned, and all copies were ordered destroyed; the author found himself opposed by such writers as Voltaire and Frederick the Great as well as by French theologians. In the book, d'Holbach wrote, "There is, in point of fact, no difference between the man that is cast out of the window by another, and the man who throws himself out of it," except that in the first case we understand what caused the man to fall, so we do not attribute it to free will, and in the second case, we do not understand the cause of the suicide, so we delude ourselves by believing the man acted out of free will—in d'Holbach's view. Neither man had a choice over their behavior. Ideas such as those of d'Holbach would find a home in behaviorism and, indeed, in all of psychology that strove to be scientific. Humanism and existentialism both arose as rebellions against viewpoints that denied free will and sought to explain human psychology and behavior in mechanistic terms.

▣ CHAPTER SUMMARY

No doubt many words have been written on behalf of humanistic and existentialist psychology, but are they compelling theories of human personality? The very strength of these perspectives as seen by their proponents is that these systems free the study of personality from the constraints of science. But that also frees them from the possibility of their being based on experimental evidence. It would be rather difficult to design an experiment to verify, for example, some of Medard Boss's (1963) ideas: "An individual's pitch . . . determines in advance the choice, brightness, and coloring of his relationships to the world" (p. 41). European existentialist psychologists, in particular, prefer the use of an evocative, almost literary, vocabulary rather than the technical terms found in most schools of psychology. This aspect of existentialist psychology reflects its close relationship with drama and literature; as we have noted, such existentialist thinkers as Sartre and Camus wrote plays and novels rather than scientific works.

As we have seen, existential psychologists specifically and completely reject the scientific method as a fit technique for studying humans. They also reject determinism and mechanism. Humanistic psychologists tend to give at least lip service to the scientific method, but they, too, reject determinism. Psychology was once a subfield of religion and philosophy, and these approaches can be seen as attempts to return psychology to an unscientific division of philosophy. Moreover, it has always been easier to define what humanistic psychology is against than what it stands for. The humanistic approach in general, and such methods associated with it as encounter groups, has been open to accusations of degenerating into a swamp of emotional subjectivity.

In addition to being open to criticism for an unrealistically optimistic view of human nature, humanistic psychology is in effect an attempt at a secular path to salvation. Existentialists tend to view science as part of the problem whereas humanists point out that humans create science—it is merely one value among others rather than the method for establishing objective knowledge. Abraham Maslow, for example, wrote about the value of science, even though his selection of self-actualized individuals and their characteristics was completely arbitrary. He noted, "Only science can progress" (Maslow, 1968, p. viii). Although Maslow was among the first to conduct seminars and popularize ashrams in the Indian style in which a humanistic guru served as a "guide for spiritual growth," he turned away from the excesses of the human potential movement in his last years to reconsider the dark side of human nature and the need to come to terms with one's own brokenness.

Chapter 12

Carl Rogers and Humanist Psychotherapy

Chapter Goals

- Explain the growth of the humanistic movement in psychology after its founding
- Provide an understanding of the importance of Carl Rogers to this growth
- Detail the profound impact Carl Rogers played in the development of both humanistic and clinical psychology
- Summarize Rogers's clinical approach and its influence on most subsequent approaches to clinical psychology
- Discuss the problems of Rogers's necessary and sufficient conditions for therapeutic cure
- Summarize the impact Rogers and subsequent humanists had on personality psychology

Carl R. Rogers deserves a chapter by himself because he may be the most influential American psychologist to date (Kirschenbaum, 2004, Smith, 1981; Warner, 1991). He helped to establish clinical psychology as a major subdiscipline within psychology, and he applied humanistic principles to create a highly influential theory of personality and clinical practice.

EARLY CAREER

At the start of Rogers's career, the psychiatric community maintained that psychologists should not be permitted to conduct psychotherapy. Rogers began his graduate education studying religion at Union Theological Seminary in New York and then transferred to Teachers College of Columbia University to study psychology. He earned a Ph.D. in clinical psychology in 1931 and

Image 12.1   Carl Rogers (1902–1987)

began work in a children's clinic in Rochester, New York. He published his first book in 1939 while working at this center. It was titled *The Clinical Treatment of the Problem Child.* Rogers's next position was at Ohio State University, where he wrote his second book, *Counseling and Psychotherapy* (1942). This work presented the core of his innovative approach, which eventually became person-centered therapy. This book can be considered the first approach to psychotherapy that offered a clear alternative to psychoanalysis.

In 1945, Rogers accepted the directorship of the counseling center of the University of Chicago. During his time there, he wrote his major work, *Client-Centered Therapy* (1951), which formally established a major new psychotherapeutic approach as well as the foundation of an original theory of personality. Rogers's theory was founded on his work as a clinician. He viewed each person as a unique individual whose dignity and identity was paramount in the therapeutic process. As *Time* reported in its July 1, 1957 issue ("Person to Person," 1957):

As Rogers describes his method: "The therapist has been able to enter into an intensely personal and subjective relationship with this client—relating not as a scientist to an object of study, not as a physician expecting to diagnose and cure, but as person to person. The therapist has been able to let himself go in understanding this client, satisfied with providing a climate which will free the client to become himself."

Far more than the analytic schools, Rogers emphasizes empathy:

To sense the client's private world as if it were your own, but without ever losing the "as if quality"—this is empathy, and this seems essential to therapy. To sense the client's anger, fear or confusion as if it were your own, yet without your own anger, fear or confusion getting bound up in it. ("Person to Person," 1957)

When this condition has been established, Rogers felt, a single interpretive remark by the counselor can work wonders in clarification for the client. There is never any attempt at actual guidance; always the aim is to enable the client, through greater insight, to accept experiences as they are.

Rogers's optimism about human personhood stands in distinct contrast to Freud's inherent pessimism. Rogers saw people as being able to exercise conscious control over their lives as long as personality pathology is not so severe as to prevent it. Rogers (1961) stated that the emotionally disturbed person "finds that he cannot behave in the fashion that he chooses. He is determined by the factors in the existential situation, but these factors include his defensiveness, his denial or distortion of some of the relevant data" (p. 193). In contrast to the disturbed person is the fully functioning person: "The fully functioning person, on the other hand, not only experiences, but utilizes, the most absolute freedom when he spontaneously, freely, and voluntarily chooses and wills that which is also absolutely determined" (Rogers, 1961, p. 193).

The Basis of Rogers's Beliefs

Carl Rogers was born into a fundamentalist Protestant family in Oak Park, Illinois. At one point, after his family moved to a farm, he thought of becoming an agricultural scientist. Rogers went to a missionary conference in China in 1922; he was one of a handful of college students sent to a Christian Federation conference in what was then called Peking and today is Beijing. But during his half-year in China, Rogers came into contact with people committed to many religious doctrines other than his own. He came to the conclusion that while issues regarding the meaning of life are of central importance, no one has the right to tell another person how to live his life.

Rogers later described the changes he underwent: "It struck me one night . . . that perhaps Jesus was a man like other men—not divine! . . . it became obvious to me that I could never in any emotional sense return home" (Rogers, 1961, p. 351). Rogers came to see the source of psychological problems as being cut off from one's true self through trying to live up to rigid and unchanging values imposed by society. Examples of these imposed rules as given by Rogers are: (1) sexuality is bad; (2) unquestioning obedience to authority is good; (3) making money is very important.

Rogers would later write:

If the line of reasoning I have been presenting is valid, then it opens new doors to us. If we frankly face the fact that science takes off from a subjectively chosen set of values, then we are free to select the values we wish to pursue. We are not limited to such stultifying goals as producing a controlled state of happiness, productivity, and the like. Suppose we start with a set of ends, values, purposes, quite different from the type of goals we have been considering. Suppose we do this quite openly, setting them forth as a possible value choice to be accepted or rejected. Suppose we select a set of values which focuses on fluid elements of process, rather than static attributes.

We might then value:

- Man as a process of becoming; as a process of achieving worth and dignity through the development of his potentialities;
- The individual human being as a self-actualizing process, moving on to more challenging and enriching experiences;
- The process by which the individual creatively adapts to an ever new and changing world;
- The process by which knowledge transcends itself, as for example the theory of relativity transcended Newtonian physics, itself to be transcended in some future day by a new perception. (Rogers 1961, pp. 395–396)

▣   MAJOR CONCEPTS IN ROGERS'S PSYCHOLOGY

Personality and Phenomenology

It is clear that Rogers saw people as capable of emotional adjustment and happiness (see accompanying box). Notably, Rogers (1961) referred to human behavior as "exquisitely rational" (p. 194) and stated that the "the core of man's nature is essentially positive" (p. 73). Rogers's view of each person as distinct and possessing a unique understanding and experience of the world is linked to his being influenced by phenomenology, an approach to philosophy that relies on immediate experience and perception without interpretation. Its goal is to have the thinker rid the mind of assumptions, inductions, or deductions. By doing so there can be no category errors or distortions of life experience that arise from analyzing one's sensations and perceptions. Rogers posited that we grow from experience, which includes every event and sensation available to us during every moment of life. According to Rogers, many of our experiences are perceived unconsciously in the sense that they are being processed outside conscious awareness (Rogers, 1977, p. 244). Experience fosters our growth as we interact with the world and observe the changes effected through our actions.

Rogers' phenomenology takes an idiographic approach to personality theory in that he believed that a person can be understood only when that person's unique perception of the world is appreciated. He once said that clinical diagnoses have no other purpose than to make the therapist feel secure (Rogers, 1957). This approach is in contrast to nomothetic theorists, who propose that a person must be understood in terms of dimensions, traits, or other general measures. Rogers's move to a phenomenological approach began in part from his reading of such philosophers as Søren Kierkegaard (1813–1855) and Martin Buber (1878–1965), which led to a shift in his view of personality and the person. Rogers seems to have been influenced by Kierkegaard's *Sickness unto Death,* in which the Danish theologian wrote that the goal of a person's life is "to be that self which one truly is" (Decarvalho, 1991; Rodríguez & Silva, 2002). In Rogers's subsequent writing, he interpreted this statement to mean that most people in psychological distress suffer because they seek to be like someone else rather than taking the risk of becoming who they really want to be.

Rogers also agreed with Martin Buber, who emphasized the importance of experiencing relationships without playing roles—an approach that leads to deeper and more meaningful interactions. Buber believed that such genuine relationships have a healing effect (Decarvalho, 1991, p. 63). This is also the essence of Roger's theory of the development of a healthy personality. He maintained that within each of us there is a self that develops as we interact with the world. The self that is the essence of our personality is both unique and private and is never completely available to others (Rogers, 1951, pp. 483–484, 494–497).

Phenomenal Field, Self, and Self-Concept

Rogers viewed the self as the personal identity portion of the phenomenal field, which represents the sum total of the organism's experiences. This position stands in contrast to his earlier view that the concept of a self is too amorphous and difficult to define (Rogers, 1959,

p. 200). At a later point in his career, Rogers said that his clinical work led him to conclude that the self is comprised of conscious sensations, perceptions, and the awareness that leads to such self-descriptions as "I" or "me." Rogers believed that all learning and personal development is mediated by changes in the organization of the phenomenal field brought about by the perceptual field. Although the self is a distinct portion of the phenomenal field, Rogers believed that the phenomenal field acts as a whole to help us satisfy our needs.

According to Rogers, the self must accommodate to the demands of the environment. The **self-concept,** which Rogers defined as the organized set of characteristics that we recognize as belonging to ourselves, develops through these interactions. By interacting with others and the challenges of life, we develop an awareness of who we are. The self-concept can also be described as the product of these experiences and any values mediated by others that the individual may adopt. Accordingly, the self-concept includes our image of ourselves in relation to our overall environment, "a fluid and changing gestalt," as Rogers put it. Rogers proposed that the self-concept has both conscious and unconscious elements. He also believed that an individual's personality is based on interaction with a "continually changing world of experience of which (the person) is the center" (Rogers, 1951, p. 483). Moreover, we alone have complete access to our private world, which exists through our conscious or unconscious interaction with our phenomenal field. He also postulated the existence of an **ideal self,** which loosely corresponds to Freud's ego ideal. The ideal self is the standard we set for ourselves; it is the person we believe we should be.

Rogers maintained that each person creates a unique reality based on the world's interaction with the individual's phenomenal field (the person's reality). Thus, the way we react to the world around us is based not on any objective reality but rather on our personal apprehension of the world. This apprehension can change as we continue to test our models of the world. According to Rogers, we react to our phenomenal field as a whole individual rather than a collection of traits, structures, or conditioned responses. And this reaction has a direction: "The organism has one basic tendency and striving—to actualize, maintain, and enhance the experiencing organism" (Rogers, 1951, p. 487). As we strive to actualize our selves, we will tend to perceive any event inconsistent with our self-concept as a threat. Rogers resembled Freud in suggesting that the reaction to such threats is to develop defenses against them. It follows that the more inconsistent our self-concept is with objective reality, the more defenses we will need. And a person with a great number of defenses will tend to develop emotional disturbances.

Organismic Valuing and Conditions of Worth

According to Rogers, a healthy personality is a product of supportive affirmation given without constraints by parents or other important people in a person's life. He referred to this type of affirmation as unconditional positive regard. He warned against limited approval, which he called **conditional positive regard**. If we receive only conditional positive regard, we are likely to form a self-concept based on external values rather than on what Rogers called the **organismic valuing process.** The organismic valuing process is a built-in guide that we have for determining what we need to grow; otherwise put, it could be defined as a subconscious process that guides us toward growth experiences.

VIGNETTE

As a child, Thomas Edison (1847–1931) found it difficult to pay attention in school. His lack of focus frustrated his teachers, who saw little promise in the boy; one of them even called him "addled." His concerned mother took him out of public school and began to educate Tom at home. Fortunately for Edison, his mother turned out to be an excellent and patient teacher. He later said that he was grateful for her work on his behalf and vowed never to disappoint her. Mrs. Edison's efforts to educate her son were aided by Thomas's insatiable appetite for knowledge, which he satisfied by methodically reading each book in each row on the shelves of the local library. By adolescence, his level of knowledge and the scope of his questions had surpassed his mother's ability to teach him. From that point on, Edison was instructed by a tutor, who helped him to understand the classics of literature as well as science, which he assiduously attempted to master.

Edison's zeal for knowledge and its applications to new inventions would define his adult life. Yet, despite his penchant for systematizing most of his tasks, he sometimes let himself go off in odd directions. Some of these were both rational and profitable, like his starting a small publishing operation. Others, however, were grandiose failures, such as preparing thousands of films to help do away with books in public schools, or more mundane ventures like finding more uses for cement or more efficient ways to mine iron ore. With each failure, Edison bounced right back with some new creative notion for a new business. And along the way he generated scores of patents, some of which were productive enough to fund his own laboratory in New Jersey. In that laboratory, Edison commonly worked 20 hours per day, arduously repeating his efforts to solve the problems of each new project. Within a decade of its construction, Edison's laboratory in Menlo Park had expanded to cover two entire city blocks.

Like Leonardo DaVinci, Edison's exuberant creativity led to many new creations that benefited people. These included an early motion picture device that was successfully marketed, an improved telegraph that allowed four separate messages to be transmitted simultaneously over the same wire, and a telephone that came a bit later than Alexander Graham Bell's celebrated invention. It was the incandescent light bulb, however, that made Edison into a legend. Persevering through thousands of trials, he developed a practical and marketable light bulb. With this success, the name of Thomas Alva Edison was assured lasting historical stature.

Like many creative figures in history, Thomas Edison had a distinctive personality that ultimately facilitated his many positive accomplishments. His personality included a large component of obsessive-compulsiveness, some grandiosity, and a slightly schizoid style. But whatever the particular mix of characteristics he possessed, they made him sufficiently different from the typical person to be assured a place in the pantheon of great inventors. Edison, like many other geniuses, might have been relegated to mediocrity, had he not had a personality that drove his intellect in a productive manner.

Vignette Questions

1. How might Rogers have assessed Edison's personality differently from Freud?

2. Do you believe that Edison suffered from a personality or psychological disorder, if so why?

3. If not, why not?

The Role of Experience. According to Rogers, there is no need for people to learn what is or is not actualizing. Intrinsic to the primarily unconscious aspects of experience is an innate capacity to value positively whatever we perceive as actualizing and to value negatively that which we perceive as non-actualizing. Rogers believed that this unconscious process represented the core of personality in that it guides us to know what will best facilitate our actualization. Moreover, it denotes that people have within themselves the ability to know their own organismic values; they do not require parental or professional guidance to achieve their actualization. They merely have to be in touch with their inner motives and their life experiences. Experience was Rogers's primary guide to self-actualization. He once acknowledged that experience is fallible, "but I believe it to be less fallible than my conscious mind alone" (Rogers, 1961, pp. 22–23).

Introjection. Many people have life experiences associated with conditional positive regard. In such cases, parents or other major figures offer accolades, support, or affection only as rewards for achievement or acceptable behavior. Rogers believed that this attitude places people in a state of conflict between accepting their own experiences of what is good or bad versus those that are imposed on them by others. The conflict is frequently resolved in favor of the imposed values because of children's great fear of losing their parents' positive regard. Acceptance of imposed values leads in turn to the individual's importing the external standards into his or her self-concept, which then impedes the organismic valuing process.

The external values that we adopt are called introjected values. These introjects add foreign conditions of worth to the personality. If we introject the values of another person, we must conform to them before feeling worthwhile. As a result of introjection, we will feel affirmed only when living according to the values of another rather than the values we have learned from our own experience—values that promote full functioning.

Congruence and Incongruence. In Rogers's theory, the process of introjection leads to a separation between a person's self-concept and the process of self-actualization. Rogers referred to this separation as **incongruence**. To be **congruent** rather than incongruent, our self-concept must be composed primarily of personal experience.

What we learn through experience, especially open receptive experience, leads to the development of a healthy personality. Our desire for positive regard, Rogers believed, can lead to distortions in the apprehension of experience, as our lived experiences will be filtered through the lens of the conditions of worth imposed on them. Consequently, if we have introjected the values of someone else, most notably those that contradict our experiences, we will be incongruent. In other words, we will have a personality at odds with itself. Incongruence leads to an incomplete development of the self, as we cannot fully express all the aspects of our being because doing so in the past led to disapproval.

Actualizing Tendencies and Self-Actualization

Rogers, like Abraham Maslow and Gordon Allport, believed that all people are driven toward a common goal, that of actualization. Rogers (1961) defined actualization as

> the directional trend which is evident in all organic and human life—the urge to expand, extend, develop, mature—the tendency to express and activate all the capacities of the organism, or the self. This tendency may become deeply buried under layer after layer of encrusted psychological defenses; it may be hidden under elaborate facades which deny its existence; it is my belief, however, based on my experience, that it exists in every individual, and awaits only the proper conditions to be released and expressed. (p. 351)

Rogers posited a universal imperative called the **actualizing tendency,** described in the preceding passage; unlike Maslow, however, he considered the motive of self-actualizing to be a subset of the actualizing tendency. Self-actualizing for Rogers is the portion of the actualizing tendency of which the person is consciously aware. If the person is not burdened by psychological conflicts, psychological defenses, or distortions of self-perception, self-actualization and the actualizing tendency will tend to be the same.

Rogers did not believe the actualizing tendency is the exclusive domain of human beings; rather, all living things are invariably driven toward self-improvement and development to the fullest of their organic potential. Humans, however, are the species most susceptible to having this natural state of affairs thrown off course by the creation of psychological defenses or conflicts that can mask or derail their actualizing tendency. The actualizing tendency is a fundamental life force that roughly corresponded to Freud's concept of libido. Table 12.1 summarizes its characteristics.

Rogers believed that the actualizing tendency is a robust process. It may be temporarily impaired by unfavorable life events, but such traumas will not destroy or eliminate it. If we face adversity that inhibits our ability to grow, we will still strive as best we can while making adjustments for the severity of the adversity. Rogers (1980) used the model of a potato plant growing in unfavorable circumstances to demonstrate this process:

> The conditions were unfavorable, but the potatoes would begin to sprout—pale white sprouts, so unlike the healthy green shoots they sent up when planted in the soil in the spring. But these sad, spindly sprouts would grow 2 or 3 feet in length as they reached toward the distant light of the window. The sprouts were, in their bizarre futile growth, a sort of desperate expression of the directional tendency I have been describing. They would never become plants, never mature, never fulfill their real potential. But under the most adverse circumstances, they were striving to become. Life would not give up, even if it could not flourish. (p. 118)

This directional trend toward improvement and development exists in all things, according to Rogers. He believed that the entire cosmos is guided by an evolutionary force toward

Table 12.1	Rogers's Account of the Actualizing Tendency

The actualizing tendency is the fundamental source of motivation in the person. Although it can manifest itself in many forms, it maintains its gestalt or form.

Every person is driven by the actualizing tendency, yet despite its universality it takes a unique form in every person.

The actualizing tendency is a constant force within the person, beginning at birth and ending only with death.

Every person is driven in a single direction by the actualizing tendency—toward personal fulfillment and perfection.

The uniquely human quality of consciousness (Rogers, 1980) serves to enhance the actualizing tendency. The ability to make decisions to guide behavior allows humans alternatives that are not afforded to other organisms.

In contrast to psychoanalysis, in which drive reduction is essential, the actualizing tendency does not require the reduction of instinctual drives. It is a force creating a positive drive toward actualization.

The actualizing tendency leads people toward autonomy and away from societal, normative, and cultural influences. It therefore leads to independence in thought and action.

The actualizing tendency is a force toward positive social action and creativity.

greater development and complexity. He referred to this force as the **formative tendency.** In humans, the formative tendency is expressed in seeking to reach our most positive potential. This motivational force is innate; it varies only if impeded by external forces or neurotic disturbance. Unlike Maslow, Rogers (1980) did not accept the prepotency of needs, as he observed that we can reduce the demands of our basic appetites while still seeking to create, innovate, explore, and establish ourselves as people:

> Whether the stimulus arises from within or without, whether environment is favorable or unfavorable, the behaviors of an organism can be counted on to be in the direction of maintaining, enhancing, and reproducing itself. This is the very nature of the process we call life. This tendency is operative at all times. Indeed, only the presence or absence of this total directional process enables us to tell whether a given organism is alive or dead. The actualizing tendency can, of course, be thwarted or warped, but it cannot be destroyed without destroying the organism. (p. 118)

> My main thesis is this: there appears to be a formative tendency at work in the universe, which can be observed at every level. This tendency has received much less attention than it deserves. Physical scientists up to now have focused primarily on "entropy," the tendency toward deterioration, or disorder. They know a great deal about this tendency. Studying closed systems, they can give it a clear mathematical description. They know that order tends to deteriorate into randomness, each stage less organized than the last. (p. 124)

What part does our awareness have in this formative function? I believe that consciousness has a small but very important part. The ability to focus conscious attention seems to be one of the latest evolutionary developments in our species. This ability can be described as a tiny peak of awareness, of symbolizing capacity, topping a vast pyramid of nonconscious organismic functioning. Perhaps a better analogy, more indicative of the continual change going on, is to think of the pyramid as a large fountain of the same shape. The very tip of the fountain is intermittently illuminated with the flickering light of consciousness, but the constant flow of life goes on in the darkness as well, in nonconscious as well as conscious ways. It seems that the human organism has been moving toward the more complete development of awareness. It is at this level that new forms are invented, perhaps even new directions for the human species. It is here that the reciprocal relationship between cause and effect is most demonstrably evident. It is here that choices are made, spontaneous forms created. We see here perhaps the highest of the human functions. Some of my colleagues have said that organismic choice—the nonverbal, subconscious choice of way of being—is guided by the evolutionary flow. I agree; I will even go one step further. I would point out that in psychotherapy we have learned something about the psychological conditions that are most conducive to increasing this highly important self-awareness. With greater self-awareness, a more informed choice is possible; a choice more free from introjects, a conscious choice that is even more in tune with the evolutionary flow. Such a person is more potentially aware, not only of the stimuli from outside, but of ideas and dreams, and of the ongoing flow of feelings, emotions, and physiological reactions that he or she senses from within. (pp. 126–127)

Clearly Rogers viewed the formative tendency in people as part of a universal process in which simpler systems evolve into more complex and superior ones. He saw evolution as a directional process in which all things move toward completion and individual perfection. This notion, of course, is not what Darwin's theory proposed and not at all what biologists mean by evolution. Rogers's concept of actualization and the formative tendency conformed to his personal notions of good and bad. He generally saw actualization as a positive process because it is humane and constructive; thus, people who are violent or cruel are not innately so but were acted upon by external factors. Absent these factors, Rogers believed people would naturally seek to help, create, and contribute to others. It follows that the actualizing and formative principles make human personality essentially good and benign.

The Fully Functioning Person

The personality that has been allowed to develop with unconditional positive regard, and that possesses a high degree of positive self-regard, can reach the state that Rogers defined as fully functioning. Achieving this state of being is similar to Maslow's concept of the self-actualized person. The essential characteristics of the fully functioning person are presented in Table 12.2 below. According to Rogers, such people do not pursue life to satisfy introjected conditions of worth. Instead, they are motivated by their organismic valuing process. In such people, there is congruence between the actualizing and self-actualizing tendencies. Their union allows continual progress toward maximizing people's potential. The fully functioning person has little need for defenses, as he or she is open to experience and can accept setbacks by accurately understanding mistakes, correcting them, and moving forward.

Rogers thought that the fully functioning person would be liked by most people and inclined to express deep and sincere concern for others. Fully functioning people would instinctively help others achieve their need for positive regard by expressing genuine concern through congruent relationships. Rogers saw fully functioning as a continual process of growth, not a state of being, which differs from Maslow's view of the actualized person.

PRINCIPLES OF ROGERIAN PSYCHOTHERAPY

Rogers (1942) initially proposed that the innate tendency in humans toward actualization or natural growth is the curative factor in psychotherapy. He wrote, "Therapy is not a matter of doing something to the individual, or of inducing him to do something about himself. It is instead a matter of freeing him for normal growth and development" (p. 29).

Toward the end of his career, however, Rogers (1980) modified his earlier position by adding the principle of the formative tendency as the basis of healing in the client-centered

Table 12.2	Characteristics of Rogers's Fully Functioning Person
Openness to experience	Their experiences are encountered completely, without denial or distortion. Reality, including their own feelings and those of others, can be accepted, even when negative, without the need for defenses and the anxiety resulting from the conditions of worth imposed by others.
Existential living	They live in and fully experience the moment at hand, in contrast to living in the past or future. They experience the present without bias from past events or future expectations. Doing so provides a greater sense of reality and objectivity.
Organismic trusting	They trust themselves and their instincts; thus, the opinions and dogmas of others will rarely distract them. They feel comfortable doing what comes naturally. They are acting on their actualizing tendency, which means that what comes naturally to them will tend to be productive.
Experiential freedom	They take action with a sense of personal responsibility. They have a sense of freedom in most situations and even in a situation with restrictions will act on those aspects over which they have control.
Creativity	They are creative in their professional and social realms and will act on their feelings of freedom. Always moving toward actualization, they will naturally help others to achieve the same. This is typically associated with effecting positive creative changes in the world.

approach. As a practical matter, this addition is more an issue of nomenclature than theoretical development. In general, Rogers's therapeutic approach can be summarized in four concepts:

1. The actualizing (or formative) tendency is the essential motivating force in all people.
2. The actualizing tendency invariably directs people toward personal development, fulfillment, and growth.
3. Expression of the actualizing tendency can be thwarted by adverse life events.
4. The effects of adverse life events can be ameliorated by client-centered therapy, which heals by stimulating the person's actualizing tendency through the unique relationship it fosters.

Thus, human personality is driven by a single all-powerful vector, namely, the actualizing tendency. If the actualizing tendency is free to do its work, the person will be free to develop a healthy and socially productive personality. Rogers could certainly not be called a pessimist in his view of human personality and the ability to change it. He was confident that most personality and emotional disorders can be ameliorated by reestablishing the person's organismic valuing process and thereby fully activating the process of actualization. Rogers believed that even people with the most damaging collections of experiences could be brought to full functioning through his client-centered or nondirective therapy. This conceptual approach to psychotherapy was formalized when Rogers published *Client-Centered Therapy: Its Current Practice, Implications and Theory* in 1951. In this book, Rogers emphasized his premise that all living things are directed by a primal force that, when uninhibited, will direct them to grow to their natural potential.

In humans, this growth can be derailed by threats to a person's self-concept, by conflicts between the self-concept and the ideal self, or by similar impediments to organismic experiences that reduce the person's congruence. Because these impediments usually result from inadequate positive regard during the person's youth, client-centered therapy seeks to correct this lack by providing positive regard in therapy. Rogers set forth six conditions for successful therapeutic remediation of incongruence, discussed in the following section and summarized in Table 12.3.

Conditions for Psychotherapeutic Change

Rogers made a major advance in the nascent field of psychotherapy by outlining its functional aspects. Prior to Rogers, there were two disparate theories of change in psychotherapy. The first was the psychoanalytic notion that patients get better when they uncover repressed unconscious forces. The second approach was behaviorist, which held that patients improve when they learn to extinguish inefficient behaviors and reinforce more adaptive ones. Rogers added conditions that were somewhat independent of theoretical constructs and very much dependent on the therapeutic environment and the relationship between therapist and client. Rogers (1951) saw the conditions he enumerated as always necessary and entirely sufficient for therapeutic efficacy.

Congruence. People whose self-image, values, and motives are in synchrony with what they actually do and present to the world are said to be congruent in Rogers's terminology. Such individuals will be genuine in their interactions with others and have all their faculties integrated. Similarly, congruent therapists present their real self to the client. Their reactions will be sincere and genuine, reflecting their sincere inner nature and values.

Unconditional Positive Regard. Rogers indicated that he sought to allow himself to experience positive attitudes toward the client, such as warmth, caring, liking, interest, and respect (Rogers, 1958). Note what Rogers chose to call his therapy. The key term for him was *client.* He considered the people who sought his help to be clients rather than "patients," because he believed they were not sick. Neither were they subservient to an all-knowing "doctor"; the term *patient,* he felt, conveys the notion of passivity as well as illness or suffering. Rogers thought that the term *client* conveyed a more positive message—that the people sitting in his office were mature human beings, equal in importance to Rogers. Rogers drew on his personal experience in stating his conviction that offering unconditional positive regard leads to a reciprocal feeling of affinity between therapist and client.

Moreover, the more distress that clients had been feeling in the form of shame, rebuke, alienation, or anger, the more relief they experienced during client-centered therapy. They would increasingly come to reject the values imposed on them by others and trust their own organismic valuing process. Unconditional positive regard would create a climate in the consulting room that would release their natural tendency toward productiveness, trustworthiness, and creativity—all the qualities that Rogers believed to be the default characteristics of humans. Once freed from external impositions, clients could begin to discern, evaluate, and ultimately solve their own problems.

Empathy. Rogers' expression *empathic understanding* is central to his third necessary condition for effective psychotherapy. Empathy as Rogers uses it refers to the suspension of the therapist's own values and perspectives in order to enter as fully as possible into the client's emotions, biases, needs, and cognitions. An empathically understanding therapist cannot disagree with or judge the client because the two share a common perspective. Rogers viewed diagnoses, evaluations, or judgments to be barriers to the therapeutic process; empathic understanding is a fundamental facilitator. He believed that clients are directly helped when they sense that the therapist completely understands and shares their point of view.

Rogers maintained that the core elements of the therapeutic process must be presented in the proper setting for maximal efficacy, as summarized in Table 12.3.

Table 12.3   Rogers's Conditions for Successful Psychotherapy

1. Two persons are in psychological contact.

2. The first person, the client, is in a state of incongruence, being vulnerable or anxious.

3. The second person, termed the therapist, is congruent or integrated in the relationship.

4. The therapist is experiencing unconditional positive regard toward the client.

5. The therapist is experiencing an empathic understanding of the client's internal frame of reference.

6. The communication to the client of the therapist's empathic understanding and unconditional positive regard is, to a minimal degree, achieved.

Thus, the client and the therapist must be in physical proximity and experience a sense of open communication. Rogers changed the physical setting of the therapeutic process of therapy. The appearance of the Freudian consulting room is so well-known that it has become an iconic image, familiar enough to be recognized by a child and the stuff of cartoons. The patient lies on a couch while the therapist sits on a throne-like chair, out of the patient's line of sight, taking notes, and occasionally making noncommittal noises like "hmm." Rogers had therapist and client sit on chairs facing each other, eye to eye.

Let us look more closely at Rogers's second condition: Clients must be suffering emotional distress as a result of incongruence. That is, clients have difficulty reconciling their life experiences with their values, self-concept, or ideal self. In response to the client's state of intrapsychic conflict, the therapist's thoughts and actions must correspond as closely as possible to those of the client. Therapists must not be a blank screen or hide behind a therapeutic mask; rather, they must be genuine people. In addition, they must make no negative judgments regarding the client's values, lifestyle, or personal presentation. Therapists must also be able to imagine what it must be like to be feeling what this client feels; and the client needs to be aware that the therapist perceives the client in this way. Therapists must avoid confrontation, challenges, or agenda-setting. Finally, clients must feel that they are the center of the therapeutic process; it is the therapist's task to convey this sense through actions and responses to the client.

▣ THE PROCESS OF ROGERIAN PSYCHOTHERAPY

Client- or person-centered therapy is nondirective, which means that therapists do not make interpretations of their clients' statements or offer advice; the course of therapy is determined primarily by the clients. The efforts of therapists are focused on creating an environment of acceptance and comfort for their clients, a place where clients can come to feel that they are the center of attention and importance. Therapists convey to their clients that the clients' beliefs, attitudes, and emotions are legitimate and meaningful simply because they have them.

An essential means to achieving this sense of acceptance is to allow clients to introduce the topics and themes of the session. Therapists never direct the content of therapy, but instead reflect to their clients the emotional tone of what the clients have expressed. Therapists should not judge, criticize, or discuss inconsistencies in their clients' comments. The typical manifestation of client-centered therapy involves the empathic showing of understanding by therapists, or what has been referred to as the empathic understanding response process (Moon, 2007).

Therapists convey empathy through summarizing; expressing inferences that convey an understanding of the theme in therapy, and asking questions intended to promote better understanding. Therapists have the overall task of communicating to their clients that they are being understood or that the therapist is seeking in earnest to understand, without setting goals or making judgments. The nondirective nature of the client-centered approach also serves to minimize the imbalance of power typical in a therapeutic relationship. Client-centered therapists seek to maintain as much equality in the relationship as possible in order to minimize the harm that Rogers believes a power relationship can inflict by stifling people's need to experience the world in their own way and from their own unique perspective.

The essential requirement that therapists be genuine requires reasonable openness and disclosure. If, for example, the client asks a question about the therapist, the therapist is encouraged to answer if the query is not too personal, irrelevant, or an attempt by the client to avoid legitimate discussion. And if the therapist prefers not to answer because the question falls into one of those categories, he or she is encouraged to state that directly and honestly, without disguising the refusal as part of the client's treatment or therapeutic process. Rogerian therapists are generally discouraged from talking about themselves, as this amount of self-disclosure would detract from the client's position at the center of the therapeutic process. On the other hand, the client's questions about the therapist's life, opinions, or values should either be answered if they are relevant to the client or the therapist should be honest in giving reasons for not answering.

It is axiomatic that therapists, in their demeanor and responses, should indicate unconditional regard for their clients. This quality requires that clients are never rebuked or criticized. Therapists should never betray feelings of aversion or surprise. According to Rogers, the ideal client-centered therapist must actually feel positive regard for clients, no matter how different the clients' lifestyle, behavior, or views of the world.

Therapists are also required to be congruent within themselves. That is, to become legitimate client-centered therapists, they must be fully aware and accepting of their own feelings, beliefs, and values. Conflicts must be minimal or nonexistent. With these conditions satisfied, Rogers apparently believed that psychotherapy would be a natural process that did not demand elaborate techniques or a diagnostic nosology. His statement, "Diagnostic knowledge and skill is not necessary for good therapy" (Rogers, 1946, p. 421) strongly suggests the principle that all that is necessary are the elements that Rogers defined as essential.

The Therapist's Attitudes

As indicated above, client-centered therapy, in contrast to many other therapies in which the actions or verbalizations of the therapist provide the basis of therapeutic change, heals through communication of the therapist's attitudes toward the client. Rogers posits that such internal mental states of the therapist as congruence, empathy, and unconditional positive regard are all that are required for healing. Rogers never offered a precise explanation of how the therapist's attitudes and mental states could treat such emotional problems as anxiety disorders. Nevertheless, he maintained that these inner states are absolutely essential to the healing process. Therapists must be fully aware of their inner strivings and motives, and these must be congruent with their actions in life.

Rogers resembled traditional psychoanalysts in requiring therapists to be conscious of their inner motives as a prerequisite to helping others. Unlike psychoanalysts who required that prospective therapists be extensively analyzed, however, Rogers was not very clear on an evaluation process for determining congruence in clinical trainees.

Rogers eschewed therapeutic masks or facades. He required therapists to be the same people in the therapy relationship that they are in all other relationships. They must be complete, real, and sincere. They must avoid condescension or any attempts toward hegemony in the relationship. Ideally, this egalitarian attitude comes naturally. Consequently, therapists must never feign affinity with the patient; rather, they must really feel it. They must both feel and convey complete acceptance of their clients' beliefs, actions, and history. Rogers never set limits to his unconditional acceptance, which implies that client-centered therapists treating a pedophile or antisocial predator must accept the client's desires and actions on a visceral level. They are never to judge or correct, just provide unconditional positive regard.

As noted earlier, each of us lives in a world of personal experiences and is the center of that world. We react to the world as we experience it, in Rogers's view, because this phenomenal field is our unique reality. The only way in which therapists can appreciate the client's unique experience of the world is through empathy. Rogers requires that therapists experience their clients' world as if it were their own. Empathy includes feeling what clients are feeling about their world. This feeling must be conveyed by the therapist's choice of words in responding to the client. The therapist's tone and apparent attitude toward the client must give the client the sense that the therapist is not judging but rather is feeling what the client is feeling.

Therapeutic Goals

If the ultimate goals of psychotherapy could be placed on a dimensional scale, one end would be labeled **supportive** and the other **reconstructive**. The latter goal is typically associated with psychoanalytically derived psychotherapies and involves the reconstitution of a disordered personality. Reconstructive psychotherapy attempts to recapitulate the development of the client's personality through the therapeutic relationship and then restructure it through the release of misdirected life energies. To take an example described in Freudian terms, a person with an **oral personality** who is childish and dependent would be guided to release the libido that was fixated in the oral stage of development. The freed energy could then be used for better purposes, such as rational secondary-process thinking. The Freudian psychoanalyst proposes to help the patient accomplish this task through a process of free association, which will ultimately result in **hypermnesia** of repressed memories and emotions that occurred during the oral stage of the patient's childhood. These recovered memories will express themselves through anxiety-producing dreams and similar manifestations. The energy used to protect the patient's neuroses must be redirected in the form of transference toward the therapist. The therapist will, over an extended period of time, interpret the transference and other responses, leading to the freeing of the patient's fixated life energy. The patient's personality will thus be free to assume a higher level of maturity.

Rogers clearly did not believe that the Freudian approach was effective in treating psychological distress. He did advocate attempting the reconstruction of personality, but only to free clients to actualize themselves. The means that Rogers adopted to effect personality change is generally described as a supportive approach. In general, supportive psychotherapies are those in which problems are directly addressed through the interventions of the therapist. This group of therapies is in contrast to depth therapies, which purport to address the client's problem indirectly but at a deeper level, by revealing and eliminating the underlying cause(s) of the patient's problem. Supportive therapies are based on the tacit premise that the presenting problem is the actual problem and that it can be addressed by supporting the client's attempts to live fully. The support offered in person- and client-centered therapy is such that the clients, their goals, ambitions, worldviews, and beliefs, are validated. This supportive approach allows clients to become congruent and move more effectively toward actualization.

Interactions in Person-Centered Therapy

All psychotherapies require interactions between therapists and their clients. These can range from the very minimal interactions of traditional psychoanalysis to the more active dialogues that characterize cognitive-behavioral approaches. Rogers's approach lies toward the middle of the spectrum. He wanted therapists to react like real people but always to be cognizant that their clients are the center of the process. Rogers outlined and examined (Rogers & Roethlisberger, 1974) several ways in which people typically respond in direct communications.

Evaluative. When therapists evaluate a client's discourse, they are in effect judging or rating that client. An evaluation generally imposes the therapist's personal values on the client and represents an implicit demand that the client live according to the values of the therapist. A direct evaluation in therapy might include a comment like: "It was unwise of you to leave your old job prior to finding a new one." Or it might take the form of a leading question such as: "Do you think it was appropriate to say that to her?" Client-centered therapists typically avoid evaluative responses to client disclosures but are encouraged to carefully provide them when directly asked. To avoid doing so at that point would not be genuine. In his earliest works on client-centered therapy, Rogers (1946) specifically stated, "the counselor refrains from any expression or action which is contrary to [client-centered] principles. This means refraining from questioning, probing, blame, interpretation, advice, suggestion, persuasion, reassurance" (p. 416).

Interpretive. In an interpretive response, therapists tell their client what they really mean by their expressions. Such a response presupposes conscious denial or unconscious motives driving the client's relationship with the therapist. In addition, interpretative responses assume that the therapeutic process requires clients to become aware of their true motivations. In client-centered therapy, however, therapists are encouraged to trust their clients' actualizing tendency; thus, interpreting client disclosures would only disrupt the therapeutic process by possibly discouraging congruity on the client's part. Interpretation will tacitly encourage clients to accept the therapist's understanding of their actions or desires rather than to trust their own. Despite Rogers's proscriptions against therapists making interpretations, in practice, this type of **intervention** seems to be practiced routinely by client-centered therapists (Gazzola, 2003; Gazzola, Iwakabe, & Stalikas, 2003; Gazzola & Stalikas, 1997, 2004).

Reassuring. Reassuring interventions seek to persuade clients that they have been overestimating the magnitude of a problem and its consequences, or even misunderstanding its basic nature. The act of reassuring, however, may actually invalidate the client's perception of the situation. The therapist in effect is stating that the problem is not as bad as the client perceives it. This type of comment runs contrary to the organismic valuing process, which requires people to trust their own reactions and perceptions. Consequently, reassurance is contrary to the client-centered approach and is advocated only in rare instances. Client-centered therapy presupposes that reassurance will be conveyed effectively through the therapist's empathy, congruence, and unconditional acceptance. There is no necessity to communicate it to the client in so many words.

Probing. Therapists who are probing are seeking more information. This type of response is predicated on the premise that the therapist will use the additional information to make an interpretation, enlighten the client, or make a recommendation for action. Probing responses were generally eschewed by Rogers, as they tended to change the course of the therapy. The center of the Rogerian process is always the client. If therapists feel the need to ask a probing question, it must be done in such a way as to allow the client to ignore it.

Reflective. Reflective responses are the *sine qua non* of client-centered therapy. This type of response recapitulates the client's statement or monologue in such a way as to demonstrate a complete understanding of what was said. A reflective response should not add to or clarify the client's statement, just demonstrate the therapist's empathic understanding. The reflective response has been most the most caricatured aspect of client-centered therapy. The overworked phrase "What I hear you saying is. . . ." is an example of a client-centered response that has become part of popular speech and serves to demonstrate the reflective type of response in the most blatant way. In 1966, a computer scientist named Joseph Weizenbaum developed a therapy emulator modeled on client-centered therapy, which he called Eliza. It was an advance in computer science but only reinforced many people's impression of client-centered therapy as a series of repetitive restatements. Below is a transcript of an actual Eliza session (Weizenbaum, 1966):

Eliza: Hello. How do you do? Please state your problem.

Client: I need help with feeling sad.

Eliza: What would it mean to you if you got help with feeling sad?

Client: I would hope it would help me feel better.

Eliza: You say you would hope it would help you feel better?

Client: Yes.

Eliza: You seem to be quite positive.

Client: I want to believe you can help me.

Eliza: Why do you want to believe I can help you?

Client: Because I think I might be depressed.

Eliza: Is that the real reason?

Client: Yes.

Eliza: You are sure?

Client: Yes, I am sure.

Eliza: I see.

Client: I have been feeling this way for a while.

Eliza: Can you elaborate on that?

Client: For several months, I have had trouble getting going.

Eliza: Do you say for several months you have had trouble getting going for some special reason?

Client: I think so.

Eliza:	That's quite interesting.
Client:	Can you help me?
Eliza:	You believe I can help you, don't you?
Client:	I hope so.
Eliza:	You say you hope so?
Client:	Yes, I hope so.
Eliza:	I understand.
Client:	I really need help.
Eliza:	Can you elaborate on that?
Client:	I can't stand feeling this way.
Eliza:	Do you say you can't stand feeling this way for some special reason?
Client:	It's been going on for too long.
Eliza:	I'm not sure I understand you fully.
Client:	I have been depressed for a very long time.
Eliza:	That's quite interesting.
Client:	I don't think you are listening.
Eliza:	Don't you really think I am listening?
Client:	You are supposed to listen to me.
Eliza:	Does it please you to believe I am supposed to listen to you?

This truncated "session" with Eliza is rigid and mechanical, as one would expect from a fairly simple bit of software. On the other hand, it also mirrors what many think Rogers's intentions were: to merely reiterate what the client expresses. Whether or not Rogers's theory of personality or therapy was correct, nevertheless there is a greater skill required of client-centered therapists than simple rephrasing. Rogers required therapists to continually reveal through their replies that they are satisfying the core conditions for effective therapy. Mindless repetition or paraphrasing of the client's statements would be counterproductive and would most likely alienate the client. Empathic understanding surely would not be engendered by a therapist who persistently repeats only what the client says. Reflective statements must assure the client that the therapist has considered and understood what the client meant and felt when speaking to the therapist. A more appropriate approach is illustrated below from a famous demonstration session with Gloria conducted by Carl Rogers; in this exchange, a 35-year-old divorced woman discusses her guilt over initiating sexual relationships with men (Thorne, 2003, p. 54).

Rogers:	If she [her daughter] really knew you, would she, could she accept you?
Gloria:	This is what I don't know; I don't want her to turn away from me. I don't even know how I feel about it because there are times when I feel so guilty like when

I have a man over, I even try to make a special set-up so that if I were ever alone with him, the children would never catch me in that sort of thing. Because I am real leery about it. And yet, I also know that I have these desires.

Rogers: And so it is quite clear that it isn't only her problem or the relationship with her, it's in you as well.

Gloria: In my guilt. I feel guilty so often.

Rogers: "What can I accept myself as doing?" And you realize that with sort of subterfuges, so as to make sure that you're not caught or something, you realize that you are acting from guilt, is that it?

Gloria: Yes, and I don't like the. . . . I would like to feel comfortable with whatever I do. If I choose not to tell Pammy [Gloria's daughter] the truth, to feel comfortable that she can handle it, and I don't. I want to be honest, and yet I feel there are some areas that I don't even accept.

Rogers: And if you can't accept them in yourself, how could you possibly be comfortable in telling them to her?

Gloria: Right.

Rogers: And yet, as you say, you do have these desires and you do have your feelings, but you don't feel good about them.

Gloria: Right. I have a feeling that you are just going to sit there and let me stew in it and I want more. I want you to help me get rid of my guilt feelings. If I can get rid of my guilt feelings about lying or going to bed with a single man, any of that, just so I can feel more comfortable.

Rogers: And I guess I'd like to say, "No, I don't want to let you stew in your feelings," but on the other hand, I also feel that this is the kind of very private thing that I couldn't possibly answer for you. But I am sure as anything [I] will try to help [you] work toward your own answer. I don't know whether that makes any sense to you, but I mean it.

The difference between this typical client-centered session and the Eliza session is evident. Rogers diligently follows the content of the client's communications and the affect associated with them. Rogers's responses do more than merely reframe the client's statements; they exhibit the empathic understanding that Rogers regarded as essential. A common problem in conducting this type of therapy, however, is that there is a fine line between demonstrating empathy and making inferences or drawing conclusions that are not appropriate to a client-centered approach. In general, if done properly, the paraphrasing or reflective responses are subtle and tend to be heard as affirmations by the client.

According to Rogers, when therapy is conducted in an appropriate manner, the client's organismic valuing process is invoked and the client begins to grow as a person. The process that Rogers described is detailed in Table 12.4.

Table 12.4   Rogers's Principles of Client Growth

1. Clients are increasingly free in expressing their feelings, through verbal and/or motor channels.

2. Their expressed feelings increasingly have reference to the self, rather than nonself.

3. They increasingly differentiate and discriminate the objects of their feelings and perceptions, including their environment, other persons, their self, their experiences, and the interrelationships of these. Their experiences are more accurately symbolized.

4. Their expressed feelings increasingly have reference to the incongruity between certain of their experiences and their concept of self.

5. They come to experience in awareness the threat of such incongruence. This experience of threat is possible only because of the continued unconditional positive regard of the therapist, which is extended to incongruence as much as to congruence—to anxiety as much as to absence of anxiety.

6. They experience fully, in awareness, feelings that have in the past been denied to awareness or distorted in awareness.

7. Their concept of self becomes reorganized to assimilate and include these experiences that have previously been distorted in or denied to awareness.

8. As this reorganization of the self-structure continues, their concept of self becomes increasingly congruent with their experience; the self, now including experiences that previously would have been too threatening to be in awareness. A corollary tendency is toward fewer perceptual distortions in awareness, or denials to awareness, since there are fewer experiences which can be threatening. In other words, defensiveness is decreased.

9. They become increasingly able to experience without a feeling of threat the therapist's unconditional positive regard.

10. They increasingly feel unconditional positive self-regard.

11. They increasingly experience themselves as the locus of evaluation.

12. They react to experience less in terms of their conditions of worth and more in terms of an organismic valuing process.

▣ ROGERS AND PERSONALITY THEORY

Carl Rogers did not construct an elaborate theory of personality because he regarded each human personality as unique and not well described by combinations of traits or other abstract entities. In addition to its quality of uniqueness, human personality is also inscrutable. Only as individuals do we have full access to our own nature and personal phenomenological experience of our world. For this reason, Rogers did not believe that researchers can make meaningful rules or generalizations about human personality. He did believe that all people shared some qualities that are uniquely human. These include the desire to be free, creative, constructive, and benign. These desires will lead to actualization unless frustrated by external forces, he thought.

For Rogers, the drive toward actualization involves every aspect of our being. If the drive toward actualization is permitted free expression and we feel that we have free agency, we will progress to become an integrated whole. Rogers did not posit distinct structures, traits, or facets of personality. He did, however, make numerous references to unconscious forces within personality. For example, Rogers (1977) said, "The great puzzle that faces anyone who delves at all into the dynamics of human behavior . . . [is] that persons are often at war within themselves, estranged from their own organisms" (p. 243).

Although Rogers regarded the organismic valuing process as nonconscious, he did not place a great deal of emphasis on the role of hidden forces in defining a person's identity. He, somewhat like Pierre Janet (1859–1947) two generations before, envisioned unconscious psychic forces as the pathological isolation of motives and emotions, not essential factors of the personality. Because actualization involves the total organism, Rogers saw little need to define specific structural constructs. Like Karen Horney, he believed that personality can be altered by painful intrapsychic conflicts. But unlike Horney and any of the theorists classified as neo-Freudian, he did not believe that these conflicts must be addressed directly. Rogers maintained instead that people exposed to client-centered therapy that meets the core conditions for a sufficient length of time will find their way back to the organismic valuing process and self-actualization.

▣ RESEARCH IN AND CRITIQUES OF ROGERS'S WORK

Rogers's theories have substantial face validity and are quite elegant. Unfortunately, there is little research to directly support his central propositions. This situation is to no small extent a problem of definition. Rogers never clearly operationalized terms like genuineness, congruity, empathy, or unconditional positive regard. All of these terms have an intuitive appeal, but none are particularly amenable to research, as they do not lend themselves to operational definitions. For example, as a theoretical foundation, Rational Emotive Behavioral Therapy holds that a reduction in irrational beliefs will reduce the intensity and frequency of such emotional disturbances as depression. This theory can be tested by measuring an individual's irrational beliefs with a scale designed for that purpose, treating the person with an appropriate form of psychotherapy, and then retesting the person to see whether a reduction in irrational beliefs and depression has taken place. Rogers's resistance to psychological testing and other nomothetic techniques led to a dearth of operational measures for his methods. For example, he objected to the use of other professionals to rate a client's improvement, as he believed that clients had to be the arbiters of their own well-being.

Jeffrey Moussaieff Masson (1941–), a Sanskrit scholar who served for a time as projects director of the Sigmund Freud Archives, has become a harsh critic of all forms of psychotherapy. Masson (1984) was discharged after reporting that Freud intentionally concealed information about childhood sexual abuse to make his theory more acceptable. Masson (1992) believes that all psychotherapy is essentially exploitative, with client-centered therapy being no exception. Masson (1992) suggests that the core conditions articulated by Rogers can never truly be met because the "circumstances of therapy are artificial." He states that this is so because therapists can suspend their normal human reactions to other people during the infrequent and brief contact inherent in psychotherapy. For this reason, in their professional capacity, therapists are not real people reacting to others in a genuine way. Masson asserts that if client-centered therapists were to have more authentic interactions with their clients, they would not continually offer empathic understanding, lack of judging, or unconditional acceptance because these qualities do not occur in human interactions in the real world. Masson (1994) goes on to say:

> No real person really does any of the things Rogers prescribes in real life. So if the thera-pist manages to do so in a session, if he appears to be all-accepting and all-understanding, this is merely artifice; it is not reality. I am not saying that such an attitude might not be perceived as helpful by the client, but let us realize that the attitude is no more than play-acting. It is the very opposite of what Rogers claims to be the central element in his therapy: genuineness. (p. 232)

Rogers believed that the ties he formed with his clients were central motivating forces in their lives. But this claim is totally at variance with the theories he espoused. Rogers posited three necessary and sufficient conditions for effective psychotherapy: unconditional positive regard, empathic understanding, and congruence. For Rogers's theory to have a valid clinical basis, this essential premise must be verified (Lockhart, 1984). To date, there is little evidence to support the hypothesis that a therapist's providing these three qualities is sufficient to cure psychological problems (Cramer, 1990a, 1990b). The landmark study of psychotherapy out-comes by Mary Smith and Gene Glass (1979) indirectly refutes some of Rogers's key premises. These researchers statistically combined the results of 375 studies of the effective-ness of psychotherapy. They found that people receiving some form of psychotherapy were better off than 75% of the people who remained untreated. What is most interesting for pre-sent purposes is the failure of these researchers to find any difference in efficacy between client-centered therapy and any of the other major therapeutic approaches. By demonstrating that client-centered therapy is no more and perhaps slightly less effective than behavioral therapies, their work strongly suggests that the necessary conditions outlined by Rogers might not be absolutely necessary. This conclusion is supported by a study by Elliott (2001). He conducted a meta-analysis of 86 outcome studies of humanistic psychotherapies and found that all of them brought about some improvement in the treated clients.

In a study that directly tested Rogers's core conditions (Truax, 1970), 32 people hospitalized with schizophrenia were assigned to two groups. The experimental group was provided with supportive therapy emphasizing empathy, nonpossessive warmth, and genuineness. The second, group, the controls, received no therapy at all. The **outcome measure** of the study was the amount of time during the 9 years following discharge that the participants would remain without subsequent hospitalizations. The results were not at all in line with what Rogers might have predicted. The control group did just as well as the group treated with the client-centered approach. Similar results were obtained by researchers (Garfield & Bergin, 1971) who performed a study examining the relationship of Rogers's core conditions to outcomes. Tape recordings of the session were reviewed, and the therapists were rated on their empathy, warmth, and genuineness. In addition, the therapists were administered the Edwards Personal Preference Schedule (EPPS), a forced-choice test that measures individuals according to 15 normal needs or motives. The therapists were evaluated regarding the degree to which they possessed Rogers's core characteristics. The authors found no relationship between the degree to which the therapists provided the core conditions and the outcome of the psychotherapy. Interestingly, the authors of the study found that the therapists' tendency toward empathy and warmth was negatively correlated with their tendency toward genuineness.

Doubtful results were also obtained in a study (Meyer, Stuhr, Wirth, & Ruster, 1988) of three client groups: a no-treatment control group, a group treated with client-centered therapy, and one treated with short-term psychodynamic therapy. All the clients in the two groups that received treatments received 30 weekly sessions of therapy and were followed for 12 years. Cramer (1994) found that therapists who provided the core conditions elevated their clients' self-esteem. This researcher performed a path analysis (a type of multiple regression analysis) to examine the degree to which a person who has a current close friend considered unconditionally accepting, empathic, and congruent experiences improvement in self-esteem. The study included 38 female and 28 male university students. The results indicated that providing unconditional acceptance alone and the core conditions combined were associated with improvements in self-reports of self-esteem. What the study did not demonstrate is the role that these conditions play in psychotherapy and whether they are indeed necessary or sufficient for helping clients resolve their psychological problems.

Truax (1966) suggested that it may not be the core conditions that are the client-centered therapist's mediator of change. He found that Rogers was more likely to exhibit empathy and unconditional positive regard when the clients responded in the ways he was hoping for. Specifically, if clients showed insight, continued to focus on the presenting problem, or expressed themselves in a client-centered framework, Rogers was more likely to reward these behaviors with core behaviors. In effect, clients were being reinforced for making changes. The findings of this study are similar to the conclusion reached by two of the authors of this text (Abrams & Abrams, 1997). In reviewing transcripts of numerous psychoanalytic sessions, they concluded that the efficacy of psychodynamic therapies does not result from exposing or relieving unconscious conflicts but from challenging the irrational thinking of the clients. Just as Truax (1966) suggested that the core conditions outlined by Rogers are used as reinforcers for positive change exhibited in therapy, psychoanalytic interventions actually may be acting to challenge the client's irrational beliefs or cognitive distortions.

Most of the other studies that tested Rogers's theories by evaluating the effectiveness of client-centered therapy did not have adequate controls and actually tested the effect of only a single clinical intervention. For example, in a study of 142 hospitalized patients with both personality disorders and depressive, anxiety, or eating disorders who were treated with client-centered therapy, the researchers reported that the clients demonstrated significant improvements in depression, self-esteem, and social adjustment (Teusch, Bohme, Finke, & Gastpar, 2001). Other researchers found that 118 observers who watched a reenacted client-centered therapy session rated therapists who exhibited the core conditions through such behaviors as physical closeness and prolonged eye contact as being more skilled than those therapists who did not demonstrate the core qualities in those ways (Sherer & Rogers, 1980). Similarly, in a study of 42 clients who received client-centered therapy and were compared to a control group of wait-listed patients, the author concluded that client-centered therapy is effective on the basis of about 30 outcome variables (Pinter, 1993). Maisiak and his coworkers examined the efficacy of client-centered therapy for people diagnosed with systemic lupus erythematosus (SLE) or rheumatoid arthritis (RA), both of which are autoimmune disorders (Maisiak, Austin, West, & Heck, 1996). Thirty-six of the clients received client-centered counseling by telephone, and 37 received their usual care without the counseling. Clients with SLE who received the client-centered counseling experienced significant improvement, as measured by the Arthritis Impact Measurement Scales, while those with rheumatoid arthritis did not.

When comparative studies were performed, client-centered therapy rarely demonstrated an advantage over other approaches. What follows are several studies that are representative of those in which client-centered therapy is compared to another modality. When client-centered therapy was compared to training in problem-solving skills in 112 children with conduct disorders, only the client-centered treatment was found to be ineffective (Kazdin, Bass, Siegel, & Thomas, 1989). In a similar vein, a study comparing client-centered therapy to focused cognitive therapy for clients with panic disorder found that after 8 weeks, 71% of the clients treated with cognitive therapy were panic-free, compared to 25% of those receiving the client-centered approach (Stiles, 1979). Teusch and his coworkers compared behavioral therapy combined with client-centered therapy to client-centered therapy alone for clients suffering from panic disorder and agoraphobia (Teusch, Bohme, & Gastpar, 1997). The results indicated that both the client-centered therapy and the combined exposure treatment reduced panic attacks, avoidance behaviors, and depressive symptoms significantly. For several months, the combined treatment was superior in helping the patients cope actively with anxiety and improving agoraphobic symptoms. After a year, however, both treatment groups were equivalent in the reduction of anxiety and depressive symptoms.

In another study, client-centered therapy was compared to dialectical behavior therapy-oriented treatment for 24 clients diagnosed with borderline personality disorder (Turner, 2000). Outcome measures included blinded independent rater evaluations and a battery of patient self-report measures. The results of the study showed that clients receiving dialectical behavioral therapy improved more on most measures than the group receiving client-centered treatment.

In the last representative study discussed here, women with family histories of breast and ovarian cancer were treated with either client-centered therapy or problem-solving therapy to help reduce the life stresses associated with their condition (Inerney-Leo et al., 2004). The psychological status of 212 women with a family history of ovarian or breast cancer was assessed at baseline and again 6 to 9 months after they were tested for the BRCA genetic mutation. Women with this gene have a markedly increased risk of developing breast cancer. A comparison group consisted of women who had a family history of cancer but chose not to undergo testing for the BRCA gene. The women were assessed for depressive symptoms, intrusive thoughts about illness, worries about cancer, and general self-esteem. The results showed that the subjects who were offered problem-solving therapy had a significantly greater improvement in well-being than those receiving client-centered therapy.

The extant research on Rogers's theories suggests that the client-centered approach offers benefits to many people, but not as a result of Rogers's theory of the person. It seems that psychotherapy can be helpful without meeting the specific requirements set forth by Rogers. Most psychotherapists, whatever their theoretical orientation, strive to develop a working alliance with their client. They do not, however, all work to act as though they completely accept their client's views and predilections. Cognitive-behavioral therapists and rational-emotive behavior therapists will directly challenge their client's behaviors and beliefs and thereby violate Rogers's tenet of unconditional acceptance. Despite this practical challenge to

Rogers's most basic principles, these therapies work at least as well as client-centered therapy. And as shown in subsequent chapters, some of them might offer superior outcomes for many disorders. Because Rogers's theory of personality and his theory of therapy are inextricably intertwined, these data cast some doubt on the validity of his theories.

▣ CHAPTER SUMMARY

The Phenomenological Background. Rogers believes that we all exist in a **phenomenal field** of which we are the center. Phenomenologists consider that what is important in understanding behavior is not the object or event in itself but how it is perceived and understood by the individual. The phenomenal field is defined as everything that the individual is experiencing at a given moment. The determinant of our actions is, therefore, not objective reality but our view of reality. Openness and responsiveness to both inner experience and the external environment are needed to move in the direction of personal growth and actualization. If people were freed from restrictive systems of social rules when growing up, Rogers thought, they could achieve a high level of functioning and avoid distortions of reality.

Determinism Versus Free Will. Existentialism, discussed in Chapter 11, is based on the notion that we are free and that in fact, we cannot avoid freedom, which is a burden as much as a blessing. Humanism, also discussed in the last chapter, is based on the idea that human beings must be free to create and fulfill their potential and that they strive to do so. Rogers acknowledges that determinism—the philosophical doctrine that holds that all observable phenomena are causally determined by preceding events or natural laws—is a necessary foundation for science. As a therapist and a humanist, however, he believes that people have freedom of choice; that individuals are solely responsible for themselves; and that the goal of therapy and of life is to maximize freedom and to grow, create, and choose on the basis of our uniqueness, as free as possible from the rigid patterns others attempt to impose on us.

The Basic Nature of Human Beings. Rogers assumes that human nature is inherently healthy and constructive. The primary motive behind all human activities is the **actualizing tendency**, which is an innate tendency to enhance the organism and to develop our inherent potentialities. There is nothing inherently negative or evil about humankind, he thought. The two basic aspects of the actualizing tendency are maintenance of the organism (survival) and enhancement (growth and fulfillment). People who are free to develop their potential differ greatly in the goals they strive to achieve, but in general, they are characterized by flexibility, openness to life, and autonomy. The actualizing tendency is the source of human energy, and anything bad that people do results from the subversion of the actualizing tendency by the social order.

The Organismic Valuing Process. According to Rogers, human beings have a built-in guide, the organismic valuing process. Through its guidance, we know what is good for us, we will seek experiences that actualize the organism, and we will avoid experiences that do not. The organismic valuing process can also be understood as the inner evaluation of experience as desirable or undesirable for the individual. Rogers believes that people lose touch with this inner "barometer" as they grow up. They then become inflexible, living according to external standards imposed on them. Thus cut off from their inner selves, they fail to find fulfillment. Why does this happen? Because it is the price society forces people to pay for positive regard.

The Need for Positive Regard. As the self develops, it needs love, acceptance, and affection (positive regard) from others. Others (parents, teachers, other relatives, other adult authority figures) give positive regard only when we please them—in other words, conditionally. The result is that in order to obtain positive regard, we must cut ourselves off from our organismic valuing process. Rogers believes that we eventually incorporate the standards forced on us (similar to Freud's account of the formation of the superego) and must adhere to those standards to maintain positive self-regard. As a result of abandoning the organismic valuing process, dissociation (incongruence) may develop between a person's self-concept and his inner experience. In other words, the person develops a neurosis.

Unconditional Positive Regard. Unconditional positive regard, which Rogers considered the universal antidote to the problems caused by conditional positive regard, is the central contribution of his theory of personality and the cornerstone of his view of psychotherapy. Unconditional positive regard is a state in which we are prized for ourselves instead of being subjected to conditions of worth. Unconditional positive regard does not mean, however, that because we are prized unconditionally, all of our behaviors must be prized. For example, Rogers would maintain that parents can still discipline a child for inappropriate behavior—they should simply refrain from threatening to take away their love because of the behavior. Unconditional positive regard is essential in a therapeutic relationship because it allows the client to feel free enough to get in touch with inner experiences promoting actualization.

The Fully Functioning Person. The fully functioning person is an ideal rather than a reality because such an individual would have had to experience unconditional positive regard from significant others. Rogers (1959) conceived of full functioning as a process rather than a static achievement. He described the fully functioning person as manifesting the five attributes summarized in Table 12.2.

Chapter 13

Early Cognitive Views
of Personality

Chapter Goals

- Explore the early development of cognitive psychology
- Show the relationship of the introspectionist, gestalt, and social psychology theorists to early personality theory
- Examine the trend away from psychodynamic perspectives to those based on cognition
- Discuss in some detail the contributions of Gordon Allport, George Kelly, Solomon Asch, and Albert Bandura to personality theory

The dominant theme in personality research and clinical psychology in the early 21st century is cognition. As previous chapters have explained in more detail, the psychological explanations and explorations of the 19th century were essentially cognitive in their approach. William James sought to explore the nature of human consciousness, as did Wilhelm Wundt, Edward Titchener, and most influential psychologists of that era. Their goal was to understand the way people think, how they learn, and what motivates them to take action.

This trend was abruptly halted with John Watson's assault on some of the more inefficient methods—such as introspection—used to study consciousness. Watson and his followers, most significantly B. F. Skinner, waged a very effective campaign, described in Chapter 9, to make the behaviorist approach to psychology the one that most psychologists engaged in research and theory development would apply. Behaviorism made consciousness irrelevant; it maintained that universal laws of behavior can be constructed without any regard for internal states such as consciousness or emotions. Cognitive perspectives were related to the clinical realm, which was a very minor field in psychology until the latter part of the 20th century, and to the parallel field of psychoanalysis.

Psychologists who subscribed to a cognitive perspective were very much at odds with the behaviorists as they studied the processes within the so-called **black box**, the entity that behaviorists pointedly disavowed as being irrelevant to the study of the human mind. Cognitivists sought to understand how the brain processed sensory information to create the perceived world. Most operated under the assumption that there is far more going on within the human psyche than learning responses to various stimuli. Instead, the brain, which exists in physical isolation from the world, must rely on the sense organs to create models of reality. Those taking a cognitive perspective have endeavored to understand the processes by which each of us creates our reality. Just as we create our own reality in terms of our perspective on the external world, our personalities are similarly constructed. That is, rather than being the sum of all stimulus-response (S-R) connections, human personality according to the cognitive perspective is created by our unique and individual interpretations of social or interpersonal events and our chosen responses to these interpretations. Most of the time—but not always—people construct a reality that will be quite similar to the reality constructed by most others.

Generations before cognitive psychology became a dominant movement in the field, researchers studying cognition made significant contributions to the understanding of personality. Psychological concepts that are now nearly universally accepted were first advanced by the early cognitive psychologists. Such concepts—that people learn through observing others, that memory has specific limits, or that perceptions of the world may differ among people—are all derived from the early cognitive psychologists. While psychoanalysis ruled the clinical realm and behaviorism dominated academic psychology, the cognitive movement began with a school of thought called Gestalt psychology.

▣   THE GESTALT PSYCHOLOGISTS

Gestalt Psychology and Gestalt Therapy

A common error is the confusion of **Gestalt therapy** with Gestalt psychology. They are not at all the same and are only distantly related. Gestalt therapy was founded by Fritz Perls (1893–1970), a German-born psychiatrist and psychotherapist who developed a range of therapeutic techniques with the objective of helping the client more effectively integrate his personality. Perls was influenced by the Gestalt psychologists' premise that a person's perception of the world is self-created. He subsequently developed a clinical approach that purportedly treats each person as an entity that creates his or her own reality in the moment, a reality that can become uncoordinated. The goal of Perls's brand of therapy was to bring the person back into wholeness through various highly directed and somewhat eccentric techniques. This quest for wholeness is the only connection between Gestalt therapy and the Gestalt psychologists who brought a fresh cognitive perspective to psychological research.

Like the Gestalt therapists who adopted some of their principles, the Gestalt psychologists proposed that the psyche needs to be understood as a system that forms its own reality. Originating in Germany in the early 20th century, the Gestalt approach to psychology focused on the ways in which perception is constructed in the brain—ways that differ markedly from the data that the senses convey. The Gestalt psychologists maintained that human perception forms a reality that differs from the sum of the sensory data and must be viewed as a whole. *Gestalt* is the German noun that means "form" or "shape."

This paradigm is largely the product of the work of three psychologists, Max Wertheimer, Wolfgang Köhler, and Kurt Koffka, who shared Watson's rejection of structuralism. In direct contrast to the structuralist view that consciousness must be explored by breaking it down into fundamental units of consciousness (Koffka, 1922), the Gestalt psychologists worked in the opposite direction. They argued that the units that compose consciousness combine to create a whole that is distinct from its components. These psychologists studied the way that the mind organizes information conveyed by the senses in a way that creates meaning—often in a form that does not correspond to any objective reality.

What is generally regarded as the first publication of the Gestalt school was a paper published by Wertheimer in 1912 that explored the means by which the visual system can infer and interpret movement. In the paper, he explained that the brain creates the impression of movement from complex and ambiguous stimuli on the retina. By defining perception as a function of specialized brain areas that interpret data delivered to them by the sense organs, the Gestalt psychologists went far beyond both the behaviorist and structuralist psychologists of their era. They sought to discover the means by which human reality is created. In contrast, the behaviorists sought only to predict and understand behavior, while the structuralists were looking for the elementary units of perception and consciousness. Neither of the latter two approaches attempted to link the functions of mind to the structures and operations of the brain.

Isomorphism

This quest became expressed as the Gestalt doctrine of **isomorphism** (Koffka, 1935), which refers to a correspondence between a stimulus array and the brain state created by that stimulus. Isomorphism indicates that perception is a direct function of the structure of the brain centers that interpret sensory information. The Gestaltists were quite prescient in this postulation, which was eventually corroborated by neuroscientists such as David H. Hubel (1926–) and Torsten N. Wiesel (1924–), whose collaborative research on the visual system of the cat won them the Nobel Prize in physiology or medicine in 1981.

Hubel and Wiesel demonstrated half a century after Wertheimer that the visual cortex creates an isomorphic map of visual sensations (Hubel, 1995; Hubel & Wiesel, 1959). For example, if a person looks at a drawing of a circle, a set of neurons in the visual cortex is activated in a pattern that physically resembles the circle. Of course, the process does not end there; the neuronal activation that took the form of the circle is affected by many other brain regions that contribute to the processing of sensory information. The ultimate conscious perception of the circle is very much contingent on these interconnected brain structures.

In a similar fashion, the Gestalt psychologists anticipated the research of neuroscientists such as John O'Keefe (O'Keefe & Dostrovsky, 1971), who demonstrated that cells in the hippocampus of the rat are activated in a way homologous to recently learned movements. In effect, the nerve cells construct a type of map of recently learned movements. Despite the conceptual support of subsequent neurocognitive research, however, the human brain has not been shown to be directly isomorphic. The numerous modules of the brain interact to suppress, enhance, or refine the activities of other brain areas.

One interesting study demonstrated that once the brain finds meaning in an ambiguous stimulus—for example, Figure 13.1—neural connections in the temporal cortices undergo permanent change, which facilitates future recognition of the image (Tovee, Rolls, &

Figure 13.1	Optical Illusion: Two identical figures appear markedly different in size

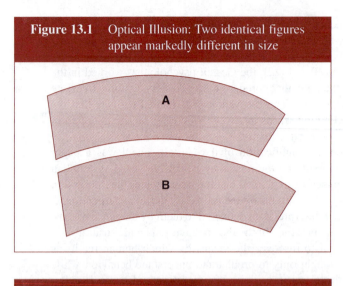

Figure 13.2	Optical Illusion: Squares A and B appear to be different colors but are actually the same shade

Ramachandran, 1996). This finding most likely explains why once we have discerned a partially obscured image, we can easily recognize it if we look again at the original picture. Findings like these demonstrate that brain operations are vastly more complex than a direct system of perceptual mapping or coordination. These operations also are more than the sum of their parts.

Optical Illusions

Gestalt theory postulates that the innate inclination for humans to impose order on the sensory world follows six laws of organization. These laws state in essence that humans impose order on the world. They make observations leading to familiar patterns that are not necessarily accurate. Why should our senses be prone to such inaccuracies? The reason seems to be that the brain finds it most efficient to organize the barrage of stimuli that besiege our senses in ways that are usually, but not always, correct.

Our brains can apprehend only a small portion of the sights, sounds, smells, tactile sensations, or other impulses that continuously trigger our sensory neurons. The distillation of this small portion would be most useful if the brain rapidly made "best guesses" about what is taking place. And these guesses would be biased in favor of finding the most familiar or probable events. The brain's estimates are typically guided by the context and setting, which are usually adequate guides to meaningful representations of reality. Optical illusions, however, can exploit these innate propensities to make guesses by leading the brain to draw incorrect conclusions about visual stimuli. Figures 13.1 and 13.2 offer two examples of visual miscues. One leads the observer to an inaccurate assessment of the relative size of two objects and the other to a mistaken judgment about color. The fact that judgments about reality are usually quite accurate is directly related to the principles of the Gestalt psychologists, who noted that the human mind effectively imposes structure on the sensory world.

A fascinating study that shed some light on the neural processes involved in some of these illusions was conducted by Aglioti and his coworkers (Aglioti, DeSouza, & Goodale, 1995), using a variation of the Titchener circles illusion. In Figure 13.3, the central circle on the left appears distinctly smaller than the circle on the right, although they are exactly the same size. As the Gestalt psychologists maintained, perception is a constructive process in which any mental image is a gestalt composed of the image itself and its milieu. Thus, people nonconsciously form an impression of the size of each central circle by using the surrounding circles as benchmarks.

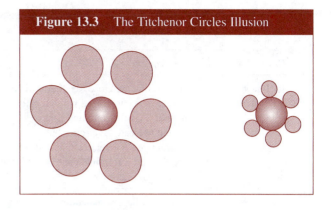

Figure 13.3   The Titchenor Circles Illusion

In Aglioti's experiment, he presented participants with plastic discs arranged in the configuration presented in Figure 13.3. As expected, most participants succumbed to the illusion and thought that the disc surrounded by the larger discs was smaller than the disc surrounded by the smaller ones. What Aglioti did not expect, however, was what happened when the participants were asked to pick up the central discs. As participants reached for the central disc, the space between their fingers was measured. The measurements revealed that the space between the fingers was the same whether the subject reached for the central disc that appeared larger or the one that appeared smaller. This and subsequent research (e.g., Smeets & Brenner, 2006; Vishton, Rea, Cutting, & Nuñez, 1999) strongly suggest that the visual cortex is deceived by optical illusions but that the subcortical structures that also process visual information are not deceived.

Why is our conscious visual system prone to these visual illusions while the phylogenetically older portions of the brain are not? The reason is probably found in the role of consciousness itself, which allows for the apprehension and processing of ambiguous information and situations. A conscious entity (like a human being) will be able to respond to vague or novel situations by extending or generalizing from past experience. This ability to make inferences from incomplete data sets would make humans better able to survive new and changing environments. But it also has the shortcoming of any intelligent system that makes inferences; it can make them incorrectly. It follows that a snake, whose visual system is roughly equivalent to the human subcortical visual system, would not be fooled by optical illusions, but the snake would do very poorly when confronted with novel visual situations. The human brain makes educated guesses.

Laws of Sensory Organization

Optical illusions like the figures presented above and other sensory phenomena were summarized by the Gestalt psychologists in the form of six laws of sensory organization, which are detailed in Table 13.1.

Table 13.1   The Six Gestalt Laws of Sensory Organization

Gestalt Law	Description	Example
1. Law of proximity	Images that are close together will be perceived as organized wholes, often as meaningful shapes and figures. To the right are 72 circles, but most neurologically intact people will tend to see them as a forming a square and three sets of parallel lines.	
2. Law of similarity	Items that have some common attribute will tend to be perceived as being grouped together. The figure to the right contains a grid of gray and blue circles. The tendency to see the blue circles as forming a triangle is an example of grouping by similarity.	
3. Law of good continuation	People will innately create an impression of vector or direction when viewing a contoured shape. This law will lead to the figure at right being seen as being composed of two flowing lines rather than, for example, four poorly formed V's.	
4. Law of closure	The figure at right will tend to be viewed as a triangle embedded within three circles rather than three circles each missing a wedge. This law is a result of the human inclination to fill in the gaps in lines that seem to describe a familiar shape.	
5. Law of prägnanz (good form)	Humans have a tendency to impose symmetry and order on images that are irregular or vague. Irrelevant or distracting aspects tend to be removed. For example, the two-dimensional Necker cube creates a perception of either of two cubes (focus on the dot and the image will shift), because our perceptual system tends to create the best fit for otherwise ambiguous images.	
6. Law of figure/ground	People are innately inclined to perceive an image as having a foreground and a background. The image to the right can be seen as a vase or as faces in profile, but it cannot simultaneously be seen as both.	

All six of the Gestalt laws of perception imply that the human brain imposes order on our senses, an order that is often useful but not necessarily accurate. The reality we perceive may not be objective but rather the one that our brain imposes on the sensory data. Given the limitations of the human senses, the brain's organizing capacity is highly beneficial. Humans can see only a small slice of the electromagnetic (EM) spectrum. More specifically, what we perceive as visible light falls in the range of 400 to 700 nanometers in wavelength, about 2% of the full EM spectrum.

A human ear in good working order can detect vibrations in the range of about 20 to 20,000 hertz (Hz; cycles per second), but the upper range is low in humans compared to those of other species; dogs can hear vibrations as high as 45,000 Hz, cats 64,000 Hz, and bats 110,000 Hz. But whatever the species, these vibrations do not become sounds until processed by the brain and are perceived accordingly. So the tree that falls in the forest does not make a sound; it creates vibrations that, if produced within the range of a hearing animal, will be perceived as a sound.

As the foregoing indicates, many auditory and electromagnetic vibrations fall outside the range that human senses can detect. Humans have a natural tendency to believe that their senses are providing the absolute truth about the world around them. The truth, however, is found in understanding how the senses help us survive. For example, the smells of decomposing animal and plant matter, which usually produce disgust in humans, will arouse the appetites of scavengers and insects. Humans who avoid rotting meat will be more likely to survive to reproduce, but organisms that can safely ingest them will have an adaptive advantage if drawn to them. So, in effect, there are no "bad" smells, tastes, or images. Such judgments about sense perceptions are created for us in our central nervous systems. We can perceive only a small slice of all that exists, and the way we perceive that slice is very much based on the way the brain interprets the information it receives from the sense organs. This key finding of the Gestalt psychologists is that all qualitative aspects of our experience in the world are manifestations of brain function.

The Gestalt movement had a lasting influence on psychology and the beginning of the cognitive era in research. It gave a new perspective to the study of learning and memory in that it rejected the behaviorist understanding of learning as a composite of stimulus-response (S-R) connections. Instead, the Gestalt psychologists suggested that learning may result from a sudden insight that can occur when the brain makes connections between apparently unrelated concepts. In this context, the gestalt is the synthesis of all the components of a problem into a new whole that contains the solution.

The Gestalt psychologists also offered a different perspective on how people view one another. We view other people not as collections of traits, isolated behaviors, or remarks but as integrated wholes. This emphasis on integration has been the principal contribution of the Gestalt school to personality psychology. That is, because people apprehend others as whole beings rather than viewing them as collections of traits, attributes, and situational responses, personality psychologists would be well served to study them in this way also.

▣ KURT LEWIN

The personality psychology of Kurt Lewin (1890–1947) was basically Gestalt psychology applied to personality theory and clinical psychology. Lewin called his approach field theory, which stated in short that a person's behavior is a function of all the person's attributes act-ing as a unity with the person's environment (Lewin, 1935, 1936). Lewin stated his theory in the form of a mathematical equation: $B = f(LS)$. This equation means that behavior is a func-tion of the life space. Another of Lewin's equations is $B = f(P, E)$, or behavior is a function of the person and the environment. Lewin called the entire entity a field because he believed that looking at the separate components of the person or situation would not describe the whole, much the same way as looking at the smaller elements of a visual field will not reveal what the person perceives.

Lewin maintained that behaviors and social interactions are guided by a person's perception of the world, which itself is derived from the totality of the individual's understanding of the relationships among the objects, events, and other people in their realm. People see the world and others around them as a gestalt—a whole formed from all their sensory and social components. They impose order on the world around them, which can result in different realities for different people.

Lewin, like many psychologists who developed original theories, used idiosyncratic nomenclature and developed quasi-scientific charts and mathematical equations to validate his models. Like many others who have done so, he framed ideas that were creative and original but not yet validated as scientific truths.

Gestalt psychology's influence on psychology has been more pervasive than just field theory. It has guided many educational psychologists to emphasize the importance of learning concepts rather than disparate facts. This emphasis is largely a result of Wolfgang Köhler's work with primates in the early 20th century. Köhler's paradigmatic study was done with four chimpanzees on Tenerife, one of the Canary Islands off the coast of Africa, during World War I. The chimpanzees were named Chica, Grande, Konsul, and Sultan. They were challenged with problems related to obtaining food placed out of their immediate reach. Köhler found that the chimpanzees would often discover ways to obtain the fruit after what appeared to be sudden bursts of insight.

Moreover, when one of the animals found a method to obtain the fruit, the others would learn it by observation. For example, Köhler placed a banana near the top of Sultan's cage far out of his reach. Sultan made repeated efforts to grab the banana, but then took a box and placed it under the banana to extend his reach. This maneuver failed, leading Sultan to kick and look at other boxes lying around the cage. As he was grabbing one of the boxes, he paused and appeared to have an insight. He then stacked the boxes on top of each other, getting far closer to the banana. Two of the other chimpanzees, Chica and Grande, observed Sultan using one box and were able to apply his method when presented with the same problem. They also discovered during a period of frustration that the boxes could be stacked, allowing them to get far closer to their goal (Köhler, 1925).

In a related study, Köhler placed a banana outside the cage beyond the reach of the chimpanzees. Within the cage, he positioned several hollow bamboo rods, each of which was too short by itself to reach the banana. Sultan first recognized that the stick could be a tool to reach the banana but was not able to extend his reach far enough to pull the fruit into the cage. He then used one stick to push a second stick to touch the banana, but of course, this maneuver would not allow him to obtain the fruit itself. Sultan did, however, react strongly to coming close to his goal. Köhler helped Sultan a bit by sticking his finger into the hollow opening at the end of a stick while the animal watched him. Shortly thereafter Sultan had an insight; he placed one stick inside the other to create a tool he could use to drag the banana into the cage. These results were particularly noteworthy, given that they were published when behaviorism was on its way to becoming the dominant school in psychology. The reader should recall that behaviorism did not allow for insights or **observational learning**. According to the behaviorists, animals and humans learn through reinforcement. In Köhler's experiments, however, there were no identifiable reinforcers guiding the chimpanzees to these solutions.

▣ SOLOMON ASCH

In addition to its influence on learning theory, Gestalt psychology influenced both social and clinical psychology. Solomon Asch (1907–1996) was among the first researchers to draw connections between social and Gestalt psychology and, in doing so, demonstrated important cognitive aspects of personality judgment. In a classic article, Asch (1946) demonstrated through 10 related experiments that people form assessments of other people by creating a unified impression that includes all salient traits. Asch's paradigm involved giving a group of subjects seven words describing a hypothetical person. The two groups of participants received word lists that differed in only one descriptive term. The results showed that the participants developed a distinct impression of the hypothetical person and created a complete personality, not merely a list of traits. It is also noteworthy that a change in only one term resulted in marked differences in the personality as described by the subjects. Asch concluded that people implicitly rate certain traits as more significant to personality than others, and they group traits into related clusters. Through these implicit processes, people form unified **schemas,** or cognitive conceptual frameworks, of others. Thus, according to Asch, people implicitly process information about others to form judgments about their personality.

Asch also proposed that individuals form social judgments on the basis of external cues, just as the Gestalt psychologists showed in regard to visual perception. Asch and his colleague Herman Witkin (1916–1979) performed several experiments (Asch &Witkin, 1948; Witkin & Asch, 1948) in which participants had to make judgments about the spatial orientation of a rod. Asch found that people's conclusions about the orientation of the rod were influenced by their perceived position and their judgments about the orientation of the room. These experiments demonstrated that a person's own location and orientation in space, as well as the relative position of other objects, are used to assess qualities like the size and position of an object. Our perception of the world is a relative process and is profoundly influenced by other factors used to orient the self and obtain a frame of reference.

Asch emphasized that the impression that we form of another person is a Gestalt or whole that includes the actions of the person, the setting in which those actions take place, and our state of mind (Asch & Zukier, 1984). This principle was exemplified by Asch's famous research in social conformity (Asch, 1951). In this study, the participants were told they would be asked questions related to visual perception. They were then shown cards with lines like those in Figure 13.4 and were asked to announce out loud which line in the second panel is the same length as the line in the first panel. In most of the 18 experimental trials, Asch had between six and eight confederates grouped with one naïve participant. Asch's confederates were told in advance which lines to select when making the comparisons. The naive participant was placed so that he or she would be the penultimate one to respond, forcing him or her to listen to most of the others announce their choices.

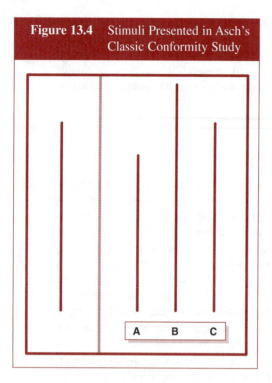

Figure 13.4 Stimuli Presented in Asch's Classic Conformity Study

Despite the apparent ease of making the correct selection, Asch observed that 75% of the naive participants yielded to the incorrect majority at least once, and 50% conformed to the majority in more than half of the trials. When the participants were interviewed after the study, many of those who yielded to the majority stated that they knew that the majority was wrong, but they felt compelled to go along. A substantial portion, however, denied that they yielded out of social pressure. Rather, they seemed to have actually adjusted their perception of the length of the line to conform to the majority's view.

Asch thus provided evidence that our perception of reality is influenced in social settings by our perception of the majority view. This finding is in general agreement with the work of the Gestalt psychologists, who found that human perception is constructed in the brain and strongly guided by context. Asch showed that this context can include the opinions of others.

Asch's research, however, needs to be considered in light of theorists such as Walter Mischel (1968, 1973) and Stanley Milgram (1974), who take a situationist view of personality. Situationists argue that our traits, temperaments, and other enduring qualities are less predictive of our behavior than the situation in which we are placed (Alker, 1972). For example, a person who appears shy in one setting may very well seem outgoing in another. By demonstrating that perception can be altered by social pressure, Asch's work provides support for this perspective.

The weight of evidence, however, seems to support the view that personality is produced by interactions between enduring traits and life situations (Bem & Allen, 1974; Endler, 1975; Furnham & Jaspars, 1983). This interaction between traits and situations is also found in all human measures from height to food preference. That is, innate characteristics interact with environmental variables to produce individual differences for almost every human quality.

The salient question in personality theory is: how much does personality change in cross-situational settings? This question was answered in a unique way by the theorist George Kelly, who did away with most innate traits while downplaying the importance of the situation. As he saw it, the answer to personality was found in the way an individual creates **personal constructs** about the world.

GEORGE KELLY

George Kelly is generally considered an early cognitive theorist. Although he refused the label of cognitive psychologist and his theories differed in some respects from what is considered cognitive psychology in the early 2000s, the label still fits him to an extent. Deriding

Freudian theory as nonsense and behaviorism as a meaningless jumble of stimulus-response connections, Kelly saw that personality emerges from the ways in which people predict and interpret the events around them. He called these interpretations personal constructs. While personal constructs are tested by people's interactions with the world, they also generate characteristic ways of acting—in other words, they shape the individual's personality.

Kelly specifically rejected the label *cognitive* because he felt it was too restrictive. "I have been so puzzled over the early labeling of personal construct theory as cognitive that. . . . I set out to write another short book to make it clear that I want no part of cognitive theory," Kelly (1969, p. 216) once wrote. In fact, Kelly rejected all labels for his theory (Winter, 1992).

Nevertheless, just as Kelly refused the cognitive label, the leaders of the so-called cognitive revolution spurned him. Kelly was primarily interested in conscious constructs, described in more detail below, and their applications in therapy, whereas contemporary cognitive psychology is interested in conscious and nonconscious cognitive processes in experimental settings.

Early Career

George Kelly was born on a farm in Perth, Kansas, in 1905. His father was a Presbyterian minister who became a farmer. Kelly embodied a certain pioneer spirit throughout his life, leaving home at the age of 13 to attend high school. He earned a bachelor's degree in physics and mathematics from Park College but decided to work toward his master's in educational sociology. Completing his M.A. at the University of Kansas in 1928, Kelly then studied at the University of Edinburgh in 1929. In 1931, he completed a Ph.D. in psychology from the State University of Iowa, writing his dissertation on speech and reading disabilities. Returning to Kansas, Kelly worked for awhile as a school psychologist, teaching at Fort Hays Kansas State College and running a traveling clinic to identify and treat problems in public school students. This pioneering clinical work forced him to seek different and innovative techniques rather than limiting himself to one approach.

Kelly entered educational psychology at a propitious time. World War II broke out in Europe in September 1939, and the United States entered the war in December 1941. The need for psychological assessment and treatment of servicemen and veterans increased dramatically. Kelly joined the Navy as an aviation psychologist, helping to screen and train pilots; through his work, he defined clinical psychology as an essential service that should be offered to military personnel. After the war, Kelly became director of clinical psychology at the Ohio State University. He remained at the university for about 20 years, developing its program in clinical psychology into one of the best in the United States. In 1955, Kelly published his most important work, *The Psychology of Personal Constructs: A Theory of Personality*. Kelly wrote little else, although a set of papers was compiled by his editor in 1969. Unlike most of the theorists discussed in this text, Kelly was not a prolific writer; however, he traveled around the world lecturing extensively, and he had a significant influence on his field through the students he trained. He was elected president of both the Clinical Division and the Consulting Division of the American Psychological Association. He was also influential as a consultant on many projects related to clinical psychology. Kelly was eventually appointed to an endowed chair at Brandeis University in 1965 but died shortly after the appointment in March 1967.

Early in his career, Kelly found behaviorism an unsatisfactory explanation of the human psyche and psychoanalysis too labyrinthine to effectively resolve emotional conflicts. His own answer became one of the first cognitive approaches to personality. As the title of his best-known book implies, Kelly's basic premises agreed with many of those of the Gestalt psychologists. Kelly did not, however, restrict his research to perception; he also attempted to devise a comprehensive psychological theory that found its locus in the mind of the individual rather than in external forces. The linchpin of Kelly's system is the notion that each of us creates and continually modifies a model of the world based on our life experience, our environment, and our style of interpreting both. He described his system as follows:

> Man looks at his world through transparent patterns or templates which he creates and then attempts to fit over the realities of which the world is composed. The fit is not always very good. Yet without such patterns the world appears to be such an undifferentiated homogeneity that man is unable to make any sense out of it. Even a poor fit is more helpful to him than nothing at all. Let us give the name *constructs* to these patterns that are tentatively tried on for size. They are ways of construing the world. They are what enables man, and lower animals too, to chart a course of behavior, explicitly formulated or implicitly acted out, verbally expressed or utterly inarticulate, consistent with other courses of behavior or inconsistent with them, intellectually reasoned or vegetatively sensed. (Kelly, 1955, p. 7)

Thus, Kelly, like the Gestalt psychologists, implies that each of us is an experimental scientist as we construct our own realities. Kelly's saying that people see the world through transparent patterns or templates implies that our perception of reality is structured by organizing principles that each of us develops for ourselves. Hence, all the events and interactions that people refer to as reality are actually personal models made up of a selected portion of sensory data. Kelly's model, although largely compatible with that of the Gestalt system, differed from it by focusing on our proclivity to create our own reality, in contrast to the Gestalt psychologists' focus on universal tendencies that guide and structure reality.

The Fundamental Postulate and Constructive Alternativism

Kelly (1955) set forth a **fundamental postulate** denoting the method by which people organize the world: "A person's processes are psychologically channelized by the ways in which he anticipates events" (p. 32). Therefore, according to Kelly, personality and all human behavior begin with the person seeking to predict future events. Our ongoing quest to make predictions about the world is guided by a network of interpretations that we acquire through life experience. People observe events and then infer—or construe in Kelly's terms—general rules about them that he called constructs.

Kelly emphasized that an individual's constructs about the world are a work in progress. In rejecting both psychoanalysis and behaviorism, Kelly also rejected the term *unconscious,* which to him implied dynamic processes. Instead, he used the term **preverbal** (Kelly, 1955, p. 344) to describe those constructs that are developed outside a person's conscious awareness. For example, a person may have constructs for predicting events and guiding behavior without being consciously aware of having them. This notion of preverbal constructs implies that Kelly believed that the process of construct formation is implicit or automatic, which is consistent with the work of recent cognitive psychologists (e.g., Abrams & Reber, 1988; Litman & Reber, 2005).

Constructive Alternativism. As we grow and develop, so too do our constructs about the world in which we live. Kelly's philosophy is one of **constructive alternativism,** which he describes as follows:

> Like other theories, the psychology of personal constructs is the implementation of a philosophical assumption. In this case the assumption is that whatever nature may be, or howsoever the quest for truth will turn out in the end, the events we face today are subject to as great a variety of constructions as our wits will enable us to contrive. This is not to say that one construction is as good as any other, nor is it to deny that at some infinite point in time human vision will behold reality out to the utmost reaches of existence. But it does remind us that all our present perceptions are open to question and reconsideration and it does broadly suggest that even the most obvious occurrences of everyday life might appear utterly transformed if we were inventive enough to construe them differently. (quoted in Bannister & Fransella, 1986, p. 5)

Essentially, Kelly proposes that people interpret life events and construct their own realities in piecemeal fashion from these events. Each of us is like a researcher who gathers data and develops hypotheses. Our research will replace old hypotheses when they fail to account for new data. We are also like researchers in having presuppositions or biases that guide the construction of our hypotheses. For example, a psychoanalyst observing someone making a series of misstatements will likely hypothesize that unconscious conflicts are resulting in parapraxis. A behaviorist observing the same events will hypothesize that the individual had been improperly reinforced. In the same way, we create explanations or models of the world based on our biases or expectations (Kelly 2003, p. 5).

Models. The concept of constructive alternativism is similar to the process in which Kelly sees people constructing models of the world. These models will differ from person to person, even if everyone experiences the same external data. Despite each model being equally real for the experiencing individual, not all models are equally good or valid. But Kelly states that until we are able to apprehend reality perfectly, we can never know for certain which construction of reality is best. It follows that because we have the ability to construct our own reality, we also have the power to view the world in ways that can be more or less pleasing. This principle was stated in a compelling manner in a summary chapter written late in his career:

> Who can say what nature is? Is it what now exists about us, including all the tiny hidden things that wait so patiently to be discovered? Or is it the vista of all that is destined to occur, whether tomorrow or in some distant eon of time? Or is nature infinitely more varied than this, the myriad trains of events that might ensue if we were to be so bold, ingenious, and irreverent as to take a hand in its management? Personal construct theory is a notion about how man may launch out from a position of admitted ignorance, and how he may aspire from one day to the next to transcend his own dogmatisms. It is, then, a theory of man's personal inquiry, a psychology of human quest. It does not say what has been or will be found but proposes rather how we might go about looking for it. (Kelly, 2003, p. 3)

Kelly asserted that his theory was both necessary and sufficient for all inquiries into personality and applied psychology. Although he is classified by most writers as an early cognitive psychologist, he rejected all affiliations with extant schools of thought, including the nascent cognitive school (Bannister & Fransella, 1986, p. 4). Kelly's rejection of classifying his personal construct theory within the subdiscipline of cognitive psychology seems to have stemmed from his literal interpretation of the term *cognitive*. Kelly maintained that his system included both reason and emotion; to label it as cognitive would have limited its scope. He believed that his system stood alone in its ability to elucidate the human condition. People, he thought, could be understood as empirical beings continually creating constructs to model the world around them, testing these models for their efficacy for functioning in life, and continually modifying them with new constructs when the old models fail in daily matters.

Eleven Corollaries

Kelly (1963) proposed 11 corollaries to describe the means by which people create and maintain models of the world that help them understand and predict the events around them. In so doing, Kelly seems to have anticipated some of the principles of cognitive psychology. Specifically, cognitive psychology has demonstrated that people can attend to only a small portion of the sounds, sights, and other sensations that they experience. Thus, our reality is constructed from a selected set of life events and sensory data. In addition, that construction is a function of the way in which we understand and manipulate the portion of the world to which we can attend.

Construction. "A person anticipates events by construing their replications" (Kelly, 1955, p. 35). In other words, people develop models of the world based on recurring or salient events in their lives, and these models are used to predict future events. For example, a student who has done well in school for a number of years usually expects to complete her remaining course work satisfactorily. The models are what Kelly means by constructs. Kelly suggested that nothing in life has an inherent meaning; rather, all meaning is constructed by the observer. The process of construing requires us to make interpretations about our experiences and fit them into a framework of other constructs that we have developed. In the case of a competent student, she will interpret her track record of successful course completion in the light of her other constructs about developing good study habits, taking care of her physical health, making friendships with other serious students rather than "party animals," and so on. Kelly stated that creating a construct requires that we construe its replication. Because most events are not repeated, however, this construal is itself a construction. Kelly's tendency to make his principles as universal as possible often leads him to be a bit labyrinthine, as the definition that follows indicates:

> By construing we mean "placing an interpretation": a person places an interpretation upon what is construed. He erects a structure, within the framework of which the substance takes shape or assumes meaning. The substance which he construes does not produce the structure; the person does. The structure which is erected by construing is essentially abstractive, though the person may be so limited in the abstraction that his construing may, in effect, be relatively concretistic. (Kelly, 1955, p. 35)

Individuality. "Persons differ from each other in their construction of events" (Kelly, 1955, p. 38). Just as people differ from one another, so too will their constructions of the world, the events therein, and the behavior of others. If people create different constructions or explanations about what they encounter in life, their behavior will typically differ, even in very similar situations. Thus, Kelly believed that each person is unique. Like such humanistic psychologists as Carl Rogers and Abraham Maslow, Kelly further believed that personality can only be understood idiographically.

Organization. "Each person characteristically evolves, for his convenience in anticipating events, a construction system embracing ordinal relationships between constructs" (Kelly, 1955, p. 39). After developing a system of constructs that organize and explain their experiences of the world, people will organize these constructs in order of importance and relevance to their life problems. Kelly proposed that an ordinal ranking of constructs is required, as an individual's constructs will often lead to contradictory conclusions about a situation. In addition, people may organize their constructs according to ethical, survival-based, or personal themes.

Dichotomy. "A person's construction system is composed of a finite number of dichotomous constructs" (Kelly, 1955 p. 39). In addition to organizing them into an ordinal hierarchy, we pair our constructs in a finite number of dichotomies. Kelly's constructivism viewed all beliefs about the world as subjective and relative. For example, if someone has a construct of himself as brave, he must be making this construct relative to a construct of fearfulness. If another person has a construct of herself as good-humored, she is defining herself in contrast to a construct of moodiness or irritability. This corollary of dichotomies is quite similar to the Gestalt law of figure and ground, in which visual perceptions are understood in terms of their settings. All constructs are, therefore, bipolar (Kelly, 1955, p. 74); that is, humans cannot conceive of black without white or good without bad. To illustrate this point in practice, Kelly used the example of a navigator:

> Ever since he left his point of departure he has been observing various events. He has made records of chronometer readings, of the declinations of astral bodies, of magnetic and gyroscopic compass readings, and of track. To these events he applies constructs from his professional repertory. For example, he may apply the constructs of longitude and latitude. Next, in relation to these navigator's coordinates, he creates a special construct of movement, tailor-made to the situation. The construct will be dichotomous, of course; one pole refers to the direction of which he is going and the other to the direction he is coming from. With this construct in hand, together with the coordinates of the hypothetical North Pole and certain other constructs, he arrives at a prediction that twenty-nine days hence he will reach the Pole. To predict is to construe movement or trend among surrounding events. The particular movement construed is always a construct tailor-made for a particular situation; nevertheless, it is one based on a standing system of coordinate axes having more general applicability. The point of convergence of all relevant constructs—time, the movement construct, and the coordinate readings of the hypothetical event—constitute the prediction. The next step is to see whether any event falls smack on this imaginary point so as to fulfill all of its presupposed conditions. That is validation. (Kelly, 1955, p. 86)

Choice. "A person chooses for himself that alternative in a dichotomized construct through which he anticipates the greater possibility for extension and definition of his system" (Kelly,

1955, p. 45). This corollary posits that when we encounter a situation in which we must respond, we will tend to make the response that will enhance our understanding of the world, thereby increasing our chances of making even better choices in the future. This corollary, like the individuality corollary, has a strong humanistic coloration. It implies that each of us is striving for self-actualization through our choices rather than merely meeting basic biological needs.

Range. "A construct is convenient for the anticipation of a finite range of events" (Kelly, 1955, p. 49). People create constructs to understand the world and make it more predictable, but no construct can apply to all situations. Some constructs might have comprehensive applications like the construct of good versus evil, but this construct would rarely be useful in judging a musical performance or the outcome of a baseball game. Fundamentally, Kelly's range corollary stipulates that any construct used to explain and react to situations does not work in all cases.

Experience. "A person's construction system varies as he successively construes the replications of events" (Kelly, 1955, p. 50). As each of us "successively construes the replication of events," we are continuously testing the efficacy of our constructs to predict events and explain the world. In performing this task, we will find some of our constructs are useful, and some are inadequate predictors of situational outcomes. The useful constructs will be left intact and the inadequate ones will be modified. A commonplace example of testing our constructs and discarding those that prove inadequate is the way that children starting to ride bicycles learn to use their brakes skillfully; they may make a tentative prediction that it will be fun to ride down a steep slope without braking, but a painful spill or two will cause them to modify that prediction. In short, Kelly stated that we continually learn from experience.

Modulation. "The variation in a person's construction system is limited by the permeability of the constructs within whose range of convenience the variants lie" (Kelly, 1955, p. 54). The more permeable a construct is, the more amenable it is to changes based on experience. Thus, if we have a construct for intelligence versus dullness but that construct is based only on standardized test scores, then it is relatively impermeable. In contrast, if our construct for intelligence takes social behavior, lifetime achievement, or other measures of intellectual ability into account, then it would tend to be more permeable or changeable. The modulation corollary depends on the experience corollary insofar as it requires the individual to establish a system to accommodate change—which is itself a construct.

Consequently, to have permeable constructs, we must have developed constructs that construe, or understand change, and thereby guide the modification of other constructs. As Kelly (1955) explains it,

> If we are to see a person's psychological processes operating lawfully within a system which he constructs, we need also to account for the evolution of the system itself in a similarly lawful manner. Our Experience Corollary states that a person's construction system varies as he successively construes the replications of events. Next, we must note that the progressive variation must itself take place within a system. If it were not so, we would be in the position of claiming that little everyday processes are

systematically governed but that the system-forming processes are not subordinate to any larger, more comprehensive system. We cannot insist upon the personal lawfulness of the elements of human behavior and at the same time concede that the patterns of human behaviour are unlawful. Nor can we insist that the elements follow a personal system but that the patterns can evolve only within a suprapersonal system. (pp. 54–55)

Fragmentation. "A person may successively employ a variety of construction subsystems which are inferentially incompatible with each other" (Kelly, 1955, pp. 54–55). With this postulate, Kelly points out that we cannot necessarily derive one construct from another in logical fashion; new constructs cannot always be inferred from prior ones. He posits that all constructs are influenced by the overall system of constructs but that no single construct can be assumed to be the precursor of any new one. In an apparent challenge to behaviorism, Kelly (1963) stated:

> This is an important corollary. It should make even clearer the assumed necessity for seeking out the regnant construct system in order to explain the behavior of men, rather than seeking merely its immediately antecedent behavior. If one is to understand the course of the stream of consciousness, he must do more than chart its headwaters; he must know the terrain through which it runs and the volume of the flood which may cut out new channels or erode old ones. (p. 83)

Commonality. "To the extent that one person employs a construction of experience which is similar to that employed by another, his psychological processes are similar to those of the other person" (Kelly, 1963, p. 90). Here Kelly states that people are essentially alike, with the only major difference among them being the way in which they construe events: "If two persons employed the same construction of experience, their psychological processes would have to duplicate each other" (Kelly, 1963, p. 90). Thus, if we develop constructs similar to those of another person, we will act and feel much as that person does. Kelly challenged the behaviorists by emphasizing that shared experiences do not necessarily lead to the same constructs. This phenomenon is explained by the experience corollary, which posits that constructs are a function of both immediate experience and all other relevant constructs that the person has developed in the past. Thus, two people can be exposed to an identical stimulus and generate very different responses. For example, studies of survivors of transportation disasters indicate that people's responses to the disaster are influenced in part by their previous experiences of trauma (Gil, 2005).

Sociability. "To the extent that one person construes the construction processes of another, he may play a role in a social process involving the other person" (Kelly, 1955, p. 8). Kelly believed that the 11th was his most significant corollary because it is the foundation on which people can relate to and understand one another. For social relationships to exist at all, people must be able to understand the actions and motives of others. Kelly did not require that people construe the same event in the same way, but he did state that they "must effectively construe the other person's outlook" (Kelly, 1963, p. 95). This corollary represents all theories or schemas that a person uses to understand and predict the actions of others. Such schemas are essential for all collaborative efforts in society, even those as mundane as driving through heavy traffic.

Approach to Therapy

Therapeutic Optimism. Kelly (1969) was an optimist who saw people as rational beings capable of using the scientific method in forming a set of personal constructs through which to make sense of reality. His optimism, however, was tempered by the understanding that some people cannot function in such a manner without special help. Kelly believed that humans are ultimately free: free from the past, their parents, and their upbringing, and free to adapt to reality in a way that maximizes rewards. But sometimes people lose sight of that freedom and box themselves in with maladaptive personal constructs. The goal of therapy is to help clients to regain their psychological freedom.

Therapy as Laboratory. Kelly was forced by circumstance to use innovative therapeutic techniques in his early years of running a traveling clinic for public schoolchildren in rural Kansas. Kelly came to describe therapy as a laboratory in which clients can perform experiments in behavioral change. Kelly thought that therapists should provide a permissive environment in which their clients are free to explore new behaviors and thereby change their personal construct system. Kelly also used self-characterization sketches, now known as **role-playing.** In this procedure, clients were asked to write a character sketch for themselves as if they were a character in a play. Role-playing has become an important technique in contemporary psychotherapy, particularly in group therapy settings.

In addition, Kelly introduced **fixed-role therapy**, which is in effect role-playing for a more extended but still limited period of time, usually 2 weeks. In fixed-role therapy, a client is asked to write out a sketch of his or her own character. The therapist then writes a sketch of a new character, not completely different from the client but different enough in some respects that the client will need to enact new behaviors outside the therapy room. For example, a person who describes herself as shy and not particularly physically active might be given a character sketch of someone who enjoys group sports, hiking, dancing, and going to social events. Kelly's use of fixed-role therapy was not to change the client permanently into the "new" character outlined by the therapist, but rather to encourage experimentation and provide "one good, rousing, construct-shaking experience" (Kelly, 1955, p. 412). Kelly is said to have gotten the idea for fixed-role therapy from seeing a friend "living" on stage the role that the friend was performing in a play.

Assessment. As Kelly believed that humans are rational and straightforward, his primary mode of assessment was the interview. As Kelly (1955) put it, "If you don't know what's wrong with a client, ask him; he may tell you!" (p. 140). As this approach indicates, Kelly had more in common with Harry Stack Sullivan than with either Freud or Skinner.

Kelly also devised a test to enable therapists to discover their clients' personal constructs, namely, the Role Construct Repertory Test or Rep Test for short. Clients list 22 people in their life who fit various roles, such as a sibling, primary care physician, closest friend of the same sex, former friend, the most intelligent person they know, the most successful person they know, a liked teacher, a disliked teacher, an employer, the present neighbor they know best, and so on.

After listing the 22 people, clients are then asked to compare them in groups of three. For each group, the client must describe which two of the three in the group are alike in some important way and which one is different. The way in which two of the three are alike is one pole of the construct, known as the emergent pole, and the way in which the third is different is the other pole of the construct, known as the implicit pole. When the client is finished, the therapist can see which constructs the client tends to use most frequently.

One of the listed roles is the name of the client. Suppose that the group of three people in one of the comparisons on the Rep Test includes you, someone you feel sorry for, and the most successful person you know. Which two are more nearly alike, and how are they similar? The reader can readily see that despite the limitations of the Rep Test, it can uncover items of interest and open up possibilities for self-exploration. For example, one subject might describe the most successful person he knows as someone who has earned large sums of money or has won a number of professional honors, whereas another subject might describe a model of success in terms of overcoming a physical handicap or some other hardship. Thus, the two test-takers have different personal constructs of "success" that they may wish to question or explore further. Kelly did not design the Rep Test to be standardized, nor did he intend it to be objectively scored. It has, however, come to be widely used in Europe and the United Kingdom to evaluate candidates for positions in the business world. In fact, it was used in two studies (Levy, 1956; Levy & Dugan, 1956) to test Kelly's premise that constructs are used by people to make predictions about the world. The results were supportive of Kelly's premises.

Goals of Therapy. Kelly saw what he was doing with clients as reconstruction rather than therapy in that he was helping them reconstruct or remodel their personal constructs. Kelly also used group therapy, which is an approach that works well in establishing a shared construction of the world. By creating new constructions, people can deal with life situations in new and more adaptive ways. People must be granted freedom, most of all freedom to change their constructs. And the therapist's task is to convince the client of such freedom and provide for its exercise (Landfield, 1988).

Summary

Kelly's work initially provoked a great deal of interest and research in psychology, which began to wane as result of his iconoclastic and highly independent approach. He sedulously resisted being classified or associated with any school or system of psychology. Kelly intended personal construct psychology to be a self-sufficient discipline, a new way of studying and conducting psychology. His model has been criticized, however, for lacking any explanation or theories regarding human development. For example, he does little to explain how children develop the ability to create constructs and how this ability matures once it is established. Kelly also failed to explain how basic drives and motivations interact with construct development. What motivates people to create constructs? Are there any attentional biases in selected life events that influence the development of constructs? Are there factors that discourage or distort construct formation? These questions are addressed only obliquely by Kelly.

More important, Kelly objected to classification within cognitive psychology because he saw that field focusing on thought at the expense of emotion. Despite this position, Kelly failed to explain the role of emotions in construct formation or personality development although subsequent researchers (Parkinson & Lea, 1991) did find personal construct theory to have some explanatory utility in understanding emotions. Kelly's emphasis on viewing each of us as a unique being who creates our own reality seems to have prevented him from postulating any universals about the formation of constructs. If there are constructs common to all people across history or constructs that are more likely to develop at certain times, places, or among certain people, Kelly did not expound on this possibility.

One last criticism in this vein: Kelly's work is based on a person-as-scientist model in which people are continually observing the world, creating hypotheses about it, and testing them for validity. The research of Tversky and Kahneman (1974), however, provides compelling evidence that people are very poor scientists when it comes to formulating constructs using probability estimates according to **Bayesian** principles. Instead, people use rules of thumb or cognitions influenced by evolution that guide behavior without the need for deduction or induction. The neurological researcher V. S. Ramachandran (Ramachandran & Blakeslee, 1999) made this same point quite emphatically:

> It astonishes me when I sometimes hear developmental psychologists assert that babies are "born scientists," because it is perfectly clear to me that even adults are not. If the experimental method is completely natural to the human mind—as they assert—why did we have to wait several thousand years for Galileo and the birth of the experimental method? Everyone believed that big, heavy objects fall much faster than light ones; all it took was a five-minute experiment to disprove it. (In fact, the experimental method is so completely alien to the human mind that many of Galileo's colleagues dismissed his experiments on falling bodies even after seeing them with their own eyes!) And even to this day, three hundred years after the scientific revolution began, people have great difficulty in understanding the need for a "control experiment" or "double-blind" studies. (p. 266)

Related to Kelly's assertion that people construct their own reality, he was a prime mover of the philosophical perspective called social constructionism, which is discussed in Chapter 16. Its essential premise is that truths about the world are constructed, not discovered. Even in fields as concrete as mathematics, social constructionists argue that the manner and means of representing quantities are socially directed fabrications that may be biased by the mathematician's point of view.

Kelly's iconoclastic approach to psychology did, however, stimulate a great deal of thought and research into personality and other disciplines of psychology. In fact, many of his fundamental premises have been validated. For example, Ryle and Breen (1972) found that people classified as neurotic had personal constructs that were less organized than those of people not so afflicted. Another early study showed that personal constructs as measured by Kelly's Rep Test were found to be the basis by which people select friends (Duck, 1973). Interestingly, this same study found that people tend to overestimate the similarity of their friend's constructs to their own.

In an interesting synthesis of the work of Kelly and Albert Ellis, researchers (Tobacyk & Downs, 1986) conducted studies that examined constructs relating to a person's competence and irrational beliefs as predictors of performance anxiety. The results supported the hypothesis that both inaccurate constructs regarding one's own ability and irrational beliefs that exaggerate the negative consequences of performing badly contributed to anxiety. McKain and his coworkers (McKain, Glass, Arnkoff, & Sydnor-Greenberg, 1988) performed a study of shy people and obtained comparable results. That is, shyness and social anxiety are strongly related to results on the Rep Test. More specifically, shy and socially phobic adults were found to have very few functionally independent constructs, which suggests that these people do not have a high degree of cognitive complexity. That is, they possess fewer distinct constructs to help understand the world around them, leading to a tendency to fear what they are less able to understand.

The results of research on Kelly's theories may be summarized as follows: People have different beliefs about themselves, about others, about the world, and about the way all three interact; and these beliefs play a role in the way a person performs in life. What the researchers do not explore is exactly how these beliefs or constructs develop, what may alter their development, and what role they play relative to other factors in personality. Kelly's importance has much to do with timing—namely, the period in which he put forth his ideas. He presented his theories when there were two dominant schools of clinical practice and personality theory: psychoanalysis and behaviorism. Both models negated the role of conscious beliefs or attitudes in daily life. In contrast, Kelly made the foundation of personality largely overt and reasonable. It is based on flexible and continually adjusting representations of reality that can be changed if the person is so inclined. And these representations can be consciously appraised and modified if life circumstances make it necessary.

▣ GORDON W. ALLPORT

We have encountered Gordon Allport in two previous chapters—an indication of the wide range of his interests and influence. Unlike many early theorists, Allport explored personality by studying psychological healthy people. He believed that information gained from researching psychopathology could not necessarily be generalized to the normal personality. In addition, he focused on traits, which is why he is often classified as a trait theorist. Allport's perspective could just as easily be classified as humanistic, phenomenological, or cognitive because he regarded personality as a function of a unique combination of characteristics that guide the way a person views and understands the world. Allport, like Maslow and Rogers, studied the factors that support high-level functioning in people. This interest meant that he did not study animals as the behaviorists did or base his theories on people in distress as the psychoanalysts did. Instead, his interest was in personality per se. As a result, Allport was one of the first psychologists to focus on this subject.

The Social Dimension of Personality

Allport viewed personality as the product of a composite of traits unique to each individual. Although allowing for social influences on personality, he saw personality as the "true nature" (Allport, 1961, p. 24) of the individual, which arises from within and changes gradually over the person's life span. Allport

Photo 13.1 Gordon W. Allport (1897–1967)

acknowledged that social interaction is required for an individual's personality to find full expression:

> We are incapable of giving a complete popular description of personality without indicating the manner in which the personality in question stimulates or influences other human beings and the manner in which the behavior of other human beings produces adjustments or responses in the personality in question. In describing this personality we inevitably take the view-point of those "other human beings." Robinson Crusoe, alone on a desert island, undoubtedly displayed a very measurable degree of intelligence in his adaptation to his environment. It was only with the advent of Friday, however, that his personality could be said to stand forth in its full significance. Not only is the language of personality a social one, but, the problems arising from the interaction of various personalities are in the truest sense social problems. They include every form of social maladjustment—from the whims of the eccentric to the worst deeds of the criminal. In general it may be said that the aim of personality measurements is the establishing of adjustments between an individual and his fellows which are a benefit to both. (Allport & Allport, 1921)

According to Allport's perspective, Robinson Crusoe would have possessed the same essential personality whether or not Friday had arrived on the castaway's island. Friday's presence was required, however, for Crusoe's personality to be more fully expressed. In effect, traits and other inherent aspects of personality are only potential guides for behaviors requiring interpersonal interaction for complete expression. In contrast to the more recent theorists who take a situationist view, however, Allport believed that our personality exists even in isolation. Each of us possesses a unique configuration of traits shaped by life events and vicissitudes. While we are unique, the traits that make up our personality are universal. In a similar fashion, each musical composition is unique while at the same time using the notes of the scale common to all pieces of music.

Allport's work in refining the concept of personality as a function of distinct traits was sufficient to make him a significant figure in personality psychology for that alone. Allport and Odbert (1936) identified about 17,953 words in English used to describe human attributes or traits. This list was distilled to 4,500 by removing terms they deemed redundant or immeasurable. Allport reasoned that the presence of such adjectives in natural language provides evidence of the existence of the characteristics they describe.

Allport's view of human beings as unique entities led to his rejection of the psychodynamic premise that biological drives are the primary source of personality and motivation:

> The doctrine of drive is a rather crude biological conception . . . inadequate to account for adult motivation, useful to portray the motives of young children. . . . After infancy primitive segmental drive rapidly recedes in importance, being supplanted by the more sophisticated type of motives characteristic of the mature personality. (cited in Guntrip, 1971, p. 82)

Instead, humans are motivated by a combination of social and individual factors. Although Allport did not deny the existence of biological needs underlying some human behavior, he viewed the biological dimension of personality as far less important then a person's traits. In his view, a trait is "a generalized and focalized neuropsychic system (peculiar to the individual), with the capacity to render many stimuli functionally equivalent, and to initiate and guide consistent (equivalent) forms of adaptive and expressive behavior" (Allport, 1937, p. 295).

In simpler terms, traits arise within the human brain but differ in their expression from person to person. They allow us to process complex events that we all are exposed to in daily life. Although many of these sensory, personal, or interpersonal events may differ in type or degree, many of them may also necessitate similar actions from the person to accommodate or adjust to them. Allport's use of the term *neuropsychic* was intended to allow for the eventual association of traits with behavioral inclinations and the brain. This was also the view of other theorists, such as Harry Stack Sullivan and Sigmund Freud. Allport viewed traits as mechanisms that allow individuals to respond to complex and divergent life events in a consistent and adaptive way. For example, if a person has the trait of friendliness and is engaged by a salesperson, he will be likely guided by this trait to respond to the salesperson with a greeting and to pay attention to the sales offering. If this same person is in a very different situation, perhaps being stopped by a police officer for speeding, his trait would still guide his behavior to react in a way that most people would describe as friendly. These two events, being approached by a salesperson and being stopped by a police officer, are different stimuli, but the trait of friendliness makes them functionally equivalent. That is, both incidents become interpersonal encounters requiring social amenities and polite discussion.

Individual and Common Traits

In addition to defining the preceding characteristics, Allport divided traits into two essential categories, individual and common. Because Allport saw traits as "peculiar to the individual," he believed that no trait would manifest itself in the same way in different people. Traits that define the unique organization of a particular individual's personality are individual traits. (In Allport's later career, he used the term *disposition* to refer to individual traits.) Typically, individual traits are consistent within each person. An illustrative example might be extreme suspiciousness, which makes the person hesitant and hostile in all social encounters. A nomothetic approach to personality study requires that people have some commonalities, which Allport included in his description. He stated that despite numerous differences, normal people developing in similar cultures will evolve similar styles of adjusting to life events (Allport, 1937). These similarities in adjustment styles are what he termed **common traits**. Allport emphasized that both individual and common traits need to be explored if the personality of any individual is to be understood.

Allport's two larger categories of traits included three subcategories: cardinal traits, central traits, and secondary dispositions. Allport believed that few people actually possess cardinal traits, but when they exist within a person they thoroughly dominate the personality. Virtually everything the person does can be seen to originate from this trait. Because such dominating traits are usually maladaptive, few people have them. Instead, Allport (1937) proposed, most personality differences among individuals result from central traits, which he described as follows:

> The foci of personality (though not wholly separate from one another) lie in a handful of distinguishable central traits. Central traits are those usually mentioned in careful letters of recommendation, in rating scales where the rater stars the outstanding characteristics of the individual or in brief verbal descriptions of a person. (p. 338)

Table 13.2   Characteristics of a Trait According to Allport

Characteristic	Explanation
Traits have a more than nominal existence.	Traits describe enduring behavioral attributes of a person. They are produced by the same mechanisms that produce generalized habits, but traits are more consistent and enduring.
A trait is more generalized than a habit.	Habits tend to be evoked by specific situations or stimuli. In contrast, traits are inclinations that cross situations and can be evoked by divergent stimuli.
A trait is dynamic, or at least determinative.	Unlike responses in classical or operant conditions, traits do not require a stimulus to exist. They are potentials within the person that motivate and direct behavior.
The existence of a trait can be established empirically or statistically.	Because traits can be observed across situations or even without eliciting stimuli, they are best inferred from statistical techniques that can extract information from a variety of behavioral indicators.
Traits are relatively independent of one another.	The characteristics that traits describe should be statistically unrelated or uncorrelated. That is, a person should be able to have one trait without having the features of another. For example, one can be extraverted with or without being neurotic.
A personality trait, psychologically considered, is not the same as a moral quality.	Constructs that are socially defined and differ among societies are not the same as traits. The former tend to be transient, arbitrary, and independent of the person, while the latter are characteristics of the person.
Acts and even habits that are inconsistent with a trait do not prove the nonexistence of the trait.	People can act against their inclinations in certain circumstances. For example, a person with the trait of introversion can behave in an extraverted fashion among people he or she knows well. This behavior would not necessarily disprove the existence of the trait of introversion.

SOURCE: Allport (1960).

Secondary dispositions are also consistent personality inclinations, but they are less obvious and less consistent in their influence in behavior. They can be described as attitudes and may only appear in a few specific situations. Overall, Allport believed that most people have no cardinal traits, between 5 and 10 central traits, and a little more than a dozen secondary dispositions.

Functional Autonomy

In basing his theory of personality on traits that are largely conscious or accessible to consciousness, Allport rejected all explanations of adult human behavior founded on instinctual or innate drives. These theories included the transitory instincts proposed by William James (Allport, 1950b), the neurologically based drives of Robert Woodworth, and the unconscious motives of the psychoanalysts. According to Allport, people must cope with too many complex social situations and life adversities to survive using only innate or instinctual behaviors. Instead, he proposed a personality system based in the traits that begin as responses to life demands and then develop **functional autonomy** (Allport, 1937). What Allport meant by functional autonomy is that these traits become part of the individual's personality and function independently of the stimuli that initiated their development. For example, a child who grows up in a family of musicians may take piano lessons to please the parents or to fit in with the rest of the family and then continue to sing or play a keyboard instrument in adult life because he or she genuinely enjoys making music.

Allport's concept of functional autonomy effectively challenged the prevailing behaviorist position that humans have no autonomy but are purely the products of conditioning. In effect, our traits can manifest in the absence of the original events that motivated them, and our actions and decisions are under our control to develop over our life span. This concept, in its rejection of psychoanalytic and behavioral models of personality, provoked a controversy in psychology. Allport's assertion that our motives change throughout our life effectively challenged the behaviorist principle that our motives or actions will not change if the eliciting stimuli do not change. Allport similarly dispensed with psychoanalytic theory when he rejected the psychoanalytic preoccupation with libido or thanatos as the sole sources of human motivation and proposed that personality is a dynamic and growing system. Allport commented on the controversy:

> I had no idea [functional autonomy] would become controversial over the years. To me it was simply a way of stating what was perfectly obvious to me, that motives change and grow in the course of one's life. Our motivational structure is not today functionally dependent upon what we were at the age of three or four, or even fifteen. Motives change and grow, and I still can't understand why a person would challenge that basic proposition unless he were a die-hard believer in reactivity instead of proactivity, of homeostasis instead of transcendence, of balance or equilibrium instead of growth. But a person who is totally devoted to a stimulus-response view, I could understand, would not like the concept at all. To me it is more or less self-evident. I realized that it wasn't self-evident to others when I had to defend it and try to answer the very difficult question of how functional autonomy comes about. That leads us into the technical side of the picture. It seems to me to be an essential element to a sound theory of personality. Most theories stress the importance of events which occur early in life through conditioning, and the analytical theory requires that the life be traced backward in time. But people are busily living their lives forward. (quoted in Evans, 1970, p. 29)

Allport's contention that personality develops across the life span required him to tacitly reject all theories of personality predicated on preordained stages of development. Thus, the developmental theories of Freud, Erikson, and even Piaget are not fully compatible with Allport's theory. In this sense, Allport was a strongly humanistic or phenomenological thinker. Like the humanists who would follow him, and like Adler who preceded him, Allport considered social factors and other life events to be essential forces in personality development.

The personality according to Allport is a composite of all mental processes within the boundary of the person:

> Without the coordinating concept of person (or some equivalent, such as self or ego), it is impossible to account for the interaction of psychological processes. Memory affects perception, desire influences meaning, meaning determines action, and action shapes memory; and so on indefinitely. This constant interpenetration takes place within some boundary, and the boundary is the person. (Allport, 1961, p. 553)

The person or personality according to Allport is a unity that emerges from the sum of its parts, which include our physical attributes, our temperament, and our intellectual capabilities. Allport considered **temperament** to be a function of our tendency to respond to environmental events, the typical intensity of that response, and our prevailing mood. He considered temperament to be largely hereditary but also shaped to some degree to meet situational or social demands. Allport clearly anticipated many concepts that would later be known in cognitive psychology as information processing. And his vision of personality was essentially a cognitive view, in which a person consists of all the dynamically interactive mental modules brought into unity in the person.

VIGNETTE

Brian was a popular figure on his college campus; he played the piano in the student lounge, was popular with the women, and had more party invitations than he could accommodate. Somewhat sedate in nature, Brian was still an engaging conversationalist and could talk intelligently about a wide range of topics. In addition to his love of music, he was fascinated by history and current politics. He was able to combine these passions in a remarkably creative fashion by writing a musical play about a political figure. The musical was actually performed by a major theater company and received good reviews.

The future looked very promising for Brian at his college graduation. He had been accepted by a graduate program in the fine arts at a prestigious university, and he had found a new girlfriend who intended to go to the same graduate school. There seemed to be no barriers to a happy and successful life.

In the first weeks of graduate school Brian seemed to accommodate quite nicely. He was sharing an apartment with his girlfriend; he was doing well in class, had written several new pieces of music, and was working on a new musical. But then the changes began. Brian's temperament changed from quiet to withdrawn. While he did not appear to be depressed, he seemed to have lost interest in things that had formerly given him pleasure—including his girlfriend.

Brian became indifferent to her; it was as though he found it hard work to even talk to her. She pleaded with him to explain what was going on. He denied that there was anything wrong. After failing at repeated efforts to draw him out, she left the relationship. Brian reacted to her leaving by stating that he was feeling tired—as he would assert when facing almost any life stressor.

Brian's new indifference to his graduate work led to his being placed on academic probation and a strong recommendation to visit the school's mental health department. It would have been an understatement to say that Brian was not receptive to counseling. He was hostile and uncommunicative with the counselor. When she suggested that he was depressed, he responded by calling her a quack and strongly denying that he was unhappy with anything. Within a few weeks, Brian left graduate school. His withdrawal from the university was followed by a brief stay with his parents, which amounted to a brief civil war in which he parried all of their statements of concern with attacks on their parenting. They could not bear his rage and asked him to leave the house; but they also offered to help defray the costs of renting an apartment.

Indeed, Brian was not depressed, but he was a different person. For the next few years, he moved from one menial job to another. His avocation was seeking alternative health care for the chronic fatigue and muscle tension he experienced. And there was no shortage of fringe practitioners who would treat him for these ailments. His rejection of mainstream medical care shortly became an obsession with him. Medicine, he thought, was an evil conspiracy that enriched a few people by poisoning others with drugs and chemotherapy. So Brian continued to seek health care from fringe practitioners who gladly took his money and provided treatments that were bizarre at best.

When Brian reached his forties, he was still apparently schizotypal but able to focus enough to go back to graduate school. He completed his degree, became a music teacher in a middle school, and actually established a stable relationship with a woman a few years older than himself. Brian's difficult life is an example of a radical personality change. Although personality is usually stable across a person's lifespan, there are cases like Brian's in which a striking change profoundly alters the person's life.

Vignette Questions

1. How might Kelly and Allport explain the personality changes that Brian exhibited?

2. Can you think of other reasons for his change that do not fit into their theories of personality?

3. If not, detail why you think they offer a complete explanation; if so, explain.

The Proprium and Propriate Striving

The person, then, is the unifying force that makes a whole of all sensory, perceptive, and motivational functions. Allport (1961) viewed personality as a force within the person that is always striving for a more perfect unity of its many components; this search is a lifelong process. Consequently, the more unified a personality is, the better functioning Allport would consider it to be. He coined the term proprium to describe the unifying aspect of personality. Allport's proprium is roughly equivalent to Freud's ego, differing in that Allport rejected Freud's notion of powerful unconscious forces underlying the ego. Thus, the proprium is the core or essence of the self and is capable of guiding us to make constructive changes in our lives. Allport saw the proprium as a product, not of the brain alone, but of interactions between the brain and all other body organs. Our sense of our body and its physical condition play a significant role in personality in Allport's model.

The Proprium. The proprium consists of eight components that arise in the course of development. Allport, like most personality theorists, believed that personality develops incrementally during maturation, and that events during this time can alter the shape of the personality. Although firm in his belief that personality has a strong heritable component, he also saw the environment as a powerful force that shapes or molds inherited dispositions. The eight aspects of the proprium are listed in order of their development (a fuller discussion can be found in Chapter 9:

1. *Sense of bodily self*

2. *Sense of continuing self-identity*

3. *Self-esteem*

4. *Self-extension*

5. *Self-image*

6. *Self as rational coper*

7. *Propriate striving*

8. *Self as knower*

Propriate Striving. The proprium or self, according to Allport, is the sum of all of a person's inclinations that are activated by a person's motivation. Here Allport disagreed significantly with the Freudian model, which holds that all motivation is derived from a fixed quantity of sexual or aggressive energy. Allport believed that people are motivated by a combination of their basic appetites, their conscious desires, and the demands of the environment. But people can shape or alter their environments to effectively alter what motivates their behavior. In fact, Allport proposed that people seek to stimulate the appetites that motivate them. He regarded this characteristic as a conscious and volitional process, required for psychological health. That is, he believed that we have a basic need to shape the world around us proactively. Propriate striving is manifested by exploring, interacting with, and shaping the world around us. Ideally, such striving leads to a process of continual growth of the proprium throughout life. Accordingly, personality is not a static entity but a dynamic and growing system.

Proper growth of personality requires the development of skills to meet the demands of living and psychological well-being. Thus, we are both reactive to environmental demands and proactive in making personal changes. To Allport, mental health meant the attainment of psychological maturity, which included having a well-developed proprium, manifested by the following characteristics:

1. Extension of the sense of self such that we are involved in some vital issue that gives purpose to our life.

2. The ability to develop close, trusting, and dependable relationships with significant others.

3. Emotional security and self-acceptance.

4. The development of a realistic assessment of the world.

5. The ability to focus on and solve life problems.

6. The ability to be objective about ourselves while keeping a sense of humor.

7. Acceptance of a unifying life philosophy with ethical or religious values.

Clearly, Allport's concept of a mature individual agrees with that of most laypeople. What is significant is that he emphasized people's ability and desire to strive toward maturity. His position is particularly interesting in light of more recent evolutionary psychology, whose proponents maintain that most human traits are innate. Allport, as an early trait theorist, is perfectly consistent with this perspective. He also considered traits to be inclinations rather than an absolute destiny. We are not the prisoners of our traits; with effort, we can overcome those that are barriers to emotional health.

Summary

Despite being best-known as a trait theorist, Allport developed a relatively comprehensive theory of personality that viewed each person as unique because there is an infinite potential combination of traits and degrees to which each trait is manifested in a person. Allport believed that people could consciously apprehend their traits and modify them as necessary. This is why his theory can be considered a cognitive approach. Allport's proprium—the essence of a person—is self-aware and eager to reach toward personal excellence. We consciously seek to suppress our undesirable traits and emphasize those that enhance our life. Allport did not view personality as the tip of an iceberg with most of its components below the surface, but rather like the humanists, he regarded it as a conscious force striving for self-development. This desire for emotional health and stability is a primary source of motivation in human life. Allport broke with the traditional psychoanalytic view by deemphasizing the role of childhood in personality development. Equally important, his theories were not founded on case studies, as he was not a clinician, but on research, statistics, and scientific principles.

🔲 SOCIAL COGNITIVE VIEWS: JULIAN ROTTER AND ALBERT BANDURA

Prior to any formal discussions of social learning, John Dollard and Neal Miller, who were discussed in Chapter 10, proposed that personality is guided by learning in ways that are more complex than the more simplistic stimulus-response (S-R) models. They, like some other early behaviorists, allowed for rudimentary cognitive evaluations as mediators for learning how to respond to the world. That is, Dollard and Miller maintained that the thoughts and judgments of learners play a role in what they learn and consequently in how they behave. Like several other like-minded psychologists of the 1940s and 1950s, they emphasized the role of internal drives, traits, or other psychic or physical structures that guide personal development of the person.

None of these theorists, however, emphasized social forces as a factor in personality formation. This perspective has been set forth most compellingly by Julian Rotter (1916–) and Albert Bandura. These men conceived of personality as arising from interactions between people and their social environment. This approach is called the social learning perspective of personality, which, like other theories that followed behaviorism, does not require direct reinforcement to explain learning and personality development. Social learning theorists believe that people learn social behavior through observing others and that this learning plays an essential role in personality formation. **Social learning theory** is a cognitive approach because it maintains that human beings reflect on and decide what social events are relevant to their lives.

Julian Rotter

Julian Rotter (1954, 1960) constructed one of the earliest cognitive approaches that became the foundation of most social learning theories, which in turn strongly influenced psychology for the latter part of the 20th century. Rotter, who was primarily a clinical psychologist, did not view people as simple subjects of reinforcement. Instead, he saw a great degree of complexity and volition in a person's behavior. In contrast to his behaviorist contemporaries, Rotter viewed personality as a very real construct, derived from internal forces interacting with social and environmental factors. Unlike the behaviorists, Rotter (1960) saw people as having choices in their behavior, choices often based on the need to achieve and our expectations of success or failure in our endeavors to improve our position in life. Rotter's experience of the Depression of the 1930s made him aware of the effects of the social and economic environment on people, as did his work with Alfred Adler during his undergraduate years at Brooklyn College and his graduate studies with Kurt Lewin at the University of Iowa in the 1940s.

Rotter received a Ph.D. in clinical psychology from Indiana University, one of the few institutions that conferred a doctorate in clinical psychology at the time. After serving in the military in World War II, Rotter joined the faculty of Ohio State University in 1946, becoming a colleague of George Kelly. In 1963, he became director of the clinical psychology program at the University of Connecticut and retired from that institution in 1987.

Expectancies and Reinforcement Values

Rotter asserted that expectancies, or the anticipation of being rewarded for our actions, play an important role in directing behavior. In essence, we learn that certain actions will result in reward and others will not from observing the outcome of our own and others' behavior. We then develop expectancies that guide our decisions regarding future behavior in similar situations. Rotter's model is similar to that of Edward Tolman, but it allows the individual a higher degree of freedom in choosing behavior. One of Rotter's most important insights is his proposal that expectancies do not have to result from our own success or failure but can also result from observing others. Thus, people do not need to be reinforced; they need only to watch others obtaining rewards or punishments for their actions. According to Rotter, people learn through social contacts and observation how to behave, what to expect from their actions, and even how to regard themselves.

Consequently, Rotter (1954) asserted that any study of personality must include an analysis of the way an individual interacts with his or her environment. He also pointed out that the study of personality should be scientific. Although personality constructs need not be based on constructs in any other science, they should at least be consistent with the basic principles established in other sciences. Rotter acted on this premise by conducting several experiments to test his hypothesis that personality is a function of biological dispositions and cognitive assessments regarding the outcome of a person's actions. Personality in Rotter's system is explained in terms of behavior potential, expectancies, **reinforcement value,** and social situation. Behavior potential is the likelihood of engaging in a particular behavior in a specific situation. In other words, what is the probability that we will exhibit a particular behavior in a given situation? In any given situation, there are multiple behaviors we can exhibit. Rotter expressed behavior potential (BP) in the form of an equation: $BP = f(E \& RV)$, where E is **expectancy** and RV is reinforcement value.

Rotter (1954) defined expectancy as the "probability held by the individual that a particular reinforcement will occur as a function of a specific behavior on his part in a specific situation" (p. 107). This simple definition had profound implications during the behaviorist era. In suggesting that people make subjective estimates about the outcome of engaging in some action, Rotter strongly implied that we have some control over our lives. For example, a person contemplating applying for a new job will most likely do so if she has a high expectancy that the application will be accepted. The probability is increased further if she considers the job to be particularly appealing; that is, if the job has high reinforcement value. Thus, we choose our actions based on our assessment of (1) the probability of being rewarded for taking an action and (2) the quality of the expected reward. In Rotter's terms, reinforcement value is "the degree of preference for any reinforcement . . . if the possibility of their occurring were all equal" (Rotter, 1954, p. 107).

Rotter proposed that expectancies can be unrealistic and that assignments of reinforcement value can be inaccurate. Because sound life decisions are based on reasonable judgments of the value of an endeavor and the likelihood of success, an individual who develops inaccurate expectancies or reinforcement values will tend to behave irrationally. This irrationality is the primary source of neurotic behavior, according to Rotter's social learning theory. Thus, Rotter explained that people act in neurotic ways either because they had developed unrealistic expectations about the outcome of their actions or because they were poor judges of what would be pleasurable. Neurotically avoidant individuals, for example, may have strong expectancies of rebuke or rejection in social situations while anticipating minimal feelings of satisfaction if they challenge their fears.

Locus of Control

A core theme of Rotter's (1966) view of personality is based on his concept of **locus of control.** Because most of Rotter's theoretical work was done during the behaviorist era, he used the term *reinforcement* when discussing any type of motivation or goal seeking. His personality theory is based on people's setting of subjective values and probabilities on reinforcements; it follows that locus of control is also related to a person's judgments about the sources of reinforcement. According to Rotter, we develop through our early experiences a set of beliefs about the source of the reinforcers that we will receive in our life. Specifically, we decide that reinforcers are awarded as a result of external forces or as a result of our actions. "These generalized expectancies will result in characteristic differences in behavior in a situation culturally categorized as chance-determined versus skill-determined," Rotter (1966) said, "and may act to produce individual differences with a specific situation" (p. 2).

The locus of control, therefore, refers to our convictions about whether or not we are the primary agent of control over the reinforcers in our life. People with a strong internal locus of control will believe that their successes and failures in life result primarily from their own abilities and efforts. In contrast, people with a strong external locus of control will tend to feel that most efforts will not yield positive reinforcement, as they are perpetually victims of forces beyond their control. People who believe in fate or subscribe to conspiracy theories about the world tend to have external loci of control. Our locus of control will play a compelling role in our behavior. And according to Rotter (1975), the locus of control also explains differences in responses among people facing similar situations. People with a strong internal locus of control, for example, are more likely to take appropriate safety measures quickly when the National Weather Service is predicting a strong hurricane for their part of the country, whereas people with an external locus of control may wait to evacuate their house until compelled to do so by local officials.

The concept of locus of control is essential to Rotter's view of human personality. Our reactions to others, our behavior in any situation, and our general approach to life are based on our beliefs about our efficacy to make changes in our life. If we believe we are powerless to affect our own life, we will be disinclined to act in the face of others' decisions, to disagree with them, or to confront a difficult or upsetting situation head-on. In contrast, if we believe that most outcomes in our life are ultimately based on our own decisions and actions, we will usually tend to try a bit harder and confront problems more forcefully and persistently. Consider the situation of a college examination: a student with an internal locus of control will persist a bit longer with a difficult question while one with an external locus of control will be more likely to give up quickly if the question appears too hard. It follows that Rotter's concept of the person is founded on free will combined with the person's belief in that freedom.

Rotter's concept of locus of control developed out of his supervision of Jerry Phares, a psychotherapist in training. Phares had a male patient who complained of loneliness and inability to get a date. Karl S., as this patient is known, had no friends and no significant social relationships. Urged by Phares to attend a dance, this patient had an initial success, but instead of being motivated to continue in these efforts, he said his pleasant evening was just luck and would not happen again. From these and similar situations, Rotter (1954) worked out the concept of locus of control. Together with Phares, Rotter developed scales to measure it, and literally thousands of studies have used these scales. In one early study conducted during the civil rights movement (Gore & Rotter, 1963), it was found that African American students with an internal locus of control were more active in civil rights advocacy. A scale that is commonly used is Rotter's (1966) LOC scale, the Internal-External Control Scale. Some have criticized this scale for using a forced-choice format rather than a Likert scale (typically, one with opposing poles, e.g., from 1 = not at all to 5 = always), and questions have arisen about whether the LOC scale is truly unidimensional (Gurin, Gurin, Lao, & Beattie, 1969). Other LOC scales have been developed since Rotter's 1966 version (Levenson, 1974; Paulhus, 1983).

Locus of control is in effect a trait, and as it affects many aspects of personality, it is roughly equivalent to a central trait in Gordon Allport's terminology and a source trait in Raymond Cattell's lexicon. For Rotter, locus of control is a continuum, and individuals can be classified along this continuum from strongly internal to strongly external. Those with a strong internal locus of control believe that success or failure is primarily due to talent and work, so they believe they must use their talent and work hard to succeed. At the other end of the scale are people with an external locus of control. Such individuals credit their success or failure to luck or the influence of others and thus feel that they can accomplish little by their own efforts.

One way of looking at Rotter's concept is to see locus of control as a generalized expectancy regarding our ability to control our supply of reinforcement. People with an internal locus regard obtaining reinforcement as something in their control, a product of their efforts. Externals, on the other hand, see reinforcement as appearing by chance or depending on the whims of others. This difference leads to experimental predictions that internals will work toward their goals and tend to succeed while externals regard effort on their part as pointless, are likely to fail, and then will find themselves trapped in a self-fulfilling prophecy. Findley and Cooper (1983) reviewed 98 research studies on locus of control and academic achievement and found a remarkably consistent positive correlation between an internal locus of control and a high level of achievement. At the other end of the spectrum, Benassi, Sweeny, and Dufour (1988) reviewed 97 research studies on locus of control and depression; they reported that all of these studies showed that a high degree of external locus of control was positively correlated with increased susceptibility to depression.

Rotter has repeatedly made clear that locus of control is not an absolute dichotomy; the world is not cleanly divided into externals and internals, and most of us fall somewhere in the middle. Furthermore, the whole point of the concept of locus of control is that it is a generalized expectancy influencing behavior across a wide variety of situations. There may be, however, specific situations in which an external person acts like an internal one and vice versa. For example, a child may believe that grades in school are a matter of luck or being liked by the teacher and be an external in most other areas of life, too, but the same child may view success in sports to be a matter of skill and under her personal control.

Rotter's View of Psychotherapy

As an early clinical psychologist, Rotter was an influential voice in advocating for the training of therapists within departments of psychology rather than in medical schools. Rotter, thus, also rejected the medical model of mental problems as diseases. To Rotter, psychological problems are created by poor learning experiences leading to faulty expectancies. Treatment involves learning adaptive behaviors and cognitions. The therapist-patient relationship is fundamentally a teacher-student relationship.

Summary

In 1947, when psychology was dominated by psychoanalysis and behaviorism, Rotter made the innovative proposal that people are guided by social learning, not by unconscious conflicts or external reinforcers. Personality and behavior can be explained by such cognitive factors as expectancies and beliefs about our locus of control. And unlike many psychologists, Rotter was precise in defining his terms, making them operational and amenable to experimental validation, much of which he did himself. This approach stands in direct contrast to the work of theorists who constructed systems based on intuition and introspection. Rotter developed hypotheses, most of which are testable and many of which he tested himself. Although Rotter is not a personality theorist per se, he contributed to the field of personality study through his work on social learning and locus of control.

Albert Bandura

Albert Bandura, born and educated in Canada, taught for many years at Stanford University. He extended the social cognitive perspective advanced by Rotter when he coauthored *Social Learning and Personality* with Richard H. Waters (Bandura & Waters, 1963). The book represented the first personality theory founded on social cognition—that is, the way people learn to think from social interactions. People behave the way they do based on both personal experience and the observation of the outcome of others' behavior. This point seems self-evident in the early 2000s, but the 1960s were still heavily influenced by behaviorism. Many psychologists held firm to the principle that all behavior must be directly reinforced to be learned.

Bandura was influenced by the work of John Dollard and Neal Miller, stating, "I was attracted to Miller and Dollard's work on the assumption that human development requires a much more powerful mode of transmitting competencies than does trial and error" (quoted in Evans, 1989, p. 4). Bandura thus rejected the need for direct reinforcement and proposed that people can be reinforced vicariously by seeing others get reinforced. Observation by itself, however, is not sufficient to direct human behavior. Bandura proposed that people's beliefs about their own ability or efficacy are also essential for action. For example, if a child observes another child receiving accolades for class participation, he will be vicariously reinforced to participate himself. Whether the child actually does participate, however, is contingent on his beliefs about his ability to state his ideas in class effectively. In other words, learning and evoking what is learned are cognitively mediated. We can acquire an inclination to behave in some way, but the decision to act on this inclination depends on our worldview.

Reinforcement and Human Freedom

People's ability to decide to allow themselves to be reinforced and to select the reinforcers to which they will respond allows for a much greater degree of human freedom than the radical behaviorists acknowledged. Bandura directly challenged Skinner's (1971) contention that "a person does not act upon the world, the world acts upon him" (p. 211) by pointing out that people have a large degree of control to shape the environment that reinforces them. The ability to decide what stimulus will reinforce us effectively means that we are capable of reinforcing ourselves. Bandura (1974) stated his viewpoint in this way:

Explanations of reinforcement originally assumed that consequences increase behavior without conscious involvement. The still prevalent notion that reinforcers can operate insidiously arouses fears that improved techniques of reinforcement will enable authorities to manipulate people without their knowledge or consent. Although the empirical issue is not yet completely resolved, there is little evidence that rewards function as automatic strengtheners of human conduct. Behavior is not much affected by its consequences without awareness of what is being reinforced After individuals discern the instrumental relation between action and outcome, contingent rewards may produce accommodating or oppositional behavior depending on how they value the incentives, the influencers and the behavior itself, and how others respond. Thus reinforcement, as it has become better understood, has changed from a mechanical strengthener of conduct to an informative and motivating influence. People do not function in isolation. As social beings, they observe the conduct of others and the occasions on which it is rewarded, disregarded, or punished. They can therefore profit from observed consequences as well as from their own direct experiences. Acknowledgment of vicarious reinforcement introduces another human dimension—namely, evaluative capacities—into the operation of reinforcement influences. People weigh consequences to themselves against those accruing to others for similar behavior. The same outcome can thus become a reward or a punishment depending upon the referents used for social comparison. (p. 860)

This conclusion of Bandura is profound, as it implies that we have a great deal more free agency than was assumed by either behaviorism or psychoanalysis. He asserted that people are inundated by reinforcers and consciously attend to some while ignoring others. People decide what will influence their behavior and what will not. They make social judgments about what is important to others, what is expected of them socially, and what they expect of others in turn. Consequently, we are less likely to allow ourselves to be reinforced by something that is socially unacceptable. Bandura's position is in direct contrast to the radical behaviorist perspective, in which a reinforcer has a hedonic (pleasure-related) value independent of any social pressures, situations, or conscious judgments.

Bandura, like Rotter, Allport, and Kelly, believes that people are capable of regulating their own behavior with conscious control and motives. People set goals in life and can direct their behavior to pursue them. During this undertaking, they are capable of reinforcing themselves when meeting self-created standards or goals. Personal standards are acquired through inference or through observational learning, especially from significant figures in our life. We are, therefore, capable of acting with a feeling of personal agency (Bandura, 1982) or a sense of control over our lives. This sense develops early in life when we see a connection between our intentions and their actualization, leading to our belief in self-efficacy and a sense that we are responsible for the outcomes of our life experiences.

Bandura (1989) specifies that people possess an **emergent interactive agency,** in which our conscious intentions arise from brain structures that are, in turn, shaped by conscious experiences with our environment and with the decisions and plans we make for our lives. Like the Gestalt psychologists, Bandura believes that the mind is different from the sum of its parts. In addition, the brain can effectively shape itself through intention and experience. Bandura emphasized that the ability to control the quality and type of life that we lead is the essential human characteristic.

Self-Reinforcement

Self-reinforcement is a major concept in Bandura's work. The ability to self-initiate reward is a key element of successful coping, and it marks an important difference between those who are able and those who are not able to engage in adaptive behaviors and navigate successfully through their environment. If we wait for the environment to provide reinforcement, that reinforcement may be long in coming. In addition, the environment may reinforce behaviors that are detrimental along the way. Students from the high school level and beyond are familiar with this situation. It takes years of hard work to qualify for a diploma or complete an academic degree and therefore obtain reinforcement, but behavior that interferes with completing that degree, such as peer pressure to go to parties instead of the library or laboratory, is reinforced immediately.

There are abundant examples of the importance of self-reinforcement in preventive medicine and health care. Such behaviors as smoking, heavy drinking, overeating, unsafe sexual practices, and overexposure to sunlight yield immediate short-term satisfactions ranging from pleasure and mood alteration to a fashionable suntan and are therefore reinforced, whereas the consequences of these behaviors may be years or even decades in the future. Self-reinforcement rewards progress toward long-term goals or standards; it helps to promote behavior toward those goals (Wehmeyer, Agran, & Hughes, 1998), whether a specific goal be completing our education or lowering our risk of so-called lifestyle diseases.

Fundamental Attributes of Agency

Bandura has proposed that human agency includes four fundamental attributes:

- *Intentionality.* Free agents act according to their own intentions. That is, their behaviors are based on their conscious will as opposed to a mechanical stimulus-response connection or raw internal drives.
- *Forethought.* Forethought refers to the ability to plan for the future, set goals, and choose a path for our life. Therefore, people who act as free agents can decide for themselves what direction their life will take.
- *Self-reactiveness.* A life plan without the motivation to see it through would represent a hollow agency. Thus, people with agency must be able to motivate themselves to carry out the plans they have developed with forethought and pursue them to completion.
- *Self-reflectiveness.* Any of the preceding constituents of agency could effectively be carried out by a robot or automaton, but what a robot cannot do is engage in metacognition; that is, it cannot think about or evaluate its own intentions or thinking processes. People with agency can, and do, contemplate their own thoughts and judge their place in the world.

Agency—the ability to choose when and how to act, and to be instrumental in shaping our environment—is the essence of human free will. Moreover, the idea that people act as free agents in directing their own lives is a fundamental facet of Bandura's theory. Bandura recently (2006) proposed that people apply three forms of agency to manage the events in their lives. These are personal, proxy, and collective agency.

Personal agency refers to our capacity to attend to those aspects of the world that have the capacity to motivate us to take some constructive action. If we take a letter to the nearest mailbox or post office, we are exercising personal agency. Not all situations or goals are under the direct control of the individual, however. Often, we will have to seek the assistance of others to reach some goal in life; that is, we will have to exercise proxy agency. An example of this type of agency would be a person in a legal conflict who engages an attorney with the skills and knowledge to act on behalf of that person. In short, if we seek help to solve a problem from someone who has expertise, influence, or power, we are exercising proxy agency. Collective agency refers to the agency of a group of people seeking to achieve a goal. Just as some tasks require help from experts, others require a collective effort to achieve. A familiar example would be the group effort required for a baseball team to win the World Series.

By emphasizing free will and conscious control, Bandura simultaneously rejected mechanistic views of human behavior and emphatically embraced cognitive ones. According to his theory, people are thinking and judging beings who can regulate the development of their own personalities by deciding what behavioral models they will learn or imitate. In addition, they are capable of judging their own behavior and if it fails to meet their personal standards, they can change the way they act to create new behavioral styles. Bandura's emphasis on agency or free will as a predicate of psychological health appears to have unquestionable face validity. It would seem that all people are capable of free will and, if unable to exercise it, will suffer psychological problems.

Bandura's theory, however, does not agree with the findings of some recent neuroscientists, who have challenged the very concept of human free will in favor of emphasizing unconscious processes. Unlike Freud, they do not postulate the existence of **homunculi** censoring aggressive or sexual impulses from a socially conscious ego. Instead, these researchers provide experimental evidence that some brain structures largely operate outside of conscious awareness, and these structures often guide actions and make decisions on their own. In addition, these neuroscientists propose that the human brain is innately structured always to convey a sense of wholeness and free will, even if that free will is illusory.

For example, Benjamin Libet (1996, 1999; Libet, Gleason, Wright, & Pearl, 1983) performed neurological studies that undermined the very concept of free will. In the prototypical experiment, participants who were connected to an electroencephalogram (EEG) were asked to sit in front of an oscilloscope screen that displayed a moving dot to signal elapsed time. Each subject was then asked to perform a simple movement such as pressing a button, moving the wrist, or bending a finger within the interval indicated by the oscilloscope. Button presses were timed, and other movements were recorded using an electromyogram, a device that measures muscle activity. The subjects were also asked to note the location of the moving dot when they were first aware of their decision to make one of the movements described above. While these actions were taking place, the EEG detected a premotor or readiness potential (RP) in each participant's brain waves. These particular brain-wave signatures are generated by the motor cortex in the brain and usually precede a volitional movement of the body. What was remarkable in Libet's studies is that the RP preceded by nearly half a second the participants' reports of their decision to act. That is, their motor cortex began the action, and half a second later the person believed they had decided to move.

A conceptually similar series of studies was conducted by Michael Gazzaniga (1985, 1992), a researcher who worked with so-called split-brain patients. Split-brain patients are people who have undergone surgical treatment for epilepsy that did not respond to available medications. The surgery consists of severing the corpus callosum, a thick band of neurons connecting the brain's two hemispheres. Without this connecting structure, each person is effectively left with two separate brains. In numerous experiments, people who have split brains consistently attribute actions verbally to free will when the verbal left hemisphere had no knowledge of the actions.

In a representative experiment, split-brain participants will be shown an array of objects and asked to point to the one that is most relevant to an image flashed on a screen. They are presented with two objects on the screen, one on the right, which can be seen only by the verbal left hemisphere, and one on the left, which is viewed only by the nonverbal right hemisphere. The left hemisphere is presented with the picture of a house and car covered with snow, and the right hemisphere sees a picture of a chicken's foot, for example.

What happened next is quite remarkable. One patient pointed to a drawing of a shovel with his left hand—controlled by the right hemisphere of the brain, and pointed to the picture of a chicken with his right hand—controlled by the left hemisphere. The patient's explanation for his behavior, however, was even more remarkable. Because his left hemisphere was the one that controlled speech but could not know what motivated the right hemisphere (which saw the snow scene) to point to a shovel, he confabulated an answer. He explained that he pointed to a chicken since he saw a chicken foot and pointed to the shovel because it was needed to clean out the chicken shed. From these and numerous related studies, Gazzaniga concluded that our left hemisphere has an interpreter that makes inferences about our numerous nonconscious behaviors and then attributes it to free will.

The work of researchers such as Libet and Gazzaniga implies that there is much work to be done to fully understand the nature of free will or agency. What is reasonably evident is that people have a bit less of it than meets the eye. Is Bandura wrong, then, in stating that emergent agency is essential for psychological health or growth? Unfortunately, the complete answer is not yet available, but perhaps, it will suffice to say that humans require a perception of agency, even if a substantial portion of behavior only seems to be—but is not actually—under their control.

Social Learning Through Imitation

According to Bandura, a large proportion of learning takes place when people observe the behavior of other people, typically in social encounters. Put most simply, those actions that are judged by an observer to be fruitful are most likely to be imitated. This imitation of other people's actions, whether incidental or intentional, is the foundation of social learning. Bandura noted that before we can use imitation to learn, we must first develop a cognitive representation of the actions to be imitated. To learn through observation, we need to assess why the agent is performing the act, what the agent is attempting to achieve, what the agent is likely to obtain, and what obstacles stand in the way of completing the act. The representation that we develop is influenced by our state of mind, desires, and needs. For example, a man watching another man courting a woman would be less attentive and would form a less coherent model of the event if he himself is not interested in dating, is not interested in women, or is already married. Naturally, events that we consider more salient, more intense, more novel, or more vivid are more likely to be noticed and imitated (Bandura, 1969). Consequently, we are more likely to imitate the actions of a person we regard as important, influential, or competent. Bandura used the term observational learning to describe this process of personal development. He proposed four factors that can promote this type of learning: attention, retention, motor reproduction, and motivation.

Attention. Bandura (1969) saw it as self-evident that we must pay attention to the actions of others to imitate or learn from them. He wrote:

Simply exposing persons to distinctive sequences of modeled stimuli does not in itself guarantee that they will attend closely to the cues, that they will necessarily select from the total stimulus complex the most relevant events, or that they will even perceive accurately the cues to which their attention has been directed. An observer will fail to acquire matching behavior at the sensory registration level, if he does not attend to, recognize, or differentiate the distinctive features of the model's responses. To produce learning, therefore, stimulus contiguity must be accompanied by discriminative observation. (p. 136)

Stimuli that are more salient or novel will, of course, elicit more attention. People who are more attuned to external events, more experienced in their observations, or in a state more relevant to the stimulus (a hungry person will pay closer attention to a cooking demonstration than someone who has just finished a meal) will be more prone to attend to stimuli. In addition, Bandura pointed out that there can be interactions between the state of the observer and the nature of the stimulus. For example, people with low self-esteem will attend more assiduously to an individual they perceive as having high status.

Mirror Neurons: Brain-Based Social Learning

In 1998, researchers observed that neurons in the precortex of monkeys would fire while they observed other monkeys or even humans grasping or manipulating objects. These cells were labeled mirror neurons by Giacomo Rizzolatti of the University of Parma in Italy and Michael A. Arbib of the University of Southern California (Rizzolatti & Arbib, 1998). It was well known that cells in the premotor cortex are activated when primates such as humans and monkeys perform tasks of grasping, tearing, opening, or otherwise manipulating an object.

These researchers also discovered, however, that neurons in the same region of the brain become active when the subject is merely watching another primate perform such actions. The researchers proposed that learning by observation preceded language as a means of communication and instruction (Arbib & Rizzolatti, 1999). In addition, functional MRI (fMRI) studies show that humans, too, have a mirror system in which the parietal cortex of people watching someone perform an action is activated as though the observers were doing it themselves (Rizzolatti, Craighero, & Fadiga, 2002).

Subsequent research further linked mirror neurons to social learning when it was discovered that people can both infer the intentions of others, predict their behavior, and even feel empathy for them through the mirror neuron system (Iacoboni & Dapretto, 2006). In fact, the mirror neuron system appears to be so essential to learning that autistic disorder has been linked to a deficiency in the mirror neuron system (Iacoboni & Lenzi, 2002). In essence, people with autism have impairments in the social cognitive tasks of reading the intentions or emotions of others through their bodily cues. They are impaired in social learning.

In contrast, unimpaired people nonconsciously read the actions and demeanor of other people, intuit their intentions and feelings (Oberman & Ramachandran, 2007), and are able to use this information to learn socially appropriate behavior.

Retention. Bandura has noted that learning is facilitated by integrating new information into our preexisting models of the world. An obvious example is the ease we have in learning new words in a language we already speak fluently compared to learning words in an unfamiliar language. Possessing a mental framework of information about a subject facilitates learning about that subject and allows us to both memorize relevant facts and associate these memories with relevant prior memories.

Bandura appears to have integrated research about memory organization into his theory. Human memory is organized in sense-specific schemas, such that as we observe another person walking or jogging along the street, we will parse the event into the colors, smells, images, sounds, and related senses to be stored in different regions of the brain. The white color of the jogger's shirt, the smell of the next-door neighbor's lilacs, the visual impression of the jogger's gait and speed, the sound of his huffing and puffing if he is out of shape—all will be recorded in different brain regions. But the conscious apprehension of the event will be coded in the form of a schema. Schemas are explanatory models of the world; they include stereotypes, social roles, and behavioral procedures, ranging from swinging a golf club to using a scalpel.

Motor Reproduction. After we attend to some action or event deemed worthy of learning, the next step is for us to be able to perform it ourselves. A short man might very well attend carefully to a professional basketball player slam-dunking a ball. He might also memorize all components of the task in the proper sequence. Sadly for him, however, he will not likely be able to use this information if he is not very tall and cannot jump very high. Another example of the diligence that may be needed in motor reproduction would be a left-handed person watching a right-handed person knit or crochet. To reproduce the movements of the knitter's hands, needles, and yarn, the southpaw will have to make allowances for the difference in handedness.

Motivation. According to Bandura, reinforcement plays a significant role in life motivation. Reinforcement in his system, however, includes not only direct rewards and punishment but also the reinforcements obtained by observing others who are reinforced for their behaviors and the rewards and punishments we bestow upon ourselves—self-reinforcement, which was discussed earlier. This third source of reinforcement is the most liberating, as it allows us the freedom to motivate ourselves and evade the behavioral control of others: "It is true that behavior is regulated by its contingencies, but the contingencies are partly of a person's own making. By their actions, people play an active role in producing the reinforcing contingencies that impinge upon them," Bandura (1974, p. 866) said.

Thus, if we are motivated to learn, we attend to a meaningful action, and we are physically capable of repeating the action, we will learn merely by observing. As noted earlier, Bandura requires that if we are to learn, we must be reinforced, but in contrast to traditional behavioral theory, he sees this reinforcement as possibly coming from within. We can effectively reinforce ourselves by imagining that we get the same reinforcement afforded to the person we are observing. Or we can provide our own reinforcement directly through thought. It is important to note that this ability of human beings to reinforce themselves either vicariously or directly is the essence of both the cognitive and agentic views of Bandura (1982, 1989, 2001). Prior to Bandura's presentation of the social learning perspective, psychologists assumed that people learned primarily through being reinforced by others. In effect, learners were at the mercy of "teachers" who could reward or punish them. The social learning psychologists challenged this picture of the learning process by asserting that people can choose to be reinforced and can even do it to themselves.

Self-Efficacy

Bandura asserts that if we have been reinforced for some action and are thereby learning it, we create a mental representation of the task. This representation includes the specifics for its performance, its purpose, and its social implications. Once the representation is completed, we can generalize it to similar situations in the future. Whether or not we choose to generalize the representation in future situations, however, is predicated on our beliefs about our ability to carry it out effectively. This constellation of beliefs relating to our ability to achieve our goals, form friendships, or gain status, represents our **self-efficacy**. People with strong feelings of self-efficacy tend to have pursued and accomplished goals or have achieved experiences of mastery. Or they can obtain self-efficacy through modeling by watching others pursue and achieve goals or mastery of tasks. In addition, they can achieve it through social persuasion in which others provide consistent positive criticism of their efforts.

In contrast to these paths to mastery, our self-efficacy is the force behind our motivation to accomplish goals, to create, and to establish ourselves in the world. Bandura (1997) described it this way:

> People make contributions to their own psychosocial functioning through mechanisms of personal agency. Among the mechanisms of agency, none is more central or pervasive than beliefs of personal efficacy. Unless people believe they can produce desired effects by their actions, they have little incentive to act. Efficacy belief, therefore, is a major basis of action. People guide their lives by their beliefs of personal efficacy. (pp. 2–3)

Self-efficacy is the *sine qua non* of Bandura's social cognitive theory in that it predicts that virtually all human action is controlled or at least mediated by a person's beliefs about outcomes. According to self-efficacy theory, people are motivated by their thoughts and beliefs, not by external reinforcers. The very belief that we can succeed at some task will motivate us to embark on it—a concept very much at odds with the behavioral view. Notably, our beliefs about our ability to accomplish a goal is often more important than our actual abilities. One unhappy manifestation of this can be gamblers who persist in playing the slots or blackjack after repeated losses because they have strong beliefs in their efficacy to beat the house. Conversely, there are many talented or knowledgeable people who refrain from speaking their minds or acting on their abilities out of inadequate self-efficacy. This outcome is commonly seen in the classroom when well-prepared students fear to answer a question or make a comment in front of the class as a result of grave doubts about their mastery of the material. The same students will often listen in frustration to a peer talking confidently and at length despite an obvious dearth of topical information.

Bandura introduced his highly influential concept of self-efficacy in 1977. It has been shown over the years since that self-efficacy is positively correlated with a person's general level of health, perceived degree of control over situations, and effective behavior (Holden, 1991; Schunk, 1989).

Since first formulating the concept, Bandura (1986) himself has fine-tuned and slightly modified his definition of self-efficacy, emphasizing its relation to social influence (1986) and

Table 13.3	Sources of Self-Efficacy
Mastery	Success is the primary basis of self-efficacy. When people achieve repeated successes or major accomplishments, they may experience what Bandura calls an enactive mastery experience. Having accomplished this, people will have the strongest feeling of self-efficacy.
Vicarious Experience	Watching others succeed at tasks can also lead to feelings of potential success, especially when the person observed is a peer rather than an expert. Vicarious experience can lead to self-efficacy, especially if observers have had prior successes or have other reasons to believe that they can succeed at the task they are observing.
Verbal Persuasion	Self-efficacy can be instilled through the verbal persuasion of individuals who appear to sincerely believe in the capabilities of the listener. The persuaders need to promote the person's beliefs in his or her own abilities and in the feasibility of the goal at hand. Bandura stressed that although positive persuasion was a means to self-efficacy, negative persuasion was even more effective in diminishing it.
Physiological and Affective States	Bandura proposed that people's physical gifts or limitations are fundamental factors in their self-efficacy. For example, verbal persuasion or vicarious experience is unlikely to instill a strong sense of self-efficacy for professional basketball if the person is of short stature. Bandura also noted that people with emotional limitations such as anxiety, depression, or life stress will tend to have impaired self-efficacy. He pointed out that regimens to strengthen physical or emotional status can offset these barriers.

SOURCE: Bandura (1997).

sociocognitive factors (1997). Three decades of research have strongly supported the construct. Deficits in self-efficacy have been found related to such clinical problems as phobias (Bandura, 1983), addictions (Marlatt, Baer, & Quigley, 1995), and depression (Davis & Yates, 1982). Self-efficacy was also found to be beneficial in the academic area. Collins (1985) found that higher levels of academic performance were positively correlated with self-efficacy, independent of the subjects' actual ability. Bouffard-Bouchard, Parent, and Larivée (1991) found, when holding ability constant, that students with high self-efficacy used more self-regulatory strategies. Lent, Brown, and Larkin (1984, 1986) found self-efficacy positively correlated with persistence in college students. Multon, Brown, and Lent (1991) used 36 studies conducted between 1977 and 1988 on the relationship between self-efficacy and academic performance in a meta-analysis and found that self-efficacy accounted for about 14% of the variance in academic performance

In particular, mathematics phobia is a common student malady from first grade through graduate school. Many researchers have found a relationship between performance in mathematics courses and mathematics self-efficacy (Betz & Hackett, 1983; Pajares, 1996; Pajares & Miller, 1994).

Studies have shown self-efficacy to be related to success in many endeavors. High self-efficacy was shown to be associated with success in smoking cessation (Solomon, Bunn, Pirie, Worden, & Flynn, 2006). Moreover, people with high self-efficacy who are afflicted with chronic pain can function better and suffer less depression than those with lower self-efficacy (Turner, Ersek, & Kemp, 2005). Similarly, there is evidence that high self-efficacy helps people recover after exposure to traumatic events (Benight & Bandura, 2004). These and hundreds of other studies have demonstrated that self-efficacy is related to the outcome of many of life's pursuits. These findings have left little doubt that our beliefs about our abilities play a compelling role in our ability to function in life. The salient question, however, is whether self-efficacy is a discrete construct. To begin, Bandura's concept of self-efficacy is quite similar to Rotter's internal versus external locus of control dimension. For example, a person with a highly external locus of control would naturally tend to have a poor sense of self-efficacy. Such a person would not be likely to try challenging or new ventures, nor would she persist in the face of adversity. How could she, when she does not believe that her efforts are instrumental in effecting desirable outcomes in her life? Also evident is conceptual similarity between self-efficacy and Martin Seligman's learned helplessness theory of depression (Alloy, Peterson, Abramson, & Seligman, 1984; Seligman, 1973, 1975). People who feel that their efforts will usually lead to defeat or failure will tend to feel despair. In a similar vein, Seligman proposed that people who are subjected to aversive stimuli that continue despite all efforts to avoid them will feel and act defeated.

The problem of self-efficacy as a distinct construct was examined by researchers (Judge, Erez, Bono, & Thoresen, 2002), who studied the relationship of self-efficacy, locus of control, self-esteem, and neuroticism. They found a strong relationship among all four of these constructs, concluding that a single factor may subsume all four. If this is the case, then self-efficacy may simply be one aspect of a more general ability to persevere.

Another potential problem with self-efficacy as a personality construct is its likely sensitivity to other personality attributes. For example, we might expect that a person with narcissistic traits would develop beliefs of self-efficacy after only a modicum of success. And this person's premature evaluation of self-efficacy would probably be quite robust in the face of failure. In contrast, a person with a depressive personality style might take some years of successful accomplishment to achieve feelings of self-efficacy, even if that person possesses a high degree of actual mastery. Bandura (1997) addresses the role of self-deception in self-efficacy and generally remains firm that self-efficacy is a distinct construct. Its distinctiveness is an open question, however; the possibility remains that self-efficacy is a function of other cognitive and personality styles rather than a foundation.

Bandura noted that achieving the best understanding of behavior requires distinguishing between outcome expectations and self-efficacy (Bandura, Kihlstrom, & Harackiewicz, 1990). Whereas self-efficacy describes the set of beliefs that we hold about our own ability to accomplish a task, outcome expectations describe our assessment of the barriers in the world that we must overcome to complete the task. For example, if a person has developed a strong sense of self-efficacy in selecting investments but is seeking to invest at a time when the market is slumping, he can maintain his belief in his investment skills, but his expectations about the results of investing in such an economic climate can be quite negative. Bandura noted that distorted outcome expectations can lead to such dysfunctional behaviors as those seen in learned helplessness (Seligman, 1975). In such a case, a person who has repeatedly failed despite what he judges to be adequate efforts will assume a helpless demeanor. In extreme cases, the person comes to believe that he has no control over the outcomes of his efforts and will stop trying, in effect becoming depressed. In contrast, a person—even one with a lower degree of self-efficacy—may engage in challenging tasks if her outcome expectations are high. This counterexample is illustrated in the case of a woman who may see herself as a weak tennis player but observes an opponent playing ineptly. The poor performance of her opponent leads to high outcome expectations and is likely to outweigh her weak feelings of self-efficacy related to playing tennis.

Aggression: Bandura and Others

If the preponderance of learning and hence behavior is the result of social learning, then it follows that a major bane of human society, namely aggression, is similarly learned. In a classic psychological study, Bandura (Bandura, Ross, & Ross, 1961) had children witness adults acting either aggressively or nonaggressively. He hypothesized that the children exposed to the aggressive adults would model that aggressive behavior. In addition, he predicted that witnessing the nonaggressive adults would lead to inhibition of aggressive behavior in the other children. That is, aggressive behavior can be mitigated or even stopped, he thought, if children are not exposed to aggressive acts and if they are given the chance to observe nonaggressive alternatives to conflict. The results showed that the children tended to imitate the behavior of the adults, including the aggressive behavior. Based on these and similar studies (Bandura & Huston, 1961; Bandura, Ross, & Ross, 1963a, 1963b), Bandura developed a theory that aggressive behavior was essentially the result of vicarious learning. Moreover, if people were directly or vicariously reinforced to resolve conflicts nonviolently, humans would largely become rational nonviolent beings. According to Bandura (1973), violent behavior is learned essentially the same way as other vicariously learned behaviors. That is, people who observe others achieving some form of success through violence are consequently reinforced to use violence. Those who receive verbal persuasion that violence is an effective strategy will also be more inclined to violence. Those who have been subjected to socially sanctioned violence such as corporal punishment (Bandura & Waters, 1963) are likewise encouraged to be violent, and those who have been reinforced by the previous methods and believe that they are physically capable of violence will be the most likely to use violence as a solution to conflict or frustration.

Of course, the notion that aggression is predominantly the result of early learning is very appealing, but many psychologists and biologists would strongly differ. And they differ with a great deal of evidence. Subsequent to Bandura's landmark work on aggression, evolutionary psychologists such as David Buss and his coworkers (Buss & Dunkley, 2006) have proposed that aggression is both innate and adaptive. In fact, their conclusion that humans have an innate aggressive drive is closer to Freud's notion of a death instinct or thanatos than to the social cognitive perspective presented by Bandura.

According to the evolutionary psychology perspective, the human tendency toward aggression developed as an adaptation to minimize the risks to males of investing resources in rearing another male's offspring. This type of behavior is observed most often in vertebrates, where males of the species battle—sometimes to the death—to preserve reproductive dominance in a territory. Primates like the gorilla often have only one male who has exclusive access to females. A male silverback gorilla, after continual battles with competing males, will acquire a harem of females, which precludes all lesser males from mating at all (Harcourt,

Fossey, Stewart, & Watts, 1980). Evolutionary psychologists point out that many murderers are men who kill in response to a humiliation that would cost them status in their social group. Such status was extremely important in early humans as it would be instrumental in allowing the male access to females (Buss, 2005).

Buss and another colleague, Todd Shackelford (1997b, p. 608), proposed that aggression evolved as an adaptation to seven survival problems:

- Co-optation of resources held by others
- Defense against attack
- Inflicting costs on same-sex rivals
- Negotiation of status and power hierarchies
- Deterrence against future aggression
- Deterrence against sexual infidelity on the part of the mate
- Reduction of resource allocation to genetically unrelated offspring

Although murderous violence to ensure a wife's fidelity or to stave off potential competition would seem maladaptive today, such behaviors evolved when the only consequences of violence were retaliation from the victims or their kin. There were no laws or complex social standards to prevent such actions. Consequently, evolutionary psychologists theorize that people who indulged in such acts would almost surely have produced more offspring, endowing them with an advantage in natural selection. Buss and Shackelford (1997a) point out that vestiges of such aggression are found today in spousal violence. Evolutionary psychologists maintain that many recent psychologists mistakenly view modern moral behavior as good or adaptive when it is not so from a survival point of view. A man who killed others to prevent being cuckolded would be more likely to pass on his genes to future generations. His descendants might not be considered kind and likable, but their offspring may well represent a large percentage of the contemporary population.

Given this view of aggression, some researchers argue (Wilson & Daly, 1996) that marital violence is an atavistic manifestation of such behavior. That is, females in early human history were not influenced by religious or cultural pressures to remain faithful; rather, their fidelity was jealously and violently enforced by their mates. Thus, some men today, having this trait, may react with violence when threatened with infidelity. Others take the view that modern violence is often a vestige from an era without laws, a time when individuals had to wield the threat of violence to ward off theft, violence, or threats to social status (Nisbett & Cohen, 1996; Shackelford, 2005). According to this perspective, those who were less capable of a violent defense of their property would not have survived, making violence an essential human trait.

Do these studies suggest that Bandura is wrong? The answer is yes and no. Indeed, if humans have an innate inclination to violence, its expression would still be shaped by social learning. The degree of violence, the weapons involved, the situations in which violence is considered legitimate, and those against whom it is directed would all be subject to shaping by society. For this reason, violent behavior does vary based on culture, economic need, and social stability.

Learned Psychopathology

The proposition that psychological disorders are learned from others is implicit in Bandura's theory. After all, if people are motivated by and learn from observing others, it follows that they can also learn aberrant ways of thinking and acting in the very same manner. If children are exposed to people being reinforced for acting aggressively or behaving in other apparently maladaptive ways, they will be inclined to integrate these behaviors into their personal style. For example, if a child observes an aggressive bully receiving deferential treatment in response to his behavior, he will be vicariously reinforced to act aggressively himself.

Bandura, therefore, rejected the notion of hidden forces underlying neurosis. Instead, he thought the behavior itself was the problem, and as such, it could be treated directly by teaching new and more effective behaviors. The solution to most neurotic behavior is to expose the neurotic individual to people with better coping skills, he asserted. According to Bandura, this exposure will allow for vicarious learning and modeling, which will in turn facilitate more adaptive behavior.

回 CHAPTER SUMMARY

The early cognitive theorists made thought, contemplation, and evaluation key components of personality. Although their concepts may seem self-evident in the early 21st century, they were not so regarded at the time that many of these theorists put pen to paper. Behaviorism envisioned human behavior to be motivated by the same fundamental forces that shape the behavior of a rat. Both are collections of reinforced responses. Psychoanalytic theories did allow for an essential difference between humans and other animals; but this difference was a dismal one. According to the psychoanalytic school, human personality is driven by a perpetual war between reproductive and aggressive drives, on the one hand, and the constraints of social mores on the other. The internal civil war would never be won by the ego, which is charged with adjusting primitive drives to the external standards of civilized society. At best, there could be a tense truce. Consciousness and cognition are negligible factors in psychoanalytic theory because they are largely subservient to the unconscious.

The Gestalt psychologists, along with George Kelly, Gordon Allport, Julian Rotter, and Albert Bandura, added a new element to personality, that of information processing. The common factor among all of these psychologists is the belief that personality is derived at least in part from the processes by which humans perceive and interpret the world.

Chapter 14

Biology, Genetics, and the Evolution of Personality

Chapter Goals

- Show how the eugenics movement created resistance to genetic explanations of behavior
- Highlight the role of Charles Darwin in the development of modern evolutionary principles
- Trace the origins of modern evolutionary biology and evolutionary psychology
- Discuss some of the major controversies in behavioral genetics
- Outline the basic principles of genetics and behavioral genetics
- Provide a basic outline of brain functioning as it relates to behavior
- Demonstrate the connection between genes, the brain, behavior, and personality

Personality theorists, like most other theorists in psychology, continue to debate variations of the mind-body problem. That is, they discuss what portion of our psyche can be directly attributed to the machinations of our various organs and the substances that underlie them, and what portion can be attributed to a mind that may be a function of the body but is in some ways distinct and separate from it? The notion that there can be an aspect of the physical body that somehow is more than or different from the other functions of the body is a vexing one. Perhaps the only parallel in science is found in quantum physics, in that the operation of the physical world cannot be directly linked to the functions of its component parts. Concepts like Werner Heisenberg's uncertainty principle, which states that the act of measuring the energy of a subatomic particle makes it impossible to know its location with certainty and vice versa, are difficult and confusing for many people. Quantum physics maintains that physics of the whole at the atomic and subatomic level is knowable, but the precise physics of the components of that whole is not.

Researchers who suggest that psychological constructs such as personality are distinct from the physical components and processes that underlie them take a position similar to that of quantum physicists. Those who are averse to reducing human qualities such as personality to biological functions suggest that studying biochemical processes, genes, neurons, or neurotransmitters cannot fully explain the vastly complex products of their interaction. Adherents of this point of view hold that this complex interplay yields an entity distinct and different from the sum of its constituent parts. Such psychologists often advocate an idiographic approach to the study of personality, as opposed to the nomothetic approach employed by most experimentalists. The idiographic method focuses on the unique aspects of the individual as opposed to seeking general or universal rules about people and personality. The more extreme idiographic theorists reject the notion of overarching human traits, whether biological, genetic, or learned. The notion that personality has genetic bases is anathema to many psychologists of this bent. Their research makes use of case studies, in which each individual is analyzed and presented as unique.

In contrast to the idiographic psychologists are the nomothetically oriented theorists who seek universal or at least common characteristics that people share. Psychologists following the nomothetic approach employ what is called the **hypothetico-deductive method or model**. That is, these researchers observe individuals or groups and infer general hypotheses about human nature. These hypotheses are then tested by one or more of the many ways that science has developed for objective and critical review.

The hypothetico-deductive method is the most widely accepted approach for studying the foundations of human personality. The evidence obtained through the use of this method points strongly to the existence of innate or genetic bases of human personality. The present chapter will examine the evidence for this conclusion as well as the arguments against it. There are still many psychologists who find the idea that human personality is even a partial product of genes and biochemistry to be completely unacceptable. This bias is, in part, a reaction against the cruel applications of social Darwinism in the direction of racism and even genocide.

▣ THE EUGENICS MOVEMENT

Social Darwinism

The negative associations that many people have with the notion that behavior has a genetic foundation can be traced to a cousin of Charles Darwin named Francis Galton. Galton was a man of great intellect who, like many in his time, did not have a great deal of sympathy for those less gifted. Galton made discoveries in fields as diverse as meteorology (weather forecasting), forensic science, and anthropology, and he is considered to be a founder of the field of biostatistics. In the early 2000s, however, he is probably best known as the 19th-century originator of eugenics. Galton coined the word to describe all scientific efforts to increase the ratio of people with superior genetic traits to those with less desirable ones. He set forth his principles in a book he published in 1869, called *Hereditary Genius*, in which he attributed superior intellect to innate traits that could be enhanced by selective breeding. His notion that mental traits are just as innate as physical features was quite controversial; it is still not fully accepted today.

Galton's efforts to apply these principles to society took form in 1883, when he first proposed the term *eugenics*, an English word derived from the Greek adjective meaning "well-born." Galton advocated two variations of eugenics, positive and negative. The former involves encouraging the marriage and reproduction of people with traits deemed to be superior, and the latter involves discouraging or preventing the breeding of those with traits deemed inferior. Galton and his wife—who, like Galton himself, came from an intellectually distinguished family—were childless.

Although eugenics was supported by the Nobel Prize-winning playwright George Bernard Shaw and some other British intellectuals, it became even more popular in the United States in the first half of the 20th century. Below are some excerpts from a book published by a professor of economics at Yale University named Ellsworth Huntington (1876–1947) in 1935, titled *Tomorrow's Children: The Goal of Eugenics*:

> The discovery that man is able to guide his own evolution by means of eugenics appears to be one of the five most momentous human discoveries.
>
> Now, for the first time, through the scientific use of genetic principles and social processes man is able consciously and purposefully to select the types of human beings that will survive. . . . In the later part of this evolutionary process the Greeks allowed weak infants to perish; the Jews expelled persons who would not conform to strict religious regulations; the Romans put conquered cities to the sword; the Puritans would not tolerate dissenters like the Quakers; and the Arabs still disown young men who lack bravery. All these and a thousand other practices represent crude, haphazard and unconscious attempts to create racial stocks conforming to a definite pattern. Today all these attempts assume a new significance. They are gropings toward a great plan of conscious evolution. We are often told that since the dawn of civilization the human race has made no real biological evolution. Today, however, we are beginning to thrill with the feeling that we stand on the brink of an evolutionary epoch whose limits no man can possibly foretell. . . . Although we cannot foretell the ultimate results of this new eugenic movement, we can vaguely see their general nature. Eugenics gives man a marvelous instrument whereby in due time a whole nation may be elevated. Many and grievous mistakes will doubtless be made, and wrong steps will have to be retraced. Nevertheless, in the long run we have reason to hope that man will use the art of eugenics as well as he has used the arts connected with tools, speech, fire, and writing. (Huntington, 1935, p. 105)

What Huntington was encouraging is the selective breeding of human beings by advanced societies. The eugenics movement involved restricting the reproduction of people considered inferior and the encouragement and support of the reproduction of the gifted and able. Although the eugenics movement reached its peak in the early 20th century, it can be traced backward to the 19th, to the **social Darwinism** of Herbert Spencer (1820–1903). Spencer's application of Darwin's theory of natural selection justified or even encouraged human suffering by proposing that such misery helped to cull individuals and groups who were not "fit" enough to live in an advanced industrial society. The social Darwinian model was used to justify the most severe forms of laissez-faire capitalism, social inequality, and colonialism during the period of rapid industrial growth in the late 19th century.

Social Darwinism stated, in effect, that the captains of industry had obtained their status because of superior genetic endowments and that those who labored under harsh conditions were in that position because they were less gifted by nature. Moreover, helping to improve their lot would only encourage reproduction of less "fit" humans to the detriment of society as a whole. So, the thinking went, the shortened life spans of factory workers, indigenous people in Africa and Asia, and other poorly paid laborers helped the human race as a whole to evolve to higher levels.

In the Courtroom: *Buck v. Bell* (1927)

Social Darwinism entailed a passive culling of those believed to be less fit whereas eugenics theorists advocated a more active stance. This position, sometimes called negative eugenics, became increasingly acceptable in the United States, as exemplified by the decision of the U. S. Supreme Court in *Buck v. Bell* (1927).

This Supreme Court ruling upheld a Virginia statute instituting compulsory sterilization of the mentally retarded "for the protection and health of the state." *Buck v. Bell* was largely seen as an endorsement of negative eugenics in which "inferior" people would be prevented from

Image 14.1   Eugenics Tree

passing on their genes to the next generation. Toward this end, the Supreme Court found that the Commonwealth of Virginia had the right to forcibly sterilize a 20-year-old woman named Carrie Bell. The doctors who examined Carrie in 1924 had concluded that she was the offspring of a "feeble-minded" mother and, therefore, was likely to be so, too.

Associate Justice Oliver Wendell Holmes, Jr., wrote the opinion for the 8 to 1 majority in support of his argument that the interest of the states in a "pure" gene pool outweighed the interest of individuals in the integrity of their bodies:

> It is better for all the world, . . . if instead of waiting to execute degenerate offspring for crime, or to let them starve for their imbecility, society can prevent those who are manifestly unfit from continuing their kind. The principle that sustains compulsory vaccination is broad enough to cover cutting the Fallopian tubes. In the case of Carrie Buck, her mother, and her daughter, the requirement of sterilization was glaringly self-apparent. Three generations of imbeciles . . . are enough. (quoted in Quinn, 2003, p. 35)

Within a few years of this 1927 decision, 28 states had passed laws permitting compulsory sterilization of the mentally or physically handicapped. Some states also enacted laws limiting the rights of "undesirables" to marry. The Virginia law mandating sterilization of the mentally retarded was not repealed until 1974.

The eugenics movement in the United States was aided or abetted by such notables as President Woodrow Wilson, social critic William Graham Sumner, and inventor Alexander Graham Bell. The growth of the movement led to states incorporating eugenic principles into their marriage laws. Connecticut was the first state to enact a marriage law based on eugenic principles in 1896. This enactment marked the beginning of a trend—which accelerated after 1927—in which numerous states enacted marriage laws intended to prevent the "epileptic, imbecile, or feeble-minded" from marrying.

The Eugenics Record Office

In 1898, a biologist named Charles Benedict Davenport (1866–1944) became the director of a biological research station based in Cold Spring Harbor, New York, where he conducted research into the evolution of animals and plants. In 1904, the Carnegie Institution funded Davenport to found the Station for Experimental Evolution, which itself evolved by 1921 into the Carnegie Institution Department of Genetics.

Davenport later sought funds from a local donor, Mary Harriman, to create what would be named the Eugenics Records Office (ERO). The plan was to make this office the genetic registry for the entire United States. All of the "unfit" and the "inferior" would be located and recorded so that future action could be taken expeditiously. In one effort toward these ends, Davenport had workers go door-to-door with questionnaires to record and enumerate the characteristics of the respondents and their families. A fundamental goal of this project was identification of genetically inferior human strains so that they could ultimately be prevented from reproducing. The statistics gathered by the ERO were also used to show that immigrants, African Americans, and members of such white ethnic minority groups as the Irish and Polish were genetically inferior.

The eugenics movement gradually gained support among the general population as well as government leaders. It reached a critical threshold in 1907, when the state of Indiana passed a law permitting the forced sterilization of people considered unworthy to reproduce. The targeted groups included those with mental impairments, those receiving public assistance, and convicted felons. Indiana was followed by Washington, which permitted the sterilization of habitual criminals; Connecticut, which enacted a law allowing the staff of psychiatric institutions to sterilize patients if they were thought to have a family history of insanity or feeblemindedness; California, which legislated the compulsory sterilization of convicts and the feebleminded; and New York and New Jersey, both of which enacted laws mandating the formation of Boards of Examiners of Feebleminded, Epileptics, and Other Defectives. These boards had the authority to order compulsory sterilization.

Davenport's associate, Harry Hamilton Laughlin (1880–1943), was a high school teacher before he turned to eugenics research. He served as managing director of the ERO and used its research to advocate the forced sterilization of "inferiors" and the creation of barriers to immigration—particularly to immigration from southern and eastern Europe. Laughlin provided extensive statistical testimony to Congress in support of the Johnson-Reed Immigration Act of 1924. An inherently dangerous flaw in this hunt for the unfit, however, was that there were no fixed and scientifically based criteria for determining unfitness. The unfit were those who were considered such by the leaders of the eugenics organizations. They included the mentally impaired, unwed mothers, alcoholics, people with seizure disorders or visual problems, deaf persons, or deformed persons. In fact, virtually any trait deemed offensive or undesirable by the leaders of this movement seemed to be a basis for declaring a person's pedigree undeserving of reproduction. In addition to supporting mandatory sterilization of the "unfit," Laughlin also supported the passage of Virginia's Racial Integrity Act, which outlawed marriage between white and black Americans. It was not until 1967 that this act was overturned by the Supreme Court.

The research of the ERO and other pro-eugenic organizations was used to justify more than 60,000 forced sterilizations. The policies of the eugenicists were reflected in mainstream medical publications such as the *Journal of the American Medical Association*, which referred to eugenics as "an event of great importance to the history of evolution (Black, 2003, p. 73). The eugenics movement also had its own publications, one of which was the *Eugenical News*, published by the American Eugenics Research Association. The *Eugenical News* published several articles endorsing Nazi policies intended to eliminate the Jewish people. The favor was returned by Adolf Hitler, who praised the American eugenics movement in its efforts to limit immigration of "inferior" peoples:

> I know that one does not like to hear all this; but there exists hardly anything that is more thoughtless, even more stupid than our present State citizenship law. There is at present one State where at least feeble attempts of a better conception are perceptible. This is of course not our German model republic, but the American Union where one endeavors to consult reason at least partially. The American Union, by principally refusing immigration to elements with poor health, and even simply excluding certain races from naturalization, acknowledges by slow beginnings an attitude which is peculiar to the national State conception. (Hitler, 1939, p. 658)

Hitler's approval of the American eugenics movement was reflected in the fact that Laughlin was awarded an honorary degree by the University of Heidelberg in 1936 for his work on behalf of the "science of racial cleansing." Ironically, Laughlin later discovered that he suffered from epilepsy, one of the criteria for forced sterilization by his standards. Although he had married in 1902, he and his wife had no children.

As the extreme measures of the Nazi government began to surpass the programs in the United States—as many as 350,000 people were sterilized (Lifton, 2000) in the first few years of the German program—they were actually met with envy in some quarters. For example, the American eugenicist Joseph DeJarnette (1866–1957), who served as the superintendent of Virginia's Western State Hospital, stated in 1934 that "Hitler is beating us at our own game" (Black, 2003, p. 7). Stefan Kühl (1994), the author of a history of the eugenics movement in the United States, suggests that Nazi racial policies were actually guided and abetted by American eugenicists. The German legislation mandating the sterilization of the unfit was modeled on American laws, and American publications on eugenics were often reprinted in Germany. Kühl states that in 1934, a member of Hitler's staff requested that Leon Whitney of the American Eugenics Society send Hitler a copy of Whitney's book *The Case for Sterilization*. Hitler received the book and sent Whitney a personal letter of thanks. In addition, Madison Grant, a eugenics advocate and trustee of the American Museum of Natural History, sent Hitler a copy of his racist book, *The Passing of the Great Race,* and received a grateful letter from Hitler reporting that the book had become his "Bible." The book stated that the Nordic races "were the white man par excellence" (Black, 2003).

Birth Control and Eugenics

Margaret Sanger (1879–1966), who is best remembered as the founder of Planned Parenthood, was also the founder of a number of groundbreaking organizations that advocated women's reproductive rights. In 1916, Sanger opened the first birth control clinic in the United States. A few years later, she founded the American Birth Control League, which later merged with the Birth Control Clinical Research Bureau to form the Birth Control Federation of America, forerunner of the Planned Parenthood Federation of America. In 1930, Sanger set up a birth control clinic in Harlem and, shortly thereafter, founded the "Negro Project," which sought to provide African Americans in the rural South with birth control information.

She is less well known for her ardent support of the eugenics movement. Sanger's only area of contention with Davenport and the other proselytizers of eugenics was their resistance to making birth control an issue. They insisted that members of the superior races should be encouraged to have a high birth rate, while Sanger (1938) insisted that the birth rate should be limited for all groups. She stated in her diary:

> Eugenics without birth control seemed to me a house built upon sands. It could not stand against the furious winds of economic pressure which had buffeted into partial or total helplessness a tremendous proportion of the human race. The eugenists wanted to shift the birth control emphasis from less children for the poor to more children for the rich. We went back of that and sought first to stop the multiplication of the unfit. This appeared the most important and greatest step towards race betterment. (pp. 374–375)

Sanger first endorsed eugenics in 1919 when she proclaimed, "More children from the fit, less from the unfit—that is the chief issue of birth control" (quoted in Kennedy, 1970, pp. 115–116). Sanger's use of the word *unfit* referred to the mentally and physically impaired as well as immigrants from eastern and southern Europe. What is now viewed as bigotry and racism were the prevailing attitudes among the educated elites in the United States in the early 20th century. The goal of improving the country's racial stock was regarded as reproductive efficiency, not bias. It took a nightmare of excess before the implications of this policy would become clear to most people in the United States.

The Cultural Rebound

The government of Nazi Germany helped to discredit eugenics in the United States by taking it to its ultimate monstrous extreme. Official government policy mandated the sterilization of alcoholics, epileptics, the mentally retarded, and all the usual categories of people considered "unfit," then went further to require euthanasia of the retarded and people with genetic disorders. Elimination by mass killing was extended to whole races and religious creeds. The vagueness of the concept of unfitness was employed to exterminate all people whose existence was deemed politically or socially unacceptable, ranging from homosexuals, Jehovah's Witnesses, and Jews to Roma (Gypsies), political opponents of the regime, and Soviet prisoners of war. The repugnance of genocide as practiced by the Nazis in the name of eugenics led to a rejection of this ugly practice in the Western world.

It also led, however, to a strong suspicion regarding all research topics—and all researchers—believed to be supportive of eugenics. The reaction to William Bradford Shockley (1910–1989), the winner of the 1956 Nobel Prize in physics, exemplifies the cultural change the United States underwent in half a century. Shockley won his Nobel for his contributions to the development of the transistor. Unfortunately, he became best known for his speeches against what he called **dysgenics**, a term he used to describe the regression of society through genetically disadvantaged people reproducing at a higher rate (Shockley, 1972).

The climate was far different in the second half of the 20th century than it was in the first, however. Shockley was almost always met by protesters, often exceeding in number the size of his audience. Equally often, he was shouted down or even barred from speaking. For example, Harvard Law School cancelled his speech in 1973 as a result of angry protests; in that same year, he was shouted off the stage at Staten Island Community College. These outbursts became the modal response to Shockley for more than a decade. In fact, in 1983, the protests prior to his scheduled speech at Stanford University were so vehement that the university apologized for having invited him. The climate had radically changed.

Shockley was not the only researcher attacked for holding views considered tainted by eugenics. Raymond Cattell, the eminent psychologist who was discussed in Chapter 9 on trait theory, was targeted in 1997 when he was chosen to receive a gold medal from the American Psychological Association for lifetime achievement in the field of psychology. Before the medal was presented, a former student named Barry Mehler launched a publicity campaign against Cattell, accusing the older man of harboring racist and fascist ideas. Mehler (1997) published an article in *Genetica* denouncing Cattell as an early advocate of the Nazi movement. In addition, Cattell had founded a movement called "Beyondism," which Mehler referred to as neo-fascist in its perspectives. Mehler (1997) cited Cattell: "Hitler actually shared many values of the average American. He aimed at full employment, family values, and raising the standard of living, and countless other things, including the Volkswagen, which he designed himself for the average family" (p. 2).

An instance of Cattell's admiration of Nazi ideals was seen in the following quotation:

> The vast majority of humans are "obsolete" and . . . the earth will be choked with the more primitive forerunners unless a way is found to eliminate them. . . . Clarity of discussion . . . would be greatly aided if genocide were reserved for the literal killing off of all living members of a people. (cited in Newnes, 2004, pp. 360–361)

Although Cattell stated that he "abhor[red] racism and discrimination based on race. Any other belief would be antithetical to my life's work," he chose to refuse the American Psychological Association's award to end the controversy.

EDWARD OSBORNE WILSON

E. O. Wilson (1929–), a naturalist who began his career with the study of insects, is best known for his major work, *Sociobiology: The New Synthesis* (1975). In that book Wilson systematized the connections among genetics, biology, and behavior, suggesting that behaviors that seem at first glance to be maladaptive from the standpoint of evolution are actually genetically based. For example, altruistic or unselfish behavior, which would appear to diminish the reproductive capacity of those engaging in it, can be genetically advantageous, he thought. It can even be seen as selfish. Wilson explained that altruistic behavior occurs most frequently when the **altruism** benefits a close relative of the altruist. Through their actions, altruists increase the probability that their genes— as manifested in their close relatives—will survive.

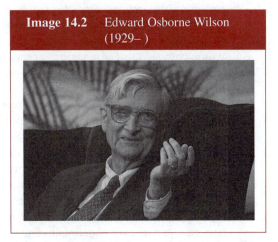

Image 14.2   Edward Osborne Wilson (1929–)

Wilson also maintains that differences in sexual behavior between males and females might be innate insofar as different reproductive strategies maximize the genetic potential of each sex. For example, males of a species typically take little risk and expend little energy in the nurturance of offspring. Thus, the male maximizes his genetic potential by mating with the greatest possible number of females. In contrast, the female maximizes her genetic potential by mating only with males who indicate by some measure of accomplishment that they possess superior genetic material.

It now seems that seeking the genetic or biological foundations of intelligence or other abilities has become controversial even if it is not associated with race or other categories. Drawing associations between ability and innate qualities has become distasteful to many.

When Wilson's *Sociobiology* was first published in 1975, its initial reception among biologists was quite positive, but when it began to circulate among social scientists, it generated an angry controversy. What some academics found questionable was Wilson's extension of his conclusions from insects—his specialty—to humans. At the time that Wilson published his work, the distaste for a concept that could be even remotely linked to eugenics or racism was so intense that the topic would not be considered for discussion in many quarters. Wilson's book was seen as a provocation to those who insist that human behavior is based largely on learning and culture. To many in this group, the proposal that genes are the basis of human personality, behavior, or nature is a throwback to the eugenics movement.

Wilson was scheduled to give a talk at a meeting of the American Association for the Advancement of Science (AAAS) in 1978. He was met by protesters holding placards with swastikas. While he was waiting to give his presentation, a woman poured a pitcher of ice water on his head while her cohorts chanted, "Wilson, you're all wet." Wilson completed his talk despite the assault, but this event denoted the tenor of the attitude of many about both the man and his message.

Wilson's message is similar to Darwin's, with the exception that Wilson addresses behavioral and mental development rather than somatic structure. He proposes that natural selection has guided the development of both animal and human behavior. That is, Wilson maintains that the behavior of both animals and humans has itself evolved. Even more controversial is his contention that actions characterized as selfless or altruistic are actually adaptive for the altruistic individual. Conversely, selfishness and violence, characteristics that most societies hold in disdain, can be evolved and innate inclinations that provide advantages for survival. Wilson postulates that as organisms engage in numerous actions, they will ultimately be forced by the environment to act in a way that maximizes their **inclusive fitness** by increasing their chances of passing on their **genotype** to future generations, either directly by reproduction or indirectly by aiding the survival of relatives who will transmit their genetic material. Human beings, like all other living things, will conduct themselves accordingly even if society regards the maximization of their inclusive fitness as undesirable, immoral, or even criminal.

Not surprisingly, heated controversy often ensues when researchers associate intelligence or other fundamental human abilities with genetic factors. This has been the case when researchers apply evolutionary theory to human racial classifications. J. Philippe Rushton (1943–) is an example of such a researcher. After examining the research literature on human brain size, maturation, family life, and reproductive style, Rushton concluded that people from eastern Asia have larger brains and higher IQs, reach physical maturity more slowly, are less fertile, and are less sexually active than Africans. He also noted that Caucasians tend to fall between these two groups on all such measures. He explains these differences by applying the r/K selection theory, first enunciated by evolutionary biologists, to humans (Rushton, 1992, 1996, 1988).

According to evolutionary biologists, animals that apply the r-strategy (sometimes called r-selected species) tend to produce a large number of offspring that receive relatively little care from the parents. Such offspring must mature quickly because they receive little nurture. Examples of such species include most insects, fish, and amphibians. In contrast, K-selected organisms produce smaller numbers of offspring, which are cared for by the parents. K-selected organisms tend to have larger brains, longer life spans, and longer maturational periods. In addition, unlike the simpler r-selected organisms, K-selected species usually have some kind of social organization. Humans and domesticated animals are examples of K-selected organisms.

Rushton's application of r/K selection theory to human racial categories resulted in tremendous controversy. Some challenges were cool headed, like those of the psychologist Richard Nisbett (2005), who rebutted Rushton by pointing out that the recent narrowing of the gap between black and white IQ scores and the improvements resulting from educational programs point to social rather than genetic factors as the basis of the difference. Rushton was also calmly answered by people like the anthropologist Leonard Lieberman (2001), who argued that the very concept of race is more of a socioeconomic construct than a genetic one.

Unfortunately, however, many professionals chose to make their arguments against Rushton's ideas in an *ad hominem* manner (Whitney, 2004). Shortly after Rushton

Image 14.3   J. Philippe Rushton (1943–)

presented his ideas at a meeting of the American Association for the Advancement of Science, the premier of Ontario called for Rushton to be fired from his university teaching position. The premier also asked Ontario police to commence a criminal investigation to determine whether Rushton's ideas violated any laws of the province. Rushton was attacked in the Canadian press as a bigot and likened to a Nazi; his faculty rating suddenly dropped from excellent to unsatisfactory. He weathered a 4-year criminal investigation, which faded along with his unsought notoriety. Rushton ultimately returned to his teaching position; however, his experiences demonstrate the changes in social norms regarding the discussion of race and ability that took place over only a few generations. Some social psychologists (G. Bear, personal communication, 2006) point out that the extreme reactions to Rushton and others who have taken unpopular positions in evolutionary, biological, or social psychology have been displaced onto others who state their opinions in far less controversial terms within these subject domains.

▣ CHARLES DARWIN

Sociobiology, **ethology**, even the less desirable theories associated with eugenics are all based on the principles developed by Charles Darwin. He was responsible for credibly demonstrating the notion that all life on Earth evolved from earlier life forms through the process of natural selection. Darwin was not the first naturalist to propose that species have evolved. His grandfather, Erasmus Darwin, proposed that life evolves by acquiring characteristics that are necessary for survival. Similarly, Jean-Baptiste de Lamarck (1744–1829), a French naturalist, also suggested that living creatures adapt to environmental demands and pass these adaptations along to their offspring. Charles Darwin, however, amassed a monumental amount of

Image 14.4   Charles Darwin (1809–1882)

evidence that supported his contention that all life forms compete in an ongoing struggle for survival. This struggle ultimately favors those that are born with variations that make them more suited to survive in the competition for life. These variations are not the result of adaptations to changes in the environment. They are random, and only in rare circumstances do they provide the bearer with an advantage for survival. Darwin gathered the evidence for this process during the 5 years that he served as a naturalist on an extended voyage of exploration.

The Voyage of the *Beagle*

Darwin was chosen by Captain Robert FitzRoy to accompany him on a 5-year journey, from 1831 to 1836, to survey the coastal regions of South America—Patagonia, Tierra del Fuego, and the Straits of Magellan. Despite having some initial doubts about Darwin because he thought the shape of the latter's nose suggested a lack of determination, Captain FitzRoy eventually selected the young Darwin for the journey. Darwin kept detailed records of the animal life he encountered during the years of the *Beagle*'s voyage. In doing so, he discovered numerous patterns of life among the many islands he visited. For example, he observed the fossils of extinct large mammals like the megatherium (an elephant-sized ground sloth) in geographic strata that revealed a climatic basis for their extinction. He found mussel beds located above the highest level of tides on the Cape Verde islands, indicating that the land mass of these islands had risen over time.

Specifically, Darwin noticed that animals of similar species differed according to the environmental demands of each location he visited. He made his most important speciation discoveries on the Galápagos Islands, an archipelago of volcanic islands lying along the equator just west of Ecuador. As a result of the geographical isolation of these islands, they developed populations of distinctive plant and animal life. Each island in the archipelago had species that were different from similar species on neighboring islands. Prior to his journey, Darwin had no reason to question the immutability of species, which he had been taught during his theological education. His teachers held that all varieties of extant life came into being during the 6 days of creation described in the book of Genesis and had remained constant since they had been directly created by God. What Darwin observed on the Galápagos Islands presented him with contradictory evidence.

Darwin noted that both plants and animals existed in forms that were sufficiently similar to be grouped into species, but they differed enough to be unique individuals within that species. He also observed that living species resembled extinct species known to have lived in the same area (Himmelfarb, 1959, p. 149). These observations led him to ask why some species thrive and others become extinct and why some distinct species closely resemble other species and how they came about. If all species were created at the same time, why do some thrive and some pass out of existence? The distribution of similar species on the

Image 14.5	Galápagos Finches: Darwin bases his theory of evolution on observed differences among the same species

1. Geospiza magnirostris   2. Geospiza fortis
3. Geospiza parvula   4. Certhidea olivacea

Finches from Galapagos Archipelago

Galápagos Islands provided a clue to the answer.

In the 1830s, about 20 species of birds lived on the archipelago, of which 14 were finch species. As Darwin traveled from one island to another, he noticed that there were distinct species of finches whose differences seemed related to the environmental demands of the particular island where they were living (Charlesworth & Charlesworth, 2003, p. 58). Examples included the woodpecker finch, which compensates for not having the long tongue of a true woodpecker by using a sharp stick or spine from a cactus plant to probe fissures in tree branches to impale grubs; and the ground finch, which steals the eggs of the booby bird. The beak of the ground finch is shaped to facilitate securing its body while it strikes the egg against a rock to access its contents. In each of these two cases, the finches had beaks that seemed to conform to their preferred foods. Darwin proposed that, at some earlier time, there was one species of finch that had colonized the islands, each island having different environmental demands. Over time, random changes in the offspring of the finches would occasionally produce an individual whose difference from its progenitors would endow it with a competitive advantage. The finch with the advantageous trait would ultimately procreate at a higher rate and supplant other less well-adapted finches.

Publication of *The Origin of Species*

The data Darwin collected on the voyage of the *Beagle* led him to a radical conclusion—that a process of natural selection accounts for the diversity of life far better than does a literal interpretation of the account of creation in Genesis. Darwin decided that a common ancestor whose descendants evolved into several disparate new species is a more logical explanation of such phenomena as the Galápagos finches than a deity creating numerous similar but distinct species.

Darwin pointed to the existence of vestigial organs in humans and other animals as evidence of natural selection. He noted that a creator was not likely to form human beings with such unnecessary structures as the coccyx (tail bone) and the vermiform appendix; whales with a pelvis; or ostriches with nonfunctional wings. He presented an alternative scientific explanation, proposing that these structures were once functional in earlier versions of the species, but through natural selection, they had become irrelevant. So humans had ancestors with tails, whales developed from walking animals, and ostriches had ancestors that took flight. The changes took place gradually over many millennia as the environment placed changing demands on life forms facing adversity and limited resources. As evidence for the numerous changes of species over time, Darwin pointed to the fossil record, which preserves an abundance of extinct life forms. Why, he asked, would a deity create a world with traces of living things that had never existed? A better explanation is that the fossils represent organisms that failed to adapt to the changing demands of their respective environments. They may have produced progeny that lived on as new and better adapted species, but their own demise left only fossils denoting a species that gradually became unviable.

Darwin believed that the process of natural selection linked human beings and the great apes. Contrary to many accounts, he did not believe that humans are descended from apes. Rather, he hypothesized that both humans and apes are the distant progeny of a common primate ancestor. This early progenitor no longer exists and, like many fossilized animals, did not fare as well as its evolved offspring. Because humans share a common origin with all other living things, Darwin did not believe that they are qualitatively different from other organisms. Accordingly, humans differ in degree but not in kind from other animals. Darwin pointed out that other animals possess characteristics associated with being human, such as intelligence, emotions, and communicative ability. He also rejected the notion that qualities such as morality, empathy, or love are anything more than naturally selected traits that exist because they provide humans with adaptive advantages. The natural selection of these adaptive advantages is the only process that determines which species live and which die. Darwin rejected the notion that the choice of life and death is made by a benevolent creator. Instead, he viewed the mechanical and noncognizant process of natural selection as the only arbiter of life and death.

In essence, Darwin stated that Thomas Malthus (1766–1834), a clergyman known for his studies of population growth, was correct in concluding that the growth of the population of any species will typically lead to an overwhelming of the resources it needs to survive. This process then leads to a struggle for scarce resources in which those organisms that are most successful in acquiring those resources will live longer and in better health. Their survival will, in turn, facilitate their ability to reproduce. Because organisms, even within the same species, tend to differ, those with differences that offer even slight advantages in obtaining food, water, or even mates will reproduce at a greater rate. These differences will be inherited by the offspring until, in many cases, only the descendants of the advantaged organisms will survive. This process in essence is the natural selection that Darwin described.

Because organisms possessing differences that provide competitive advantages are more likely to survive and reproduce at a greater rate than others, those traits that differ will tend to become more pronounced. The result is that organisms with that trait are likely to mate with others possessing the same trait. Chance exaggerations of that trait will then produce even greater advantages to the descendants. Over generations, the entire species will undergo a gradual change in its form, which is called evolution. Evolution exists in all life forms at all times, although people often miss its significance. For example, when a doctor describes a cancer that fails to respond to chemotherapy, a bacterium that becomes resistant to an antibiotic, or a virus that jumps the species barrier from a pathogen that infects only animals to one that can infect humans, the doctor is talking about evolutionary processes. The stereotypical picture of upward progress from apes to human beings left many researchers thinking in a box. The process of natural selection, however, does not require improvement in intelligence or any other functional measure. Instead, it is a system without values or mercy in which changes in an organism endow it with an advantage that allows it to reproduce at a greater rate. If this increase in reproductive capacity is even minutely advantageous, those within a species possessing it will completely supplant those of the same species who are not so gifted.

回 THE GENETIC DIMENSION OF EVOLUTION

The Contributions of Lamarck and Mendel

A problem that vexed Darwin through the numerous editions of the *Origin of Species* was his inability to explain the process that produced the changes in species that would endow them with more adaptive qualities than their forebears. A solution to this problem had been advanced a generation before Darwin's birth by Jean-Baptiste Pierre Antoine de Monet, Chevalier de Lamarck. In a book titled *Philosophie Zoologique*, published in 1809, Lamarck proposed that organisms could adapt their structures, even to the point of developing new organs, in response to environmental demands. Moreover, Lamarck believed that these acquired characteristics could be inherited by the organism's offspring, and this idea became known as **Lamarckism**.

Lamarck's paradigm had strong face validity and still does, as we often see corresponding changes in individuals who endure continued life demands. For example, most would conclude that the enhanced musculature of athletes or people who perform physical labor is an adaptation to their environment of hard exercise or hard work. So intuitive was the logic of Lamarck's explanation of change that it became the generally accepted model of evolution. In fact, Darwin gradually adopted an increasing number of Lamarckian principles with each subsequent edition of the *Origin of Species*. He was compelled to make these alterations as a result of his inability to explain why organisms should change at random. Even if they could change in that way, some would argue, why wouldn't the change be absorbed and diluted by subsequent generations?

The answer that Darwin never found came from the work of an Austrian botanist and Augustinian monk, Gregor Mendel (1822–1884). Although he never passed the national examination for his teacher's license in physics, Mendel laid the foundation for the science of genetics. His work with pea plants revealed a pattern of dominant and recessive inheritance. It would have bolstered Darwin's original contention that individual traits can be inherited. Unfortunately for Darwin, Mendel's findings were published in an obscure Austrian botany journal in 1866. His work did not become widely known until 1900, when the botanists Carl Erich Correns, Erich Tschermak von Seysenegg, and Hugo de Vries independently came to similar conclusions. When reviewing prior research in the field, they discovered Mendel's original article outlining his discoveries and theory.

Of course, all this work took place before genetics and the role of germ cells were understood. What Lamarck and others like Erasmus Darwin could not know is that there are genes in reproductive or germ cells that are separate from the cells in the rest of the organism.

Thus, if the organism or the environment acts to change the structure or cells or the genes in a body part, there is no reason for these changes to occur in the germ cells. For example, if a blacksmith builds up his arms and thereby changes the nature of the muscle cells in his arms and chest, these changes will have no effect on his germ cells. Consequently, the children of blacksmith are not born with larger muscles. The functional separation of germ cells means that adaptations to life demands could not easily—if at all—be conveyed through reproduction.

Lamarck had concluded that our hypothetical blacksmith's robust physique would be conveyed to his offspring. We now know, however, that the process of evolutionary change does not work in this fashion. The blacksmith's sperm cells are quite separate from the cells in the muscle tissue that have responded to the nature of his work. The new research said that the blacksmith's (male) children were no more likely to be well-muscled than if their father had been a clerk—although some recent evidence suggests that this might, in fact, not be entirely true. There was no knowledge of genetics during the time when Darwin wrote the *Origin of Species*. Gregor Mendel's work, which paved the way for an understanding of the laws of genetic inheritance, was in preparation but was two generations away from general acceptance.

In sum, Darwin and his proponents were at a loss to explain how the changes that would be necessary for an organism to adapt to the surrounding environment could take place. We now know that the process involves variations, which usually occur by chance, in the genes that guide an organism's development. Changes to the deoxyribonucleic acid (DNA)—the molecule of nucleic acid responsible for the transmission of an organism's genetic "blueprint"— in genes are called **mutations**.

DNA and Genes

Deoxyribonucleic acid, or DNA, is a generally stable molecule that is capable of both replication and encoding of all information necessary to design a complex organism. In humans and most other organisms, the DNA is stored in the nucleus of the cell in the form of chromosomes. Chromosomes are threadlike chains of genes, which themselves are chainlike arrangements of nucleic acids. The DNA molecule is shaped like a double helix, or spiral, in which two strands of a sugar-phosphate molecule wind around each other. The stability of the DNA molecule results in part from the unique bonds between the nucleic acids. The four nucleic acids that represent the core of the DNA molecule are arranged in base pairs of nucleotides joined by hydrogen bonds, such that adenine always pairs with thymine and guanine with cytosine. This pattern of pairing allows for the DNA molecule to replicate itself reliably. When the hydrogen bond that links the paired nucleotides is broken, the single strand effectively creates a template for a new strand.

The role of DNA in encoding the structure and nature of the organism is based on the specific sequence of **nucleotides**. A gene consists of a large sequence of nucleotides that commonly encode proteins. The proteins that are the foundation of the structure of the cell as well as enzymes and hormones are all encoded by specific genes. Proteins are composed of combinations of 20 different amino acids. They are constructed according to the unique combination of nucleic acids that determines both the shape of the protein and its constituent amino acids.

A gene always has a counterpart on the homologous or corresponding chromosome called an **allele.** In most cases, only one allele is active in the construction of proteins; this is called the dominant allele, whereas the inactive one is the recessive allele. Our **phenotype** denotes our expression of all dominant or expressed genes; it is sometimes described as the outcome of our genotype interacting with our environment. In contrast, our genotype refers to our complete complement of both dominant and recessive genes; that is, the full amount of our hereditary information. Genotypes are important because recessive genes can be passed along to offspring, and if not paired with a dominant gene, they will then be expressed in the phenotype. For example, if a woman has brown eyes and a recessive gene for blue eyes and has four children by a man who also has a brown-eye phenotype and a genotype for brown and blue eyes, one of the four children is likely to have blue eyes. It is important to remember, however, that few traits are governed by a single allele.

The role of genes in governing both human bodies and human behavior is quite complex. For example, besides coding proteins, genes can also regulate one another; that is, genes can activate or deactivate other genes. This function makes the actions of genes more complex than merely coding for proteins. There is an intricate interplay among genes in which the estimated 25,000 to 30,000 genes in human beings can produce the vast number of cells, organs, biochemical substances, and other components of the human being. This number seems surprisingly low and is exceeded by the gene count of several plants. But rather than disqualify our genes as a basis for determining who we are, it actually speaks to the complexity of their interactions. The human **genome** is not a static blueprint but a living document that interacts with itself and the world it encounters as the species develops.

This complex and dynamic system, however, sometimes leads to errors. The processes by which genes are replicated, self-regulate, and produce all the organism's proteins are very reliable, but complexity almost always leads to some mistakes. When a mistake occurs, it often disrupts the construction of some key components of an organism. On very rare occasions, it can actually bestow an advantageous change or even add a new feature to the organism. These mistakes are called mutations; they represent changes in single genes or sections of a chromosome. In general, for a mutation to be meaningful in an evolutionary sense, it must take place in a **gamete** (a germ or reproductive cell). If a mutation occurs in somatic (body) cells, the result may be dysfunction, cancer, or cell death, but there is no direct way in which the change can be passed along to the offspring of the individual undergoing the mutation.

Mutations can be caused by such chemicals as solvents (benzene) or medications, such forms of ionizing radiation as x-rays or ultraviolet light, or by errors in DNA replication. Common types of mutations include **point mutations** or substitutions, which occur when one nucleotide is replaced or inserted in the DNA molecule in error. An **inversion mutation** takes place when a segment of a chromosome breaks away during mitosis or **meiosis.** The disconnected segment then reattaches to the chromosome in an inverted position. A similar type of mutation is the **translocation mutation,** in which a segment of a chromosome breaks away during cell duplication but reattaches to a different chromosome or the wrong portion of the same chromosome. Should a segment of the chromosome break away and fail to reattach at any point, resulting in a loss of genetic material, it is called a **deletion mutation.** In contrast, genetic material can be added to an organism when a portion of a chromosome is duplicated, usually during the process of cell division, and attaches itself to a chromosome. This is a **duplication mutation.**

In addition to mutations, changes in a genome can take place through the recombination of genes on a chromosome. This process is believed to result in faster changes in a species than random mutations. Recombination takes place during meiosis, which is the process of producing gamete cells containing half of the parent's genetic material. In meiosis, the order of genes on a chromosome is changed as a result of an exchange of DNA between homologous chromosomes.

Genetic Drift

Genetic drift is another process that is believed to result in evolutionary changes to a genome. Genetic drift occurs when segments of a species population are separated from the rest of the species. For example, monk parrots, which are indigenous to Central America, have been brought to North America as pets. Enough of these birds have escaped captivity to establish wild colonies in the northeastern United States. According to the principle of genetic drift, the gene pool or the total number of available alleles for all monk parrot traits will be more limited in the colonies of escaped birds in the United States than what would be found in the larger population back home in Central America. Smaller populations, which have a smaller selection of alleles, are more likely to produce animals with traits determined by less common alleles because each individual's alleles now constitute a larger portion of a smaller gene pool.

If this hypothesis is correct, the monk parrots in North America would diverge from their progenitors in Central America. There is evidence that this divergence is in fact happening. These tropical birds appear to have been naturally selected to survive the frigid winters in cities like Chicago. The monk parrots are an example of how speciation or the development of a new species can take place without mutations. It is important to understand that genetic drift is *not* a response to environmental demands but a result of small populations breeding in isolation. Thus, genetic drift can result in marked changes in species that are not necessarily adaptive.

A related evolutionary theory is **punctuated equilibrium** (Gould & Eldredge, 1993), which challenges Darwin's theory that natural selection is a gradual and fairly continuous process. According to Darwin, species change over many millennia, leaving intermediate species existing for extended periods. In fact, Darwin spent a full chapter in the *Origin of Species* explaining why so few missing evolutionary links had been found. According to this variant of evolution by natural selection, species will often remain static in form for thousands of centuries and then undergo a rapid period of adaptive change. In addition, only a subset of a species will evolve in this way, so that the fossil record may not record the intermediate species. Punctuated equilibrium typically takes place when a population becomes physically separated from the rest of the species. According to its main proponents, a new species can evolve in these circumstances as quickly as a few thousand years, and changes at this rate would not leave evidence in the geologic strata that preserve fossils.

Lysenko and Marxist Evolutionary Dogma

Many who reject natural selection may do so without the knowledge of a bizarre era for science in the former Soviet Union that resulted from the doctrinaire rejection of Darwin's concepts. Trofim Denisovich Lysenko (1898–1976) was an expert in plant breeding. He developed a rigid belief in the principles of Lamarck on the basis of his personal experience; he therefore rejected natural selection as the foundation of species change. Lysenko rose to a high position as a biologist in the Soviet Union. He achieved prominence when he claimed to discover the vernalization of wheat. This process shortened the growing period of winter crops of wheat by wetting and cooling the germinated seeds of the summer crop.

Image 14.6　Trofim Denisovich Lysenko (1898–1976)

Lysenko's growing stature in the Soviet Union endowed him with extraordinary power, given that he was working during the regime of Josef Stalin, a tyrant who summarily executed millions. The fear of being labeled a dissident extended to every realm of society, including that of science. This fear made it difficult for many scientists who researched evolution by natural selection because Lysenko completely rejected virtually all of Darwin's and Mendel's concepts. Everything that could have been done to prevent the development of the science of genetics was carried out in the Soviet Union under Lysenko's rule. Lysenko went as far as to condemn Mendelian genetics as reactionary and decadent. He referred to scientists who pursued related lines of research as enemies of the Soviet people.

For a 5-year period, from 1948 to the year of Stalin's death in 1953, Lysenko dominated all biological research and applications. His theories, known as **Lysenkoism,** were based entirely on personal intuition and included the notion that rye plants could be obtained by altering the environment in which wheat plants are grown. Using similar logic, Lysenko stated that the demands of living in the wild would result in domestic dogs giving birth to foxes. In essence, he was an extremist defender of Lamarck. His rejection of Darwin had a powerful appeal to Soviet leaders,

(Continued)

(Continued)

who advocated an egalitarian and noncompetitive society. The idea that competition for limited resources was the force powering species development was rejected as capitalist dogma. The principle of survival of the fittest was seen as the justification of capitalists for oppressing the working class.

Unfortunately, Lysenko's extremism was not limited to theoretical abstractions. Russian farmers were actually forced to act on his ideas. For example, in an effort to cultivate trees, Lysenko mandated planting the trees in a cluster based on the idea that the seedlings would not be competing for the limited access to sunlight and nutrients, but like good communists, they would grow cooperatively. This program, which cost nearly a billion rubles, resulted in fewer than 15% of the trees surviving (Watson & Berry, 2003). These and similar programs were based on an idiosyncratic theory of heredity that rejected the existence of genes but asserted that each cell had the capacity to change in response to environmental demands.

Under Lysenko's guidance, the historic principles of the science of inheritance were ignored. Instead, dogma and politics guided the applications of technology with disastrous results. The Soviets had rejected evolution by natural selection because it conflicted with the Marxist creed, which holds that the collective determines the history as well as the formation of people and their personalities. Marxism was absurdly extended to basic biology by proponents who held that the Marxist dialectic can control nature. After all, it was anathema to Marxist doctrine that the individual can evolve or develop even partially, independent of social forces. Their dogma was exacerbated by the correlation fallacy—the notion that events that occur in succession do so because of a causal relationship. In most cases, however, there are hidden confounding variables that create the apparent causal link. Is Lysenkoism completely dead? In its strongest form yes, but we can find some remnants in the use of psychological interventions based on the intuition of practitioners rather than on research evidence.

Sociobiology, Evolutionary Psychology, and Personality

A central issue in the understanding of personality development is the significance of the role that genes play in determining the characteristics of a person. Many researchers, for example, David Buss (1995) and Steven Pinker (1997, 2002), suggest that many traits are directly governed by the genome. They would argue that humans, like many other animals, have genes that directly endow the organism with innate knowledge and prepare it for action without any shaping through experience. Thus, for some traits or behaviors, the environment surrounding the individual has little or no importance. This position is in contrast to those like Blumberg (2005), who posit that there are far too few genes in the human genome to account for the wide variations observed in human personality. Advocates of this position suggest that genetics plays a relatively small role, perhaps no more than guiding some basic inclinations.

Instead, people are shaped by their experiences, environmental forces, and their interactions with others.

Sociobiologists and evolutionary psychologists lean more toward the former view. They see most aspects of human nature as having evolved in the face of shifting environmental demands. Consequently, the essential path that we must take to understand personality and all other human qualities is to infer what advantages each would bestow in the various settings in which people find themselves. This perspective largely originated from the work of the sociobiologists, who focused primarily on the role biology and genetics played in animal social behavior. As noted at the beginning of the chapter, the consensus founder of the field is Edward O. Wilson, who provoked a great deal of controversy by suggesting that human behavior evolves. Such a notion is disturbing to some observers because it appears to suggest that many behaviors that are regarded as socially disruptive are in fact naturally selected and adaptive—in some environments, at least.

EVOLUTIONARY PSYCHOLOGY

The preceding section summarizes the abundant evidence that many human behavioral and cognitive characteristics have a genetic basis, but it does not answer the question of the origins of this development. The answer, according to evolutionary psychologists, is that behavioral characteristics come about by the very same processes as physical traits. Evolution by natural selection is a directionless and nonjudgmental process that results in changes to species when chance mutations provide even a minimal advantage in reproduction. It is directionless in the sense that organisms are not necessarily developing toward greater complexity, intelligence, or beauty. Thus, evolution does not push development in any particular direction unless that direction allows the organism to reproduce at a higher rate. As Steven Pinker (1997, pp. 163–164) points out, if an organism that constitutes 0.1% of a species develops a mutation that allows it to have 1% more offspring, its descendants will replace 99.9% of the original species in just 4,000 generations.

This example represents the essence of all evolutionary processes: If a change that can be passed along to offspring enhances an organism's ability to reproduce, the organism is on its way to evolving. Such a change does not have to make the organism more complex, smarter, or bigger; it merely has to increase its efficiency in reproducing. It is reasonable to assume that, after a sufficiently large number of generations, virtually every aspect of an organism is in service to its reproductive capacity. And cognitive capacities are no exception to this principle. Evolutionary psychology is founded on this principle. Specifically, it seeks to understand behaviors and cognitions in terms of their contribution to the inclusive fitness of the organism.

Since Darwin's landmark proposition, there has been little doubt among life scientists that the human body is the product of eons of evolution. When the various components of the body are studied, from the most basic organic compounds to organ systems, their role in aiding human survival is fundamental to understanding them fully. Each of the components and organs of the body plays a precise role in an orchestration of functions facilitating life and reproduction. Their contribution to human viability is considered in terms of homeostasis and evolutionary viability. That is, how does each of the many specialized components of the human body assist the human species in the Darwinian competition for life?

Image 14.7   Leda Cosmides

Evolutionary biologists have explored such human attributes as opposable thumbs, the upright spine, or the enlarged brain with its dense convolutions to understand how each of these has endowed us with competitive or adaptive advantages. Natural selection implies that individuals who possess any physical attribute that bestows even a minuscule advantage in reproductive fitness will replace most of their environmental competitors over time. Any trait that aids in survival naturally aids in reproduction. Evolutionary psychologists take an analogous approach, but instead of studying physical attributes, they study behavior and cognition.

Evolutionary psychologists seek to understand how specific behaviors and cognitions improve the fitness of the individual. The discipline further seeks to understand the environmental setting that encouraged the development of these beneficial attributes. Evolutionary psychologists also explore the functionally specialized areas of the brain and examine the ways in which they contribute to the competition for life and reproduction. The brain, like the rest of the body, is seen as a complex of specialized and interacting modules. Although the evidence for this hypothesis is not as distinct as that related to the organs of the body, evolutionary psychologists propose that the brain is organized into functionally specialized organs or modules (Cosmides & Tooby, 1999; Duchaine, Cosmides, & Tooby, 2001). The function of each of these modules is best understood in terms of its contribution to the process of living and reproduction.

John Tooby (1953–) and Leda Cosmides (1957–) are generally credited with formalizing the field of evolutionary psychology. They refer to the modularization of the brain as the "adapted mind" (Barkow, Cosmides, & Tooby, 1992), meaning that the brain consists of an assemblage of modules that have evolved to solve the problems of survival that humans faced during their evolutionary past. The brain may be said to function more like a multifunction calculator than a computer. It has many preprogrammed innate functions, which can act alone or, more typically, make use of life experience. Such brain programs help us to interpret facial expressions, encourage altruistic behavior, and define what we find attractive in a mate.

Many have misunderstood this model of the brain to mean that evolutionary psychologists see people as enslaved by their genes. This is not the case. The genome provides direction and guidance but also interacts with life events and experience to form the person. Only the most rudimentary functions are completely outside the control of individuals and the lives they lead. The complex cortex of the human brain evolved to endow us with the ability to make choices, to learn and to apply that learning. Few deny that we have free agency and can choose to apply or nullify our modules in most cases.

Evolutionary psychologists also take a distinctly teleological view of the brain. Like other organs of the body, the brain has an ultimate purpose or goal, which is to assist reproduction or the dissemination of its genome. This goal is accomplished through the natural selection of cognitive abilities that are best suited for many of the problems humans encountered during their evolutionary history. Thus, humans would be more capable of performing the innate complex calculations required to toss a rock or projectile accurately than to calculate the area of a triangle. Similarly, people would be more inclined to fear a snarling dog or an aggressive wasp than a speeding automobile. The reason is that the brain modules for throwing projectiles helped early humans to down prey, and the modules for fearing potentially dangerous fauna gave those who possessed them a bit more fitness in the competition for survival than those who lacked them.

Tooby and Cosmides (1992) have proposed several principles that define this discipline:

1. Every organ in the human body evolved to serve a function that promotes life and survival. The brain's function is to process environmental information to direct behavior and to regulate bodily functions. Tooby and Cosmides state that the brain is an organic computer with programs designed by natural selection.

2. Every human decision or action is a function of this organic computer. The function is based on innate programs that use inputs from our internal state and our external and social environment.

3. The programming of the brain's computer took place during the long period of human evolution. Thus, many of the programs are constructed to accommodate and facilitate survival within the environments in which our distant ancestors resided. As a result, many of the brain's programs are poorly adapted to our current environment.

4. The evolved programs can generally be assumed to be adaptive in the environments of our progenitors. They may no longer be so, however, as we now live in complex societies that are starkly different from the small nomadic bands of hunter-gatherers from whom we are descended.

5. The process of natural selection has developed a brain with many distinct cognitive programs, most which are specifically adapted for solving problems of survival. This concept is in contrast to the notion that the human brain is a general-purpose problem-solving device.

Advocates of these principles posit that the primary means for studying and understanding the nature of any organism is examination of the environment in which the organism evolved. The organism's behavior, temperament, or personality is believed to have evolved through natural selection, just as any physical feature did. The way to understand personality is to view each trait in terms of any adaptive advantage it may endow. For example, evolutionary psychologists would not necessarily consider fearfulness a deficit in humans. Instead, they would seek to find circumstances in which being fearful or even panicky might provide an individual with a survival advantage over someone who is bold.

Evolutionary psychologists warn against social value judgments in assessing the adaptive value of traits. Such socially endorsed behaviors as sexual fidelity are viewed radically differently by evolutionary psychologists. Men who commit to their spouses and have children with only one woman may put their genetic legacy in grave danger. The man who is not swayed by social norms and mores might have to face scorn and rebuke, but by fathering children with numerous women, he will likely have his genes better represented in future generations.

Evolutionary psychologists view the brain as an information processing system whose features evolved to meet the demands of the environment. The brain is composed of modules that essentially are regions of the brain that have evolved to allow the organism to respond to specific events or situations that our distant ancestors confronted.

Natural Selection of Psychological Mechanisms

Tooby and Cosmides (1990) suggest that most of us miss the subtle but profound workings of evolutionary psychology, as these workings result in competencies that we are likely to take for granted. Humans are replete with cognitive capacities that Tooby and Cosmides would classify as **evolved psychological mechanisms** (EPMs). EPMs can be defined as any aspect of a human or other animal's psychology that serves a specific purpose and was created and selected by evolutionary pressures. Some EPMs evoke little controversy, such as visual abilities like depth and distance perception or object constancy. Similarly, our olfactory sense and inclinations, which includes aversion to the smells of decay and fecal matter, are generally regarded as innate and adaptive. So, too, are the human faculties that permit the interpretation of verbal intonation or facial cues that indicate emotion, social attraction, or aversion (Frith & Frith, 1999).

The ability to communicate social attraction or revulsion is an adaptive attribute that is seen in such other primates as the great apes. Interestingly, people who are deficient in this ability, such as children with **Asperger's disorder** or autistic disorder, tend to fare quite poorly in most competitive social settings. Because all EPMs provided a reproductive advantage at some time, many deal with mating strategies. Age preferences in mating for each gender have been shown to follow the pattern of an EPM (Isaacson, 2001). Authors of one study consistently found that males seek younger females and females seek older males. This bias increases with older males, who tend to seek women progressively younger than themselves as they age. Conversely, the age bias declines with females, with older females seeking males closer in age to themselves. This finding supports the notion that males seek reproductive viability, which is most likely to be found in younger females, whereas females seek males who can provide the most parental resources, which are most likely to be greater in older males. Interestingly, the authors found that female fantasies centered around a liaison with a short-term partner commonly included a male younger than their ideal marriage partner.

Some researchers have argued that evolved psychological mechanisms can go awry when they are at odds with a changing cultural milieu (Barber, 1998). For example, the greater proportion of body fat to bone and muscle in females, which is relatively fixed, can become maladaptive when the evolved psychological mechanism that determines female attractiveness changes based on economic conditions. According to this model, corpulent women, who would be considered attractive in times of scarcity, are considered less desirable during times of plenty. The ideal image can change rather rapidly, too; a number of commentators have noted that Marilyn Monroe, considered the archetype of female beauty in the late 1950s, would be considered unattractively heavy in the early 2000s. Another EPM related to mating strategy was supported in a study that indicated that mechanisms exist to prevent conflict between same-sex friends who become rivals for the same mate (Bleske & Shackelford, 2001). For example, women are disinclined to become friends with other women they perceive as promiscuous.

EPMs for disease avoidance have been suggested in studies that examined bias against people with physical disabilities (Park, Faulkner, & Schaller, 2003). According to this theory, asymmetries following an amputation or structural differences, as in cases of paraplegia, cause observers to react as if the person with the disability had a contagious disease. This

EPM may have developed because many deformities or physical abnormalities in our evolutionary past resulted from disease. Our ancestors would have been well served if they avoided others who were obviously suffering from some type of infection. In the contemporary situation, however, this atavistic reaction leads to inaccurate assessments of and reactions to people who pose no threat to others' health.

Evolved psychological mechanisms operate under the principle of **domain specificity**. That is, they deal with recurrent problems in adaptation over the course of human evolutionary history.

Genes and Behavior

Evolutionary psychology and other systems that explain behavior in terms of innate characteristics all explain, at least in part, individual differences in terms of genes. Genes represent codes or templates for the production of either proteins or RNA. In doing so, genes can act to activate or suppress other genes but they can neither regulate behavior directly nor determine specific traits. They do play an indirect role in both behavior regulation and trait expression. The production of all somatic chemicals, from neurotransmitters and neuropeptides to hormones, are guided by each organism's genome. The intricate interactions among genes also guide the specific structure of the organism, including the arrangement and connection of neurons. The nature of these connections defines who we are and the nature of our personalities. Any individual neuron can only signal another neuron to increase or decrease the probability of that neuron sending a signal to still another neuron, but that complex symphony of signals serves to represent the outer world, our inner desires and fears, all combining to create the person.

An individual gene, like an individual neuron, has an unremarkable function. The neuron can send a chemical signal, and the gene can make a protein. The proteins can be used to build complex tissues or simpler substances like hormones or neurotransmitters. The proteins can act to regulate other genes' production of proteins by either inhibiting or increasing their level of activity.

Humans have far too many attributes for each to be governed by a specific gene. Thus, many traits must rely on multiple genes, while some genes may play roles in multiple traits. The influence of individual genes on multiple traits of an organism is referred to as **pleiotropy**. Pleiotropy is in contrast to **epistasis,** in which multiple genes interact to influence a single trait or characteristic. In humans, epistasis is at work in such traits as body shape, skin color, and height. Complicating this situation further is the fact that the expression of many genes is contingent on the environment. They can be compared to conditional statements as opposed to blueprints. Such complexities make it very difficult to separate the roles of genetics and of the environment in producing a specific characteristic in an organism. Genes regulate one another, and the expression of each gene can be influenced by environmental factors, producing a complex network of interactions.

In 1975, Amotz Zahavi (1928–), an Israeli evolutionary biologist, proposed that animals engage in self-handicapping behaviors as a means of demonstrating genetic fitness (Zahavi, 1975). The classic example of self-handicapping is the peacock, whose cumbersome plumage saddles him with greater caloric needs and increased susceptibility to predators. The advantage is the message to peahens that only a genetically superior bird could maintain such costly plumage. Similarly, gazelles, which respond to predators by fleeing, then slowing and jumping, demonstrate to the predator that they possess genes that make

Table 14.1	Genes Related to Behavior and Personality Traits

Gene	Examples of Characteristics Guided by a Single Gene
neuroD2	In mice, this gene has been linked to reduced fearfulness, and in humans, it is believed to be associated with diminished risk aversion.
DRD4	DRD4 produces the receptor for dopamine, a neurotransmitter. One allele, known as 7R, was strongly associated with ADHD. By analyzing the variations in DRD4, they also found that the 7R allele was created recently and may have provided an evolutionary advantage at some time in human history. The study could not determine, however, if that evolutionary selection is still occurring.
DTNBP1	The dysbindin-1gene is associated with intelligence and schizophrenia. One single nucleotide polymorphism of this gene, known as a haplotype, was demonstrated to be linked to a higher IQ, whereas other haplotypes appear to increase the risk of schizophrenia.
AGTR2	This gene, which codes for the receptor of angiotensin II, a peptide that regulates fluid levels, is associated with higher levels of mental retardation in a variant form.
TRP2	In mice, this gene allows for pheromone recognition. Without it, mice will not act aggressively toward invading males but instead will attempt to mate with them.
AVPR1a and SLC6A4	People possessing variants of a gene that codes for the arginine vasopressin 1a receptor and the serotonin transporter gene have enhanced abilities of social communication and feelings of spirituality, both of which are linked to the ability to dance.
GABABR2	This gene is a variant of the gene that codes for gamma-aminobutyric acid type B. It inclines those possessing it toward nicotine dependence.
BNDF	The brain-derived neurotrophic factor gene plays a role in the development of social aversions in mice
hSERT	A mutation in the human serotonin transporter gene has been linked to more severe forms of obsessive compulsive disorder

them too costly to chase. In essence, the **Zahavian handicap** describes evolutionary traits that would at first glance appear to be maladaptive but actually bestow a paradoxical evolutionary advantage.

For example, testosterone is a hormone that carries with it survival costs, such as reduced immunity to disease and shortened life span, so that those whose physique suggests high levels of the hormone could be less attractive to females. One study suggests, however, that the faces of males that are highly masculinized by testosterone are more attractive to females—Zahavian paradox. In this study, photographs of 45 men were analyzed for jaw size and eyebrow ridge development, which are considered indicators of masculinization. Sixty women were presented with 10 randomly chosen pairs of male faces and asked to rate them for attractiveness. As a whole, the women revealed no preference for more masculine faces unless they had scored highly on a sociosexuality scale, which indicates a preference for short-term mating. These findings suggest that women seeking males likely to offer parental investment or long-term marriage are not drawn to men who evidence high levels of testosterone, while those seeking only brief sexual encounters ostensibly will seek those with the best genome. In other words, a man who can flourish with high levels of testosterone signals to women that he possesses a superior genome (Pawlowski & Jasienska, 2005).

These principles have also been applied to male homosexuality (Dickemann, 1995), a characteristic that on first glance might appear to offer a distinct disadvantage in natural selection. However, if male homosexuals, who tend not to be invested in reproduction, offer nurturance or support to close relatives, such as nieces or nephews, they will be effectively enhancing their inclusive fitness. By selflessly aiding the survival of two nephews, each of whom bears 25% of his genes, the homosexual uncle has effectively lent support to the same number of his genes as if he had aided in the support of his own child, who would carry 50% of his genes.

Epigenetics and the Person

In most discussions of human traits, there are usually two dichotomous explanations: nurture or nature. (The phrase "nature or nurture" was coined by Francis Galton.) In essence, the idea is that our genes provide our basic blueprint, and the environment determines how the finished product of that blueprint develops. However, research into **epigenetics** suggests a more fundamental interaction between genetics and environment. This issue dates back to Larmarck's theory, which proposed that adaptation was evoked by environmental necessity as opposed to natural selection. Although the theory was fundamentally incorrect, the notion that environmental conditions may play a role in the structure of offspring may not have been entirely wrong. Darwin defined his principles of evolution by natural selection before the discovery of genes. He and his contemporaries inferred that there was some mechanism by which life forms transmit their characteristics to their offspring. We now know that DNA in the form of genes and chromosomes transmits all heritable traits from parent to offspring. The main problem for Lamarck's and similar theories is that they fail to account for the way in which any organism that makes adaptive changes during its lifetime can convey these changes to its germ cells. Without being able to do so, the organism's offspring cannot benefit from its accommodations to environmental demands.

For example, it is conceivable that the predecessors of the modern giraffe expanded their necks slightly by tenaciously reaching for leaves on high tree branches. But even if they did so, their offspring could not have benefited because the gametes of the parent animals would not have been changed by changes to the neck muscles or vertebrae. With the advent of the science of genetics, the barrier between the genome and environmental demands grew even higher. Natural selection prescribes that random changes or mutations to the genes in the gametes lead to occasional advantages for the bearer of these genes. Any giraffe with a chance mutation that led to a slightly longer neck would eat more easily and thereby be more likely to live to produce more offspring.

But studies of the development of genetically identical animals and humans with identical genomes—**monozygotic twins**—have produced a conundrum for genetic researchers: such twins are never exactly the same. There is no personality trait or psychological disorder that has perfect concordance in identical twins. The heights, intellects, and body weights of monozygotic twins are very similar but never identical. Even psychiatric illnesses such as schizophrenia and bipolar disorder, which are believed to be primarily genetic in origin, have high but never exact concordances. How is it that twins with identical genetic material can have so many differences in traits that are so highly genetically contingent?

This conundrum can be partially explained by the process of epigenesis. Epigenesis, which literally means "above the genome," refers to processes that alter or regulate the function of DNA but are not part of the DNA itself. Studies of the DNA molecule have revealed thousands of sites that researchers call *marks*. Molecules of hydrogen and carbon called methyl groups (CH_3) bind to these marks. Methylation (the attachment of methyl groups) occurs when enzymes link to methyl group points on DNA where there are links between the nucleotides cytosine and guanine. Methylation typically takes place at the beginning of a gene; thus, the attachment of a methyl group may have the effect of shutting down the entire gene. In addition to methylation, studies have shown that epigenesis can occur as a result of organic molecules binding to the histones—the coils around which DNA coils when it forms chromosomes. Histone acetylation, in which an acetyl group (CH3CO-) binds to the histone proteins of the chromosome, serves to promote the expression of certain genes.

Fraga and his colleagues (Fraga et al., 2005) studied DNA methylation and histone acetylation in 40 pairs of monozygotic twins. They found that in about a third of the twin pairs, there were measurable differences in the twins' epigenetic patterns. These differences were associated with twins who had lived in different environments and had experienced different degrees of health. Thus, the human genetic blueprint is not a static template but is dynamic and can interact with environmental agents, leading to variations in phenotypes even in people with identical genotypes. Studies suggest that many psychiatric and behavioral differences in identical twins result from epigenesis (Mill et al., 2006). Several teams of researchers have proposed that epigenesis explains some of the discordance in schizophrenia in monozygotic twins (Tsujita et al., 1998). A common explanation is that epigenetic histone modifications occur that alter frontal lobe functioning (Akbarian et al., 2005; Stadler et al., 2005).

Epigenetic modifications of the genome are a fundamental means by which the environment may shape personality, but even more significant, it may do so in a heritable manner (Kramer, 2005). This heritability stands in contrast to all the environmental insults that can change or damage genes: ionizing radiation, drugs, smoking, and so on. Environmental insults will not result in changes passed on to offspring unless they produce changes in the gametes. On the other hand, epigenesis, especially if it occurs early in development, can produce changes to the genes in germ cells—changes that can be passed to subsequent generations.

Heritability

Much of the prior discussion of the evolution and genetics of traits is predicated on determining how much of a characteristic of an organism is described by its genome and how much by the environment. The term **heritability** refers to a statistic that measures the portion of a characteristic that is inherited; that is, the portion that is associated with the genome. The heritability ratio for a trait is expressed as follows: $h^2 = (r_m - r_d) \times 2$, where r_m is the correlation of the trait in monozygotic twins and r_d is the correlation of the trait in dizygotic twins. The example set forth in Table 14.2 represents the calculation of the heritability of body weight. In this case, the correlation of the body weight of samples of monozygotic and dizygotic twins are calculated and subtracted. The remainder is multiplied by two, and the heritability coefficient is the result. Thus, if the correlation of body weight in monozygotic twins is .75 and in dizygotic twins is .25, the heritability (h^2) is $(.75 - .40) \times 2 = .7$

There are some problems with the calculation of heritability, however, in that the computation represents a ratio of genetic to environmental factors in a phenotype. This is not a problem if we are comparing people who are coming from a reasonably similar environment. If the role of the environment were to be substantially more consequential in the development of a characteristic, the role of the genome tends to shrink. For example, if we sought to determine the heritability of infant mortality, we would obtain a substantially different heritability ratio in Singapore than we would in Angola. The reason is that Singapore's infant mortality is slightly more than 2 per 1,000 births, while Angola's is close to 190 per 1,000. Consequently, infant mortality in Angola would be calculated to have a low heritability, whereas in Singapore, the ratio would suggest a high heritability because Angola's high number due to poverty, poor sanitation, and other factors would so increase the denominator of the ratio that genetic factors would seem inconsequential. In comparison, Singapore, with its very low rate of infant mortality, would serve to increase the importance of the genetic portion, which should be similar across human cultures.

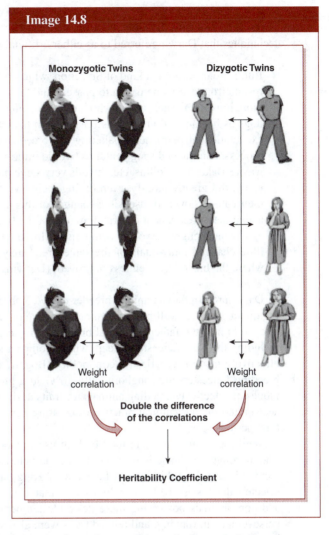

Image 14.8

Monozygotic Twins   Dizygotic Twins

Weight correlation   Weight correlation

Double the difference of the correlations

Heritability Coefficient

Genetics of Traits in Other Species

The discussion of eugenics at the beginning of the chapter failed to elaborate on a widespread, ongoing, and uncontested eugenics movement: animal breeding. The earliest human civilizations selectively bred animals to produce strains that had desirable physical and behavioral characteristics. The shift from hunting and gathering to farming led to efforts to breed animals that would produce more meat, milk, or labor. Evidence of animal breeding dates back to 11,000 years ago in what is now northern Iraq. Cattle were bred in what is now southwestern Iran 7,500 years ago, and the horse was domesticated in Russia as early as 5,000 years ago. Humans did not wait for natural selection to modify animals. They applied techniques that Darwin referred to as either artificial selection or unconscious selection:

> But, for our purpose, a kind of Selection, which may be called unconscious, and which results from every one trying to possess and breed from the best individual animals, is more important. Thus, a man who intends keeping pointers naturally tries to get as good dogs as he can, and afterwards breeds from his own best dogs, but he has no wish or expectation of permanently altering the breed. Nevertheless I cannot doubt that this process, continued during centuries, would improve and modify any breed, in the same way as Bakewell, Collins, etc., by this very same process, only carried on more methodically, did greatly modify, even during their own lifetimes, the forms and qualities of their cattle. Slow and insensible changes of this kind could never be recognised unless actual measurements or careful drawings of the breeds in question had been made long ago, which might serve for comparison. In some cases, however, unchanged, or but little changed individuals of the same breed may be found in less civilised districts, where the breed has been less improved. (Darwin, 1859/1996, p. 30)

Darwin referred to an animal breeder named Robert Bakewell (1725–1795) in the preceding quotation. Bakewell became famous for developing breeding techniques that led some to refer to him as the father of animal breeding. His techniques led to many breeds of animals including the New Leicesters sheep, whose compact size, small bones, and rapid maturation effectively made sheep flesh a commodity (Bogart, 1942, p. 9). He had similar success in breeding Leicestershire longhorn cattle to yield a greater amount of edible flesh. His techniques of selectively breeding animals for traits desired for human commerce or consumption accelerated the agricultural practice of creating new breeds of animals over relatively short time periods.

While some animals were modified for use as wool or meat, others were bred for speed. The thoroughbred horse is in shape, form, and behavior quite different from horses found in the wild. Breeding this animal began with King James I of England (1566–1625), who selected the fastest 10% of stallions and mated them with the fastest 50% of mares. In addition, animals possessing more desirable temperaments in terms of affinity to humans, perseverance in running, and related traits were also selected more often for breeding. Thus, both the physical and behavioral attributes of the horse were shaped by breeding.

Temperament is important to breeders of thoroughbred horses but even more critical to breeders of dogs. It is well established that canine behavior has a genetic component (Saetre et al., 2006), and it is also well known that behavior or personality differs according to the breed of dog. These differences are not likely to be accidents; dogs were bred for aggression, in the case of pit bulls and Doberman pinschers, and loyalty and intelligence in the case of collies. Each breed of dog exhibits a range of characteristic behaviors and temperaments, resulting from centuries of selective breeding for these very specific traits (Hart & Miller, 1985). Early hunters would not want an animal that would compete for prey, nor would they want one that would disrupt the hunt. Shepherds would not tolerate dogs that hunted the sheep they were supposed to guard. The gradual selection of animals that met the needs of their human hosts was unconscious, as Darwin called it. That is, the individual animals that best met the needs of their human hosts were allowed to remain and breed. Those that didn't were killed or expelled. Thus, a conscious goal of changing the behavior of the animal was not required to eventually produce one with the desired behavior.

People have been able to breed animals of many species for specific behaviors, appearances, or temperaments. Some mice have been selectively bred for aggressiveness (Gariépy & Lewis, 1996), and some rats have been bred to enthusiastically run mazes and passively accept human contact (Barnett, 2001, pp. 117–125). Current research indicates that virtually any behavioral characteristic in an animal can be enhanced or diminished by selective breeding. Given these findings, is it a logical conclusion that humans can be bred for specific behaviors? The evolutionary psychologists enthusiastically say yes, and they point to the natural environment as the breeder that has indeed selected humans for specific behavioral tendencies.

Evidence in Humans: Twins and Beyond

Resolving the question as to how much of human behavior is encoded in or guided by genes is confounded by a complex interplay of environmental and genetic variables. The question could be partially resolved by studying people who have identical genes, so that the greatest portion of variations among these people could be linked to environmental factors. Monozygotic (identical) twins share the same genome; thus, any difference in their phenotype must be primarily due to environmental factors. In most cases, the developmental environment of each member of a monozygotic twin pair is quite similar. Most are reared by the same set of parents, at the same location, in identical socioeconomic situations, and so on. It is particularly interesting, therefore, to study monozygotic twins who have not developed within the same environment.

Whether the subjects are raised together or apart, however, twin studies provide convincing evidence of the genetic basis of behavior. One such study examined the degree to which heritability explained something as basic as gender identity (Coolidge, Thede, & Young, 2002). In this study, the researchers examined 157 twin pairs, of which 96 were monozygotic and the remainder dizygotic. The authors of the study concluded that 62% of the subjects' gender identity was explained by genetic factors. Our gender identity is instrumental in choosing a mate. Whether or not this is a matter of volition, of inborn nature, or somewhere between the two remains a point of contention. Another group of psychologists studied the heritability of mating preferences. These researchers (Rushton & Bons, 2005) compared 174 pairs of monozygotic twins, 148 pairs of dizygotic twins, and 563 pairs of best friends in their preferences for social partners. The results indicated that 34% of the preferences for social partners can be explained by genetic factors, leading the authors to conclude that people are genetically inclined to choose people who resemble themselves as friends and lovers.

Even an existential characteristic of life like loneliness has been linked to genes. In a Dutch investigation of trait inheritance, 8,383 twins were given such self-rating items as "Others don't like me," "I lose friends very quickly," "I feel lonely," and "Nobody loves me." These items measured the participants' feelings of belonging and social affiliation (Sterelny & Fitness, 2003). The results led the authors to the conclusion that genetic factors explained 48% of the tendency to feel lonely.

In stark contrast to the human need for affiliation is the tendency to move against others with aggression. Not surprisingly, this, too, has been found to have a genetic connection in several studies of twins (Brendgen et al., 2005). For example, one study (Eley, Lichenstein, & Stevenson, 1999) recruited 1,022 pairs of Swedish twins and 501 pairs of British twins; about a third of the Swedish pairs and half of the British pairs were monozygotic. The researchers found no differences between the Swedish and British participants in the study, but they found that twins were more alike in aggressive antisocial behavior. They also found that aggressive antisocial behavior has a much stronger genetic component than nonaggressive antisocial behavior.

A genetic link has also been found in the construct of self-esteem. This study included 363 monozygotic and 238 dizygotic female twin pairs, who completed the Rosenberg Self-Esteem Questionnaire twice to quantify the stability of self-esteem over time. It was found to be relatively stable (test-retest reliability, 0.75). Significantly, heritability accounted for 52% of the variance in self-esteem scores (Roy et al., 1995).

Evolutionary psychologists have proposed that social behaviors such as reciprocal altruism (Aoki, 1983; Godfray, 1992), appropriate mating rituals, or aggressive displays are highly adaptive and tend to bestow survival advantages on those with the most effective manifestations. For example, if altruism is to be adaptive for survival, it must offer a benefit to altruists that will accrue to their offspring. This benefit may, in fact, accrue if members of a species have evolved a tendency to expect a reciprocal altruistic act when necessary. The evolutionary anthropologist Robert Trivers (1943–) elaborated on this concept in a classic work (Trivers, 1971) by proposing that altruism can be an evolved trait if it occurs reciprocally. Reciprocity is most likely to occur in small social groups. In contrast, in settings in which people are in infrequent contact with one another, altruistic acts would rarely be reciprocated and would thus be maladaptive.

Trivers went on to say that for altruism to be adaptive the payoff for altruism must exceed the cost to the individual for being altruistic. In short, all reciprocating altruistic individuals must end up better off for their altruism. An example of this benefit could occur in small groups of hunter-gatherers when a successful hunter would share his kill. Because there was no refrigeration in that period of human history, any meat he could not consume would be lost to decay; thus, his altruistic sharing came with little cost to him. When the act is reciprocated by another hunter in his group at a time when he needs food, both would have a net gain in their survivability.

The evolution of reciprocal altruism has been modeled in experiments based on the so-called prisoner's dilemma (Axelrod & Dion, 1988; Axelrod & Hamilton, 1981; Milinski, 1987; Shimizu, 1997), a classic teaching device in game theory, originally framed by Merrill Flood and Melvin Dresher working at the RAND Corporation in 1950. The dilemma is that of two suspects who have been detained for a crime about which they are being questioned separately. Confident of their guilt, the police present each of them with an ultimatum. If the prisoner cooperates, he will be given a reduced sentence, and the other prisoner will suffer the maximum punishment. Conversely, if the prisoner refuses to cooperate and his accomplice does, he will face the maximum punishment while his counterpart serves only a minimal sentence. Both prisoners are aware, however, that if neither of them cooperates, the police will most likely have to free both of them. In experiments based on this dilemma, participants are given points instead of prison time. The decisions and the resulting points are presented in a payoff matrix, an example of which is presented in Table 14.2.

If this game is played only once, the player can either testify against his colleague or remain silent. If a player testifies, he can score either 1 or 5, and if he remains silent, he can score 3 or –1. The obvious rational choice is to testify against his cohort. Because testifying is the obvious rational choice for both players, the likely outcome of the initial trial of the

	Player 1 Silent	Player 1 Testifies
Player 2 Silent	Both get off; score 3 each	Player 2 gets punished; score -1. Player 1 released: score 5
Player 2 Testifies	Player 2 released: score 5 (Player 1 punished with score –1)	Both get a light punishment: score 1

Table 14.2   Sample Prisoner's Dilemma Payoff Matrix

game is a score of 1. Notably, Axelrod (Axelrod & Hamilton, 1981) performed experiments in which participants played a prisoner's dilemma game repeatedly. He found that those who maintained a selfish strategy earned lower scores over time than those that adopted a less selfish or altruistic strategy. Axelrod and others (e.g., Boyd, 1988) have used this as a model of the way in which reciprocal altruism could have evolved in human communities without any awareness of moral values. Instead, altruism could have evolved because those who were inclined to adopt less selfish strategies would, in the long run, be more likely to survive and consequently pass on more of their genes.

In two separate experiments, Rilling et al. (2002) used functional magnetic resonance imaging (fMRI) to scan the brains of 36 women while they played the prisoner's dilemma game. Two players independently chose either to cooperate with each other or not (defect), and each was awarded a sum of money that depended on the interaction of both players' choices in that round. In the first experiment, 19 subjects were scanned in four game sessions designed to observe neural function during cooperation and non-cooperation in both human interactions (social) and interactions with a computer (non-social). The results of the first experiment revealed different patterns of neural activation depending on whether the playing partner was identified as a person or a computer. In the second experiment, 17 subjects were scanned during three game sessions that focused specifically on human interaction.

Mutual cooperation was the most common outcome in games played with presumed human partners in both experiments, even though a player was maximally rewarded for defecting when the other player cooperated. During the mutually cooperative social interactions, activation was noted in those areas of the brain that are linked to reward processing: the nucleus accumbens, the caudate nucleus, the ventromedial frontal and orbitofrontal cortex, and the rostral anterior cingulate cortex. Based on these studies, Rilling observed that people are innately rewarded for social cooperation. This is because there appear to be reward circuits in the brain that are activated by reciprocal altruism. And these circuits are so reinforcing that the temptation to accept altruistic behavior without reciprocating is suppressed. It simply feels better to maintain mutual cooperation.

This line of research has led evolutionary psychologists to conclude that altruism is not a form of selflessness but rather a biological tendency that can aid the altruist to survive in a hostile and competitive world—as long as the altruism is reciprocated. This was the observation of a graduate student named W. D. Hamilton (1964), who hypothesized that altruism could evolve as a behavioral trait if altruists are related to the beneficiaries of their generosity. This trait is exhibited in animals who sound an alarm when a predator approaches. Animals sounding

Image 14.9   Meerkat standing in vigilant position watching for predators

the alarm attract the attention of the predator, thus risking their lives for their fellows. Hamilton pointed out that even if the alarm-sounding animals become the prey, the act is worthwhile if they save relatives who share a high proportion of their genes.

For example, meerkats, animals similar to the mongoose, are known for their apparently altruistic behavior. When a colony of meerkats gathers, one assumes a vigilant posture by standing on hind legs watching for predators. By doing so, the altruistic meerkat becomes an easy target for any nearby predators. Research has shown that these seemingly altruistic behaviors in meerkats and other animals increase in proportion to the genetic related-ness of the animals being guarded. In effect, an alarm call is more probable if nieces and nephews are nearby than if cousins are.

Altruism in this form aids the inclusive fitness of the self-sacrificing animals. That is, they may not be able to transmit their genes directly, but they will do so indirectly by allowing relatives to live long enough to reproduce. But how does altruism of the form modeled in the prisoner's dilemma survive if relatives are not involved? The prisoner's dilemma experiment shows that a tendency toward altruism evolves if expectation of the altruism of others is likely. The experiment, however, raises an evolutionary problem, namely cheating. If people had evolved a tendency to depend for survival on the exchange of altruistic acts, what is to prevent the evolution of a line of individuals who adapt by cheating? These people would thrive by accepting the altruism of others and would offer nothing but gloating in exchange.

Cosmides (1989) put forth a compelling solution, that of cheater detection. Cosmides theorized that a natural selection for altruism would have to be associated with selection for the ability to detect cheaters in implicit social contracts. To test for the existence of a cheater detection module in the human brain, Cosmides and her coworkers devised a series of experiments based on the so-called Wason selection task, which tests propositional logic in the form of: *If P, then Q.* In this selection task, participants are asked to solve a problem like one presented below. Each of four cards has a letter on one side and a number on the other. Participants must determine which cards would have to be turned over to test the validity of the proposition that if a card has a D on one side then it must have 5 on the other side, or put in the form of the proposition: If P (D), then Q (5) (see Figure 14.1).

Most people will first turn D over to check to see if there is a 5 on the other side, understanding that it will demonstrate that *If P, then Q* is violated, if P is true but Q is false,

Figure 14.1

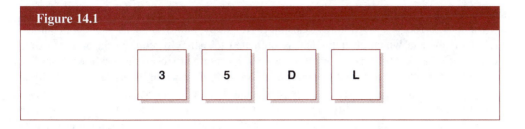

that is, if we have a D on one side and there is no 5 on the other side. However, most participants also tend to turn over the 5, apparently making the assumption that if a D is not on the other side of the 5, then the proposition is false. The proposition, however, sets no condition for cards with 5s on them, only those with Ds. So if the card has a D on the back, the statement is true, but if it doesn't, all we have shown is that 5s don't have to have Ds on the back—which is not part of the proposition.

It is obvious to most participants that if L is turned over, it will offer no help in proving the truth of the proposition. But most participants tend to miss that the 3 must be turned over. For the proposition to be true, there must be a letter other than D on the other side of the 3. This can be presented in the form of the contrapositive *If not-Q, then not-P* which is the logical equivalent of the proposition If P, then Q. Thus, the D and the 3 have to be turned over to prove the truth of the proposition. It is no surprise that most people have difficulty solving this problem, as it is not presented in a way that humans are evolutionarily prepared to comprehend or resolve.

However, when Cosmides and other evolutionary psychologists conducted experiments using logical problems like the one presented above, but based them on social judgments similar to the one in Figure 14.2, the results were quite different.

In such a task participants would be asked to decide the truth of the proposition: *If a person drinks gin, she has to be over 21 years old.* The cards have a drink on one side and an age on the other. The solution is conceptually identical to the first problem—that is, both the Gin and 16 cards would have to be turned over. Not surprising was the finding that problems that tested logical reasoning without a social basis were beyond the skills of most participants; only about 10% arrived at the correct solution. When the solution was founded on a real-world matter like the drinking problem presented above, about 75% of the subjects were correct.

This content effect showed that problems having nearly identical logical form but differing only in their content yielded radically different results. Tooby and Cosmides proposed that the

Figure 14.2

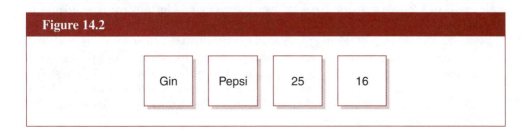

content effect results from the fact that the drinking problem models a social contract rule (Cosmides & Tooby, 1989; Fiddick, Cosmides, & Tooby, 2000). A social contract is defined as "a situation in which an individual is obligated to satisfy a requirement of some kind, usually at some cost to him- or herself, in order to be entitled to receive a benefit from another individual (or group)" (Barkow, Cosmides, & Tooby, 1992, p. 180). In this case, the ability to drink gin without being subject to arrest is a social benefit for those who are least 21 years old. Thus, if we have the ability to detect cheating in tacit social contracts, then this type of problem should be more easily solved than equally difficult problems that do not deal with social contracts. This is what Cosmides and her coworkers consistently found.

The work of evolutionary psychologists like Cosmides and Tooby demonstrates that human personality is based at least partially on evolved and heritable social behaviors. It follows that many social behaviors should be heritable. That was the conclusion of a study of twins. The parents of twins in 670 families were given questionnaires about the social behaviors of their children. The authors concluded that 68% of social skills can be explained by hereditable factors (Scourfield, Neilson, Lewis, & McGuffin, 1999).

Further evidence that sociability has a genetic or biological basis is supported by two highly disparate infirmities that can be viewed as extremes in a dimension of sociability. People with Asperger's disorder typically cannot "mind read" or apprehend another's affective state through observing facial expressions and bodily posture. In stark contrast to people with Asperger's are those with **Williams syndrome,** who, despite cognitive deficits, are often perceived as intelligent because they typically display highly appropriate social behavior, are gregarious, and read others' emotional states quite accurately. For this reason, the disorder is sometimes called "cocktail party syndrome."

Religion is a highly social practice, and a person's experience of a spiritual connection or a desire to affiliate with an organized religion is often fundamental to that person's identity. This characteristic of personality seems to have a significant heritable component. Unlike religious affiliation, which seems to be culturally based, some religious attitudes (D'Onofrio, Eaves, Murrelle, Maes, & Spilka, 1999) can be explained by genetic factors. For example, in one study of religiosity (Koenig, McGue, Krueger, & Bouchard, 2005), 169 monozygotic and 104 dizygotic twins were administered a self-report inventory of the importance of religion in their lives and those of their parents. The results indicated a significant heritability of religiosity. It also suggested that monozygotic twins maintain similar levels of religious interest whereas dizygotic twins tend to diverge over their lifetimes. Such results imply that religious beliefs learned or enforced in childhood that do not correlate with inherent religious feelings will tend to diminish as the person grows older.

Given that there is often an indirect relationship between any trait and any gene or set of genes, it follows that the behavior of an organism is not easily associated with its genome. In a Finnish study, 1,180 male and 1,315 female pairs of monozygotic twins along with 2,765 male and 2,613 female pairs of dizygotic twins were studied for lifetime concordance of schizophrenia. The authors concluded that the heritability of schizophrenia is about 83% (Cannon, Kaprio, Lonnqvist, Huttunen, & Koskenvuo, 1998). In other words, even though monozygotic twins have identical genetic structures and schizophrenia is strongly associated with the genome, 17 percent of the illness has to be explained by environmental factors. This study is unusual because it found a particularly strong genetic connection for the disorder. In fact, virtually no human behavioral characteristic has a heritability much higher than 60% (Benjamin, Ebstein, & Lesch, 1998).

This previous research shows that a significant portion of the human personality is constructed from heritable traits, behaviors, or brain modules. Do these findings mean that we are defined by our genes? Again, the simple answer is no. Our genes develop in an environment that includes every event, action, person, and place we encounter as we develop. Genes would produce the most efficient organism if they interacted with and responded to these environmental events during the development of the organism. These interactions are most likely to make us who we are.

Genetics of Personality

Traits and Temperament. Much of the research on the genetic basis of personality has centered on personality traits and temperament. Temperament and trait are closely related constructs in that both describe fundamental and enduring aspects of a person. In 1961, Gordon Allport provided a compelling definition of temperament:

> Temperament refers to the characteristic phenomena of an individual's nature, including his susceptibility to emotional stimulation, his customary strength and speed of response, the quality of his prevailing mood, and all the peculiarities of fluctuation and intensity of mood, these being phenomena regarded as dependent on constitutional make-up, and therefore largely hereditary in origin. (p. 34)

Temperament, therefore, refers to fundamental emotional responses, especially those that are long-standing or originate in childhood (Molfese & Molfese, 2000). The common usage of the adjective *temperamental*, which describes a person as moody, easily offended, or sensitive to slights, captures the essence of the term. In contrast to the temperaments are traits, which have been reviewed in Chapter 9. According to the *Diagnostic and Statistical Manual of Mental Disorders IV-TR* published by the American Psychiatric Association (2000), personality traits are "prominent aspects of personality that are exhibited in a wide range of important social and personal contexts" (p. 826). The psychologist's definition is similar. A personality trait is an enduring feature of a person that results in observed consistencies in behavior. Thus, a person who is consistently anxious, fearful, and suspicious would be judged to have the trait of neuroticism, without implying that neuroticism is either learned or innate. In contrast to more specifically defined traits, temperament is viewed as a more fundamental and organically based behavioral inclination. McCrae and his coworkers (2000) suggest that the essential difference between trait and temperament research is that temperament researchers are concerned with the underlying processes of behavioral inclinations, whereas trait researchers examine the outcomes of these inclinations with particular regard to their origins. Thus, there is no meaningful explanatory value in making the distinction between a trait and a temperament. We are inclined to agree. Until such time as the evidence shows that there is an actual psychological or biological basis that allows for a precise distinction between the two, they can be considered variations of a single theme.

Eysenck's Scales. Hans Eysenck and his coworkers (Eysenck & Eysenck, 1985) argued that there is a physiological, neurological, and genetic foundation of personality traits (Eysenck,

1990). Eysenck posited that a neural tract called the ascending reticular activating system endows people with diverse degrees of brain stimulation. According to Eysenck, introverts will generally have a higher baseline of internal stimulation, thereby making them more sensitive to external events. Accordingly, "introverts are characterized by higher levels of activity than extraverts and so are chronically more cortically aroused than extraverts" (Eysenck & Eysenck, 1985, p. 197). According to Eysenck, neuroticism is mediated by varying thresholds of arousal in the sympathetic nervous system and in the limbic structures that regulate the fight-or-flight response. Consequently, the trait of neuroticism is most evident and measurable in times of stress. Eysenck posits that an introvert with low neuroticism will have a higher baseline level of arousal but will react less dramatically to a stressful situation than a neurotic extravert. A neurotic extravert will be inclined toward verbal and physical aggression, deception, and theft. In contrast, the neurotic introvert will be prone to depression, unfulfilled daydreaming, and professional inefficiency.

Eysenck's third personality dimension, psychoticism, is conceptualized as being **orthogonal** to (statistically independent of) the extraversion and neuroticism dimensions. Those afflicted with its extreme form are prone to such psychotic conditions as schizophrenia, bipolar disorder, and antisocial personality disorder. This dimension's link to three somewhat disparate conditions has resulted in questions about its legitimacy as a distinctive dimension of personality (Block, 1977a, 1977b). Despite these conceptual problems, however, there is sufficient evidence of genetic and statistical associations with Eysenck's measure of psychoticism and psychotic illness to provide a reasonable degree of legitimacy (Gattaz, 1981; Gattaz, Seitz, & Beckmann, 1985; Gentry, Polzine, & Wakefield, 1985). An individual with a high degree of this dimension lacks empathy, is aggressive, has strange preferences in regard to food and pleasure, and tends to view the world in idiosyncratic ways. Eysenck believed that less pronounced elevations in this dimension inclined people to be creative or innovative. A recent study that examined the relationship between Eysenck psychoticism scores and creativity, however, failed to find a link (Reuter et al., 2005). Eysenck proposed that differences in hormone production, most notably of testosterone, and levels of catecholamines like norepinephrine are responsible for variations in psychoticism. There is, however, only weak evidence to support this hypothesis.

VIGNETTE

For the first few years of her life, Jeanine was an affectionate but quiet child. She idolized her brother, Billy, whom she followed around like a puppy. Her parents were attentive but not overly demonstrative. The parents divorced, however, when Jeanine was 15. She and Billy remained in their home with her mother, where they fared well without their father—who had become involved with another woman. His visits, infrequent to begin with, became even less frequent over the next few years when his paramour became his second wife.

Jeanine was an adequate although not outstanding student in high school. Her dream was to find an office job after graduation and earn enough money to buy nice things for herself and her family. It never occurred to her to marry and leave home.

Dates with young men were rare events for her, and sexual overtures made her feel very anxious. Her first job after high school was in the billing department of a small company a few miles from her home. Although the position did not pay very well, Jeanine was happy. After all, she had achieved her goal of finding steady employment and bringing home money to help her mother and Billy, who was now receiving disability payments as a result of severe sciatica.

In the beginning of the second year of employment, however, Jeanine began to feel anxious even when she was not around young men. In fact, she began to fear that men in her workplace were going to hurt her or rape her. She told Billy that she heard them talking about her whenever she turned her back. Billy's way of reassuring her, however, was rather unsympathetic. He would tell her to stop saying stupid things and would harshly remark that no one would want to rape her because she was not attractive to men. Reassurances of this type, as one could predict, did little to mitigate Jeanine's fears, which escalated to the point of incapacitating her.

Her fears were intensified further by the growing cacophony of voices she began to hear. The voices followed her wherever she went, criticizing her behavior or warning her about the people in her life. Sometimes, she would hear Billy or her mother giving her admonitions or commands—and she had no way of telling whether the voices came from outside or inside her head.

Tragically, Jeanine's situation did not improve; she had developed schizophrenia, which completely disabled her. "The people of the neighborhood," as she had come to call her voices, were always with her, distracting and tormenting her. She could no longer work in the billing office, but remarkably, her life was not destroyed by her illness. Jeanine, despite her profound infirmity, was still Jeanine—she was the loving sister and daughter she had been in earlier years, and she had many of the same interests. She continued to go to church and to participate in various church activities in spite of occasional distress. Her anxiety made movies, a prior passion, difficult to attend in a public theater; however, she still enjoyed watching movies at home and discussing them with Billy or her mother.

The fact that Jeanine was in many respects the same person she had been before the onset of the schizophrenia was apparent to both Billy and their mother. In a way, the continuity of her personality was both a consolation and a source of anguish for them as it made her suffering more evident. Had the disease completely stolen her identity, perhaps it would not have been as painful to see her lose some of her intellectual capacities. Several times after the onset of the illness, Jeanine tried to return to office work, only to be forced to leave again when her hallucinations or anxiety made her employment impossible. But her motivation and desires had been much the same as they were before her illness. This essential core of her being—her personality—had been damaged by schizophrenia but was still intact in many respects.

Jeanine's plight indicates that, in many cases, personality is a highly robust aspect of a human being that retains much of its integrity despite severe psychiatric or neurological disease. People like Jeanine raise the question as to how much of the

(Continued)

(Continued)

human brain must be changed or destroyed before a person loses the essence of his or her personality.

Vignette Questions

1. Could Jeanine's problems have been a result of childhood experience or trauma?

2. If so, what personality theorist would best explain how she became ill?

3. If not, what other etiology explains her extreme personality change.

A number of studies have provided support for the genetic basis of Eysenck's neuroticism and extraversion dimensions (Ebstein, 2006; Rauch et al., 2005; Tambs, Sundet, Eaves, & Hornberg, 1991). For example, a study by the psychologist Mohammed Milad and his coworkers (2005) found a connection between the size of the medial orbitofrontal cortex and the ability to suppress fear. Exposure to life situations that are reminiscent of prior frightening events tend to lead to some degree of reliving the fear. People who don't succumb to this reaction have a greater degree of memory extinction; that is, they are better able to eliminate their fearful response to the traumatic event. The trait that is the obverse of fearfulness is aggression or sociopathy. People possessing this characteristic tend to experience less fear and related emotions.

Scientists have studied the existence of genetic susceptibility to antisocial behavior and have focused on the monoamine oxidase A (*MAOA*) gene on the X chromosome, which controls the metabolism of three neurotransmitters, norepinephrine, serotonin, and dopamine. For example, a rare mutation resulting in no *MAOA* expression was associated with violent antisocial behavior (Stamps, Abeling, van Gennip, van Cruchten, & Gurling, 2001).

As with most genetic inclinations, however, life events tend to sculpt the resulting personality trait. This was the finding of researchers who identified a variation of the gene that produces the enzyme monoamine oxidase A (*MAO-A*) in 1,037 men in New Zealand. As noted previously, other studies have shown that genetic deficiencies in this enzyme are associated with aggression in humans and other mammals. But numerous studies in social and clinical psychology have also linked similar behavior to early abuse. When the participants in this study were between the ages of 3 and 11 years, 8% experienced severe maltreatment, 28% experienced probable maltreatment, and 64% experienced no maltreatment. These men were longitudinally studied from age 3 to age 26 for evidence of antisocial behavior. Such behaviors were determined by several methods, including *DSM* criteria, objective measures such as arrest records, and school classifications of conduct disorder. Notably, the low-activity variant of the gene did not always produce antisocial behavior but was strongly associated with such behavior when the man had been abused in childhood. Only 12% of the study subjects had both the low-activity *MAO-A* allele and suffered abuse, but these men accounted for 44% of violent convictions. In addition, 85% of the men with low-activity *MAO-A* exhibited some type of antisocial behavior (Caspi et al., 2002).

Mapping the Brain for Personality Traits

The deciphering of the human genome has revealed that humans have far fewer genes than was previously believed. Current estimates of the number of human genes range between 25,000 and 35,000. This is far too low a number for there to be one gene for each trait or behavior. There is little contention, however, that the human genetic blueprint is the foundation of a significant portion of human personality. Exactly what that proportion is remains a matter of contention and research. Prior to the human genome projects of the 1990s, which identified most human genes (their number and location on chromosomes, but few of their functions), there were more theorists who hypothesized that the human brain is genetically prewired to express most personality functions. Just as Noam Chomsky proposed that there is a language organ in the brain, as explained in Chapter 10, other scientists propose that the human cortex contains organs, as it were, for most human personality traits.

The evidence for such organs is still inconclusive. The cortex appears to be more localized than specialized (Efron, 1990). In 1909, Korbinian Brodmann (1868–1918), a German neurologist, identified 52 functional areas of the cerebral cortex based on structural differences. A century later, there remains little doubt that many cognitive functions are localized to specific brain regions. What remains open to question in the early 2000s is whether the cortex is genetically programmed to develop dedicated functional areas, or whether these regions acquire these specialized functions through genetic-experiential interactions (Blumberg, 2005; O'Leary, 1989). Jeff Hawkins (Hawkins & Blakeslee, 2005), who has theorized about the functions of the human cortex, points out that the cortex has a surprisingly uniform structure despite the fact that specific regions seem dedicated to specific functions.

The notion that the brain acquires much of its specialization during development is not new. Psychologists researching patients recovering from brain injury have documented a large degree of neural plasticity. That is, some functions of the brain that are lost to traumatic injury can be recovered when nearby regions adapt to acquire that function (Celnik & Cohen, 2003; Robertson & Murre, 1999; Thickbroom, Byrnes, Archer, & Mastaglia, 2004). The ability of the brain to relocate functions after injury diminishes with age (Johnson, 1999), suggesting that localization of function in the brain is at least partly a developmental process. That is, the disposition for the brain to typically allocate motor control to the parietal lobe, speech to the left frontal lobe, and so on is partially guided by processes that emerge during development (Elman, Bates, Johnson, & Karmiloff-Smith, 1996).

Steven Pinker, the author of *How the Mind Works* (Pinker, 1997), is a strong advocate of genetically guided specialization in the brain. He asserts that the human brain is built of functional modules that evolved to produce behaviors that serve to improve reproductive capacity. He rebukes those who argue that the plasticity of the cortex and recovery of brain function in children prove that humans are tabulae rasae or blank slates. Pinker maintains that cases like that of an infant who recovered nearly normal brain function after losing an entire hemisphere, or animals who had their optic tracts rewired to the auditory centers and still demonstrate brain equipotentiality, do not substantively refute modularity of the brain. He argues that although the modules of the brain are somewhat plastic in early development, radical changes do not produce equivalent brains, even if some functions seem to be maintained.

Pinker (1994) explains that facilities like spoken language, which manifests with little or no prompting, are genetically programmed and adaptive. Written language, on the other hand, takes years of teaching and encouragement; it is not so clearly innate and genetically prepared. It follows that spoken language is innate and part of the language organ in the brain, whereas lexical skills are developed by coaxing brain centers to adapt to new functions through nurture.

An interesting example of the genetic guiding of brain function is biological preparedness. This term refers to an evolutionarily prepared tendency to more readily learn to fear, enjoy, or in other ways react to some stimuli rather than others (Dellarosa & Cummins, 1999). The biological preparedness model is in contrast to those of associationists and behaviorists, who posit that humans begin as blank slates and accrue knowledge by forming meaningful associations through their experiences. Accordingly, our brains are unbiased repositories for information, and the only prejudices in learning are found in the particular reinforcements associated with the information or the salience of the information in the environment. For example, if we are encouraged or rewarded by acquiring some information, we will learn that information. Information not so reinforced will be lost.

In contrast, being biologically prepared means that the mind is not a level playing field for all information. Instead, natural selection has endowed us with the tendency to attend to and learn or make connections with certain events. According to this view, we are more likely to learn to fear things that were dangerous to our distant ancestors. Our predecessors who successfully avoided poisonous snakes, sudden falls, aggressive canines, or venomous spiders were more likely to transmit the genes that now constitute us. Those who did not avoid dangerous situations had genomes that are largely extinct. It is interesting to note the high rate of phobias for animals or situations that are not particularly dangerous and the low rate of phobias for things that are.

Phobias for cars, for pesticides, or for guns are rare. Show any number of lethal firearms on a movie screen, and you will hear few shudders or expressions of disgust. But have an adventurer find a pit of snakes or a field of spiders in the movie, and the distress in the audience will be audible. In fact, in one survey, 22.4% of respondents acknowledged irrational fears of insects, rodents, or snakes; 18.2% fear of heights; and 12.5% fear of water. In contrast, only 10.5% of the respondents expressed fear of public transportation (Cartwright, 2001, p. 98). There is evidence that prepared or innate fears tend to resist extinction more than fears that are not innate.

In fact, researchers identified genes that encode two peptides that play differential roles in the innate versus non-innate fear systems (Shumyatsky et al., 2002, 2005). The gene that encodes gastrin-releasing peptide (GRP) and the gene that encodes the peptide stathmin play complementary roles in regulating fears arising from the amygdala. The GRP gene encodes a protein that acts to inhibit learned—but not innate—fear responses in the brain. In contrast, stathmin was found to be instrumental in both innate and learned fears. This finding provided evidence of two distinct fear systems in the brain, one for learned fears and one for innate fears. Both are genetically regulated.

Innate fears are evident in many animal species. For example, Sackett (1966) raised monkeys in complete isolation from both other monkeys and humans. He then projected images of other monkeys with aggressive postures or facial expressions. Notably, despite the fact that the experimental monkeys had never seen other monkeys or observed their social interactions, they responded with fear to these aggressive displays. The innate fear of snakes in humans and other primates has been proposed as a result of an evolutionary race between primates that evolved more sensitive visual systems to detect snakes and snakes that evolved better camouflage (Isbell, 2006). The importance of these innate fears becomes immediately apparent if one looks for birds on the island of Guam (Savidge, 1987). Prior to the introduction of the brown tree snake, Guam was replete with birds such as the Mariana fruit dove and the cardinal honeyeater. These and other varieties of birds had evolved in an environment without predatory snakes. During World War II, the brown tree snake was inadvertently brought to the island, where it found birds with no natural fear of it. In a quarter of a century, 9 of 18 bird species became extinct in the wild, and the populations of the remaining nine have been severely depleted.

▣ THE HUMAN BRAIN AND PERSONALITY

The preceding section presented evidence of inborn behavioral traits in several animals. This raises two essential questions for students of personality. First, what portion of human personality is inborn or innate? Second, what portion of it is directly attributed to structures of the brain that develop through life? The degree to which the brain defines the essence of the person has been a point of debate in philosophy and psychology since the fields began. The premise that an incorporeal force exists within or independent of a person's brain exists today in many religious and spiritual quarters. The evidence of faith for this entity exists apart from the scientific evidence. Science is confident and robust in showing that everything that makes us aware, unique, and active originates in the organ within our skulls. This is not a point of serious debate.

What *is* debatable, however, is how much of our identity is based on the pure structure of the brain, and how much is a result of the brain's interaction with experience during its development. The brain demonstrates a high degree of plasticity or flexibility in its development. For example, if an infant receives damage to the areas of the brain associated with speech control—typically, the left hemisphere—the opposite hemisphere will commonly take over that function. This is true for many functions believed to be hard-wired. It appears that the specialization of function observed in the cortex of the brain develops over time. Should this process be derailed early enough, the cortex seems flexible enough to reassign that function.

This flexibility does not mean that the brain is a general-purpose computer that can run different programs as needed. It appears, as the evolutionary psychologists would argue, that many functions are innate. As explained earlier, the evolutionary psychologists support the idea that the human brain is composed of naturally selected modules that direct or encourage behaviors or functions. The function of many of these modules can be significantly altered by environmental demands. Some have very specific functions that are almost identical in humans and animals with much less complex brains.

This is especially true of the **subcortical** structures that process information, usually outside of conscious awareness. Several of these subcortical structures are often grouped together as the limbic system. The neurologist Paul MacLean (1954, 1977a) first presented the concept that the human brain evolved by developing newly adapted regions that formed layers above the phylogenetically older ones. The limbic system, according to MacLean, lies under the cortex. It is roughly equivalent to the complete brain of a simpler animal, one that need be concerned only with basic survival. MacLean referred to this system as the paleomammalian brain. It lies under the neomammalian brain and above the reptilian brain in MacLean's (1990) system of classification. In humans as well as animals, the limbic system guides rudimentary survival behaviors. That is, it contains the basic modules for aggression, fear, sexuality, and the satisfaction of hunger or thirst. In fact, most emotional experience can be traced at least in part to these brain centers (Adolphs, Baron-Cohen, & Tranel, 2002; Moll et al., 2002; Murphy, Nimmo-Smith, & Lawrence, 2003; Phan, Wager, Taylor, & Liberzon, 2004).

There has been some debate, however, as to whether MacLean's divisions are as distinct in function as he proposed. MacLean viewed the three brains as evolutionarily distinct brain structures. Pinker (1997) questions MacLean's threefold division by using the logic of evolutionary psychology. He points out that the driving force of evolution is adaptation, and adaptations are not likely to occur in discrete layers. All organs or even neuronal nuclei are subject to change; if that change yields an increase in fitness, then that trait is likely to be passed on. There is little doubt, however, that these nonverbal and typically nonconscious parts of the brain are responsible for a good portion of emotion and behavior that we associate with personality. The major structures that MacLean associates with the limbic system are the amygdala, the hippocampus, the hypothalamus, the mammillary bodies, the caudate nucleus, the fornix, and the cingulate cortex. These comprise the major limbic structures, although neuroanatomists include other structures.

The Limbic System

The Cingulate Cortex. The cingulate cortex is a part of the brain that lies between the phylogenetically older limbic structures and the neocortex. It links the hippocampus and the thalamus, playing a role in the storage of long-term memories, especially those dealing with strong emotions or traumatic life events. The cingulate cortex appears to help focus attention, especially to events that may pose a risk to survival, and is therefore crucial for decision making. Thus, it plays an important role in storing memories as well as coordinating the emotional input from other brain structures in the assessment of potential risks and rewards. In addition, it appears to play a role in the conscious apprehension of pain and emotion.

The Amygdala. The amygdala, which is named for its almond shape, resides bilaterally within each hemisphere; it is the primary source of feelings of fear and rage. As with most organs in the human body, it functions within certain ranges. Thus, people who are characteristically fearful rather than daring, or hostile rather than complacent, can be understood at least in part as having different levels of activity in their amygdalae. Damage to the amygdala can result in severe deficits in the ability to learn what to fear or even to understand the meaning of fear (Adolphs, Tranel, Damasio, & Damasio, 1995; Adolphs et al., 1999). Similarly, lesions in this part of the brain can lead to a lack of anger, and even the most aggressive and hostile person can be reduced to one who is relatively passive and calm (Albert & Walsh, 1984; Blanchard, Blanchard, Lee, & Nakamura, 1979; Emery et al., 2001).

The role of the amygdala in personality is particularly notable because this primeval and nonverbal brain center is instrumental in making social judgments (Bechara, Damasio, & Damasio, 2003; Beeckmans & Michiels, 1996), especially those dealing with the interpretation of emotions in other people's facial expressions (Arnold, Hyman, Van Hoesen, & Damasio, 1991).

The Hippocampus. The hippocampus is the nexus of several important cognitive functions, the most important of which is assimilation of short-term memory by long-term stores and the retrieval of memory from these stores (Henke, Buck, Weber, & Wieser, 1997; Henke, Weber,

Kneifel, Wieser, & Buck, 1999; Winocur, 1985). This memory function of the hippocampus creates the most cogent point of contention with MacLean's view of the limbic system as a relatively old system that operates largely separately from the neocortex. The close interaction between the hippocampus and the cortex in memory consolidation suggests that it is playing a more recent evolutionary role in the human brain.

It appears that when we are exposed to sensory data, our brains try to make sense of it by asking in effect, "Have I seen this before?" If the answer is yes, the brain triggers the appropriate memory locations and a reference to the input is found. If, however, the stimulus is new, it will be processed by the hippocampus for long-term storage—especially if it is considered significant.

This finding indicates that this portion of the limbic system is not processing information beneath or in parallel to the cortex; instead, it is collaborating at a very high level with the cortex and actually receives input after it has been processed at very high levels in the brain. In addition to its role in consolidating long-term memories, the hippocampus is the portion of the brain that appears to be responsible for our memory of spatial locations; that is, our cognitive maps (Cave & Squire, 1991; Kumaran & Maguire, 2005).

The Insula or Insular Cortex. This structure resembles a small brain residing deep within each hemisphere. It appears to be instrumental in many mental functions that underlie both the conscious experience of emotions and the personality. For example, there is evidence that the insula works with the mirror neurons to beget feelings of empathy (Iacoboni & Lenzi, 2002). It plays a role in processing sensory information that can lead to the emotion of disgust (Calder et al., 2007). However, most significant is the recent evidence that reveals the insula serves to integrate sensations from the body and use them as a basis for both decision making and motivation (e.g., Adolphs, Tranel, & Damasio, 2003; Contreras, Ceric, & Torrealba, 2007). This function of the insula is the basis of its central role in the somatic marker hypothesis, which was first proposed by Antonio Damasio (1996). He theorized that conscious decision making is powerfully influenced by bodily states. We may experience this type of bodily influence if we feel uneasy when asked to do something risky or socially inappropriate.

The Hypothalamus. The limbic system as a whole regulates all life functions essential for survival. Our sexual and gustatory appetites; our ability to detect, record, recall, and respond to danger; our skills in socializing and mating; and our capacity to find our way around and recall the relevant aspects of our environment are all mediated by the limbic system. Within this system, a relatively tiny portion of the brain called the hypothalamus plays an important role in most of these functions by itself. Damage to this structure, depending on the location of the injury, can result in hyperphagia (overeating), anorexia, passivity, aggression, hypersexuality, or asexuality.

The hypothalamus also regulates the pituitary gland and its release of most major hormones. To summarize the role of the hypothalamus in a single word, it would be homeostasis. The hypothalamus serves to keep all the body's organ systems in balance. The fact that such an old structure (in the evolutionary sense) plays such an important regulatory role leads to the question of its interactions with the other brain areas that mediate these functions. The answer is that the hypothalamus usually interacts smoothly with these areas, but sometimes, there are conflicts. One example of a conflict is obesity, a condition in which the person's conscious goal of weight loss is often trumped by compelling feelings of hunger. Another example is found in the paraphilias, sexual disorders in which **ego-dystonic** appetites often lead to personal ruin.

The Caudate Nucleus. The caudate nucleus is a part of the basal ganglia that plays several essential roles in the coordination of movement, emotional control, and thought. The function of the basal ganglia can be inferred from illnesses that arise from its dysfunction. These include Tourette syndrome, Parkinson's disease, and obsessive-compulsive disorder (OCD). The caudate nucleus lies between the amygdala and the globus pallidus. The basic function of the caudate nucleus is to link the physical condition of the body with the person's emotional state. This role is consistent with António Damásio's theory of emotion, which holds that human emotions evolved as a means for consciousness to apprehend the state of the viscera or internal organs. According to Damásio, emotions originate in the subcortical brain as bodily responses to events relevant to survival. Such somatic responses as increased respiration, digestive slowdown, or speeded-up heart rate lead to conscious feelings about the events.

The Mammillary Bodies. These structures are so named because they resemble the shape of female breasts (*mammae* in Latin). The mammillary bodies play a role in the consolidation of memory. People suffering from Korsakoff's dementia, an illness associated with severe anterograde amnesia, confabulation, and cognitive deficits, usually have evidence of damage to the mammillary bodies (Shear, Sullivan, Lane, & Pfefferbaum, 1996). Papez's circuit, also known as the hippocampal/mammillothalamic tract, was originally proposed as the locus of

Image 14.10 Caudate Nucleus

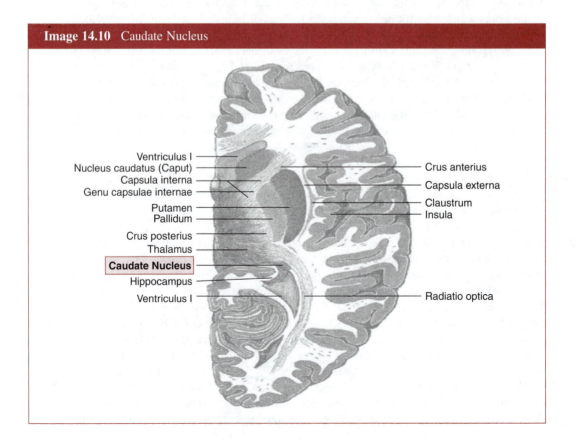

- Ventriculus I
- Nucleus caudatus (Caput)
- Capsula interna
- Genu capsulae internae
- Putamen
- Pallidum
- Crus posterius
- Thalamus
- **Caudate Nucleus**
- Hippocampus
- Ventriculus I
- Crus anterius
- Capsula externa
- Claustrum
- Insula
- Radiatio optica

emotional processing in the brain. Later, a more complex integration of limbic structures became part of the Papez-MacLean model of emotions. In both the older and the current model, the mammillary bodies appear to play a role in coordinating memories with the affective content of the memories.

Examination of the brain structures classified as the limbic system reveals how much of human cognition takes place outside of conscious awareness. What we remember, how we assess risks, how we feel sexual attraction, what we fear, what angers us, and many fundamental aspects of our personalities are processed without conscious awareness. It is likely that the core of altruism, reciprocal altruism, and the mechanisms to detect cheaters who violate these innate norms are found in these limbic structures. Why would humans evolve a brain center that works in this way? It is because decisions regarding survival must draw on prior experience as rapidly as possible and make a decision that in the times of our earliest progenitors meant life or death.

The Executive Region: The Cerebral Cortex

From the information presented in the preceding sections on the limbic system it is evident that a great deal is taking place in brain structures that are quite old in an evolutionary sense. The location in which the ghost in the machine lives, however, is likely to be the cortex. Overlying the limbic and all phylogenetically older structures is the cortex and the neocortex, the outermost region of the cortex. The cortex of the human brain lies above the limbic and other subcortical structures and is intimately connected with them. That is, it is important to avoid regarding the cortex as independent of the lower brain structures; rather, it is dynamically interacting with them at all times. We are who we are as a result of the interplay between the cortex and all other structures of the brain. Without the emotional and sensory information from the centers below it, the cortex becomes a vastly complex but soulless computer. It would be unable to employ the **mirror neurons** that have been shown to apprehend and duplicate the actions of others. It would not be able to learn from mistakes that led to emotion-laden events. Nor would it be able to draw on the vast repository of memories that are encoded in the limbic structures. Limbic and other subcortical memories are conveyed in the form of feelings or intuitions, which tacitly guide human behavior. Without these subcortical memories, the cortex would not be able to draw on the vast repository of sensory and memory data to make decisions. Many of our judgments seem to be based on these nonverbal conscious repositories of emotional memories.

Chapter 16 contains a description of Elliot, a man who suffered damage to the neuronal pathways connecting the limbic structures to the frontal lobes of his brain. This individual suffered a profound change to his personality. His cognitive capacity was largely unimpaired, but he was no longer recognizable to those who had known him as Elliot. His moral values had changed, his social judgment was that of a sociopath, and his ability to relate to others was radically impaired. A brain tumor that had been surgically removed to save his life left Elliot no longer Elliot. This case study makes clear that our personalities exist somewhere, and that place is our brain. Although the human personality has not been localized to specific brain regions, it is clear that if critical brain areas are damaged or injured, the individual's personality will change.

Another commonplace example is the impact of such organic brain disorders as Alzheimer's on personality. It may be a subtle change or a profound one as Elliot suffered. Based on the sum total of the evidence, the human personality is a product of dynamically interacting modules throughout the brain. The limbic structures, which produce raw drives, emotions, and memories, interact with cortical structures in producing awareness, consciousness, and a sense of identity. The cortex appears to be the most recent addition to the brain in terms of evolution, and it correlates with intelligence and complex thought. The cortex acting alone, however, would produce a very bland personality.

Interactions With the Environment

The evidence that a major portion of human personality is genetic or biological in origin and adapted to physical survival is quite compelling. Nevertheless, virtually all inherited traits are, at least in part, shaped by the environment in an interactive fashion. That is, humans can shape their environments, which in turn may lead to changes in the environmental milieu that affects the developing personality.

Although few researchers deny that genetic factors play a central role in our development, some assert that genes alone cannot explain the diversity observed in both human and animal development. This is cogently set forth in genetically similar or identical organisms. In humans, the most prominent example is that of monozygotic or identical twins. Notably in terms of personality, they are generally similar but never identical. Thus, even with identical genes, people differ, indicating that environment must play a role. But the role the environment plays is far from simple. People can alter their environment and that can result in changes to the people that performed that shaping. Humans, more than any other animal, have the power to change their own environment, which adds a complex variable to the nature-versus-nurture question. We modify the environment that is instrumental in shaping the expression of our genes. Alteration of the environment is accomplished in numerous ways that involve everything from the layout of our cities to the types of foods we grow and prepare. For example, humans build cities, which create a new environment—one that may require very different attributes for survival than a tropical forest. Conversely, we change our environment based on our needs; for example, we level forests to create farmland, which in turn reduces the need for hunting and gathering.

▣ CHAPTER SUMMARY

During the past quarter century, there has been a marked change in the way personality and psychology as a whole is studied. This model began more than 150 years ago with Charles Darwin, but it came to a near standstill due to abuses by individuals who distorted the content of Darwin's principles. This distortion led to the eugenics movement, which justified social oppression in the name of improving the human species. This movement came to its logical if very ugly conclusion in the mass murder of genetically "inferior" people perpetrated by the Nazi regime in Germany. In reaction to these horrors, there was a backlash against all theoretical systems that maintained the existence of inborn or innate human differences. These theories were not only rejected but virtually banned as subjects of discussion in English-speaking countries.

E. O. Wilson began the debate anew in 1975 with his landmark work on sociobiology. Prior to the movement accelerated by Wilson, environment and culture formed the leitmotif for the study of psychological characteristics. Prior to the advent of evolutionary or biological psychology, human culture was viewed as a type of overarching organism that guides the individuals who constitute it.

In contrast to cultural psychologists, evolutionary psychologists view most human culture and cultures as products of the evolution of human nature. Culture is viewed as an artifact of a common human nature that metamorphoses to accommodate to different environments. Thus, humans in New Guinea are just as aggressive as those in Washington, D.C., but differ as a result of divergent technologies in the intensity and style of expressing their aggression. This approach sharply contradicts the cultural relativity model that many psychologists prefer. These psychologists see most differences between people as driven by differences in their culture. Although evolutionary psychologists see culture as playing a role in personality formation, they find it secondary to the evolutionarily adapted mechanisms or modules that compose the human brain.

The evolutionary and biological approaches are compatible, even synergistic, with other models of personality. Psychoanalytic personality theory subsumes an evolutionary theory in devising its mental structures, topology, and drives. Existential and humanistic theorists, although less interested in the physical basis of our humanity or existence, do not deny that human nature is influenced by the workings of the body's various systems. This is the case for the cognitive theorists who choose to focus on the workings of the processes of thought and perception rather than the organic equipment that makes these processes possible. No one denies, however, that the hardware is an essential predicate of all cognition.

In contrast to these other schools and systems, which primarily take a bottom-up approach to understanding personality, the biological and evolutionary theories take more of a reverse-engineering approach. The bottom-up approach involves observing and measuring human behavior, interactions, expressions of affect, and the like and then developing theories of personality based on those observations. In reverse engineering, the theorist observes the structures of the brain and evolutionary environments and infers the traits, behaviors, or cognitive styles that would arise from these environments. For example, if evolutionary psychologists find that our ancestors spent numerous millennia within small nomadic groups, they would develop and test theories about the personal qualities that would have been most beneficial to the survival of the people in those groups.

The biological and evolutionary psychologist's view of human personality is that of adaptation. Personality is the outward manifestation of brain modules that evolved to cope with problems that confronted our ancestors during the generations of natural selection that created us. Of course, not every trait, temperament, or behavior can be identified as an evolutionary adaptation, but that is the starting point for the psychologist's efforts to understand them.

Chapter 15

Abnormal Personality and Personality Disorders

Chapter Goals

- To be able to distinguish between normal and abnormal personalities
- To explore the various bases for making the distinction between a high- and a low-functioning personality
- To examine the research and methodology in distinguishing a normal from a disordered personality
- To provide an overview of some of the salient perspectives on personality disorders

The preceding chapters detailing the numerous views of personality and its development make it clear that the concept of personality itself remains open to debate. Most of us believe that we are encountering different personalities among our friends and acquaintances, but we have trouble defining precisely what a personality is. And just as personality is a complex concept, the disordered personality is even more difficult to define. To classify a personality as dysfunctional or pathological requires a social and pragmatic judgment. Moreover, all judgments of human affairs are at least somewhat subjective. Thomas Szasz (1960) produced a virtual library of works accusing the mental health field of conflating social judgments with medical diagnoses. His sentiments, although sometimes dogmatic and extreme, may serve as useful warnings to both clinicians and researchers in classifying personality as either normal or disordered.

Clinicians, researchers, and epidemiologists, in categorizing a personality as pathological, typically face the risk of labeling someone as disordered who may be only eccentric or socially offensive. It would be convenient if we could invoke a paraphrase of U.S. Supreme Court Justice Potter Stewart's comment about pornography to the effect that we cannot define personality disorders but we know one when we see it. Psychology as a science, however, cannot be this informal. The requirements for diagnosis or categorization of personality disorders must be precise and specific. Without such a requirement, people would be labeled pathological if they strayed too far from the standards of any particular social order. Given the vast number of societies, each with its own set of norms, allowing deviations from community standards to be the basis of diagnosis would lead to diagnostic chaos.

🔳 THE SPECTRUM OF PERSONALITY DISORDERS

The *Diagnostic and Statistical Manual of Mental Disorders* (DSM) and the *International Classification of Diseases* (ICD) have taken a categorical approach to the diagnosis of personality disorders. Prior to the American Psychiatric Association's publication of the first edition of the DSM (DSM-I) in 1952, personality disorders were described in such psychoanalytic terms as oral character, anal character, and so on. Chapter 7 detailed the first set of personality disorders that the DSM established as diagnostic guidelines. The DSM-I did not include, however, a list of criteria for establishing a diagnosis. What it did provide is a dichotomous system in which a person either has or does not have a personality disorder.

This approach, which has continued through the most recent edition, DSM-IV-TR (American Psychiatric Association, 2000), belies the usual layperson's observation that most human qualities are points along a continuum rather than absolutes. People can be slightly shy to very shy, slightly antisocial to downright sociopathic, mildly anxious some of the time to highly anxious most of the time, and so on. Defining the disordered personality as differing in degree but not in kind from the high-functioning personality tacitly implies that disordered personalities develop in much the same way as normal ones. That is, personality disorders may arise as a result of an excess or deprivation of critical life events that guide interpersonal development. These differences may be amplified by such constitutional differences as easy arousability or hyperemotionality. This approach to personality disorders is known as a dimensional approach.

Despite the potential advantages of dimensions versus categories, the complexity of applying either to diagnosis or research still requires much work before a consensus is reached on the origin and exact nature of these disorders. What is *not* in dispute, however, is the existence of people whose own personalities cause distress to themselves or others around them. Moreover, the fact that some personality styles allow for better life functioning than others is hard to deny.

Many people are endowed with personalities that readily facilitate their social and professional functioning, to the point that some researchers argue that personality is at least as critical to organizational success as intelligence (Miner, 1962; Ridgell & Lounsbury, 2004; Terman, 1942). Conversely, there are other people who fare poorly in life as a result of deficiencies in personality despite an abundance of talents. These people present themselves to the world and process information in ways that result in their ongoing misery or frequent suffering to those around them.

Interestingly, unlike most psychological disorders, disorders relating to personality are the least likely to be recognized by those who have them. In contrast, depressed or anxious people are often well aware that they are having emotional problems simply because these disorders cause subjective suffering, in contrast to personality disorders, which typically do not. Thus, self-insight, however, is typically lacking in people with personality disorders because personality as such, whether normal or disordered, is our gateway to the world. It is the psychological mechanism that guides our interpretation of all the events in our lives. In effect, personality is the lens through which reality is perceived. So when personality is impaired, it is the world that seems to be out of joint for afflicted individuals, not themselves.

Consequently, people with disordered personalities will tend to view the world and those in it as acting badly, rather than seeing themselves as the problem. To such individuals, the world tends to seem less fair and more frightening than to people with higher functioning personalities. Coworkers, family, and friends will be more difficult to get along with and their behavior will be difficult to interpret. This aspect of personality disorders raises a problematic nosological issue—namely, can something be a disorder—an illness in one sense—if it does not trouble the afflicted individuals but largely serves to annoy or disturb those around them?

Perhaps the best justification for calling a disturbing personality a disorder is that it is guided by the primary hallmark of the personality disorder—inflexibility. That is, people who cannot change their style of behavior to meet social or environmental demands are likely to perform poorly in life. Such people rarely even try to change their attitudes or behaviors because they do not feel a need to fix what does not seem broken to them. As a result, such people will seem perversely to persist in the same self-defeating or socially alienating behaviors. In fact, they may even get worse with time because the disordered personality style may provide an illusory sense of security or defense. For example, a narcissist whose arrogant solipsism leads to social isolation might very well retreat further into narcissism for comfort in what would seem to him as irrational and cruel rejecting behavior on the part of others. To be sure, narcissists have elicited the rejection by their manipulative or exploitative treatment of others in the first place, but they typically will not see their own conduct as a contributing factor.

This chapter will describe and discuss people with abnormal or disordered personalities. Although the standard for discriminating normal from disordered personality is the DSM-IV-TR (American Psychiatric Association, 2000), we will include several other personality styles that are not included in the manual but that are nevertheless sufficiently unusual to merit discussion. Each personality style or disorder will be examined from several theoretical perspectives. The reader should bear in mind that as theories of personality are diverse, so, too, are their explanations of how human personalities go awry. The numerous perspectives span a wide spectrum, with some psychologists viewing the disordered personality as an exaggeration of the normal whereas others regard disordered personalities as fundamentally different in kind. For this reason, DSM-IV allows for some cultural relativity in its definition of personality disorder.

Some researchers, however, would extend this relativity to the temporal or historical plane as well as the cultural. Thus, they would maintain that covetous and aggressive sociopaths might very well have been normal in the time when Cro-Magnon people faced off with Neanderthals. In addition, some theorists suggest that personality characteristics labeled as disordered may be quite functional in some settings. For example, a person who has a defensive and hostile personality style, leading to the loss of friends and family, might do very well in a time of conflict or war. Similarly, a person whose extreme attention to detail impedes her spontaneity and social functioning could have a distinct advantage in occupations or situations in which great precision is required—as in some surgical specialties or pharmaceutical research. Could the personality disorders as presently defined refer to little more than specific personalities in the wrong place and the wrong time? The answer is not clear as of the early 2000s, but we will examine the evidence for this view.

What Is a Personality Disorder?

A nearly universal ability found among human beings is a capacity for understanding the behavior, implied intentions, and emotional states of others. In fact, evidence was presented in Chapter 13 indicating that some aspects of this ability have been localized in portions of the prefrontal cortex of the human brain and are mediated by mirror neurons. An extension of the ability to "read" others is seen in the widespread ability to detect if a person is in some way aberrant (Haselton & Funder, 2006; Mahaffey & Marcus, 2006). Although such factors as generational, social, or cultural differences may result in false alarms, most often people can nevertheless detect a psychological **outlier** (Malloy, Albright, Diaz-Loving, Dong, & Lee, 2004; Oltmanns, Friedman, Fiedler, & Turkheimer, 2004). There is significant face validity for this phenomenon because it surely would have been adaptive for our forebears to be able to detect a potentially dangerous individual quickly and heuristically.

What is it that both lay people and professionals take into account in determining a personality to be abnormal? It is likely that both the DSM and the layperson look for much of the same features. First, a person's aberrant behavior or style of perception must develop in parallel with the maturation of the individual's personality. Consequently, a sudden change in behavior in which the person is "not herself" would *not* apply. For example, someone who is generally self-controlled but gets into a shouting match at work after a series of crises in the office would not be considered as having a personality disorder, nor would the elderly person showing the first changes in emotional stability related to Alzheimer's disease.

Second, once an aberrant personality style has established itself, it must operate consistently across virtually all situations. This criterion would rule out atypical behaviors seen among people suffering from grief and stress reactions or those placed in new or challenging settings. For example, people who have survived disasters often find it difficult to return to the site of the tragedy or to use a particular means of transportation—a man who survived a train wreck in Australia in 1977, for example, has not been able to go near a railway bridge ever since. He is, however, able to function perfectly well at work and with his family and so would not be considered as having a personality disorder.

Third, most components of the personality are affected by a personality disorder. That is, people with personality disorders will have aberrations of cognition, interpersonal relations, impulse control, and social behavior; and these disturbances will usually lead to long-standing problems in academic pursuits, work, and relationships. Aberrations of cognition, however, most cogently qualify personality disorders as a category of mental illness. Persistent or severe cognitive distortions represent breaks with reality. Narcissists who judge their mediocre performance as superb, paranoids who regard most people as enemies conspiring against them, and obsessive-compulsives who can focus only on trivial details at the expense of the larger picture are examples of the ways in which personality disorders lead to distortions of reality. Most important, people who have a disordered personality will resist efforts to change their behavior or to help them learn from experience—further evidence of the maladaptive nature of many personality disorders.

Personality pathology that is not severe often becomes apparent only when the person is under stress. Someone with a disordered personality can be likened to a patient with frail health. Such a person can be physically healthy for extended periods but will suffer a severe and rapid decline when exposed to a disease organism. Similarly, people with personality pathology who are not exposed to any life stressors may function quite well most of the time but will tend to collapse emotionally when encountering harsh challenges—or a group of minor problems occurring close together. Personality disorders deprive individuals of the capacity to adapt to stressful and novel situations, thus creating a psychological vicious circle in which stressors are left unresolved, thereby raising the stress level in the person's life, leading to further dysfunction, and so on. Because the *sine qua non* of personality disorders is inflexibility, novel or stressful situations are particularly vexing for those that suffer them.

▣ PERSONALITY DISORDERS ACCORDING TO DSM-IV

The *Diagnostic and Statistical Manual of Mental Disorders* was discussed at some length in Chapter 7. Within the present edition (American Psychiatric Association, 2000) is a listing of 10 personality disorders and disorders related to mental retardation, which fall under the rubric of DSM's Axis II. As discussed in Chapter 7, DSM-IV uses five diagnostic components or axes. The basic premise of this edition of the manual is that any mental disorder is best understood by exploring the primary disorder along with any **comorbid** personality pathology, medical disorders, all major psychosocial stressors, and the individual's general level of life functioning.

The definitions of the personality disorders, as with all DSM pathologies, were worked out through research review and a consensus interpretation of the relevant medical literature by the committee responsible for the inclusion of personality disorders in DSM-IV. Although a worthy effort, nosologies constructed in this way must be approached with a bit of caution and skepticism. They are approximations and condensed versions of reality—not literal and comprehensive descriptions of every possible aberration or variation of personality.

Moreover, each personality disorder represents more of a general theme than a distinct construct. This quality of generality is a result of the nature of diagnosis. Each personality disorder is more of a Platonic archetype than a representation of an actual person. That is, people may have many of the characteristics that are identified as those of the narcissist, the borderline, or the obsessive-compulsive, but each patient or client differs in varying degrees from the model that the framers of DSM–IV had in mind.

The DSM-IV Diagnostic Process

Some researchers describe the DSM-IV classification as the family resemblance approach (McElroy, Davis, & Blashfield, 1989). This concept of family resemblance becomes clearer when we observe that siblings may all look quite different from one another but still be recognizable as coming from the same family. In fact, siblings can share a striking family resemblance to one another, even though some might be said to be attractive and others rather homely. For example, the sisters of the late President Kennedy are clearly siblings from the same family, but Kathleen, the oldest sister, was considered beautiful, whereas Patricia and Jean were considered moderately attractive and Eunice was regarded as plain. There is little doubt that part of the **gestalt** of both face recognition and personality categorization includes the tendency to find themes and commonalities.

The diagnostic process of DSM is predicated on deconstructing these personality archetypes into diagnostic symptoms and then having the clinician make a best match. If we take the family resemblance metaphor a bit further, however, and imagine trying to determine whether a person comes from a particular family, the problem with this approach becomes more apparent. Such a task would require that a family type be broken down into facial and muscular or bone structure criteria. This list might include features like medium height, slender build, aquiline nose, prominent chin, narrow face, blue eyes, and so on. Suppose that people were assigned to a family based on possessing five out of nine salient family characteristics: How accurate would such a classification be? In all likelihood, it would be significantly better than chance, but there surely would be many misses and many inaccurate assignments. This is the fundamental problem with the categorical approach to diagnosis. That is, by using dichotomous categories—even if they are very specific and detailed—the clinician runs the risk of assuming that a person who fits a certain category suffers from the disorder associated with it. Why then are the DSM-IV categories used? Simply because they are easier to apply, minimize subjectivity, reduce the so-called **halo effect,** and save time.

Diagnostic Subtypes

Further complicating interpretation of the DSM personality disorders is the high degree of overlap among the various personality disorders. Many of the 10 that are listed in the manual have diagnostic criteria so similar that people could be diagnosed as having multiple disorders, or at least elements of several disorders. According to DSM-IV, a personality disorder is an "enduring pattern of inner experience and behavior that deviates markedly from the expectations of the individual's culture, is pervasive and inflexible, has an onset in adolescence or early adulthood, is stable over time, and leads to distress or impairment" (American Psychiatric Association, 1994, p. 686). The DSM describes 10 disorders of personality, none of which completely excludes any of the others. That is, a person can be afflicted with more than one personality disorder.

Further blurring diagnostic precision is the selection of criteria used for diagnosis. To qualify for each personality disorder in DSM-IV-TR (American Psychiatric Association, 2000), the patient or client must meet a minimum number of diagnostic criteria associated with that disorder. For example, a person diagnosed with borderline personality disorder, or BPD, must demonstrate a minimum of five of the following nine symptoms or diagnostic criteria:

1. Frantic efforts to avoid real or imagined abandonment

2. A pattern of unstable and intense interpersonal relationships characterized by alternating between extremes of idealization and devaluation

3. Identity disturbance: markedly and persistently unstable self-image or sense of self

4. Impulsivity in at least two areas that are potentially self-damaging (e.g., spending, sex, substance abuse, reckless driving, binge eating)

5. Recurrent suicidal behavior, gestures, or threats, or self-mutilating behavior

6. Affective instability due to a marked reactivity of mood (e.g., intense episodic dysphoria, irritability, or anxiety usually lasting a few hours and only rarely more than a few days)

7. Chronic feelings of emptiness

8. Inappropriate, intense anger or difficulty controlling anger (e.g., frequent displays of temper, constant anger, recurrent physical fights)

9. Transient, stress-related paranoid ideation or severe dissociative symptoms

For example, a person with BPD might show a moderate degree of the symptoms listed in criteria 1, 3, and 7, and show severe symptoms listed in criteria 2 and 9. Obviously, this assortment would result in a markedly different outward manifestation of the disorder than that in someone who displayed all of these characteristics with equal severity. Thus, although the DSM personality disorder criteria describe well-defined themes, they can still classify very different people as suffering from the same disorder.

Table 15.1 presents a calculation of the total number of combinations of borderline diagnostic criteria, or, in other words, how many different ways these criteria can be combined to yield what could be markedly different personalities.

This example demonstrates that DSM-IV tacitly allows for 256 different subtypes of borderline personality disorder, even if a diagnostician is precise in application of the DSM-IV

Table 15.1   Possible Combinations of Borderline Personality Disorder Diagnostic Criteria

To be diagnosed with borderline personality disorder one must exhibit a minimum of five of the nine diagnostic criteria. Since five is the minimum number, it follows that a specific individual may also meet six, seven, eight, or even all nine criteria. Thus, the number of possible ways to meet the diagnostic criteria for borderline personality disorder would be the sum of all possible combinations of five to nine diagnostic criteria:

$$C(n,r) = n!/(r!*(n-r)!)$$

In the preceding formula, n is the total number of criteria, and r is the number of criteria to be used to make a diagnosis. By applying the formula, one obtains the following results:

No. of Criteria	Total Criteria	Combinations
5	9	126
6	9	86
7	9	36
8	9	9
9	9	1
Total BPD Combinations:		256

criteria. But the possibilities do not end there. Although each criterion was worded to imply a relatively specific degree of severity, there can still be a great degree of diversity among people meeting any one criterion. Therefore, within any individual, each criterion can vary in degree of severity, leading to an even greater number of borderline subtypes. To illustrate this diversity, suppose that two individuals are diagnosed with BPD on the basis of meeting criteria 1 through 5. Suppose further that the first person experiences continual and intense fears of abandonment (criterion 1) and the second suffers from such fears only occasionally. This single difference would lead to two similarly diagnosed individuals manifesting their disorders quite differently. This issue was examined by Clarkin and his coworkers (Clarkin, Widiger, Frances, Hurt, & Gilmore, 1983) for a previous edition of DSM. The group found that DSM-III allowed for 93 possible combinations of BPD. Moreover, they found that each of the diagnostic criteria was indeed expressed with significantly different frequencies. These authors reported that 10% of people diagnosed with BPD met all eight DSM-III criteria for the disorder; 25% met seven; 40% met six criteria; and 25% met only five.

Category Overlap

Eligibility for multiple diagnoses adds to the complexity of DSM-IV personality diagnosis. The high incidence of individuals meeting the criteria for several personality disorders (Oldham et al., 1992; Stuart et al., 1998) makes both diagnosis and treatment far more problematic. With the high degree of overlap among the diagnostic criteria for the personality disorders, it is quite common for people to meet the criteria for two or more of them. Is this degree of overlap an artifact of the method of diagnosis? Or do people actually suffer from multiple discrete disorders of personality? This issue is not yet resolved, but on its face, it would seem unlikely that people will display aberrant personalities in a neatly circumscribed fashion. What is more likely is that disturbances in personality, especially severe disturbances, will affect so many areas of functioning as to appear to meet the criteria of more than one personality disorder.

In effect, severely disturbed people will have generalized deficits in all areas of personality functioning in the same way as a person suffering from major depression will also often meet the criteria for numerous disorders—including those involving social, emotional, and cognitive functioning. Thus, a single but severe pathology can manifest in such a way as to make the afflicted person seem to have numerous disorders.

Diagnostic Stability

In addition to the personality disorders defined by DSM-IV, several disorders are currently being researched, such as the sadistic, self-defeating, and passive-aggressive personality disorders. Still other pathologies cause profound disturbances of personality. These include the problematic dissociative identity disorder (DID; formerly called multiple personality disorder or MPD) and such organic disorders as Pick's disease (dementia caused by degeneration of the frontotemporal lobe of the brain). Of course, the problem of generalized deficits still confounds the understanding of personality disorders because any acute pathology will alter personality functioning. A person in chronic pain may become quite avoidant, for example; similarly, a person who has suffered several major traumas may behave as though he is paranoid or even

| **Table 15.2** | DSM-IV-TR Personality Disorders and Diagnostic Requirements |

Disorder	*Diagnostic Requirements (minimum of total criteria)*
Cluster A (disorders characterized by odd or eccentric behavior)	
Paranoid personality disorder	4 of 7
Schizoid personality disorder	4 of 7
Schizotypal personality disorder	5 of 9
Cluster B (disorders characterized by dramatic or erratic behavior)	
Antisocial personality disorder	3 of 7
Borderline personality disorder	5 of 9
Histrionic personality disorder	5 of 8
Narcissistic personality disorder	5 of 9
Cluster C (disorders characterized by anxious or fearful behavior)	
Avoidant personality disorder	4 of 7
Dependent personality disorder	5 of 8
Obsessive-compulsive personality disorder	4 of 8

borderline. This phenomenon raises the issue of the stability of a personality disorder. As has been discussed at length, personality is generally fairly stable across the life span (e.g., Costa & McCrae, 1986; Haan & Day, 1974; Hampson & Goldberg, 2006; Helson & Moane, 1987; Roberts, Caspi, & Moffitt, 2001; Vaillant 1977).

The same degree of stability, however, has not been clearly established for disorders of personality (Grilo & McGlashan, 2005). In one longitudinal study of this issue (Lenzenweger, Johnson, & Willett, 2004), the researchers found a high degree of variability over time among individuals diagnosed with personality disorders. A similar result was found with the putative depressive personality (Laptook, Klein, & Dougherty, 2006), as well as with personality disorders among people diagnosed with mood disorders (Durbin & Klein, 2006).

The failure of research to support the stability of personality disorders across time strongly implies that disorders of personality are different in nature from personality traits or dimensions. The fact that personality disorders have been shown to improve over time (Grilo, Becker, Edell, & McGlashan, 2001) implies that at least some disorders are transient disturbances of the basic personality, which remains stable at its core.

Table 15.3   Overview of the DSM-IV Personality Disorders

Disorder	Description of Disorder
Cluster A: Disorders characterized by odd or eccentric behavior	
Paranoid	Suspicious of others, unforgiving, easily insulted, hostile, emotionally withholding, guarded about intimacy
Schizoid	Socially detached, emotionally constricted, indifferent to the emotions of others, prefers to be alone
Schizotypal	Socially uncomfortable, eccentric style of speaking, odd thoughts and unusual or distorted perceptions
Cluster B: Disorders characterized by dramatic, emotional, or erratic behavior	
Antisocial	Impulsive, reckless, manipulative, deceptive, feels rules do not apply, irresponsible, aggressive, lacks remorse
Borderline	Prone to intense and unstable relationships, unstable self-image, suicidal behavior, labile emotions, feelings of emptiness, angry and impulsive
Histrionic	Dramatic in most social settings, seeks attention, overly emotional, sexually seductive, emotionally shallow, vague, and suggestible
Narcissistic	Exaggerated feeling of self-importance, solicits or demands admiration, rages when criticized, lacks empathy, feelings of entitlement, exploitative
Cluster C: Disorders characterized by anxious or fearful behavior	
Obsessive-Compulsive	Parsimonious, perfectionistic regarding self and others, extremely controlled, rigid in thought and behavior, stubborn, and demanding of others
Avoidant	Feels inadequate, dreads criticism, excessively fears rejection, continually anticipates embarrassment and is socially inhibited
Dependent	Indecisive, low self-confidence, emotionally vulnerable, feelings of helplessness, fear of acting independently, overly compliant

▣ DIMENSIONAL AND FACTORIAL DIAGNOSTIC MODELS

The alternative dimensional approach to the diagnosis of personality disorders is still quite problematic although it offers some advantages over the DSM-IV categories (O'Connor, 2005; Widiger, 1992). To diagnose people based on a dimensional approach, the clinician must address several problems (Trull, Tragesser, Solhan, & Schwartz-Mette, 2007), including the most obvious: What dimensions should be used? The dimensions of pathology can be specific to a disorder, like those seen in the diagnostic criteria of DSM-IV-TR. In this case, the diagnosis is based on an algorithm that assigns people to a specific category on the basis of a required number of pathological criteria or traits. An entirely different approach could be used, one in which all pathologies are based on factors of personality, like the extensively researched Five-Factor Model.

Factorial models of personality are based on a statistical method called **factor analysis**. First developed by Karl Pearson in 1901, factor analysis is a technique in which observations or measures of any kind are grouped together into closely correlated factors. This technique looks for underlying relationships among variables that may contribute to some more comprehensive or universal explanation of events or behavior. What factor analysis does is to identify all the items that are closely correlated. Thus, factor analysis begins with a matrix of correlations among the variables. In personality research, factor analysis would generally consist of a matrix of correlated personality traits or qualities. From this matrix, the analyst would then find the underlying linear relationships that best explain the connections among the variables.

Most factor analytical techniques attempt to successively reduce the number of variables. A mathematical value that guides this process is called the eigenvalue, which denotes the proportion of the variance each factor explains. Accordingly, factors with low eigenvalues are dropped from an explanatory model. The best-known personality factor model is the "Big Five" or the Five-Factor Model of personality. One can assume that the original calculations yielded more than five factors, but only those with meaningful eigenvalues were considered to be meaningful summaries of personality.

For example, suppose an experimental psychologist wishes to determine which attitudes are most strongly related to a positive psychological outlook. A large number of subjects are asked to endorse numerous questionnaire items about life. People with a positive mind-set might endorse items like: "The future holds positive challenges," "I have the ability to control my emotions," "I rarely stay down for very long," "Adversities are challenges to be overcome," and so on. People who do not possess a positive outlook will not endorse these statements but are more likely to endorse pessimistic statements, which we will not enumerate here. With factor analysis, statisticians will find that several of these statements cluster together. In this case, the positive statements enumerated above are likely to cluster. Researchers then look at all the items in the cluster and find a common thread. They ask themselves, what underlying personality characteristic causes people to respond in the affirmative to this cluster of questions? They will likely conclude that it is a positive attitude toward life that causes those particular subjects to endorse this group of statements. People who see the future as holding positive opportunities will typically regard setbacks as challenges to be overcome. They also tend to expect good things to happen in their future, and so on. A simple correlational analysis would then determine that people who tend to respond positively on one item will also respond positively to one other item.

The new factor variable that contains the two items mentioned above could be called an "optimistic sense of control." This is the essence of factor analysis: to summarize closely correlated variables or manifest variables to create a new summary variable or latent variable that contains most of the information contained in the numerous original items. The correlation that each manifest variable has with the factor is called its factor loading. Thus, variables with a high factor loading are closely linked to the factor and contribute significantly to the factor's ability to explain some phenomenon. Factor analysis can be calculated with several statistical techniques, all of them seeking to find factors composing measures that are closely related to one another while also being minimally related to measures that constitute other factors.

The most commonly used contemporary model is the Five-Factor Model (Costa & McCrea, 1990). It was constructed using the natural language approach developed by Gordon Allport and the statistical methodology of Raymond Cattell (1990). This method compiles people's evaluations of their own or others' personalities from surveys or questionnaires. These responses are then analyzed using any of a number of statistical techniques that find the personality traits or qualities which are most closely correlated with one another. This type of analysis is depicted in Table 15.4, in which three factors are derived from a fictional questionnaire. A personality characteristic would be placed into a factor because it is highly correlated with the other characteristics in that factor and minimally correlated with characteristics in the other factors.

Once the terms are compiled into factors, the next requirement is to find the meaning of those factors (Goldberg & Digman, 1994). For example, suppose researchers conduct a survey of a large sample of people who are asked to rate themselves on 15 personal qualities that result in three factors (see Table 15.4). These factors will be correlative groups and will not be named or explained by the statistical procedures that identified them. This is the task of the researchers, who must impose meaning on the factors. In the model factor analysis displayed in Table 15.4, three factors are derived from the hypothetical personality survey. Researchers contemplating these factors would look for logical commonalities among the items in each factor. This investigation might lead to the first factor being called Bellicosity, the second factor Intellectualism, and the third Sociality. They could, however, have also been called Aggressiveness, Openness, and Congeniality. This freedom of nomenclature is the case for all of the factor models of personality. Experimental psychologists analyzed the results from numerous natural language personality instruments and distilled them into factors. The names we now use were intuitive and logical, but arbitrary nonetheless.

The dimensional and factor analytical approaches are predicated on the notion that personality is best understood and described by people in real-life situations. These approaches stand in direct contrast to the committee and consensus approach found in DSM-IV. Thus, the personality disorders defined by DSM-IV are based on the clinical and experimental data of mental health professionals. In comparison, the factor analytic approach effectively lets people

---

Table 15.4   Personality Factors Derived from a Hypothetical Survey

Factor I	Factor II	Factor III
• Suspicious • Easily angered • Believes revenge is justified	• Interested in new things • Likes to read • Believes all views have some legitimacy • Dislikes intellectual rigidity • Finds mental challenges pleasurable • Considers meeting new people desirable	• Laughs easily • Likes to socialize • Works best in groups • Enjoys public speaking • Prefers being the leader • Would like to be an actor

define their own personality in ordinary terms and then finds those terms that best summarize all the components of human personality. Factor analytic approaches have resulted in several well-known models of personality. The numerous dimensional or factor models of personality include the 16 personality factors (16 PF) of Cattell (1990), the "Big Five" of Costa and McCrea, the P-E-N three-factor model of Eysenck (1991), and the two factors of Digman (1997), who found that two higher order factors account for most of the variance in the "Big Five." All of these models use one form of factor analysis to find correlated personality traits and then name the factors according to personal judgment.

The most widely accepted factor model of personality as of 2007 is the "Big Five." As its appellation implies, this five-factor model posits that any personality can be expressed as a point in a five-dimensional space because each factor represents a continuum that can be expressed from a high to low degree in each person. Because it is difficult to envision five dimensions in spatial terms, tests that measure these five factors yield a score for each factor. One such test is the Revised NEO Personality Inventory (Costa & McCrea, 1992) or NEO-PI-R. The five dimensions can be summarized as shown in Table 15.5.

Diagnosing personality pathology using the five factors implies that normal and abnormal personalities differ quantitatively rather than qualitatively; that is, an individual diagnosed with a personality disorder is at the extreme range of at least one of the factors. Researchers applying this concept (Bagby, Costa, Widiger, Ryder, & Marshall, 2005; Costa & McCrae, 1990; De Fruyt, De Clercq, van de Wiele, & Van Heeringen, 2006; Saulsman & Page, 2004) have found that the five-factor model of personality can be used to both elucidate and diagnose personality disorders.

Much research remains to be done, however. Although factor models have been demonstrated to have correlative relationships with most of the personality disorders, they have yet to completely explain these disorders. Of course, this lack of explanatory power could very

---

Table 15.5   Dimensions Measured in the Five-Factor Model of Personality

Characteristics of Low Range	*Factor*	*Characteristics of High Range*
Lacks curiosity; is resistant to change, unoriginal in thought, and rigid in approaches to adversity	**Openness to experience**	Attracted to intellectual pursuits; is nonconforming and accepting of novel ideas
Indolent, readily surrenders to adversity, and unreliable	**Conscientiousness**	Persistent, diligent, and scrupulous in interpersonal affairs
Aloof, uncomfortable in social settings, laconic, and reserved	**Extroversion (surgency)**	Outgoing, attracted to social situations, confident, and garrulous
Suspicious of others' intentions, uncooperative, and antagonistic	**Agreeableness**	Helpful to others, trusting, and cooperates in social settings
Emotionally labile, prone to negative emotions, and easily traumatized	**Neuroticism**	Calm, readily recovers from trauma, and emotionally secure

well be a result of the nature of the diagnoses themselves. That is, the 10 personality disorders as currently defined may turn out to be poor approximations of real-life disturbances of personality. If this is the case, then even a perfect factor model of normal personality will fail to account for imperfect categories of abnormality. In addition, factor models of personality have been formulated from samples of predominantly normal individuals. So although they have been shown to be robust in explaining variations in normal personality, they have not performed equally well in explaining personality disorders, which may in fact be drawn from a different population distribution (Miller, Pilkonis, & Clifton, 2005; Shedler & Westen, 2004)

CAUSAL EXPLANATIONS OF PERSONALITY DISORDERS

Trait and factor models of personality disorders typically make no explicit statement regarding the causes of the disorder; they are merely methods of classifying or describing them. There is, however, no shortage of hypothetical explanations for personality disorders. In fact, virtually every one of the numerous clinical schools has its own causal explanation of personality disturbances. In reading about the theories of personality disorders, the student will find many points of contention as well as many overlapping concepts. The best-known etiology of personality disorders is Freud's, which attributes them to libidinal fixations during the various psychosexual stages of development. This model has largely been supplanted in modern psychodynamic or psychoanalytic schools, which stress social, self-concept, and ego factors more than such constructs as drives and libido. In fact, despite the continued use of psychoanalytic nomenclature on the part of writers in the **psychodynamic** tradition, more recent writers from this school have incorporated concepts drawn from cognitive psychology in their work (Abrams & Abrams, 1997).

Despite the movement of psychodynamic theorists toward either a more cognitive perspective or a biological one (Schore, 1994), however, there still remains a diverse assortment of theories. This is true to a lesser extent among those writers who adopt cognitive, biological, and interpersonal theories of personality. That is, within each of the major perspectives there are theorists with different opinions regarding the origins of personality disorders. Fortunately, most of these can be understood by reviewing some of the more salient theoretical positions.

Ego Psychology

As a partial response to Freud's explanation of personality as primarily a function of unconscious sexual and aggressive drives, several clinicians advocated a greater focus on the person's conscious identity, namely the ego. These writers proposed that personality is derived from social strivings, the personal quest for excellence, and the search for personal identity.

The ego psychologists proposed that the essential core of the human psyche is the rational and largely conscious ego. They examined its role in controlling primitive impulses, in reality testing, and in regulating the emotions. An early proponent of this view was Heinz Hartmann, who hypothesized that a properly functioning ego can maintain memory, test reality adequately, and cope with traumatic experiences in a satisfactory fashion. Moreover, the ego can be examined as an independent mental construct without the need for assuming conflicts arising from the id or superego. Hartmann, who was deeply influenced by the principle of natural selection, believed that a properly functioning ego would be well adapted to the demands of life (Mitchell & Black, 1995). This adaptation includes adequate management of the primitive impulses arising from the id. Hartmann was the catalyst of a movement that refocused psychoanalysis by defining human beings as conscious volitional agents. The essential difference between the traditional Freudian view of the ego and that of Hartmann is that for Hartmann, the ego is not necessarily in a perpetual battle with the id's impulses or the superego's restraints. Instead, the ego has the primary function of adjusting to the demands of one's social life, job, and other matters in the world. Like Horney and Adler, Hartmann attempted to make psychoanalysis more relevant to social problems and everyday concerns of life rather than focusing on intrapsychic conflicts (Lifschutz, 1964).

In the perspective of ego psychology, personality disorders arise when an individual has persistent emotional intrusions, largely conscious, that impair thought, functioning, and interpersonal relationships. Hartmann and subsequent ego psychologists were most concerned with a person's ability to adapt to the demands of life (Hartmann, 1958). The ability to consciously focus one's intellect, knowledge, and strengths to meet changing social demands represents the core of a healthy personality.

Object-Relations Theories

The object-relations perspective is largely the result of the work of Melanie Klein (1984), who proposed that developing infants are shaped by stimulating objects. They do not see people as a whole but relate to their parts; for example, the infant sees the mother's breast rather than mother as a whole as a source of sustenance and nurturance. Klein inferred that infants have an innate aggressive drive that leads them to fantasize about sadistic acts against their objects or their mental models of significant things. In the first year of life, according to Klein, the infant fantasizes that the mother has a good breast that is completely good and loving, and a bad breast that the child desires to attack and consume. Since the breast is the first external object that the baby notices, his first experience effectively involves splitting his mother into an all-good and an all-bad object. Klein referred to this **splitting** as the paranoid-schizoid position (Klein, 1946), which continues until the age of two, when the child is able to apprehend his mother as a complete object.

With the recognition that the good and bad breasts are both part of one mother, Klein (1946) asserted that the child suffers

> extreme feelings of grief, guilt and fear of loss, and, as a result, seeks to make reparation for her/his damages to what once was the idealized, good breast. In exchange for this bitter realization, the infant's anxieties lose in strength; objects become both less idealized and less terrifying, and the ego becomes more unified. All this is interconnected with the growing perception of reality and adaptation to it.

Klein's idiosyncratic understanding of mental objects evolved into a psychodynamic school that regards personality and pathology as arising from early relationships, particularly the relationships between the developing child and significant others in his early life. In the course of these relationships the child develops representations of others that become part of her psyche. These representations become the core of her personality.

Margaret Mahler (1897–1985) proposed that the mother-child relationship is instrumental in the formation of both normal and pathological personalities (Mahler, 1972; Mahler, Pine, & Bergman, 1994). Her theories, which have been influential among both ego and object-relation psychologists, are founded on the premise that severe pathologies arise when the child has not bonded adequately with her mother. Normal development, according to Mahler, first requires that a bond between mother and child bond be formed through a series of stages. In the first phase, which covers only the first few weeks of life, the child is aware only of itself. In the normal symbiotic phase, which begins in the fourth or fifth month, the child becomes aware of things beyond itself but is limited to seeing them only as extensions of its own body. In the separation-individuation phase, which lasts until the child's third year, Mahler maintained that the child forms an identity separate from its mother and ideally develops a medley of objects that will consistently and realistically model social relationships. Personality disorders, according to Mahler, result from disruptions in this process of separation-individuation.

Mahler, like most other object-relation theorists, believed that objects serve as points of reference for behavior and sources of solace during times of distress. Consequently, this perspective suggests that what might appear to be a reaction to flesh-and-blood people in the present (sometimes called external objects) is actually a response to one's internal objects. This is especially the case if the internal object is somehow related to or similar to the external object. For example, in the case of a boss who reminds an employee of his rejecting father, the worker may react with disproportionate anger to a minor rebuke by the boss. The appellation object raises the question as to why this perspective is not called personal or interpersonal relations. The answer is that the child, according to Mahler's model, is neither able to apprehend people as wholes nor to separate people from other objects in his world that appear to meet his needs.

More recently, object-relations theorists have moved away from a focus on primitive and aggressive drives toward a greater emphasis on objects as models that provide stability and consistency to personality (Greenberg & Mitchell, 1983). In addition, some prominent object-relations theorists like Otto Kernberg have reemphasized the limits of metaphorical language in describing mental processes—a point that Freud made clear in many of his early writings; for example: "we must recollect that all of our provisional ideas in psychology will someday be based on organic substructure" (Freud, 1949a, p. 36). More recently, Kernberg (1993) wrote: "Psychoanalysis increases an understanding, for example, of the early development of the human infant, affect theory, and the neuropsychology of memory at its boundary with biological sciences" (p. 46).

Thus it would seem that object-relations theory is based on metaphorical representations of human propensities and behaviors. However, whether biological, metaphorical, or based in the more traditional psychoanalytic perspective, object-relations psychologists essentially believe that personality pathology results from poorly formed internal objects. That is, the person with a personality disorder has failed to construct healthy or stable internal representations of other people within his or her psyche. The failure to have reliable objects to guide behavior is believed to result in inconsistent relationships, anxiety, impulsive behavior, and many of the behavioral characteristics observed in those with personality disorders. For example, an individual with a dependent personality disorder is believed (Bornstein, 1996) to have failed in creating a cogent parental representation at the time the infant was developing his own identity during the separation-individuation period. This separation-individuation phase, first elaborated by Mahler (1971; Mahler et al., 1994), essentially states that the neonate perceives herself and her caretaker (usually the mother) as one being. As the normal development of the infant progresses she will begin to discern boundaries between herself and her mother, ultimately conceiving of herself as a separate being.

An individual with borderline personality disorder is also believed by object-relations theorists to suffer from inadequately constructed mental objects. Accordingly, the borderline individual, who typically experienced inconsistent nurturance or even abuse, develops separate internal objects: one for the good parent and one for the bad. This development leads to what psychoanalysts have called splitting (Kernberg, 1968; Klein, 1946), a psychological mechanism in which people are viewed as either all good or all bad. The borderline lacks the ability to see shades of gray in relationships; thus he regards others only in terms of his most recent interaction with them. Should that interaction have been positive or beneficial, the borderline regards the other with deep affection; should it have been unsatisfying, however, the borderline will regard the other with loathing or intense anger. In addition, the absence of a well-defined internal object also leads to the chronic feelings of emptiness and emotional **lability** that characterize persons with borderline personality disorder.

Object-relations theorists view all personality pathology as following this pattern. Early relationships foster the maturation of representational objects that guide future relationships. Each personality disorder is viewed as a manifestation of a particular deficiency in the person's pantheon of internal objects. In general, object-relations adherents do not attempt to coordinate their concepts of personality disorders with DSM-IV's definitions.

Self Psychology

The **self psychology** perspective is a derivative of both the psychoanalytic and object-relations schools. Self psychology is largely based on the work of Heinz Kohut (1971), who emphasized the interactions between an individual's mental objects and her self. Kohut and those who subscribe to his self psychology emphasize a person's ability to empathize with others as the essential measure of the stability of his or her personality. They use the term *empathize* literally, that is, to be able to feel vicariously what others are feeling and to be able to comprehend what led the others to experience those feelings. This ability to empathize is believed to be fostered through empathic parents who guide the developing infant to withstand the emotional conflicts and turmoil he will face in adult life (Kohut & Wolf, 1978). Kohut, like Carl Rogers, proposed that psychotherapy can facilitate healing if the individual feels understood by an empathic

Image 15.1   Heinz Kohut (1913–1981)

therapist (Kohut, 1984b). A central concept in the self-psychology theory of personality disorders is the notion of the **selfobject**. According to Kohut (who dropped the hyphen from the term), each person develops a selfobject through her developmental experiences with significant others. Thus salient emotion-laden events with others become integrated into one's own psyche and become the core of the personality. It is this core that is essential for emotional stability and healthy interpersonal functioning. Selfobjects, like objects in traditional object-relations theory, are representations of the world that are the fundamental building blocks of a person's identity. According to the principles of self psychology, these selfobjects do not necessarily correspond to any external reality. Kohut described selfobjects as relatively impersonal, once defining a selfobject as "that dimension of our experience of another person that relates to the person's functions in shoring up our self" (Kohut, 1984a, pp. 49–50). Selfobjects are based on people or events but can be sufficiently reconstructed so as to be unique to the individual holding them. When functioning properly, selfobjects provide the person with a consistent level of self-esteem and appropriate emotional responses to persons and events.

Although the self is based on selfobjects, Kohut makes a distinction between the self and the selfobject. The former represents the person's developing identity and the latter the external life events that guide it. According to Kohut, the self can take several forms, including the virtual self, which is the reflection of one's identity in the eyes of the parents. There is the early grandiose self, which represents an immature narcissistic phase of development. He also proposed the fragmented self, a condition in which a person's identity is unstable due to inadequate selfobject development. The final self that Kohut defined is the cohesive self, found in the person who achieves a healthy integration of the components of their personality.

Kohut maintained that a certain degree of narcissism is both healthy and necessary to a high-functioning personality; however, healthy narcissism can be acquired only through proper selfobject experiences. The first of these requires a child's exposure to people (who will be made into selfobjects) who strongly affirm the child's early feelings of strength, perfection, and energy. The second necessary experience requires exposure to people who are perceived as powerful and to whom "the child can look up and with whom he can merge as an image of calmness, infallibility, and omnipotence" (Kohut & Wolf, 1978, p. 414). The third essential experience requires that the child be exposed to people with whom the child can strongly identify and who provide a sense of similarity and belonging.

Through these selfobject forming experiences and relationships, the child's early grandiose narcissism evolves into a healthy self-esteem. This growth process facilitates the management of frustration and conflict. Importantly, Kohut believed that selfobjects develop and are modified throughout the lifespan. Conceptually, Kohut's theory is quite reminiscent of Bandura's, especially if selfobjects are replaced by cognitive models. The continual modification of selfobjects is quite compatible with Bandura's concept of observational learning and modeling. The individual creates representations through observing significant others and develops theories about the best way to respond in like situations. In comparison, Kohut's selfobjects are formed through observation and interaction with significant others who also become the basis of future behavior in similar situations. This similarity is especially apparent when Kohut's theory of therapeutic transferential relationships is examined.

Like both Bandura and Carl Rogers, Kohut did not recommend that the therapist offer interpretations in therapy. Instead, the therapist allows the client to augment or strengthen his selfobjects by accepting the client's transference. This process can be accomplished by providing a supportive and caring therapeutic environment (as in Rogers's theory), which evokes a mirroring transference. Or the therapist can serve as an idealized role model (as in Bandura's model), who bestows feelings of strength and significance through her association with the client. Kohut called this development an idealizing transference. Alternately, the client can identify with the therapist directly and thereby shore up his selfobjects. This form of identification is called alter ego transference.

A developmental psychoanalyst named Allan Schore (1994) has constructed a comprehensive model in a novel synthesis that applies neuropsychology, developmental physiology, and biochemistry to current understandings of brain development. His proposal, which is concordant with most neurodevelopmental views, states that the development of the infant's brain is guided by her interaction with key figures, most prominently the mother. According to this view, the genetic templates that structure the growth of the brain require external cues to allow for emotional control, self-concept, and a model of social relations. This growth is accomplished by an interactive feedback between the burgeoning limbic structures and the more slowly developing frontal lobes. This interactive process is innately guided by emotional feedback in the form of physical contact, facial expressions, and later verbal cues from the mother.

According to Schore, the child's cognitive representation of the mother is the foundation of selfobjects that ultimately provide emotional stability and coherent self-image in later life. Explaining unconscious conflicts in neurological terms, however, undermines the basis of psychoanalytic treatment, in which transference and insight produce healing. If indeed a person's internal conflicts become neurologically integrated in youth, mere insight is unlikely to resolve them in adult life.

According to self psychology, personality disorders result from poorly developed selfobjects and failure to receive empathy during early development. For example, borderline personality disorder can develop when the individual suffered empathic failures and presently lacks an integrated selfobject (Wolf, 1988). The nurturance and empathy that fosters the development of selfobjects allows the growing child to develop a selfobject that provides motivation, the ability to soothe itself in stressful situations, and feelings of affiliation (Wastell, 1992). Without these foundations, a person must continually seek security and stability from external sources. Such a person will collapse in the face of adversity, experience wild mood swings under stress, and easily swing from loving to loathing intimates in his life. In addition, since judgments of other people's behaviors are referenced against one's selfobject, an inadequate selfobject fails to provide this grounding, which leads in turn to splitting—namely the inability to judge the actions of others in the context of terms of an overall relationship. Thus a person who is acting badly (in the borderline's judgment) is seen as a bad person, and when acting kindly is deeply loved. The borderline patient therefore tends to behave as though each person in their life is split into different people.

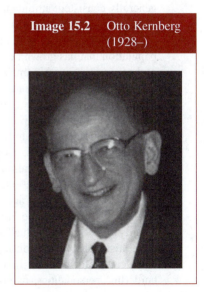

Image 15.2   Otto Kernberg (1928–)

Although borderline personality disorder is the most severe personality disorder, Kohut saw it as a severe and special case of the narcissistic personality. According to Kohut, narcissism is a healthy aspect of human personality that arises from selfobject growth with the support of strong and supportive caregivers. The narcissistic personality disorders arise when the caregivers fail to help the selfobject mature so that the child can form a realistic view of him- or herself. According to Kohut, this outcome is the direct result of the parents' failure to provide mirroring or affirmative responses that bolster the child's selfobject. The shame and rejection inherent in the caregivers' lack of support leads to the child's growing into an adult who craves adoration to compensate for his own underlying fragility (Siomopoulos, 1988). In contrast, the healthy individual progresses from infantile grandiosity to more mature feelings of realistic self-esteem.

Otto Kernberg (1928–) and his coworkers (Kernberg, 2005; Kernberg & Caligor, 2005) further expanded the object-relations explanations of personality disorders with a special focus on the narcissistic and borderline disorders. Kernberg, like Freud, sees the sex drive as central to personality organization and personality disorders. According to Kernberg, human personality develops with children's acquisition of increasingly mature object representations of themselves and of key figures in their lives. At first the child cannot represent himself separately from his caregiver, nor can he construct objects with gradations of good and bad, so the child represents the world by fusing his identity with his mother as being all good or all bad. With further maturation the child can distinguish himself from his mother or other caregiver, but cannot represent these objects with shades of gray. Consequently he has an all-good self, an all-bad mother, and so on. With additional maturation the child can represent separate people along a qualitative continuum, which allows him to model the world with different people all having good, bad, and in-between qualities. Once this level of maturity is achieved, the individual is capable of responding to others appropriately. That is, he can view another person's actions as separate from the permanent worth of that person. He is capable of positive, negative, or conflicted feelings toward a specific person while maintaining a generally consistent attitude toward that person.

Like Kohut, Kernberg has focused on narcissistic and borderline personality disturbances—in part because patients with these two types of disturbance represent a segment of the clinical population that has grown rapidly since the 1950s (Lasch, 1978). Those with the more severe of these two disorders, namely borderline patients, are unable to maintain stable relationships because they cannot form stable objects with shades of gray. They are able to separate the self from others but lack the ability to see others as three-dimensional beings with multiple qualities. Borderline individuals tend to be intensely drawn to those they find attractive because of their tendency to first formulate an all-good object. When that person fails in some way to meet their needs, they experience intense rage because they now have formed a completely bad representation of the other person. This splitting of the other person into an all-good or all-bad representation leads to a relationship that alternates between clinging adoration and homicidal rage.

Because Kernberg, like Freud, views personality as driven by sexual energy or libido, he regards borderline individuals, with their attendant instability, as tending toward aggressive or masochistic sexual relationships. In his system, the individual with narcissistic personality disorder has focused her libido on herself instead of on another person. Like people with borderline personalities, narcissists have unstable and incomplete objects, unlike the stable objects that endow healthy people with the ability to both understand and engage the vicissitudes of life. This deficit leaves narcissists feeling insecure and angry at a world that they perceive as hostile and unpredictable (Kernberg, 1975). Their insecurity in turn leads to a state of pathological narcissism in which the afflicted person devalues his unreliable objects and compensates by inflating his own object to a grandiose state. According to Kernberg, the pathological narcissist loses the ability to love others in a mature fashion because she has directed her essential and limited libido toward herself. In effect, she has become her own love object. And according to psychoanalysis, the amount of sexual energy or love that anyone can have is limited; thus the more one loves oneself, the less love one can give to others.

Most of the psychological theories derived from psychoanalysis, including both object relations and self psychology, are burdened by the heavy use of metaphors in explaining both normal and pathological human development. Exacerbating this difficulty is the fact that most of the early proponents of these views based their metaphors on simple observation and very little research. Very few of their testable theories have ever been subjected to scientific scrutiny. There is no doubt that as the child's brain develops, it becomes increasingly capable of understanding the world. The child becomes increasingly able to comprehend the purpose of various items and the intentions and roles of the different people in its life. The complex phantasmagoria of many of the early objection theorists has not withstood the test of time or scientific scrutiny—especially in light of our growing understanding of organic brain development. Much of what is said in object-relations theory can be stated far more precisely with the use of terminology that facilitates scientific study. In fact, there is no evidence that children or adults represent the world through the use of objects in the way described by early writers like Melanie Klein or Margaret Mahler. Instead, people do form increasingly complex representations of the world that include all sensory modalities. Current research in cognition, however, indicates that the link between these representations and individual personality are quite different from those suggested by the schools of thought derived from psychoanalysis.

Cognitive Perspectives on Personality Disorders

Cognitive psychology and cognitive therapies have a common foundation but also diverge in many important ways. The most salient difference between the two is their essential goals. Cognitive therapists seek to understand and treat psychological problems by addressing problems in the client's thinking. These problems include irrational modes of thought, arbitrary inference, magnification of minor problems, and so on. In contrast, cognitive psychology represents a comprehensive school that includes the study of the way the brain perceives the world, the way it processes information from the senses, the way it forms conclusions, and the way it stores and retrieves memories. Consequently, cognitive psychologists are far less concerned with treating problems than they are with discovering how the mind works.

It is the cognitive therapists who have been largely responsible for investigating and explaining the etiology of personality disorders. These explanations are largely the product of Aaron Beck and Albert Ellis. Beck has been a bit more explicit in his formulation of the cognitive therapy of personality disorders, having written a text (Beck, Freeman, & Davis, 2004) on the subject. Although Ellis did not formally present an explanation of personality disorders prior to this text, it has been implicit in his clinical writings (e.g., Ellis, 1962, Ellis & Bernard, 1986). The perspectives of both of these founders are presented below.

AARON BECK'S COGNITIVE THERAPY

Early Career

Aaron Beck, who was originally trained as a psychoanalyst, drew on his own experience to derive some of his insights about the role of cognition in treating emotional disorders. As a child, he suffered a broken arm in a playground accident, and the shattered bone became infected, causing him to miss several months of school while the injury healed slowly in those pre-penicillin days. He was then forced to repeat first grade, which led him at first to feel stupid and incompetent. He decided, however, to work hard to overcome his feelings. He proved to himself that he could succeed in school, "that I could do things, that if I got into a hole I could dig myself out" (quoted in Weishaar, 1993, p. 10). In other words, Beck discovered at an early age that he could change his moods and feelings by a kind of cognitive self-help treatment. He later cured himself of phobias related to tunnels, high places, and suffocation by working through his fears cognitively.

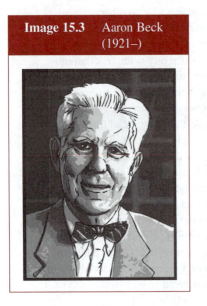

Image 15.3   Aaron Beck (1921–)

In medical school, Beck disliked the Freudian approach to psychotherapy but was not able to test alternative views until he took a faculty position at the University of Pennsylvania and began to conduct research with colleagues in the department of psychology. Beck was fortunate to move to Penn just as the dominant school in psychology was changing from behavioral to cognitive. At this time, psychologists were breaking away from the premise that consciousness and thinking are too subjective to be the subjects of scientific study. They proposed that mental activities could be scientifically modeled and experimentally inferred. Out went the dynamic unconscious of Freud and in came the notion of automatic or nonconscious processing of information. The mind was now conceived as an information-processing device that manipulated some information in an aware fashion and other data automatically and nonconsciously. Beck applied these concepts to his clinical research, particularly his work with depressed patients.

Concept of Schemas

Beck used the concept of schemas and automatic thoughts to explain depression, anxiety, and other psychological disturbances. Schemas, which Beck likens to George Kelly's notion of personal constructs (Beck, Freeman, & Davis, 2004, p. 27), are models or templates that individuals use to interpret the world and the events they encounter.

According to Beck and other cognitive theorists, people are bombarded with far too much information to easily process. The term *schema* in its current usage was coined by Frederic C. Bartlett (1886–1969), a British psychologist investigating memory. Bartlett wrote in 1932:

Schema refers to an active organization of past reactions, or of past experiences, which must always be supposed to be operating in any well-adapted organic response. That is, whenever there is any order or regularity of behavior, a particular response is possible only because it is related to other similar responses which have been serially organized, yet which operate, not simply as individual members coming one after another, but as a unitary mass. Determination by schemata is the most fundamental of all the ways in which we can be influenced by reactions and experiences which occurred some time in the past. All incoming impulses of a certain kind, or mode, go together to build up an active, organized setting: visual, auditory, various types of cutaneous impulses and the like, at a relatively low level; all the experiences connected by a common interest: in sport, in literature, history, art, science, philosophy and so on, on a higher level. There is not the slightest reason, however, to suppose that each set of incoming impulses, each new group of experiences persists as an isolated member of some passive patchwork. They have to be regarded as constituents of living, momentary settings belonging to the organism, or to whatever parts of the organism are concerned in making a response of a given kind, and not as a number of individual events somehow strung together and stored within the organism. (p. 201)

Bartlett performed a classic experiment on the effect of schemas on memory by giving his adult British subjects a Native American folk tale called "The War of the Ghosts" to read. He deliberately chose a narrative that would not be familiar to or easily fitted within the cultural background of these subjects. Here is the story when first presented to the subjects (Bartlett, 1932):

There were two young Indians who lived in Egulac, and they went down to the sea to hunt for seals. And where they were hunting it was very foggy and very calm. In a little while they heard cries, and they came out of the water and went to hide behind a log. They heard the sound of paddles, and they saw five canoes. One canoe came towards them, and there were five men within, who cried to the two Indians and said: "Come with us up the river and war on the people there."

But one of the Indians replied: "We have no arrows."

"There are arrows in the canoe."

"But I might be killed, and my people have need of me. You have no parents," he said to the other, "you can go with them of you wish it so; I shall stay here."

So one of the Indians went, but the other stayed behind and went home. And the canoes went on up the river to the other side Kalama, and fought the people there. Many of the people were killed, and many of those from the canoes also.

Then one of the warriors called to the young Indian and said: "Go back to the canoe, for you are wounded by an arrow." But the Indian wondered, for he felt not sick.

And when many had fallen on either side they went back to the canoes, and down the river again, and so the young Indian came back to Egulac.

Then he told them how there had been a battle, and how many fell and how the warriors had said he was wounded, and yet he felt not sick. So he told them all the tale, and he became weak. It was near daybreak when he became weak; and when the sun rose he fell down. And he gave a cry, and as he opened his mouth a black thing rushed from it. Then they ran to pick him up, wondering. But when they spoke he answered not.

He was dead. (p. 120)

Bartlett asked his subjects to recall the story for him several times over the course of the following year. He found that the retellings reflected the use of various schemas. First, the subjects shortened the story and made it more coherent. Second, they tended to pick up on a few details of the story and used those details to organize or anchor their retelling. Third, they retold the story in ways that reflected their own cultural norms and expectations. Below is the story after the tenth retelling.

Two Indians were out fishing for seals in the Bay of Manpapan, when along came five other Indians in a war-canoe. They were going fighting.

"Come with us," said the five to the two, "and fight."

"I cannot come," was the answer of the one, "for I have an old mother at home who is dependent upon me." The other also said he could not come, because he had no arms. "That is no difficulty," the others replied, "for we have plenty in the canoe with us;" so he got into the canoe and went with them.

In a fight soon afterwards this Indian received a mortal wound. Finding that his hour was come, he cried out that he was about to die. "Nonsense," said one of the others, "you will not die." But he did. (Bartlett, 1932, p. 124)

Bartlett proposed that the radical change in the recounting of the story was a result of memory being organized in the form of schemas. That is, the classification and storage of new memories is guided by prior memories of similar items or events, which in turn guide our reaction to novel life events. Thus, people develop working models of the world that act as rules of thumb that allow for more efficient interpretation of life events. These rules of thumb or schemas can be simple, such as "Houses have rooms," or they can describe more complex events, such as "When you enter a restaurant, wait to be seated and to be given a menu, and then select the food you desire" (Anderson, 1985). This second schema would be sufficiently general as to guide behavior in most establishments from neighborhood diners to five-star establishments. Because schemas are fairly generic, they provide frameworks for understanding and behaving in many diverse but conceptually related settings.

Beck essentially used the concept of schemas to propose that virtually all psychological problems result from faulty information processing. Like Ellis, Beck has been far less concerned with the history of an individual's distortion of reality and consequent **dysphoria** than he is in finding and correcting disordered cognitions.

Cognitive Therapy in Clinical Practice

Beck's cognitive therapy is intended to guide people to discover their particular problematic schemas or automatic thoughts and replace them with new modes of information

VIGNETTE

Schoolwork came easily to Gianni. He was endowed with a remarkable memory and a talent for integrating new information. Needless to say, he always did well in all of his subjects. Complementing his scholastic gifts, he was a natural athlete. Gianni became an expert skier, a highly competitive tennis player, and a capable participant in most other sports that did not involve teamwork. Team activities of any kind were something that never appealed to him.

Even in his youth, Gianni seemed driven to prove his worth. He was never satisfied with anything he did; he always thought he could do better. Never being satisfied was the basis of his chronically brooding personality style. This aspect of his nature did not appear to be related either to his parents or his three brothers, all of whom were close to one another and mutually supportive. Gianni's father was a successful orthodontist and his mother a former teacher who left work to raise her family. He was the second of four sons with markedly different styles and interests. Thus, there was little competition among the members of Gianni's family in their suburban New England home.

Gianni did well in college and began a committed relationship with Marlene, whom he married shortly after graduation. After college, Marlene entered a graduate degree program in child psychology while Gianni began dental school. Despite doing extremely well, Gianni was never content while he was in dental school; he seemed to think he should be doing "something better." As the years passed, Gianni found a solution for his chronic dissatisfaction: drugs, all types of drugs. Marijuana, sedatives, painkillers, and alcohol were his favorites, which he used daily. His weekends were often wild binges of drug-induced euphoria. Marlene, who virtually worshipped her husband, followed his lead with drugs, albeit to a lesser extent. This was the pattern they followed all through Gianni's years in dental school, his additional year of training to be a dental anesthesiologist, and his residency in oral surgery.

Gianni was accepted into one of the most prestigious oral surgery programs in the country, and as soon as he was eligible for the position, he became chief resident. As always, however, he was not satisfied with his achievements. Gianni could compare himself only to people he felt were superior. It was irrelevant how high he rose; he could only look upward to identify other people who were more successful, more respected, "better" than he was. This pattern led him to hate and resent himself and to make his drug habit even more necessary to numb the negative feelings. His growing dread of being discovered as the imposter he felt he really was further exacerbated his drug abuse. Gianni did not feel like a surgeon; he did not really believe that he was particularly smart. That early drive to prove his worth actually intensified with each additional achievement.

Upon completing his residency, Gianni began work as an oral surgeon at a major medical center. There he convinced himself that the surgeons who were medical

(Continued)

(Continued)

doctors did not respect him because he was "only" a dentist. Within a year, Gianni was back in school in an accelerated program to earn an M.D., which he accomplished in 2 years. Now, Gianni was a professionally certified dentist, an anesthesiologist, an oral surgeon, and a medical doctor. Not surprisingly, he was offered a position at one of the most prestigious university-related hospitals in New England. He was now a professor of medicine and dentistry at an Ivy League institution and was also making a name for himself as a brilliant facial surgeon. People with the most horrendous facial deformities or traumatic injuries were made whole by Gianni's gifted hands.

Unfortunately, Gianni's drug use escalated along with his increasing prestige and income. The feelings of being an imposter only worsened, as did the need to deaden them. Prior to a major operation on a woman with jaw cancer that Gianni was about to perform, he was seen injecting himself by a nurse. She reported Gianni to his superiors. The incident was kept in-house so that Gianni could continue to work as long as he submitted to voluntary drug testing and attended a program for drug-impaired physicians. He complied assiduously. Within a year, he was back to work unencumbered by any restrictions with the exception of those he continued to impose on himself. Gianni had reached the point where there were very few people he could look upward to compare himself with.

His high attainments did not help. At the pinnacle of his profession, his fears and self-doubts only increased. His narcotic injections increased to the point where he was medicating himself several times a day. It was no surprise that Gianni was caught again. This time, he was reported to the state medical and dental boards. Sadly, he lost both his faculty position and his professional licenses. He was found out and disgraced, but not in the way he had always feared. Gianni's self-destruction was largely the by-product of a personality style in which he masked grave feelings of inadequacy by striving for increasingly noteworthy achievements.

Vignette Questions

1. How much of a role do you think Gianni's personality played in his self-destructive behavior?

2. What beliefs about himself and his role in life do you think might have exacerbated his behavior?

3. Do you feel these beliefs were more or less important than his personality style? Explain.

processing. With regard to depression, Beck's first area of research, he identified the schemas that he believes to underlie depression as the **cognitive triad** (Beck, 1976). The cognitive depressive triad includes negative views of ourselves, a poor view of our life situation, and dire forecasts for our future. Beck allows for the fact that many depressed people suffer genuine failures and setbacks in life; however, a tendency to become depressed requires a person's subjective evaluation of misfortunes to be considerably more negative than the actual situation warrants. According to Beck, personality disorders are essentially produced by one or more distortions in schemas or other aspects of thinking. Typical cognitive distortions include:

Arbitrary inference: Drawing a self-deprecating conclusion with minimal or no evidence to support it. For example, a worker is told by her boss that he wants to meet with her privately. The worker then concludes that she is not competent because the boss wants to meet with her and not other employees. Her conclusion, however, is not based on substantive information. She was simply asked to come to the boss's office but concludes from this fact alone that she is going to be reprimanded for incompetence. For all she knows, the boss may be planning to give her a raise or ask her if she would accept a promotion.

Selective abstraction: This cognitive distortion involves focusing on one aspect of a situation that generally confirms some self-defeating notion and tending to disregard information that would disconfirm that conclusion. For example, an artist berates himself as incompetent because one of his paintings has a discolored area in one corner. He fails to notice the quality of the rest of the painting, however, and he also ignores the overall high quality of his other works.

Overgeneralization: In this cognitive distortion, a person forms a comprehensive evaluation of himself or his life based on a single or isolated event. For example, a man forgets his daughter's birthday and concludes, "I forget everything important."

Magnification: Exaggerating the significance of failing or other negative event. For example, a generally good student gives a poor presentation in one class meeting and concludes that "I am a complete failure as a student."

Minimization: The devaluation or negation of accomplishments or positive outcomes as insignificant. For example, a woman who is told by a man that he finds her attractive comments, "He probably says that to every woman he meets."

Personalization: This cognitive distortion represents a type of inverse narcissism in which a person thinks the world revolves around him in order to criticize or attack him. For example, a person borrows a friend's notes to study for an exam and fails the test. The personalizing friend is likely to think, "He failed because of me and my lousy notes."

Absolutistic dichotomous thinking: This distortion requires black-and-white thinking on the part of the thinker. For example, a person who is turned down for a job promotion thinks, "I am a total failure without the promotion." In effect, the person ties his complete worth as a human being to one outcome in one area of life.

In addition to identifying cognitive distortions like those set forth above, Beck hypothesizes that people with personality disorders develop early maladaptive schemas (EMSs), which are "extremely broad, pervasive themes regarding oneself and one's relationships with others, developed during childhood and elaborated throughout one's lifetime, and dysfunctional to a significant degree" (Beck et al., 2004, p. 65). EMSs are believed to be deeply ingrained and to become part of the individual's sense of self. In Beck's model of information processing as the source of emotional dysphoria, early maladaptive schemas, automatic thoughts, and cognitive distortions conspire to produce dysfunctional feelings and behaviors. Beck points out that a person's style of information processing can lead to cognitive distortions that are particular to each psychological disorder. Some of the more common distortions associated with personality disorders are presented in Table 15.6; Beck's research (Beck et al., 2001) has shown that these distortions differ among the personality disorders in a consistent fashion.

Beck, like Albert Ellis and other cognitive theorists, believes that aberrant cognitions like the ones listed in Table 15.6 underlie the personality disorders, but he also thinks that such disorders require some preexisting disposition in the client to develop (Weishaar & Beck, 2006).

In recent years, Beck has increasingly emphasized information processing in his model of personality. In this conceptualization, the stages of information processing are mediated by biological, neurological, historical (learning), and cognitive factors. Like most other cognitive or cognitive-behavioral clinicians, however, Beck recognizes that factors like biology, temperament, or the person's life history cannot be changed, although he maintains that the person's thinking and behavior can be altered. His approach to cognitive therapy, therefore, is predicated on patiently illuminating the client's dysfunctional automatic thoughts and distorted cognitions and challenging their legitimacy. When clients can accept or even endorse that their thought patterns are a major source of their pathology, they can begin to change their cognitive style to one that is more functional.

One of Beck's examples concerns a radiologist diagnosed with paranoid personality disorder (PPD) who was fearful of making mistakes on the job and regarded his competence as an all-or-nothing matter. He also saw his nervousness about making mistakes as an indication that he was incompetent. The therapist worked on a number of cognitive distortions with this client, including his tendency to expect the worst from others (including other doctors in his hospital) as well as his absolutistic dichotomous thinking ("I am either a competent physician or a total screw-up") and his interpretation of his worrying about errors as automatic proof that he was "a total screw-up" (Beck et al., 2004, pp. 125–136).

ALBERT ELLIS AND RATIONAL EMOTIVE BEHAVIOR THERAPY (REBT)

Innate Irrationality of Human Beings

The Rational Emotive Behavior Therapy view of personality disorders holds that disturbances in both innate temperament and styles of thinking are the basis of personality disorders. Albert Ellis (1958a, 1962), the originator of this perspective, saw people as intrinsically irrational, a characteristic that invariably leads to psychological problems, varying only in degree and duration. Moreover, Ellis held that individual differences in the degree and expression of irrationality are the basis of almost all psychopathology. According to Ellis (1994b), these individual differences derive from a combination of heredity, organic variations, and environmental influences. He rejected the common tendency to explain particular personality pathologies as functions of single traits or characteristics:

Humans tend to attribute special reasons to various events and behaviors. Because they feel comfortable (the Gestalt psychologists would say they feel "completed" or that they have effected "closure") with these reasons, they then wrongly believe that they

Table 15.6   Cognitive Distortions in Personality Disorders

Paranoid	• I am vulnerable to other people and must always be on my guard. • Other people cannot be trusted. • People have bad intentions towards me. • I must be careful to avoid people taking advantage of me.
Schizoid	• I am basically alone. • I can do things better without being burdened by other people. • Close relationships are unrewarding and messy. • Close relationships will interfere with my freedom.
Schizotypal	• I am different, worthless, uninteresting, and abnormal. • If I have unusual experiences, then others will notice me. • It is better to be isolated from others. • I believe in such magical things as telepathy and clairvoyance.
Antisocial	• If I am not the aggressor, I will be the victim. • I need to look out for myself. • Other people are suckers and patsies. • People are exploitative, so I am entitled to exploit them.
Borderline	• I can't cope on my own. • I need someone to rely on. • I deserve to be punished. • I cannot bear unpleasant feelings. • If I rely on someone, I'll be mistreated, found wanting, and abandoned.
Histrionic	• I need others to admire me in order to be happy. • I am entitled to admiration. • I am basically inadequate. • People exist to admire me and take care of me.
Narcissistic	• I am special and deserve special treatment and privileges. • I am superior to others, and they should acknowledge my greatness. • I am above the rules that apply to others. • Others should be punished if they don't recognize my superiority.
Obsessive-Compulsive	• I need organization, procedures, and rules in order to survive. • If I don't follow systems and procedures, everything will collapse. • If I and others don't perform perfectly, we will fail. • People should do better and try harder.
Avoidant	• I am worthless, no good, or unlovable. • I am incompetent in social interactions and work settings. • If others really get to know me, they will reject me. • I must avoid uncomfortable situations at all costs.
Dependent	• I am completely helpless. • I cannot survive without the help of someone really competent. • I cannot be happy without the support of someone strong. • I must be subservient in order to bind my caretaker to me.

SOURCE: Adapted from Beck, Freeman, & Davis (2004).

"proved" the validity of their "explanations." Primitive people pray for rain and, when it eventually does rain, they see their prayers as the "cause" of the rain. [All people] enjoy simple explanations . . . and we don't want to bother ourselves with all the complex factors that constitute the causal conditions of some event. So with personality theories. If I murder someone and you want to explain the cause of my act, you are likely to focus on one or two outstanding "influences"—for example, that my mother taught me the value of aggression or that some early religious teachings taught me the value of an eye for an eye. Certainly these "influences" *may* have affected me. But it seems most likely that out of a hundred children whose mothers or whose early religious training favored aggression, very few will murder people later in life! In fact it is unlikely that any of them will. Therefore, if I murdered someone, countless things might have contributed to my act. There might have been, for example, my innate tendency to demand that things go my way; my rebellion against social teachings which oppose murder; my low frustration tolerance when someone balks me; my being particularly sensitive to my victim's insults. . . . My theory of personality development . . . holds that any special reason for personality development or disturbance rarely if ever exists. (Ellis, 1979, p. 7)

Ellis (1995a) pointed out that many theorists are inclined to interpret salient actions as markers or evidence of personality pathology, often finding relationships where none exist. He maintained that any behavior, even one as shocking or repugnant as murder, may have a number of contributing factors, many of them quite unremarkable. The tendency to impose arbitrary meaning on any particular behavior runs the risk of missing alternative explanations or even of bending the available data to confirm a particular personality theory. Ellis argued that this arbitrary imposition of meaning is a common practice among psychological theorists, who tend to be strongly humanistic in their belief systems and are therefore attracted to theories founded on a belief in essential human virtue or those that allow maximal personal betterment. For this reason, Ellis always strongly advocated employing hypotheses that are testable and amenable to change to explain personality disorders.

Ellis (1976) differed from Beck in his emphasis on the innate irrationality in all people. Unlike Beck, who generally refers to cognitive distortions as an index or marker of psychopathology, Ellis (2004) considered irrationality as innately and invariably human and as lying within the person's control with some effort. In addition, he diverged widely from the psychodynamic and attachment theorists, who strongly emphasize the role of relationships in the development of personality pathology. Although acknowledging that environmental and developmental factors have some effect on personality pathology, Ellis asserted that most psychodynamic theories have overemphasized these factors. Ellis supported his position with the following observations from more than half a century of clinical practice and research.

1. Severely neglected and abused children often turn out to be remarkably hardy and less disturbed than non-abused children, including some of their own siblings who are also abused.

2. Millions of children who are treated exceptionally well by their parents and other family members develop severe personality disorders and even psychoses.

3. Many children, because they show emotional vulnerability from their earliest years, are therefore actually favored by their caretakers and are treated with unusual kindness, yet they still develop severe personality disorders.

4. Considerable evidence keeps turning up that, unlike common neurotics, individuals with personality disorders have biological deficits—such as serotonin deficiencies—which, if and when corrected with proper medication, help them think, feel, and behave much better than they ever did previously.

5. Effective psychotherapy frequently helps many normal neurotics to make appreciable improvements in a relatively short period of time, while it takes much longer to achieve minimal gain and sometimes no gain at all with clients with severe personality disorders. This finding again raises the possibility that these individuals are sometimes innately different from neurotics.

6. Individuals with severe personality disorders frequently have close relatives, especially parents, with similar or related disorders, and could therefore easily be genetically prone to emotional disturbance, no matter how well or badly they are raised.

7. A higher percentage of adopted individuals, who are usually very much wanted by their parents and therefore treated unusually well, significantly more often develop personality disorders than do non-adopted children, who are often less well treated.

8. When people who have personality disorders and who were abused by their parents later abuse their own children—which they sometimes do—it may not be their early learning that leads them to be abusive. It may be largely their genetic predisposition to be like their parents—severely disturbed.

The Two Sources of Personality Disorders

Ellis (1976, 2004) proposed that personality disorders often represent exaggerations of common irrational patterns of thought. He strongly emphasized the innate biological nature of irrationality in people as a fundamental component of both normal and disordered personality. And he frequently criticized the early trauma hypothesis of many psychotherapists (Ellis, 1995a), stating that innate tendencies play a far greater role than early trauma. In addition, Ellis anticipated the perspective of evolutionary psychology, which was also ultimately adopted by Beck. As will be explained further in Chapter 16, Ellis hypothesized that irrational beliefs about our behavior or the actions of others might very well have been quite adaptive in simpler times. In addition to his emphasis on the contribution of irrational beliefs to dysphoria and maladaptive behavior, Ellis has integrated the evidence that many temperaments and behavioral inclinations are genetically shaped. He proposed that an unfortunate combination of distorted thinking and genetic vulnerability is the foundation of personality disorders. Ellis believed that although personality disorders are predominantly innate, they have characteristic patterns of irrational thoughts associated with them. These are predicated on:

1. *Musts* about ourselves, others, or the world. Musts amount to tacit demands on people or the world to provide desirable outcomes. If these are not forthcoming, the individual experiences dysphoria. Beliefs based on musts effectively result in emotional extortion directed at the self. If we insist on our musts, we are stating that unless things happen the way we want, we will make ourselves miserable.

2. *Awfulizing* about undesirable events. In awfulizing, the person apprehends a setback or an undesired event as absolutely bad. Thus, a picnic postponed or canceled on account of rain is not a minor disappointment but a major catastrophe.

3. *Irresoluteness* (I-can't-stand-it-itis). People afflicted with this inclination have low tolerance of frustration and tend to believe that life must be easy. A common example is people who "can't stand it" when there is a line of people waiting to be seated at their favorite restaurant.

4. *Damning.* This irrational attitude includes excessively strong rebuke of ourselves or others for failings or disapproved actions. For example, toddlers who briefly forget their toilet training when a new brother or sister is born are scolded as "the worst child in the world."

5. *Absolutistic thinking.* In this irrational style, people draw negative global conclusions about others, themselves, or the world at large based on limited data or evidence. Thus, a minor fluctuation in the stock market is an indicator that another Great Depression is just around the corner.

Ellis (1977c) pointed out that most of the irrational beliefs underlying personality disorders are present to some extent in all people. Personality disorders, therefore, require a person's irrational belief system to follow a consistent and enduring pattern. Ellis noted that all people have patterns of thinking that could be classified as paranoid, dependent, narcissistic, or schizoid on occasion; however, those who could be classified as having a personality disorder will have such thought patterns consistently and across different situations. For example, the radiologist in Beck's case study described earlier not only expected his superiors at the hospital to pounce on the smallest flaws in his work but also expected his girlfriend to criticize him harshly over minor matters.

Ellis's emphasis on the dual origin of personality disorders holds especially true for the more severe disorders, such as the borderline and schizotypal personality disorders. The latter disorder has a high prevalence among the relatives of schizophrenia sufferers (Maier, Lichtermann, Minges, & Heun, 1994), which suggests that this personality disorder shares both genetic and neurological factors with schizophrenia. Interestingly, there is evidence that the relatives of people diagnosed with schizophrenia tend to be more creative than average (Kinney, Richards, Lowing, LeBlanc, & Zimbalist, 2001). This finding raises the possibility that disorders in the schizophrenic spectrum are exaggerated versions of an adaptive trait. It may be that a gene or genes that guide the connections among the many modules of the brain to think creatively are more active in those with these disorders. An abnormally large array of neural connections might lead to disordered cognition and emotions, whereas possessing only a slightly greater number of such connections might actually facilitate original or creative thinking. This hypothesis might explain why the relatives of schizophrenics are more creative than most people.

Although schizoid personality disorder is commonly associated with schizophrenia, it probably has a biological and presentational foundation more in common with disorders of the autistic spectrum (Tantam, 1988; Wolff & McGuire, 1995; Wolff, Narayan, & Moyes, 1988). For this reason, Ellis saw irrational thinking as a less crucial diagnostic criterion of such disorders. In contrast, he saw irrational beliefs as fundamental in the etiology of dependent, narcissistic, and avoidant personalities. The greater significance of irrationality as a criterion of these disorders does not mean that he would have asserted that biology does not play a role. The reader should recall that Ellis believed that irrationality is intrinsically human and part of human biology. Thus, all personality disorders involve both irrational thought patterns and biological predispositions. For example, the irrational beliefs associated with the dependent personality disorder (see Table 15.6)—combined with high levels of social anxiety, strong aversive emotions upon perceived setbacks, and feelings of serenity in the presence of a dominant supportive figure—would combine and interact to produce the disorder.

Thus, according to Ellis, irrational beliefs do not necessarily produce personality disorders by themselves. Rather, they are often assisted in the generation of pathology by neurological or physical vulnerabilities. Consequently, even in personality disorders that are predominantly learned, Ellis maintained that people usually suffer from some kind of constitutional weakness that manifests as the enduring style of dysfunction seen in personality disorders. Ellis also proposed, however, that based on current evidence, several of the DSM-IV personality disorders result primarily from learned or acquired irrational beliefs, whereas others are forms of irrationality arising from genetic or constitutional factors. More specifically, he saw histrionic, narcissistic, obsessive-compulsive, avoidant, and dependent personality disorders as owing more to irrational thinking than biology. And as Table 15.7 sets forth, he thought the reverse is true of the remainder.

This is Ellis's explanation for the apparent paradox in which all people are inherently prone to irrational thinking yet not all develop personality disorders. Interestingly, studies by Ellis and his associates (e.g., Leaf, Ellis, DiGiuseppe, & Mass, 1991) that have compared scales of irrational thinking with tests of personality disorders have shown some associations between the two. Additional research needs to be done, however, to trace the connections between irrational beliefs and biological predispositions. One such study was performed by Schnell and Herpertz (2007), who found that dialectical behavioral therapy helped to regulate pathology involving a brain circuit that includes the amygdala, cingulated cortex, and left insula in individuals with borderline personality disorder. This report implies that a personality disorder as severe as BPD has neurological substrates that are exacerbated by dysfunctional thinking (e.g., Butler, Brown, Beck, & Grisham, 2002).

Ellis proposed that several major irrational styles of thought underlie personality disorders as well as most other psychological disturbances. These include **musturbation**, in which people either overtly or covertly believe that certain conditions must be in place in order for them to be content. Another is "shoulding." In this pattern, people make demands regarding outcomes on the sole justification that they believe this is the way the world "should" work. Just as Karen Horney (1950) described the "tyranny of the shoulds," Ellis pointed out that shoulding is irrational because any event that has actually occurred is what should have happened, simply because it did. In other words, for someone to state that "I should have invested more wisely" or "he should have treated me more kindly" is really making an absolute demand that things should have happened differently because that is what the speaker wanted. Because there is no reason for the world to conform to any individual's values or desires, imposing shoulds on others or the world in general is irrational.

Catastrophizing or **awfulizing** is another essential element of human irrationality, according to Ellis. These cognitive distortions involve the perception of unpleasant or bad things as maximally or intolerably bad. An irrational style found in many troubled individuals is often prominent in personality disorders, namely self-downing.

Ellis noted that most people with personality disorders are aware that there is something wrong with the way in which they engage the world. This awareness can be summarized in two basic misconceptions: "I am terrible for being deficient" or "It is completely awful that people always treat me badly." According to Ellis, the first self-conception is primarily found

Table 15.7	Etiology of Personality Disorders According to Ellis	

Disorder	*Irrational Beliefs*	*Examples of Biological or Innate Factors*
Paranoid	• I cannot stand seeing people get away with things. • People are always mocking or judging me. • People should not bother me.	Higher rate in relatives with unipolar depression (Maier, Lichtermann, Minges, & Heun, 1994), with delusional disorder (Kendler, Masterson, & Davis, 1985), and schizophrenia (Kendler & Gruenberg, 1982; Kendler et al., 1985)
Schizoid	• It is too hard to deal with people. • I can never understand other people. • Solitary tasks are always most satisfying. • People always distract me from important work.	Excessive left versus right hemisphere activity (Raine & Manders, 1988); link with Asperger's syndrome (Wolff, 1998, 2000; Wolff & McGuire, 1995) and hereditary blood disorders (Zucca, Puzella, & Bersani,1994)
Schizotypal	• The world is run by magical forces. • Other people always make me feel bad. • Nothing happens by chance. • I am very special/I am very defective.	Inappropriate or excessive number of limbic and cortical connections (Nakamura et al., 2005); dysfunctions of temporal lobe; dysfunction of uncinate fasciculus (Gurrera et al., 2007); reduced hippocampal volume and increased size of cavum septum pellucidum (Dickey et al., 2007)
Antisocial	• I deserve to be exempt from rules. • I must be entertained at all times. • I must have what I want when I want it.	Underarousal in reticular activating system; anterior cingulate and orbitofrontal dysfunction (Rudebeck, Buckley, Walton, & Rushworth, 2006); dysfunction in dorsolateral and ventromedial prefrontal cortex (Dolan & Park, 2002); reduced gray matter in prefrontal lobe (Bigler, 2001)
Borderline	• People who let me down are totally bad. • It is unbearable to be alone. • I deserve to be hurt. • I must hurt those who hurt me.	Improper amygdala-frontal lobe function (Beblo et al., 2006); orbito-frontal cortex dysfunction (Berlin, Rolls, & Iversen, 2005); frontal cortex immaturity, (Meares, Melkonian, Gordon, & Williams, 2005); reduced amydala and hippocampal volume (Tebartz van Elst et al., 2003)
Histrionic*	• People must pay attention to me. • I am special and should be noticed. • If I feel upset, I must be sick (conversion symptoms).	Conversion aspect associated with reduced lentiform and caudate nuclei volume (Atmaca, Aydin, Tezcan, Poyraz, & Kara, 2006)

Table 15.7 (Continued)

Disorder	Irrational Beliefs	Examples of Biological or Innate Factors
Narcissistic*	• I am special and must be appreciated. • If I fail in front of others, I will be completely worthless. • I cannot stand to have my special qualities unappreciated. • I must always be noticed.	No cogent neurological or physiological correlates in evidence
Obsessive-Compulsive*	• Others must do things my way. • I can't stand leaving things unfinished or being late. • I must keep all important things in mind. • It would be terrible to forget something important. • I cannot trust anyone to do something for me.	Dorsolateral or mesial prefrontal cortex dysfunction (Ayçiçegi, Dinn, & Harris, 2002)
Avoidant*	• Being shamed is absolutely awful. • I cannot stand to be judged. • It is completely awful to fail in front of others.	Linked with childhood motor impairments (Kristensen & Torgersen, 2007); associated with social phobia and shyness (Schneider, Blanco, Antia, & Liebowitz, 2002)
Dependent*	• I absolutely can't do anything without someone strong to help me. • It would be terrible to try things on my own and fail. • People should help me with difficult things in life.	No cogent neurological or physiological correlates in evidence

* Disorders that are predominantly a result of learning or development rather than innate characteristics

in people with these disorders: schizoid, schizotypal, avoidant, dependent, and obsessive-compulsive. They will tend to see the consequences of their personality disorder as arising from defects within themselves. Consequently, they will compound their problems with self-deprecation and will often suffer such secondary problems as depression or anxiety.

In essence, secondary problems involve people making themselves more upset over their fundamental problem. For example, if a person suffers from an avoidant personality and then irrationally thinks, "I am totally worthless because I get nervous in front of others" or "I will be a complete loser unless I get over this problem immediately," he will be setting himself up to suffer secondary symptoms of depression or anxiety because of his irrational beliefs regarding his personality disorder.

Finally, Ellis throughout his long career witnessed changes in the nomenclature and diagnostic criteria of most personality disorders. Accordingly, he proposed that personality disorders are tentative models of personality pathology that need further research. Despite his emphasis on the irrational beliefs that underlie all personality disorders, he was open to the idea that biological or genetic inclinations underlie these irrational beliefs. For example, a person with a genetic tendency to fearfulness would most likely develop irrational beliefs along the lines that the world is a very dangerous place or that people will always try to do harm, and so on. The beliefs might be the consequence of innate factors. Once these beliefs are established, however, they will tend to exacerbate the person's fearfulness. Whether their disorder is biological or learned, Ellis emphasized that people have the power to diminish or eliminate these irrational beliefs by strongly and consistently disputing them. Thus, his REBT approach to treating a personality disorder would be, first, to identify the unique beliefs maintained by the disordered individual and then assist the person in systematically challenging them. Moreover, Ellis would identify the behaviors concordant with the personality disorder and motivate the individual to confront and change them.

For example, Evelyn, a middle-aged woman, sought treatment with one of the authors for help with conflicts she was having with her fiancé. Her depictions of events in her life, discussions of her beliefs about others, and her results on both the MMPI and MCMI indicated that she suffered from paranoid personality disorder. Her personality led Evelyn to be preemptively hostile in her encounters with new people in her life and to erode all longstanding relationships over time. This outcome was a result of her belief that the motives of others would be inevitably discovered to be bad, so she would "get" them before they had the chance to hurt her. Any ambiguous statement made to Evelyn would almost always be interpreted as mocking or hostile. In addition, she tended to overestimate the potential dangers of any activity because she believed that virtually all people necessary for her to complete a trip or social activity had bad intentions—including airline pilots, ticket agents, and even close friends.

Evelyn's thinking was dominated by beliefs such as the following:

"All people will do me harm if given a chance."

"People will wish me harm if they discover that I have anything they want or need."

"If I provoke anyone, even accidentally, they will inevitably seek to do me great harm."

"If anything bad happens anywhere, it will definitely happen to me."

"Trusting anyone will lead them to believe they have an advantage over me, which they will invariably exploit."

Evelyn's REBT treatment involved a gradual exposure of her beliefs as they were tacitly expressed in her autobiographical statements. When Evelyn made such statements, she was questioned until she would ultimately express the irrational belief directly. For example, she once said that she was enraged at her fiancé but would not tell him she was angry because he often cooks her meals. The therapist questioned her until she openly expressed her conviction that her fiancé would poison her if she ever overtly criticized him. At that point, she was further queried to support the rationality of such thinking. She was then able to dispute the irrationality of the belief that all people would want to do her great harm if she offended them.

Over several sessions, Evelyn was systematically exposed to the irrational quality of her own thinking, and she became increasingly capable of recognizing such thinking before it led to fear or rage. She was also guided to make behavioral changes that included increasing the range of her social activities, beginning a course of bibliotherapy (the use of books for self-education in problem-solving), and keeping REBT disputation journals. Evelyn maintained a strong tendency toward paranoid thinking but was able to recognize it and moderate it to significantly improve her life functioning.

▣ ARNOLD LAZARUS AND MULTIMODAL THERAPY

Early Career

Arnold Lazarus (1932–) is a psychologist who is often grouped together with Beck and Ellis because of his background in cognitive behavioral therapy. He was born in Johannesburg, South Africa, on January 27, 1932, the youngest of four children. He quit school for a brief period in his late teens, thinking he might open a training center for weight lifters. After 2 years, he returned to school, completing his undergraduate degree in psychology in 1955. While he was completing his Ph.D. in clinical psychology at the University of the Witwatersrand in Johannesburg, the dominant orientation of the department was Freudian. Lazarus, however, came to identify with the neo-behaviorist group thanks to the influence of Joseph Wolpe (1915–1997), who became Lazarus's dissertation adviser. Wolpe had been a pioneer in using the methods of behaviorism to change clients' behavior as part of clinical treatment; he regarded personality disorders as primarily behavioral disorders, and thought that they were treatable because behavior can be changed. Wolpe (1952, 1956, 1961, 1977) considered personality disorders and neuroses to be persistent maladaptive habits that could be both learned and unlearned.

Image 15.4   Arnold Lazarus (1932–)

Lazarus was the first psychologist to use the term *behavior therapy*. In 1958, while still a graduate student, Lazarus described his approach to behavior therapy. He started a private practice in South Africa in 1959. In 1966, Lazarus coauthored *Behavior Therapy Techniques* with Wolpe, who had moved to the United States in the meantime. In 1967, Lazarus followed Wolpe to the United States and joined him on the faculty of Temple University Medical School in Philadelphia. Lazarus was a pioneer in using systematic desensitization and imagery in treating phobias; the use of this technique was the subject of his doctoral dissertation. However, his growing emphasis on interpersonal relationships as a factor in maladaptive behavior represented a move in the direction of behavior therapy more in line with cognitive psychology; thus, Lazarus developed what he first called broad-spectrum behavior therapy and later termed multimodal therapy.

Evolution of Multimodal Therapy

It became clear to Lazarus that simply using the techniques of behaviorism limited what needed to be accomplished in psychotherapy. In 1971, he published *Behavior Therapy and Beyond*, which outlined his view of **cognitive behavioral therapy** or CBT. After moving from Temple to Rutgers University in the mid-1970s, Lazarus (1971) became dissatisfied with the results of behavior therapy, particularly the high relapse rate among patients with anxiety and panic disorders, obsessive-compulsive disorders, and depression. He observed that Ellis's adding cognitive interventions to behavior therapy added a large degree of durability to psychotherapy efficacy. Lazarus (1973) became convinced that an adequate appraisal of personality and the treatment of psychological disorders needed to include a range of approaches in addition to simply modifying behavior. He therefore proposed seven interated modalities: *b*ehavior, *a*ffect, *s*ensation, *i*magery, *c*ognition, *i*nterpersonal relationships, and the individual's biology (referred to in this case as *d* for drugs) that are necessary for appropriate treatment and understanding of psychological problems.

Arnold called his new approach **multimodal therapy**, which involves examining and treating seven different but interconnected attributes, which form the acronym **BASIC ID**. Lazarus published *Multimodal Behavior Therapy* in 1976 and opened his Multimodal Therapy Institute in Kingston, New Jersey, the same year.

Multimodal Therapy in Clinical Practice

Lazarus (1992) has championed what he calls **technical eclecticism** in his therapy. He uses a treatment method that he considers effective without regard to the theory that generated it. Lazarus (1995) rejects the unsystematic combining of therapeutic techniques without the research to support that their combination actually improves therapeutic outcome. He therefore recommends to the large number of therapists who categorize their approach as eclectic that they empirically support the basis of their eclecticism (Lazarus, 1996). Alternatively, he proposes technical eclecticism, which systematically culls the best of psychotherapies after demonstrating experimentally that their combination enhances their efficacy.

Lazarus's strong preference for a basis for psychotherapy is social and cognitive learning theory. In fact, Lazarus (Lazarus & Shaughnessy, 2002) has asserted that the efficacy of any effective psychotherapy can be explained in terms of social learning and cognitive theory. From these principles, he developed his own brand of cognitive behavior therapy.

Multimodal therapy involves treatments designed specifically for each individual, after extensive analysis of each client's unique situation and favored modalities within the BASIC ID. A client under the care of a multimodal therapist will typically be given a modality profile, which outlines the client's basic problems and proposed course of treatment; and a structural profile, which evaluates the relative prominence of each of the seven modalities in the client's personality. The treatment itself will incorporate **bridging**, which is Lazarus's term for a technique in which the therapist starts with the client's preferred modality and gradually "bridges" into other modalities of the BASIC ID that the client finds more difficult. For example, a client who likes to think in pictures or images (the "I" modality) may not be accustomed to examining his or her thoughts (the "C" modality) or monitoring bodily sensations when upset (the "S" modality). In this instance, the multimodal therapist will begin with the client's use of imagery and use the recurrent images presented by the client as bridges into the other modalities.

Another technique used by multimodal therapists is tracking, which refers to monitoring the order in which the seven modalities appear in the client's behavior and attitudes. Lazarus calls this order of appearance the **firing order**. He has found that most people have a relatively stable firing order over time. Tracking allows the therapist to see how the interaction of all or some of the seven modalities are interacting to produce the client's problems and to devise interventions to interrupt or rearrange the client's firing order.

Some of Lazarus's later writings fall into the category of self-help books. These include *I Can If I Want To* (Lazarus & Fay, 1975); *In the Mind's Eye: The Power of Imagery for Personal Enrichment* (Lazarus, 1984a); and *Don't Believe It for a Minute!: Forty Toxic Ideas That Are Driving You Crazy* (Lazarus, Lazarus, & Fay,1993). The basic concept outlined in these books is the use of mental imagery to lead to more adaptive behavior and the elimination of such maladaptive thoughts as "Life should be fair."

📖 BIOLOGICAL AND GENETIC MODELS OF PERSONALITY DISORDERS

The biophysical foundation of personality, explained in Chapter 14, holds that most personality traits have a significant degree of heritability. This genetic linkage is just as true for personality disorders as it is for normal personality traits. In fact, evolutionary psychologists often find the line dividing the two quite blurred (Buss, 2005). Evolutionary psychologists commonly maintain that aggressive sociopaths might very well be quite normal in a society that existed 20,000 years ago or in a more recent society undergoing violent turmoil. For example, this type of thuggish individual adapted easily to the conditions of the Soviet Union under Stalin or Cambodia under Pol Pot. In contrast, the anxious or obsessive individual might be well suited to eras or situations in which timidity or fastidiousness would represent a survival advantage; for example, a person who was obsessive about personal cleanliness might well have been more likely to survive the Black Death or other medieval epidemics than people who were more casual in their personal habits. Whether adaptive or pathological, the consensus among both biological and evolutionary psychologists is that personality disorders are a function of both genetic factors and environmental shaping of the developing brain.

Developmental Factors

Because the heritability coefficient of any personality characteristic rarely exceeds .5, it is evident that a person's genetic complement is shaped by developmental events. Consequently, people may be born with genetic inclinations toward a personality disorder, but the degree and particular expression of those inclinations will be a partial function of developmental advantages or **insults**. Many psychological theorists, such as Freud, Erikson, Kohlberg, and

Piaget, have all set forth different specific stages that individuals move through in the course of development. There is little compelling evidence, however, that people develop personality disorders as a result of trauma or excessive nurturance during any specific stage of development. Rather, severe stress or deprivation during early life may trigger genetic inclinations that contribute to a disturbed personality. Some researchers (Cozolino, 2006; Schore, 1994) have suggested that parental nurturance and affective feedback guide the development of the neuronal connections between the frontal lobe and limbic structures in the brain. Thus, anxiety-provoking experiences or emotional isolation through early development may result in diminished prefrontal development and exaggerated development of the amygdala and the hypothalamic structures that govern the emotion of fear. Overdevelopment of these parts of the limbic system (Yu, Fu, & Cao, 2006) may very well be the underpinning of such fear-based personality disorders as borderline, dependent, and avoidant personality disorders as well as those in Cluster B disorders (shown in Table 15.2).

In contrast, it does not seem that people with antisocial personality require any particular trauma to develop this disorder, which is quite **prevalent** among adoptees (Roth & Finley, 1998), ranging from 13% to 47.6%, depending on the study. These findings strongly suggest that antisocial parents are most likely to abandon their children to be reared by others. Of course, there may be adverse effects in the experience of adoption itself that may contribute to bringing this personality to fruition (Crowe, 1974), possibly spending time in institutional or foster settings prior to adoption. Nevertheless, it would appear that antisocial personality disorder is a robust condition that requires a minimum of environmental influences to emerge. The evolutionary adaptive basis for such findings has strong face validity. People who are aggressive, fearless, and lacking in remorse or social responsibility would do well in settings in which acting like a bully endows an adaptive advantage. Such an advantage would become apparent in both primitive societies at all times and technologically advanced societies during times of war.

Disorders of Attachment in Personality Disorders

Theorists like John Bowlby, Donald Winnicott (1896–1971), and Mary Ainsworth (1913–1999) viewed a positive parent-child attachment as crucial to the development of a healthy personality. Similarly, research has shown that deprived early environments often lead to permanent personality and emotional pathology (Kreppner et al., 2007; Le Mare, Audet, & Kurytnik, 2007; MacLean, 2003). An unfortunate and inadvertent test of this premise was carried out in the orphanages in Romania. Under the regime of Nicolae Ceauşescu, women were mandated to produce at least five children, irrespective of their economic means, and abortion was forbidden. With the economic collapse that followed his overthrow in 1989, many impoverished women were forced to surrender their newborns and infants to an underfinanced system of orphanages. Newborns and infants in these institutions were commonly deprived of all but the most perfunctory human contact, essentially confined to cribs and provided with only a minimum of nutrition and stimulation. Not surprising is the devastating and lasting effects of the extreme deprivation that children suffered in these institutions. For more than a decade after adoption, many of these children had trouble bonding with parents or siblings, had difficulty sleeping, exhibited such stereotyped behavior as rocking back and forth, had frequent emotional outbursts, and were observed to commit a number of antisocial acts (Iftene & Roberts, 2004; Marcovitch, Goldberg, Gold, & Washington, 1997; O'Reilly, Lacey, & Lancioni, 2001).

The relationship between attachment or bonding and subsequent personality development was dramatically illustrated by the plight of these Romanian orphans. Their development provides evidence for the theory that early relationships are required to guide the formation of the proper neuronal connections between the frontal lobe and the emotional centers in the limbic system of the brain (Cozolino, 2006; Schore, 1994). Orphans and other children who are deprived of the emotional contact and feedback necessary for proper brain development apparently suffer permanent personality pathology. Therefore, constitutional factors include more than genetic endowments. Our genes lay a foundation for personality that is guided by the environmental events and scenarios that we encounter as we develop. This interactive process of personality development explains the differences in personality between monozygotic twins (Kandel & Squire, 2000) because, despite having identical genomes, each twin will experience different challenges, events, and settings as he or she develops.

Evolutionary psychologists and others who take a biological perspective tend to see personality disorders as arising in three ways. The first is the way discussed earlier; that is, personality disorders develop as the result of trauma or deprivations that precluded proper neurological development. The second pathway represents the end result of vulnerabilities in temperament, emotional regulation, or brain structure exacerbated by traumatic or demanding events over the course of the individual's life. The third way, which implicitly challenges the very concept of a disorder, maintains that the individual has inherited a trait that was once adaptive and is now dysfunctional.

🔲 CHAPTER SUMMARY

The study of and hypotheses regarding the development of disordered personalities has largely remained within the field of clinical psychology, which has used a far different approach to theory and research than that of experimental psychology or social psychology, which focuses on the normal personality. To some extent, this separation of fields has left open the question as to whether personality disorders represent a distinct pathology or merely a difference in degree from normal personality. Freud believed that personality disorders or neuroses are largely the result of developmental perturbations that weaken a person's ability to resist the primitive impulses that exist in all of us. Subsequent to Freud, especially among such departed followers as Adler and Horney, these disorders were seen as the outcome of social conflicts, alienation, striving, or personal deficiencies.

Along with the more recent modifications of the psychoanalytic tradition came an increasing emphasis on the complexity of the psychic structures required to explain personality. Consequently, the descriptions and analyses of personality disorders, of necessity, became as complex as the theories explaining them. This, at least in part, led clinicians such as Aaron Beck and Albert Ellis to incorporate recent findings from the field of cognitive psychology regarding the brain's processing of information within their approaches to the treatment of personality disorders. Along with other clinicians, they sought scientific and evidence-based explanations and treatments of personality disorders. This work continues.

Chapter 16

Albert Ellis and the Rational Emotive Behavioral Theory of Personality

Chapter Goals

- Place Albert Ellis in the historical context to best understand the impetus behind his original perspective
- Explain why Ellis broke with psychodynamic theory and therapy to develop the first cognitive behavior system
- Discuss Ellis's theory of innate irrationality and show how it relates to personality
- Detail Ellis's view of personality development and the life forces that can lead it astray
- Develop an overview of Ellis's Rational Emotive Behavior Therapy
- Present Ellis's own theory of personality

The Rational Emotive Behavioral theory of personality is based on the work of one of the first authors of this text, Albert Ellis, who set forth a model of personality based on two synergistic factors: more than a half-century of direct clinical experience and a substantial body of research that explains and expands on the conclusions of his clinical practice.

Albert Ellis was born in Pittsburgh in 1913 and was raised in New York City. He entered the field of clinical psychology after first earning a degree in business from the City University of New York. He began a brief career in business, followed by a stint as a writer. His first forays into the workplace took place during the Great Depression, which began in 1929, making a business career difficult. He also found that writing fiction was not his calling, but he had some success in writing nonfiction. This talent led him to write about human sexuality, a field in which he had developed some expertise.

Image 16.1   Albert Ellis (1913–2007)

The dearth of experts in this area in the 1930s led to his being sought out for advice on the subject, and he counseled a number of people. His lay counseling led him to discover his true work as a therapist, convincing him to seek a new career in clinical psychology. In 1942, he began his studies for a Ph.D. in clinical psychology at Columbia University, which at that time trained psychologists in the psychoanalytic and Rogerian traditions. On completion of his M.A. in clinical psychology from Teachers College in June 1943, Ellis started a part-time private practice while still working on his Ph.D. He could practice legally because there was no state licensure procedure for psychologists in New York at that time. Ellis began publishing innovative articles even before receiving his Ph.D. For example, in 1946, he wrote a critique of many widely used pencil-and-paper personality tests, which had not been sufficiently validated. He concluded that only the Minnesota Multiphasic Personality Inventory (MMPI) met the standards of a research-based instrument (Ellis, 1946).

▣   EARLY CAREER

After the completion of his doctorate, Ellis sought additional training in psychoanalysis. Like most psychologists of that time, he had been initially impressed by the mystique and complexity of Freudian theories. Shortly after receiving his degree in 1947, Ellis began a personal analysis and program of supervision with Richard Hulbeck (whose own analyst had been Hermann Rorschach), who was a leading training analyst at the Karen Horney Institute. Horney proved to be the single greatest influence in Ellis's thinking, although the writings of Alfred Adler, Erich Fromm, and Harry Stack Sullivan also played a role in shaping his psychological models.

Break With Psychoanalysis

As Ellis's knowledge and experience in psychoanalysis grew, so too did his questions about its efficacy and scientific foundations. As early as 1947, Ellis published an article titled "Telepathy and Psychoanalysis: A Critique of Recent Findings," the first of a series of writings critical of antiscientific mysticism and cultism in psychology. Ellis expressed his opinion clearly in his 1950 monograph by commenting on the need for scientific support of psychoanalysis:

Although the art of psychoanalysis is now over a half century old, a comprehensive formulation of its scientific principles is still far from being realized. Such a formulation, which will strip from analytic theory and practice all trappings of dogmatism, unverified speculation, bias, and cultism, and which will leave standing only those principles and procedures which are, or seem well on their way to becoming, clinically validated, has been partially attempted, but by no means as yet systematically executed, by several neo-Freudians. . . .

It would be impertinent to assume, at the start, that psychoanalysis must be scientifically based and oriented. Some analysts, notably Jung, have at times been frankly unscientific, even antiscientific, and have contended that there are more things to analysis than are dreamed of in scientific ideologies. Other analysts, like [Otto] Rank and [Theodore] Reik, have offered doughty lip-service to scientific ideals, but have in practice advocated semi-mystical theories of analysis that are antithetical to scientific viewpoints.

With advocates of unscientific psychoanalysis there can be essentially no argument—as long as they frankly admit that science is not their goal, and that faith, religion, mental healing, or some other non-scientific object is in all frankness, to espouse some other kinds of analytic viewpoints, that is their democratic right—as long as they do not call their views scientific. . . . Most contemporary psychologists and psychiatrists agree, however, that thorough-going scientific knowledge is the only valid basis for analytic (and other) therapy, and that rigorous criticism of non-scientific psychological methods is quite justified. (Ellis, 1950, p. 147)

While conducting his part-time practice in New York, Ellis worked full-time as a psychologist for the state of New Jersey and became chief psychologist of the state in 1950. By 1952, however, he had left his position with the state and expanded his private practice to full time. His task of building a full-time practice was aided by his growing reputation as a sexologist, especially on the basis of his books, which included *The Folklore of Sex* (1951a), *The American Sexual Tragedy* (1954), and *Sex Without Guilt* (1958b). He also achieved a degree of notoriety by defending publishers of sex materials, gay people, and alleged sex offenders in court. In one prominent case, Ellis collaborated with a well-known attorney, O. John Rogge, to defend the Reverend Ilsley Boone, a Protestant minister and the publisher of magazines for the American Nudist Association. Boone was prosecuted by the U.S. Attorney's office for sending "obscene" magazines through the mail and placing them on newsstands. Ellis ultimately helped to write the brief that led to the case being won on appeal before the U.S. Supreme Court.

Ellis's growing reputation as an advocate of sexual freedom came with some costs, however. His undergraduate school, the City College of New York, and his graduate school, Teachers College of Columbia University, both refused to offer him teaching positions because of his then-controversial writings about human sexuality. Many psychology departments banned or canceled his presentations, even after he had achieved national prominence as a psychologist. In 1951, Ellis became the American editor of the *International Journal of Sexology* and began to publish a number of articles advocating sexual liberation (Benjamin & Ellis, 1954; Ellis, 1951b; Ellis, Doorbar, Guze, & Clark, 1952). He also wrote the introduction to Donald Webster Cory's (1951) controversial book *The Homosexual in America* and thereby became the first prominent psychologist to advocate tolerance of gay people.

The prominence that Ellis achieved from his publications and expertise in matters relating to human sexuality led to his being one of a handful of psychologists in New York City who were able to earn their entire income from their clinical practice. Although Ellis continually modified his technique, he was still primarily using psychoanalytic methods with his clients in the early 1950s. The growth of his client base made the passivity and marginal efficacy of the psychoanalytic approach increasingly apparent, however. Having a penchant for efficiency, Ellis began exploring new methods that would be more active as well as more effective.

He worked out an approach that was based on a consistent pattern he deduced in his clients. He had noted that virtually all people labeled as neurotics had in common a tendency toward **irrationality** and rigid thinking. What Ellis noted was a major advance over the stupidity-misery syndrome identified by John Dollard and Neal Miller (Dollard & Miller, 1950). In their integration of psychoanalytic and behavioral concepts, Dollard and Miller proposed that neuroses are caused by the conditioned repression of thoughts or behaviors that resulted in anxiety. Consequently, a nominally intelligent person will act in ways that seem self-defeating and foolish.

In contrast, Ellis observed that people are fully aware that their beliefs are irrational but tend to tenaciously maintain them despite their leading to continual problems. This important observation, combined with the philosophical tradition of **Stoicism** with its tacit **hedonism**, formed the foundation of a new psychotherapy. Stoicism holds that emotions must be strictly controlled, with hedonism as the ultimate motivation. Ellis was led to his conclusions based in part on his readings of such philosophers in the Stoic tradition as Epictetus (c. 55–135 CE) and Marcus Aurelius (121–180 CE), emperor of Rome from 161 to 180. The Stoics held that disruptive emotions like fear or jealousy arise from false judgments and that the sage—a person who has attained moral and intellectual perfection—will not undergo them. We attain wisdom, according to the Stoics, by accepting the principles implied in the quotations that follow. In other words, all extreme, disturbing, or neurotic emotions result from the individual's distorted perception of the situation, not the situation itself.

> If you are distressed by anything external, the pain is not due to the thing itself but to your own estimate of it; and this you have the power to revoke at any moment.
>
> —Marcus Aurelius

> For freedom is not acquired by satisfying yourself with what you desire, but by destroying your desire.
>
> —Epictetus

Deeply influenced by personal experience, reading, and the unscientific nature of psychoanalysis, by January 1953, Ellis made a complete break with psychoanalysis. He now began to call himself a rational therapist, advocating a new, more active, and more directive type of psychotherapy (Ellis, 1955). In 1955, he dubbed his new approach Rational-Emotive Therapy, or RET. Ellis's new approach required the therapist to help clients understand and act on the understanding that their personal philosophy contains beliefs that lead to their own emotional pain. This new approach stressed the importance of working actively to change the client's self-defeating beliefs and behaviors by illuminating and demonstrating their irrationality or rigidity. The next year, Ellis began teaching his new technique to other therapists; by 1957, he formally set forth the first cognitive behavioral psychotherapy by proposing that therapists help people to adjust their thinking and behavior as the most effective treatment for neuroses (Ellis, 1957a, 1957c, 1958a).

Going Public With RET

In 1957, Ellis published a book titled *How to Live with a Neurotic* (Ellis, 1957a), which elaborated on his new method of therapy. The next year, Ellis presented a paper on his new approach at the American Psychological Association convention in Chicago. There was mild interest, but few recognized the paradigm that would become normative within a generation. The prevailing school in experimental psychology in the mid-1950s was behaviorism; in clinical psychology, it was the psychoanalytic school of Freud or the alternatives to strict Freudianism introduced by Carl Jung, Alfred Adler, and Friedrich Perls. Despite the fact that Ellis's approach represented a combination of cognitive, emotive, and behavioral methods, his strong emphasis on cognition provoked almost everyone at the conference with the possible exception of the followers of Adler. Ellis was often received with hostility at professional conferences and maligned in print. Interestingly, there were several occasions at symposia or APA conventions when Perls, the founder of gestalt therapy, would refer sarcastically to Ellis's "rationality," while completely ignoring the experiential and behavioral components of RET.

Despite the slow adoption of his approach, Ellis founded his own institute. The Institute for Rational-Emotive Therapy was founded as a nonprofit organization in 1959. By 1968, it was chartered by the New York State Board of Regents as a training institute and psychological clinic. This charter was no minor accomplishment, as New York State had a Mental Hygiene Act that mandated psychiatric management of mental health clinics. Ellis had broken ground by founding an institute that was based purely on psychological principles and governed by psychologists.

The 1957 Outcome Study

Ellis conducted an early psychotherapy outcome study in 1957 in which he compared his nascent rational psychotherapy to psychoanalytically oriented psychotherapy. Then, as in the early 2000s, Ellis's approach demonstrated to clients that such strong negative feelings as anger, depression, anxiety, or guilt are not remedied by extensive explorations into the past. Rather, these negative, self-defeating emotions are generated afresh in each life situation via the individual's irrational attitudes or beliefs about the situation. Ellis (1957b) wrote in a landmark report:

Rational therapy, though usually a briefer procedure than psychoanalysis, is in some respects more depth-centered and intensive because it seeks to reveal and assail the basic ideas or philosophies or values which may underlie irrational behavior or neurosis. It is an application of the theory that much of what we call emotion is nothing more than a certain kind—a biased, prejudiced—kind of thought, and that human beings can be taught to control their feelings by controlling their thoughts—or by changing their internalized sentences, or self-talk, with which they largely created these feelings in the first place. (p. 344)

Ellis set forth this approach in opposition to psychoanalysis, which theorizes that negative emotions arise from conflicts that developed during the individual's maturation and require extensive biographical review to understand and discharge. On this hypothesis, he wrote:

> Where in the psychoanalytic techniques, considerable time is spent on showing the patient how he originally became neurotic, in rational analysis much more emphasis is placed on how he is *sustaining* his disturbance by still believing the nonsense or illogical ideas, which first led him to feel and act in an aberrated [*sic*] fashion. (1957b, p. 345)

To test the relative efficacy of psychoanalytic and rational methods, Ellis used his detailed records and notes and assigned prior clients to three groups. The two primary groups each contained 78 clients, closely matched as to diagnosis, age, sex, and level of education. The clients in the first group received at least 10 sessions of psychoanalytically oriented psychotherapy, with an average treatment length of 35 sessions. The second group consisted of clients who received at least 10 sessions of rational psychotherapy with an average treatment length of 26 sessions. A third group containing 16 clients received orthodox psychoanalysis for an average treatment length of 93 sessions. Ellis provided all treatments himself and also used outcome ratings he determined after each client completed therapy. Clients were rated as to whether they had made (a) little or no progress, (b) some distinct improvement, or (c) considerable improvement. Ellis (1957b) concluded that "therapeutic results appear to be best for clients treated with rational analysis and poorest for orthodox analysis" (p. 345–346). The actual proportions of cases showing distinct or considerable improvement were 90% for rational-emotive psychotherapy, 63% for psychoanalytically oriented psychotherapy, and 50% for orthodox psychoanalysis. Ellis pointed out that these results should be considered instructive, given the fact that orthodox psychoanalysis was carried on for three times as many sessions as rational psychotherapy.

This early study has the obvious weakness of having the ratings carried out by the same clinician who is conducting all of the therapy and advocating a particular form of therapy. Ellis cannot be commended for his research design in this case, but he deserves credit for making the effort to perform one of the first studies comparing the outcomes of different therapeutic approaches.

▣ ELLIS'S SOCIAL AND PHILOSOPHICAL WORLDVIEW

Like many other personality theorists, Ellis grounded his view of humanity in his perspectives of many aspects of social and individual life. Although many of his concepts are distributed throughout his large body of publications, a review of them yields a comprehensive theory covering most aspects of human and social development. What follows are the essentials of his view of growth and the components of a person.

Basic Theory of Personality

Although Ellis (1962, 1984) is often cited as defining personality in terms of his **ABC model**, which will be explained below, a review of his writings makes clear that he has formulated a more comprehensive conception. According to Ellis, human personality consists of all biological drives, impulses, and styles of information processing, both rational and irrational. This latter aspect is particularly important because it includes the way in which an individual organizes information about the world. The same environment may lead to one person's being an optimistic Pollyanna and another's becoming a hostile paranoiac, depending on the way in which each processes information.

Ellis's emphasis on beliefs, although central to his concept of personality, does not completely define it. Rather, he posits that a person's beliefs interact with many other cognitive, emotional, and biological attributes to create a relatively consistent style of relating to the world and other people in it. Thus, according to Ellis, personality is the generally consistent behavioral, communicative, and reactive style of an individual, which results from the continual interaction of his or her biology, cognitive propensities, and emotional inclinations.

In addition, he believes that personality develops throughout the life span but assumes a distinctive shape in early adulthood. Furthermore, he proposes that it can be changed through focused effort or will, but significant changes require even greater efforts. Like most theorists, Ellis sees personality as a phenomenon that arises from preceding processes that make each of us unique in the way we behave, perceive, and contemplate the world and those in it. Because Ellis sees irrationality in thinking as an invariant aspect of humanity, he includes the unique configuration of an individual's irrationality as central to the person's identity.

Human Development

Ellis does not subscribe to the notion of fixed developmental stages but has adapted many of the principles of Jean Piaget and other psychologists who take a neurodevelopmental perspective. According to Ellis, children's personalities gradually unfold with the maturation of their brain, as the limbic system reaches a balance with the regulating frontal cortex. There is, however, an initial stage of imbalance, which is the reason that Ellis believes that children are particularly irrational. The prefrontal cortex, which is one of the last brain regions to fully develop, leaves the more phylogenetically primitive limbic system with more control over the behavior of the child and adolescent. Therefore, children are even more prone to demandingness, musturbation, awfulizing, and absolutistic thinking—the personality disorders Ellis distinguishes. Like Piaget, Ellis sees children becoming more rational as their brains progress across major developmental thresholds.

Ellis (1976, 1987) proposes that personality is genetically prone to developing emotional vulnerabilities. He said:

> I am still haunted by the reality, however, that humans . . . have a strong biological tendency to needlessly and severely disturb themselves, and that, to make matters much worse, they also are powerfully predisposed to unconsciously and habitually prolong their mental dysfunctioning and to fight like hell against giving it up. (Ellis, 1987, p. 365)

Ellis (1976) believes that individuals have inborn tendencies to react to events in certain patterns, regardless of environmental factors, by damning themselves and others when they do not get what they want. In addition, Ellis (1994a) believes that many mental disturbances are innate; that is, they have strong biological components. For example, it is well established that first-order relatives of schizophrenics will often exhibit characteristic patterns of personality. These variations may range from enhanced creativity to such **schizotypal** personality features as **magical thinking** and **ideas of reference**. These distinct personality qualities appear without regard to whether the individuals have contact with or are raised by the relatives with schizophrenia. Ellis holds that the development of irrational thinking works in a similar way.

This concept has been supported by numerous recent studies. Researchers at the National Institute of Mental Health (NIMH) reported finding a genetically based brain mechanism responsible for people's social behavior (Meyer-Lindenberg et al., 2005). These researchers performed a study that compared normal individuals with patients diagnosed with Williams syndrome, a genetic disorder resulting from alterations of approximately 21 genes on chromosome 7. This disorder is characterized by a subnormal IQ and by distinct personality traits that include an empathic gregariousness, a large vocabulary, and an absence of social phobia. People with this syndrome, however, also tend to exhibit increased fearfulness of creatures or objects that commonly elicit phobic responses. These include insects, dogs, or such loud noises as thunder.

In this study, researchers used functional magnetic resonance imaging (fMRI) to examine the differences between the brain activity of subjects with Williams syndrome and activity in healthy controls. With their brain activity being monitored, participants were shown pictures of people with angry or fearful faces. Normal people have strong visceral reactions to pictures of other human beings who are visibly distressed. In this study, however, the fMRI revealed that the subjects with Williams syndrome had markedly less activity in their amygdalas than the normal participants.

The researchers hypothesized that the muting of the negative emotions produced by the amygdala to potentially threatening social stimuli is the basis of the social fearlessness of people with Williams syndrome. Interestingly, in the same study, the researchers then presented the subjects with photos of such dangerous situations as a plane crash or a burning building. In this case, the subjects with Williams syndrome had stronger reactions in the amygdala. In addition to the activity in the amygdala, the researchers found differences in function in three areas of the prefrontal cortex: the dorsolateral, the medial, and the orbitofrontal cortex. Notably, the dorsolateral area is thought to establish and maintain social goals governing interactions; the medial area has been associated with empathy and mediation of negative emotions; and the orbitofrontal region assigns emotional values to a situation.

Even though Ellis emphasizes innate or biological factors in personality, he asserts that the specific events that people respond to emotionally are primarily learned during youth, but the process is organically nonconscious. In his earlier writings, Ellis (1958a, 1962) credited the hypothalamus with the regulation of nonconscious emotions. More recently, he has maintained that many components of personality are nonconscious and mediated by a network of modules like the phylogenetically old brain structures, the hippocampus and the amygdala. These brain regions operate nonverbally and largely nonconsciously, mediating the storage of memory. The amygdala records events or images associated with danger. Connected to other more primitive fear centers like the lateral hypothalamus and the paraventricular nucleus, the amygdala is the logical source of aversion learning.

The amygdala receives sensory input from both the thalamus, a structure in the phylogenetically older part of the brain that mediates all sensory input independent of consciousness, and from the cortex. Consequently, the amygdala can associate events, images, sounds, and other stimuli with a feeling of dread without any conscious awareness. The evidence is strong that the amygdala plays a critical role in the learning of fear by association. For example, a rat can be classically conditioned to fear a light source by pairing the light with an electric shock.

When a rat with a lesion in its amygdala is similarly conditioned, however, it will show a fear response to the shock but will not exhibit a response of conditioned fear to the light. Humans with natural damage to the amygdala will display a similar deficit. Human beings, however, would generally be able to express a conscious awareness of the connection in words despite their lack of a physiological response to the conditioned stimulus (LeDoux, 1996).

Neuropsychological research has supported Ellis's view that the majority of an individual's emotional proclivities are innate, especially those that predispose people toward irrationality. He has been consistent in maintaining, however, that these are inclinations and not destinies. That is, we can learn to mitigate our tendencies toward irrationality when necessary through learned cognitive change. Ellis also distinguishes between the explanatory power of describing the brain as a multimodular system and the individual's personal experience. Specifically, the brain will often be divided against itself internally, leading to irrational or self-defeating thinking or behavior. People, however, almost always experience themselves as an integrated whole. Ellis (1978) wrote,

> While RET sees people as having units or elements (e.g., high sexuality or low energy) that influence their whole lives, it also sees them as having interacting parts (including cognitions, emotions, and behaviors) that cannot be separated, and it primarily sees them as having a holistic or central "consciousness" or "will" that tends to direct these various parts. (p. 306)

And in a similar vein, Ellis (1977b) wrote, "Human cognition, emotion, and behavior do not constitute separate entities but all significantly interrelate and importantly affect each other" (p. 6).

Thus, Ellis the personality theorist explains human behavior in terms of brain modules, whereas Ellis the clinician views people as the Gestalt psychologists would—as integrated wholes that are different from or more than the sum of their parts.

Cognition and Traits

From his earliest writings, Ellis has tacitly proposed that personalities include distinct and largely enduring traits. He has, however, described traits more as propensities rather than forces. These propensities result in meaningful emotions and behaviors only when they are mediated by cognitions or beliefs. Thus, if we have a tendency toward greater arousability or emotionality, we will experience more intense psychological disturbance when an irrational belief is triggered by a disappointing personal performance. The traits that have most concerned Ellis are emotionality, irrationality, and the ability to reason. In recent years, he has acknowledged the **five-factor model** as an acceptable if incomplete explanation of personality. Ellis's emphasis on innate irrationality has led him to conclude that the five-factor model is a good basic model but fails to account for intellectual differences, varying degrees of irrationality, creative abilities, and several other dimensions that contribute to a complete human personality.

Defense Mechanisms

Like Anna Freud, who coined most of the terminology related to defense mechanisms, and current theorists (Miceli & Castelfranchi, 2001; Simeon, Guralnik, Knutelska, & Schmeidler, 2002), Ellis holds that people do indeed use defense mechanisms. They do so when their actions, status, or other measures of personal worth do not hold up to their irrational demands for excellence or prestige. The most important distinction between the psychodynamic view of defense mechanisms and that of Ellis is that Ellis maintains that defenses are always initially conscious or volitional. He points out that people will defend only against events that lead to disturbing emotions. Because we usually have to learn the standards by which life events are judged, we must first set the stage for those adversities that will require self-defense. For example, if a person plays sports but has learned to place no import on the outcome of the game or match, then it follows that defeat will not require any type of defense mechanism. In contrast, for someone who has adopted the belief that she must do well at golf and believes herself to be an excellent player, a poor outcome will often lead to rationalization, denial, or any of the numerous defenses that will cushion this individual against poor performance.

Underlying the use of defenses are our irrational beliefs and the tendency to feel strong emotional arousal. Thus, a setback, failure, or a poor performance in any task will result in aversive emotional consequences if we have such beliefs as "I must always do well in important endeavors," "It is a terrible thing to fail," or "I can't bear it if others think less of me for doing poorly." These beliefs will almost always lead to negative emotions if we have a propensity to strong emotions. An exemplary contrast would be the case of the person with a schizoid personality style or Asperger's syndrome, who would usually not be prone to strong emotions, especially those related to interpersonal interactions. In such people, the irrational beliefs mentioned above are not likely to cause major emotional upsets.

Ellis holds that defense mechanisms are inelegant and inefficient solutions to emotional disturbances because they do nothing to change the irrational belief system that necessitates their use. To illustrate his point, the athlete who rationalizes a loss by saying that "I really didn't care about winning this particular game" will find temporary relief from his disappointment, but because his basic philosophy of life continues to make winning essential to happiness, he will continue to feel perturbed each time he loses. If, however, he has the insight that winning is desirable and pleasurable but not an absolute necessity of life, then his defense mechanism will no longer be necessary.

Hedonism and Human Appetites

Ellis is in agreement with the strict behaviorists and to a lesser extent with Freud in his belief that humans are motivated by pleasure or by actions that become strongly associated with pleasure. In fact, Ellis, along with Epictetus and the Stoic philosophers, proposes that the pursuit of pleasure is a primary goal of human existence. Pursuing pleasure in a socially responsible manner with the ability to appropriately defer gratification is a marker of a healthy and productive personality. Thus, Ellis advocates long-term responsible hedonism and suggests avoiding short-term indulgence. He regards pleasure as including creative acts and socially responsible endeavors as well as satisfaction of the more basic appetites. He sees no conflict between hedonism and responsibility, as the mature and psychologically healthy individual will seek pleasure through activities that yield positive social standing and approval. Ellis refers to this attitude as responsible hedonism. He asserts that both maturity and emotional stability are indicated by the ability to confront frustration and delay gratification. He considers low frustration tolerance to be a fundamental cause of poor functioning in life. Implicit in low frustration tolerance are the beliefs that lead to impulsivity. Such beliefs are typically the equivalent of "I can't stand waiting for what I want" or "I must have it now."

Humanism

Ellis has defined himself as an ethical humanist. He personally rejects all religious beliefs but maintains that people with religious convictions can be well-adjusted provided their beliefs are not rigid or dogmatic, wherever they may stand on the spectrum of beliefs. His approach emphasizes the role of human beings over that of any deity. Originally highly critical of any form of religious faith, Ellis softened his view over the years, yielding to research findings that people adhering to religious beliefs do not present with increased pathology (Bergin, 1983; Pfeifer & Waelty, 1999). His therapeutic approach is compatible with most religious doctrines. He is primarily opposed to extreme forms of religiosity, not to religious belief or practice as such. He asserts that extreme and inflexible views lead to hostility toward others as well as the risk of emotional distress when God fails to immediately rescue the person from the vicissitudes of life.

A basic tenet of Ellis's (1994a) humanism is his belief that a healthy individual has **unconditional self-acceptance.** Individuals possessing this attribute will be less sensitive to self-rating and the judgments of others. Ellis points out that rating ourselves is pointless because it is necessarily an overgeneralization and is virtually impossible to perform accurately. We are composed of literally millions of acts, deeds, characteristics, and traits exhibited during a lifetime. It would be impossible for us to assign a value to each of these, even if we could be fully aware of all these performances and characteristics simultaneously. It would be just as impossible to combine all these ratings to yield a meaningful global value of our worth. And even if this rating were somehow accomplished, we would be faced with daily fluctuations in these valuations and with having to continually modify our worth based on our latest performance in each life function. Finally, we would have to wait until death to be able to compile a complete list of all of our characteristics and actions on which to base rating and self-esteem.

Instead of rating ourselves, Ellis proposes that we find our value inherent in our existence, our living, and our humanity. If we accomplish this task, self-esteem becomes irrelevant, as external accomplishments are no longer necessary for a feeling of worth. If we unconditionally accept both our good and undesirable aspects, we come to believe that our worth is predicated on our existence as a sentient and volitional being. Having reached a condition in which self-rating is minimal or nonexistent, we will have less need to make interpersonal comparisons and judgments. This lack of interest in comparative evaluation, according to Ellis, leads to **unconditional acceptance of others,** which is the state of mind in which others are considered acceptable as human beings, even if some of their traits and behaviors are not. Thus, a person's actions can be viewed as bad, even a majority of them perhaps, but the individual is never rated as a bad human being overall, because we simply cannot assume that any human being is totally lacking in any positive characteristics. Such an assumption would lead, according to Ellis, to fearfulness, hostility, and bigotry. On the other hand, judging the behaviors and not the person allows for better interpersonal relations and ultimately a more emotionally balanced and satisfying life for the person who accepts others unconditionally.

Free Will

As suggested in his definition of personality, Ellis is somewhat pessimistic about the degree of free will we possess. He has said, "A soft determinism or the belief that humans have some degree of choice that is limited by environmental situations and by innate biological predispositions, seems much more realistic" (Ellis, 1985, p. 286).

Some have said that his view of personality is in conflict with his psychotherapeutic approach, which, he has stated, acknowledges free will. Specifically, Ellis maintains that one of the distinctive features of his therapy is that it stresses the importance of our ability to choose. This apparent contradiction fades when we understand that Ellis strongly endorses personal responsibility as an essential means to sound mental health. Despite his belief in innate irrationality and the consequent emotional disturbance it brings, his therapy directs individuals to make every effort through a will derived from reason and logic to overcome their innate irrationality. Ellis recognizes that this innate tendency complicates emotional maturation, but he believes that most of us can decide to work hard enough to learn new ways to react to life events. The more rationally we learn to behave, says Ellis (1978), the more free will we exercise.

VIGNETTE

In his youth, Benjamin was short, slight in build, and somewhat effeminate in appearance. He was continually bullied by his peers; when he asked his parents for help, however, they responded with disgust at his inability to fight his own battles. To add to Benjamin's pain, his older brother Manny was much larger physically than he was and had reached most developmental milestones at an earlier age. Manny was clearly his parents' favorite. He used to join his parents in the family practice of ridiculing Benjamin for his weaknesses, especially his tendency to cry. Years later, when Benjamin was in therapy, he reported that his fear that he would cry in response to being bullied was greater than his dislike of the beatings he often received.

In addition to being ridiculed and bullied outside of his home, Benjamin suffered nearly nightly humiliation when he was trying to sleep. He shared a bedroom with Manny, who delighted in degrading and terrorizing his younger brother. Manny's abuse included punching Benjamin while he slept, slapping him for no apparent reason, and verbally humiliating him about his slow sexual development as a result of late puberty. Benjamin was terrified by these nightly episodes of abuse, and he tried twice to tell his parents about the situation. His mother simply ignored him or repeated the platitude: Boys will be boys. His father actually became angry at Benjamin for being so weak as to complain.

Manny's abuse was duplicated by the treatment Benjamin received at school. The relentless physical and emotional abuse led to ongoing episodes of intense anxiety combined with obsessive behaviors. Sadly, the nuns at Benjamin's parochial school failed to recognize his jitteriness and obsessions as symptoms of distress and viewed them as signs of a conduct disorder. Because the school permitted corporal punishment, Benjamin received a good deal of paddling. He was subjected to a range of other disciplinary measures that included having to stand by the waste basket in front of the class or being forced to sit under the teacher's desk like a dog during class.

The relentless humiliations, beatings, and isolation that Benjamin experienced in his youth led him to believe he was worthless. He entered his teens anxious, depressed, and hopeless about his future. Redemption came when he was encouraged to try out for a high school sport—wrestling—that requires great endurance as well as muscular strength. He joined the junior varsity wrestling team and immersed himself in weight and endurance training. With near obsessive diligence he developed a new and well-muscled physique, which soon affected the way others saw him. Benjamin marveled at the way people now responded to him. Since he had become physically imposing, he was treated with deference and respect for the first time in his life. Notably, his brother stopped abusing him. The changes in his body build meant that Benjamin had metamorphosed into someone who was feared rather than mocked.

Unfortunately, Benjamin made up for his earlier suffering by treating others as he had been treated. And for a while he behaved in a way that he later reported caused him some guilt. He became something of a thug, intimidating his peers and those who were weaker than he was, just as his brother had intimidated him. This behavior became especially problematic when he became a police officer, a position that allowed him to impose his will on almost anyone who got in his way. His angry acting out began to abate, however, when he witnessed a group of his fellow officers humiliating a mentally ill man. Benjamin's fit of rage at their abuse was the epiphany he needed to make a major change. He was aware that he often acted like his brother and his fellow officers, and he hated this fact. He made a highly motivated effort to stop behaving like a bully.

As Benjamin matured emotionally, so did his apparent confidence. The thuggish behavior was virtually gone; it was replaced with far more patience and reflection. Through conscious effort, he worked on his thoughts and feelings about himself until he no longer felt like the diminutive and vulnerable victim he had once been. To his great satisfaction, his brother now treated him with deference, and his family took pride in his professional success as he moved up the ladder of the police force.

Unfortunately, and in spite of his promotions, Benjamin was increasingly plagued by the residue of his years of trauma. He suffered from both panic attacks and obsessive compulsive disorder, which increased in severity during times of emotional stress. Benjamin had made major alterations in his personality, but he now had to overcome an increasingly debilitating complex of anxiety disorders. This work was possible for him because there was a personality of integrity, consciousness, and focused will underlying all of the pathological symptoms. With the help of a therapist, he began a regimen of cognitive behavior therapy to help him face his fears in a constructive way. His treatment brought Benjamin back to a point where he was able to function adequately again. He still suffered bouts of obsessive behavior and anxiety from time to time, but he coped with them more effectively, as he had also matured into a less hostile and fearful person.

(Continued)

(Continued)

Benjamin's case illustrates the ways in which personality can be both adversely affected by events during a person's early development and repaired with professional help and personal effort. His early humiliations and traumas led him to adopt the persona of a hostile and vengeful man, a persona that he was able to overcome when he understood the sources of his emotional impulses. There was an aspect of Benjamin's personality that his victimizers were not able to damage. This conscientious, resilient, and moral individual essentially restored himself to healthy maturity and undid much of the damage he had suffered early in life.

Vignette Questions

1. What irrational beliefs do you think Benjamin developed as a result of his childhood experiences?

2. What philosophical changes do you think he had to make about himself and others to overcome his emotional problems?

Ellis's View of the Person

Ellis's theory and his Rational Emotive Behavior Therapy (REBT) are founded on several key conceptions of human personality. Ellis proposes that personality is a function of many innate dispositions and traits that are genetically based, although not necessary tied to a specific gene. This distinction has been discussed in Chapter 14. Because these genetically based traits are fundamental aspects of each individual's personality, they tend to be enduring but can nonetheless be shaped to varying degrees throughout the life span. That is, these innate dispositions predispose people to certain styles of thinking and feeling. Ellis has consistently held that an individual's personality is a function of both emotion and cognition. From his earliest writings (1958a), Ellis has maintained that cognition and reason, on the one hand, and emotion on the other are closely interwoven and that any model of personality must consider both as interacting elements of the mind. As noted earlier, this view has received increasing support from numerous neuroscientists who have studied the interplay of cognition and emotion.

Nearly half a century ago, Ellis proposed that human emotional responses result from complex interactions of sensations, perceptions, bodily actions, and emotions. He stated that these are not discrete entities but exist in their interaction:

The theoretical foundations of RT (Rational Therapy)[1] are based on the assumption that human thinking and emotion are *not* two disparate or different processes, but they significantly overlap and are in some respects, for all practical purposes, essentially the same thing. Like the other basic life processes, sensing and moving, they are integrally interrelated and never can be seen wholly apart from each other. In other words: none of the four fundamental life operations—sensing, moving, emoting, and thinking—is experienced in isolation. . . . Emotion, then, has not a single cause or result, but can be said to have three main origins and pathways: (a) through the sensori-motor processes;

(b) through biophysical stimulation mediated through the tissues of the autonomic nervous system and the hypothalamus and other subcortical centers; and (c) through the cognitive or thinking processes. We may also, if we wish, add a fourth pathway and say that emotion may arise through the experiencing and recirculating of previous emotional processes (as when a recollection of a past feeling of anger triggers off a renewed surge of hostility). (Ellis, 1962, pp. 38–40)

These early foundations of Ellis's theory are highly concordant with the more recent conclusions of neuroscientists who investigate emotions. For example, António Damásio (see box) has proposed a **somatic marker hypothesis**, which states that emotions are provoked by some external event that produces arousal and other bodily changes. We then interpret these bodily changes as emotions. So one perhaps original function of emotions is to provide a representation of our bodily states. According to Damásio, this role has expanded such that bodily states represented in the form of emotions guide our decisions by providing us with aversive or supportive feelings. Remarkably, this is very similar to what Ellis (1962) wrote nearly half a century before:

A good deal—though not necessarily all—of what we call emotion, therefore, would seem to be a kind of appraisal or thinking that (a) is strongly slanted or biased by previous perceptions or experiences; that (b) is highly personalized; that (c) is often accompanied by gross bodily reactions; and (d) that is likely to induce the emoting individual to take some kind of positive or negative action. (p. 48)

Thus, Damasio and Ellis both theorize that thought, emotion, and physical sensation are all interlinked, and emotion serves the role of guiding cognition or decision making.

António Damásio: Somatic Markers and Emotional Learning

Damásio's research has dealt with the role of the brain centers that regulate emotion and their role in consciousness and decision making. He has concluded that the limbic system of the brain records a vast amount of data that are conveyed from our senses in a quantity far too great to be consciously processed. Once stored in our brain's emotional centers, these experiential data are used to guide our behavior through emotional feedback. That is, we will get a bad feeling when we do something that was stored with negative associations. This is Damásio's somatic marker hypothesis, which states that when an individual needs to make a judgment, each choice elicits a body sensation (a somatic marker) that corresponds to an emotional reaction. Damásio proposes that these markers guide our decisions and can lead to choosing the appropriate choice even in the absence of conscious knowledge of the choices. Damásio illustrated this process through the case of Elliot, a man whose brain injury altered the normal function of his emotional feedback system.

(Continued)

(Continued)

Elliot was an educated professional in his thirties who had exhibited a radical change in personality and a consequent inability to work. He had undergone surgery for the removal of a brain tumor, a meningioma, which had been growing just under his frontal lobes. The nonmalignant tumor was successfully removed, along with some portions of his frontal lobes that it had damaged. The man that awoke after the operation was, according to Damásio, "no longer Elliot." Despite obtaining normal scores on the MMPI and tests of intellectual functioning, he suffered some grievous losses that would soon become apparent. The once-industrious self-starting business and family man now could not begin his day unless prompted. He could no longer reliably make decisions; he would typically become fixated for an entire day deciding on the method to apply to a task without ever beginning it. Not surprisingly, he lost his job. His response was to pursue a series of risky and irrational business ventures, all leading to severe financial losses. Bankrupt and oblivious to his new destructive approach to life, Elliot suffered personal losses; his wife and children left him. He remarried, only to be divorced again shortly thereafter.

When evaluating Elliot for disability, Damásio noticed that he experienced his emotions on a very superficial level. His speech revealed no affect, no impatience with prolonged questioning, and no sorrow about his condition. As part of Elliot's evaluation, Damásio presented him with photos of natural disasters and people with severe injuries. Elliot exhibited no emotional reaction to these. Interestingly, Elliot was aware of his own lack of response and informed Damásio that prior to the surgery, he would have found the photos upsetting.

Damásio describes Elliot's case as a failure of the functions that emotions normally play in decision making and apprehension of the world. Our feelings about the world both enhance our knowledge of it and guide our interactions with it. Damásio points out that the amount of data about the world that our senses take in is far too great to consciously process and apply. Despite this limitation, a great deal of information is stored nonconsciously in the form of emotional associations. These associations, which can be conscious or unconscious, are represented in the internal states of the body. Thus, emotions begin as physiological responses that may later end as conscious appraisals of the sensory event that led to the physical sensation.

Similarly, Ellis's integrated model of thought, body, and emotion is compatible with the work of prominent emotion researcher, Joseph LeDoux (1949–). LeDoux is a neuropsychologist who studies the biological basis of emotions and has concluded that emotions and cognition are inseparable and continuously interacting aspects of cognition. LeDoux's research has demonstrated that the amygdala mediates almost all emotional arousal in mammals, including humans, of course. His studies of rats have provided evidence that they respond with fear or alarm to potential environmental dangers before the structures of their forebrains ever receive information about the dangers. LeDoux points out that this has strong face validity from an evolutionary perspective. Organisms that require higher processing of fear-producing sensations would be at a distinct disadvantage compared to those who process such sensations quickly and automatically. But these, like many evolutionary adaptations, might yield disadvantages in a changing environment. In a complex world that requires more careful social judgments, these rapid or automatic emotional reactions may cause dysfunction in many of us. Some people dread the height above the ground involved in aircraft travel, while being fully aware of its safety; or they rage at someone crossing into "their" highway lane despite their knowledge that it is the other person's right to do so. These reactions may be atavistic adaptations that may very well lie at the root of any emotional problems.

LeDoux and his coworkers have focused on the nonconscious, nonverbal amygdala as the brain structure that governs the learning, storage, and manifestation of all fears. They propose that this brain center rapidly recognizes dangers specific to each species and conveys these recognitions to higher brain centers, which can in turn modulate these impulses, leading to a feedback system that primarily involves the amygdala and the frontal cortex. In addition, LeDoux emphasizes that emotion and cognition are not separate processes but one larger interrelated whole. Indirectly supporting Ellis, LeDoux proposes a theory of a cognitive-emotional interplay. Although his work centers primarily on fear, he concludes that most emotions have both evolutionary and learned components that can operate both nonconsciously

Image 16.2   Joseph LeDoux (1949–)

and consciously. His work with animals indicated that emotions have genetic as well as learned components. Emotions once learned, however, can take the same subcortical path as those that reflect genetic predispositions. Specifically, the thalamus, a nonconscious area of the brain that processes and routes sensory inputs, will signal the amygdala, which can produce a strong emotional reaction well before the conscious cortex is notified (LeDoux, 1994).

More recently, LeDoux and his colleagues have suggested that active coping responses to emotional learning in the form of "memories that seize control of mental life and behavior" allow humans to minimize fearful passivity following a traumatic experience and return to "successful engagement with the environment" (LeDoux & Gorman, 2001, p. 1955). LeDoux and his research team discovered that rats could learn to cope actively to avoid electric shocks after classical conditioning by rerouting messages from the amygdala to other parts of the brain:

> After being fully conditioned, the rats can be given the option of moving to another place during the occurrence of the conditioned stimulus. If they do so, the conditioned stimulus is terminated, a condition that signals that the shock will not be coming. The learning of this response requires the diversion of the flow of information leaving the lateral nucleus of the amygdala. Rather than going to the central nucleus and engaging the passive fear response, the information is sent from the lateral nucleus to the basal nucleus of the amygdala, which does not project to the brain stem but instead to motor circuits in the ventral striatum. By engaging these alternative pathways, passive fear responding is replaced with an active coping strategy. This diversion of information flow away from the central nucleus to the basal nucleus, and the learning that takes place, do not occur if the rat remains passive. It requires that the rat take action. It is "learning by doing," a process in which the success in terminating the conditioned stimulus reinforces the action taken. When the rat shifts from passive to active coping, it is performing the neurological equivalent of "getting on with life." (LeDoux & Gorman, 2001, p. 1954)

LeDoux then applies these findings to people traumatized by the events of September 11, 2001:

> In practice, then, the approach suggested from the laboratory studies requires that patients develop strategies that enable them to "do something" whenever they are entertaining dysphoric thoughts or are avoiding necessary or meaningful activities. . . . The goal should simply be to successfully carry out activities, especially ones that lead to pleasure or that prevent displeasure. The rats in the experiments described above did not have to perform a difficult action—they only had to move across the chamber in order to succeed in ending their conditioned stimulus. If they had been required to perform some complex task, they might have reached a state of helplessness before figuring out how to succeed. Hence, an individual should be asked, "Instead of watching CNN, what other shows might you watch, or what other things do you think you could do that would engage you but not be too difficult?" Similarly, if the person is dwelling on the events of September 11, it might be helpful to step into another place mentally by thinking about what happened the day before, the week before, or even several months before. (LeDoux & Gorman, 2001, p. 1954)

Current cognitive research indicates that emotions represent the conscious apprehension of the guidance offered by phylogenetically old structures like the amygdala. These nonconscious brain structures regulate our basic survival behaviors: appetite satisfaction, reproduction, defense, and aggression. They can help our survival, consciously or nonconsciously, by responding to environmental events by triggering physiological arousal, the conscious apprehension of which can be experienced as fear, dread, disgust, rage, and so on.

Ellis has long held that these nonconscious affective reactions exist, but he has also stressed that they can be mediated by conscious cognitive learning and practice. He points to the classic studies by Stanley Schachter and Jerome Singer (1962). In a series of experiments ranging over 17 years, Schachter and Singer gave their subjects injections of adrenaline (norepinephrine). Some participants were informed that the injection they received contained adrenaline while others were not informed. Adrenaline is a stress-related hormone that produces rapid heart rate, dilation of the pupils, perspiration, and a general condition of physiological arousal. All participants were asked to enter a room and complete a questionnaire.

Each participant was joined in the room by a confederate of the experimenters; however, they were led to believe that the confederate was another subject. This individual either acted hostile and complained about the experimental conditions or acted elated and pleased about his participation. Participants who did not know they had received adrenaline tended to interpret the effects of the drug with either hostility or elation according to the way the confederate behaved. In contrast, the subjects who had been told that they had been injected with adrenaline did not reflect the affect of the confederate. This line of research has provided support for Ellis's premise that despite any tendencies individuals may have toward affective sensitivity, their cognitive interpretations have a powerful effect on how they feel and behave.

Social Constructionism

In his early writings, Ellis took a logical positivist view of personality, but his perspective changed: "I myself, though one of the early phenomenologists in the field of therapy . . . was indeed a logical positivist up to the mid 1970s. But Bartley . . . Mahoney . . . and Popper . . . showed me that I was wrong, and therefore I have been a nonpositivist, a constructionist, and even a postmodernist since then" (Ellis, 1996, p. 18).

Logical positivists assert that knowledge can be acquired in two ways: logical reasoning and empirical testing. They believe that all fundamental truths can be discovered through these methods. Implicit in their position is that there is a single reality; subjective realities and metaphysical entities are meaningless. In terms of personality, a logical positivist approach implies that there can be an absolute determination of sanity or insanity, good traits and bad traits. As the foregoing quotation indicates, however, Ellis shifted his view of human nature to one of a modified **social constructionism**, a view that has its recent origins in the work of George Kelly, with his model of personal constructs.

Kelly thought that people organize the world by creating bipolar dimensions of meaning, which is what he meant by personal constructs. These are personal models that guide our behavior by organizing our view of reality. Kelly believed that we continually modify our personal constructs based on how well the constructs predict experiences. Kelly and likeminded theoreticians have in common the concept that human information processing involves more than the sum of the information acquired. Instead, each individual constructs a unique structure of personal knowledge and meaning of the world. In other words, a classroom of

30 students presented with exactly the same information will yield 30 unique representations and interpretations of that information.

Social constructionism originated in the philosophical tradition of constructivism. This approach posits that our reality is a function of our context, environment, and culture. Even apparently absolute sciences like mathematics are viewed as constructed, on the basis of the social perspectives of the mathematicians and the culture in which they live. Constructivists maintain that there are a vast number of methods by which computations can be constructed and an equal number of choices as to what to compute. Furthermore, they would argue that the mathematicians are guided by their social context and biases in their selection of specific approaches to analyze and develop. Constructivism holds that reality is created in the human perception of it and that we can never determine an absolute truth or reality because each of us is continuously constructing our own reality.

Social constructionists reject many psychological approaches that presuppose an absolute truth which can be discovered if persistently pursued through the use of scientific procedures. They further reject the principle that a psychotherapist uses objective reason to uncover the clients' true problems and designs objectively valid treatments for the clients, who are identified as resistant or in denial if they do not agree. Social constructionists suggest an either/or approach in which therapists work to understand and develop the client's reality without imposing their own.

The defining distinction between constructivism and the social constructionism is the distinction between the individual and the larger group or society. That is, constructivism proposes that each of us contrives our own unique reality, whereas social constructionism holds that reality is created through social consensus. The creative process is, therefore, a function of our culture (Mahoney, 1991) and the culture's collective perception of it. Accordingly, social constructionism views the person as a function of linguistic norms, social context, and social values. Furthermore, knowledge is not absolute but derived from a continually changing consensus among people. Social constructionists believe that different cultures and societies can have legitimately different realities and systems of knowledge. Thus, reality does not exist independently of its social creation. Constructionists also believe the development of moral values and learning processes are socially and contextually based.

Personality is, thus, regarded as the result of a social consensus. An individual cannot have a personality that exists independently of his or her social milieu. Ellis's modified social constructionism, which he refers to as an *and-also position*, allows for some external reality that exists apart from the social consensus. For example, Ellis maintains that most rules of reason and logic exist independently of social convention. He also holds that believing we absolutely must be loved in return by anyone we love is inherently irrational. This position is in contrast to radical social constructionism or constructivism, which avows that there is no absolute rationality or irrationality, that logic and reason are constructed by the individual, and that no person can be the arbiter of error or correctness.

Ellis criticizes the many contemporary constructionists and postmodernists in psychology who advocate dispensing with diagnoses of pathology. He refutes strict social constructionists such as Jeffrey Guterman who take this position. For example, Guterman (1994) wrote that realist epistemologies

tend to define problems in terms of some objective domain (irrational beliefs, repressed complexes, arid environmental contingencies). In contrast, social constructionist approaches eschew the notion that it is possible to obtain such objective criteria and, instead, contend that problems are linguistic creations which are maintained and perturbed in the domain of intersubjective conversation. (p. 228)

Ellis rejects the notion that irrational beliefs are not objective in the sense that they exist in the perspective of the therapist. Ellis maintains that such beliefs are unrealistic and antiempirical because they contradict both social and personal realities. He pointed out that the belief, "I must at all times win significant people's approval," contradicts the social reality that "no matter how hard I try, a number of significant people most likely will not approve of me." Ellis explains that, in his theory, irrational beliefs are illogical or semantically false in some kind of social setting. So that the statement, "Because I love you greatly, you have to love me," is logically or linguistically false because no matter how much someone loves another person, that person has the choice to reciprocate or not. Ellis emphasizes that irrational beliefs underlying virtually all emotional disturbance are not arbitrary edicts solely from the point of view of a therapist but are socially impractical. They are dysfunctional because the people who hold them live in a social system that is set up to make such beliefs impractical.

Definitions: Beliefs, Personality, and Rationality

Ellis proposes that the beliefs that we develop about the world, ourselves, others, and our relationship to these entities is the defining core of our personality. As will be explained below, these beliefs can be rational or irrational. Without regard to the ratio between the two, they define the ways in which we view our role in society, interpret events, appraise behavior, and choose our responses to life events. The expression of personality is largely a social phenomenon, although Ellis points out that we can still exhibit a consistent personality in isolation. Self-talk, sexual fantasy, self-rating, or choices for solitary recreation are examples of personality expression that do not arise out of interpersonal interactions. We can spend a great deal of time alone and still be inclined toward melancholy or self-aggrandizement without any immediate social cues.

Ellis defines irrationality in two ways. The first is the definition of irrationality according to formal logic, such that an argument is irrational if its conclusion does not follow from overtly stated or implied premises. The second approach is a practical one, defining beliefs that are dysfunctional and emotionally disturbing as intrinsically irrational. In other words, beliefs that will consistently lead to undesirable outcomes if acted on are irrational. These include beliefs that create barriers to achieving our goals; beliefs that lead to distorted views of reality, beliefs that lead to unrealistic views of the self; or beliefs that are rigid or inflexible. Thus, rational people, according to Ellis, are continually testing their hypotheses about life and readily adjusting these ideas when the world shows them they are wrong.

Ellis has proposed numerous categories of irrational beliefs. Some examples are:

1. *Irrational beliefs derived from custom and conformity.* These may include yielding to fads or insisting on outdated customs that fail to serve any present-day purpose. An example would be a hospital that insisted that nurses must rise when a physician enters the room because this custom was common in the 1940s.

2. *Ego-related irrationalities that include self-deification or the perceived need to believe that we are superior to others.* This type of irrational belief is one of the criteria of narcissistic personality disorder.

3. *Prejudice-based irrationalities that include political dogmas and social biases.* An example would be a person who refuses to talk to others in the workplace because the others voted for the "wrong" political candidate.

4. *Irrationalities that represent errors in logic or reason.* These include **overgeneralization**, non sequiturs, utopian or mystical beliefs, and the like. Overgeneralization is a logical fallacy or cognitive distortion caused by making an overly broad assumption on the basis of a small sample or other type of insufficient evidence. An example would be the sports fan who assumes that because his team lost the first two games of its season, it will finish at the bottom of its division.

5. *Irrationality regarding emotions and emotion-based reasoning.* These include the belief that strong feelings about a topic always indicate its truth or reality; that authentic and deeply experienced events are always good; or that a conviction associated with strong emotions is more valid than one based on empirical investigation. Many arguments between people over politics or social policies are sparked by this type of irrationality.

6. *Irrational beliefs used to justify or support habits.* These include labeling a habit a disease to avoid making an effort to change it. An example might be a person who says that he has a disease called "shopaholism" in order to avoid learning money management skills.

7. *Irrationalities that maintain or encourage the development of personality disorders.* These include vilifying people we find displeasing, self-pity, and the elevation of moderate dangers into horrors. An example of the third would be the person who is convinced that every new disease reported by the Centers for Disease Control will turn into an epidemic that will kill millions.

8. *Dogmatic religious irrationalities.* These include insistence on fundamentalist approaches to religion and vilification of people who belong to other faith traditions or hold different beliefs.

9. *Political, social, and economic irrationalities.* Examples of these are the belief that acts of terrorism, horrifying environmental changes, or the irresponsible use of resources can be justified.

10. *Social irrationalities.* These include beliefs justifying hostility, inappropriate dependency on others, antisocial acts, or elevation of social rejection into a catastrophe. Common examples would include damaging the property of neighbors over a disagreement with their opinions; vandalizing public buildings; or stalking someone who has ended a relationship.

Self-Talk and Personality Development

Ellis views personality as predicated on continual **self-talk**. We are always evaluating the world and making judgments about our own actions and the results of these actions.

Accordingly, the beliefs that we have or acquire about the world determine whether this self-talk is positively motivating, discouraging, or emotionally disturbing. Ellis considers conscious cognition as primarily verbal. The verbal centers of the brain are the loci of the representations of the world required for mental manipulation, the induction of generalities from specific events, rational and irrational beliefs, and most other higher order cognitions. Therefore, Ellis's view of personality implies the development of verbal ability. Accordingly, prior to the development of verbal ability, personality is limited to such fundamental human characteristics as extraversion, stimulus seeking, or neuroticism (emotional stability and regulation). As children develop verbal ability, their style of self-talk is either emphasized or mitigated by their innate characteristics. Ellis believes that as children move from representing the world in terms of images to using verbal and conceptual representations, they will develop their own unique style of thinking. Along with the development of their unique style, unfortunately, comes the growth of the tendency toward irrationality. Ellis believes that our personality becomes partially crystallized in early adulthood when we have formulated a conception of ourselves, significant others, and the operations of the world. These formulations become the lens through which temperaments and traits express themselves.

Ego and Self

According to Ellis, there is no ego, per se; however, we possess a number of qualities that have been associated with that term. For example, people are unique entities, and they are aware of this existence and its limited duration. What we call our "self" or "totality" or "personality," on the other hand, has a vague, almost indefinable quality. People may well have "good" or "bad" traits—that is, characteristics that help or hinder them in their goals of survival or happiness—but they really have no "self" that "is" good or bad. Self-aware people can evaluate their own effectiveness in thought, deeds, or affect. Once they choose their goals and purposes, they can rate their skill and efficiency in achieving these goals. As a number of experiments by Albert Bandura and his students have shown, their belief in their efficacy will often help make them more productive and achieving. But when people yield to the inclination to make a global rating of their self, ego, or personality, they typically create self-defeating thoughts, feelings, and behaviors.

Ellis has emphasized that the ego is central in personality in that people are continually being egoistic in rating themselves. He believes this is an innate tendency that has several adaptive advantages in certain settings, situations that are, however, no longer typical. The tendency to rate ourselves by comparing our achievements to others in a peer group can be a positive motivating force. Moreover, when we can achieve a high social rating, it may serve to impress others and possibly improve our social standing further. Finally, self-rating may have survival value in that it can motivate us to acquire more assets, such as money or the educational credentials that may lead to opportunities for lucrative employment.

On the other hand, Ellis believes that continual self-rating was more effective when people lived in small competitive groups on the Arctic tundra during the Ice Age or on the savannahs of Africa eons ago. In a complex society that provides abstract as well as concrete rewards, self-rating is usually more emotionally draining than motivating. That is, for self-rating to be useful in a contemporary society, we must be extraordinarily gifted in intellect, talent, and appearance. According to Ellis, if we elevate our ego only when we do well and conversely deflate it when we do poorly, we will tend to be emotionally unstable when self-rating. Ellis emphasizes that a strong ego or high self-esteem requires us to be above average in almost all measures—something very few people are.

Innate Irrationality

Having evolved throughout eras mostly characterized by privation, violence, or predation, people have become inclined to absolute "musts" about what they perceive to be legitimate needs or goals. Such "musts" are surrogates for survival needs. That is, as primates, people have absolute needs for such fundamental necessities as air, sustenance in the form of food and fluids, and shelter. For survival of the species, most individuals need access to opportunities for reproduction. As society has become more complex and needs are defined in more abstract terms, the strategies that were efficient, quick, and potentially life saving have frequently become impediments. In the contemporary world, we are not facing imminent death if food is not immediately acquired. Nor are most people confronted by predatory animals and lethal competitors on a daily basis. To be sure, such situations do occur during wars, famines, pandemics, or other crises; and in those cases, some irrational beliefs might be reinstated as being adaptive. For example, in the case of hand-to-hand combat with an armed criminal, a person's belief that she must do well and that it would be monumentally bad if she lost might very well be a rational conviction.

The problem for most of us in most situations is that through early learning, such social achievements as educational attainments, social approval, or material possessions become surrogates for actual needs. Their actual necessity is illusory, but most people develop very strong emotions about obtaining them or losing them if they have acquired them. When these emotions are strong enough to result in disturbed behaviors, then the people who are acting in these dysfunctional ways can be presumed to make irrational demands on themselves and the world.

Although there is little research in behavioral genetics regarding irrational thinking, there is sufficient indirect evidence to conclude that it is the case. For example, the Nobel Prize-winning work of Daniel Kahneman, which is largely based on his collaboration with Amos Tversky, essentially concludes that people are indeed irrational. Kahneman and his colleagues proposed that virtually all people use heuristics to organize the world around them in a way that commonly leads to incorrect conclusions (Kahneman, Slovic, & Tversky, 1982). Notably, prior to Kahneman and Tversky's work, economics from the time of Adam Smith operated under the assumption that people make economic decisions on a rational basis. Apparently, however, people can be as irrational in economic matters as they can in all others.

Kahneman and Tversky were conceptually preceded by Newell and Simon, with their principle of **bounded rationality,** which states that people have increasingly greater rates of irrational decision as situations grow more complex. Several large-scale environmental and transportation disasters have been attributed to "errors made by people [under stress] in crucial circumstances" (McCreary, Pollard, Stevenson, & Wilson, 1998). The worst disaster in the history of civil aviation to date, a runway collision between two jumbo jets in 1977 that cost the lives of 583 people, has been attributed in part to "separate small failures" in decision making "chained together so that they result in a disastrous outcome" (Weick, 1990). The separate small failures in this particular case included air traffic controllers whose command of English was not the best, a Dutch pilot in a hurry to take off because of deteriorating weather conditions and company regulations about crew overtime, and an American pilot who misunderstood the controllers' numbering of the airport's taxiways.

Because most of us cannot apprehend and integrate the vast amount of information available to us when making decisions, we focus on just a few sources of information. Having done so, we tend to apply a simplified model to make a decision. Such a model is called a schema, which is a cognitive conceptual framework. For example, a social schema might hold that all well-dressed students pay better attention in class. Or a self-schema could be stated to the effect that "I am a well-liked and articulate person." Although simple and often efficient, applying schemas can result in the exclusion of additional relevant information. For example, let us suppose that someone uses a schema for the purchase of a car that requires using evaluations from a consumer magazine. Once equipped with the evaluation, the individual selects the most highly recommended car equipped in the recommended configuration. At the dealership, the individual may be offered a different but better car at an even better price. Bounded rationality predicts that he is likely to turn down the better deal because his schema covers only the specific car recommended by the magazine.

Some Heuristics of Kahneman and Tversky

Daniel Kahneman and Amos Tversky conducted research on the way people make decisions. Their work led to a Nobel Prize for Kahneman (Tversky died in 1996 before the prize was awarded). Their research revealed that people frequently use irrational heuristics to make decisions. A heuristic is a replicable method or approach for directing our attention in learning, discovery, or problem-solving. In effect, we use rules of thumb based on observation or experience that on the surface seem sound but are actually based on poor reasoning and ignorance of the rules of probability. In addition, we neither consciously acquire nor apply information about the probability of prior events; we do not adjust our decisions based on sample size; and we are poor at distinguishing rare from typical events. In short, Kahneman and his colleagues have found that people are consistently and universally irrational.

Availability Heuristic

Most judgments are made on the basis of what we can remember about a subject, not the complete amount of information available. This is particularly common when we estimate the frequency or probability of events. This can be seen in the precautions parents take regarding their children after seeing news reports of a kidnapped child. Because the news reports are recent and readily available and overall mortality statistics are not, parents will tend to be far more concerned about the risk of their child being snatched by a kidnapper than the risk to their child when riding in a car. The National Incidence Studies of Missing, Abducted, Runaway, and Throwaway Children estimated that in 2002, 115 children in the United States were abducted by strangers—far fewer than the approximately 3,000 children killed in automobile accidents in that year.

(Continued)

(Continued)

Anchoring and Adjustment

When it is necessary to make an estimate of some kind, we to tend to base such estimates on "anchors" or familiar positions or quantities. We will then adjust the estimate upward or downward on the basis of additional information. But we base increments or decrements on the original **anchoring**, even if it is a very poor estimator. For example, if we were asked to estimate the age of an unseen college student, we would probably estimate something close to 20. When told the person is considerably older, we might increase the age to 22 or 23, basing our increase on the anchor, not on the possibility that the anchor might not even be close. So if the student were 40 years old, we might never get close to getting the correct age, even with several prompts.

Representativeness Heuristic

When we attempt to predict the likelihood of an event occurring, we compare it to a similar event for which we have some knowledge of the likelihood of occurrence and then make the irrational assumption that the two events have similar probabilities. The fallacy is based on the irrational assumption that if two events have some salient similarity, they will be similar in all other ways. This heuristic is the basis of the gambler's fallacy. An example of this would be the roulette player who concludes that "black is due," after a run of eight red numbers. The gambler is forgetting, of course, that each roll of the wheel is independent of all others, and the run of eight reds has no effect on the next outcome. In addition, we might falsely intuit that a series of seemingly symmetrical outcomes like red, red, red, black, black, black, black is less likely than a seemingly "random" run like red, black, black, red, black, red, red. In fact, both outcomes have equal a priori probabilities. But because the second series comes closer to many people's conception of what a stochastically independent series looks like, they will conclude that it is indeed more probable. Another example of this heuristic would be the case of the individual who meets three people from Russia who are computer scientists and then concludes that most Russians are computer scientists.

Conjunction Fallacy

People frequently fail to grasp that if two events can occur separately or together, the conjunction—the point at which they overlap—cannot be more likely than the likelihood of either of the two separate events. Instead, people assign a higher likelihood to combination events, irrationally associating the quantity of events with the level of probability. Kahneman and Tversky demonstrated this fallacy with a problem presented to a number of people: A hypothetical person named Linda is 31, single, outspoken, and very bright. She majored in philosophy in college. As a student, she was deeply concerned with issues of discrimination and social justice, and she also participated in antinuclear demonstrations. The researchers then asked whether Linda was more likely to be (a) a bank teller or (b) a bank teller and activist in the feminist movement. About 86% answered (b). They believed that the probability of her meeting two constraints (bank teller and active feminist) is greater than the probability of meeting only one (bank teller). This is contrary to logic and probability theory. The fallacy was detected more often if the subjects were asked: Of those women who have the same background of Linda, how many are bank tellers and how many are both bank tellers and active in the feminist movement?

Cognitive psychologists like Newell and Simon or Kahneman and Tversky were not alone in documenting the extent of human irrationality. Psychology is replete with other examples of irrational thinking. An oft-cited psychological principle is the **Barnum** or **Forer effect**. This is a form of irrationality that makes the work of fortune tellers, astrologers, and psychics much easier. It explains that people will endorse descriptions of their traits or personalities when the descriptions are vague, mostly flattering, and general. In fact, most people will state that such descriptions are highly accurate and describe them quite well.

Social psychologists have coined the phrase fundamental attribution error to describe the universal tendency to associate some undesirable behavior of another person as representing that individual's innate nature while attributing the same behavior in ourselves to the specific situation. In other words, we all tend to be trait theorists when condemning others but situationists when explaining our own imperfect behavior. For example, if someone cuts us off while we are driving, we are likely to believe the person is a dangerous antisocial individual; but if we cut someone off while driving, we believe that we are a good responsible driver who was in an inescapable dilemma or perhaps just having an off day.

The psychologists Dale Miller and Michael Ross (1975) describe a robust bias in people called the *self-serving bias.* They maintain that we tend to attribute successes to our abilities and volition and our failures to external factors or unfairness. For example, if someone gets a promotion at her job, she is likely to believe she earned it as a talented and capable worker. If she is passed over for the same promotion, she is likely to attribute the outcome to bias on the part of her boss. A similar irrational view of the world is observed with the **false consensus effect.** This pervasive thinking error leads us to believe that most others agree with us. This distortion is particularly common among people who socialize within a like-minded group.

The regression fallacy is another source of irrational thinking in most people in which we fail to understand regression to the mean. It is a statistical fact that in virtually all measures of natural events, extreme or outlying measurements will tend to move closer to the mean when measured again. That is, there is regression to the mean. Despite this, people tend to attribute this regression, which is an almost invariable outcome, to some failure of the individual or some innate quality of the event being measured. For example, if a baseball player achieves a batting average of .400 (that is, he is successful in hitting the pitched ball sufficiently well to get on base 40% of the time), he has accomplished an extraordinary feat. If in the subsequent season he were to drop to .300—a very satisfactory average—many fans would seek an explanation for the decline in his performance. It is also typical for the player himself to become dejected for merely playing excellently after an extraordinary year. This is a result of the fans' and the player's failure to understand regression to the mean—which ordains that it is the most probable outcome to perform at a level closer to the average after performing either extraordinarily well or extraordinarily badly. In fact, the more unusual the performance, the more likely it is that the next measure will be closer to the mean, less unusual.

The Confounding Factor of Personal History

Ellis's emphasis on the constitutional or genetic basis of many personality characteristics led him to dispute the learned or traumatic basis of many personality characteristics. He points out that many learning and developmental theorists point to traumatic events or poor parental behavior as the cause of certain personality characteristics, especially pathological ones. Ellis has asserted that this conclusion might very well be an example of the **post hoc ergo propter hoc** fallacy. This fallacy is a logical error that confuses temporal sequence with causality; that is, if one event happens after another in time, the first is often assumed to be the cause of the second. The Latin phrase means "after this, therefore, because of this." Ellis points out that this apparent connection might very well be the result of an illusory correlation. For example, suppose a sexually and emotionally disturbed father abuses his daughter, and she subsequently becomes an emotionally ill adult. The most common psychological explanation is that her disturbance is the direct result of her father's abuse.

Ellis proposed an alternative explanation that would need to be ruled out before a cause-and-effect relationship can be inferred between abuse and pathology. Suppose that the abusive father is suffering from extreme psychopathology, which, Ellis says, is almost requisite before committing such an act. Furthermore, such a disturbed individual will generally seek the path of least resistance, which in this case would be selecting the most vulnerable child in the family to exploit. This particular child might be anxious, withdrawn, or otherwise vulnerable because she inherited some of the disturbed parent's psychological characteristics. A perpetrator would choose an emotionally vulnerable child for two reasons. The first is that she would be less capable of defending herself or seeking intervention. The second reason would be greater ease in blaming the victim. That is, the perpetrator will feel that it is less morally offensive to harm a child who is already damaged. Of course, the act of abuse would exacerbate this victim's innate vulnerabilities, but it is not their direct cause.

Ellis criticizes therapists who conclude a priori that there is a cause-and-effect relationship in cases like this for several reasons. First, it tends to encourage a therapeutic approach that focuses on past events, which does nothing to liberate the person from the aftereffects of these events. Second, if indeed the individual is suffering from some constitutional emotional problems, a therapy that concentrates on an illusory cause will miss the point, which should be to show the woman that she can be empowered to control her disturbed emotions without changing her personal history. This position is supported by research showing that abusive parents tend to have poorly integrated personalities (Anderson & Lauderdale, 1982) or personality and Axis I disorders (Francis, Hughes, & Hitz, 1992; Sloan & Meier, 1983).

Another problem with attributing a cause-and-effect relationship between present-day pathology and abuse in childhood is that the typical source of evidence is the afflicted individual. As memory researchers have repeatedly shown, autobiographical memory is flawed. Individuals who are suffering emotional problems tend to be motivated to be inaccurate as they are commonly faced with a dilemma of attribution. They can either attribute their neurosis to some intrinsic aspects of themselves or find some external explanation. The latter is certainly more palatable. And given the pervasive influence of dynamic theories that have associated almost all psychopathology with early development, attributing their problems to parental abuse is not only palatable but ostensibly plausible. What Ellis recommends is to make the cause of the disturbance irrelevant to the therapy process and to look for the person's current perception of it.

Irrational Beliefs

The irrational beliefs that people can maintain cover a wide range of human affairs, but they commonly fall into several categories. These include demands for personal competency, social standing, adulation, or possessions. The irrationality of such demands can be obvious. These demands are commonly phrased as conditional statements founded on emotional reasoning to the effect: "Because I very much want something to be, it therefore should be." To the person making such a demand on reality, the demand seems rational, but on examination, it can be seen to be based on poor logic.

It cannot be rational to cause ourselves to feel intensely disturbing emotions about failing to have something that is not absolutely necessary for survival. Of course, it is rational to be sad or disappointed if our desire is not satisfied. But if that desire crosses the line to become an absolute must or an illusory need, then we are indulging an irrational belief. Irrational beliefs or rigid, self-defeating demands commonly lead to distortions in social interpersonal perceptions, attributions, or inferences. For example, if someone adopts the irrational belief that it is absolutely essential for the boss to think highly of them, when confronted with the reality that this is not the case, the individual will commonly torment himself with cognitions that are extreme variants. Thus, he might then strongly believe that the boss thinks that he is completely incompetent, that the boss hates him, or even that no employer will ever hold him in positive regard. The principle here is that irrational thinking is extremely emotionally provocative, thereby leading to even more irrational thinking.

Human personality is the result of a complex interplay of cognitions, emotions, and behaviors. That is, a thought, emotion, or behavior is at least partially contingent on the situation in which it arises; and a situation includes the individual's actions, emotion, and cognitions. Consequently, feelings and behaviors have an important influence on beliefs; beliefs affect feelings and behaviors; and feelings affect beliefs and behaviors (Ellis, 1962, 1988, 1991). Thus, an individual's personality is constructed from a dynamic interplay of multiple internal and external factors. Despite the complexity of human personality, virtually all humans, however reared, have two opposing creative tendencies: (a) to damn or deify themselves and others, as noted earlier and thereby to make themselves disturbed and dysfunctional; and (b) to change and actualize themselves as healthier and less distressed.

People are innately creative and constructive, and whenever they needlessly upset themselves, they also have the tendency and ability to think about their dysfunctional thinking, feeling, and behaving and to reverse the self-defeating ways they have largely constructed. Ellis has also hypothesized that once people upset themselves, their emotional reactions—especially their panic, depression, and self-hatred—are often so strong and consuming that these emotions interfere with their curative powers and sabotage some of their constructiveness. Also, as noted earlier, their disturbance about being disturbed often blocks them from changing.

Robert Zajonc (1984) and Richard Lazarus (1984b) wrote cogent although competing arguments on the primacy of affect or cognition. In Ellis's view, Zajonc and Lazarus might well agree that such disturbed feelings as severe anxiety, depression, hostility, and self-pity are complex emotions that almost invariably have a substantial cognitive component. Considerable clinical and experimental data would seem to support the following hypotheses about these special kinds of emotions. Rarely if ever do disturbed emotions exist independently of cognitions. They largely (although not invariably) are preceded by and include strongly held ("hot") thoughts—especially (a) powerful preferences such as, "I really wish that I would succeed and be approved of by significant others"; and (b) insistent demands, such as "Because I would like very much to succeed and be approved of, I must be, and it would be horrible if I weren't" (Ellis, 1962, 1977a). Many of the cognitions that lead to and are included in emotional disturbance are conscious. Many, however, are unconscious or implicit philosophies of which people may be unaware, but they can usually bring these to consciousness and then work on changing them (Beck, 1976; Ellis, 1962). Some forms of emotional disturbance, such as endogenous depression, mania, and schizophrenia, appear to be sparked by physiological or neurological processes and hardly by cognitive factors alone. When this is true, the physiological processes appear to affect and to interact with cognitions, so that the resulting emotional disturbance includes important cognitive elements (Ellis, 1962, 1979; Meehl, 1962).

Ellis predicates a number of his premises on nonconscious processes. The nonconscious he refers to, however, is consistent with cognitive psychology as opposed to the nonconscious of psychoanalysis. Nonconscious beliefs, according to Ellis, are those that are innate or are so deeply learned that they require no conscious mediation to process. All nonconscious beliefs that are learned began as conscious beliefs or attitudes, but rehearsal and repetition make them unconscious in the same way that a well-practiced gymnast will unconsciously process the complex tumbles and jumps that were learned over many thousands of hours of practice. Such unconscious cognitions can readily be made conscious if the individual needs to attend to them or is directed to them.

Those that are not learned have a genetic basis. Ellis does not propose that there are genes that code for specific irrational beliefs. Instead, he proposes that tendencies such as arousal, learning aversion rapidly, or feeling an emotion more deeply are all likely to have strong heritabilities. These genetic tendencies are the basis for the universal irrationality he believes is a central aspect of personality. Their development requires social reinforcement. People are all irrational, says Ellis, but not all to the same degree or about the same beliefs.

Origins of Irrationality

As noted earlier, Ellis believes that as children develop, they will innately have temperamental tendencies toward extraversion, introversion, stimulus-seeking, fearfulness, and so on. Temperaments that involve exaggerated emotionality act to amplify innate irrational thinking. Adversity early in a person's life will also serve to increase the tendency toward irrational thinking. In addition, irrationality is exaggerated by the social events or milieu in which a person develops. This environment-temperament model of Ellis does not differ significantly from those of many other personality theorists except that Ellis postulates that there are several primal irrational styles inherent in human beings. These are primarily absolutism, demandingness, and musturbation. These are the innate foundations of irrationality, which can be minimal or acutely dysfunctional depending on developmental trends. They are innate and universal because at one time, they were adaptive for humans. Being demanding during times when humans lived in loosely cooperative tribal groups, when they were nomadic, or when privation was nearly continual would be far more helpful than rational flexibility.

These innate thinking styles, according to Ellis, are basic and primitive. Whether or not they become particularly problematic is contingent on the individual's development. Absolutism, demandingness, and musturbatory thinking can be exaggerated or mitigated by our developmental milieu and social life. Irrationality will be shaped by the environment—of which the parents are only one part—resulting in various types and degrees of irrational

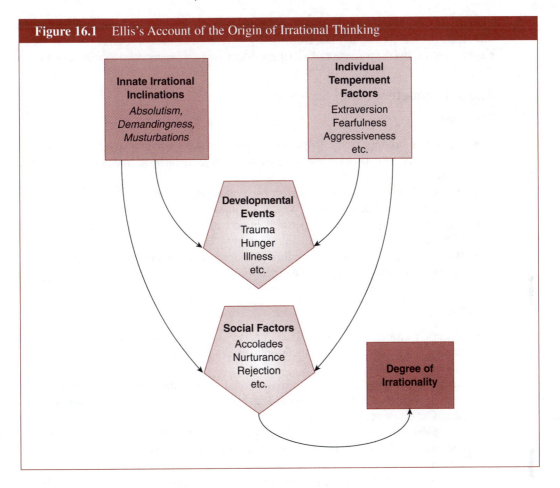

Figure 16.1   Ellis's Account of the Origin of Irrational Thinking

thinking. For example, a child may be shy, easily scared, and prone to be strongly reinforced from nurturance. If he is given excessive nurturance and protection, he will be encouraged to be dependent and believe that he absolutely needs this support. In this case, he is likely to become more demanding about receiving comfort following adverse life events. In addition, during development, the individual will tacitly be encouraged or discouraged in his expression of these tendencies through environmental events. An individual growing up hungry is likely, for example, to become more absolutistic in his thinking as a result of facing a survival threat. As the schematic diagram in Figure 16.1 indicates, the three factors that conspire to increase (or diminish irrationality) can be synergistic, complementary, or mutually inhibitory.

⧉ SOME SPECIFIC IRRATIONAL BELIEFS

The foundation of all of Ellis's work is the elucidation and reduction of irrational thinking. He has set forth literally hundreds of examples of such beliefs. Here we describe several that cover a significant portion of those that he has discussed. They are divided into obvious and subtle irrational beliefs. The obvious ones are self-evident and are readily exposed as self-defeating. The subtle ones, according to Ellis, are typically more difficult to expose and change. They are more deceptive, and the possessor of such beliefs tends to be more resistant to abandoning them.

About Competence and Success

Obvious

- Because I strongly desire to perform important tasks competently and successfully, I *absolutely must* perform them well (and I am an inadequate incompetent person if I don't).
- Because I strongly desire to perform important tasks competently and successfully, I *absolutely must* perform them well at all times.
- Because I strongly desire to perform important tasks competently and successfully, I *absolutely must* perform them outstandingly well.
- Because I strongly desire to perform important tasks competently and successfully, I *absolutely must* perform them perfectly well.

Subtle

- Because I strongly desire to perform important tasks competently and successfully, and because I want to succeed at them only *some of* the time, I *absolutely must* perform these tasks well.
- Because I strongly desire to perform important tasks competently and successfully, and because I really try hard to succeed at these tasks, I deserve to perform well and *absolutely must* perform that way.
- Because I strongly desire to perform important tasks competently and successfully, and because I have failed so many times to perform well in the past, I *absolutely must* perform well now.
- Because I strongly desire to perform important tasks competently and successfully, and because I am quite competent and successful in several other ways, I *absolutely must* perform well now.
- Because I strongly desire to perform important tasks competently and successfully, and because I am a special kind of person who has unusual abilities, I *absolutely must* perform well now.
- Because I strongly desire to perform important tasks competently and successfully, and because I am handicapped in some other ways, I *absolutely must* perform well in this area.
- Because I strongly desire to perform important tasks competently and successfully, and because I feel so anxious and depressed when I do not, my powerful feelings of worthlessness prove that I *absolutely must* perform well.

About Love and Approval

Obvious

- Because I strongly desire to be approved by people I find significant, I *absolutely must* have their approval (and I am worthless if I do not).

- Because I strongly desire to be approved by people I find significant, I *absolutely must* always have their approval.
- Because I strongly desire to be approved by people I find significant, I *absolutely must* have their total approval.

Subtle

- Because I strongly desire to be approved by people I find significant, and because I *very* strongly want to be, I *absolutely must* have their approval.
- Because I strongly desire to be approved by people I find significant, and because I only want *a little* approval from them, I *absolutely must* have it.
- Because I strongly desire to be approved by people I find significant, and because I haven't had much love and approval for a long period of time, I *absolutely must* have their approval.
- Because I strongly desire to be approved by people I find significant, and because I am a *special kind* of person, I *absolutely must* have their approval.
- Because I strongly desire to be approved by people I find significant, and because I have been *so* deprived in other areas of my life (as I *must* not be), I *absolutely must* have their approval.
- Because I strongly desire to be approved by people I find significant, and because I feel so anxious and depressed when I am not approved, my powerful feelings of neediness prove that I *absolutely must* have their approval.

About Fairness

Obvious

- Because I strongly desire people to treat me considerately and fairly, they *absolutely must* do so (and they are evil, damnable people who deserve to be severely condemned and punished when they don't).
- Because I strongly desire people to treat me considerately and fairly, they *absolutely must* at all times and under all conditions do so.

Subtle

- Because I very strongly desire people to treat me considerately and fairly, they *absolutely must* do so.
- Because I strongly desire people to treat me considerately and fairly, and because people have treated me very well in the past, they *absolutely must* now treat me that way.
- Because I strongly desire people to treat me considerately and fairly, and because so many people have treated me very unfairly during my past life, people *absolutely must* treat me well now.
- Because I strongly desire people to treat me considerately and fairly, and because I am unusually weak and unable to take care of myself, people *absolutely must* treat me well.
- Because I strongly desire people to treat me considerately and fairly, and because I feel so greatly upset and angry when they don't do this, my powerful upset and angry feelings prove that it is absolutely right that they treat me well and that they *absolutely must* do so.

About Safety and Comfort

Obvious

- Because I strongly desire to have a safe, comfortable, and satisfying life, the conditions under which I live *absolutely must* be easy, convenient, and gratifying (and it is *awful,* and I *can't bear it* and *can't be happy at all* when they are unsafe and frustrating).
- Because I strongly desire to have a safe, comfortable, and satisfying life, the conditions under which I live *absolutely must* at all times be easy, convenient, and gratifying.

Subtle

- Because I strongly desire to have a safe, comfortable, and satisfying life, and because I am a nice person who tries to help others lead this kind of life, the conditions under which I live *absolutely must* be easy, convenient, and gratifying.
- Because I strongly desire to have a safe, comfortable, and satisfying life, and because in the past I have had a hard and unsatisfying existence, the conditions under which I live *absolutely must* now be easy, convenient, and gratifying.
- Because I strongly desire to have a safe, comfortable, and satisfying life, and because I am weak and handicapped (as I *should not* be), the conditions under which I live *absolutely must* be easy, convenient, and gratifying.
- Because I strongly desire to have a safe, comfortable, and satisfying life, and because I am a special person who deserves to have one, the conditions under which I live *absolutely must be* easy, convenient and gratifying.
- Because I strongly desire to have a safe, comfortable, and satisfying life, and because it is so unfair when I suffer trouble and discomfort, the world must not be that unfair and has to grant me conditions that are easy, convenient, and gratifying.

⊡ ELLIS'S ABC MODEL OF PERSONALITY AND PATHOLOGY

Albert Ellis proposes a simple, yet profound model of emotional functioning. Ellis's ABC model is the foundation of both personality and psychopathology. Ellis asserts that people are inherently irrational and prone to emotional malfunctioning, but he also acknowledges that the human personality is more complex than this. According to the ABC model, when we are confronted with some adversity or any activating life event, we will almost always experience an emotional consequence of having done so. As current research indicates, emotions serve an essential regulatory role in human cognition. Researchers like Joseph LeDoux and António Damásio point out that the subcortical structures that mediate emotion are capable of learning and can offer the benefits of this learning to guide our conscious mentation.

Despite the innate and universal irrationality in people, Ellis strongly asserts that with effort and guidance, people can become far more rational. They can in effect override their innate irrationality through *in vivo* practice and mental rehearsal. Ellis's single most compelling contribution to personality theory is the ABC model. He proposed that most emotional reactions, especially dysfunctional ones, can be explained with this model. Emotional responses begin with an activating event, which ultimately results in an emotional consequence. A fundamental

Figure 16.2   Ellis's ABC Model

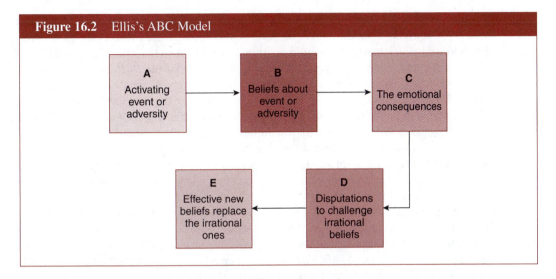

aspect of Ellis's therapeutic approach is the fallacious causal connection most people make between the activating event and the emotional consequence. In fact, the belief that the person maintains about the meaning of such events is the cause of the emotion.

The *sine qua non* of Ellis's REBT is the illumination of the connection between beliefs and emotional responses and the changing of irrational beliefs that lead to neurotic or dysfunctional emotions. One of the key themes of irrationality is absolutistic thinking. This cognitive process occurs when an individual takes a wish or preference and elevates it into an essential need. For example, we can rationally state that it is highly preferable for everyone on a highway to drive safely and courteously. This preference becomes irrational, however, when we think that because we believe it is preferable to do so, everyone therefore *must* drive in this way.

Ellis demonstrates that this thinking is irrational because people undoubtedly do not always drive safely and courteously; and therefore, this absolute edict that they must *always* do so cannot hold. Ellis refers to this type of absolutistic thinking in which we impose our personal musts (or absolute values) on the world as musturbation. By musturbation, Ellis refers to a belief that leads to the creation of illusory imperatives. Musturbation by its nature precludes finding alternatives or rational solutions. Someone who "must" be loved by someone, or "must" get the promotion they want at work fails to see that these are strong desires and preferences but not absolute requirements. If something is indeed an absolute imperative for their existence or well-being, then it would follow that it is pointless to find an alternative path to happiness, just as it would not make sense for a person dying of thirst to try to find a good meal as they will be dead before they could consume it. Ellis suggests that people who musturbate cause themselves emotional distress for two reasons; they lament excessively over the object or achievement that they "must" but do not have; and they lose the opportunity to improve themselves by achieving other goals that *are* within their grasp.

A variant of musturbation that Ellis has described as a fundamental irrational thinking style is *demandingness*. In demandingness, we issue imperatives to the world that satisfy our personal standards of fairness, propriety, or desire. The demanding individual will commonly use the word *should* irrationally. Here the influence of Karen Horney and her "tyranny of the shoulds" on Ellis is evident. He has repeatedly emphasized that any statement about what "should" be is irrational unless it takes the form of a conditional statement. That is, if we state, "I should treat people fairly if I want to be treated in kind," then that statement has a kind of **syllogism**-like self-evidence. In contrast, if we make statements like, "He *should* give me the promotion," or "I *should* have been treated better by my parents," then we are being irrational. The reason why this is so is that the first statement requires justification. Because the term *should* in English denotes a duty or absolute propriety, we must find the basis of such a duty or propriety. Specifically, why *should* the boss give this person the promotion? Ellis points out that *should* implies here something like the following: "The boss should give me the promotion because I want it." Because there is no universal standard requiring that a person absolutely must do something merely because someone else strongly wants it, it is irrational to demand it in the form of a *should*. In the case of the second statement, which refers to a past event, to say that the past should have happened otherwise than it did is on its face illogical. As Ellis has explained, if the past should have been different, then it would have been different; but because it came out the way we remember it, no imposed duty or propriety can change it. What happened *should* have happened because it indubitably did.

Another fundamental type of irrational thinking that Ellis focuses on is awfulizing. This common penchant has people labeling events as maximally bad and consequently experiencing exaggerated or neurotic emotional reactions to the events. Awfulizing can include self-statements such as "It is terrible that I am lost and will be late getting to the airport" or "I am a complete failure as a human being because I failed one examination."

The Role of Diagnosis and Testing

Ellis has long been an advocate of the use of scientifically validated psychological tests. He has argued that most psychotherapists are blinded by their narcissistic belief that their initial personality and pathology appraisals are always or most often correct. Psychotherapists who usually work without oversight are particularly prone to both the **expectancy effect** and the **confirmation bias.** In other words, having diagnosed and evaluated a client, therapists will naturally pay attention only to those expressions and behaviors that confirm their initial assessment. For this reason, testing adds an important element of objectivity to the process.

Ellis's Method of Psychotherapy

REBT as prescribed by Ellis is far more humanistic than the therapy that has been practiced by many of his acolytes. The reason for this discrepancy is the deceptive simplicity of the ABC model. Just as some adherents of Carl Rogers's client-centered therapy believe that they are practicing psychotherapy well if they mindlessly paraphrase their client's statements, so, too, some misguided REBT practitioners falsely believe that they merely have to throw invectives against what they believe are irrational beliefs. In fact, Ellis has advanced a far more subtle and collaborative process.

REBT begins with the development of a therapeutic relationship. To accomplish this, therapists initially will soften or even avoid the active directive interventions that are the hallmark of REBT therapy. Clients are encouraged to express their understanding of their problem as well as its origin. Therapists will generally demonstrate an understanding of the client's point of view, perceived needs, and desires.

Only after a considerable degree of trust and rapport is established does the therapist begin the process of exploring and modifying the client's dysfunctional philosophy. The first step in doing so is to understand the client's worldview sufficiently well to find the aspects of it that are rigid, excessively dogmatic, demanding, or absolutistic, resulting in psychological problems. This understanding is usually accomplished by asking clients to define their goals in therapy and in each session and then to find the irrationalities that are the prime barrier to achieving those goals. The client's history and development are explored to the extent that they might clarify beliefs and philosophy, but they are not the central focus. Ellis points out that biographical memory tends to be unreliable, and making attributions about the origin of an irrational belief does little in the end to eliminate it.

Having achieved a collaborative understanding of the client's goals and problems, the therapist's next step involves helping clients challenge their own irrational beliefs. Ellis points out that this can be accomplished in a number of ways. It can include direct challenges to the irrational beliefs and then placing the burden on the clients to provide some evidence or proof of their beliefs. The therapist may do so by using the Socratic method, in which the therapist makes focused inquiries about the client's beliefs with the goal of having the client ultimately discover their irrationality. Or the therapist may use a paradoxical approach, supporting the client's irrational beliefs in an exaggerated fashion so that the client softens his or her position and so examines in a new light these previously strongly held values. REBT allows for numerous approaches like those discussed, and it encourages therapists to be creative in their development. The limits preclude therapist narcissism, attacks on clients or their behavior, mocking of the client's beliefs even if they are irrational, or dogmatism on the part of the therapist.

In essence, REBT is indeed a humanistic therapy, and clients are unconditionally accepted as human beings, even though their values and beliefs may not be accepted. Illuminating the irrationality of these values or beliefs, however, is better accomplished in a sensible and flexible fashion, and the client's values that are not irrational are unconditionally accepted. REBT does not work with such absolutes as labeling people or behavior good or bad. Instead, it seeks to determine functional versus nonfunctional cognitions, behaviors, and emotions. Ellis maintains that the goal of psychotherapy is not to eliminate unhappiness, sadness, or other normal if unpleasant emotions. Consequently, he does not advocate unrealistic positive thinking or Pollyannaism. Rather, he strives for a healthy and realistic worldview, even if it necessitates accepting the painful emotions that are intrinsic to human existence. The imparting of a new worldview is done collaboratively so that clients learn to dispute their beliefs on their own without the therapist's ongoing intervention. Usually, this collaboration is achieved by helping people understand that their emotions and actions are primarily caused by their beliefs and their thinking. This end is achieved with Ellis's ABC model, in which an event from the client's own life that led to a disturbed emotion or dysfunctional behavior is explored within its framework. The goal is to provide the epiphany that the client's behavior and emotions resulted from the belief that came between the activating life event and the emotional consequence. This process is enhanced by reading, practicing disputing irrational beliefs, and learning to construct new and more effective beliefs and behaviors.

Specific techniques suggested by Ellis include shame attacks, in which clients act in a manner that would typically cause them a great deal of embarrassment or social discomfort. Clients are taught to explore the beliefs that are implicit in their disturbed emotional reactions. Similarly, clients are encouraged to engage in risk taking. These risks are predominantly actions that the client perceives as far more dangerous, either materially or socially, than they actually are. These risks can range from public speaking to asking someone for a date to ordering a meal in a fancy restaurant to getting on an aircraft.

EXCERPT OF A THERAPY SESSION WITH ALBERT ELLIS

What follows is a portion of a psychotherapy session that Ellis provided to a young professional man who was suffering panic attacks and anxiety. This individual had sought medical help repeatedly for what he believed to be heart attacks. His physician referred him for psychological help when no medical problem could be found. The man's anxiety permeated most aspects of his life. His panic attacks had become so severe he all but lost his ability to perform sexually with his wife. The session begins with the client telling Dr. Ellis about his resistance to taking the anxiolytic medication that brought him some relief but gave him discomfort about needing pharmacotherapy.

Client:	But the one thing I don't like is to take pills. I know that sometimes you need medication, but I hate it.
Therapist:	Well, if we can help you to change your ideas and attitudes about taking trains and about having a heart attack, that will really help you, and you won't need medication. You see, you said you were a perfectionist. So you're first making yourself anxious about doing things perfectly well. "I must do well! I must do well!" Instead of telling yourself, "I'd like to do well, but if I don't, I don't. . . . It's not the end of the world." You see, you're rarely saying that. You're saying, "I've got to! I've got to!" And that will make you anxious—about your work, about sex, about having a heart attack, or about almost anything else. Then, once you make yourself anxious, you often tell yourself, "I must not be anxious! I must not be anxious!" That will make you more anxious—anxious about your anxiety. Now, if I can help you to accept yourself with your anxiety, first, and stop horrifying yourself about it; if we can help you, second, to give up your perfectionism—your demandingness—then you would not keep making yourself anxious. But you're in the habit of demanding that things have to go well and that, when they don't, you must not be anxious about them. "I must not be anxious! I must be sensible and sane!" That's exactly how people make themselves anxious—with rigid, forceful shoulds, oughts, and musts.
Client:	Like yesterday. Yesterday was my worst day in a long time.
Therapist:	Yes, because?
Client:	What I did is when I was going to the train, I said: "I need to put something in my mind."
Therapist:	To distract yourself from your anxiety that you expected to have when you got on the train?
Client:	Yes. I said, "I am going to buy some sports things for the children." So I went to one of the stores, and I bought some things, and as soon as I got on the

train, I started deliberately reading. Ten minutes after I was on the train, I still didn't have any anxiety. I was OK. But then I remembered, and I said, "Jesus, I feel OK." At that moment, I started feeling panicked again.

Therapist: That's right. What you probably said to yourself was, "Jesus, I feel OK. But maybe I'll have another attack! Maybe I'll get an attack!" You will if you think that way! For you're really thinking, again, "I must not get another attack! What an idiot I am if I get another attack!" Right?

Client: Yes.

Therapist: Well, let me explain to you in a little more detail how humans disturb them-selves—what they think and do to make themselves anxious and panicked. They don't get disturbed because of the happenings in their early childhood. That's largely psychoanalytic hogwash. They almost always needlessly dis-turb themselves by first listening to their nutty parents and, more important, taking the goals and standards they are taught and insisting that they absolutely have to live up to them, that they completely must do well. They are born with the tendency to "musturbate"; that's their nature. But they can teach themselves not to do so and mainly remain with their preferences. Let me give you a model of most neurotic disturbance, and I know you'll under-stand it. Suppose you go out of this building at the end of this session into the streets of New York, and you don't know how much money you have in your pocket. It could be a dollar or it could be $50,000. You're ignorant of how much you have. And the one and only thing you think to yourself is, "I wish, I'd like, I'd prefer to have in my pocket a minimum of $10. Not $100, not $200, just $10. I'd like to have $10 in my pocket because I might eat, take a cab, or go to a movie." Then you actually look in your pocket and you find $9, one less than $10. Now, how would you feel if you preferred $10 and had $9, one less? What would your feeling be?

Client: That I don't have enough of what I want.

Therapist: Yes, but how would you feel about not having enough of what you want? You'd like to have $10, but then you have $9, one less than $10.

Client: Slightly disappointed.

Therapist: Fine. That's a very appropriate feeling because we wouldn't want you to feel good about not having what you want.

Client: Yeah.

Therapist: OK. Now the second time you're going out, this time you're saying foolishly to yourself—you know it's foolish but you still say and believe it—"I must, I must, I must, at all times, at all times have a minimum guarantee of $10. I have to! I've got to! I must!" That's what you believe in your head. Then again, you look in your pocket and you find only $9 and you can't get the tenth. Now how would you feel?

Client: I would feel very upset.

Therapist: Yes, because of your must. It's the same $9, but this time, you're insisting that you absolutely must have it—and, of course, you don't. You see, we humans don't get upset by a bad condition that occurs in our lives. We only get upset—or upset ourselves—because of our musts. We take our preferences, our wishes, our desires and we often make them into absolute demands, musts, shoulds, oughts. That—your musts—would be what's upsetting you.

Client: I see. My musts.

Therapist: Now finally, the third time, you go out again and you're still saying to yourself the same thing as the second time: "I must at all times have a minimum guarantee of $10 in my pocket!" And you look in your pocket and this time you find $11—more than enough. Now how would you feel?

Client: I'd feel OK.

Therapist: That's right. But a minute later, something would occur to you to make you anxious. Now, why would you be anxious a minute later? First you say to yourself, "Great! I've got $11—more than enough!" Then something would occur to make you anxious. Now why would you become anxious a little later? You've still got the $11. You haven't lost it, and you haven't said, "I must have $12" or "I must have $13." You're still saying, "I must have a minimum of $10. Great, I've got $11!" Now what would make you anxious?

Client: Well, I—I don't really know.

Therapist: Well, don't forget: You're saying to yourself: "I must have a minimum of $10 at all times. I now have $11. But suppose I spend $2. Suppose I lose $2. Suppose I get robbed!' All of which could happen, you see, because there are no guarantees in the universe! They don't exist, and you're demanding one.

Client: Yes, I see. So I'm still anxious.

Therapist: Right! Now this model shows that anybody in the whole universe—and it doesn't matter what their status is, black or white, young or old, male or female, rich or poor—anybody who takes any desire, any goal, any preference for anything and makes it into a must, a "got to," first is miserable when they don't have what they must have; and second, they're anxious when they do have it—because they could always lose it. Now do you see how that applies to you?

Client: Yes, I do. Any must, any real demands.

Therapist: Yes, and you've got two main musts that make and keep making you anxious: (1) "I must do well; I must be perfect. I must do the right thing and not bring on a heart attack!" And (2) "I must not be anxious! I must not be panicked! I must not be panicked!" With these two musts, you're really going to be off the wall. You see?

Client: I never thought of that before.

Therapist: But can you see it now?

Client: Yes, I think I can.

Therapist: Fine. Now if we can just help you to think, "I don't like being anxious, but if I am, too damned bad, it won't kill me," you'll then get rid of your anxiety about your anxiety, your panic about your panic. If you can convince yourself that anxiety is uncomfortable, but it won't kill me—it won't lead to a heart attack, and it won't make me an idiot for bringing on my anxiety, it's just uncomfortable, it's not awful—then you'll get rid of most of your problem. Then, as you rid yourself of your anxiety about your anxiety, you can much more easily go back to your original perfectionism—your demand that you always do well and not make serious errors. Then you'll work on being less perfectionistic. You'll still very much want to do well, prefer to do well, but you'll give up the idea that you *have* to. There's no necessity, you see in doing well; no necessity for you to be unanxious.

Client: What is the best way to react—when you feel that stress is too strong? How can you overcome it?

Therapist: When you're anxious?

Client: Yes.

Therapist: You say to yourself very strongly, until you really mean it: ". . . So I'm anxious! It'll pass; it'll pass in a few minutes. It won't kill me. It won't turn my hair gray. It won't send me to the loony bin, nothing will happen if I'm anxious! Just go with the anxiety and relax." So you relax. You sit down and you relax. And you strongly tell yourself "Too damned bad—so I'm anxious. But it's not the end of the world." Anxiety won't kill you.

Client: Well, I know that. But—

Therapist: Well, you don't know that well enough. You're probably saying to yourself, "Yeah, it won't kill me. But maybe it will! Maybe it will. Maybe it will!" Then, you'll be more anxious!

Client: Yeah, I think that I need to be anxious to keep living, to stay alive.

Therapist: Well, you don't! You'd better accept the fact that at times we're all anxious, depressed, or upset. Too bad; tough; that's the way it is. That's the human condition—humans often make themselves anxious. But all you have to do is relax—do some deep breathing or other relaxation exercises. Do you know any relaxation exercises?

Client: Yes, I bought a tape the other day. I think I have it here. It shows how to breathe freely.

Therapist: What's it called? *How to Turn Stress into Energy.* That may be all right. If you really follow this tape, or one of our own relaxation tapes that you can get downstairs, then you'll learn to immediately relax, and your anxiety will temporarily go away. But if you go back to being a perfectionist and insist that you must do well, you must not be anxious, your anxiety will come back.

Client:	Someone told me that when you have great stress, if you do a lot of exercise, you can drain it out.
Therapist:	You can distract yourself and feel better. That will temporarily work. But you'd better also change your philosophy—that will work much better. You'd better do two things: (1) distract yourself with some exercise, then your anxiety will go away temporarily. But it will come back because you're still telling yourself, "I must do perfectly well. I must not be anxious! I must not be upset!" (2) You therefore had better change your attitude, as well as relax. Show yourself that you don't have to do that well and that your anxiety won't kill you. Relaxation alone will help, but it will not cure you. Changing your basic musturbatory philosophy will help you permanently.
Client:	So you have to do it physically and mentally?
Therapist:	Exactly! You have to do it physically and mentally. And you really have to tell yourself—and believe—"So what! If I'm anxious, I'm anxious. Too damned bad! This too will pass. And if I work on it and change my philosophy, I can make it rarely come back."
Client:	You see, that's what I'm trying to do in regard to the train. I think that my problem is that I think that if I have an attack on the train, it will be awful.
Therapist:	So suppose you do have an attack on the train? What's going to happen to you then?
Client:	Something will happen to me.
Therapist:	What?
Client:	Most of the time I've said to myself, "OK, nothing will happen. Because I know that whatever I have is not a heart problem—it's a mental problem, and I create it myself." So I then relax. But what's getting to me is that I have to deal with the same thing every day. Every day I have to deal with it.
Therapist:	I know. Because you're saying, "I must not be anxious! I must not be anxious!" Instead of, "I don't like being anxious, but if I am, I am!" You see, you're terrified of your own anxiety.
Client:	That's exactly what it is!
Therapist:	OK. But anxiety is only a pain in the neck. That's all it is. It doesn't kill you. It's only a pain. Everybody gets anxious, including you. And they live with it!
Client:	It's a big pain!
Therapist:	I know. But that's all it is. Just like—well, suppose you lost all the money you had with you. That would be a real pain, but you wouldn't worry about it too much because you know you'd get some more money. But you're making yourself terrified. "Something awful will happen. Suppose people see I'm so anxious! How terrible!" Well, suppose they do.
Client:	I don't care about that.

Therapist:	Well, that's good. Most people are afraid of that, and it's good that you're not.
Client:	When I walk to the train, I know that I am going to start feeling anxious.
Therapist:	You know it because you're afraid of it happening. If you said to yourself strongly and really believed—"So what! If it happens, it happens!"—then it won't even happen. Every time you say, "I must not be anxious! I must not be anxious!"—then you'll be anxious.

In the portion of the session presented above, Ellis practices the active-directive methodology he espouses. The client is continually confronted with his own irrational thinking, and Ellis proposes new alternative ways of thinking. Ellis uses didactic, experiential, and behavioral methods with the client. He eschews discussions of the origins of the client's beliefs; rather, he focuses on their irrationality and enlists the client in their elimination by logical disputation and behavioral change.

🔲 DISTINCTIVE FEATURES OF REBT

Ellis's REBT has several distinctive features. These are essentially philosophical propositions that differentiate REBT from most other psychotherapeutic techniques. Some of those that are particular to Ellis are presented below.

Absence of Self-Evaluation

A consistent feature of Ellis's vast body of writing is his rejection of the concept of self-esteem. As detailed earlier, he states that self-esteem requires us to continually rate and compare ourselves to others. Instead, he suggests that people avoid rating themselves altogether. Rather than maintaining an ongoing evaluation of the self, he proposes accepting our value as immutable and unchanging—that as sentient, existing human beings, we have a worth that does not ebb and flow according to our latest accomplishments or failures. Instead of evaluating ourselves, we should strive toward a state of unconditional self-acceptance. Ellis says that people who rate themselves invariably set themselves up for pain and disappointment. In contrast, he advocates working toward goals, improving social relationships, and minimizing neurotic reactions to life's vicissitudes.

Secondary Problems

Ellis notes that just as people make themselves emotionally disturbed by their views of life events, they can upset themselves about their very disturbance. He refers to this phenomenon as a secondary problem. He suggests that guilt is a prime example of such a secondary problem. Another is feeling shame about being ashamed—a vicious circle in which people with social phobias berate themselves for fearing shame or humiliation in social situations, thereby compounding the problem. Ellis's approach involves helping the individual accept these secondary flaws and deficits, as well as accept feelings of shame as a first step on the way to achieving well-being.

Discomfort Disturbance Versus Ego Disturbance

Ellis admonishes against people making global ratings of themselves. His theory holds that overall self-evaluation almost invariably leads to emotional dysfunction. He refers to this dysfunction from self-rating as ego disturbance. Notably, Ellis proposes an additional type of disturbance, which he refers to as discomfort disturbance. In discomfort disturbance, people create emotional dysfunction over their resistance to tolerating discomfort or sustained effort. Ellis refers to this as low frustration tolerance (LFT). LFT is a function of people's beliefs about their own adequacy, as when someone says, "I might as well give up, I am not capable or worthy of this task," or denies personal responsibility, as in saying, "I shouldn't have to work this hard." Ellis acknowledges that, indeed, sustained effort or some endeavors might indeed be more difficult for some people than for others, but their beliefs about this discomfort is what leads to both direct disturbance and secondary disturbances related to it.

Personality Change in REBT

REBT posits that human personality can change through prolonged and consistent effort alongside professional guidance to revise our beliefs or personal philosophy. In addition, Ellis proposes that consistent behavioral change will yield long-term changes to enduring traits like neuroticism or introversion. Such changes require thoroughgoing revision of a person's individual philosophy. Although Ellis repeatedly emphasized that the preponderance of personality is biological (e.g., Ellis, 1987; Ellis & Whitely, 1979), he proposed that a significant portion of a person's biological propensities can be altered by sustained effort. Ellis (1974) holds that people's innate predisposition to irrational thinking is a key element in personality and the reason why all people often behave in ways that are inefficient, self-defeating, or hurtful to others. Naturally, these are the aspects of personality that would be the most beneficial to change. To do so requires that people identify an aspect of their personal philosophy or belief system that is irrational. Having done so, they must continually dispute and challenge these philosophies or beliefs; if not, they tend to recur as a result of their innate nature. Thus, new rational beliefs that are developed through disputings must be maintained through committed effort. Using this method, even a person who is shy and fearful can learn to behave in an outgoing and serene manner through continual disputation of his or her irrational beliefs as they arise. Over time, Ellis posits, the effort required to sustain personality change may diminish, but it must be kept up to some extent for most of the person's life.

REBT Contrasted With Other Models

Ellis has criticized other clinical personality models for emphasizing the impact of early childhood on later development. He accepts that neurotic states are sometimes originally learned or aggravated by early teaching of irrational beliefs in a person's family and by society. He stresses, however, that these early-acquired irrationalities are not automatically sustained over time by the individual. In contrast, Ellis asserts that people must actively sustain and re-create their irrational belief. This position stands in stark contrast to that of the psychodynamic schools, which hold that by exposing the origins of emotional disturbances, the individual will discharge or release the repressed psychic energy and be freed from the neurotic behavior. Ellis requires a therapist to demonstrate that the client's basic approach to life is irrational, not to investigate when and how the client acquired it. Clients are presently disturbed because they still harbor a self-defeating view of self and world. If they will pay close attention to exactly what they are irrationally thinking in the present, and will challenge and question these self-statements, they will usually reduce their symptoms.

Ellis and his REBT place a strong emphasis on philosophical change at a deep level and an analytic or scientific style of thinking. It follows that Ellis believes that human neurotic disturbance is largely ideologically or philosophically based. This position stands in contrast to other theorists' positions that unconscious mechanisms or dysfunctional interpersonal relationships cause neurosis. Ellis accepts that sadness and regret are inevitable and healthy aspects of living when we are faced with genuine loss, deprivation, or rejection. As in the scientific method, clients are shown how to interrogate the questionable hypotheses that they construct about themselves and others. Similarly, when people perceive, sometimes correctly, that the acts of others were unfair or malicious and express anger toward their victimizers, Ellis suggests that they be shown how to control their anger and to explore their unspoken premise that these historical adversaries are intrinsically bad people. Instead, he suggests accepting them as fallible human beings who are neither evil nor bad, but people who in that circumstance acted badly.

In contrast to subsequent cognitive and cognitive behavior therapies, Ellis's REBT encourages the teaching of unconditional self-acceptance and the parallel acceptance that other people are fallible. The cognitive therapies of Aaron Beck, for example, seek to expose a client's cognitive distortions and automatic thoughts. Ellis points out, however, that very often clients will not be unthinkingly magnifying their problems or selectively abstracting the negative aspects of themselves or their situation. He states that people may very well be psychologically disturbed after accurately assessing very bad situations. His approach accepts the accuracy of their perceptions but challenges their philosophical interpretation of the event.

For example, in the case of a client undergoing a severe illness or the loss of a loved one, Ellis advocates acknowledging the magnitude of the adversity while all the while accepting it as part of life. By changing the way people characterize even the most painful life events, they will change the way they react emotionally to what happens. For example, dying people who focus obsessively on what will happen to them when they die will fail to make the most of the time they have left. Ellis counsels the dying to accept that while a shortened life is unfair, they can still dispute the belief that it is a direct assault on them and focus on the tasks or challenges facing them in the time they have left. This approach is supported by the range of reactions expressed by people facing virtually the same extreme adversity.

Studies of cancer patients' survival rates indicate that personality makes a difference in length of survival, as does participation in support groups (Siegel, 2001, 2003). Some patients diagnosed with cancer experience profound despair or rage whereas others show equanimity and acceptance. Ellis's theory holds that the explanation of the differences in attitude lies in the patients' beliefs and their resulting self-talk.

Ellis acknowledges that enlightenment about the sources of our emotions can sometimes be acquired by psychoanalytic therapies; however, he has strongly denied that this kind of enlightenment by itself is effective in diminishing neurosis or emotional disturbance. Instead, he stresses intellectual insight instead of the historical insight into emotions sought by psychoanalysts. A client's discovery of the historical origins of his or her neurosis can be fascinating, according to Ellis, but not curative. Intellectual maturation, however—in which clients discover that their current beliefs, philosophies, or attitudes conspire to cause misery and their concomitant discovery that they can argue against their illusory logic—is curative.

Ellis emphasizes the role of philosophy in his model, as he holds that neurotic disturbance is largely ideologically or philosophically based. As such, his REBT strives for a thoroughgoing philosophic reorientation of clients' outlook on life rather than a mere removal of any of their psychological symptoms. He advocates teaching people that most perceived needs are actually preferences; for example, the wish to be loved, or even accepted, despite its obvious desirability, is not a need. Similarly, Ellis encourages individuals to be healthily sad or regretful when they are rejected, frustrated, or deprived. He seeks to teach people to overcome feelings of intense hurt, self-deprecation, and depression. As in science, he wants clients to be shown how to question the questionable hypotheses that they construct about themselves and others. If they believe that they are worthless because they perform certain acts considered bad, they are taught to ask, "What is really bad about my acts?" and "Where is the evidence that they are wrong or unethical?"

He states that it is even more important that people be shown how to ask themselves, "Granted that my acts may be mistaken, why am I a totally bad person for performing them? Where is the evidence that I must always be right in order to consider myself worthy? Assuming that it is preferable for me to act well rather than badly, why do I have to do what is preferable?" His overarching goal is to teach people that to be human is to be fallible and that if people are to get on in life with minimal upset and discomfort, they would do better to accept this reality and then work hard—without anxiety—to become a little less fallible.

A final component of Ellis's psychotherapeutic approach is the use of psychological homework. He agrees with most Freudian, neo-Freudian, Adlerian, and Jungian schools that acquiring insight, especially so-called emotional insight, into the source of a neurosis can be an important part of people's corrective teaching, but he believes that such insight is far less important than the outcomes obtained by working in a determined and energetic manner to apply this knowledge to the solution of these problems. Ellis maintains that therapists should help clients to acknowledge that there is usually no other way to get better than by continually observing, questioning, and challenging their own belief systems and by working and practicing to change their own irrational beliefs by verbal and behavioral counter-propagandizing activity.

He prescribes actual homework assignments that are frequently agreed on in individual and group therapy. Assignments may include asking a person for a date in spite of fear of rejection; looking for a new job; experimentally returning to live with a husband with whom one has previously continually quarreled; and similar tasks. The therapist quite actively tries to encourage clients to undertake such assignments as an integral part of the therapeutic process.

▣ CRITICISMS OF ELLIS AND REBT

Albert Ellis has been a controversial figure throughout his career. Never hesitating to criticize opposing theories and theorists in very direct terms, he has predictably acquired numerous critics of his own. As is the case with theorists who are both prominent and controversial, his critics often confuse the individual and his work. That is, many people who have found Ellis's personal style confrontational or harsh have criticized his theories on the assumption that his theories and method of psychotherapy are inextricably linked to his personal style.

Throughout his career, he has endeavored to communicate his theories about personality and therapy to the general public as opposed to professional or academic audiences. This has resulted in a large lay following but cost him by not establishing a reputation in the academic community.

Also, in Ellis's attempts to reach a wider audience, he has given hundreds of in-person demonstrations of his therapy. Some have criticized these presentations for being histrionic or strident, and then they have drawn the erroneous conclusion that his theory and psychotherapy must be similarly flawed. Specifically, some have criticized REBT as being harsh, formulaic, or overly directive. By extension, many have falsely concluded that Ellis's approach is superficial and fails to address "deep" or "underlying" problems. A careful reading of his work cogently refutes this misperception. His psychotherapy is humanistic and individualized. In addition, recent research into the cognitive unconscious has supported his premise that psychotherapy cannot address unconscious processes, as they are largely biological and nonverbal. He has pointed out that his use of behavioral methods is the only way to address issues of nonconscious functioning.

Some, like the radical constructivists, have taken Ellis to task for operating with a vague or arbitrary definition of rationality. These critics suggest that there is nothing that is inherently rational but that reason and logic are subjective properties of the individual and cannot be imposed by a system of psychotherapy. Those who accept that reason can be objectively determined have stated that REBT fails to base its judgments of rationality on sufficient evidence. These do not appear to be valid criticisms, as Ellis requires that practitioners of REBT should raise objections to a client's irrational choice or conclusion as a working hypothesis and, with that client's collaboration, demonstrate the irrationality of the client's notions on functional, social consensual, or practical grounds.

Ellis has long maintained that the first step in psychotherapy is to establish a collaborative alliance, with the therapist expressing an understanding of the client's point of view. Only after this working alliance is established is the therapist to challenge any of the client's beliefs, values, attitudes, or philosophies. Ellis has always used *rational* and *irrational* in the context of a practical social consensus. That is, rational acts are those that produce consistently positive outcomes in life.

Ellis has been criticized for moral relativism, as he has maintained that there need be no higher purpose in life than responsible hedonism. He has, however, always advocated social responsibility because that is the wisest and most efficient long-term strategy. He completely rejects any absolutes in terms of moral right or wrong. Despite this, he has pointed out that his approach is not incompatible with any theological or moral system. He notes that accepting our human frailty and vulnerability is far from an automatic endorsement of immoral or antisocial behavior. He likens himself to the Christian who rejects the sin while accepting the sinner. Overall, his most enduring caveat is the avoidance of rigid or absolute thinking but not rejection of spiritual or religious commitments as such.

Those with a more experimental orientation have criticized Ellis for not being sufficiently empirically based. This criticism is partially valid, in that Ellis founded his model of personality and psychotherapy on the basis of his own observations and induction. In addition, he has strongly endorsed science as a means to validate or invalidate his models whenever possible. As was mentioned earlier in the chapter, one of his first efforts after originating his rational psychotherapy was to perform a clinical outcome study. One of his fundamental premises has been to be always open to challenges. Ellis asserts that he has always been open to being proven wrong and has openly acknowledged any errors in his theories and practices.

🔲 CHAPTER SUMMARY

Albert Ellis began his career as a sex therapist and evolved into the first therapist applying what today would be called cognitive behavior therapy. Ellis views personality as the result of the dynamic interaction of perceptions, emotions, cognitions, and actions. His REBT model, therefore, does not view emotions as being distinct from thought, behavior, or even physical activity. Instead, the person is the whole that results from the interaction of these components of being. Consequently, psychological problems must be addressed by helping the person with all four of these processes.

According to Ellis, personality is predicated primarily on a person's style of self-talk. Of course, such other factors as sensitivity to arousal, perceptual style, and intelligence all play roles, but self-talk is the defining factor. Self-talk, rational or irrational, sustains or suppresses emotions, enhances or depletes motivation, and is the regulating force behind most human behavior. The core of Ellis's method is derived from this premise—that is, people create their own feelings and actions through their beliefs. These beliefs are prone to be irrational because human thinking is guided by an evolutionary development that began in settings quite different from those of recent times. The environmental settings of early humans favored people who were demanding, absolutistic, and fiercely competitive. Therefore, most of us still harbor these proclivities despite far more complex and forgiving social and cultural settings. Irrational thinking leads to illusory needs for social approval, punishment for adversaries we have never met, status, and the like. Ellis does not state that wanting these things is problematic but that elevating them to needs and demands leads to emotional and personality dysfunction.

He presents what is an ultimately optimistic view of humanity. Despite his theory of universal and innate irrationality, he also strongly proposes that people can overcome this tendency through repeated decisions and acts of will. They can learn, according to Ellis, new and more effective beliefs that will supplant the old less functional beliefs. Ellis believes that the pursuit of pleasure and the consequent desire to live happily will ultimately assist people in accepting rationality and fulfilling their potential. His ABC model of thinking and therapy is profound in its simplicity. Through it, Ellis states that people can learn to regulate their own behavior despite powerful innate or genetic tendencies. People, according to Ellis, are composed of biological impulses and tendencies, learned behaviors, and styles of thinking. Nonetheless, the person exists as a whole, a gestalt of all the subordinate parts, which is greater than the sum of its parts. Ellis asserts that this gestalt endows the individual with a will or free agency that can overcome, sometimes with external help, the problems that some of the individual's components present.

His method requires that people be made aware that they have a personal philosophy, a set of beliefs, and attitudes that are the foundation of all their emotions. The more complex or social the emotion, the more it is based on the individual's beliefs. Once aware of the beliefs, Ellis says that the individual must learn to disavow those that are irrational in the sense that they lead to inefficient or self-harming behaviors or emotions. By strongly disputing those beliefs that are found to be irrational, people, if assiduous in their efforts, can effectively reshape portions of their personality.

NOTE

1. Rational Therapy was Ellis's first name for his approach, which is now called Rational Emotive Behavior Therapy or REBT.

Chapter 17

Religious, New Age, and Traditional Approaches to Personality

Chapter Goals

- To acquire a basic understanding of several different alternative approaches to personality theory and psychotherapy

- To be able to situate each of these approaches within a general outline of world history

- To compare these alternative approaches with the major schools of personality theory discussed in earlier chapters and to identify both similarities and differences

Up to this point, the authors of this book have concentrated on mainstream Western approaches to personality theory, particularly those that developed in the 19th and 20th centuries. This chapter will introduce the reader to alternative approaches that psychologists in North America are likely to encounter in the 21st century in the course of research or clinical practice. These approaches include a variety of different systems of thought, ranging from Asian and Native American medical systems dating back several millennia to mainstream Christianity (and Judaism) to New Age beliefs. These alternative approaches have become more widespread in both Canada and the United States since the 1960s, partly as a result of immigrants from China and India bringing their traditional medical systems with them, partly because of growing disillusionment with Western science and medicine, and partly because of increased interest in holistic or integrative medicine and psychotherapy.

▣ TRADITIONAL MEDICAL SYSTEMS

Ayurveda

Ayurveda or Ayurvedic medicine is the traditional medical system of India, in use for thousands of years. Its name comes from two Sanskrit words meaning "knowledge of life." Ayurveda is classified by the National Center for Complementary and Alternative Medicine (NCCAM) as an alternative medical system because it is based on a set of theories about health, illness, and treatment; it is not simply a collection of isolated practices without an underlying rationale.

Ayurveda is based on Hinduism and on ancient religious notions from Persia; however, a person does not have to be a Hindu to become a practitioner of Ayurvedic medicine or to consult one. About half the population of India still makes use of Ayurveda, particularly in rural areas. A survey taken by NCCAM in 2004 found that about 750,000 people in the United States have tried Ayurveda at some point, and more than 150,000 had used it within the previous 12 months (NCCAM, 2007).

Origins

Ayurveda is thought to have originated around 3500 BCE in northern India and is considered the oldest medical system in the world in continuous use (Pelletier, 2002). It was the medical system used and recommended by Gautama Buddha (c. 500 BCE), who supported the study of Ayurvedic medicine (Svoboda & Lade, 1995). Traditionally, Ayurveda was attributed to a divine revelation from Brahma, the Hindu creator god, who passed it down to other deities and then to human sages or gurus. The principles and practice of Ayurveda were handed down orally from gurus to their students for some centuries; the oldest written texts are about 3,000 years old.

Even in ancient times, students of Ayurveda were required to train for a period of 7 years and pass an examination before being licensed to practice (Svoboda & Lade, 1995). Practitioners were required to adopt a lifestyle of chastity, vegetarianism, and honesty; to avoid the use of alcohol and drugs; to dress modestly; to keep patient confidentiality; to continue studying and improving their skills; and to focus on each patient's welfare at all times. This code of ethics is similar in several respects to the principles expressed in another ancient code of good practice for physicians, the Hippocratic oath.

The primary texts of Ayurvedic medicine are the *Charaka Samhitā*, a treatise on internal medicine compiled about 1000 BCE, and the *Susruta Samhitā*, a book on surgery written by Susruta, an eminent ancient surgeon, about 600 BCE. These two treatises contain discussions of medical ethics and nursing as well as descriptions of diseases, diagnostic techniques, and treatments.

Basic Beliefs

Ayurveda is considered a holistic approach to treatment; that is, it considers people as having three basic dimensions—body, mind, and spirit—that should be kept in proper balance (similar to the Western concept of homeostasis) to maintain psychological well-being and prevent physical illness. It does, however, also prescribe specific treatments for physical or emotional disorders. A distinctive characteristic of Ayurvedic medicine is its emphasis on cleansing the body of substances believed to cause disease and cleansing the mind of anger, fear, envy, and other negative emotions that interfere with emotional stability and healthy relationships with other people (Chopra & Doiphode, 2002).

Some of the core beliefs underlying Ayurvedic medicine are as follows:

- Human beings are part of the universe and made up of the same five elements as the rest of the universe. These Five Great Elements are earth, water, fire, air, and ether (the source of all matter and the space in which it exists).
- All people are born in a condition of basic balance within themselves and in harmony with the rest of the universe.
- This state of balance can be disrupted by life processes and events. The disruptions may be physical, emotional, spiritual, or a combination of these.
- People become susceptible to physical disease or mental disorders when they lose their inner balance or are out of harmony with the universe.

Ayurvedic Practices

Ayurvedic medicine has eight major branches, sometimes referred to as the eight-armed Ayurveda or Ashtanga Ayurveda. The eight branches are internal medicine; surgery; eye, ears, nose, and throat; pediatrics; toxicology; purification of the male and female sex organs; health and longevity; and spiritual care/psychiatry.

Because the focus of treatment in Ayurveda is restoring people to harmony with themselves and with the universe, diagnosis is different from the usual Western pattern. The Ayurvedic practitioners will try to determine a patient's constitution, or **prakriti**, from observation of the patient's general appearance, facial expression, body build, skin condition, gait, and so on. Although practitioners do not take samples of body fluids for laboratory tests, they will examine a sample of the patient's urine for color and smell, believing that the patient's prakriti will be influenced by digestion and other body functions. Practitioners will also look closely at the patient's teeth and tongue for discoloration or other irregularities that may provide clues to the condition of the prakriti, and they will take three pulses on each wrist. The three pulses correspond to the three **doshas,** or basic qualities that are present in all things, including the human body. The **tridosha system** and the specific *doshas* will be further described in the section on personality below.

In addition to examining the patient's body, Ayurvedic practitioners will take an extensive history of the patient's family, social life, personal history, diet and nutrition, most recent illnesses, and other aspects of his or her present environment.

The treatments given by Ayurvedic practitioners reflect the holistic approach of this form of traditional medicine. The basic purposes of these treatments are to eliminate impurities from the body through perspiration or the digestive tract; lower patients' stress level and increase emotional harmony in their life; and restore psychological as well as physical balance:

- *Poorvakarma. Poorvakarma* is a 3-to-7-day preparatory regimen that involves taking herbal medicines and receiving a form of therapeutic massage intended to help the patient release toxins stored in the joints and muscles as well as to relieve joint pain, lower stress, and improve the patient's quality of sleep.

- *Panchakarma*. *Panchakarma* is an intensive program of digestive detoxification that lasts for 1 or 2 weeks and includes the use of laxatives, induced vomiting, medicated enemas, sweat baths, therapeutic massage, and cleansing of the nasal passages. Traditionally, *panchakarma* included bloodletting, which is sometimes done through donation to a blood bank (Pelletier, 2002).
- *Shaman*. Sometimes called "palliation" in English, *shaman* is a form of treatment that emphasizes spiritual healing. It can be used as preventive health care and also as a form of treatment for those who are too ill or frail to undergo *panchakarma*. *Shaman* includes gentle yoga stretches, fasting, breathing exercises, and sunbathing for limited periods of time.
- *Basayana*. This is considered a rejuvenation treatment and follows detoxification. The patient performs yoga and breathing exercises and takes herbal medicines intended to restore vitality.
- *Satvajaya*. *Satvajaya* is a form of psychotherapy intended to reduce stress and calm the patient's mind. Patients spend time in meditation and are given mantras to chant to change their mental patterns (or what George Kelly would term their personal constructs).

In addition to being holistic, Ayurveda's view of human psychology is idiographic rather than nomothetic; that is, it emphasizes the uniqueness of each person. Thus, treatments are tailored to the prakriti of the individual patient and his or her combination of the *doshas*.

Theory of Personality

The Tridosha *System.* The basic principle underlying the Ayurvedic theory of personality is the *tridosha* system. Ayurveda holds that three essential qualities, the *doshas*, are present in all things, including human bodies and psyches. The three *doshas* represent combinations of the Five Great Elements; the relative proportion of the *doshas* in a person determines that person's body type and unique personality characteristics. The body types governed by the three *doshas* are similar to the three somatotypes described by William Sheldon (see Chapter 7).

The first *dosha* is *vata*, which is a combination of ether and air. It is the dominant *dosha* in people who are active, restless, and unpredictable. The second *dosha* is *pitta*, a combination of fire and water that typifies people who are temperamental, inclined to anger, and highly organized. The third *dosha*, *kapha*, is a compound of earth and water, and predominates in people who are sluggish, inclined to overweight, and stable in temperament. According to practitioners of Ayurveda, it is rare for a person to be constituted by only one *dosha*; most people are combinations of two or all three. Keeping the *doshas* in balance is the key to good health and long life, and most Ayurvedic interventions—particularly those related to nutrition and exercise—are intended to restore this balance.

In addition to influencing body type and personality, the *doshas* are also associated with specific parts of the body, seasons of the year, time of day, and phases of the human life cycle. These are summarized in Table 17.1.

Treatment of Emotional and Personality Disorders. An Ayurvedic practitioner begins with the assumption that each patient is unique; therefore, even though the person's constitution and the relative proportion of each *dosha* in it will be evaluated, the practitioner tailors the treatments intended to balance the three *doshas* to the individual. For example, two people whose prakritis are basically *pitta/kapha* combinations and need to have their *vata dosha* strengthened may have

Table 17.1   The Three Doshas in Ayurvedic Medicine

Association	*Dosha*		
	Vata	*Pitta*	*Kapha*
Basic elements	Ether and air	Fire and water	Earth and water
Body build (somatotype)	Tall and slender	Medium build	Heavy; tendency toward overweight
Hair	Dry, coarse, curly	Fine, light in color, often straight; goes gray early	Lustrous, thick, and oily
Eye color	Gray or violet	Blue, green, or hazel	Brown, occasionally blue
Function within the body	Movement and activity	Digestion of food and other metabolic processes	Physical stability and lubrication of joints and organs
Activity level/habits	Moves/works quickly and hastily; restless; wasteful	Moves/works with moderate speed; well-organized and efficient	Slow-moving; tends to accumulate or hoard
Sleep and digestion	Irregular	Regular	Digests slowly; sleeps easily and deeply
Psychological traits	Anxious, erratic, alert, restless, easily bored, moody	Irritable, temperamental, aggressive, sarcastic	Calm, stubborn, stable, tends to procrastinate
Emotional disorders	Fear and anxiety-related disorders	Angers easily	Tends toward depression, avoidance, and dependence
Memory and cognition	Learns quickly; forgets quickly	Learns quickly; forgets slowly	Learns slowly; forgets slowly
Body organs	Large intestine, pelvis, skin, ears, thighs	Small intestine, stomach, sweat glands, blood, eyes	Chest, lungs, spinal fluid, mouth, kidneys
Time of day/seasons of the year	Evening, summer	Midday, autumn, and late spring	Morning, winter, and early spring
Human life cycle	Old age	Adulthood	Childhood and adolescence
Climate and weather preferences	Prefers warm climates and seasons	Prefers cool climates and seasons	Enjoys seasonal changes

SOURCE: Based on Svoboda and Lade (1995) and Pelletier (2002).

developed their imbalances for very different reasons; the proportion of *pitta* and *kapha* in their constitutions may vary considerably, with one person having a 60/40 proportion and the other 80/20; and the climates in which they live, their family situations, their daily schedules, their nutritional patterns, and their recent medical histories may also be very different.

Ayurvedic programs in the United States typically treat psychological disorders with a combination of nutritional evaluation, therapeutic massage, heat treatments, and mild herbal enemas. Clients are instructed in meditation techniques, yoga workouts designed for their specific issues, and dietary regimens intended to correct nutritional deficiencies—all of these to be used after they return home to maintain good health. Tranquilizers, antidepressants, and similar psychotropic medications are not used.

Research

According to Dr. Kenneth Pelletier, the former director of the program in complementary and alternative medicine at the medical school of Stanford University, Ayurveda is one of the least researched traditional systems of medicine. This has been the result in part of language barriers, as well as the fact that Western researchers tend to focus on individual drugs or methods of therapy when conducting clinical trials, which makes it difficult to evaluate a holistic system of medicine tailored to each individual (Pelletier, 2002). Much of the recent research carried out in India concerns the application of Western methods of chemical analysis to the herbal products used in Ayurveda.

Clinical research on Ayurveda has been encouraged by the government of India since 1969, when its Ministry of Health and Family Welfare established the Central Council for Research in Ayurveda and Siddha (CCRAS). Much of this research, however, does not meet the World Health Organization's standards for clinical studies. In the United States, NCCAM (2007) has stated that "most clinical trials of Ayurvedic approaches have been small, had problems with research designs, lacked appropriate control groups, or had other issues that affected how meaningful the results were" (p. 7). NCCAM itself, as of 2007, was sponsoring two clinical trials of Ayurvedic medicine, including three herbal formulas under investigation at the University of Arizona and an Ayurvedic medicine that may be useful in the treatment of Parkinson's disease at the Cleveland Clinic.

Indian physicians agree that more research is necessary to establish the safety and effectiveness of Ayurvedic herbal preparations as part of the system of medicine. An article published in the *Journal of the American Medical Association* in 2004 reported that 20% of Ayurvedic herbal medicines purchased at various stores in the Boston area contained potentially harmful levels of heavy metals (lead, mercury, and arsenic) (Saper et al., 2004). Since the early 2000s, clinical pharmacologists in India have been calling for increased safety testing of Ayurvedic formulations: "We still have a long way to go. The conflict between the traditional practitioners and the purists demanding evidence of safety and efficacy needs to be addressed" (Gogtay, Bhatt, Dalvi, & Kshirsagar, 2002, p. 1018).

Critiques

The basic critique of Ayurveda as practiced in the United States is that it is difficult for people interested in it as an approach to psychology in general or personality theory in particular to conduct rigorous clinical studies. Ayurveda has the smallest number of trained practitioners of any medical system in the United States as of 2007. A few hundred American physicians trained in mainstream Western medicine have studied Ayurveda, some naturopaths have also studied it, and there are Indian physicians trained in Ayurveda as well as Western medicine who have come to the United States to practice. The present Indian system of training in Ayurveda requires a minimum of 5 years to complete. There are as of 2007 no licensing standards in the United States, although several organizations of Ayurvedic practitioners are in the process of drawing up certification standards. NCCAM (2007) recommends that anyone interested in Ayurveda should inquire about the practitioner's training and experience.

Relatively little contemporary research has been done on Ayurveda as an intervention in psychological disorders, even though it has been used for centuries in India to treat depression (Rao, 2000). Studies of Ayurveda in elderly patients diagnosed with depression (Krishnamurthy & Telles, 2007) and cardiovascular patients with anxiety (Mamtani & Mamtani, 2005) indicate that the most effective part of the Ayurvedic program in treating emotional disturbance is the yoga exercises, including yogic breathing.

Traditional Chinese Medicine

Traditional Chinese medicine, or TCM, is a medical system whose earliest written records date back to 200 BCE; however, its practice dates back several millennia before that time. Like Ayurveda, TCM is considered a complete medical system with its own set of theories about health and disease as well as specific practices. As of 2007, TCM is used by a quarter of the world's population, including 12 million to 15 million people in the United States. Although TCM is based on a combination of religious concepts derived from Confucianism, Taoism, and Buddhism, it is not necessary to follow any of these faith traditions to practice TCM or to consult a TCM practitioner.

TCM resembles Ayurveda in several respects: It is based on a holistic view of the relationship between body and mind or psyche; it emphasizes the importance of preventive health care as well as the treatment of disease; it regards the universe as an energy system with human beings as smaller centers of energy who should live in harmony with the larger whole; and its treatments are highly individualized. While TCM, like Ayurveda, makes use of therapeutic massage, herbal formulations, and dietary adjustments in the treatment of illness, it also has some unique treatment modalities:

- *Acupuncture.* Acupuncture is a technique in which thin needles are inserted at various points along meridians, or energy channels in the body, to stimulate or redirect the patient's life force or qi.
- *Moxibustion.* Moxibustion is a technique in which an herb called mugwort *(Artemisia vulgaris)* is beaten to a fluffy fibrous mass, formed into a wick, and then lit a few inches away from the patient's skin to warm it before acupuncture.
- *Qigong.* Qigong is a form of energy therapy that combines body movements, breathing exercises, and meditation. It is used as a form of preventive medicine in TCM.
- *Martial arts* and *tai chi.*
- *Chinese astrology* as a form of psychotherapy.

Origins

TCM is thought to have developed out of tribal folk medicine and **shamanism** as they were practiced in ancient China. According to legend, an emperor named Shen Nong, who lived about 3490 BCE, introduced agriculture to his people and investigated the medicinal properties of various herbs (Reid, 1994, p. 10). The earliest textbook of TCM, the so-called *Yellow Emperor's Inner Classic*, was compiled around 200 BCE. The *Inner Classic*, which is still used in Chinese schools of traditional medicine, is a treatise that discusses a variety of religious and philosophical traditions as well as shamanic healing, human anatomy, theories about the circulation of blood, and various diseases and their treatments. "The ancient authors [of the *Inner Classic*] clearly felt no need to synthesize all the various traditions, or to propagate just one doctrine. Their effort was rather to attempt to reconcile opposing interpretations. This inclusion of sometimes antagonistic views and approaches is an early and enduring trait of Chinese medicine" (Svoboda & Lade, 1995, p. 10).

Basic Beliefs

The basic beliefs underlying TCM were enunciated by Lao Tzu (also transliterated as Laozi or Lao Tse), the possibly legendary founder of Taoism, and by Confucius (551–479 BCE), China's revered moral teacher. According to tradition, Lao Tzu wrote the central document of Taoism, the *Tao Te Ching* (*The Book of the Way and Its Virtue*) around the 6th century BCE; however, its actual date of composition is debated by modern scholars.

The *Tao Te Ching* opens with a poetic description of the Tao (usually translated as "way" or "path") as an ineffable first principle, the source of all reality, which goes beyond all human conceptual distinctions and contains both active and passive principles within itself. Later interpreters of the *Tao Te Ching* formulated a dualistic theory of nature based on one of the sayings attributed to Lao Tzu: "The Tao gave birth to the One, the One gave birth to Two, the Two gave birth to Three, and Three gave birth to the ten thousand things; the ten thousand things carry Yin and embrace Yang and through their blending of forces they achieve harmony" (*Tao Te Ching*, Chapter 42, sentence 1). In other words, the Tao was understood as the right path or way within the proper order and harmony of the universe. "Along that path the two basic expressions of the Tao lay locked in their perpetual embrace—the positive, active, and even aggressive yang, and the negative, passive, receptive yin, their correlation and balance determining the universal order" (Reid, 1994, p. 12). This notion of balance was reflected in traditional Chinese medicine's use of food as medicine: Foods are chosen for therapeutic qualities as well as for nutrition and are categorized as "cold" or "hot" and additionally classified according to their flavors in order to regulate both mind and body according to the individual's needs.

The physician's task is understood as keeping yin and yang in balance and harmony (a kind of homeostasis) as well as maintaining a smooth flow of vital energy within the specific patient's body and mind. "Taoism encourages cooperative work with all aspects of mental, emotional, physical, and spiritual health to promote a long, peaceful life" (Hagen, 2002, p. 174).

What Confucius added to the Taoist concept of a universal order based on the balance and harmony of two opposing forces was a moral or ethical dimension. Human beings are responsible for practicing the Five Virtues (benevolence, justice, wisdom, sincerity, and proper conduct) in order to keep the universe in moral balance.

In addition to the Tao and the opposing principles of yin and yang, TCM also posits the existence of **qi** (sometimes spelled chi), understood as vital energy or the life principle, and the Five Elements, which represent various phases in the eternal cycle of yin and yang. Qi travels through the body through the system of meridians (energy channels), and disease can be understood as the result of blocked or unbalanced qi.

The Five Elements are fire, earth, metal, water, and wood: in their endless cycle, fire turns into earth; earth turns into metal; metal turns into water; water turns into wood; wood turns into fire. The five elements are reflected in the various seasons of the year, the organs of the human body, and various dimensions of human personality.

Diagnosis

The process of diagnosis in TCM is similar to that in Ayurveda, in that the practitioner scrutinizes the patient's outward appearance, including the smell of the breath, the appearance of the tongue, the texture of the patient's skin as well as its color, and the quality of the patient's voice. The practitioner will also take the patient's family health history and personal health history. As in Ayurveda, the patient's pulse is taken more than once, although in TCM it is taken at six locations and three depths on each wrist. In TCM, the human pulse is considered to have 28 different qualities (slow, tense, thin, etc.) that reveal the condition of the patient's qi. The TCM practitioner will then examine the patient's muscles and joints to locate the diagnostic points along the energy **meridians** in the patient's body (Pelletier, 2002, p. 119). These points will be used if acupuncture is part of the patient's treatment.

The TCM practitioner will evaluate the patient's condition according to the Eight Guiding Principles, which consist of four pairs of opposites: yin and yang; interior and exterior; cold and heat; and deficiency or excess. The yin/yang dichotomy denotes the general character of the patient's disease. For example, diseases that produce high fevers or are associated with summertime heat are generally considered yang diseases, whereas those that produce chills in the patient or are associated with cold or damp weather are usually classified as yin diseases. Interior/exterior refers to the depth of the disease's activity within the body. Yang diseases are those that affect the part of the body above the waist and the superficial layers of skin and connective tissue; the lower part of the body and its inner structures are considered yin. Deficiency/excess refers to the state of the patient's qi in comparison to the strength of the disease. Therapy consists of treating yang diseases with yin remedies (such as sour, bitter, or salty foods or medicines) whereas yin diseases are treated with yang remedies (hot, warm, pungent, sweet, or bland foods or medications).

Theory of Personality

Basic Concepts of Emotional Health in TCM. The concepts of emotional health and a balanced personality in traditional Chinese medicine are largely derived from its Taoist component. The following is a summary of these basic concepts (Marin, 2006, pp. 4–5):

- The mind and body cannot be separated. That is, physical symptoms have an emotional dimension and a specific emotional charge.
- Emotions are not rational. They cannot be "solved" but must be digested and outgrown.
- Emotions are carried in the body as energetic charges that must be processed physically.

Table 17.2   The Five Elements in Traditional Chinese Medicine

	Fire	*Earth*	*Metal*	*Water*	*Wood*
Season	Summer	Late summer	Autumn	Winter	Spring
Direction	South	Center	West	North	East
Growth pattern	Active growth	Transformation	Maturation	Decay/storage	Germination
Colors	Red, purple	Orange, gold, yellow	White, silver, blue-gray	Deep blue, turquoise	Green, brown
Planet	Mars	Saturn	Venus	Mercury	Jupiter
Taste	Bitter	Sweet	Pungent	Salty	Sour
Climate/ weather	Heat	Dampness	Dryness	Cold	Wind
Yin body organ	Heart	Spleen	Lung	Kidneys	Liver
Yang body organ	Small intestine	Stomach	Large intestine	Bladder	Gallbladder
Sense organ	Tongue	Mouth	Nose	Ears	Eyes
Body fluid	Sweat	Saliva	Stool	Urine and reproductive fluids	Tears
External body feature	Facial color	Lips	Skin and body hair	Teeth and head hair	Nails
Positive emotions	Joy and happiness	Satisfaction and comfort	Courage, honesty, and pride	Gentleness, caring	Kindness and generosity
Negative emotions	Rage, hatred	Worry and anxiety	Sadness and depression	Fear, terror	Anger, aggression
Character virtue	Humility	Faithfulness	Fairness	Wisdom	Kindness
Mental aspect	Wisdom, guidance, spirit	Cleverness, practicality	Emotional maturity, elegance, sensitivity	Creativity, instinct, vision	Intelligence, problem-solving

Table 17.2 (Continued)					
	Fire	*Earth*	*Metal*	*Water*	*Wood*
Fields of study	Religion, philosophy	Geography, earth science	Fine and performing arts	History	Science
Occupations	Medicine, nursing, religious service, teaching	Farming, engineering, construction work, architecture, restaurant and hotel work	Fashion and design, tailoring, interior decoration, landscaping, public relations	Finance, banking, real estate, retail sales, travel and tourism	Administration, politics, law and law enforcement, civil service, military, consulting, research and development

SOURCE: Based on Svoboda and Lade (1995) and Pelletier (2002).

- Healing can take place only in the presence of conscious awareness.
- Healing is determined by spirit, which can be defined as a sense of guidance and connection with a reason for being alive.

The Five Elements and Human Personality. In TCM, as is summarized in Table 17.2, each of the five elements in Taoist cosmology represents a specific dimension of the mind and emotions. In terms of mental powers, fire represents wisdom and guidance; earth represents cleverness and practical "know-how"; metal symbolizes sensitivity, elegance, and emotional maturity; water represents creativity and instinct; and wood symbolizes problem-solving abilities and what most Westerners mean by intelligence. In the mentally healthy person, wisdom manifests itself as practicality and nurturing; nurturing produces sensitivity and awareness of one's feelings; emotional sensitivity and receptiveness leads to vision and inspiration; vision and inspiration turn to study, research, and the pursuit of knowledge; knowledge in turn becomes wisdom and nourishes the spirit (Marin, 2006, p. 77).

Each element is also associated with two or three positive emotions and two or three negative emotions, as noted in Table 17.2. The positive emotions are experienced when a person's qi is abundant or flowing smoothly, and the negative emotions take over when qi is deficient or blocked (Marin, 2006, p. 75). The terms *positive* and *negative* do not imply a moral judgment about the feelings; they are simply markers of the quality of the energetic charge. Personality traits can also be understood as excesses or deficiencies of one of the five elements; for example, a person who suffers from chronic anxiety has excessive (or destabilized) earth, whereas a fearful person has uncontrolled water. Excessive fire leads to an impatient personality, whereas too much wood results in chronic anger. Too much metal produces depression.

In terms of psychiatric disorders, TCM generally distinguishes two major types: yin types, considered more chronic and characterized by withdrawal, passivity, and antisocial behavior; and yang types, considered more acute and associated with rapid movement, agitation, aggression, and violence. In some cases, psychiatric disturbances are attributed to loss of equilibrium among the 10 key internal organs. For example, the dizziness that indicates panic disorder in DSM-IV's nosology is attributed by TCM practitioners to disturbances in one of the yin or yang body organs listed in Table 17.2 as well as lack of harmony or stability in the patient's social or family situation (Park & Hinton, 2002).

Treatment of personality disorders or psychiatric disturbances in TCM is based on the notion that deficiencies or excesses in the person's energy system must be corrected and balanced. **Acupuncture** is a common treatment modality, as are **moxibustion**, dietary adjustment, Chinese herbal remedies, and recommendation of certain types of exercise regarded as suitable for a particular condition. One practitioner of TCM treating adolescents with schizophrenia gave the youths specific Chinese medicines intended to transform phlegm (the body fluid involved in the disorder), moderate the element of fire, open the orifices of the body, and quiet the patient's spirit. He then gave the patients one treatment of acupuncture per day along the meridians associated with mania and chaotic behavior, applying moxibustion at each point for 3 minutes (Wolfe, 2004). Some TCM practitioners use various herbal medicines to treat such conditions as senile dementia (Meng et al., 2005).

In general, a personality issue related to any of the five elements will be treated by selective use of the element regarded as the problem element's natural corrective. To treat anger, for example, the TCM practitioner will suggest activities or practices related to metal, which is the element that controls wood, the element underlying anger. The following is a sample set of recommendations for "treating the pattern of anger":

Anger is Wood, and therefore, can only grow and grow. Anger is a Yang emotion, very hot, consistent, superficial, and powerful. It is at the surface of things and generally protects us from more deeply-seated negative feelings such as sadness, grief, fear, and terror that can rob us of our power. Anger is then an emotion that needs to be treated with respect because it is the ultimate protection against depression.

To outgrow anger, in Taoist terms, we need to "sharpen and polish our [metal] sword." This consists of breathing more fully and getting in touch with feelings and emotions. It takes strength to be sensitive. [Practice] breathing exercises daily, listening to music, and even studying music. . . . Also spending more time on personal grooming, or getting into design, home décor, antiques, and spending more time refining yourself.

If you have a chronic state of anger, and are in a Wood profession such as legal, political, or civic [work], military, or law enforcement, it is advisable to make a change of profession toward Metal activities such as advertising, design, fashion, and landscaping. (Marin, 2006, p. 81)

Research

Most research in the West involving TCM has focused on specific techniques or treatment modalities used in TCM (Chinese herbal formulae, acupuncture, qigong, dietary therapy, and the like) rather than the system as a whole. In the United States, acupuncture is the most widely used TCM therapy, with massage growing in popularity. Chinese herbal medicines are used less frequently, partly because unlike acupuncture, their cost is not covered by most health insurance plans (Pelletier, 2002).

A major difficulty in evaluating research done on TCM is the difference between Chinese and Western philosophical assumptions about research:

> TCM clinicians, for example, prefer to use complex individualized combinations of herbal ingredients. Also, they consider it unethical to give an ineffective placebo to a patient who is suffering. When they do use placebos, they object to randomization of patients in clinical studies, because they feel that patients should have the right to choose whether they will receive the treatment or the placebo. . . . Chinese double-blind studies generally compare two agents that are both presumed to be effective. TCM clinicians also tend to believe that Western research relies too heavily on laboratory test results, and not enough on the patient's relief of symptoms and the quality of life. (Pelletier, 2002, p. 129)

As with Ayurveda, TCM's description of health or diseases in terms of energy patterns unique to the individual (rather than symptom clusters identified with a particular disease or mental disorder) also complicates the recruitment of subjects for clinical trials. One positive aspect of the TCM approach, however, is that Chinese herbal formulae and acupuncture have relatively few side effects precisely because they are chosen to fit the individual's symptom pattern and biorhythms. In contrast to Western pharmaceuticals, which are usually produced by refinement of raw materials and extraction and concentration of the active ingredients, Chinese medicines use herbs in their natural state, and are thus less potent than Western drugs (Lake, 2004). The patient may take the herbal combinations as a broth, tea, flavored wine, powder, or paste. The Chinese practitioner will tell the herbalist what method of preparation to use for the prescription as well as the appropriate ingredients (Reid, 1994, p. 50). Because Chinese medicines are not "standard formulas for presumed average disorders," the TCM practitioner is "trained to continue rethinking and refining a patient's herbal prescription until desired effects are achieved with few or no side effects" (Lake, 2004, p. CE).

Critiques

Some practices associated with TCM have been generally accepted in Canada and the United States as acceptable on the basis of mainstream clinical studies, particularly acupuncture and acupressure (a modified version of acupuncture in which the practitioner puts pressure on the diagnostic points along the meridians rather than stimulating them with needles). In 1997, the National Institutes of Health (NIH, 1997) issued a consensus statement that included the following:

> Promising results have emerged, for example, showing efficacy of acupuncture in adult postoperative and chemotherapy nausea and vomiting and in postoperative dental pain. There are other situations such as addiction, stroke rehabilitation, headache, menstrual cramps, tennis elbow, fibromyalgia, myofascial pain, osteoarthritis, low back pain, carpal tunnel syndrome, and asthma, in which acupuncture may be useful as an adjunct treatment or an acceptable alternative or be included in a comprehensive management program. Further research is likely to uncover additional areas where acupuncture interventions will be useful. (p. 11)

In addition, such low-impact forms of physical exercise as tai chi have also been found useful in maintaining flexibility and muscle strength as well as relaxation and a sense of improved well-being in older adults (Kuramoto, 2006; Wang, Collet, & Lau, 2004). The general emphasis in TCM on integrating regular physical activity with diet and nutrition as part of preventive health care is certainly in line with mainstream Western recommendations regarding healthful lifestyles.

On the other hand, some components of TCM, particularly its reliance on herbal medications, have been criticized as potentially dangerous. Ephedra (*Ephedra sinica*), an herb known in China as *ma huang*, is used to treat yin diseases caused by cold and wind, particularly asthma, hay fever, and certain skin allergies (Reid, 1994, p. 50). Ephedrine, a compound isolated from this plant, has been used in the West to treat asthma, but it is currently banned in the United States because its abuse in weight loss products caused the Food and Drug Administration (FDA) to decide that it posed a risk to consumers (Guharoy & Noviasky, 2003). Moreover, Chinese versions of patent medicines (as distinct from the unprocessed herbs used by Chinese pharmacists to make up prescriptions for individual patients) have sometimes been found to be contaminated by heavy metals or even Western pharmaceuticals (Pelletier, 2002).

Studies carried out in China itself have discovered evidence of insecticide contamination in Chinese herbs (Wu, Li, & Zou, 2005). Damage to the liver has been traced to Chinese herbal medicines sold over the counter in the United Kingdom as well as in Singapore (McRae, Agarwal, Mutimer, & Bassendine, 2002; Wai et al., 2007). As with Ayurvedic practitioners in India, some practitioners of TCM in China are calling for the institution of good manufacturing practices for Chinese patent medicines, good agricultural practices for the growing and harvesting of raw herbs, and better reporting of the findings of clinical trials. One 2006 study found that only one of 167 randomized clinical trials carried out in China discussed quality control of the drugs under investigation, and the general quality of reporting was poor (Leung et al., 2006).

There are very few studies of patients' attitudes toward the Taoist beliefs underlying TCM or of the Five Elements theory of personality. Most such studies concern differences between Chinese and Western attitudes toward mental disorders, with Chinese patients typically placing greater emphasis on harmony within the family and feeling intense guilt and shame over disrupting this harmony (Hsiao, Klimidis, Minas, & Tan, 2006). One group of Western researchers maintains that people drawn to alternative medical systems and the religious traditions underlying them tend to differ from those who follow mainstream Western religions along several different dimensions of personality (Saucier & Skrzypi ska, 2006). In addition, most Western psychologists appear to regard TCM's theory of personality as unscientific superstition on a par with astrology or phrenology.

Japanese Therapies: Morita Therapy

A Japanese approach to psychotherapy and personality disorders that has become influential in the West in recent years is Morita therapy, developed by Sh ma Morita (also known as Masutake Morita) (1874–1938), a contemporary of Sigmund Freud. This approach, as well as another Japanese therapy called Naikan, was known to Karen Horney and Albert Ellis; the two Japanese systems have been brought together in an educational self-help approach for Westerners called **constructive living** (Reynolds, 1984). The reader should recognize some of the echoes of Morita's work in Ellis's psychology from Chapter 16.

Origins

Both Morita therapy and Naikan emerged from the changes in Japanese society brought about by the opening of Japan to the West in the mid-19th century and the subsequent fall of the Tokugawa shoguns, military leaders who had ruled Japan (with a succession of emperors as ceremonial figureheads) since the unification of the country in 1600. In 1867, the emperor was reinstated as the titular ruler of Japan, and the country entered on a period of intense industrialization and modernization, seeking to catch up with the Western powers as rapidly as possible. Part of Japan's modernization program was the construction of universities on the Western, and particularly the German model. For many years, Japanese medical students sought residencies in German hospitals and clinics for advanced postgraduate training, and the German psychiatric tradition became the basic model for Japanese psychiatry at the beginning of the 20th century. Morita's knowledge of Freud's approach to emotional disturbances and his eventual rejection of it can thus be understood in the context of the medical education he received as a young man.

Morita's Early Career. After completing his training, Morita became the chair of the Department of Psychiatry at the Jikei University School of Medicine in Tokyo. This institution was notable at the time of its founding in 1881 for its rejection of the German authoritarian model of medical training, which dominated the medical school of its competitor, the University of Tokyo. Jikei's approach to medical education and patient care was based on the English and American models of treating patients (including those with mental disorders) as people suffering from illness rather than as raw material for medical research. Even in the 21st century, the spiritual basis of this university and its teaching hospital is the "compassionate heart" of the Buddhist religious tradition. Morita himself was influenced by the psychological principles of Zen Buddhism, although he did not consider acceptance of Zen to be essential for learning his method or benefiting from treatment.

Basic Principles of Morita Therapy. Morita therapy was initially developed as a treatment for a type of anxiety neurosis called **shinkeishitsu,** which includes most of the anxiety and obsessional disorders defined in 2000 by DSM-IV and some of the post-traumatic syndromes. According to a contemporary Japanese psychiatrist, Morita thought that the basic symptom underlying shinkeishitsu was *toraware,* a Japanese word that meant "to be bound or caught, as by some intense preoccupation" (Doi, 1978, p. 213). Morita's basic approach to treating these neuroses was to focus on strengthening the patient's character through purposeful action rather than concentrating on symptom reduction or the person's feelings as such—which would have only reinforced the patient's preoccupation with internal feelings.

Character is developed through behavior, Morita believed, by doing what needs to be done at the moment out of a sense of purpose rather than allowing ourselves to be overwhelmed by emotions. Patients' improvement is measured by their growing ability to take constructive action when needed and not being controlled by emotional states; it is not measured by whether they "feel better" or have attained peak experiences or some other idealized emotional state.

Morita's approach can be summarized in three basic principles:

1. *Accept the Existence of Feelings.* Morita did not ask patients to suppress feelings or pretend that they didn't have them. Such feelings as anxiety, shyness, sadness, and anger are

normal parts of human experience, he thought. Morita believed that preoccupation with feelings, trying to manipulate them, led people to be overwhelmed by them and to experience life as a roller coaster of emotional highs and lows. "Trying to control the emotional self willfully by manipulative attempts is like trying to choose a number on thrown dice or to push the water of the Kamo River back upstream. Certainly, people end up aggravating their agony and feeling unbearable pain because of their failure in manipulating the emotions" (Morita, 1998, p. 22).

Morita referred to accepting one's feelings as *arugamama* or acceptance of reality. It is natural to feel sad when a loved one dies or to feel pleased when one wins a prize or award of some kind. We do not need to try to "fix" feelings; most feelings, even strong ones, will fade by themselves in a few hours. A saying of Morita's that is often quoted is as follows: "My way of doing things is simple. It's not necessary to make impossible efforts when troubled. Put simply, when you are vexed just be vexed, and say, 'Yes, and what shall I do?' Just be in suspense about the outcome and move forward a little at a time" (quoted in Reynolds, 1987, p. 89).

2. *Develop a Purpose-Orientation.* Morita believed that people need to take responsibility for their behavior because they can control what they do no matter how they feel at the moment. The purpose of any activity or behavior is to meet the requirements of the real situation at hand in an appropriate manner. For example, the person with panic disorder leaves her house to go to the supermarket in spite of fearful feelings because her purpose is to purchase food for the next week. The shy person goes to the job interview in spite of his social anxieties because his purpose is to find a better employment situation than his present one. A purpose-orientation gradually shifts the patient's focus of attention away from inner feeling states to the requirements of the immediate situation. In time, the patient feels considerably less anxious.

3. *Do What Needs Doing.* Morita believed that people with neurotic disturbances often postpone or ignore small daily tasks because they don't see any grand meaning or significance in them. He often prescribed specific activities for his patients as a way to help them see that doing even such minor actions as washing dishes, taking out the trash, or brushing one's teeth with attentiveness and care build character. "The accumulated effect [of doing many 'small' tasks well] is powerful and visible, both to ourselves and others. . . . Life is built on moment-by-moment doing" (quoted in Reynolds, 1987, p. 37).

Stages in Morita Therapy. Morita's original program of treatment had four stages designed for Japanese life in the 1920s. In the first stage, patients were admitted to the hospital for a rest phase, in which they were completely alone for a week without any sources of outside stimulation. The second phase consisted of doing light work (usually writing in a journal or helping out in the hospital kitchen) in silence and reconnecting with the natural world by taking outdoor walks. The third phase, sometimes called the "chopping wood" phase, involved heavier physical work intended to move patients from being passive recipients of physical therapy to active participants in their ongoing healing, whether physical or psychological. These first three phases usually took a total of 3 or 4 weeks to complete. In Phase 4, patients returned from the clinic to their job and family, integrating what had been learned in the first three phases into their new life in the outside world. Contemporary Morita therapists follow this basic four-phase program, with the exception that patients are generally not sent to a hospital as inpatients now. In addition to individual therapy, Morita's principles have also been used in group therapy, particularly for groups of patients diagnosed with social phobia, a disorder that is more common in Japan than in most Western countries (Takahashi & Aizawa, 1973).

Moral Dimension of Morita Therapy. One distinctive aspect of Morita therapy is its emphasis on the importance of moral wisdom in recovery from neurosis. For example, a commonplace behavioral exercise for shy or socially avoidant people in Morita therapy is to greet neighbors and workplace colleagues on first meeting them every single day. The point of this exercise is not intellectual insight or the uncovering of deep unconscious impulses but to bring patients back into a better social or moral alignment with others. As Reynolds (1987) explains:

> The assignment to greet one's neighbors is built on the recognition that neurosis grows as much from social/moral errors as from wrong understandings and unpleasant feelings (that is, psychological difficulties). The shy person has been neglecting social responsibilities. He has been avoiding simple social courtesies. When he does what is "proper," the social relations are more likely to be smooth and the client is more likely to feel good about them. . . . The performance of the greeting puts him back on the social track. . . . To put it baldly, greetings are "good," "right," "proper," "moral" behaviors. Morita therapists don't assign just any behaviors when working with clients. They never assign behaviors that are considered "wrong" or "immoral" by society. When they are in doubt about the rightness of a behavior, they leave the choice up to the client or else advise against the behavior. (p. 21)

This moral dimension is also an important dimension of Naikan practice, to which we now turn.

Japanese Therapies: Naikan

Naikan is perhaps better described as a structured method of self-reflection rather than a therapy in the strict sense. Many people, however, find it helpful in gaining a deeper perspective on family and social relationships. Its name means "inside-looking" or "seeing oneself with the mind's eye" in Japanese.

Origins

Naikan was developed by Yoshimoto Ishin, a devout member of the Jōdo Shinshu or True Pure Land sect of Japanese Buddhism. Jōdo Shinshu was founded in the 12th century by Shinran Shonin, a member of an aristocratic family who had become a Buddhist monk. Shinran popularized a devotional practice known as *nembutsu*, which is the repetition of the Japanese phrase *Namu Amida Butsu*, or "I take refuge in Amida Buddha." The phrase is understood as an expression of gratitude to Buddha, and the practice of gratitude is a core component of contemporary Naikan. Jōdo Shinshu became popular in Japan because the simple ritual chanting of *nembutsu* could be carried out by peasants and laborers, who did not have long periods of free time to devote to the elaborate religious practices of other Buddhist sects.

Yoshimoto Ishin continued this aspect of Jōdo Shinshu in his development of Naikan. Ishin had learned a rigorous and difficult method of introspection that met his own spiritual needs but was not accessible to most laypeople. Naikan emerged from Ishin's desire to devise a form of introspection that people could use in their ordinary life circumstances. He began to teach others his simplified form of introspection in 1935. A businessman at the time that he began teaching Naikan to others, Ishin eventually became a lay priest of Jōdo Shinshu.

Basic Principles of Naikan Therapy

Naikan is intended to redirect people's attention outward toward others and what they owe the world rather than what they can take from it. Its emphasis on moral virtue, particularly the virtue of gratitude and "giving back." is similar to the moral dimension of Morita therapy. As Reynolds (1987) says, "it is important to be able to see oneself as 'one-who-gives' rather than 'one-who-takes' from the world. . . . Miserable people see themselves as 'takers,' as burdens or as exploiters of those about them" (p. 34). Naikan therapy seeks to lead clients to accept responsibility for selfish and irrational behavior toward others and to live from a sense of gratitude to others and the universe in general for nurture and support. It is significant that this gratitude should extend to objects as well as other people; clients in Naikan therapy may be asked to reflect on the specific services that such apparently simple objects as eyeglasses, pens and pencils, or coffee mugs perform for them, not to mention cars, computers, and other machines or equipment (Krech, 2002, pp. 54–56). And as will be seen in the case study below, significant others include animals as well as other humans.

The core of Naikan therapy is self-examination according to three questions:

1. What have I received from (X)?

2. What have I given to (X)?

3. What troubles and difficulties have I caused (X)?

Naikan intentionally leaves aside consideration of the troubles and difficulties others cause the client, on the grounds that most people are all too conscious of these and that focusing on the problems others cause us is the source of a good deal of everyday misery (Kamilar, 2002, p. 119). By listing what a specific person in our life has done for us (without regard to his or her attitude or motivation), according to Naikan thought, we begin to understand that we are supported and cared for in many "little" ways in daily life. Making a list for the second question often prompts some painful recognition that we give significantly less to the world than we demand from the world as our "due" or "right." The third question is the most difficult for most clients in Naikan therapy because it compels a hard look at the problems we cause others. Ishin suggested that people performing a Naikan meditation should spend 60% of their time on this third question (France, 2000).

Forms of Naikan Practice

There are three basic forms of Naikan practice. The first is called *nichijo Naikan* or daily Naikan. In *nichijo Naikan,* people spend about 20 to 30 minutes in a quiet place before bedtime and write out three lists of answers corresponding to the three questions. The items on the list should be as specific as possible, including those that clients might be tempted to dismiss as "trivial"—those are precisely the things it is important to notice.

Here is a partial example of one person's daily Naikan practice:

- What did I receive today?
  - The letter carrier delivered my mail.
  - The plumber came by to fix the leaky faucet.
  - The clerk at the supermarket wrapped my deli purchases and weighed them.
  - My car got me to the store and back safely and efficiently.
  - My neighbor smiled and waved to me when I took my daily walk.
  - The seeds I planted in the back yard showed their first sprouts today.
  - The weather was sunny and pleasant.
  - The electric company supplied the energy that lights my office, powers my computer and microwave, and generally makes my life more comfortable.
  - I wore a shirt that was a birthday gift from my brother.
- What did I give today?
  - I fed the cats and changed their litter box.
  - I took a package to the post office for my sister.
  - I sent a donation to the United Way.
  - I weeded the back yard garden and watered the new shoots.
  - I thanked the supermarket clerk for her courteous service.
  - I paid my dentist's bill.
  - I smiled back at my neighbor.
- What troubles did I cause others today?
  - I ignored several e-mails that deserved replies.
  - I kept a friend waiting at lunch.
  - I yelled at a driver who made a left-hand turn in front of me at a traffic light.
  - I frightened a rabbit in the park where I take my walks.
  - I wasted half a sandwich at lunch.
  - I took two spaces in the parking lot at the office by parking over a dividing line.
  - I used up all the hot water even though my roommate was waiting to take a shower.
  - I put off calling a friend who needs some support right now.
  - I scolded one of the cats for throwing up a hairball.
  - I left a nasty comment on someone's weblog.

The second form of Naikan practice is called reflection on a person and involves spending 50 or 60 minutes reflecting on that relationship. In some situations, clients may choose to focus on a stressful period in their life (such as the 3 years following a parent's death or a divorce) rather than on an individual person, answering the same questions.

The third form of Naikan practice is a week-long retreat known as *shuchu Naikan*. Clients go away to a Naikan retreat center for a week of total immersion in meditation and solitude. In some centers, they may speak with therapists at intervals during the day for guidance in meditation and introspection, but for the most part, the clients are alone from 4:30 a.m. to about 7:00 p.m.

After the intensive retreat, clients may choose to undergo further counseling through weekly or monthly visits to a Naikan therapist. An example of treatment with a Naikan therapist is given in the case study below. Clients are usually asked to keep a journal and to complete "homework" assignments, such as writing a letter of gratitude to a specific person thanking them for specific deeds of kindness that the recipient of the letter performed for the writer. The letter is to be as concrete and detailed as possible, listing such kindnesses as driving the writer to the emergency room when he ran a high fever; taking time out of a busy schedule to provide a listening ear; covering the cost of a meal when the writer had left her wallet at home; and similar acts of concern or generosity. The writer of the letter is not to mention what he or she did for the recipient or anything that the recipient did that caused trouble for the writer. "It is strictly a letter of gratitude" (Reynolds, 1987, p. 61). In other cases, the client's assignment might be to write and send a letter of apology. Still another exercise might be to thank a husband, wife, or roommate 10 times during the day for something, whether the client feels grateful at the moment or not.

A Case Study in Naikan Therapy

The following case study is an application of Naikan therapy in a Western setting (France, 2000). The patient was a 35-year-old Canadian who was upset by the breakup of his marriage:

M came to therapy with the desire to reduce stress and overcome a generally "blue" feeling. M reported that he felt a great deal of anger, yet even after expressing his anger, he felt "stuck." [After Naikan had been explained to him], M was invited by the therapist to share his feelings. He talked for over an hour about his state of mind and how he thought he had been coping. . . . M described his existence as: "Going down the road of life, minding my own business, and being attacked by colleagues who disagreed with me. The viciousness of their attacks was a real surprise and I felt myself being knocked down in the mud. The sorrow of their attacks seems to have somehow paralyzed me. . . . I don't feel that I can get up, yet I see the uselessness of staying and wallowing in the mud."

[M then practiced meditation for several weeks, after which the therapist asked him to look at several significant relationships in his life.] Of the many people he felt were significant in his life, he chose to "work" on a relationship involving a colleague who he felt had treated him in an unfair way. Rather than focus on the negative aspects of his relationship with the person, he was asked to focus on what he had learned in the encounter with that person. Although he found it difficult to explore the positive parts, he listed a number of things he had learned about himself and how the experience had changed his life. After considerable time exploring this experience . . . he was surprised at what he had learned [particularly] the "little kindnesses" of acquaintances and how much "closer" he had been drawn to his family. . . .

Generally, the therapist focused on actions and meaning. In every case, M was asked to make sense of what was given and what he did to repay others. . . . Over the next two sessions, M explored a number of other relationships from the past, including the relationship with his parents, siblings, and ex-spouse. In each case, he was asked to meditate on how these people had influenced and given "something" to him. This was followed by an exploration of how he had given back to others. After tying all these themes together, M was asked to write out how, when, where, and to whom he would return the "gifts" that he had been given. A clear theme was his pleasure at "taking care" of his pets [cats] and house plants. In fact, he learned that he was happier in "nurturing" than in controlling his relationships with others. . . .

Specific living strategies for giving back to others were discussed and clarified so M had a clearer idea of what he could do. The two follow-up sessions evaluated how well the strategies were working for him. It was not surprising that a motto he developed and promised to repeat everyday consisted of this thought: "The best way to receive is to give."

VIGNETTE

Sil grew up in a lower middle-class neighborhood in a suburb of New York City. His parents were kind and simple people, neither of whom had been particular adept in school. Despite not having a tradition of higher education in his family, Sil became the first member of his family to attend college. He was a good student as an undergraduate, but his major distinction was his active participation in school politics. A member of several student groups working for social justice, Sil always found time to remember the impoverished, the disenfranchised, and the oppressed.

Ironically, some of the people who benefited from Sil's advocacy had easier lives than he did. His tuition at the public college he attended was defrayed by student loans and part-time work. At the end of each day, he returned to his parents' small apartment, where he studied and worked on his social justice programs. Despite all the hard work that filled his typical day, Sil maintained a consistent attitude of optimism about his own future and those of his fellow human beings. This attitude was maintained throughout his college years; he became the editor of the college newspaper and an officer of three public service groups on campus.

After college, Sil became a reporter for a small trade newspaper. Within 5 years, he became a feature reporter and columnist for a large regional paper. Although he occasionally expressed some frustration that he was unable to get so much as an interview at a national paper like the *Washington Post* or *New York Times*, he pressed onward toward his goal of making the world a more just and equitable place. Sil's columns about crime and the inequities of the criminal justice system led a judge he had come to know to suggest that he go to law school. The judge's suggestion and promise of a recommendation was the push Sil needed to move into a field that he had found increasingly attractive.

A few years later, Sil graduated summa cum laude from the law school of a state university. To the astonishment of his parents and close friends, he turned down all the offers he received from corporations and prestigious law firms to take a job as a public defender that paid only a bit more than a quarter of the highest salary he had been offered. Sil was excited by the opportunity to make the law work well for all people. He was now participating in the system that he had once covered as a reporter. For the next decade, Sil persevered in his efforts to represent people who were rejected, even loathed, by virtually everyone. Sil believed that every defendant deserved the best representation, and he intended to resolutely provide it. He never

(Continued)

(Continued)

revealed even a hint of envy of peers who now lived in wealth while he made do with a slender salary. Nor did he yield to a growing tide of judicial conservatism that had made defending certain categories of accused felons far more difficult.

Sil suffered numerous personal adversities over the next 15 years. He lost both of his parents, his fiancée left him for a man earning far more money, and his niece developed a chronic illness. In spite of all these setbacks, he maintained his hopefulness about his life and his role in the world. Each painful event was viewed as a challenge to surmount and move beyond. Refusal was never an option for Sil; he was always available to help a friend, and he maintained his devotion to public service organizations. Sil was gifted with a personality that endowed him with focus and equanimity in life.

Vignette Questions

1. Although Sil seemed happy, some might say his high level of dedication might be indicative of a personality flaw. What might some say it is?

2. If you don't think he had a personality problem, how would you explain his resistance to adversity?

Japanese Therapies: Research and Critique

Research

Understandably most research into both Morita therapy and Naikan has been carried out in Japan and other countries in East Asia. The Society of Morita Therapy in Japan publishes its own periodical, the *Journal of Morita Therapy*. In addition, Western psychotherapists who have studied Morita therapy and Naikan have published in mainstream Western medical and scientific journals, sometimes with Japanese coauthors (Chang, 1974; Gibson, 1974; Iwai & Reynolds, 1970; Murase & Johnson, 1974).

Japanese research in both forms of therapy is conducted according to standard Western models of clinical research and statistical analysis. In many cases Japanese psychiatrists use the diagnostic categories of DSM-IV or the ICD in publishing their findings; it is understood that outcome studies of these two Japanese psychotherapies should proceed according to the same rigorous criteria as clinical research in other branches of medicine. Specific outcome studies of Morita therapy include its benefits in treating social phobia (Takahashi & Aizawa, 1973), depersonalization and other dissociative symptoms (Mizuno, Nakamura, & Ushijima, 1973), insomnia (Yamadero et al., 2005), and schizophrenia. With regard to schizophrenia, Morita therapy is still considered an experimental treatment that shows promise, particularly in regard to treating the isolation and low level of social functioning of many patients with schizophrenia (He & Li, 2007).

Recent outcome studies of Naikan therapy include research with depressed patients (Tashiro, Hosoda, & Kawahara, 2004) and patients with generalized anxiety disorder or panic disorder (Nukina, Wang, Kamei, & Kawahara, 2005), using Western diagnostic categories and Western personality inventories modified for the Japanese population. Another area of clinical research with Naikan therapy is the treatment of attachment disorders between mothers and infants. One case study of an attachment disorder gave the following rationale for choosing Naikan as the form of treatment:

> Mother-to-infant attachment is thought to be influenced by how the mother was brought up. Naikan therapy reflects the relationships with one's relatives from childhood up to the present, providing an important element concerning attachment formation. Through Naikan therapy, mothers may recall that they themselves have received love from their parents, which strengthens the feeling of basic trust. Consequently, they are encouraged to love their children. Therefore, Naikan therapy is suggested to be one of the effective therapies to treat attachment disturbances between mothers and infants. (Furuichi, Mizobe, Nukina, & Kawahara, 2006)

Critiques

Morita therapy is generally better known in the West than Naikan, perhaps because some of its principles resemble those of both Beck and Ellis, particularly its emphasis on purposeful action in the present as the key to changing character rather than ruminating about the past. Some researchers have compared Morita therapy to the cognitive behavioral therapy (CBT) of Joseph Wolpe and others (Gibson, 1974). Several clinicians in Canada and the United States have recommended Morita therapy as an effective bridge between Western and Eastern approaches to psychotherapy because of its compatibility with cognitive psychology. One researcher, a Japanese psychologist working in Australia, maintains that Morita therapy offers possibilities for resolving differences in cross-cultural information processing (Matsuda, 2003).

As Matsuda's reference to differences in information processing indicates, a common critique of the two Japanese psychotherapies is that they may not be adequate to treat mental disorders and personality disorders affecting people who have grown up in the West. Some observers have taken issue with Naikan's focus on gratitude to specific people in our lives, particularly parents. The reader should note that this is a typically Western critique: Asian religions, philosophies, and systems of thought in general place more emphasis on the groups to which an individual belongs than on individuals per se. "The emphasis in Oriental systems [of psychology] is mainly on the structure of family, clan, class, and state through which individuals relate to one another" (Pedersen, 1977, p. 368). Naikan retreats in Japan customarily begin with a reflection on a person, usually the client's mother or father. Westerners who have had abusive or dysfunctional relationships with a parent may find spending 60% of their meditation time focusing on what she or he did for them to be counterproductive, particularly if the parent had abandoned the family or was jailed or institutionalized for long periods. In such cases, the person in treatment is usually invited to focus on a significant relationship outside the family; the point of the exercise is to lead participants to a clearer recognition of the support they have received and still receive from others in their lives, not to instill guilt or shame regarding anger toward a parent.

On the positive side, some Western clinicians maintain that Morita therapy and Naikan offer useful correctives to the one-sided Western focus on the individual and a succession of so-called "values-free" theories of human behavior. For a variety of cultural and institutional reasons, Western modernity has produced a notion of the human person as "the disengaged, particular self, whose identity is constituted [primarily] in memory" (Taylor, 1989, p. 288). Individualism has been described by Robert Bellah and his colleagues as residing "at the very core of American culture" (Bellah, Madsen, Sullivan, Swidler, & Tipton, 1986, p. 142). This individualism, they note, is reinforced by the dominant forms of psychotherapy in the contemporary United States, particularly the school of Carl Rogers, and the current emphasis on the primacy of emotion over a sense of duty or obligations to others:

> The [standard American] therapeutic attitude liberates individuals by helping them get in touch with their own wants and interests, freed from the artificial constraints of social rules, the guilt-inducing demands of parents and other authorities, and the false promises of illusory ideals such as love. Equally important, the therapeutic attitude redefines the real self. Money, work, and social status are not central to the authentic self, which instead consists of the experience and expression of feelings. (Bellah et al., 1986, pp. 101–102)

Writing 3 years after Bellah, another American clinician quoted an observation by William James: "The hell we make for ourselves in this world is the hell we create by habitually fashioning our characters in the wrong way" (James, 1890, p. 130). The clinician then urged the importance of what he calls ethical therapy:

> Deliberately reforming our characters, "assuming the virtue," as Shakespeare put it, is the essence of effective self-help. This begins with an awareness of the kind of ethical violation which usually causes the emotional problem we suffer from—to see that depressed feelings, for example, stem from resentful attitudes or that chronic frustration with others comes most often from our attempts to manipulate them. (Andrews, 1989, p. xiv)

Moreover, it is not surprising that some clinicians regard the "relatively group-centered, ritualistic, and behavioristic" qualities of Morita therapy as providing a needed balance to excessive focus on the self and a tendency to allow momentary emotions to control behavior. The growing acceptance of Morita therapy and Naikan in North America "suggests that previously popular Western techniques may not be optimum for handling certain problems of the post-industrial American" (Reynolds & Kiefer, 1977, p. 405). Other clinicians note that the multidimensional model of causality of mental disorders in Morita therapy and its effectiveness in redirecting anxious feelings toward constructive action is helpful in the North American context (Ishiyama, 2003).

Native American Healing

Native Americans (called First Nations in Canada) and their healing rituals have become a subject of interest to many North Americans looking for alternatives to traditional methods of psychotherapy or personality assessment. For obvious historical reasons, traditional Native American medicine is not usually studied by European or Asian clinicians. The relationship between mainstream Western medicine and Native American/First Nations practices is more complicated, however, than the relationship between mainstream medicine and either Ayurveda or traditional Chinese medicine (TCM), for political as well as historical reasons.

Native American methods of healing are now considered a distinctive type of traditional medical system that can be grouped together with Ayurveda and TCM (Go & Champaneria, 2002). Native American traditional medicine, however, covers a wider variety of tribal cultures and practices than either Ayurveda or TCM. As of 2008, the U.S. federal government recognizes 561 different Native American tribes, and there are many smaller groups that have not obtained formal governmental recognition, with an estimated (as of 2005) 1% to 2% of the U.S. population being of Native American (including Alaska Native) descent.

With regard to the variety of tribal cultures, even a brief glance at the geography of North America as well as the history of Native Americans before the arrival of Europeans shows that climate, animal migration patterns, and the location of waterways affected the hunting and farming patterns of the different tribes. The Iroquois, Susquehanna, Delaware, and other tribes living in what is now the northeastern United States had settled agricultural villages that were different from the subsistence agriculture of the Pueblo Indians of the Southwest, the semi-settled or fully nomadic lifestyle of the Plains Indians, or the seafaring ventures of the Indians of the Pacific Northwest. Most tribes had their own spoken dialects, most of which were completely unintelligible to other tribal groups living only a few miles away (Richter, 2001, p. 6).

Long-term climatic changes also affected the movement and settlement patterns of Native Americans. During the so-called Medieval Warm Period (roughly 900 to 1350 CE), the tribes living along the East Coast and in the Mississippi River valley cultivated maize, squash, and beans and practiced selective breeding and improvement of the wild varieties of these plants. Some Native American cities in what are now Alabama, Georgia, and Missouri had as many as 20,000 inhabitants. When the climate changed around the beginning of the 14th century to what is now called the Little Ice Age, the large population centers dispersed, and many tribes moved southward while others moved further north to join the tribes that hunted and fished in the Great Lakes area. In the Southwest, the Little Ice Age brought about such severe climate changes that many of the Pueblo communities had to give up settled agriculture; they began a period of intense warfare with one another because of competition for increasingly scarce resources (LeBlanc, 1999).

Origins

In general, Native American beliefs about health, disease, and the place of spirituality in restoring health go back about 30,000 to 60,000 years, when the ancestors of the various tribes migrated across a land bridge that then connected northeastern Asia with North America. These ancestors brought with them shamanism, beliefs in spirits, ceremonial practices related to animals, and hunting taboos. Some details of early Native American beliefs about healing mental as well as physical disorders remain unclear because the traditions were passed down orally. Common patterns of belief, however, include the following:

- Beliefs about religion and healing are closely related to the natural world.
- Local geography (mountains, canyons, rivers, and the like) acquires sacred significance.
- Natural objects (e.g., rocks and minerals) are regarded as tokens or manifestations of the supernatural.
- Ceremonies and rituals are used to secure community and individual well-being or healing.

Tribes that were only semi-settled or purely nomadic placed greater emphasis on the role of shamans, on ceremonies involving animals, on belief in a male supreme god, and on human need for spiritual power. They had relatively few sacred places. Tribes that had a settled agri-cultural way of life had priests (male or female) rather than shamans, annual fertility rituals with less emphasis on animal magic, and more permanent shrines or holy places. In both types of tribal culture, ceremony and ritual were important parts of community life in general and became associated with medicine and healing. A physician trained in both Western med-icine and Native American healing summarizes the traditional practices as

> a dynamic energy system. Within this [Native American] theoretical framework, physical illness, which is viewed as simultaneously spiritual, mental, and physical, can be treated by counseling and ceremony. Due to the interaction and hierarchical nature of these levels, intervention at any one level affects the others. (Mehl-Madrona, 1999, p. 39)

With regard to Native American shamans, it is important to note that the shamans themselves do not attribute their role as healers to their own efforts—in contrast to typical Western medical students, who generally regard completion of their education and training as the outcome of a deliberate career choice followed by years of hard work. Even shamans who had a conscious desire to become shamans maintain that their transformation into healers happened in spite of their wishes, not as the result of their pursuing a personal goal. An Iglulik Eskimo described the process of his becoming a shaman:

> I endeavored to become a shaman by the help of others; but in this I did not succeed. I visited many famous shamans. . . . I sought solitude, and here I soon became very melancholy. I would sometimes fall to weeping. . . . Then, for no reason, all would sud-denly be changed, and I felt a great, inexplicable joy, a joy so powerful that I could not restrain it, but had to break into song, a mighty song. . . . And I had to use the full strength of my voice. And then in the midst of such a fit of mysterious and over-whelming delight I became a shaman, not knowing myself how it came about. But I was a shaman. I could see and hear in a totally different way. I had gained my *quamanEq*, my enlightenment, the shaman-light of brain and body . . . it was not only I who could see through the darkness of life, but the same light also shone out of me, imperceptible to human beings, but visible to all the spirits of earth and sky and sea, and these now came to me and became my helping spirits. (Dossey, 2001, p. 28)

Relationship to Western Medicine and Psychology

Traditional Native American methods of healing are not regarded by either their practitioners or their clients as necessarily incompatible with mainstream Western medicine—although one 1998 study reported that Native Americans who use traditional healers (most commonly for spiritual rather than physical problems) are likely (61.4%) to regard their healer's advice more highly than their physician's, and only 15% said that they told their physician about their use of traditional remedies (Marbella, Harris, Diehr, Ignace, & Ignace, 1998). Another study comparing the attitudes of different racial and ethnic groups in the United States toward the use of alternative therapies found that Native Americans (along with Hispanics) were more likely to regard complementary and alternative medicine therapies as alternatives to mainstream treatment rather than complementary to it (Tom Xu & Farrell, 2007). This attitude on the part of Native Americans may be due in part to awareness of mainstream medicine's long-standing suspicion of or hostility toward traditional medical systems. A 1994 survey of Canadian physicians found that while a majority was open to the use of Native healing practices for health maintenance, end-of-life care, or minor illnesses, most physicians were opposed to their use in treating serious illnesses (Zubek, 1994). Another reason for this attitude is a desire to keep some traditional practices secret from non-Indians, often combined with resentment of so-called **New Age** misunderstandings and exploitation of Native American spirituality, which will be discussed in more detail below.

On the other hand, the growing number of Native Americans in medical and nursing schools reinforces the general willingness on the part of many Native Americans to accept mainstream medications and surgical techniques when they serve the community's health. A Hopi premed student expressed his belief that studying to become a physician was not an act of disloyalty to the ancestral ways:

> I mean, I *am* studying to be a doctor and not a medicine man. But I'm no apple Indian— red outside and white underneath. . . . What I'm saying is that I've lived on Hopi land and I've lived away. . . . To me, being Indian means being responsible to my people. Helping with the best tools. Who invented penicillin doesn't matter. . . . A Hopi learns that he belongs to two families, his natural clan and that of all things. As he gets older, he's supposed to move closer to the greater family. In the Hopi Way, each person tries to recognize his part in the whole. . . . My heritage is the Hopi Way, and that's a way of the spirit. Spirit can go anywhere [including technological medicine]. In fact, it has to go places so it can change and emerge. . . . That's the whole idea. (Least Heat Moon, 1982, pp. 182–186)

Larry Dossey, an internist and the former director of what is now the NCCAM, tells of the time he was consulted by Rolling Thunder, a famous Native American shaman, who had a severe neck ache and was scheduled to give a lecture in Dallas in just a few hours. Dr. Dossey was initially worried about the situation; it seemed paradoxical that a famous healer who had nothing in common with mainstream medicine would want to see a Western-trained physician. After examining the patient and deciding that Rolling Thunder's neck pain was caused by muscle spasms resulting from having to stand in an unnatural position to use a microphone, Dr. Dossey (1993) asked the shaman what he thought about the use of drugs:

> He went on to explain his personal philosophy of healing. There is a time for the shaman's chants, prayers, and herbs, he said. There is also a place for a modern approach, including the use of synthetic chemical medications. A wise healer uses what works. He does not confine himself to a single methodology. All things considered, Rolling Thunder believed the use of drugs was the best treatment for his neck ache in this situation. I went to the area where we kept sample medications and returned with two, a pain reliever and a muscle relaxant. I handed them to Rolling Thunder and he beamed. . . . The drugs worked. Rolling Thunder was in fine form at his lecture that night, speaking—through the microphone he despised—to a packed house. (p. 144)

In some fields of medicine, such as the treatment of substance abuse disorders, integrated programs combining Western approaches (medications, Twelve-Step programs, and cognitive behavioral interventions) with Native healing practices (sacred dances, sweat lodges, and massage) have had positive results (Abbott, 1998). Long-term studies of alcohol problems on four reservations in the United States and five in Canada found "empirical evidence that traditional practices and traditional spirituality play an important role in alcohol cessation and . . . maintaining sobriety" (Stone, Whitbeck, Chen, Johnson, & Olson, 2006, p. 236).

Another area in which traditional Native American practices have proved helpful is the treatment of posttraumatic stress disorder (PTSD), particularly in combat veterans (Johnson, Feldman, Lubin, & Southwick, 1995; Scurfield, 1995). The Navajo tribe has a specific ceremony called the Enemy Way, a curing ritual intended to bring a warrior returning from battle back into harmony with the universe. The Enemy Way (sometimes called the Squaw Dance) is a 3-day ceremony in which healers, herbalists, and medicine men take part. While the herbalist burns sage or other purifying herbs, the medicine man makes a bundle containing anything that belonged to the enemy (usually pieces of cloth from an enemy uniform or eyeglasses or other objects found in the pockets). The bundle is then placed in a hole and buried while a rifle is shot four times. This symbolic action is intended to "cut off all bad communication between the mind of the Navajo and the enemy—feelings of guilt or regret that are causing the [posttraumatic] sickness. . . . [The returnee] is thus brought back into harmony with nature" (Paul, 1973, p. 105). A non-Native writer describes his encounter with a group of Navajos performing the Enemy Way ceremonial:

> It was July, 1945. I was just back from World War II, a very senior private first class with a patch over a damaged eye. . . . I had a sixty-day convalescent furlough and I found a job . . . driving a truckload of pipe from Oklahoma City to an oil well drilling site north of Crownpoint. . . . Suddenly, a party of about twenty Navajo horsemen (and women) emerged from the piñons and crossed the dirt road in front of me. They were wearing ceremonial regalia and the man in front was carrying something tied to a coup stick. . . . I was fascinated. . . . What I had seen was the stick carrier's camp of an Enemy Way ceremonial making its ritual delivery of the [symbolic] "scalp" to the camp of the patient. He turned out to be a just-returned serviceman like myself—who was being restored to beauty with his people and cured of the disharmony of exposure to foreign cultures. (Hillerman & Bulow, 1991, p. 25)

The importance of traditional healing ceremonials became even more evident with Vietnam veterans. According to the National Center for Posttraumatic Stress Disorder, American Indians were twice as likely as Caucasian or Asian American veterans to suffer from PTSD, in part because they were more likely than men from any other ethnic group to serve in the Marines, the branch of service that saw the most combat in Vietnam. Those who participated in healing ceremonials, however, were less likely to develop PTSD, and if they did so, they recovered more rapidly. The Center's fact sheet advises veterans to "become involved with traditional teachers and healing ceremonies in your community. Rediscover traditions that have helped countless warriors return home, heal the wounds of war, and become vital members of their families and communities" (National Center for PTSD, 2007). The fact sheet closes with a traditional Native American prayer for a returning warrior:

> Oh Grandfather, there is one war left that is raging, worse than all the wars I have survived. Oh Grandfather, I need guidance, patience, understanding as this final war rages

within me. Oh Grandfather, help me overcome this turmoil within my heart and mind, bring peace to my mind, end these feelings of hatred, of hurt, of death, of revenge, and replace them with love, compassion, and caring for my people. So I can live the rest of my life in peace.

Diagnostic and Therapeutic Techniques

Native American healers use a range of practices in treating patients suffering from emotional as well as physical disorders. Cohen (1998) lists these as prayer, music, the use of herbal remedies, ritual purifications, massage, ceremonies of various types, and spontaneous innovations (including humor) on the part of a shaman. Mehl-Madrona (1998) describes the Native American shaman's willingness to move the client a bit off-center, so to speak, as part of the diagnostic process.

Change sometimes must begin with a surprise, with a sudden break from everyday life. At the beginning of a treatment, a shaman doesn't know (any more than a [mainstream] physician does) exactly what will heal a sick person. She takes it on faith that the person "knows" at some deeper level of consciousness but isn't able to access the knowledge. Sometimes what the shaman will do is throw her client psychically off balance, so that he, while metaphorically "falling," will reach out and grab for something, anything, to stop the fall. Once he has caught hold of something, the shaman has that something to work with, to base a healing experience upon. (pp. 283–284)

Use of Western Psychological and Psychiatric Nosologies

DSM-IV categories as well as mental health inventories used by primary care physicians have been applied to Native Americans, who appear to have high rates of depression or generalized anxiety disorder (Parker et al., 1997). Some studies carried out by the National Institute of Mental Health (NIMH) on shamans and other healers found that these practitioners are frequently psychologically healthier than nonhealer members of their respective communities (Cohen, 2003, pp. 212–213). On the other hand, Western diagnostic categories do not address the question of loss of meaning that lies at the root of many psychiatric disturbances. A Cherokee trained in Western psychiatry as well as traditional healing practices comments on this modern affliction of the human spirit:

The depressed person, or the person suffering from psychotic disorders of the self, is suffering from a lack of absolute reference points. Without limits or boundaries, emotion becomes unbearable—it is out of control. Few are strong enough to survive without reference points. Those of us who try suffer from a loss of meaning, or loss of world, or loss of self. . . . Today when I am able to help people heal themselves, it is often because I have been able to do one thing: coax them back into a view of life where their soul exists. Where there are forces with agency and will overseeing and guiding life on earth. Where the absolute reference point is that our lives are purposeful. . . . Finding direction means recognizing that life actually has a purpose. Once we believe that it does, then we have it in our power to heal ourselves. (Mehl-Madrona, 1998, pp. 164–165)

Traditional Native American Psychological Interventions

Cohen (2003) describes the following practices as common to most Native American healers' approach to personality disorders or other mental illnesses:

- *Talking Circles.* A talking circle is a basic feature of many types of Native American gatherings, not just healing rituals. It can be used for problem-solving as well as a kind of group therapy. The talking circle is based on the belief that expressing ourselves "from the heart" helps us to break through obsessive thoughts or behavior patterns. The participants in a talking circle may pass a sacred object (usually a stone, feather, or small carved stick) around the circle to each speaker in turn.
- *Confession and Prayer.* Native Americans rarely criticize one another for moral failings or mental disorders because such criticism implies an attitude of superiority. It is, however, considered an important first step to healing for patients to confess their misdeeds to the healer (or simply to the Creator) because violating the moral order of the community is an invitation to disease to enter the body or mind. This belief is similar to the emphasis on moral wisdom in Morita therapy and Naikan.
- *Humor.* Native American shamans may tell jokes or humorous anecdotes even during healing ceremonies. Laughter is considered a form of empathic communication in many Native tribes; among the Navajo, a baby's first laugh is considered an important milestone in the child's development. As therapy, humor is considered a way to loosen up overly rigid thought patterns and help patients to see their problems from a fresh perspective.
- *Dream Interpretation.* Most Native American healers encourage patients to discuss their dreams, which may be considered either personal dreams (about their own life or present situation) or visitation dreams—that is, a dream that represents a visit or message from the spirit world. Dreams about animals are often interpreted as visitation dreams.
- *Participation in a Healing Ceremonial or Ritual.* The sweat lodge is one of the best-known Native American healing rituals. Although the details vary somewhat from tribe to tribe, in most cases, the lodge is a thick-walled structure intended to hold heat and be completely dark inside. Oriented to the four cardinal directions, it has a low door and a central fire pit. People must crawl on hands and knees to enter the low door. Tobacco and herbs are usually burnt on the heated stones as offerings to the ancestors. In some sweat lodges, there is complete silence; in others, chanting, music, or ritual prayers are part of the ceremony. Some tribes permit men and women to use the lodge at the same time whereas others separate the sexes. Traditionally the participants were naked, but nowadays, cotton shorts and T-shirts are usually worn.

One important difference between the Native American approach to psychotherapy and conventional mainstream medicine is a relaxed approach to time. Native American healers rarely use the Western pattern of scheduled weekly appointments at fixed hours. They generally follow a time-intensive approach tailored to the individual patient:

The Native American healers told us that they typically worked with the client until the job was done. They typically treated one client at a time, and some clients traveled great distances to see them. Sometimes they traveled far to see a patient, and needed to put in maximum effort over a short period of time. Partly because of long distances traveled, they would concentrate their work over a number of days with multiple hours being spent each day. When they felt progress had been made, the client would be sent home with instructions to return at a later date for further treatment, and often with specific instructions for tasks to complete during the interval between treatments. (Mehl-Madrona, 1999, p. 40).

Research

Research in North America into Native American healing generally focuses on one of four topics: use of alternative therapies in conjunction with mainstream treatments; effectiveness of Native American rituals in specific patient populations; chemical analysis of herbs used in Native American rituals; and epidemiological studies of specific mental disorders among Native Americans. Large-group statistical studies are difficult to carry out among Native Americans because of the variety of tribal traditions and practices. In addition, the acceptance of a shaman's freedom to improvise or innovate to diagnose or treat a patient's problem complicates setting up a rigorously controlled outcome study because there is no one "school" of psychology or psychotherapy among these healers. Last, many researchers have strong ethical concerns about violating Native American beliefs about secrecy in regard to traditional practices.

Critiques

Most critiques of Native American healing have to do with misappropriation of tribal customs and practices by non-Indians rather than with the rituals themselves. Beginning shortly after 1900, when the construction of passenger railroads across the Southwest made visits to Native villages and pueblos possible for many middle-class Americans, people began to regard the West in general as "an exotic destination" newly accessible to those looking for spiritual adventure as well as the beautiful weaving, pottery, jewelry, and other handicrafts produced by the Indians. As early as 1902, the Santa Fe Railway used images of Native Americans to advertise round-trip tours (costing a total of $50) between Chicago and Los Angeles by way of the Grand Canyon (Howard & Pardue, 1996). The middle-class tourists were followed in the 1920s by the first wave of artists and intellectuals seeking an escape from what they perceived as the dullness of ordinary American life, on the one hand, and the overpriced sophistication of postwar Paris, on the other. New Mexico was perceived as mysterious, primitive, affordable, and therefore ideal (Baca, 2000).

One of these visitors was Carl Jung, who was fascinated by Native American lore as well as the traditions of most other cultures he considered "primitive," but whose knowledge of Native Americans had been secondhand. In January 1925, Jung visited Taos Pueblo for himself and interpreted the culture of its inhabitants in terms of his own analytical psychology. Years later, Jung's remarks were published in his book, *Man and His Symbols*:

> It is the role of religious symbols to give a meaning to the life of man. The Pueblo Indians believe that they are the sons of Father Sun, and this belief endows their life with a perspective (and a goal) that goes far beyond their limited existence. It gives them ample space for the unfolding of personality and permits them a full life as complete persons. Their plight is infinitely more satisfactory than that of a man in our own civilization who knows that he is (and will remain) nothing more than an underdog with no inner meaning to his life. (quoted in Baca, 2000, p. 8)

There were several problems in Jung's approach to Native Americans, not the least of which was European snobbery. One of Jung's analysands, a Spanish physician who had received his medical degree from Johns Hopkins University, arranged for Jung to meet Mountain Lake, a Hopi elder who was willing to discuss some of his people's creation stories and other myths with Jung but not to disclose information that his people considered sacred secrets. Jung told his analysand that when he was talking to Mountain Lake, he had "the extraordinary sensation that [he] was talking to an Egyptian priest of the fifteenth century before Christ" (Bair, 2003, p. 336). Later, however, Jung dismissed Mountain Lake as no more than "a man of above-average intelligence, i.e., above average in comparison to the [other] Indians" (Bair, 2003, p. 337). Another problem was Jung's attempt to force his understanding of the psychology of the Pueblo Indians into his categories of personality types rather than to approach his interviewees without preconceptions. His Spanish analysand later broke with "Mountebank Jung," saying that Jung had destroyed his relationships with the Indians "through his Teutonic stupidity" (Bair, 2003, p. 337).

Perhaps the most damaging aspect of Jung's interpretation of Native American religion as a "space for the unfolding of personality" (Bair, 2003, p. 337), however, was its contribution to the human potential movement of the 1960s and the emergence of New Age spirituality in the 1970s and 1980s. Jung became a guru to an entire generation of spiritually homeless Westerners, looking for "a sense of how to effectively pursue a richer, more authentic, and more complete life" (Schwartz, 1996, p. 11). And Jung's superficial discussion of Native American traditions led many of these seekers to look for authenticity and healing in tribal rituals, ceremonies, and sacred places. Some non-Indians desecrated sacred places. For example, the Cahuilla Indians in California felt compelled to close Tahquitz Canyon to the public in 1969 after a rowdy crowd left a rock concert and descended into the canyon for several days of drug and alcohol consumption. In other instances, Native Americans were offended by the self-centered attitudes of non-Natives toward their traditions. An article written by a member of the Lakota tribe stated:

> All American Indian people must consider if it is worth the consequences of letting non-Indians partake in the ancient religious ceremonies of our originally great nations. Many of the non-Indians are lost or alone, but each of us must decide for ourselves if it is our responsibility to save them. Too many times have we found that our compassion is psychoanalyzed, dissected, and commercialized to eventually become the Sunday movie of the week or locked up in the homes of collectors or the Smithsonian. (Housden, 1999, p. 31)

The peculiar mingling of New Age fascination with alternative forms of spirituality and Native American traditions produced what one writer has termed "plastic shamans and Astroturf sun dances," or crude commercialized exploitation of Native American practices (Aldred, 2000, p. 330). In 1993, a group of Lakota elders issued a formal "Declaration of War against Exploiters of Lakota Spirituality," noting that

> individuals and groups involved in "the New Age Movement," in "the men's movement," in "neo-paganism" cults and in "shamanism" workshops all have exploited the spiritual traditions of our Lakota people by imitating our ceremonial ways and by mixing such imitation rituals with non-Indian occult practices in an offensive and harmful pseudo-religious hodgepodge. (Stampede Mesteth, Standing Elk, & Swift Hawk, 1993, p. 22).

Unsurprisingly, careless borrowing of Native American ritual practices by non-Indians has led to medical as well as psychiatric misadventures: There have been several cases of death from dehydration and heat exposure following amateur sweat lodge ceremonies. As two forensic examiners have reported, "Unfortunately, the adoption of rituals and practices from other cultures may not be a completely safe undertaking" (Byard & Riches, 2005, p. 236).

▣ RELIGIOUS APPROACHES TO PERSONALITY: CHRISTIANITY

This section of the chapter will discuss a religious—as distinct from a spiritual—approach to personality and psychotherapy. Although the boundary between religion and spirituality is not always easy to define, religion generally implies adherence to a communally defined set of beliefs and practices rather than a completely individualized approach to faith. The English word *religion* comes from the Latin *religare,* which means "to tie" or "to bind fast." Spirituality, on the other hand, implies a less formal and less clearly defined interest in the supernatural. In North America, it is not unusual for people to maintain that they are "spiritual but not religious," implying that they feel a need for some sense of connection to a being, force, power, or purpose greater than themselves, but not for participation in a church or synagogue. Some researchers think that people who are active members of a mainstream religious tradition have a different set of psychological traits from those who are interested in nontraditional spirituality (Granqvist, Ivarsson, Broberg, & Hagekull, 2007).

Space does not allow treatment of all the major religious traditions represented in North America. This section of the chapter will focus on Christianity, partly because it is still the dominant religion in Canada and the United States and partly because of its lengthy and complex history of involvement with psychology and psychotherapy. It is important, when studying the relationship between any major religion (whether Western or Eastern) and Western psychology, to distinguish carefully between that religion's teachings about human nature and human personality, on the one hand, and clinical practice by members of that religion, on the other. There are a wide variety of personality theories and approaches to psychotherapy that are compatible with mainstream Christianity (and Judaism), and a given practitioner's religious faith does not necessarily commit him or her to a specific school of psychology.

One remaining caution is in order. Christianity in North America includes a bewildering variety of denominations, from those with elaborate forms of worship (Roman Catholics, Eastern Orthodox, Lutherans, and Episcopalians) to those with less formal styles (Amish and Mennonites, Baptists, Methodists, Pentecostals, Holiness groups, and the Black churches); from those that require long years of academic study on the part of future clergy to those that ordain people to the ministry on the basis of spiritual gifts or a sense of calling. Some Christian traditions have highly centralized forms of church government, with bishops or a comparable hierarchy responsible for the teaching and personal conduct of parish clergy. In other churches, local congregations choose their pastors and allow them to be an intellectual as well as spiritual guide. This variety should be kept in mind because the discussion that follows is necessarily a general overview.

Origins

Christianity cannot be understood apart from its Jewish roots and heritage. The two religions had largely become separate faiths by the end of the first century CE, partly because of the early Church's missionary activities among Gentiles as well as Jews, and partly because Judaism was regarded by imperial Rome as a *religio licita*, or tolerated religion, whereas Christianity was not. In the early 80s, the Emperor Domitian (51–96 CE) officially declared Christianity a *religio illicita*, or outlawed religion, on the grounds that it was a *superstitio Iudaica* or Jewish superstition. The emperor's condemnation indicates both that Roman officials recognized the origins of Christianity within Judaism and also that the new faith had developed its own distinctive teachings and forms of worship.

Scriptural Foundations. The Church retained the Hebrew Bible, or Old Testament, as part of its own sacred scriptures. This acceptance meant that the ancient Hebrew understanding of the human person (and the human person in relation to God) passed into Christianity. Very briefly, the teachings of the Old Testament regarding humans can be summarized as follows:

- Humans were created by God to live in a relationship with him. They are not cosmic accidents or chance by-products of natural processes. God is separate from nature and stands above it; he cannot be simply identified with it (as in some forms of Hinduism or Buddhism). His relationship to human beings has a personal dimension. The various writers of the Old Testament speak of God as a king (Psalm 99:1), a shepherd (Psalm 23), a husband (Hosea 2:2), a warrior (Psalm 18:14), a physician (Exodus 15:26), a comforter (Isaiah 51:3), a mother (Isaiah 49:15), and a teacher (Psalm 119:33), even though they also recognize that God is beyond all categories of race, sex, or occupation and that he cannot be fully comprehended by humans (Isaiah 55:8–9).
- God created matter as well as spirit. He blessed the world he had made (Genesis 1:31), including the heavenly bodies and other physical features of the universe as well as living creatures. Humans are, therefore, beings with bodies as well as souls and minds. The body as well as the mind deserves care and respect because God created it.
- Although humans were created "in God's image" (Genesis 1:27), they also have the potential to commit evil deeds. This falling away from God is known as sin. Humans can choose between good and evil acts and thoughts (Deuteronomy 30:15ff) and are therefore responsible before God for their choices.
- God entered into a **covenant**, or special reciprocal relationship, with the patriarch Abraham, the forebear of the Jewish people (Genesis 17). The covenant committed Abraham and his descendants to worship God alone (rather than the many gods of the Egyptians or Babylonians) and to follow the rules God gave them for a holy way of life. In return, God promised to bless Abraham and his descendants and to give them a homeland, the Promised Land. A contemporary Jewish psychotherapist has said that "the importance of relationship is pivotal in a Jewish psychology. The covenant—the relationship that God has with humanity—is the core of Judaism. Also important is the relationship that people have with each other, for this reflects their relationship with God" (Hartsman, 2002, p. 217).
- These rules for holy living were restated 400 years later, when Moses led Abraham's descendants out of slavery in Egypt. On Mount Sinai, God gave Moses (Exodus 20)

what Christians were to call the Ten Commandments; the Hebrew phrase *'aseret ha-dibroth*, however, is more accurately translated as "the Ten Words." The Ten Words are guidelines to help people choose the good and avoid doing evil.

- People who commit sin can be forgiven by God and restored to right relationships with humans they have wronged through *t'shuva* or repentance. *T'shuva* involves not only asking for forgiveness but also committing oneself not to repeat the sin and to make restitution when possible.

This brief summary offers necessary background for understanding the distinctive aspects of Christian teaching concerning human nature and personality theory as well as what Christians hold in common with Jews.

The books of the Christian New Testament were written toward the end of the first and the beginning of the second century CE. They continue and build on the understanding of human beings set forth in the Old Testament; however, there are also some changes and new emphases:

- The relationship between God and humans is not only personal but deeply loving; Jesus addressed God as his Father (the Aramaic word he used actually means *Daddy*) and taught his disciples to pray to God as Father (Matthew 6:9).
- Jesus' ministry of healing reflects God's concern for people's bodies as well as minds and hearts. Jesus' followers should, therefore, care for all dimensions of a person's needs (James 2:14). In addition, people with special abilities as healers are serving God as well as their fellow humans by caring for them (1 Corinthians 12:9) because God wills health and well-being for all his creatures. Physical disease and mental disorders should not be interpreted as punishment for personal sin (John 9:3) or as evidence of bad **karma** from a previous life but as human needs deserving of good care and treatment.
- Jesus is the mediator of a new covenant between God and humankind that includes Gentiles as well as Jews. This universalism means that any person can become a Christian without regard to race, sex, nationality, or citizenship (Galatians 3:28). As in Judaism, faithfulness to the covenant requires just and ethical relationships with other people as well as with God (Romans 13).
- The Ten Commandments are still binding on Christians as guides for holy living (Romans 13:9). As in Judaism, people can be forgiven for sins provided they repent. They should, however, also be forgiving of one another according to Jesus' words (Matthew 6:12) and example (Luke 23:34).

Later Developments

The Meaning of Person in Early Christianity. As is obvious from the foregoing summary of the New Testament, the person of Jesus is central to Christianity in a way that no single patriarch, lawgiver, or prophet is central to Judaism. As early as the beginning of the second century, Christian teachers had to explain how the traditional Jewish emphasis on the oneness of God (Exodus 3:13ff) could be reconciled with references in the Gospels and other New Testament books to Jesus as God's Son (John 1:34) and to Jesus' promise to send a Holy Spirit (Luke 24:49) as an ongoing guide for the Church. It took several centuries for the bishops and other teachers to work out what is now known as the doctrine of the Trinity.

What is important for our purposes in this chapter is that this process required several generations of leaders trained in both Greek philosophy and Roman law to think through what it means to say that there are three persons in the Godhead. These people had to carefully sort out the differences between Greek (the common language of the eastern Roman Empire) and Latin (the common language of the western provinces) terminology to prevent misunderstanding. They did this to define what it means to say that God is personal and that human beings are persons. Thus, although the philosophical and legal systems of the ancient world may seem remote from contemporary psychology and personality theory, they did provide the best tools available in the third through the fifth centuries for a systematic attempt to define *person*. In the European languages derived from or influenced by Latin—including English—*person* acquired a religious dimension in addition to its theatrical and legal roots.

The writer who contributed the most to the use of *person* as a Latin theological term was not a priest or bishop but a lawyer from North Africa named Tertullian (c. 155–230 CE). Tertullian originated the phrase *tres personae, una substantia* to define the three persons in the Godhead. A modern church historian explains:

> In respect to supremacy God is one; but in respect to administrative action we distinguish three beings within the Godhead which we may call *personae*. Like *substantia*, *persona* is a legal term. In the Roman law courts it meant a party to a legal action—for instance, one of the parties to a contract, whether it be an individual or a partnership or a corporation, or an estate or a unit of government. For the purposes of the contract, each party is considered an individual being and can be called, therefore, *persona*. (In [American] law courts, the word *person* is still used in that manner). The term means primarily a functioning unity. The same general sense is familiar in the Roman theater, where *dramatis personae* are the roles to be performed. Sometimes one actor will play one role throughout the drama; sometimes he will play two or more roles, and then there are a number of *personae*, though only one actor; and the parts will be identified by masks which also may be called *personae*. (Calhoun, 2008, p. 128)

The connection between the doctrine of the Trinity and the application of the word *person* to human beings was the identification of Jesus, an individual human person, with the Son, the second person of the Trinity. What this meant in the daily life of ordinary believers was that human personhood acquired a new dignity. If God became a human being in the person of Jesus of Nazareth, then no human being henceforth could be reduced to a subhuman object. A contemporary Christian psychologist asserts that respect for human dignity is an "irreducible aspect" of any ethically acceptable theory of personality (Van Leeuwen, 1989, p. 192).

Personality Theory and Pastoral Care in Early Christianity. Regard for human dignity led eventually to a new interest in human personality differences. This interest was primarily pastoral, concerned with the care of men and women in local congregations rather than with abstract speculation for its own sake. As the early Church's system of penance for sin evolved, clergy increasingly recognized that spiritual guidance tailored to each person's areas of moral weakness was needed. In addition, the clergy noted that people differ in their responses to various approaches: Some require firm instruction, others are more receptive to gentleness; some respond to intellectual discussion, others are more emotional. By the fourth century, there were manuals of advice for parish clergy on discerning these differences among their parishioners.

An early form of personality theory also evolved within the monastic orders that came into being in the fourth century, first in Egypt and shortly thereafter in the West. Although some early monastics were hermits, others formed communities under the guidance of abbots. Inevitably, communal life led to reflection on personality issues as a potential cause of friction within the community. John Cassian (c. 360–433 CE) was a monk who had visited the Egyptian monasteries and brought their traditions of community life with him when he was asked to establish monasteries (one for women as well as one for men) near Marseilles in southern France about 400 CE. Cassian wrote two books on communal living, the *Institutes* and the *Conferences*, both of which dealt with differences of individual personality and their beneficial as well as their potentially negative aspects.

Another area of pastoral concern involving personality was the spiritual care of the mentally retarded and the insane. Like Judaism, Christianity developed a set of teachings that required a certain level of intellectual understanding as well as emotional commitment. What should be done with those incapable of mastering the basics of belief? Could they be considered full members of the Church? By the 13th century, the Western Church had worked out an understanding of the fullness of human personhood that identified reason and cognition as mental powers that should control the emotions but were not the sole determinants that define a human being. Thus, those whose cognitive capacities are limited by developmental or emotional disorders are nonetheless fully human. The 18th-century Enlightenment, not mainstream Christianity, made critical reason the central defining characteristic of what it is to be human (Keck, 1996).

The Church and Academic Psychology. In the heated controversies that developed within American university faculties after the American Civil War concerning the place of science (and the new discipline of psychology) in the university, Christianity was often caricatured as the enemy of scientific inquiry into the workings of the mind. In historical perspective, however, Christian thinkers had made some noteworthy contributions to theoretical psychology. St. Augustine (354–430 CE), the bishop of a small town in what is now Algeria, has been called the "first modern man" because of his reflections in his autobiography, the *Confessions*, on the nature of human memory, the scope of the human will, and the significance of the human sense of time. No opponent of reason, Augustine also produced arguments against astrology and other magical practices.

The Middle Ages saw the foundation of the first European universities. In the 13th century, an English scholar at Oxford, Robert Grosseteste (c. 1175–1253), was one of the most outstanding researchers of his day, with wide-ranging interests that included what would now be considered psychology and astronomy as well as philosophy and theology. Grosseteste was part of an intellectual revolution that urged mathematics as a tool for understanding nature as well as empiricism (testing a hypothesis through experience, experimentation, and close observation of the natural world). He was the first Western European to fully grasp Aristotle's notion of the dual path of scientific reasoning, from observing particular events to formulating general laws and then using general laws to predict particular events. Grosseteste was the forerunner of Galileo's use of this method in the 17th century.

In the 14th century the most influential contributor to the study of psychology was Nicholas Oresme (1323–1382), a French scholar at the University of Paris who became a bishop. Like Grosseteste, Oresme regarded mathematics as the key to discoveries in the natural sciences. He was a gifted translator who translated many of Aristotle's scientific works into Latin, even though he disagreed with some of Aristotle's statements about physics. On the basis of his experiments in psychology, Oresme anticipated some of the findings of Hermann von Helmholts about auditory and visual perception and the psychophysics of Gustav Theodor Fechner. Oresme maintained that psychological processes could be measured in the same way as physical processes in the external world. Oresme was, like Augustine, an opponent of astrology and maintained that people should look for natural causes underlying surprising natural events (such as comets or unusual weather patterns) rather than automatically assuming supernatural interventions.

What cut short the study of psychology in the medieval universities was not religious opposition—several popes donated books and helped to fund the schools—but the Black Death, which struck Western Europe in 1349 and is thought to have killed a third of the population. Cities, in which most of Europe's universities were located, were particularly vulnerable to the plague because of population crowding.

It was the 19th century, not the 15th or the 17th, which ended in a separation of the natural sciences from the social sciences and the humanities in the universities. In many schools, especially the major research universities of the United States, the natural sciences gained a position of dominance in terms of funding as well as representation on the faculties after the Civil War. Eventually, many academics came to think of science as the only form of genuine knowledge, while literature, theology, and the other humanities were viewed as "art forms," necessary to intellectual polish and well-roundedness, but not as sources of knowledge about the "real world." Such fields as sociology and psychology, which seemed more amenable to empirical testing than history or philosophy, tried to become as objective as physics or chemistry. As was noted in Chapter 10, behaviorism dominated American experimental psychology from the 1920s through the 1950s, not least because of the desire of many psychologists to be regarded as scientists on a par with astronomers or physicists. In the process, many derided the study as well as the practice of religion as intellectually disreputable.

The Impact of Freud. Sigmund Freud was a pivotal figure in the "culture wars" of the 1920s on the popular as well as the academic level. Freud's relationship to the religion of his birth, Judaism, had been fraught with tension and unhappiness. On the one hand, he regarded himself as an enlightened Jew in the cosmopolitan society of the prewar Austro-Hungarian empire. The orthodox Jews of the empire's eastern provinces struck him as backward, with their strange dress and ritual observances. Although Freud's father came from this type of background, the young Sigmund was embarrassed by it. On the other hand, Freud could not deny that he was Jewish by birth. He determined to become a scientist because it was a sure path to professional advancement even in anti-Semitic Vienna; however, he was forced into the clinical practice of medicine because certain positions on the faculty of the university were closed to Jews. When Freud first began to work on what became the psychoanalytic method, he fitted religion into it as an example of "obsessional neurosis."

In Freud's later years, he returned to questions of religion and tradition, viewing religions as widespread patterns in human cultures as well as systems of belief held by individuals. In 1939, he published *Moses and Monotheism,* a book in which he sought to attribute guilt and neuroses to the laws given through Moses on Mount Sinai:

> [Freud] claimed that Moses was a Gentile, son of the pharaoh, and that Moses had been an imposter in Israel. The Jews had been deceived into believing that Moses was one of

them, and the laws he forced upon them had been the source of their misery. Because the Jews had bequeathed the Mosaic laws to Christians, they too were its victims. . . . Freud believed this was the origin of anti-Semitism. Believing that he had exposed the deception, Freud also believed that he could lift the burden of the law from . . . modern civilization. In the process of psychoanalytic insight, the weight of the law is lifted, and the analysand comes to see that guilt is unnecessary. (Vander Goot, 1989, pp. 61–62)

Freud's writings on religion, particularly in simplified form for public consumption, convinced many Christians in the United States that psychology as well as other branches of science was an enemy of faith. The sudden changes in social mores (short skirts for women, jazz music, and drinking and smoking in public, for example) that accompanied the popularization of Freud during the so-called Roaring Twenties did not help matters (Marsden, 1991, pp. 55–56). Freud, thus, played a major part in a growing perception on both sides of the divide that Christian belief and scientific psychology are incompatible.

Rapprochement. Since the heyday of behaviorism, there have been several developments leading to more fruitful discussions between Christian scholars (in a variety of fields, not just academic theology) and scientific psychology. One reason for these positive exchanges was the rediscovery of the importance of the *cura animarum*, or the cure of souls, as part of parish ministry. Priests and pastors in the mainstream churches, Roman Catholic as well as Protestant, discovered that some knowledge of psychology is beneficial in ministering to troubled men and women. Harry Emerson Fosdick (1878–1969), for many years the pastor of Riverside Church in New York City, suffered an emotional and nervous breakdown during his seminary years. Convinced of the value of psychological counseling in restoring his own mental health, he devoted much of his later ministry to counseling members of his congregation. By the 1950s, courses in psychology were offered as electives in many seminaries, Jewish as well as Christian. By the 1970s, summer hospital programs (usually called clinical pastoral education programs) were mandatory for candidates for ordination in the mainstream churches.

Another factor in the changing relationship between psychology and religion was the emergence of alternatives to Freudian psychoanalysis within clinical psychology. Carl Jung's analytical psychology, with its eclectic borrowing of religious symbols and its recognition that the 20th-century crisis of European culture was in part a religious crisis, was appealing to a number of Christian clergy (although others recognized the lack of coherence in Jung's system, not to mention his flirtations with Nazism; Rieff, 1966). In addition to publishing articles on such topics as a psychological interpretation of the doctrine of the Trinity (Jung, 1948), Jung also lectured to gatherings of Swiss clergy (Jung, 1932) on the relationship between spiritual care (*Seelsorge* in German) and psychotherapy. In the United States, the interpersonal psychology of Harry Stack Sullivan, the humanistic psychologies of Abraham Maslow and Carl Rogers, and the cognitive behavioral approaches of Aaron Beck and Albert Ellis offered congenial alternatives to Freud.

Still a third reason for the changing relationship between psychology and religion was the work of such researchers as Gordon Allport, who made psychology of religion a legitimate subdiscipline. Allport's distinction between mature and immature religion (Allport, 1950a) and his creation of a scale for measuring religiosity helped researchers to recognize that people differ from one another in the depth to which they internalize religious faith as well as in the specific religious tradition they accept. A later generation of researchers has studied the relationship of adult religious faith, both Christian and Jewish, to subjects' congregations of origin as well as families of origin, and has uncovered a rich variety of material related to ritual practices as well as religious education in forming mature personalities (Wuthnow, 1999). Thus, psychologists came to accept a distinction between religious convictions that contribute to healthy personality structures and those that appear to confirm Freud's negative judgment of religion as nothing more than an obsessional neurosis.

Research

The relationship between Christianity and psychology has stimulated research in a number of fields since the 1990s. These can be summarized as follows:

History of Ideas. Historians of ideas study such subjects as the role of Christianity in preserving and transmitting ancient medical and scientific texts during the 5th-century barbarian invasions; its involvement in the foundation of the medieval universities and the preconditions of modern science; and the concepts of individual theologians on will, memory, insight, cognition, personality, and other topics of interest in contemporary psychology. In recent years, these studies have helped to correct earlier stereotypes of the Middle Ages as a period of hostility to science and the life of the mind.

Religion and Personality Structure. This field includes research into such subjects as the impact of religious conversion on personality change (Paloutzian, Richardson, & Rambo, 1999); the relationship of religious faith to certain personality traits or personality styles; and the relationship between different levels of personal maturity and religious faith. Some psychologists have attempted to formulate typologies or scales of religious maturity; Fowler's (1981) *Stages of Faith* is one of the best known of these.

Psychological Implications of Specific Religious Practices. Some researchers study the effects of specific ritual observances on participants (Wuthnow, 1999). Some rituals, such as baptism (Meador & Shuman, 2000) and the Eucharist or Holy Communion (Joncas, 1983), are specific to Christians; however, such others as prayer are observed by adherents of all the major religions. Although controlled experiments involving prayer—especially prayer for healing—were at one time uncommon, there is a growing research literature in this area. By 1990, there were reports of at least 131 controlled experiments on prayer for healing—of plants and animals as well as humans (Benor, 1990). Whatever the weaknesses of some of these studies, the important point is that religious practice and its effects on humans are no longer off limits as topics for research in psychology.

Critiques

Critiques by psychologists in this field generally focus on study design—the size of the study sample and method of recruiting subjects; the reliability and validity of questionnaires or personality measures used, if any; or the adequacy of statistical analysis—rather than specific outcomes. In 1997, a report on 30 studies of religious practice published in peer-reviewed scientific journals between 1972 and 1997 stated that only 12 of these studies could be considered rigorously designed (Pelletier, 2002, p. 253). More recent studies have been better designed, in part because they tend to focus more narrowly on a specific attitude or practice (forgiveness, confession, prayer, and worship attendance are common examples) rather than such broad or general categories as "faith." In any event, however, research in the psychology of religious practice is no longer the career-ender it would have been for a physician or psychologist only a few decades ago (Dossey, 1993).

Critiques by Christian theologians and psychologists interested in systematic questions focus on the issue of incompatibility between specific schools of personality theory and mainstream Christian doctrine. That is, are there certain approaches to psychology that conflict with a traditional Christian understanding of human nature and human dignity? There are two major schools that come in for the heaviest contemporary criticism: behaviorism and Jungian analytical psychology. Behaviorism is rejected because of its failure to examine its underlying assumptions as well as its reductionistic view of the human psyche. "The difficulties inherent in behaviorism make it clear that their root lies not in the scientific or experimental methods themselves, but in the philosophical assumptions that determine not only how they are employed, but also what they mean" (Burke, 1989, p. 17).

Jungian psychology is a particularly interesting example of theological critiques of personality theory because there are a number of therapists who consider themselves Christian Jungian analysts. Most of these practitioners make heavy use of dream inter-pretation as well as analysis of their patients' references to symbolic images or objects (Sanford, 1992). On the other hand, there are other researchers who regard Jung's fascination with the occult and his tendency to mix together symbols from a variety of religious traditions in an uncritical and unsystematic fashion to be fundamentally incompatible with Christianity. Even in Jung's lifetime, some clergy, such as the British Roman Catholic priest Victor White (1902–1960), parted ways with Jung after an initial period of interest in his analytical psychology because they recognized that Jung's notion of God as having a shadow is alien to the Old as well as the New Testament; and that Jung's reduction of Jesus to an archetype of the Self is equally unbiblical (Bair, 2003, pp. 544–546). A recent writer states that "my own experience with Jungian Christians is that Jungian categories have commonly overshadowed their Christianity" (Vitz, 1989, p. 66).

▣ NEW AGE THEORIES OF PERSONALITY: THE ENNEAGRAM

New Age thought or spirituality refers to a heterogeneous collection of alternative religions, beliefs, and health practices, interest groups, and artistic or musical styles characterized by indi-vidualism and a do-it-yourself approach to psychology as well as spiritual practice. The term *New Age* itself dates back to 1970 or 1971, when the phrase was first used as a catchall category for people or groups considered part of an alternative spiritual subculture. The New Age move-ment is also known as self-spirituality, new spirituality, or the mind-body-spirit movement.

There are no precise boundaries defining New Age thought; its emphasis on individualism means that it attracts people who may combine beliefs and practices from a wide variety of thought systems. One American scholar has suggested that people who sample many diverse teachings and practices from both mainstream and fringe traditions on the basis of experience rather than intellectual analysis can be considered New Age (Melton, 2000). Thus "New Age" can include believers in such paranormal phenomena as UFOs, channeling, and other psychic phenomena; interest in alternative medical systems or the integration of mainstream Western medicine with traditional medical systems; fascination with such occult or esoteric traditions as the Tarot, astrology, the kabbalah, magic, or alchemy; the use of crystals, color therapy, or other healing modalities thought to have mystical properties; belief in reincarnation or other teachings considered unacceptable in mainstream Judaism or Christianity; or an attachment to the environmental movement as a kind of alternative religion. Some observers estimate that as many as 20% of adults in Canada and the United States accept at least some beliefs or practices of New Age thought.

New Age beliefs draw from a wide variety of religious and spiritual traditions, including Zen Buddhism, Taoism, Sufism (a mystical form of Islam), Hinduism, shamanism, and neo-paganism. Although very few adherents of New Age thought would subscribe to all of the following beliefs, they may be useful to the reader in mapping the main features of the movement as well as its relationship to the systems of traditional medicine discussed in earlier sections of this chapter:

- All forms of life (including humans) are interconnected with one another and with the universe as a whole. The universe is thus a living superorganism with its own consciousness. This belief is sometimes called **cosmic consciousness**.
- The human mind is capable of transcending or transforming material reality, although it is subject to the law of spiritual karma or cause-and-effect.
- There are spiritual beings—angels, **ascended masters**, other benevolent spirits, or space aliens—who will guide humans who open themselves to such guidance.
- Nothing happens by chance or coincidence. Events can be connected in a meaningful manner without direct causality. This notion of synchronicity was first described within academic psychology by Carl Jung (1952), and is related to Jung's notions of the collective unconscious and archetypes (Main, 2000).
- The ultimate level of human potential is theoretically open to everyone; however, it has been realized only by a few ascended masters.
- The afterlife is a series of reincarnations or rebirths meant to educate (rather than reward or punish) the individual soul. All human relationships are part of a person's education and will be repeated in successive reincarnations until the appropriate lesson is learned.
- Intuition or spiritual guidance is a more appropriate method of inquiry than rationalism or the scientific method.
- All religions have a mystical core that is essentially the same; there are no significant differences among the major religions. Some New Age writers maintain that Jesus was either a reincarnation of Gautama Buddha or that he traveled to India to study under Hindu gurus.
- When a certain critical mass of people becomes enlightened, the entire population will undergo a spiritual transformation.
- Some geographic locations have unique energy fields, as do certain minerals and crystals. These places or objects can be used for psychic attunement or healing.
- There were ancient civilizations (such as Atlantis) that left behind monuments (Stonehenge, the Great Pyramid, Aztec temples, Indian burial mounds, etc.) containing secrets ignored by mainstream historians.

The one major theory of personality that has emerged from New Age thought is the **Enneagram**; most of the remainder of this section will focus on its features and contemporary use. The name of the Enneagram, which is a nine-pointed geometric figure used to explain personality theory, comes from the Greek words for "nine" and "drawing" or "writing."

Origins

The Enneagram is usually traced back to a Greek/Armenian mystic named Georges Gurdjieff (1866?–1949), who promoted a program of self-development that he called the Fourth Way, in contrast to systems of thought that emphasize body, intellect, or emotions as separate entities. Gurdjieff maintained that humans lead their lives in a kind of sleepwalking state and that they can attain to higher forms of consciousness, higher bodies, and higher levels of inner development (Needleman & Baker, 1996).

It is important to understand that Gurdjieff himself was part of a larger wave of interest in the occult, **esoteric** teachings of various types, spiritualism, **theosophy**, and alchemy that began in the 19th century. The notion of ascended masters, of secret teachings handed down via **channeling** to human mediums, of wisdom from Eastern religions that was superior to anything Western science could offer, all began around the turn of the 20th century. Such older practices as astrology, Tarot readings, and palmistry also began to reemerge during this period. What is most noteworthy about the small splinter groups of spiritualists and believers in secret teachings that formed in the early 1900s was their near-total lack of a sense of history. Most adherents of these groups even in the early 21st century tend to regard history as "begin[ning] anew for the participant with the contact that she or a particular teacher makes with the higher invisible realms, and all that preceded that contact is dismissed as irrelevant" (Melton, 2000, p. 3). Thus, there is little about New Age thought that is actually new; and the various theories about Gurdjieff's role in formulating the Enneagram or introducing it to the West reflect this lack of interest in history or difficulty in critical evaluation of historical records.

According to some contemporary teachers of the Enneagram, Gurdjieff derived his knowledge of the Enneagram from Sufi mysticism. The Sufis are a mystical sect of Islam that began sometime in the 10th century. Gurdjieff himself, however, never disclosed to his disciples where the figure originally came from; he simply claimed that it was the emblem of certain secret societies. Some maintain that the ultimate source of the Enneagram is "a brotherhood of wise men" in Mesopotamia who preserved the mystic teachings associated with the diagram from about 2000 BCE until the 6th century BCE, when they taught the Enneagram to Zoroaster and the Greek mathematician Pythagoras. After the Persian king Cambyses conquered Egypt in 524 BCE, the keepers of the Enneagram tradition migrated westward and northward until they reached Bokhara (or Bukhara), a city in present-day Uzbekistan. There they transmitted the diagram and its meaning to Muslim mathematicians, who discovered that the nine-pointed figure had some additional interesting mathematical properties. "[The Enneagram] proved to have amazing significance. It could be used to represent every process that maintains itself by self-renewal, including, of course, life itself" (Bennett, 1983, p. 3).

Gurdjieff is generally credited with introducing the Enneagram, whatever its remote sources may (or may not) have been, to the West. In the years following World War I, Gurdjieff opened a school outside Paris that he named the Institute for the Harmonious Development of Man. From that school, the Enneagram was transmitted to small study groups in London, New York City, and Paris. Gurdjieff did not, however, develop the descriptions of the nine personality types that are now associated with the Enneagram.

That further step was taken by Oscar Ichazo (1931–), the founder of the Arica School, named for a city in Chile where Ichazo once taught. The Arica School is best described as a collection of techniques for consciousness-raising and a process called protoanalysis.

Members of Arica believe that protoanalysis is analysis of the complete human being, from the lowest aspects of being human and progressing systematically to higher states of consciousness and full enlightenment.

Ichazo had a disciple named Claudio Naranjo (1997), an anthropologist and psychiatrist who split with Ichazo over the correct interpretation of the Enneagram. Naranjo worked with Fritz Perls, the founder of Gestalt therapy, in the 1960s, and is still considered one of the leading figures in the human potential movement. Naranjo also taught at the Esalen Institute in Big Sur, California, in the early 1970s. Some of his students were American Jesuit priests, who began to adapt the Enneagram for use in their counseling programs with seminarians and laypeople. Although the nine personality types outlined in Tables 17.3 and 17.4 were initially passed down orally from teachers to students, at some time in 1972 or 1973, the types were written down in the form of brief one-page descriptions of each personality type (Riso, 1987, p. 17).

Naranjo had another disciple, Helen Palmer, a former antiwar activist who had worked as a psychic intuitive in San Francisco for several years before taking one of Naranjo's classes in 1973. Palmer has written several books on the Enneagram for a popular audience, focusing on self-analysis and applying the Enneagram to family and workplace relationships (Palmer, 1988, 1995; Palmer & Brown, 1998).

There is no unified school of thought regarding the proper use of the Enneagram or the interpretation of the nine personality types associated with the system. Ichazo has disowned Naranjo, Palmer, and the Jesuit writers on the Enneagram on the grounds that his descriptions of the nine types represent ego fixations that develop in early childhood in response to trauma. These fixations then become the core of a personality attempting to protect itself from repeated traumas through mechanistic and unexamined patterns of thought and behavior. Ichazo maintains that his typology is intended to help people understand their fixation so that they can reduce their suffering and eventually move beyond the fixation. He believes that Naranjo and his followers are misguided and are essentially reinforcing their clients' personality disorders. Even within Naranjo's group of followers, there are different inter-pretations of the nine types. Some teachers felt that the original notes on the nine types overemphasized the negative traits of each type and so developed lists of "healthy" and "average" traits for each type (Riso, 1987, p. 20).

As a result, some people regard the Enneagram as a tool for "meaningful" self-discovery or self-exploration rather than a method for uncovering the source of their suffering and a guide to overcoming it. One such writer states, "[The Enneagram] provides a route not just to more adaptive behavior in short but to an experience of a truer self" (Schwartz, 1996, p. 377). Another says, "The ultimate purpose of the Enneagram is to help each of us become a fully-functioning person. It helps us to see ourselves more clearly so we can become better balanced and integrated individuals" (Riso, 1987, p. 45). The reader will note the use of a key phrase from Carl Rogers to describe the purpose of the Enneagram.

The nine Enneagram personality types, their major qualities, and the childhood experiences and defensive strategies attributed to each type are summarized in Table 17.3.

There have been attempts on the part of some of Naranjo's followers to correlate the Enneagram with other theories of personality or other diagnostic nosologies, as outlined in Table 17.4.

Table 17.3   The Nine Enneagram Personality Types

Type	Positive Traits	Negative Traits	Childhood Experience	Defensive Strategy
1. Reformers	Rational, realistic, conscientious, highly principled	Self-righteous, intolerant, inflexible, severe	Severe parental criticism	Behaving perfectly in order to avoid criticism
2. Helpers	Unselfish, altruistic, empathetic, compassionate	Manipulative, self-deceived, overbearing, coercive	Rewarded for being pleasing and self-sacrificing	Putting others first in order to get affection in return
3. Status Seekers	Self-assured, energetic, adaptable, ambitious	Exploitative, opportunistic, deceitful, exhibitionistic	Valued by parents only for successes and accomplishments	Maintaining an image of superiority in order to impress others
4. Artists	Inspired, creative, sensitive, emotionally honest	Depressive, self-hating, impractical, unproductive	Early parental abandonment and loss	Escaping depression through intense and passionate experiences
5. Thinkers	Visionary, knowledgeable, perceptive, insightful	Tendency toward reclusiveness and withdrawal	Overly intrusive or detached and distant parents	Cultivating detachment and minimizing needs; using knowledge as power
6. Loyalists	Trusting, committed, responsible, trustworthy	Insecure, clinging, anxious, self-disparaging	Untrustworthy or humiliating parents	Paying close attention to the motives of others to ward off harm or attack
7. Generalists	Enthusiastic, vivacious, lively; does many things well	Rude and insensitive, impulsive, infantile; acts out	Childhood deprivation or other frightening circumstances	Seeking pleasures and satisfaction to ward off future deprivation
8. Leaders	Courageous, heroic, self-confident	Aggressive, ruthless, combative, bullying	Domineering or tyrannical parents	Dominating others and denying vulnerability as keys to safety
9. Peacemakers	Emotionally stable, peaceful, patient, good-natured	Repressed, underdeveloped, ineffectual; ignores real problems	Overshadowed by siblings or reared by neglectful parents	Discounting own needs and accepting others' agendas

SOURCE: Based on Naranjo (1997) and Palmer (1995).

Table 17.4 The Nine Enneagram Personality Types and Other Typologies

Type	Basic Characteristics	DSM-IV Categories	Freud's Typology	Jung's Typology
1. Reformers	Principled, perfectionistic, orderly	Obsessive-compulsive personality disorder	Anal retentive	Extraverted thinking type
2. Helpers	Caring, manipulative, possessive	Histrionic personality disorder	Anal expulsive	Extraverted feeling type
3. Status Seekers	Narcissistic, hostile, self-confident	Narcissistic personality disorder	Phallic receptive	No corresponding Jungian type
4. Artists	Creative, intuitive, tendency toward depression	Avoidant personality disorder	Oral retentive	Introverted intuitive type
5. Thinkers	Perceptive, analytic, eccentric	Corresponds partly to paranoid and partly to schizotypal personality disorder	Oral expulsive	Introverted thinking type
6. Loyalists	Dutiful, dependent, self-sacrificing	Dependent personality disorder	Anal receptive	Introverted feeling type
7. Generalists	Accomplished, impulsive, tends to be manic	Histrionic personality disorder with manic features	Phallic retentive	Extraverted sensation type
8. Leaders	Forceful, combative, self-assured	Antisocial personality disorder	Phallic expulsive	Extraverted intuitive type
9. Peacemakers	Reassuring, passive, neglectful	Dependent personality disorder	Oral receptive	Introverted sensation type

SOURCE: Based on Riso (1987).

Theory of Personality

The basic theory of personality underlying the Enneagram as it is currently used is developmental in the sense that each personality type is understood to emerge from specific patterns of childhood experience combined with genetic factors (Riso, 1987, p. 27). On the other hand, teachers of the Enneagram maintain that we cannot change our basic personality type even though "people do change in many ways throughout their lives" (Riso, 1987, p. 28). We can become aware of the automatic behaviors characteristic of our type, strive to maximize the highest qualities of our type, and guard against the negative qualities, but we cannot exchange our Enneagram type for another.

Other aspects of Enneagram personality theory include the following:

- The descriptions of the personality types apply equally to men and women; there is no such thing as a masculine or feminine Enneagram type.
- Not everything in the description of a person's basic type will apply to that person all the time. People fluctuate among the healthy and unhealthy characteristics belonging to their type.
- No personality type is inherently superior or inferior to any of the others; some, however, are valued more highly in Western society than others.

Research

Relatively little clinical research has been done on the Enneagram. This is partly the result of the number of different interpretations of the system, which makes it difficult to evaluate data on any of the nine personality types. One confounding factor that is often mentioned in discussions of the types is that some people don't recognize themselves in any of the nine (Riso, 1987, pp. 29–34; Schwartz, 1996, p. 393). Another is the fact that many proponents of the Enneagram maintain that it is too "spiritual" or complex to be measured by clinical methods. There have been a few attempts to correlate the Enneagram with neuroscience; some have speculated that the nine personality types can be grouped into three sets corresponding to the three parts of Paul MacLean's model of the triune brain. Others have theorized that the nine types can be correlated to high, medium, or low levels of three neurotransmitters in the brain: serotonin, norepinephrine, and dopamine.

Still others have attempted to relate the Enneagram to quality-of-life research. Some European proponents of holistic medicine maintain that the Enneagram's identification of a person's life mission enables that person to "improve and develop health, the ability to function, [and] all aspects of quality of life. . . . To know yourself, your purpose of life (life mission), and talents, and taking these into full use and becoming coherent with life inside and reality outside is what human life is essentially about" (Ventegodt, Flensborg-Madsen, Andersen, & Merrick, 2005).

Most recent research on the Enneagram, however, is in the area of organizational psychology (Haynes, 1994). The Enneagram has been used in nursing schools to evaluate the compatibility of staff members with one another (Wright & Sayre-Adams, 2007). According to the website of the Enneagram Institute in Stone Ridge, New York, SHL, an occupational testing service based in the United Kingdom, invited Don Riso and Ross Hudson in 2004 to "explore the connections" between SHL's personality tests and the Enneagram:

> After a year of testing, independent researchers at SHL, led by Prof. David Bartram, found that the nine personality types of the Enneagram are "real and objective," and that they stand on a par psychometrically with the Myers-Briggs system, the Big Five, and other well-known, accepted psychological systems. In short, the Enneagram is now "scientifically supported" by preliminary tests, and two more years of research are being planned to further validate the Enneagram scientifically. (Enneagram Institute, 2005)

As of 2008, however, there are no references to the Enneagram on the main SHL website.

Critiques

Critiques of the Enneagram are plentiful. Some observers consider it pseudoscience, no more scientifically valid than the Myers-Briggs or similar personality inventories. In addition, the nine personality types cannot be falsified and therefore cannot be empirically validated. For these observers, the Enneagram is an example of "the reliance upon individual, emotion-based evaluations (e.g., "my truth," "whatever works for you") [that] renders New Age spirituality science-proof, and has enabled it to expand massively in an age of science" (Charlton, 2006, p. 433).

Other researchers suggest that the Enneagram, like newspaper astrology columns, is an example of the Forer effect (or Barnum effect): that is, the tendency for people to believe that a description supposedly tailored to them is applicable, even when the description has been worded in very broad terms.

Last, although there are few studies of people who are attracted to the Enneagram, one such study reported in 2007 that young adults attracted to the Enneagram and other forms of New Age spirituality were more likely to have been rejected by their parents and to have insecure attachments to others than young adults who were religious in a traditional fashion (Granqvist et al., 2007).

▣ CHAPTER SUMMARY

The purpose of this chapter has been to introduce readers to some alternative approaches to human psychology and psychotherapy, which they may encounter in research as well as clinical work. As the populations of the United States and Canada become more diverse as well as larger, it becomes increasingly important to have a basic understanding of the different belief systems that may influence clients' psychometric profiles or their response to treatment.

Biographical Index

Alfred Adler (1870–1937), born in Austria, emigrated to the United States. Medical doctor and founder of individual psychology, Adler is sometimes classified as a social psychologist. He is best known for his studies of birth order and his concept of the creative self.

Mary Ainsworth (1913–1999), American. Ainsworth was a developmental psychologist who studied patterns of mother-child interaction. She introduced a procedure called the "Strange Situation," which allowed an observer to study the nature of the attachments between mothers and children.

Gordon W. Allport (1897–1967), American. Usually classified as a trait theorist, Allport also made notable contributions to social psychology—particularly studies of prejudice—and the psychology of religion.

John Robert Anderson (1947–), born and educated in Canada, moved to the United States in 1968. Influenced by the work of Allan Newell, Anderson is known for his development of a theory of human cognition (ACT-R) specific enough to be simulated on a computer.

James Rowland Angell (1869–1949), American. A student of John Dewey, Angell was also influenced by William James. Generally classified as a functionalist, he served as president of Yale University from 1921 to 1937, strengthened the psychiatry department of the School of Medicine, and helped to establish the Institute of Human Relations in 1933.

Aristotle (384–322 BCE), Greece. Aristotle was an ancient Greek philosopher, pupil of Plato, and tutor of Alexander the Great.

Solomon Asch (1907–1996), born in Poland, emigrated to the United States as a teenager. Asch, a social psychologist, became famous in the 1950s for his experiments on social conformity.

Augustine of Hippo (354–430 CE), North African. One of the greatest theologians of Western Christianity, Augustine wrote some of the earliest analyses of human memory, time, free will, and other topics of interest in psychology. His *Confessions* is regarded as the first Western autobiography. His interest in Neoplatonic philosophy helped to bring Greek thought into the European intellectual tradition.

Marcus Aurelius Antoninus (121–180 CE), Italy, Emperor of Rome from 161 to 180 CE, Marcus Aurelius was the last of the so-called "Five Good Emperors." He was known for his philosophical writings, particularly the *Meditations* (written between 170 and 180), which had considerable influence on Albert Ellis.

Avicenna (980–1037 CE), Persian. Avicenna is the Latinized name of Abu Ali Sina, a philosopher and physician who wrote *The Canon of Medicine* and *The Book of Healing*. He is sometimes called the "father of modern medicine" for his accounts of various brain diseases and the impact of emotional stress on the human body.

Francis Bacon (1561–1626), English. Bacon began his professional life as a lawyer but is best known for his defense and advocacy of what came to be known as the scientific revolution. Bacon popularized an inductive approach to scientific inquiry known as the Baconian method. His method included gathering information from natural phenomena through observation, experimenting, and testing hypotheses.

Albert Bandura (1925–), Canadian. Educational psychologist noted for his work on self-efficacy and social learning theory.

Frederic Charles Bartlett (1886–1969), English. Best known for his studies of memory and his introduction of the concept of schemas, Bartlett was a noted experimental psychologist and a forerunner of cognitive psychology. He was elected a Fellow of the Royal Society in 1932, a rare honor for a psychologist.

Aaron T. Beck (1921–), American. Trained as a psychoanalyst, Beck parted company with Freudian theories to develop his own form of cognitive therapy, originally applied to the treatment of depression, later to the treatment of personality disorders and even schizophrenia.

Ludwig Binswanger (1881–1966), Swiss. Considered the father of existentialist psychology, Binswanger studied under both Eugen Bleuler and Carl Jung. He moved away from Freud's theories as a result of reading Edmund Husserl and Martin Buber, and he began publishing books on existential psychology in the 1940s.

Paul Eugen Bleuler (1857–1940), Swiss. A psychiatrist who first gave schizophrenia the name by which it is still known, he also identified autism (in a journal article in 1912). Bleuler is perhaps best known, however, for having employed Carl Jung as an intern at the Burghölzli, the famous university hospital in Zurich.

Medard Boss (1903–1990), Swiss. Another theorist who studied under Bleuler and Jung, Boss is often paired with Ludwig Binswanger as the father of existential psychology. More than other existential psychologists, Boss found dreams useful in therapy, although he did not "interpret" them but allowed them to reveal their own messages to his clients. He called his approach to therapy *Daseinsanalysis*.

John Bowlby (1907–1990), English. A developmental psychologist in the psychoanalytic tradition, Bowlby is best known for his work in attachment theory. He regarded children's attachment behavior as an evolutionary survival strategy that protected human infants from predators.

Josef Breuer (1842–1925), Austrian. Medical doctor and psychoanalyst, Breuer is best known for his collaboration with Sigmund Freud.

Jerome S. Bruner (1915–), American. Bruner is a cognitive psychologist who has written a number of books on cognitive learning theory and educational psychology.

Martin Buber (1878–1965), born in Austria, emigrated to Israel. A biblical translator as well as a philosopher, Buber is best known for his book *I and Thou* (first published in 1923), in which he set forth his understanding of existence as encounter. Buber was a major influence on Ludwig Binswanger, Rollo May, and other existential psychologists.

Cyril Burt (1883–1971), English. An educational psychologist, Burt was controversial in his lifetime for his views on the importance of heredity in determining intelligence and for his advocacy of eugenics. After his death, he was accused of scientific fraud in his twin studies.

Albert Camus (1913–1960), French. A writer and philosopher rather than a psychologist, Camus was often linked with Jean-Paul Sartre even though he rejected the label of existentialism. He was awarded the Nobel Prize in literature in 1957.

James McKeen Cattell (1860–1944), American. A student of Francis Galton as well as Wilhelm Wundt, Cattell was a publisher and editor as well as an academic psychologist. One of his goals was to have psychology considered as a science on a par with the physical and biological sciences. For this reason, he emphasized the importance of the experimental method and quantitative measurements in psychology.

Raymond Cattell (1905–1998), born in England, emigrated to the United States. Known for his application of factor analytical methods to psychological research and his identification of 16 basic source traits as the building blocks of personality. Cattell was accused of racism toward the end of his life because of his views on eugenics and evolution.

Ugo Cerletti (1877–1963), Italian. Trained as a neurologist, Cerletti introduced the use of electroconvulsive therapy (ECT) in the treatment of schizophrenia, depression, and manic-depressive illness. He was influenced by the work of Manfred Sakel and Ladislas Meduna in using chemical agents to induce seizures, and he is said to have gotten the idea to use electrical shocks by watching pigs being anesthetized with electroshock in slaughterhouses.

Jean-Martin Charcot (1825–1893), French. Trained as a medical doctor, Charcot specialized in neurology. He identified several neurological and vascular disorders but is best known for his work in hypnosis and the treatment of hysteria. Both Sigmund Freud and William James visited Charcot's neurology clinic at the Salpêtrière.

Noam Chomsky (1928–), American. Best known for his work in theoretical linguistics, Chomsky has been credited with initiating the "cognitive revolution" in psychology through his critique of B. F. Skinner's behaviorism.

António C. R. Damásio (1944–), born in Portugal, emigrated to the United States. Trained as a medical doctor, Damásio is known for his research on the neurobiology of the mind, particularly the subsystems of the nervous system that govern language, memory, emotion, and decision-making.

Charles Darwin (1809–1882), English. Famed for his theory of evolution as the best available explanation for diversification in nature, Darwin published his landmark *The Origin of Species* in 1859. His best-known contribution to psychology is *The Expression of the Emotions in Man and Animals,* published in 1872, one of the first books to be published with photographs.

René Descartes (1596–1650), French. Noted for his many contributions to mathematics as well as philosophy, Descartes' chief contribution to psychology is his emphasis on the limitations of sense perception and his acceptance of only rational deduction as a method for acquiring knowledge.

John Dewey (1859–1952), American. Known as a philosopher and educational reformer as well as a psychologist, Dewey is usually considered a functionalist.

John L. Dollard (1900–1980), American. Dollard's original training was in sociology and anthropology, although he later studied psychoanalysis; he worked together with Neal Miller at the Institute of Human Relations at Yale University on combining behaviorist psychology with psychoanalytic theory. Dollard is also well known for his studies of race relations in the Deep South.

Herman Ebbinghaus (1850–1909), German. Experimental psychologist noted for his studies of memory and his discovery of the forgetting curve (decline of memory retention over time).

Albert Ellis (1913–2007), American. Originally trained in the psychoanalytic tradition of psychotherapy, Ellis developed Rational Emotive Behavioral Therapy as a more effective and time-efficient approach to neurotic problems. He is often categorized with Aaron Beck as a cognitive therapist.

Epictetus (c. 55–135 CE), born in Greece, taken to Rome as a slave. While in Rome, Epictetus studied philosophy under Musonius Rufus. Exiled by the emperor Domitian, Epictetus returned to Greece and founded a famous school of Stoic philosophy.

Erik Homburger Erikson (1902–1994), born in Germany, emigrated to the United States. A developmental psychologist, Erikson is best known for his coining of the term "identity crisis" and his outline of eight stages of human psychosocial development.

Hans Eysenck (1916–1997), born in Germany, emigrated to England. His work was controversial because of his research on IQ differences among different racial groups and because of an early paper in which he maintained that there is no acceptable evidence for the effectiveness of psychotherapy.

William Ronald Dodds Fairbairn (1889–1964), Scottish. A psychoanalyst who spent his entire career in Scotland, Fairbairn belonged to the group of postwar object relations theorists represented by Donald Winnicott and John Bowlby.

Gustav Theodor Fechner (1801–1887), German. An experimental psychologist, Fechner began his career as a professor of physics. He turned to the study of mind-body relations when a temporary eye disorder in the 1830s curtailed his studies of color and other visual phenomena. He tried to work out mathematical equations for the relationship between the intensity of physical stimuli and the corresponding intensity of conscious perception of stimuli.

Leon Festinger (1919–1989), American. A student of Kurt Lewin, he was best known for his work in social psychology, particularly his theory of cognitive dissonance.

Jean Pierre Flourens (1794–1867), French. Flourens was a medical doctor and physiologist who was asked by the Academy of Sciences in Paris to test Frans Gall's hypothesis of the localization of brain functions. Flourens performed a series of experiments in 1825 on living rabbits and pigeons, demonstrating that different regions of the brain do indeed govern different functions, but not in the way that Gall had proposed.

Jerry Fodor (1935–), American. Fodor is a philosopher and cognitive psychologist influenced by Noam Chomsky and Jerome Bruner. He is known for his theories about the modularity of human thought and the language of thought in the mind.

Viktor Frankl (1905–1997), Austrian. A neurologist and psychiatrist, Frankl survived 3 years in a Nazi concentration camp. After his release in 1945, he developed an existentialist approach to psychotherapy known as logotherapy.

Walter Jackson Freeman II (1895–1972), American. Known as the psychiatrist who popularized leucotomy in the United States as a treatment for mental illness, Freeman invented the transorbital or "ice pick" leucotomy, in which he inserted an ice pick through the back of the eye socket into the brain. He performed almost 3,500 such operations before the death of a patient in 1967 ended his career.

Anna Freud (1895–1982), born in Austria, emigrated to England. The sixth and youngest child of Sigmund Freud, she collaborated with her father until his death in 1939. She then specialized in child psychology and development.

Sigmund Freud (1856–1939), born in Austria, emigrated to England. Trained as a medical doctor and neurologist, Freud became the founder of the psychoanalytical school of psychology.

Erich Fromm (1900–1980), born in Germany, emigrated to the United States. Classified as both a humanistic and a social psychologist, Fromm was interested in the social and political dimensions of human nature as well as individual personality and character orientation.

Frieda Fromm-Reichmann (1889–1957), born in Germany, emigrated to the United States. Trained as a medical doctor, Fromm-Reichmann trained to become a psychoanalyst in Berlin, where she met and married Erich Fromm in 1926. The couple separated in 1933. Fromm-Reichmann came to the United States in 1935 and spent the remainder of her career as an analyst at Chestnut Lodge in Rockville, Maryland.

Claudius Galen (c. 130–c. 200 CE), born in Pergamum, a Greek city in Asia Minor, moved to Rome. Galen was a medical doctor and writer who served four Roman emperors as their personal physician. His theory of the four humors was partially derived from Hippocrates.

Franz Josef Gall (1758–1828), born in Germany, emigrated to France. Considered the father of phrenology, Gall was a neuroanatomist who was one of the first researchers to localize mental functions in the brain. He discovered that the gray matter of the brain contains the bodies (neurons) of nerve cells and that the white matter contains the nerve fibers (axons).

Francis Galton (1822–1911), English. Half-cousin of Charles Darwin, Galton was known as a statistician, geographer, and explorer as well as a psychologist. He is credited with establishing the field of psychometrics as well as coining the term *eugenics*. Galton is also the originator of the fundamental lexical hypothesis.

Michael S. Gazzaniga (1939–), American. A neuropsychologist and colleague of Roger Sperry, best known for his studies of split-brain patients, that is, people with severe epilepsy who have had an operation known as a commissurotomy, which severs the corpus callosum. Split-brain research has demonstrated that the two halves of the brain have distinctive characteristics and specialized activities.

Kurt Goldstein (1878–1965), born in Germany, emigrated to the United States. An eminent neuropsychiatrist who studied World War I soldiers with brain injuries, Goldstein developed organismic psychology, a holistic approach that emphasized the unity of the organism rather than its separate parts.

Wilhelm Griesinger (1817–1868), German. Trained as a medical doctor, Griesinger conducted research into infectious diseases and pathology as well as mental illness and mental retardation. He founded a medical-psychological society in Berlin and published several editions of a textbook on mental illness. He pioneered the study of structural abnormalities of the brain as a cause of mental disorders.

Robert Grosseteste (c. 1170–1253), English. Bishop of Lincoln after 1235, Grosseteste was one of the most outstanding scholars of the Middle Ages, with wide-ranging interests that included psychology and astronomy as well as philosophy and theology. Grossteste's insistence on experimentation in answering scientific questions has been regarded as an early anticipation of the scientific method.

Adolf Grünbaum (1923–), born in Germany, emigrated to the United States. A research professor of psychiatry and a historian of science, Grünbaum is known for his critiques of Freudian psychoanalysis

Georges Gurdjieff (1866?–1949), Greek/Armenian. Gurdjieff was a mystic and spiritual teacher who is generally credited with the transmission (or invention) of the Enneagram and some esoteric traditions associated with it. He is a controversial figure, with some observers considering him the founder of a spiritual psychology that offers insights superior to those of Western science and others dismissing him as an attention-seeking charlatan.

G. Stanley Hall (1844–1924), American. Hall, who studied under both William James and Wilhelm Wundt, became the first president of the American Psychological Association (APA) and the first president of Clark University, where he taught psychology from 1899 to 1920. Hall was well known for his studies of the psychology of adolescence and for inviting Freud to lecture at Clark in 1909.

Heinz Hartmann (1894–1970), born in Austria, emigrated to the United States. Hartmann was a psychologist who was analyzed by Freud himself and considered one of the outstanding psychoanalysts in Vienna in the late 1920s and early 1930s. Leaving Austria in 1938 to escape the Nazis, Hartmann eventually settled in New York City and became one of the best-known members of the New York Psychoanalytic Society. He specialized in the field of ego psychology.

Starke R. Hathaway (1903–1984), American. Hathaway originally intended to become an engineer but eventually earned a Ph.D. in psychology at the University of Minnesota. He collaborated with J. Charnley McKinley, a psychiatrist, on the construction of the Minnesota Multiphasic Personality Inventory (MMPI), perhaps the most widely used objective psychological test in the world. The first edition of the MMPI was published in 1943. Hathaway is considered an exceptional therapist as well as a researcher and teacher.

Martin Heidegger (1889–1976), German. An existentialist philosopher who had considerable influence on French existentialism, Heidegger also influenced such German-speaking psychologists as Medard Boss and Ludwig Binswanger.

Hermann von Helmholtz (1821–1894), German. Originally trained in medicine, Helmholtz became a physicist whose studies of auditory and visual perception, including the perception of motion, provided the basis for the work of Wilhelm Wundt.

Hippocrates of Cos (c. 460–c. 380 BCE) Ancient Greek physician known as the "father of medicine," generally regarded as the founder of a scientific rather than a magical approach to healing. The theory of the four bodily humors as keys to personality traits passed down from the Hippocratic Corpus (a collection of about 60 treatises attributed to Hippocrates) to Galen in the 2nd century BCE.

d'Holbach, Paul-Henri Thiry, baron (1723–1789), born in Germany, moved to France. A philosopher and encyclopedist, d'Holbach is considered one of the earliest self-proclaimed atheists in Europe.

Karen Horney (1885–1952), born in Germany, emigrated to the United States. Variously classified as a neo-Freudian or social psychologist, she broke with Freud's psychology of women and is considered the first feminist psychoanalyst. She concentrated on the study of neurotic behavior and introduced the concept of basic anxiety as a central experience in childhood.

David Hunter Hubel (1926–), born in Canada, moved to the United States. A graduate of the medical school of McGill University, Hubel shared the 1981 Nobel Prize with Torsten N. Wiesel for his work on the visual system of cats. Their work on visual neurophysiology has confirmed the hypotheses of the Gestalt psychologists of the 1930s.

Clark L. Hull (1884–1952), American. Generally classified as a behaviorist psychologist, Hull started out as a student of engineering before he became a psychologist. This early training influenced his development of mathematic equations to explain quantifiable behaviors related to learning and motivation. Hull was also known for his investigation of hypnosis; he demonstrated, among other things, that it is not a form of sleep.

Yoshimoto Ishin (1916–1988), Japanese. The founder of Naikan therapy, Ishin was a devout Buddhist businessman who eventually gave up his business to become a lay Buddhist priest and practitioner of Naikan.

William James (1842–1910), American. Originally intending to be a physician, James turned to philosophy and psychology, establishing the first laboratory in experimental psychology in the United States in 1875. James is best known for his 1902 Gifford Lectures, published as *The Varieties of Religious Experience*.

Pierre Janet (1859–1947), French. Originally trained as a philosopher, Janet earned his medical degree studying under Charcot. He published some innovative studies in dissociative phenomena and post-traumatic disorders.

Smith Ely Jelliffe (1866–1945), American. Jelliffe began his career as a botanist and pharmacist but switched to neurology in the 1890s and then to Freudian psychoanalysis. He founded and edited an influential monograph series that published English translations of Freud, Jung, Adler, and other European psychiatrists. He was also one of the pioneers of psychosomatic medicine in the United States.

Carl Gustav Jung (1875–1961), Swiss. Interested in archaeology as a young man, Jung became a psychiatrist instead. Initially friendly with Freud, he broke with him over the nature of the unconscious. Jung is best known for his concept of the collective unconscious and his interest in dream interpretation and mythological symbolism.

Daniel Kahneman (1934–), born in Israel, emigrated to the United States. A colleague of Amos Tversky in developing prospect theory, Kahneman was awarded the Nobel Prize in Economics in 2002, even though he is a research psychologist.

George Kelly (1905–1966), American. Kelly began his career as an educational psychologist but switched to aviation psychology during World War II and then to clinical psychology, a field that he brought into the mainstream of American psychology. He is best known for his personal construct theory.

Otto Kernberg (1928–), born in Austria, emigrated to Chile and then to the United States. A psychoanalyst in the object relations tradition, Kernberg has written extensively on narcissism and borderline personality disorder.

Søren Kierkegaard (1813–1855), Danish. Variously described as a theologian, a Christian existentialist, an existential psychologist, or the first existentialist philosopher, Kierkegaard had a profound influence on such 20th-century psychologists as Ludwig Binswanger and Rollo May.

Melanie Klein (1882–1960), born in Austria, emigrated to England. One of the cofounders of object relations theory, Klein split with orthodox Freudianism over the possibility of psychoanalyzing children and pioneered the use of play therapy in understanding children's emotional development. She is also known for her emphasis on the centrality of envy and aggression in child development.

Kurt Koffka (1886–1941), born in Germany, emigrated to the United States. One of the founders of the Gestalt school of psychology, he helped to introduce its principles to American students and researchers.

Wolfgang Köhler (1887–1967), born in Estonia, emigrated to the United States. A Gestalt psychologist, Köhler pioneered the use of anthropoid apes as laboratory subjects rather than dogs (Ivan Pavlov) or cats (Edward Thorndike). Köhler's most famous work was done between 1913 and 1917, when he studied a group of chimpanzees on Tenerife in the Canary Islands. After moving to the United States, Köhler taught at several colleges and served as president of the American Psychological Association.

Emil Kraepelin (1856–1926), German. Trained as a psychiatrist, Kraepelin is best known for his attempt to create a diagnostic system for mental illnesses based on patterns of symptoms (rather than single symptoms in isolation) and for his conviction that mental disorders have specific biological causes. He made important contributions to the diagnosis of Alzheimer's disease, schizophrenia (which he called dementia praecox), and bipolar disorder.

Ernst Kretschmer (1888–1964), German. A psychiatrist, Kretschmer first identified the condition known as a persistent vegetative state. He is better known, however, for his classificatory system that linked personality differences to body types. Kretschmer identified pyknics (stocky, overweight, and inclined toward mood disorders); asthenics (tall, thin, and inclined toward schizophrenia); and athletics (relatively free from mental illness).

de La Mettrie, Julien Offray (1709–1751), French. Trained as a physician and philosopher, de La Mettrie is considered the first of the materialist thinkers of the European Enlightenment. His work has also been called a forerunner of cognitive science.

Jean-Baptiste de Monet, Chevalier de Lamarck (1742–1829), French. Lamarck was a zoologist who served as a curator of plant and invertebrate life at the Museum of Natural History in Paris. He was an early proponent of evolution, which he saw as proceeding according to natural laws, but he is largely remembered for the discredited notion that acquired traits can be inherited.

Richard T. LaPiere (1899–1986), American. A professor of sociology at Stanford University for many years, LaPiere specialized in social psychology. His most-cited study was an article published in 1934 on the discrepancy between verbal reports of attitudes and actual behavior in social situations.

Arnold Lazarus (1932–), born in South Africa, emigrated to the United States. Generally grouped together with Albert Ellis and Aaron Beck as a cognitive psychotherapist, Lazarus modified cognitive behavioral therapy into what he calls multimodal therapy, an approach to treatment that involves seven different but related modalities.

Joseph LeDoux (1949–), American. A cognitive neuroscientist who has studied the amygdala as the focal point of the learning and storage of fear in humans, LeDoux emphasizes the interrelationship of cognition and emotion.

Kurt Lewin (1890–1947), born in Germany, emigrated to the United States. Known for his introduction and development of field theory, Lewin was also a pioneer in the study of group dynamics, T-groups, sensitivity training, and action research.

John Locke (1632–1704), English. Trained as a physician, Locke is better known as a political philosopher. His chief contribution to personality theory is his empiricism, or the notion that all human knowledge originates in experience.

Cesare Lombroso (1835–1909), Italian. Lombroso was an army surgeon who later became a psychiatrist and criminologist. He believed that criminality is inherited and that criminals can be identified by their physical features. Many of Lombroso's theories are now considered pseudoscience.

Niccolò di Bernardo dei Machiavelli (1469–1527), Italian. Generally regarded as a political theorist, his observations about human nature have made his name a synonym for the belief that the ends justify the means.

Paul D. MacLean (1913–2008), American. A physician who specialized in neurology and served as director of the National Institute of Mental Health, MacLean has made many contributions to brain research and psychiatry, particularly his evolutionary model of the triune brain.

Margaret Mahler (1897–1985), born in Hungary, later moved to England and then to the United States. Trained as a psychoanalyst in Vienna in the 1930s, Mahler began to focus on the treatment of disturbed children after her move to the United States in 1938. She is best known for her separation-individuation theory of child development.

Bronislaw Malinowski (1884–1942), Polish. Considered one of the most important anthropologists of the 20th century, Malinowski's fieldwork with the Trobriand Islanders during World War I helped to show that Freud's concept of the Oedipus complex is not universally applicable.

Abraham Maslow (1908–1970), American. A humanistic psychologist, Maslow introduced the notion of a hierarchy of human needs. He is considered one of the intellectual fathers of the human potential movement of the 1960s.

Jeffrey Moussaieff Masson (1941–), Canadian. Trained as a Sanskrit scholar as well as a psychoanalyst, Masson turned away from the field after he became the central figure in a controversy involving his use of the Freud archives. After writing several books attacking all forms of psychotherapy as essentially exploitive, Masson has produced several others on the emotional lives of animals.

William McDougall (1871–1938), born in England, emigrated to the United States. Best known for an approach that he called hormic psychology, a subtype of functionalism, he was a notable opponent of behaviorism.

John Charnley McKinley (1891–1950), American. A neuropsychiatrist, McKinley earned his medical degree from the University of Minnesota in 1919 and his Ph.D. in 1921. Although he was well known in the 1940s for his research in poliomyelitis and writing the first major textbook in neuropsychiatry, McKinley is chiefly remembered for his work with Starke R. Hathaway on the Minnesota Multiphasic Personality Inventory (MMPI).

Ladislas Joseph Meduna (1896–1964), born in Hungary, emigrated to the United States. He pioneered the use of convulsive therapy as a treatment for schizophrenia. Meduna began with camphor dissolved in oil but then used Metrazol (pentylenetetrazol), a respiratory stimulant, to produce convulsions in his patients.

Adolf Meyer (1866–1950), born in Switzerland, emigrated to the United States. Trained in Europe as a neuropathologist, Meyer was influenced by the functionalist psychologists at the University of Chicago after he moved to Illinois. Serving as a professor of psychiatry at Cornell University and later at Johns Hopkins University, Meyer introduced the term *psychobiology* to American psychiatry.

Stanley Milgram (1933–1984), American. A student of Gordon Allport, Milgram was best known for his experiment demonstrating what he called "the perils of obedience" and for his "small world experiment" of 1967.

George A. Miller (1920–), American. Miller is a cognitive psychologist best known for his paper: *The Magical Number Seven, Plus or Minus Two: Some Limits on Our Capacity for Processing Information*, which explored the limits of human capacity to process information. He founded the Center for Cognitive Studies at Harvard University in 1960 with Jerome Bruner.

Neal E. Miller (1909–2002), American. Miller was trained as an experimental psychologist but also studied psychoanalysis at the Institute of Psychoanalysis in Vienna before accepting a position at the Institute of Human Relations at Yale University. He worked together with John Dollard, co-authoring several important books on the applications of personality theory to psychotherapy.

Walter Mischel (1930–), born in Austria, emigrated to the United States. Currently a professor of psychology at Columbia University, Mischel has written two widely used textbooks on personality psychology. He is sometimes termed a cognitive-affective psychologist because he emphasizes the role of cognitive processes in shaping personality.

António Egas Moniz (1874–1955), Portuguese. Trained as a neurologist, Egas Moniz received the Nobel Prize in Medicine in 1949 for his work in psychosurgery, particularly his introduction of a technique known as a prefrontal leucotomy for the relief of severe depression or psychotic disorders.

Shōma Morita (Masutake Morita) (1874–1938), Japanese. Trained as a psychiatrist in Western medicine, Morita developed Morita therapy in the 1920s as a method for treating anxiety disorders through character building.

Ulric Neisser (1928–), born in Germany, emigrated to the United States. Also a cognitive psychologist, Neisser specializes in the study of human memory and intelligence measurement.

Allen Newell (1927–1992), American. Best known for his work in cognitive psychology and artificial intelligence (AI), Newell worked together with Herbert Simon on two of the earliest AI programs, the Logic Theory Machine (1956) and the General Problem Solver (1957).

Nicholas Oresme (1323–1382), French. One of the outstanding mathematicians and scientific researchers of the high Middle Ages, Oresme wrote a number of treatises on the psychology of perception.

Ivan Pavlov (1849–1936), Russian. Winner of the 1904 Nobel Prize in medicine, Pavlov was the first researcher to describe conditioned reflexes in his experiments with dogs. His work is sometimes considered a forerunner of behaviorism in psychology.

Karl Pearson (1857–1936), English. Pearson founded the first university department of statistics. Deeply influenced by Francis Galton, he later published a three-volume biography of his hero. Pearson's later views on eugenics were quite controversial, as he urged "war" upon "inferior races." He regarded these racist views, however, as the logical outcome of his scientific work on human measurement.

Friedrich (Fritz) Perls (1893–1970), born in Germany, moved to South Africa and eventually to the United States. Trained as a medical doctor, Perls served as a military psychiatrist in the South African army before moving to New York in 1946. Considered the founder of Gestalt therapy, Perls was associated with the human potential movement of the 1960s.

Jean Piaget (1896–1980), Swiss. Piaget was a developmental psychologist who became famous for his work with children and his theory of the stages of children's cognitive development.

Philippe Pinel (1745–1826), French. Trained as a medical doctor at a provincial university, Pinel became interested in the study of mental illness after he moved to Paris. He pioneered what would now be called psychotherapy for mental disorders instead of the bleeding and purging used in the 18th century. Pinel published a treatise on mental illness in 1801; translated into English in 1806, it became a standard psychiatric textbook for 19th-century medical students.

Plato (427–347 BCE), Greek. Plato was a philosopher and teacher of Aristotle. His notion of innate forms or ideas (most of them mathematical) was combined with a theory of recollection to explain how human beings acquire knowledge.

Morton Prince (1854–1929), American. Prince was trained as a physician and decided to specialize in neurology after meeting Jean-Martin Charcot. He founded the *Journal of Abnormal Psychology* and pioneered the study of the dissociative disorders.

Claudius Ptolemy (c. 90–c. 168 BCE), most likely an Egyptian who had become a Roman citizen. Ptolemy was one of the most eminent geographers and astronomers of the ancient world.

Wilhelm Reich (1897–1957), Austrian, emigrated to the United States. Reich studied in Vienna under Freud himself, becoming a psychoanalyst and eventually the assistant director of Freud's clinic. He was expelled from the mainstream psychoanalytic community for such therapeutic techniques as touching his patients and asking them to strip down to their underwear during analytic sessions. In the United States, Reich developed some eccentric theories about a form of universal life energy that he called orgone energy. Reich died in prison, where he had been sent in early 1957 for violating federal injunctions against the production and sale of orgone therapy equipment and literature.

Carl Rogers (1902–1987), American. Rogers is regarded, along with Abraham Maslow, as one of the founders of humanistic psychology. He is best known for his style of nondirective psychotherapy. Originally called client-centered therapy, it is now known as person-centered psychotherapy.

Hermann Rorschach (1884–1922), Swiss. Rorschach was a medical doctor and psychiatrist who studied under Paul Bleuler and Carl Jung and devised the projective inkblot test that bears his name.

Julian B. Rotter (1916–), American. Rotter published the first edition of the Rotter Incomplete Sentences Blank, the 40-question projective test for which he is best known, in 1950. Rotter is also known for his social learning theory of personality and his concept of locus of control.

Benjamin Rush (1745–1813), American. A signer of the Declaration of Independence as well as a professor of medicine at the University of Pennsylvania, Rush is considered the "father of American psychiatry." He published the first textbook on the subject of mental illness in the United States in 1812, *Medical Inquiries and Observations upon the Diseases of the Mind*.

John Philippe Rushton (1943–), born in England, moved to South Africa and then to Canada. Rushton is an evolutionary psychologist who has published studies of altruism and the heritability of intelligence.

Manfred Sakel (1900–1957), born in Poland, emigrated to the United States. Trained as a neurologist, he discovered insulin shock therapy in 1927 as a treatment for drug addicts as well as patients with psychotic disorders. The treatment is still used in Europe, where it is known as "Sakel therapy."

Jean-Paul Sartre (1905–1980), French. Existentialist author, philosopher, and playwright who influenced American as well as European existential psychologists.

William Sheldon (1899–1977), American. Sheldon pioneered the study of anthropometry and is best known for his theory of somatotypes (body types).

Herbert A. Simon (1916–2001), American. Simon published in many fields, from computer science to public administration and philosophy as well as cognitive psychology. He worked together with Allen Newell on artificial intelligence. He is credited with the concept of organizational decision-making as it is known today. Simon was awarded the Nobel Prize in economics in 1978.

Burrhus Frederic (B. F.) Skinner (1904–1990), American. A behaviorist psychologist, Skinner also wrote some popular controversial books about social engineering and about child rearing based on operant conditioning. He is also known as the inventor of the Skinner box, a laboratory chamber large enough to hold a rodent or small primate and used to study animal cognition.

Paul Slovic (1938–), American. Known for his work in psychological heuristics with co-editors Amos Tversky and Daniel Kahneman, Slovic is a professor of psychology at the University of Oregon and president of the Decision Research Group.

Charles Spearman (1863–1945), English. A former student of Wilhelm Wundt, Spearman entered psychology after 15 years as an officer in the British Army. He pioneered the use of statistics in psychology, particularly factor analysis, and also did important work on models of human intelligence.

George Sperling (1933–), American. Trained as a cognitive psychologist, Sperling is best known for his work on iconic memory traces, which he demonstrated in a 1960 monograph called *The Information Available in Brief Visual Presentations*.

Roger W. Sperry (1913–1994), American. Winner of the 1981 Nobel Prize in Medicine for his work in split-brain research, Sperry had originally specialized in primate biology before working at the National Institutes of Health and later teaching at the California Institute of Technology.

Saul Sternberg (1932–), American. Sternberg is a cognitive psychologist best known for his studies of short-term memory.

J. Ridley Stroop (1897–1973), American. Inventor of a landmark color-word cognitive task that has been used for more than half a century to demonstrate interference with attention, Stroop was a professor of biblical studies as well as an academic psychologist.

Harry (Herbert) Stack Sullivan (1892–1949), American. Trained as a Freudian psychoanalyst, Sullivan became interested in interpersonal relationships as the basis for understanding individuals, and he is generally grouped together with Karen Horney and Erich Fromm as a social psychologist. He was one of the founders of the William Alanson White Institute.

Thomas S. Szasz (1920–), born in Hungary, emigrated to the United States. Trained as a psychiatrist, Szasz is perhaps the most outspoken critic of contemporary psychiatry. He published a controversial book, *The Myth of Mental Illness,* in 1960.

Theophrastus (372–287 BCE), Greek. Theophrastus was a philosopher and successor of Aristotle as the head of the Peripatetic School. His book *The Characters* is considered the first recorded attempt at systematic personality analysis.

Edward L. Thorndike (1874–1949), American. Thorndike, who was associated with Teachers College of Columbia University, was best known for his studies of animal behavior and learning. He originated the concept of the learning curve.

Edward B. Titchener (1867–1927), born in England, emigrated to the United States. A student and translator of Wilhelm Wundt, Titchener based his theory of structuralism on what he took to be Wundt's ideas. Titchener conceived of sensations and thoughts as structures of the mind.

Edward C. Tolman (1886–1959), American. A behaviorist psychologist, although less radical than B. F. Skinner, Tolman was known for his studies of rats in mazes. His concept of the cognitive map foreshadowed later developments in cognitive psychology.

Amos Tversky (1937–1996), American. A cognitive psychologist and colleague of Daniel Kahneman, he developed prospect theory as an explanation of irrational human economic choices.

Philip E. Vernon (1905–1987), born in England, emigrated to Canada. Best known for his collaboration with Gordon Allport on the Study of Values (SOV) personality measure, Vernon also worked with Allport on studies of expressive movement. In his later career, he researched the influence of genetic factors on intelligence and concluded that they play a larger role in human development than environmental factors.

John B. Watson (1878–1958), American. Founder of the behaviorist school of psychology, later known as a popular writer on childrearing and a consultant to the advertising industry. He conducted a controversial classical conditioning experiment on an 11-month-old infant known as the "Little Albert" experiment.

James W. Watts (1904–1994), American. A trained neurosurgeon, Watts worked together for several years with Walter Freeman in performing lobotomies, including the operation on Rosemary Kennedy, sister of the late President John F. Kennedy, which he carried out under Freeman's supervision. Watts ended his partnership with Freeman (who had no formal training in surgery) when he discovered that Freeman was performing lobotomies on his own without the presence of a board-certified surgeon.

Max Wertheimer (1880–1943), born in Czechoslovakia, emigrated to the United States. Together with Wolfgang Köhler, he is considered one of the founders of the Gestalt school of psychology.

Torsten Nils Wiesel (1924–), born in Sweden, moved to the United States. Wiesel graduated from medical school in Sweden, intending to become a psychiatrist like his father. After working as a researcher in neurophysiology at the Karolinska Institute in Stockholm, he came to join a research team at Johns Hopkins, where he met David Hubel and worked with him on the properties of cells in the central visual pathways of the brain. Wiesel and Hubel shared the 1981 Nobel Prize in physiology or medicine for their work on the neurophysiology of the visual system.

Edward Osborne (E. O.) Wilson (1929–), American. A biologist and naturalist who began his career as a researcher in insect life, Wilson is best known for his work in sociobiology and his insistence that the human mind is shaped more by genetic factors than by culture. Thus, he maintains that there are limits to the power of society to shape or alter human behavior.

Donald Winnicott (1896–1971), English. A pediatrician as well as a psychoanalyst, Winnicott was an influential figure in the post-Kleinian school of object relations theory. He is best known for his concept of the "good-enough mother" and of therapy as a holding environment.

Herman A. Witkin (1913–1979), American. A specialist in cognitive psychology and learning psychology, Witkin conducted a series of notable experiments with Solomon Asch on people's perception of spatial orientation.

Lightner Witmer (1867–1956), American. A student of Wilhelm Wundt, Witmer coined the term *clinical psychology* and helped to found the first psychological clinic in 1896 at the University of Pennsylvania in Philadelphia. He is regarded as an early pioneer in the field of educational psychology.

Joseph Wolpe (1915–1997), born in South Africa, emigrated to the United States. Wolpe was trained as a psychiatrist and developed an approach to treatment known as behavior therapy. He is best known for his experiments in systematic desensitization.

Robert Sessions Woodworth (1869–1962), American. A colleague of Edward Thorndike at Columbia, Woodworth wrote textbooks that were used by generations of undergraduates, most notably *Psychology: A Study of Mental Life* (first edition, 1921) and *Experimental Psychology* (first edition, 1938). Woodworth also pioneered the psychological evaluation of American military recruits during World War I. A functionalist, he was noted for his opposition to the behaviorism of John Watson.

Wilhelm Wundt (1832–1920), German. Considered the father of experimental psychology, he is often described as a structuralist—although this classification was heavily influenced by the English translations of his works by one of his American students, Edward Titchener.

Robert B. Zajonc (1923–), American. Zajonc is a social psychologist who focuses on the basic processes involved in social behavior, with special emphasis on the relationships between affect and cognition.

Glossary

ABC model: The model used in Albert Ellis's approach to explain the connection between irrational beliefs and real-world results: an activating event (A) triggers an irrational belief (B), which then has consequences (C).

actor-observer bias: The tendency to attribute other people's behaviors to their dispositions but to attribute our own behavior to the immediate situation.

actual neurosis: In Freudian psychoanalysis, a psychological syndrome with a contemporary somatic or physical explanation, usually related to sexual functioning.

actualizing tendency: In Carl Rogers's system, a basic characteristic of human beings that seeks to develop all of the capacities that maintain our personality and helps us to move toward autonomy; a force that enhances growth rather than stability.

acupuncture: A treatment modality in traditional Chinese medicine in which fine needles are inserted through the skin at specific points along the meridians to relieve pain or cure disease.

affect(s) (noun): An expressed or observed emotional response to a stimulus.

allele: Any of the alternative forms of a gene that may occur at a given locus on a chromosome.

altruism: Selfless concern for the welfare of others. Some evolutionary biologists consider altruism to be a heritable trait as well as one that is beneficial to the survival of a species.

amygdala: An almond-shaped structure in the limbic system of the brain, which is associated with the emotions of aggression and fear. Its name comes from the Greek word for almond.

anal personality: In Freudian psychoanalysis, a personality shaped by fixation at the anal stage of psychosexual development. There are two subtypes of this personality pattern, anal-retentive, characterized by preoccupation with order, control, and precision; and anal-expulsive, characterized by carelessness, lack of emotional self-control, and general untidiness.

anal stage: The second of Sigmund Freud's stages of psychosexual development, during which the libido is directed toward the anus. In this phase, defecation or the control thereof is the primary source of sexual stimulation. According to Freudian theory, fixations in this stage can result in anal-retentive (obsessive-compulsive) or anal-expulsive (disorganized or labile) personalities.

analysand: A person undergoing a course of psychoanalysis.

analytical psychology: The school of psychology started by Carl Jung in the early 20th century.

anchoring: A term used in psychology to describe the human tendency to rely too much on one trait or item of information when making estimates or decisions. It is also called *focalism*.

anima: In Jungian psychology, the inner feminine dimension of a male's personality.

animism: A general term used to refer to the belief that inanimate objects as well as animals and humans have souls or are inhabited or indwelt by supernatural beings. In simpler terms, animism is the belief that everything is alive or that everything has some form of spiritual consciousness.

animus: In Carl Jung's psychological system, the inner masculine dimension of a female's personality.

anxiety neurosis: In Freudian theory, a chronic feeling of dread or apprehension in which the sufferer has no conscious basis for his or her distress. The Freudian etiology is a weakening of the process of repression such that id impulses become dangerously close to intruding into the conscious ego.

aphasia: Impaired speech production, usually resulting from damage to the cerebral hemisphere. It is sometimes caused by emotional conflicts.

approach-approach conflict: A situation in which people need to choose between one of two mutually exclusive desirable situations. Often, as they get closer to pursuing the chosen situation, the loss of the other opportunity becomes increasingly distressing.

approach-avoidance conflict: The discord people experience when offered a desirable opportunity that has undesirable aspects. Thus, if we are offered a job promotion, we may fear the exposure the job will bring. Thus, we will eagerly approach the job, but as we get closer to accepting it, our fear will increase our desire to avoid it.

archetype(s): In Jungian psychology, one of the basic structures of the collective unconscious; an inherited unconscious thought pattern, image, or idea present in all individual psyches. Carl Jung derived his concept of the archetype from Plato's theory of forms.

artificial intelligence: The ability of a computer to perform operations normally thought to require intelligence. The term is also used to refer to the branch of computer science that investigates the construction of machines that have this ability.

ascended master: A term used in theosophy to refer to spiritually enlightened teachers who were ordinary human beings in previous incarnations but have overcome their negative karma and have been spiritually transformed into higher beings. Jesus, Buddha, Confucius, Mary (the mother of Jesus), and Pope John Paul II have all been regarded as ascended masters by American theosophists.

Asperger's disorder: A specific type of pervasive developmental disorder that is characterized by problems in development of social skills and behavior. Most children with Asperger's disorder, however, have normal intelligence.

associations: Learned connections between two or more elements of mind, such as sensations, images, or perceptions, that relate the function or meaning of these elements to one another. The most basic association is that of stimulus and response.

associationism: A theory that explains complex psychological phenomena as built up from simple sensory perceptions or behaviors.

attachment theory: A term coined by the English psychologist John Bowlby to explain children's tendency to seek closeness to a parental figure and to feel secure in the presence of that person. Bowlby regarded human attachment as an evolutionary survival strategy that developed to protect human infants from predators.

attitude: A readiness to respond in a characteristic way to an object, person, or situation; a positive or negative feeling toward an object. Attitudes are often correlated with traits.

attunement: In Medard Boss's existentialist psychology, a term used to describe moods or emotions. Cheerful people, for example, are in a happy mood because they are attuned to cheerful events, objects, or thoughts.

authenticity: A concept borrowed from existential philosophy, generally understood to include retaining our own individuality and character in spite of external pressures to conform to alien or imposed standards.

automaticity: The ability to perform an action without occupying the mind with minor details required to carry out the action. Automaticity is the result of learning, repetition, and practice. Common examples include walking and playing a musical instrument.

automaton conformity: Erich Fromm's term for escaping the demands of freedom by accepting the personality type preferred by our culture or social group.

avoidance-avoidance conflict: A situation in which we are forced to select between two undesirable choices. This type of conflict leads to vacillation as we move toward what seems to be the lesser of the two evils; our anxiety will increase, and we will then move to the other choice only to experience the same increasing anxiety, ultimately leading to anxious indecision.

awfulizing: Albert Ellis's term for a type of irrational thought that exaggerates the negative aspects of a situation or event, often to the point that the person becomes unable to cope with it.

Ayurveda: The traditional medical system of India, in use since the 6th century BCE. The name comes from two Sanskrit words meaning "knowledge of the life principle."

B-needs: Abraham Maslow's term for being-needs (also called *meta-needs* or *growth needs*). When these needs are met, they do not go away but rather motivate the person to pursue the satisfaction of higher needs.

Barnum effect: A type of validation in which a subject regards a statement that could apply to many people as personally meaningful, as with astrology readings or Chinese fortune cookie messages. It is also known as the Forer effect.

basal ganglia: A group of tissue nuclei located beneath the cerebral cortex, connected to it and to the thalamus and the brainstem. The basal ganglia have several functions in humans and other mammals, including learning, cognition, emotions, and motor control.

basic anxiety: In Karen Horney's thought, the primary emotion experienced by children when they see themselves as isolated and helpless in a fundamentally hostile environment. It is not necessarily the result of abuse but can be produced by anything that disturbs children's sense of security with their parents.

basic evil: According to Karen Horney, parental cruelty, indifference, or abuse is the basic evil that a child may encounter.

basic hostility: This is the response of children who are subjected to basic evil in early development, in Karen Horney's formulation. Because children cannot express their distress at the parent upon whom they are dependent, they will displace the frustration on to others.

BASIC ID: The acronym for the seven modalities or dimensions of personality in Arnold Lazarus's multimodal therapy: behavior, affect, sensation, imagery, cognition, interpersonal relations, and drugs/biology.

Bayesian: Referring to or involving statistical methods assigning probabilities to future events based on past experience or best guesses before experimentation and data collection. These methods are named for the Reverend Thomas Bayes (1702–1761), an English mathematician.

behavior modification: A set of techniques used in some forms of psychotherapy to modify a person's reactions to certain stimuli through positive reinforcement and the correction of maladaptive behavior.

behaviorism: The school of psychology started by John Watson, which focuses on an organism's objectively observable and quantifiable behaviors rather than inner mental states.

being-beyond-the-world: In existentialist psychology, an expression that refers to our possibilities for transcending the conditions of our present existence and realizing our full potential.

beyondism: A quasi-religion that Raymond Cattell attempted to derive from science that presupposed natural selection and eugenics. His publication of a book on beyondism in 1987 led to his being accused of racism and fascism.

biotypology: The notion that human beings can be classified according to their body types or constitutions.

bipolar: Having or involving two opposite qualities; in George Kelly's psychology, a characteristic of personal constructs such that each quality that is important to an individual is defined by its opposite.

black box: A phrase sometimes used to refer to the human mind as an entity whose internal workings are mysterious to either the user or an external observer. It is often associated with radical skepticism regarding the possibility of ever successfully describing the underlying structure, mechanisms, or dynamics of the mind.

borderline personality disorder: A personality disorder characterized by extreme mood swings, emotional dysregulation, chaotic relationships with others, and a tendency toward splitting. The term *borderline* originated in the 1930s, when psychiatrists thought of patients with this disorder as being on the border between neurosis and psychosis.

bounded rationality: A term used to describe behavior that is rational (in the sense of using available information in a reasonable manner) but not optimal because of built-in limitations in the amount of information available or the person's capacity to use it.

bridging: A technique used in multimodal therapy that involves beginning with the modalities of personality used most frequently by the client and using them as bridges to the modalities that the client finds less congenial.

case study: A detailed narrative of the travails a person experiences as a result of a significant life event or psychological problem. Usually, the individual's pre-illness history, course of treatment, and response to treatment are provided.

catharsis: A term used in psychoanalysis to describe the release of emotional tension or anxiety through reliving past events. The English word is derived from the Greek word for purification.

cathexis: Sigmund Freud's term for attaching emotional significance to an object or idea. The reverse process is called decathexis.

channeling: The practice of communicating with or conveying thoughts or energy from a disembodied or nonphysical being or spirit.

cingulate gyrus: A ridge of tissue in the medial region of the brain that functions as part of the limbic system. *Cingulate* is derived from the Latin word for belt; the cingulate gyrus wraps around the corpus callosum like a belt.

classical conditioning: A type of associative learning that involves the pairing of an originally neutral stimulus with an unconditioned (automatic) response to elicit a conditioned response acquired through learning. The best-known example of classical conditioning is Ivan Pavlov's dogs, which were presented with a neutral stimulus (the sound of footsteps, a metronome, or vanilla) at the same time that they were fed. Eventually, the dogs would salivate when presented with the stimuli they associated with food, even though no food was given. Classical conditioning is also called *Pavlovian conditioning* or *respondent conditioning*.

client-centered therapy: Carl Rogers's original name for his approach to psychotherapy. It is now called person-centered therapy.

coefficient of determination: In statistics, the square of the correlation coefficient; it is used in regression analysis.

cognition: A general term that covers the mental processes involved in memory, thinking, and learning.

cognitive behavioral therapy (CBT): An approach to psychotherapy based on modifying a person's thoughts and behaviors to change their emotional response to a certain stimulus or activity. CBT typically includes questioning assumptions or habits of thought about the self, gradually attempting activities previously avoided, and trying out new sets of behaviors.

cognitive dissonance: Anxiety produced by holding two contradictory beliefs at the same time. The term was coined by Leon Festinger.

cognitive psychology: An American school of psychology associated with Ulric Neisser that compares human cognition to a computer's stages of information processing.

cognitive triad: Aaron Beck's term for the three beliefs that he considers the underpinnings of depression: negative views of the self, hopelessness about the present, and negative expectations of the future.

collective unconscious: A term in Carl Jung's system of analytical psychology that refers to the part of the unconscious common to all human beings. The collective unconscious contains the archetypes (forms or symbols that Jung regarded as common to all cultures).

common trait: In Gordon Allport's theory, a hypothetical concept that allows for the comparison of different individuals within the same culture.

comorbidity: A condition in which a patient has two or more coexisting but unrelated disease processes or psychiatric disorders.

complex: In Carl Jung's system, a group or collection of repressed thoughts, feelings, perceptions, and memories that exerts a strong pull or influence on a person's behavior and personality.

conditional positive regard: An aspect of the theory of Carl Rogers in which a significant individual in a person's life indicates that positive feelings, which will provide the person with feelings of worth, will ensue only if the person behaves in a specified manner. This is in direct contrast to unconditional positive regard.

confabulation: In psychiatry, a term that describes filling in a gap in memory with false or bizarre statements that the patient believes to be true. Confabulation should not be confused with intentional lying.

confirmation bias: A type of cognitive bias involving a tendency to look for or interpret new information in a way that confirms our preconceptions and avoids information and interpretations that contradict prior beliefs.

confounding: A situation in which the effects of two or more processes are not separated; the distortion of the effect of a risk factor resulting from the association of other factors that might influence the outcome.

congruence: In Carl Rogers's psychology, the extent of agreement between a person's real self, ideal self, and self-concept. The greater the degree of congruence, the greater the person's psychological health.

conscience: In psychoanalysis, a subsystem of the superego that governs a person's capacity for self-evaluation and self-criticism.

construct validity: A term that refers to whether a psychometric scale measures the unobservable social concept (e.g., inferiority feelings or introversion) that it purports to measure.

constructive alternativism: In George Kelly's psychology, the notion that any given event may be interpreted in a variety of ways.

constructive living: A version of Morita therapy adapted for Westerners.

conversion disorder: A mental disorder in which an unconscious emotional problem is expressed as a loss of or change in physical functioning.

corpus callosum (plural, corpora callosa): A thick band of nerve fibers that connects the cerebral hemispheres of the brain.

correlation coefficient: In statistics, a number that indicates the strength and direction of a linear relationship between two random variables.

cortex: In anatomy, the outer part of any organ, such as the kidney, brain, or adrenal gland. The cerebral cortex of the brain is the gray mantle covering the entire surface of the cerebral hemisphere in humans and other mammals.

cosmic consciousness: The belief, found in some forms of New Age thought, that the universe is a living superorganism with its own consciousness in which humans, animals, and other life forms are interconnected.

countertransference: In psychoanalysis, the analyst's present responses to the manifestations of the analysand's transference.

covenant: In mainstream Judaism and Christianity, the word used to describe the relationship between God and humankind, based on God's promises to humans as set forth in the Old and New Testaments. A covenant is distinguished from a contract (in the legal sense) by its solemnity, usually taking the form of an oath or seal.

cue: In John Dollard and Neal Miller's personality theory, a specific stimulus that tells the organism when, where, and how to respond. An example is an alarm in a fire station that tells the crew on duty that a fire is occurring (when), the location of the fire (where), and that the crew is needed (how to respond).

D-needs: Abraham Maslow's term for deficit or deficiency needs. If D-needs are not met, the individual typically feels anxious.

daimonic: In Rollo May's existential psychology, any natural force or function, such as sex, anger, or ambition, that is strong enough to take over a person. The word comes from the Greek for "little god" or "spirit."

Dasein: In existentialist philosophy, the basic word for existence or being-in-the-world. It means "being there" in German.

Daseinsanalysis: The German name of the existential approach to psychotherapy advocated by Medard Boss.

death instinct: In Freudian theory, a drive toward death or destruction that counterbalances the pleasure principle. Later Freudians sometimes use the term *Thanatos* to refer to the death instinct, although the term does not occur in Sigmund Freud's own work.

debriefing: An intervention following a psychological trauma intended to relieve stress by allowing the people involved to discuss the event and express feelings. The term is also used to refer to the practice of reviewing an experiment with participants after its completion to disclose any deception that may have been involved.

deduction: A process of reasoning that moves from the general to the particular.

Deese-Roediger-McDermott (DRM) paradigm: A model or pattern for psychological experiments involving the use of phonologically and semantically related word lists to test true and false recall.

defense: In Freudian psychoanalysis, any psychological mechanism intended to ward off anxiety by preventing its conscious perception.

defense mechanism: Any of a number of unconscious mental strategies, hypothesized by Anna Freud, that protect the ego from unconscious impulses that the conscious mind would find threatening or morally undesirable.

deindividuation: A state of lowered self-awareness or loss of personal identity. It is commonly invoked as an explanation of the lack of self-restraint in members of a mob.

deletion mutation: A genetic mutation resulting from the loss of genetic material during the process of cell division.

denial: A specific defense mechanism that reduces anxiety by excluding intolerable thoughts, feelings, or facts from conscious awareness.

dependent variable: The factor whose value is determined by that of one or more other factors in an experiment. The dependent variable is sometimes called the response variable or regressand.

desensitization: A therapeutic technique for reducing and eventually extinguishing a fearful or anxious response to stimuli that formerly induced it.

differential reinforcement: A pattern of reinforcement in which reinforcement is provided for behaviors when these behaviors occur at certain times and places, whereas reinforcement is not provided when the behaviors occur in other times and places.

determinism: The philosophical doctrine that holds that all observable phenomena, including social and psychological events as well as natural occurrences, are causally determined by preceding events or natural laws.

discrimination: In B. F. Skinner's behaviorism, an organism's learned ability to distinguish among different stimuli.

disposition: A term that Gordon Allport used in his later work to refer to traits in individuals. He distinguished three types: cardinal dispositions, which govern almost all aspects of an individual's personality and behavior (few people have this type of disposition); central dispositions (major aspects of an individual's personality; most people have between 5 and 10); and secondary dispositions (which include tastes and preferences and may be situation-specific).

dissociation: An unconscious separation of a group of mental processes from the others, resulting in the independent functioning of the dissociated processes. Dissociation is a symptom of post-traumatic stress disorder and certain types of amnesia.

distributed practice: A technique for improving retention of study material or motor skills by distributing effort over many study or practice sessions, as compared to massed practice.

domain specificity: In evolutionary psychology, a term that is used to describe evolved psychological mechanisms (EPMs) that deal with recurrent adaptive problems over the course of human evolutionary history. EPMs that deal with a general ability to adapt to novelty are called domain-general EPMs.

dopamine: A neurotransmitter produced in the brain that helps to regulate movement and emotion.

dosha: In Ayurvedic medicine, the Sanskrit word for one of the three essential principles that determine a person's basic constitution and personality.

double bind: A term used to describe a psychological dilemma in which a person is given conflicting messages from a single source and cannot make an appropriate response. At one time, parents who put their children in double binds were believed to cause schizophrenia.

double-blind: A term used to refer to a clinical trial or experiment in which neither the subjects nor the researchers know which subjects are receiving a specific treatment or medication; the goal is to eliminate bias.

drive(s): In Sigmund Freud's system, a basic compelling urge, such as sexuality or aggression. Freud's emphasis on drives as the central factor in human development is sometimes referred to as drive theory. In John Dollard and Neal Miller's work, a drive is a stimulus that impels a person to act but does not specify behavior.

duplication mutation: A mutation that results from the duplication of a portion of a chromosome during cell division and the attachment of the duplicated genetic material to a chromosome.

dynamism: In Harry Stack Sullivan's theory, a recurrent pattern of energy transformation that characterizes our interpersonal relationships.

dysgenics: A term that refers to behaviors or policies that promote the survival or reproduction of weak or diseased individuals of a species at the expense of healthier and stronger individuals.

dysphoria: A condition of feeling unhappy or unwell.

ego: In Sigmund Freud's system, the part of the personality attuned to the reality principle; it operates according to reality testing and secondary process thinking. In Carl Jung's system, a person's conscious perception of him- or herself.

ego-dystonic: An adjective used to describe aspects of our behavior or attitudes that are viewed as inconsistent with our fundamental beliefs and personality. It is the opposite of ego-syntonic, a term used to describe aspects of our behavior or attitudes viewed as acceptable to and consistent with our fundamental personality and beliefs.

ego-ideal: In Freudian psychoanalysis, a subsystem of the ego that constructs an ideal image of the self.

ego psychology: A school of psychology started by Anna Freud that emphasizes the importance of expanding the conflict-free sphere of ego functioning rather than focusing on internal mental conflicts.

Electra complex: A concept used in Freudian psychoanalysis, modeled on the Oedipus complex, to denote a girl's desire for the exclusive love of her father and the wish to eliminate her mother. It is named after the daughter of Agamemnon, King of Mycenae, who helped to plot the murder of her mother, Clytemnestra. Sigmund Freud disapproved of the introduction of the term.

electroconvulsive therapy (ECT; also called *electroshock therapy*): A form of treatment of mental disorders (most commonly severe depression) in which an electric current is passed through the brain to produce convulsions.

emergent interactive agency: In Albert Bandura's system, a definition of human cognitive processes as emergent brain activities that exert determinative influence on behavior. Emergent properties differ qualitatively from their constituent elements and therefore are not reducible to them.

empathy: One of six conditions that Carl Rogers considered essential for successful psychotherapy; it refers to the therapist's ability to suspend his or her own judgments and beliefs and enter as fully as possible into the client's perspective. Empathy is also an important concept in Heinz Kohut's self psychology.

empiricism: The philosophical position, associated with John Locke, that human knowledge is gained from sense experience, observation, and experimentation.

enculturation: The process by which we learn the traditions of our culture and absorb its attitudes and values.

Enneagram: A nine-pointed geometric figure inscribed in a circle used to represent a typology of personality based on nine principal ego archetypes. The nine personality configurations are sometimes called Enneatypes.

environment of evolutionary adaptedness (EEA): A term first used by John Bowlby that refers to the environment to which a particular evolved psychological mechanism was adapted. The human EEA is generally considered to be the Pleistocene era, which lasted from about 1.8 million years ago to about 12,000 years ago. Human society in the EEA consisted of small tribes of hunter-gatherers whose members knew one another well.

epidemiology: The branch of medicine that deals with the incidence of disease (including mental illnesses) in large populations and tracks the sources and causes of epidemics.

epigenetic: Related to or involving any change in gene function that does not involve a change in DNA sequence.

epinephrine: A hormone secreted by the adrenal gland in response to stress or anger. It increases heart rate, blood pressure, and the body's metabolism of carbohydrates.

epistasis: In genetics, a condition in which the action of one gene is modified by one or several genes that assort independently.

erg(s): In Raymond Cattell's theory, an innate or constitutional dynamic trait similar to an instinct.

ergonomics: The application of scientific information concerning the human body and psyche to the design of objects, systems, and environments for human use.

eros: In Freudian psychoanalysis, the life instinct; all the impulses or drives that maintain life and the reproduction of the species.

esoteric: A term applied to knowledge or teachings considered to be specialized or advanced in nature, available only to a narrow circle of enlightened or highly educated initiates. Many New Age groups form around esoteric teachings. The Enneagram is supposedly derived from esoteric forms of Middle Eastern mysticism or mathematical speculation.

ethology: The study of human character, its formation, and its evolution.

eugenics: The pursuit of policies or practices, such as mate selection for people with desired genetic traits or selective sterilization of people with undesirable traits, intended to improve the human stock. The encouragement of reproduction on the part of those with desirable traits is known as positive eugenics, whereas the discouragement or prohibition of reproduction by the "unfit" is known as negative eugenics.

evolved psychological mechanism (EPM): In evolutionary psychology, any aspect of a human or other animal's psychology that serves a specific purpose and was created and selected by evolutionary pressures.

existentialism: A 20th-century philosophical movement that studies the meaning of existence and emphasizes our responsibility for our own life choices.

expectancy: In Julian Rotter's social learning theory, our subjective estimation of the probability that a specific reinforcement will occur if we behave a certain way in a given situation.

expectancy effect: A type of cognitive bias that occurs when a researcher or therapist expects a certain result and therefore unconsciously manipulates the experiment or patient in order to find it.

expressive psychoanalytically oriented psychotherapy: Otto Kernberg's term for an approach to treating borderline patients that differs from classical psychoanalysis in that a complete transference is not allowed to develop; the therapist confronts the patient with his or her distortions of reality.

external validity: A form of experimental validity. An experiment is said to have external validity if its results hold across different experimental settings and participants. Its results can be generalized to the larger population.

extinction: The tendency of a response to a stimulus to disappear when it is not reinforced.

extraversion: A term coined by Carl Jung to describe interest in the external environment rather than in our internal thoughts or feelings.

extroversion: The tendency to be outgoing, to actively engage others in most settings, and to vigorously set forth our ideas and values.

face validity: A term that refers to what a test or experiment appears to measure rather than what it actually measures.

factor: An element that contributes to a particular result or situation. In personality theory, factor is roughly equivalent to dimension or trait.

factor analysis: In statistics, a data reduction technique used to explain variability among random observed variables in terms of fewer unobserved variables called factors. Factor analysis was introduced into psychology by Charles Spearman.

false consensus effect: A term used to describe the tendency for people to overestimate the degree to which others agree with them. It is strongest among people who work and socialize within a group of like-minded colleagues or friends.

falsifiability: Capable of being disproved or shown to be false.

fetishism: A paraphilia characterized by displacement of sexual interest and satisfaction onto an inanimate object or nonsexual part of the body.

field theory: A term that refers to Kurt Lewin's social psychological system. Lewin thought that an individual's field (or life space) was built up from a number of factors, including the person's motives, values, needs, moods, goals, and ideals.

firing order: In multimodal therapy, the order in which the seven modalities of the BASIC ID appear in the client's behavioral repertoire.

five-factor model: A model of human personality structure developed by Paul Costa and Robert McCrae that classifies 30 personality traits under five factors known as the Big Five: openness, conscientiousness, extraversion, agreeableness, and neuroticism. They can be remembered by the mnemonic OCEAN.

fixation: A term used in Freudian psychoanalysis to refer to arrested growth and excessive neediness reflecting an earlier stage of development.

fixed-ratio reinforcement: In behaviorism, a schedule of reinforcement in which the number of responses before each reinforcement is identical.

fixed-role therapy: A technique introduced by George Kelly in which clients are asked to write a sketch of their personality and then asked (usually for a 2-week period) to enact a new character created for them by the therapist. The goal is not to effect permanent changes in the clients' personality but to help them become more open to changes in their personal constructs.

fixed-schedule reinforcement: In behaviorism, a schedule of reinforcement in which the time period before each reinforcement is identical.

Forer effect: Another name for the Barnum effect. It is named for Bertram Forer, the psychologist who first reported on it in 1948.

formative tendency: In Carl Rogers's later psychology, the notion that the entire universe is evolving in the direction of greater complexity and fullness.

fourth force: A term coined by Abraham Maslow for transpersonal psychology, of which he was an early proponent.

free association: A technique used in classical psychoanalysis in which the client talks about whatever comes to mind without controlling or organizing the flow of ideas or thoughts.

fully functioning person: Carl Rogers's term for a self-actualized person; in his view, full functioning represented a process rather than a state of being.

functional autonomy: Gordon Allport's term for a behavior that has become detached from its motive in the person's earlier life and is now a goal in itself.

functionalism: A largely American school of psychology associated with William James that regarded such mental functions as memory, perception, imagination, and judgment as the proper subject matter of psychology. Functionalists studied both the ways in which mental processes operated and the ways in which they thought these processes helped organisms adapt to their environments.

fundamental attribution error: A term used to describe a human tendency to overemphasize the role of personality traits in someone else's observed behavior and underemphasize the role and strength of situational factors. It is also known as correspondence bias or overattribution effect.

fundamental postulate: In George Kelly's theory, the basic assumption that our psychological processes are channeled by the ways in which we anticipate events.

fuzzy set: A set in which each member of a group of objects is given a number (usually between 0 and 1) that indicates the degree to which the member belongs to the set.

g factor: Charles Spearman's term for a general intelligence factor that governs an individual's performance across a series of different cognitive tests.

gamete: A mature male or female germ cell, possessing half of the organism's genetic material.

Gemeinschaftsgefühl: A German word coined by Alfred Adler and used by Abraham Maslow that refers to a capacity for empathy or compassion for human beings in general. Maslow considered Gemeinschaftlsgefühl to be a major characteristic of self-actualizing people.

gene(s): The basic physical unit of heredity; a linear sequence of nucleotides along a segment of DNA that the cell transcribes into RNA.

genetic drift: The fundamental tendency of any of an organism's alleles to vary randomly in frequency over time due to statistical variation alone.

genome: The genetic material of an organism.

genotype: The full genetic makeup of an individual or group; the full hereditary information of an organism.

gestalt: In psychology, a form or figure with properties that cannot be derived from a summary of its separate parts. The term was taken into English from German.

Gestalt psychology: A school of psychology that began in the 1920s; it holds that behaviors and other psychological phenomena cannot be explained by analyzing their separate parts but must be studied and understood as wholes.

Gestalt therapy: A holistic existentialist approach to psychotherapy developed by Fritz Perls and his wife, Laura, in the 1940s and associated with the human potential movement. It should not be confused with Gestalt psychology.

group dynamics: A term coined by Kurt Lewin to refer to the processes that form groups and distinguish them from random collections of individuals. Group dynamics include such topics as roles within the group, social interactions, norms, and the effects of group membership on individual members.

guilt: In psychology, a conflicted feeling related to having done something that violates our moral standards or failing to do something we should have done. In Freudian theory, guilt results from a struggle between the ego and the superego.

halo effect: A form of cognitive bias in which the perception of a specific trait in a person is influenced by our previous perceptions of the person's other traits. For example, if our initial perception of someone is favorable, our evaluation of specific traits in that individual is likely to be also favorable. The reverse of the halo effect is sometimes called the devil effect.

hedonic: Related to or characterized by pleasure.

hedonism: A term that can be applied to any philosophy or view of human nature that emphasizes the centrality of pleasure or maintains that the key to human behavior is seeking pleasure and avoiding pain. Albert Ellis's approach to therapy has sometimes been described as responsible hedonism.

heritability: In genetics, a term that refers to the proportion of variations in phenotypes in a population that is due to genetic variations among individuals. Heritability analyses estimate the relative contributions of differences in genetic and nongenetic factors to the total phenotypic variance in a population.

heuristics: Replicable methods or approaches for directing our attention in learning, discovery, or problem-solving. In psychology, the term is often used to refer to rules of thumb hard-coded by evolutionary processes. These rules have been proposed to explain how we make decisions, arrive at judgments, and solve problems, typically when confronted by incomplete information.

hierarchy of needs: A psychological theory first proposed by Abraham Maslow in 1943 to explain the human drive toward what he termed self-actualization. Maslow outlined four deficiency needs (for biological survival, safety, love/belonging, and status) and a fifth need, for psychological growth and transcendence. Maslow believed that people can focus on higher needs only when the lower needs in the hierarchy have been satisfied.

hierarchy of response: In John Dollard and Neal Miller's learning theory, an innate tendency for certain responses to stimuli to occur before others.

hippocampus (plural, hippocampi): A curved ridge of tissue located inside the temporal lobes of the brain, one on each side in humans. The hippocampi are part of the limbic system and play a part in memory and the sense of direction.

holistic: Referring to a belief or system that regards living beings as interacting wholes rather than as collections of separate parts. Holistic views generally situate humans within the larger universe or pattern of nature as well as treating individual people as whole entities.

homeostasis: The property of an open system, especially living organisms, to regulate its internal environment to maintain a stable equilibrium.

homunculus (plural, homunculi): A hypothesized miniature person that doctors of the 16th and 17th centuries assumed to exist inside the human sperm or ovum. The term is also used to refer to the human figure projected onto a map of the brain's surface to illustrate the parts of the body supplied by the various motor and sensory regions of the cortex.

hormic psychology (also called *purposive psychology*): An approach to psychology associated with William McDougall, which holds that human behavior is driven by a goal or purpose (as opposed to Sigmund Freud's pleasure principle). McDougall thought that human striving may be either instinctual or intentional.

human potential movement: A movement that emerged in the United States in the 1960s from humanistic psychology and existential thought. It was heavily influenced by Abraham Maslow's concept of self-actualization, which it regarded as the highest expression of a person's life.

humanistic psychology: A movement that emerged in the late 1950s in the United States in opposition to both psychoanalysis and behaviorism. Sometimes called the third force, humanistic psychology emphasizes the qualities that are unique to humankind and the real problems of human life.

humor(s): In ancient medicine, one of four body fluids (blood, phlegm, yellow bile, or black bile) regarded as determining a person's basic constitution and personality.

hypermnesia: Complete or abnormally vivid recall of our past.

hypothalamus (plural, hypothalami): A region in the diencephalon (the posterior section of the forebrain) of the brain that regulates sleep cycles, body temperature, the sensations of hunger and thirst, and the activity of the pituitary gland.

hypothesis (plural, hypotheses): A provisional theory offered to explain a group of phenomena or data and accepted as a guide to future research and investigation.

hypothetico-deductive method or model: A method of scientific inquiry that proceeds by formulating a hypothesis in a form that could conceivably be falsified by a test of observable data. A test result that could but does not run contrary to the hypothesis is considered to corroborate the theory.

hysteria: A term used in the 19th century to describe various neurotic disorders most commonly found in women and characterized by violent emotional outbursts and physical symptoms caused by psychological factors. It has generally been replaced by the categories of somatization disorder and conversion disorder.

iconic memory: A type of short-term visual memory first identified by George Sperling in 1960. Sperling's experiments showed that iconic memory decays quite rapidly, lasting for only 1,000 milliseconds after the offset of a display. Some researchers think that iconic memory may be governed by the retina of the human eye.

id: In Sigmund Freud's system, the oldest component of the personality. It lies completely in the unconscious, is unorganized, serves as a reservoir of psychic energy, and operates under the influence of primary processes.

ideal self: In Carl Rogers's theory, the self that a person would like to be.

ideas of reference: The concern, usually driven by social anxiety, that events or conversations in our general vicinity refer to us directly. For example, if we enter a room immediately after a person already in the room has told a joke, we may wonder whether those present are laughing at us.

identification: In Freudian psychoanalysis, one of the fundamental defense mechanisms, in which we reduce anxiety by emphasizing the characteristics that we have in common with a stronger or more powerful person.

identity crisis: Erik Erikson's term for the critical phase of human identity formation during adolescence. Some later followers of Erikson have criticized his use of the word *crisis* to describe what they consider a slow process that extends well beyond adolescence.

identity statuses: A term used by James Marcia, an Eriksonian developmental psychologist, to categorize four phases of adolescent identity formation defined by completion (or incompletion) of an identity crisis and commitment (or lack of commitment) to a social role or set of social values. Marcia's four identity statuses are identity diffusion, identity foreclosure, identity moratorium, and identity achievement.

idiographic: In psychology, the study of what is unique to each individual. The terms *idiographic* and *nomothetic* were invented by the German philosopher Wilhelm Windelband to describe two different approaches to knowledge.

implicit learning: A process in which a person learns complex information without being able to consciously describe in words what has been learned.

inclusive fitness: A concept used by evolutionary biologists to explain the benefits of altruistic behavior, in that an organism can be genetically successful through guaranteeing the survival of its relatives (who share most of its genetic material) as well as by reproducing itself directly.

incongruence: In Rogerian psychotherapy, a condition in which our symbolized experiences are separated from our experiences.

independent variable: The factor whose values are independent of the other factors in an experiment and whose value determines the value of the other factors. The independent variable is sometimes called the predictor or the regressor.

induction: A process of reasoning that moves from the particular to the general, usually by extending a statement that is true about some members of a group to the entire group. Conclusions reached by inductive reasoning do not necessarily have the same degree of certainty as the initial premises.

infantile sexuality: A major component of Sigmund Freud's theory of human development. For Freud, infants from the moment of birth have drives toward physical/sexual pleasure, derived first from the mouth, then from the anus, and finally from the genitals. These stages are known as oral, anal, and phallic respectively.

insult: A general term in medicine or psychotherapy for an injury to the body or psyche.

intellectualization: A defense mechanism in which we use reason, logic, technical jargon, or an excessive focus on intellectual fine points to avoid confronting an objectionable emotion or impulse. It is sometimes called a "flight into reason."

internal validity: The degree of confidence that any change in the dependent variable in an experiment is due to the experimental manipulation of the independent variable(s). In the case of a test, it refers to the degree of correlation each item has with the overall score.

interpersonal psychiatry: The theoretical and clinical system of Harry Stack Sullivan, which stressed external and social sources of psychological or emotional problems. This approach was in direct contrast to Sigmund Freud's view that internal conflicts are the basis of such problems.

intervention: In medicine and psychology, any action that produces an effect or is intended to affect the course of a disease process. Interventions may include medications, surgical procedures, physical therapy, various types of counseling, or other treatments.

intrapsychic: Occurring or existing within the individual's mind or psyche.

introjection: An unconscious process in which we take the characteristics of another person or object into our own psyche. A value or idea thus incorporated into the personality is called an introject.

introspection: In psychology, the act of looking inward to scrutinize our own mental processes. Both structuralist and functionalist psychologists made heavy use of introspection in constructing their theories of personality.

introversion: In Jungian psychology, a withdrawn attitude in which people are concerned primarily with internal thoughts and processes rather than the external world.

intuition: In Carl Jung's system, the perceiving function that receives data primarily from the unconscious rather than the senses and understands relationships via insights.

inversion mutation: A genetic mutation that occurs when a portion of a chromosome breaks away during the process of cell division.

irrationality: In Albert Ellis's system, a characteristic of beliefs that either violate the rules of formal logic, distort the external realities of a situation or event, or are dysfunctional and emotionally disturbing.

isomorphism: In Gestalt psychology, a correspondence between a stimulus array and the brain state created by that stimulus.

karma: The Sanskrit word for action or deed. In Hinduism and some forms of New Age thought, it refers to cause and effect; specifically, the effects of our past deeds in causing future consequences in our next reincarnation.

lability: A state or condition of rapid emotional change or breakdown.

Lamarckism: The notion, first propounded by Jean Baptiste Pierre Antoine de Monet, Chevalier de Lamarck, that acquired characteristics can be inherited.

language acquisition device (LAD): An inborn "organ" or capacity in the human brain for learning symbolic language. Noam Chomsky hypothesized the existence of the LAD in the late 1950s and early 1960s in opposition to B. F. Skinner's extreme behaviorist theories of language acquisition.

law of acquisition: In B. F. Skinner's thought, the principle that the strength or frequency of an operant behavior increases when followed by a reinforcer.

law of effect: A law proposed by Edward Thorndike that states that a response to any stimulus is more likely to be repeated if it is accompanied or followed by a positive reinforcement.

lay analyst: A therapist who practices psychoanalysis without a medical degree. Erich Fromm and Melanie Klein are examples of lay analysts.

libido: In Sigmund Freud's theory, emotional and psychic energy derived from biological sexual desire; in Carl Jung's theory, a general form of psychic energy, not necessarily sexual.

life space: In Kurt Lewin's system, our field of perception and action or ourselves and our psychological or behavioral environment.

limbic system: The second part of Paul MacLean's triune brain, consisting of the amygdala, the hippocampus, the hypothalamus, and a few minor structures located near the edge (limbus) of the cerebral hemisphere. The limbic system affects the autonomic motor system as well as motivation and emotions.

locus (plural, loci) of control: Julian Rotter's term for people's belief about their control over reinforcements. Those who believe that reinforcements are controlled by their own behavior are said to have an internal locus of control, whereas those who think that their reinforcements are controlled by outside forces are said to have an external locus of control.

lure word: Also known as a critical lure, a lure word is a word used in memory experiments that is not presented to the test subjects but appears on word recall lists because the words that were actually presented to the subjects are associated with the lure word.

Lysenkoism: A pseudoscientific biological doctrine that holds that heredity is influenced by somatic and environmental factors rather than genetic transmission. It is named for Trofim Lysenko, a Russian biologist-turned-politician.

Machiavellianism: A term used by some personality psychologists to describe a tendency on the part of some people to manipulate or deceive others for advantage or gain. The results are the goal of the Machiavellian person; the means by which one achieves the results are only important insofar as they affect the results.

magical thinking: A general term for nonscientific causal reasoning, such as the notion that our thoughts can influence events or that words can bring about changes. In general, magical thinking confuses correlation (or coincidence in time) with causation.

mandala: In Jungian psychology, a graphic or symbolic pattern divided into four quadrants that serves to represent the self during the process of self-realization. The English word is derived from the Sanskrit for circle.

masculinity complex: In Freudian theory, the notion that women suffer from deeply repressed envy and resentment of men and depreciate their own gender identity. Sigmund Freud thought that the masculinity complex is essentially biological in origin and emerges in various forms ranging from dysmenorrhea and infertility to rejection of marriage and a desire for academic or professional accomplishment.

massed practice: The practice of using few but lengthy study or practice sessions to master a subject to be learned. It is the opposite of distributed practice.

meiosis: The cellular process of reduction division involved in the production of gamete cells, each containing only half of the organism's genetic material.

memantine: A drug that targets the brain's glutamatergic system. Originally developed in the 1990s to treat Alzheimer's disease, memantine has been used in psychological experiments to test whether the personality differences between extroverts and introverts are related to differences in the central nervous system.

mentalism: Any approach to psychology that is distinguished from behaviorism by its use of subjective data (such as information gained from introspection) in researching and explaining behavior.

meridian: In traditional Chinese medicine, any of the pathways (or energy channels) through the body that conduct the flow of *qi*. Certain points along the meridians are stimulated during acupuncture or acupressure.

meta-analysis: A statistical analysis of several separate but similar studies or experiments to pool the data and test them for statistical significance.

metacognition: Awareness or analysis of our own learning or thinking processes.

Metrazol (also called *Cardiazol*): The commercial name of pentylenetetrazol (PTZ), a respiratory and cardiovascular stimulant used to cause convulsions as part of shock therapy for schizophrenia. It was first used by Ladislas Meduna for this purpose in 1934. Metrazol is still used by pharmaceutical companies to test the effectiveness of antiepileptic drugs in animals.

mirror neurons: Specialized nerve cells in the brains of humans and other primates that are activated when the subject watches another primate perform an action. Mirror neurons appear to be essential to observational learning.

modularity of mind: A hypothesis introduced by Jerry Fodor to refer to modules, or "organs," in the human mind that he regards as relatively independent of each other as well as of the central processing part of the mind.

monozygotic twins: Twins derived from a single fertilized egg.

moral anxiety: In Freudian psychoanalysis, anxiety arising from a conflict between impulses coming from the ego or the id, on the one hand, and the moral dictates of the superego, on the other.

Morita therapy: A form of psychotherapy that originated in Japan with Dr. Sh ma Norita, a psychiatrist who treated patients with anxiety disorders through building strength of character. Morita therapy is focused on enabling patients to take action responsively in life regardless of symptoms, natural fears, and wishes.

moxibustion: A therapeutic technique used in traditional Chinese medicine in which the practitioner uses a burning herbal wick prior to acupuncture to warm the patient's skin and open the flow of *qi* in the meridians.

multimodal therapy: A modified form of cognitive behavioral therapy developed by Arnold Lazarus, based on the notion that therapy should address each of seven modalities of the human person. These are behavior, affect, sensation, imagery, cognition, interpersonal relationships, and drugs/biology (corresponding to the acronym BASIC ID).

musturbation: Albert Ellis's term for any belief that escalates a preference into an absolute imperative; for example, people who think they must have something or achieve a certain goal rather than merely wanting to have or achieve it.

mutation: A relatively permanent change in an individual's genetic material, involving either a physical change (transposition or deletion) in the relationships between chromosomes or a biochemical change in the genes themselves.

Naikan: A structured method of introspection developed by Yoshimoto Ishin, a devout Japanese Buddhist. It has been used in mental health counseling and addiction treatment.

narcissism: A state or condition in which a person interprets or regards everything in relation to themselves and not to other people or objects in the external world.

nativism: A term that refers to any view that holds that certain ideas or faculties are innate or inborn in human beings. Plato's concept of innate ideas is one form of nativism.

neocortex: The newest part of the human brain to develop over the course of human evolution, according to Paul MacLean's model of the triune brain. The neocortex includes the cerebral hemispheres; it governs the ability to speak, write, think rationally, and make plans for the future.

neurasthenia: A psychological condition characterized by lack of motivation, psychosomatic symptoms, and a tendency to become easily fatigued; Sigmund Freud and other late 19-century doctors attributed the condition to overindulgence in sex. The word is no longer used as a diagnostic term.

neuron: The medical name for nerve cell. A neuron consists of a nerve cell body, dendrites, and an axon.

neurosis (plural, neuroses): A mental or behavioral disorder with anxiety as the central characteristic and defenses or phobias as the person's coping mechanisms. In contrast to patients with psychotic disorders, people with neuroses do not usually exhibit gross distortions of reality or disorganization of personality.

neurotic anxiety: In Freudian psychoanalysis, anxiety arising from impulses from the id intruding into consciousness.

neurotransmitter: A chemical produced by the body that serves to transmit, amplify, or modulate the electrical signals that pass from one neuron (nerve cell) to another in the human nervous system. Neurotransmitters include such chemicals as dopamine, serotonin, vasopressin, and noradrenaline.

New Age: A general term used to cover various spiritualities that emerged in the West in the 1970s and later as alternatives to both scientific positivism and mainstream Judaism and Christianity. New Age thought is usually characterized by an interest in mysticism and a belief in the interconnectedness of all living beings.

nomothetic: In psychology, the study of large groups of individuals to infer general characteristics or universal principles.

nonconscious: A term used by Albert Ellis to describe beliefs that are innate or so basic that they do not require conscious attention to process. Nonconscious beliefs should not be confused with the Freudian concept of the unconscious.

nondirective: An approach to psychotherapy in which the course of therapy is determined primarily by the client or patient. The term originated with Carl Rogers.

norm: A set standard of achievement or development, usually derived from the average or median scores of a large group of test subjects.

nosology: The branch of medicine that deals with the classification of physical and mental disease.

nucleotide: One of several chemical compounds that are the structural units of DNA and RNA.

numinosum: Carl Jung's term for a transcendent entity that serves as the ground for a religious attitude toward life.

object: In Freudian psychoanalysis, anything through which an instinct can achieve its aim. *Object* is often used as a synonym for *person* in classical psychoanalysis. Good object refers to the supportive or positive aspects of an important person in the analysand's life—usually (though not always) a parent.

object constancy: The capacity of the human mind to perceive objects accurately, even though they change their apparent shape or size as they move in space or as the observer moves while viewing them.

object relations theory: An approach to psychotherapy based on the notion that the ego or self exists only in relation to other objects (people, pets, or material objects), which may be either internal or external. Object relations themselves are the intrapsychic experiences of these early relationships.

objective test (also called structured test): In psychology, a test that is designed to measure one or more specific variables according to scientific standards of reliability and validity. Objective tests are derived from the psychometric tradition of American psychology.

observational learning: In Albert Bandura's psychology, learning that occurs when one person observes another perform an action without any direct reinforcement of the observer.

Oedipus complex: A concept used in Freudian psychoanalysis to explain the childhood origins of some adult neuroses. The complex is defined as a male child's desire to possess his mother exclusively, his jealousy of his father, and his unconscious wish for the father's death. It is named for Oedipus, a mythological Greek king who killed his father and married his mother. According to the Freudian model, this complex should be resolved by the time a child is about 7 years old.

operant conditioning: A concept in B. F. Skinner's psychology that refers to changes in an organism's behavior brought about over time by the consequences of the behavior. It is distinguished from Pavlovian conditioning in that it applies to voluntary rather than involuntary behavior.

oral personality: In Sigmund Freud's system, a personality type originating in fixation at the oral stage of psychosexual development. There are two major subtypes of the oral personality: *oral-dependent*, characterized by a focus on such oral pleasures as eating, drinking, or smoking; and *oral-aggressive* (also known as *oral-sadistic*), characterized by verbal cruelty and a generally sarcastic or "biting" style of interaction.

organismic psychology: A holistic approach to psychology associated with Kurt Goldstein, a neuropsychiatrist who was influenced by the Gestalt school. Goldstein emphasized the unity of the human organism and held that anything that occurs in a part of it affects the whole.

organismic valuing process: Carl Rogers's term for a subconscious process that guides a person toward growth experiences.

orthogonal: Statistically independent.

outcome measure: Data used to evaluate changes in a person's condition or the achievement of a program's objectives and goals.

outlier: In statistics, a datum or observation that differs markedly from others in the data set or sample.

overgeneralization: A logical fallacy or cognitive distortion caused by making an overly broad generalization on the basis of a small sample or other type of insufficient evidence.

paraphilia: A condition in either men or women in which the person requires an unusual or socially unacceptable external stimulus or internal fantasy to achieve sexual gratification. The most recent edition of the *Diagnostic and Statistical Manual of Mental Disorders* (DSM-IV) lists such conditions as *pedophilia* (sexual desire for prepubertal children), *necrophilia* (sexual interest in corpses), *voyeurism* ("Peeping Tom" behavior), *zoophilia* (sexual interest in animals), *exhibitionism* (a compulsive need to display one's genitals to members of the opposite sex), and *fetishism* (the use of inanimate objects or nonsexual parts of the body to stimulate sexual arousal) as paraphilias. Some paraphilias, most notably pedophilia, voyeurism, necrophilia, and (male) exhibitionism, are considered criminal offenses in most jurisdictions in Canada and the United States.

parapraxis: The formal name for a Freudian slip or "slip of the tongue," usually thought to reveal a repressed motive or thought. Sigmund Freud himself usually used the German word *Fehlleistung,* which means "faulty action" in English.

parataxic experience: Sullivan's term for an intermediate level of cognition in which a person perceives a causal relationship between two events but not necessarily on the basis of logic or reality.

part-object: In object relations theory, one body part or psychological aspect of a person that plays a decisive part in a subject's development. An example of a part-object is the mother's breast, which represents the entirety of the mother for the infant.

passive aggression: A term used to describe forms of hostile behavior, usually in response to a request or command from an authority figure, adopted by people who are afraid to express anger directly. Passive aggression takes such forms as procrastination, dawdling, sulkiness, resentment, or failure to complete requested tasks.

pathology: The study of the processes underlying physical disease or other harmful abnormalities, including psychological problems.

Pavlovian conditioning (also called *classical conditioning*): The modification of reflexive or involuntary behavior through the pairing of a neutral stimulus with an unconditioned stimulus.

peak experience: A term coined by Abraham Maslow to describe an intense experience in which the individual transcends the self or temporarily loses the sense of self and feels at one with the universe.

penis envy: A term used by Sigmund Freud to account for women's envy of men's social advantages and privileges. Freud assumed that women believe they are castrated males and consequently desire to have a penis.

percept: The impression of an object obtained through use of the senses; the subjective correlate of a physical stimulus.

perception: In psychology, the process in which humans acquire, select, organize, and interpret sensory information.

person-centered therapy: The current name given to Carl Rogers's nondirective approach to psychotherapy. It was originally called client-centered therapy.

persona: In Jungian psychology, the social mask or outward appearance that a person shows to the world.

personal construct: In George Kelly's psychology, a pattern through which we organize our view of reality through a set of bipolar or dichotomous dimensions. We continually test, revise, and rearrange our personal constructs on the basis of our ongoing life experiences, he thought.

personal unconscious: In Carl Jung's analytical psychology, the second of the three components of the psyche, containing a reservoir of material unique to the individual, material that was once conscious but has been forgotten or suppressed.

personality disorder: A term that refers to a group of behavioral disorders, defined by DSM-IV as lifelong patterns of distorted internal experience and maladaptive external behaviors that cause recurrent difficulties for patients in the areas of judgment, impulse control, and interpersonal functioning.

personology: A term coined by Henry Murray as a partial replacement for the phrase *personality psychology.* Personology emphasizes the study of individual lives over a period of time from a variety of angles; it stresses the importance of the whole person rather than experimental studies of thinking, perception, or other variables divorced from real life. Personology in psychology should not be confused with a New Age pseudoscience, also called *personology,* which purports to teach people how to predict someone's character and behavior from a reading of their facial features.

phenomenal field: In Carl Rogers's theory, the sum total of an organism's experiences.

phenomenology: A school of philosophy that studies human consciousness of objects (whether mental or physical), particularly its quality of intentionality. Modern phenomenology is most closely associated with the philosopher Edmund Husserl (1859–1938), although John Locke and René Descartes are considered its forerunners.

phenotype: The observable properties or characteristics of an organism produced by the interaction of its genotype and the environment.

phi phenomenon: An illusion of movement created by a rapid succession of still images. It was first described by Max Wertheimer in *Experimental Studies on the Seeing of Motion* (1912).

phobia: An objectively unfounded fear of an object or situation that produces a state of panic. Specific phobias are often named for the stimulus of the fear; thus, agoraphobia refers to fear of open or public spaces, aviophobia to fear of flying, acrophobia to fear of heights, and so on. Most specific phobias can be traced back to a traumatic experience, usually at an early age.

phrenology: A 19th-century theory that held that a person's intelligence, character, and personality traits could be determined by studying the shape of the head.

phylogeny: The evolutionary history of an organism or species.

pineal gland (also called the *pineal body*): A small cone-shaped organ located in the forebrain that secretes melatonin and is involved in biorhythms. Its name is derived from the Latin word for "pine" because it is shaped like a pine cone. Descartes thought that the pineal gland was the seat of the human soul and the place in which all human thoughts are formed.

placebo: An inactive substance administered as if it were an active medication. The name comes from the Latin *placebo,* which means "I shall please." Placebos are commonly administered to a control group in clinical trials of new medications while the experimental group receives the new drug.

pleasure principle: In Freudian psychoanalysis, a concept that holds that humans tend to seek pleasure and avoid pain. The pleasure principle has also been defined as the id's seeking of pleasure to reduce tension.

pleiotropy: A condition in which a gene affects multiple traits in an organism's phenotype. The English word is formed from two Greek words meaning *many* and *changes.*

point mutation: A genetic mutation in which a single base nucleotide is replaced by another nucleotide. Point mutations are also known as substitutions.

polymorphous perversity: Sigmund Freud's term for a young child's tendency to seek sexual gratification from various bodily parts. He thought that education from the parents quickly suppresses the child's desire for such gratification, so much so that when the child becomes an adult, he or she will have amnesia about his or her childhood desires.

positive self-regard: A phrase coined by Carl Rogers to refer to self-acceptance without judgment.

post hoc ergo propter hoc fallacy: A logical error that confuses temporal sequence with causality; that is, if one event happens after another in time, the first is often assumed to be the cause of the second. The Latin phrase means "after this, therefore, because of this."

prakriti: In Ayurvedic medicine, the Sanskrit term for a person's basic constitution.

preattentive processes: Mental processes that occur without the subject's conscious attention. Some experimenters believe that they precede conscious attention, others that they operate in parallel with it. The term comes from the work of Ulric Neisser.

preconscious: In Sigmund Freud's topographic picture of the psyche, the division of the psyche that lies between the unconscious and the conscious. The preconscious includes all ideas, past experiences, and other memory contents that can be consciously recalled with effort.

prefrontal leucotomy: A psychosurgical procedure in which the surgeon cuts the nerve fibers joining the frontal lobes of the brain to a structure called the thalamus. It is generally called a lobotomy in the United States.

prepotency: The state or condition of being more powerful, influential, or forceful than another or others. In Abraham Maslow's hierarchy of needs, a prepotent need is one that is stronger than others (usually the higher needs).

prevalence: In epidemiology, the proportion of people with a particular disease or mental illness at a given point in time. It should not be confused with incidence, which refers to the number of new cases of disease that occur over time.

preverbal: George Kelly's preferred term for constructs developed outside our conscious awareness.

primary drive: In John Dollard and Neal Miller's psychology, an innate drive associated with physiological processes necessary to survival, such as hunger, thirst, or the need for sleep.

primary process(es): In Freudian psychoanalysis, the mental processes directly related to the primitive life forces associated with the id and characterized by illogical thinking, disorganization, and a tendency to seek or demand immediate gratification.

projection: A defense mechanism in which we unconsciously attribute our own belief, attitude, or feeling to someone or something else.

projective test: A type of psychological test in which people are given an ambiguous picture or other stimulus and invited to project aspects of their personality into the answer. Projective tests are derived from the psychoanalytic and Gestalt schools of European psychology.

propriate striving: In Gordon Allport's psychology, the aspect of personality that emerges in adolescence and is required for setting and pursuing long-term goals.

proprium: A term used by Gordon Allport for the self, characterized by seven key functions: sense of body, self-identity, self-esteem, self-extension, self-image, rational coping, and propriate striving. Allport later added an eighth function, the self as knower.

prosopagnosia: A condition in which a person loses the ability to recognize faces; it is also known as face blindness. Derived from the Greek words for *face* and *not knowing,* prosopagnosia is variously thought to result from injury to a part of the brain called the fusiform gyrus or possibly to be a hereditary disorder.

prototaxic experience: In Harry Stack Sullivan's theory, the lowest level of cognition, characteristic of infants, in which the individual perceives the world as a disconnected series of sense impressions without any causal connection or symbolic meaning.

psyche: The ancient Greek word for *breath* or *life principle.* In contemporary usage, it generally refers to our mind, personality, self, or soul in contrast to our bodily nature. In Jungian psychology, it refers to the totality of the human personality.

psychoanalysis: A system of theories and therapeutic procedures devised by Sigmund Freud for the treatment of mental illness through the uncovering of unconscious material.

psychobiology: A term coined by Adolf Meyer to emphasize the biological bases of behavior and mental states. Psychobiology is also known as biopsychology, physiological psychology, and behavioral neuroscience.

psychodynamic: Referring to any school or technique of psychotherapy that regards personality as the result of interactions between conscious and unconscious factors.

psychogenic: Originating in the mind or in a mental condition or process.

psychometric(s): The quantitative measurement of psychological characteristics by means of statistical calculations and techniques.

psychoneurosis: A category of psychological disorder that Sigmund Freud distinguished from actual neuroses on the basis of their origin in dysfunctional personality structures produced by attempts to deal with childhood traumas.

psychophysics: An experimental discipline related to physics that deals with the relationship between physical stimuli and their subjective correlates, or percepts. Psychophysicists usually employ experimental stimuli that can be objectively measured, such as musical tones or lights of varying intensity or color.

psychosis (plural, psychoses): A mental disorder, typically characterized by delusions or hallucinations, that causes gross distortions in a person's ability to recognize reality and respond appropriately.

psychosomatic: Referring to a physical disorder caused or strongly influenced by emotional factors.

psychosurgery: The treatment of mental disorders by a brain operation, such as leucotomy.

Psychotherapy: Any of a number of nonmedical interventions for psychological problems that employ education, guided insight, expressions of understanding and sympathy, or behavioral change. Although based on sometimes contentious theoretical orientations, most psychotherapies have in common a confidential, sympathetic relationship in which the client is guided to a new way of thinking, emoting, or reacting to the world via the interactions that occur in that relationship.

punctuated equilibrium: A theory in evolutionary biology that states that most sexually reproducing species will show little change for most of their history. It is opposed to the concept of phyletic gradualism, which holds that evolution is generally smooth and continuous.

qi (or *chi*): In traditional Chinese medicine, the word for vital energy or life force.

quasi-experiment: A type of experiment in which there is manipulation of an independent variable but no random selection of subjects, no random assignment of subjects to groups, and/or no control group.

radical behaviorism: The psychological perspective which rejects everything that cannot be observed or directly measured as irrelevant. This is in contrast to derived approaches like neo-behaviorism or cognitive behaviorism, which apply behavioral principles while accepting that processes that can be inferred or deduced are also relevant to human behavior and personality.

rationalization: A defense mechanism characterized by logical or intellectual analysis of a behavior or impulse to avoid experiencing the emotions associated with it.

reactance: In social psychology, an emotional reaction in direct contradiction to rules or regulations that threaten or eliminate specific behavioral freedoms.

reaction formation: A defense mechanism in which we unconsciously develop behaviors and attitudes that are the opposite of unacceptable repressed desires and impulses.

realistic anxiety: In Freudian psychoanalysis, anxiety elicited by an objectively present external threat.

reality principle: In Freudian psychoanalysis, the way in which the ego satisfies the desires and impulses of the id through awareness of and adjustment to the demands of the external environment.

reconstructive: An approach to therapy that emphasizes the restructuring of the client or patient's personality, often through such insight-oriented approaches as psychoanalysis.

regression: In Sigmund Freud's system, a defense mechanism in which a person reverts to behaviors characteristic of an earlier stage of development.

reincarnation: The belief that the human soul separates from the body after death and is reborn in another human body or other form of life.

reinforcement: The process of increasing or decreasing the likelihood of a subject's response to a particular stimulus.

reinforcement value: In Julian Rotter's personality theory, the importance of a specific reinforcement for an individual in a given situation.

reinforcer: In B. F. Skinner's behaviorist theory, any event that increases or decreases the likelihood of a specific response. A positive reinforcer is one that increases the frequency or likelihood of an operant's being repeated whereas a negative reinforcer is any event that increases the frequency or likelihood of an operant's occurrence when it is removed.

reliability: The quality of consistently yielding the same or compatible results in different clinical experiments or trials or in the same trial over time.

reliability coefficient: A measure of correlation of two scores achieved on the same test taken at different times.

replicability: The quality of allowing successful repetition or reproduction.

repression: The most important psychological defense mechanism in Sigmund Freud's system, in which a wish or desire is so completely blocked from expression that it cannot be experienced consciously or acted out in behavior.

resistance: In Freudian psychoanalysis, a psychological defense mechanism in which the analysand rejects, denies, or otherwise opposes the analyst's interpretations or other comments.

reticular formation: A somewhat poorly defined area in the brain stem that controls such stereotyped actions as walking or sleeping. The ascending reticular activating system, or ARAS, which figures in Hans Eysenck's distinction between introverts and extroverts, is a set of nerves that connects the reticular formation to various areas in the thalamus, hypothalamus, and cerebral cortex.

return of the repressed: In Freudian psychoanalysis, a term that refers to the emergence of repressed material in the form of a symptom or series of symptoms.

role-playing: A technique introduced by George Kelly for individual or group therapy in which clients are asked to temporarily assume another person's role in a situation to explore alternative ways to handle the situation or to better understand the other person.

schema: A cognitive conceptual framework; a plan or model.

schizophrenia: A psychotic disorder characterized by hallucinations, delusions, and abnormalities of perception and thought content. It is now considered a group or spectrum of disorders. Schizophrenia should not be confused with a so-called "split personality" or with multiple personality disorder.

schizotypal: A term used to refer to a personality characterized by a need for social isolation, strange behavior and thought patterns, and often unconventional beliefs.

scientific method: A five-step method of inquiry in which the researcher describes a problem formulates a hypothesis, predicts the results of a trial, tests the hypothesis through experimentation, and draws an appropriate conclusion.

secondary drive: In John Dollard and Neal Miller's psychology, an elaboration of a primary drive that may eventually replace the primary drive.

secondary process(es): In Sigmund Freud's system, the mental processes related to learned or acquired functions of the ego and characterized by preconscious or conscious thought. Secondary processes are marked by logical thinking and the capacity to delay gratification.

security operation: In Harry Stack Sullivan's theory, an interpersonal behavioral device that a person uses to ward off anxiety related to other people.

self-actualization: In humanistic psychology, an innate tendency of human beings to fulfill and enhance their potential, provided that basic physical and social needs are met. The term originated with Kurt Goldstein but was popularized by Abraham Maslow.

self-concept: In Carl Rogers's theory, the organized set of characteristics that we recognize as belonging to us.

self-efficacy: In Albert Bandura's psychology, our perception of our effectiveness in dealing with life.

self psychology: A post-Freudian variant of psychoanalysis pioneered by Heinz Kohut that emphasizes the importance of empathy and mirroring in human development rather than Sigmund Freud's drive theory.

self-system: In Harry Stack Sullivan's interpersonal theory, a dynamism made up of a set of security operations that protects a person against anxiety.

self-talk: The automatic internal dialogue that most people carry on that affects their emotions and eventually actions. It is also known as mind chatter, mind-set, or inner belief system.

selfobject: Heinz Kohut's term for a person's impersonal experience of a function that is provided by someone else. Kohut later defined the selfobject (no hyphen) as "that dimension of our experience of another person that relates to the person's functions in shoring up our self."

sensation(s): In Carl Jung's analytical psychology, a way of gathering information based on the perception of facts in the external world.

sentiment(s): In Raymond Cattell's psychology, a source trait molded by the person's environment (as distinct from a hereditary source trait).

shadow: In Carl Jung's psychology, the part of the unconscious mind that lies relatively close to the conscious mind but is often unacceptable to it. The shadow typically contains the disowned aspects of the conscious personality.

shaman/shamanism: A priest-like spiritual leader who acts as an intermediary between the natural and the spirit world, using magic to cure the sick, determine the hidden meaning of events, or control the weather and other natural forces. Most shamans regard animals as omens and message-bearers. Shamanism refers to any form of spirituality in which shamans play a central role.

shame: An intensely painful feeling of humiliation, dishonor, or condemnation. It is sometimes contrasted with guilt as associated with our self or fundamental being rather than our deeds or specific actions.

shaping: In behaviorist psychology, a process of gradually molding an organism's behavior to approximate a desired behavior as closely as possible.

shinkeishitsu: In Morita therapy, a term that refers to stress-related anxiety, particularly an anxious mind-set that feeds on itself.

situationism: A school of psychology that holds that behavioral differences are due less to individual dispositional differences than to situational ones; that people often behave without the consistency required for trait attributions; and that inconsistent dispositions may coexist within a single personality. Situationism is generally opposed to trait psychology.

social constructionism: An approach to psychology that holds that our perception of reality is a function of our social context, environment, and culture.

social Darwinism: The view that the principles of natural selection first described by Charles Darwin can be applied to human society. Most often associated with the theories of Francis Galton and Herbert Spencer, social Darwinism holds that competition and conflict are inevitable in human societies and that the fittest individuals and groups (including races) will win the battle for survival.

social facilitation: A term in social psychology used to describe the tendency for people to perform simple tasks (or tasks in which they are expert) more effectively in the company of others than when they are alone. Recent research in social facilitation is associated with the work of Robert Zajonc.

social learning theory: An approach to personality psychology that attempts to explain personality development within the context of the individual's society.

somatic marker hypothesis: A hypothesis about decision making first proposed by António Damásio. It suggests that when a person is confronted with a decision, each alternative elicits a bodily state (somatic marker) that corresponds to an emotional reaction. These markers supposedly influence decision making and can guide the individual to make an advantageous choice, even in the absence of conscious knowledge to guide the decision.

somatization disorder: A mental disorder in which the patient has a long and complicated medical history and physical symptoms involving several different organ systems, but with no known organic basis. The term has generally replaced hysteria as a diagnostic category in contemporary psychiatric practice.

somatotype: In William Sheldon's classification system, one of three basic body types (ectomorph, mesomorph, or endomorph) based on anthropometric data.

source trait: In Raymond Cattell's psychology, one of 16 basic temperamental and ability-related traits that underlie surface traits and serve to structure the individual's personality. He subdivided them into environmental and hereditary traits and also categorized them as ability, temperament, and dynamic traits.

spiritualism: A religious movement that was most popular in English-speaking countries in the period between 1840 and 1920. Its distinctive feature is the belief that the spirits of the dead can be contacted by and deliver messages to survivors through mediums (people with a special ability to communicate between the human and spirit worlds).

splitting: A psychological defense mechanism in which the ego compartmentalizes difficult or traumatic experiences rather than integrating them within the personality. Splitting is also used to refer to the tendency of people with narcissistic or borderline personality disorders to see other people as either all good (unrealistic idealization) or all bad (unrealistic devaluation).

Stoicism: A school of philosophy associated with the Hellenistic thinker Zeno of Citium and the Roman emperor Marcus Aurelius, which teaches the importance of self-control and detachment from emotional distractions. It emphasizes virtue, reason, and natural law.

Stroop effect: A demonstration of interference in the reaction time of a task. It is named for John Ridley Stroop, an American psychologist who discovered in the 1930s that subjects asked to say the color of a word printed in a different color from the word's meaning (e.g., "red" printed in blue ink) had longer reaction times and made more mistakes.

structuralism: In psychology, a 19th-century school of thought represented by Wilhelm Wundt and Edward Titchener, which held that conscious mental activity can be broken down into simpler elements. These can then be combined to form more complex mental structures. The term *structuralism* was coined by Titchener.

stupidity-misery syndrome: A phrase coined by John Dollard and Neal Miller to refer to neuroses.

subconscious: A term employed by Pierre Janet that referred to lesser mental processes that were split off from consciousness as a result of pathological states such as hysteria. This is in contrast to Sigmund Freud's use of the term *unconscious* to refer to the preponderance of mental functioning, which is naturally separate from the conscious mind.

subcortical: Referring to a part of the brain lying underneath the cerebral cortex.

subjective: Existing in the mind or referring to the thinking subject rather than the object of thought.

sublimation: In Sigmund Freud's system, a defense mechanism in which a wish that cannot be directly expressed is diverted toward socially or morally acceptable behavior.

superego: In Freudian psychoanalysis, the part of the personality that represents internalized or introjected ideals, values, and moral standards.

supportive: Referring to a type of psychotherapy with limited goals, intended to strengthen the patient's defenses and ability to adapt rather than confronting resistance or challenging the patient.

surface trait: In Raymond Cattell's usage, a cluster of overt behaviors that appear to belong together and can be observed by outsiders.

syllogism: In logic, an argument that takes the form of a major premise and a minor premise connected by a middle term and a conclusion. It is commonly used in deductive reasoning.

symbiosis: In psychology, the mutual cooperation or emotional interdependence of two people, as parent and child or husband and wife.

synchronicity: The notion, often attributed to Carl Jung, that events can be connected in a symbolic or otherwise meaningful manner without direct causality.

syntality: In Raymond Cattell's system, a term that refers to the behavior of a group as a whole; its collective personality.

syntaxic experience: In Harry Stack Sullivan's theory, the highest level of human cognition, dependent on language and other shared symbol systems. Syntaxic experience makes interpersonal communication possible.

technical eclecticism: In Arnold Lazarus's therapy, the use of effective treatment methods drawn from a variety of sources without regard to the theory that produced them.

teleological: Referring to or demonstrating a design or purpose; in psychology, the view that human beings have a purpose, destiny, or orientation toward a goal.

temperament: The psychological biologically based structures belonging to a specific individual; a person's characteristic manner of thinking, perceiving, and acting.

thalamus (plural, thalami): A brain structure that forms the major part of the diencephalon and relays sensory signals to the cerebral cortex. It also regulates sleep and wakefulness.

thanatos: In Freudian psychoanalysis, the death instinct; the source of aggression and all other instinctual impulses ending in death.

theory: A scientifically acceptable general principle or body of principles offered to explain a set of natural phenomena.

theosophy: A modern movement that began in the 1870s and represents a mixture of esoteric Hindu and Buddhist teachings with Western notions of individual personality and human potential. Its doctrines include reincarnation and karma, as well as a notion that each person has a higher self.

therapeutic alliance: The working relationship between therapist and patient, usually understood to include agreement on the goals of treatment, the tasks involved in treatment, and a personal bond between therapist and patient.

third force: A phrase sometimes used to define humanistic psychology in contrast to psychoanalysis (the second force) and behaviorism (the first force).

thrownness: The English word most commonly used to translate philosopher Martin Heidegger's term *Verworfenheit,* which refers to the condition of finding oneself in and having to respond to the external world.

topological theory of mind: A term that refers to Sigmund Freud's view of the mind as containing three structures: id, ego, and superego.

trait: A component or distinguishing characteristic of an individual's personality that is stable across time and external situations.

trait psychology: An approach to the study of personality that emphasizes the existence, identifiability, and significance of personality traits. Trait psychology is sometimes called differential psychology.

transference: In Freudian theory, the process in which an analysand transfers to the analyst emotions experienced in childhood toward parents or other important figures.

translocation mutation: A mutation in which a segment of a chromosome breaks away during the process of cell division and either reattaches itself to a different chromosome or to a wrong location on its original chromosome.

transorbital: A term that refers to surgery carried out through the bony cavity (the orbit) surrounding the eyeball. A transorbital lobotomy is one performed by cutting or penetrating through the patient's eye socket.

transpersonal psychology: A school of psychology that grew out of humanistic psychology in the late 1960s and focuses on the spiritual or transcendent dimension of humanity. Sometimes called the fourth force, it emphasizes mystical experiences, peak experiences, and the possibility of developing beyond the boundaries of the individual ego.

tridosha system: In Ayurvedic medicine, the use of the three doshas (vata, pitta, and kapha) to diagnose a person's health condition, including assessment of their personality.

triune brain: A phrase that refers to Paul MacLean's model of the human brain as consisting of three parts or modules representing different stages of human evolution: the R-complex (brain stem and cerebellum; controls basic survival processes), the limbic system (amygdala, hypothalamus, and hippocampus; governs emotions, some memories, and some aspects of personality), and the neocortex (cerebral hemispheres; governs higher-order thinking, speech, and reasoning).

true experiment: An experiment in which participants are randomly selected and randomly assigned to an experimental group or a control group.

unconditional positive regard: In Carl Rogers's psychology, supportive affirmation that is not contingent on specific behaviors.

unconscious: In Freudian theory, the portion of the psyche that is usually inaccessible to the subject even though it has a profound influence on his or her behavior. The unconscious holds socially unacceptable ideas or wishes, painful emotions, and traumatic memories that have been repressed.

vagina envy: A concept used in Karen Horney's psychology to explain men's envy of women's ability to bear children and men's consequent striving to find compensation through their work, income, or social status. Some feminist psychologists prefer the term *vagina envy.*

validity: The extent to which a psychological test measures what it claims to measure.

variable interval reinforcement: In behaviorism, a schedule of reinforcement in which the timing of each reinforcement varies, without regard to the number of responses.

variable-ratio reinforcement: In behaviorism, a schedule of reinforcement in which the number of responses before each reinforcement is allowed to vary.

verification: The process of proving the truth or accuracy of experimental or test results.

virtù: The Italian word for leadership quality that Niccoló Machiavelli used to describe his ideal prince. It has been variously translated as *skill, strength,* or *prowess.*

virtue: In Erik Erikson's usage, a strength (or potency) of personality that people acquire when they successfully resolve the crisis associated with their present stage of development. The virtues that Erikson assigned to his eight life stages are hope, will, purpose, competence, fidelity, love, caring, and wisdom.

whole-object: In object relations theory, the entirety of a person (or other object) that is the locus of satisfaction for a developing child.

Williams syndrome: A rare genetic disorder in which patients appear to be more intelligent than they are in actuality because they possess excellent social skills. The disorder is sometimes called "cocktail party syndrome" for this reason.

Zahavian handicap: In evolutionary biology, a phrase used to describe a trait that would seem to place individuals possessing it at an evolutionary disadvantage but that actually confers an advantage on such individuals.

References

Abbott, P. (1998). Traditional and Western healing practices for alcoholism in American Indians and Alaska Natives. *Substance Use and Misuse, 33,* 2605–2646.

Abrams, M., & Abrams, L. D. (1997). The paradox of psychodynamic and cognitive-behavioral psychotherapy. *Journal of Rational-Emotive & Cognitive Behavior Therapy, 15,* 133–156.

Abrams, M., & Reber, A. (1988). Implicit learning: Robustness in the face of psychiatric disorders. *Journal of Psycholinguistic Research, 17,* 425–439.

Adams, F. (1891). *The genuine works of Hippocrates.* New York: William Wood.

Adams, G., & Jones, R. (1983). Female adolescents' ego development: Age comparisons and childrearing perceptions. *Journal of Early Adolescence, 1,* 423–426.

Adler, A. (1917). *A study of organ inferiority and its psychical compensation* (S. E. Jelliffe, Trans.). New York: Nervous and Mental Disease Publishing. (Original work published 1907)

Adler, A. (1927). *The practice and theory of individual psychology.* New York: Harcourt.

Adler, A. (1930). Individual psychology. In C. Murchison (Ed.). *Psychologies of 1930.* Worcester, MA: Clark University Press.

Adler, A. (1931). *What life should mean to you.* Boston: Little, Brown.

Adler, A. (1956). *The individual psychology of Alfred Adler* (H. L. Ansbacher & R. R. Ansbacher, Eds.). New York: Harper & Row. (Original work published 1912)

Adler, A. (1964). *Problems of neurosis.* New York: Harper & Row.

Adler, K, & Deutsch, D. (1959). *Essays in individual psychology.* New York: Grove Press.

Adolphs, R., Baron-Cohen, S., & Tranel, D. (2002). Impaired recognition of social emotions following amygdala damage. *Journal of Cognitive Neuroscience, 14,* 1264–1274.

Adolphs, R., Tranel, D., & Damasio, A. (2003). Dissociable neural systems for recognizing emotions. *Brain and Cognition, 52*(1), 61–69.

Adolphs, R., Tranel, D., Damasio, H., & Damasio, A. R. (1995). Fear and the human amygdala. *Journal of Neuroscience, 15,* 5879–5891.

Adolphs, R., Tranel, D., Hamann, S., Young, A. W., Calder, A. J., Phelps, E. A., Anderson, A., Lee, G. P., & Damasio A. R. (1999). Recognition of facial emotion in nine individuals with bilateral amygdala damage. *Neuropsychologia, 37,* 1111–1117.

Aglioti, S., DeSouza, J., & Goodale, M. (1995). Size-contrast illusions deceive the eye but not the hand. *Current Biology, 5,* 679–685.

Akbarian, S., Ruehl, M. G., Bliven, E., Luiz, L. A., Peranelli, A. C., Baker, S. P., Roberts, R. C., Bunney, W. E., Jr., Conley, R. C., Jones, E. G., Tamminga, C. A., & Guo, Y. (2005). Chromatin alterations associated with down-regulated metabolic gene expression in the prefrontal cortex of subjects with schizophrenia. *Archives of General Psychiatry, 62,* 829–840

Albert, D. J., & Walsh, M. L. (1984). Neural systems and the inhibitory modulation of agonistic behavior: A comparison of mammalian species. *Neuroscience & Biobehavioral Reviews, 8,* 5–24.

Aldred, L. (2000). Plastic shamans and astroturf sundances: New Age commercialization of Native American spirituality. *American Indian Quarterly, 24,* 329–352.

Alexander F. G., & Selesnick S. T. (1966). *The history of psychiatry.* New York: Harper and Row.

Alker, H. (1972). Is personality situationally specific or intrapsychically consistent? *Journal of Personality, 40,* 1–16.

Alloy, L., Peterson, C., Abramson, L., & Seligman, M. (1984). Attributional style and the generality of learned helplessness. *Journal of Personality and Social Psychology, 46*(3), 681–687.

Allport, F. H., & Allport, G. W. (1921). Personality traits: Their classification and measurement. *Journal of Abnormal and Social Psychology, 16,* 6–40.

Allport, G. (1937). *Personality: A psychological interpretation.* New York: Henry Holt.

Allport, G.W. (1950a). *The individual and his religion.* New York: Macmillan.

Allport, G. W. (1950b). *The nature of personality: Selected papers.* Cambridge, MA: Addison-Wesley.

Allport, G. (1954). The roots of religion. *Pastoral Psychology, 5*(43), 13-24.

Allport, G. W. (1955). *Becoming: Basic considerations for a psychology of personality.* New Haven, CT: Yale University Press.

Allport, G. W. (1960). *Personality and social encounter.* Boston: Beacon Press

Allport, G. W. (1961). *Pattern and growth in personality.* New York: Holt, Rinehart & Winston.

Allport, G. W. (Ed.). (1965). Letters from Jenny. New York: Harcourt, Brace & World.

Allport, G. W. (1967). Autobiography. In E. G. Boring & G. Lindzey (Eds.), *A history of psychology in autobiography.* New York: Appleton-Century-Crofts.

Allport, G. W., & Odbert, H. S. (1936). Trait names: A psycholexical study. *Psychological Monographs, 47,* 171–220.

American Psychiatric Association. (1952). *Diagnostic and statistical manual of mental disorders* (1st ed.). Washington, DC: American Psychiatric Association.

American Psychiatric Association. (1968). *Diagnostic and statistical manual of mental disorders* (2nd ed.). Washington, DC: American Psychiatric Association.

American Psychiatric Association. (1980). *Diagnostic and statistical manual of mental disorders* (3rd ed.). Washington, DC: American Psychiatric Association.

American Psychiatric Association. (1987). *Diagnostic and statistical manual of mental disorders* (3rd revised ed.). Washington, DC: American Psychiatric Association.

American Psychiatric Association. (1994). *Diagnostic and statistical manual of mental disorders* (4th ed.). Washington, DC: American Psychiatric Association.

American Psychiatric Association. (2000). *Diagnostic and Statistical Manual of Mental Disorders* (4th ed., text revision). Washington, DC: Author.

American Psychological Association. (2002). *Ethical* principles of psychologists and code of conduct: 2002. American Psychologist, *57,* 1060–1073.

Ammons, R. B. (1962). Psychology of the scientist: IV. Passages from the Idea Books of Clark L. Hull. *Perceptual and Motor Skills, 15,* 807–882.

Andersen, P., & Nordvik, H. (2002). Possible Barnum effect in the five factor model: Do respondents accept random NEO Personality Inventory-Revised scores as their actual trait profile? *Psychological Reports, 90*(2), 539–545.

Anderson, J. R.(1983). *The architecture of cognition.* Cambridge, MA: Harvard University Press.

Anderson, J. R. (1985). *Cognitive psychology.* New York: W. H. Freeman.

Anderson, S. C., & Lauderdale, M. L. (1982). Characteristics of abusive parents: A look at self-esteem. *Child Abuse & Neglect, 6,* 285–293.

Andrews, L. (1989). *To thine own self be true: The relationship between spiritual values and emotional health.* New York: Doubleday.

Ansbacher, H. (1972). Adlerian psychology: The tradition of brief psychotherapy. *Journal of Individual Psychology, 28,* 137–151.

Aoki, K. (1983). A quantitative genetic model of reciprocal altruism: A condition for kin or group selection to prevail. *Proceedings of the National Academy of Sciences, 80,* 4065–4068.

Arbib, M., & Rizzolatti, G. (1999). Neural expectations: A possible evolutionary path from manual skills to language. In P. Van Loocke (Ed.), *The nature of concepts: Evolution, structure, and representation* (pp. 128–154). Florence, KY: Taylor & Frances/Routledge.

Archer, S. (1982). The lower age boundaries of identity development. *Child Development, 52,* 1551–1556.

Arnold, S. E., Hyman, B. T., Van Hoesen, G. W., & Damasio, A. R. (1991). Some cytoarchitectural abnormalities of the entorhinal cortex in schizophrenia. *Archives of General Psychiatry, 48,* 625–632.

Aronson, E., Ellsworth, P. C., Carlsmith, J. M., & Gonzales, M. H. (1990). *Methods of research in social psychology.* New York: McGraw-Hill.

Asch, S. (1946). Forming impressions of personality. *Journal of Abnormal and Social Psychology, 41,* 258–290.

Asch, S. (1951). Effects of group pressure upon the modification and distortion of judgments. In H. Guetzkow (Ed.), *Groups, leadership, and men: Research in human relations* (pp. 177–190). New York: Carnegie Press.

Asch, S., & Witkin, H. (1948). Studies in space orientation: I. Perception of the upright with displaced visual fields. *Journal of Experimental Psychology, 38*(3), 325–337.

Asch, S., & Zukier, H. (1984). Thinking about persons. *Journal of Personality and Social Psychology, 46*(6), 1230–1240.

Atkinson, L. (1986). The comparative validities of the Rorschach and MMPI: A meta-analysis. *Canadian Psychology, 27,* 238–247.

Atmaca, M., Aydin, A., Tezcan, E., Poyraz, A., & Kara, B. (2006). Volumetric investigation of brain regions in patients with conversion disorder. *Progress in Neuro-Psychopharmacology & Biological Psychiatry, 30*(4), 708–713.

Axelrod, R., & Dion, D. (1988). The further evolution of cooperation. *Science, 242,* 1385–1390.

Axelrod, R., & Hamilton, W. D. (1981). The evolution of cooperation. *Science, 211,* 1390–1396.

Ayçiçegi, A., Dinn, W., & Harris, C. (2002). Neuropsychological function in obsessive-compulsive personality with schizotypal features. *Klinik Psikofarmakoloji Bülteni, 12*(3), 121–125.

Baars, B. J. (1986). *The cognitive revolution in psychology.* New York: Guilford Press.

Babkin, B. P. (1974). *Pavlov: A biography.* Chicago: University of Chicago Press.

Baca, E. (2000). *Mabel's Santa Fe and Taos: Bohemian legends 1900–1950.* Salt Lake City, UT: Gibbs-Smith.

Bachrach, A. J., Erwin, W. J., & Mohr, J. P. (1965). The control of eating behavior in an anorexic by operant conditioning techniques. In L. Ullmann & L. P. Krasner (Eds.), *Case studies in behavior modification* (pp. 153–163). New York: Holt, Rinehart, and Winston.

Bacon, F. (1994). *Novum Organum: With other parts of the great insaturation* (Vol. 3). Peru, IL: Carus. (Original work published 1620)

Bagby, R., Costa, J., Widiger, T., Ryder, A., & Marshall, M. (2005). DSM-IV personality disorders and the five-factor model of personality: A multi-method examination of domain- and facet-level predictions. *European Journal of Personality, 19*(4), 307–324.

Bair, D. (2003). *Jung: A biography.* Boston & New York: Little, Brown.

Balay, J., & Shevrin, H. (1988). The subliminal psychodynamic activation method: A critical review. *American Psychologist, 43,* 161–174.

Bandura, A. (1969). *Principles of behavior modification.* New York: Holt, Rinehart & Winston.

Bandura, A. (1973). *Aggression: A social learning analysis.* Englewood Cliffs, NJ: Prentice Hall.

Bandura, A. (1974). Behavior theory and the models of man. *American Psychologist, 29,* 859–869.

Bandura A. (1977). *Social learning theory.* Englewood Cliffs, N.J.: Prentice Hall.

Bandura, A. (1982). Self-efficacy mechanism in human agency. *American Psychologist, 37*(2), 122–147.

Bandura, A. (1983). Self-efficacy determinants of anticipated fears and calamities. *Journal of Personality and Social Psychology, 45*(2), 464–469.

Bandura, A. (1986). *Social foundations of thought and action: A social cognitive theory.* Englewood Cliffs, NJ: Prentice Hall.

Bandura, A. (1989). Human agency in social cognitive theory. *American Psychologist, 44*(9), 1175–1184.

Bandura, A. (1997). *Self-efficacy: The exercise of control.* New York: W. H. Freeman.

Bandura, A. (2001). Social cognitive theory: An agentic perspective. *Annual Review of Psychology, 52,* 1–26.

Bandura, A. (2006). Toward a psychology of human agency. *Perspectives on Psychological Science, 1*(2), 164–180.

Bandura, A., & Huston, A. (1961). Identification as a process of incidental learning. *The Journal of Abnormal and Social Psychology, 63,* 311-318.

Bandura, A., Kihlstrom, J. F., & Harackiewicz, J. M. (1990). An evolutionary milestone in the psychology of personality. *Psychological Inquiry, 1*(1), 86–92.

Bandura, A., Ross, D., & Ross, S. (1961). Transmission of aggression through imitation of aggressive models. *Journal of Abnormal & Social Psychology, 63*(3), 575–582.

Bandura, A., Ross, D., & Ross, S. A. (1963a). Imitation of film-mediated aggressive actions. *Journal of Abnormal and Social Psychology, 66,* 3–11.

Bandura, A., Ross, D., & Ross, S. (1963b). Vicarious reinforcement and imitative learning. *The Journal of Abnormal and Social Psychology, 67,* 601-607.

Bandura, A., & Waters, R. H. (1963). *Social learning and personality development.* New York: Holt, Rinehart, & Winston.

Bannister, D., & Fransella, F. (1986). *Inquiring man: The psychology of personal constructs.* London: Routledge.

Barber, N. (1998). The slender ideal and eating disorders: An interdisciplinary 'Telescope' model. *International Journal of Eating Disorders, 23,* 295–307.

Bardo, M. T., Bowling, S. L., Robinet, P. M., Rowlett, J. K., Lacy, M., & Mattingly, B. A. (1993). Role of dopamine D1 and D2 receptors in novelty-maintained place preference. *Experimental and Clinical Psychopharmacology, 1*(1–4),101–109.

Barkow, J. H., Cosmides, L., & Tooby, J. (1992). *The adapted mind: Evolutionary psychology and the generation of culture.* New York: Oxford University Press.

Barnett, S. A. (2001). *The story of rats: Their impact on us, and our impact on them.* Crows Nest, N.S.W.: Allen & Unwin.

Bartlett, F. C. (1932). *Remembering: A study in experimental and social psychology.* Cambridge, UK: Cambridge University Press.

Bates E., & Carnevale, G. (1993). New directions in research on language development. *Developmental Review, 13,* 436–470.

Bateson, G., Jackson, D., Haley, J., & Weakland, J. (1956). Toward a theory of schizophrenia. *Behavioral Science, 1,* 251–264.

Baumeister, R. (1991). Identity crisis. In R. M. Lerner, A. C. Petersen, & J. Brooks-Gunn (Eds.), *Encyclopedia of adolescence.* New York: Garland.

Baumrind, D. (1964). Some thoughts on ethics of research: After reading Milgram's "Behavioral Study of Obedience." *American Psychologist, 19,* 421–423..

Beblo, T., Driessen, M., Mertens, M., Wingenfeld, K., Piefke, M., Rullkoetter, N., Silva-Saavedra, A., Mensebach, C., Reddemann, L., Rau, H., Markowitsch, H. J., Wulff, H., Lange, W., Berea, C., Ollech, I., & Woermann, F. G. (2006). Functional MRI correlates of the recall of unresolved life events in borderline personality disorder. *Psychological Medicine, 36*(6), 845–856.

Bechara, A., Damasio, A. R., Damasio, H., & Anderson, S. W. (1994). Insensitivity to future consequences following damage to human prefrontal cortex. *Cognition, 50,* 7–15.

Bechara, A., Damasio, H., & Damasio, A. R. (2003). Role of the amygdala in decision-making. *Annals of the New York Academy of Sciences,, 985,* 356–369.

Beck, A. T. (1976). *Cognitive therapy and the emotional disorders.* Madison, CT: International Universities Press.

Beck, A., Butler, A., Brown, G., Dahlsgaard, K., Newman, C., & Beck, J. (2001). Dysfunctional beliefs discriminate personality disorders. *Behaviour Research and Therapy, 39*(10), 1213–1225.

Beck, A. T., Freeman, A., & Davis, D. D. (2004). *Cognitive therapy of personality disorders* (2nd ed.). New York: Guilford Press.

Beck, A. T., & Hollon, S. (1993). Controversies in cognitive therapy: A dialogue with Aaron T. Beck and Steve Hollon. *Journal of Cognitive Psychotherapy, 7*(2), 79–93.

Beck, A., Ward, C., Mendelson, M., Mock, J., & Erbaugh, J. (1961). An inventory for measuring depression. *Archives of General Psychiatry, 4,* 561–571.

Beeckmans, K., & Michiels, K. (1996). Personality, emotions, and the temporolimbic system: A neuropsychological approach. *Acta Neurologica Belgica, 96,* 35–42.

Bellah, R., Madsen, R., Sullivan, W., Swidler, A., & Tipton, S. (1986). *Habits of the heart: Individualism and commitment in American life.* New York: Harper & Row.

Bem, D., & Allen, A. (1974). On predicting some of the people some of the time: The search for cross-situational consistencies in behavior. *Psychological Review, 81*(6), 506–520.

Benassi, V., Sweeney, P., & Dufour, C. (1988). Is there a relation between locus of control orientation and depression? *Journal of Abnormal Psychology, 97*(3), 357–367.

Benight, C., & Bandura, A. (2004). Social cognitive theory of posttraumatic recovery: The role of perceived self-efficacy. *Behaviour Research and Therapy, 42*(10), 1129–1148.

Benjamin, H., & Ellis, A. (1954). An objective examination of prostitution.. *International Journal of Sexology, 8,* 100-105.

Benjamin, J., Ebstein, R. P., & Lesch, K. P. (1998). Genes for personality traits: Implications for psychopathology. *International Journal of.Neuropsychopharmcology, 1,* 153–168.

Benjamin, J., Li, L., Patterson, C., Greenberg, B., Murphy, D., & Hamer, D. (1996). Population and familial association between the D4 dopamine receptor gene and measures of novelty seeking. *Nature Genetics, 12,* 81–84.

Bennett, J. (1983). *Enneagram studies.* York Beach, ME: Samuel Weiser.

Benor, D. (1990). Survey of spiritual healing research. *Complementary Medical Research, 4,* 9–33.

Bensberg, G. (Ed.). (1965). *Teaching the mentally retarded: A handbook for ward personnel.* Atlanta, GA: Southern Regional Education Board.

Bergin, A. E. (1983). Religiosity and mental health: A critical reevaluation and meta-analysis. *Professional Psychology: Research & Practice, 14,* 170–184.

Berlin, H., Rolls, E., & Iversen, S. (2005). Borderline personality disorder, impulsivity, and the orbitofrontal cortex. *American Journal of Psychiatry, 162*(12), 2360–2373.

Betz, N., & Hackett, G. (1983, December). The relationship of mathematics self-efficacy expectations to the selection of science-based college majors. *Journal of Vocational Behavior, 23*(3), 329–345.

Bigler, E. (2001). Frontal lobe pathology and antisocial personality disorder. *Archives of General Psychiatry, 58*(6), 609–611.

Binswanger, L. (1958). The case of Ellen West. In R. May, E. Angel, & H. Ellenberger (Eds.), *Existence: A new dimension in psychiatry and psychology.* New York: Basic Books.

Black, E. (2003). *War against the weak: Eugenics and America's campaign to create a master race.* New York: Four Walls Eight Windows.

Blacker, K., & Tupin, J. (1991). Hysteria and hysterical structures: Developmental and social theories. *Hysterical personality style and the histrionic personality disorder (Rev. ed.)* (pp. 17–66). Lanham, MD: Jason Aronson.

Blanchard, D. C., Blanchard, R. J., Lee, E. M., & Nakamura, S. (1979). Defensive behaviors in rats following septal and septal—amygdala lesions. *Journal of Comparative Physiological Psychology, 93,* 378–390.

Blanck, G., & Blanck, R. (1974). *Ego psychology: Theory and practice.* New York: Columbia University Press.

Bleske, A. L., & Shackelford, T. K. (2001). Poaching, promiscuity, and deceit: Combatting mating rivalry in same-sex friendships. *Personal Relationships, 8,* 407–424.

Bleuler, E. (1950). The fundamental symptoms. In E. Bleuler (Ed.), *Dementia praecox; or the group of schizophrenias* (J. Ziskin, Trans.) (pp. 14–54). New York: International Universities Press.

Block, J. (1977a). The Eysencks and psychoticism. *Journal of Abnormal Psychology, 86,* 653–654.

Block, J. (1977b). P scale and psychosis: Continued concerns. *Journal of Abnormal Psychology, 86,* 431–434.

Block, J. (2001). Millennial contrarianism: The five-factor approach to personality description 5 years later. *Journal of Research in Personality, 35*(1), 98–107.

Blumberg, M. (2005). *Basic instinct: The genesis of behavior.* New York: Thunder's Mouth Press.

Bogart, E. L. (1942). *Economic history of Europe, 1760-1939.* London: Longmans, Green.

Bond, M. H., Nakazato, H., & Shiraishi, D. (1975). Universality and distinctiveness in dimensions of Japanese person perception. *Journal of Cross-cultural Psychology, 6,* 346–357.

Borgatta, E. F. (1964). The structure of personality characteristics. *Behavioral Science, 12,* 8–17.

Boring, E. (1942). *Sensation and perception in the history of experimental psychology.* New York: Appelton.

Bornstein, R. (1996). Beyond orality: Toward an object relations/interactionist reconceptualization of the etiology and dynamics of dependency. *Psychoanalytic Psychology, 13*(2), 177–203.

Boss, M. (1963). *Psychoanalysis and* Daseinsanalysis (L. Lefebre, Trans.). New York: Basic Books.

Boss, M. (1977). *Existential foundations of medicine and psychology* S. Conway & A. Cleaves, Trans.). New York: Jason Aronson.

Bouchard, T. J., Lykken, D. T., McGue, M., Segal, N. L., & Tellegen, A. (1990). Sources of human psychological differences: The Minnesota study of twins raised apart. *Science, 250,* 223–250.

Bouffard-Bouchard, T., Parent, S., & Larivée, S. (1991). Influence of self-efficacy on self-regulation and performance among junior and senior high-school age students. *International Journal of Behavioral Development, 14*(2), 153–164.

Bowlby, J. (1969). *Attachment* (2nd ed.). New York: Basic Books.

Bowlby, J. (1982). *Attachment and loss.* New York: Basic Books.

Bowlby, J. (1988). *A secure base: Parent-child attachment and healthy human development.* London: Routledge.

Boyd, R. (1988). Is the repeated prisoner's dilemma a good model of reciprocal altruism? *Ethology & Sociobiology, 9*(2), 211–222.

Bradsher, K. (2002). *High and mighty.* New York: Perseus Books.

Brehm, J. W. (1966). *A theory of psychological reactance.* New York: Academic Press.

Breland K., & Breland, M. (1961). The misbehavior of organisms. *American Psychologist, 16,* 681–684.

Brems, C., Thevinin, D., & Routh, D. (1991). History of clinical psychology. In C. E. Walker (Ed.), *Clinical psychology: Historical and research foundations* (pp. 3–35). New York: Plenum Press.

Brendgen, M., Dionne, G., Girard, A., Boivin, M., Vitaro, F., & Pérusse, D. (2005). Examining genetic and environmental effects on social aggression: A study of 6-year-old twins. *Child Development, 76,* 930–946.

Breuer, J., & Freud, S. (1957). *Studies on hysteria* (J. Strachey, Trans.). New York: Basic Books. (Original work published 1895)

Briggs, I., & Briggs, P. (1995). *Gifts differing:Understanding personality type.* Mountain View, CA: Davies-Black.

Brill, A. A. (Ed.). (1938). *Basic writings of Sigmund Freud.* New York: The Modern Library.

Broadbent, D. E. (1958). *Perception and communication.* New York: Pergamon Press.

Bromberg, W. (1959). *The mind of man: A history of psychotherapy and psychoanalysis.* New York: Harper.

Brown, B. L., Strong, W. J., & Rencher, A. C. (1974). Fifty-four voices from two: The effects of simultaneous manipulations of rate, mean fundamental frequency, and variance of fundamental frequency on ratings of personality from speech. *Journal of the Acoustical Society of America, 55,* 313–318.

Bryant-Tuckett, R., & Silverman, L. H. (1984). Effects of the subliminal stimulation of symbiotic fantasies on the academic performance of emotionally handicapped students. *Journal of Counseling Psychology, 31,* 295–305.

Buck v. Bell, 274 U.S. 200 (1927).

Bugental, J. F. T. (1967). *Challenges of humanistic psychology.* New York: McGraw-Hill.

Burke, T. (1989). Psychology, theology, and the liberal arts: Toward the unity of knowledge. In T Burke (Ed.), *Man and mind: A Christian theory of personality* (pp. 1–18). Hillsdale, MI: Hillsdale College Press.

Buss, D. M. (1995). Psychological sex differences: Origins through sexual selection. *American Psychologist, 50*(30), 164–171.

Buss, D. (2005). *The murderer next door: Why the mind is designed to kill.* New York: Penguin Press.

Buss, D., & Duntley, J. (2006). The evolution of aggression. In M. Schaller, J. A. Simpson, & D. T. Kenrick (Eds.), *Evolution and social psychology: Frontiers of social psychology* (pp. 263–285). Madison, CT, US: Psychosocial Press.

Buss, D., & Shackelford, T. K. (1997a). From vigilance to violence: Mate retention tactics in married couples. *Journal of Personality and Social Psychology, 72*(2), 346–361.

Buss, D., & Shackelford, T. K. (1997b). Human aggression in evolutionary perspective. *Clinical Psychology Review, 17,* 605–619.

Butcher, J. N. (1990). *MMPI-2 in psychological treatment.* New York: Oxford University Press.

Butler, A., Brown, G., Beck, A., & Grisham, J. (2002). Assessment of dysfunctional beliefs in borderline personality disorder. *Behaviour Research and Therapy, 40*(10), 1231–1240.

Byard, R., & Riches, K. (2005). Dehydration and heat-related death: Sweat lodge syndrome. *American Journal of Forensic Medicine and Pathology, 26,* 236–239.

Calder, A., Beaver, J., Davis, M., van Ditzhuijzen, J., Keane, J., & Lawrence, A. (2007). Disgust sensitivity predicts the insula and pallidal response to pictures of disgusting foods. *European Journal of Neuroscience, 25*(11), 3422–3428.

Calhoun, R. (2008). *Lectures on the history of Christian doctrine.* Eugene, OR: Wipf & Stock.

Cannon, T. D., Kaprio, J., Lonnqvist, J., Huttunen, M., & Koskenvuo, M. (1998). The genetic epidemiology of schizophrenia in a Finnish twin cohort: A population-based modeling study. *Archives of General Psychiatry, 55,* 67–74.

Cartwright, J. (2001). *Evolutionary explanations of human behaviour.* Hove, England: Routledge.

Caspi, A., McClay, J., Moffitt, T. E., Mill, J., Martin, J., Craig, I. W., Taylor, A., & Poulton, R. (2002). Role of genotype in the cycle of violence in maltreated children. *Science, 297,* 851–854.

Castelnuovo-Tedesco, P. (1975). Studies of superobesity: I. Psychological characteristics of superobese patients. *International Journal of Psychiatry in Medicine, 6,* 465–480.

Castiglioni, A. (1946). *Adventures of the mind.* New York: Knopf.

Cattell, J. (1890). Mental tests and measurements. *Mind, 15,* 373–381.

Cattell, R. B. (1950). *Personality: A systematic, theoretical, and factual study.* New York: McGraw-Hill.

Cattell, R. B. (1959). Foundations of personality measurement theory in multivariate expressions. In B. M. Bass & I. A. Berg (Eds.), *Objective approaches to personality assessment* (pp. 42–65). Princeton, NJ: Van Nostrand.

Cattell, R. B. (1972). *A new morality from science: Beyondism.* New York: Pergamon.

Cattell, R. B. (1979). *Personality and learning theory.* New York: Springer.

Cattell, R. B. (1987). *Beyondism: Religion from science.* New York: Praeger.

Cattell, R. B. (1990). Advances in Cattellian personality theory. In L. A. Pervin (Ed.), *Handbook of personality: Theory and research* (pp. 101–110). New York: Guilford Press.

Cave, C. B., & Squire, L. R. (1991). Equivalent impairment of spatial and nonspatial memory following damage to the human hippocampus. *Hippocampus, 1,* 329–340.

Ceci, S. J., Huffman, M. L. C., Smith, E., & Loftus, E. F. (1994). Repeatedly thinking about a non-event: Source misattributions among preschoolers. *Consciousness & Cognition: An International Journal, 3,* 388–407.

Ceci, S. J., Loftus, E. F., Leichtman, M. D., & Bruck, M. (1994). The possible role of source misattributions in the creation of false beliefs among preschoolers. *International Journal of Clinical & Experimental Hypnosis, 42,* 304–320.

Celnik, P., & Cohen, L. G. (2003). Functional relevance of cortical plasticity. In S. Boniface & U. Ziemann (Eds.), *Plasticity in the human nervous system: Investigation with transcranial magnetic stimulation* (pp. 231–245). Cambridge, UK: Cambridge University Press.

Cerletti, U. (1950). Old and new information about electroshock. *American Journal of Psychiatry, 107,* 87–94.

Chang, S. (1974). Morita therapy. *American Journal of Psychotherapy, 28,* 208–221.

Charlesworth, B., & Charlesworth, D. (2003). *Evolution: A very short introduction.* Oxford, UK: Oxford University Press.

Charlton, B. (2006). Despite their inevitable conflicts—science, religion, and New Age spirituality are essentially compatible and complementary activities. *Medical Hypotheses, 67,* 433–436.

Choca, J., Bresolin, L., Okonek, A., & Ostrow, D. (1988). Validity of the Millon Clinical Multiaxial Inventory in the assessment of affective disorders. *Journal of Personality Assessment, 52,* 96–105.

Chomsky, N. (1957). *Syntactic structures.* The Hague: Mouton.

Chomsky, N. (1959). A review of B.F. Skinner's *Verbal Behavior. Language, 1,* 26–58.

Chopra, A., & Doiphode, V. (2002). Ayurvedic medicine: Core concept, therapeutic principles, and current relevance. *Medical Clinics of North America, 86,* 75–89.

Church, A. T., Katigbak, M. S., & Reyes, J. A. (1996). Toward a taxonomy of trait adjectives in Filipino: Comparing personality lexicons across cultures. *European Journal of Personality 10,* 3–24.

Clark, R. W. (1980). *Freud, the man and the cause.* New York: Random House.

Clarkin, J., Widiger, T., Frances, A., Hurt, S., & Gilmore, M. (1983). Prototypic typology and the borderline personality disorder. *Journal of Abnormal Psychology, 92*(3), 263–275.

Cohen, K. (1998). Native American medicine. *Alternative Therapies in Health and Medicine, 4,* 45–57.

Cohen, K. (2003). *Honoring the medicine: The essential guide to Native American healing.* New York: Ballantine Books.

Colby, K. (1960). *An introduction to psychoanalytic research.* Oxford, UK: Basic Books.

Collins, J. (1985, July). Self-efficacy and ability in achievement behavior. *Dissertation Abstracts International, 46*(1-A), 103–104.

Conn, S. R., & Rieke, M. L. (1994). The 16PF fifth edition technical manual. Champaign, IL: Institute for Personality and Ability Testing.

Contreras, M., Ceric, F., & Torrealba, F. (2007). Inactivation of the interoceptive insula disrupts drug craving and malaise induced by lithium. *Science, 318*(5850), 655–658.

Coolidge, F. L., Thede, L. L., & Young, S. E. (2002). The heritability of gender identity disorder in a child and adolescent twin sample. *Behavior Genetics, 32,* 251–257.

Cory, D. W. (1951). The homosexual in America: A subjective approach. New York: Greenberg.

Cornwell, D., Hobbs, S., & Prytula, R. (1980). Little Albert rides again. *American Psychologist, 35,* 216–217.

Cosmides, L. (1989). The logic of social exchange: Has natural selection shaped how humans reason? Studies with the Wason selection task. *Cognition, 31,* 187–276.

Cosmides, L., & Tooby, J. (1989). Evolutionary psychology and the generation of culture: II. Case study: A computational theory of social exchange. *Ethology & Sociobiology, 10,* 51–97.

Cosmides, L., & Tooby, J. (1999). Toward an evolutionary taxonomy of treatable conditions. *Journal of Abnormal Psychology, 108,* 453–464.

Costa, P., & McCrae, R. (1986). Personality stability and its implications for clinical psychology. *Clinical Psychology Review, 6*(5), 407–423.

Costa, P. T., & McCrae, R. R. (1990). Personality disorders and the five-factor model of personality. Journal of Personality Disorders, 4, 362–371.

Costa, P. T., & McCrae, R. R. (1992). *NEO PI-R professional manual.* Odessa, FL: Psychological Assessment Resources.

Cote, J., & Levine, C. (1988). On critiquing the identity status paradigm: A rejoinder to Waterman. *Developmental Review, 8,* 209–218.

Cozolino, L. (2006). *The neuroscience of human relationships.* New York: W. W. Norton.

Craig, R. J. (1999*).* Overview and current status of the Millon Clinical Multiaxial Inventory. *Journal of Personality Assessment, 72,* 390–406.

Craig, R. J. (2005). *New directions in interpreting the Millon Clinical Multiaxial Inventory-III: Essays on current issues.* Hoboken, NJ: John Wiley.

Cramer, D. (1990a). The necessary conditions for evaluating client-centered therapy. In G. Lietaer & J. Rombauts (Eds.), *Client-centered and experiential psychotherapy in the nineties* (pp. 415–428). Louvain: Leuven University Press.

Cramer, D. (1990b). Toward assessing the therapeutic value of Rogers's core conditions. *Counselling Psychology Quarterly, 3*(1), 57.

Cramer, D. (1994). Self-esteem and Rogers' core conditions in close friends: A latent variable path analysis of panel data. *Counselling Psychology Quarterly, 7,* 327–337.

Crowe, R. (1974). An adoption study of antisocial personality. *Archives of General Psychiatry, 31*(6), 785–791.

Damasio, A. (1995). *Descartes' error: Emotion reason and the human brain.* New York: Quill.

Damasio, A. (1996). The somatic marker hypothesis and the possible functions of the prefrontal cortex. *Philosophical Transactions of the Royal Society of London. Series B, Biological Sciences, 351*(1346), 1413–1420.

Damásio, A. (1999). *The feeling of what happens: Body, emotion, and the making of consciousness.* New York: Harcourt.

Darley, J. M., & Batson, C. D. (1973). "From Jerusalem to Jericho": A study of situational and dispositional variables in helping behavior. *Journal of Personality and Social Psychology, 27,* 100–108.

Darwin, C. (1996). *The origin of species* (G. Beer, Ed.). Oxford, UK: Oxford University Press. (Original work published 1859)

Davis, F., & Yates, B. (1982, March). Self-efficacy expectancies versus outcome expectancies as determinants of performance deficits and depressive affect. *Cognitive Therapy and Research, 6*(1), 23–35.

Davis, S. E., & Hays, L. W. (1997). An examination of the clinical validity of the MCMI-III Depressive Personality scale. *Journal of Clinical Psychololgy, 53,* 15–23.

Decarvalho, R. J. (1991). *The founders of humanistic psychology.* New York: Praeger.

De Fruyt, F., De Clercq, B., van de Wiele, L., & Van Heeringen, K. (2006). The validity of Cloninger's psychobiological model versus the five-factor model to predict DSM-IV personality disorders in a heterogeneous psychiatric sample: Domain facet and residualized facet descriptions. *Journal of Personality, 74*(2), 479–510.

Delhees, K. H., & Cattell, R. B. (1970). Obtaining 16PF scores from the MMPI, and MMPI scores from the 16PF. *Journal of Projective Techniques and Personality Assessment, 34,* 251–255.

Dellarosa, C. D., & Cummins, R. (1999). Biological preparedness and evolutionary explanation. *Cognition, 73,* B37–B53.

Descartes, R. (1649). *Les passions de l'âme*. Paris: Henri le Gras.

Deutsch, J. A., & Deutsch, D. (1963). Attention: Some theoretical considerations. *Psychological Review, 87,* 80–90.

Dickemann, M. (1995). Wilson's Panchreston: The inclusive fitness hypothesis of sociobiology re-examined. *Journal of Homosexuality, 28*(1–2), 147–183.

Dickey, C., McCarley, R., Xu, M., Seidman, L., Voglmaier, M., Niznikiewicz, M., Connor, E., & Shenton, M. E. (2007). MRI abnormalities of the hippocampus and cavum septi pellucidi in females with schizotypal personality disorder. *Schizophrenia Research, 89*(1), 49–58.

Dickson, D. H., & Kelly, I. W. (1985). The "Barnum effect" in personality assessment: A review of the literature. *Psychological Reports, 57*(2), 367–382.

Diener, E., & Crandall, R. (1978). *Ethics in social and behavioral research.* Chicago: University of Chicago Press.

Digman, J. M. (1997). Higher-order factors of the Big Five. *Journal of Personality and Social Psychology, 73,* 1246–1256.

Doi, T. (1978). Amae: A key concept for understanding Japanese personality structure. In R. Corsini (Ed.), *Readings in current personality theories* (pp. 213–219). Itasca, IL: F. E. Peacock.

Dolan, M., & Park, I. (2002). The neuropsychology of antisocial personality disorder. *Psychological Medicine, 32*(3), 417–427.

Dollard, J., & Miller, N. E. (1950). *Personality and psychotherapy: An analysis in terms of learning, thinking, and culture.* New York: McGraw-Hill.

Dollard, J., Miller, N., Doob, L., Mower, O., Sears, R., Ford, C., Hovland, C., & Sollenberger, R. (1939). *Frustration and aggression.* New Haven, CT: Yale University Press.

D'Onofrio, B. M., Eaves, L. J., Murrelle, L., Maes, H. H., & Spilka, B. (1999). Understanding biological and social influences on religious affiliation, attitudes, and behaviors: A behavior genetic perspective. *Journal of Personality, 67,* 953–984.

Dossey, L. (1993). *Healing words: The power of prayer and the practice of medicine.* San Francisco: HarperSanFrancisco.

Dossey, L. (2001). *Healing beyond the body: Medicine and the infinite reach of the mind.* Boston: Shambhala.

Dowd, E., & Kelly, F. (1980). Adlerian psychology and cognitive-behavior therapy: convergences. *Journal of Individual Psychology, 36,* 119–135.

Doyle, A. C. (2002). *The adventures of Sherlock Holmes.* http://publicliterature.org/ pdf/advsh12.pdf

Duchaine, B., Cosmides, L., & Tooby, J. (2001). Evolutionary psychology and the brain. *Current Opinion in Neurobiology, 11,* 225–230.

Duck, S. (1973). Similarity and perceived similarity of personal constructs as influences on friendship choice. *British Journal of Social & Clinical Psychology, 12,* 1–6.

Durbin, C., & Klein, D. (2006). Ten-year stability of personality disorders among outpatients with mood disorders. *Journal of Abnormal Psychology, 115*(1), 75–84.

Ebbinghaus, H. (1913). *Memory: A contribution to experimental psychology* (H. A. Ruger & C. A. Bussenius, Trans.). New York: Teachers College, Columbia University. (Original work published 1885)

Ebstein, R. P. (2006). The molecular genetic architecture of human personality: Beyond self-report questionnaires. *Molecular Psychiatry, 11,* 427–445.

Ebstein, R., Novick, O., Umansky, R., Ebstein, R., Novick, O., Umansky, R., Priel, B., Osher, Y., Blaine, D. Bennett, E. R., Nemanov, L., Katz, M., & Belmaker, R. H.. (1996). Dopamine D4 receptor (D4DR) exon III polymorphism associated with the human personality trait of novelty seeking. *Nature Genetics, 12,* 78–80.

Efron, R. (1990). *The decline and fall of hemispheric specialization.* Hillsdale, NJ: Lawrence Erlbaum.

Eley, T. C., Lichenstein, P., & Stevenson, J. (1999). Sex differences in the etiology of aggressive and nonaggressive antisocial behavior: Results from two twin studies. *Child Development, 70,* 155–168.

El-Hai, J. (2005). *The lobotomist: A maverick medical genius and his tragic quest to rid the world of mental illness.* New York: John Wiley.

Ellenberger, H. F. (1970). *The discovery of the unconscious: The history and evolution of dynamic psychiatry.* New York: Basic Books.

Ellenberger, H. (1972). The story of "Anna O": A critical review with new data. *Journal of the Behavioral Sciences, 8,* 267–279.

Ellenberger, H. F. (1974). Psychiatry from ancient to modern times. In S. Arieti (Ed.), *The foundations of psychiatry* (pp. 11–27). New York: Basic Books.

Elliott, R. (2001). The effectiveness of humanistic therapies: A meta-analysis. In D. J. Cain & J. Seeman (Eds.), *Humanistic psychotherapies: Handbook of research and practice* (pp. 57–81). Washington, DC: American Psychological Association.

Ellis, A. (1946). The validity of personality questionnaires. *Psychological Bulletin, 43*(5), 385–440.

Ellis, A. (1947). Telepathy and psychoanalysis: A critique of recent "findings." *Psychiatric Quarterly, 21,* 607–659.

Ellis, A. (1950). An introduction to the principles of scientific psychoanalysis. *Genetic Psychology Monographs,* 147–212.

Ellis, A. (1951a), *The folklore of sex,* Oxford, UK: Charles Boni.

Ellis, A. (1951b). The influence of heterosexual culture on the attitudes of homosexuals. *International Journal of Sexology, 5,* 77–79.

Ellis, A. (1952). A critique of systematic theoretical foundations in clinical psychology. *Journal of Clinical Psychology, 8,* 11–15.

Ellis, A. (1954), *The American sexual tragedy.* New York: Twayne.

Ellis, A. (1955). New approaches to psychotherapy techniques. *Journal of Clinical Psychology, 11,* 207–260.

Ellis, A. (1957a). *How to live with a neurotic.* New York: Crown.

Ellis, A. (1957b). Outcome of employing three techniques of psychotherapy. *Journal of Clinical Psychology, 13,* 344–350.

Ellis, A. (1957c). Rational psychotherapy and individual psychology. *Journal of Individual Psychology, 13,* 38–44.

Ellis, A. (1958a). Rational psychotherapy. *Journal of General Psychology, 59,* 35–49.

Ellis, A. (1958b).*Sex without guilt.* New York: Hillman.

Ellis, A. (1962). Reason and emotion in psychotherapy. Secaucus, NJ: Citadel Press.

Ellis, A. (1974). Rational-emotive theory: Albert Ellis. In A. Burton (Ed.), *Operational theories of personality* Oxford, England: Brunner/Mazel.

Ellis, A. (1976). The biological basis of human irrationality. *Journal of Individual Psychology, 32*(2), 145–168.

Ellis, A. (1977a, July). Emotional disturbance and its treatment in a nutshell. *Indian Journal of Psychiatric Social Work, 6,* 29–30.

Ellis, A. (1977b). Personality hypotheses of RET and other modes of cognitive behavior therapy. *The Counseling Psychologist, 7,* 2–42.

Ellis, A. (1977c). Rational-emotive therapy: Research data that supports the clinical and personality hypotheses of RET and other modes of cognitive-behavior therapy. *Counseling Psychologist, 7*(1), 2–42.

Ellis, A. (1978). Toward a theory of personality. In R. J. Corsini (Ed.), *Readings in current personality theories.* Itasca, IL: Peacock.

Ellis, A. (1979). Toward a new theory of personality. In A. Ellis & J.M. Whiteley (Eds.), *Theoretical and empirical foundations of rational-emotive therapy* (pp. 7–32). Monterey, CA: Brooks/Cole.

Ellis, A. (1984). Expanding the ABCs of RET. *Journal of Rational-Emotive Therapy, 2*(2), 20–24.

Ellis, A. (1985). Free will and determinism: A second story. *Journal of Counseling and Development, 64,* 286.

Ellis, A. (1987). The impossibility of achieving consistently good mental health. *American Psychologist, 42*(4), 364–375.

Ellis, A. (1988). *How to stubbornly refuse to make yourself miserable about anything—yes, anything!*. Secaucus, NJ: Lyle Stuart.

Ellis, A. (1991). The revised ABC's of rational-emotive therapy (RET). *Journal of Rational-Emotive & Cognitive Behavior Therapy, 9*(3), 139–172.

Ellis, A. (1994a). Reason and emotion in psychotherapy (rev.). New York: Carol Publishing Group.

Ellis, A. (1994b). The treatment of borderline personalities with rational emotive behavior therapy. *Journal of Rational-Emotive & Cognitive Behavior Therapy, 12*(2), 101–119.

Ellis, A. (1995a). Psychotherapy is alarmingly encumbered with disposable myths. *Psychotherapy: Theory, Research, Practice, Training, 32*(3), 495–499.

Ellis, R. D. (1995b). *Questioning consciousness: The interplay of imagery, cognition, and emotion in the human brain.* Amsterdam: John Benjamins.

Ellis, A. (1996). "A social constructionist position for mental health counseling": Reply. *Journal of Mental Health Counseling, 18*(1), 16–28.

Ellis, A. (2004). Expanding the ABCs of rational emotive behavior therapy In A. Freeman, M. J. Mahoney, & P. DeVito (Eds.), *Cognition and psychotherapy* (2nd ed., pp. 185–196). New York: Springer.

Ellis, A., & Bernard, M. (1986). *What is rational-emotive therapy (RET)?* New York: Springer.

Ellis, A., Doorbar, R., Guze, H., & Clark, L. (1952). A study of sexual preferences: preliminary report. *International Journal of Sexology, 6,* 87–88.

Ellis, A., & Whitely, J. M. (Eds.). (1979). *Theoretical and empirical foundations of rational-emotive therapy.* Belmont, CA: Wadsworth.

Elman, J. L., Bates, E. A., Johnson, M. H., & Karmiloff-Smith, A. (1996). *Rethinking innateness: A connectionist perspective on development.* Cambridge: MIT Press.

Emery, N. J., Capitanio, J. P., Mason, W. A., Machado, C. J., Mendoza, S. P., & Amaral, D. G. (2001). The effects of bilateral lesions of the amygdala on dyadic social interactions in rhesus monkeys (Macaca mulatta). *Behavioral Neuroscience, 115,* 515–544.

Emotional rats. (1939, April 10). *Time Magazine* [Electronic version]. Retrieved April 15, 2008, from http://www.time.com/time/magazine/article/0,9171,761000,00.html

Endler, N. (1975). The case for person-situation interactions. *Canadian Psychological Review, 16,* 12–21.

Ennegram Institute. (2005, August 1). *Independent researchers conclude first validation study of the enneagram system* [press release]. Retrieved April 17, 2008, from http://www.enneagraminstitute.com/articles/SHLrelease_brief.asp

Erdelyi, M. H. (1985). *Psychoanalysis: Freud's cognitive psychology.* New York: W. H. Freeman/Times Books/Henry Holt.

Erdelyi, M. H. (2001). Defense processes can be conscious or unconscious. *American Psychologist, 56,* 761–762.

Erikson, E. H. (1964). *Insight and responsibility.* New York: W. W. Norton.

Erikson, E. H. (1968). *Identity: Youth and crisis.* New York: W. W. Norton.

Erikson, E. H. (1969). *Gandhi's truth: On the origins of militant nonviolence.* New York: W. W. Norton

Erikson, E. H., Erikson, J. M., & Kivnick, H. Q. (1986). *Vital involvement in old age.* New York: W. W. Norton.

Evans, C. (1996). *The casebook of forensic detection.* New York and Toronto: John Wiley.

Evans, R. I. (1964). *Conversations with Carl Jung.* Princeton, NJ: D. Van Nostrand.

Evans, R. I. (1970). *Gordon Allport: The man and his ideas.* New York: E. P. Dutton.

Evans, R. I. (1989). *Albert Bandura: The man and his ideas—a dialogue.* New York: Praeger.

Exner, J. E. (1993). *The Rorschach: A comprehensive system: Vol. 1. Basic foundations* (3rd ed.). New York: John Wiley.

Eysenck, H. J. (1952). The effects of psychotherapy: an evaluation. *Journal of Consulting Psychology, 16*(5), 319–324.

Eysenck, H. (1965). *The causes and cures of neurosis.* London: Routledge & Kegan Paul.

Eysenck, H. J. (1967). *The biological basis of personality.* Springfield, IL: Charles C Thomas.

Eysenck, H. J. (1986). Failure of treatment—failure of theory? *Behavioral and Brain Sciences, 9,* 236.

Eysenck, H. J. (1990). Genetic and environmental contributions to individual differences: The three major dimensions of personality. *Journal of Personality, 58,* 245–261.

Eysenck, H. J. (1991). Dimensions of personality: 16, 5, or 3? Criteria for a taxonomic paradigm. *Personality & Individual Differences,* VI, *12*(8), 773–790.

Eysenck, H. J. (1992). Four ways five factors are not basic. *Personality & Individual Differences,* VI, *13*(6), 667–673.

Eysenck, H. J. (1994). The big five or giant three: Criteria for a paradigm. In C. Halverson, G. A. Kohnstamm, & R. P. Martin (Eds.), *The developing structure of temperament and personality from infancy to adulthood* (pp. 37–51). Hillsdale, NJ: Lawrence Erlbaum

Eysenck, H. J. (1997). *Rebel with a cause: The autobiography of Hans Eysenck.* New Brunswick, NJ: Transaction.

Eysenck, H. J., & Eysenck, S. B. (1969). *Personality structure and measurement.* London: Routledge.

Eysenck, H. J., & Eysenck, S. B. (1971). The orthogonality of psychoticism and neuroticism: A factorial study. *Perceptual & Motor Skills, 33*(2), 461–462.

Eysenck, H., & Eysenck, S. (1985). *Personality and individual differences.* San Diego, CA: R. R. Knapp.

Eysenck, S. B. G., & Eysenck, S. J. (1967). Salivary response to lemon juice as a measure of introversion. *Perceptual and Motor Skills, 24,* 1047–1051.

Eysenck, S. B. G., & Long, F. Y. (1986). A cross-cultural comparison of personality in adults and children: Singapore and England. *Journal of Personality and Social Psychology, 50,* 124–130.

Fairbairn, R. (1954). *An object-relations theory of the personality.* New York: Basic Books. (Previously published as *Psychoanalytic studies of the personality*)

Fairbairn, B. E., & Scharff, D. E. (Eds.). (1994). *From instinct to self. Selected papers of W. R. D. Fairbairn: Vol. 2. Applications and early contributions.* Northvale, NJ: Jason Aronson.

Farrell, B.A. (1981). *The standing of psychoanalysis.* Oxford, UK: Oxford University Press.

Fatzer, R., Gandini, G., Jaggy, A., Doherr, M., & Vandevelde, M. (2000). Necrosis of hippocampus and piriform lobe in 38 domestic cats with seizures: A retrospective study on clinical and pathologic studies. *Journal of Veterinary Internal Medicine 14,* 100–104.

Festinger, L. (1950). Informal social communication. *Psychological Review, 57,* 271–282.

Festinger, L., & Carlsmith, J. M. (1959). Cognitive dissonance as a consequence of forced compliance. *Journal of Abnormal and Social Psychology, 58,* 203–211.

Festinger, L., Pepitone, A., & Newcomb, T. (1952). Some consequences of de-individuation in a group. *Journal of Abnormal and Social Psychology, 47,* 382–389.

Fiddick, L., Cosmides, L., & Tooby, J. (2000). No interpretation without representation: The role of domain-specific representations and inferences in the Wason selection task. *Cognition, 77,* 1–79.

Findley, M., & Cooper, H. (1983). Locus of control and academic achievement: A literature review. *Journal of Personality and Social Psychology, 44*(2), 419–427.

Fischer, R., & Juni, S. (1982). The anal personality: Self-disclosure, negativism, self-esteem, and superego severity. *Journal of Personality Assessment, 46,* 50-58

Fiske, D.W. (1949). Consistency of the factorial structures of personality ratings from different sources. *Journal of Abnormal and Social Psychology, 44,* 329–344.

Flor-Henry, P. (1975). Psychiatric surgery—1935–1973: Evolution and current perspectives. *Canadian Psychiatric Association Journal, 20,* 157–167.

Flugel, J. C. (1964). *A hundred years of psychology: 1833–1933.* New York: Basic Books.

Fodor, J. A. (1975). *The language of thought*. New York: Crowell.

Fodor, J. A. (1983). *The modularity of mind: An essay on faculty psychology*. Cambridge, MA: MIT Press.

Forer, B. (1949). The fallacy of personal validation: A classroom demonstration of gullibility. *Journal of Abnormal and Social Psychology, 44,* 118–123.

Fowler, J. (1981). *Stages of faith: The psychology of human development and the quest for meaning.* San Francisco: Harper & Row.

Fraga, M. F., Ballestar, E., Paz, M. F., Ropero, S., Setien, F., Ballestar, M. L., Heine-Suñer, D., Cigudosa, J. C., Urioste, M., Benitez, J., Boix-Chornet, M., Sanchez-Aguilera, A., Ling, C., Carlsson, E., Poulsen, P., Vaag, A., Stephan, Z., Spector, T. D., Wu, Y. Z., Plass, C., & Esteller, M. (2005). Epigenetic differences arise during the lifetime of monozygotic twins. *Proceedings of the National Academy of Sciences of the United States of America, 102,* 10604–10609.

France, M. (2000). *Naikan: A Buddhist approach to psychotherapy.* Victoria, Canada: University of Victoria.

Francis, C. R., Hughes, H. M., & Hitz, L. (1992). Physically abusive parents and the 16-PF: A preliminary psychological typology. *Child Abuse & Neglect, 16,* 673–691.

Freeman, W. (1971): Frontal lobotomy in early schizophrenia. Long-term follow-up in 415 cases. *British Journal of Psychiatry, 119,* 621–624.

Freud, A. (1936). *The ego and the mechanisms of defense* (rev. ed.). Madison, CT: International Universities Press, 1966.

Freud, A. (1937). *The ego and the mechanisms of defence.* (C. Baines, Trans.). London: Leonard and Virginia Woolf at the Hogarth Press.

Freud, S. (1910). The origin and development of psychoanalysis. *American Journal of Psychology, 21,* 181–218.

Freud, S. (1916a). *Psychopathology of everyday life* (A. A. Brill, Trans.). New York: Macmillan.

Freud, S. (1916b). *Some character-types met with in psychoanalytic work* (Standard edition, Vol. 14, pp. 309–333). London: Hogarth Press.

Freud, S. (1920a). *Dream psychology: Psychoanalysis for beginners* (M. D. Eder, Trans.). New York: James A. McCann.

Freud, S. (1920b). *A general introduction to psychoanalysis* (G. S. Hall, Trans.). New York: Horace Liveright.

Freud S. (1924). The passing of the oedipus-complex. In *Collected papers* (Vol. 2, pp. 269–282). London: Hogarth Press.

Freud, S. (1927). *The ego and the id.* London: Hogarth Press.

Freud, S. (1928). *The future of an illusion* (W. D. Robson-Scott, Trans.). New York, Liveright.

Freud, S. (1930). *A general introduction to psychoanalysis* (G. S. Hall, Trans.). New York: Horace Liveright.

Freud S. (1933). *New introductory lectures in psychoanalysis.* New York: W. W. Norton.

Freud, S. (1936). *The problem of anxiety* (H. A. Bunker, Trans.). New York: Psychoanalytic Quarterly Press; W. W. Norton.

Freud, S. (1938). The masturbatic sexual manisfestations. In A. A. Brill (Ed.), *The basic writings of Sigmund Freud.* New York: Modern Library.

Freud, S. (1949a). On narcissism: an introduction. In J. Riviere (Trans.), *Collected papers* (Vol. 4, pp. 30–59). London: Hogarth Press.

Freud, S. (1949b). *An outline of psychoanalysis.* New York: W. W. Norton.

Freud, S. (1949c). *Three essays on the theory of sexuality* (J. Strachey, Trans.). London: Imago. (Original work published 1905)

Freud, S. (1950). *Entwurf einer Psychologie.* In M. Bonaparte, A. Freud, & E. Kris (Eds.). *Aus den anfangen der psychoanalyse. Briefe an Wilhelm Fliess, Abhandlungen und Notizen aus den Jahren 1887–1902.* London: Imago. (Original work published 1895)

Freud, S. (1954). A project for a scientific psychology. In M. Bonaparte, A. Freud, & E. Kris (Eds.), The origins of psycho-analysis: Letters to Wilhelm Fliess, drafts and notes, 1887–1902 (pp. 283–387) (J. Strachey, Trans.). London: Imago. (Original work published 1895)

Freud, S. (1957). The psychotherapy of hysteria. In J. Strachey (Ed., Trans.), *Studies on hysteria*. New York: Basic Books.

Freud, S. (1959). *Collected papers* (J. Riviere, Trans.). (Vol. 2). New York: Basic Books. (Original work published 1908)

Freud, S. (1960). The psychopathology of everyday life. In J. Strachey (Ed., Trans.), Standard edition of the works of Sigmund Freud (Vol. 6, pp. 1–310). London: Hogarth Press. (Original work published 1901)

Freud, S. (2000). *Three essays on the theory of sexuality* (J. Strachey, Trans.). New York: Basic Books. (Original work published 1905)

Freud, S., & Jung, C. (1974). *The Freud/Jung letters* (William McGuire, Ed.; Ralph Mannheim & R. F. C. Hull, Trans.). Princeton, NJ: Princeton University Press. (Original work published 1906–1913)

Freud, S., & Oppenheim, D. E. (1958). *Träume im Folklore* [Dreams in folklore].New York: International Univeisities Press. (Original work published 1911)

Friedman, A. F. (2004). *Psychological assessment with the MMPI-2*. Mahwah, NJ: Lawrence Erlbaum.

Friedman, H., & Schustack, M. (2006). *Personality: Classic theories and modern research* (3rd ed.). Boston: Pearson/Allyn & Bacon.

Frith, C. D., & Frith, U. (1999). Interacting minds—a biological basis. *Science, 286,* 1692–1695.

Fromm, E. (1941). *Escape from freedom*. New York: Rinehart.

Fromm, E. (1955). *The sane society*. New York: Rinehart.

Fromm, E. (1973). *The anatomy of human destructiveness*. New York: Holt, Rinehart and Winston.

Fromm-Reichmann, F. (1948). Notes on the development of treatment of schizophrenics by psychoanalytic therapy. *Psychiatry: Journal for the Study of Interpersonal Processes, 11,* 263–73.

Fullerton, G. S. (1906). *An introduction to philosophy*. New York: MacMillan.

Funder, D. C., & Ozer, D. J. (1983). Behavior as a function of the situation. *Journal of Personality and Social Psychology, 44,* 107–112.

Furnham, A., & Jaspars, J. (1983). The evidence for interactionism in psychology: A critical analysis of the situation-response inventories. *Personality and Individual Differences, 4,* 627–644.

Furnham, A., & Schofield, S. (1987). Accepting personality test feedback: A review of the Barnum effect. *Current Psychological Research & Reviews, 6*(2), 162–178.

Furuichi, A., Mizobe, K., Nukina, S., & Kawahara, R. (2006). Case of bonding disorder effectively treated by Morita therapy. *Seishin Shinkeigaku Zasshi, 108,* 449–458.

Gall, F. J. (1810). *Anatomie et physiologie du sy*stème nerveux [The anatomy and physiology of the nervous system] (Vol. 1). Paris: Librairie Grecque-Latine-Allemande.

Garb H. (1998). The validity of the Rorschach and the Minnesota Multiphasic Personality Inventory: Results from meta-analyses. *Psychological Science. 5,* 402–404

Garfield, S. L., & Bergin, A. E. (1971). Therapeutic conditions and outcome. *Journal of Abnormal Psychology, 77,* 108–114.

Gariépy, J.-L., & Lewis, M. (1996). Genes, neurobiology, and aggression: Time frames and functions of social behavior in adaptation. In D. M. Stoff & R. B. Cairns (Eds.), *Aggression and violence: Genetic, neurobiological, and biosocial perspectives*. Mahwah, NJ: Lawrence Erlbaum.

Gattaz, W. F. (1981). HLA-B27 as a possible genetic marker of psychoticism. *Personality and Individual Differences, 2,* 57–60.

Gattaz, W. F., Seitz, M., & Beckmann, H. (1985). A possible association between HLA B-27 and vulnerability to schizophrenia. *Personality and Individual Differences, 6,* 283–285.

Gaylin, W. (1984). *The rage within: Anger in modern life*. New York: Simon & Schuster.

Gazzaniga, M. (1970). *The bisected brain*. New York: Appleton-Century-Crofts.

Gazzaniga, M. S. (1985). *The social brain: Discovering the networks of the mind*. New York: Basic Books.

Gazzaniga, M. S. (1992). *Nature's mind: The biological roots of thinking, emotions, sexuality, language, and intelligence.* New York: Basic Books.

Gazzola, N. (2003). *Therapist interpretations and client change: An investigation of process in non-dynamic psychotherapies.* Ann Arbor, MI: University Microfilms International.

Gazzola, N., Iwakabe, S., & Stalikas, A. (2003). Counsellor interpretations and the occurrence of in-session client change moments in non-dynamic psychotherapies. *Counselling Psychology Quarterly, 16,* 81–94.

Gazzola, N., & Stalikas, A. (1997). An investigation of counselor interpretations in client-centered therapy. *Journal of Psychotherapy Integration, 7,* 313–327.

Gazzola, N., & Stalikas, A. (2004). Therapist interpretations and client processes in three therapeutic modalities: Implications for psychotherapy integration. *Journal of Psychotherapy Integration, 14,* 397–418.

Geen, R. G. (1984). Preferred stimulation levels in introverts and extraverts: Effects on arousal and performance. *Journal of Personality and Social Psychology, 46,* 1303–1312.

Gelernter, J., Kranzler, H., Coccaro, E., Siever, L., New, A., & Mulgrew, C. (1997). D4 dopamine receptor (DRD4) alleles and novelty seeking in substance-dependent, personality-disorder, and control subjects. *American Journal of Human Genetics, 61,* 1144–1152.

Geller, D. M. (1982). Alternatives to deception: Why, what, and how? In J. E. Sieber (Ed.), *The ethics of social research: Surveys and experiments* (pp.39–55). New York: Springer-Verlag.

Gentry, T. A., Polzine, K. M., & Wakefield, J. A. (1985). Human genetic markers associated with variation in intellectual abilities and personality. *Personality and Individual Differences, 6,* 111–113.

Gerdes, E. P. (1979). College students' reactions to social psychological experiments involving deception. *Journal of Social Psychology, 107,* 99–110.

Gibson, H. (1974). Morita therapy and behaviour therapy. *Behaviour Research and Therapy, 12,* 347–353.

Gil, S. (2005). Evaluation of premorbid personality factors and pre-event posttraumatic stress symptoms in the development of posttraumatic stress symptoms associated with a bus explosion in Israel. *Journal of Traumatic Stress, 18,* 563–567.

Gilbert, D. G., & Hagen, R. L. (1985). Electrodermal responses to noise stressors: Nicotine extraversion interaction. *Personality and Individual Differences, 6,* 573–578.

Gilbert, J. (1980). *Interpreting psychological test data.* New York: Van Nostrand Reinhold.

Go, V., & Champaneria, M. (2002). The new world of medicine: Prospecting for health. *Nippon Naika Gakkai Zasshi, 91,* 159–163.

Godfray, H. C. (1992). The evolution of forgiveness. *Nature, 355,* 206–207.

Gogtay, N., Bhatt, H., Dalvi, S., & Kshirsagar, N. (2002). The use and safety of non-allopathic Indian medicines. *Drug Safety, 25,* 1005–1019.

Goldberg, L. R. (1981). Language and individual differences: The search for universals in personality lexicons. In L. Wheeler (Ed.), *Review of personality and social psychology* (pp.141–165). Beverly Hills, CA: Sage.

Goldberg, L. R., & Digman, J. M. (1994). Revealing structure in the data: Principles of exploratory factor analysis. In S. Strack & M. Lorr (Eds.), *Differentiating normal and abnormal personality* (pp. 216–242). New York: Springer.

Goleman, D. (2006). *Emotional intelligence.* New York: Bantam Books.

Gomez, R., & Gerken, L. (1999). Artificial grammar learning by 1-year-olds leads to specific and abstract knowledge. *Cognition, 70*(2), 109–15.

Gore, P., & Rotter, J. (1963). A personality correlate of social action. *Journal of Personality, 31,* 58–64.

Gottheil, E., & Stone, G. (1974). Psychosomatic aspects of orality and anality. *Journal of Nervous and Mental Disease, 159,* 182–90

Gould, S. J., & Eldredge, N. (1993). Punctuated equilibrium comes of age. *Nature, 366,* 223–227.

Grandin, T. (2005). *Animals in translation.* New York: Scribner.

Granqvist, P., Ivarsson, T., Broberg, A., & Hagekull, B. (2007). Examining relations among attachment, religiosity, and New Age spirituality using the Adult Attachment Interview. *Developmental Psychology, 43,* 590–601.

Greenberg, J. R., & Mitchell, S. A. (1983). *Object relations in psychoanalytic theory*. Cambridge, MA: Harvard University Press.

Greenberg, M. (1967). Role playing: An alternative to deception? *Journal of Personality and Social Psychology, 7,* 152–157.

Griesinger, W. (1965). *Mental pathology and therapeutics*. New York: Hafner. (Original work published 1867)

Grigsby, J., & Schneiders, J. L. (1991). Neuroscience, modularity, and personality theory: Conceptual foundations of a model of complex human functioning. *Psychiatry, 54,* 21–38.

Grilo, C., Becker, D., Edell, W., & McGlashan, T. (2001). Stability and change of DSM-III-R personality disorder dimensions in adolescents followed up 2 years after psychiatric hospitalization. *Comprehensive Psychiatry, 42*(5), 364–368.

Grilo, C., & McGlashan, T. H. (2005). Course and outcome of personality disorders. In J. M. Oldham, A. E. Skodol, & D. S. Bender (Eds.), *The American Psychiatric Publishing textbook of personality disorders* (pp. 103–115). Washington, DC: American Psychiatric Publishing.

Grosskurth, P. (1986). *Melanie Klein: Her world and her work*. New York: Random House.

Grünbaum, A. (2001). A century of psychoanalysis: Critical retrospect and prospect. *International Forum of Psychoanalysis, 10*(2), 105–112.

Grünbaum, A. (2002). Critique of psychoanalysis. In E. Erwin (ed.), *The Freud encyclopedia: Theory, therapy, and culture* (pp. 117–136). New York & London: Routledge.

Grünbaum, A. (2006). Is Sigmund Freud's psychoanalytic edifice relevant to the 21st century? *Psychoanalytic Psychology, 23*(2), 257–284.

Grünbaum, A. (2007). The reception of my Freud-critique in the psychoanalytic literature. *Psychoanalytic Psychology, 24*(3), 545–576.

Guharoy, R., & Noviasky, J. (2003). Time to ban ephedra—now. *American Journal of Health-System Pharmacy, 60,* 1580–1582.

Guntrip, H. (1971). *Psychoanalytic theory, therapy, and the self: A basic guide to the human personality in Freud, Erikson, Klein, Sullivan, Fairbairn, Hartmann, Jacobson, and Winnicott*. New York: Basic Books.

Gurin, P., Gurin, G., Lao, R., & Beattie, M. (1969). Internal-external control in the motivational dynamics of Negro youth. *Journal of Social Issues, 25*(3), 29–53.

Gurrera, R., Nakamura, M., Kubicki, M., Dickey, C., Niznikiewicz, M., Voglmaier, M., McCarley, R. W., Shenton, M. E., Westin, C., Maier, S. E., & Seidman, L. J. (2007). The uncinate fasciculus and extraversion in schizotypal personality disorder: A diffusion tensor imaging study. *Schizophrenia Research, 90*(1), 360–362.

Guterman, J. T. (1994). A social constructionist position for mental health counseling. *Journal of Mental Health Counseling, 16,* 226–244.

Haan, N., & Day, D. (1974). A longitudinal study of change and sameness in personality development: Adolescence to later adulthood. *International Journal of Aging & Human Development, 5*(1), 11–39.

Haas, L. (2001). Phineas Gage and the science of brain localisation. *Journal of Neurology, Neurosurgery, and Psychiatry, 71,* 761.

Hagen, L. (2002). Taoism and psychology. In R. Paul Olson (Ed.), *Religious theories of personality and psychotherapy: East meets west* (pp. 141–210). Binghamton, NY: Haworth Press.

Haggard, H. W. (2004). *From medicine man to doctor: The story of the science of healing*. New York: Dover.

Hagmann, M. (2000). In Europe, hooligans are prime subjects for research. *Science, 289,* 572.

Hall, C., & Lindzey, G. (1970). *Theories of personality* (2nd ed.). New York: John Wiley.

Hamilton, W. D. (1964). The genetical evolution of social behaviour I and II. Journal of Theoretical Biology, 7, 1–16, 17–32.

Hamilton-Giachritsis C., & Browne, K. (2005). A retrospective study of risk to siblings in abusing families. *Journal of Family Psychology, 19,* 619–624.

Hamlin, J. (2005, October 31). Family grief: A suicide leaves a legacy of anguish. *San Francisco Chronicle,* p. A1.

Hampson, S., & Goldberg, L. (2006). A first large cohort study of personality trait stability over the 40 years between elementary school and midlife. *Journal of Personality and Social Psychology, 91*(4), 763–779.

Harcourt, A. H., Fossey, D., Stewart, K. J., & Watts, D. P. (1980). Reproduction in wild gorillas and some comparisons with chimpanzees. *Journal of Reproduction and Fertility 28,* 59–70.

Harris, B. (1979). Whatever happened to little Albert? *American Psychologist, 34,* 151–160.

Hart, B., & Miller, M. (1985). Behavioral profiles of dog breeds. *Journal of the American Veterinary Medical Association, 186,* 1175–1180.

Hart, S. D. F. (1991). The MCMI-II and psychopathy. *Journal of Personality Disorders,* 318–327.

Hartmann, H. (1958). *Ego psychology and the problem of adaptation* (D. Rapaport, Trans.). New York: International Universities Press.

Hartsman, E. (2002). Jewish anthropology: The stuff between. In R. Paul Olson (Ed.), *Religious theories of personality and psychotherapy: East meets west* (pp. 211–246). Binghamton, NY: Haworth Press.

Haselton, M. G., & Funder, D. (2006). The evolution of accuracy and bias in social judgment. In M. Schaller, D. T. Kenrick, & J. A. Simpson (Eds.), *Evolution and social psychology* (pp. 15–37). New York: Psychology Press.

Hasher, L., Goldstein, D., & Toppino, T. (1977). Frequency and the conference of referential validity. *Journal of Verbal Learning & Verbal Behavior, 16,* 107–112.

Hasher, L., & Zacks, R. T. (1979). Automatic and effortful processes in memory. *Journal of Experimental Psychology: General, 108,* 356–388.

Hathaway, S. R., & McKinley, J. C. (1942). *The Minnesota Multiphasic Personality Schedule.* Minneapolis: University of Minnesota.

Hawkins, J., & Blakeslee, S. (2005). *On intelligence.* New York: Times Books, Henry Holt.

Haynes, C. (1994). The Enneagram: Perspective on ourselves, each other, and our clients. *Beginnings 14,* 1–4.

He, Y., & Li, C. (2007, January 24). Morita therapy for schizophrenia. *Cochrane Database of Systematic Reviews,* Issue 1, Article CD006346. Retrieved April 17, 2008, from http://dx.doi.org/10.1002/14651858.CD006346"\t"_blank

Hebb, D. O. (1958). *A textbook of psychology.* Philadelphia: Saunders.

Heilbrun, K. S. (1980). Silverman's subliminal psychodynamic activation: A failure to replicate. *Journal of Abnormal Psychology, 89,* 560–566.

Helson, R., & Moane, G. (1987). Personality change in women from college to midlife. *Journal of Personality and Social Psychology, 53*(1), 176–186.

Henke, K., Buck, A., Weber, B., & Wieser, H. G. (1997). Human hippocampus establishes associations in memory. *Hippocampus, 7,* 249–256.

Henke, K., Weber, B., Kneifel, S., Wieser, H. G., & Buck, A. (1999). Human hippocampus associates information in memory. *Proceedings of the National Academy of Sciences, 96,* 5884–5889.

Herbst, J., Zonderman, A. B., McCrae, R. R., & Costa, P. T. (2000). Do the dimensions of the temperament and character inventory map a single genetic architecture? Evidence from molecular genetics and factor analysis. *American Journal of Psychiatry, 157,* 1285–1290.

Hergenhahn, B. R. (2001). *An introduction to the history of psychology* (4th ed.). Belmont, CA: Wadsworth Thomson Learning.

Hiller J. (1999). A comparative meta-analysis of Rorschach and MMPI validity. *Psychological Assessment* (3):278–296

Hillerman, T., & Bulow, E. (1991). *Talking mysteries: A conversation with Tony Hillerman.* Albuquerque: University of New Mexico Press.

Himmelfarb, G. (1959). *Darwin and the Darwinian revolution.* Garden City, NY: Doubleday.

Hippocrates of Cos. (1978). *Hippocratic writings* (G. E. R. Lloyd, Ed., & J. Chadwick, Trans.). New York: Penguin Books.

Hitler, A. (1939). *Mein kampf.* New York: Reynal & Hitchcock.

Holden, G. (1991). The relationship of self-efficacy appraisals to subsequent health related outcomes: A meta-analysis. *Social Work in Health Care, 16*(1), 53–93.

Hollingworth, H. L. (1930). *Abnormal psychology: Its concepts and theories.* New York: Ronald Press.

Holmes, D. S. (1976a). Debriefing after psychological experiments: 1. Effectiveness of postdeception dehoaxing. *American Psychologist, 31,* 858–867.

Holmes, D. S. (1976b). Debriefing after psychological experiments: 2. Effectiveness of postdeception desensitizing. *American Psychologist, 31,* 868–875.

Holmes, J. (2004). Disorganized attachment and borderline personality disorder: A clinical perspective. *Attachment & Human Development, 6,* 181–190.

Horney, K. (1937). *The neurotic personality of our time.* New York: W. W. Norton.

Horney, K. (1939). *New ways in psychoanalysis.* New York: W. W. Norton.

Horney, K. (1942). *Self-analysis.* New York: W. W. Norton.

Horney, K. (1945). *Our inner conflicts.* New York: W. W. Norton.

Horney, K. (1950). *Neurosis and human growth. The struggle toward self-realization.* New York: W. W. Norton.

Horowitz, I. A., & Rothschild, B. H. (1970). Conformity as a function of deception and role playing. *Journal of Personality and Social Psychology, 14,* 224–226.

Housden, Roger. (1999). *Sacred America: The emerging spirit of the people.* New York: Simon & Schuster.

Howard, K., & Pardue, D. (1996). *Inventing the Southwest: The Fred Harvey Company and Native American art.* Flagstaff, AZ: Northland Publishing and the Heard Museum.

Hsiao, F., Klimidis, S., Minas, H., & Tan, E. (2006). Cultural attribution of mental health suffering in Chinese societies: The views of Chinese patients with mental illness and their caregivers. *Journal of Clinical Nursing, 15,* 998–1006.

Hubel, D. H. (1995). *Eye, brain, and vision.* New York: Scientific American Library.

Hubel, D. H., & Wiesel, T. N. (1959). Receptive fields of single neurones in the cat's striate cortex. *Journal of Physiology, 148,* 574–591.

Hull, C. L. (1951). *Essentials of behavior.* New Haven, CT: Yale University Press.

Hull, C. L. (1952). *A behavior system.* New Haven, CT: Yale University Press.

Hunsley, J., Lee, C., & Wood, J. (2004). Controversial and questionable assessment techniques. In S. Lilienfeld, J. Lohr, & S. Lynn (Eds.), *Science and pseudoscience in clinical psychology.* New York: Guilford Press.

Hunt, M. (1993). *The story of psychology.* New York: Anchor Books.

Hunt, M. (1999). *The new know-nothings: The political foes of the scientific study of human nature.* New Brunswick, NJ: Transaction.

Huntington, E. (1935). *Tomorrow's children: The goal of eugenics.* New York: John Wiley.

Iacoboni, M., & Dapretto, M. (2006). The mirror neuron system and the consequences of its dysfunction. *Nature Reviews Neuroscience, 7*(12), 942–951.

Iacoboni, M., & Lenzi, G. (2002). Mirror neurons, the insula, and empathy. *Behavioral and Brain Sciences, 25*(1), 39–40.

Iftene, F., & Roberts, N. (2004). Romanian adolescents: Literature review and psychiatric presentation of Romanian adolescents adopted in Romania and in Canada. *Canadian Child and Adolescent Psychiatry Review, 13*(4), 110–113.

Inerney-Leo, A., Biesecker, B. B., Hadley, D. W., Kase, R. G., Giambarresi, T. R., Johnson, E., Lerman C., & Struewing, J. P. (2004). BRCA1/2 testing in hereditary breast and ovarian cancer families: Effectiveness of problem-solving training as a counseling intervention. *American Journal of Medical Genetics A, 130*, 221–227.

Isaacson, S. S. (2001). *The influence of sex, age, and personality on mate-age preferences: An evolutionary perspective.* Ann Arbor, MI: University Microfilms International.

Isbell, L. A. (2006). Snakes as agents of evolutionary change in primate brains. *Journal of Human Evolution, 51,* 1–35.

Ishiyama, F. (2003). A bending willow tree: A Japanese (Morita therapy) model of human nature and client change. *Canadian Journal of Counselling, 37,* 216–231.

Iwai, H., & Reynolds D. (1970). Morita psychotherapy: The views from the West. *American Journal of Psychiatry, 126,* 1031–1036.

Jackendoff, R. (1994). *Patterns in the mind.* New York: Basic Books.

Jacobi, F., Wittchen, H., Hölting, C., Höfler, M., Pfister, H., Müller, N., & Lieb, R. (2004). Prevalence, co-morbidity, and correlates of mental disorders in the general population: Results from the German Health Interview and Examination Survey (GHS). *Psychological Medicine, 34*(4), 597–611.

James, W. (1890). *Principles of psychology* (Vol.1). Cambridge, MA: Harvard University Press.

James, W. (1905). *The principles of psychology* (2nd ed.). New York: Henry Holt.

Jelliffe, S. E. (1918). The epileptic attack in dynamic pathology. *New York Medical Journal 108,* 139–141. Reviewed in *Journal of Nervous and Mental Disease, 49,* 156–57.

Jenkins, H. M., & Moore, B. R. (1973). The form of autoshaped response with food or water reinforcers. *Journal of the Experimental Analysis of Behavior, 20,* 163–181.

John, O. P. (1990). The big-five factor taxonomy: Dimensions of personality in the natural language and in questionnaires. In L. Pervin (Ed.), *Handbook of personality theory and research* (pp. 66–100). New York: Guilford Press.

Johnson, D., Feldman, S., Lubin, H., & Southwick, S. (1995). The therapeutic use of ritual and ceremony in the treatment of posttraumatic stress disorder. *Journal of Traumatic Stress, 8,* 283–298.

Johnson, M. H. (1999). Cortical plasticity in normal and abnormal cognitive development: Evidence and working hypotheses. *Development and Psychopathology, 11,* 419–437.

Joncas, J. (1983). The Eucharist in health care settings: Some pastoral care issues. *Hospital Progress, 64,* 66–68.

Jones, E. (1953). *The life and work of Sigmund Freud.* New York: Basic Books

Jones, E. (1955). *The life and works of Sigmund Freud* (Vol. 2). New York: Basic Books.

Judge, T., Erez, A., Bono, J., & Thoresen, C. (2002). Are measures of self-esteem, neuroticism, locus of control, and generalized self-efficacy indicators of a common core construct? *Journal of Personality and Social Psychology, 83*(3), 693–710.

Jung, C. (1932). *Die Beziehungen der Psychotherapie zur Seelsorge.* Zürich: Rascher.

Jung, C. (1933). *Modern man in search of a soul.* London: Kegan Paul.

Jung, C. (1939). *The integration of the personality.* New York: Farrar & Rinehart.

Jung, C. (1946). *Psychological types.* New York: Harcourt, Brace.

Jung, C. (1948). Versuch zu einer psychologischen Deutung des Trinitätsdogmas. In *Gesammelte Werke: Vol. 11. Symbolik des Geistes* (pp. 321–446). Zürich: Rascher.

Jung, C. (1952). Synchronicity: An acausal connecting principle. In *Collected works: Vol. 8. The structure and dynamics of the psyche.* London: Routledge & Kegan Paul.

Jung, C. (1954). *Collected works of C. G. Jung: Vol. 17. The development of personality* (G. Adler & R. F. C. Hull, Trans.). Princeton, NJ: Princeton University Press.

Jung, C. (1959a). *Collected works of C. G. Jung: Vol. 9, part 1. Archetypes and the collective unconscious* (G. Adler & R. F. C. Hull, Trans.). Princeton, NJ: Princeton University Press.

Jung, C. (1959b). *The collected works of C.G. Jung: Vol. 16. The practice of psychotherapy* (H. Read, M. Fordham, G. Adler, & W. McGuire, Eds.; R.F.C. Hull, Trans.). Bollingen, New Jersey: Princeton University Press.

Jung, C. G. (1959c). *Flying saucers: A modern myth of things seen in the skies.* New York: Harcourt, Brace.

Jung, C. (1959d). *Mandala symbolism* (R.F.C. Hull, Trans.). Princeton, NJ: Princeton University Press.

Jung, C. (1961). *Memories, dreams, reflections.* New York: Pantheon.

Jung, C. G. (1966). *The practice of psychotherapy: Essays on the psychology of the transference and other subjects.* London: Routledge.

Jung, C. (1969). *The archetypes and the collective unconscious* (2nd ed., R.F.C. Hull, Trans.). Princeton, NJ: Princeton University Press.

Jung, C. (1970). *Collected works of C. G. Jung: Vol. 10, Civilization in Transition* (G. Adler & R.F.C. Hull, Trans.). Princeton, NJ: Princeton University Press.

Jung, C.G. (1977). *C. G. Jung speaking* (W. McGuire & R.F.C. Hull, Eds.). Princeton, NJ: Princeton University Press

Jung, C. G. (1983). *Memories, dreams, and reflections.* London: Fontana. (Original work published 1963)

Jung, C. G. (2002). *Answer to Job.* London: Routledge. (Original work published 1954)

Juni, S. (1982). Person perception as a function of orality and anality. *Journal of Social Psychology,* 118, 99–103.

Kahneman, D., Slovic, P., & Tversky, A. (1982). *Judgment under uncertainty: Heuristics and biases.* Cambridge, UK, and New York: Cambridge University Press.

Kahneman, D., & Tversky, A. (Eds.). (2000). *Choices, values, and frames.* New York: Russell Sage Foundation.

Kamilar, S. (2002). A Buddhist psychology. In R. Paul Olson (Ed.), *Religious theories of personality and psychotherapy: East meets west* (pp. 85–139). Binghamton, NY: Haworth Press.

Kandel, E. R., & Squire, L. R. (2000). *Memory: From mind to molecules.* New York: Henry Holt.

Kantor, J. R. (1963). *The scientific evolution of psychology* (Vol. 1). Chicago: Principia Press.

Kaplan, H. I., & Sadock, B. J. (1996). *Concise texbook of clinical psychiatry.* Baltimore, MD: William & Wilkins.

Kaufmann, W. (1980). *Discovering the mind: Vol. 3. Freud Versus Adler and Jung.* New York: McGraw-Hill.

Kazdin, A. E., Bass, D., Siegel, T., & Thomas, C. (1989). Cognitive-behavioral therapy and relationship therapy in the treatment of children referred for antisocial behavior. *Journal of Consulting & Clinical Psychology,* 57, 522–535.

Keck, D. (1996). *Forgetting whose we are: Alzheimer's disease and the love of God.* Nashville, TN: Abingdon Press.

Keith, R., & Vandenberg, S. (1974). Relation between orality and weight. *Psychological Reports,* 35, 1205–1206.

Kelln, B. R. C. (1998). An MCMI-III discriminant function analysis of incarcerated felons: Prediction of subsequent institutional misconduct. *Criminal Justice & Behavior,* 177–189.

Kelly, G. A. (1955). *The psychology of personal constructs.* New York: Norton.

Kelly, G. A. (1963). *A theory of personality.* New York: W. W. Norton.

Kelly, G. (1969). *Clinical psychology and personality: The selected papers of George Kelly* (B. Mahler, Ed.). New York: John Wiley.

Kelly, G. A. (1991). *The psychology of personal constructs* (Vol. 1). London: Routledge.

Kelly, G. A. (2003). A brief introduction to personal construct theory. In F. Fransella (Ed.), *International handbook of personal construct psychology* (pp. 3–20). New York: John Wiley.

Kelman, H.C. (1967). Human use of human subjects: The problem of deception in social psychological experiments. *Psychological Bulletin,* 67(1), 1–11.

Kendler, K., & Gruenberg, A. (1982). Genetic relationship between paranoid personality disorder and the "schizophrenic spectrum" disorders. *American Journal of Psychiatry*, *139*(9), 1185–1186.

Kendler, K. S., Jacobson, K. C., Myers, J., & Prescott, C. A. (2002). Sex differences in genetic and environmental risk factors for irrational fears and phobias. *Psychological Medicine, 32*(2), 209–217.

Kendler, K., Masterson, C., & Davis, K. (1985). Psychiatric illness in first-degree relatives of patients with paranoid psychosis, schizophrenia, and medical illness. *British Journal of Psychiatry, 147*, 524–531.

Kendler, K. S., Myers, J., & Prescott, C. A. (2002). The etiology of phobias: An evaluation of the stress-diathesis model. *Archives of General Psychiatry, 59*(3), 242–248.

Kendler, K. S., Myers, J., Prescott, C. A., & Neale, M. C. (2001). The genetic epidemiology of irrational fears and phobias in men. *Archives of General Psychiatry, 58*(3), 257–265.

Kennedy, D. M. (1970). *The career of Margaret Sanger*. New Haven, CT: Yale University Press.

Kenrick , D. T., & Springfield, D. O. (1980). Personality traits and the eye of the beholder: Crossing some traditional philosophical boundaries in the search for consistency in all of the people. *Psychological Review, 87*, 88–104.

Kernberg, O. F. (1968). The treatment of patients with borderline personality organization. *International Journal of Psycho-Analysis*, *49*(4), 600–619.

Kernberg, O. F. (1975). *Borderline conditions and pathological narcissism*. New York: Jason Aronson.

Kernberg, O. (1976). *Object relations theory and clinical psychoanalysis*. New York: Jason Aronson.

Kernberg, O. (1992). *Aggression in personality disorders and perversions*. New Haven, CT: Yale University Press.

Kernberg, O. F. (1993). The current status of psychoanalysis. *Journal of the American Psychoanalytic Association*, *41*(1), 45–62.

Kernberg, O. F. (2005). Identity diffusion in severe personality disorders. In S. Strack (Ed.), *Handbook of personology and psychopathology* (pp. 39–49). New York: John Wiley.

Kernberg, O. F., & Caligor, E. (2005). A psychoanalytic theory of personality disorders. In J. F. Clarkin & M. F. Lenzenweger (Eds.), *Major theories of personality disorder* (2nd ed., pp. 114–156). New York: Guilford Press.

Kessler, R. (1996). *The sins of the father: Joseph P. Kennedy and the dynasty he founded*. New York: Warner Books.

Kessler, R., McGonagle, K., Zhao, S., & Nelson, C. (1994). Lifetime and 12-month prevalence of DSM-III-R psychiatric disorders in the United States: Results from the National Comorbidity Study. *Archives of General Psychiatry*, *51*(1), 8–19.

Kihlstrom, J. F., Cantor, N., Albright, J. S., Chew, B. R., Klein, S. B., & Niedenthal, P. M. (1988). Information processing and the study of the self. *Advances in Experimental Social Psychology, 21*, 145–178.

Kimble, G. A., Wertheimer, M., & White, C. (Eds.). (1991). *Portraits of pioneers in psychology*. Washington, DC: American Psychological Association.

King, B. (2006). Amygdaloid lesion-induced obesity: Relation to sexual behavior, olfaction, and the ventromedial hypothalamus. *American Journal of Physiology. Regulatory, Integrative and Comparative Physiology, 291*, R1201–R1214.

Kinney, D., Richards, R., Lowing, P., LeBlanc, D., & Zimbalist, M. (2001). Creativity in offspring of schizophrenic and control parents: An adoption study. *Creativity Research Journal*, *13*(1), 17–25.

Kirschenbaum, H. (2004). Carl Rogers's life and work: An assessment on the 100th anniversary of his birth. *Journal of Counseling & Development, 82*, 116–124.

Klein D. (1970). *A history of scientific psychology: Its origins and philosophical backgrounds*. New York: Basic Books.

Klein, M. (1932). *The psychoanalysis of children*. London: Hogarth Press.

Klein, M. (1946). Notes on some schizoid mechanisms. *International Journal of Psycho-Analysis*, *27*, 99–110.

Klein, M. (1984). The psycho-analysis of children (A. Strachey, Trans.). In R. Money-Kyrle (Ed.), *The writings of Melanie Klein* (Vol. 2). New York: Free Press.

Klein, M., & Riviere, J. (1964). *Love, hate, and reparation*. New York: W. W. Norton.

Kline, P., & Storey, R. (1977). A factor analytic study of the oral character. *British Journal of Social & Clinical Psychology, 16,* 317-328

Kline, P., & Storey, R. (1978). Oral personality traits and smoking. *British Journal of Projective Psychology & Personality Study, 23,* 1–4.

Kline, P., & Storey, R. (1980). The etiology of the oral character. *Journal of Genetic Psychology, 136,* 85–94.

Knowles, J. A., Mannuzza, S., & Fyer, A. J. (1995). Heritability of social anxiety. In M. B. Stein (Ed.), *Social phobia: Clinical and research perspectives* (pp. 147–161). Washington, DC: American Psychiatric Press.

Koch, S., & Leary, S. E. (Eds.). (1985). *A century of psychology as a science.* New York: McGraw-Hill.

Koenig, L. B., McGue, M., Krueger, R. F., & Bouchard, T. J. J. (2005). Genetic and environmental influences on religiousness: Findings for retrospective and current religiousness ratings. *Journal of Personality, 73,* 471–488.

Koffka, K (1922). Perception: An introduction to the Gestalt-theorie. *Psychological Bulletin, 19,* 531–585.

Koffka, K. (1935). *Principles of gestalt psychology.* New York: Harcourt, Brace & World.

Köhler, W. (1925). *The mentality of apes* (E. Winter, Trans.). New York: Harcourt, Brace.

Kohn, D. F., Wixson, K., White, W. J., & Benson, G. J. (Eds.). (1997). *Anesthesia and analgesia in laboratory animals.* New York: Academic Press.

Kohut, H. (1971). *The analysis of the self: A systematic approach to the psychoanalytic treatment of narcissistic personality disorders.* New York: International Universities Press.

Kohut, H. (1977). *The restoration of the self.* New York: International Universities Press.

Kohut, H. (1981). Introspection, empathy, and mental health. *Journal of the American Psychoanalytic Association, 63,* 395–408.

Kohut, H. (1984a). *How does analysis cure?* Chicago: University of Chicago Press.

Kohut, H. (1984b). Introspection, empathy, and semicircle of mental health. *Emotions & Behavior Monographs, 3,* 347–375.

Kohut, H., & Wolf, E. (1978). The disorders of the self and their treatment: An outline. *International Journal of Psycho-Analysis, 59*(4), 413–425.

Kraepelin, E. (1921). *Clinical psychiatry: A textbook for students and physicians.* New York: Macmillan.

Kraepelin, E. (1971). *Dementia praecox and paraphrenia* (R. M. Barclay, Trans.). Edinburgh, Scotland: Livingston. (Original work published 1919)

Kramer, D. A. (2005). Commentary: Gene-environment interplay in the context of genetics, epigenetics, and gene expression. *Journal of the American Academy of Child and Adolescent Psychiatry, 44,* 19–27.

Kramer, H., & Sprenger, J. (2000). *Malleus maleficarum.* Escondido, CA: The Book Tree. (Original work published 1486)

Krech, G. (2002). *Naikan: Gratitude, grace, and the Japanese art of self-reflection.* Berkeley, CA: Stone Bridge Press.

Kreppner, J., Rutter, M., Beckett, C., Castle, J., Colvert, E., Groothues, C., Hawkins, A., O'Connor, T. G., Stevens, S., & Sonuga-Barke, E. J. S, (2007). Normality and impairment following profound early institutional deprivation: A longitudinal follow-up into early adolescence. *Developmental Psychology, 43*(4), 931–946.

Kretschmer, E. (1970). *Physique and character.* New York: Cooper Square.

Krishnamurthy, M., & Telles, S. (2007). Assessing depression following two ancient Indian interventions: Effects of yoga and Ayurveda on older adults in a residential home. *Journal of Gerontological Nursing, 33,* 17–23.

Kristensen, H., & Torgersen, S. (2007). The association between avoidant personality traits and motor impairment in a population-based sample of 11-12 year-old children. *Journal of Personality Disorders, 21*(1), 87–97.

Kroenke, K. (2007). Somatoform disorders and recent diagnostic controversies. *Psychiatric Clinics of North America, 30,* 593–619.

Kühl, S. (1994). *The Nazi connection: Eugenics, American racism, and German national socialism.* New York: Oxford University Press.

Kumar, A., & Geist, C. (2007). A case report of bilateral autoenucleation and its prevention. *Orbit, 26,* 309–313.

Kumaran, D., & Maguire, E. A. (2005). The human hippocampus: cognitive maps or relational memory? *Journal of Neuroscience, 25,* 7254–7259.

Kuramoto, A. (2006). Therapeutic benefits of tai chi exercise: Research review. *Wisconsin Medical Journal, 105,* 42–46.

Lachman, R., Lachman, J. L., & Butterfield, E. C. (1979). *Cognitive psychology and information processing: An introduction.* Hillsdale, NJ: Lawrence Erlbaum.

Lah, M. (1989). New validity, normative, and scoring data for the Rotter Incomplete Sentences Blank. *Journal of Personality Assessment, 53*(3), 607–620.

Lake, J. (2004). The integration of Chinese medicine and Western medicine: Focus on mental illness. *Integrative Medicine 3,* CB–CJ.

Langer, W. (1972). *The mind of Adolf Hitler: The secret wartime report.* New York: Basic Books.

Landfield, A. (1988). Personal science and the concept of validation. *International Journal of Personal Construct Psychology, 1,* 237–249.

LaPiere, R. T. (1934). Attitudes versus action. *Social Forces, 13,* 230–237.

Laptook, R., Klein, D., & Dougherty, L. (2006). Ten-year stability of depressive personality disorder in depressed outpatients. *American Journal of Psychiatry, 163*(5), 865–871.

Lasch, C. (1978). *The culture of narcissism: American life in an age of diminishing expectations.* New York: W. W. Norton.

Lazarus, A. (1971). Notes on behavior therapy, the problem of relapse, and some tentative solutions. *Psychotherapy: Theory, Research & Practice, 8*(3), 192–194.

Lazarus, A. (1973). Multimodal behavior therapy: Treating the "BASIC ID." *Journal of Nervous and Mental Disease, 156*(6), 404–411.

Lazarus, A. (Ed.). (1976). *Multimodal behavior therapy.* New York: Springer.

Lazarus, A. (1984a). *In the mind's eye: The power of imagery for personal enrichment.* New York: Guilford Press.

Lazarus, R. (1984b). On the primacy of cognition. *American Psychologist, 39*(2), 124–129.

Lazarus, A. (1985). *Casebook of multimodal therapy.* New York: Guilford Press.

Lazarus, A. (1992). *Multimodal therapy: Technical eclecticism with minimal integration.* New York: Basic Books.

Lazarus, A. (1995). Different types of eclecticism and integration: Let's be aware of the dangers. *Journal of Psychotherapy Integration, 5*(1), 27–39.

Lazarus, A. (1996). The utility and futility of combining treatments in psychotherapy. *Clinical Psychology: Science and Practice, 3*(1), 59–68.

Lazarus, A., & Fay, A. (1975). *I can if I want to.* Essex, CT: FMC Books.

Lazarus, A., Lazarus, C., & Fay, A. (1993). *Don't believe it for a minute! Forty toxic ideas that are driving you crazy.* San Luis Obispo, CA: Impact.

Lazarus, A., & Shaughnessy, M. (2002). An interview with Arnold A. Lazarus. *North American Journal of Psychology, 4*(2), 171–182.

Leaf, R., Ellis, A., DiGiuseppe, R., & Mass, R. (1991). Rationality, self-regard, and the "healthiness" of personality disorders. *Journal of Rational-Emotive & Cognitive Behavior Therapy, 9*(1), 3–37.

Least Heat Moon, W. (1982). *Blue highways: A journey into America.* Boston: Little, Brown.

LeBlanc, S. (1999). *Prehistoric warfare in the American Southwest.* Salt Lake City: University of Utah Press.

Le Bon, G. (1896). *The crowd.* London: Ernest Benn.

LeDoux, J. E. (1994). Emotion, memory, and the brain. *Scientific American, 12,* 62–71.

LeDoux, J. (1996). *The emotional brain: The mysterious underpinnings of emotional life.* New York: Simon & Schuster.

LeDoux, J., & Gazzaniga, M. (1981). The brain and the split brain: A duel with duality as a model of mind. *Behavioral and Brain Sciences, 4*(1), 109–110.

LeDoux, J., & Gorman, J. (2001). A call to action: Overcoming anxiety through active coping. *American Journal of Psychiatry 158,* 1953–1955.

Legault, E., & Laurence, J. (2007). Recovered memories of childhood sexual abuse: Social worker, psychologist, and psychiatrist reports of beliefs, practices, and cases. *Australian Journal of Clinical & Experimental Hypnosis, 35*(2), 111–133.

Le Mare, L., Audet, K., & Kurytnik, K. (2007). A longitudinal study of service use in families of children adopted from Romanian orphanages. *International Journal of Behavioral Development, 31*(3), 242–251.

Lent, R., Brown, S., & Larkin, K. (1984, July). Relation of self-efficacy expectations to academic achievement and persistence. *Journal of Counseling Psychology, 31*(3), 356–362.

Lent, R., Brown, S., & Larkin, K. (1986, July). Self-efficacy in the prediction of academic performance and perceived career options. *Journal of Counseling Psychology, 33*(3), 265–269.

Lenzenweger, M., Johnson, M., & Willett, J. (2004). Individual growth curve analysis illuminates stability and change in personality disorder features: The longitudinal study of personality disorders. *Archives of General Psychiatry, 61*(10), 1015–1024.

Lester, D. (1990). Galen's four temperaments and four-factor theories of personality: A comment on "Toward a four-factor theory of temperament and/or personality." *Journal of Personality Assessment, 54*(1–2), 423–426.

Leung, K., Bian, Z., Moher, D., Dagenais, S., Li, Y., Liu, L., Wu, T., & Miao, J. (2006). Improving the quality of randomized controlled trials in Chinese herbal medicine: part III. Quality control of Chinese herbal medicine used in randomized controlled trials. *Zhong Xi Yi Jie He Xue Bao, 4,* 225–232.

Levenson, H. (1974). Activism and powerful others: Distinctions within the concept of internal-external control. *Journal of Personality Assessment, 38*(4), 377–383.

Levitt, S. D., & Dubner, S. J. (2005). *Freakonomics.* New York: William Morrow

Levy, L. (1956). Personal constructs and predictive behavior. *Journal of Abnormal & Social Psychology, 53*(1), 54–58.

Levy, L., & Dugan, R. (1956, February). A factorial study of personal constructs. *Journal of Consulting Psychology, 20,* 53–57.

Lewicki, P., Czyzewska, M., & Hill, T. (1997). Nonconscious information processing and personality. In D. C. Berry (Ed.), *How implicit is implicit learning?* (pp. 48–72).New York: Oxford University Press.

Lewicki, P., Hill, T., & Czyzewska, M. (1992). Nonconscious acquisition of information. *American Psychologist, 47*(6), 796–801.

Lewin, K. (1935). *A dynamic theory of personality.* New York: McGraw-Hill.

Lewin, K. (1936). *Principles of topological psychology.* New York: McGraw-Hill.

Lewis, C. (1994). Anal personality traits and science A-levels: A failure to replicate. *Psychological Reports, 74,* 157–158.

Libet, B. (1996). "Free will in the light of neuropsychiatry": Commentary. *Philosophy, Psychiatry, & Psychology, 3*(2), 95–96.

Libet, B. (1999). Do we have free will? *Journal of Consciousness Studies, 6*(8), 47–57.

Libet, B., Gleason, C. A., Wright, E. W., & Pearl, D. K. (1983). Time of conscious intention to act in relation to onset of cerebral activity (readiness potential): The unconscious initiation of a freely voluntary act. *Brain, 106,* 623–642.

Lichtenberg, J., Bornstein, M., & Silver, D. (Eds.). (1984). *Empathy* (2 vols.). Hillsdale, NJ: The Analytic Press.

Lieberman, L. (2001). How "Caucasoids" got such big crania and why they shrank: From Morton to Rushton. *Current Anthropology, 42,* 69–95.

Lifschutz, J. (1964). A brief review of psychoanalytic ego psychology. *Social Casework, 45*(1), 3–9.

Lifton, R. J. (2000). *The nazi doctors: Medical killing and the psychology of genocide.* New York: Basic Books.

Litman, L., & Reber, A. (2005). Implicit cognition and thought. In *The Cambridge handbook of thinking and reasoning* (pp. 431–453). Cambridge, UK: Cambridge University Press.

Lockhart, W. H. (1984). Rogers' "necessary and sufficient conditions" revisited. *British Journal of Guidance & Counselling, 12,* 113–123.

Loevinger, J. (1998). *Technical foundations for measuring ego development: The Washington University Sentence Completion Test.* Mahwah, NJ: Lawrence Erlbaum.

Loftus, E. F. (1979a). The malleability of human memory. *American Scientist, 67,* 312–320.

Loftus, E. F. (1979b). Reactions to blatantly contradictory information. *Memory & Cognition, 7,* 368–374.

Loftus, E. F., & Loftus, G. R. (1980). On permanence of information in the human brain. *American Psychologist, 35,* 409–420

Loftus, E. F., & Pickrell, J. E. (1995). The formation of false memories. *Psychiatric Annals, 25,* 720–725.

Ludvigh, E. J., & Happ, D. (1974). Extraversion and preferred level of sensory stimulation. *British Journal of Psychology, 65,* 359–365.

Lynn, D. J., & Vaillant, G. E. (1998). Anonymity, neutrality, and confidentiality in the actual methods of Sigmund Freud: A review of 43 cases, 1907–1939. *American Journal of .Psychiatry, 155,* 163–171.

Machiavelli, N. (1935). *The prince* (W. K. Marriott, Trans.). New York: E. P. Dutton. (Original work published 1546)

Machover, K. (1949). *Personality projection in the drawing of the human figure.* Oxford, UK: C. C. Thomas.

Machover, K. (1953). *Personality projection in the drawing of the human figure: A Method of Personality Investigation.* Springfield, IL: Charles C Thomas.

MacKinnon, D. W. (1965). Personality and realization of creative potential. *American Psychologist, 20,* 273–281.

MacLean, K. (2003). The impact of institutionalization on child development. *Development and Psychopathology, 15*(4), 853–884.

MacLean, P. D. (1954). Studies on the limbic systerm "visceral brain" and their bearing on psychosomatic problems. In E. D.Wittkower & R. A. Cleghorn (Eds.), *Recent developments in psychosomatic medicine* (pp. 101–125). London: I. Pittman.

MacLean, P. (1972). Cerebral evolution and emotional processes: new findings on the striatal complex. *Annals of the New York Academy of Sciences, 193,* 137–149.

MacLean, P. (1977a). On the evolution of three mentalities. In S.Arieti & G. Chrzanowski (Eds.), *New dimensions in psychiatry: A world view* (pp. 305–328). New York: John Wiley.

MacLean, P. (1977b). The triune brain in conflict. *Psychotherapy and Psychosomatics, 28*(1–4), 207–220.

MacLean, P. (1985). Evolutionary psychiatry and the triune brain. *Psychological Medicine, 15*(2), 219–221.

MacLean, P. (1990). *The triune brain in evolution: Role in paleocerebral functions.* New York: Plenum Press.

Macmillan, M. (1992). Freud and his empirical evidence. *Australian Journal of Psychology,* 171–175.

Mahaffey, K., & Marcus, D. (2006). Interpersonal perception of psychopathy: A social relations analysis. *Journal of Social & Clinical Psychology*, 25(1), 53–74.

Mahler, M. (1971). A study of the separation-individuation process and its possible application to borderline phenomena in the psychoanalytic situation. *The Psychoanalytic Study of the Child*, 26, 403–424.

Mahler, M. (1972). On the first three subphases of the separation-individuation process. *International Journal of Psycho-Analysis*, 53(3), 333–338.

Mahler, M., Pine, F., & Bergman, A. (1994). Stages in the infant's separation from the mother. In G. Handel & G. G.Whitchurch (Eds.), *The psychosocial interior of the family* (pp. 419–448). Hawthorne, NY: Aldine de Gruyter.

Mahoney, M. (1991). *Human change processes: The scientific foundations of psychotherapy.* New York: Basic Books.

Maier, W., Lichtermann, D., Minges, J., & Heun, R. (1994). Personality disorders among the relatives of schizophrenia patients. *Schizophrenia Bulletin*, 20(3), 481–493.

Main, R. (2000). Religion, science, and synchronicity. *Harvest: Journal for Jungian Studies*, 46, 89–107.

Maisiak, R., Austin, J. S., West, S. G., & Heck, L. (1996). The effect of person-centered counseling on the psychological status of persons with systemic lupus erythematosus or rheumatoid arthritis: a randomized, controlled trial. *Arthritis Care and Research, 9,* 60–66.

Malik, R., Apel, S., Nelham, C., Rutkowski, C., & Ladd, H. (1997). Failure to uncover the effects of unconscious symbiotic fantasies on heart rate and fine motor performance. *Perceptual and Motor Skills, 85,* 1231–1241.

Malinkowski, B. (1929). *The sexual life of savages.* London: Routledge.

Malloy, T., Albright, L., Diaz-Loving, R., Dong, Q., & Lee, Y. (2004). Agreement in personality judgments within and between nonoverlapping social groups in collectivist cultures. *Personality and Social Psychology Bulletin*, 30(1), 106–117.

Mamtani, R., & Mamtani, R. (2005). Ayurveda and yoga in cardiovascular diseases. *Cardiology in Review, 13,* 155–162.

Marbella, A., Harris, M., Diehr, S., Ignace, G., & Ignace G. (1998). Use of Native American healers among Native American patients in an urban Native American health center. *Archives of Family Medicine, 7,* 182–185.

Marcel, A. J. (1983a). Conscious and unconscious perception: Experiments on visual masking and word recognition. *Cognitive Psychology, 15,* 197–237.

Marcel, A. J. (1983b). Conscious and unconscious perception: An approach to the relations between phenomenal experience and perceptual processes. *Cognitive Psychology, 15,* 238–300.

Marcia, J. (1994). The empirical study of ego identity. In H. A Bosma, T. L. G. Graafsma, H. D. Grotevant, & D. J. De Levita (Eds.), *Identity and development.* Thousand Oaks, CA: Sage.

Marcovitch, S., Goldberg, S., Gold, A., & Washington, J. (1997). Determinants of behavioural problems in Romanian children adopted in Ontario. *International Journal of Behavioral Development*, 20(1), 17–31.

Marin, G. (2006). *Five elements, six conditions: A Taoist approach to emotional healing, psychology, and internal alchemy.* Berkeley, CA: NorthAtlantic Books.

Mark, M., & Reichardt, C. (2004). Quasi-experimental and correlational designs: Methods for the real world when random assignment isn't feasible. In C. Sansone, C. C. Morf, & A. T. Panter (Eds.), *The Sage handbook of methods in social psychology* (pp. 265–286). Thousand Oaks, CA: Sage.

Marlatt, G., Baer, J., & Quigley, L. (1995). Self-efficacy and addictive behavior. In A. Bandura (Ed.), *Self-efficacy in changing societies* (pp. 289–315). New York: Cambridge University Press.

Marsden, G. (1991). *Understanding fundamentalism and evangelicalism.* Grand Rapids, MI: Wm. B. Eerdmans.

Maslow, A. (1943). A theory of human motivation. *Psychological Review, 50,* 370–396.

Maslow, A. (1954). *Motivation and personality.* New York: Harper.

Maslow, A. H. (1968). *Toward a psychology of being.* New York: Van Nostrand.

Maslow, A. H. (1970). *Motivation and personality* (2nd ed.). New York:Harper & Row

Masserman, J. H. (1961). *Principles of dynamic psychiatry.* Philadelphia, PA: W. B. Saunders.

Masson, J. (1988). *Against therapy: Emotional tyranny and the myth of psychological healing.* New York: Atheneum.

Masson, J. (1984). *Assault on the truth.* New York: Farrar Straus & Giroux.

Masson, J. (1992). The tyranny of psychotherapy. In W. Dryden & C. Feltham (Eds.), *Psychotherapy and its discontents* (pp. 7–29). Berkshire, UK: Open University Press.

Masson, J. (1994). *Against therapy.* Monroe, MA: Common Courage Press.

Matsuda, Y. (2003). Cognition and mental health. *Seishin Shinkeigaku Zasshi, 105,* 576–588.

Matthews, R. (2000). Storks deliver babies ($p = 0.008$). *Teaching Statistics, 22*(2), 36–38.

May, R. (1950). *The meaning of anxiety.* New York: Ronald Press.

May, R. (1953). *Man's search for himself.* New York: W. W. Norton.

May, R. (1958). Contributions of existential psychology. In R. May, E. Engel, & E. F. Ellenberger (Eds.), *Existence: A new dimension in psychiatry and psychology.* New York: Simon & Schuster.

May, R. (Ed.). (1961). *Existential psychology.* New York: Random House.

May, R. (1969). *Love and will.* New York: W. W. Norton.

May, R. (1981). *Freedom and destiny.* New York: W. W. Norton.

May, R. (1991). *The cry for myth.* New York: W. W. Norton.

May, R., Angel, E., & Ellenberger, H. (Eds.). (1958). *Existence: A new dimension in psychiatry and psychology.* New York: Basic Books.

McDougall, W. (1923). *Outline of psychology.* New York and Chicago: Charles Scribner's Sons.

McCrae, R. R., & Costa, P. T. (1987). Validation of the five-factor model of personality across instruments and observers. *Journal of Personality and Social Psychology, 52,* 81–90.

McCrae, R. R., & Costa, P. T. (1994). The stability of personality: Observations and evaluations. *Current Directions in Psychological Science, 3,* 173–175.

McCrae, R. R., Costa, P. T., Ostendorf, F., Angleitner, A., Hrebícková, M., Avia, M. D., Sanz, J., Sánchez-Bernardos, M. L., Kusdil, M. E., Woodfield, R., Saunders, P. R., & Smith, P. B. (2000). Nature over nurture: Temperament, personality, and life span development. *Journal of Personality and Social Psychology, 78,* 173–186.

McCrae, R. R., Costa, P. T., & Yik, M. S. M. (1996). Universal aspects of Chinese personality structure. In M. H. Bong (Ed.), *The handbook of Chinese psychology* (pp. 189–207). Hong Kong: Oxford University Press.

McCrae, R. R., & John, O. P. (1992). An introduction to the five factor model and its applications. *Journal of Personality, 60,* 175–215.

McCreary J., Pollard M., Stevenson, K., & Wilson, M. (1998). Human factors: Tenerife revisited. *Journal of Air Transportation World Wide, 3,* 23–31.

McElroy, R., Davis, R., & Blashfield, R. (1989). Variations on the family resemblance hypothesis as applied to personality disorders. *Comprehensive Psychiatry, 30*(6), 449–456.

McKain, T., Glass, C., Arnkoff, D., & Sydnor-Greenberg, J. (1988). Personal constructs and shyness: The relationship between rep grid data and therapy outcome. *International Journal of Personal Construct Psychology, 1*(2), 151–167.

McRae, C., Agarwal, K., Mutimer, D., & Bassendine, M. (2002). Hepatitis associated with Chinese herbs. *European Journal of Gastroenterology and Hepatology, 14,* 559–562.

Meador, K., & Shuman, J. (2000). Who/se we are: Baptism as personhood. *Christian Bioethics, 6,* 71–83.

Meares, R., Melkonian, D., Gordon, E., & Williams, L. (2005). Distinct pattern of P3a event-related potential in borderline personality disorder. *Neuroreport: For Rapid Communication of Neuroscience Research, 16*(3), 289–293.

Meehl, P. (1962). Schizotaxia, schizotypy, schizophrenia. *American Psychologist, 17*(12), 827–838.

Mehler, B. (1997). Beyondism: Raymond B. Cattell and the new eugenics. *Genetica, 99,* 153–163.

Mehl-Madrona, L. (1998). *Coyote medicine: Lessons from Native American healing.* New York: Simon & Schuster.

Mehl-Madrona, L. (1999). Native American medicine in the treatment of chronic illness: Developing an integrated program and evaluating its effectiveness. *Alternative Therapies in Health and Medicine, 5,* 36–44.

Melton, J. (2000, July 17). *Beyond millennialism: The New Age transformed.* Paper presented at the conference on the "New Age in the Old World," Caligny, Switzerland.

Meng, R., Li, Q., Wei, C., Chen, B., Liao, H., & Zhou, Y. (2005). Clinical observation and mechanism study on treatment of senile dementia with Naohuandan. *Chinese Journal of Integrative Medicine, 11,* 111–116.

Merenda, P. F. (1987). Toward a four-factor theory of temperament and/or personality. *Journal of Personality Assessment, 51*(3), 367–374.

Messina, N., Wish, E., Hoffman, J., & Nemes, S. (2001). Diagnosing antisocial personality disorder among substance abusers: the SCID versus the MCMI-II. *American Journal of Drug Alcohol Abuse, 27,* 699–717.

Meyer, A. (1957). *Psychobiology: A science of man.* Springfield, IL: Charles C Thomas.

Meyer, A. E., Stuhr, U., Wirth, U., & Ruster, P. (1988). 12-year follow-up study of the Hamburg short psychotherapy experiment: An overview. *Psychotherapy and Psychosomatics, 50,* 192–200.

Meyer-Lindenberg, A., Hariri, A. R., Munoz, K. E., Mervis, C. B., Mattay, V. S., Morris, C. A., & Berman, K. F. (2005). Neural correlates of genetically abnormal social cognition in Williams syndrome. *Nature Neuroscience, 8*(8), 991–993.

Micale, M. (1995). *Approaching hysteria: Disease and its interpretations.* Princeton, NJ: Princeton University Press.

Miceli, M., & Castelfranchi, C. (2001). Further distinctions between coping and defense mechanisms? *Journal of Personality, 69,* 287–296.

Michell, J. (1999). *Eccentric lives and peculiar notions.* New York: Black Dog and Leventhal.

Milad, M. R., Quinn, B. T., Pitman, R. K., Orr, S. P., Fischl, B., & Rauch, S. L. (2005). Thickness of ventromedial prefrontal cortex in humans is correlated with extinction memory. *Proceedings of the National Academy of Sciences, 102,* 10706–10711.

Milgram, S. (1963). Behavioral study of obedience. *Journal of Abnormal Psychology, 63,* 371–378.

Milgram, S. (1964). Issues in the study of obedience: A reply to Baumrind. *American Psychologist, 19,* 848–852.

Milgram, S. (1974). *Obedience to authority: An experimental view.* New York: Harper & Row.

Milinski, M. (1987). TIT FOR TAT in sticklebacks and the evolution of cooperation. *Nature, 325,* 433–435.

Mill, J., Dempster, E., Caspi, A., Williams, B., Moffitt, T., & Craig, I. (2006). Evidence for monozygotic twin (MZ) discordance in methylation level at two CpG sites in the promoter region of the catechol-O-methyltransferase (COMT) gene. *American Journal of Medical Genetics.* Part B, *Neuropsychiatric Genetics, 141,* 421–425.

Miller, D., & Ross, M. (1975). Self-serving biases in the attribution of causality: Fact or fiction? *Psychological Bulletin, 82*(2), 213–225.

Miller, G. A. (1956). The magical number seven plus or minus two: Some limits on our capacity for processing information. *Psychological Review, 63,* 81–97.

Miller, J., Pilkonis, P., & Clifton, A. (2005). Self- and other-reports of traits from the five-factor model: Relations to personality disorder. *Journal of Personality Disorders, 19*(4), 400–419.

Miller, L. (1988). Behaviorism and the new science of cognition. *Psychological Record, 38*(1), 3–18.

Miller, N. E., & Dollard, J. (1941). *Social learning and imitation.* New Haven, CT: Yale University Press.

Miller, N. E., Mowrer, O. H., Doob, L. W., Dollard, J., & Sears, R. R. (1958). Frustration-aggression hypothesis. In C. L. Stacey & M. DeMartino (Eds.), *Understanding human motivation* (pp. 251–255). Cleveland, OH: Howard Allen.

Miller, R., & Forbes, J. (1990). Camptocormia. *Military Medicine, 155,* 561–565.

Miner, J. (1962). Personality and ability factors in sales performance. *Journal of Applied Psychology, 46*(1), 6–13.

Mischel, W. (1968). *Personality and assessment.* New York: John Wiley.

Mischel, W. (1973). Toward a cognitive social learning reconceptualization of personality. *Psychological Review, 80,* 252–283.

Mischel, W., & Shoda, Y. (1995). A cognitive-affective system theory of personality: Reconceptualizing situations, dispositions, dynamics, and invariance in personality structure. *Psychological Review, 102,* 246–268.

Mitchell, S. A. (2000). *Relationality: From attachment to intersubjectivity.* London: Routledge.

Mitchell, S. A., & Black, M. J. (1995). *Freud and beyond: A history of modern psychoanalytic thought.* New York: Basic Books.

Mizuno, K., Nakamura, K., & Ushijima, S. (1973). An experience in Morita therapy for a case with depersonalization syndrome. *Journal of Morita Therapy 10,* 135–140.

Molfese, V., & Molfese, D. (Eds.). (2000). *Temperament and personality development across the life span.* Mahwah, NJ: Lawrence Erlbaum.

Moll, J., de Oliveira-Souza, R., Eslinger, P. J., Bramati, I. E., Mourao-Miranda, J., Andreiuolo, P. A., & Pessoa L. (2002). The neural correlates of moral sensitivity: A functional magnetic resonance imaging investigation of basic and moral emotions. *Journal of Neuroscience, 22,* 2730–2736.

Moniz, E. (1964). Essay on a surgical treatment for certain psychoses. *Journal of Neurosurgery, 21,* 1108–1114. (Original work published 1936)

Montag, I., & Lewin, J. (1994). The five-factor personality model in applied settings. *European Journal of Personality, 8,* 1–11.

Moon, K. (2007). A client-centered review of Rogers with Gloria. *Journal of Counseling & Development, 85*(3), 277–285.

Moray, N. (1959). Attention in dichotic listening: Affective cues and the influence of instructions. *Quarterly Journal of Experimental Psychology, 12,* 214–220.

Morgan-Gillard S. (2003). Predictive validity of MMPI-2 and Rorschach in the diagnosis of depression and schizophrenia. *Dissertation Abstracts International*: Section B: The Sciences & Engineering, 9, 4380

Morita, S. (1998). *Morita therapy and the true nature of anxiety-based disorders* (Shinkeishitsu) (Akihisa Kondo, Trans.). Albany: State University of New York Press.

Moscovitch, M. (1995). Recovered consciousness: A hypothesis concerning modularity and episodic memory. *Journal of Clinical and Experimental Neuropsychology, 17,* 276–290.

Multon, K., Brown, S., & Lent, R. (1991). Relation of self-efficacy beliefs to academic outcomes: A meta-analytic investigation. *Journal of Counseling Psychology, 38*(1), 30–38.

Murase, T., & Johnson, F. (1974). Naikan, Morita, and Western psychotherapy. *Archives of General Psychiatry, 31,* 121–128.

Murphy, F. C., Nimmo-Smith, I., & Lawrence, A. D. (2003). Functional neuroanatomy of emotions: A meta-analysis. *Cognitive, Affective, & Behavioral Neuroscience, 3,* 207–233.

Nachson, I. (1995). On the modularity of face recognition: The riddle of domain specificity. *Journal of Clinical and Experimental Neuropsychology, 17,* 256–275.

Nakamura, M., McCarley, R., Kubicki, M., Dickey, C., Niznikiewicz, M., Voglmaier, M., Seidman, L. J., Maier, S. E., Westin, C., Kikinis, R., & Shenton, M. E. (2005). Fronto-temporal disconnectivity in schizotypal personality disorder: A diffusion tensor imaging study. *Biological Psychiatry, 58*(6), 468–478.

Naranjo, C. (1997). *Transformation through insight: Enneatypes in life, literature, and clinical practice.* Prescott, AZ: Hohm Press.

National Center for Complementary and Alternative Medicine (NCCAM). (2007). *Backgrounder: What is Ayurvedic medicine?* Bethesda, MD: Author.

National Center for PTSD. (2007). *The legacy of psychological trauma from the Vietnam War for American Indian military personnel* [fact sheet]. Retrieved April 17, 2008, from http://www.ncptsd.va.gov/ncmain/ncdocs/fact_shts/fs_native_vets.html

National Institutes of Health. (1997). Acupuncture: NIH consensus statement. Bethesda, MD: Author.

Neagoe, A. (2000). Abducted by aliens: A case study. *Psychiatry, 63,* 202–207.

Needleman J., & Baker, G. (Eds.). (1996). *Gurdjieff: Essays and reflections on the man and his teaching.* New York: Continuum.

Neher, A. (1991). Maslow's theory of motivation: A critique. *Journal of Humanistic Psychology, 31*(3), 89–112.

Neisser, U. (1967). *Cognitive psychology.* New York: Appleton-Century-Crofts.

Neisser, U. (1976). *Cognition and reality: Principles and implications of cognitive psychology.* San Francisco: W. H. Freeman.

Newell, A., Shaw, J. C., & Simon, H. A. (1958). Elements of a theory of human problem solving. *Psychological Review, 65,* 151–166.

Newman, L., & Stoller, R. (1971). The oedipal situation in male transexualism. *British Journal of Medical Psychology, 44,* 295–303.

Newnes, C. (2004). Psychology and psychotherapy's potential for countering the medicalization of everything. *Journal of Humanistic Psychology, 44*(3), 358–376.

Nietzsche, F. (1969). *Thus spake Zarathustra* (R. J. Hollingdale, Trans.). Harmondsworth, UK: Penguin Books. (Original work published 1883)

Nisbett, R. E. (1980).The trait construct in lay and professional psychology. In L. Festinger (Ed.), *Retrospections on social psychology* (pp. 109–130). New York: Oxford University Press.

Nisbett, R. E. (2005). Heredity, environment, and race differences in IQ: A commentary on Rushton and Jensen (2005). *Psychology, Public Policy, and Law, 11,* 302–310.

Nisbett, R. E., & Cohen, D. (1996). *Culture of honor.* Boulder, CO: Westview Press.

Noll, R. (1997). *The Aryan Christ: The secret life of Carl Jung.* New York: Random House.

Norman, D. A. (1968). Toward a theory of memory and attention. *Psychological Review, 57,* 522–536.

Norman, W. T. (1963). Toward an adequate taxonomy of personality attributes: Replicated factor structure in peer nomination personality ratings. *Journal of Abnormal and Social Psychology, 66,* 574–583.

Nukina, S., Wang, H., Kamei, K., & Kawahara, R. (2005). Intensive Naikan therapy for generalized anxiety disorder and panic disorder: Outcomes and background [in Japanese]. *Seishin Shinkeigaku Zasshi, 107,* 641–666.

Oberman, L., & Ramachandran, V. (2007). The simulating social mind: The role of the mirror neuron system and simulation in the social and communicative deficits of autism spectrum disorders. *Psychological Bulletin, 133*(2), 310–327.

O'Brien, G., & Jureidini, J. (2002). Dispensing with the dynamic unconscious. *Philosophy, Psychiatry, & Psychology, 9,* 141–153.

O'Connor, B. (2005). A search for consensus on the dimensional structure of personality disorders. *Journal of Clinical Psychology, 61*(3), 323–345.

O'Keefe, J., & Dostrovsky, J. (1971). The hippocampus as a spatial map. Preliminary evidence from unit activity in the freely-moving rat. *Brain Research, 34,* 171–175.

Oldham, J., Skodol, A., Kellman, H., Hyler, S., Rosnick, L., & Davies, M. (1992). Diagnosis of DSM-III-R personality disorders by two structured interviews: Patterns of comorbidity. *American Journal of Psychiatry, 149*(2), 213–220.

O'Leary, D. D. (1989). Do cortical areas emerge from a protocortex? *Trends in Neuroscience, 12,* 400–406.

Oliver, J. M., & Burkham, R. (1982). Subliminal psychodynamic activation in depression: A failure to replicate. *Journal of Abnormal Psychology,* 91, 337–342.

Oltmanns, T., Friedman, J., Fiedler, E., & Turkheimer, E. (2004). Perceptions of people with personality disorders based on thin slices of behavior. *Journal of Research in Personality,* 38(3), 216–229.

Ono, Y, Manki, H, Yoshimura, K, Muramatsu, T., Mizushima, H., Higuchi, S., Yagi, G., Kanba, S., & Asai, M. (1997). Association between dopamine D4 receptor (D4DR) exon III polymorphism and novelty seeking in Japanese subjects. *American Journal of Medical Genetics, 74,* 501–503.

O'Reilly, M., Lacey, C., & Lancioni, G. (2001). A preliminary investigation of the assessment and treatment of tantrums with two post-institutionalized Romanian adoptees. *Scandinavian Journal of Behaviour Therapy,* 30(4), 179–187.

Ozer, D. J. (1986). *Consistency in personality: A methodological framework.* New York: Springer-Verlag.

Pajares, F. (1996, December). Self-efficacy beliefs in academic settings. *Review of Educational Research,* 66(4), 543–578.

Pajares, F., & Miller, M. (1994, June). Role of self-efficacy and self-concept beliefs in mathematical problem solving: A path analysis. *Journal of Educational Psychology,* 86(2), 193–203.

Palmer, H. (1988). *The Enneagram: Understanding yourself and the others in your life.* San Francisco: Harper & Row.

Palmer, H. (1995). *The Enneagram in love and work: Understanding your intimate and business relationships.* San Francisco: HarperSanFrancisco.

Palmer, H., & Brown, P. (1998). *The Enneagram advantage: Putting the 9 personality types to work in the office.* New York: Harmony Books.

Paloutzian, R., Richardson, J., & Rambo, L. (1999). Religious conversion and personality change. *Journal of Personality,* 67, 1047–1079.

Park, J. H., Faulkner, J., & Schaller, M. (2003). Evolved disease-avoidance processes and contemporary anti-social behavior: Prejudicial attitudes and avoidance of people with physical disabilities. *Journal of Nonverbal Behavior,* 27, 65–87.

Park, L., & Hinton, D. (2002). Dizziness and panic in China: Associated symptoms of zang fu organ disequilibrium. *Culture, Medicine, and Psychiatry,* 26, 225–257.

Parker, T., May, P., Maviglia, M., Petrakis, S., Sunde, S., & Gloyd, S. (1997). PRIME-MD: Its utility in detecting mental disorders in American Indians. *International Journal of Psychiatry in Medicine,* 27, 107–128.

Parkinson, B., & Lea, M. (1991). Investigating personal constructs of emotions. *British Journal of Psychology,* 82(1), 73–86.

Patrick, P., & Léon-Carrión, J. (2001). Mood and organic personality disorder following brain injury. In J. Léon-Carrión & M. Pontón (Eds.), *Neuropsychiatry and the Hispanic patient: A clinical handbook* (pp. 243–274). Mahwah, NJ: Lawrence Erlbaum.

Paul, D. (1973). *The Navajo code talkers.* Pittsburgh, PA: Dorrance.

Paulhus, D. (1983). Sphere-specific measures of perceived control. *Journal of Personality and Social Psychology,* 44(6), 1253–1265.

Pavlov, I. P. (1927). *Conditioned reflexes: An investigation of the physiological activity of the cerebral cortex.* London: Oxford University Press.

Pawlowski, B., & Jasienska, G. (2005). Women's preferences for sexual dimorphism in height depend on menstrual cycle phase and expected duration of relationship. *Biological Psychology, 70,* 38–43.

Peabody, D., & Goldberg, L. R. (1989). Some determinants of factor structures from personality-trait descriptors. *Journal of Personality and Social Psychology, 57,* 552–567.

Pearson, K. (1909). *Treasury of human inheritance.* London: Dulau.

Pedersen, P. (1977). Asian personality theory. In R. Corsini (Ed.), *Current personality theories* (pp. 367–397). Itasca, IL; F. E. Peacock.

Pelletier, K. (2002). *The best alternative medicine.* New York: Simon & Schuster.

Penrod, S. (1986). *Social psychology.* Upper Saddle River, NJ: Prentice Hall.

Person to person. (1957, July 1). *Time Magazine* [Electronic version]. Retrieved April 15, 2008, from http://www.time.com/time/magazine/article/0,9171,809592,00.html

Pervin, L. A., Cervone, D., & John, O. P. (2005). *Personality: Theory and research.* New York: John Wiley.

Pervin, L., & John, O. (1999). *Handbook of personality: Theory and research* (2nd ed.). New York: Guilford Press.

Peterson, L. M. (1980). Why men have pockets in their pants: A feminist insight (or if Freud had been a woman). *Society for the Advancement of Social Psychology Newsletter, 6,* 19.

Pfeifer, S., & Waelty, U. (1999). Anxiety, depression, and religiosity—a controlled clinical study. *Mental Health, Religion, & Culture, 2,* 35–45.

Phan, K. L., Wager, T. D., Taylor, S. F., & Liberzon, I. (2004). Functional neuroimaging studies of human emotions. *CNS Spectrums, 9,* 258–266.

Piaget, J. (1962). *Le développement des quantities physiques chez l'enfant: Conservation et atomisme.* Neuchâtel, Switzerland: Delachaux et Niestlé.

Piedmont, R. L., & Chae, J. H. (1997). Cross-cultural generalizability of the five-factor model of personality. *Journal of Cross-Cultural Psychology, 28,* 131–155.

Pinker, S. (1994). *The language instinct.* London: Penguin.

Pinker, S. (1997). *How the mind works.* New York: W. W. Norton.

Pinker, S. (2002). *The blank slate: The modern denial of human nature.* New York: Viking.

Pinter, G. (1993). Effectiveness of client-centered therapy: Part I. *Psychiatria Hungarica, 8,* 139–152.

Pizzagalli, D., Bogdan, R., Ratner, K., & Jahn, A. (2007). Increased perceived stress is associated with blunted hedonic capacity: potential implications for depression research. *Behaviour Research and Therapy 45,* 2742–2753.

Plomin, R. (1994). *Genetics and experience: The interplay between nature and nurture.* Thousand Oaks, CA: Sage.

Popper, K.R. (1963). *Conjectures and refutations* London: Routledge.

Popper K. (1986a). *How I see philosophy.* In S. G. Shanker (Ed.), *Philosophy in Britain today* (pp. 198–212). London: Croom Helm.

Popper, K. (1986b). Predicting overt behavior versus predicting hidden states. *Behavioral and Brain Sciences, 9,* 254–255.

Posner, M. I. (1982). Cumulative development of attentional theory. *American Psychologist, 37,* 168–179.

Posner, M. I., & Boies, S. J. (1971). Components of attention. *Psychological Renew, 78,* 319–408.

Posner, M. I., & Snyder, C. R. R. (1975). Attention and cognitive control. In R. L. Solso (Ed.), *Information processing and cognition: The Loyola symposium* (pp. 160-174). Hillsdale, NJ: Lawrence Erlbaum.

Prince, M. (1921). *The unconscious, the fundamentals of human personality: Normal and abnormal* (2nd ed.). New York: Macmillan.

Quinn, P. (2003, February-March). Race cleansing in America. *American Heritage, 54,* 34–43.

Raine, A., & Manders, D. (1988). Schizoid personality, inter-hemispheric transfer, and left hemisphere over-activation. *British Journal of Clinical Psychology, 27*(4), 333–347.

Rajmohan, V., Thomas, B., & Sreekumar, K. (2004). Case study: Camptocormia, a rare conversion disorder. *Journal of the American Academy of Child and Adolescent Psychiatry, 43,* 1168–1170.

Ramachandran, V. S., & Blakeslee, S. (1999). *Phantoms in the brain.* New York: HarperCollins.

Rao, A. (2000). Depression in Indian history. *Journal of the Indian Medical Association, 98,* 219–223.

Rapaport, D., Gill, M., & Schafer R.(1946). *Diagnostic psychological testing: The theory, statistical evaluation, and diagnostic application of a battery of tests*, Baltimore: Waverly Press.

Rauch, S. L., Milad, M. R., Orr, S. P., Quinn, B. T., Fischl, B., & Pitman, R. K. (2005). Orbitofrontal thickness, retention of fear extinction, and extraversion. *Neuroreport, 16,* 1909–1912.

Reber, A. (1967). Implicit learning of artificial grammars. *Journal of Verbal Learning and Verbal Behavior, 5,* 855–863.

Reber, A. (1989). Implicit learning and tacit knowledge. *Experimental Psychology: General, 118,* 219–235.

Reber, A., Walkenfeld, F., & Hernstadt, R. (1991). Implicit learning: individual differences and IQ. *Journal of Experimental Psychology: Learning, Memory, and Cognition, 17,* 888–896.

Reber, A. (1992). The cognitive unconscious: An evolutionary perspective. *Consciousness and Cognition, 1,* 93–133.

Reber, A. (1993). *Implicit Learning and Tacit Knowledge: An Essay on the Cognitive Unconscious.* New York: Oxford University Press.

Reber, P., & Squire, L. (1994). Parallel brain systems for learning with and without awareness. *Learning and Memory, 1,* 217–229.

Reich, W. (1948). The genital character and the neurotic character. In R. Fliess (Ed.), *The psychoanalytic reader.* New York: International Universities Press. (Original work published 1929)

Reid, D. (1994). *Chinese herbal medicine.* Boston: Shambhala.

Reuter, M., Panksepp, J., Schnabel, N., Kellerhoff, N., Kempel, P., & Hennig, J. (2005). Personality and biological markers of creativity. *European Journal of Personality, 19,* 83–95.

Reynolds, D. (1984).*Constructive living.* Honolulu: University of Hawaii Press.

Reynolds, D. (1987). *Water bears no scars: Japanese lifeways for personal growth.* New York: William Morrow.

Reynolds, D., & Kiefer, C. (1977). Cultural adaptability as an attribute of therapies: The case of Morita therapy. *Culture, Medicine, and Psychiatry, 1,* 395–412.

Richter, D. (2001). *Facing east from Indian country: A native history of early America.* Cambridge, MA: Harvard University Press.

Ridgell, S., & Lounsbury, J. (2004). Predicting academic success: General intelligence, "Big Five" personality traits, and work drive. *College Student Journal, 38*(4), 607–619.

Rieff, P. (1966). *The triumph of the therapeutic: Uses of faith after Freud.* New York: Harper & Row.

Rilling, J., Gutman, D., Zeh, T., Pagnoni, G., Berns, G., & Kilts, C. (2002). A neural basis for social cooperation. *Neuron, 35,* 395–405.

Rilling, M. (2000). John Watson's paradoxical struggle to explain Freud. *American Psychologist, 55,* 301–312.

Riso, D. (1987). *Personality yypes: Using the Enneagram for self-discovery.* Boston: Houghton Mifflin.

Rizzolatti, G., & Arbib, M. (1998). Language within our grasp. *Trends in Neurosciences, 21*(5), 188–194.

Rizzolatti, G., Craighero, L., & Fadiga, L. (2002). The mirror system in humans. In M. I. Stamenov & V. Gallese (Eds.), *Mirror neurons and the evolution of brain and language* (pp. 37–59). Amsterdam, Netherlands: John Benjamins Publishing Company.

Roback, A. A. (1928). *The psychology of character: With a survey of temperament* (2nd ed.). New York: Harcourt, Brace.

Roberts, B., Caspi, A., & Moffitt, T. (2001). The kids are all right: Growth and stability in personality development from adolescence to adulthood. *Journal of Personality and Social Psychology, 81*(4), 670–683.

Robertson, I. H., & Murre, J. M. J. (1999). Rehabilitation of brain damage: Brain plasticity and principles of guided recovery. *Psychological Bulletin, 125,* 544–575.

Rodríguez, J., & Silva, S. (2002). Sören Kierkegaard, Carl Rogers y la relación terapéutica. *Anales de Psiquiatría, 18*(8), 375–377.

Roediger, H. L., & McDermott, K. B. (1995). Creating false memories: Remembering words that were not presented in lists. *Journal of Experimental Psychology: Learning, Memory, & Cognition, 21,* 803–814.

Rogers, C. (1942). *Counseling and psychotherapy: Newer concepts in practice.* Boston and New York: Houghton Mifflin.

Rogers, C. (1946). Significant aspects of client-centered therapy. *American Psychologist, 1,* 415–422.

Rogers, C. (1951). *Client-centered therapy, its current practice, implications, and theory.* Boston: Houghton Mifflin.

Rogers, C. (1957). The necessary and sufficient conditions of therapeutic personality change. *Journal of Consulting Psychology, 21,* 95–103.

Rogers, C. (1958). The characteristics of a helping relationship. *Personnel & Guidance Journal, 37,* 6–16.

Rogers, C. (1959). *A therapist's view of personal goals.* Wallingford, PA: Pendle Hill.

Rogers, C. (1961). *On becoming a person: A therapist's view of psychotherapy.* Boston: Houghton Mifflin.

Rogers, C. (1977). *Carl Rogers on personal power.* New York: Delacorte Press.

Rogers, C. (1980). *A way of being.* Boston: Houghton Mifflin.

Rogers, C., & Roethlisberger, F. (1974). Barriers and gateways to communication. In D. A. Kolb, I. M. Rubin, & J. M. McIntyre (Eds.), *Organizational psychology: A book of readings* (2nd ed.). Oxford, UK: Prentice Hall.

Rorschach, H. (1998). *Psychodiagnostics: A diagnostic test based on perception* (10th ed.). Cambridge, MA: Hogrefe & Huber (Original German edition published 1921)

Rosenberg, C. (1968). *The trial of the assassin Guiteau: Psychiatry and law in the Gilded Age.* Chicago: University of Chicago Press.

Rosenthal, R., & Rubin, B. D. (1982). A simple, general-purpose display of the magnitude of experimental effect. *Journal of Educational Psychology, 74,* 166–169.

Ross, L. (1977). The intuitive psychologist and his shortcomings. Distortions in the attribution process. In L. Bekowitz (Ed.), *Advances in experimental social psychology.* New York: Academic Press.

Roth, W. E., & Finley, G. E. (1998). Adoption and antisocial personality: Environmental factors associated with antisocial outcomes. *Child and Adolescent Social Work Journal, 15,* 133–150.

Rowan, J. (1988). Maslow amended. *Journal of Humanistic Psychology, 38*(1), 81–92.

Rotter J. (1954). *Social learning and clinical psychology.* Englewood Cliffs, NJ: Prentice Hall.

Rotter, J. (1960). Some implications of a social learning theory for the prediction of goal directed behavior from testing procedures. *Psychological Review, 67,* 301–316.

Rotter, J. (1966). Generalized expectancies for internal versus external control of reinforcements. *Psychological Monographs, 80,* 1–28.

Rotter, J. (1975). Some problems and misconceptions related to the construct of internal versus external control of reinforcement. *Journal of Consulting and Clinical Psychology, 43,* 56–67.

Rotter, J. B., & Willerman, B. (1947). The Incomplete Sentence Test as a method of studying personality. *Journal of Consulting Psychology, 11,* 43–48.

Roy, M. A., Neale, M. C., & Kendler, K. S. (1995). The genetic epidemiology of self-esteem. *British Journal of Psychiatry, 166,* 813–820.

Rudebeck, P., Buckley, M., Walton, M., & Rushworth, M. (2006). A role for the macaque anterior cingulate gyrus in social valuation. *Science, 313*(5791), 1310–1312.

Rush, B. (1812). *Medical inquiries and observations upon the diseases of the mind.* Philadelphia: Kinker & Richardson.

Rushton, J. P. (1988). Do r/K reproductive strategies apply to human differences? *Social Biology, 35,* 337–340.

Rushton, J. P. (1992). Contributions to the history of psychology: XC. Evolutionary biology and heritable traits (with reference to oriental-white-black differences): the 1989 AAAS paper. *Psychological Reports, 71,* 811–821.

Rushton, J. P. (1996). Race, genetics, and human reproductive strategies. *Genetic, Social, and General Psychology Monographs, 122,* 21–53.

Rushton, J. P., & Bons, T. A. (2005). Mate choice and friendship in twins: Evidence for genetic similarity. *Psychological Science, 16,* 555–559.

Ruth, W. J. (1992). Irrational thinking in humans: An evolutionary proposal for Ellis' genetic postulate. *Journal of Rational-Emotive & Cognitive Behavior Therapy, 10*(1), 3–20.

Rychlak, J. (1981). *Introduction to personality and psychotherapy: A theory-construction approach* (2nd ed.). Boston: Houghton Mifflin.

Ryle, A., & Breen, D. (1972). Some differences in the personal constructs of neurotic and normal subjects. *British Journal of Psychiatry*, *120*(558), 483–489.

Sackett, G. (1966). Monkeys reared in isolation with pictures as visual input: Evidence for an innate releasing mechanism. *Science, 154,* 1468–1473.

Saetre, P., Strandberg, E., Sundgren, P. E., Pettersson, U., Jazin, E., & Bergstrom, T. F. (2006). The genetic contribution to canine personality. *Genes, Brain, & Behavior, 5,* 240–248.

Sakel, M. (1937). A new treatment of schizophrenia. *American Journal of Psychiatry, 93,* 829–841.

Sanford, J. (1992). *Healing body and soul: The meaning of illness in the New Testament and in psychotherapy.* Louisville, KY: Westminster/John Knox Press.

Sanger, M. (1938). *Margaret Sanger: An autobiography.* New York: W. W. Norton.

Saper, R., Kales, S., Paquin, J., Burns, M., Eisenberg, D., Davis, R., & Phillips, R. (2004). Heavy metal content of Ayurvedic herbal medicine products. *Journal of the American Medical Association, 292,* 2868–2873.

Sartre, J. P. (1947). *The republic of silence* (R. Guthrie, Trans.; A. J. Liebling, Ed.). New York: Harcourt, Brace,

Sass, L. (1982, August 22). The borderline personality. *New York Times Magazine*, p. 12.

Saucier, G., & Skrzypi ska, K. (2006). Spiritual but not religious? Evidence for two independent dispositions. *Journal of Personality, 74,* 1257–1292.

Saulsman, L., & Page, A. (2004). The five-factor model and personality disorder empirical literature: A meta-analytic review. *Clinical Psychology Review, 23*(8), 1055–1085.

Savidge, J. A. (1987). Extinction of an island forest avifauna by an introduced snake. *Ecology, 68,* 660–668.

Schachter, S., & Singer, J. (1962). Cognitive, social, and physiological determinants of emotional states. *Psychological Review, 69*(5), 379–399.

Scharff, D. (1996). *Object relations theory and practice.* Northvale, NJ: Jason Aronson.

Schneider, F., Blanco, C., Antia, S., & Liebowitz, M. (2002). The social anxiety spectrum. *Psychiatric Clinics of North America, 25*(4), 757–774.

Schnell, K., & Herpertz, S. (2007). Effects of dialectic-behavioral-therapy on the neural correlates of affective hyperarousal in borderline personality disorder. *Journal of Psychiatric Research, 41*(10), 837–847.

Schore, A. N. (1994). *Affect regulation and the origin of the self: The neurobiology of emotional development.* Hillsdale, NJ: Lawrence Erlbaum.

Schunk, D. (1989). Self-efficacy and achievement behaviors. *Educational Psychology Review, 1*(3), 173–208.

Schwartz M. A., Wiggins, O. P., & Norko, M. A., (1995). Prototypes, ideal types, and personality disorders: the return to classical phenomenology. In W. John Livesley (Ed.), *The DSM-IV personality disorders* (pp. 417–432). New York: Guilford Press.

Schwartz, T. (1996). *What really matters: Searching for wisdom in America.* New York: Bantam Books.

Scourfield, J., Neilson, M., Lewis, G., & McGuffin, P. (1999). Heritability of social cognitive skills in children and adolescents. *British Journal of Psychiatry, 175,* 559–564.

Scurfield, R. (1995). Healing the warrior: Admission of two American Indian war-veteran cohort groups to a specialized inpatient unit. *American Indian and Alaska Native Mental Health Research, 6,* 1–22.

Segal, H. (1979). *Melanie Klein.* New York: Viking Press.

Seligman, M. (1973). Fall into helplessness. *Psychology Today, 7*(1), 43–48.

Seligman, M. (1975). Generality of learned helplessness in man. *Journal of Personality and Social Psychology, 31*(2), 311–327.

Shackelford, T. (2005). An evolutionary psychological perspective on cultures of honor. *Evolutionary Psychology, 3,* 381–391.

Shear, P., Sullivan, E., Lane, B., & Pfefferbaum, A. (1996, November). Mammillary body and cerebellar shrinkage in chronic alcoholics with and without amnesia. *Alcoholism, Clinical and Experimental Research, 20*(8), 1489–1495.

Shedler, J., & Westen, D. (2004). Dimensions of personality pathology: An alternative to the five-factor model. *American Journal of Psychiatry, 161*(10), 1743–1754.

Sheldon, W., Stevens, S., & Tucker, W. (1940). *The varieties of human physique: An introduction to constitutional psychology.* New York: Harper.

Sherer, M., & Rogers, R. W. (1980). Effects of therapists' nonverbal communication on rated skill and effectiveness. *Journal of Clinical Psychology, 36,* 696–700.

Shiffrin, W., & Schneider, R. M. (1977). Controlled and automatic processing: II. Perceptual learning, automatic attending, and a general theory. *Psychological Review, 84,* 127–190.

Shimizu, T. (1997). Evolution of cooperation in the finitely repeated prisoner's dilemma. *Japanese Journal of Behaviormetrics, 24,* 101–111.

Shockley, W. B. (1972). Dysgenics, geneticity, raceology. *Phi Delta Kappan,* (Suppl.), 297–312.

Shorter, E. (1997). *A history of psychiatry.* New York: John Wiley.

Shumyatsky, G. P., Malleret, G. L., Shin, R. M., Takizawa, S., Tully, K., Tsvetkov, E., Zakharenko, S. S., Joseph, J., Vronskayam S., Yinm D., Schubart, U. K., Kandel, E. R,. & Bolshakov, V. Y. (2005). Stathmin, a gene enriched in the amygdala, controls both learned and innate fear. *Cell, 123,* 697–709.

Shumyatsky, G. P., Tsvetkov, E., Malleret, G. l., Vronskaya, S., Hatton, M., Hampton, L., Battey, J. F., Dulac, C., Kandel, E. R., & Bolshakov, V. Y. (2002). Identification of a signaling network in lateral nucleus of amygdala important for inhibiting memory specifically related to learned fear. *Cell, 111,* 905–918.

Siegel, B. (2001). Cancer patients who participate in support groups. *Advances in Mind-Body Medicine, 17,* 231.

Siegel, B. (2003). Personality and survival. *Advances in Mind-Body Medicine, 19,* 4.

Silverman, L. H. (1978). Unconscious symbiotic fantasy: A ubiquitous therapeutic agent. *International Journal of Psychoanalytic Psychotherapy, 7,* 562–585.

Silverman, L. H., Bronstein, A., & Mendelsohn, E. (1976). The further use of the subliminal psychodynamic activation method for the experimental study of the clinical theory of psychoanalysis: On the specificity of the relationship between symptoms and unconscious conflicts. *Psychotherapy: Theory,* 13, 2–16.

Silverman, L. H., Martin, A., Ungaro, R., & Mendelsohn, E. (1978). Effect of subliminal stimulation of symbiotic fantasies on behavior modification treatment of obesity. *Journal of Consulting & Clinical Psychology, 46,* 432–441.

Silverman, L. H., Spiro, R. H., Weisberg, J. S., & Candell, P. (1969). The effects of aggressive activation and the need to merge on pathological thinking in schizophrenia. *Journal of Nervous & Mental Disease, 28,* 39–51.

Silverman, L., & Weinberger, J. (1985). Mommy and I are one: Implications for psychotherapy. *American Psychologist, 40,* 1296–1308.

Simeon, D., Guralnik, O., Knutelska, M., & Schmeidler, J. (2002). Personality factors associated with dissociation: Temperament, defenses, and cognitive schemata. *American Journal of Psychiatry, 159,* 489–491.

Simons, C. W., & Piliavin, J. A. (1972). Effect of deception on reactions to a victim. *Journal of Personality and Social Psychology, 21,* 56–60.

Sinclair, W. J. (1909). *Semmelweis: his life and doctrine: A chapter in the history of medicine.* Manchester, UK: University Press.

Siomopoulos, V. (1988). Narcissistic personality disorder: Clinical features. *American Journal of Psychotherapy, 42*(2), 240–253.

Skinner, B. F. (1938). *The behavior of organisms: An experimental analysis.* New York: D. Appleton-Century.

Skinner, B. F. (1948a). "Superstition" in the pigeon. *Journal of Experimental Psychology, 38,* 168–172.

Skinner, B. F. (1948b). *Walden two.* New York: Macmillan.

Skinner, B. F. (1953). *Science and human behavior.* New York: Free Press.

Skinner, B. F. (1956). A case history in scientific method. *American Psychologist, 11,* 221–233.

Skinner, B. F. (1957). *Verbal behavior.* New York: Appleton-Century-Crofts.

Skinner, B. F. (1959). *Cumulative record.* New York: Appleton-Century-Crofts

Skinner, B. (1963). Operant behavior. *American Psychologist, 18*(8), 503–515.

Skinner, B. F. (1971). *Beyond freedom and dignity.* New York: Knopf.

Sloan, M. P., & Meier, J. H. (1983). Typology for parents of abused children. *Child Abuse & Neglect, 7,* 443–450.

Smeets, J., & Brenner, E. (2006). 10 years of illusions. *Journal of Experimental Psychology: Human Perception and Performance, 32*(6), 1501–1504.

Smith, C. P. (1981). How (un)acceptable is research involving deception? *IRB: A Review of Human Subjects Research, 3,* 1–4.

Smith, G. M. (1967). Usefulness of peer ratings of personality in educational research. *Educational and Psychological Measurement, 27,* 967–984.

Smith, M. L., & Glass, G. V. (1979). Meta-analysis of psychotherapy outcome studies. In C. A. Kiesler & N. A. Cummings (Eds.), *Psychology and national health insurance: A sourcebook* (pp. 530–539). New York: American Psychological Association.

Snyder, C. R., Shenkel, R. J., & Lowery, C. R. (1977). Acceptance of personality interpretations: the "Barnum Effect" and beyond. *Journal of Consulting and Clinical Psychology, 45,* 104–114.

Sohlberg, S., Billinghurst, A., & Nylén, S. (1998). Moderation of mood change after subliminal symbiotic stimulation: Four experiments contributing to the further demystification of Silverman's "Mommy and I Are One" findings. *Journal of Research in Personality, 32*(1), 33–54.

Solomon, L., Bunn, J., Pirie, P., Worden, J., & Flynn, B. (2006). Self-efficacy and outcome expectations for quitting among adolescent smokers. *Addictive Behaviors, 31*(7), 1122–1132.

Solso, R. (1979). Twenty-five years of recommended readings in psychology. *American Psychologist, 34*(8), 703–705.

Somer, O., & Goldberg, L. R. (1999). The structure of Turkish trait-descriptive adjectives. *Journal of Personality and Social Psychology, 76,* 431–450.

Spangler, W. (1992). Validity of questionnaire and TAT measures of need for achievement: Two meta-analyses. *Psychological Bulletin, 112*(1), 140–154.

Spearman, C. (1904). General intelligence objectively determined and measured. *American Journal of Psychology, 15,* 201–292.

Sperling, G. (1960). The information available in brief visual presentations. *Psychological Monographs, 74,* 1–29.

Sperry, R. (1993). The impact and promise of the cognitive revolution. *American Psychologist, 48*(8), 878–885.

Spinoza, B. (1883). *Ethics, Part II. On the nature and origin of the mind* (R.H.M. Elwes, Trans.). London: G. Bell and Sons. (Original work published 1677)

Stadler, F., Kolb, G., Rubusch, L., Baker, S. P., Jones, E. G., & Akbarian, S. (2005). Histone methylation at gene promoters is associated with developmental regulation and region-specific expression of ionotropic and metabotropic glutamate receptors in human brain. *Journal of Neurochemistry, 94,* 324–336.

Stampede Mesteth, W., Standing Elk, D., & Swift Hawk, P. (1993). Declaration of war against exploiters of Lakota spirituality. *Eyapaha* (newsletter), *2,* 22.

Stamps, V. R., Abeling, N. G. G. M., van Gennip, A. H., van Cruchten, A. G., & Gurling, H. M. D. (2001). Mild learning difficulties and offending behaviour—is there a link with monoamine oxidase A deficiency? *Psychiatric Genetics, 11,* 173–176.

Sterelny, K., & Fitness, J. (2003). *From mating to mentality: Evaluating evolutionary psychology.* New York: Psychology Press.

Sternberg, R. J. (2003). *Cognitive psychology.* Belmont, CA: Wadsworth.

Sternberg, S. (1966). High-speed scanning in human memory. *Science, 153,* 652–654.

Stiles, W. B. (1979). Verbal response modes and psychotherapeutic technique. *Psychiatry, 42,* 49–62.

Stone, G., & Gottheil, E. (1975). Factor analysis of orality and anality in selected patient groups. *Journal of Nervous and Mental Disease, 160,* 311–323.

Stone, R., Whitbeck, L., Chen, X., Johnson, K., & Olson, D. (2006). Traditional practices, traditional spirituality, and alcohol cessation among American Indians. *Journal of Studies on Alcohol, 67,* 236–244.

Strozier, C. (2001). *Heinz Kohut: The making of a psychoanalyst.* New York: Farrar, Strauss, and Giroux.

Stuart, S., Pfohl, B., Battaglia, M., Bellodi, L., Grove, W., & Cadoret, R. (1998). The cooccurrence of DSM-III-R personality disorders. *Journal of Personality Disorders, 12*(4), 302–315.

Sullivan, H. S. (1953). *The interpersonal theory of psychiatry.* New York: W. W. Norton.

Sullivan, H. S. (1954). *The psychiatric interview.* New York: W. W. Norton.

Sullivan, H. S. (1964). *The fusion of psychiatry and social science.* New York: W. W. Norton.

Sullivan, P. F., Fifield, W. J., Kennedy, M.A., Mulder, R., Sellman, J., & Joyce, P. (1998). No association between novelty seeking and the type 4 dopamine receptor gene (DRD4) in two New Zealand samples. *American Journal of Psychiatry; 155,* 98–101.

Sulloway, F. J. (1991). Reassessing Freud's case histories: The social construction of psychoanalysis. *Isis, 82,* 245–275.

Sulloway, F. (1996). *Born to rebel: Birth order, family dynamics, and creative lives.* New York: Pantheon.

Svoboda, R., & Lade, A. (1995). *Tao and Dharma: Chinese medicine and Ayurveda.* Twin Lakes, WI: Lotus Press.

Szasz, T. (1960). *The myth of mental illness: Foundations of a theory of personal conduct.* New York: Harper & Row.

Szasz, T. (1988). *The myth of psychotherapy.* Syracuse, NY: Syracuse University Press.

Szasz, T. (2007). *Coercion as cure: A critical history of psychiatry.* New Brunswick, NJ: Transaction.

Takahashi, T., & Aizawa, S. (1973). Morita-oriented group psychotherapy for *Taijin-kyofu-sho* (or the Japanese type of social phobia) cases characterized by withdrawal tendencies. *Journal of Morita Therapy, 10,* 1–12.

Tambs, K., Sundet, J. M., Eaves, L., & Hornberg, M. (1991). Pedigree analysis of Eysenck Personality Questionnaire (EPQ) scores in monozygotic (MZ) twin families. *Behavior Genetics, 21,* 369–382.

Tantam, D. (1988). Lifelong eccentricity and social isolation: II. Asperger's syndrome or schizoid personality disorder? *British Journal of Psychiatry, 153,* 783–791.

Tashiro, S., Hosoda, S., & Kawahara, R. (2004). Naikan therapy for prolonged depression: Psychological changes and long-term efficacy of intensive Naikan therapy. *Seishin Shinkeigaku Zasshi, 106,* 431–457.

Taylor, C. (1989). *Sources of the self: The making of the modern identity.* Cambridge, MA: Harvard University Press.

Tebartz van Elst, L., Hesslinger, B., Thiel, T., Geiger, E., Haegele, K., Lemieux, L., Lieb, K., Bohus, M., Hennig, J., &Ebert, D. (2003). Frontolimbic brain abnormalities in patients with borderline personality disorder: A volumetric magnetic resonance imaging study. *Biological Psychiatry, 54*(2), 163–171.

Terman, L. (1942). The vocational successes of intellectually gifted individuals. *Occupations, 20,* 493–498.

Teusch, L., Bohme, H., Finke, J., & Gastpar, M. (2001). Effects of client-centered psychotherapy for personality disorders alone and in combination with psychopharmacological treatment. An empirical follow-up study. *Psychotherapy and Psychosomatics, 70,* 328–336.

Teusch, L., Bohme, H., & Gastpar, M. (1997). The benefit of insight-oriented and experimental approach on panic and agoraphobia symptoms. *Psychotherapy and Psychosomatics, 66,* 293–301.

Thickbroom, G. W., Byrnes, M. L., Archer, S. A., & Mastaglia, F. L. (2004). Motor outcome after subcortical stroke correlates with the degree of cortical reorganization. *Clinical Neurophysiology, 115,* 2144–2150.

Thorndike, E. L. (1898). *Animal intelligence: An experimental study of the associative processes in animals* (Psychological Review, Monograph Supplements, No. 8). New York: Macmillan.

Thorne, B. (2003). *Carl Rogers.* Thousand Oaks, CA: Sage.

Titchener, E. B. (1899). *An outline of psychology.* New York: Macmillan.

Tobacyk, J., & Downs, A. (1986). Personal construct threat and irrational beliefs as cognitive predictors of increases in musical performance anxiety. *Journal of Personality and Social Psychology, 51*(4), 779–782.

Todd, C., & Still, A. (1993). General practitioners' strategies and tactics of communication with the terminally ill. *Family Practice 10,* 268–276.

Tolman, E. C. (1932). *Purposive behavior in animals and men.* New York: Century.

Tolman, E. C. (1948). Cognitive maps in rats and men. *Psychological Review, 55,* 189–208.

Tom Xu, K., & Farrell, T. (2007). The complementarity and substitution between unconventional and mainstream medicine among racial and ethnic groups in the United States. *Health Services Research, 42,* 811–826.

Tooby, J., & Cosmides, L. (1990). On the universality of human nature and the uniqueness of the individual: The role of genetics and adaptation. *Journal of Personality, 58,* 17–67.

Tooby, J., & Cosmides, L. (1992). The psychological foundations of culture. In J. Barkow, L. Cosmides, & J. Tooby (Eds.), *The adapted mind: Evolutionary psychology and the generation of culture* (pp. 19–136). New York: Oxford University Press.

Torgersen, S. (1980). The oral, obsessive, and hysterical personality syndromes: A study of hereditary and environmental factors by means of the twin method. *Archives of General Psychiatry, 80,* 1272–1277.

Tovee, M., Rolls, E., & Ramachandran, V. (1996). Rapid visual learning in neurones of the primate temporal visual cortex. *Neuroreport, 7*(15–17), 2757–2760.

Trivers, R. L. (1971). The evolution of reciprocal altruism. *Quarterly Review of Biology, 46,* 35–57.

Truax, C. (1966). Reinforcement and nonreinforcement in Rogerian psychotherapy. *Journal of Abnormal Psychology, 71,* 1–9.

Truax, C. (1970). Effects of client-centered psychotherapy with schizophrenic patients: Nine years pretherapy and nine years posttherapy hospitalization. *Journal of Consulting & Clinical Psychology, 35,* 417–422.

Trull, T., Tragesser, S., Solhan, M., & Schwartz-Mette, R. (2007). Dimensional models of personality disorder: Diagnostic and Statistical Manual of Mental Disorders Fifth Edition and beyond. *Current Opinion in Psychiatry, 20*(1), 52–56.

Tsujita, T., Niikawa, N., Yamashita, H., Imamura, A., Hamada, A., Nakane, Y., & Okazaki, Y. (1998). Genomic discordance between monozygotic twins discordant for schizophrenia. *American Journal of Psychiatry; 155,* 422–424.

Turner, J., Ersek, M., & Kemp, C. (2005). Self-efficacy for managing pain is associated with disability, depression, and pain coping among retirement community residents with chronic pain. *Journal of Pain, 6*(7), 471–479.

Turner, R. M. (2000). Naturalistic evaluation of dialectical behavior therapy-oriented treatment for borderline personality disorder. *Cognitive & Behavioral Practice, 7,* 413–419.

Tversky, A., & Kahneman, D. (1973). Judgment under uncertainty: Heuristics and biases. *Science, 185*(4157), 1124–1131.

Tversky, A., & Kahneman, D. (1974). Judgment under uncertainty: Heuristics and biases. *Science, 185,* 1124–1131.

Tversky, A., & Kahneman, D. (1983). Extensional versus intuitive reasoning: The conjunction fallacy in probability judgment. *Psychological Review, 90*(4), 293–315.

Vaihinger, H. (1924). *The philosophy of as-if.* London: Routledge & Kegan Paul.

Vaillant, G. E. (1977). *Adaptation to life.* Boston: Little, Brown.

Valenstein, E. S. (1986). *Great and desperate cures: The rise and decline of psychosurgery and other radical treatments for mental illness.* New York: Basic Books.

Vander Goot, M. (1989). Has modern psychology secularized religion? In T. Burke (Ed.), *Man and mind: A Christian theory of personality* (pp. 43–64). Hillsdale, MI: Hillsdale College Press.

Van Hoof, A. (1999). The identity status field re-reviewed: An update of unresolved and neglected issues with a view on some alternative approaches. *Developmental Review, 19,* 497–565.

Van Leeuwen, M. (1989). Personality theorizing within a Christian world view. In T. Burke (Ed.), *Man and mind: A Christian theory of personality* (pp. 171–198). Hillsdale, MI: Hillsdale College Press.

Ventegodt, S., Flensborg-Madsen, T., Andersen, N., & Merrick, J. (2005). The life mission theory VII. Theory of existential (Antonovsky) coherence: a theory of quality of life, health, and ability for use in holistic medicine. *ScientificWorldJournal, 5,* 377–389.

Vincent de Paul, Saint. (1851). *Maximes spirituelles de saint Vincent de Paul.* Tours: A. Mame et compagnie.

Vishton, P., Rea, J., Cutting, J., & Nuñez, L. (1999). Comparing effects of the horizontal-vertical illusion on grip scaling and judgment: Relative versus absolute, not perception versus action. *Journal of Experimental Psychology: Human Perception and Performance, 25*(6), 1659–1672.

Vitz, P. (1989). Secular personality theories: A critical analysis. In T. Burke (Ed.), *Man and mind: A Christian theory of personality* (pp. 65–94). Hillsdale, MI: Hillsdale College Press.

von Mayrhauser, R. (1989). Making intelligence functional: Walter Dill Scott and applied psychological testing in World War I. *Journal of the History of the Behavioral Sciences, 25*(1), 60–72.

Wahl, O. (1999). *Telling Is Risky Business: Mental Health Consumers Confront Stigma.* New Brunswick, NJ: Rutgers University Press.

Wai, C., Tan, B., Chan, C., Sutedja, D., Lee, Y., Khor, C., & Lim, S. (2007). Drug-induced liver injury at an Asian center: A prospective study. *Liver International, 27,* 465–474.

Walster, E. (1965). The effect of self-esteem on romantic liking. *Journal of Experimental Social Psychology, 1,* 184–197.

Walster, E., Berscheid, E., Abrahams, D., & Aronson, V. (1967). Effectiveness of debriefing following deception experiments. *Journal of Personality and Social Psychology, 6,* 126–131.

Wang, C., Collet, J., & Lau, J. (2004). The effect of tai chi on health outcomes in patients with chronic conditions: A systematic review. *Archives of Internal Medicine, 164,* 493–501.

Warner, R. E. (1991). A survey of theoretical orientations of Canadian clinical psychologists. *Canadian Psychology, 32,* 525–528.

Warwick, D. P. (1982). Types of harm in social research. In T. L. Beauchamp, R. R. Faden, R. J. Wallace, Jr. & L. R. Walters (Eds.), *Ethical issues in social science research* (pp. 101–124). Baltimore: Johns Hopkins University Press.

Wastell, C. (1992). Self psychology and the etiology of borderline personality disorder. *Psychotherapy: Theory, Research, Practice, Training, 29*(2), 225–233.

Watson, J. B. (1913). Psychology as the behaviorist views it. *Psychological Review, 20,* 158–177.

Watson, J. B. (1916). Behavior and the concept of mental disease. *Journal of Philosophy, Psychology, and Scientific Methods, 13,* 589–597.

Watson, J. B. (1919). *Psychology: From the standpoint of a behaviorist.* Philadelphia: J. B. Lippincott.

Watson, J. B. (1926). What the nursery has to say about instincts. In C. Murchison (Ed.), *The psychologies of 1925.* Worcester, MA: Clark University Press.

Watson, J. B. (1930). *Behaviorism.* New York: W. W. Norton.

Watson, J. B., & Rayner, R. (1920). Conditioned emotional reactions. *Journal of Experimental Psychology, 3,* 1–14.

Watson, J. D., & Berry, A. (2003). *DNA: The secret of life.* New York: Knopf.

Watson, J. P. (1975). An experimental method for the study of unconscious conflict. *British Journal of Medical Psychology, 48,* 299–301.

Webster, R. (2004). *Why Freud was wrong: Sin, science, and psychoanalysis.* New York: Basic Books.

Wehmeyer, M., Agran, M., & Hughes, C. (1998). *Teaching self-determination to students with disabilities: Basic skills for successful transition.* Baltimore, MD: Paul H. Brookes.

Weick, K. (1990). The vulnerable system: An analysis of the Tenerife air disaster. *Journal of Management, 16,* 571–593.

Weishaar, M. (1993). *Aaron T. Beck.* Newbury Park, CA: Sage.

Weishaar, M., & Beck, A. (2006). Cognitive theory of personality and personality disorders. In S. Strack (Ed.), *Differentiating normal and abnormal personality* (2nd ed., pp. 113–135). New York: Springer.

Weizenbaum, J. (1966). ELIZA—A computer program for the study of natural language communication between man and machine. *Communications of the ACM, 9*(1), 36–45.

Wertheimer, M. (1912). Experimentelle studien über das Sehen von Bewegung. *Zeitschrift für Psychologie, 61,* 161–265.

Wertheimer, M. (1925). *Über Gestalttheorie. Vortrag gehalten in der Kant-Gesellschaft, Berlin, am 17. dezember 1924.* Erlangen, Germany: Philosophische Akademie.

Weyer, J. (1967). *De praestigiis daemonum.* Amsterdam: E. J. Bonset. (Original work published 1563)

Whalen, P. J., Shin, L. M., McInerney, S. C., Fischer, H., Wright, C. I., & Rauch, S. L. (2001). A functional MRI study of human amygdala responses to facial expressions of fear versus anger. *Emotion, 1*(1), 70–83.

Whitney, G. (2004). The return of racial science. *PsycCRITIQUES, 41,* 1189–1191.

Widiger, T. (1992). Categorical versus dimensional classification. *Journal of Personality Disorders, 6,* 287–300.

Widiger, T. A., Verheul, R., & van den Brink, W. (1999). *Handbook of personality: Theory and research* (2nd ed.). New York: Guilford Press.

Williams, D. E., & Page, M. M. (1989). A multi-dimensional measure of Maslow's hierarchy of needs. *Journal of Research in Personality, 23,* 192–213.

Willis, R. H., & Willis, Y. A. (1970). Role playing vs. deception: An experimental comparison. *Journal of Personality and Social Psychology, 16,* 472–477.

Wilson, E. O. (1975). *Sociobiology: The new synthesis.* Cambridge, MA: Belknap Press.

Wilson, M. I., & Daly, M. (1996). Male sexual proprietariness and violence against wives. *Current Directions in Psychological Science, 5,* 2–7.

Winocur, G. (1985). The hippocampus and thalamus: Their roles in short- and long-term memory and the effects of interference. *Behavioural Brain Research, 16,* 135–152.

Winter, D. A. (1992). *Personal construct psychology in clinical practice: Theory, research and applications.* London: Routledge.

Witkin, H., & Asch, S. (1948). Studies in space orientation. III. Perception of the upright in the absence of a visual field. *Journal of Experimental Psychology, 38*(5), 603–614.

Wolf, E. S. (1988). *Treating the self.* New York: Guilford Press.

Wolfe, H. (2004). Ding De-zheng's acupuncture treatment of psychiatric disorders. *Townsend Letter for Doctors and Patients, 21,* 150–151.

Wolff, S. (1998). *Schizoid personality in childhood: The links with Asperger syndrome, schizophrenia spectrum disorders, and elective mutism.* New York: Plenum Press.

Wolff, S. (2000). *Schizoid personality in childhood and Asperger syndrome.* New York: Guilford Press.

Wolff, S., & McGuire, R. (1995). Schizoid personality in girls: A follow-up study: What are the links with Asperger's syndrome? *Journal of Child Psychology and Psychiatry, 36*(5), 793–817.

Wolff, S., Narayan, S., & Moyes, B. (1988). Personality characteristics of parents of autistic children: A controlled study. *Journal of Child Psychology and Psychiatry, 29*(2), 143–153.

Wolpe, J. (1952). Experimental neuroses as learned behavior. *British Journal of Psychology, 43,* 243–268.

Wolpe, J. (1956). Learning versus lesions as the basis of neurotic behavior. *American Journal of Psychiatry, 112,* 923–927.

Wolpe, J. (1961). The systematic desensitization treatment of neuroses. *Journal of Nervous and Mental Disease, 132,* 189–203.

Wolpe, J. (1969). *The practice of behavior therapy.* New York: Pergamon Press.

Wolpe, J. (1977). The acquisition, augmentation and extinction of neurotic habits. *Behaviour Research and Therapy, 15*(3), 303–304.

Wolpe, J., & Lazarus, A. (1966). *Behavior therapy techniques: A guide to the treatment of neuroses.* New York: Pergamon Press.

Wright, S., & Sayre-Adams, J. (2007). Who do you think you are? *Nursing Standard, 21,* 20–23.

Wu, J., Li, L., & Zou, Y. (2005). Determination of carbamate insecticides in Chinese medicinal herbs by gas chromatography with a nitrogen-phosphorus detector. *Journal of AOAC International, 88,* 1261–1264.

Wundt, W. (1904). *Principles of physiological psychology* (E. B. Titchener, Trans.). New York: Macmillan. (Original work published 1873/1874)

Wuthnow, R. (1999). Growing up religious: Christians and Jews and their journeys of faith. Boston: Beacon Press.

Yadav, R. S. (1990). Interview as a means of personality assessment: Some baffling dilemmas. *Indian Journal of Psychometry & Education, 21*(2), 67–79.

Yamadera, W., Sato, M., Ozone, M., Nakamura, K., Itoh, H., & Nakayama, K. (2005). Psycho-physiological evaluations of clinical efficacy in outpatients: Morita therapy for psychophysiological insomnia [in Japanese]. *Seishin Shinkeigaku Zasshi, 107,* 341–351.

Yang, K. S., & Bond, M. H. (1990). Exploring implicit personality theories with indigenous or imported constructs: The Chinese case. *Journal of Personality and Social Psychology, 58,* 1087–1095.

Yinon, Y., Shoham, V., & Lewis, T. (1974). Risky-shift in a real vs. role-played situation. *Journal of Social Psychology, 93,* 137–138.

Yu, H., Fu, W., & Cao, W. (2006). Childhood traumatic experiences of cluster-B personality disorders in college students. *Chinese Journal of Clinical Psychology, 14*(6), 593–595.

Zacks, R. T., Hasher, L., & Sanft, H. (1982). Automatic encoding of event frequency: Further findings. *Journal of Experimental Psychology: Learning, 8,* 106–116.

Zahavi, A. (1975). Mate selection—a selection for a handicap. *Journal of Theoretical Biology, 53,* 205–214.

Zajonc, R. B. (1965). Social facilitation. *Science, 149,* 269–274.

Zajonc, R. (1984). On the primacy of affect. *American Psychologist, 39*(2), 117–123.

Zubek, E. (1994). Traditional native healing. Alternative or adjunct to modern medicine? *Canadian Family Physician, 40,* 1923–1931.

Zucca, C., Puzella, A., & Bersani, G. (1994). Anomalie di G-6-PD in due soggetti con disturbo schizoide di personalità. *Rivista di Psichiatria, 29*(6), 59–62.

Index

About the Authors

Albert Ellis, Ph.D., was the intellectual founder of all clinical approaches that now fall under the rubric of cognitive behavior therapy, and he is generally regarded as one of the most influential psychologists of the 20th century. His Rational Emotive Behavior Therapy is now practiced and taught throughout the world, along with the numerous similar therapies that it spawned. Dr. Ellis wrote 70 books and more than 600 journal articles and monographs. At the Albert Ellis Institute, which he founded and managed for more than half a century, he personally trained or supervised thousands of clinicians. As a practicing psychologist, he personally helped more than 10,000 people lead less painful and more productive lives. Dr. Ellis received dozens of awards from organizations like the American Psychological Association and American Counseling Association for his tireless work in advancing psychology, counseling, and social work. When he received his Ph.D. from Columbia University in 1947, he had already established himself as the most renowned sex therapist in the first half of the 20th century, and he then went on to revolutionize the field of clinical psychology. Dr. Ellis died July 24, 2007, while this book was in the final stages of preparation.

Mike Abrams, Ph.D., has been a practicing clinician in New Jersey for more than 20 years. He is also on the graduate counseling faculty of William Paterson University and is a fellow and supervisor of the Albert Ellis Institute. Dr. Abrams studied and worked closely with Dr. Ellis, with whom he published several books, chapters, and articles. Dr. Abrams has received commendations from the New Jersey governor, the Hudson County executive, and the Jersey City mayor for his volunteer efforts. His commitment to pro-bono work includes his being among the first psychologists to counsel people with AIDS at the Gay Men's Health Crisis in the early 1980s. Dr. Abrams has degrees from Queens College, Brooklyn College, the Graduate Center of City University of New York, and New York University. He also did postdoctoral study at Columbia University and the Albert Ellis Institute. Prior to becoming a psychologist, he earned an MBA and worked in organizations such as the New York Stock Exchange, Merrill Lynch, and Citicorp.

Lidia Dengelegi Abrams, Ph.D., is the executive director of Resolve Community Counseling Center, Inc., a private, nonprofit mental health agency. She also maintains a private clinical psychology practice and consults for the New Jersey Division of Youth and Family Services, the New Jersey Office of Parental Representation, and the New Jersey Division of Vocational Rehabilitation. Dr. Abrams has co-authored one other book with Dr. Ellis and has published research in the areas of AIDS education and prevention, eating disorders, and comparative psychotherapy efficacy. For several years, she conducted research on health care utilization at Rutgers University's Institute for Health, Health Care Policy, and Aging Research. She has a master's degree in psychology from New York University and a Ph.D. in psychology from Temple University. She is a fellow and supervisor of the Albert Ellis Institute. Dr. Abrams has taught at New Jersey City University.